CHILDHOOD DISORDERS DIAGNOSTIC DESK REFERENCE

Childhood Disorders Diagnostic Desk Reference
Cecil R. Reynolds and Elaine Fletcher-Janzen, Editors

CHILDHOOD DISORDERS DIAGNOSTIC DESK REFERENCE

Edited by

Elaine Fletcher-Janzen
University of Northern Colorado

Cecil R. Reynolds
Texas A&M University and
Bastrop Mental Health Associates

WILEY
John Wiley & Sons, Inc.

This book is printed on acid-free paper. ♾

Published by John Wiley & Sons, Inc., Hoboken, New Jersey.
Published simultaneously in Canada.

For general information on our other products and services please contact our Customer Care Department within the U.S. at (800) 762-2974, outside the United States at (317) 572-3993 or fax (317) 572-4002.

Wiley also publishes its books in a variety of electronic formats. Some content that appears in print may not be available in electronic books.

Library of Congress Cataloging-in-Publication Data:

Childhood disorders diagnostic desk reference / edited by Elaine Fletcher-Janzen and Cecil R. Reynolds.
p. cm.
Includes bibliographical references and index.
ISBN 0-471-40428-4 (cloth : alk. paper)
1. Children—Diseases—Diagnosis. 2. Pediatrics. I. Fletcher Janzen, Elaine. II. Reynolds, Cecil R., 1952–

RJ50.C483 2003
618.92′0075—dc21

2002032387

Printed in the United States of America

10 9 8 7 6 5 4 3 2 1

This book is dedicated to all parents of exceptional children and to our own parents,

Winifred and Peter Fletcher
and
Cecil C. and Daphne Reynolds,

teachers and mentors extraordinaire, with our gratitude for their guidance, love, and nurturance.

CONTENTS

PREFACE

The growth of knowledge about neurodevelopmental disorders, genetic disorders, and the implications of many other, even common childhood disorders for cognitive and behavioral functions has been nothing short of phenomenal in the past 15 years. The number of disorders identified and known to exist has grown geometrically during this time period and continues to do so. It has become increasingly difficult to stay fully abreast of this literature and the many subtle nuances of diagnosis. It is a boon to children and their families to see that heretofore unrecognized disorders now have specific diagnoses and treatment regimens. Many children with the disorders listed in this work will also require special education services. Clinicians, however, need assistance in tracking and understanding the broad growth of literature in this area and need to do so efficaciously. It is in this spirit that the present work is proffered.

The object of a desk reference is functional. The book sits on the desk or on the bookcase close to the desk and is picked up frequently for consultation. When a clinician needs just a nugget of information (especially in differential diagnosis), out comes the desk reference to solve the immediate problem. The reference work is concise; it provides just the right amount of information, and it requires little effort on the part of the reader to perform the needed function.

This Diagnostic Desk Reference was born out of a repeated need, on the part of our editors and authors working in the field of child psychology, neurology, and pediatrics, to have a source of information that contained just the basic facts associated with various childhood disorders. Most students and clinicians will first refer to the American Psychiatric Association's current *Diagnostic and Statistical Manual of Mental Disorders* for facts and then move on to the internet databases or books such as Smith's Recognizable Patterns of Human Malformation to gather information about a client. This process is cumbersome and often frustrating. There is also no guarantee that after this effort the clinician will have the information that he or she needs! Hence, the Childhood Disorders Diagnostic Desk Reference speaks to the clinician who simply wants to know the basic facts with reference to further sources of information.

There are approximately 700 entries describing different childhood disorders in this work. There are not enough entries! We would have very much liked to include 2,000 entries in this work and incorporate all of the orphan or rare diseases. However, at some point, we had to decide how heavy a desk reference should be, and the determination to stop at 700 entries was purely pragmatic—there is no use in having a desk reference that one cannot simply lift off the desk!

The text of each entry is organized in a standardized format so that the reader knows exactly where to look for a specific piece of information. The entry format is as follows:

- Definition of the disorder
- Incidence and prevalence rates
- Characteristics of the disorder (placed in a box and divided into numbered points for easy reference)
- Treatment
- Special education concerns
- Prognosis and future research
- References

The intended audience for this book was initially professionals in the school, clinical, medical, and private practice settings. However, parents and family members of children who are experiencing difficulties also may find this work useful. Authors were instructed to use limited jargon, deliver culturally competent incidence and prevalence rates as well as treatment considerations, and provide online as well as hardcopy references. Children are always diagnosed and treated in the context of the systems within which they live; therefore, each entry attempts to address the disorder in a holistic fashion. We intend these considerations to translate into a seamless and flexible treatment of the subject matter that appeals to a wide audience.

The reader of this work will find that it contains disorders and diseases that span the pediatric medical, psychiatric, and educational fields. We have included some symptoms that clinicians may observe (i.e., perseveration) just for convenience in differential diagnosis. However, for the most part, the entry list contains high and low incidence disorders and syndromes of childhood. At some point, editors had to make difficult decisions about rare disorders (e.g., 14 cases worldwide) and the utility of adding these entries at the expense of leaving other, more frequently observed, disorders aside. Another unexpected and cumbersome process was deciding which medical name to use for many entries. Any blending of the medical and psychiatric fields would naturally have this problem, so much time was taken in listing entries by their most popular title and using "See" and "See also" citations to guide the reader around the indexes. The reader may note that citations of disease/disorder names that have been traditionally possessive (e.g., Tourette's Syndrome and Down's Syndrome) are slowly being changed to nonpossessive. This text reflects the field as it changes from one convention to another; therefore, some authors quote possessive names and others do not. Subsequent editions of this text will reflect a complete change to nonpossessive names.

With regard to thanking those who contributed to this desk reference: Elaine would like to thank, as usual, David, Emma, and Leif for their patience and support. Many thanks also to Carla Cde Baca, who wrestled endlessly with the 700 electronic files without complaint! Cecil once again acknowledges his debt to Julia, who keeps him more centered than anyone thought possible and who allows him the unencumbered pursuit of the work he loves. As always, we thank Tracey Belmont, our editor at John Wiley & Sons, for her patience and enthusiastic support of this project.

This work would not have been possible if it had not been for the contributing editors and their authors. The myriad of details required for keeping track of the manuscript (hardcopy and electronic) were formidable. Every one of our contributing editors—Bob Brown, Elaine Clark, Rik D'Amato, Barry Davidson, James Kaufman (and Allison), Antolin Llorente, Joan Mayfield, Nancy Nussbaum, Peg Semrud-Clikeman (with assistance from U.S. Department of Education, Educational Leadership Grant H325D000038), Cyndi Riccio, and Rachel Toplis—were motivated, timely, and patient with the process of producing a detailed reference work. We are very grateful to this wonderful team of professionals.

We also wish to thank Dr. Wiedemann and Kunze for their work in producing the outstanding graphics in the book *Clinical Syndromes* (3rd ed.) published by Times Mirror International Publishers Limited. Their years of difficult work collecting photographs of rare clinical syndromes allowed us to provide illustrations for our readers in this current volume. In addition, many thanks to Diana Jones, editor for Elsevier Publishing, who arranged the international effort to gain permission for these graphics. Our thanks also goes to Susan Dodson at Graphic Composition, Inc., for keeping us on the straight and narrow in the production of this and other works.

Elaine Fletcher-Janzen
University of Northern Colorado

Cecil R. Reynolds
Texas A&M University and
Bastrop Mental Health
Associates

CONTRIBUTOR LIST

Acree, William M.
University of Northern Colorado
Greeley, Colorado

Aguire, Theresa T.
Texas A&M University
College Station, Texas

Anderson, Kari
University of North Carolina
Wilmington, North Carolina

Anhalt, Karla
Texas A&M University
College Station, Texas

Anselene, Stephanie
University of North Carolina
Wilmington, North Carolina

Arnstein, Laura
State University of New York
Binghamton, New York

Athanasiou, Michelle S.
University of Northern Colorado
Greeley, Colorado

Ballatore, Melanie E.
University of Texas at Austin
Austin, Texas

Bates, Stacey L.
University of Texas at Austin
Austin, Texas

Baxter, Emily R.
University of Colorado
Colorado Springs, Colorado

Beckham, Melissa L.
Citadel
Charleston, South Carolina

Bender, Karen
University of Northern Colorado
Greeley, Colorado

Bjoraker, Kendra J.
University of Northern Colorado
Greeley, Colorado
Kennedy Krieger Institute
Johns Hopkins University School of Medicine

Boada, Richard
University of Denver
Denver, Colorado

Branan, Tammy
University of Northern Colorado
Colorado Springs, Colorado

Bristol, Adam S.
Yale University
New Haven, Connecticut

Brown, Robert T.
University of North Carolina at Wilmington
Wilmington, North Carolina

Brumm, Virdette L.
Children's Hospital Los Angeles
Keck/USC School of Medicine
Los Angeles, California

Bubonic, Elizabeth A.
Texas A&M University
College Station, Texas

Bunner, Melissa R.
Austin Neurological Clinic
Austin, Texas

Burkholder, Leslie
Idea Infusion Consulting and Contracting
Denver, Colorado

Caldwell, Catherine M.
University of Texas at Austin
Austin, Texas

Cde Baca, Carla
University of Northern Colorado
Colorado Springs, Colorado

Cde Baca, Christine D.
University of Northern Colorado
Greeley, Colorado

Cheng, Nina
University of Texas at Austin
Austin, Texas

Chernoff, Robert A.
Harbor–UCLA Medical Center
Los Angeles, California

Chittooran, Mary M.
Saint Louis University
St. Louis, Missouri

Christiansen, Elizabeth
University of Utah
Salt Lake City, Utah

Clark, Elaine
University of Utah
Salt Lake City, Utah

Compton, Sarah
University of Texas at Austin
Austin, Texas

Cooper, Carey E.
University of Texas at Austin
Austin, Texas

Corlett, Mary
University of Texas at Austin
Austin, Texas

Cornforth, Emily
University of Colorado
Colorado Springs, Colorado

Corriveau, Barbara
Laramie County School District #1
Cheyenne, Wyoming

Crepeau-Hobson, M. Franci
University of Northern Colorado
Greeley, Colorado

Crowley, Jill E.
Saint Louis University
St. Louis, Missouri

Cutillo, Juliette
Fountain-Fort Carson School District 8
Colorado Springs, Colorado

D'Amato, Rik Carl
University of Northern Colorado
Greeley, Colorado

Dahlstrom, Amy J.
University of Northern Colorado
Greeley, Colorado

Davis, Andrew S.
University of Northern Colorado
Greeley, Colorado

Davison, Barry H.
Ennis, Texas

Dekeyzer, Lori
University of Utah
Salt Lake City, Utah

Downs, Darrell L.
Mount Sinai Medical Center and Miami Heart Institute
Miami, Florida

Drummond, Jonathan T.
Princeton University
Princeton, New Jersey

Durkin, Abbey-Robin
University of Colorado
Colorado Springs, Colorado

Edens, Retha M.
Saint Louis University
St. Louis, Missouri

Edgel, Heather
University of Utah
Salt Lake City, Utah

Estep, Kimberly M.
University of Houston–Clear Lake
Houston, Texas

Evans, Carol Anne
University of Utah
Salt Lake City, Utah

Fasko, Sharla
Rowan County Schools
Morehead, Kentucky

Fasnacht-Hill, Lisa A.
Keck University of Southern California School of Medicine
University of Southern California/ University Affiliated Program at Children's Hospital of Los Angeles
Los Angeles, California

Fassig, Elizabeth I.
University of Northern Colorado
Greeley, Colorado

Ferguson, Laurie L.
Wright Institute
Berkeley, California
The Children's Hospital
Denver, Colorado

Filaccio, MaryLynne D.
University of Northern Colorado
Greeley, Colorado

Fletcher, Kiely Ann
Ohio State University
Columbus, Ohio

Fletcher-Janzen, Elaine
University of Northern Colorado
Colorado Springs, Colorado

Forness, Stephanie R.
University of Northern Colorado
Greeley, Colorado

Franklin, Leslie Coyle
University of Northern Colorado
Greeley, Colorado

Frederick, Brigitte N.
Texas A&M University
College Station, Texas

French, Christine L.
Texas A&M University
College Station, Texas

Gallagher, Sherri L.
University of Northern Colorado
Greeley, Colorado

Gallo, Cynthia A.
University of Colorado
Colorado Springs, Colorado

Garcia de Alba, Roman
Texas A&M University
College Station, Texas

George, Carrie
Texas A&M University
College Station, Texas

Gillis, Jennifer M.
Center for Educational Partnerships
University of California, Irvine
Irvine, California

Gisi, Theresa M.
Colorado Neurological Associates, PC
Denver and Colorado Springs, Colorado

Gonzales, Maricela P.
Texas A&M University
College Station, Texas

Gonzales, Rex
University of Utah
Salt Lake City, Utah

Graf, Elizabeth Ann
University of Northern Colorado
Greeley, Colorado

Guli, Laura A.
University of Texas at Austin
Austin, Texas

Guy, Kathryn L.
University of Texas at Austin
Austin, Texas

Hannan, Monika
University of Northern Colorado
Colorado Springs, Colorado

Hargrave, Jennifer
University of Texas at Austin
Austin, Texas

Harvey, Melissa M.
University of Colorado at Colorado Springs
Colorado Springs, Colorado

Heathfield, Lora Tuesday
University of Utah
Salt Lake City, Utah

Hess, Robyn S.
University of Colorado at Denver
Denver, Colorado

Higgins, Kellie
University of Texas at Austin
Austin, Texas

Hoadley, Sarah L.
Appalachian State University
Boone, North Carolina

Holland, Andrea
University of Texas at Austin
Austin, Texas

Hourmanesh, Najmeh
University of Utah
Salt Lake City, Utah

Janzen, Emma
Colorado Springs, Colorado

Jenne, Helen G.
Alliant International University–California School of Professional Psychology
San Diego, California

Jensen, Jenise
University of Utah
Salt Lake City, Utah

Johnson, Brian D.
University of Northern Colorado
Greeley, Colorado

Johnson, Judy A.
Goose Creek Consolidated Independent School District
Baytown, Texas

Kamens, Michele Wilson
Rider University
Lawrenceville, New Jersey

Karnik, Dilip
'Specially for Children Children's Hospital of Austin
Austin, Texas

Katz, Allison
Rutgers University
New Brunswick, New Jersey

Kaufman, James C.
Educational Testing Service
Princeton, New Jersey

Kaufmann, Elizabeth
University of Texas at Austin
Austin, Texas

Keith, Jennifer
University of Northern Colorado
Greeley, Colorado

Kelly, Theresa
University of Northern Colorado
Greeley, Colorado

Kilpatrick, Paula
University of North Carolina
Wilmington, North Carolina

Kirchner, Bob
University of Northern Colorado
Greeley, Colorado

Kirson, Donald A.
Counseling Center, University of San Diego
San Diego, California

Konter, Dana R.
University of Wisconsin–Stout
Menomonie, Wisconsin

Krach, S. Kathleen
Texas A&M University
College Station, Texas

Krichner, Bob
Larame City School District #1
Cheyenne, Wyoming

Kruschwitz, Moana
University of Texas at Austin
Austin, Texas

Kuhn, Loni
University of Utah
Salt Lake City, Utah

Kutz, Alexandra S.
University of Texas at Austin
Austin, Texas

La Conte, Michael
District 11 Public Schools
Colorado Springs, Colorado

Lahroud, Iman Teresa
University of Texas at Austin
Austin, Texas

Lassiter, Kerry S.
Citadel
Charleston, South Carolina

Lee, Donghyung
Texas A&M University
College Station, Texas

Leverett, J. Patrick
Citadel
Charleston, South Carolina

Lewis, Lucy
University of North Carolina at Wilmington
Wilmington, North Carolina

Llorente, Antolin M.
Baylor College of Medicine
Houston, Texas

Lyle, Teresa M.
University of Texas at Austin
Austin, Texas

Maricle, Denise E.
University of Wisconsin–Stout
Menomonie, Wisconsin

Mathie, Heidi
University of Utah
Salt Lake City, Utah

Mathis, Jill
Laramie School District #1
Cheyenne, Wyoming

Matthews, T. Darin
Citadel
Charleston, South Carolina

Mayfield, Joan W.
Baylor Pediatric Specialty Services
Dallas, Texas

McCallister, Heidi A.
University of Texas at Austin
Austin, Texas

McCarthy, Cristina
University of Utah
Salt Lake City, Utah

McCloskey, Dalene M.
University of Northern Colorado
Greeley, Colorado

McDaniel, Ryan E.
Citadel
Charleston, South Carolina

McHugh, Stacy E.
The Children's Hospital
Denver, Colorado

Melvin, Brenda
New Hanover Regional Medical Center
Wilmington, North Carolina

Moore, Melanie
University of North Carolina
Wilmington, North Carolina

More, Susannah
University of Texas at Austin
Austin, Texas

Morrow, Amy
University of North Carolina
Wilmington, North Carolina

Muenz, Tracy A.
Alliant University
San Diego, California

Nebel, Diana L.
University of Northern Colorado
Greeley, Colorado

Nelson, R. Brett
University of Northern Colorado
Greeley, Colorado

Nicholls, Jennifer
Dysart Unified School District
El Mirage, Arizona

Nock, Matthew K.
Yale University
New Haven, Connecticut

Nussbaum, Nancy L.
Austin Neurological Clinic
Austin, Texas

O'Donnell, Louise
University of Texas Health Science Center
San Antonio, Texas
University of Texas at Austin
Austin, Texas

Olympia, Daniel
University of Utah
Salt Lake City, Utah

Parrino, Maryann Toni
Montclair University
Upper Montclair, New Jersey

Pelletier, Shelley F.
Dysart Unified School District
El Mirage, Arizona

Perfect, Michelle
University of Texas at Austin
Austin, Texas

Perrill, Paula
University of Northern Colorado
Greeley, Colorado

Phillips, Lindsey A.
University of Utah
Salt Lake City, Utah

Plotts, Cynthia A.
Southwest Texas State University
San Marcos, Texas

Pompa, Janiece
University of Utah
Salt Lake City, Utah

Powell, Shawn
United States Air Force Academy
Colorado Springs, Colorado

Radcliff-Lee, Shannon
University of North Carolina
Wilmington, North Carolina

Rae, William A.
Texas A&M University
College Station, Texas

Ramos, Christine D.
University of Northern Colorado
Colorado Springs, Colorado

Razo, Nancy Peña
Texas A&M University
College Station, Texas

Reynolds, Cecil R.
Texas A&M University and Bastrop Mental Health Associates
College Station, Texas

Rhodes, Robert L.
New Mexico State University
Las Cruces, New Mexico

Riccio, Cynthia A.
Texas A&M University
College Station, Texas

Richards, Laura
University of Utah
Salt Lake City, Utah

Rioth, Matthew
University of Colorado
Colorado Springs, Colorado

Rollins, Dahl A.
Texas A&M University
College Station, Texas

Romine, Cassandra Burns
Texas A&M University
College Station, Texas

Rosenstein, Leslie D.
Neuropsychology Clinic, PC
Austin, Texas

Rosenthal, Eve N.
Texas A&M University
College Station, Texas

Rybicki, Daniel J.
ForenPsych Services
Agoura Hills, California

Sage, Susan
Dysart Unified School District
El Mirage, Arizona

Satre, Derek D.
University of California
San Francisco, California

Scammacca, Nancy K.
University of Texas at Austin
Austin, Texas

Schamber, Walter R.
University of Northern Colorado
Greeley, Colorado

Schmitt, Carol
San Diego Unified School District
San Diego, California

Schnoebelen, Sarah
University of Texas at Austin
Austin, Texas

Semrud-Clikeman, Margaret
University of Texas at Austin
Austin, Texas

Sessoms, Amy
University of North Carolina at Wilmington
Wilmington, North Carolina

Sherman, Vedia
Austin Neurological Clinic
Austin, Texas

Shine, Agnes E.
Barry University
Miami Shores, Florida

Singer, Jennifer Kaufman
California Department of Corrections, Region 1 Parole Outpatient Clinic
Sacramento, California

Singleton, Jessica L.
University of Northern Colorado
Greeley, Colorado

Slappey, Jaime
University of North Carolina at Wilmington
Wilmington, North Carolina

Smith, April M.
Yale University
New Haven, Connecticut

Snider, Mary Helen
Devereux Cleo Wallace
Colorado Springs, Colorado

Soorya, Latha V.
Binghamton University and Institute for Child Development
Binghamton, New York

Spradling, Vicky Y.
Austin State Hospital
Austin, Texas

Steinman, David R.
Austin Neurological Clinic and Department of Psychology
University of Texas at Austin
Austin, Texas

Sullivan, Jeremy R.
Texas A&M University
College Station, Texas

Svien-Senne, Lana
University of South Dakota
Vermillion, South Dakota

Swan, Tricia
University of Colorado
Colorado Springs, Colorado

Tobin, Renée M.
Texas A&M University
College Station, Texas

Toplis, Rachel
University of Northern Colorado
Colorado Springs, Colorado

Tucker, David M.
Austin Neurological Clinic and University of Texas at Austin
Austin, Texas

Urquhart, Marilyn
University of South Dakota
Vermillion, South Dakota

Vaurio, Rebecca
Austin Neurological Clinic and University of Texas at Austin
Austin, Texas

Warnygora, Nicole R.
University of Northern Colorado
Greeley, Colorado

Webber, Sharine
Laramie County School District #1
Cheyenne, Wyoming

Webster, Lauren M.
Department of Psychology
Wake Forest University

Whitman, Susie
Immune Deficiency Foundation
Odessa, Texas

Wiley, Karen
University of Northern Colorado
Colorado Springs, Colorado

Wilkening, Greta N.
University of Colorado Health Sciences Center
The Children's Hospital
Denver, Colorado

Wilson, Kimberly D.
University of Texas
Austin, Texas

Wolfe, Monica E.
Texas A&M University
College Station, Texas

Wolfe, Wendy
University of Utah
Salt Lake City, Utah

Work, Patricia
University of South Dakota
Vermillion, South Dakota

Zupancic, Kathryn
University of Northern Colorado
Colorado Springs, Colorado

A

AARSKOG SYNDROME

Aarskog syndrome, or Aarskog-Scott syndrome, is a genetic disorder characterized by short stature and musculoskeletal, facial, and genital abnormalities. This inherited disorder of unknown etiology involves either an autosomal recessive or semidominant X-linked transmission.

Aarskog syndrome is a rare condition, although precise estimates of incidence are lacking. Estimates of prevalence range from 100 cases worldwide (Gandy, 2000) to 180 cases in one research study of reported males (Teebe et al., 1993). Although Aarskog syndrome affects primarily males, females may carry some of the symptoms (Meschede, Rolf, Neugebauer, Horst, & Nieschlag, 1996). Because males are typically more severely affected than females and females lack the characteristic genital anomalies, incidence in females may be underreported (Teebe et al., 1993). Many of the reports in the literature are case studies, often involving multiple family members. The phenotype varies with age and across cases, which may further contribute to inconsistency in diagnosis and in incidence estimates (Berry, Cree, & Mann, 1980; Teebe et al., 1993).

Characteristics

1. Short stature (may not be obvious until child is 1–3 years of age), with height at or below 3rd percentile until puberty, when a growth spurt results in height at or below 10th percentile
2. Hypertelorism (wide-set eyes with droopy eyelids), enlarged corneal diameter, and down-slanting palpebral fissures, with possible strabismus or astigmatism
3. Rounded face, broad forehead with widow's peak at hairline, anteverted nares with long philtrum, and crease below lower lip
4. Orthodontic problems such as dental malocclusion and delayed eruption of teeth
5. Thick, fleshy earlobes with top portion of the ear folded over slightly
6. Genital anomalies, particularly "shawl scrotum" (overriding scrotum) and undescended testicles
7. Protruding umbilicus, inguinal and umbilical hernia
8. Joint hyperlaxity, tissue webbing between fingers, and possible fifth finger clinodactyly and simian crease
9. Broad, flat, and small feet with bulbous toes
10. Spina bifida occulta, cervical vertebral defects, and scoliosis

Although there is no treatment for Aarskog syndrome itself, genetic counseling is recommended for affected families as a preventive measure. Trials of growth hormone have not been found effective to treat short stature in this disorder. Specific treatments will depend upon individual symptoms and may include surgery for cryptorchidism and inguinal hernia, orthodontic treatment for facial abnormalities, and ophthalmologic consultation. Children with Aarskog syndrome will likely have multiple X rays to examine for musculoskeletal abnormalities. In some cases, cystic changes in the brain and generalized seizures may occur, resulting in a need for referral to a neurologist and pharmacotherapy (National Library of Medicine [NLM], 1999).

Special education considerations include the possibility of cognitive impairment and attention deficit disorder with or without hyperactivity (NLM, 1999). Although estimates vary across studies, 70–90% of affected individuals can be expected to have normal or low normal intelligence (Teebe et al., 1993). Fryns (1992) reported that in a study of 52 males from one center, 30% of affected males were mentally retarded. Puberty is frequently delayed (Fryns, 1992). Although detailed information regarding developmental and school functioning is lacking in reported case studies, it appears that at least some affected individuals experience delayed speech, language, and gross motor milestones but are able to succeed in regular education classrooms (Teebe et al., 1993). One reported case (Berry et al., 1980) exhibited learning problems in mathematics. Children with Aarskog syndrome may be eligible for special education services, with the specific handicapping condition depending upon the nature and severity of symptoms. Findings from the literature suggest that the most likely handicapping conditions are Mentally Retarded or Other Health Impairment.

Individuals with Aarskog syndrome can be expected to have a normal life span, with varying degrees of

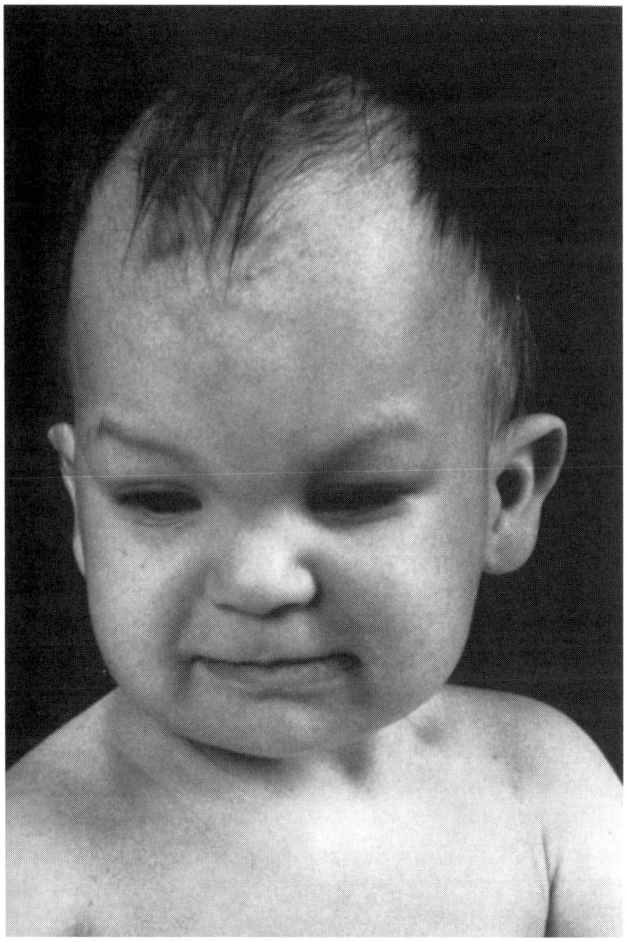

Aarskog Syndrome
Reprinted from *Clinical Syndromes,* Wiedemann and Kunze, 1997, by permission of the publisher Mosby

independence depending upon level of cognitive functioning. One case study reported sperm abnormalities and reduced fertility in an affected male (Meschede et al., 1996), with the implication that other adult males with Aarskog syndrome could be screened for sperm abnormalities. Future research is focused upon differential diagnosis, particularly with disorders that share similar symptoms, specific mode or modes of genetic transmission, and prevention through genetic counseling. Greater attention to developmental differences among children with Aarskog syndrome is needed to better inform school-based interventions for this population.

REFERENCES

Berry, C., Cree, J., & Mann, T. (1980). Aarskog's syndrome. *Archives of Disease in Childhood, 55,* 706–710.

Fryns, J. P. (1992). Aarskog syndrome: The changing phenotype with age. *American Journal of Medical Genetics, 43,* 420–427.

Gandy, A. (2000). Aarskog syndrome. Retrieved from http://www.pedianet.com/news/illness/disease/files/aarskogs.htm

Meschede, D., Rolf, C., Neugebauer, D., Horst, J., & Nieschlag, E. (1996). Sperm acrosome defects in a patient with Aarskog-Scott syndrome. *American Journal of Medical Genetics, 66,* 340–342.

National Library of Medicine. (1999, October 27). Aarskog syndrome. In *Multiple congenital anomaly/mental retardation (MCA/MR) syndromes.* Retrieved from http://www.nlm.nih.gov/mesh/jablonski/syndromes/

Cynthia A. Plotts
Southwest Texas State University

ACALCULIA (ACQUIRED DYSCALCULIA)

Acalculia, also known as acquired dyscalculia, is the loss of arithmetic skills due to brain injury. The arithmetic difficulties may involve the reading or writing of numbers or arithmetic signs and misaligning or rotating digits or numbers, as well as inaccurately solving problems requiring calculation (Keller & Sutton, 1991). Traumatic brain injury and cerebrovascular disease are the most common causes; however, demyelinating disease, neoplasm, and degenerative disease can also produce acalculia (Stringer, 1996).

Characteristics

Acalculia is an injury to the brain that results in a loss of mathematical skills. The loss of skills may include the following (Stringer, 1996):

1. Inaccurate reading of arithmetic signs or numbers. For example, individual digits are read aloud incorrectly (e.g., *2* as *8*), multidigit numbers are read incorrectly (e.g., *53* as *503*), or arithmetic signs are read incorrectly (e.g., + for –).
2. Inability to understand the meaning of arithmetic signs or numbers, as evidenced by inability to match a number with the actual quantity or errors using the wrong arithmetic sign (e.g., adding instead of subtracting) on written math problems.
3. Inability to write numbers or produce recognizable numbers. This may include writing digits out of order or different digits than requested.
4. Incorrect alignment of number columns, rotation (vertically or horizontally) of individual digits, incorrect spacing of digits, or transposition of digits (e.g., *89* written as *98*).
5. Inaccurate solution of written or oral addition, subtraction, division, or multiplication problems.

The majority of youth with brain injuries have some spontaneous cognitive recovery for several months after their injuries; however, often a rehabilitation program is needed. A comprehensive evaluation of the student's mathematical strengths and weaknesses (including how these limitations affect the student) should be completed to guide the treatment plan (Rosselli & Ardila, 1997). The retraining of number concepts and writing numbers is accomplished through practice and repetition. Calculation deficits can be addressed by encouraging a student to use a calculator. "Fingermath," a technique that teaches students to do quick calculations using their fingers, can also be taught to those with acalculia. Fingermath can be used on all basic mathematical operations, including those with multidigit numbers (Stringer, 1996). Computer technology has been used in acalculia assessment and rehabilitation; in rehabilitation, it allows for standardized procedures, more training time, and self-training (Guyard et al., 1997). In addition, youth with acalculia may develop anxiety regarding arithmetic. Relaxation strategies can be taught to address this anxiety (Stringer, 1996) and improve math performance.

Youth with acalculia may receive special education services under the classification of Traumatically Brain Injured if a physician can provide eligibility documentation of a brain injury. If this documentation is not possible, a student may qualify as Mentally Retarded or Learning Disabled in the areas of mathematics calculation, mathematics reasoning, or both, depending on the severity of his or her brain injury. Modifications implemented in the classroom may involve the use of a calculator, mathematical fact tables, or computer technology. Instructional techniques should include numerous repetitions of basic mathematical concepts and calculations.

Future research is focusing on effective interventions for those with acalculia. Additionally, technological advances will continue to assist those with acalculia in educational, occupational, and personal settings.

REFERENCES

Guyard, H., Masson, V., Quiniou, R., & Siou, E. (1997). Expert knowledge for acalculia assessment and rehabilitation. *Neuropsychological Rehabilitation, 7*(4), 419–439.

Keller, C. E., & Sutton, J. P. (1991). Specific mathematics disorders. In J. E. Obrzut & G. W. Hynd (Eds.), *Neuropsychological foundations of learning disabilities* (pp. 549–571). San Diego, CA: Academic Press.

Rosselli, M., & Ardila, M. (1997). Rehabilitation of calculation disorders. In J. Leon-Carrion (Ed.), *Neuropsychological rehabilitation: Fundamentals, innovations and directions* (pp. 353–370). Delray Beach, FL: GR/St. Lucie Press.

Stringer, A. Y. (1996). *A guide to adult neuropsychological diagnosis.* Philadelphia: F. A. Davis.

Judy A. Johnson
Goose Creek Consolidated Independent School District

See also Dyscalculia

ACHONDROPLASIA

Achondroplasia is the most common form of skeletal dysplasia or chondrodystrophy. It is a bone disorder that is characterized by a defect in the formation of the cartilage of the long bones. People with achondroplasia often refer to themselves as dwarfs or little people. Achondroplasia usually results from a spontaneous mutation (chemical change) within a single gene. The condition may be passed on to future generations. For example, a couple with one achondroplasic spouse and an average-statured spouse has a 50% chance of having an average-statured child (Telzrow, 2000).

Achondroplasia occurs in all races and with equal frequency in females and males. It affects approximately 1 in 25,000 children in the United States.

Characteristics

1. By adulthood, an individual with achondroplasia generally does not exceed 1.4 m in height.
2. Characteristics of this condition are usually apparent at birth and include attenuation of extremities. This shortness is particularly noticeable in the upper arms and thighs.
3. A reverse curvature (kyphosis) of the lower spine may be apparent in infancy, and bowed legs may develop any time after the child begins to walk.
4. Short hands and feet. Fingers tend to be equal in length (trident hands).
5. Normal truck and head size.
6. A prominent bulging forehead and flattened, "saddle" nose.
7. Intelligence is usually not affected.
8. Children with achondroplasia may reach motor milestones of development slowly.
9. Children have a tendency toward middle-ear infections in the first 5 or 6 years of life, and dental problems may be caused by overcrowded teeth.

At present there is no specific treatment to promote growth in achondroplasia. Surgery to lengthen legs and arms of people with this condition is being performed on an experimental basis in some centers in the United States (e.g., Kashiwagi, Suzuki, Seto, & Futami, 2001). However, it is not common practice because complications are frequent and the process is long and arduous. Current treatment is aimed at preventing and treating complications of achondroplasia. For example, the spinal kyphosis may require surgery or bracing, and bowlegs may be treated by orthopedic bracing. Ear infections should be treated promptly to avoid sustaining significant hearing loss.

Although intelligence is not usually affected by this

condition, children with achondroplasia may qualify for special services under the Individuals with Disabilities Education Act (1997) within the physical disability category. Children with this condition may require adaptive equipment to accommodate their short stature. Older children may require pain management techniques to adjust to the pain often experienced in the lower back with spinal cord and nerve problems. Ear infections need to be recognized and treated promptly, and frequent hearing checks may be necessary to avoid hearing problems. Children with this condition may require counseling to recognize that their condition need not prevent them from leading a full and satisfying life. Contact with other well-adjusted short people through a support group may help build self-esteem and confidence.

The prognosis for an individual with achondroplasia is very good. This condition is not life threatening. However, it is important for children with achondroplasia to recognize that a wide range of occupation choices exists for them and that their condition does not prevent them from living a fulfilling life. For more information on this condition, contact Little People of America, Inc., P.O. Box 745, Lubbock, TX, 79408, telephone: (888) 572–2001; or National Organization for Rare Disorders, Inc., at P.O. Box 8923, New Fairfax, CT, 06812-8923.

REFERENCES

Kashiwagi, N., Suzuki, S., Seto, Y., & Futami, T. (2001). Bilateral humeral lengthening in achondroplasia. *Clinical Orthopedic, 391,* 251–257.

Telzrow, C. F. (2000). Achondroplasia. In C. Reynolds & E. Fletcher-Janzen (Eds.), *Encyclopedia of special education* (2nd ed., p. 33).

Rachel Toplis
University of Northern Colorado

See also Hypochondroplasia; Dwarfism

ACNE VULGARIS

Acne vulgaris (AV) is a skin disorder seen primarily in adolescents (Burkhart, Burkhart, & Lehmann, 1999). It is the most common skin disease treated by physicians (Krowchuk, 2000). AV is characterized by a pilosebaceous follicular eruption of the comedo that starts an inflammatory reaction. A pilosebaceous follicle consists of a follicle or pore, the sebaceous gland, and a hair. These specialized follicles are concentrated on the face, chest, and back. Formation of papules, pustules, and cysts can result from the inflammation. AV is a chronic condition that may last for years and may cause emotional distress and permanent facial scarring (Krowchuk, 2000). Clinical characteristics of AV vary with age, stage of puberty attained, gender, and race (White, 1998).

There are four basic reasons that adolescents are at risk for AV: hormonal surges that take place both before and during puberty, bacteria, comedogenesis, and genetic predisposition (Krowchuk, 2000). In adolescents, cycling hormones cause gonadal development and adrenal maturation, which increases androgen production, leading to sebaceous gland enlargement and higher sebum. Higher levels of androgen dehydroepiandrosterone sulfate (DHEAS) cause more sebum to be produced, which leads to the oily face and chin with scattered comedones that are the hallmark of puberty production (White, 1998). Bacteria are also involved with increased acne production. Krowchuk (2000) reports that *Propionibacterium acnes* (*P. acnes*) begin to colonize after sebum production increases. This bacteria uses the sebum as a nutrient that allows this normal facial bacteria to multiply so that it increases the inflammatory reaction that causes the pustules, papules, and cysts characteristic of AV. Finally, although it is not possible to predict the severity of AV based on genetic factors, there does appear to be a genetic predisposition for AV (Krowchuk, 2000).

AV affects an estimated 17 million people in the United States, affecting 85% of adolescents and young adults (Krowchuk, 2000), although a higher percentage of teenage boys than teenage girls are affected by AV (White, 1998). Krowchuk (2000) reports that AV severity correlates with sebum secretion, which is caused by adrenal and gonadal androgens. Therefore, both sebum secretion and AV peaks during adolescence and begins to decline after age 20.

Characteristics

1. Obstructive lesions are blackheads or whiteheads. Blackheads are open comedones, or follicles with a wide, dark opening. Whiteheads are closed comedones, or small, white papules. They are follicles that have become dilated with cellular and lipid debris but have only a microscopic opening into the skin.
2. Some patients with acne will develop scars or cysts when inflammatory lesions have resolved.

The first step in treating AV is conducting a global assessment of acne severity that states the number, size, location, and extent of lesions and scarring (Krowchuk, 2000). Next, the patient should be given information that will help him or her avoid behaviors and factors that worsen AV. This information list should include advice such as do not pick at acne, avoid wearing athletic gear over areas with acne, avoid cosmetics and moisturizers containing oils, use only noncomedogenic or nonacnegenic products, and avoid working in an environment where one comes into contact with grease.

Acne is a chronic condition, and treatment efforts generally take 6–8 weeks before therapeutic benefit is seen (Krowchuk, 2000). Both topical and systemic treatments are recommended for AV. Topical therapies include benzoyl peroxide, topical antibiotics, and azelaic acid, which when used alone or in combination with each other have an antibacterial effect on mild to moderate inflammatory acne. Topical retinoids (Retin-A) and salicylic acid are indicated in the treatment of mild to severe obstructive lesions. Severe inflammatory acne is best treated with oral antibiotics, such as erythromycin or tetracycline. Other treatments include isotretinoin (Accutane), which can help in some severe cases of inflammatory lesions that do not respond to milder treatments, because Accutane can have adverse effects. Oral contraceptives are generally seen as adjunctive therapy and should be utilized in combination with other treatments for AV.

In the classroom, AV can affect student performance because of the emotional distress that generally accompanies active lesions on the face. These adolescents may be distracted from learning because of a preoccupation with their face. In addition, these students may be vulnerable to peer teasing. Therefore, teachers should be sensitive to adolescents who may have severe cases of AV, and a referral to the school counselor may be appropriate.

There are several areas of future research in the area of AV. Certain forms of AV may be resistant to oral and topical antibiotics. According to Krowchuk (2000), researchers in the United Kingdom found that cases of acne resistant to antibiotics rose from 34.5% in 1991 to 60% in 1996. Because multiple factors influence effectiveness of antibiotic treatment, studies clarifying what strains of AV are actually treatment resistant are needed. New treatments or therapies for treatment-resistant AV are also needed. Another area for future research is investigating and clarifying the exact relationship between microbial organisms and the inflammation that creates AV. *P. acnes* is the predominant microorganism in the pilosebaceous follicle, and although *P. acnes* is not pathogenic, it is the main target of oral and topical antibiotic treatments. Burkhart et al. (1999) suggest that future research should clarify how *P. acnes* and other microorganisms are involved in acne inflammation via its interaction with other chemical properties.

REFERENCES

Burkhart, C. G., Burkhart, C. N., & Lehmann, P. F. (1999). Acne: A review of immunologic and microbiologic factors. *Postgraduate Medical Journal, 75*(884), 328–331.

Krowchuk, D. P. (2000). Treating acne: A practical guide. *Adolescent Medicine, 84*(4), 811–828.

White, G. M. (1998). Recent findings in the epidemiologic evidence, classification, and subtypes of acne vulgaris. *Journal of the American Academy of Dermatology, 39*(2/3), S34–S37.

Jennie Kaufman Singer
California Dept. of Corrections, Region 1 Parole Outpatient Clinic

ACROCALLOSAL SYNDROME

Acrocallosal syndrome (ACS) is a genetic disorder that is apparent at birth. The disorder is typically characterized by underdevelopment or absence of the corpus callosum and by mental retardation. However, other associated symptoms may be variable, even among affected members of the same family.

ACS is believed to be a rare condition, but prevalence is unknown and has not been studied in detail. Considered at first to be sporadic, the syndrome has more recently been ascribed to an autosomal recessive gene, on the basis of its observation in two siblings (Schinzel, 1988) and in two unrelated patients, each born to consanguineous parents (Salgado, Ali, & Castilla, 1989; Temtamy & Meguid, 1989). True and confirmed etiology remains unknown.

There have been no reports of prenatal diagnosis of this syndrome. However, certain manifestations such as polydactyly and cerebral malformations can be detected by ultrasound examination during the second trimester (Hendricks, Brunner, Haagen, & Hamel, 1990). In view of the variability of the major clinical manifestations, prenatal detection of this syndrome may not be possible in all cases.

Characteristics

1. Macrocephaly, large anterior fontanel, epicanthal folds, prominent occiput, and bulging forehead
2. Low-set posteriorly rotated ears
3. Down-slanting palpebral fissures, exotropia, protruding eyeballs, and hypertelorism
4. Broad and short nose and anteverted nostrils
5. Short upper lip and high arched cleft palate
6. Umbilical and inguinal hernia
7. Postaxial polydactyly of the fingers and toes, bifid terminal phalanges of the thumbs, and tapered fingers
8. Hypotonia
9. Hypoplasia or agenesis of corpus callosum, seizures, and hyperreflexia
10. Hypospadias and hypogonadism
11. Mental, motor, and speech retardation

Treatment of ACS is entirely symptomatic, and diagnosis of the disorder is difficult due to similarities with other conditions. ACS is most often compared with Greig syndrome (Greig, 1926), which is characterized by similar finger anomalies. However, the higher frequency and severity of syndactyly and the rarity of mental retardation in Greig syndrome have distinguished this condition from ACS (Schinzel, 1982).

Special education approaches 100% in cases of ACS, but learning and academic skills vary across individuals with the disorder. A child with ACS typically qualifies for special education services under multiply handicapped due to health problems and speech and language delays accompanied by mental retardation. In addition, occupational therapy is often required.

Prognosis is poor for children with ACS, and future research focuses on etiology and prevention of this serious disorder.

REFERENCES

Greig, D. M. (1926). Oxycephaly. *Edinburgh Medical Journal, 33,* 189–218.

Hendricks, H. J. E., Brunner, H. G., Haagen, T. A. M., & Hamel, B. C. J. (1990). Acrocallosal syndrome. *American Journal of Medical Genetics, 35,* 443–446.

Salgado, L. J., Ali, C. A., & Castilla, E. E. (1989). Acrocallosal syndrome in a girl born to consanguineous parents. *American Journal of Medical Genetics, 32,* 298–300.

Schinzel, A. (1982). Acrocallosal syndrome. *American Journal of Medical Genetics, 12,* 201–203.

Schinzel, A. (1988). The acrocallosal syndrome in first cousins: Widening of the spectrum of clinical finding and further indication of autosomal recessive inheritance. *Journal of Medical Genetics, 25,* 332–336.

Temtamy, S. A., & Meguid, N. A. (1989). Hypogentialism in the acrocallosal syndrome. *American Journal of Medical Genetics, 32,* 301–305.

Carey E. Cooper
University of Texas at Austin

ACRODYSOSTOSIS

Acrodysostosis is also called acrodysplasia, Arkless-Graham syndrome, or Maroteaux-Malamut syndrome. It is an extremely rare disease in which bones and skeleton are deformed. The hands and feet are short with stubby fingers and toes (National Organization for Rare Disorders [NORD], 2000; PDR, 2000). The cause of the disease is unknown at this time (Medlineplus, 2000; PDR, 2000)

Both sexes are equally likely to be affected. It tends to occur with older parental age (Medlineplus, 2000).

Characteristics (Medlineplus, 2000; National Library of Medicine [NLM] 1999; NORD, 2000)

1. Abnormally short and malformed bones of the hands and feet (peripheral dysostosis).
2. Underdevelopment of the nose (nasal hypoplasia)—short nose with low bridge, broad and dimpled tip, anteverted nostrils, long philtrum, and epicanthal folds.
3. Mild to moderate growth deficiency—short stature and unusual head and facial (craniofacial) features.
4. Characteristic facial features may include a flattened, underdeveloped (hypoplastic) pug nose, an underdeveloped upper jaw bone (maxillary hypoplasia), widely spaced eyes (ocular hypertelorism), and an extra fold of skin on either side of the nose that may cover the eyes' inner corners (epicanthal folds).
5. Mental deficiency in approximately 90% of affected children.
6. Short head, measured front to back (brachycephaly).
7. Other abnormalities of the skin, genitals, teeth, and skeleton.
8. It frequently co-occurs with middle ear infections.

There is no treatment or cure for this syndrome. It is recommended that the child be referred to a geneticist (specialist in inherited diseases) and the child should be monitored by a medical professional (NORD, 2000).

If the skeletal deformities are severe enough to interfere with academic progress, children with this disorder would receive services under orthopedically impaired. Depending on the extent of the cognitive deficiency, the child may receive services for Learning Disability, Mental Retardation, or both. Services could include resource classes, physical therapy, and occupational therapy. If the child's cognitive or physical impairment is not severe enough, the 504 modifications with technology to modify the regular curriculum might be sufficient.

The prognosis of the children who have acrodysostosis varies depending on the degree of skeletal involvement and mental retardation (Medlineplus, 2000). The treatment should be provided according to the child's condition.

REFERENCES

Medlineplus. (2000). Acrodysostosis condition. Retrieved from http://medlineplus.adam.com/ency/article/001248.htm

National Library of Medicine. (1999, October 27). Acrodysostosis condition. Retrieved from http://www.nlm.nih.gov/mesh/jablonski/syndromes/syndrome005.html

National Organization for Rare Disorders. (2000). Acrodysostosis condition. Retrieved from http://www.stepstn.com/cgi-win/nord.exe?proc=Redirect&type=rdb_sum&id=613.htm

PDR medical dictionary (2nd ed.). (2000). Montvale, NJ: Medical Economics.

Nina Cheng
University of Texas at Austin

ACROMEGALY

Acromegaly is characterized by excessive growth due to oversecretion of growth hormone, which is produced in the liver and other tissues and is secreted by the anterior pituitary gland. Oversecretion of growth hormone is often caused by the presence of a benign pituitary tumor (adenoma) but can also be caused by lung and pancreas tumors that stimulate the excessive production of substances similar to growth hormone (Berkow, Beers, & Fletcher, 1997).

The prevalence of acromegaly is approximately 50–70 cases per million. Three or four infants who will develop acromegaly are born per million births (Novartis Pharmaceuticals Corporation, 1999). It has been estimated that there are 15,000 cases of acromegaly within the United States. Its onset most commonly occurs between the ages of 30 and 50 years (Berkow et al., 1997), but it is not usually diagnosed until 10 years after increased hormone secretion has begun (Novartis Pharmaceuticals Corporation, 1999). Reasons accounting for this delay of diagnosis include slow development of symptoms, a variety of clinical signs and symptoms, and the need to rule out other medical conditions with similar signs and symptoms (Novartis Pharmaceuticals Corporation, 1999). If excessive growth of the same nature occurs by the age of 10 years, it is referred to as gigantism (accelerated growth).

Acromegaly is diagnosed through the presence of elevated blood levels of growth hormone (GH) or insulin-like growth factor I (IGF-I). X rays confirm the thickening of bones. Pituitary tumors are the cause of acromegaly in 90% of cases (Tierny, McPhee, & Papadakis, 2000). A CT scan or magnetic resonance imaging (MRI) examines the site and size of possible tumors. If there is no tumor, these same tests can be used to detect the enlargement of organs or the source of excessive growth hormone excretion.

Additional symptoms associated with acromegaly include carpal tunnel syndrome, sleep apnea, goiter, colon polyps, and hypertension. Weight gain is frequent and largely attributable to muscle and bone growth. Diabetes sometimes occurs due to insulin resistance, and arthritis and joint pain are common. The heart may become enlarged, increasing the chance of heart failure. Headaches are common due to pressure caused by the tumor. As tissues enlarge, they may compress nerves including the optic nerve, sometimes resulting in loss of vision.

Characteristics

1. Enlarged hands, feet, jaw, facial features, and internal organs
2. Coarsening facial features and deeper voice
3. Excessive perspiration
4. Amenorrhea
5. Sweaty handshake

Treatment of acromegaly is primarily medical. Initially, the tumor is either removed through surgery or destroyed through radiation therapy. Medication such as octreotide or bromocriptine slow or block the production of growth hormone (Berkow et al., 1997). When surgical treatment is successful, normal pituitary function returns, resulting in the decrease of soft tissue swelling. Bone enlargement, however, is permanent (Tierney et al., 2000). In children, because excessive growth hormone is secreted before the bones stop growing, the result is abnormal height and excessive bone growth.

Acromegaly, referred to as gigantism when seen in children, is not necessarily accompanied by cognitive deficiencies. Special education issues are most often related to physical accommodations or services such as occupational therapy.

Unlike adults with acromegaly, children who are treated for gigantism do not become deformed. Other symptoms persist, however, such as swollen tissue around bones, delayed puberty, and incomplete development of the genitals (Berkow et al., 1997). One study has shown that the life expectancy of individuals with acromegaly is approximately 10 years lower than that of nonacromegalic individuals (Novartis Pharmaceuticals Corporation, 1999).

REFERENCES

Berkow, R., Beers, M. H., & Fletcher, A. J. (Eds.). (1997). *Merck manual of medical information: Home edition.* Whitehouse Station, NJ: Merck Research Laboratories.

Novartis Pharmaceuticals Corporation. (1999). The acromegaly infosource. Retrieved from http://www.acromegalyinfo.com

Tierney, L. M., Jr., McPhee, S. J., & Papadakis, M. A. (Eds.). (2000). *Current medical diagnosis and treatment* (39th ed.). New York: Lange Medical Books/McGraw-Hill.

Kathryn L. Guy
University of Texas at Austin

Nancy L. Nussbaum
Austin Neurological Clinic

ACROMESOMELIC DYSPLASIA (ACROMESOMELIC DWARFISM)

Acromesomelic dysplasia is a form of dwarfism characterized by premature fusion of the areas of growth (epiphyses) in the long bones of the arms and legs. Affected individuals have severely shortened forearms, lower legs, and short stature (short-limbed dwarfism).

Acromesomelic dysplasia is extremely rare. It is inherited in an autosomal recessive manner. Two distinct clinical forms, distinguished by different X-ray and biochemical findings, have been described. The Maroteaux type is caused by an abnormal gene in Chromosome 9. The Hunter-Thompson type has been traced to Chromosome 20.

Characteristics

1. Prominent forehead, slightly flattened face, and short nose
2. Short limbs, especially the forearms and lower leg below the knee
3. Progressive inward curving of the lower spine (kyphosis) as the child ages
4. Linear growth deficiency that becomes more obvious with increasing age
5. Short, broad hands and feet
6. Mild lag in motor development
7. Normal intelligence

There is no specific treatment or cure for this disorder. In the future, therapy directed toward correcting the defective gene offers some promise.

Children with acromesomelic dysplasia may benefit from modifications in the classroom, such as provision of an appropriately sized desk and chair. Evaluation and treatment by occupational and physical therapists may be needed to address the lag in the motor development. These children should be treated in an age-appropriate manner and not according to their short stature.

Evaluation of a small number of adults with this problem showed that they had normal intelligence. Final heights in these individuals ranged from 38 to 49 inches.

Families may benefit from additional emotional support as they learn coping strategies and problem solving abilities to help integrate their child into society. For more information and support, please contact

- Restricted Growth Association: P.O. Box 8, Countesthorpe, Leicestershire, LE8-5ZS, United Kingdom (44) 116-2478913.
- Little People of America, Inc.: P.O. Box 745, Lubbock, TX 79408, (888) 572-2001, e-mail: lpadatabase@juno.com.
- International Center for Skeletal Dysplasia: Saint Joseph's Hospital, 7620 York Road, Towson, MD 21204, (410) 337-1250.

REFERENCES

Jones, K. L. (1997). *Smith's recognizable patterns of human malformation* (5th ed.). Philadelphia: W. B. Saunders.

National Organization for Rare Disorders (1999). Acromesomelic dysplasia. Retrieved from http://www.stepstn.con/cgiwin/nord.exe?proc=GetDocument&rectype=0&recnum=1087

Barry H. Davison
Ennis, Texas

Joan W. Mayfield
Baylor Pediatric Specialty Services
Dallas, Texas

ACROMICRIC DYSPLASIA

Initially described by Spranger (1971), acromicric dysplasia is a rare bone deformity mainly characterized by reduced bone growth; this results in facial anomalies, short limbs, and abnormally limited growth. It is very closely linked to geleophysic dysplasia, sharing many of the same characteristics, and there has been speculation as to whether these two are in fact the same disorder but have different methods of inheritance. It is possible that acromicric dysplasia is inherited through a dominant gene: There have been a few cases in which the disorder was present in multiple family members; however, these cases were the minority, and the possibility of genetic inheritance is still debated.

Biochemically speaking, acromicric dysplasia is caused by disorganization at the site of bone growth—abnormal cells, isolated clusters of cells, and abnormal levels of collagen forming rims around the cells (Maroteaux, Stanescu, Stanescu, & Rappaport, 1986).

Characteristics

1. Facial deformities
2. Shortened limbs
3. Abnormally short stature
4. Cell disorganization at growth sites

Children with acromicric dysplasia display normal intelligence levels. Accordingly, these children will mostly likely be placed in inclusive programming if chronic health issues and treatment do not prevent regular school attendance. The physical anomalies may present some issues in terms of social acceptance and self-esteem; therefore, counseling may be supportive for individual problems as they arise. It may be necessary for a parent, teacher, or nurse to educate a child's class on acromicric dysplasia to help with the adjustment and socialization.

This condition may well include progressive cardiac involvement, but such involvement can be mild and asymptomatic in some children (Jones, 1997); therefore, ongoing medical monitoring is a natural course.

REFERENCES

Jones, K. L. (1997). *Smith's recognizable patterns of human malformation.* Philadelphia: W. B. Saunders.

Maroteaux, P., Stanescu, R., Stanescu, V., & Rappaport, R. (1986). Acromicric dysplasia. *American Journal of Medical Genetics, 24,* 447–459.

Spranger, J. W. (1971). Geleophysic dwarfism: A "focal" mucopolysaccharidosis? *Lancet, 2,* 97.

Allison Katz
Rutgers University

ADDISON'S DISEASE

First described by Dr. Thomas Addison in the mid-1800s, Addison's disease (adrenocortical insufficiency, hypocortisolism) is an endocrine disorder characterized by a lack of production of the hormones *cortisol* and *aldosterone,* both of which are produced by the adrenal cortex. Each individual has two adrenal glands, one above each kidney. Each adrenal gland has two parts. The inner part is called the medulla, and the outer part is called the cortex. Thus, the outer part of the adrenal gland is responsible for producing the hormones cortisol and aldosterone. Cortisol has many effects on the body, including maintaining blood pressure, maintaining cardiovascular functions, and slowing the immune system's inflammatory response. In addition, cortisol balances the effects of insulin in breaking down sugar for energy and regulating the metabolism of proteins, carbohydrates, and fats. Aldosterone helps the body maintain blood pressure, water, and salt balance. Together these two hormones have a role in the proper functioning of our major organs. Thus, Addison's disease has a significant impact on the body's functions.

Although there are no exact statistics on the incidence of Addison's disease, most studies report that this disease effects between 1 and 4 individuals per 100,000 (Merck Research Laboratories, 1992). Addison's disease occurs in all age groups and occurs slightly more frequently in females than in males (Marguiles, 1998). In approximately 70% of the cases, onset is due to the gradual destruction of the adrenal cortex by the body's own immune system. Tuberculosis is the second leading cause, accounting for another 20% of the cases. The remainder of cases are caused by chronic infections (especially fungal and cytomegalovirus infection in association with AIDS), cancer metastasis, and surgical removal of the adrenal glands.

Characteristics

1. Fatigue that may steadily worsen
2. Loss of appetite
3. Weight loss
4. Low blood pressure
5. Lightheadedness, especially upon standing
6. Nausea
7. Vomiting
8. Diarrhea
9. Muscles that are weak and spasm
10. Irritability
11. Depression
12. Craving for salty foods
13. Darkening of the skin in exposed and unexposed areas of the body

Treatment of Addison's disease consists of hormone replacement therapy. Cortisol is replaced orally in the form of hydrocortisone tablets divided into morning and afternoon doses. Aldosterone is replaced by fludrocortisone (a synthetic steroid) tablets taken daily. The doses of each of these hormones are adjusted for the individual's size and any coexisting medical conditions. Because the disease is chronic, replacement hormones must be taken for life.

Children with this disorder may be classified under Other Health Impairment. They may need a school schedule that includes rest periods, a shortened school day, or both. Peer helpers may be needed to assist students during the day. Also, easy access to restrooms and the health or nurse's office should be available to the student. In addition, psychological services may be needed to deal with chronic health concerns and other mental health issues. Parents should consult with the school psychologist in their district to discuss any academic needs with respect to chronic illness.

The prognosis for Addison's disease is good, and patients can lead a normal, crisis-free life as long as replacement hormones are taken properly and absorbed. Individuals with Addison's disease should wear an identification bracelet or necklace to ensure proper treatment in an emergency because additional doses of hydrocortisone may be needed so the body can effectively deal with the additional stress associated with trauma.

REFERENCES

Merck Research Laboratories. (1992). Addison's disease. *Merck manual* (16th ed.). New Jersey: Merck Research Laboratories.

Marguiles, P. (1997–1998). National Addison's Disease Foundation. Retrieved from http://www.medhelp.org/nadf

MaryLynne D. Filaccio
Rik Carl D'Amato
University of Northern Colorado

ADRENAL HYPERPLASIA, CONGENITAL

Congenital adrenal hyperplasia is a family of inherited disorders that result from the inability of the adrenal glands to sufficiently synthesize hormones known as corticosteroids. The various types of congenital adrenal hyperplasia are caused by enzyme deficiencies in different stages of hormone production.

The most common enzyme deficiency is 21-hydroxylase, which is necessary for the production of two adrenal steroid hormones, cortisol and aldosterone. Cortisol is responsible for maintaining the body's energy supply, blood sugar level, and reaction to stress. Aldosterone is a salt-retaining hormone, which maintains the balance of salt and water in the body. In response to the low cortisol levels, the anterior pituitary gland produces high amounts of adrenocorticotropin hormone (ACTH) to activate the adrenal glands to produce cortisol. The high levels of ACTH result in the overproduction of cortisol precursors, which are used to produce an excessive amount of androgens. Excess androgens cause abnormal sexual development, such as masculinized external genitalia in female newborns. An additional defect in aldosterone synthesis may be present, resulting in the inability to conserve urinary sodium. Deficient aldosterone in addition to insufficient cortisol production is labeled the salt-wasting form of the disorder. Individuals with only deficient cortisol production have the non-salt-wasting form of congenital adrenal hyperplasia. The third type of congenital adrenal hyperplasia is the milder, nonclassic form, which has a later onset between early childhood and puberty (McKusick, 1994; Plum & Cecil, 1996).

About 95% of cases of congenital adrenal hyperplasia are caused by 21-hydroxylase deficiency, affecting one in 13,000–15,000 births in the general population. About half the cases have the salt-wasting form of the disorder (McKusick, 1994). Nonclassical adrenal hyperplasia affects approximately 1 in 20 Ashkenazi Jews, 1 in 40 Hispanic persons, 1 in 50 Yugoslavians, and 1 in 300 Italians. Congenital adrenal hyperplasia is an autosomal recessive disorder. The defective gene that causes 21-hydroxylase deficiency is located on the short arm of Chromosome 6 (Carlson, Obeid, Kanellopoulou, Wilson, & New, 1999).

Characteristics

1. Symptoms include muscle weakness, nausea, vomiting, anorexia, irritability, depression, hyperpigmentations of the skin, hypotension, lack of tolerance to cold temperatures, and the inability of the body to effectively respond to stress (Pang, 2000).
2. A child will grow rapidly and develop pubic hair during early childhood.
3. Female newborns may have an abnormally enlarged clitoris and joining labial folds, resulting in ambiguous external genitalia. In rare cases females are raised as males.
4. Male newborns do not exhibit physical signs except for pigmentation around the genitalia (Wynbrandt & Ludman, 2000).
5. An infant with the salt-wasting form may experience vomiting, poor weight gain, poor feeding, drowsiness, diarrhea, dehydration, and circulatory collapse. Without treatment the infant will go into shock and die (Plum & Cecil, 1996).
6. During puberty girls with the mild form of the disorder will develop excess body hair, acne, menstrual irregularity, and in some cases infertility and polycystic ovaries.

Early diagnosis and treatment of congenital adrenal hyperplasia is extremely important, especially for the salt-wasting form of the disorder, which is life threatening. Treatment is aimed at providing the body with the ability to maintain energy, normal growth, and a balance between salt and water. In the non-salt-wasting form of the disease, only cortisol replacement is needed. In the salt-wasting form, it is necessary to replace cortisol, aldosterone, and salt with synthetic hormones such as hydrocortisone and fludrocortisone (Florinef), a salt-retaining hormone. Extra doses of hydrocortisone are important when the child experiences injury, infection, or surgery because the body cannot respond to stress without cortisol (Pang, 2000).

With treatment, children with congenital adrenal hyperplasia can have normal growth and development. However, they must continue receiving cortisol therapy. Without treatment, the child may experience dehydration, electrolyte imbalance, and adrenal crisis. Children under stress such as high fever, serious injury, or vomiting usually need additional cortisol treatment and possibly emergency care (Pang, 2000). Thus, medication may need to be managed at school. Special education services may be available to children with congenital adrenal hyperplasia under Other Health Impairment. A health care plan should be implemented in the child's individual educational plan so that school personnel understand the necessary actions during an emergency (Plumridge, Bennett, Dinno, & Branson, 1993).

If congenital adrenal hyperplasia continues to be treated and monitored throughout life, an individual with the disorder is expected to have a normal life expectancy and live a healthy, productive life. Many individuals do not reach the height potential indicated by family height because they have premature growth spurts and bone aging. The effectiveness and safety of certain drug treatments continue to be investigated. Female fetuses affected with the 21-hydroxylase deficiency form of congenital adrenal hyperplasia may be treated with dexamethasone, a long-acting corticosteroid, early in the pregnancy until birth. As a result, the adrenal glands are suppressed and the external genitalia develop normally (Carlson et al., 1999). In the future researchers will investigate whether enzyme replacement by gene therapy is possible.

REFERENCES

Carlson, A. D., Obeid, J. S., Kanellopoulou, N., Wilson, R. C., & New, M. I. (1999). Congenital adrenal hyperplasia: Update on prenatal diagnosis and treatment. *Journal of Steroid Biochemistry and Molecular Biology, 69,* 19–29.

McKusick, V. A. (Ed.). (1994). *Mendelian inheritance in man: A catalog of human genetic disorders* (11th ed.). Baltimore: Johns Hopkins University Press.

Pang, S. (2000). Congenital adrenal hyperplasia. Retrieved from http://www.magicfoundation.org/cah.html

Plum, F., & Cecil, R. L. (Eds.). (1996). *Cecil textbook of medicine* (20th ed., Vol. 2). St. Louis, MO: W. B. Saunders.

Plumridge, D., Bennett, R., Dinno, N., & Branson, C. (1993). *The student with a genetic disorder.* Springfield, IL: Charles C. Thomas.

Wynbrandt, J., & Ludman, M. D. (2000). *The encyclopedia of genetic disorders and birth defects* (2nd ed.). New York: Facts on File.

Susannah More
University of Texas at Austin

ADRENOCORTICOTROPIC HORMONE (ACTH) DEFICIENCY

Adrenocorticotropic hormone (ACTH) deficiency, sometimes referred to as secondary adrenal insufficiency, is a rare (affecting fewer than 1 in 100,000) and potentially life-threatening form of adrenocortical failure in which there is partial or complete lack of ACTH production and secretion by the anterior pituitary gland (Schmidli, Donald, & Espiner, 1989). ACTH acts to stimulate release of cortisol from the adrenal cortex during both the diurnal rhythm and exposure to stressors. Onset may occur throughout the life span.

Characteristic signs and symptoms of ACTH deficiency include weight loss, anorexia (lack of appetite), vomiting, hyponatremia (sodium deficiency), hypoglycemia, postural hypotension, muscular fatigue or stiffness, hypotonia (loss of muscle tone), muscle weakness, lethargy, general fatigue, and subtle attentional or memory deficits (Brown, 1994). In contrast to Addison's disease, abnormal skin pigmentation and aldosterone hyposecretion are not present (Schmidli et al., 1989). More easily diagnosed in conjunction with various other conditions (see later discussion), ACTH deficiency is more difficult to diagnose when isolated; across a number of studies, a sizable minority of cases display an idiopathic etiology. Additionally, clinician awareness may not be high, and some complex diagnostic work may require referral to specialists (Schmidli et al., 1989).

A number of tests may be administered to diagnose ACTH deficiency. The insulin-induced hypoglycemia test is sometimes considered the gold standard, but it requires close supervision and may not be as safe for children as the metyrapone test (Erturk, Jaffe, & Barkan, 1998). The metyrapone test is very effective, but it may induce adrenal crisis, it requires overnight hospitalization, and metyrapone is at times difficult to obtain for diagnostic use. See Rose et al. (1999) for an outstanding comparison of the metyrapone, high-dose ACTH, and low-dose ACTH tests. Hypothyroidism may mask ACTH deficiency, and it may not be revealed by the aforementioned tests until L-thyroxine therapy has been initiated (Nanao, Miyamoto, Anzo, Tsukuda, & Hasegawa, 1999). The cause of ACTH deficiency may be of hypothalamic (rather than pituitary) origin, and a corticotropin-releasing hormone (CRH) test may be indicated. CT scans or other imaging procedures are often employed as a check for tumors, lesions, or trauma.

There are many likely causes of ACTH deficiency. It has been observed in association with familial history of ACTH deficiency, hypopituitarism (and short stature), pituitary or brain tumor, head trauma, benign intracranial hypertension, cranial radiation therapy, long-term pharmacologic steroid therapy, intermittent high-dose steroid therapy, autoimmune disorders, diabetes mellitus, a likely cleavage enzyme defect, hypothalamic and pituitary lesions, birth injury, infection, and neurosurgery (Rose et al., 1999).

Characteristics

1. Weight loss, anorexia, or vomiting
2. Hypocortisolism, hypoglycemia, or hyponatremia
3. Postural hypotension
4. Muscular fatigue or stiffness, hypotonia, or muscle weakness
5. Lethargy and general fatigue
6. Subtle attentional or memory deficits

Treatment of ACTH deficiency involves replacing cortisol that the adrenal cortex is not being stimulated to produce; this is most often done with daily oral administration of hydrocortisone and additional "stress dosing" as required (Rose et al., 1999). In partial ACTH deficiency, only stress dosing may be needed. In severe cases, intravenous injections of hydrocortisone may be needed during high stress or other crises.

Although treatment is quite effective and many treated children will require no special education support, the period during which ACTH deficiency was untreated may have generated some conditions requiring such services and support (Rose et al., 1999; Schmidli et al., 1989). Being of short stature, underweight, and physically weaker, as well as experiencing delayed growth and development, may require both educational and psychological support. Cognitive (attentional and memory) deficits in the past or present may generate some special educational considerations. Finally, educators should be somewhat knowledgeable about daily and stress dosing requirements, should crises arise in the educational setting. All of these concerns can be exacerbated by the presence of other diseases or conditions with which ACTH deficiency is often associated.

Further research continues on ACTH deficiency and hypothalamic-pituitary-adrenal function across the fields of psychology, psychiatry, neurology, endocrinology, and immunology. The greatest promise of such research is further insight into the etiology and prompt, precise diagnosis of the condition, especially in cases of isolated ACTH deficiency.

REFERENCES

Brown, R. E. (1994). *An introduction to neuroendocrinology.* New York: Cambridge University Press.

Erturk, E., Jaffe, C. A., & Barkan, A. L. (1998). Evaluation of the integrity of the hypothalamic-pituitary-adrenal axis by insulin hypoglycemia test. *Journal of Clinical Endocrinology and Metabolism, 83*(7), 2350–2354.

Nanao, K., Miyamoto, J., Anzo, M., Tsukuda, T., & Hasegawa, Y. (1999). A case of congenital hypopituitarism: Difficulty in the diagnosis of ACTH deficiency due to high serum cortisol levels from a hypothyroid state. *Endocrine Journal, 46*(1), 183–186.

Rose, S. R., Lustig, R. H., Burstein, S., Pitukcheewanont, P., Broome, D. C., & Burghen, G. A. (1999). Diagnosis of ACTH deficiency. *Hormone Research, 52,* 73–79.

Schmidli, R. S., Donald, R. A., & Espiner, E. A. (1989). ACTH deficiency: Problems in recognition and diagnosis. *New Zealand Medical Journal, 102,* 255–257.

Jonathan T. Drummond
Princeton University

ADRENOLEUKODYSTROPHY

Adrenoleukodystrophy (ALD) is an inherited, serious, progressive neurological disorder effecting the adrenal gland and white matter of the nervous system. The defective gene is located within the Xq28 region (Moser, 1997) and is inherited in an X-linked, recessive fashion; only males demonstrate the classic disease. The biochemical defect, an abnormal accumulation of very long chain fatty acids (VLCFA) is common to all forms of the disease, although there are multiple presentations (phenotypes) of the disorder.

Estimates of the incidence of ALD vary, with a range of 1.1 to 1.6 per 100,000 live births (Bezman & Moser, 1998). There is not complete agreement regarding the relative frequency of the different phenotypes of ALD (also discussed in this section), although the childhood cerebral phenotype and adrenomyeloneuropathy (AMN) are consistently found to be the most frequently occurring (Bezman & Moser, 1998). It is reported that up to two thirds of those who have the genetic abnormality escape the most severe phenotype, childhood cerebral form of ALD (CCALD) (Moser, 1997) The rate of occurrence appears to be the same worldwide. ALD has been identified in many ethnic groups, and there appears to be no racial predilection

Characteristics

1. Childhood cerebral form of andrenoleukodystrophy (CCALD):
   - Most common (40% of all cases) and severe form (Melhem, Barker, Raymond, & Moser, 1999).
   - Male child, normal until 4–8 years of age when he presents with attentional and behavioral difficulties and school failure. Poor coordination may be noted.
   - Symptoms rapidly progress, with evidence of increasing motor deficits (progressive ataxial and spasticity, including loss of ambulation), swallowing problems, visual loss (cortical blindness), personality changes, seizures, and dementia. Ongoing deterioration results in a vegetative state, generally within 2 to 3 years of the emergence of initial symptoms.
2. Adolescent cerebral form of adrenoleukodystrophy:
   - Signs and symptoms of cerebral involvement, as in the childhood cerebral form, but are evident between 10 and 21 years.
3. Adult cerebral form of adrenoleukodystrophy:
   - Rapid regression of neurological status presenting after 21 years of age, including dementia, psychiatric disturbances, and spasticity (more in the lower extremities than in the upper extremities (Garside, Rosebush, Levinson, & Mazurek, 1999).
   - Often present with symptoms that are similar to multiple sclerosis; differentiation is important for identification of at-risk family members.

4. Adrenomyeloneuropathy:
   - This is a more indolent form of the disorder, with later age of onset, generally between 20 and 30 years of age.
   - Neurological changes are generally preceded by symptoms of adrenal insufficiency (inability to tolerate mild illnesses, hyperpigmentation; Brett & Lake, 1998)
   - Primary pathology is the white matter of the spinal cord (Sakkubai, Theda, & Moser, 1999). Patients present with progressive spastic paraplegia, sphincter disturbances, peripheral neuropathy, and ataxia (Melhem et al., 1999).
   - Progression is slower than in CCALD; the interval from onset to vegetative state or death is more than 13 years (Brett & Lake, 1998).
5. ADL with Addison's disease only, asymptomatic patients with the biochemical defect of ADL, symptomatic heterozygotes:
   - Five of eight patients followed for Addison's disease only have the biochemical marker for ADL but do not have neurological deterioration (Sakkubai et al., 1999). Identification is important for counseling purposes.
   - Asymptomatic children with ALD (identified biochemically because of their genetic relationship to a known patient) may have evidence of neuropsychological deficits and have MRI changes prior to disease progression (Riva, Mova, & Brussone, 2000).
   - Women who are carriers of the gene may have neurological symptoms (20%, Melhem et al., 1999)—generally motor involvement—late in life (Sakkubai et al., 1999), and up to 50% have abnormalities on neurobehavioral testing (Melhem et al., 1999).

The results of treatment of ADL have been disappointing. The adrenal insufficiency is readily responsive to treatment with oral corticosteroids (Melhem et al., 1999). The neurological manifestations of the disease have not been responsive. Documentation of raised VLCFAs in patients with ALD raised hopes that neurological deterioration could be altered via dietary restriction. Dietary restriction of VLCFAs were unsuccessful in decreasing serum levels of VLCFAs or in halting disease progression (Moser, 1997). Use of Lorenzo's oil, a mixture of glyceryl trioleate (GTO) and glyceryl trierucate (GTE), proved successful in lowering plasma levels of VCLA but has no efficacy upon the neurological progression of the disease in individuals already demonstrating neurological progression (Moser, 1997). There are ongoing attempts to evaluate the efficacy of preventative treatment via Lorenzo's oil in presymptomatic effected individuals. Given the variability of the progression of the disease (e.g., the multiple phenotypes that occur both within and among families), this research is difficult and requires long term follow-up. Initial results indicate that the treatment is not an absolute preventative (Moser, 1997). Bone marrow transplantation (BMT) has been utilized in treating patients with overt, rapid deterioration secondary to ALD. Initial attempts revealed that transplantation was contraindicated in these individuals, with yet more rapid progression of the disease subsequent to transplantation (Moser, 1997). More recent reports of improved neurological outcome in ALD patients' post-BMT has renewed hope that this treatment can be successful for individuals who show early evidence of cerebral involvement (Moser, 1997). Immunosuppression, as a treatment for ALD, has been attempted to reduce the inflammatory brain response that is thought to be a major pathogenic factor in cerebral ALD. This treatment has been unsuccessful to this point (Moser, 1997).

It is difficult to know how best to provide education to children with a severe degenerative neurological disease. Identification is currently important for genetic purposes and presumably will ultimately be important for treatment. Overt, persistent deterioration (loss) in skills and behavior requires medical evaluation. It is important to remember that after the genetic abnormality associated with ALD is identified, the outcome is not clear or predictable.

REFERENCES

Bezman, L., & Moser, H. W. (1998). Incidence of X-linked adrenoleukodystrophy and the relative frequency of its phenotypes. *American Journal of Medical Genetics, 76,* 415–419.

Brett, E., & Lake, B. D. (1997). Progressive neurometabolic brain diseases. In E. Brett (Ed.), *Pediatric neurology* (3rd ed.). New York: Churchill Livingstone.

Garside, S., Rosebush, P. I., Levinson, J. J., & Mazurek, M. F. (1999). Late-onset adrenoleukodystrophy associated with long-standing psychiatric symptoms. *Journal of Clinical Psychiatry, 60,* 460–468.

Melhem, E. R., Barker, P. B., Raymond, G. V., & Moser, H. W. (1999). X-linked adrenoleukodystrophy in children: Review of genetic, clinical and MR imaging characteristics. *American Journal of Roentgenology, 173*(6), 1575–1581.

Moser, H. W. (1997). Adrenoleukodystrophy: Phenotype, genetics, pathogenesis, and therapy. *Brain, 120,* 1485–1508.

Riva, D., Mova, S. M., & Brussone, M. G. (2000). Neuropsychological testing may predict early progression of asymptomatic adrenoleukodystrophy. *Neurology, 54,* 1651–1655.

Sakkubai, N., Theda, C., & Moser, H. W. (1999). Perioxisomal disorders. In Swaiman & Ashwal (Eds.), *Pediatric neurology: Principle and practice* (3rd ed.). St. Louis, MO: Mosby.

Greta N. Wilkening
University of Colorado Health Sciences Center
The Children's Hospital

AFIBRINOGENEMIA, CONGENITAL

Congenital afibrinogenemia is a rare blood disorder that causes improper clotting of the blood. It is also referred to as hypofibrinogenemia. Afibrinogenemia is an inherited condition that is caused by an autosomal recessive gene. It is found in both males and females.

Congenital afibrinogenemia is characterized by problems with the functionality of fibrinogen, a protein in the body that is necessary for the clotting of blood. This condition can be due to a lack of fibrinogen or to a defect in existing fibrinogen.

Diagnosis at birth is common because uncontrollable bleeding from the umbilical cord is often found. Later in life, bleeding in the cerebrum and spleen areas is also found to be common (Neerman-Arbez, Honsberger, Antonarakis, & Morris, 1999).

Patients diagnosed with congenital afibrinogenemia show no major mutations or deletions in the vicinity of the gene responsible for the production of fibrinogen (Duga et al., 2000). It is most likely that this disorder is caused by missense mutations in the gene and the corresponding problems with fibrinogen secretion. It is also likely that there are multiple mutations causing the condition. Affected people tend to respond well to fibrinogen replacement techniques, and the breakdown times of this substance in the body are normal.

Characteristics

1. Failure of blood to clot
2. Absence or malfunction of fibrinogen
3. Possible uncontrolled bleeding from umbilical cord at birth
4. Possible spontaneous bleeding in areas of the cranium, spleen, or both

Treatment for congenital afibrinogenemia is usually preventive. Patients may be transfused with plasma (the liquid portion of the blood) or cryoprecipitate (a blood product containing concentrated fibrinogen) to treat bleeding episodes or in preparation for surgery needed to treat other conditions. Children with this condition should be immunized with the hepatitis B vaccine because of the increased risk of developing hepatitis due to transfusion.

Because this disorder is genetic, children born with the condition will most likely be born into families in which multiple people have the disorder; from a psychological standpoint, this may be much better for the child's mental outlook. Seeing others who are affected could help normalize the situation for someone with a disorder this rare and this unusual. Children who are in school must of course take many precautions against routine cuts and scrapes that could begin to bleed excessively. Additionally, teachers, nurses, and other responsible adults in the school system should be made aware of the situation. However, much worry can be eliminated with preventive care and the administration of fibrinogen on a regular basis so that there is always some present in the patient's system. However, some patients may develop antibodies (inhibitors) to fibrinogen with treatment, or they may develop other complications such as gastrointestinal bleeding, cranial bleeding, or bleeding from the mucous membranes. Therefore, the prognosis for children with this condition is dependent on consistent and appropriate medical management. Genetic counseling may be helpful for families and the child when he or she reaches childbearing age.

REFERENCES

Duga, S., Asselta, R., Santagostino, E., Zeinali, S., Simonic, T., Malcovati, M., et al. (2000). Missense mutations in the human beta fibrinogen gene cause congenital afibrinogenemia by impairing fibrinogen secretion. *Blood, 95,* 1336–1341.

Neerman-Arbez, M., Honsberger, A., Antonarakis, S. E., & Morris, M. A. (1999). Deletion of the fibrogen alpha-chain gene (FGA) causes congenital afibrogenemia. *Journal of Clinical Investigation, 103,* 215–218.

Allison Katz
Rutgers University

AGAMMAGLOBULINEMIAS, PRIMARY

Primary agammaglobulinemias are a group of rare immune deficiencies characterized by a lack of antibodies to fight disease and by dysfunction of B lymphocytes (specialized white blood cells that produce antibodies). Other names for this syndrome include antibody deficiency, gammaglobulin deficiency, and immunoglobulin deficiency. There are many subdivisions of primary agammaglobulinemia that describe the specific deficiency in a given patient. Acquired immunodeficiency syndrome (AIDS) is perhaps the most well known of these subdivisions.

Antibodies, which are vital to the body's ability to fight disease, are responsible for killing any foreign cells that enter the body, such as bacteria, viruses, and other toxic substances. Thus, they protect the body from disease and form the basis of the immune system. These antibodies are composed of immunoglobulins—proteins that are produced internally by cells such as B lymphocytes. These B lymphocytes, in addition to T lymphocytes (better known as killer T cells), search out these foreign cells and produce antibodies that are tailored to kill the specific invading cell. When the function of these lymphocytes is suppressed due to an immunoglobulin deficiency such as in the case of primary agammaglobulinemia, the body is increasingly subject to infection.

In some cases, this condition has been linked to genetic

inheritance (Smart & Ochs, 1997). It can also be caused by the presence of a secondary condition that impairs the immune system, by an autoimmune disease, or by abnormally excessive cell growth.

Characteristics

1. Weakened immune system
2. Susceptibility to infection and illness
3. Lack of gammaglobulins
4. Inability to produce antibodies

Treatment for primary agammaglobulinemia ranges with the specific subdivision of the disease. The overall goal, however, is to reduce the number and severity of infections—without treatment, a minor infection can become severe and eventually fatal. Patients are usually given gamma globulins to supplement the immune system. These may come in injection form, or in cases in which gamma globulins are needed quickly, they may be given by plasma transfusion directly into a vein, because many antibodies are contained in plasma. In cases in which an infection is already in progress, patients can be given high-titer gamma globulin in high doses and antibiotics in the case of bacterial infections. The lives of many people with primary agammaglobulinemia have been improved with proper treatments.

Schoolchildren with primary agammaglobulinemia will need special care and special precautions. These children may be undergoing regular treatments to receive gamma globulins to boost their immune systems; therefore, they may need to miss abnormally large amounts of school for doctor's appointments, tests, and hospital stays. However, perhaps more important is that the parents and teachers of children with primary agammaglobulinemia will have to be extraordinarily vigilant to minimize the chances of exposure to sickness and infection for the child; this is indeed a very daunting task. Additionally, it requires the child to be aware of his or her condition, to be able to explain it, to have the confidence to refuse contact with peers who may be sick, and to be able to take steps to prevent infections in day-to-day life. Peers of a child with primary agammaglobulinemia may need to be educated about the disorder, and an affected child will most certainly need family support and counseling to aid in attempts to normalize day-to-day life.

REFERENCE

Smart, B. A., & Ochs, H. D. (1997). The molecular basis and treatment of primary immunodeficiency disorders. *Current Opinions in Pediatrics, 9,* 570–576.

Allison Katz
Rutgers University

AGENESIS OF THE CORPUS CALLOSUM

Agenesis of the corpus callosum (ACC) is a congenital disorder characterized by partial to complete absence of the corpus callosum. The incidence of the disorder is difficult to estimate because many individuals with ACC are relatively asymptomatic and may never present for evaluation. However, Ashwal (1994) reports that ACC occurs in approximately 1–3 births per 1,000.

Characteristics

1. The central diagnostic features on magnetic resonance imaging (MRI) or CT scan are partial to total absence of the corpus callosum. The septum pellucidum is also typically absent. The lateral ventricles are shifted laterally, leaving a large subarachnoid interhemispheric space. The third ventricle is enlarged. The occipital horns of the lateral ventricles are dilated, creating an appearance resembling rabbit ears or teardrops.
2. Commissural fibers that form remain ipsilateral, creating large bundles of Probst.
3. In isolation, ACC is not life threatening and may produce little if any clinically significant symptomatology.
4. ACC is often associated with or the consequence of other congenital anomalies that can result in a wide variety of symptoms ranging from mild cognitive dysfunction to severe mental retardation to failure to thrive and death.

Multiple etiologies have been reported for ACC. Sporadic cases may result from vascular or inflammatory lesions; those occurring prior to the 10th–12th week of gestation result in complete agenesis, whereas later-occurring lesions result in partial dysgenesis (Gupta & Lilford, 1995). Sporadic cases have also been found in association with fetal alcohol syndrome, Dandy-Walker syndrome, Leigh's syndrome, Arnold-Chiari II syndrome, maternal toxoplasmosis, maternal rubella, and inborn errors of metabolism (Gupta & Lilford, 1995). Callosal lipoma has been reported to mechanically block the decussation of callosal fibers. Factors affecting neuronal differentiation and migration can affect callosal development as well (Utsunomiya, Ogasawara, Hayashi, Hashimoto, & Okazaki, 1997). ACC can be transmitted as an autosomal dominant or sex-linked trait, or by means of genetic abnormalities of Chromosomes 8, 11, and 13–15. Given these multiple etiologies, ACC can be found to occur (a) in isolation, (b) in combination with other CNS and somatic anomalies, or (c) as a central feature of another syndrome.

When ACC occurs in isolation (Type I), it is relatively asymptomatic. Often, the diagnosis is made as a coincidental finding. However, on very detailed cognitive tasks, subtle difficulties with bimanual coordination and interhemispheric transfer of sensorimotor information have been reported (Klaas, Hannay, Caroselli, & Fletcher, 1999;

Sauerwein & Lassonde, 1994). In keeping with Rourke's theory of white matter dysfunction as a potential cause of nonverbal learning disability (NVLD), an association between ACC and NVLD has been suggested, but thus far, a causal association has not been substantiated (Smith & Rourke, 1995). Several mechanisms have been suggested for the relative lack of symptoms in these individuals, including (a) less hemispheric specialization, leading to bilateral representation of cognitive functions; (b) simple behavioral compensation (e.g., "crossed" self-cueing); (c) greater reliance on ipsilateral pathways; (d) greater reliance on subcortical pathways (e.g., collicular, thalamic, etc.); and (e) greater reliance on the anterior and posterior commissures (Smith & Rourke, 1995).

ACC can also occur in combination with a variety of other congenital anomalies (Type II). Gupta and Lilford (1995) report that up to 85% of postmortem cases of ACC also show other CNS abnormalities. Seizures occur in approximately 42% of Type II cases. Associated neurological problems include hydrocephalus, heterotopias, cortical dysplasia, porencephaly, pachygyria, and micrencephaly (Utsunomiya et al., 1997). ACC is a characteristic feature of Aicardi, Andermann, and Sharpiro syndromes (Ashwal, 1994). In general, the constellation of neurological and neuropsychological findings in the Type II group is more dependent on the comorbid abnormalities than on ACC per se.

ACC and associated anomalies can be identified prenatally by transvaginal sonography and CT scan. After ACC is identified, genetic testing and counseling are recommended. Children identified with ACC in isolation have an excellent prognosis for normal intellectual development and for living a normal and productive life. When severe CNS and somatic abnormalities are identified, difficult questions regarding continuation of pregnancy may arise (Gupta & Lilford, 1995). Often, symptoms of Type II ACC are easily observable at birth and are generally diagnosed by the age of 2 years. Children who manifest developmental delays and seizures should also be screened for metabolic disorders (National Institute of Neurological Disorders and Stroke [NINDS], 2000). Treatment and special education considerations of ACC are largely dependent on the nature and severity of the associated anomalies in a given individual.

REFERENCES

Ashwal, S. (1994). Congenital structural defects. In S. Manning (Ed.), *Pediatric neurology: Principles and practice* (pp. 440–442). St. Louis, MO: Mosby.

Gupta, J. K., & Lilford, R. J. (1995). Assessment and management of fetal agenesis of the corpus callosum. *Prenatal Diagnosis, 15,* 301–312.

Klaas, P. A., Hannay, J. H., Caroselli, J. S., & Fletcher, J. M. (1999). Interhemispheric transfer of visual, auditory, tactile, and visuomotor information in children with hydrocephalus and partial agenesis of the corpus callosum. *Journal of Clinical and Experimental Neuropsychology, 21*(6), 837–850.

National Institute of Neurological Disorders and Stroke. (2000, August 1). Agenesis of the corpus callosum. Retrieved from http://www.ninds.nih.gov/health and medical/disorders/agenesisdoc.htm

Sauerwein, H. C., & Lassonde, M. (1994). Cognitive and sensorimotor functioning in the absence of the corpus callosum: Neuropsychological studies in callosal agenesis and callosotomized patients. *Behavioural Brain Research, 64,* 229–240.

Smith, L. A., & Rourke, B. P. (1995). Callosal agenesis. In B. P. Rourke (Ed.), *Syndrome of nonverbal learning disabilities: Neurodevelopmental manifestations* (pp. 45–92). New York: Guilford Press.

Utsunomiya, H., Ogasawara, T., Hayashi, T., Hashimoto, T., & Okazaki, M. (1997). Dysgenesis of the corpus callosum and associated telencephalic anomalies: MRI. *Neuroradiology, 39,* 302–310.

David M. Tucker and Rebecca Vaurio
Austin Neurological Clinic and University of Texas at Austin

AGORAPHOBIA

Agoraphobia (Greek for *fear of the market*) is fear of being alone in places or situations in which the individual believes that escape might be difficult or embarrassing or in which help may not be available in the event that the individual experiences panic-like symptoms. The fear leads to an avoidance of a variety of situations that could include riding a bus, going into a school building, maintaining attendance for the complete school day, being on a bridge or in an elevator, and riding in cars or attendance at special events like field trips or performances. Children in particular may come up with their own "treatment" for the disorder, in the form of rules—not riding in other people's cars, not waiting in lines, not going to birthday parties, and so on—that are difficult for family members to accommodate.

The 1-year prevalence rate for anxiety disorders in children ages 9–17 is 13% (U.S. Department of Health and Human Services, 2000). In 95% of clinical populations, agoraphobia is frequently diagnosed with a concurrent panic disorder. Two thirds of individuals with agoraphobia are female. Symptoms typically develop in later adolescence (ages 17–18) into midadulthood, so agoraphobia is infrequently diagnosed in young children. The median age for onset of agoraphobia is 27 years of age. The onset may be sudden or gradual in nature. People with agoraphobia often develop the disorder after first experiencing one or more panic attacks without warning; this makes it impossible for them to predict what situation will trigger such a reaction, so the fear is often tied to many possible situations.

Characteristics (adapted from American Psychiatric Association, 1994)

1. Focus of anxiety is on being in situations or places from which escape may not be available in the event an individual experiences incapacitating or extremely embarrassing panic-like symptoms. Fears typically involve clusters of situations.
2. Situations are endured under great duress or with anxiety associated with the fear of experiencing a panic attack. The individual may require the presence of a companion in order to move about normally.
3. Symptoms are not due to the direct physiological effects of medications or other substances or to a medical condition.
4. If an associated medical condition is present (e.g., severe allergy), the fear of being incapacitated or embarrassed by the development of symptoms is clearly in excess of that usually associated with the condition.

The most widely used treatments for phobias consist of behavioral, cognitive-behavioral, and pharmacological interventions. There is relatively little research on the efficacy of traditional psychotherapy in the treatment of agoraphobia (Kendall et al., 1997). The most recent large sample trials of treatments for all anxiety disorders point to the efficacy of behavioral and cognitive-behavioral therapy (CBT). For childhood-onset phobias, contingency management was the only intervention deemed to be well established. Other therapies showing good support in the literature include systematic desensitization, modeling and observational learning, and several cognitive-behavior therapies (CBT). These treatments often incorporate the individual's progressive exposure to fear- or anxiety-provoking stimuli. Graduated exposure, response prevention, and relaxation training have shown consistent positive treatment effects for the disorder. Cognitive therapy, which addresses patterns of cognitive distortions and their relationship to worsening symptoms, has also been effective when the child or adolescent is motivated and able to identify his or her own thoughts and feelings and when extended time is available for treatment. Recently, a parent-training component added to CBT intervention significantly enhanced treatment outcomes when compared with CBT alone (Barrett, Dadds, & Rapee, 1996).

Medical treatments for agoraphobia may involve the use of selective serotonin reuptake inhibitors (SSRIs) such as Prozac, Paxil, Celexa, Zoloft, and Luvox. They generally require 6–8 weeks to achieve effectiveness and need to be periodically monitored for effectiveness. Neither trycyclic antidepressants (Aventyl, Norpramine, and imipramine) nor benzodiazpines have been shown to be more effective than placebo in children, although they may be used to a lesser extent for relief of multiple symptoms.

Special education services may be available to students diagnosed with agoraphobia under specific categories of Other Health Impaired, Severe Emotional Disurbance, or Behavior Disorder if an impact on the child's education can be established; this may be particularly important if the disorder is chronic in nature. Accommodations may also be requested and provided under Section 504 of the Rehabilitation Act of 1973. Due to the nature and scope of the disorder, school attendance may become problematic. Families can benefit from additional counseling and support to effectively implement a treatment plan across both school and home settings.

There is some speculation that early onset of separation anxiety disorder in children is associated with the development of agoraphobia in adolescence and adulthood. Although data on the course of agoraphobia are lacking, retrospective patient accounts indicate that it appears to be a chronic condition that waxes and wanes in severity. Unfortunately, the chronicity of the disorder may be due in part to the lack of appropriate treatment.

REFERENCES

American Psychiatric Association. (1994). *Diagnostic and statistical manual of mental disorders* (4th ed.). Washington, DC: Author.

Barrett, P. M., Dadds, M. R., & Rapee, R. M. (1996). Family treatment of childhood anxiety: A controlled trial. *Journal of Consulting and Clinical Psychology, 64,* 333–342.

Kendall, P. C., Flannery-Schroeder, E., Panicelli-Mindel, S. M., Southam-Gerow, M., Henin, A., & Warman, M. (1997). Therapy for youths with anxiety disorders: A second randomized clinical trial. *Journal of Consulting and Clinical Psychology, 65,* 366–380.

U.S. Department of Health and Human Services. (1999). *Children and mental health in mental health: A report of the Surgeon General.* Rockville, MD: Author.

Daniel Olympia
University of Utah

AGRAPHIA

Agraphia is the loss or impairment of the ability to produce written language and is the result of acquired central nervous system dysfunction (Hinkin & Cummings, 1999). The term *agraphia* is often used interchangeably with dysgraphia. Agraphia may occur in isolation, but more often it is associated with disorders such as aphasia (disordered speech), dyslexia (disorder of reading), and acalculia (disorder of mathematical calculation).

Several classification systems for agraphia exist; however, none is universally accepted. The neurological model characterizes agraphia according to five categories based on the presence or absence of accompanying symptomatology. These categories are pure agraphia, aphasic agraphia, agraphia with alexia, apraxic agraphia, and spatial agraphia (Roeltgen, 1993). The cognitive neuropsychological model classifies agraphias according to patterns of errors in writing and spelling and associated anatomic regions. Lexical agraphia is related to a disturbance in retrieval of information based on visual whole word images and is associated with lesions at the junction of the posterior angular gyrus and the parieto-occipital lobule. Phonological agraphia refers to difficulty decoding word and speech sounds and converting them into letters. It is related to lesions of the supramarginal gyrus or the insula medial to it. Motor agraphia is associated with an impairment in motor functions necessary for writing and has been linked to lesions in the basal ganglia, cerebellum, and corticospinal tracts (Roeltgen, 1993).

The prevalence and incidence rates of agraphia have not been well established. Newman (1998) indicated that at least 10% of the population experiences difficulty with acquiring written language and that agraphia is the primary problem referred to occupational therapists in the school setting.

Characteristics

1. Loss or impairment of the ability to produce written language.
2. Writing may be agrammatical, sparse, fluent, illegible, and messy, and it may contain few substantive words.
3. Intimately associated with aphasia.
4. Deficits in linguistic, visuospatial, or motor components of writing or some combination thereof.

Treatment of agraphia should be tailored to the needs of each child according to a thorough assessment of linguistic, sensorimotor, visuospatial, and cognitive abilities, as well as psychosocial and environmental factors that may affect writing ability (Newman, 1998). It should be determined whether the written language disorder parallels similar oral speech or language problems and whether individual children learn more effectively with phonemic or whole-word approaches (Elbert, 1999). Treatment usually progresses according to three general stages. In the first stage, activities are focused on recall and motor production of graphic and graphemic patterns; this is accomplished by having children reproduce presented letters while their view of the result is shielded. In this way, children develop a kinesthetic sense of letters that is independent of visual control (Newman, 1998). Next, the spelling of single words is emphasized. The final stage involves tasks that require semantic and syntactic linguistic processing, such as forming phrases, sentences, and paragraphs (Shewan & Bandur, 1986). During this stage, Elbert (1999) emphasized the importance of monitoring and regulating planning, drafting, revision, and editing. Children should reproduce symbols by copying first, by dictation second, and by spontaneous writing third. It is recommended that children practice writing skills 30 min per day for a period of 2 years for lasting success (Newman, 1998). Modeling of accurate writing and the use of traceable letter tiles may be used to address agraphia (Elbert, 1999). Elbert (1999) also suggests that teachers reduce and space the introduction of new spelling words and provide agraphic children with structured peer tutoring.

In the special education setting, children with agraphia typically qualify for services as students with learning disabilities (Newman, 1998), as needing occupational therapy, or both. Some students are served under the classification of students with traumatic brain injuries. Occupational therapists and others may devise exercises for individual children to develop necessary writing skills and may provide teachers with strategies to improve academic performance. Children with agraphia are likely to experience feelings of frustration and shame. School psychologists may assess the emotional ramifications of agraphia and design appropriate interventions. Teachers can use peer coaching, aides, and volunteers to help address the needs of agraphic children and provide ample time for the completion of assignments to prevent frustration and failure (Shewan & Bandur, 1986). For children who do not respond to handwriting instruction, compensatory strategies such as the use of a computer or typewriter may be employed.

The prognosis for recovery from agraphia is related to several factors. Younger patients usually recover premorbid levels of functioning to a greater degree than do adults. Consistency and appropriate individualization of treatment that is started in the early stages of the disorder may lead to better outcomes. The site and severity of the lesion also determine the degree of recovery to some extent. Finally, the presence and severity of comorbid disorders such as aphasia may affect the obtained level of previous functions.

Future research will probably focus on the application of computer technology in the retraining of writing abilities and also in the compensation for a lack of those abilities. Ongoing research studies are using neuroimaging techniques to determine the specific anatomic substrates of agraphia and aphasia as a means of achieving a more useful and accurate classification and diagnostic system. Research will also continue in the area of devising and refining treatments of agraphia.

REFERENCES

Elbert, J. C. (1999). Learning and motor skills disorders. In S. D. Netherton, D. Holmes, & E. C. Walker (Eds.), *Child and adolescent psychological disorders* (pp. 24–50). Oxford, England: Oxford University Press.

Hinkin, C. H., & Cummings, J. L. (1999). Agraphia. In J. G. Beaumont, P. M. Kenealy, & M. J. C. Rogers (Eds.), *The Blackwell dictionary of neuropsychology* (pp. 21–31). Boston: Blackwell.

Newman, R. M. (1998). Dysgraphia: Causes and treatment. Retrieved from http://www.dyscalculia.org/Edu563.html

Roeltgen, D. P. (1993). Agraphia. In K. M. Heilman & E. Valenstein (Eds.), *Clinical neuropsychology* (3rd ed., pp. 63–89). New York: Oxford University Press.

Shewan, C. M., & Bandur, D. L. (1986). *Treatment of aphasia: A language oriented approach.* San Diego, CA: College Hill Press.

William M. Acree
Brian D. Johnson
University of Northern Colorado

AICARDI SYNDROME

Aicardi syndrome is a very rare genetic disorder that was first identified and reported in 1965 by Jean Aicardi, a French neurologist (Aicardi, Lefebvre, & Lerique-Koechlin, 1965). It was originally described as consisting of a triad of primary features: infantile spasms, chorioretinal lacunae, and agenesis of the corpus callosum. The condition has been given several other names, generally by combining descriptions of the primary features (e.g., chorioretinal anomalies–corpus callosum agenesis–infantile spasms syndrome or corpus callosum agenesis–ocular anomalies–salaam seizures syndrome). Modern imaging techniques have revealed that corpus callosum agenesis does not occur in all cases and that the presence of several other brain abnormalities (see characteristics) are more characteristic of the disorder than is isolated agenesis of the corpus callosum (Aicardi, 1999). Severe mental and motor developmental delays usually occur, with only a limited number of affected children able to develop some language or to ambulate independently or with assistance. Additional features that may be seen include skull abnormalities; ocular abnormalities; absent or abnormal ribs; vertebral abnormalities, including scoliosis and hemivertebrae; hypotonia; unilateral hip dysplasia; telangiectasia; and recurrent pneumonia (National Library of Medicine, 2001).

The cause of Aicardi syndrome is currently thought to be an X-linked dominant gene mutation occurring postfertilization. The disorder is normally seen only in females due to embryonic lethality in heterozygous males, although two cases of boys with XXY genotype have been reported. The condition is not inherited, with all cases representing new mutations. Birth and early development appear normal. Onset of symptoms is usually between the ages of 3 and 5 months. Initial clinical presentation is commonly flexion spasms in the infant. Severe mental and motor developmental delays are common, although rare cases of normal development have been reported (National Center for Biotechnology Information, 2001).

The incidence rate of Aicardi syndrome is unknown. The number of identified cases is 300–500 worldwide. It has been estimated from a series of cases at tertiary referral centers that 1% to 4% of cases of infantile spasms may be due to Aicardi syndrome (Aicardi, 1999).

Characteristics

1. Classic triad
   - Infantile spasms
   - Chorioretinal lacunae
   - Agenesis of the corpus callosum (complete or partial)
2. New major features (present in most patients studied by magnetic resonance imaging)
   - Cortical malformations (mostly microgyria)
   - Periventricular and subcortical heterotopia
   - Cysts around the third ventricle, choroid plexuses, or both
   - Papillomas of choroid plexuses
   - Optic disc and nerve coloboma
3. Supporting features (present in some cases)
   - Vertebral and costal abnormalities
   - Microphthalmia and other eye abnormalities
   - Split-brain electroencephalogram (dissociated suppression-burst tracing)
   - Gross hemispheric asymmetry

Source: Aicardi (1999)

There is currently no specific treatment for Aicardi syndrome. Seizures and infantile spasms may be treated with medications, including hydrocortisone, adrenocorticotropic hormone (ACTH), and anticonvulsants. In addition to medical management, early and ongoing interventions for mental and motor developmental delays are usually necessary.

Special education services are often needed for severe developmental delays. These services may include physical and occupational therapy, provision of adaptive equipment, and instruction for skill development at the appropriate developmental level for the individual child. The Aicardi Syndrome Foundation and the Aicardi Syndrome Newsletter provide support and information for families with an Aicardi syndrome child and also provide funding for ongoing research (Aicardi Syndrome Foundation, 2001).

Prognosis for children with Aicardi syndrome varies with the severity of the disorder. A more favorable course is associated with milder initial symptoms and later onset. Symptoms tend to worsen with age. Upper respiratory infections can be life threatening. Recurrent pneumonia is a frequent complication. The survival rate of affected children has been estimated at 76% at age 6 years and 40% at age 14 (Aicardi, 1999). Life expectancy is currently thought to be up to 30 years. Research is continuing to determine the precise location of the genetic abnormality and how its effects can be treated or prevented.

REFERENCES

Aicardi, J. (1999). Aicardi syndrome: Old and new findings. *International Pediatrics, 14,* 5–8.

Aicardi, J., Lefebvre, J., & Lerique-Koechlin, A. (1965). A new syndrome: Spasms in flexion, callosal agenesis, ocular abnormalities. *Electroencephalography and Clinical Neurophysiology, 19,* 609–610.

Aicardi Syndrome Foundation. (2001). What is Aicardi syndrome. Retrieved from http://www.aicardi.com/

National Center for Biotechnology Information. (2001). Corpus callosum, agenesis of, with chorioretinal abnormality. Retrieved from http://www3.ncbi.nlm.nih.gov/htbin-post/Omim/dispmim?304050

National Library of Medicine. (2001). Multiple congenital anomaly/mental retardation (MCA/MR) syndromes. Retrieved from http://www.nlm.nih.gov/mesh/jablonski/syndromes/syndrome015.html

David R. Steinman
Austin Neurological Clinic and Department of Psychology, University of Texas at Austin

AIDS DYSMORPHIC SYNDROME

The National Organization for Rare Disorders (2000) describes AIDS dysmorphic syndrome (ADS) as a rare disorder of infancy that can result from a mother's infection with the human immunodeficiency virus (HIV) during pregnancy. HIV is the retrovirus that causes acquired immune deficiency syndrome (AIDS). This syndrome has many synonyms, such as dysmorphic AIDS, fetal AIDS infection, HIV embryopathy, and perinatal AIDS. ADS is caused by the transmission of HIV-1 or HIV-2, both forms of the human immunodeficiency virus. The transmission can occur during fetal development or during the birth of the child. Current data suggest that the most likely time for transmission of HIV between mother and infant occurs late in pregnancy or during delivery (Milosevic, 1998).

Most infants born to HIV-positive mothers have passively acquired maternal antibodies against this virus. An infant with passive antibodies is protected because the antibodies help fight the infection by neutralizing or destroying certain foreign proteins called antigens, thus fighting off HIV. If the antibodies prevent the infant from getting ADS, they will no longer be present in the infant's bloodstream by about 12 to 16 months of age. ADS can be accurately diagnosed when the infant is 18 months of age and the presence or absence of the passive antibodies can be clearly tested (National Organization for Rare Disorders [NORD], 2000). NORD (2000) reports that current estimates suggest that the risk of an infant's contracting HIV from his or her infected mother is approximately 13–39% of infants who are born to HIV-positive mothers in developed countries who have not undergone treatment with antiviral medications during pregnancy. Milosevic (1998) reports that the incidence of perinatal transmission of ADS varies from 25–48% for developing countries. ADS is believed to affect equal numbers of male and female infants (NORD, 2000). Statistics provided from Centers for Disease Control and Prevention (CDC) show that in the early 1990s, approximately 1,000–2,000 new cases of ADS were contracted each year in the United States. Between 1992 and 1998, these numbers have declined 75% in the United States, largely because of utilized preventive measures unknown prior to the later 1990s. CDC (1999) also reports that HIV transmission from infected mother to infant during pregnancy, during labor, during delivery, or by breast-feeding has accounted for 91% of reported AIDS cases in children in the United States. These children are differentially affected by racial background. CDC (1999) reports that 84% of children with AIDS were African American and Hispanic. This number is particularly concerning because only 31% of the U.S. population of children are African American or Hispanic.

Characteristics

1. Unusually small head (microencephaly) with a prominent boxlike forehead
2. Prominent and widely set eyes (ocular hypertelorism)
3. Flattened nasal bridge and shortened nose
4. An unusual bluish tint to the tough, outermost layer of the eyes (sclerae)
5. An unusually pronounced vertical groove (philtrum) in the center of an abnormally prominent upper lip

The best treatment for ADS is the use of preventive measures (CDC, 1999; Milosevic, 1998; NORD, 2000). These measures would include utilizing or creating programs that would work to prevent infection in women. These programs would dispense knowledge of how to have safe sex and avoid activities such as needle sharing if a woman is an intravenous drug user. After a woman is infected with HIV, education can help her understand the risks of pregnancy and help with birth control methods. If a woman is both infected with HIV and pregnant, the best treatment is early prenatal care, which would include HIV testing, counseling, and treatment with AZT and additional antiviral medications. In addition, delivery by cesarean section may reduce the risk of transmission of HIV to the newborn. The mother would also be told to refrain from breast-feeding her child, and the child would receive AZT during the first 6 weeks of life.

HIV-infected mothers with newborns should consult specialists in infants and children with HIV. Specific drug therapies suggested for the child may include AZT, didanosine (ddI), or lamivudine (3TC; nucleoside analog reverse transcriptase inhibitors) in combination with protease inhibitors. The child will need continued monitoring to assess the effectiveness of the drug therapy.

Teachers working with students affected with ADS will have to be aware of these children's potential for lowered intelligence and problems in psychomotor functioning. Special education teachers should help students with ADS learn skills that will help them with activities requiring a coordination between physical and mental tasks. Children with ADS who are performing below grade level would be good referrals to school psychologists who could assess the child's intellectual, psychomotor, and psychological functioning. The psychological reports can aid teachers in developing a better learning program by utilizing a child's strengths to combat his or her weaknesses.

Children with ADS may look smaller and more immature than their classmates; they may also need a referral to a school counselor or social worker in order to help them develop better social skill so that they can fit in better with same-age peers. Aside from their potentially small stature, their facial abnormalities may prompt severe teasing from their peers. Teasing can be extremely hurtful, and counseling may help the child build necessary coping skills.

Children with ADS are at chronic risk for developing life-threatening illnesses such as non-Hodgkins B-cell lymphoma, brain lymphoma, and Pneumocystis carinii pneumonia (NORD, 2000). An exact percentage of how many ADS children survive into adulthood and older age is unknown. Survival depends on medication therapy and individual treatment for all infections that are likely to assault the child's immune system. Future research should also focus on exactly how and when transmission occurs and on improving methods for preventing transmission between HIV-positive mothers and their infants. Most beneficially, however, future research should focus on continued efforts to find better treatment medications until a cure or vaccine for HIV is developed.

REFERENCES

National Organization for Rare Disorders. (2000). *Aids dysmorphic syndrome.* New Fairfield, CT: Author.

Milosevic, S. (1998). Perinatal infection with the human immunodeficiency. *Medicinski Pregled, 51,* 325–328.

Center for Disease Control and Prevention. (1999). *Status of perinatal HIV prevention: U.S. declines continue.* Atlanta, GA: Author.

Jennie Kaufman Singer
California Department of Corrections, Region 1 Parole Outpatient Clinic
Sacramento, California

ALBERS-SHÖNBERG DISEASE (OSTEOPETROSIS, MARBLE BONE DISEASE)

Albers-Schönberg disease is one form of osteopetrosis, which is a hereditary disorder affecting bone density and formation. In persons with osteopetrosis, decreased skeletal resorption leads to improper bone formation inside the bone marrow space, which leads to increased bone density (Carolino, Perez, & Popa, 1998). Osteopetrosis can have onset in infancy, childhood, or adulthood, with childhood and infant onset leading to the most serious forms of the disease. Which form of osteopetrosis is technically called Albers-Schönberg disease is not always consistent in the literature (i.e., www.osteopetrosis.org and Bénicho et al., 2001). For this reason, the childhood and infant forms of the disease will be referred to as simply osteopetrosis for this article. The forms affecting children are autosomal recessive, meaning that both parents must carry the gene for osteopetrosis in order for the disease to manifest in the child. In the less serious adult form, the disease is autosomal dominant (Carolino et al., 1998). The location of the gene that causes Albers-Schönberg disease has been mapped to Chromosome 16p.13.3 (Bénicho et al., 2001).

Because osteopetrosis is autosomal recessive, it is a rare disorder. It is estimated that it affects only 1 in 200,000 children (www.stjude.org). There have been no epidemiological studies performed on osteopetrosis (Manusov, Douville, Page, & Trivedi, 1993).

Characteristics

1. Child is usually diagnosed by age 1 year, after having multiple fractures, having multiple infections, or being diagnosed with failure to thrive (Manusov et al., 1993).
2. Child may experience thickening at the base of the skull, which can lead to vision loss, deafness, and hydrocephalus (Carolino et al., 1998). Vision loss is also caused by retinal degeneration (Manusov et al., 1993).
3. Child may have bone marrow failure, leading to more frequent infections and severe anemia. Because other systems are attempting to compensate for the bone marrow failure, a child with osteopetrosis may have an enlarged spleen and liver (Carolino et al., 1998).
4. Other symptoms may include growth retardation, "rugger jersey" spine, brittle bones, delayed dentition, and psychomotor retardation (Manusov et al., 1993).

The only known cure for autosomal recessive osteopetrosis is bone marrow transplant (Carolino et al., 1998). Transplants from siblings are the most successful, and the child must have the transplant early in life to avoid permanent, irreversible effects of osteopetrosis (www.stjude.org). Because bone marrow transplants are expensive and donors can be difficult to find in time, other forms of treatment are being researched.

Special education concerns for children with osteopetrosis will revolve around physical concerns and the physical safety of the child. Because they are prone to bone fractures, children with osteopetrosis may need special supervision in certain situations to help them avoid injury. Special testing situations and classroom setup may need to be considered for children with vision or hearing loss. Children with osteopetrosis may miss many days of school because of their medical problems.

Without successful treatment of the disease, autosomal recessive osteopetrosis is usually fatal within the first 10 years of life. Children with osteopetrosis usually die of severe anemia or infections. Current research is examining the effectiveness of a drug called interferon-gamma on osteopetrosis (www.stjude.org). Some researchers have also tried a nutritional supplement called 1,25 dihydroxy vitamin D, with limited results (Carolino et al., 1998). As research on the location of the gene that causes osteopetrosis continues, gene therapy is also an option that many hope will be available in the future (www.stjude.org).

REFERENCES

Bénicho, O., Cleiren, E., Gram, J., Bollerslev, J., de Vernejoul, M., & Van Hul, W. (2001). Mapping of autosomal dominant osteopetrosis type II (Albers-Schöenberg Disease) to chromosome 16p13.3. *American Journal of Human Genetics, 69,* 647–654.

Carolino, J., Perez, J. A., & Popa, A. (1998). Osteopetrosis. *American Family Physician, 57,* 1293–1296.

Manusov, E. G., Douville, D. R., Page, L. V., & Trivedi, D. V. (1993). Osteopetrosis ("marble bone" disease). *American Family Physician, 47,* 175–180.

Osteopetrosis. (n.d.). Retrieved August 1, 2001, from http://www.osteopetrosis.org/home.htm

Osteopetrosis. (n.d.). Retrieved August 1, 2001, from http://www.stjude.org/medical/osteopetrosis.htm

Whyte, M. P. (1995). Chipping away at marble bone disease. *The New England Journal of Medicine, 332,* 1639–1640.

Mary Helen Snider
Devereux Cleo Wallace
Colorado Springs, Colorado

See also Myelofibrosis, Idiopathic; Osteopetrosis

ALBINISM

Albinism refers to a group of inherited conditions. Individuals with albinism have a deficiency or absence of pigment in the skin, hair, and eyes (or eyes only) due to an abnormality in production of a pigment called melanin (King, Hearing, Creel, & Oetting, 1995).

Albinism affects individuals from all races. The prevalence of this disorder is approximately 5 in 100,000 people in the United States, but it is much higher in certain parts of the world (e.g., approximately 20 in 100,000 people in southern Nigeria; Clayman, 1989).

Characteristics

1. Little or no pigment of the eyes, skin, or hair.
2. Usually autosomal recessive inheritance.
3. There are several types of albinism:
   - Type 1 (tyrosinase-related albinism) involves almost no pigmentation.
   - Type 2 (defect in the "P" gene) involves slight pigmentation.
   - Hermansky-Pudlak syndrome is a less common form of albinism that can involve problems with bleeding and lung and bowel disease.
4. Vision problems are usually present in albinism because of abnormalities of the retina and optic nerve connections to the brain.

One of the primary treatment concerns regarding albinism is vision rehabilitation. Surgery may be carried out to improve strabismus (crossed eyes or lazy eye). However, because surgery does not correct the misrouting of the optic nerves from the eyes to the brain, surgery does not provide fine binocular vision.

Individuals with albinism are sensitive to glare because the iris, the colored area in the center of the eye, does not have enough pigment to screen stray light coming into the eye. Sunglasses or tinted contact lenses help with outdoor light. It is helpful to place indoor light sources for reading behind rather than in front of the individual.

There are a variety of optical aids for individuals with albinism, such as bifocals with strong reading lenses, prescription reading glasses or contact lenses, handheld magnifiers, and special small telescopes. Some individuals use bioptics, eyeglasses that have small telescopes mounted on in, or behind their regular lenses. Some states allow the use of bioptic telescopes for driving. The American Foundation for the Blind (1-800-AFB-LIND) maintains a directory of low vision clinics, where the individual's needs can be assessed and treated by an ophthalmologist or optometrist experienced in working with people who have low vision.

Other medical problems may affect the individual with albinism. People with Hernansky-Pudlak syndrome may have significant problems with lung disease, bowel disease, or hemorrhaging. If a child with albinism shows unusual bruising or bleeding, Hernansky-Pudlak syndrome should be suspected.

People with albinism are at increased risk for skin cancers because of the lack of the protective melanin pigment.

Appropriate skin protection is necessary, such as sunscreen lotions rated 20 or higher and opaque clothing.

Also, individuals with albinism are at risk for social isolation because the condition is often misunderstood. Social stigmatization can occur, especially within communities of color, where the race or paternity of a person with albinism may be questioned. Support and information groups can be very helpful for the individual and his or her family (e.g., the National Organization for Albinism and Hypopigmentation [NOAH], 2000, 1-800-473-2310).

The child with albinism may qualify for special education services under the category of Visually Handicapped. Due to the vision problems previously noted, the child with albinism may require certain individual accommodations in order to meet his or her educational needs. These accommodations may include large-print text, adequate lighting, books on tape, low-vision aids, and extended test-taking time. In addition, supportive counseling and sensitive education of the school community may be needed if social ostrasization is observed.

In the United States, people with albinism live normal life spans and have the same types of general medical problems as the rest of the population. Lung disease or other problems can shorten the lives of people with Hernansky-Pudlak syndrome. Also, those who do not use skin protection may develop life-threatening skin cancers (NOAH, 2000).

REFERENCES

Clayman, C. B. (1989). *The American Medical Association encyclopedia of medicine.* New York: Random House.

King, R. A., Hearing, V. J., Creel, D. J., & Oetting, W. S. (1995). Albinism. In C. R. Scrivner, A. L. Beaudet, W. S. Sly, & D. Valle (Eds.), *The metabolic and molecular bases of inherited disease* (7th ed., pp. 4353–4393). New York: McGraw Hill.

The National Organization for Albinism and Hypopigmentation (2000). What is albinism? Retrieved from http://www.albinism.org

Nancy L. Nussbaum
Austin Neurological Clinic

ALBRIGHT HEREDITARY OSTEODYSTROPHY (PSEUDOHYPOPARATHYROIDISM)

Hypoparathyroidism is a disorder of the parathyroid glands, which are located in the front of the neck along the periphery of the thyroid gland. Parathyroid glands synthesize and secrete parathyroid hormone (PTH), which is a principal regulator of calcium metabolism. Hypoparathyroidism has a variety of causes, but constant findings in this disease are inadequate levels of PTH and correction of the related biochemical abnormalities by PTH administration.

Albright hereditary osteodystrophy (AHO) causes calcium peculiarities similar to those found in hypoparathyroidism, but these problems do not respond to PTH. Therefore, the defect of this disorder is felt to be at hormone receptor sites on the cell membrane. Consequently, PTH measures in patients with AHO are either normal or elevated.

AHO is a rare disorder. Its true incidence is unknown. Its pattern of inheritance is autosomal dominant. There is a female-to-male sex ratio of 2:1. This observation has no clear explanation. AHO has four distinct clinical types, with Type Ia accounting for more than 50% of patients with this disease.

Characteristics

1. The initial symptom is often tetany, a state of central and peripheral nervous system hyperexcitability, caused by inadequate levels of ionized calcium in the fluid surrounding nerve cells. Tetany manifests as painful spasms of the wrists and ankles, spasm of the vocal cords, numbness and tingling of the extremities, and (occasionally) seizures.
2. Abnormal anatomic findings include short stature (adult height 54–60 inches), moderate obesity, round face, short neck, cataracts, delayed tooth eruption, absent or malformed teeth, shortened bones of the hands and feet, and calcification of tissue under the skin and within the brain.
3. Moderate degrees of mental retardation (mean IQ around 60) are common, but intelligence may occasionally be normal.
4. Other endocrine abnormalities such as hypothyroidism and gonadal dysfunction may be present.

Treatment of AHO is focused on the detrimental effects of abnormal calcium metabolism. Careful administration of high doses of vitamin D may be necessary to correct ionized calcium deficits. Periodic cessation of this therapy is indicated to determine whether spontaneous remission of the tendency toward the calcium-related biochemical aberrations has occurred. As some of these patients grow older, they may experience some amelioration of this feature of the disorder.

Because the average intellectual functioning is around 60, many individuals with this disorder require some form of special education support services. Providing an educational program that focuses on functional academic abilities as well as life skills training is important. At the child enters junior high school, it is important to develop a transition plan to prepare the child for an appropriate vocation and living environment. Students may experience peer difficulties because of physical differences, so care should be taken to provide for social adjustment skills for these children.

The prognosis for AHO is guarded. The outlook for patients who are diagnosed in the first few years of life is more favorable than is the prognosis for children whose condition is not detected until a later age. In the latter group, moderate degrees of mental retardation, cataracts, and brain calcifications are common findings.

REFERENCES

Doyle, D. A., & DiGeorge, A. M. (2000). Disorders of the parathyroid glands. In R. E. Behrman, R. M. Kleigman, & H. B. Jenson (Eds.), *Nelson's textbook of pediatrics* (16th ed., pp. 1718–1719). Philadelphia: W. B. Saunders.

Jones, K. (1997). *Smith's recognizable patterns of human malformations* (5th ed.). Philadelphia: W. B. Saunders.

Barry H. Davison
Ennis, Texas

Joan W. Mayfield
Baylor Pediatric Specialty Services
Dallas, Texas

ALCOHOL ABUSE

Alcohol abuse is defined as a maladaptive pattern of alcohol use leading to clinically significant impairment or distress. Prevalence increases with age, leveling off in the early 20s. For example, a large national survey conducted in 2000 found that 14% of eighth graders and 30% of 12th graders reported binge drinking (having five or more drinks at a time) in the preceding 2 weeks (Johnston, O'Malley, & Bachman, 2001). Risk factors for alcohol abuse include early use of alcohol, parental alcohol abuse or dependence, aggressive behavior, delinquent activity, and temperament factors such as low attention span and high emotionality (National Institute for Alcohol Abuse and Alcoholism [NIAAA], 2000).

Characteristics

A maladaptive pattern of substance use leading to clinically significant impairment or distress, as manifested by one or more of the following symptoms occurring within a 12-month period:

1. Recurrent alcohol use resulting in a failure to fulfill major role obligations at school, work, or home
2. Recurrent use in situations in which it is physically hazardous
3. Recurrent substance-related legal problems
4. Continued use despite having persistent or recurrent social or interpersonal problems caused or exacerbated by the effects of alcohol (American Psychiatric Association, 1994)

Alcohol abuse has been associated with poor performance in school, behavior problems, and reduced self-esteem. Students may miss school days recovering from the effects of alcohol or may experience decrements in concentration while in class. Professional treatment by a counselor experienced in substance abuse problems is recommended. Such treatment may include individual and family psychotherapy. Prevention efforts have included school-based programs designed to increase students' communication with parents, examine their perceptions of peer alcohol use, and resist peer influence. Results have been mixed: One large longitudinal study found that such programs seemed to delay adolescent drinking but did not reduce alcohol consumption among students who were already drinking (NIAAA, 2000).

REFERENCES

American Psychiatric Association. (1994). *Diagnostic and statistical manual of mental disorders* (4th ed.). Washington, DC: Author.

Johnston, L. D., O'Malley, P. M., & Bachman, J. G. (2001). *Monitoring the future: National results on adolescent drug use.* Washington, DC: National Institute on Drug Abuse.

National Institute for Alcohol Abuse and Alcoholism. (2000). *10th special report to the U.S. Congress on alcohol and health.* Rockville, MD: U.S. Department of Health and Human Services.

Derek D. Satre
University of California
San Francisco, California

ALEXANDER DISEASE

Alexander disease is a rare, genetic, degenerative disorder of the nervous system. It is one of a group of genetic disorders called the leukodystrophies that affect growth of the myelin sheath on nerve fibers in the brain. The myelin sheath is the fatty covering that acts as an insulator (National Institute of Neurological Disorders and Stroke [NINDS], 2000; PDR, 2000)

This disease can occur at any age, including adulthood. The most frequent form of Alexander disease is the infantile form. It has an average onset at 6 months of age. The onset of the disease ranges any time from shortly before birth to as late as 2 years of age (Goetz & Pappert, 1999; NINDS, 2000; Rudolph, Hoffman, Julien, & Rudolph,

1996). In addition to the infantile form of Alexander disease, juvenile and adult onset forms of the disorder have been reported. These forms occur less frequently and have a longer course of progression (NINDS, 2000). Juvenile form usually occurs between 7 and 14 years of age. The duration is approximately 8 years (Goetz & Pappert, 1999). Alexander affects mostly males.

Characteristics (Goetz & Pappert, 1999; McKusick, 1998; NINDS, 2000; Rudolph et al., 1996; Rowland, 2000)

Infantile form:

1. The mental and physical retardation exist initially.
2. Dementia, enlargement of the brain and head, and spasticity (stiffness of arms and legs).
3. Seizures in younger children.
4. Children with this disease eventually become mute, bedridden, and totally dependent.

Source: NINDS (2000)

Juvenile form:

1. Dysphagia.
2. Full facial palsy.
3. Tongue atrophy.
4. Generalized spasticity and weakness may also occur.
5. Unlike the severe mental retardation characteristic of the infantile form, mentation tends to remain intact.

There is neither a cure nor a standard course of treatment for Alexander disease; however, much support care is necessary, including good nutrition and generous use of antibiotics and antiepileptics (Goetz & Pappert, 1999; NINDS, 2000). The treatment of Alexander disease is symptomatic and supportive.

Children with this disease would probably initially qualify for Early Childhood services (special education services for children under the age of 3). Under Early Childhood, children could receive any type of service (speech, physical, and occupational therapy). Depending on the extent of mental retardation and their life span, they may then qualify as Mentally Retarded and enter life skills classes. The other services would continue. They may also qualify as Other Health Impaired for the seizures, Physically Handicapped or Speech Impaired depending on the areas of delay. If multiple designations exist, they would probably qualify as multiply handicapped.

The prognosis for patients with Alexander disease is generally poor. The younger the age of onset, the more rapid the neurological deterioration (Rudolph's Pediatrics, 1996). Children with the infantile form of Alexander disease usually do not survive past the age of 6. In the juvenile form, death usually occurs within 10 years after the onset of symptoms (Goetz & Pappert, 1999; NINDS, 2000). Recent findings in positron-emission tomography (PET) scanning and single-photon emission computed tomography (SPECT) indicate that there is an abnormal flow of spinal fluid through the blood-brain barrier. This may be an important knowledge in fully understanding these disorders. Furthermore, such findings may aid in developing intervention (Goetz & Pappert, 1999).

REFERENCES

Goetz, C. G., & Pappert, E. J. (1999). *Textbook of clinical neurology.* Philadelphia: W. B. Saunders.

McKusick, V. A. (1998). *Mendelian inheritance in man: A catalog of human genes and genetic disorders* (24th ed.). Baltimore: Johns Hopkins University Press.

PDR medical dictionary (2nd ed.). (2000). Montvale, NJ: Medical Economics.

Rowland, L. P. (2000). *Merritt's neurology* (10th ed.). Philadelphia: Lippincott Williams & Wilkins.

Rudolph, A. M., Hoffman, Julien, I. E., & Rudolph, C. D. (1996). *Rudolph's pediatrics* (20th ed.). Stamford, CT: Appleton & Lange.

The National Institute of Neurological Disorders and Stroke. (June 9, 2000). Alexander disease. Retrieved from http://www.ninds.nih.gov/health_and_medical/disorders/alexand_doc.htm

Nina Cheng
University of Texas at Austin

ALEXIA

Alexia is an acquired neurological disorder characterized by a partial or complete inability to read. The etiology of alexia is typically associated with a lesion behind and beneath the left occipital lobe, which damages the visual pathways within the hemisphere. Alexia can also be caused by the combination of a lesion on the corpus callosum, which disconnects the right-to-left visual information transfer, or a lesion in the left occipital lobe, which disconnects the left visual association cortex from the left language cortex. This results in a disconnection of visual information in the right hemisphere from the word-recognition system in the left hemisphere (Behrman, 1999; Benson & Ardila, 1996; Coslett, 1997; Friedman, Ween, & Albert, 1993).

Although several subtypes of alexia have been identified, all types have the common feature that the affected patient cannot read normally. Reading rate is slow and comprehension of read material is impaired. Pure alexia or alexia without agraphia involves an isolated impairment in reading without impaired ability to write. In other words, individuals with pure alexia are able to write normally but then are unable to read what they have just written. Alexia, an acquired disorder following brain injury, is not to be confused with dyslexia, a developmental reading disorder, which typically manifests during childhood (Benson & Ardila, 1996).

Alexia can occur in anyone suffering from a brain injury. Although anyone receiving a brain injury can acquire alexia, it most commonly affects adults who have suffered a stroke. Cerebral tumors, inflammatory processes, and head injuries are less common causes of alexia. In some cases, alexia is seen as an early feature of some degenerative diseases such as Alzheimer's disease (Friedman et al., 1993). Thus, it is difficult to estimate the incidence and prevalence rates of alexia in the United States. According to the Bureau of the Census (1999), of all children and youth with disabilities who were served by selected programs in 1998, approximately 19.8% had speech or language impairments. Of that percentage, it is unclear how many had pure alexia, although it is likely to be a relatively small percentage.

Characteristics

1. Acquired reading impairments in an individual who was previously literate.
2. Inability to read most words and sentences, and in some cases reading of single letters is also impaired.
3. No disturbances in the ability to write words or sentences or in any other aspects of speech and language functioning.
4. In order to read, individuals name each letter of the word in serial order and use auditory input to decode the word (also called letter-by-letter reading).
5. Words spelled aloud to the individual are recognized with no apparent difficulty.

Treatment involves using compensatory techniques to teach individuals to read faster and with greater accuracy. One such treatment method is the multiple oral reading (MOR) technique developed by Moyer (1979). In this method, an individual reads and rereads the same short text passage every day for about 1 week. The individual is given a second short text passage for the next week and so on. Moyer (1979) found this repetitive practice of the same text to be successful in terms of text reading speed with alexic patients. The MOR technique has been shown to be most effective for text reading speed compared to performance on list of single words. One reason for this finding is that word processing may be facilitated using concurrent context, whereas no context is available to aid in decoding single-word lists (Behrman, 1999).

A second approach to remediation of alexia is kinesthetic facilitation. In this method, the individual is taught to trace each letter by using a finger or by moving the head or eyes. The body movement provides feedback that enables the individual to identify the letter. Although this method appears to improve accuracy in reading, the reading speed remains slow and laborious. Nitzberg and Friedman (1999) attempted to increase speed of reading while implementing a tactile-kinesthetic strategy to improve reading accuracy in the treatment of David, an alexic patient. They showed in their case study that the speed of letter-by-letter reading can be increased without sacrificing accuracy of reading words by reinforcing and encouraging the patient to practice letter-by-letter reading as quickly as possible until David's daily mean letter-naming time reached a plateau. In both methods of remediation of alexia, treatment does not focus on the damaged area of the brain causing alexia; rather, it focuses on compensatory strategies to retrain word recognition (Behrman, 1999).

Children with alexia will most likely require speech and language services from trained professionals; thus, they should be able to qualify for special education under Speech and Language Impairments, Specific Learning Disabilities, or Traumatic Brain Injury. The aforementioned compensatory strategies are recommended for treatment of pure alexia (Behrman, 1999). Other therapies are emerging that better target specific subtypes of alexia (see Friedman et al., 1993). Children with alexia may also experience emotional and behavioral problems that often occur in children with developmental reading disorders such as dyslexia. They will probably need psychological services such as counseling.

Overall, prognosis for recovery from alexia becomes more guarded as the child gets older when considering a reversal of the effects of brain damage. However, the prognosis for regaining word recognition and reading skills is good when the patient uses compensatory strategies to circumvent the reading deficits. Although individuals may not return to their previous reading ability level, with practice and determination, reading ability usually improves to a useful level (Benson, 1996). Research in the area of alexia is limited, and further research is warranted to continue identifying new interventions for improving reading skills among individuals with alexia (Friedman et al., 1993).

REFERENCES

Behrman, M. (1999). Pure alexia: Underlying mechanisms and remediation. In R. Klein & P. McMullen (Eds.), *Converging methods for understanding reading and dyslexia* (pp. 153–189). Cambridge, MA: MIT Press.

Benson, F., & Ardila, A. (1996). *Aphasia: A clinical perspective.* New York: Oxford University Press.

Coslett, H. (1997). Acquired dyslexia. In T. Feinberg & M. Farah (Eds.), *Behavioral neurology and neuropsychology* (pp. 197–208). New York: McGraw-Hill.

Friedman, R., Ween, J., & Albert, M. (1993). Alexia. In K. Heilman & E. Valenstein (Eds.), *Clinical neuropsychology* (pp. 37–60). New York: Oxford University Press.

Moyer, S. (1979). Rehabilitation of alexia: A case study. *Cortex, 15,* 139–144.

Nitzberg, L. S., & Friedman, R. (1999). Can treatment for pure alexia improve letter-by-letter reading speed without sacrificing accuracy? *Brain and Language, 67,* 188–201.

U.S. Department of Education, Office of Special Education Programs, Data Analysis Systems. (1999). *Statistical abstract of the U.S.: 1999.* Washington, DC: Bureau of the Census.

Jennifer Keith
Brian D. Johnson
University of Northern Colorado

ALLERGY DISORDERS

Allergies are inflammatory conditions resulting from an allergen (or antigen) producing an adverse immune reaction involving the antibody immunoglobulin E (IgE). Hypersensitivity disorders mediated by IgE include: atopic diseases (i.e., allergic rhinitis, allergic conjunctivitis, atopic dermatitis, and allergic asthma), some cases of urticaria, some cases of digestive allergy, and systemic anaphylaxis (Merck Research Laboratories, 2000). The response to the allergen is determined by the duration, route (i.e., by inhalation, contact, ingestion, or injection), amount of exposure, and other environmental and host factors (e.g., genetic susceptibility). Allergies affect more than 20% of the population in the United States, with allergic rhinitis having a prevalence rate of 59.7 cases per 1,000. Rhinitis is the most common condition in children under the age of 18 years. Asthma, which occurs at a rate of 42.5 cases per 1,000, frequently co-occurs with allergic rhinitis. The prevalence for digestive allergies is 25.1 cases per 1,000, and for eczema and other skin allergies it is 32.9 cases per 1,000 (Fireman, 2000).

Characteristics

1. Symptoms of allergic response include hives, wheezing, coughing, itching, digestive disorders, and in severe cases, anaphylaxis.
2. Affects more than 20% of the U.S. population.
3. Treatments range from elimination of allergen or reducing exposure to drug therapy and immunotherapy.
4. First-generation drugs are highly potent but cause drowsiness, fatigue, and performance impairment. Second-generation drugs are as potent but do not cause the side effects.

The preferred method of treatment is to eliminate the allergen (e.g., change of diet, residence, removal of a house pet) or reduce the exposure (e.g., wet mopping and dusting frequently to reduce house dust). Reducing exposure is often impractical given the prevalence of certain allergens (e.g., dust, mites, mold, and pollen). When an allergen cannot be avoided or sufficiently controlled, antihistamines, corticosteroids, or allergen immunotherapy have been used (Merck Research Laboratories, 2000).

Most individuals are familiar with the physical discomforts caused by wheezing, coughing, and itching that accompany allergic reactions, but few realize the potential for cognitive and psychosocial disability. Allergic rhinitis, for example, has been shown to cause both systemic and localized symptoms (e.g., weakness, malaise, irritability, fatigue, headache, and anorexia). These symptoms can affect a child's ability to perform at his or her normal level and can also interfere with regular school attendance. Some estimates put the number of lost school days to 2 million a year (Marshall, O'Hara, & Steinberg, 2000). In addition, individuals with ragweed allergies have been shown to experience slowing of process speed (Marshall et al., 2000).

Not only do allergies have the potential to diminish energy, cognition, and mood, but the treatments also do. Antihistamines, the most effective treatment, are categorized as first-generation drugs that are available over-the-counter but sedating, or as second generation drugs that require a prescription but are nonsedating. The first-generation drugs are highly potent histamine antagonists, acting at the histamine H_1-receptors on the target cells. The drugs are lipophilic and easily cross the blood-brain barrier in order to occupy the H_1-receptors on the frontal lobes and deeper brain structures. Research has demonstrated that the level of cognitive dysfunction correlates with brain-receptor occupancy. First-generation antihistamines have been shown to occupy 75% of the H_1-receptors in the brain, resulting in central nervous system side effects including fatigue, drowsiness, and performance impairment. This also explains why the first-generation antihistamines (e.g., Dimetapp, Chlor-Trimeton, and Benadryl) are required to carry a label to warn users against potential ill effects. The newer and more costly antihistamines (i.e., second-generation drugs) are as effective as their predecessors but have fewer sedative effects. These antihistamines are made up of larger lipophobic molecules with different ionic charge, thus unable to freely cross the blood-brain barrier. These drugs occupy only 20% of H_1-receptors in the brain, which explains why they do not have the same effects as the first-generation drugs and why drugs like Allegra and Claritin are not required to carry warning labels (Kay, 2000).

Elementary-age children with seasonal allergic rhinitis who are treated with sedating drugs have been shown to perform more poorly on learning tasks than do children who use the nonsedating antihistamines (Kay, 2000). Tasks that are particularly affected include those requiring divided attention, working memory, and vigilance. Understandably, children treated with sedating drugs report more fatigue and lower levels of motivation than do peers using nonsedating drugs. Unfortunately, the negative effects of first-generation drugs affect children not only on the day of ingestion but also on the day after (e.g., show diminished awareness of functional problems).

Educators need to be aware of the potential adverse effects of sedating antihistamines on mood, alertness, cognitive performance, and psychomotor speed. Some accommodations educators can make for students with allergies include adjusting the pace at which information is presented and the timelines for completing work assignments (e.g., giving more breaks and allowing more time for assignment completion). Educators may also review safety factors with students and parents, including the sedating effects of certain antihistamines and the impact on performance. Although not a problem in elementary school, in adolescence students need to be informed about the potential impact on driving.

REFERENCES

Fireman, P. (2000). Therapeutic approaches to allergic rhinitis: Treating the child. *Journal of Allergy and Clinical Immunology, 6,* 16–20.

Kay, G. G. (2000). The effects of antihistamines on cognition and performance. *Journal of Allergy and Clinical Immunology, 6,* 22–27.

Marshall P. S., O'Hara, C., & Steinberg, R. (2000). Effects of seasonal allergic rhinitis on selected cognitive abilities, *Ann Allergy Asthma Immunology, 4,* 403–410.

Merck Research Laboratories. (2000). Hypersensitivity disorders. In *Merck manual of diagnosis and therapy* (17th ed., pp. 1041–1048). Whitehouse Station, NJ: Author.

Najmeh Hourmanesh
Elaine Clark
University of Utah

ALOPECIA AREATA

Alopecia areata is an unpredictable autoimmune skin disease resulting in the loss of hair on the scalp and sometimes elsewhere on the body. The affected hair follicles are mistakenly attacked by the person's own immune system (white blood cells), impeding hair growth. Heredity plays a role in the development of this condition. At least 1 in 5 persons with alopecia areata have a family member with the condition. Alopecia areata often occurs in families whose members have asthma, hay fever, atopic eczema, or other autoimmune diseases such as thyroiditis.

Alopecia areata occurs in males and females of all ethnicities and ages. Onset is often in childhood. Approximately 1.7% of the overall population is affected by this condition (more than 4 million U.S. citizens).

Characteristics

1. Alopecia areata usually starts in childhood with one or more small, round, smooth bald patches on the scalp.
2. Progression to total scalp hair loss (alopecia totalis) or complete body hair loss (alopecia universalis) is possible.
3. In some people, the nails develop stippling that looks as if a pin had made rows of tiny dents.
4. The hair can grow back even after years of hair loss. However, it can also fall out again at a later date.

Several treatments are available, and choice of treatment depends upon the individual's age and extent of hair loss. Treatments available for mild hair loss include such things as cortisone injections into the areas of the scalp affected by hair loss. Or solutions (e.g., topical minoxidil or anthralin cream) can be applied to the affected areas. For more severe cases, cortisone pills, topical immunotherapy (which consists of producing an allergic rash to trigger hair growth), or wigs can be used.

Because the general public is still generally unfamiliar with this disorder, students diagnosed with alopecia areata may find that this disease can have a profound impact upon their school life (e.g., Smith, 2001). Due to its sudden onset, recurrent episodes, and unpredictable course, alopecia areata can be life altering. Therefore, students may require counseling to be able to come to terms with this disorder. School personnel may benefit from information about this disorder to help them understand the condition and support the student. Contact with other individuals with this condition may help to bolster student's self-esteem.

The prognosis for someone with this condition is varied. For some individuals, hair growth can return to normal. For some people, however, recurring hair loss can occur. The National Alopecia Areata Foundation (NAAF) funds research into this disorder and holds research workshops to exchange knowledge and further alopecia areata research in the field. For more information, contact NAAF, P.O. Box 150760, San Rafael, CA, 94915, telephone (415) 456-4644; or National Organization for Rare Disorders, P.O. Box 8923, New Fairfax, CT 06812-8923.

REFERENCE

Smith, J. A. (2001). The impact of skin disease on the quality of life of adolescents. *Adolescent Medicine, 12*(2), 343–353.

Rachel Toplis
University of Northern Colorado

See also Monilethrix

ALPERS DISEASE

Alpers disease, also known as progressive infantile poliodystrophy, is a neurological condition occurring in infants and children. The degeneration of cerebral gray matter results in motor disturbances, seizures, and dementia (Adams, Victor, & Ropper, 1997; Boyd, Harden, Egger, & Pampiglione, 1986). It is also common for patients with Alpers disease to develop liver damage. Although a familial form has been identified, the etiology is still unknown for most cases (Thoene & Coker, 1995). Males and females are affected equally. There are very few cases of Alpers disease reported in the United States.

Characteristics

1. Infant or child shows signs of partial paralysis, spasticity, motor and growth retardation.
2. Infant or child may often have myoclonic seizures or sometimes intractible seizures.
3. Progressive mental deterioration may occur.
4. Blindness, deafness, and liver damage are also associated with this disease.

Currently Alpers disease is untreatable; thus, treatment plans involve attempting to alleviate the various symptoms. For example, anticonvulsant drug therapy can be used to prevent seizures.

Children with Alpers disease may qualify for special education services under the category of Other Health Impaired due to their seizures, motor problems, and possible liver damage. If characteristics of blindness or deafness occur, the child may qualify for services under these categories. Physical and occupational therapy may be required to help with motor problems. Psychoeducational testing should occur annually to monitor the effects of the disease on the child's cognitive and motor functioning.

Alpers disease is fatal, usually resulting in death a few months after its onset.

REFERENCES

Adams, R. D., Victor, M., & Ropper, A. H. (1997). *Principles of neurology* (6th ed.). New York: McGraw-Hill.

Boyd, S. G., Harden, A., Egger, J., & Pampiglione, G. (1986). Progressive neuronal degeneration of childhood with liver disease (Alpers' disease): Characteristic neuropysiological features. *Neuropediatrics, 17,* 75–80.

Thoene, J. G., & Coker, N. P. (Eds.). 1995. *Physicians' guide to rare diseases* (2nd ed.). Montvale, NJ: Dowden.

Jennifer Hargrave
University of Texas at Austin

ALPHA-1-ANTITRYPSIN DEFICIENCY

Alpha-1-antitrypsin deficiency (A-1-AD) is caused by an inadequate amount of the enzyme alpha-1-antitrypsin in the blood. Affected individuals have 10–20% of normal levels of this serum protein. As a result, they experience early-onset emphysema (blebs and cysts replacing normal lung tissue), usually in the third or fourth decade. A-1-AD can also cause liver disease in infants and children.

Alpha-1-antitrypsin inactivates protreases, which are substances released from dead bacteria and white blood cells. Accumulation of proteases in the lung leads to destruction of normal architecture and emphysema.

A-1-AD is an hereditary disorder. Symptomatic individuals are homozygous for the abnormal gene. A-1-AD is one of the most common fatal genetic diseases in people of European descent. The incidence in white populations is 1:200–1:4,000.

Characteristics

1. Highly variable course of liver disease in infants. Jaundice and liver enlargement may occur in the first week of life. These findings may resolve completely or progress to chronic liver disease with diffuse scarring (cirrhosis) and liver failure.
2. Lung disease in childhood is rare. A few pediatric patients experience chronic cough, wheezing, or shortness of breath. Passive smoke exposure enhances early development of emphysema.
3. Symptoms of chronic lung disease usually do not begin until the third or fourth decade.

General therapy includes aggressive treatment of lung infections, immunization with pneumococcal and influenza vaccines, inhaled medications for wheezing, and avoidance of smoke exposure as well as other environmental irritants. Intravenous administration of alpha-1-antitrypsin can raise blood levels into the normal range, at least temporarily.

Children with A-1-AD may meet eligibility criteria to receive support services as Other Health Impaired if an educational need is demonstrated. There is no research to indicate cognitive delay as a result of this disease; however, the child's ability to function in the classroom may be impaired by his or her illness. Providing additional emotional support to help the child develop age-appropriate coping mechanisms would be helpful.

A-1-AD patients have a guarded prognosis. Liver transplantation can be curative for young children with cirrhosis and liver failure, but that procedure is no stroll through the park. Older patients with chronic lung disease must deal with their illness every day. They are susceptible to pneumonia and bronchitis, which can cause swift, catastrophic deterioration in their respiratory status. In the future, gene insertion therapy offers the best hope for prolonged survival and improved quality of life.

For more information and support, contact the Alpha 1 National Association at 1-800-521-3025 or e-mail AIN@alpha1.org.

REFERENCES

Balistreri, W. F. (2000). Metabolic disease of the liver. In R. E. Behrman, R. M. Kleigman, & H. B. Jenson (Eds.), *Nelson's textbook of pediatrics* (16th ed., pp. 1207–1212). Philadelphia: W. B. Saunders.

Orenstein, D. M. (2000). Emphysema and overinflation. In R. E. Behrman, R. M. Kleigman, & H. B. Jenson (Eds.), *Nelson's textbook of pediatrics* (16th ed., pp. 1302–1305). Philadelphia: W. B. Saunders.

What is alpha 1. (n.d.). Retrieved from http://www.alpha2alpha.org/whatisalpha1.htm

Barry H. Davison
Ennis, Texas

Joan W. Mayfield
Baylor Pediatric Specialty Services
Dallas, Texas

ALPORT SYNDROME

Alport syndrome is an inherited (usually X-linked) disorder. It involves damage to the kidneys, blood in the urine, and loss of hearing in some families—and in some cases, loss of vision. In cases in which there is no family history of kidney disease, Alport syndrome is caused by a mutation in a collagen gene.

This uncommon disorder affects about 2 out of 10,000 people (MEDLINE Plus Health Information, 2000). Although approximately 1 in 50,000 Americans carry the Alport Syndrome gene, twice as many females as males carry the gene. However, a greater percentage of males with the gene have symptoms. Before the age of 50, nearly all of the males carrying the gene show symptoms. They eventually develop chronic renal failure and end-stage renal disease (ESRD), which is the final stage in chronic renal failure. Even though most females with the gene manifest the same symptoms, the progression and severity of the disease is less severe. Only about 20% of the females carrying the gene will develop ESRD, but usually at an older age (National Organization for Rare Disorders [NORD], 2001).

Alport syndrome is classified by mode of inheritance, age, and features other than kidney abnormalities. The age of onset of ESRD determines whether Alport Syndrome is classified as a juvenile form or an adult form of the disease. If ESRD occurs before the age of 31, it is classified as the juvenile form; after the age of 31, it is classified as the adult form (NORD, 2001).

There are six subtypes of Alport syndrome:

1. Type I is a dominantly inherited juvenile form. The symptoms include kidney disease, nerve deafness, and eye abnormalities.
2. Type II is an X-linked dominant juvenile form. Symptoms are the same as in the Type I subtype.
3. Type III is an X-linked dominant adult form. Symptoms include kidney disease and nerve deafness.
4. Type IV is an X-linked dominant adult form. It primarily involves kidney disease. There are no vision or hearing impairments.
5. Type V (Epstein syndrome) is an autosomal dominant form of the disease. Symptoms include nerve deafness and thrombocytopathia (disorders of blood platelets). It is so rare that it has not been classified as either adult or juvenile. The incidence of ESRD in the reported cases seems to be the same for males and females.
6. Type VI is an autosomal juvenile form. Symptoms include kidney disease, nerve deafness, and eye abnormalities (NORD, 2001).

Characteristics

1. Abnormal urine color
2. Blood in the urine
3. Loss of hearing (more common in males)
4. Decrease or loss of vision (more common in males)
5. Cough
6. Ankle, feet, and leg swelling
7. Swelling, overall
8. Swelling around the eyes
9. Upset stomach
10. Peculiar-smelling breath
11. Fatigue and excessive need for sleep
12. Shortness of breath
13. Dry, often itchy skin

Source: MEDLINE Plus Health Information (2000)

Treatment of Alport syndrome includes vigorous treatment of the chronic renal failure. Hemodialysis may be used to treat this problem. This treatment would involve removing blood from the patient's artery, cleaning it of unwanted substances that would be normally excreted in the urine, and returning the cleansed blood to a vein (NORD, 2001). It is also important to aggressively treat urinary tract infections and control blood pressure; this can be done through diet by restricting salt and protein intake. High blood pressure can also be controlled with medication. Cataracts may be surgically repaired (MEDLINE Plus Health Information, 2000). Genetic counseling is also recommended.

Hearing loss may be permanent. It is therefore important to learn new skills such as sign language or lip reading. Hearing aids are helpful, and it is recommended that young men use hearing protection in noisy environments. Counseling and education can help to increase coping skills (MEDLINE Plus Health Information, 2000).

If diagnosed during school age, the child may be eligible for special education services under the classification of Hearing Impaired, Visually Impaired, or Other Health Impaired. They may benefit from services to address these impairments.

Prognosis for females is that they usually have a normal life span with little or no manifestation of the disease. Some complications may arise during pregnancy. Males, however, are likely to develop permanent deafness, a decrease in or total loss of vision, chronic renal failure, and ESRD by the age of 50. Investigational therapies include the use of a new drug, calcium acetate, during ESRD, to treat hyperphosphatemia.

REFERENCES

MEDLINE Plus Health Information. (2000, September 5). Alport syndrome. Retrieved from http://medlineplus.adam.com/ency/article/000504.htm

National Organization for Rare Disorders. (2001, January 30). Alport syndrome. Retrieved from http://www.rarediseases.org

VEDIA SHERMAN
Austin Neurological Clinic

ALSTRÖM SYNDROME

Alström syndrome is an autosomal recessive genetic disorder characterized primarily by retinitis pigmentosa beginning during infancy and progressive sensorineural hearing loss beginning in early childhood. There is typically infant or childhood obesity that may normalize somewhat later, and individuals with this disorder frequently develop diabetes mellitus by early adulthood. In contrast to Bardet-Biedl syndrome, which shares several symptoms, in Alström syndrome there are normal intelligence and normal extremities (Online Mendelian Inheritance in Man, 2000).

Characteristics

1. Retinitis pigmentosa from infancy; nystagmus and photosensitivity
2. Mild to moderate sensorineural hearing loss, starting in childhood
3. Cardiomyopathy, in infancy or later
4. Moderate obesity in infancy and childhood, possibly normalizing
5. Insulin resistance syndrome, with associated acanthosis nigricans
6. Diabetes mellitus (non-insulin-dependent diabetes mellitus), typically juvenile onset
7. Renal disease; early signs of urine retention, incontinence, or both
8. Possible hepatic disease
9. Possible short stature, scoliosis, and hypothyroidism
10. Normal intellectual range

Other symptoms of Alström syndrome can include progressive renal disease, hepatic dysfunction, congestive heart failure (appearing at any age), growth retardation, and insulin resistance syndrome along with its related dark pigmentation of skin flexures (acanthosis nigricans). Alström syndrome in childhood is typically difficult to recognize without the presence of infantile cardiomyopathy, and it is often not identified until the development of diabetes in the second or third decade. Homozygotic carriers appear to be asymptomatic.

First described in 1959 by Swedish physician and researcher Carl-Henry Alström, the syndrome is quite rare. To date there have been only about 76 cases of Alström syndrome reported in the medical literature. Current incidence is estimated as about 117 worldwide, including cases in 18 countries (Jackson Laboratory, 2000). The disorder occurs in males and females with equal probability. It has relatively increased frequency in French Acadian or Amish groups in which couples often have common ancestors. The largest numbers of diagnosed cases have been in the United States and the United Kingdom, likely due to increased availability of informed health care.

The degeneration of the retina (retinitis pigmentosa) may be apparent in the first year of life. Nystagmus and photosensitivity (so-called photophobia) can be early indicators. There is early loss of central vision, in contrast to initial loss of peripheral vision as is typically seen with other pigmentary retinopathies. The electroretinogram is absent or attenuated, with better-preserved rod than cone function early on. The retinal dystrophy is progressive, leading to total blindness. Visual acuity is typically 6/60 or less by age 10 and absence of light perception occurs by about age 20. When a patient presents with infantile cone and rod retinal dystrophy—especially if the weight is above the 90th percentile or there is infantile cardiomyopathy—then the diagnosis of Alström syndrome should be considered (Russell-Eggitt et al., 1998).

Because of the syndrome's effects on endocrine functioning, growth can be stunted, leading to short stature, and there may be scoliosis and hypothyroidism (Alter & Moshang, 1993). Renal and hepatic dysfunction can lead to serious complications. Screening for bladder dysfunction signs of urinary retention and/or incontinence has been suggested to help identify renal disease earlier and allow more timely preventive care (Parkinson & Parkinson, 2000).

General intelligence is not affected. Although some studies suggest there may be developmental delays, such effects seem most likely secondary to the visual and aural deficits. Intellectual functioning is typically within the normal range, and the prognosis to lead full productive lives is very good. Special education services may be available to children with Alström syndrome under the classification of Other Health Impaired or Physical Disability. Classroom modifications for visual and hearing deficits should be made (including for the photophobia). Most children can be mainstreamed if accommodations are made successfully and supported with appropriate supplemental programming. It is suggested that Braille be learned early to prevent the child from falling behind in school as vision deteriorates. Incorporating regular physical activity is very important in regulating weight and managing diabetes.

Alström syndrome has been linked to Chromosome 2p13, but the gene has not yet been identified (Collin et al., 1999). Study of the Alström gene may contribute to knowledge about the regulation of body weight and blood glucose and about how these processes may be related to maintenance of sight and vision.

At present there is no prenatal screening for Alström syndrome available. Diagnosis is typically made on the basis of presenting features. There is no cure; treatment is focused on ameliorating the symptoms. Interventions include monitoring and controlling metabolism, weight, and diabetes and providing compensatory audio-visual aids.

REFERENCES

Alter, C., & Moshang, T. (1993). Growth hormone deficiency in two siblings with Alström syndrome. *American Journal of Disabled Children, 147*(1), 97–99.

Collin, G., Marshall, J., Boerkoel, C., Levin, A., Weksberg, R., Greenberg, J., et al. (1999). Alström syndrome: Further evidence for linkage to human chromosome 2p13. *Human Genetics, 105,* 474–479.

Jackson Laboratory. (2000, December 14). *Alström.* Retrieved from http://www.jax.org/alstrom

Online Mendelian Inheritance in Man. (2000, December 14). Alström syndrome. Retrieved from http://www3.ncbi.nlm.nih.gov/htbin-post/Omim/dispmim?203800

Parkinson, J., & Parkinson, K. (Eds.). (2000, September 5). *Alström UK Newsletter, No. 7.* Retrieved from http://www.alstrom.org.uk

Russell-Eggitt, I., Clayton, P., Coffey, R., Kriss, A., Taylor, D., & Taylor, J. (1998). Alström syndrome: Report of 22 cases and literature review. *Ophthalmology, 105*(7), 1274–1280.

Vicky Y. Spradling
Austin State Hospital

ALTERNATING HEMIPLEGIA OF CHILDHOOD

Alternating hemiplegia of childhood (AHC) is a rare but serious neurological disorder. The hallmark of AHC is the onset of frequent, recurrent, transient episodes of hemiplegia (paralysis of a body part). Hemiplegia manifestations run the gamut from numbness to complete loss of movement and feeling. Hemiplegia may affect either side of the body and may occasionally affect both sides simultaneously. These attacks may last a few minutes or may go on for days. In most cases, sleep induces resolution of a hemiplegia episode.

AHC is a relatively new addition to the list of neurological diseases. Fewer than 100 cases have been reported in the United States. Worldwide, there appear to be only about 250 cases. The exact cause of AHC is not known. However, the appearance of more than one case in sibling groups suggests that—at least in some situations—there may be an autosomal dominant mode of transmission.

Characteristics

1. Onset of symptoms no later than 18 months of age.
2. Episodic hemiplegia affecting both sides of the body.
3. The existence of other paroxysmal neurological abnormalities not related to hemiplegia. This list includes dystonia (exaggerated muscle contraction), choreoathetosis (sudden, involuntary movement of limb or facial muscles), and temporary paralysis of muscles that control eye movement.
4. Autonomic abnormalities (excessive sweating, changes in skin color, and changes in body temperature).
5. Diminished intellectual function.
6. Exclusion of other causes responsible for recurrent neurological deficits.

AHC has no known cure. Because the frequency and duration of attacks appear to have a cumulative damaging effect on the brain, therapy is directed toward ameliorating their severity. Because sleep usually ends an episode, one strategy is to use sedatives. Seizures, which frequently complicate the clinical picture, respond to anticonvulsants.

A few clinical trials, involving small groups of patients, show that the drug flunarizine may decrease the severity of hemiplegic episodes. However, the results of these studies have been deemed inconclusive.

Children with AHC will require support services from an early age. Because of the delay in development, children will be eligible to receive support services from the early childhood intervention (ECI) program. Therapy services provided through ECI in the areas of occupational, physical, and speech therapy may help the child attain developmental milestones. As the child develops and the deficits become more evident, support services will need to be modified to meet the changing needs of the child. There also may be cognitive deficits as a result of the medication needed to help control the seizure activity. Careful monitoring of the educational strategies will be required to continue to help the child attain his or her academic potential.

AHC is a serious neurological disorder with a rather poor prognosis. There is no evidence that the disease shortens life expectancy, but there are insufficient data from long-term follow-ups of affected children to be confident about that assumption. Symptoms persist into adulthood, but as many of these patients grow older, they tend to handle attacks better. The younger the child is at the time of diagnosis, the more likely he or she is to acquire permanent neurological impairment and arrested intellectual development as he or she approaches maturity.

For more information and support, please contact

- International Foundation for Alternating Hemiplegic of Childhood (IFAHC), 239 Nevada Street, Redwood City, CA 94062, e-mail:laegan@aol.com, home page: http://www.ahckids.org
- NIH/National Institute of Neurological Disorders and Stroke, 31 Center Drive MSC 2540, Building 31 Room 8806, Bethesda, MD 20892, (301) 496-5751, (800) 352-9424, home page: http://www.ninds.nih.gov?

REFERENCES

Haslam, R. H. A. (2000). Acute stroke syndromes. In R. E. Behrman, R. M. Kleigman, & H. B. Jenson (Eds.), *Nelson's textbook of pediatrics* (16th ed., pp. 1854–1856). Philadelphia: W. B. Saunders.

What Is AHC? (n.d.). Retrieved from http://www.ahckids.org/ahc_whatis.htm

National Organization for Rare Disorders. (1996). Alternating hemiplegia of childhood. Retrieved from http://www.stepstn.com/cgi-win/nord.exe?proc=GetDocument&rectype=0&recnum=1027

Roach, E. S., & Riela, A. R. (1995). *Pediatric cerebrovascular disorder* (2nd ed.). New York: Futura.

Silver, K., & Andermann, F. (1993). Alternating hemiplegia of childhood: A study of 10 patients and results of flunarizine treatment. *Neurology, 43,* 36–41.

Barry H. Davison
Ennis, Texas

Joan W. Mayfield
Baylor Pediatric Specialty Services
Dallas, Texas

See also Hemiplegia

AMBLYOPIA

Amblyopia is a term used to describe a loss of vision in an eye that appears to be physically healthy. It is commonly known as lazy eye. Amblyopia can occur for a variety of reasons, including strabismus (crossed or turned eye), congenital cataracts, cloudy cornea, droopy eyelid, nearsightedness, farsightedness, or astigmatism. Amblyopia may occur in various degrees depending on the severity of the underlying problem. The visual system is fully developed between approximately the ages of 9 and 11. If it is caught early, amblyopia can be corrected, however, after age 11 it is difficult if not impossible to train the brain to use the eye normally.

It is estimated that 2–3% of the population has amblyopia. Prevalence appears to be consistent across race and gender.

Characteristics

1. Poor vision in one or both eyes.
2. Squinting or closing one eye while reading or watching TV.
3. Crossed or turned eye.
4. Turning or tilting the head when looking at an object.
5. Children with amblyopia lack binocular vision (stereopsis), which impairs the ability to judge distances.

The treatment for amblyopia depends on the underlying problem. Glasses are often prescribed to improve focusing or misalignment of the eyes. Surgery may be performed to straighten eye muscles. Eye exercises may be recommended to correct faulty visual habits. Patching or covering the stronger eye may be required to force the weaker eye to work. Medication, such as eye drops, to blur the stronger eye may also be used to force the weaker eye to work. Routine eye exams should be performed to detect potential problems.

A child diagnosed with amblyopia may qualify for special services depending on the severity of the underlying visual disorder. It may be necessary to follow the guidelines for the provision of special services to visually impaired individuals and to provide visual aids such as books with large text. Children who are required to wear patches over their strong eye are likely to find reading and other predominantly visual activities difficult initially and may require accommodations (e.g., more time to complete activities and tests). The student and school personnel should be informed about the importance of compliance with patch wearing. It may help if children's fears concerning the reaction of peers and classmates are addressed. Therefore teachers—with the students' permission—may want to incorporate fun activities discussing how the eye works and the importance of patch wearing to correct vision difficulties.

The prognosis for an individual with amblyopia is positive if the problem is discovered early. However, if amblyopia goes untreated, the amblyopic eye may never develop good vision and may even become functionally blind as the child's brain learns to permanently suppress or ignore the eye. Research into amblyopia is ongoing. Areas of research include the importance of early diagnosis (e.g., Juttmann, 2001; LaRoche, 2001).

REFERENCES

Allen, T. E. (2000). Amblyopia. In C. R. Reynolds & E. Fletcher-Janzen (Eds.), *Encyclopedia of special education* (2nd ed., p. 85). New York: Wiley.

Juttmann, R. (2001). The Rotterdam AMblyopia Screening Effectiveness Study (RAMSES): Compliance and predictive value in the first 2 years. *British Journal of Ophthalmology, 85*(11), 1332–1335.

LaRoche, G. R. (2001). Amblyopia: Detection, prevention and rehabilitation. *Current Opinions in Ophthalmology, 12*(5), 363–367.

Rachel Toplis
University of Northern Colorado

AMNESIA

The term amnesia refers to memory loss, either partial or total. Classification of amnesia types may be according to temporal factors, etiology, or extent of memory loss. Amnesia may occur after a neurological injury or illness, or it may represent a psychological reaction to a traumatic event. Amnesia may occur after head injury, electroshock therapy, drug or alcohol intoxication, anoxia, or other conditions affecting the memory systems of the brain. It may also occur as a symptom of psychological disorders such as major depression, posttraumatic stress disorder, or dissociative identity disorder. Children who have been physically or sexually abused, survivors of war or other catastrophe, or victims of violence may develop psychological amnesia.

Characteristics

1. Anterograde amnesia—loss of ability to store and encode newly learned information, associated with damage to the hippocampus.
2. Retrograde amnesia—loss of ability to retrieve information learned in the past, associated with damage to the mammillary bodies and thalamus.
3. Transient global amnesia—the sudden onset of an inability to form new memories or retrieve old information from memory, with no apparent cause (Kolb & Whishaw, 1996).
4. Posttraumatic amnesia (PTA)—memory disturbance following brain injury, up to the point at which continuous memory for events is regained. May include a period of coma as well. Is often used as an index of severity of injury, with PTA $<$ 5 min representing very mild injury; 5–60 min, mild injury; 1–24 hours, moderate injury; 1–7 days, severe injury; 1–4 weeks, very severe injury; and more than 4 weeks, extremely severe injury (Lezak, 1995).
5. Traumatic or dissociative amnesia—memory loss associated with psychological trauma. Research suggests that trauma and stress can cause disturbances in hippocampal activation and arousal. Secretion of corticosteroids can also impair memory and learning processes and result in hippocampal atrophy (Miller, 1998).

The treatment of posttraumatic amnesia in children may include medications designed to enhance memory functioning or improve attention, thus enhancing the encoding and storage of information in memory. Compensatory techniques such as using a personal organizer to keep track of appointments, setting a beeper watch to remind the child to take medications, and so forth are frequently used. Spontaneous improvement in memory is also expected as a part of the child's recovery process. Research indicates that the recovery curve for memory is steepest in the first 6 months after brain injury, with continuing recovery occurring at a slower rate for several years or more afterwards.

Psychological amnesia is best treated by a psychotherapist experienced in therapy of children who have suffered psychological trauma. Individual, group, and family therapy may be beneficial in the treatment of this disorder. Although hypnosis and sodium amytal (so-called truth serum) interviews have been used in the past to help recover "lost memories," this treatment has fallen into disfavor due to the risk of precipitating the recovery of false memories, and lawsuits have resulted.

Children suffering from amnesia may be eligible for special education services under the classification of Traumatic Brain Injury or Other Health Impaired if the condition is due to brain trauma or neurological illness. Curriculum modification as well as the use of compensatory devices or strategies may be necessary to help compensate for the amnesic child's impairment in retrieving old information or learning new information. If the amnesia is psychological in origin, the child may be eligible for special education services under the classification of Emotional Disturbance. Support by the school psychologist may be necessary to help the child cope with and reduce memory blocks caused by anxiety secondary to specific triggers.

REFERENCES

Kolb, B., & Whishaw, I. (1996). *Fundamentals of human neuropsychology* (4th ed.). New York: W. H. Freeman.

Lezak, M. (1995). *Neuropsychological assessment* (3rd ed.). New York: Oxford University Press.

Miller, L. (1998). *Shocks to the system: Psychotherapy of traumatic disability syndromes.* New York: W. W. Norton.

Janiece Pompa
University of Utah

See also Memory Disorders

AMYOPLASIA CONGENITAL DISRUPTIVE SEQUENCE (ARTHROGRYPOSIS MULTIPLEX CONGENITAL)

Amyoplasia congenital disruptive sequence (ACDS) is a congenital neuromuscular disease. Patients with ACDS are born with markedly diminished muscle mass and multiple joint contractures that are generally symmetrical. These malformations usually affect all four extremities, but they may involve only the arms or only the legs.

The etiology of ACDS is unclear. One plausible explanation for this unique set of anomalies is poor blood flow to the developing fetal spinal cord.

The occurrence of this disorder is sporadic. Its frequency is higher than expected in identical twins, although only one of the pair is affected. This disorder is considered rare; however, more than 500 case reports of ACDS have appeared in the medical literature.

Characteristics

1. Diminished muscle mass and severe, symmetrical joint contractures present at birth.
2. Round face, small jaw, small upturned nose.
3. Rounded, sloping shoulders with decreased muscle mass.
4. Elbows are fully extended. Severe contractures of the wrists, hands and fingers are usually present.
5. Lower extremity findings include fixed dislocation of the hips and bilateral clubfoot.
6. The spine is usually straight and stiff, but scoliosis is common as children age.

Therapy for ACDS patients requires multiple orthopedic procedures to obtain the best functional results. With good physical therapy, almost all of these individuals become ambulatory and self-supportive. However, treatment must be started early to mobilize and strengthen what muscle mass there is. Casting and splinting may be necessary to correct clubfeet and knee contractures.

A child with ACDS may require modifications in the physical environment such as assistive devices or technology of the classroom to allow them to achieve their academic potential in light of their physical limitations. There is no research to support cognitive deficits. Providing a positive environment that builds good self-images will facilitate peer relationships.

The prognosis for this disorder is generally favorable. Intelligence is usually normal. There may be diminished bone growth in affected extremities. Occasionally the joint contractures worsen with age. However, with aggressive management of the orthopedic abnormalities, ACDS patients can achieve a considerable degree of self-sufficiency.

REFERENCES

Thompson, G. H., & Scoles, P. V. (2000). Arthrogryposis. In R. E. Behrman, R. M. Kleigman, & H. B. Jenson (Eds.), *Nelson's textbook of pediatrics* (16th ed., pp. 2094–2095). Philadelphia: W. B. Saunders.

Jones, K. (1997). *Smith's recognizable patterns of human malformations* (5th ed.). Philadelphia: W. B. Saunders.

Barry H. Davison
Ennis, Texas

Joan W. Mayfield
Baylor Pediatric Specialty Services
Dallas, Texas

ANEMIA, APLASTIC

There are various types of anemias that differ in severity and etiology (e.g., aplastic, sickle cell, and Fanconi). The first description of aplastic anemia was offered by Ehrlick in 1888 and later named by Vaquez in 1904 (Young, 1995). In general, aplastic anemia is the failure of bone marrow to reproduce new blood cells. Specifically, there is a low production of (a) red blood that carries the oxygen to all parts of the body, (b) white blood cells that help the body fight off infection, and (c) platelets that involve the controlling of bleeding by forming blood clots. Production of new blood is of critical importance because blood cells have very limited life spans (e.g., red about 120 days, platelets about 6 days, and white less than 24 hours). The diagnosis of aplastic anemia is usually done through blood and bone marrow tests, and as blood count decreases, severity and morbidity increase.

Aplastic anemia is a rare disorder; about two per 1 million individuals are diagnosed each year in the United States. The incidence of aplastic anemia varies; more cases are identified in Asia (e.g., Thailand about four per million new cases each year) than on other continents. Both males and females are equally affected. Although the median age of onset is 20–25 years, newborns have been diagnosed with the disorder. The underlying etiology in about 50% of the cases is unknown, and the other known 50% may be due to physical or chemical damage to the bone marrow, viral infection, cytotoxic drugs used in chemotherapy, prescription and over-the-counter drugs, or heredity.

Characteristics

1. Fatigue.
2. Bleeding of the mucus membranes.
3. Headaches.
4. Dizziness.
5. Nausea.
6. Shortness of breath.
7. Heart palpitations.
8. Underside of eyelids, nails, and lips may become very pale.
9. May bruise easily.
10. High risk for infection.

Aplastic anemia is generally considered a medical emergency, and the individual is immediately hospitalized. In cases in which the cause is known, the cause is removed if possible, and the individual is given a transfusion. For more severe cases and for children, the first line of treatment is bone marrow transplantation. The bone marrow of one person is extracted and then grafted into the bone marrow of the affected individual; the ideal donor is a sibling. If a sibling donor is not viable, other individuals in the family or community may potentially become donors. While waiting for a donor, the child may be given a blood transfusion (not from family or any potential donor) and is carefully monitored because such children are highly susceptible to infections. The transplantation is successful if the recipient's body does not reject the transplant and new blood is reproduced. If a donor cannot be found, treatment with immunosuppressant drugs is prescribed. Immunosuppressant drugs such as cyclosporine are often used with bone marrow transplantations to lessen the possibility of rejection (March & Gordon-Smith, 1998).

Children diagnosed with aplastic anemia may need special education services, including home-based tutoring and psychological services. They may be classified as Other Health Impaired. The classroom and school of the child may also need psychological services with a focus on supportive peer and family counseling.

In the past, for individuals with severe aplastic anemia, prognosis has been grim—about 30–50% of individuals died within 6 months of diagnosis. Therefore, research on aplastic anemia has focused on understanding the underlying physiological structure of the disorder and on developing new treatment protocols that can increase survival rate (Foulade et al., 2000). For example, in an 8-year follow-up study of children with aplastic anemia treated with bone marrow transplant or a regiment of immunosuppressant drugs, the survival rate was 80% (Pitcher, Hann, Evans, & Veys, 1999). The educational or psychological effects of the diagnosis of aplastic anemia have not been adequately addressed in the literature.

REFERENCES

Aplastic Anemia Foundation of America. Retrieved from http://www.teteport.com/nonprofit/aafa

Aplastic Anemia & MDS International Foundation, Inc. Retrieved from http://www.aplastic.org

Foulade, M., Herhan, R., Rolland-Grehton, M., Jones-Wallace, D., Blanchette, V., Calderwood, S., et al. (2000). Improved survival in severe acquired aplastic anemia in childhood. *Bone Marrow Transplant, 26*(11), 1149–1156.

March, J. C., & Gordon-Smith, E. C. (1998). Treatment options in severe aplastic anemia. *Lancet, 351*(9119), 1830–1831.

Pitcher, L. A., Hann, I. M., Evans, J. P., & Veys, P. (1999). Improved prognosis for acquired aplastic anemia. *Archives of Disease in Childhood, 80*(2), 158–166.

Young, N. S. (1995). Aplastic anemia. *Lancet, 346*(8969), 228–238.

Agnes E. Shine
Barry University

Darrell L. Downs
Mount Sinai Medical Center and Miami Heart Institute

ANEMIA, DIAMOND-BLACKFAN

Diamond-Blackfan anemia (DBA) is a congenital deficiency in the precursor mechanism of red blood cells causing failure or low production rates of new blood cells in the bone marrow. The disease is usually present at birth or develops during the first year of life, with 50% of males developing the disease by 2 months of age and 3 months for females. The ratio of males to females is 1.1 to 1.

The etiology and pathogenesis of DBA is unknown. Researchers have studied the possible link between DBA and mutations of ribosomal protein RPS 19; the presence of a second gene on Chromosome 8p (Willig, Gazda, & Sieff, 2000) and Chromosome 19. The characteristics of individuals with DBA vary, and a consistent pattern has not been established due to the small number of cases seen.

Characteristics

1. Weakness and fatigue
2. Slow growth
3. Webbing or shortness of the neck
4. Hand deformities
5. Congenital heart defects
6. At risk for developing leukemia
7. Facial dysmorphic features such as wide-set eyes, thick upper lip, micro- or macrocephaly
8. Upper limb malformations
9. Cataracts, epicanthal folds
10. Renal structural anomalies
11. Short stature

Individuals with DBA are usually treated with corticosteroids such as prednisone (DeCosta, Willig, Fixer, Mohandas, & Tchernia, 2001). Side effects of prednisone therapy may include growth retardation, hypertension, diabetes, fluid retention, gastric ulcers, cataracts, and weight gain. For individuals who do not positively respond to prednisone, red blood cell transfusion may be an option. Transfusions are generally needed every 3 weeks. Side effects associated with transfusion include adverse reactions and the possibility of contracting hepatitis. Bone marrow transplantation may be utilized in cases in which the individual does not response to other forms of treatment. With advances in bone marrow transplantation and immunosuppressant drug therapy, survival rates after transplantation have increased. However, because the child's bone marrow is destroyed prior to transplantation, rejection or poor functioning of the new grafted bone marrow generally results in death. In about 15% of the individuals with DBA, spontaneous remission occurs, and the median age of survival for individuals with DBA is approximately 31 years.

Educational needs of children with DBA change dependent upon their general health and treatment protocol. Children may receive special education services under the Other Health Impaired category. At times, homebound services may be needed. Children who received successful bone marrow transplantation (i.e., child has not rejected the marrow and the new marrow is normally functioning) may be considered cured and may only need minimal medical supervision. Predisone treatment or blood transfusion involves many more risks, and frequency of the treatment (3–6 hours for blood transfusion) may result in missed educational opportunities. Fatigue, physical problems, and treatment side effects can have a negative impact on the child's physical and cognitive growth. Because children with DBA may be very fragile, their ability to engage in age appropriate play and to interact with age mates may be limited.

REFERENCES

DeCosta, L., Willig, T. N., Fixer, J., Mohandas, N., & Tchernia, G. (2001). Diamond-blackfan anemia. *Current Opinion in Pediatrics, 13*(1), 10–15.

Diamond Blackfan Anemia Online. Retrieved from http:// www.Diamondblackfan.com.

National Organization for Rare Disorders. Retrieved from http://www.rarediseases.org

Willig, T. N., Gazda, H., & Sieff, C. A. (2000). Diamond-blackfan anemia. *Current Opinion in Hematology, 7*(2), 85–94.

Darrell L. Downs
Mount Sinai Medical Center and Miami Heart Hospital

Agnes E. Shine
Barry University

ANEMIA, FANCONI

Fanconi anemia (FA) was first reported by Guido Fanconi, a Swiss pediatrician, in 1927. Because FA is an autosomal recessive disorder that leads to bone marrow failure, both parents must carry the recessive gene for the child to have the disorder. People with FA do not produce a protein necessary for cell functioning; as the cells die and are not reproduced, the individual develops aplastic anemia. Because FA is a recessive gene disorder, after a sibling is diagnosed with FA, all siblings should be tested for FA.

FA occurs equally in males and females and can affect all ethnic groups. The prevalence rate is unknown, but there are about 3,500 known cases; estimates of carrier frequency are approximately 1 in 600. Birth defects occur in approximately 75% of the children born with FA, and the disorder affects all body systems (Alter, 1996). Of major concern for children with FA is the high rate of aplastic anemia, leukemia, and cancers (DeKerviler, Guermazi, Zagdanski, Gluckman, & Frija, 2000). Although FA may be diagnosed at birth, age of onset is typically between 3 and 12 years of age, and in rare cases, adults may be diagnosed with FA. Children with the disorder rarely live to adulthood; their life expectancy is about 22 years.

Characteristics

1. Short stature
2. Anomalies of the thumb and arm
3. Skeletal anomalies (e.g., hip and spine)
4. Structural renal malformations
5. Mental or learning disabilities
6. Gastrointestinal difficulties
7. Heart defects, cancer, and leukemia
8. Hyperpigmentation of the skin (café-au-lait spots)
9. Urinary malformations

In children with FA, treatment is usually bone marrow transplantation, androgen therapy, synthetic growth factor therapy, and gene therapy. Androgen and synthetic growth therapies (drug therapies) are used to stimulate blood growth and can be very effective (Frohnmayer & Frohnmayer, 2000). They are not a cure, and most FA patients eventually fail to respond to drug therapy. Bone marrow transplantation is an effective therapy; the best prognosis is seen in young children who are relatively healthy and have received no or few blood transfusions. Five years after transplantation with a sibling donor, the survival rate is about 70%, whereas the survival rate with nonrelated donors is negligible (Bosch, 2000). At the present time, researchers are investigating at least eight different genes involved in FA.

Children with FA should be allowed to engage in age-related activities as much as possible. Some children may need special education services such as hospital or homebound instruction, individualized instruction focusing on learning problems, or support given through classes for Other Health Impaired children. Children with FA and their families need psychological support, and the child must feel accepted and cared for while attending school. Because about 50% of children with FA are short in stature, care should be given that they are treated as any other child their age and not treated as if they were much younger children.

REFERENCES

Alter, B. P. (1996). Aplastic anemia, pediatric aspects. *Oncologist, 1*(6), 361–366.

Bosch, X. (2000). Setbacks and hopes for patients with Fanconi's anaemia. *Lancet, 355*(9200), 291–295.

DeKerviler, E., Guermazi, A., Zagdanski, A. M., Gluckman, E., & Frija, J. (2000). The clinical and radiological features of Fanconi's anaemia. *Clinical Radiology, 55*(5), 340–345.

Fanconi Anemia Research and Family Support Network, Fact Sheet. Retrieved from http://www.2.cybernex.net/~jj/fa/fa_facts.htm

Agnes E. Shine
Barry University

Darrell L. Downs
Mount Sinai Medical Center and Miami Heart Institute

ANEMIA, HEREDITARY NONSPHEROCYTIC HEMOLYTIC

Hereditary nonspherocytic hemolytic anemia describes a group of blood disorders that may result from defects in red blood cell membranes, chemical abnormal metabolism, and approximately 16 enzyme deficiencies in the cells, such as glucose-6-phosphate dehydrogenase deficiency (Fiorelli, Martinez di Montemuros, & Cappellini, 2000). The shape of the red blood cell is not changed as a result of the disorder. The two most common disorders are Glucose-6-Phosphate Dehydrogenase deficiency and Pyruvate Kinase Deficiency.

Glucose-6-phosphate dehydrogenase deficiency (G-6-PD) is a hereditary X-linked recessive enzyme disorder. When an individual with the disorder is exposed to stress of infection or some drugs, the G-6-PD enzyme in the red blood cells is reduced and the red blood cells begin to break down. The incidence for G-6-PD is higher in African Americans; 10–14% of African American males are affected. Individuals with the disorder can remain undiagnosed until their red blood cells are exposed to infections or oxidants such as antimalarial drugs and antibiotics. However, new blood cells do not have decreased levels of G-6-PD and so episodes of anemia may be brief.

Characteristics

1. Fatigue
2. Pale color
3. Shortness of breath
4. Rapid heart rate
5. Yellow skin tone
6. Dark urine
7. Enlarged spleen

If the decrease in red blood cell G-6-PD is a result of infection, the infections is treated, and if the cause is drugs, the drugs are stopped. This form of treatment generally returns the individual to a more normal healthy state.

Pyruvate kinase deficiency is the second most common cause of enzyme related nonspherocytic hemolytic anemia and is an inherited autosomal recessive trait which results in a decrease of the enzyme pyruvate kinase in red blood cells. Evidence of pyruvate kinase deficiency can be found in all ethnic groups, but it appears to affect some groups of people more than others (e.g., Amish). The deficiency can cause mild to severe hemolysis (cell death) and anemia and can be identified in infancy.

Characteristics

1. Family history
2. Pallor
3. Jaundice

Treatment for the disorder depends on severity; some individuals experience few if any symptoms, whereas others may need blood transfusions and a splenectomy to decrease the destruction of red blood cells.

For individuals with G-6-PD or pyruvate kinase deficiency family and genetic counseling may be appropriate. Children and adolescents with these disorders may not need any additional special educational support unless they develop chronic anemia, which may restrict their activities and result in missed school days. The category of Other Health Impaired may need to be considered if the student's activities are restricted. Providing the individual with information about their disorder is important, since the individual may need emotional support when dealing with life long conditions. Additional research is needed to understand etiology and treatment.

REFERENCES

Fiorelli, G., Martinez di Montemuros, F., & Cappellini, M. D. (2000). Chronic non-spherocytic haemolytic disorders associated with glucose-6-phosphate dehydrogenase variants. *Best Practices in Research Clinical Haematology, 13*(1), 39–55.

Medline Plus Medical Encyclopedia. Retrieved from http://medlineplus.nlm.nih.gov/medlineplus/ency

Rare Disease Database. Retrieved from http://www.stepstn.com/cgi-win/nord

Vanderbilt University Medical Center. Retrieved from http://www.mc.vanderbilt.edu/peds/

Agnes E. Shine
Barry University

Darrell L. Downs
Mount Sinai Medical Center and Miami Heart Institute

ANEMIA, HEREDITARY SPHEROCYTIC HEMOLYTIC

The blood cells in individuals with hereditary spherocytic hemolytic anemia (HSHA) are sphere-shaped due to a defect within the blood cell as a result of a metabolic defect. Because of the cells' shape, they are not readily passed through the small blood vessels of the spleen and are often prematurely destroyed by the spleen. The incidence rate of HSHA in the United States is estimated to be approximately 1 in 5,000 individuals and usually affects Caucasian individuals of northern European ancestry; it is rarely found in other racial groups. The disorder is autosomal dominant, with 50% of the siblings affected. However, in a small number of cases, neither parent has the defect and the expression of the disorder may be due to a recessive form of the disorder or to spontaneous mutation. The severity of the disorder depends upon whether the individual can compensate for the loss of red blood cells by producing more cells. If the bone marrow temporarily halts production of new blood cells due to infection, the individual may experience an aplastic crisis as a result of the loss of blood.

Characteristics

1. Jaundice, causing skin and whites of the eyes to turn yellow
2. Fatigue
3. Enlarged spleen

Treatment for the disorder for a young child consists of folic acid supplements, and in emergencies transfusions may be provided. For individuals older than 5 years of age, a splenectomy (removal of the spleen, which allows the blood cells to live longer) may be needed (Beutler & Luzzatto, 1999). However, removal of the spleen is not considered a cure, and the individual must take precautions to prevent serious infections that may increase the risk of anemia.

The educational and social-emotional needs of the individual will depend upon the severity of the disorder. In mild cases, the individual may need to avoid infections and stress-related activities. In more severe cases, physical activities may be restricted and the individual may constantly feel fatigued. Children and adolescents should be instructed about their condition and play a vital role in the management of their care. Special education services may need to be provided in the Other Health Impaired category. Psychological counseling and education may also be needed.

REFERENCES

Beutler, E., & Luzzatto, L. (1999). Hemolytic anemia. *Seminar in Hematology, 36*(4 Suppl. 7), 38–47.

Medline Plus Medical Encyclopedia. Retrieved from http://medlineplus.nlm.nih.gov/medlineplus/ency

Rare Disease Database. Retrieved from http://www.stepstn.com/cgi-win/nord

Vanderbilt University Medical Center. Retrieved from http://www.mc.vanderbilt.edu/peds/

Agnes E. Shine
Barry University

Darrell L. Downs
Mount Sinai Medical Center and Miami Heart Institute

ANENCEPHALY

Anencephaly is a neural tube defect (NTD) resulting in the incomplete development of part of the neural tube that usually develops between the 23rd and 26th days of pregnancy (National Institute of Neurological Disorders and Stroke [NINDS], 2000). Specifically, the cephalic or head end of the neural tube does not close, which results in a failure to form major portions of the brain, skull, and scalp. Infants with anencephaly are born without a forebrain, and the rest of the brain tissue is often exposed. Etiology is unknown, but it is thought that anencephaly can be influenced by genetic conditions or by environmental influences on the mother during pregnancy such as antiseizure medication use, maternal insulin-dependent diabetes, prolonged maternal fevers, environmental toxins, or exposure to radiation (Centers for Disease Control and Prevention [CDC], 2000b; NINDS, 2000a).

Anencephaly is detectable during pregnancy through the use of ultrasound and amniocentesis. It occurs in approximately 5 out of 1,000 pregnancies, but only one third of these pregnancies is carried to full term (Clayman, 1989). Another estimate approximates 1,000 to 2,000 American births with anencephaly each year, with more females affected by the disorder than males (NINDS, 2000a). Ninety-five percent of the time, neural tube defects occur in women who have no family history of them. After a woman has had a neural tube defect pregnancy, however, her chances of having another such pregnancy are increased 20 times (CDC, 2000b). It has been found that neural tube defects are more common among European American women than among African American women and more common among Hispanic women than among non-Hispanic women (CDC, 2000b).

Characteristics

1. Incompletely formed brain, including lack of forebrain and cerebrum
2. Brain tissue not covered by bone or skin
3. Blindness, deafness, unconsciousness, inability to feel pain
4. Sometimes reflex actions of rudimentary brainstem, such as breathing
5. Miscarriage, stillbirth, or death usually within a few hours or days after birth

There is no cure or standard treatment for anencephaly (NINDS, 2000b). Prognosis is poor because most infants do not survive infancy; many are miscarried, are stillborn, or die within a few hours or days after birth (NINDS, 2000a). Some recent studies have shown a 50–70% prevention rate of NTDs when a small dosage of folic acid is consumed daily during pregnancy (CDC, 2000). Research has even suggested that including folic acid in the diet of all women of childbearing age would reduce the incidence of neural tube defects because they occur very early in pregnancy, often before many women know they are pregnant (CDC, 2000b; NINDS, 2000a). Future research will continue to focus on normal fetal brain development as well as on the causes and prevention of neural tube defects (NINDS, 2000a).

REFERENCES

Centers for Disease Control and Prevention. (2000a, September 19). Preventing neural tube birth defects: A national campaign. Retrieved from http://www.cdc.gov/nceh/cddh/folic/prof.htm

Centers for Disease Control and Prevention. (2000b, September 25). Folic acid now. Retrieved from http://www.cdc.gov/nceh/cddh/fact/folicfaqs.htm

Clayman, C. B. (Ed.). (1989). *The American Medical Association encyclopedia of medicine.* New York: Random House.

National Institute of Neurological Disorders and Stroke. (2000a, June 14). Cephalic disorders fact sheet. Retrieved from http://www.ninds.nih.gov/health_and_medical/pubs/cephalic_disorders.htm

National Institute of Neurological Disorders and Stroke. (2000b, June 27). Anencephaly. Retrieved from http://www.ninds.nih.gov/health_and_medical/disorders/anencephaly_doc.htm

Kathryn L. Guy
University of Texas at Austin

Nancy L. Nussbaum
Austin Neurological Clinic

ANGELMAN SYNDROME

Angelman syndrome, formerly known as happy puppet syndrome due to a resemblance of children with the disorder to the movement and appearance of a marionette, is a rare congenital neurodevelopmental disorder with complex genetic etiology. It is manifested by mental retardation, speech impairment, movement disorder, and easily-provoked laughter. Dysmorphic facial features frequently occur. The condition was first reported by the English pediatrician, Harry Angelman (Angelman, 1965). The condition is usually not recognized at birth or in infancy due to nonspecific features. Average age of diagnosis is 6 years.

The incidence of Angelman Syndrome is not precisely known and is estimated to be 1 in 10,000 to 1 in 20,000. Several genetic etiological mechanisms of the disorder have been identified, most commonly deletion of chromosome region 15q 11–13. High-resolution chromosome testing, fluorescent in situ hybridization analysis, and DNA methylation testing help determine the diagnosis when Angelman syndrome is suspected.

Characteristics

Consistent (100%)

1. Developmental delay, functionally severe
2. Speech impairment, no or minimal use of words, better receptive and nonverbal communication skills than expressive
3. Movement or balance disorder, usually ataxia of gait or tremulous movement of limbs
4. Unique behaviors: any combination of frequent smiling or laughter; apparent happy demeanor; easily excitable personality, often with hand flapping movements; hypermotoric behavior; short attention span

Frequent (more than 80%)

1. Delayed, disproportionate growth in head circumference, usually resulting in microcephaly (absolute or relative) by age 2
2. Seizures, onset usually before age 3
3. Specific EEG abnormalities

Associated (20–80%)

1. Dysmorphic features: flat occiput, horizontal occipital groove, mandibular prognathia, wide mouth, widely spaced teeth
2. Protruding tongue, tongue thrusting
3. Sucking-swallowing disorders, feeding problems during infancy
4. Frequent drooling, excessive chewing-mouthing behavior
5. Strabismus
6. Hypopigmented chin, light hair and eye color (relative to family)
7. Uplifted, flexed wrists and elbows, especially during ambulation
8. Increased sensitivity to heat
9. Sleep disturbance
10. Attraction to or fascination with water (Williams et al., 1995)

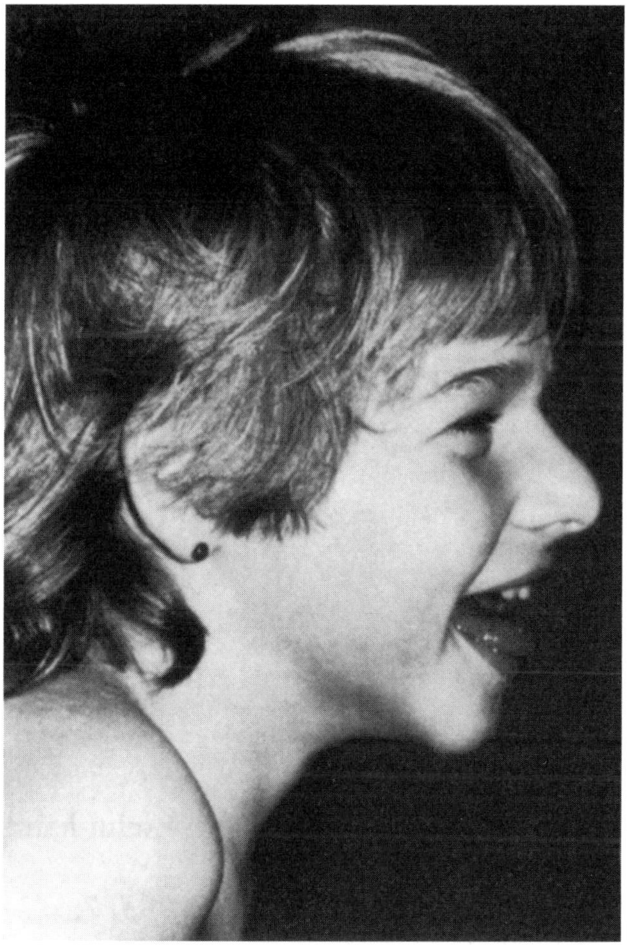

Happy Puppet Syndrome
Reprinted from *Clinical Syndromes,* Wiedemann and Kunze, 1997, by permission of the publisher Mosby

There is no specific treatment for Angelman syndrome at this time other than management of symptoms. Seizures require medication. Valproic acid and clonazepam are usually effective. Stimulant medication may improve short attention span. Physical therapy is helpful for improving gait and balance. Surgery or bracing may be needed to properly align the legs. Life span is not thought to be substantially affected by Angelman syndrome (Laan, Haeringen, & Brouwer, 1999).

Severe developmental delay necessitates intensive education and rehabilitation efforts. Managing hyperactivity and inattention improves opportunities for learning. Behavior modification techniques are utilized to reduce or eliminate undesirable behaviors. A teacher aide may be needed to help manage hyperactive and inattentive behavior and to administer a behavior modification plan. Occupational therapy may help fine motor and oral motor control. Because expressive speech is very limited, speech or communication therapy is important for developing nonverbal communication methods. Incorporating communication aids, such as picture boards, at the earliest appropriate time is advisable. Consistency in techniques used at school and home facilitates development of skills for activities of daily living (National Angelman Syndrome Foundation, 2000).

Additional research is needed for better understanding and control of seizures. Future research in genetics holds promise for reversing the abnormal gene processes that cause Angelman syndrome and other disorders with similar etiology.

REFERENCES

Angelman, H. (1965). "Puppet" children: A report on three cases. *Developmental Medicine and Child Neurology, 7,* 681–688.

Laan, L. A. E. M., Haeringen, A. V., & Brouwer, O. F. (1999). Angelman syndrome: A review of clinical and genetic aspects. *Clinical Neurology and Neurosurgery, 101,* 161–170.

National Angelman Syndrome Foundation. (2000). Facts about Angelman syndrome. Retrieved from http://asclepius.com/angel/asfinfo.html

Williams, C. A., Angelman, H., Clayton-Smith, J., Driscoll, D. J., Hendrickson, J. E., Knoll, J. H. M., et al. (1995). Angelman syndrome: Consensus for diagnostic criteria. *American Journal of Medical Genetics, 56,* 237–238.

DAVID R. STEINMAN
Austin Neurological Clinic and Department of Psychology, University of Texas at Austin

ANGIOEDEMA (HEREDITARY)

Angioedema (hereditary) is a genetic disorder associated with the deficiency of C1 inhibitor, a protein in the blood. This disorder is characterized by episodes of swelling in areas of the skin and the tissue beneath or in mucous membranes that line the openings of the body, such as the mouth, throat, genitalia, or gastrointestinal tract (Anderson, Anderson, & Glanze, 1998; Berkow, Beers, Bogin, & Fletcher, 1997). Hands, feet, face, and lips may also be affected.

C1 esterase inhibitors are part of a group of proteins that help fluids to move through the capillaries, affecting allergic and immune reactions in the body (National Organization for Rare Disorders [NORD], 1999). These complex proteins are known as *complement* and help to regulate the flow of body fluids in and out of cells.

Angioedema is also sometimes known as angioneurotic edema (hereditary; HAE), C1-INH, complement component 1 inhibitor deficiency, complement component C1, regulatory component deficiency, esterase inhibitor deficiency, or HAE (NORD, 2000). The most common form of hereditary angioedema is Type I, when C1 esterase inhibitors are found in abnormally low levels in the blood. In Type II, the C1 esterase inhibitors produced by the body are abnormal; this form of the disease is more rare.

Symptoms of angioedema are caused by an accumulation of body fluids that results in the blockage of lymphatic vessels or veins (NORD, 1999). The obstruction of the normal flow of blood or lymphatic fluid causes the swelling of the skin and mucous membranes.

Episodes of angioedema are usually short and can be triggered by injury, viral illness, or emotional stress. Patients may have areas of painful swelling that is accompanied by hives and sometimes itching. Nausea, vomiting, and cramps may also accompany the skin irritation. Severity of angioedema can vary greatly among individuals. The most serious complication of angioedema occurs when the upper airways become swollen, making it difficult for the patient to breathe. Without appropriate treatment, blocked airways have been fatal in approximately 25–30% of patients with hereditary angioedema (Bowen, Hawk, Sibunka, Hovick, & Weiler, 2001).

Angioedema may be diagnosed by checking the levels or activity of C1 inhibitor in the blood. The patient may exhibit respiratory or gastrointestinal symptoms. It is recommended that the physician check the family history to confirm that the angioedema is of hereditary origin.

Characteristics

1. Episodes of swelling in areas of the skin and the tissue beneath, or in mucous membranes that line the openings of the body, such as the mouth, throat, genitalia, or gastrointestinal tract.
2. Hands, feet, face, and lips may also be affected.
3. Episodes are usually short.
4. Areas of painful swelling accompanied by hives and sometimes itching.
5. Nausea, vomiting, and cramps may also accompany the skin irritation.
6. Upper airways may become swollen, making it difficult for the patient to breathe.

An attack of angioedema can sometimes be treated with aminocaproic acid (Berkow et al., 1997). Sometimes medications such as antihistamines, corticosteroids, and epinephrine are given, but there is no conclusive proof that these are effective.

During an acute attack of angioedema, it may be necessary to place an endotracheal tube in the trachea to facilitate respiration. In severe cases, a tracheotomy may need to be performed to prevent obstruction of the respiratory tract (Anderson et al., 1998).

To prevent an attack before minor surgery or dental work, a plasma transfusion may be needed to increase the C1 inhibitor levels in the blood. According to Berkow et al. (1997), purified C1 inhibitor can prevent attacks, but this is not currently available for general use. Prevention of angioedema attacks can be facilitated by administering oral anabolic steroids (androgens) such as stanozolol or danazol, which can stimulate the body to produce more C1 inhibitor. However, dosage of these drugs for women must be carefully monitored due to masculinizing side effects (Berkow et al., 1997). Local treatments rarely work but may help to make the patient more comfortable.

Angioedema does not have any direct relationship to a need for special education. However, children with more severe cases may have to be monitored for respiratory difficulty.

Currently, research is being conducted to identify the gene mutations that cause hereditary angioedema (Bowen et al., 2001).

REFERENCES

Anderson, K. N., Anderson, L. E., & Glanze, W. D. (Eds.). (1998). *Mosby's medical dictionary* (5th ed.). St. Louis, MO: Mosby.

Berkow, R., Beers, M. H., Bogin, R. M., & Fletcher, A. J. (Eds.). (1997). *The Merck manual of medical information.* Whitehouse Station, NJ: Merck Research Laboratories.

Bowen, B., Hawk, J. J., Sibunka, S., Hovick, S., & Weiler, J. M. (2001). A review of the reported defects in the human C1 esterase inhibitor gene producing hereditary angioedema including four new mutations. *Clinical Immunology, 98*(2), 157–163.

National Organization for Rare Disorders. (1991). Angioedema. Retrieved from http://www.stepstn.com/cgi-win/nord.exe?proc=GetDocument&rectype=0&recnum=98

Michele Wilson Kamens
Rider University

ANIRIDIA CEREBELLAR ATAXIA MENTAL DEFICIENCY

Aniridia cerebellar ataxia mental deficiency, also known as Gillespie syndrome, is characterized by mental retardation, partial absence of the iris of the eye (partial aniridia), and incoordination of voluntary movements due to underdevelopment of the brain's cerebellum (cerebellar ataxia; National Organization of Rare Disorders, 1998).

Aniridia cerebellar ataxia mental deficiency is an extremely rare autosomal recessive condition, with approximately 16 cases reported in the literature (McKusick, 1997). It affects males and females equally.

Characteristics

1. Child may have slow and halting speech, hypotonia, and an unsteady gait (Nevin, 1990).
2. Child may show developmental delays with certain motor skills, such as walking or speaking.
3. Mild to moderate retardation is usually present.
4. The pupillary margin of the iris and the sphincter pupillae may be absent, resulting in poor vision and photophobia (Wittig, Moreira, Freire-Maia, & Vianna-Morgante, 1988).
5. Child may develop glaucoma, which could lead to loss of vision.

Treatment for aniridia cerebellar ataxia mental deficiency depends on the individual's symptoms. A team of ophthalmologists and optometrists is necessary to treat visual problems. Surgery may be required for the child's visual difficulties, such as diplopia. Glasses or contact lenses may be necessary to alleviate problems caused by partial aniridia. The child should also be monitored for glaucoma to prevent possible vision loss. Physical therapists may assist the child with gross motor skills, and speech therapists may be necessary to address speech delays. In rare cases, individuals with the disorder have heart abnormalities or skeletal malformations that require treatment (McKusick, 1997).

Children with aniridia cerebellar ataxia mental deficiency have mental retardation, cerebellar ataxia, visual impairments, health problems, and possible speech delays that may interfere with their education. To help them reach their maximum learning potential, most children with this disorder need special education services and early intervention programs. The services required depend on the child's symptoms and needs. Psychoeducational assessments can help school personnel develop an appropriate individual educational plan for each child. Physical therapy and speech therapy may also be necessary for young children with motor impairments or speech delays (Plumridge, Bennett, Dinno, & Branson, 1993).

Individuals with aniridia cerebellar ataxia mental deficiency may require some form of assisted living, depending on the severity of their symptoms. There does not appear to be a decrease in functioning with age, and in some cases motor performance improves (McKusick, 1997). Future research is focusing on the etiology, prevention, and treatment of this disorder.

REFERENCES

McKusick, V. A. (Ed.). (1997, August). Online Mendelian inheritance in man: A catalog of human genes and genetic disorders. Retrieved from http://www.ncbi.nlm.nih.gov

National Organization for Rare Disorders. (1998, February 28).

Aniridia cerebellar ataxia mental deficiency. Retrieved from http://www.rarediseases.org

Nevin, N. C., & Lim, J. H. (1990). Syndrome of partial aniridia, cerebellar ataxia, and mental retardation—Gillespie syndrome. *American Journal of Medical Genetics, 35,* 468–469.

Plumridge, D., Bennett, R., Dinno, N., & Branson, C. (Eds.). (1993). *The student with a genetic disorder.* Springfield, IL: Charles C. Thomas.

Wittig, E. O., Moreira, C. A., Freire-Maia, N., & Vianna-Morgante, A. M. (1988). Partial aniridia, cerebellar ataxia, and mental deficiency (Gillespie syndrome) in two brothers. *American Journal of Medical Genetics, 30,* 703–708.

Susannah More
University of Texas at Austin

ANOREXIA NERVOSA

The literal translation of anorexia nervosa is lack of appetite (Cassell, 1994). The first case of anorexia nervosa cited in the literature was in 1686 by Dr. Richard Morton. He described "nervous consumption" of a woman who appeared as if she were a skeleton with skin and had coldness of the body, diminished appetite, uneasy digestion, and fainting spells (Costin, 1999). Anorexia nervosa is defined in Costin (1999) as an eating disorder that is often life-threatening. A person with anorexia nervosa engages in a relentless pursuit of thinness. Also according to the *Sourcebook,* there are two types of anorexia nervosa. The restricting type involves low nutritional intake; the binge-purge type involves alternate episodes of binge eating or purging behavior. The disorder qualifies as a mental disorder according to criteria set forth in the *Diagnostic and Statistical Manual of Mental Disorders–Fourth Edition* (American Psychiatric Association, 1994).

Anorexia nervosa is more commonly diagnosed among females, but accurate female-male ratios are difficult to determine for several reasons. Admitting to having an eating disorder is more difficult for males because of the preconceived notion that only females are affected by this disorder. Males also report the fear that if they are diagnosed with an eating disorder, they would also be suspected of homosexuality (Costin, 1999). Onset can be as early as age 10 or as late as the postmenopausal years (Costin, 1999).

Characteristics

1. Child or adolescent refuses to maintain body weight consistent with that considered normal weight for age and height (i.e., total body weight only 85% of that expected to be within normal range).
2. Although severely underweight, child has intense fear of gaining weight or becoming obese. Fear does not diminish with weight loss.
3. Disturbance in body image—seeing oneself as fat even when emaciated.
4. Cessation of menstrual cycle.
5. Hyperactivity, especially in initial stages.
6. Fasting, vomiting, or laxative use, often following a binge.
7. Preoccupation with thoughts of food, weight, and exercise.

In severe cases or latter stages:

1. Disturbance in cognitive ability
2. Deterioration of family and social relationships
3. Overt increase in depression
4. Development of fine body hair
5. Sensation of feeling cold
6. Low blood pressure and slow pulse
7. Electrolyte imbalance
8. Dental problems

There is no known specific cause, but researchers agree that anorexia nervosa is more likely a negative response to a number of psychological, environmental, and physiological factors. Individuals with anorexia appear to lack the skills necessary to cope with such psychological factors (Cassell, 1994).

Effective treatment revolves around therapy. Although virtually every type of therapy has been tried, there is not one type that has proven to be more effective than any other. The difficulty with treatment is that most individuals with anorexia tend to deny the presence of the disorder. Development of trust between the therapist and the client is therefore crucial to treatment in order to reduce the resistive tendencies of the client. In the most severe cases, in which the client's weight has fallen to 25% or more below normal, hospitalization is suggested. The urgency of hospitalization depends on whether there is the presence of severe metabolic disturbance, severe depression or suicide risk, severe purging, psychosis, or symptoms of starvation (Cassell, 1994). Drug therapy, group therapy, and family counseling have also been recommended as part of treatment.

According to the Individuals With Disabilities Education Act (1997), a student with anorexia nervosa would probably qualify for special education services under the category of Other Health Impairment. The school psychologist should provide direct services for students with anorexia nervosa in the form of counseling. Collaboration by the school psychologist with the parents and the student's mental health provider is crucial to the academic success of the student, along with close monitoring while the student is at school.

Currently, the National Institutes of Health (NIH) are

researching causes, methods of treatment, and early identification of those at risk of developing anorexia nervosa. Studies are ongoing at the NIH regarding the biological aspects of appetite, hypothalamic and pituitary aspects of anorexia nervosa, and potassium levels in persons with anorexia nervosa (Cassell, 1994).

REFERENCES

American Psychiatric Association. (1997). *Diagnostic and statistical manual of mental disorders* (4th ed.). Washington, DC: Author.

Cassell, D. (1994). *Encyclopedia of obesity and eating disorders.* New York: Facts on File.

Costin, C. (1999). *The eating disorder sourcebook: A comprehensive guide to the causes, treatments, and prevention of eating disorders.* Los Angeles: Lowell House.

Christine D. Cde Baca
University of Northern Colorado

ANOXIA

All cellular functions in the body including the neuronal cells in the brain are dependent on adequate oxygenation. A healthy human brain utilizes 20% of total oxygen inhaled. Brain cells have a low threshold for oxygen deprivation, because they are unable to respire anaerobically or store oxygen for later use. If the cerebral blood flow drops to 20% of its normal rate, consciousness will be lost within 10 s, followed by interruption of nerve cell metabolism within 30 s, and manifestation of electrophysiological abnormalities within 60 s. Although immediate and adequate perfusion of the brain with oxygen will restore its normal functions, anoxic-hypoxic conditions persisting longer than 4–8 min can result in diffuse neuronal cell death.

Characteristics

1. Hypoxia and anoxia are often used interchangeably; however, anoxia implies near-total deprivation of oxygen with adequate blood supply.
2. Hypoxia often results in general cognitive deficits, poor memory, impaired executive functioning, visual-perceptual deficits, and mood problems.
3. Acute hypoxia often causes decreased concentration, short-term memory, motor-processing speed, and verbal fluency.
4. Chronic hypoxia tends to affect abstract reasoning, motor strength, and psychomotor speed.

Both states of hypoxia—reduced oxygen delivery to cells in spite of normal blood flow and anoxia, in which almost no oxygen is delivered although blood supply is adequate—can lead to brain dysfunction. Although these conditions are different, the two terms are often used interchangeably. Hypoxemia, low level of oxygen in blood, is associated with such pathologies as carbon monoxide (CO) poisoning, cardiopulmonary arrest, cerebral ischemia, in-utero asphyxiation, near drowning, obstructive sleep apnea, congenital heart disease, asthma, and chronic lung disease.

The brain regions most affected by poor oxygenation are those areas at the end of the vascular reach comprised of hippocampus, basal ganglia, cerebellum, occipital cortex, and some frontal regions. The neuropsychological sequalae of anoxic injury, regardless of the etiology, include general cognitive deficits, memory problems, impaired executive functions, visual-perceptual problems, apperceptive agnosia, and affective changes (e.g., anxiety, depression, irritability, and personality changes). Permanent cerebral structural changes demonstrated by several radiological studies corroborate these regions' involvement following an anoxic-hypoxic episode (Bigler & Alfano, 1988).

There are significant differences in manifestations of acute versus chronic hypoxia. In acute hypoxia (e.g., in CO poisoning) the abilities reported to be most sensitive are concentration, short-term memory, new learning, critical judgment, motor speed, and verbal fluency, whereas in chronic hypoxia (e.g., in obstructive lung disease), the emerged deficits are on tasks requiring abstract reasoning, visuomotor abilities, motor strength, and psychomotor coordination (Berry, Webb, Block, Bauer, & Switzer, 1986).

Four mechanisms by which neurons can incur damage or death following hypoxia-anoxia are: (a) lowered neuronal pH environment due to lactic acidosis, (b) increased intracellular calcium following ionic pump failure in the nerve cell membrane, (c) increased firing rate of neurons due to extensive release of excitatory amino acids such as glutamate, and (d) formation of oxygen-free radicals upon neuronal membrane reoxygenation (Hopkins, 2000).

The National Institute of Neurological Disorders and Stroke (NINDS, 2000) outlines the treatment strategy for anoxia-hypoxia. NINDS suggests promptly establishing an adequate airway, assuring blood oxygen saturation, supporting the cardiovascular system, and preventing (or treating) pneumonia. Even with proper and immediate support provided to the respiratory and cardiovascular systems, prognosis for recovery is often tenuous. Factors that have been shown to be associated with poorer prognosis include the rate at which hypoxia develops, the extent and duration of oxygen depletion, and the degree to which other organ systems (e.g., heart) are compromised due to such factors as vascular and circulatory insufficiency.

Special education services are often required for children who have suffered an hypoxic episode. With the exception of those with milder degrees of hypoxia, such as asthma and cardiac problems, many children with hypoxic brain damage will require comprehensive services (e.g., special education placement and speech and language and physical-occupational therapies). These children often receive services under the category Intellectual Disabilities; however, in cases of an acquired head injury or near-drowning, Traumatic Brain Injury services may be more appropriate. Regardless of the classification of special education assistance, careful assessment to identify strengths and weaknesses is needed. Furthermore, ongoing monitoring is necessary to determine the adequacy of service. Home-school collaboration is particularly important, given the impact that hypoxic brain injuries have on the entire family and the needs of each individual member (e.g., education and supportive counseling).

REFERENCES

Berry, D. T. R., Webb, W. B., Block, A. J., Bauer, R. M., & Switzer, D. A. (1986). Nocturnal hypoxia and neuropsychological variables. *Journal of Clinical and Experimental Neuropsychology, 8,* 229–238.

Bigler, E. D., & Alfano, M. (1988). Anoxic encephalopathy: Neuroradiological and neuropsychological findings. *Archives of Clinical Neuropsychology, 3,* 383–396.

Hopkins, R. O., Weaver, L. K., & Bigler, E. D. (2000). Longitudinal outcome following carbon monoxide poisoning: Psychological changes. *Journal of the International Neuropsychological Society, 6,* 393.

National Institute of Neurological Disorders and Stroke. (2000). Anoxia/Hypoxia. Retrieved from www.nih.gov

Najmeh Hourmanesh
Elaine Clark
University of Utah

See also Hypoxia

ANTISOCIAL PERSONALITY DISORDER

Antisocial personality disorder (ASPD) is characterized by a pervasive pattern of disregard for and violation of the rights of others. This pattern begins in childhood or adolescence, continues into adulthood (American Psychiatric Association [APA], 2000), and often involves criminal behavior (Millon, 1996). It is estimated that less than 3% of the males in the general population have ASPD. Far fewer females are given the diagnosis; they are thought to make up less than 1% of all cases. In clinical populations, prevalence estimates vary from 3% to 30%. Unlike other personality disorders, in order to be diagnosed with ASPD, the individual must be at least eighteen years of age. According to *Diagnostic and Statistical Manual of Mental Disorders–Fourth Edition, Text Revision (DSM-IV)* criteria (APA, 2000), however, antisocial behaviors must be present before the age of 15, despite the delay in actual diagnosis.

Characteristics

1. Failure to conform socially with respect to lawful behavior (e.g., repeated delinquent and criminal acts that lead to arrests)
2. Display of deceitfulness (e.g., repeated lying and conning of others for personal gain)
3. Frequent irritability and aggressiveness, including physical fighting and assaults
4. Failure to express remorse for wrongdoing
5. Demonstration of a reckless disregard for self and others
6. Irresponsible acts as noted by the failure to achieve as expected in school, maintain employment, and honor financial obligations, to name a few

A pattern of antisocial behavior needs to be established prior to making a diagnosis of ASPD. According to Taylor, Iacono, and McGue (2000), antisocial behaviors that are first evident during adolescence tend to be more transitory and are less likely to be predictive of a personality disorder (i.e., than are antisocial behaviors occurring earlier in life). The onset of antisocial behaviors during early childhood often denotes a more serious and persistent disorder (e.g., repeated lifelong criminal activity). When first evident during childhood, a diagnosis of conduct disorder is often made, and the likelihood of developing ASPD is much greater. Establishing a pattern of chronicity not only helps to predict the course, but it can also be used to rule out other non-ASPD conditions that may lead to a disturbance in conduct (e.g., substance abuse disorders).

In terms of comorbid personality disorders, individuals with ASPD may have narcissistic and sadistic personality disorders or traits (Millon, 1996). For example, individuals with ASPD may be overly self-focused and narcissistic, may gain sadistic pleasure from inflicting pain, or both. What distinguishes this group, however, from others with personality disorders is the pattern of offending behaviors. Although offending behaviors improve with age, considerable harm can be inflicted before the individual gets too old to commit crimes.

The conduct problems and antisocial behaviors of children and adolescents who develop ASPD often warrant special attention in the schools, including special education services. Given the high rate of comorbid learning problems (with conduct disturbance), many times these students are served in programs for children with learning disabilities. Some, however, have such serious problems of conduct early on that services under the category of Emotional Disturbance are warranted. When the structure of the school is not sufficient, alternative programs need to be considered, including day treatment programs and residential placements. Adolescents, like adults, are often treated while in custody and at the insistence of legal authorities. This situation as well as the fact that individuals with ASPD often lack insight into their own role in offending behaviors (e.g., unable or unwilling to accept responsibility) can seriously impede treatment. Exploiting others for personal gain may be reduced if these individuals gain a better understanding of the impact of their behavior on others.

Both genetic and environmental factors have been implicated in the etiology of ASPD. Researchers have shown that antisocial behaviors tend to occur in families (e.g., Goldstein, Prescott, & Kendler, 2001); however, this has not been shown to be the case so much with late-onset behaviors (e.g., delinquent behaviors among adolescents). Genetics have been thought to play more of a role when conduct disturbance occurs early in childhood. Nonetheless, distinguishing genetic from environmental influences is difficult. More research is needed to understand risk factors and what can be done early in a child's life to prevent criminal behaviors from occurring.

REFERENCES

American Psychiatric Association. (2000). *Diagnostic and statistical manual of mental disorders* (4th ed., text revision). Washington, DC: Author.

Goldstein, R. B., Prescott, C. A., & Kendler, K. S. (2001). Genetic and environmental factors in conduct problems and adult antisocial behavior among adult female twins. *The Journal of Nervous and Mental Disease, 189*(4), 201–209.

Millon, T. (1996). *Disorders of personality:* DSM-IV *and beyond* (2nd ed.). New York: Wiley.

Taylor, J., Iacono, W. G., & McGue, M. (2000). Evidence for a genetic etiology of early-onset delinquency. *Journal of Abnormal Psychology, 109*(4), 634–643.

Rex Gonzales
Elaine Clark
University of Utah

ANTLEY-BIXLER SYNDROME

This syndrome is a rare hereditary disorder. It causes distinctive deformities of the head and face. There are also other skeletal anomalies of the extremities.

Only a few cases have appeared in the medical literature. One instance of affected siblings suggests an autosomal recessive pattern of inheritance.

Characteristics

1. High, arched skull with flattening of the back of the skull
2. Craniosynostotis (premature closure of the sutures between the skull bones)
3. Protruding forehead
4. Flattened, underdeveloped midfacial area, including the bridge of the nose and the eye sockets
5. Choanal atresia (very small nasal openings)
6. Lowset, malformed ears; bulging eyes
7. Limb deformities, including fusion of the bones of the forearm (radioulnar synostosis), joint contractures, arachnodactyly (long, thin fingers) and femoral bowing (curvature of the thigh bone)

These infants have a very dysmorphic appearance. However, plastic surgeons who specialize in the repair of craniofacial anomalies can transform their appearance in an almost magical way. Several operations may be necessary to achieve acceptable cosmetic results. Babies who survive past the first few months of life may need tracheostomy to relieve severe upper airway obstruction and gastrostomy (a surgical opening into the stomach through the abdominal wall) to overcome feeding difficulties. Joint contractures usually improve with age and respond to physical therapy.

There is no research to support the need for educational modifications due to the rarity of the disorder and the poor prognosis.

Prognosis for the disorder is rather dismal. There is an 80% mortality rate in the first few months, secondary to breathing difficulties, including apneic episodes. After these patients survive infancy, their outlook improves. One 10-year-old child with this problem is currently a normal fifth grader who functions well both socially and intellectually.

For more information, please contact FACES: The National Craniofacial Association, P.O. Box 11082, Chattanooga, TN, 37401, (423) 266-1632, (800) 332-2373, home page: http://www.faces-cranio.org.

REFERENCES

Jones, K. (1997). *Smith's recognizable patterns of human malformations* (5th ed.). Philadelphia: W. B. Saunders.

Barry H. Davison
Ennis, Texas

Joan W. Mayfield
Baylor Pediatric Specialty Services
Dallas, Texas

ANXIETY DISORDERS

According to Bernstein and Borchardt (1991), anxiety disorders are very common in children. There are nine major disorders that have anxiety as a salient feature (Albano, Chorpita, & Barlow, 1996). These disorders include but are not limited to separation anxiety, obsessive-compulsive disorder, panic disorder, generalized anxiety disorder, post-traumatic stress disorder (PTSD), and social phobia. Although the aforementioned disorders are all considered anxiety disorders, only separation anxiety falls under the category of "Disorders Usually Diagnosed in Infancy, Childhood, or Adolescence" in the *DSM-IV* (American Psychiatric Association [APA], 1994). Anxiety disorders contain many common features like fears, irritability, nervousness, insomnia, inattentiveness, and hypervigilance (APA, 1994). Research in the area supports an integrated etiological model for the development of anxiety. It is believed that there are multiple factors (e.g., genetics, learned behaviors) working together that lead to the onset of the disorder (Barlow, 1988).

As mentioned, anxiety is a common condition in children. Estimates of prevalence reveal that 5–18% of children have an anxiety disorder (Labellarte, Ginsberg, Walkup, & Riddle, 1999). It is unclear, however, how socioeconomic status, gender, and ethnicity affect the onset of the disorder. Similarly, research does not provide clear evidence concerning socioeconomic, gender, or ethnic differences (Albano et al., 1996). In addition, overall prevalence rates may be hard to ascertain due to problems in diagnosing the disorder. Diagnosing a child with an anxiety disorder can be controversial because "anxiety is considered normal for young children [especially when they] . . . confront situations such as the dark, separation from caretakers, or the first day of school" (Albano et al., 1996, p. 213). Adolescents also can experience anxiety when applying for college or finding a date for the prom. Distinguishing normal anxiety from abnormal anxiety can be a difficult task. When determining whether a child is disordered, it is important to identify whether anxiety is causing impairment in everyday functioning. Diagnostic decisions also can be problematic because of the significant amount of symptom overlap between anxiety and other disorders and the high amounts of comorbidity (Albano et al., 1996; Labellarte et al., 1999).

Characteristics

1. Recurrent fears or phobias
2. Nervousness
3. Insomnia
4. Irritability
5. Hypervigilance
6. Inattentiveness
7. Clinging behaviors
8. Avoidance of fearful situations and people
9. Agitated or on-edge behavior
10. Crying

Treatment for childhood anxiety can include medication in the form of hypnotics and sedatives. However, psychopharmacological interventions are not substantiated in the literature (Brown & Sawyer, 1998). Children also can be treated with psychosocial interventions like individual, group, or family therapy. Cognitive-behavioral therapy is thought to be a promising intervention for anxiety disorder in children (Ollendick & King, 1998). Through this form of treatment children can identify distorted thought patterns and irrational beliefs as these thoughts and beliefs relate to their fears and phobias. Unfortunately, cognitive-behavioral techniques may not be appropriate for all children. Not all children are insightful, especially at young ages, so other behavior modification techniques may be necessary.

Special education placement will vary. Because anxiety is an internalizing disorder, children with anxiety disorders may go unnoticed in the classroom. Children who do receive special education services are most likely to be diagnosed with severe emotional disturbance. For those in need of special education placement, services can vary from behavioral monitoring in the classroom to residential placement. Children who remain in the public school setting often need supplementary aids and services such as counseling, social skills training, or both. Children also may need extra academic support in the form of resource or content mastery services. Children with milder forms of anxiety can function well with minimal support.

Children who receive this diagnosis may or may not continue to meet criteria as an adult. With proper treatment, children can learn to compensate for or alleviate their fears. Anxiety disorders are complex and need to be properly understood. Future research needs to focus on the etiology and the specific treatments that are effective for anxiety disorders.

REFERENCES

Albano, A. M., Chorpita, B. F., & Barlow, D. H. (1996). Childhood anxiety disorders. In E. J. Mash & R. A. Barkely (Eds.), *Child psychopathology.* New York: Guilford Press.

American Psychiatric Association. (1994). *Diagnostic and statistical manual of mental disorders* (4th ed.). Washington, DC: Author.

Barlow, D. H. (1988). *Anxiety disorders: The nature and treatment of anxiety and panic.* New York: Guilford Press.

Bernstein, G. A., & Borchardt, C. M. (1991). Anxiety disorders of childhood and adolescence: A critical review. *Journal of the American Academy of Child and Adolescent Psychiatry, 30,* 519–532.

Brown, R. T., & Sawyer, M. G. (1998). *Medications for school age children: Effects on learning and behavior.* New York: Guilford Press.

Labellarte, M. J., Ginsberg, G. S., Walkup, J. T., & Riddle, M. A. (1999). The treatment of anxiety disorders in children and adolescents. *Biological Psychiatry, 46,* 1567–1578.

Ollendick, T. H., & King, N. J. (1998). Empirically supported treatment for children with phobic and anxiety disorders: Current status. *Journal of Clinical Child Psychology, 27,* 156–167.

Carrie George
Texas A & M University

APECED SYNDROME

APECED is also known as autoimmune polyglandular disease Type I or autoimmune-polyendocrinopathy-candidias. APECED stands for autoimmune polyendocrinopathy (APE), candidiasis (C), and ectodermal dysplasia (ED). It is a very rare genetic syndrome that involves the autoimmune system. It is a combination of several distinct disorders and is defined as the subnormal functioning of several endocrine glands at the same time (National Organization for Rare Disorders [NORD], 2000; Tierney, McPhee, & Papadakis, 2000; Ward et al., 1999). There are three types of APECED: polyglandular autoimmune syndrome, Type I; polyglandular autoimmune syndrome, Type II; and polyglandular autoimmune syndrome, Type III. Type I affects children and adults younger than age 35. Type II more frequently strikes adults, with peak incidence at about 30 years.

APECED syndrome affects people of all ages. It usually begins in childhood. However, it can develop as late as the fifth decade. The syndrome affects equal numbers of males and females. It is a very rare disease that occurs in only about 170 persons worldwide. The majority of the affected persons live in Finland (NORD, 2000).

APECED is defined as a combination of at least two of the following disorders: hypoparathyroidism (a disorder that causes lower than normal levels of calcium and phosphate in the blood), candidiasis (harmless yeast infection that occurs in the mouth, intestinal tract, skin, nails, and genitalia), ectodermal dysplasia (a group of hereditary nonprogressive syndromes that affects tissues derived from the ectodermal germ layer).

Characteristics

1. Children with hypoparathyroidism have symptoms such as weakness, muscle cramps, and abnormal sensations such as tingling, burning, and numbness of the hands. Excessive nervousness, loss of memory, headaches, and uncontrollable cramping muscle movements of the wrists and feet are also present.
2. Children with hypoparathyroidism may have inability to adequately absorb nutrients (malabsorption), and diarrhea can result. Anemia and autoimmune thyroid disease may also occur.
3. Children with candidasis have the symptoms of yeast infection of either the mouth or nails.
4. Dystrophy of the teeth and nails.

The treatment of APECED syndrome is directed toward the specific diseases that are apparent in each patient. Hypoparathyroidism (low plasma levels of calcium and phosphate) is treated with calcium, ergocalciferol, or dihydrotachysterol (forms of Vitamin D). There is no known cure for ectodermal dysplasia. Treatment is directed at symptoms. Over-the-counter creams may relieve skin discomfort. Dentures, hearing aids, and so forth may be required. Heat and overexercise are to be avoided due to impaired sweating. Cleft lip and palate, syndactyly, and other limb deformations are treated by surgery (NORD, 1999). Genetic counseling is important for patients with APECED and for their relatives.

This syndrome would probably not necessitate special education services. Classification under Section 504 of the Vocational Rehabilitation Amendment of 1973 would be appropriate to release the child from physical education requirements. Furthermore, modifications can be made if the child is frequently absent from school.

The researchers showed that mutations in the gene AIRE (autoimmune regulator) are responsible for the pathogenesis of APECED. The identification of the gene defective in APECED should facilitate finding a potential treatment for the disease. Some studies (Ward et al., 1999) have supported the use of cyclosporine (CyA) therapy for the treatment of severe APECED.

REFERENCES

National Organization for Rare Disorders. (November 30, 1999). APECED syndrome. Retrieved from http://www.medica.com/kbase/nord/nord835.htm

Tierney, E. M., McPhee, S. J., & Papadakis, M. A. (2000). *Current medical diagnosis and treatment* (39th ed.). Los Altos, CA: Lange Medical Publications.

Ward, L., Paquette, J., Seidman, E., Huot, C., Alvarez, F., Crock, P., et al. (1999). Severe autoimmune polyendocrinopathy-candidiasis-ectodermal dystrophy in an adolescent girl with a novel AIRE mutation: Response to immunosuppressive therapy. *Journal of Clinical Endocrinology and Metabolism, 84,* 844–852.

Nina Cheng
University of Texas at Austin

See also Ectodermal Dysplasia

APERT SYNDROME

Apert syndrome is a genetic defect that is classified as a craniofacial and limb anomaly. It can be either inherited or sporadically occurring. Apert is one of four autosomal dominant disorders and is a result of de novo mutations (Ferreira et al., 1999). It results in specific distortions of the head, face, hands, and feet during fetal development, including abnormal skull development (craniosynostosis), concave face (midface hypoplasia), and fusion of the fingers and toes (syndactyly). The presence of syndactyly separates Apert syndrome from other similar syndromes.

Apert syndrome is caused by a mutation of fibroblast growth-factor receptor-2 (FGFR2; Wilkie et al., 1995). Ninety-nine percent of patients identified with Apert syndrome had mutations on chromosomes S252W or P253R of the fibroblast growth factor gene. Infants with P253R mutations generally have better craniofacial appearance after surgery than do infants with S252W mutations.

In a study involving 53 affected children, approximately 50% of fathers were over the age of 35, whereas in approximately 20% of cases, both parents were over 35 (Tolarova, Harris, Ordway, & Vargervik, 1997). This finding suggested that mutations may be more associated with paternal alleles. Rare cases in offspring of healthy couples can be explained by germinal mosaicism (Allanson, 1986).

Since its discovery in the late 19th century, more than 300 cases of Apert syndrome have been reported (Cohen, 1991). The prevalence was found to be 12.4 cases per million births (Tolarova et al., 1997). Asians were found to have the highest prevalence rate (22.3 per million live births), and Hispanics had the lowest prevalence rate (7.6 per million live births). Both genders seem to be affected equally.

Characteristics

1. At birth or during sonogram, the following features are found:
   - Craniosynostosis—distortions of the head and face, primarily with a large skull, widely spaced and slanted eye sockets, and crowding of the teeth
   - Midface hypoplasia
   - Syndactyly of the hands and often the feet—webbed or "mitten" hands
2. Brain scans reveal malformations of the corpus callosum, limbic system, gyral abnormalities, hypoplastic white matter, and heterotopic gray matter.
3. Cleft palate occurs in 30% of cases.

For infants with Apert syndrome, premature fusion of plates in the skull restricts brain growth and causes increased pressure in the brain as it develops. Early surgery can detach the plates to relieve the pressure. Craniofacial surgery results in some healing of features (vonGernet, Golla, Ehrenfels, Schuffenhauer, & Fairley, 2000). Surgery is needed to separate the fingers to maximize functionality, but this procedure is performed on the feet only if walking will otherwise be impaired. Surgery normally takes place between 5 and 8 months.

In the past, diagnosis was made at birth, but advances within the last decade have made prenatal diagnosis possible. In mothers with Apert syndrome, detection as early as 20 weeks has been made (Lyu & Ko, 2000). In unaffected mothers, prenatal diagnosis is typically in the third trimester (Kaufmann, Baldinger, & Pratt, 1997). Prenatal diagnosis is generally based on findings of craniosynostosis and syndactyly originally using fetoscopy and more recently using sonograms (Lyu & Ko, 2000).

Although cases of normal cognitive functioning are common, varying degrees of mental retardation are found in 50% of patients (Sarimski, 1998). Psychosocial functioning of children with Apert syndrome is similar to that of children with facial disfigurement in general, with children with more severe cognitive deficits experiencing more severe psychosocial impairment (Sarimski, 1998). Twenty percent of patients were found to suffer from emotional lability, social competence deficits, hyperactivity, or attentional problems. Psychosocial intervention is implicated for children with Apert syndrome as well as their parents, but little research on specific interventions has been conducted.

Prognosis and complications vary between patients. Additional reconstructive surgeries may be needed and congenital abnormalities may exist that require additional treatment. More research is needed in order to improve treatment and early detection of Apert syndrome.

REFERENCES

Cohen, M. M., & Kreiborg, S. (1991). Genetic and family study of the Apert syndrome. *Journal of Craniofacial Genetic Developmental Biology, 11,* 7–17.

Ferriera, J. C., Carter, S. M., Bernstein, P. S., Jabs, E. W., Glickstein, J. S., Marion, R. W., et al. (1999). Second-trimester molecular prenatal diagnosis of sporadic Apert syndrome following suspicious ultrasound findings. *Ultrasound in Obstetrics and Gynecology, 14,* 426–430.

Kaufmann, K., Baldinger, S., & Pratt, L. (1997). Ultrasound detection of Apert syndrome: A case report and literature review. *American Journal of Perinatology, 14,* 427–430.

Lyu, K. J., & Ko, T. M. (2000). Prenatal diagnosis of Apert syndrome with widely separated cranial sutures. *Prenatal Diagnosis, 20,* 254–256.

Sarimski, K. (1998). Children with Apert syndrome: Behavioural problems and family stress. *Developmental Medicine and Child Neurology, 40,* 44–49.

Tolarova, M. M., Harris, J. A., Ordway, D. E., & Vargervik, K. (1997). Birth prevalence, mutation rate, sex, ratio, parents' age, and ethnicity in Apert syndrome. *American Journal of Medical Genetics, 72,* 394–398.

vonGernet, S., Golla, A., Ehrenfels, Y., Schuffenhauer, S., & Fairley, J. D. (2000). Genotype-phenotype analysis in Apert syndrome suggests opposite effects of the two recurrent mutations on syndactyly and outcome of craniofacial surgery. *Clinical Genetics, 57,* 137–139.

Wilkie, A. O. M., Slaney, S. F., Oldridge, M., Poole, M. D., Ashworth, G. J., Hockley, A. D., et al. (1995). Apert syndrome results from localized mutations of FGFR2 and is allelic with Crouzon syndrome. *Nature and Genetics, 9,* 165–172.

Elizabeth Kaufmann
University of Texas at Austin

APHASIA, BROCA'S

Often called expressive or motor aphasia, Broca's aphasia is characterized by difficulties with the motor production of speech, problems with articulation, and a paucity of spoken language. Broca's aphasia can vary in severity from a slight difficulty in the reproduction of a spoken word to a complete inability to produce spoken language.

Broca's aphasia occurs in children who either fail to or have difficulty in expressing themselves despite normal cognitive abilities and normal linguistic comprehension. Developmental language disorders and mental retardation should be ruled out when screening for this disorder. The main cause is a traumatic brain injury resulting in a lesion to the left hemisphere of the brain in either the frontal operculum or the corticocortical association pathways in the white matter of the temporal, parietal, and frontal lobes that relate to the motor speech areas (Martin, 1989).

Characteristics

1. Difficulties in the production of spoken language, accompanied by a varying impairment in language comprehension.
2. Verb forms are often reduced to the infinitive or participle; nouns are usually expressed in singular form and conjunctions; and adjectives, adverbs, and articles are often omitted. This type of speech is often labeled telegraphic speech (Goodwin, 1989).
3. Speech tends to be slow, nonfluent, effortful, and poorly articulated.
4. Repetition of single words is effortful but usually accomplished.
5. Although Broca's aphasia is associated with language expression, difficulties in language reception and comprehension may accompany this disorder. This symptom can be observed in deficits in comprehension, reading, naming, and memory (Hynd & Willis, 1988).
6. May be associated with hemiplegia, a weakness or paralysis on the right side of the body. This tends to be manifested by motor weakness and sagging or drooping of the lower right side of the face. There also may be weakness in the right arm and leg (Goodwin, 1989).

The treatment of Broca's aphasia focuses on retraining the child to recover or gain the ability to produce spoken language; this is done by addressing the child's deficits by symptom, such as intense retraining using picture cards to improve naming ability. It is hoped that retraining will have the effect of shifting language expression to an area of the brain that is not impaired. Because Broca's aphasia tends to be associated with left-hemisphere damage, the expectation is that the right hemisphere will assume the responsibility of producing expressive language.

The effect of treatment on Broca's aphasia in children can vary greatly. Children tend to have greater success in recovery than do adults, due to their increased brain plasticity. Many predictive factors can influence a child's level of recovery. The size and type of lesion in the brain is the most critical variable. For example, a minor closed head injury that results in slight swelling of the brain could produce signs and symptoms of Broca's aphasia that could later disappear completely. A traumatic brain injury that involves extensive bilateral damage could produce a case of Broca's aphasia resulting in a complete loss of language expression, from which the child would never recover.

Another major predictive recovery factor is the age of the child when the lesion occurs. It is thought that younger children have increased plasticity of the brain, the ability to reorganize actions within levels of functioning, and the ability to shift functioning to different areas of the brain that have not been impaired (Goodwin, 1997). A problem can emerge, however, with shifting functions from one area of the brain to another. It may be that when an area of the brain not yet specialized in function assumes a new responsibility, a compromise in meeting later developmental milestones may emerge (Fletcher-Janzen & Kade, 1997).

Special education placement can be a very important issue for children with Broca's aphasia. If their impairment is severe, they will probably be classified as a child with a traumatic brain injury. If their difficulties are related to academic problems, they could be served as children with learning disabilities or as children needing speech and language services. Difficulties with expression of language can inhibit many educational, emotional, and social aspects of a child's development. The special education teacher will need to be cognizant of a number of special considerations that these children require. For example, the ability to learn to read can be severely affected by Broca's aphasia, even if the child's receptive language skills are intact. The child may have difficulty exchanging and expressing thoughts and ideas and asking questions; this could result in a significantly reduced vocabulary and an inability to obtain phonemic awareness of words and rules of grammar. The child's social skills can also be affected because the child may have problems with positive, normal peer interactions; this can also lead to a deficit in the development of social skills and nuances as well as the development of appropriate behavior. Children with Broca's aphasia may demonstrate signs of depression, especially those children with localized impairment, because they have no other cognitive difficulties and are fully aware of their deficits.

The future for children with Broca's aphasia appears to be promising. Improved technology helps emergency services respond more quickly to accidents involving brain trauma and new medical technology such as the positron-emission tomography (PET) scan is helping neurologists understand more about how the brain operates. Although prognosis for recovery still remains guarded for children with severe lesions and diffuse damage, improved understanding of Broca's aphasia is offering increasing amounts of hope for children with expressive language problems.

REFERENCES

Fletcher-Janzen, E., & Kade, H. D. (1997). Pediatric brain injury rehabilitation in a neurodevelopmental milieu. In C. R. Reynolds & E. Fletcher-Janzen (Eds.), *Handbook of clinical child neuropsychology* (2nd ed., pp. 452–481). New York: Plenum Press.

Goodwin, D. M. (1989). *A dictionary of neuropsychology.* New York: Springer-Verlag.

Hynd, G. W., & Willis, W. G. (1988). *Pediatric neuropsychology.* Orlando, FL: Grune & Stratton.

Martin, J. H. (1989). *Neuroanatomy: Text and atlas.* Norwalk, CT: Appleton and Lange.

Andrew S. Davis
University of Northern Colorado

APHASIA, JARGON

Jargon aphasia (JA) is an acquired language disorder in the comprehension and use of words, in which patients use incorrect words or sounds in place of intended words. The speech jargon in JA can be (a) paraphasic—grammatically intact with the inclusion of misused, semantically related words; (b) asemantic—intact speech with the inclusion of nonsense words, or neologisms; and (c) phonemic, a stream of nonsense syllables. Given the intact ability to produce speech, JA is considered a form of fluent aphasia.

In children and adults, JA results from brain damage due to infection, tumors, cerebrovascular disturbance, or head trauma. Although early conceptualizations assumed a right-hemisphere damage bias in childhood aphasias, more recent analyses have found that childhood aphasias are usually the result of left-hemisphere damage, which is consistent with the etiology of adult aphasias (Woods & Teuber, 1978). The trauma responsible for the acquired aphasias may initially lead to other symptoms, such as headaches, muscle weakness or paralysis, visual field deficits, and personality changes. It is important to note that children with JA may have difficulties in auditory comprehension, despite their ability to produce speech.

Characteristics

1. Language disorder involving use of incorrect words or sounds and auditory comprehension.
2. Result of severe brain damage.
3. Prognosis is good, but some language and educational deficiencies persist.

Recovery from JA depends on a number of interrelated factors, such as etiology, the site and size of the brain damage, age at which the brain insult occurred, and the presence of other neurological disturbances (Murdoch, 1990). It is generally believed that younger children show more complete and rapid recovery from acquired aphasias, reflecting the plasticity of the developing brain. However, several reports have documented slow (months to years) and incomplete recovery in children, resulting in persistent language deficits. There are numerous treatments available for JA and other aphasias, such as speech or writing therapies, but their efficacy is variable. Often, language ability exhibits spontaneous recovery, in which the natural healing of the brain restores some speech capacity—that is, in the absence of any intervention, children with acquired aphasias show improvement over time. This tendency underscores the fact that the defining symptoms of a form of acquired aphasia (such as the jargon in JA) may subside as the recovery process unfolds, but that other subtle language and cognitive impairments may persist.

In general, children with JA and other acquired aphasias show lower levels of scholastic achievement due at least in part to persistent language impairments. Cooper and Flowers (1987) tested individuals on a variety of language and academic achievement tests 1 to 10 years after suffering childhood aphasias. They found that although these individuals were competent verbal communicators, they performed more poorly than did age-matched controls on tasks of word, sentence, and paragraph completion, naming, production of complex sentences, and word fluency. Other academic difficulties included arithmetic and spelling skills. Accordingly, two thirds of the group were receiving special education services at the time of testing. Thus, regular monitoring of JA children after apparent clinical recovery is crucial for supporting educational achievement.

REFERENCES

Cooper, J. A., & Flowers, C. R. (1987). Children with a history of acquired aphasia: Residual language and academic impairments. *Journal of Speech and Hearing Disorders, 52,* 251–262.

Murdoch, B. E. (1990). *Acquired speech and language disorders: A neuroanatomical and functional neurological approach.* London: Chapman and Hall.

Woods, B. T., & Teuber, H. L. (1978). Changing patterns of childhood aphasia. *Annals of Neurology, 3,* 273–280.

Adam S. Bristol
Yale University

Jennifer M. Gillis
University of California, Irvine

APHASIA, TRANSCORTICAL

Three types of transcortical aphasia were identified by Goldstein in 1948, including transcortical sensory aphasia, transcortical motor aphasia, and mixed transcortical aphasia. In transcortical motor aphasia, the damage occurs in the frontal lobe, anterior to Broca's area along the motor speech cortex. The lesion is often deep in the cortical matter. In transcortical sensory aphasia, the damage occurs in the occipito-temporal area, posterior to Wernicke's area. Some authorities believe the two types are actually deficits to the same semantic accessing system and that they simply differ in the anatomical levels that are involved (Rothi, 1998). They can result from trauma, stroke, or disease. In mixed transcortical aphasia, the damage can occur in both areas or in the association cortex; it often occurs as a result of diffuse damage (i.e., carbon monoxide poisoning, dementia, multiple infarctions). The incidence of transcortical aphasia is not reported in the literature, and prevalence likely depends on the etiology of the disorder. However, in children it is considered rare.

Characteristics

Transcortical motor aphasia:

1. Able to maintain a simple conversation.
2. Speech may be somewhat disfluent as a result of lack of connector words and is often characterized as having phonemic and global paraphasias.
3. The ability to repeat is very good; often they are echolalic and visual and auditory comprehension is adequate.

Transcortical sensory aphasia:

1. Often have anosognosia, meaning it is difficult for children to recognize that they have deficits.
2. Speech is often quite fluent but may have paraphasias.
3. Often able to repeat and may be echolalic, which distinguishes them from Wernicke aphasia.
4. The primary concern is the very poor comprehension.

Mixed transcortical aphasia:

1. The speech is often disfluent.
2. Diminished quantity of speech.
3. Poor comprehension.
4. Adequate ability to repeat.
5. Individuals with the mixed variety may be able to correct syntactic errors but not semantic errors.

Treatment of aphasias generally follows one of two major regimes, including restoration of functioning or development of compensatory strategies. The treatment of transcortical motor aphasias tends to follow the restoration philosophy, often because the transcortical variety is believed to be a less severe form of aphasia and more likely to show improvement. For example, treatment may focus on restoring volitional initiation of motor acts through practice and self-cueing techniques. The use of pharmacology has also been reported to improve functioning in some individuals. The treatment of transcortical sensory aphasia is highly dependent on the etiology of the aphasia. For example, when the aphasia results from dementia, therapy is different from that used to treat aphasia resulting from a stroke. Rothi (1998) reported that therapy of transcortical sensory aphasia has received no attention in the rehabilitation literature. Treatment of the mixed variety has also not been discussed in the literature.

In children, the terms *acquired aphasia* and *developmental aphasia* must be distinguished. Acquired aphasia refers to language disorders that are the result of identifiable neurological insults (tumor, stroke, trauma, etc.). Developmental aphasia, also known as developmental language disorders, has no known neurological etiology, but the child fails to develop language and speech in an expected manner (Aram, 1998). Depending on the degree of deficit and concomitant problems, the child will likely qualify for special education. Acquired aphasia will likely be identified in the schools under the Traumatic Brain Injury or Physical or Other Health Disorders labels, but depending on the presence of other symptoms, it could be identified as a Speech and Language Disorder. If the disorder is acquired, revision of the child's educational plans should parallel gains. Developmental aphasia will likely be treated under the category of Speech and Language Disorder. Special education plans should be reviewed at least annually, and monitoring of academic progress is highly encouraged.

Generally, the best prognosis is reserved for transcortical motor aphasia, followed by sensory aphasia, and then by mixed transcortical aphasia. Based on several single-case studies, the prognosis for TMA is good; however, with studies that have larger sample sizes, the results have been less encouraging. Wernicke aphasia patients often recover into a condition of transcortical sensory aphasia. When this occurs, the prognosis is considered favorable. Future research dealing with treatment efficacy and future theoretical models will add much to the knowledge based in aphasiology.

REFERENCES

Aram, D. M. (1998). Acquired aphasia in children. In M. T. Sarno (Ed.), *Acquired aphasia* (pp. 451–480). New York: Academic Press.

Rothi, L. J. G. (1997). Transcortical motor, sensory, and mixed aphasia. In L. I. LaPointe (Ed.), *Aphasia and related neurogenic language disorders* (2nd ed., pp. 91–111). New York: Thieme.

Dalene McCloskey
University of Northern Colorado

APHASIA, WERNICKE (SENSORY APHASIA)

Wernicke aphasia is characterized by the inability to comprehend speech or to produce meaningful speech following lesions to the posterior cortex. Individuals with Wernicke aphasia rarely experience muscular weakness affecting one side of the body, or hemiparesis. In most cases, its etiology involves a lesion affecting the dominant temporal lobe, particularly the auditory association cortex of the posterior-superior portion of the first temporal gyrus (Benson, 1993; Kolb & Whishaw, 1990).

Although anyone can acquire Wernicke aphasia, it most often affects people in their middle to late years of life. It has been estimated that 80,000 adults and 1,400 children acquire some type of aphasic disorder each year; this results in an estimated 1 million Americans that currently live with some type of aphasia. Although the exact prevalence of Wernicke aphasia is unknown, Wernicke is one of the more commonly recognized aphasic syndromes. Men and women appear to be equally affected, and common causes include stroke, severe head trauma, brain tumors, and infections (National Institute on Deafness and Other Communication Disorders, 2000).

Characteristics

1. This disorder is acquired following a period of normal language functioning.
2. The key feature of the disorder is a striking disturbance in comprehension of verbal and/or written language.
3. Deficits in the ability to repeat information (e.g., when patients are instructed to repeat "no ifs, ands, or buts") and to name common objects are frequently noted.
4. Verbal output is fluent, but it is almost always contaminated by unintended syllables, words, or phrases (paraphasias) and by made-up words (neologisms).

Some individuals with Wernicke aphasia will experience a spontaneous recovery within a few hours to a few days following the injury, and no additional treatment will be necessary. In most cases, however, language recovery is neither quick nor complete. In these instances, the most common treatment involves some form of language therapy. Although there are various approaches to conducting language therapy, all approaches attempt to help individuals utilize remaining abilities, restore impaired abilities, compensate for lost abilities, and learn alternative methods of communicating. It is widely believed that language therapy is most effective early in the recovery process. Additional treatment modalities may include medications, such as the anticoagulant Heparin, and in some instances, surgery (Richman & Wood, 1999).

Children with Wernicke aphasia will likely require speech and language services and frequently qualify for special education services for individuals with speech and language impairments, traumatic brain injuries, or learning disabilities. For severely impaired children, compensatory strategies intended to maximize the amount of communication they can regain will be indicated. Children with less severe deficits will probably have phonemic segmentation weaknesses. They may benefit from reading instruction that focuses on phonemic awareness and synthesis activities such as being presented with the same and different sounds through headphones in a repetitive manner. Placement in the regular education classroom with full inclusion will probably be problematic. Individual services in a special education resource room will probably be needed. Some children may have such difficulty with phonemic awareness activities that whole-word approaches will be necessary for reading instruction. Deficits in listening or reading comprehension are also likely to be present, and instructional modifications will probably be necessary (Richman & Wood, 1999).

Children with significant language deficits have also been found to be at increased risk for both internalizing and externalizing behavior problems (Cantwell & Baker, 1991). Consequently, children with Wernicke aphasia may also qualify for special education services under the Serious Emotional Disturbance or Other Health Impaired categories. Treatment for these comorbid psychological and behavioral problems will probably need to be addressed in order for speech and language therapy to be effective. Due to problems with language comprehension, traditional "talk therapies" are likely to be of limited benefit. Behavior modification techniques and highly structured, and repetitive exercises that address specific topics (e.g., social skills training, impulse control) may be most beneficial for managing the comorbid behavior problems associated with language deficits in children (Richman & Wood, 1999). Parent training and parent education will also probably be important treatment interventions.

In general, the prognosis for recovery from Wernicke aphasia is influenced by a number of factors. The first is related to the severity and location of the lesion. The more isolated and limited the lesion, usually the better the prognosis. The age of the individual is also an important factor. Younger patients—usually no older than early adulthood—tend to recover prior levels of functioning more fully than do older patients. Healthier patients also tend to recover more fully. Finally, the time at which educational interventions are initiated also appears to be important. The sooner services can be provided, the better the outcome.

Research activities that investigate new combinations of medications to improve recovery or decrease the risk of the vascular accidents that frequently result in Wernicke aphasia are currently in progress. Research activities that investigate the use of new gene therapies to actually regenerate neural pathways are on the horizon. Studies investigating new diagnostic devices such as positron-emission tomography (PET) and functional magnetic resonance imaging (fMRI) are ongoing. It is hoped that with these new devices, more accurate diagnostic techniques will be identified. Investigations concerning which language therapy techniques work best and how computer-aided interventions can help aphasic patients are also currently underway.

REFERENCES

Benson, D. F. (1993). Aphasia. In K. M. Heilman & E. Valenstein (Eds.), *Clinical neuropsychology* (3rd ed., pp. 17–36). New York: Oxford University Press.

Cantwell, D. P., & Baker, L. (1991). *Behavior problems and developmental disorders in children with communication disorder.* Washington, DC: American Psychiatric Press.

Kolb, B., & Whishaw, I. Q. (1990). *Fundamentals of human neuropsychology* (3rd ed.). New York: W. H. Freeman.

National Institute on Deafness and Other Communication Disorders. (2000, September 20). Aphasia. Retrieved from http://www.nih.gov.nidcd/textonly/health/pubs_vsl/aphasia.htm

Richman, L. C., & Wood, K. M. (1999). Psychological assessment and treatment of communication disorders: Childhood language subtypes. In S. D. Netherton, D. Holmes, & C. E. Walker (Eds.), *Child and adolescent psychological disorders* (pp. 51–75). New York: Oxford University Press.

Brian D. Johnson
University of Northern Colorado

APNEA

Sleep apnea is a sleep disorder—specifically, hypersomnia that is associated with apnea, hypoventilation, or both. The disorder causes temporary cessation of breathing that occurs several times a night. Sleep apnea is typically classified as central or obstructive (Baum, 1998). In central apnea, blood oxygen levels decrease to the point breathing ceases and the sleeper awakens in order to start breathing normally. The individual typically recalls being awake in the night, therefore, more likely to report sleep as a problem. Individuals with obstructive sleep apnea (OSA), the most common type of apnea, often attribute their fatigue during daytime to depression or other medical problems (e.g., Nordenberg, 1998). OSA involves either a partial or a complete blockage of the airway during sleep. Respiratory effort either is reduced significantly or ceases entirely during that period; this causes a desaturation of oxyhemoglobin and in some cases cardiovascular problems. Heavy snoring and lack of adequate airflow reduce the amount of deep (and satisfying) sleep an individual receives—hence the increased daytime sleepiness. Although periods of awakening occur, they are often so brief there is no memory of this. As a result, OSA is often difficult to diagnose and inadequately treated.

Sleep apnea is much more common in adults than in children; however, it has been estimated to affect 1–3%, with highest rates during the preschool and elementary years (Owens & Opipari, 1998). It is not clear whether overweight male children, like their adult counterparts, are more prone to developing OSA; however, children with apnea have been found to have enlarged tonsils and adenoids, mandibular abnormalities, and narrower pharyngeal airway space (Kawashima et al., 2000).

Characteristics

1. More common in adults, but when apnea occurs during childhood, it is seen more often in preschool- and elementary-age children (and males).
2. Children with obstructive sleep apnea tend to have enlarged tonsils and adenoids, mandibular abnormalities, and narrower airways.
3. Sleep apnea has been associated with impaired daytime functioning due to sleepiness and with behavior problems.

Sleep apnea usually occurs at the onset of sleep or during rapid eye movement (REM). The episodes of apnea are, on average, 10–15 s in length. In order to meet diagnostic criteria, there must be a minimum of 30 episodes a night. Assessment, therefore, must include a complete sleep history (preferably provided by a reliable observer). Examiners must inquire as to the individual's snoring behaviors; daytime level of arousal and daytime somatic complaints (e.g., sleepiness, headaches, memory impairment, and depression); nighttime sleep problems, including insomnia; cognitive functioning, including slow processing and poor judgment; and changes in mood and personality (Baum, 1998).

It is recommended that children suspected of having sleep apnea be referred to a sleep clinic for consultation. In addition, pediatricians and pediatric dentists need to be consulted regarding treatment options; this includes consideration for tonsillectomy and adenoidectomy, as well as dental treatments for mandibular problems. It is not likely that a child who suffers from sleep apnea will need special education for problems associated with the sleep disorder; however, sleepiness and reduced cognitive efficiency from a lack of sleep can interfere with learning. There is also the likelihood of increased behavior problems in children who have sleep disorders (Owens & Opipari, 1998). Educators need to be aware of such problems and provide interventions to assist these children. In more severe cases, services under Specific Learning Disabilities may be needed, but Other Health Impaired is more likely because the school nurse may be the first person involved to evaluate the child and determine what needs to be done (e.g., opportunities for rest during the school day). School psychologists may also be helpful in providing information about ways to improve a child's or adolescent's sleep hygiene (e.g., maintaining a regular bedtime) and avoid substances that may decrease satisfying sleep (e.g., alcohol, tobacco, and sleep sedatives). School psychologists may also be needed to assess academic and behavioral functioning and to determine what interventions are needed (e.g., contracts, reduced workload, and tutoring).

With early, appropriate interventions, the prognosis for sleep apnea should be good. Research, however, is needed to determine how best to diagnose sleep apnea in a child, especially the preschool- and early-elementary-age child who seems to be most likely to suffer from the problem. Investigations as to what treatments will offer the best outcomes are also needed; this includes many of the treatments that have been found to help adults with apneas—for example, surgical procedures to correct narrow air passageways, nasal sprays, weight loss programs, drug therapies (e.g., antidepressant drugs), and nasal masks to force air (Victor, 1999).

REFERENCES

Baum, G. L., Crapo, J. D., Celli, B. R., & Karlinsky, J. B. (Eds.). (1998). *Textbook of pulmonary diseases* (6th ed.). Philadelphia: Lippincott-Raven.

Kawashima, S., Kiikuni, N., Chia-Hung, L., Takahasi, Y., Kohno, M., Nakajima, I., et al. (2000). Cephalometric comparisons of craniofacial and upper airway structures in young children with obstructive sleep apnea syndrome. *Ear, Nose & Throat Journal, 79*(7), 499–505.

Nordenberg, T. (1998). Tossing and turning no more. *FDA Consumer, 32*(4), 8–13.

Owens, J., & Opipari, L. (1998). Sleep and daytime behavior in children with obstructive sleep apnea and behavioral sleep disorders. *Pediatrics, 102*(5), 1178–1184.

Victor, L. D. (1999). Obstructive sleep apnea. *American Family Physician, 60*(8), 2279–2286.

Cristina McCarthy
Elaine Clark
University of Utah

APRAXIA, DEVELOPMENTAL

Developmental apraxia refers to a sensory integration problem that involves praxis and motor planning deficits. It can affect gross and fine motor performance as well as speech. The disorder is one of higher cortical process and results in problems with planning and executing learned, volitional movements. These children, however, show normal strength, tone, reflex, sensation, and coordination. Developmental apraxia can affect a broad range of functioning, including self-care and academic performance. There are also social implications for children with this disorder (Ripley, Daines, & Barrett, 1997).

Extensive searching of the literature failed to provide prevalence data. There is, however, evidence to suggest that developmental apraxia is a function of immature brain development, or fewer connections between nerve cells (Portwood, 1999). There is also evidence of low weight gain during pregnancy and infant feeding problems. In these cases, neural pathways may be poorly developed, causing problems with neurosynaptic transmission.

The Diagnostic and Statistical Manual of Mental Disorders–Fourth Edition (*DSM-IV*) uses the term *Developmental Coordination Disorder* to refer to developmental apraxia (American Psychiatric Association [APA], 1994). Children with this disorder may qualify for special education services under the Individuals with Disabilities Education Act (IDEA). Typically, these services are provided under the category of Other Health Impaired. In order to qualify for services, the child must demonstrate a marked impairment in the development of motor coordination that significantly interferes with academic achievement or activities of daily living. Coordination difficulties cannot be due to a general medical condition, such as cerebral palsy, muscular dystrophy, or hemiplegia. Furthermore the diagnosis is not made when problems with sensory integration are a function of a pervasive developmental disorder (PDD). It can, however, be made concurrent with a diagnosis of mental retardation (MR); however, motor difficulties must be in excess of those found in children with MR. Associated features include phonological disorder, expressive language disorder, and mixed receptive-expressive disorder (APA, 1994). Developmental apraxia has also been found among children diagnosed with attention-deficit/hyperactivity disorder and specific learning disorders such as dyslexia, dyspraxia, and dyscalculia (House, 1999). According to House, it is important to consider developmental apraxia as a possible comorbid diagnosis in children with dyscalculia or mathematics disorder, both of which are linked to nonverbal learning disabilities.

Characteristics

1. Delayed development of motor skills, with tasks performed slowly and inefficiently
2. Visuospatial deficits and a poor sense of body and objects in space
3. A tendency to fall and bump into objects
4. Heightened sensitivity to sensory input (e.g., noise and lights)
5. Difficulty carrying out a sequence of movements causing oral production (articulation) and fine and gross motor problems (illegible handwriting)
6. Associated problems with attention, concentration, hyperactivity, following directions, and interacting socially

Depending on the severity and nature of the problem, a number of professionals may be involved in the assessment process; this includes the school psychologist, speech-language pathologist, and occupational (and sometimes physical) therapists. Pediatric neurologists may also be involved in order to rule out alternative explanations for the apraxia (e.g., acute or degenerative central nervous system disorder). Tools that are used to evaluate developmental apraxia include the Sensory Integration and Praxis Tests, Bruininks-Oseretsky Test of Motor Proficiency, Comprehensive Apraxia Test, and the Movement Assessment Battery for Children (see Portwood, 1999). In addition to administering standardized measures such as these, it is important to obtain an in-depth developmental history and comprehensive evaluation of the child's cognitive skills and academic performance. Behavioral observations should be a part of the assessment process in order to identify specific deficits that might interfere with the child's classroom performance and extracurricular activities (e.g., recreation).

Treatment often includes speech and language services and occupational therapy involving sensory integration techniques. There are a number of classroom accommodations that may prove beneficial, including allowing extra time to complete assignments, requiring smaller amounts of information to be worked on at any given time, providing extra structure and organization (e.g., line up columns for math assignments), and offering alternative tests and assignments such as dictated rather than written homework.

With appropriate accommodations and services, the prognosis should be good. Further research, however, is needed to provide information about the incidence of this disorder and ways to best remedy the problem.

REFERENCES

American Psychiatric Association. (1994). *Diagnostic and statistical manual of mental disorders* (4th ed.). Washington, DC: Author.

House, A. E. (1999). DSM-IV *diagnosis in the schools.* New York: Guilford Press.

Portwood, M. (1999). *Developmental dyspraxia: Identification and intervention: A manual for parents and professionals* (2nd ed.). London, England: David Fulton.

Ripley, K., Daines, B., & Barrett, J. (1997). *Dyspraxia: A guide for teachers and parents.* London, England: David Fulton.

Lindsey A. Phillips
Elaine Clark
University of Utah

APRAXIA, OCULAR MOTOR COGAN TYPE

Ocular motor apraxia, Cogan type (OMA) is a rare congenital eye disorder. This is also referred to as congenital oculomotor apraxia (COMA). Cogan (CaF Directory, 1997) first reported this disorder in 1952. It is thought to be inherited as an autosomal recessive genetic trait. However, school-age children, as a secondary problem to neurological and metabolic diseases, may acquire this condition. Ocular motor apraxia can be associated with a wide array of brain malformations, metabolic disorders, and perinatal problems (OMA Homepage, 2000).

Ocular motor apraxia effects the mechanism that controls horizontal eye movement, both voluntary and responsive. This disorder is characterized by defective or absent horizontal ocular attraction movements or absence of horizontal voluntary or responsive eye movements. Infants with the disorder may appear to be blind at first because they do not seem to respond to visual stimuli, but later they may develop head movements to shift their gaze (Kearney, Groenveld, Sargent, & Poskitt, 1998). In addition, there have been some reports of infants with the disorder having colic during their first few months of life. Many children fail hearing tests when there is nothing wrong with their hearing because traditional hearing tests do not account for the impact of visual impairment on a child's responses.

The condition and its causes are relatively unexplored because of the rarity of its occurrence. Additionally, due to the rarity of this congenital disorder, its epidemiology was difficult to obtain. The National Organization for Rare Disorders (2000) stated that there were only 50 reported cases in the medical literature.

Characteristics

1. Infant may seem visually unresponsive from birth, behaving as if he or she were blind.
2. There is difficulty with horizontal eye movement. The child will develop a jerking of the head or excessive blinking, which helps to break and then realign focus.
3. The child will have to turn his or her head for side vision instead of using peripheral vision.
4. Low muscle tone is common but is usually due to the secondary condition of being developmentally delayed.
5. The child may reach developmental milestones more slowly than do his or her peers.

There is no direct treatment for ocular motor apraxia. Most treatment is related to the secondary effects of the disorder. Regular visits to a physiotherapist to assist in the development of muscle tone and the use of special toys and equipment in an attempt to correct the effects of ocular motor apraxia are examples of treatments for this condition (CaF Directory, 1997; OMA Homepage, 2000). Parents of children with OMA may find a valuable support system by registering with the OMA organization (http://wwweb.org/oma/). This is a helpful site to interact with other families and gather information regarding this disorder.

Children with OMA may be eligible for special services at school. These children, due to the nature of their disorder, typically have poor reading skills that require remedial assistance. Many of these individuals also display speech apraxia and require speech and language services. Secondary to OMA itself, there may be gross and fine motor difficulties that may make the child appear clumsy. In an effort to cope with such clumsiness, a child may develop behavior problems.

OMA is not a progressive disease. Generally it is thought that the prognosis of this disorder is good and has a developmental resolution. This disorder typically improves or disappears between the ages of 5 and 10. However, there are cases still apparent in adulthood (Prasad & Nair, 1994).

REFERENCES

CaF Directory. (1997, December). Congenital ocular motor apraxia. Retrieved from http://www.cafamily.org.uk

Kearney, S., Groenveld, M., Sargent, M., & Poskitt, K. (1998). Speech, cognition, and imaging studies in congenital ocular motor apraxia. *Developmental Medicine and Child Neurology, 40,* 95–99.

National Organization for Rare Disorders. (2000). Apraxia, ocular motor, Cogan type. Retrieved from http://www.rarediseases.org

OMA Homepage. (2000, July). Investigating and dealing with ocular motor apraxia. Retrieved from http://wwweb.org/oma

Prasad, P., & Nair, S. (1994). Congenital ocular motor apraxia: sporadic and familial: Support for natural resolution. *The Journal of Neuroophthalmology, 14,* 102–104.

Theresa Kelly
William M. Acree
University of Northern Colorado

ARACHNOID CYSTS

Arachnoid cysts are benign cerebrospinal fluid-filled sacs that develop between the surface of the brain and cranial base or attach to the arachnoid membrane (National Institute of Neurological Disorders and Stroke [NINDS], 2000). The cysts may develop anywhere along the cerebrospinal axis but have a predilection for the Sylvian fissure. Arachnoid cysts account for approximately 1% of all intracranial space-occupying lesions (Wester, 1999). Although most are slow growing and asymptomatic at first, if untreated, they can have devastating effects as a result of increased intracranial pressure.

Symptoms are often dependent on the size and location of the cyst. Common symptoms, however, include headache, vomiting, and papilloedema (i.e., problems associated with hypertension). Other symptoms associated with increased pressure include hydrocephalus and subsequent changes in the cranial vault. Gait can also be disturbed, and both endrocrine problems and seizures can occur (Adan et al., 2000). Although epilepsy occurs more often in adults than children with cysts, in 20% of pediatric cases a seizure disorder is diagnosed (compared to 80% in adults; Artico, Cervoni, Salvati, Fiorenza, & Caruso, 1995).

Most arachnoid cysts are congenital; however, they can be acquired. Head injury is often responsible for acquired cysts. Ultrasound is often used to make the diagnosis, even in utero. Males seem to be more prone to developing arachnoid cysts, and the cysts most often occur in the left temporal lobe (Wester, 1999). No sex differences have been found for other cyst locations.

Characteristics

1. Common symptoms include those associated with hypertension (headache, vomiting, papilloedema).
2. Less common problems include gait disturbance, endrocrine abnormalities, and epilepsy.
3. Cognitive problems are often associated with etiology (e.g., head injury causing poor verbal memory, visuospatial deficits, difficulty shifting sets, and slowed processing).

Arachnoid cysts must be treated in order to avoid severe brain damage from increased pressure, hemorrhaging, or both. Treatment depends on the size and location of the cyst, but most interventions are intended to drain the cyst and prevent the accumulation of fluid. Surgical procedures typically include cyst fenestration and shunt placement. Although fenestration appears to be preferred over shunt placements (i.e., to avoid shunt dependency and infection), when arachnoid cysts communicate with the subarachnoid space to cause increased pressure (and hydrocephalus), shunts are used (Artico et al., 1995).

Although there is little indication that these cysts have any long-term physical or cognitive sequelae, some problems appear to be associated with the cause of the cyst (e.g., traumatic brain injury). Other symptoms, however, that have been related to arachnoid cysts include problems as verbal memory and learning, visual-perceptual skill, cognitive flexibility, and psychomotor speed (Soukup, Patterson, Trier, & Chen, 1998). The impact on learning, beyond the acute phase, is unclear. Neuropsychological assessments are, therefore, in order to identify potential deficits in order to design effective interventions. Special education may in these cases be necessary and provided under the category of Other Health Impaired. In cases in which a traumatic brain injury causes the cyst, however, services may be more appropriately provided under that category. More often than not, Section 504 services or classroom accommodations will suffice (e.g., assistance to catch up on missed assignments or reduction of homework to assist the child in completing work in a reasonable time frame).

Prognosis appears to be good when arachnoid cysts are treated early—that is, before they cause further neurological damage (NINDS, 2000). Research, however, is needed to better diagnose the cyst in utero and in infants. Further investigations of preferred treatment strategies are also needed in order to maximize treatment outcome and reduce negative side effects (e.g., problems associated with shunts).

REFERENCES

Adan, L., Bussieres, L., Dinand, V., Zerah, M., Pierre-Kahn, A., & Brauner, R. (2000). Growth, puberty and hypothalamic-pituitary function in children with supresellar arachnoid cyst. *European Journal of Pediatrics, 159*(5), 348–355.

Artico, M., Cervoni, L., Salvati, M., Fiorenza, F., & Caruso, R. (1995). Supratentorial arachnoid cysts: Clinical and therapeutic remarks on 46 cases. *Acta Neurochirurgica, 132,* 75–78.

National Institute of Neurological Disorders and Stroke. (2000, September 16). NINDS arachnoid cysts information page. Retrieved from http//www.ninds.nih.gov/health-and-medical/disorders/aracysts-doc.htm

Soukup, V., Patterson, J., Trier, T., & Chen, J. (1998). Cognitive improvement despite minimal arachnoid cyst decompression. *Brain Development, 20*(8), 589–593.

Wester, K. (1999). Peculiarities of intracranial arachnoid cysts: Location, sidedness distribution in 126 consecutive patients. *Neurosurgery, 45*(4), 775–779.

Wendy Wolfe
Elaine Clark
University of Utah

ARTERIOVENOUS MALFORMATIONS

Arteriovenous malformations (AVMs) of the central nervous system are a set of vascular abnormalities. These congenital lesions are typified by the failure of development of the capillary network normally separating arteries and veins. Lack of a capillary bed allows exaggerated blood flow through the malformation, shunting and stealing blood from other areas of the vascular system, potentially hemorrhaging, and at times growing, so as to lead to obstructive hydrocephalus. The clinical features of the malformation depend on the site, size, and integrity of the malformation. The most common presentation is related to the hemorrhage of an AVM (Humphreys, 1999). Less than 15% of children with AVMs present with seizures, and the remainder are identified secondary to symptoms that include evidence of ischemia, congestive heart failure, developmental delay, or chronic headaches (Humphreys, 1999). AVMs may be divided into three subtypes: true AVMs, AVMs involving the vein of Galen (aneurysms of the vein of Galen), and cavernous hemangiomas (Brett, 1997).

Arteriovenous malformations of the brain or spinal cord are reported to be rare (Hubbard & Meyer, 1998). Prevalence and incidence rates are not reported, however, probably because these lesions are identified only when there is a clinical event (e.g., hemorrhage or seizure). Humphreys (1999) reported that AVMs are rarely discovered as an incidental finding, except in the context of trauma.

Characteristics

1. True AVMs
   - These are structural defects in the formation of the capillary network.
   - The etiology of the abnormality is unclear.
   - Classic AVMs may expand their bulk, causing obstructive hydrocephalus. They may present when they hemorrhage. The gliotic cortex may become a seizure focus.
2. AVMs involving the vein of Galen
   - AVMs involving the vein of Galen are marked by direct communication between the cerebral arterial circulation and the vein of Galen
   - Congestive heart failure is the usual presentation in infants and occurs when massive amounts of blood are shunted to the malformation leading to progressive high-output heart failure.
   - In toddlers, presentation is frequently that of obstructive hydrocephalus. A reversible hemiplegia, secondary to a *steal effect* (blood being shunted away from one hemisphere), may be present.
   - Older children may present with headaches, pyramidal and cerebellar signs, hydrocephalus, or mental retardation.

3. Cavernous hemangiomas
   - Cavernous malformations (also called angiographically occult vascular malformations) are comprised of dilated thin-walled vascular channels.
   - Cavernous angiomas may be inherited as an autosomal dominant disorder. The genetic abnormality is not the same between pedigrees (e.g., there is genetic heterogeneity; Labauge, Lagerge, Brunereau, Levy, & Tournier-Lasserve, 1998).

AVMs are treated when they become symptomatic. Treatment goals are to preserve life and limit neurologic compromise while achieving complete removal of the AVM and maintaining cerebral circulation (Humphreys, 1999). AVMs can be ablated via surgical resection, intravascular embolization, radiosurgery, or a combination of these modalities. The choice of modality is dependent on the size and site of the lesion. Seizures, which often persist after surgical resection, are treated with anticonvulsant medication but may require repeat surgery for seizure control (Humphreys, 1999). The natural history of cavernous angiomas is less clear, so treatment decisions are difficult (Humphreys, 1999; Labauge et al., 1998).

Educational needs are dependent on the degree of neurologic dysfunction. A full neuropsychological evaluation is required to identify current needs and establish areas of deficit and strength. The mechanism of damage (e.g., hemorrhage vs. hydrocephalus vs. ischemia, etc.), as well as location and age of symptom onset, will mediate educational needs. There is some suggestion that the less invasive nature of radiosurgery will mitigate cognitive consequences for those children in whom it is an appropriate treatment modality (Humphreys, 1999).

Prognosis depends on the type of AVM involved. Eighty percent of children who have symptomatic AVMs will require neurosurgery (Humphreys, 1999). History of a previous bleed, a single draining vein, and diffuse AVM morphology are the most important risk factors predicting additional hemorrhage in those with classic AVMs (Kondziolka, Pollack, Lunsford, 1999). There is some suggestion that mortality from hemorrhage is higher in children than in adults (Kondziolka et al, 1999). The risk of hemorrhage in children with cavernous angiomas is unclear (Humphreys, 1999). Functional outcome depends on the site of a cavernous lesion (Labauge et al., 1998). Vein-of-Galen malformations are associated with high morbidity, and treatment is difficult (DeVeber, 1999). Progress in imaging and treatment of AVMs has decreased mortality and morbidity and will be the focus of continued investigation (Humphreys, 1999).

REFERENCES

Brett, E. M. (1997). Vascular disorders of the nervous system in childhood. In E. M. Brett (Ed.), *Pediatric neurology.* New York: Churchill Livingstone.

DeVeber, G. (1999). Cerebrovascular disease in children. In K. F. Swaiman & S. Ashwal (Eds.), *Pediatric neurology: Principles and practice* (3rd ed.). St. Louis, MO: Mosby.

Hubbard, A. M., & Meyer, J. S. (1998). Magnetic resonance imaging of the fetus. In A. Milunsky (Ed.), *Genetic disorders and the fetus: Diagnosis, prevention and treatment.* Baltimore: John Hopkins Press.

Humphreys, R. P. (1999). Vascular malformations: Surgical treatment. In A. L. Albright, I. F. Pollack, & P. D. Adelson (Eds.), *Principles and practice of pediatric neurosurgery.* New York: Theime Medical.

Kondziolka, D. S., Pollack, B. E., & Lunsford, L. D. (1999). Vascular malformations: Conservative management, radiosurgery, and embolization. In A. L. Albright & I. F. Pollack (Eds.), *Principles and practice of pediatric neurosurgery.* New York: Theime Medical.

Labauge, P., Lagerge, S., Brunereau, L., Levy, C., & Tournier-Lasserve, E. (1998). Hereditary cerebral cavernous angiomas: Clinical and genetic features in 57 French families. *Lancet, 352,* 1892–1897.

Greta N. Wilkening
University of Colorado Health Sciences Center
The Children's Hospital

ARTHRITIS, JUVENILE RHEUMATOID

Arthritis is a chronic inflammatory disease of the joints and is a general term that refers to more than 100 rheumatic diseases. The most common type of arthritis in children is called juvenile rheumatoid arthritis (JRA) in the United States and is known as juvenile chronic arthritis (JCA) in Europe. Juvenile rheumatoid arthritis is an autoimmune disorder, which means that the body mistakenly identifies some of its own cells and tissues as foreign. The disorder is defined as arthritis that causes joint inflammation and stiffness for more than 6 weeks in a child of 16 years of age or less. Inflammation causes redness, swelling, warmth, and soreness in the joints. Any joint may be affected, and inflammation may limit the mobility of the affected joints.

There are three types of JRA, which are classified according to the number of joints involved, the symptoms, and the presence or absence of certain antibodies in the blood (Cassidy & Petty, 1995; Robinson, 1998). The first type is pauciarticular JRA (also known as oligoarticular JRA). Pauciarticular JRA is the mildest and most common form, affecting about 50% of children diagnosed with JRA (Cassidy & Petty, 1995; Robinson, 1998). The second type, polyarticular JRA, affecting approximately 30–40% of all children diagnosed with JRA, is considered to be the same as adult rheumatoid arthritis (Cassidy & Petty, 1995;

Robinson, 1998) except that it typically appears before puberty and is more likely to remain in remission (Hatt, Puig, & Wright, 2000). The last form is known as systemic JRA or Still's disease. The systemic form affects approximately 10–20% of children diagnosed with JRA (Cassidy & Petty, 1995; Robinson, 1998). In addition to joints, this form of JRA may also affect internal organs such as the heart, liver, spleen, and lymph nodes.

Juvenile rheumatoid arthritis affects as many as two individuals per 1,000 children with overall estimates ranging from 100,000 to 200,000 youth per year (Hatt et al., 2000; Robinson, 1998). The disorder is twice as common in girls. The main difference between juvenile and adult rheumatoid arthritis is that many children with JRA outgrow the illness, whereas adults have lifelong symptoms.

Characteristics

1. The most common symptom is persistent joint swelling with pain and stiffness that are typically worse in the morning or after a nap. Some children may have little or no pain.
2. Juvenile rheumatoid arthritis commonly affects the knees and joints in the hands and feet, but any joint may be affected.
3. Children with systemic JRA may have a high fever and light pink rash.
4. Eye inflammation is a potentially severe complication.
5. Juvenile rheumatoid arthritis follows a course of flare-ups and periods of remission.
6. Medical interventions include nonsteroidal anti-inflammatory drugs such as aspirin, as well as disease-modifying antirheumatic drugs. In some cases, surgery (joint replacement) may be necessary.
7. There is no known cure for JRA. It is a chronic lifelong condition.

There is no known cure for JRA. Medical intervention concentrates on nonsteroidal anti-inflammatory drugs (NSAIDs) including aspirin, ibuprofen, and naproxen. A trial of aspirin therapy is usually the first course of action. If aspirin therapy is ineffective, other NSAID medications (e.g., Celebrex and Viox) may be tried. If NSAIDs are not effective, disease-modifying antirheumatic drugs (DMARDs) may be prescribed. Exercise is essential to relieve stiffness, maintain flexibility, and prevent joint deformity. Physical and occupational therapies are frequently recommended. The major goal of physical and occupational therapy is to maintain range of motion, muscle strength, and flexibility. Surgery, including joint replacement, may sometimes be necessary and can be beneficial.

Children with JRA may be eligible for special education services under the Other Health Impairment classification of the Individuals with Disabilities Education Act or for accommodations under Section 504 of the Rehabilitation Act of 1973. Children with JRA are not typically at risk for academic difficulties, but JRA can affect a child's mobility, strength, and endurance (Robinson, 1998), and some children may be at risk for emotional and behavioral problems (Wilkinson, 1981). Academic performance may be affected because children may miss school frequently due to pain, stiffness, and medical appointments. Certainly, limitations on physical activities need to be addressed. Generally speaking, competitive sports such as football, hockey, or running are not suitable. Physical education requirements may need to be modified or adaptive physical education provided. Classroom modifications may also need to be developed to address physical limitations (Robinson, 1998). Because of pain and stiffness, some students may have difficulty with fine motor tasks (e.g., writing quickly and often, using scissors, typing on a computer), whereas others may have more difficulty with weight-bearing activities (e.g., moving quickly in hallways, climbing stairs, carrying books, or sitting in one position for a period of time).

Juvenile rheumatoid arthritis is a chronic disease. An individual's prognosis depends on both the type of disease and the response to treatment. Generally, one third of children recover completely, another third continue to have symptoms well into adulthood, and with the remaining one third the condition worsens (Hatt et al., 2000; Robinson, 1998). Death occurs in approximately 2–4% of children with JRA worldwide (Robinson, 1998). In the United States the majority of deaths associated with JRA occur with children experiencing systemic onset of the disease and are often related to infection (Cassidy & Petty, 1995).

REFERENCES

Cassidy, J., & Petty, R. (1995). *Textbook of pediatric rheumatology* (3rd ed.). Philadelphia: W. B. Saunders.

Hatt, D., Puig, N., & Wright, L. (2000). Arthritis, juvenile. In C. R. Reynolds & E. Fletcher-Janzen (Eds.), *Encyclopedia of special education* (2nd ed., Vol. 1). New York: Wiley.

Robinson, E. (1998). Arthritis (juvenile rheumatoid). In L. Phelps, *A guidebook for understanding and educating: Health-related disorders in children and adolescents.* Washington, DC: American Psychological Association.

Wilkinson, V. A. (1981). Juvenile chronic arthritis in adolescence: Facing the reality. *International Rehabilitation Medicine, 3,* 161–176.

Denise E. Maricle
Dana R. Konter
University of Wisconsin-Stout

ASPERGERS SYNDROME

Aspergers syndrome (AS) is a pervasive developmental disorder considered to be at the higher end of the autistic spectrum. The main distinction between a child with autism and a child with AS is in cognitive ability. Children with AS typically have an IQ within the normal to very superior range (Bauer, 2001). Another distinction can be identified in language ability: Children with AS often have normal basic language skills but will have problems with pragmatic-social language (Bauer, 2001). Children with AS typically have impairments in three areas of functioning: social skills, language, and behavior (Bauer, 2001). With respect to behavior, children with AS display repetitive routines and compulsions that can be confused with a diagnosis of obsessive-compulsive disorder (OCD). The difference between AS and OCD would be in the purpose it serves the child. For a child with AS, the repetitive routines and compulsions may serve as self-stimulatory behavior or high arousal (Szatmari, 1991).

Aspergers syndrome is considered to be more common than autism with the prevalence of AS ranging from 20 to 25 per 10,000 children (Bauer, 2001). The syndrome is also more common in boys than girls, with ratios ranging from 2.3:1 (Ehlers & Gillberg, 1993) to 4:1 (Bauer, 2001). Aspergers syndrome is considered a neurologically based disorder that has a genetic link, but the true etiology of AS is still unknown (Bauer, 2001). It typically occurs in association with tic disorders, attention problems, and mood problems (Bauer, 2001). There is no indication of ethnic differences.

Characteristics (Gillberg & Gillberg, 1989):

1. Social impairment (extreme egocentricity) that may include an inability to interact with peers, a lack of desire to interact with peers, a lack of appreciation of social cues, or socially and emotionally inappropriate behavior
2. Narrow interest that may involve exclusion of other activities, repetitive adherence, and more rote than meaning
3. Repetitive routines that may be on self, in aspects of life, or on others
4. Speech and language peculiarities that may include delayed development, superficially perfect expressive language, formal pedantic language, odd prosody (peculiar voice characteristics), or impairment of comprehension, including misinterpretation of literal versus implied meanings
5. Nonverbal communication problems that may consist of a limited use of gestures, clumsy or gauche body language, limited facial expression, inappropriate expression, or a peculiar, stiff gaze
6. Motor clumsiness that includes poor performance on neurodevelopmental examination

Treatment of AS will not provide a cure for the disorder; instead, it only helps to manage AS. Some methods that have been found to be effective in treating AS consist of psychotherapy, pharmacology, or a combination of both (Gillberg & Ehlers, 1998). Increasing adaptive skills, improving communication and socialization, educating parents on AS (including the differences between AS and autism), undergoing social skills training, and participating in group therapy for older children are several interventions that have been found helpful for children with AS (Szatmari, 1991).

Children with AS are eligible for special education services under the Autism category, but these services might not be necessary for children with mild symptoms. In fact, many children can function well in general education classrooms without the need of special education services (Bauer, 2001). For those children who do need special education services, speech services can be extremely beneficial, as can receiving instruction in a resource room for those children with significant learning difficulties or behavior problems (Bauer, 2001).

Aspergers syndrome is a disorder that will not be with a child for his or her entire life. As a child progresses through adolescence and adulthood, different aspects of the disorder will become problematic. Whereas social interaction, behavior, and language may be problematic for a child, this might not be the case when he or she reaches adolescence and adulthood. Once children with AS become adults, they can potentially lead very "normal" lives (Bauer, 2001). There is some controversy as to whether AS is an actual disorder or whether it is just a variation of high-functioning autism (HFA; Gillberg & Ehlers, 1998). As research in this area increases, perhaps a clearer distinction will be made and a decision will be reached as to whether AS and HFA are different disorders. Another area of future research in this area will focus on making a differential diagnosis. Children with AS are often misdiagnosed or underdiagnosed (Bauer, 2001). In order for children to receive more effective interventions and treatment, they will have to be diagnosed appropriately.

REFERENCES

Bauer, S. (2001). Asperger syndrome. Retrieved from http://www.asperger.org/asperger/asperger_bauer.htm

Ehlers, S., & Gillberg, C. (1993). The epidemiology of Asperger syndrome: A total population study. *Journal of Child Psychology and Psychiatry and Allied Disciplines, 34,* 1327–1350.

Gillberg, C., & Ehlers, S. (1998). High-functioning people with autism and asperger syndrome: A literature review. In E. Schopler, G. B. Mesibov, & L. J. Kunce (Eds.), *Asperger syndrome or high-functioning autism?* (pp. 79–106). New York: Plenum Press.

Gillberg, I. C., & Gillberg, C. (1989). Asperger syndrome—some epidemiological considerations: A research note. *Journal of Child Psychology and Psychiatry, 30,* 631–638.

Szatmari, P. (1991). Asperger's syndrome: Diagnosis, treatment, and outcome. *Psychiatric Clinics of North America, 14,* 81–93.

Nancy Peña Razo
Texas A&M University

See also Autism; Pervasive Developmental Disorder

ASPHYXIA

Asphyxia, also called hypoxic-ischemic encephalopathy, is one of the leading causes of perinatal mortality and morbidity in infants (Kumar, 1999). Asphyxia occurs when the brain is deprived of oxygen. Although prolonged delivery can cause asphyxia, more often than not the cause is from intrauterine damage where oxygen deprivation takes place. A depletion of oxygen is caused by one of two mechanisms: *hypoxemia,* or a decrease of oxygen in blood that supplies tissue, or *ischemia,* a decrease in the actual blood supply. Hypoxia or ischemia that occurs weeks or months before birth may or may not be evident at birth. In some cases, the damage is manifest later by various neurologic signs, including seizures. In other cases, it is known at the time of birth (e.g., Apgar scores lower than 6 at 1 and 5 min postdelivery). Although the rate of occurrence is probably equal in preterm and term infants, asphyxia is more apparent in infants who have reached a gestational age of at least 35 weeks. At 34 weeks of gestational age, cortical neurons in the cerebrum, basal ganglia, brain stem, and Purkinje cells in the cerebellum are extremely vulnerable. Damage during this time often causes serious sequelae, including cerebral palsy, a nonprogressive motor disorder with associated cognitive and sensory impairments. Despite improved perinatal care, the incidence of cerebral palsy that is thought to be caused by asphyxia has not changed and is estimated to involve 20% of all cases.

Infants who have been deprived of oxygen often manifest the condition with a reduced heart rate and respiration, pale or cyanotic skin color, diminished muscle tone, and reduced or absent reflexes. Whereas the p02 in the arterial blood is low, pCO2 is elevated. There is also evidence of metabolic and respiratory acidosis.

Characteristics

1. Asphyxia is a leading cause of perinatal mortality and severe neurologic impairment in children, including cerebral palsy.
2. Hypoxemia and ischemia cause asphyxia.
3. Most often, recognizable symptoms appear in an infant who is at least 35 gestational weeks of age and has Apgar scores lower than 6 at 1 and 5 min.
4. Improved status in the first 36 hours after birth provides the best prognosis.

The most favorable prognosis is made when improvement in infant status is observed in the first 36 hr after birth. Infants who appear normal or make substantial progress (e.g., from extreme hypertonia or hypotonia to near-normal status) tend to have a favorable prognosis. Infants who improve but at a slow pace often have less favorable outcomes (i.e., less than 50% eventually achieve normal status). Among infants who develop seizures, at least 80% have persistent impairment. Electroencephalograms and brain computerized tomography (CT) are the most powerful tools for assessing damage. CT scan patterns that suggest poor prognosis (i.e., no better than 50% chance of good outcome) include patchy, decreased, and diffuse density of the cerebral gray and white matter during the first week of life.

Children who have suffered from severe asphyxia almost always require special education services under the category of Intellectual Disabilities. When asphyxia occurs as a result of a traumatic brain injury (TBI), services may be deemed more appropriate under the classification of TBI or Other Health Impairment. Ancillary services are also often required to insure that the child achieves at the expected level both academically and socially. These services often include physical and occupational therapy, speech and language, and school psychological services. Nursing assistance may also be required to assist the child depending on the extent of his or her medical needs (e.g., care of a tracheotomy tube). When a child is not found to be eligible for special education, a comprehensive assessment is still warranted to determine what accommodations, if any, are needed in the regular classroom.

Treatment depends on the severity and manifestation of the condition. For example, in cases of seizure, infants and children need to be treated with anticonvulsant medications (e.g., phenobarbital). When seizures are intractable and further oxygen loss is possible, ventilation support may be necessary. Other treatments include glucose for signs of hypoglycemia. Further research is needed to determine whether steroids can be safely used to reduce edema and cellular treatments can be effective in reducing cell death (e.g., blocking glutamate), thus improving outcome.

REFERENCE

Kumar, K. (1999). Hypoxic-ischemic brain damage in perinatal age group. *Indian Journal of Pediatrics, 66*(4), 475–482.

Najmeh Hourmanesh
Elaine Clark
University of Utah

ASTHMA

Asthma is the most common chronic disease of childhood and the leading cause for pediatric hospitalization and school absenteeism. An estimated 4.8 million children in the United States experience asthma attacks ranging from mild to severe, with the highest rate found among African Americans. Asthmatic symptoms are manifest in 80% of children by age 5. Despite new knowledge about the pathophysiology and treatment of asthma, the morbidity and mortality rates continue to climb. Mortality is often associated with the lack of proper diagnosis of asthma severity and lack of adequate treatment due to limited funds for access (Sanders, 1998).

Characteristics

1. Cardinal features are bronchial hyperactivity to various stimuli, reversible airway obstruction, and an increase in a type of white blood cell associated with allergic reactions.
2. Primary symptoms often present are wheezing, coughing, and shortness of breath, and they occur more frequently at night.
3. Onset in 80% of children with asthma is before the age of 5 years and is more common in males.
4. Asthma is often comorbid with allergic rhinitis and chronic hyperplastic sinusitis.
5. Asthma persists in three quarters of children with a history of moderate to severe disease and in some cases is associated with hypoxemia, acidosis, seizures, and death.

Asthma is a chronic respiratory disease caused by reversible airflow obstruction. The obstruction of the airway is attributed to several factors, including bronchospasm, swelling of the airway, increased mucus secretion, and lymphocytic invasion of the airway walls, to name a few (Merck Manual of Diagnosis and Therapy, 1999). Characteristic symptoms include wheezing, coughing, and shortness of breath. Symptoms tend to worsen at night; in fact, some estimates show a 15–20% variation from morning to night in expiratory flow. Asthma tends to be more severe in males (i.e., a ratio of 3 males to 2 females) and in children under 5 years of age. Atopy, a predisposition to developing an IgE-mediated response to common allergens, is the primary predisposing factor in childhood. Both allergic and atopic asthma, however, are found with eczema or allergic rhinitis.

Asthmatic attacks typically occur as a result of heightened sensitivity to airborne allergens (e.g., dust mites, animal danders, and cockroaches). Asthma can also be triggered by exercise, cold air, tobacco smoke, sudden changes in barometric pressure, pollutants, foods, and chemicals. Aspirin has not been known to cause an asthma attack in children, but it has with adults. Some conditions that exacerbate asthma in children, however, include sinusitis, gastroesophageal reflux, and psychosocial factors.

Complications associated with acute asthma include hypoxemia, acidosis, generalized seizures, and death. Regardless of severity, asthma is life threatening, and death can occur even in milder cases. Underestimating severity, thus delaying treatment, has been found to be associated with mortality.

Long-term outcome studies show that in 75% of children with moderate to severe symptoms (e.g., marked airway hyperactivity and greater susceptibility to allergens), the disease persists into adulthood (Sanders, 1998). The most effective management strategy is to reduce environmental exposure in order to prevent permanent structural and functional impairment to the respiratory system. It is imperative that the child and his or her parents and teachers learn what triggers an attack and work to avoid exposure. Using peak flow meters to monitor airflow obstruction is another way to detect respiratory problems early, that is, before permanent damage occurs.

Asthma is treated with a variety of medications, but higher doses are initially used for control. Common medications include β_2 agonists, corticosteroids, leukotriene inhibitors, theophylline, cromolyn, nedocromil, ipratropium, and epinephrine. Metered-dose inhalers have been shown to provide optimal delivery of medications, and they can reduce the side effects of steroids. Some medications are preventative and need to be used when the child is asymptomatic.

Children with severe asthma are at risk for cognitive impairment (e.g., oral corticosteroid use and episodes of respiratory arrest and hypoxia). Less severe asthma has not been associated with significant cognitive deficits (Annett, Aylward, Lapidus, Bender, & DuHamel, 2000); however, frequent school absences from even the milder cases can impact learning and achievement. It is therefore critical that early intervention be used, including anti-inflammatory medications and environmental controls. Psychologists, teachers, and other professionals need to help educate parents and children about ways to prevent and treat asthma and to collaborate to ensure adequate educational opportunities. Home-school partnerships can be used to improve the child's health and school attendance. This may serve not only to enhance achievement but also to improve the child's self-esteem (e.g., enable them to interact more with peers both in and outside the classroom).

REFERENCES

Annett, R. D., Aylward, E. H., Lapidus, J., Bender, B. G., & DuHamel, T. (2000). Neurocognitive functioning in children with mild and moderate asthma in the childhood asthma management program. *Journal of Allergy and Clinical Immunology, 105,* 717–724.

Merck manual of diagnosis and therapy–17th ed. (1999). Whitehouse Station, NJ: Merck Research Laboratories.

Sanders, N. (1998). Belief systems that affect the management of childhood asthma. *Immunology and Allergy Clinics of North America, 18,* 99–112.

Najmeh Hourmanesh
Elaine Clark
University of Utah

ASTROCYTOMAS

Astrocytomas are neoplasms of the stellate astrocytic neuroglia. Low-grade astrocytomas have a favorable prognosis in the pediatric age group. Slow-growing tumors, pediatric astrocytomas are far more benign than are those in adults. In children, astrocytomas usually occur in the posterior fossa (Brett & Harding, 1997).

The most widely used system for grading astrocytomas is the World Health Organization's four-tiered grading system. Grade I includes astrocytomas with an excellent prognosis following surgical excision, such as juvenile pilocytic astrocytomas of the cerebellum, the most common tumor of childhood (Sagar & Israel, 1998). Grade IV astrocytomas include glioblastoma multiforme, with the four features of endothelial proliferation, nuclear and cytoplasmic atypia, mitosis, and necrosis. Grade II tumors have two of the four features, whereas Grade III tumors are anaplastic, with three of the four features (Hanieh, 2000; Sagar & Israel, 1998). Unlike in adults, pediatric brain tumors are mostly infratentorial, representing 59% of all childhood neoplasms (Hanieh, 2000). The majority of cerebellar astrocytomas are histologically benign (B. Cohen & Garvin, 1996).

The histologically benign juvenile pilocytic astrocytoma of the cerebellum is the most common childhood brain tumor. Typically, this low-grade astrocytoma is well demarcated and is composed of compact, fibrillated cells alternating with looser, spongy areas (B. Cohen & Garvin, 1996; Sagar & Israel, 1998). Approximately 80% of cerebellar astrocytomas are cystic (M. Cohen & Duffner, 1999). The cyst contains straw-colored, proteinaceous fluid and has a mural nodule, the active portion of the tumor. Computerized tomography (CT) and magnetic resonance imaging (MRI) are equally sensitive in the diagnosis of cerebellar astrocytomas (B. Cohen & Garvin, 1996).

Astrocytomas affect males and females equally (Brett & Harding, 1997). They can occur at any age, with a peak incidence between ages 10 and 14 for both low- and high-grade astrocytomas, and a peak incidence between ages 5 and 9 for cerebellar astrocytomas (M. Cohen & Duffner, 1999). There is a lack of clear data regarding the link between ethnicity and incidence of low-grade astrocytomas, although malignant central nervous system (CNS) tumors are slightly more common in American Whites than in Blacks (Benardete & Jallo, 2000). Familial and genetic syndromes have been identified as most important risk factors for astrocytomas. These include the autosomal dominant conditions neurofibromatosis Types 1 and 2, tuberous sclerosis, and epidermal nevus syndrome (B. Cohen & Garvin, 1996; M. Cohen & Duffner, 1999). Environmental factors are believed to increase the risk of developing CNS tumors, including exposure to aromatic hydrocarbons, N-nitroso compounds, triazines, systemic hydrazines, and ionizing radiation (Benardete & Jallo, 2000; B. Cohen & Garvin, 1996; M. Cohen & Duffner, 1999).

Characteristics

1. There is no typical presentation of a child with an astrocytic CNS tumor. Signs and symptoms vary greatly, depending mostly on the location of the tumor and on the presence or absence of increased intracranial pressure (B. Cohen & Garvin, 1996).
2. The child is brought to the pediatrician most often due to headache. Other signs and symptoms include seizures, vomiting, weakness, dysmetria, gait disturbance, endocrinological dysfunction, decreased visual acuity, papilledema, nystagmus, abducens (6th cranial nerve) palsy, behavioral abnormalities, confusion, memory loss, emotional lability, and declining school performance (Brett & Harding, 1997; B. Cohen & Garvin, 1996; M. Cohen & Duffner, 1999).

Diagnosis of a mass lesion is confirmed by MRI, with and without gadolinium enhancement, or by high-resolution CT scans with contrast. These have replaced other forms of imaging. Arteriography provides information regarding vascularity of the tumor and helps exclude vascular malformation (M. Cohen & Duffner, 1999).

The treatment of choice is gross total surgical resection (B. Cohen & Garvin, 1996). This intervention alleviates increased intracranial pressure, relieves local compression of the tumor on functional areas, and provides a tissue diagnosis (M. Cohen & Duffner, 1999). Total surgical removal is often possible in pediatric astrocytomas, especially in the case of cystic lesions. In more solid lesions and those involving the brain stem or midbrain, excision may be dangerous or impossible (Brett & Harding, 1997). There is no universally accepted approach to treatment of optic pathway gliomas (M. Cohen & Duffner, 1999). Drainage of the cyst may relieve blockage of cerebrospinal fluid (CSF) flow and the consequences of hydrocephalus. Ventriculostomy or shunting may be required (Hanieh, 2000). As many as 30% of patients with a posterior fossa mass will require CSF diversion via shunt (M. Cohen & Duffner, 1999).

In terms of adjuvant therapy, low-grade supratentorial

astrocytomas and brain stem gliomas usually do not seed the CSF; therefore, radiation can be limited to the tumor bed alone (M. Cohen & Duffner, 1999). Radiation is not indicated for low-grade cerebellar astrocytomas. For some astrocytomas, radiation has been used only after partial removal or after partial removal of a recurrence (Brett & Harding, 1997). In some cases, chemotherapy is an alternative for patients who have progressive disease after surgery or who cannot undergo resection (B. Cohen & Garvin, 1996).

Special education services may be available to children with astrocytomas by qualifying under the Other Health Impairment handicapping conditions. The 504 plan is another alternative, allowing for classroom and learning modifications. Children with astrocytomas can expect to spend many days out of the classroom. Changes in intellectual functioning and academic performance may involve decrements in executive functioning, heightened sensitivity about performance, demoralization, and lower frustration tolerance, especially in cerebellar lesions with or without radiation therapy (Karatekin, Lazereff, & Asarnow, 2000).

Prognosis is excellent following gross total surgical resection without further treatment of low-grade astrocytomas, with a 5-year survival rate of 90–95%. Up to 85% of children with aggressive but subtotal resection will survive 5 years (Brett & Harding, 1997; B. Cohen & Garvin, 1996). In high-grade astrocytomas without postsurgical irradiation, the 5-year survival is 0–3%, compared with 15–20% in those who received radiotherapy (B. Cohen & Garvin, 1996; M. Cohen & Duffner, 1999).

REFERENCES

Benardete, E., & Jallo, G. (2000, July 10). Low-grade astrocytoma. In R. Kuljis, F. Talavera, J. Kattah, M. Baker, & N. Lorenzo (Eds.), *Medicine Journal* [Online]. Retrieved from http://www.emedicine.com/neuro/topic190htm

Brett, E., & Harding, B. (1997). Intracranial and spinal cord tumours. In E. M. Brett (Ed.), *Paediatric neurology* (3rd ed., pp. 537–553). New York: Churchill Livingstone.

Cohen, B., & Garvin, J. (1996). Tumors of the central nervous system. In A. M. Rudolph, J. E. Hoffman, & C. D. Rudolph (Eds.), *Rudolph's pediatrics* (20th ed., pp. 1900–1920). Stamford, CT: Appleton & Lange.

Cohen, M., & Duffner, P. (1999). Tumors of the brain and spinal cord including leukemic involvement. In K. F. Swaiman & S. Ashwal (Eds.), *Pediatric neurology: Principles and practice* (3rd ed., pp. 1049–1098). St. Louis, MO: Mosby.

Hanieh, A. (2000, November). Neoplasm: Pediatric brain tumors. Retrieved from http://www.health.adelaide.edu.au/paed-neuro/neoplasm.html

Karatekin, C., Lazareff, J., & Asarnow, R. (2000). Relevance of the cerebellar hemispheres for executive functions. *Pediatric Neurology, 22*(2), 106–112.

Sagar, S., & Israel M. (1998). Tumors of the nervous system. In A. S. Fauci, J. B. Martin, E. Braunwald, D. L. Kasper, K. J. Isselbacher, S. L. Hauser, J. D. Wilson, & D. L. Longo (Eds.), *Harrison's principles of internal medicine* (14th ed., pp. 2398–2409). New York: McGraw-Hill.

Greta N. Wilkening
University of Colorado Health Sciences Center
The Children's Hospital

Laurie L. Ferguson
The Wright Institute
The Children's Hospital

ATAQUE DE NERVIOS

Ataque de nervios is a culture-bound idiom of mental distress principally reported among Latinos from the Caribbean but recognized among many Latin American and Latin Mediterranean groups (American Psychiatric Association [APA], 1994). Ataque de nervios has a very broad range of diagnosis and is apparently neither age nor gender specific (Cardenas et al., 1998).

Ataque de nervios first appeared in medical literature in 1955. The initial case study focused on extreme emotional reactions seen in Puerto Rican army recruits. From this initial study, the disorder has been documented as appearing in many Latin groups from Colombian Indians (Calderon, Pineros, & Rosselli, 1998) to Puerto Rican populations in Houston, Texas (Cardenas et al., 1998). In the incidence of immigrant Puerto Rican populations, "self-report of Ataque de Nervios was the central variable; 16% of all respondents reported having experienced an Ataque de Nervios at some point in their lives" (Cardenas et al., 1998, p. 233). When this rate is compared to the total population of Puerto Rico, the 16% positive responsive rate approximated a 13.8% overall prevalence. Typically, ataques de nervios are expressions of self-labels of psychiatric symptoms that have been shaped by cultural factors such that many cases are reported within family groups. Respectively, this disorder apparently affects all age groups, although cases are initially reported at adolescence (Calderon et al., 1998).

Characteristics

1. Uncontrollable shouting
2. Attacks of crying
3. Trembling
4. Heat in chest rising to head
5. Verbal or physical aggression
6. Asphyxia
7. Fear of dying

According to the *Diagnostic and Statistical Manual of Mental Disorders–Fourth Edition* dissociative experiences are closely related to ataque de nervios. Seizure-like or fainting episodes and suicidal gestures are prominent in some attacks but absent in some others (APA, 1994). Ataque de nervios also seems to be stress related such that ataques have been known to occur typically at funerals, accidents, or family conflicts and "will call forth family or other social supports, suggesting that [ataques] may be culturally shaped and sanctioned responses to severe stress" (Cardenas et al., 1998, p. 234).

In treatment of this syndrome, diagnosticians created the Ataque de Nervios Questionnaire–Revised (ANQ-R). The ANQ-R is a "self-related questionnaire, which starts by asking subjects directly if they have ever experienced an Ataque de Nervios" (Cardenas et al., 1998, p. 234). Following completion of the questionnaire, a structured diagnostic interview is conducted with the Anxiety Disorders Interview Schedule–Revised (ADIS-R) or the Structured Clinical Interview for DSM-III (SCID) to detect the degree and frequency of the ataques (Cardenas et al., 1998). When treating and diagnosing children, a separate questionnaire is recommended, the Ataque de Nervios Questionnaire for the Child Study. Similarly, a semistructured diagnostic interview with a psychiatrist is recommended with child cases. Typically, ataque de nervios is treated with antidepressants.

When encountering a child exhibiting characteristics of ataque de nervios, utilizing the above methods of treatment is encouraged, and performing a proper family history to examine the degree of assimilation and family environment is recommended (Cardenas et al., 1998). Special education services may be needed if the condition is determined to be chronic and interfering with academic success at school.

There are no known studies of prognostic factors associated with ataque de nervios at this time. Clinicians working with students with this syndrome will need to be alert for culturally competent assessment and intervention methods in the school setting.

REFERENCES

American Psychiatric Association. (1994). *Diagnostic and statistical manual for mental disorders* (4th ed.). Washington, DC: Author.

Calderon, C., Pineros, M., & Rosselli, D. (1998). An epidemic of collective conversion and dissociation disorder in an indigenous group of Colombia: Its relation to cultural change. *Social Science and Medicine, 11,* 1425–1428.

Cardenas, D., Carrasco, J. L., Davies, S. O., Fyer, A. J., Guarnaccia, P. J., Jusino, C. M., Klein, D. F. Liebowitz, M. R., Salman, E., Silvestre, J., & Street, L. (1998). Subtypes of ataque de nervios: the influence of coexisting psychiatric diagnosis. *Culture, Medicine, and Psychiatry, 2,* 231–244.

Kiely Ann Fletcher
Ohio State University

ATAXIA, FRIEDREICH

Friedreich ataxia is one of a set of inherited diseases resulting in degeneration of the spine and cerebellum. Friedreich ataxia is the most common of the hereditary ataxias (Evidente, Gwinn-Hardy, Caviness, & Gilman, 2000), with an estimated incidence of 1 in 20,000 and a prevalence of 1 in 50,000 people (Evidente et al., 2000). It is inherited in an autosomal recessive pattern, and the carrier rate, based on molecular data, is estimated at 1:60–1:90. The incidence of the disease in Asians and in those of African descent is low (Delatycki, Williamson, & Forrest, 2000). It affects males and females equally (Zoghbi & Swaiman, 1999).

Characteristics

1. Clinical manifestations are usually evident by late childhood. Mean age of onset is 10.52 years (Delatycki et al., 2000), with progression to loss of ambulation occurring at a mean age of 25 years.
2. The initial manifestation of the disease is most often progressive difficulty with gait, including widening, wavering, slowing, and gait disorganization.
3. Deep tendon reflexes in legs are absent.
4. There is progressive dysarthria (decreased pace, slurring, and rapid, uncontrolled changes in volume of speech) and a reduction in or loss of vibratory sense and proprioception.
5. Scoliosis and evidence of cardiomyopathy are common.
6. Bladder dysfunction may occur.
7. Diabetes mellitus is associated with Friedreich ataxia.
8. Higher cortical functions are generally intact, although auditory dysfunction is common, and limited eye movements, hand deformities, slow processing speed, and dysarthria progressing to ineffective speech may make school performance problematic.
9. Death occurs after progression, with an average age of death, most often related to cardiomyopathy, of 37.5 ± 14.4 years.
10. There is clinical variability in the presentation of the disease, even within sibships (Delatycki et al., 2000; Pandolfo, 1999; Zorghbi & Swaiman, 1999).

The symptoms are secondary to cellular damage and death, thought to caused by mitochondrial iron accumulation, although the mechanism of damage continues to be debated (Evidente et al., 2000). Cellular death occurs primarily in the dorsal root ganglia, posterior columns of the spinal cord, corticospinal tracts, and the heart. There is mild cellular loss in the cerebellum (Delatycki et al., 2000). The disease is due to a genetic alteration that maps to

Chromosome 9q13. In most cases the abnormality associated with Friedreich ataxia is a large expansion of a normal guanine-adenine-adenine (GAA) repeat. There is variability in the size of the expansion, with larger expansions associated with earlier onset and more severe pathology. The abnormality is unstable, and transmission from parent to child is accompanied by change in the size of the genetic abnormality. Maternal transmission may result in either a larger or smaller area of abnormality, whereas the GAA repeat size is generally diminished in paternal transmission (Delatycki et al., 2000). The abnormality causes a reduction in frataxin, a mitochondrial protein (Pandolfo, 1999).

There is currently no treatment for Friedreich ataxia, although identification of and cloning of the gene have offered new hope (Delatycki et al., 2000). The role of antioxidant therapy is being evaluated, and the results are said to be promising. Scientists have found that residual frataxin is present in all patients with Friedreich ataxia. This suggests that gene therapy may play a role in management of Friedreich ataxia, as the therapy could be delivered without the complications of an adverse immunologic response (Delatycki et al., 2000).

Few recent studies have looked at cognitive functioning in patients with Friedreich ataxia, and these have been conducted with adult populations. Patients with Friedreich ataxia appear to have a disturbance in the speed and efficiency of information processing, and this is independent of motor abnormalities. There is no consistent evidence of global cognitive impairment (Botez-Marquard & Boetz, 1993; Hart, Kwentus, Leshner, & Frazier, 1985).

Educational services to children with Friedreich ataxia should recognize the progressive nature of the disease, the sensory abnormalities that may develop, and the need for assistive technology. These children will require help with motor performance in all domains. They should be provided with alternative modes of response, such as dictation. Simple accommodations for the mildly affected, such as additional sets of books to decrease the need to carry, which makes ambulation yet more difficult, can help in the early stages of the disease. Additional time between classes is imperative. Allowances for bathroom breaks should be included in the individual education plan, or other educational plan. Teachers should be alerted to the need for extra processing time.

REFERENCES

Botez-Marquard, T., & Botez, M. I. (1993). Cognitive behavior in hereditodegenerative ataxias. *European Neurology, 33*(5), 351–357.

Delatycki, M. B., Williamson, R., & Forrest, S. M. (2000). Friedreich ataxia: An overview. *Journal of Medical Genetics, 37,* 1–8.

Evidente, V. G., Gwinn-Hardy, K. A., Caviness, J. N., & Gilman, S. (2000). Hereditary ataxias. *Mayo Clinic Proceedings,* 75, 473–490.

Hart, R. P., Kwentus, J. A., Leshner, R. T., & Frazier, R. (1985). Information processing speed in Friedreich's ataxia. *Annals of Neurology, 17,* 612–614.

Pandolfo, M. (1999). Molecular pathogenesis of Friedreich ataxia. *Archives of Neurology, 56,* 1201–1208.

Zoghbi, H. Y., & Swaiman, K. F. (1999). Spinocerebellar degeneration. In K. F. Swaimann & S. Ashwal (Eds.), *Pediatric neurology: Principles and practice* (3rd ed.). St. Louis, MO: Mosby.

Greta N. Wilkening
University of Colorado Health Sciences Center
The Children's Hospital

ATAXIA, HEREDITARY

Hereditary ataxia is a designation for inherited disorders that involve incoordination of voluntary muscle movements as the result of spinocerebellar degeneration. There are several forms of hereditary ataxia, which are delineated according to how they are manifested genetically. Autosomal recessive forms of hereditary ataxia are expressed by means of a mutated recessive gene. For the disease to be expressed, children must inherit two affected genes, one from each parent (Evidente, Gwinn-Hardy, Caviness, Gilman, 2000). There are several identified autosomal recessive ataxias with heterogeneous etiologies and clinical features; however, the most common ataxia is Friedreich ataxia. Friedreich ataxia has a prevalence of 1 in 50,000 persons. Onset of the disorder is usually before 20 years of age, and progression is continuous (Evidente et al., 2000). Late onset of Freidreich' ataxia (this includes individuals older than 20 to 25 years) is characterized by a more benign course and lower incidence of skeletal deformities (Evidente et al., 2000).

Characteristics

Note: Symptoms for these disorders vary widely according to each specific disorder. The following are some common characteristics.

1. Incoordination of speech muscles and ataxia of all four limbs and of gait
2. Impaired eye movements
3. Sensory loss
4. Dementia
5. Swallowing difficulties
6. Motor neuron degeneration manifested as lack of coordination or muscle control
7. Skeletal abnormalities

Symptoms of Freidreich ataxia include gait and limb ataxia, dysarthria, absent muscle stretch reflexes in lower limbs, sensory loss, and skeletal abnormalities (Evidente et al., 2000). Diabetes and cardiac disease are also fairly common in persons with this disorder. Freidreich ataxia is thought to be the result of the expansion of a DNA trinucleotide repeat (guanine-adenine-adenine) that disrupts the normal assembly of amino acids into proteins (Evidente et al., 2000). This disruption eventually leads to cellular degeneration.

The autosomal dominant cerebellar ataxias (ADCAs) are the result of a mutated dominant gene. These disorders have been labeled as spinocerebellar ataxias (SCAs) and have been assigned numbers according to their chromosomal localization (Woods, 1999).

The incidence of ADCAs is 5 in 100,000 persons. Onset of these disorders occurs in childhood in only 10% of the cases, and progression is continuous. However, childhood onset is associated with a more rapid course. Similar to the autosomal recessive ataxias, genetic testing is required in order to diagnose ADCAs (Woods, 1999). Characteristics of the ADCAs differ according to genetic localization and are heterogeneous between and within affected families (Woods, 1999). In general, however, symptoms indicate involvement of peripheral nerves, spinal cord cell groups and tracts, cranial nerve nuclei, and basal ganglia (Evidente et al., 2000). These symptoms may include limb and gait ataxia, impaired eye movements, extrapyramidal tract and motor neuron degeneration, dementia, sphincter disturbances, and swallowing difficulties (Evidente et al., 2000; Woods, 1999). The ADCAs are thought to be caused by expansion of the DNA trinucleotide repeat (cytosine-adenine-guanine) that codes for polyglutamine (Woods, 1999).

The third type of hereditary ataxia is referred to as X-linked SCAs. These disorders are less common and have a heterogeneous presentation. Currently, they are not well characterized, and there is little genetic or molecular data (Evidente et al., 2000).

Presently, there is no cure for the hereditary ataxias and no effective treatments to slow the progression of the disease (Woods, 1999). Treatment may be focused on management of the symptoms and concomitant disorders such as diabetes and cardiac disease (Evidente et al., 2000). Physical therapy may prolong the use of the arms and legs.

Although inherited ataxias lead to tremendous loss of physical abilities, there is usually no impairment of cognitive functioning (Stevenson, 1987). For children enrolled in schools, special education programs should focus efforts on modifying the environment to accommodate the child's physical and emotional needs. This may involve providing close supervision, special seating arrangements, and devices such as a wheelchair or railings to increase safety for the child. Occupational, physical, and speech therapists may need to provide extensive support for the child, teachers, and family to maintain optimal functioning as long as possible. As children grow they gain insight into the progressive nature of their disease and may become vulnerable to significant depression and anxiety. Psychological counseling can be offered within the educational setting as a means of addressing these issues (Stevenson, 1987). Often, family therapy may also be warranted.

Future research will likely focus on determining the genetic and molecular substrates of these disorders as a means of developing methods of diagnosis, prevention, and treatment (Evidente et al., 2000).

REFERENCES

Evidente, V. G. H., Gwinn-Hardy, K. A., Caviness, J. N., & Gilman, S. (2000). Hereditary ataxias. *Mayo Clinic Proceedings, 75*(5), 475–490.

Stevenson, R. J. (1987). Cerebellar disorders. In C. Reynolds & L. Mann (Eds.), *Encyclopedia of special education: Reference for the education of the handicapped and other exceptional children and adults* (Vol. 1). New York: Wiley.

Woods, B. T. (1999). The autosomal dominant spinocerebellar ataxias: Clinicopathologic findings and genetic mechanisms. In A. Joseph & R. Young (Eds.), *Movement disorders in neurology and neuropsychiatry* (2nd ed.). Blackwell Science.

William M. Acree
Theresa Kelly
University of Northern Colorado

ATAXIA, MARIE'S

Ataxia is a disorder that involves incoordination of voluntary muscle movements. Marie's ataxia is a designation for hereditary conditions expressed through dominant genes and characterized by spinocerebellar degeneration. These conditions normally occur in adulthood, although the time of onset varies widely. The clinical features of Marie's ataxia are heterogeneous within and between families, so diagnosis and classification are difficult (Harding, 1982).

Marie's ataxia is thought to be a very rare condition, but there is little agreement as to its prevalence. Schoenberg (1978) estimated the prevalence of all inherited ataxias to be less than 6 cases per 100,000 people. The etiology of Marie's ataxia is thought to involve the expansion of an exonic DNA trinucleotide repeat (cytosine-adenine-guanine) that codes for polyglutamine (Woods, 1999).

Characteristics

1. Incoordination of speech muscles and ataxia of all four limbs and of gait
2. Most individuals becoming nonambulatory within 15 years of onset

3. Increased or decreased tendon reflexes
4. Impaired eye movements
5. Sphincter disturbances
6. Swallowing difficulties
7. Dementia
8. Optic atrophy

The presence of Marie's ataxia can be determined through genetic studies. Genetic counseling may allow people to prepare for the symptoms of the disease. However, at this point there is no effective treatment to reverse or halt its progression (Woods, 1999).

Early onset of Marie's ataxia can necessitate numerous environmental and educational modifications. This disorder may manifest itself as a physical handicap or as a health impairment. Special education programs need to modify the environment to accommodate the child's physical needs. This may include special seating arrangements, safety devices such as railings, and increased supervision. Occupational, physical, and speech therapists may provide support for the child, teachers, and family to maintain optimal functioning as long as possible. In addition, as children gain insight into the progressive nature of their disease, they become more vulnerable to significant anxiety and depression. Psychological counseling within the educational setting can be offered as a means of addressing these issues (Stephenson, 1987). Often, family therapy may also be warranted.

Marie's ataxia has a poor prognosis, as it is a progressive degenerative disease. With effective management of symptoms there may be 10 to 20 years of productivity following onset (Stephenson, 1987). Future research will likely focus on etiology, classification, and treatment.

REFERENCES

Harding, A. E. (1982). The clinical features and classification of the late onset autosomal dominant cerebellar ataxias: A study of 11 families, including descendants of "The Drew Family of Walworth." *Brain, 105,* 1–28.

Schoenberg, B. S. (1978). Epidemiology of the inherited ataxias. *Advances in Neurology, 21,* 15–30.

Stephenson, R. J. (1987). Cerebellar disorders. In C. Reynolds & L. Mann (Eds.), *Encyclopedia of special education: A reference for the education of the handicapped and other exceptional children and adults* (Vol. 1). New York: Wiley.

Woods, B. T. (1999). The autosomal dominant spinocerebellar ataxias: Clinicopathologic findings and genetic mechanisms. In A. Joseph & R. Young (Eds.), *Movement disorders in neurology and neuropsychiatry* (2nd ed.). Boston: Blackwell Science.

William M. Acree
Theresa Kelly
University of Northern Colorado

ATAXIA-TELANGIECTASIA (LOUIS-BAR SYNDROME)

Ataxia-telangiectasia (A-T) is an autosomal recessive neurodegenerative genetic disorder characterized by progressive ataxia due to cerebellar degeneration, oculocutaneous telangiectasia, immunodeficiency with recurrent sinopulmonary infections, significant sensitivity to ionizing radiation, and increased risk of cancers, especially lymphoma and leukemia. Incidence is estimated as 1 in 40,000 births, although this may be an underestimate due to early deaths prior to diagnosis. There are between 500 and 600 cases of A-T in the United States. Occurrence has shown no bias on racial, gender, geographic, or other lines. It is estimated that 1% of the general population is a carrier for one of the mutated A-T genes, and carrier status itself is associated with lower than normal tolerance for radiation and an increased risk of cancer for both genders. For females, it is estimated that A-T carriers comprise approximately 6–9% of all breast cancer cases, and carrier status is associated with a three- to five-times greater risk of developing breast cancer (Lavin, 1998). Thus, this disorder carries health implications for both homozygote patients as well as heterozygote parent carriers. Well siblings have a two-thirds chance for being carriers.

Patients may appear normal at birth, and even though there may be early signs of cerebellar ataxia at infancy (e.g., abnormal swaying of the head and trunk) and later in toddlerhood (e.g., wobbly gait, clumsiness), the diagnosis is typically not established until ages 4 to 6. The appearance of telangiectasia may occur early but usually appears around age 4 or 5. A common early misdiagnosis because of the ataxia is cerebral palsy, and other children are often born into the family before an A-T diagnosis is established and genetic counseling is provided for the parents.

Earlier detection may occur with the use of routine serum alpha-fetoprotein testing in children with persistent ataxia, where elevated levels often distinguish A-T from other ataxia and immunodeficiency syndromes (Cabana, Crawford, Winkelstein, Christensen, & Lederman, 1998). Less established, but offering possible earlier diagnostic assistance, is the use of magnetic resonance imaging to pick up leukodystrophic changes in the brain that may predate the appearance of many clinical symptoms (Chung, Bodensteiner, Noorani, & Schochet, 1994).

Characteristics

1. Progressive cerebellar ataxia, with early signs such as head swaying, trunk instability, and clumsiness; by age 4 to 6 more apparent balance, coordination, and gait difficulties; use of a wheelchair typically by age 10
2. Related ocular ataxia, dysarthria, dysphagia, dystonia, choreoathetosis, and tremor

3. Reddish lesions on skin, mucosa, and conjunctivas (oculocutaneous telangiectasia)
4. Sensitivity to ionizing radiation
5. Immunodeficiencies, associated with recurrent sinopulmonary infections
6. Increased risk for cancers of all types, but especially lymphoma and leukemia
7. Normal range intelligence
8. A characteristic "sweet breath" in some cases
9. Abbreviated life expectancies, with most succumbing to cancer or respiratory illness before age 20
10. Elevated radiosensitivity and increased risk of cancers, including breast cancer, in single A-T gene carriers

A-T is not associated with mental retardation. One study did report lower verbal IQ scores in A-T children (although this may be due to the indirect effects on learning from the symptoms of the disorder rather than direct effects limiting innate cognition) as well as reduced ability for judging duration of time intervals in A-T children (Mostofsky, Kunze, Cutting, Lederman, & Denckla, 2000). Cerebellar dysfunction has previously been linked to duration judgment deficits, and salient cognitive effects in A-T children may be identified as more is learned about the cerebellum's general role in cognition.

Nevertheless, the intelligence range of children with A-T is commensurate with that of the general population; thus, most A-T children should be appropriate for regular education classes, provided that appropriate accommodations related to their physical limitations and needs are made available. These would typically include speech, occupational, and physical therapies, as well as the use of classroom aids for handwriting, note taking, and even reading as progressive ocular apraxia can make reading functionally inadequate.

Although there is some variation in presentation of the disorder, progression of the ataxia is inexorable and prognosis is poor, typically leading to use of a walker by age 8, loss of writing ability by 8, wheelchair use by age 10, and loss of functional reading ability due to difficulties coordinating eye focus (e.g., fixation nystagmus). Death due to cancer or respiratory failure occurs frequently by age 20, although some patients may live into their 30s and very rarely into their 40s. Although there is no cure or treatment yet to correct the disorder, interventions have been directed toward the symptoms. These include neurorehabilitative oriented physical, occupational, and speech-swallowing therapies. Some symptoms can be managed to some degree pharmacologically (e.g., drooling with anticholinergics, basal ganglia–related movement disorders with dopamine agonists or antagonists as appropriate, weakness or fatigue with pyridostigmine; A-T Children's Project, 2000). Some benefits from nutritional supplements and diet changes for reducing symptoms have been reported.

Though a rare disorder, there is much research on A-T in part because of its possible connections to understanding other disorders such as breast cancer (A-T Project, 2000). Research includes gene therapy and stem cell transplantation, as well as areas of nutrition and diet. For example, supplementation with myoinositol has shown some positive initial effects in improved coordination in some patients. B vitamins, fatty acids, antioxidants and coenzyme Q10 are also being investigated, as is an alcohol-avoidance diet, which may reduce the ataxic symptoms in some patients through avoidance of the ethanol and methanol in many foods and beverages (National Organization to Treat A-T, 2000).

REFERENCES

A-T Project. (2000, October 16). Connection between A-T and breast cancer. Retrieved from http://www.atproject.org/PAGES/2b.breastcancer2.html

A-T Children's Project. (2000, November 1). Managing the neurological symptoms of A-T with medications. Retrieved from http://www.atcp.org/mngneuro.htm

Cabana, M., Crawford, T., Winkelstein, J., Christensen, J., & Lederman, H. (1998). Consequences of the delayed diagnosis of ataxia-telangiectasia. *Pediatrics, 102,* 98–100.

Chung, E., Bodensteiner, J., Noorani, P., & Schochet, S. (1994). Cerebral white-matter changes suggesting leukodystrophy in ataxia telangiectasia. *Journal of Child Neurology, 9*(1), 31–35.

Lavin, M. (1998, August 22). Role of the ataxia-telangiectasia gene (ATM) in breast cancer. *British Medical Journal, 317,* 486–487.

Mostofsky, S., Kunze, J., Cutting, L., Lederman, H., & Denckla, M. (2000). Judgment of duration in individuals with ataxia-telangiectasia. *Developmental Neuropsychology, 17*(1), 63–74.

National Organization to Treat A-T. (2000, November 1). The nutritional approach. Retrieved from http://www.treat-at.org/nutrition.aadietsupplement.html

Vicky Y. Spradling
Austin State Hospital

ATHETOSIS

Athetosis is characterized by uncontrollable, jerky, irregular, and twisting movements of the extremities, which result in unsteadiness, incoordination, and distortion of movement and posture (Hadra, 1966). Accuracy of release is difficult due to the lack of voluntary control or direction and is often concentrated in the hands, arms, feet, and legs (National Institute of Neurological Disorders and Stroke [NINDS], 2001a). The slow writhing movements may be combined with intermittent stiffening spells and extensor spasms. Athetoid movements are a result of the alternating flexion-extension and supination-pronation of the muscle groups and limbs (Wilson, 2000). The athetoid's walking style is characterized as a writhing, lurching, and stumbling gait accompanied by an excess of arm movement (Denhoff, 1966). The abnormal twisting movements of the muscles are often reduced or completely disappear during sleep. Emotional stress can intensify the athetoid symptoms (NINDS, 2001a).

Lesions in the midbrain involving the basal ganglia have been implicated in athetosis, and these result in difficulties in controlling the direction and completion of attempted voluntary movements (Keats, 1965; NINDS, 2001a). Damage to the basal ganglia can be caused by prenatal (e.g., maternal infections), perinatal (e.g., asphyxia), or postnatal (e.g., head trauma, poisoning) factors. Also, the role of gamma-aminobutyric acid (GABA), dopamine, acetylcholine, norepinephrine, and serotonin in movement disorders in general is being investigated (NINDS, 2001a, 2001b).

Athetosis has been associated with several different conditions such as Fahr's syndrome, Lesch-Nyhan syndrome, and cerebral palsy (CP). Abnormal deposits of calcium in areas of the brain, specifically the basal ganglia, have been associated with athetoid symptoms in Fahr's syndrome (NINDS, 2001a). In the rare genetic disorder of Lesch-Nyhan syndrome, abnormally high levels of uric acid, specifically in the central nervous system, have been implicated in the development of athetosis in these individuals (NINDS, 2001a, 2001b).

Athetosis is the second largest subtype of CP, occurring in approximately 10–20% of the CP population (NINDS, 2001a). The physical symptoms can vary from being mild to almost physically incapacitating (Denhoff & Robinault, 1960). Athetoids have a high incidence of accompanying speech deficits, which has been attributed to deficits in tongue control and difficulty controlling other speech musculature (Denhoff & Robinault, 1960; Keats, 1965; NINDS, 2001a). Athetosis is also often accompanied by hearing deficits and a muscular imbalance of the eyes and eye-movement deficits, often in the vertical direction (Cruickshank, 1966; Denhoff & Robinault, 1960). It has been noted that approximately two thirds of CP children are intellectually impaired to some degree; however, an athetoid's communicative deficits can make psychoeducational assessments very difficult (Denhoff & Robinault, 1960; NINDS, 2001a, 2001b).

Twelve different clinical types of athetoid CP have been identified (Denhoff & Robinault, 1960; Keats, 1965):

1. *Rotary athetosis:* (common) slow rotary motions; often feet move in circular motions, hands pronate and supinate, and shoulders rotate both internally and externally
2. *Tremor-like:* (common) uneven involuntary contraction and relaxation of flexor and extensor muscles as well as abductor and adductor mechanisms
3. *Dystonic athetosis:* distorted positions of extremities lasting from a few seconds to a few minutes
4. *Shudder athetosis:* ranges from mild shuddering motion moving through arms and legs to violent shuddering that can result in loss of balance
5. *Flailing athetosis:* (very rare) arms and legs thrown violently from the axial shoulder and the hip joints; fingers and toes unaffected
6. *Neck and arm athetosis:* athetosis limited to head, neck, and shoulder girdle; little or no symptoms in the legs; often the motion is dystonic, but other forms are possible
7. *Hemiathetosis athetosis:* presence of rotary, tremor-like, dystonic, or shudder athetosis on one side of the body
8. *Tension athetosis:* muscular straining and rigidity that may mask other types of athetosis, which become revealed when the tension is relieved; may be a temporary classification until the true nature is discerned
9. *Nontension athetosis:* less muscle tightness with an increased amount of contorted motions; may mask other types of athetosis; may be a temporary classification until the true nature is discerned
10. *Deaf athetosis:* athetoid symptoms plus high-pitched or high-tone hearing loss and limited vertical eye movements; displays normal lateral motions
11. *Balance-release athetosis:* sudden loss of balance without falling despite a stable floor; includes other involuntary movements
12. *Emotional-release athetosis:* often a rotary or tremor-like athetosis combined with a release of laughing, crying, and anger despite only a slight stimulation for the emotion

Traditionally, physical and occupational therapy teaching purposeful coordination of movement in conjunction with bracing and splinting to control involuntary motions has been recommended to improve motor development and teach daily living and classroom skills (Denhoff & Robinault, 1960; Keats, 1965; NINDS, 2001b, 2001c). A full assessment of the child's neuropsychological needs is recommended to assist with educational programming. Physical therapists use techniques such as active assisted motion, resisted motion, and combined motion moving from simple to complex sets of motions. Speech therapy is recommended for those exhibiting speech deficits, including learning how to use special communication devices if necessary. Behavioral and emotional counseling may also be necessary, especially as the child nears adolescence. Anticholinergic drugs such as trihexyphenidyl, benztropine, and procyclidine hydrochloride may help reduce the abnormal movements. Although orthopedic surgery and neurosurgery have been utilized for spastic CP, these procedures have not shown to be productive for athetosis (NINDS, 2001a; Wilson, 2000).

REFERENCES

Cruickshank, W. M. (1966). The problem and its scope. In W. M. Cruickshank (Ed.), *Cerebral palsy: Its individual and community problems* (pp. 3–23). Syracuse, NY: Syracuse University Press.

Denhoff, E. (1966). Cerebral palsy: Medical aspects. In W. M. Cruickshank (Ed.), *Cerebral palsy: Its individual and community problems* (pp. 24–100). Syracuse, NY: Syracuse University Press.

Denhoff, E., & Robinault, I. P. (1960). *Cerebral palsy and related disorders: A developmental approach to dysfunction.* New York: McGraw-Hill.

Hadra, R. (1966). Occupational therapy for the cerebral palsied child. In W. M. Cruickshank (Ed.), *Cerebral palsy: Its individual and community problems* (pp. 431–458). Syracuse, NY: Syracuse University Press.

Keats, S. (1965). *Cerebral palsy.* Springfield, IL: Charles C. Thomas.

National Institute of Neurological Disorders and Stroke. (2001a, July 1). NINDS cerebral palsy information page. Retrieved from http://www.ninds.nih.gov/health_and_medical/pubs/cerebral_palsyhtr.htm

National Institute of Neurological Disorders and Stroke. (2001b, July 1). NINDS dystonias information page. Retrieved from http://www.ninds.nih.gov/health_and_medical/pubs/dystonias.htm

National Institute of Neurological Disorders and Stroke. (2001c, July 1). NINDS Fahr's syndrome information page. Retrieved from http://www.ninds.nih.gov/health_and_medical/disorders/fahrs.htm

National Institute of Neurological Disorders and Stroke. (2001d, July 1). NINDS Lesch-Nyhan information page. Retrieved from http://www.ninds.nih.gov/health_and_medical/disorders/lesch_doc.htm

Wilson, J. D. (2000). Athetosis. In C. R. Reynolds & E. Fletcher-Janzen (Eds.), *Encyclopedia of special education: A reference for the education of the handicapped and other exceptional children and adults.* (2nd ed., Vol. 1, pp. 165–166). New York: Wiley.

Alexandra S. Kutz
University of Texas at Austin

Margaret Semrud-Clikeman
University of Texas at Austin

ATRIOVENTRICULAR SEPTAL DEFECT

Atrioventricular septal defect (AVSD) is a congenital heart defect (present at birth). It is also known as cor biloculare. Additionally, there are several subdivisions depending on the size and location of the defect. Specifically, these subdivisions are atrial and septal and small ventricular septal defect, atrial septal defect primum, complete atrioventricular septal defect, incomplete atrioventricular septal defect, large atrial and ventricular defect, and transitional atrioventricular septal defect.

The heart is composed of four chambers, two atria and two ventricles. The atria are separated by a wall called the atrial septum, and the ventricles are also separated by a septum. The right atrium and right ventricle are connected by valves, as are the left atrium and ventricle. In the case of the presence of atrioventricular septal defects, the septa or valves either are not fully formed or are fully developed but are deformed. This causes the septa or valves to malfunction and blood to leak between chambers or be moved in incorrect directions within the heart. The severity of the defect ranges from mild, as in a cleft mitral valve, to severe, in which there are several deformities within both the valves and the chambers of the heart. The severity of the defect is categorized into three forms: cleft mitral valve, partial atrioventricular septal defect, and complete atrioventricular septal defect. The type of defect determines the symptoms and the type of medical care needed. However, medical care and surgery are almost always going to be needed in infancy. It is interesting to note that approximately half the cases of this defect occur in children with Down syndrome.

Depending on the type of defect, atrioventricular septal defects in infants can cause different types of irregular movement of blood within the heart. This can be as straightforward as left to right movement of blood (as opposed to vertical movement) or as complicated as movement of blood between the left ventricle and right atrium.

Infants with this defect are in danger of congestive heart failure at 4–12 weeks old because of abnormal blood flow levels. Infants whose hearts are able to function despite irregular movement of blood in the heart are at risk of pulmonary vascular obstructive disease at ages of less than 1 year. Defects must be repaired surgically, a difficult procedure because of the size, age, and lack of immunities in an infant. In some cases, surgeons may opt simply to stabilize the situation and fully correct the condition at a later date when the child is larger; however, this requires two surgeries and may also further deform the heart in the process.

Characteristics

1. Malformed septa or valves in heart
2. Inability to maintain blood flow through heart efficiently

3. Risk of congestive heart failure
4. Risk of pulmonary vascular obstructive disease

Because almost all cases of atrioventricular septal defect must be corrected in infancy (Kwiatkowska, Tomaszewski, Bielinacuteska, Potaz, & Ericinacuteski, 2000), surgical procedures are not likely to interrupt the life of a school child with this defect. However, this child may still need to be examined regularly and may not be able to participate in all activities that strain the heart or lungs. Many support, resource, and educational groups are available both locally and online, and it may be beneficial for a child with atrioventricular septal defects and his or her family to participate actively in one of these groups.

REFERENCE

Kwiatkowska, J., Tomaszewski, M., Bielinacuteska, B., Potaz, P., & Erecinacuteski, J. (2000). Atrioventricular septal defect: Clinical and diagnostic problems in children hospitalized in 1993–1998. *Medical Science Monitor, 6,* 1148–1154.

Allison Katz
Rutgers University

ATTENTION-DEFICIT/HYPERACTIVITY DISORDER

It is estimated that approximately 3–6% of children have some form of attention-deficit/hyperactivity disorder (ADHD); approximately three times as many males are identified as females (Barkley, 1998). Although diagnosis of ADHD may occur at any age, most often diagnosis is made in elementary school–aged children. Subtyping of ADHD is made based on the extent to which symptoms are present in areas of inattention and hyperactivity/impulsivity with resulting subtypes of predominantly inattentive (PI), predominantly hyperactive-impulsive (PHI), and combined type (CT; American Psychiatric Association [APA], 1994). By middle childhood, the majority of children with ADHD also present with some cooccurring disorder (Barkley, 1998). Comorbid disorders with ADHD are most likely to be learning disabilities, language disabilities, oppositional defiant disorder, and conduct disorder.

A number of theories have been offered with regard to the etiology of the brain dysfunction that results in ADHD. Since the early 1900s, what is now termed ADHD has been believed to involve some form of brain dysfunction. ADHD was initially conceptualized as being the result of minimal brain damage. Brain damage as a result of infection, trauma, and complications during pregnancy or at the time of delivery has been postulated as potential causes of ADHD; however, routine neurological examination of children with ADHD is generally normal (Voeller, 1991). In the 1970s, one of the more popular theories was that food additives or refined sugar were direct causes of ADHD. Subsequent research, however, has not substantiated either of these hypotheses (see Riccio, Hynd, & Cohen, 1994, for a review).

Of the etiological theories discussed, the one for which there is the greatest evidence is that of a genetic predisposition for ADHD. Consistently, studies have demonstrated that biological relatives of children with ADHD are significantly more likely to have a history of childhood ADHD (Biederman et al., 1992). Further findings have demonstrated that family-genetic influences exist that are independent of psychosocial adversity (Biederman et al., 1992).

Characteristics (Barkley, 1998; Conners & Jett, 1999)

1. Inattention and/or hyperactivity/impulsivity criteria of APA (1994)
2. Difficulty with organization and completion of routine tasks
3. Easily fatigued or bored; easily distracted
4. Feelings of restlessness
5. Lack of persistence or decreased motivation
6. Difficulty with problem solving in social situations; impaired social functioning
7. Impaired academic performance
8. Low frustration tolerance and high emotional reactivity

ADHD is believed to have an early onset of symptoms (prior to age 7), but it may not be identified until later; symptom presentation varies across the life span (Barkley, 1998). The hyperactivity and impulsivity may become less severe in early adolescence or adulthood; the problems with inattention continue to be present through adulthood. Over time, the likelihood of social problems, academic problems, and frustration increase the likelihood of the development of internalizing disorders in adolescents and adults with ADHD (Biederman et al., 1992). Conceptually, Barkley (1998) asserted that the subtypes (PI, CT) are actually different disorders and that for CT the underlying problem is one of poor self-regulation (disinhibition) as evidenced in deficit executive functions (working memory, internalized speech, fluency, self-regulation of arousal and affect).

Treatment options for ADHD include the use of medication, strategies and modifications within the classroom, behavior management (e.g., contingency management, self-management), cognitive behavior therapy (e.g., self-talk), and parent training and education about ADHD. Research suggests that the most effective treatments include multiple components (e.g., medication, behavior management, and parent training) as opposed to any single approach to treatment (Barkley, 1998; Conners & Jett, 1999). Children with ADHD may be eligible for special education or related services if (a) they have a co-occurring disorder that meets eligibility criteria or (b) the ADHD symptoms are significantly and adversely affecting their educational progress.

Not only is it evident that differential diagnosis of ADHD, learning disability, and conduct disorder is needed, but also the research on subtypes of ADHD (PI, CT, PHI) indicates that a view of ADHD as unidimensional is questionable (Barkley, 1998). It may be most appropriate to view ADHD as a cluster of different behavioral deficits (attention, hyperactivity, impulsivity), each with a specific neural substrate of varying severity, of variable etiology, occurring in variable constellations, and sharing a common response to treatment (Voeller, 1991).

REFERENCES

American Psychiatric Association. (1994). *Diagnostic and statistical manual of mental disorders* (4th ed.). Washington, DC: Author.

Barkley, R. A. (1998). *Attention deficit hyperactivity disorder: A handbook for diagnosis and treatment* (2nd ed.). New York: Guilford Press.

Biederman, J., Faraone, S., Keenan, K., Benjamin, J., Krifcher, B., Moore, C., Sprich-Buckminster, S., Ugaglia, K., Jellinek, M. S., Steingard, R., Spencer, T., Norman, D., Kolodny, R., Kraus, I., Perrin, J., Keller, M. B., & Tsuang, M. T. (1992). Further evidence for family-genetic risk factors in attention deficit hyperactivity disorder. *Archives of General Psychiatry, 49,* 728–738.

Conners, C. K., & Jett, J. L. (1999). *Attention deficit hyperactivity disorder (in adults and children).* Kansas City, MO: Compact Clinicals.

Riccio, C. R., Hynd, G. W., & Cohen, M. J. (1994). Etiology and neurobiology of ADHD. In W. N. Bender (Ed.), *Understanding ADHD: A practical guide for teachers and parents.* Columbus, OH: Merrill.

Voeller, K. K. S. (1991). Toward a neurobiologic nosology of attention deficit hyperactivity disorder. *Journal of Child Neurology, 6,* S2–S8.

Cynthia A. Riccio
Texas A&M University

ATYPICAL CHILD SYNDROME

Atypical child syndrome, which was borrowed from the medical community and was commonly used prior to 1980, is almost never used to identify children today (Filips, 1999). This syndrome refers to children who are exceptional. Exceptional children differ from average or normal children and are now characterized more specifically in terms of their physical or behavioral disabilities. For example, children with handicaps including specific learning disabilities, mental retardation, emotional/behavior disorders, speech/language impairments, visual impairments, hearing impairments, other health impairments, multiple handicaps, autism, traumatic brain injury, and orthopedic impairments were once identified as atypical (Kamphaus, Reynolds, & Imperato-McCammon, 1999).

Prevalence rates for atypical child syndrome are undocumented and difficult to discern because of the wide variety of disorders included in the category and the lack of current use of the term (Clements, 1966). According to the Office of Special Education and Rehabilitative Services (2000), during the 1989–1999 school years 6,109,787 children from 3 to 21 years of age received special education services under the Individuals with Disabilities Education Act (IDEA).

Characteristics

1. The child has any disability that deviates from the average or normal child.
2. The atypical development can be in following areas: communication and learning disorders, sensory impairments, neurological problems, orthopedic handicaps, and emotional-behavioral disorders.

Treatment of atypical development needs to be individualized for each child depending on the particular concerns and severity of the disorder. This provides the psychologist, teacher, and other service providers with an understanding of the unique attributes of the child with school problems rather than the less meaningful broad characterization of atypical child syndrome (Levine, Brooks, & Shonkoff, 1980). Atypical children are served in a variety of special education settings from the regular education classroom with support from service providers to residential treatment centers. Their placement depends largely on the severity of the disorder. Children with mild disabilities can be serviced in regular education with support, whereas children with moderate to severe disabilities may need to receive their education in a self-contained classroom or residential treatment center.

REFERENCES

Clements, D. D. (1966). *Minimal brain dysfunction in children* (Public Health Service Publication No. 413). Washington, DC: U.S. Department of Health, Education, and Welfare.

Filips, D. (1999). Atypical child syndrome. In C. R. Reynolds & E. Fletcher-Jansen (Eds.), *The encyclopedia of special education* (Vol. 1). New York: Wiley.

Kamphaus, R., Reynolds, C., & Imperato-McCammon, C. (1999). Roles of diagnosis and classification in school psychology. In C. Reynolds & T. Gutkin (Eds.), *The handbook of school psychology* (3rd ed., pp. 292–306). New York: Wiley.

Levine, M. D., Brooks, R., & Shonkoff, J. P. (1980). *A pediatric approach to learning disorders.* New York: Wiley.

Office of Special Education and Rehabilitative Services. (2000). *Twenty-second annual report to Congress on the implementation of the Individuals with Disabilities Education Act.* United States Department of Education. Retrieved from http://www.ed.gov/offices/OSERS/OSEP/OSEP2000AnlRpt

Sherri L. Gallagher
University of Northern Colorado

AUTISM

Autism, more recently referred to as autism spectrum disorder, is classified under the umbrella of pervasive developmental disorders, which also includes Aspergers syndrome, Retts, childhood disintegrative disorder, and pervasive development disorder not otherwise specified. Autism cannot be diagnosed by physiological symptoms or medical testing, but rather is determined by how closely the child's condition fits certain criteria (Hamilton, 2000). The *Diagnostic and Statistical Manual of Mental Disorders–Fourth Edition* defines autism as essentially "the presence of significantly abnormal or impaired development in social interaction and communication accompanied by a restricted repertoire of activity and interests" (American Psychiatric Association, 1997).

According to statistics from the Mayo Clinic (2001), autism affects between 10 and 20 of every 10,000 people in the United States. Boys are affected with the disorder more often than girls at a rate of 4 to 1. The signs and symptoms of autism appear by the age of 3. Some studies have suggested that the incidence of autism is significantly higher now than in previous decades due to increased use of antibiotics, reactions to vaccinations, or pollution. However, there are now better diagnostic criteria for identification, and there is also much more awareness of the disorder, which could account for the increase in numbers (Hamilton, 2000).

Characteristics

1. Child does not respond to name.
2. Child does not make eye contact.
3. Child resists cuddling and holding.
4. Child appears to be unaware of others' feelings.
5. Child has abnormal social interaction and prefers to play alone.
6. Child starts speaking later than other children, if at all.
7. If child does speak, there is abnormal tone and rhythm in speech.
8. Child fails to initiate or maintain conversation.
9. Child may repeat words or phrases verbatim but does not know how to use them.
10. Child uses repetitive movements, such as rocking or hand twisting.
11. Child develops specific routines or rituals and becomes very upset if there is a change in routine.
12. Child may engage in self-injurious behaviors, such as head banging.
13. Child is usually hyperactive.
14. Child may be fascinated by parts of an object.

To date, there is no cure for autism. The effects of autism, however, can be overcome or reduced through a combination of treatment modalities, such as behavioral, dietary, and biomedical interventions (Hamilton, 2000).

Autism is one of the 13 categories of disabilities specified in the Individuals with Disabilities Education Act of 1997. A child with a medical diagnosis of autism would therefore qualify for special education services. The amount of support required would depend on the severity of the characteristics that the child exhibits, ranging from full, one-on-one support to minimal support at various times of the day.

There are autism research centers in virtually every major city in the United States. On October 25, 2001, the National Institute of Environmental Health Sciences and the Environmental Protection Agency announced the opening of four new children's environmental health research centers that will focus on autism and other behavioral difficulties of children.

REFERENCES

American Psychiatric Association. (1997). *Diagnostic and statistical manual of mental disorders* (4th ed.). Washington, DC: Author.

Hamilton, L. (2000). *Facing autism: Giving parents reasons for hope.* Colorado Springs, CO: Water Book Press.

Mayo Clinic [Online database]. (2001). Autism. Retrieved November 2001 from http://mayoclinic.com/findinformation/diseasesandconditions

Christine D. Cde Baca
University of Northern Colorado

See also Aspergers Syndrome

B

BABINSKI REFLEX

The Babinski reflex is a phenomenon observed when the sole of the foot is stroked from below the heel toward the toes on the lateral (outside) side resulting in the big toe flexing toward the top of the foot and the other toes fanning out (Fletcher-Janzen, 2000). The Babinski reflex is considered one of the infantile reflexes. It is normal in children under the age of 2 or 3 years but typically disappears as the child matures and the nervous system develops. In individuals older than 2 or 3, the presence of a Babinski reflex indicates damage to the pyramidal tract (the nerve paths connecting the spinal cord and the brain; American Heritage Stedman's Medical Dictionary, 1995; Royal College of Physicians of London, 1996). Even though the Babinski reflex is considered to be a normal response before children reach a certain age, medical researchers have not reached consensus as to the age at which the sign becomes abnormal. Berkow (1997) suggested that it is abnormal after 6 months of age; Neelon and Harvey (1999) consider it abnormal after 3 years of age; and the majority of medical professionals consider it abnormal after age 2 (Babinski's reflex, 1999; HealthCentral, 1998).

The Babinski reflex was first formally recognized in 1896 (Wartenberg, 1951). Joseph Francois Felix Babinski (1857–1932), a French neurologist of Polish descent, differentiated between a normal and a pathological response of the toes that subsequently became known as the Babinski reflex (also called Babinski's sign, or toe reflex) or the extensor plantar reflex (American Heritage Stedman's Medical Dictionary, 1995; Basseti, 1995). The Babinski reflex is considered the single most important sign in clinical neurology because of its reliability (Fletcher-Janzen, 2000), and its clinical utility has remained unchanged for over 100 years (Royal College of Physicians of London, 1996).

Characteristics

1. It is a reflex whereby the great toe flexes toward the top of the foot and the other toes fan out when the sole of the foot is firmly stroked.
2. It is a normal reflex in infants but is associated with a disturbance of the pyramidal or corticospinal tract in older children and adults.
3. Because the pyramidal tract is right- and left-sided, a Babinski reflex can occur on one side or both sides (HealthCentral, 1998).
4. An abnormal Babinski reflex can be temporary or permanent (HealthCentral, 1998).
5. It is commonly characteristic of an upper motor neuron lesion (Curless, 1999; Walton, Beson, & Scott, 1986). But other common causes include amyotrophic lateral sclerosis, brain tumors, Friedreich ataxia, head injury, hepatic encephalopathy, meningitis, multiple sclerosis, pernicious anemia, rabies, spinal cord injury or tumor, stroke, and syringomeyelia (Babinski's reflex, 1999; HealthCentral, 1998).
6. Lack of coordination, weakness, and difficulty with muscle control are symptoms associated with an abnormal Babinski reflex (HealthCentral, 1998).

The Babinski reflex is symptomatic of a variety of disease processes. Common diseases that may result in an abnormal Babinski Reflex include amyotrophic lateral sclerosis, brain tumors of the corticospinal tract or cerebellum, head injury, meningitis, multiple sclerosis, spinal cord injury or tumor, and stroke (HealthCentral, 1998). This list is not all-inclusive, and there are other causes of an abnormal Babinski reflex. The individual's health care provider usually finds the presence of an abnormal Babinski reflex during a medical examination. The individual is then referred for a comprehensive neurological examination, which may include computerized tomography scans of the head and spine, angiography of the head, or lumbar puncture and analysis of cerebrospinal fluid. Prognosis, treatment, and special education intervention or services are disease specific and based on individual needs and are not necessarily related to the diagnosis of an abnormal Babinski reflex.

REFERENCES

American Heritage Stedman's medical dictionary. (1995). New York: Houghton Mifflin.

Babinski's reflex. (1999). Retrieved September 20, 2000, from http://ocnow.adam.com/ency/article/003294.htm

Basseti, C. (1995). Historical perspective: Babinski and Babinski's sign. *Spine, 20*(23), 2591–2594.

Berkow, R. (1997). *The Merck manual of medical information.* New York: Merck.

Curless, R. G. (1999). A baby with a Babinski reflex. *New England Journal of Medicine, 340*(24), 1929–1930.

Fletcher-Janzen, E. (2000). Babinski reflex. In C. R. Reynolds & E. Fletcher-Janzen (Eds.), *Encyclopedia of special education* (2nd ed., Vol. 1). New York: Wiley.

HealthCentral. (1998). General health encyclopedia: Babinski's reflex. (1998). Retrieved September 20, 2000, from http://www.healthcentral.com/mhc/to/003294.cmf

Neelon, F. A., & Harvey, E. N. (1999). Images in clinical medicine. *New England Journal of Medicine, 340*(3), 196.

Royal College of Physicians of London. (1996). A hundred years of the Babinski reflex. *Journal of the Royal College of Physicians of London, 30*(1), 83.

Walton, J., Beson, P. B., & Scott, R. B. (1986). *The Oxford companion to medicine.* New York: Oxford University Press.

Wartenberg, R. (1951). Babinski: Reflex and marie-foix flexor withdrawal reflex. *AMA Archives of Neurology and Psychiatry, 65,* 713–716.

Denise E. Maricle
Dana R. Konter
University of Wisconsin-Stout

BALLER-GEROLD SYNDROME (CRANIOSYNOSTOSIS-RADIAL APLASIA SYNDROME)

This is a rare, hereditary disorder characterized by premature fusion of the sutures between the skull bones (craniosynostosis) and various malformations of the bones in the forearm, hand, and fingers.

Because of the paucity of cases (only about 20 appear in the literature), the prevalence of this syndrome is uncertain. A group of affected siblings was described a few years after the initial, unrelated case was reported in 1950. The pattern of inheritance appears to be autosomal recessive.

Characteristics

1. Craniosynostosis, malformed ears
2. Complete absence or malformation of the radius (the bone on the thumb side of the forearm)
3. Short ulna (the other bone in the forearm)
4. Missing carpals (wrist bones), metacarpals (hand bones), phalanges (finger bones) and absent or very small thumb
5. Prenatal and postnatal growth deficiency
6. 50% incidence of mental retardation in children followed beyond the first year
7. Anal anomalies, including imperforate anus (no anal opening) and anteriorly placed anus (anal opening too far forward)
8. Kidney anomalies, including underdevelopment or complete absence of the organ

Surgical treatment of craniosynostosis may be necessary to avoid disfiguring skull asymmetry. Premature fusion of all skull sutures requires operative intervention soon after the diagnosis is confirmed. Reopening the sutures allows for continuing expansion of cranial volume to accommodate brain growth. Repair of imperforate anus is undertaken soon after birth but may require two procedures. In some cases a colostomy is first done to provide an exit for fecal material. Some months later a "pull through and hook up" operation is performed, and the colostomy is taken down.

Because of a 50% incidence of mental retardation in children followed beyond the first year, there is an indication that children with Baller-Gerold syndrome will require special education support. However, the number of children who survive into school age is small, and therefore there is no research documenting specific educational strategies or behavioral problems.

The prognosis for this disorder is unfavorable. Twenty percent of affected infants die unexpectedly in the first year of life. There is a 50% incidence of mental retardation in those who survive beyond infancy. The anatomic abnormalities, although treatable, may need multiple surgeries before they are satisfactorily repaired. Occasional findings associated with this syndrome (conductive hearing loss and optic atrophy) may leave these children with significant sensory deficits.

REFERENCE

Jones, K. (1997). *Smith's recognizable patterns of human malformations* (5th ed.). Philadelphia: W. B. Saunders.

Barry H. Davison
Ennis, Texas

Joan W. Mayfield
Baylor Pediatric Specialty Services
Dallas, Texas

BALO DISEASE

Balo disease, also known as concentric sclerosis, is a childhood neurological disorder characterized by brain demyelination. Rapid and progressive loss of the fatty cover-

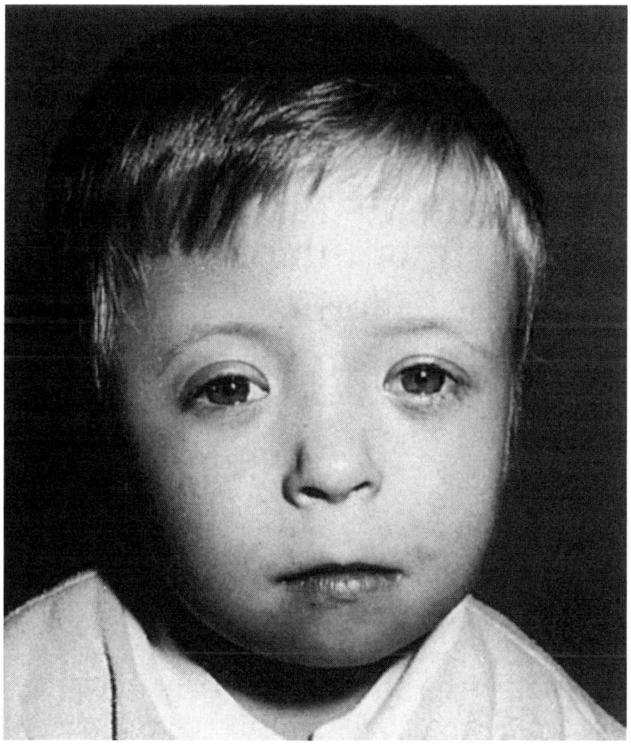

Baller-Gerold Syndrome
Reprinted from *Clinical Syndromes,* Wiedemann and Kunze, 1997, by permission of the publisher Mosby

ing around nerve fibers in the brain results in various neurological symptoms depending on the brain areas affected (Rowland, 1995; Thoene & Coker, 1995). The damage to the brain consists of irregular patches in a series of widening concentric circles. The cause of Balo disease is unknown, and symptoms can progress rapidly over several weeks or more slowly over 2–3 years. Balo disease may be the result of a slow virus or the involvement of autoimmune factors (Rowland, 1995). It may be a variant of multiple sclerosis or an unusual form of Schilder's disease (Thoene & Coker, 1995). Balo disease affects both male and female children.

Characteristics

1. Involuntary muscle spasms and gradual paralysis
2. Possibly other neurological, intellectual, or physical symptoms may develop
3. Possible impairment of regulation of physiologic functions

Balo disease has no specific treatment; thus medical care is symptomatic and supportive (Thoene & Coker, 1995). Special education services for Balo disease may be available under the multiple handicapping condition of Other Health Impairment category or Physical Disability. Children may show neurological, physical, and intellectual deficits and thus need multiple interventions for all areas. Psychoeducational testing should occur annually to determine the ongoing educational need in these areas. Occupational and physical therapy may also be required services for children with Balo disease.

Balo disease is a life-threatening disorder. Most patients survive for less than a year (Rowland, 1995). Current research is aimed at determining the cause of this disease.

REFERENCES

Rowland, L. P. (Ed.). (1995). *Merritt's textbook of neurology* (9th ed.). Baltimore: Williams & Wilkins.

Thoene, J. G., & Coker, N. P. (Eds.). 1995. Physicians' guide to rare diseases (2nd ed.). Montvale, NJ: Dowden.

Jennifer Hargrave
University of Texas at Austin

See also Schilder's Disease

BARBITURATE ABUSE

Barbiturates are depressant drugs that were initially designed to induce sleep and relieve anxiety or tension by slowing down the central nervous system (Meeks, Heit, & Page, 1996). The sedative affect is much the same as alcohol's and normally lasts for 3-6 hours at a time (Information on barbiturates, 2002). Currently, there are over 2,000 known legal and illegal barbiturates available. In small doses they are considered safe, and they may be prescribed by a physician for insomnia, anxiety, tension, or epilepsy (Information on barbiturates, 2002). Unfortunately, barbiturate dosage must continually be increased to maintain the same relaxation effect, and the use quickly establishes dependence in the user (Information on barbiturates, 2002). Higher levels of dosages are considered dangerous and may interfere with respiration (Information on barbiturates, 2002).

Legal use of barbiturates includes ingestion of a pill or tablet form; illegal use also includes pills or tablets and may include the use of a powder that is manufactured and injected. The use of barbiturates appears to have lessened in recent years. In 1968 24.7 million Americans used prescription barbiturates in comparison to 8.8 million in 1973 (DAWN barbiturates, 2002). A study dealing with workplace drug usage indicated that approximately .19% of the workers in the study had recently used barbiturates (News briefs, 1997).

Characteristics

Short-term use

1. Relief from tension, anxiety, and insomnia
2. Behaviors consistent with intoxication: slurred speech, balance difficulties
3. Memory problems

Long-term use

1. Vision problems
2. Slowed reflexes
3. Menstrual problems
4. Lack of coordination
5. Sexual dysfunction
6. Breathing problems

The use of barbiturates is considered dangerous because of the potential for dependency. It is especially dangerous in infants born to barbiturate-dependent women. The treatment involves withdrawal from the effects and use of the drug. Because withdrawal can cause serious side effects, a physician should carefully monitor the period of withdrawal. Side effects can include irritability, nervousness, fainting, nausea, convulsions, and, in rare cases, death due to respiratory problems. The same potential side effects are possible with infants who must experience withdrawal (DAWN barbiturates, 2002).

In terms of special education, the use of barbiturates does not in itself render a student eligible for special education services. Students who are using (legal or illegal) drugs may be evaluated in all areas to determine whether there is a concomitant disability, such as a learning disability, emotional disability, or other health impairment. If the student is ineligible, the team may want to consider whether the student is eligible for a Section 504 plan because of possible chemical dependence.

Best practices for the future would be to institute effective preventative measures. For example, students who are at risk for drug use should be educated about the affects of barbiturates, and at-risk pregnant women should be educated regarding the effects on their unborn child.

REFERENCES

DAWN barbiturates. (2002). Retrieved from http://www.kakourous.co.ukbarbs.html

Information on barbiturates. (2002). Retrieved from http://www.gwu.edu/~cade/barbiturates.htm

Meeks, L., Heit, P., & Page, R. (1996). *Comprehensive school health education: Totally awesome strategies for teaching health* (pp. 267–269). Blacklick, OH: Meeks Heit.

News briefs. (1997). Retrieved from http://www.ndsn.org/FEB97SKBEECH.html

Dalene M. McCloskey
University of Northern Colorado

BARDET-BIEDL SYNDROME

Bardet-Biedl syndrome is a rare disorder inherited as an autosomal recessive genetic trait. As with Laurence-Moon syndrome, Bardet-Biedl syndrome is characterized by mental retardation, hypogonadism, and progressive retinal dystrophy with vision failure. Renal failure also occurs, as does hypertension, and these represent the leading cause of death. Two symptoms specific to Bardet-Biedl syndrome include obesity and polydactyly. Alstrom syndrome and Prader-Willi syndrome exhibit similar symptoms to that of Bardet-Biedl and may be useful in terms of differential diagnosis.

Bardet-Biedl affects males and females in equal numbers. There have been over 100 cases of this disorder reported in the medical literature with an increased number of incidences among the Arabs of Kuwait (Berg, 1996).

The primary symptom in this disorder is degeneration of the retina. This typically occurs in early childhood. The course of progression of sight deterioration differs in each individual. Impairments range from loss of central vision, to day blindness, to lesions in the middle of the retina. In some cases, the degeneration of the retina may follow the course of retinitis pigmentosa with night blindness followed by tunnel vision (McKusick, 1992).

Besides obesity found in almost all individuals with Bardet-Biedl syndrome, many also suffer from abnormalities in their fingers and toes, such as additional fingers and/or toes, webbing of the digits, or abnormal shortness of the digits.

Another feature prevalent is mild to moderate retardation typically more apparent in males in early childhood than in females. Sexual maturation is often delayed or absent. Males tend to have small testes and genitalia and females are usually affected by menstrual irregularities and reproductive dysfunction. Other abnormalities include hypertension, diabetes mellitus, and short stature (McKusick, 1992).

Bardet-Biedl syndrome is inherited as an autosomal recessive genetic trait. In other words, the syndrome only affects the offspring if the defective gene is passed on by both the mother and the father. If the child receives only one defective gene from one parent, the child will be a carrier but will not display the symptoms. The risk of two parents carrying this gene and passing it on to their offspring is 25%. The risk of passing one of the defective genes is 50%, and there is a 25% chance of the parents passing on two normal genes. The risk is the same for each pregnancy (Berg, 1996).

Characteristics

1. Mental retardation
2. Hypogonadism
3. Progressive retinal dystrophy with vision failure

Other symptoms may include hypertension, obesity, abnormal fingers and toes, and sexual maturation delay or absence and occasional hearing impairment.

Treatment and diagnosis of retinal degeneration found in Bardet-Biedl syndrome can be made by an ophthalmologist through various tests. Visual aids may help as vision decreases, and special eyeglasses can be used to protect the eye from excessive light. A variety of visual and nonvisual aids can help the individual to mediate visual deficits. Treatment also includes medical responses to symptoms, urinary cultures, measurement of blood pressure, and genetic counseling (Weidemann, Kunze, Grosse, & Dibbern, 1989).

Surgery may be helpful to remedy abnormalities found in the fingers and toes. Genetic counseling may be beneficial for patients and families. Additionally, psychological counseling can be a useful tool to help individuals and their families cope with the effects of Bardet-Biedl syndrome.

Finally, early educational intervention can be extremely critical in helping those affected by mental retardation. Indeed, the course and prognosis of this disorder is determined by the degree of mental retardation and by the progression of the retino- and neuropathy (Weidemann et al., 1989). Specialized classes addressing the child's strengths and mediating weaknesses will be useful in helping the child attain social and academic potential (Berg, 1996).

REFERENCES

Berg, B. (1996). *Principles of child neurology.* San Francisco: McGraw-Hill.

McKusick, V. A. (1992). *Mendelian inheritance in man* (10th ed.). Johns Hopkins University Press.

Wiedemann, H. R., Kunze, J., Grosse, F. R., & Dibbern, H. (1989). *Atlas of clinical syndromes: A visual aid to diagnosis* (2nd ed.). St. Louis, MO: Mosby.

Lisa A. Fasnacht-Hill
Keck University of Southern California School of Medicine
University of Southern California / University Affiliated Program at Children's Hospital of Los Angeles

BATTEN DISEASE

Batten disease is one of a group of degenerative encephalopathic diseases known as the neuronal ceroid-lipofuscinoses (NCLs). Batten originally described the disease in 1903 (Cassedy & Edwards, 1993). In all the NCLs ceroid or lipofuscin accumulates within neurons and cells in other body systems. The cellular accumulations are autoflourescent, and the lipopigments distend the affected cells (Dyken, 1999). Multiple systems have been derived to categorize the set of NCLs. Although the term Batten disease sometimes is used to refer to the entire set of diseases, classically the term is used to refer only to the juvenile form of the disorder (classical juvenile NCL; Bennett & Hofmann, 1999).

Classical juvenile NCL is the most common of the NCLs, accounting for 49% of the patients with NCL (Dyken, 1999). It has an incidence of 1 in 25,000 in northern European populations (Munroe, 1996), but lower worldwide (1:100,000; Santavuori, 1988). The gene for classical juvenile NCL is located on Chromosome 16p11.2-12.1 (Bennett & Hofmann, 1999). Not all affected individuals have the classic deletion (Bennett & Hofmann, 1999). All of the NCLs have an autosomal recessive mode of inheritance. It is believed that the pathologic basis of the disorder is one of an inborn error in metabolism, leading to membrane instability (Dyken, 1999).

Characteristics

1. Slowly progressive dementia.
2. The usual age of onset is between 4 and 9 years of age (5.93 ± 1.35 years).
3. Initial symptoms are visual loss and behavioral changes. Initially, cognitive impairment is mild and is observable only at school.
4. By 10–15 years of age speech becomes indistinct, overly rapid, and dysarthric.
5. Psychomotor problems, including extrapyramidal, pyramidal, and cerebellar findings, develop.
6. Seizures develop later in the course of the disease.
7. Ocular exam demonstrates macular degeneration, optic atrophy, and retinal degeneration.
8. Death occurs by 20 years of age.

(Dyken, 1999; Santavuori, 1988)

Educational interventions should be aimed at maintaining the highest level of functioning. The anticipated deterioration must be acknowledged in educational plans. There is no current, efficacious medical treatment (Percy, 1999). Future research will focus on understanding the basic pathophysiology of the disorder and its treatment. Treatment approaches using stem-cell transplantation or genetically engineered viruses for corrective gene therapy are anticipated (Percy, 1999).

REFERENCES

Bennett, M. J., & Hofmann, S. L. (1999). The neuronal ceroid-lipofuscinoses (Batten disease): A new class of lysosomal storage diseases. *Journal of Inherited Metabolic Diseases, 22,* 535–544.

Cassedy, K. J., & Edwards, M. K. (1993). Metabolic and degenerative diseases of childhood. *Topics in Magnetic Resonance Imaging, 5,* 73–95.

Dyken, P. R. (1999). Degenerative diseases primarily of gray matter. In K. Swaiman & S. Ashwal (Eds.), *Pediatric neurology: Principles and practice* (3rd ed.). St. Louis, MO: Mosby.

Munroe, P. B. (1996). Prenatal diagnosis of Batten's disease. *The Lancet, 347,* 1014–1015.

Percy, A. K. (1999). Inherited neurodegenerative disease: The evolution of our thinking. *Journal of Child Neurology, 14*(4), 256–262.

Santavuori, P. (1988). Neuronal ceroid-lipofuscinoses in childhood. *Brain and Development, 10,* 80–83.

Greta N. Wilkening
University of Colorado Health Sciences Center
The Children's Hospital

See also Kufs Disease

BATTERED-CHILD SYNDROME

Battered-child syndrome describes children who are chronically exposed to physical, sexual, or psychological abuse or neglect. The physical abuse may range from moderate injuries to severe ones that require hospitalization. Severe cases may result in permanent physical damage or even death (Buris, Posta, Darok, & Gorombey, 2000).

Owing to unknown numbers of unreported cases of child abuse, incidence is difficult to estimate. In 1986 more than 1 million children experienced some form of abuse, yielding a rate of 16.3/1,000 U.S. children (Vadasy, 1989). The incidence of sexual abuse is thought to be frequent but often not reported. Statistically, psychological abuse is the most frequent but is often in addition to other forms of abuse, such as physical trauma (Buris et al., 2000). Mostly younger children, under age 3, are the targets of abuse (Kempe, Silverman, Steele, Droegemueller, & Silver, 1985). Assaults, of which abuse is an important component, are thought to cause 10% of cases of traumatic brain injury in children. In one study of children under 2 years of age hospitalized for head injuries, abuse was suspected in 24% of cases (see Christensen, 1996).

Characteristics

1. Child's health is below average, and child shows poor skin hygiene, multiple soft tissue injuries, and malnutrition.
2. Parents' explanation for the injuries is not plausible according to clinical findings. When in care of a hospital or other protected environment, no new lesions emerge.
3. Injuries of the appendicular skeleton are the most common.
4. Subdural hematoma, failure to thrive, soft-tissue swellings or skin bruising, and multiple unexplained fractures and lesions at different healing stages may be apparent.
5. In the majority of sexual abuse cases, the perpetrator tends to be a relative or close family friend.
6. Battered children may exhibit self-injurious behavior or suicide attempts or ideation.
7. The first warning signs tend to be neglect and malnutrition.
8. Prematurity and low birth weight are risk factors concerning child battery.

In many cases, battered children are brought to hospitals for treatment of physical injuries. Physicians and other medical professionals should be aware of battered-child syndrome characteristics so that appropriate action, legal if necessary, can be taken. They must be able to identify discrepancies between a parent's explanation of what happened and what actual features of the injury suggest happened (Buris et al., 2000). Early identification of abuse may enable intervention, including family therapy or removal of children from their dangerous environment and placement with relatives or a foster family. While the child is still in the hospital, a psychological and neuropsychological evaluation is useful to aid in planning for rehabilitation (Kempe et al., 1985).

Due to chronic abuse and maltreatment, battered infants tend to form insecure attachment styles that often hinder their adaptation to the preschool environment. Battered children usually hide their feelings and view themselves in negative ways, which could also interfere with adapting to a school environment because the child may have deficits in achievement motivation and self-efficacy (Cicchetti, Toth, & Hennessy, 1989). Problems may also arise when a battered child must form peer relationships in a school setting. Due to the child's negative models of the self and insecure attachment styles, the child often has difficulty forming positive peer relationships. Battered children often view others as hostile or rejecting, and they may direct aggressive responses at their teachers (Cicchetti et al., 1989).

Treatment varies with age of the injured child, the type and degree of abuse, and the consequent psychological and physical injury. A variety of physical and speech-language therapies may be necessary to help deal with the physical effects, and individual and group therapy, particularly cognitive-behavioral, may be helpful in treating psychological effects.

Prognosis obviously depends on the nature and extent of the abuse and consequent damage. For unreported and thus untreated cases of child abuse, prognosis is poor owing both to the continuing nature of the abuse and to the fact that the degree of abuse may escalate to irreversible physical injury or even death. Research contradicts two commonly held beliefs about the effects of abuse: that those abused as children will likely abuse their own children and that sexual abuse generally has adverse adult consequences. Most parents who were themselves abused as children do not abuse their own children, although approximately 30% do—a figure well above base rate (Kaufman & Zigler, 1989); a well-designed meta-analytic study (Rind, Tromovitch, & Bauserman, 1998) found that childhood sexual abuse did not consistently lead to intense or broad negative effects in young adults, although effects were more serious in women than in men. Prognosis for recovery from mild to moderate degrees of psychological abuse, then, may be better than is often thought. Of course, more severe degrees of physical or psychological abuse are likely to have long-term adverse consequences.

REFERENCES

Buris, L. F., Posta, J., Darok, M., & Gorombey, S. (2000). Battered children, medical forensic aspects: A 20-year review from eastern Hungary. *International Journal of Offender Therapy and Comparative Criminology, 44,* 657–666.

Christensen, J. R. (1996). Pediatric traumatic brain injury. In A. J. Capute & P. J. Accardo (Eds.), *Developmental disabilities in infancy and childhood: Vol. 2. Neurodevelopmental diagnosis and treatment* (2nd ed., pp. 245–260). Baltimore: Brookes.

Cicchetti, D., Toth, S. L., & Hennessy, K. (1989). Research on the consequences of child maltreatment and its application to educational settings. *Topics in Early Childhood Special Education, 9,* 33–55.

Kaufman, J., & Zigler, E. (1989). The intergenerational transmission of child abuse. In D. Cicchetti & V. Carlson (Eds.), *Child maltreatment* (pp. 129–150). New York: Cambridge University Press.

Kempe, C. H., Silverman, F. N., Steele, B. F., Droegemueller, W., & Silver, H. K. (1985). The battered child syndrome. *Child Abuse and Neglect, 9,* 143–154.

Rind, B., Tromovitch, P., & Bauserman, R. (1998). A meta-analytic examination of assumed properties of child sexual abuse using college samples. *Psychological Bulletin, 124,* 22–53.

Vadasy, P. F. (1989). Child maltreatment and the early childhood special educator. *Topics in Early Childhood Special Education, 9,* 56–72.

Jaime Slappey
Robert T. Brown
University of North Carolina at Wilmington

BECKWITH-WIEDEMANN SYNDROME

Beckwith-Wiedemann syndrome (BWS) is a rare disorder recognized primarily by a consistent grouping of findings of unknown etiology (Ocean State Online, 2001) and is characterized by excessive size and height at birth. For instance, in many males, birth length may be at or above the 95th percentile. Typically, their height remains within this range throughout their adolescent years. Growth closely parallels the normal growth curve. Females, however, are usually born at or about the 75th percentile, and their height increases to the 95th percentile by 18 months of age. Their height then remains at this percentile throughout adolescence. Many infants also develop advanced bone age within the first 4 years of life. Other features include an unusually large tongue within a gaping mouth; enlarged organs, such as spleen, liver, and heart; umbilical hernias; and creases in the earlobes. Infancy is a very critical period because of the possibility of severe hypoglycemia, increased tumor growth, such as Wilm's, and gonadoblastoma (National Organization for Rare Disorders, Inc., 2001).

In most cases, BWS seems to result from a spontaneous genetic change. In rare cases, approximately 15%, it appears to be familial, suggesting autosomal dominant inheritance. The risk of transmitting the disorder from the affected parent to the offspring is 50% for each pregnancy regardless of the gender of the resulting child. This risk is the same for subsequent pregnancies (National Organization for Rare Disorders, Inc., 2001). The severity at which each child is affected is highly variable. The great majority of persons who carry the gene are only minimally affected (Beckwith-Wiedemann Support Network, 2001).

BWS seems to affect males and females equally. Since J. B. Beckwith and H. R. Wiedemann concurrently described the disorder in the early 1960s, over 400 cases have been reported. The incidence of BWS has been difficult to determine because of the variance in the severity of the reported symptoms. Estimates range from 1 in 13,600 to 1 in 17,000 (National Organization for Rare Disorders, Inc., 2001).

Characteristics

1. Large newborn (large for gestational age, or LGA)
2. Large tongue, sometimes protruding
3. Large prominent eyes
4. Creases in earlobes
5. Pinna abnormalities and low-set ears
6. Umbilical hernia (omphalocele)
7. Separated abdominal muscles (diastasis recti)
8. Undescended testicles (cryptorchidism)
9. Hypoglycemia
10. Poor feeding
11. Lethargy
12. Seizures
13. Polyhydramnios
14. Enlargement of some organs and tissues

(Ocean State Online, 2000)

In families with a history of BWS, diagnostic screens can be performed prenatally. Ultrasound imaging may be used to determine fetal size or the size of the developing organs. Early detection of the syndrome allows for prompt treatment of some of the symptoms, especially neonatal hypoglycemia. The early treatment of hypoglycemia can prevent associated neurological complications, such as mental retardation. With early treatment, it seems that the hypoglycemia is usually temporary in infants, and the infant responds well to medical therapy during the first 4 months of life (National Organization for Rare Disorders, Inc., 2001). Intravenous glucose solutions and corticosteriods are used to treat the hypoglycemia. Treatment of other symptoms of BWS is directed toward the specific symptom. For instance, caregivers must pay careful attention to feeding and to the position of the child while he or she is sleeping to avoid problems with the enlarged tongue. In some children the umbilical hernias may disappear within the first year, but if the hernia becomes larger, surgery may be indicated (Ocean State Online, 2000). Medications and surgery may also be used in the cases with congenital heart defects. Tumors that develop require close observation to determine specific malignancy. Depending on the malignancy, treatment may include use of anticancer drugs, radiation therapy, or surgery (National Organization for Rare Disorders, Inc., 2001).

Children who survive infancy do well, although no long-term follow-up studies are available. Mental function seems to be normal to slightly below normal. Genetic counseling is strongly recommended for affected families. Although most treatment is symptomatic and supportive, special services such as speech therapy, social services, and vocational services may be beneficial to the affected children.

REFERENCES

Beckwith-Wiedemann Support Network. (2001, March 29). Retrieved from http://www.geocities.com/bwsn/bws.html

National Organization for Rare Disorders, Inc. (2001, January 30). Beckwith-Wiedemann syndrome. Retrieved from http://www.rarediseases.org

Ocean State Online. (2000, September 5). Beckwith-Wiedemann syndrome. Retrieved from http://oso.adam.com/ency/article/001186.htm

Vedia Sherman
Austin Neurological Clinic

BELL'S PALSY

Bell's palsy is an acute unilateral facial nerve paralysis resulting from injury or viral or spirochete infection (e.g., mumps, Lyme disease), or from postinfectious allergic or immune demyelinating facial neuritis that may have an abrupt onset of clinical manifestations about 2 weeks after infection. The age of onset can be anywhere from infancy to adolescence, and the incidence is common (Pedlynx, 2002).

Characteristics

1. Paresis of upper and lower face
2. Drop of corner of mouth
3. Unable to close eye leading to exposure keratitis at night
4. Loss of taste on anterior two thirds of tongue in 50% of cases
5. Possible signs of a neuropathy and regeneration of the facial nerve

Supportive treatment includes the protection of the cornea with methylcellulose eye drops or an ocular lubricant, as well as medical assurances of the chances for recovery. Special education services would not likely be needed for this temporary condition because 85% of cases recover spontaneously. However, in 10% of cases mild facial weakness continues, and in 5% of cases severe facial weakness continues and may require cosmetic surgery (Rothenberg & Chapman, 1994).

REFERENCES

Pedlynx. (2002). Bell's palsy. Retrieved from http://www.icondata.com/health/pedbase/files/Bell'spaHTM

Rothenberg, M., & Chapman, C. (1994). *Barron's dictionary of medical terms.* Hauppauge, NY: Barron's Educational Series.

Elaine Fletcher-Janzen
University of Northern Colorado

BENIGN ESSENTIAL TREMOR

Benign essential tremor (BET) is characterized by rapid rhythmic movements that are pronounced during active muscle innervation. The tremors are decreased or absent during rest and sleep. BET typically presents as a postural tremor that gets worse during action and sustained posturing. BET is also referred to as a familial tremor, intention tremor, and hereditary BET (senile tremor is used when the onset is much later in life).

In most cases the tremor begins in midlife (e.g., after 40 or 50 years of age) but can be found in children. The tremor has been reported to occur sporadically but is also familial. BET is considered an autosomal dominant disorder with approximately 50% of affected individuals having family members with a similar tremor (Williams, 1999). A specific gene has not been discovered, and the exact etiology of the disorder is still unknown. The tremor is suspected to be caused by a dysfunction of beta adrenergic receptors in the basal ganglia but is estimated to occur 20 times more frequently than Parkinson's disease (Marsden & Fowler, 1998). Incidence figures are difficult to obtain because many individuals are so mildly affected and do not seek medical opinions. Because the tremor is considered to be benign, it is not associated with other neurological abnormalities; however, it can be seen in cases of torsion dystonia, spasmodic torticollis, hereditary peripheral polyneuropathy, Parkinson's disease, and Charcot-Marie-Tooth disease.

Characteristics

1. Tremors tend to be bilateral and fairly symmetrical.
2. Tremors are most often present during volitional movements (e.g., holding cup) and are absent during rest.
3. In 50% of cases the head is involved, and in 33% legs are.
4. Tremors affect facial and oropharyngeal muscles causing chewing difficulty and vocal tremors.
5. Tremors are frequently exacerbated by stress and caffeine.
6. Coordination and walking are usually unaffected.

The severity of BET generally remains unchanged throughout an individual's life but in some instances worsens. Nearly half of individuals with BET respond to beta adrenoceptor blockers (e.g., propranolol and primidone; Williams, 1999). Postural arm tremors tend to respond best, whereas head tremors are more resistant to drug therapies. Drug response should be carefully monitored for side effects, including cardiac and respiratory complications. Like alcohol, benzodiazepines and barbiturates have been shown to reduce the tremor and relieve the embarrassment of having it. Drugs intended to treat Parkinson's disease have not been found to be effective with BET (Marsden & Fowler, 1998). When no drug works, deliberate lesioning of the thalamus, a procedure referred to as contralateral ventrolateral thalamotomy, has been used. Risks for this procedure are, however, serious (e.g., mutism).

Although referred to as a benign tremor, there are risks for serious social and psychological consequences, including social phobias and avoidance of potentially embarrassing situations, including eating and speaking in public (George & Lydiard, 1994). Some children also develop more generalized anxiety and mood disorders. Teachers and other professionals who are in contact with children who have BET need to be aware of this. Psychological help ranging from simple reassurance to counseling may be needed. Children with BET may qualify for special education services under Other Health Impairment if learning is affected. In most cases, however, this is not necessary, and regular classroom accommodations will suffice. Typical accommodations include allowing for oral examination and dictation of assignments and providing the child with written lecture notes. An occupational therapy evaluation, however, may help to ensure that accommodations are appropriate and that no other intervention is needed (this includes services under Section 504 of the American with Disabilities Act).

Further research is needed to determine more specifically the cause of BET and ways to prevent or effectively treat the tremor. Drug studies may be particularly beneficial.

REFERENCES

George, M. S., & Lydiard, R. B. (1994). Social phobia secondary to physical disability: A review of benign essential tremor (BET) and stuttering. *Psychosomatics, 35,* 520–523.

Marsden, C. D., & Fowler, T. J. (1998). *Clinical neurology* (2nd ed.). New York: Oxford University Press.

Williams, A. C. (1999). *Patient care in neurology.* New York: Oxford University Press.

Jenise Jensen
Elaine Clark
University of Utah

BERNARD-SOULIER SYNDROME

Bernard-Soulier syndrome is a disorder of platelet dysfunction, presenting with severe and prolonged bleeding periods, below-normal blood platelet counts, and thrombocytopenia. The underlying defect of this genetic disorder is an absence or decreased expression of the glycoprotein Ib-IX-V complex on the surface of platelets, resulting in defective platelet adhesion.

Bernard-Soulier syndrome is believed to be an extremely rare condition. Based on reported cases in Europe, North

America, and Japan, it has been estimated that the disorder has a prevalence rate of less than 1 in 1,000,000, but this is believed to be an underestimate due to underreporting and misdiagnosis (Lopez, Andrews, Afshar-Kharghan, & Berndt, 1998).

The disorder manifests itself early in childhood, and severity of symptoms varies considerably. Bernard-Soulier syndrome is almost always transmitted in an autosomal recessive manner (Lopez et al., 1998). However, autosomal dominant inheritance has been reported in several cases (Miller, Lyle, & Cunningham, 1992).

Characteristics

1. Below-normal blood platelet counts (thrombocytopenia)
2. Large platelet size
3. Prolonged bleeding (5 to greater than 20 min)
4. Epistaxis (nose bleeding) and gingival and cutaneous bleeding
5. Easy bruising
6. Severe hemorrhaging following surgery

With the high risk of hemorrhage, treatment of Bernard-Soulier syndrome is limited to treating severe bleeding episodes. In cases of surgery or life-threatening hemorrhage, platelet transfusion becomes necessary. General support involves educating the child and his or her parents about the bleeding diathesis and the importance of avoiding trauma. In addition, the child with Bernard-Soulier syndrome should be advised against the use of antiplatelet medications such as aspirin.

Special educational considerations for the child with Bernard-Soulier syndrome involve encouragement against participation in any high-contact sports. Depending on the severity of symptoms, further restriction of activity may be necessary.

The severity of Bernard-Soulier syndrome symptoms may lessen throughout puberty and adult life (Mhawech & Saleem, 2000). However, there have been incidences reported in which the severity of symptoms progressively worsened (Lopez et al., 1998). Future research plans to focus on the potential use of gene therapy in individuals with the disorder. Bernard-Soulier syndrome appears to be an ideal candidate disease for gene therapy due to the simplicity of the defective gene involved in the syndrome (Lopez et al., 1998).

REFERENCES

Lopez, J. A., Andrews, R. K., Afshar-Kharghan, V., & Berndt, M. C. (1998). Bernard-Soulier syndrome. *Blood, 91*(12), 4397–4418.

Mhawech, P., & Saleem, A. (2000). Inherited giant platelet disorders: Classification and literature review. *American Journal of Clinical Pathology, 113*(2), 176–190.

Miller, J. L., Lyle, V. A., & Cunningham, D. (1992). Mutation of leucine-57 to phenylalanine in a platelet glycoprotein Ib alpha leucine tandem repeat occurring in patients with an autosomal dominant variant of Bernard-Soulier disease. *Blood, 79,* 439–446.

Cassandra Burns Romine
Texas A&M University

BILIARY CIRRHOSIS, PRIMARY

Primary biliary cirrhosis (PBC) is a disease of the bile ducts and liver. Primarily effecting women (Fanning et al., 2000), this condition may lie dormant for years and never cause a problem. However, once triggered, PBC acts as an autoimmune disorder in which the body attacks its own cells as if they were foreign. Specifically, the body attacks the cells that line the bile ducts. This causes damage to the ducts, allowing bile acids to corrode the liver. The condition of having this corrosion of the liver is called cirrhosis.

The triggers for PBC are unknown, but it is possible that pregnancy, infection, stress, or a hereditary factor may be involved. The incidence of PBC is 3 to 15 cases per million per year (Medline, 2002).

Liver damage causes a number of serious side effects. Most common is the inability to break down toxins that enter the body. These toxins can be in the form of drugs, alcohol, and some foods. Damage can impair the liver's ability to balance the amounts of certain vitamins and minerals in the body.

Characteristics

1. Itching
2. Chronic fatigue
3. Discoloration of skin
4. Nausea, indigestion
5. Bone and joint pain
6. Aches in upper abdomen
7. Diarrhea
8. Dark urine, pale stools
9. Weakness in wrists and hands
10. Easy bruising
11. Dry eyes or mouth

There is no known cure for PBC, but doctors may prescribe drugs that decrease the activity of the immune system. PBC may also be controlled by diet: Eating small portions very often will ensure that there is always some food for the bile ducts to be digesting, thus decreasing the amount of time that liver cells are attacked. Treatment basically is targeted at symptom reduction and prevention of complications (Medline, 2002).

In an educational setting, children may need special medical and dietary care that is specific to the liver problems and complications. They may also need to be absent more often due to symptoms that interfere with their ability to attend school; therefore, they will most likely qualify for special education under the Other Health Impairment category of services.

The course is variable, but untreated the average referral for liver transplantation occurs at 7 years. Statistical models are now used to predict the best timing of transplantation (Medline, 2002).

REFERENCES

Fanning, P. A., Jonsson, J. R., Clouston, A. D., Edwards-Smith, C., Balderson, G. A., Macdonald, G. A., Crawford, D. H., Kerlin, P., Powell, L. W., & Powell, E. E. (2000). Detection of male DNA in the liver of female patients with primary biliary cirrhosis. *Journal of Hepatology, 33,* 690–695.

Medline. (2002). *Medline plus medical encyclopedia: Primary biliary cirrhosis.* Retrieved from http://www.nlm.nih.gov/medlineplus/ency/article/000282.htm

Allison Katz
Rutgers University

BIPOLAR AFFECTIVE DISORDER

Bipolar affective disorder (BAD) is a mood disorder that is characterized by distinct periods of depression and manic episodes. Manic episodes are characterized by elevated mood, grandiosity, pressured speech, racing thoughts, distractibility, decreased need for sleep, increased goal-directed behavior, and extreme involvement in pleasurable (but reckless) activities. Depressive episodes are often characterized by diminished interest, sadness, disturbed sleep and appetite, feelings of guilt and hopelessness, and problems with concentration and performance. During periods of depression, suicidal thoughts are common. In fact, among adolescents diagnosed with BAD, around 20% make serious suicide attempts; males are more likely to complete these (American Psychiatric Association [APA], 2000).

According to the *Diagnostic and Statistical Manual of Mental Disorders–Fourth Edition, Text Revision (DSM-IV-TR),* there are two types of BAD, one that is characterized by a history of at least one manic episode (or mixed episodes) and depression (Bipolar I), and the other a history of one or more episodes of both major depression and hypomania (Bipolar II). *DSM-IV-TR* criteria are essentially the same for young people and adults. The overall risk of developing Bipolar I has been estimated to be .4% to 1.6%, and .5% for Bipolar II (APA, 2000). Twenty percent of individuals diagnosed as having BAD have their first episode during adolescence, with peak onset between 15 and 19 (and overall prevalence rate about 1%; (McClellan & Werry, 1997). Sex differences have been reported, with more females being diagnosed with Bipolar II and presenting more often with depression as the first episode and the more frequent manifestation. Males are more likely to present with mania first but have equal occurrences of manic and depressive episodes over a lifetime. Compared to males, females and adolescents of both sexes are more likely to be rapid cyclers (i.e., 4 or more episodes a year).

Characteristics

1. There are distinct periods of abnormally elevated, expansive, or irritable mood lasting for at least one week (or requiring hospitalization).
2. If mood is elevated or expansive, the individual must have three or more prominent symptoms; if mood is irritable only, four or more (e.g., grandiosity, decreased need for sleep, racing thoughts, excessive involvement in reckless activities).
3. Symptoms must be distinguished from normal baseline behaviors, must have a fluctuating course, and must cause impairment in functioning (or significant distress).
4. Symptoms cannot be due to drug abuse, medication use, or medical condition.
5. Children tend to be more irritable and belligerent than euphoric, and adolescents more labile and psychotic (e.g., paranoia and frank hallucinations).
6. Long-term outcome for early versus later onset of BAD is about the same, but when occurring earlier, symptoms appear more chronic and resistant to treatment.

The risks for having an early onset of BAD include rapid onset of depression with psychomotor slowing or agitation, family history of affective disorders (especially BAD), and report of mania-hypomania after treatment with antidepressant medications (McClellan & Werry, 1997). Mania is considered rare in young children; however, current thought suggests that chronic irritability, hypersensitivity, and belligerence may be symptomatic of BAD, and not just "normal" behaviors of childhood (Sach, Baldassano, Truman, & Guille, 2000). There is no known association between earlier onset and long-term outcome of the condition; however, the course appears more chronic and less responsive to treatment. This may be explained in part by the higher rate of mixed symptoms in earlier onset BAD and greater frequency of psychosis and comorbidity.

Frequently reported comorbid conditions include attention-deficit/hyperactivity disorder, conduct disorder, and substance abuse. The unusually high rate of comorbidity not only complicates treatment but also makes diagnosis more difficult (and the prognosis worse). Differential diagnosis is also complicated by conditions that have a number of shared features. This includes children with posttraumatic stress disorder who have unstable moods, irritability, sleep disturbance, and hypervigilance, as well as adolescents who have schizophrenia and present with disturbed thinking, paranoia, and hallucinations. Measures such as the Mania Rating Scale (Fristad, Weller, & Weller, 1990) can help to distinguish BAD from other conditions; however, a complete and reliable history is critical to ensure accurate diagnosis and treatment (e.g., data on baseline functioning and symptom stability of the child and family history of mood disorders, especially BAD).

Genetics plays a critical role in BAD; in fact, 15% of individuals with BAD have first-degree relatives with the disorder. The rate is even higher for early-onset BAD. Pharmacology is the most common treatment, and lithium is the drug of choice. Lithium has been found to be particularly effective in treating mania; however, when lithium is ineffective or contraindicated (e.g., females prone to developing ovarian cysts or children with renal problems), anticonvulsants such as valproate and carbamazepine have been used. Benzodiazepines and neuroleptics are also used as adjunctive therapies for agitation and psychotic symptoms. In addition to drug therapy, psychological interventions are needed to address certain behavior problems and psychosocial concerns. Research has demonstrated that individuals who experience significant negative life events and have fewer social supports take longer to recover than do those with positive attitudes and supports (Miklowitz & Alloy, 1999).

Children and adolescents with BAD are likely to require special accommodations at school, in some cases, special education (e.g., services under the category Emotional Disturbance). Regardless of the need for special service, the school psychologist should be contacted to ensure appropriate services, including home-school collaborations regarding behavior and schoolwork (e.g., implementing strategies such as home notes to improve work completion). Education about BAD is also important for the child, parent, and teacher.

BAD is considered a recurrent condition with relapse rates as high as 40% in the first year and 73% at year five (Gitlin, Swendsen, Heller, & Hammen, 1995). Research is therefore needed to identify treatments that will reduce the relapse rates and provide more effective symptom relief. Finding ways to identify at-risk infants and children is also needed to prevent associated problems such as school failure, substance abuse, and social-legal problems and to provide more effective symptom relief. Research is also needed to determine protective factors and the long-term consequence of early-onset BAD.

REFERENCES

American Psychiatric Association. (2000). *Diagnostic and statistical manual of mental disorders* (4th ed., Text Revision). Washington, DC: Author.

Fristad, M., Weller, E., & Weller, R. (1990). The Mania Rating Scale: Can it be used in children? *Journal of the American Academy of Child and Adolescent Psychiatry, 34*(7), 867–876.

Gitlin, M., Swendsen, J., Heller, T., & Hammen, C. (1995). Relapse and impairment in bipolar disorder. *American Journal of Psychiatry, 152,* 1635–1640.

McClellan, J., & Werry, J. (1997). Practice parameters for the assessment and treatment of children and adolescents with bipolar disorder. *Journal of the American Academy of Child and Adolescent Psychiatry, 36*(10), 157–175.

Miklowitz, D., & Alloy, L. (1999). Psychosocial factors in the course and treatment of bipolar disorder: Introduction to the special section. *Journal of Abnormal Psychology, 108*(4), 555–557.

Sach, G., Baldassano, C., Truman, C., & Guille, C. (2000). Comorbidity of attention deficit hyperactivity disorder with early and late onset bipolar disorder. *American Journal of Psychiatry, 157*(3), 466–468.

Elaine Clark
Rex Gonzales
University of Utah

See also Depression

BLUE DIAPER SYNDROME

Blue diaper syndrome is a metabolic disorder caused by the incomplete breakdown of the dietary nutrient and obligatory serotonin (5-HT) precusor tryptophan. Excessive amounts of tryptophan are broken down by intestinal bacteria, thus converting the excessive tryptophan into indican. The indican is then absorbed by the intestinal wall and excreted in urine, thus causing the bluish discoloration seen in infants' diapers. Blue diaper syndrome is believed to be an inherited, autosomal, possibly X-linked, recessive trait.

Blue diaper syndrome, often occurring in infancy, is rare equally affecting females and males. The actual prevalence of blue diaper syndrome is unknown, as it has been underreported. Because tryptophan is involved in the production of serotonin, a neurotransmitter involved in the regulation of mood and other cognitive processes, blue diaper syndrome has been known to be associated with cognitive sequelae.

Characteristics

1. Bluish discoloration of the infant's urine (and bluish stained diaper)

2. Craniostenosis (a congenital deformity of the skull resulting from premature closure of the sutures between the cranial bones) and osteoscerosis (abnormal increase in bone tissue density)
3. Dwarfism, mental retardation, hypercalcemia, failure to thrive, irritability, poor appetite, constipation, and vomiting
4. Abnormally high levels of calcium in the blood (hypercalcemia), which could accumulate in the kidneys, eventually leading to possible kidney failure (nephrocalcinosis)
5. Impaired vision, as well as other ocular abnormalities, and frequent intestinal infections

Treatment of blue diaper syndrome is predominantly symptomatic, revolving around dietary adjustments to minimize the side effects on the body. To reduce the likelihood of kidney damage, children's consumption of calcium should be restricted, as should their intake of protein and vitamin D. Antibiotics may be dispensed to control intestinal bacteria. Foods, such as turkey and milk, containing high levels of tryptophan should also be avoided. Genetic counseling also may be beneficial to families.

Special education placement may become an issue; however, the range of mental deficiency is unknown at this time. Prognosis is highly dependent on individual symptomology and management via diet and medical intervention. Future research is aimed at genetic mapping, which could lead to prevention and treatment options for this rare disorder.

REFERENCES

Chen, Y., Wu, L., & Xiong, Q. (1991). The ocular abnormalities of blue diaper syndrome. *Metabolic, Pediatric, and Systemic Ophthalmology, 14,* 51–53.

Drummond, K. N., Michael, A. F., Ulstrom, R. A., & Good, R. A. (1964). The blue diaper syndrome: Familial hypercalcemia with nephrocalcinosis and indicanuria. *American Journal of Medicine, 37,* 928–947.

McKusick, V. A. (1986). Online Mendelian inheritance in man, article 211000. Retrieved June 2001 from http://www.ncbi.nlm.nih.gov/Omim

Kimberly M. Estep
University of Houston–Clear Lake

BORDERLINE PERSONALITY DISORDER

Borderline personality disorder (BPD) is characterized by instability of interpersonal relationships and mood, poor self-concept, and impulsive behaviors. Individuals with BPD often display self-destructive behaviors, including undermining goals (e.g., dropping out of school just before graduation) and behaving in reckless ways (e.g., unsafe and promiscuous sex and driving at high rates of speed). Often, the terms *borderline traits* or *borderline pathology* are used to describe young people who show symptoms of BPD. Like other personality disorders, BPD is usually not diagnosed until late adolescence or early adulthood. It can be assumed, however, that traits exist long before the disorder is firmly diagnosed (Guzder, Paris, Zelkowitz, & Feldman, 1999).

Although the symptoms of BPD are considered to vary significantly among individuals, impulsivity and self-harm behaviors are fairly common (e.g., cutting, scratching, and burning). Adolescents with borderline traits have been found to engage in more self-injurious behaviors than other clinical groups, and they are at higher risk for suicide. Fortunately, suicidal behaviors, like functional problems, decrease with age. Adults with BPD, however, continue to report significant symptomatology and are considered twice as likely to hurt themselves than are adults with other personality disorders (Dubo, Zanarini, Lewis, & Williams, 1997). For this reason, chronic self-destructive tendencies are used to discriminate individuals with BPD from individuals with other personality disorders.

Individuals diagnosed with BPD not only manifest impulsive and self-destructive behaviors but also display identity problems. Because adolescents and young adults without personality disorders have problems with identity, diagnosis is difficult and often delayed. Recognizing what issues are "normal" (e.g., indecisiveness, mood instability, conflicts about sexual identity, career choice dilemmas, and existential crises; American Psychiatric Association [APA], 2000) and what populations are more likely to develop a borderline personality is critical. Females, for example, are more likely to have the disorder than are males. In fact, two thirds of cases are female. Individuals who have received mental health services are also more likely to develop the disorder (Hampton DeCoux, 1997). Although the estimated rate of BPD in the general population is 2%, it has been shown to be as high as 20% in inpatient and 10% in outpatient populations (APA, 2000)

Characteristics

1. Pattern of unstable mood and conflicted interpersonal relationships
2. Impulsive behavior including suicidal gestures and self-mutilating behavior
3. Propensity to engage in high-risk behaviors such as promiscuity
4. Identity disturbance marked by tenuous sense of self and feelings of emptiness
5. Intense dependency on others as well as vulnerability to perceived separation from external sources of support

6. Persistent feelings of emptiness, dysphoria, and intense, inappropriate anger

Given the propensity for self-harm, borderline behaviors need to be carefully assessed in children and adolescents. Although some of the symptoms look dramatically different from that of other children with behavior disorders (Dubo et al., 1997), even the most astute clinician may have difficulty differentially diagnosing the disorder. Researchers, however, have noted that children with borderline traits are more likely to show an elevated mixture of impulsive, affective, and "cognitive" symptoms on the Child Behavior Checklist, and show more internalizing behaviors such as social withdrawal (Guzder et al., 1999).

The etiology of BPD is heavily debated, and it remains unclear as to any specific cause of this personality disorder. A biological link has been suggested due to the higher incidence rate of BPD among family members. BPD is known to be five times more likely in first-degree relatives than in the general population (APA, 2000; Hampton DeCoux, 1997). There also appears to be psychosocial correlates with BDP. For example, children who have been neglected or abused sexually or physically or who have witnessed violence are considered to be at higher risk for BPD. There is also an increased likelihood for borderline features in children whose parents commit crimes and abuse substances. According to Guzder et al. (1999), these factors are particularly relevant if children are predisposed to other psychiatric conditions.

Adults diagnosed with BPD are typically treated with long-term psychotherapy (Hampton DeCoux, 1997). There are, however, other therapeutic options, including dialectical behavior therapy (DBT; Linehan, 1993), a cognitive-behavioral treatment that involves milieu training. Many researchers consider the prognosis for BPD to be poor; however, data have shown that 10 years after treatment up to 50% of individuals no longer meet diagnostic criteria, that is, from the *Diagnostic and Statistical Manual of Mental Disorders–Fourth Edition, Text Revision* (APA, 2000). Borderline personality disorders are still challenging to treat given the intensity of emotions, degree of dependency needs, propensity to act out impulsively (even in ways that inflict self-harm), and the tendency to elicit strong negative reactions from others, even therapists. Due to these and other behaviors, including splitting between one individual and another, therapists need to be experienced. When psychological services are provided in the schools, it is critical that home-school collaborations take place to ensure a unified treatment approach (i.e., shared goals and consistent strategies). Although school psychological services or counselor services are likely to be needed, special education is often unnecessary. When services through the Individuals with Disabilities Education Act are required (e.g., emotional problems are interfering with learning and social adjustment), services are typically provided under the category Emotional Disturbance. Research is needed to provide further information about early identification and treatment of BPD. Knowing more about the causative factors may also help to design effective treatments.

REFERENCES

American Psychiatric Association. (2000). *Diagnostic and statistical manual of mental disorders* (4th ed., Text Revision). Washington, DC: Author.

Dubo, E., Zanarini, M., Lewis, R., & Williams, A. (1997). Childhood antecedents of self-destructiveness in borderline personality disorder. *Canadian Journal of Psychiatry, 42,* 63–69.

Guzder, J., Paris, J., Zelkowitz, P., & Feldman, R. (1999). Psychological risk factors for borderline pathology in school-age children. *Journal of the American Academy of Child and Adolescent Psychiatry, 38,* 206–212.

Hampton DeCoux, M. (1997). Dialectical behavior therapy in the treatment of persons with borderline personality disorder. *Archives of Psychiatric Nursing, 11*(2), 96–101.

Linehan, M. M. (1993). *Cognitive-behavioral treatment of personality disorder.* New York: Guilford Press.

Rex Gonzales
Elaine Clark
University of Utah

BORJESON-FORSSMAN-LEHMANN SYNDROME

Borjeson-Forssman-Lehmann syndrome (BFLS) is an X-linked, possibly incompletely recessive, genetic disorder characterized by numerous dysmorphic anomalies, obesity, hypogonadism, epilepsy, and mental retardation. The full expression in males results in more severe symptoms, whereas penetrance in carrier females appears to be associated with variable X-chromosome inactivation (Kubota, Oga, Ohashi, Iwamoto, & Fukushima, 1999). In heterozygous women, the phenotypic effects vary widely between apparent normality to mild or moderately evident BFLS manifestations (Ardinger, Hanson, & Zellweger, 1984).

Characteristics

1. *Facial anomalies:* enlarged but normally formed ears, hyperplastic supraorbitral ridges, deep-set eyes, narrow palpegral fissures, ptosis, swollen subcutaneous facial tissue, microcephaly
2. *Extremities:* soft fleshy hands with tapering fingers; short, widely spaced, flexed toes

3. *Neurological problems:* seizures or epilepsy, mild to severe mental retardation (more severe in males), visual abnormalities and deficits
4. *Metabolic disorders:* hypometabolism, generalized obesity, hypotonia
5. *Endocrine abnormalities:* delayed bone age, short neck, hyperkyphosis; delayed sexual development, hypogonadism, micropenis, cryptorchidism, postpubertal gynecomastia in males

Incidence is extremely rare, but BFLS is inherited with equal frequency in males and females. Three large families have been identified with the disorder, two from the United States and of European descent and one in Australia and originally from the United Kingdom. Although no more than a half dozen families have been reported in the literature, there are also several smaller families identified with less certainty. Of these, three are from the United Kingdom, two from Australia, two located in the United States, one in Mexico, and two in Belgium. There has also been one unusual female case from Japan with an extremely skewed X-inactivation pattern. Genetic mapping has pointed to region Xq26q27, but the gene itself remains unidentified (Jones, 1997).

Hypotonia, obesity, and micropenis are often noted in infancy, along with the abnormalities of the face and extremities. The unusual facial appearance typically includes a coarse, fleshy face; enlarged but not deformed ears; and deep-set eyes with prominent supraorbital ridges and narrow palpebral fissures. Distal extremities are typically shortened, with tapering fingers and widely spaced, flexed toes. Other features include generalized obesity, epilepsy, mental retardation, stunted growth, and delayed sexual development. There may also be ophthalmologic abnormalities (e.g., nystagmus, cataract, poor vision), skeletal deformities (e.g., irregular end-plates to vertebrae, hyperkyphosis, short neck, thickened calvarium), and electroencephalogram disturbances. There are developmental delays including late walking. The degree of mental retardation varies from mild to severe. Common differential diagnoses include Prader-Willi, Noonan, Coffin-Lowry, and Bardet-Biedl syndromes. Occasional association with dilated cardiomyopathy suggests the importance of cardiovascular study in this syndrome (Kaplinsky et al., 2001).

Special education services are available for mental retardation, and the degree of intellectual impairment ranges from mild to severe. Intellectual deficits are more pronounced in males because of full expression. Depending on the degree of penetrance, female carriers may exhibit normal or borderline IQ or more mild to moderate retardation. Qualification for special education services may also be available for associated health problems (e.g., epilepsy, hypotonia) as well as for the behavioral problems and speech-language delays typically seen with mental retardation. Occupational therapy services may be useful depending on the degree of hypotonia, abnormalities of the distal extremities, hyperkyphosis, or other skeletal problems.

There is no cure for this genetic disorder. Life span is predicted to be normal. Treatment focuses on the symptoms, especially seizure control and management of metabolic and endocrine dysfunction, as well as on providing special education and other services. In some cases, testosterone supplementation may enhance intellectual performance and induce loss of weight when testosterone levels are low. Depending on the degree of impairment, a sheltered environment may be needed. Genetic counseling is recommended for patients and families.

REFERENCES

Ardinger, H., Hanson, J., & Zellweger, H. (1984). Borjeson-Forssman-Lehmann syndrome: Further delineation in five cases. *American Journal of Medical Genetics, 19*(4), 653–664.

Jones, K. (Ed.). (1997). *Smith's recognizable patterns of human malformation* (5th ed.). Philadelphia: W. B. Saunders.

Kaplinsky, E., Perandones, C., Galiana, M., Fidelell, H., Favaloror, R., Carlos, V., & Perrone, S. (2001). Borjeson-Forssman-Lehmann syndrome and dilated cardiomyopathy: A previously unreported association. *Canadian Journal of Cardiology, 17*(1), 80–83.

Kubota, T., Oga, S., Ohashi, H., Iwamoto, Y., & Fukushima, Y. (1999). Borjeson-Forssman-Lehmann syndrome in a woman with skewed X-chromosome inactivation. *American Journal of Medical Genetics, 87*(3), 258–261.

Vicky Y. Spradling
Austin State Hospital

BRAIN DISORDERS, DEGENERATIVE MOTOR DISEASES

Degenerative motor diseases refers to a group of central nervous system (CNS) disorders that have an insidious onset and lead to progressive deterioration in motor functioning. These diseases are often transmitted genetically; however, infectious agents have been linked to some conditions (e.g., spongiform encephalopathatic virus causing Cruetzfelt-Jakob disease). Not all movement disorders are progressive; in fact, Sydenham's chorea, a condition associated with streptococcal infection and rheumatic fever, generally has a good outcome. But unlike Cruetzfelt's, Sydenham's is not a degenerative motor disease (DMD). Diseases in the class of DMD tend to be fatal, but only after years of slow decline. Friedreich ataxia is an example of a childhood DMD in which deterioration comes much earlier than death. In fact, death may not occur until the fifth decade of life, but confinement to a wheelchair comes a decade or two earlier (Fenichel, 1993). Death is often caused by medical problems associated with deteriorated physical functioning (e.g., years of immobility).

In many cases, emotional and cognitive changes accompany the deterioration in motor functioning. Motor symptoms, however, may be the only manifestation of the disease for years before cognitive deterioration is observed. The eventual decline in multiple functions is related in part to disease pathology. For example, DMDs often are associated with extrapyramidal system dysfunction, that is, abnormalities of the basal ganglia and cerebellum. Both are considered multifunction, parallel processing systems of the brain that are connected to areas that regulate mood and thought processes (e.g., the prefrontal cortex and limbic system) (Bradshaw, 2001). The basal ganglia, however, is known more for its inhibitory functions, and the cerebellum for its excitatory capabilities, regardless of the specific activity (e.g., motor performance, emotion, and learning; Drepper, Timman, Kolb, & Diener, 1999).

A number of DMDs occur during childhood and have broad impacts on functioning. Telzrow (2000) reviewed several of these, including some that are caused by diseases of the white and gray matter (e.g., Schilder's, which is a demyelinating disease, and Alper's, which is a gray matter disease) and lipid storage (e.g., Tay-Sachs). Two diseases are described here: juvenile Huntington's chorea (JHC) and Friedreich ataxia (FA). The reasons for choosing these is that both involve the extrapyramidal system and that both are genetically transmitted: JHC through an autosomal dominant gene and FA through an autosomal recessive gene. JHC, however, affects the basal ganglia, and FA affects the cerebellum. Movement problems in JHC are therefore characterized by rigidity and choreiform movements, whereas in FA the problem relates more with poor coordination and clumsiness. The two diseases share certain features (e.g., gait problems and speech dysfluencies), but the etiology for this differs according to the pathophysiological process. For example, weakness often underlies movement problems associated with FA, whereas rigidity and rapid jerking interfere with mobility in cases of JHC. Perhaps more consistent are the emotional and cognitive sequelae associated with these two degenerative diseases. Both, however, are incurable, and both eventually lead to death. Like other DMDs, the life span (and quality of life) is determined in part by the age at which the disease began; the earlier the onset, the more severe are the symptoms and the shorter is the life. Children with JHC often die within the decade of onset, whereas children with FA spend years confined to a wheelchair before their death, which is often in the 40s or 50s.

Diagnosis of DMD is not easy, especially if it is based only on clinical symptoms. Depending on the age of the child, the symptom picture may vary. For example, individuals with JHC tend to have more rigidity than chorea, which is the classic sign of adult-onset Huntington's. Therefore, family history is critical to distinguish these diseases. Neuroimaging such as brain magnetic resonance imaging (MRI) can be helpful as well, especially in ruling out competing diagnoses (e.g., Wilson's disease versus Parkinson's).

Children and adolescents with DMD often require special education services, particularly under the category Other Health Impairment. But in cases where severe intellectual deterioration occurs during school-age years, services for children with Intellectual Disabilities may be more appropriate. Regardless of category, Individuals with Disabilities Education Act, Section 504 services, and related services are likely to be needed for adequate learning and socialization of a student with DMD. Related services may include reading support, speech and language therapy, and occupational and physical therapy. Many of these children, as well as their families, are also likely to benefit from psychological treatment provided by the school psychologist given the degenerative nature of the condition and the impact on family functioning. The school psychologist can also help by making referrals to outside professionals to ensure that sufficient assistance is provided, including evaluations by physiatrists and neurologists familiar with DMD and the drugs that relieve certain symptoms (e.g., valproic acid, haloperidol, and baclofen, which impact the dopamineric and cholinergic systems). Psychologists can also put families in contact with community agencies that will assist them in long-term transition planning.

Despite the significant advances that have been made in genetics research and diagnostic methods (e.g., MRI), treatments have not kept pace. There is an urgent need for research that addresses the degree of debilitation caused by DMD and ways to prevent this devastating condition.

Characteristics

1. There is progressive deterioration in motor function with associated cognitive and emotional problems caused by abnormalities of the central nervous system.
2. Etiology varies, but genetic transmission is common.
3. The basal ganglia and cerebellum are often impacted by these diseases and explain the symptom manifestation (e.g., ataxia if cerebellar and chorea if basal ganglia).
4. Drug therapy provides symptom relief (i.e., motor and psychiatric).
5. Severity and life span expectancy are associated with underlying cause and age at the time of onset (i.e., earlier onset equals worse prognosis).
6. As yet there is no cure for these diseases, and death is often inevitable.

REFERENCES

Bradshaw, J. L. (2001). *Developmental disorders of the frontostriatal system.* Philadelphia: Taylor & Francis Group.

Drepper, J., Timman, D., Kolb, F., & Diener, H. (1999). Non-motor associative learning in patients with isolated degenerative cerebellar disease. *Brain, 122*(1), 87–97.

Fenichel, G. M. (1993). *Clinical pediatric neurology.* Philadelphia: W. B. Saunders.

Telzrow, C. F. (2000). Brain disorders: Degenerative motor dysfunction. In C. Reynolds & E. Fletcher-Janzen (Eds.), *Encyclopedia of special education* (2nd ed., pp. 288–289). New York: Wiley.

Elaine Clark
University of Utah

BRAIN FAG

Brain fag, or *brain fog,* is a culture-bound psychiatric syndrome found in West Africa (American Psychiatric Association, 1994). This syndrome is a condition experienced by high school or university students in response to challenges of schooling (Weber, 2000). Brain fag is also termed *brain fatigue* in certain regions of Africa and is perceived as an idiom of distress in many cultures (Weber, 2000).

Behavioral manifestations of this disorder are closely related to, and in certain cases resemble, anxiety, depressive, and somatoform disorders. In fact, some authors and clinicians classify brain fag as "somatized anxiety with hysterical features" (Cherian, Cherian, & Peltzer, 1998, p. 1187).

This disorder primarily impacts students, and there appears to be a correlation between the frequency of brain fag and the degree of westernization within the culture area of the afflicted. According to Cherian et al. (1998), this correlation may support the hypothesis that children tend to develop distress disorders, such as brain fag, due to shifting from a collective and cooperative culture environment present in many African culture groups to the highly individualistic and competitive requirements of Western education systems.

There have been no reported epidemiological studies conducted on brain fag. However, Cherian et al. (1998, p. 1187), reports that "Brain Fag is a stereotyped psychiatric syndrome that affects 20 to 40% of secondary school and university students in diverse cultures across Africa south of the Sahara." The range tends to fall within 17 to 24 years. There appear to be four major clusters of symptoms of brain fag: unpleasant head symptoms, visual difficulties, fatigue, and sleepiness. This syndrome seems to have a direct relation to stress levels such that the student's life stress could give "rise to features of distress which are expressed as physiological disturbance and subsequent symptom of Brain Fag" (Cherian et al., 1998, p. 1192).

Characteristics

1. Difficulties in concentrating
2. Difficulties in remembering
3. Head and neck pain
4. Pressure of tightness
5. Blurring of vision
6. Heat or burning sensations
7. Complaints of "tired brain"

Incidents of brain fag could possibly be identified in the United States among immigrant African populations. For proper diagnosis of incidents of brain fag, medical and psychiatric professionals utilize the Cultural Orientation Scale (Bierbrauer, Meyer, & Wolfrandt, 1994), the General Self-Efficiency Scale (Schwarzer, 1993), and a Self-Reporting Questionnaire (World Health Organization, 1994) to determine socioeconomic status, cultural orientation, stress events, self-efficiency, perceived stress, and "neurotic" disorders (Cherian et al., 1998). Mental health professionals rather than cultural or traditional health care providers typically administer treatment for this disorder. Typically, treatment coincides with that of anxiety disorders.

It is unlikely that special education services would be needed or available for this syndrome. There is little information available on the treatment outcomes with brain fag; therefore, prevention efforts have not been noted.

REFERENCES

American Psychiatric Association. (1994). *Diagnostic and statistical manual of mental disorders* (4th ed.). Washington, DC: Author.

Bierbrauer, G., Meyer, H., & Wolfrandt, U. (1994). Measurement of normative and evaluative aspects in individualistic and collective orientations: The Cultural Orientation Scale (COS). In U. Kim, H. C. Triandis, C. Kagitcibasi, S. C. Choi, & G. Yoon (Eds.), *Individualism and collectivism: Theory, method, and applications* (pp. 189–199). London: Sage.

Cherian, L., Cherian, V. I., & Peltzer, K. (1998). Brian fag symptoms in rural South African secondary school pupils. *Psychological Reports, 83,* 1187–1196.

Schwarzer, R. (1993). *Measurement of perceived self-efficacy: Psychometric scales for cross-cultural research.* Berlin, Germany: Freie Universitaet Berlin.

Weber, C. (2000). Glossary of culture-bound syndromes. Retrieved from http://weber.ucsd.edu/~thall/cbl_glos.html

World Health Organization. (1994). *A user's guide to the Self-Reporting Questionnaire (SRQ).* Geneva, Switzerland: Author.

Kiely Ann Fletcher
Ohio State University

BRAIN TUMOR

A brain tumor is a new growth of tissue in the brain in which cell multiplication is uncontrolled and progressive. It grows independent of surrounding structures and has no physiological use. Brain tumors in children are typically primary tumors; that is, the tumor originates at the site rather than having migrated from another organ (e.g., metastases from the lung such as seen in adults with brain tumors). Tumors may be classified as benign or malignant, and benign tumors have a better prognosis than do malignant tumors (i.e., they are unlikely to reoccur or to be progressive and fatal). Malignant tumors are given a grade of one to four, with one being the least malignant. Grades 1 and 2 are often called low-grade tumors, whereas Grades 3 and 4 are high-grade tumors. Brain tumors have serious consequences as they grow and crowd out—or deplete oxygen and nutrient supply for—normal cell growth. Brain tumors also put pressure on surrounding tissue that cuts off blood supply and flow of cerebrospinal fluid (CSF). Increased pressure and decreased blood supply often result in the death of surrounding tissue and in greater space for tumor growth.

Increased intracranial pressure (ICP) is common for most brain tumors. Common signs of ICP include headache, vomiting, and papilledema. Headaches are usually worse in the morning and tend to get better later in the day, as well as with physical activity and exertion. Some individuals complain of being awakened by headaches and report that vomiting relieves headache pain. Vomiting may occur with or without nausea. Papilledema, a result of swelling and increased blood flow to the vessels of the eye, also occurs frequently. Other common characteristics that may be seen, but that are more specific to the tumor site, include seizures, hemiparesis (i.e., weakness or partial paralysis on one side of the body), vision change (e.g., blurred, doubled, and reduced acuity), endocrine problems (e.g., growth problems, diabetes insipitus, and early onset of puberty), slurred speech, dysphasia (i.e., difficulty swallowing), loss of appetite and weight, and motor problems (e.g., ataxic gait, poor balance, and poor coordination). With younger children and infants, symptoms tend to be vague (e.g., irritability, crying, and failure to thrive).

Brain tumors are a common form of childhood cancer and are second only to leukemia as a cause. Brain tumors, however, have surpassed leukemia in terms of deaths. Approximately 2.5 to 4 cases are diagnosed per every 100,000 children in the United States, or 2,000 new cases each year (Packer, 1999). This represents an increase of 35% over the past 20 years, a rate thought to reflect improvements in identification procedures and increased environmental risk factors causing new cases.

The exact cause of a particular brain tumor is often unknown. Hereditary and environmental factors, however, are thought to play a major role. Environmental risk factors include exposure to radiation, chemicals, and viruses. There is also increased risk associated with certain central nervous system (CNS) disorders, including neurofibromatosis, tuberous sclerosis, and Sturge-Weber syndrome.

Characteristics

1. Intracranial pressure occurs in most types of brain tumors, with symptoms including papilledema, headache, and vomiting.
2. Depending on tumor location, seizures, hemiparesis, vision changes, endocrine problems, slurred speech, dysphagia, loss of appetite/weight, and ataxia occur.
3. Infants or young children are more likely to present with vague symptoms of irritability, crying, and failure to thrive.
4. Approximately 2,000 new pediatric cases are diagnosed in the United States each year.

Treatment options typically include surgery, radiation, and chemotherapy. Surgery is the treatment of choice; depending on tumor location, however, this may not be an option. Approximately 20% of brain tumors are successfully resected with surgery and do not require further treatment such as radiation and chemotherapy (Valentino, Conway, Shiminski-Maher, & Siffert, 1997). Cancer cells tend to be responsive to radiation therapy; however, this treatment has been shown to cause serious cognitive deficits in young children. Currently, the standard practice is to use chemotherapy first and delay or avoid radiation therapy until the child gets older and brain development is less likely to be interrupted. If possible, no radiation should be used in children under 5 years of age. Medications used to treat brain tumors (e.g., chemotherapy) can also have negative long-term sequelae including kidney and liver toxicity, cataracts and glaucoma, ulcers, cardiac problems, growth retardation, and reproductive dysfunction. Neuropsychological problems are also common but to a lesser degree than when radiation is used. Common short-term side effects from chemotherapy include nausea, vomiting, diarrhea, abdominal pain, fever, chills, hair loss, jaw pain, and fluid retention. In addition, chemotherapy (and radiation) can increase the risk of developing future cancers.

Potentially life-threatening conditions such as a brain tumor cause significant stress to the family. Not only is the child's life changed, but so is the family's. Lengthy hospitalizations, the experience of pain and illness, and prolonged school absences can seriously impact the child's quality of life. Changes in physical appearance from hair loss, weight loss or gain, and surgical scars are just one of many adjustments that the child may have to make. Having to face peers, catch up on school work, and deal with cognitive changes (e.g., attentional difficulties and diminished memory) may be more than the affected child can tolerate.

Children who have, or have had, a brain tumor often qualify for special education and related services under the category of Other Health Impairment. Services that are most often needed are intended to address various cognitive changes, attentional and memory difficulties, and language impairments.

Emotional concerns are also likely to arise and require counseling. Regular contact with the parents is critical to ensure that the child's progress is monitored and that adequate support is given. In addition, frequent parent contact can help to assess what their needs are, as well as those of the siblings. There are a number of community support services for children with brain tumors. In addition to brain tumor associations, there are special camp programs (e.g., Candlelighters). Providing opportunities for children and their families to interact with others who are faced with similar challenges is important. This provides not only opportunities for support but also resources for further (and future) assistance. Close monitoring and frequent assessment of the child is needed because many of the common difficulties of attention, cognitive changes, memory, language difficulties, and emotional concerns can vary greatly over time or show up years after treatment.

The survival rate for brain tumors at 5 years is 60%. This rate reflects a significant increase from the 1960s, when the rate was only 35% (Stewart & Cohen, 1998). Several factors have been associated with a worse outcome, including tumor location (e.g., brain stem tumors and tumors that are difficult to access), malignant tumors, the degree to which the tumor has infiltrated surrounding tissue, and the younger age of the child (e.g., under 2 years). Further research is needed to identify tumors early and find improved treatments to decrease the mortality and morbidity rates.

REFERENCES

Packer, R. J. (1999). Brain tumors in children. *Archives in Neurology, 56,* 421–425.

Stewart, E. S., & Cohen, D. G., (1998). Central nervous system tumors in children. *Seminars in Oncology Nursing, 14*(1), 34–42.

Valentino, T. L., Conway, J. R., Shiminski-Maher, T., & Siffert, J. (1997). Pediatric brain tumors. *Pediatric Annals, 26,* 579–586.

Laura Richards
Elaine Clark
University of Utah

See also Glioblastoma

BRITTLE BONE DISEASE (OSTEOGENESIS IMPERFECTA)

Osteogenesis imperfecta (OI), commonly known as brittle bone disease, is a genetic disorder in which the production of collagen is inadequate or defective collagen is produced, leading to a susceptibility of bone fractures. An individual with OI may suffer as little as a few to several hundreds of bone fractures over a lifetime. The wide variation in the severity of OI has been described and categorized as four types of OI. The most mild and common form of OI is Type I (Moriwake & Seino, 1997).

The prevalence of OI in the United States remains unknown. Reports estimate that 1 in every 20,000 to 50,000 children born each year is affected (Osteogenesis Imperfecta Foundation [OIF], 2001). In general, frequent bone fractures in infancy and childhood, some even recognized before birth, are the cardinal symptoms of this disorder. The rate of fractures decreases during puberty (Moriwake & Seino, 1997). Children with OI have bone deformities in their extremities and retarded growth, and they may experience chronic bone pain, although there can be wide variation in clinical features of OI across individuals. This holds true for individuals with OI within the same family as well. Thus, a combination of genes and environment influences the expression of the disorder.

Usually, clinical features of the different types of OI are used for diagnosis. In addition, DNA and collagen tests may be performed; however, several weeks are required to obtain the results, and the results are not always conclusive. OI patients have bones with less or poorer quality Type I collagen, the connective fibers of the bones, than of normal quality, either of which lead to bones that break easily (Moriwake & Seino, 1997). Children with OI Types I and IV often live normal life spans, and their deaths are due to unrelated causes. However, children with the most severe type of OI, Type III, are at higher risk for dying as a result of OI. Children with OI may be confined to a wheelchair and sometimes do not survive childhood. The severity of the OI contributes significantly to risk of death. Thus, minor injuries may have fatal consequences for a child with OI Type III (McAllion & Paterson, 1996).

Characteristics

1. Fragile bones leading to frequent fractures
2. Growth retardation and deformities of the arms and legs
3. Chronic bone pain

No cure for OI exists. Increasing bone mass and preventing future fractures are goals of current treatments. Aggressive physical therapy and rehabilitation programs result in increased body control and replacement of the routine use of a wheelchair with physical supports, such as a brace, to enable children to walk more independently (Binder et al., 1993). Stimulating bone growth using growth hormones can be used during childhood. Rodding of the humeral bone (lower extremities) may also be used to prevent future bone deformities and fractures (Moriwake & Seino, 1997).

It is clear that a child with OI has a physical disability, but most children with OI do not have any cognitive disabilities. It is important that educational staff be aware of the child's increased susceptibility to injury. Thus, classroom modifications, physical assistance, adaptive physical education, and other arrangements to prevent injury should be taken into consideration (OIF, 2001). It is thought that each type of OI is due to different gene mutations, making gene therapy a potential avenue for future research (Moriwake & Seino, 1997).

REFERENCES

Binder, H., Conway, A., Hason, S., Gerber, L. H., Marini, J., Berry, R., & Weintrob, J. (1993). Comprehensive rehabilitation of the child with osteogenesis imperfecta. *American Journal of Medical Genetics, 45,* 265–269.

McAllion, S. J., & Paterson, C. R. (1996). Causes of death in osteogenesis imperfecta. *Journal of Clinical Pathology, 49*(8), 627–630.

Moriwake, T., & Seino, Y. (1997). Recent progress in diagnosis and treatment of osteogenesis imperfecta. *Acta Paediatrica Japonica, 39,* 521–527.

Osteogenesis Imperfecta Foundation. (2001). OIF homepage. Retrieved from http://www.oif.org

Jennifer M. Gillis
University of California, Irvine

BRUCELLOSIS

Brucellosis is an infectious disease that is transmitted from animals to humans through infected meat or animal products. The disease is rare in the United States, although it is more prevalent in Midwestern states and rural areas. Approximately 200 cases are found in the United States each year (Clayman, 1989). It is more frequently found in other countries where precautions in meat handling and pasteurization are not common practice, and it is sometimes carried to the United States by visitors or immigrants. Brucellosis is also known as Cyprus fever, Gibraltar fever, Malta fever, Mediterranean fever, rock fever, or undulant fever (Berkow, Beers, Bogin, & Fletcher, 1997).

Brucellosis is commonly caused by six types of gram negative or rods of the *Brucella* genus of bacteria. Brucella abortus is carried by cattle, brucella suis by hogs, brucella melitensis by goats, brucella canis by dogs, brucella ovis by sheep and hares, and brucella neotomae by desert wood rats (Behrman, 1992). The disease is usually spread by contact with the excretions and secretions of infected animals (Anderson, Anderson, & Glanze, 1998). It may also be contracted by drinking infected, unpasteurized milk, eating cheese or other dairy products made from infected milk, or handling infected meat. It can also be transmitted by air (Clayman, 1989). Brucellosis is more commonly found in individuals who handle live animals or meat, such as veterinarians, farmers, and meat packers. It is rarely transmitted from person to person.

The symptoms of brucellosis can initially be subtle and mistaken for other diseases. The onset may also be acute. The patient can exhibit flu-like symptoms, with headache, fatigue, muscle and joint pain, insomnia, lack of appetite, sweating, irritability, and emotional instability. Intermittent fever may occur, which is usually higher at night and lower in the morning. Later, symptoms may include an enlarged spleen, liver, and lymph nodes. More severe complications include inflammation and infections of the heart, brain, nerves, testes, gallbladder, liver, and bones (Berkow et al., 1997).

Symptoms may become chronic, occurring in intervals followed by periods in which the patient may appear to be symptom-free, but then the symptoms will recur. Treatment is important to prevent complications and other infections such as encephalitis, pneumonia, and meningitis. Although the disease is rarely fatal, brucellosis can lead to chronic bad health, and the symptoms may persist.

Characteristics

1. Flu-like symptoms are experienced initially, with headache, fatigue, muscle and joint pain, insomnia, lack of appetite, sweating, irritability, and emotional instability.
2. Intermittent fever may occur, being higher at night and lower in the morning.
3. Later symptoms may include an enlarged spleen, liver, and lymph nodes.
4. More severe complications include inflammation and infections of the heart, brain, nerves, testes, gallbladder, liver, and bones.
5. Other symptoms may be severe constipation, profuse sweating, decreased body temperature, heart rate variability, and eye irregularities.

Incubation of brucellosis may be from a few days to several weeks, but it is usually two weeks after exposure. Often, patients do not seek treatment for some time after the disease has been contracted. The physician can detect brucellosis by checking the blood for high levels of antibodies to the bacteria. Brucellosis can also be detected in spinal fluid, urine, or bone marrow. Tissues may be sent for culture to confirm the diagnosis; these cultures need be incubated for 21 days. Negative readings are common in chronic cases.

With treatment, patients usually recover from brucellosis in 2 to 3 weeks. Treatment with a single antibiotic for patients with the disorder may result in recurrence, so a combination of antibiotics is recommended. Tetracycline plus streptomycin with bed rest has been effective. Other combinations, such as doxycycline plus rifampin or streptomycin or both and trimethoprim-sulfamethoxazole plus rifampin or streptomycin (or both) have been found to be effective in doses over 21 days. Longer courses of treatment for several months may be needed in more severe or chronic cases (Tierney, McPhee, & Papadakis, 2001). Pain reliever may be needed to make the patient more comfortable.

Although brucellosis is treatable, children with chronic symptoms may need accommodations in school. Because the symptoms are very similar to many common diseases, it may not be quickly diagnosed, and symptoms may persist over a long period of time. This may result in frequent absence from school. Students may fall behind in their work; tutoring or some kind of support may be necessary.

Research is currently being conducted to create vaccines to prevent human brucellosis (Cosivi & Corel, 1998). Prevention can be accomplished through the vaccination of young animals and the pasteurization of milk and milk products. Gloves and glasses should be worn when handling animals or animal products.

Brucellosis can be contracted through a break in the skin, so cuts in the skin should be covered. The practice of good hygiene can help to prevent spread of the bacteria that cause the disease.

REFERENCES

Anderson, K. N., Anderson, L. E. & Glanze, W. D. (Eds.). (1998). *Mosby's medical dictionary* (5th ed.). St. Louis, MO: Mosby.

Behrman, R. (Ed.). (1992). *Nelson's textbook of pediatrics* (14th ed.). Philadelphia: W. B. Saunders.

Berkow, R., Beers, M. H., Bogin, R. M., & Fletcher, A. J. (Eds.). (1997). *The Merck manual of medical information.* Whitehouse Station, NJ: Merck Research Laboratories.

Clayman, C. B. (Ed.). (1989). *The American Medical Association encyclopedia of medicine.* New York: Random House.

Cosivi, O., & Corel, M. J. (1998). WHO consultation on the development of new/improved brucellosis vaccines. *Biologicals, 26,* 361–363.

Tierney, L. M., Jr., McPhee, S. J., & Papadakis, M. A. (Eds). (2001). *Current medical diagnosis and treatment* (40th ed). New York: Lange Medical Books, McGraw-Hill.

Michele Wilson Kamens
Rider University

BRUXISM

Bruxism is the medical term for unintentional, forcible grinding and clenching of the jaw and teeth (ViaHealth, 2001). Etiology is not known, but certain anatomical and psychological factors may lead to the onset of bruxism (KidsHealth, 2001). Bruxism usually occurs at night during sleep and is often associated with stress (Teethgrinding, 2000). It also commonly occurs in children with cerebral palsy.

Approximately half of the adults in the United States grind their teeth at night, and 20% of these individuals cause damage to their teeth. Although bruxism usually develops in adults over 25, it may also occur in children (Teethgrinding, 2000). Approximately 15–30% of children grind or clench their teeth, and the highest incidence is in children under 5 years of age. Gender differences are not apparent in children (e.g., Laberge, Tremblay, Vitaro, & Montplaisir, 2000). Children usually grind because of improper alignment of top and bottom teeth or in response to pain or stress (KidsHealth, 2001). Children with bruxism show higher levels of anxiety than do unaffected controls (Laberge et al., 2000).

Characteristics

1. The child reports mild headaches or earaches in the morning after waking up.
2. At night a grinding sound is heard while the child is sleeping.
3. In more extreme cases, the child may report temperature sensitivity along with severe pain in the jaw.
4. A popping or clicking sound in the jaw is heard.
5. The tips of the child's teeth appear flat and the tooth enamel appears worn down.
6. The child appears to have damage to the inside of the cheek.

Bruxism owing to the child's growth and development apparently cannot be avoided but is frequently outgrown (KidsHealth, 2001). Regular dental visits, along with parental observations to determine if teeth are worn down, enamel is chipped, and other damage due to grinding has occurred, may be enough to control the problem. In more serious cases, a night guard or splint may be prescribed to protect the child's teeth from damage and to absorb the force of the biting. If the bruxism is caused by stress, relaxation techniques may prove helpful along with talking to the child about his or her anxiety. In the rare cases when relaxation techniques do not alleviate the child's stress, a psychological assessment may be needed to determine a course of treatment (KidsHealth, 2001). Other behavioral techniques may help treat some cases of bruxism. Behavior modification assists in teaching patients how to rest their tongue, teeth, and lips properly, alleviating discomfort in the jaw. Biofeedback involves the use of an electronic instrument that measures the amount of muscle activity that is occurring in the mouth and jaw. The instrument indicates when increased muscle activity is taking place. A biofeedback program for those who clench at night is not yet available (ViaHealth, 2001).

Childhood bruxism is usually outgrown by adolescence. Children usually stop grinding when they lose their baby teeth because permanent teeth are much more sensitive to pain (KidsHealth, 2001).

REFERENCES

KidsHealth. (2001, June). Bringing bruxism to a grinding halt. Retrieved from http://kidshealth.org/parent/general/teeth/bruxism.html

Laberge, L., Tremblay, R. E., Vitaro, F., & Montplaisir, J. (2000). Development of parasomnias from childhood to early adolescence. *Pediatrics, 106,* 67–73.

Teethgrinding. (2000). Understanding bruxism. Retrieved from http://www.teethgrinding.org/html/understanding_bruxism.html

ViaHealth. (2001, May 2). Bruxism. Retrieved from http://www.viahealth.org/disease/oralcare/bruxism.htm

Lucy Lewis
Robert T. Brown
University of North Carolina at Wilmington

BULIMIA NERVOSA

The word *bulimia* translates to "oxen appetite" or gorging. There are two types of bulimia nervosa. One involves a recurrent pattern of binge eating followed by purging, either by vomiting or using diuretics or laxatives, and the nonpurging type involves engagement in a strenuous exercise routine or other inappropriate compensatory behaviors to avoid weight gain (Cassell, 1994; Costin, 1999). The hallmark of bulimia nervosa is eating a larger amount of food than most people would eat under similar circumstances and experiencing the eating as out of control (Barlow & Durand, 1999).

Although a small percentage of those diagnosed with bulimia are male, the disorder is most commonly diagnosed in females. Most bulimics are within 10 to 15 pounds of their normal weight range and have struggled with weight fluctuation. Bulimia usually develops during late adolescent or early adult years (Costin, 1999). Some research studies have reported bulimia to be at epidemic proportions in the United States, with estimates of 18% of women between the ages of 17 and 23 suffering from bulimia in one form or another (Cassell, 1994). However, other studies have found that even though self-reported overeating and purging may be high in numbers among college-age females in the United States, actual numbers of persons clinically diagnosed with bulimia are much lower (Cassell, 1994).

Characteristics

1. Recurrent episodes of binge eating, each episode lasting approximately 1 to 1 1/2 hours, with consumption of approximately 3,500 calories per episode
2. Feeling of lack of control over eating behavior during binges
3. Regular desire to self-induce vomiting, use laxatives or diuretics, diet or fast, or vigorously exercise to prevent weight gain
4. A minimum average of two binge eating episodes per week for at least the last 3 months
5. Overly concerned with body shape and/or weight

Research suggests that the most effective treatment involves a combination of therapy and counseling, group therapy, and, more recently, use of antidepressant medication. Research also suggests that the chances for recovery increase the earlier bulimia is detected. Antidepressants are effective because those diagnosed with bulimia typically show signs of depression such as feelings of low self-esteem, lack of emotional fulfillment, and feelings of inadequacy.

Under the Individuals with Disabilities Education Act (1997), a student with bulimia could technically qualify for special education services under the category of Other Health Impairment. However, due to the nature of the disorder (i.e., the need for acceptance and approval and the constant striving for perfection, and the fact that most individuals with bulimia are 10 to 15 pounds within their normal weight range), it is likely that the school personnel would not even be aware that a student is afflicted with the disorder. If the school psychologist is aware of a student with bulimia, then he or she should obtain permission to provide direct counseling services to the student on an as-needed basis or refer the student and family for counseling specific to eating disorders.

REFERENCES

Barlow, D., & Durand, V. M. (1999). *Abnormal psychology.* Pacific Grove, CA: Brooks/Cole.

Cassell, D. (1994). *Encyclopedia of obesity and eating disorders.* New York: Facts on File.

Costin, C. (1999). *The eating disorder sourcebook: A comprehensive guide to the causes, treatments, and prevention of eating disorders.* Los Angeles: Lowell House.

Christine D. Cde Baca
University of Northern Colorado

BULLOUS PEMPHIGOID

Bullous pemphigoid is a skin disease in which the skin blisters severely. These blistered spots are most likely found in folds of skin such as the groin and armpit areas. Bullous pemphigoid is a rare disorder that is most often found in elderly persons, with the average age at onset being 65 to 75. However, it has recently been diagnosed in children along with other immunobullous diseases (Powell, Kirtschig, Allen, Dean, & Wojnarowska, 2001). Bullous pemphigoid is not a contagious condition.

Bullous pemphigoid is actually a disease of the immune system, in which the immune system begins to attack skin cells as if they were foreign cells. The reason for this immune response is not known, but it causes the layers of the skin to separate and thus form blisters.

Incidences of bullous pemphigoid begin as simple rashes on the skin but progress to itchy, inflamed areas. The skin condition is also often associated with fatigue and anxiety. Psychologically, the disease causes the patient to become lethargic and depressed. This in turn aggravates the skin condition more. A further aggravated condition may resemble other common skin diseases and thus is often misdiagnosed.

Following the initial stages, blisters develop. These blisters are fluid filled and inflamed, causing the skin to feel itchy and painfully tender. These blisters have been found to be concentrated in folds of skin where movement occurs, as well as in mucus membranes in approximately one third of cases.

This disorder most often occurs in flare-ups: An affected person can be symptom free for a period of years before having an incidence. Additionally, the disease occurs in varying levels of severity. Between flare-ups affected persons are advised to keep the skin well hydrated. Various methods from bathing to lotions to oils may be suited for this purpose, but individuals report varying preferences and tolerances. Finally, those with bullous pemphigoid are advised to use caution in sunlight, as further skin damage can worsen the condition.

Characteristics

1. Itchy, inflamed rash in folds of skin
2. Fatigue and anxiety
3. Blisters (often large) that follow rash
4. Possible blistering in the mouth

There is no cure for bullous pemphigoid, but the symptoms are controllable. Treatment for this disorder when it is at its most severe involves hospitalization. Oral treatments often involve steroids or immunosuppressants, which decrease the activity of the immune system. However, as these are potent drugs with other side effects, they are usually administered in an initially large dosage, which is subsequently decreased until a minimum effective dose is reached. This then becomes a maintenance dose, which is continued for a set amount of time, possibly as long as several years. Additionally, the use of antibiotic ointment is strongly advised due to a high risk of infection, especially when dealing with blisters that have been broken.

This is a very rare disease in children (Baykal, Okan, & Sarica, 2001). However, it is undoubtedly a psychologically damaging one due to its outwardly visible nature. Children affected by bullous pemphigoid who are between flare-ups will be able to lead a routine life. However, children experiencing flare-ups will be subject to much teasing from peers. It may be necessary to educate classmates on the condition or to provide counseling for the affected child. Additionally, children with this disorder and their teachers will need to be aware of situations that may worsen the condition in order to avoid them.

REFERENCES

Baykal, C., Okan, G., & Sarica, R. (2001). Childhood bullous pemphigoid developed after the first vaccination. *Journal of American Academic Dermatology, 44,* 348–350.

Powell, J., Kirtschig, G., Allen, J., Dean, D., & Wojnarowska, F. (2001). Mixed immunobullous disease of childhood: A good response to antimicrobials. *British Journal of Dermatology, 144*(4), pp. 769–774.

Allison Katz
Rutgers University

C

CAFE AU LAIT SPOTS

Cafe au lait spots refer to hyperpigmented areas of the skin. The spots are flat, sharply demarcated, more or less oval patches that are light to medium brown in color. The coffee-stain appearance is reflected by the name, which means "coffee with milk" in French. The long axis of the cafe au lait spot or oval is situated along a cutaneous (skin) nerve tract. The spots are usually present at birth but may become apparent in the first few years of life (Hull, 2000).

Cafe au lait spots are prevalent in approximately 10% of the normal population (National Skin Centre, 2001). They are reportedly more common in African American infants (Hull, 2000).

Characteristics

1. Flat, sharply demarcated oval patches
2. Light to medium brown in color (coffee color)
3. Present at birth or emerge during childhood
4. Commonly benign, but possibly associated with neurofibromatosis

Cafe au lait spots often represent benign birthmarks; however, they can be a manifestation of other underlying disorders (Cohen, Janniger, & Schwartz, 2000). Most commonly, they are associated with neurofibromatosis, which is a genetically transmitted neurocutaneous disorder (Spreen, Risser, & Edgell, 1995). The presence of six or more cafe au lait spots larger than 1.5 cm in diameter (the size of a quarter) prepubertal or 5 cm postpubertal may occur in neurofibromatosis. It should be noted that other symptoms are necessary to make the diagnosis of neurofibromatosis, and some individuals may have multiple cafe au lait spots without having the disorder.

Cafe au lait spots with jagged borders are associated with McCune-Albright syndrome (MAS). MAS is a rare multisystem disorder that is also characterized by displacement of normal bone tissue with areas of abnormal fibrous growth or abnormalities of the endocrine system (e.g., precocious puberty; National Organization for Rare Disorders, 2001).

In addition, there have been reports of an increased incidence of early-onset colorectal cancer in some individuals with cafe au lait spots. It was reported that patients with a variant of hereditary nonpolyposis colorectal cancer (HNPCC) who had cafe au lait spots developed their malignancies at a much earlier age than did other HNPCC patients (Oncology News International, 1999).

REFERENCES

Cohen, J. B., Janniger, C. K., & Schwartz, R. A. (2000). Cafe-au-lait spots. *Pediatric Dermatology, 66,* 22–24.

Hull, J. (2000). Parent's common sense encyclopedia. Retrieved from http://www.drhull.com/EncyMaster/C/cafe-au-lait.html

National Organization for Rare Disorders. (2001). McCune-Albright syndrome. Retrieved from http://www.rarediseases.org/

National Skin Centre. (2001). Cafe-au-lait spots. Retrieved from http://www.nsc.gov.sg/commskin/Pigment/pigment6.html

Oncology News International. (1999, August). Cafe au Lait spots linked to early onset colorectal cancer. *Copy Editor, 8*(8).

Spreen, S., Risser, A. T., & Edgell, D. (1995). *Developmental neuropsychology.* New York: Oxford Press.

David R. Steinman
Nancy L. Nussbaum
Austin Neurological Clinic

See also Neurofibromatosis, Type 1; Neurofibromatosis, Type 2

CANDIDIASIS

The *Candida* genus is opportunistic in comparison to other fungal genera and is part of the normal gastrointestinal flora. Candidiasis is an opportunistic fungal infection. Symptoms of candidiasis may resemble bacterial sepsis or necrotizing enterocolitis (NEC; Witek-Janusek, Cusack, & Mathews, 1998). In its severest form, intramural intestinal gas, intrahepatic portal vein gas, and intestinal perforation characterize NEC (Hughes, Lepow, & Hill, 1993). The clinical diagnosis of disseminated fungal infection is usually associated with one or more of the following: respiratory deterioration, abdominal distention, guaiac-positive stools, carbohydrate intolerance, candiduria, endophthalmitis, meningitis, abscesses, erythematous rash, temperature instability, lethargy, and hypotension (Baley, 1991; Van den Anker, Popele, & Sauer, 1995).

The species most common in neonates with disseminated disease is *Candida albicans,* accounting for 75% of cases. *C. tropicalis* and *C. parapsilosis* account for 10% and 6%, respectively (Hughes et al., 1993).

Opportunistic microorganisms multiply in vulnerable infants; however, they are no threat to those with a noncompromised immune system (Witek-Janusek et al., 1998). Vulnerable infants are considered to be those in whom both inadequate immune defense mechanisms and risk factors associated with clinical management are present. Invasive *C. albicans* infection is generally difficult to manage and is associated with high morbidity and mortality (Witek-Janusek et al.). Neonatal systemic candidiasis is predominantly a disease of low-birth-weight infants (Hughes et al., 1993).

The placement of intravascular catheters and endotracheal tubes in premature infants interrupts the skin and mucous membranes as a defense against candidal invasion. Catheters provide an entryway for microorganisms and initiate a site of adherence for yeast (Hughes et al., 1993).

Infants usually become colonized with *Candida* soon after birth (Witek-Janusek et al., 1998). Colonization from the maternal vaginal tract during birth is a common path of *Candida* transmission. This is particularly the case for pregnant women with vaginal candidiasis. However, the interruption of initial colonization of the infant at birth may decrease the incidence of systemic *Candida* infections in high-risk infants (Witek-Janusek et al.).

According to Hughes et al. (1993), the manifestations of candidiasis include oral, systemic, catheter-associated candidemia, urinary system, endocarditis, endophthalmitis, meningitis, and congenital.

Characteristics

1. Temperature instability
2. Respiratory distress
3. Abdominal distention
4. Other symptoms may include unstable vitals, apnea, bradychardia, lethargy, and decreased perfusion

Systemic antifungal drugs used to treat candidiasis include amphotericin B, 5-flucytosine, miconazole, fluconazole, and itraconazole (Hughes et al., 1993.). Despite good treatment, nosocomial fungal infections have become a cause of morbidity, extended hospitalization, and mortality in critically ill newborn babies (Khoory, Vino, Dall'Agnola, & Fanos, 1999). Furthermore, the high incidence of central nervous system involvement in septic newborns often results in serious neurological damage and psychomotorial sequelae (Khoory et al., 1999). *Candida* infection of the central nervous system has a significant impact on long-term neurodevelopmental outcome. Performance of cranial ultrasound examination is recommended as a part of the diagnostic investigation for these infants. Detection of brain parenchymal involvement might provide further information to predict outcome (Friedman, Richardson, Jacobs, & O'Brien, 2000).

Further research is needed to determine potential educational implications for infants with this serious infection.

REFERENCES

Baley, J. E. (1991). The current challenge. *Clinics in Perinatology, 18,* 263–280.

Friedman, S., Richardson, S. E., Jacobs, S. E., & O'Brien, K. (2000). Systemic *candida* infection in extremely low birth weight infants: Short-term morbidity and long term neurodevelopmental outcome. *Pediatric Infectious Disease Journal, 19*(6), 499–504.

Hughes, P. A., Lepow, M. L., & Hill, H. R. (1993). Neonatal candidiasis. In G. P. Bodey (Ed.), *Candidiasis: Pathogenisis, diagnosis and treatment* (pp. 261–277). New York: Raven Press.

Khoory, B. J., Vino, L., Dall'Agnola, A., & Fanos, V. (1999). *Candida* infections in newborns: A review. *Journal of Chemotherapy, 11*(5), 367–378.

Van den Anker, J. N., Popele, N. M., & Sauer, P. J. (1995). Antifungal agents in neonatal systemic candidiasis. *Antimicrobial Agents and Chemotherapy, 30*(7), 1391–1397.

Witek-Janusek, L., Cusack, C., & Mathews, H. L. (1998). *Candida albicans:* An opportunistic threat to critically ill low birth weight infants. *Dimensions of Critical Care Nursing, 17*(5), 243–255.

Helen G. Jenne
Alliant International University–California School of Professional Psychology

CARCINOID SYNDROME

Carcinoid tumors were first discovered in the 1800s, and the term *carcinoid* began being used by the medical profession in 1907. Tumors were found to arise from glandular endocrine-hormone producing cells found commonly in the small intestine. To a lesser extent, these tumors may also be found in the appendix, the rectum, the lung, and the pancreas and very rarely in the ovaries, the testes, the liver, and the bile ducts. It was not until 1954 that carcinoid syndrome was recognized by medical professionals as a specific disease (Oats, 1996).

Carcinoid syndrome is a rare, malignant disease affecting 8 out of every 100,000 persons. This rare disease affects males and females of all ages in equal numbers. The actual number may be underreported due to undetected tumors and the fact that some patients do not experience the three hallmark symptoms of carcinoid syndrome—flushing, wheezing, and diarrhea—leading to misdiagnosis (Oats, 1996).

Carcinoid syndrome begins quietly with the absence of symptoms. It is not until the tumors have been growing for years that the symptoms are noticeable. Typically, the malignant tumors affect the small bowel, stomach, or pancreas. Eventually, the tumors can spread to the liver, lungs, and ovaries. As the disease progresses, congestive heart failure associated with the right-sided valvular heart disease develops. In addition, the carcinoid tumors make deadly hormones that are commonly found in the liver and cause the notorious symptoms of flushing of the face, asthma-like wheezing attacks, and diarrhea. These symptoms can become severe to the point of being life threatening. In the beginning stages of the disease, the "carcinoid crisis," as it is commonly referred to, may be infrequent and usually associated with abrupt low blood pressure and fainting. As the disease progresses, the symptoms become more frequent and chronic (Thonene, 1995).

Characteristics

1. Flushing in the face
2. Diarrhea
3. Asthma-like wheezing
4. Loss of vital nutrients due to diarrhea
5. Stomach pain
6. Blocked arteries in the liver
7. Heart palpitations
8. Excessive peptide excretion in the liver

The first three characteristics are the hallmark symptoms of carcinoid syndrome.

At one time, the survival rate from onset of flushing was 3 years and only 2 years from the time of diagnosis with a range of 10 years. Seventy-five percent of the patients died from the potent substances released from the tumors, and 25% died from the tumor growth itself. Within the last 10 years, the prognosis of carcinoid syndrome has improved dramatically. This positive outlook is due to the effective combinations of treatments with Sandostatin, various surgeries, chemotherapy, hepatic artery injections, and biological response mediators. The average survival time from the start of treatment has increased by more than 5 years. The late diagnosis delays the start of treatment; thus, an early diagnosis may look even more favorable (Oats, 1996).

Although carcinoid syndrome does not directly affect the cognitive abilities of children, additional school service such as a private tutor may prove useful to in helping the child maintain academic abilities while undergoing different life-saving procedures. Additional individual and family support can be useful to help the family cope with the symptoms and the side effects of treatment caused by this disorder.

REFERENCES

Oats, J. (1996). *Cecil textbook of internal medicine* (20th ed.). Philadelphia: W. B. Saunders.

Thonene, J. G. (1995). *Physicians' guide to rare diseases.* Montvale, NJ: Dowden.

Lisa A. Fasnacht-Hill
Keck University of Southern California School of Medicine
University of Southern California / University Affiliated Program at Children's Hospital of Los Angeles

CARCINOMA, RENAL CELL

Renal cell carcinoma is a type of cancer of the kidney that involves cancerous changes in the lining of renal tubule cells. Prevalence of this disorder is estimated to be .03%, with 18,000 new cases diagnosed each year in the United States and approximately 8,000 deaths (U.S. National Library of Medicine, 2000). The disorder is more common in men than in women, especially men over the age of 55. Among children, renal cell carcinoma is exceedingly rare, representing only 2.6% of all renal cancers in children under 15 years old (Bernstein, Liney, Smith, & Olshan, 1995). The National Cancer Institute reported just 32 cases of renal cell carcinoma in children under age 15 in the years between 1975 and 1995 (Bernstein et al.).

Among the known risk factors for this disorder are a family history of kidney cancer, a kidney disease that requires dialysis, von Hippel-Lindau disease (an inherited condition that affects the capillaries of the brain), and smoking (U.S. National Library of Medicine, 2000). Occurrence of renal cell carcinoma in children is usually associated with tuberous sclerosis or von Hippel-Lindau disease (Henske, Thorner, Patterson, Zhuang, & Bernstein, 1999).

Characteristics

1. Evidence of blood in the urine or brown or rust-colored urine
2. Complaint of pain in the flank, back, or abdomen
3. Loss of more than 5% of body weight or an emaciated appearance
4. Enlargement of one testicle or swelling of the abdomen

The recommended treatment for this disorder is surgery to remove all or part of the kidney. The surrounding tissues, lymph nodes, and bladder also may be removed (U.S. National Library of Medicine, 2000). Renal cell carcinoma is known to metastasize quickly to the lungs and other organs. As a result, radiation therapy may be used either prior to surgery to shrink the tumor or as a treatment to prevent metastasis (U.S. National Library of Medicine). However, renal cell carcinoma often does not respond to radiation. In some cases, hormone therapy and drugs such as alpha-interferon and interleukin have been successful in limiting the growth of the cancer (U.S. National Library of Medicine).

Due to its extremely low prevalence in children, little information is available on the educational implications of renal cell carcinoma. Henske et al. (1999) reported developmental delays in the two cases of childhood renal cell carcinoma that they studied. The need for surgery and radiation therapy associated with treatment for this disorder would lead to extended absences from school for children with renal cell carcinoma. These children may qualify for special education services under the Other Health Impairment handicapping condition.

When renal cell carcinoma is diagnosed in its early stages, 60–75% survival at five years is reported in adults (U.S. National Library of Medicine, 2000). This rate drops to 5–15% if the cancer has spread to the lymph nodes and to less than 5% if other organs show signs of carcinoma. In children, a 5-year survival rate of 83% was reported in cases diagnosed between 1985 and 1994 (Bernstein et al., 1995).

REFERENCES

Bernstein, L., Liney, M., Smith, M., & Olshan, A. (1995). Renal tumors. In *Cancer incidence and survival among children and adolescents: United States SEER program 1975–1995.* National Cancer Institute. Retrieved from http://seer.cancer.gov/Publications/PedMono/

Henske, E., Thorner, P., Patterson, K., Zhuang, Z., & Bernstein, J. (1999). Renal cell carcinoma in children with diffuse cystic hyperplasia of the kidneys. *Pediatric and Developmental Pathology, 2,* 270–274.

U.S. National Library of Medicine. (2000). Renal cell carcinoma. Retrieved from http://medlineplus.adam.com/ency/article/000516.htm

Nancy K. Scammacca
University of Texas at Austin

CARDIOFACIOCUTANEOUS SYNDROME

Cardiofaciocutaneous (CFC) syndrome, also known as cardio-facial-cutaneous syndrome and facio-cardio-cutaneous syndrome, affects both males and females. It is a rare genetic disorder found in children that is diagnosed based on specific physical appearances of the head, face, chest, hands, skin, and/or heart, in addition to visual impairment, growth delays, and/or varying degrees of mental retardation.

This rare disorder has an autosomal dominant inheritance and, in circumstances where no family history of CFC syndrome is found, is thought to be the result of random sporadic mutations.

Many symptoms are associated with CFC syndrome. The head of a CFC patient may have one or more of the following characteristics: macrocephaly (unusually large in size); a prominent forehead with abnormal narrowing of both sides; a short, upturned nose with a low nasal bridge; and prominent external ears (pinnae) abnormally rotated toward the back of the head. Distinctive facial characteristics may consist of extremely sparse and brittle curly hair, a lack of eyebrows and eyelashes, palpebral fissures (downwardly slanting eyelid folds), ocular hypertelorism (widely spaced eyes), and esotropia (inward deviation of the eyes). There is also a greater chance of difficulties with oral motor/feeding/swallowing because of the increased incidence of craniofacial abnormalities.

Other symptoms include pectus carinatum or excavatum (protrusion or indentation of the breastbone), hands with pads on the fingertips, and opal-colored nails. There may also be a number of skin abnormalities, such as dermatitis (skin inflammation), generalized ichthyosis (unusually dry, thickened, scaly skin covering the entire body), generalized pigmentation, patchy hyperkeratosis (patches of thickened skin), keratosis plantaris (red skin in the soles of the feet), and keratosis pilaris (red skin surrounding the eyebrows).

Congenital heart defects are common among individuals with CFC syndrome. The defects include pulmonary stenosis (obstruction of the normal flow of blood from the lower right chamber of the heart to the lungs due to a narrowing of a valve that connects the lungs to the heart), atrial septal defect (abnormal opening in the fibrous partition, or septum, that divides the left and right atria of the heart), and hypertrophic cardiomyopathy (enlarged heart).

Visual impairment as a result of strabismus (muscle imbalance), amblyopia (lazy eye), nystagmus (involuntary eye movements), ptosis (drooping eyelid), and optic atrophy (dysfunction of the optic nerve) are often seen in case studies done on children with CFC syndrome (Levack, 1991). In addition, most people with CFC syndrome have delayed growth, mild to severe mental retardation, and psychomotor retardation (delays in mastering the skills that require the coordination of muscular and mental activity).

To date, there is no laboratory test available to diagnose someone with CFC syndrome; diagnosis is dependent on a clinician's observations. For diagnosis to occur, a person must have several of the many symptoms of CFC syndrome. The majority of the physical features indicating that a patient has CFC syndrome are often not apparent until childhood, although in some cases a newborn may be diagnosed with CFC syndrome.

Characteristics

1. *Head:* large and oddly shaped head, forehead, nose, ears
2. *Face:* extremely sparse and brittle curly hair; lack of eyebrows and eyelashes; downward slanting, widely spaced, and inwardly deviated eyes; difficulties involving oral motor/feeding/swallowing
3. *Chest:* pectus carinatum or excavatum (protrusion or indentation of the breastbone)
4. *Hands:* pads on the fingertips, opal-colored nails
5. *Skin:* inflamation of skin; dry, thickened, scaly skin covering much of the body; red skin around eyebrows and/or on soles of the feet
6. *Heart:* narrowing of the valve that connects lungs and heart, abnormal opening in septum that divides the left and right atria, hypertrophic cardiomyopathy (enlarged heart)
7. *Vision:* muscle imbalance in eye, lazy eye, drooping eyelid or other involuntary eye movements; optic atrophy (dysfunction of the optic nerve)
8. *Other:* delayed growth, mild to severe mental or psychomotor retardation

Unfortunately, there is no cure for CFC syndrome. It is a genetic change and therefore affects every cell in the body. Science has not yet found a way to repair the gene coding for CFC syndrome, nor is there a way to treat every cell in a patient. As a result, clinicians must treat the symptoms and not the source of the CFC syndrome. Treatment should not be universal, but instead individual and based on each child's needs.

There are a multitude of support groups, foundations, and associations available for those who have children with CFC syndrome. The CFC Family Network is a group run strictly by parents who collect donations to supply CFC families with newsletters, family packets, contacts to other CFC families, articles, and photo albums. Currently, donations are being put toward helping families go to a CFC Research Program where doctors are examining children with CFC syndrome in the hope of learning more about this disorder (National Organization for Rare Disorders, Inc., 2000).

Children with CFC may need special care in the classroom. They may fall behind in their lessons due to mental retardation or to missing large amounts of classes. Additionally, these children may be on pain management techniques that interfere with their schooling.

REFERENCES

Levack, N. (1991). *Low Vision, A Resource Guide with Adaptations for Students with Vision Impairments.* Texas School for the Blind.

National Organization for Rare Disorders, Inc. (2000). Retrieved from www.rarediseases.org

Maryann Toni Parrino
Montclair University

CARNITINE PALMITOYLTRANSFERASE DEFICIENCY, TYPE I

Carnitine palmitoyltransferase deficiency (CPT) is an extremely rare genetic disorder of mitochondrial fatty-acid oxidation. Two forms of this genetic defect have been described: CPT-I and CPT-II. CPT-I is a more severe form (hepatocardiomuscular syndrome) associated with onset in infancy. CPT-II is a milder form of muscle disease associated with an adult presentation.

Of the two forms of this disorder, CPT-I, the hepatic form, has been documented the most. Ten patients (5 males and 5 females) with CPT-I have been reported in 8 families. Ethnic origins of patients with the hepatic form of the disease include Caucasian, Middle Eastern, Central American Indian, Inuit, and Asian Indian.

Characteristics

1. Initial onset usually in infancy (neonatal period to 18 months)
2. CPT-I: First presenting illness usually associated with fasting (viral infection, diarrhea) with attacks of vomiting, coma, seizures, hepatomegaly, and hypoglycemia
3. No evidence of chronic muscle weakness or cardiomyopathy
4. CPT-II: muscle pain after exhaustive exercise or fasting
5. Persistent neurological deficit, probably resulting from the initial insult
6. Developmental delays and cognitive deficits associated with neurological insult

A major element in management is avoidance of fasting. Recurrent episodes are common and have been successfully treated with glucose. Frequent feeding and special diet including reduction of fat appear to be beneficial.

Many children with mitochondrial disorders might have

normal intelligence or static mental retardation or developmental delay. Children may have long periods with a stable neurologic picture simulating a static encephalopathy and later deteriorate either in an acute or in a slowly progressive manner (Nissenkorn et al., 2000). Of the 10 patients that have been reported, all but one are alive. Evaluation for special education needs is recommended. Many of these children will qualify for services under the classification of Other Health Impairment as a result of their medical condition. Future research should attempt to determine reasons behind the onset of CPT-I versus CPT-II.

REFERENCE

Nissenkorn, A., Zeharia, A., Lev, D., Watember, N., Fattal-Valevski, A., Barash, V., Gutman, A., Harel, S., & Lerman-Sagie, T. (2000). Neurologic presentations of mitochondrial disorders. *Journal of Child Neurology, 15,* 44–48.

Virdette L. Brumm
Children's Hospital Los Angeles
Keck / USC School of Medicine

CARNITINE PALMITOYLTRANSFERASE DEFICIENCY, TYPE II

Carnitine palmitoyltransferase deficiency (CPT) is a very rare autosomal recessive genetic disease created from the interaction of one gene from the mother and one gene from the father. Thus, the condition does not appear in the child unless the same defective gene for the same trait from each parent is inherited. If only one normal and one gene with the disease are passed on, the child will be a carrier of the disease but usually will not show symptoms. If both parents are carriers of the recessive disease, the child has a 25% chance of demonstrating positive symptoms of the disease, a 50% chance of being of carrier, and a 25% chance of receiving both normal genes from each parent (Schaefer, Jackson, Taroni, Swift, & Turnbull, 1997).

The defective gene responsible for CPT Type I (CPT-I) regulates the production of the enzyme CPTase I. CPT Type II (CPT-II) is a milder form of the disorder that affects adults. CPT-I is located on the long arm of Chromosome 11, and CPT-II is located on the short arm of Chromosome 1. If a member of the family is diagnosed with CPT-II, each child in the family should be tested in order to take necessary precautions to avoid the symptoms of the illness.

CPT is very rare and observed in males more frequently than in females. This disease is seen more in individuals with diabetes and those who may be malnourished. The disorder is usually detectable in adolescence and adulthood. CPT is characterized by easy fatigability after prolonged periods of strenuous exercise. Weak and disabling muscles along with stiffness and pain may last for days. Destruction of the skeletal muscles may be followed by a passage of red-brown urine. The combination of these conditions can be life threatening (Schaefer et al., 1997).

Related disorders with similar symptoms include Eaton-Lambert syndrome, S-capuloperoneal myopathy, and fibromyalgia. Like CPT, these disorders are characterized by fatigue and muscle stiffness and deterioration of muscle tissue.

Characteristics

1. Usually found more frequently in individuals with diabetes and/or malnourishment
2. Detectable in adolescence or adulthood
3. Easy fatigue after prolonged periods of strenuous exercise or activity
4. Weak and disabling muscles lasting possibly for weeks after the onset
5. Red-brown urine

CPT is usually diagnosed by enzymatic studies and muscle biopsy. Persons diagnosed with metabolic problems should be cognizant of the types of foods eaten, specifically avoid high fatty foods, avoid a highly stressful lifestyle, and exercise in moderation (Schaefer et al., 1997). To aid in controlling the severity of the symptoms associated with this disease, supportive therapies include nutritional counseling, individual or family therapy, and frequent contact with school professionals to ensure that the ramifications from this disease are not hindering the child's learning. Additionally, genetic counseling is warranted for the affected individual and the family.

REFERENCE

Schaefer, J., Jackson, S., Taroni, F., Swift, P., & Turnbull, D. M. (1997). Characterization of carnitine palmitoyltransferases in patients with carnitine palmitoyltransferase deficiency: Implications for diagnosis and therapy. *Journal of Neurology Neurosurgery and Psychiatry, 62*(2), 169–176.

Lisa A. Fasnacht-Hill
Keck University of Southern California School of Medicine
University of Southern California / University Affiliated Program at Children's Hospital of Los Angeles

CARPAL TUNNEL SYNDROME

Carpal tunnel syndrome (CTS) is a type of cumulative trauma disorder in the sense that it develops after protracted repetitive mechanical stress on musculoskeletal systems. Musculoskeletal system disorders can subdivided into three classifications, namely nerve, neurovascular, and tendon disorders. CTS is considered a nerve compression disorder. Specifically, it is the resultant neuropathy associated with restriction of the median nerve passing through the carpal tunnel. Nerve compression disorders usually result in reduction or complete loss of motor, particularly fine motor skills, sensory, and sensory perception. In severe cases, complete autonomic nerve function is lost.

Characteristics

1. Pain, numbness, reduced grip strength
2. Reduction or loss of fine motor skills in affected hand
3. Reduction or loss of sensation in afflicted hand
4. Weakness and tingling in hand
5. Dropping objects and reduced range of motion
6. Autonomic nerve function loss
7. Complete loss of hand function
8. History of prolonged, repetitive stress on afflicted hand

CTS has received special attention in recent years in children as a result of work-related injuries to children in underdeveloped countries. Children's hospital and clinics have seen a proliferation of CTS and other nerve compression disorders associated with repeated and sustained work-related activities in the United States and abroad, but particularly in nations in which child labor laws are not enforced.

Treatment for CTS varies from restriction of motion and medication to surgery in more severe cases. Future research should focus on the development of ergonomic methods capable of reducing these work-related injuries through human factor engineering and better surveillance. In the case of childhood injuries, the enforcement of child labor laws has been found to be a critical factor in reducing these injuries. Special education for these children should include the development of curriculum modification under an Other Health Impairment label. The application of technology as a way of reducing the use of the afflicted limb also is usually beneficial.

REFERENCES

Armstrong, T. J. (1986). Ergonomics and cumulative trauma disorders. *Hand Clinics, 2,* 553–565.

Gross, C. M. (1988). *Diagnostic criteria for cumulative trauma disorders of the upper extremity.* New York: Melville.

Putz-Anderson, V. (Ed.). (1988). *Cumulative trauma disorders: A manual for musculoskeletal diseases of the upper limbs.* New York: Taylor & Francis.

U.S. Department of Labor, Bureau of Statistics. (1997). *Worker injuries and illnesses by selected classification (1982–1996).* Washington, DC: U.S. Department of Labor.

Antolin M. Llorente
Baylor College of Medicine
Houston, Texas

CARPENTER SYNDROME (ACROCEPHALOPOLYSYNDACTYLY, TYPE II)

Carpenter syndrome (acrocephalopolysyndactyly, Type II) is a congenital condition that was first described in 1901 by George Carpenter, a British pediatrician (Islek, Kucukoduk, Incesu, Selcuk, & Aygun, 1998). Although Carpenter syndrome presents with marked phenotypical variability (Islek et al.), defining characteristics of this disorder include acrocephaly (peaked head), craniosynostosis (premature closure of the cranial sutures), craniofacial asymmetry, soft tissue syndactyly (webbing of the fingers and toes), and preaxial polydactyly, primarily of the toes (Ashby, Rouse, & DeLange, 1994; National Organization for Rare Disorders, Inc., 2000).

Carpenter syndrome occurs so rarely that only 43 cases, representing both isolated cases and recurrence in siblings, have been reported in the literature to date (Islek et al., 1998). There is significant intrafamilial variability as evidenced by affected siblings who present with very different profiles; in one instance, a female twin was affected while her twin brother was not (Ashby et al., 1994). Carpenter syndrome has been identified worldwide in males and females of various ethnicities. Affected individuals have ranged in age from a 20-week-old fetus to an adult male of 49 years (Balci, Onol, Eryilmaz, & Haytoglu, 1997). Parental age does not seem to be a factor in causation of Carpenter syndrome as the condition has been noted in children born to teens as well as to middle-aged parents. The fact that consanguinity of parents of affected children has been reported in six cases and suspected in one may be of potential significance (Al-Arrayed, 1999; Gershoni-Baruch, 1990).

The etiology of Carpenter syndrome is presently unknown. Although it is presumed to be the result of autosomal recessive inheritance, there is some speculation that it results from codominant or dominant inheritance, based on the fact that a father of four children with Carpenter syndrome also presented with some characteristics of the disorder (Al-Arrayed, 1999).

Characteristics

1. Essential characteristics of Carpenter syndrome are acrocephaly; soft tissue syndactyly of the fingers and toes; craniosynostosis of the sagittal, lambdoid, and coronal cranial sutures; craniofacial assymetry; and preaxial polydactyly, primarily of the toes (Islek et al., 1998; Taravath & Tonsgard, 1993).
2. Associated complications may include cardiovascular defects (seen in about a third of affected individuals), mild to moderate obesity, short stature, unusually short fingers and toes, hypogenitalism, umbilical hernia, and cryptorchidism (NORD, 2000).
3. The most frequently occurring facial features include a flat nasal bridge; dysplastic, low-set ears; a small mouth with a hypoplastic maxilla or mandible; a narrow, high-arched palate; and abnormal and missing permanent teeth (NORD, 2000). About 50% of documented cases have abnormalities of the eyes including corneal opacity and optic atrophy; other features include shallow orbits, palpebral fissures, epicanthic folds, and hypertelorism.
4. Some degree of intellectual impairment has been identified in approximately 75% of individuals with Carpenter syndrome; however, normal intelligence levels, with IQ scores of 103, have also been described. Mental retardation is common but is not necessary for a diagnosis; when it does occur, IQ scores have been reported in the mildly to profoundly retarded range (Islek et al., 1998).
5. Other problems include sensorineural hearing loss, visual impairments, delayed or impaired language, and speech problems in the areas of articulation, nasality, and resonance (Shprintzen, 1997).
6. Developmental milestones are generally acquired later than normal, and growth retardation is a constant feature of this condition.

A diagnosis of Carpenter syndrome is confirmed by examination of its phenotypic manifestations. Prenatal diagnosis has also been successfully attempted with the use of ultrasound in the second trimester and transabdominal embryoscopy in the first. The issue of differential diagnosis is particularly important because there is such variability in its expression and because there are a number of conditions that mimic this disorder. For example, Goodman and Summitt syndromes are considered to belong within the clinical spectrum of Carpenter syndrome but are associated with normal intelligence and often an absence of polydactyly (Gershoni-Baruch, 1990; Islek et al., 1998). The syndrome has also been diagnosed in individuals without acrocephaly, craniosynostosis, and congenital heart defects (Gershoni-Baruch, 1990).

Cranial computer tomography (CT) and magnetic resonance imaging (MRI) scans are used to indicate level of involvement, treatment plans, and prognosis. Treatment of Carpenter syndrome during the first year of life includes surgical intervention that is usually performed in stages. Such surgery is used mainly to correct cranial deformities, to support rapid growth of the brain, and to prevent mental retardation (Balci et al., 1997). Other treatment may include hand and foot surgery for release of syndactyly, correction of cardiac defects, and midface advancement and jaw surgery (Shprintzen, 1997).

Psychoeducational interventions for the child with Carpenter syndrome will depend on the degree of involvement as well as on its severity. Most of these children will qualify for special educational services under the handicapping conditions of physical disabilities or multiple disabilities; as such, the Individualized Educational Plan (IEP) must offer comprehensive and aggressive treatment efforts designed to address the whole range of each child's needs. Such a child may need special educational services to remediate or compensate for cognitive and academic deficits and to develop social-behavioral skills. In addition, the IEP must outline the use of support services such as physical and occupational therapy to address gross and fine motor deficits, speech and language services, and assistance for hearing or visual impairments. Self-help and socialization skills may be limited because of retardation but also because of physical deficits. As children with Carpenter syndrome age, they may exhibit developmental delays and increasing difficulty with daily tasks. Personal and vocational counseling may be beneficial, particularly for older children and adults. In addition, because Carpenter syndrome appears to be inherited, it is strongly recommended that adults with this condition undergo genetic counseling prior to marriage and pregnancy. In general, intervention efforts for individuals of all ages should be directed toward increasing self-sufficiency and independence.

The prognosis for individuals with Carpenter syndrome is variable, given its expression. There is presently no cure for this condition, but individuals with Carpenter syndrome can learn to function adequately given early intervention and adequate support. Carpenter syndrome is thought to be associated with reduced life expectancy; however, no studies have been reported in this area. Given Carpenter's marked phenotypical variability and the contradictory information regarding inheritance, it is likely that future research efforts will be directed toward clarifying these issues and improving the quality of life for individuals affected by this serious condition.

REFERENCES

Al-Arrayed, S. S. (1999). Carpenter Syndrome in eight Arab patients, dominant inheritance suspected. Retrieved from http://faseb.org/genetics/ashg99/f751.htm

Ashby, T., Rouse, F. A., & DeLange, M. (1994). Prenatal sonographic diagnosis of Carpenter Syndrome. *Journal of Ultrasound in Medicine, 13,* 905–909.

Balci, S., Onol, B., Eryilmaz, M., & Haytoglu, T. (1997). A case of Carpenter syndrome diagnosed in a 20-week-old fetus with postmortem examination. *Clinical Genetics, 51*(6), 412–416.

Gershoni-Baruch, R. (1990). Carpenter syndrome: Marked variability of expression to include the Summitt and Goodman syndromes. *American Journal of Medical Genetics, 35*(2), 236–40.

Islek, I., Kucukoduk, S., Incesu, L., Selcuk, M. B., & Aygun, D. (1998, July). Carpenter syndrome: Report of two siblings. *Clinical Dysmorphology, 7*(3), 185–189.

National Organization for Rare Disorders, Inc. (2000). Carpenter syndrome. Retrieved from http://www.rarediseases.org

Shprintzen, R. J. (1997). *Genetics, syndromes, and communication disorders.* San Diego, CA: Singular Publishing Group.

Taravath, S., & Tonsgard, J. H. (1993). Cerebral malformations in Carpenter syndrome. *Pediatric Neurology, 9*(3), 230–234.

Mary M. Chittooran
Retha M. Edens
Saint Louis University

CASTLEMAN DISEASE

Castleman disease (CD), also referred to as angiofollicular lymph node hyperplasia, is a heterogeneous group of lymphoproliferative disorders, characterized by abnormal growth of the lymph nodes. There are three histopathological variants of CD: hyaline-vascular type, which accounts for approximately 80–90% of reported cases; plasma cell type; and an intermediate, or mixed, histological type (Maslovsky & Lugassy, 1999). Clinical presentation of CD appears to be either localized or generalized (multicentric); however, there is controversy about whether the multicentric form is a distinct entity or simply a form of the plasma cell type (National Organization for Rare Disorders, Inc. [NORD], 2000; Parez, Bader-Meunier, Roy, & Dommergues, 1999). There is also some evidence that CD constitutes a spectrum of benign to malignant diseases (Malaguarnera et al., 1999) and that if left untreated, the benign form of the disease may serve as a precursor to the malignant form (Parez et al.).

Since it was first described in 1954 CD has been reported in fewer than 150 cases worldwide and appears to be more common in underdeveloped parts of Africa and southern Europe. Although the disease has been identified in both males and females, Smir, Greiner, and Weisenburger (1996) reported a male-female ratio of 1:3 in children. The disease occurs at all ages; however, its presentation in children tends to be localized, benign, and of the hyaline-vascular type (Parez et al., 1999). CD has a favorable clinical course in children, that is, low morbidity and mortality (Smir et al.). In adults, however, the disease tends to take an aggressive, often fatal course, and multicentric forms of the disease are common, particularly after age 50 (Malaguarnera et al., 1999).

The etiology of CD is presently unknown and somewhat controversial. Schulz (2000) speculated that genetic factors play an important role in this disorder. Malaguarnera et al. (1999) found that ornithine decarboxylase (ODC) gene expression varied between the localized and multicentric forms of the disease and suggested that aberrant ODC expression may be a critical factor in transforming a premalignant lesion into a malignant one. Researchers (e.g., Plaza & Gilbert-Barness, 2000) have suggested that certain environmental factors, as yet unidentified, could act as stimuli for the proliferation of lymph nodes. The association between HIV infection and multicentric CD in adults has been well established (Kumari, Schechter, Saini, & Benator, 2000), and Kaposi's sarcoma–associated herpesvirus (human herpes virus 8; HHV-8) is known to be involved in the pathogenesis of the plasma cell variant of multicentric CD in adults (Schulz, 2000). Elevated serum levels of Interleukin-6 (IL-6) have also been reported in patients with multicentric CD (Malaguarnera et al., 1999). Several medical conditions mimic CD; therefore, it is suggested that differential diagnoses of CD in children include consideration of microcytic anemia (De Heer-Groen, Prakken, Bax, & van Dijken, 1996), small round cell tumors of childhood (Fiel-Gan, Voytek, Weiss, Brown, & Joshi, 2000), and lymphoma.

Characteristics

1. Clinical presentation varies widely, but CD frequently manifests as a single mediastinal mass identified on radiographic examination. Although tumors develop most often in the chest and abdomen, they also occur in the axilla, pelvis, and pancreas. Tumors may represent abnormal enlargement of the lymph nodes normally found in these areas (lymphoid hamartoma).
2. The localized, hyaline-vascular type of CD is most common in children; affected individuals are frequently asymptomatic.
3. Multicentric, plasma cell CD, which is more common in adults, is characterized by fever, weight loss, chronic fatigue, general weakness, skin rash, and respiratory problems. Hepatosplenomegaly (abnormally large liver and spleen; NORD, 2000) may also be evident. Laboratory findings may include hemolytic anemia and hypergammaglobulinemia (increase of certain immune factors in the blood).
4. The intermediate type of CD may show features of both the hyaline-vascular and plasma cell variants.
5. Renal complications such as nephrotic syndrome have been infrequently reported.

The medical treatment of CD varies depending on its histologic variant, its clinical expression, and its severity. Surgical excision of localized tumors has been successful (Maslovsky & Lugassy, 1999) with the virtual disappearance of all symptoms following surgery; however, some recurrence of symptoms has been noted in adults (Tuerlinckx, Bodart, Delos, Remacle, & Ninane, 1997). Because multicentric CD is marked by a swift, often fatal course, treatment necessitates the use of aggressive chemotherapeutic regimens (Maslovsky & Lugassy, 1999). Some successes have been reported in the use of prednisone and retinoic acid (Parez et al., 2000; Rieu, Drooz, Gessain, Grunfeld, & Hermine, 1999), interferon-alpha (Kumari et al., 2000), and immunity-restoring methods such as HAART (Lanzafame, Carretta, Trevenzoli, Lazzarini, & Concia, 2000). Because patients present with immunosuppressive deficits, it has also been suggested (Maslovsky & Lugassy, 1999) that infections be treated promptly and that organ and blood donors be carefully screened.

Psychoeducational interventions for the child with CD depend on clinical presentation and degree of involvement. Children with localized CD may not have significant difficulties in a classroom other than those temporarily involved with surgery and postsurgical recovery. Children who present with the plasma cell multicentric variant may experience significant difficulties, particularly if the disease is not treated early or if it is inadequately managed. Many of these children will qualify for special educational services under Other Health Impairment; as such, the Individualized Educational Plan (IEP) must offer comprehensive efforts designed to address the whole range of needs, including academic, medical, social, and behavioral. As the disease progresses, children with multicentric CD may be hospitalized or homebound, and arrangements may have to be made for continued instruction as long as it is appropriate. Personal counseling may be beneficial for children and families, and vocational counseling should also be offered for adolescents.

Additional research studies are needed to clarify both the etiology and the pathophysiology of CD with a view to improving treatment options for affected individuals (Parez et al., 1999). Further, because CD has such variable clinical expression for age, it is anticipated that future research efforts will be directed toward differential management of the disease in children and adults.

REFERENCES

De Heer-Groen, T. A., Prakken, A. B. J., Bax, N. M. A., & van Dijken, P. J. (1996). Iron therapy resistant microcytic anemia in a 13-year old girl with Castleman disease. *European Journal of Pediatrics, 155,* 1015–1017.

Fiel-Gan, M. D., Voytek, T. M., Weiss, R. G., Brown, R. T., & Joshi, V. V. (2000). Castleman's disease of the left triceps in a child suspected to be a small round cell tumor of childhood. *Pedriatic and Developmental Pathology, 3,* 286–289.

Kumari, P., Schechter, G. P., Saini, N., & Benator, D. A. (2000). Successful treatment of human immunodeficiency virus-related Castleman's disease with interferon-alpha. *Clinical Infectious Diseases, 31*(2), 602–604.

Lanzafame, N., Carretta, G., Trevenzoli, M., Lassarini, L., & Concia, S. V. E. (2000). Successful treatment of Castleman's disease with HAART in two HIV-infected patients. *Journal of Infection, 40*(1), 90–91.

Malaguarnera, L., Pilastro, M. R., Vicari, L., Di Marco, R., Malaguarnera, M., & Messina, A. (1999). Ornithine decarboxylase gene expression in Castleman's disease. *Journal of Molecular Medicine, 77,* 798–803.

Maslovsky, I., & Lugassy, G. (1999). The management of Castleman's disease. *Blood, 94*(10), 4391.

National Organization for Rare Disorders, Inc. (2000). Castleman's disease. Retrieved from http://www.rarediseases.org

Parez, N., Bader-Meunier, B., Roy, C. C., & Dommergues, J. P. (1999). Paediatric Castleman disease: Report of seven cases and a review of the literature. *European Journal of Pediatrics, 158*(8), 631–637.

Plaza, M. C., & Gilbert-Barness, E. (2000). Castleman's disease: Pediatric pathology case. *Pediatric Pathology and Molecular Medicine, 19*(6), 487–490.

Rieu, P., Drooz, D., Gessain, A., Grunfeld, J. P., & Hermine, O. (1999). Retinoic acid for treatment of multicentric Castleman's disease. *Lancet, 354*(9186), 1262–1263.

Schulz, T. F. (2000). Kaposi's sarcoma-associated herpervirus (human herpesvirus 8): Epidemiology and pathogenesis. *Journal of Antimicrobial Chemotherapy, 45,* 15–27.

Smir, B. N., Greiner, T. C., & Weisenburger, D. D. (1996). Multicentric angiofollicular lymph node hyperplasia in children: A clinicopathologic study of eight patients. *Modern Pathology, 9*(12), 1135–1142.

Tuerlinckx, D., Bodart, E., Delos, M., Remacle, M., & Ninane, J. (1997). Unifocal cervical Castleman disease in two children. *European Journal of Pediatrics, 156,* 701–703.

Mary M. Chittooran
Saint Louis University

CAT EYE SYNDROME

Cat eye syndrome (CES) is a malformation involving an extra marker chromosome derived from Chromosome 22. CES shows characteristic features such as ocular coloboma of the iris, giving the appearance of a vertical pupil, hence the name. However, over half of the reported cases do not manifest this feature (Masukawa, Ozaki, & Nogimori, 1998). This chromosomal abnormality usually arises spontaneously, although there are reports of intergenerational family transmission. Transmission appears to be possible through both sexes. Some reports show the parents as mosaic for the marker chromosome but without phenotypic symptoms of the syndrome (McKusick, 1998).

CES is believed to be a very rare condition, but no reliable estimates are available. Estimates based on reported cases from northeast Switzerland during the past 20 years suggest incidence estimates ranging from 1:50,000 to 1:150,000. CES was first described in 1965 by Schachenmann and colleagues, and since then more than 40 cases have been reported in the literature (Liehr, Pfeiffer, & Trautmann, 1992). Variability in symptom manifestation is enormous, with the following characteristics listed in order of decreasing frequency. Rarer malformations can affect almost any organ, but the eyes are preferentially affected (McKusick, 1998).

Characteristics

1. Anal atresia (abnormal obstruction of the anus)
2. Unilateral or bilateral iris coloboma (absence of tissue from the colored part of the eyes)
3. Palpebral fissures (downward slanting openings between upper and lower eyelids)
4. Preauricular pits or tags (small depressions or growths of skin on outer ears)
5. Cardiac defects
6. Kidney problems (missing, extra, or underdeveloped kidneys)
7. Short stature
8. Scoliosis/skeletal problems
9. Mental retardation (mostly borderline normal to mildly retarded, a few of normal intelligence, rarely moderate to severe)
10. Micrognathia (smaller jaw)
11. Hernias
12. Cleft palate
13. Rarer malformations that can affect almost any organ

Treatment considerations include surgery for anal atresia and complex cardiac malformations. In addition, with intestinal problems malrotation, Meckel diverticulum, and biliary atresia (related to passage of bile) must be considered. Further surgical procedures may be indicated if hernias or cleft palate are present. Patients with very short stature may have additional hypothalamic growth hormone deficiency and therefore be candidates for growth hormone therapy (McKusick, 1998). Orthopedic treatment for scoliosis may be a treatment issue as well. Genetic counseling will likely be recommended for families affected by CES.

Special education considerations include the possibility of growth retardation and other physical abnormalities that may require medical treatment and interfere with regular school attendance or progress. Mental retardation is possible. Most individuals with CES function in the borderline normal to mildly retarded range; a few are within the normal range of cognitive functioning; and some are moderately to severely retarded, although the latter condition is rare. Affected individuals may be eligible for special education services as Other Health Impairment, Mentally Retarded, or Orthopedically Handicapped, depending on specific symptoms and their severities. Behavioral problems have been reported in individual cases but are not characteristic of the disorder (Schinzel et al., 1981). Information regarding neuropsychological or educational functioning in individuals affected with CES is not available in the literature.

Life expectancy is not significantly reduced in patients who do not present with life-threatening abnormalities. However, a few patients die from multiple malformations during early infancy (Schinzel et al., 1981). Future research should focus on patterns of cognitive strength and weakness in children affected with CES, both through case studies and through collections of data across reported cases, to further inform educational interventions. Issues of psychosocial development, family adjustment, and effectiveness of medical and educational interventions are also important.

REFERENCES

Liehr, T., Pfeiffer, R. A., & Trautmann, U. (1992). Typical and partial cat eye syndrome: Identification of the marker chromosome by FISH. *Clinical Genetics, 42,* 91–96.

Masukawa, H., Ozaki, T., & Nogimori, T. (1998). Cat eye syndrome with hypogonadotropic hypogonadism. *Internal Medicine, 37*(10), 853–855.

McKusick, V. A. (1998, October 9). Cat eye syndrome. In *Online Mendelian inheritance in man database* [Online]. Available from http://www.ncbi.nlm.nih.gov/htbin-post/Omim

Schinzel, A., Schmid, W., Fraccaro, M., Tiepolo, L., Zuffardi, O., Opitz, J. M., Lindsten, J., Zetterqvist, P., Enell, H., Baccichetti, C., Tenconi, R., & Pagon, R. A. (1981). The "cat eye syndrome": Decentric small marker chromosome probably derived from a 22 associated with a characteristic phenotype. Report of 11 patients and delineation of the clinical picture. *Human Genetics, 57,* 148–158.

Cynthia A. Plotts
Southwest Texas State University

CAT-SCRATCH DISEASE

Cat-scratch disease is a bacillary infection that primarily affects children and adolescents. It is caused by the bacterium *Bartonella henselae* and is transmitted via feline saliva. Felines contract the disease through fleas, and humans are infected when bitten or scratched by an infected cat, typically a very young cat. The disease is typically benign and self-limiting; that is, the symptoms are mild and tend to resolve within 2 to 4 months without treatment.

Serious complications are infrequent, that is, found in less than 10% of all cases (Busen & Scarborough, 1997). Although considered the least hazardous cause of encephalopathy (Carithers & Margileth, 1991), neurologic involvement occurs in about 2% of cases, including coma, seizures, temporary blindness, lethargy, and combative behavior (Wheeler, Wolf, & Steinberg, 1997). Other central nervous system problems include cranial and peripheral nerve palsy (e.g., facial weakness) and neuroretinitis (inflammation of the retina and optic nerve of the eye). Osteitis, which is a chronic bone infection, is another serious complication of cat-scratch disease.

Cat-scratch disease is estimated to affect 22,000 persons per year in the United States, resulting in hospitalization for 2,000 of those infected (Jackson, Perkins, & Wenger, 1993). In about 80% of cases, the age of onset is less than 21 years. Certain times of the year increase the risk factors for contracting the disease. For example, 75% of cases are reported from September through March. Males are slightly more likely to contract the disease than are females, with ratios reported to be about 3:2 (Carithers & Margileth, 1991).

Characteristics

1. Contracted through the saliva of a cat by a scratch or bite. Chronic lymphadenitis (i.e., swollen and tender lymph nodes) is the hallmark feature.
2. The disease is typically self-limiting, and symptoms remit spontaneously within 2 to 4 months without treatment except in cases of a compromised immune system.
3. Neurologic involvement such as encephalopathy may occur, but full recovery is expected.
4. The disease is considered nonfatal, but death has been implicated in .03% of cases.

Treatment depends on the severity of the sequelae. For example, in cases where fevers, conjunctivitis, and seizures occur, medications are likely to be used. Antibiotics are frequently prescribed to treat the disease (e.g., lymphadenopathy); however, there is considerable debate as to their effectiveness (Busen & Scarborough, 1997).

Prognosis for recovery is generally excellent. Even in cases where there is central nervous system involvement (e.g., seizures and blindness), recovery typically occurs within 12 months of onset (Wheeler et al., 1997). Although cat-scratch disease is considered nonfatal, some researchers have reported deaths. For example, Jackson et al. (1993) reported mortality in .03% of cases.

Special education is not likely to be required, except in cases where complications occur and achievement is affected. In these cases, services are likely to be provided under the category Other Health Impairment. Regular monitoring will be needed to determine how best to meet the child's educational needs. Because most recovery of neurologic problems occurs within the first year, short-term interventions are likely to be sufficient. In most cases, however, symptoms remit within the first few months; therefore, interventions need to be directed to facilitating recovery, including reduction of assignments and stimulation in and outside the classroom (e.g., playground). Parents should be involved so that information about the child's progress can be communicated among all professionals involved, including the child's treating physician.

Research is needed to increase understanding regarding the efficacy of antibiotic treatment. Further information about morbidity is also needed.

REFERENCES

Busen, N. H., & Scarborough, T. (1997, July 1). Diagnosis and management of cat-scratch disease in primary care. *Internet Journal of Advanced Nursing Practice, 1*(2). Retrieved July 1, 1997, from http://www.ispub.com/journals/IJANP/Vol1N2/catscratch.htm

Carithers, H., & Margileth, A. M. (1991). Cat-scratch disease. *American Journal of Diseases of Children, 145*(1), 98–101.

Jackson, L., Perkins, B., & Wenger, J. (1993). Cat scratch disease in the United States: An analysis of three national databases. *American Journal of Public Health, 83*(12), 1707–1711.

Wheeler, S., Wolf, S., & Steinberg, E. (1997). Cat-scratch encephalopathy. *Neurology, 49*(3), 876–878.

Heather Edgel
Elaine Clark
University of Utah

CATARACTS

A cataract is an ocular disease of the lens (a flexible, transparent structure located posterior to the pupil and iris that focuses light rays on the retina) or of the connective tissue capsule that encloses it (Gale Encyclopedia of Medicine, 1999). Opacity (cloudiness) caused by a cataract can lead to decreased vision and may eventually result in blindness if left untreated; in fact, cataracts have been identified as the major cause of blindness and visual impairment in adults (Harding, 1999). Cataracts can occur in various areas of the lens and capsule; they may be located in the center of the lens (nuclear cataracts), in the area surrounding the nucleus (cortical cataracts), or within the capsule (posterior subcapular cataracts; Gale Encyclopedia of Medicine).

Although cataracts occur in people of all ages, they are

most common among the elderly. An individual has a 50% chance of developing a cataract between the ages of 52 and 64, and this risk increases to 70% in those 70 and older (Gale Encyclopedia of Medicine, 1999). Congenital cataracts occur rarely, with a reported incidence that ranges between 1 and 6 for every 10,000 live births (Francis, Berry, Bhattacharya, & Moore, 2000; National Organization for Rare Disorders, Inc., 2000). The terms *congenital* and *infantile* cataract are often used interchangeably in clinical practice (Rahi & Dezateux, 2000).

The etiology of cataracts tends to vary, depending on the age of the affected individual. Cataracts in adults are often associated with the normal aging process; among infants and children, cataracts may be caused by ocular disorders, maternal infections, metabolic disorders, hereditary disorders, or idiopathic (unknown) factors (Rahi & Dezateux, 2000). The majority of congenital and infantile cataracts are caused by idiopathic and hereditary disorders (Rahi & Dezateux). Genetic mutations in eight genes have been implicated in the formation of autosomal dominant congenital cataracts (Francis et al., 2000). Additional causes of cataracts include exposure to toxic agents, trauma, radiation, and nutritional deficiencies (Ayala, Michael, & Söderberg, 2000). Chronic steroid use in the treatment of juvenile rheumatoid arthritis can also cause cataracts (Weiss, Wallace, & Sherry, 1998). Cataracts may also develop in association with systemic illnesses, such as diabetes mellitus (Falck & Laatikainen, 1998). In a 20-year longitudinal study, researchers determined that 1% of a population comprised of 600 diabetic patients ranging in age from 9.1 to 17.5 years of age eventually developed cataracts (Falck & Laatikainen). It has been suggested (e.g., Scarpitta, Perrone, & Sinagra, 1997) that elevated blood glucose levels are associated with biochemical changes within the lens that can result in the formation of cataracts.

Characteristics

1. Vision becomes blurred during cataract development. Cataract size and density may remain stable or increase.
2. The lens may become swollen.
3. As the cataract matures, the lens may lose fluid and shrink.
4. In a final stage of development, the lens may either solidify or become filled with fluid.
5. Blindness may result if the cataract is left untreated.

Cataracts that do not interfere with vision are often left untreated but are monitored and assessed by an optometrist or ophthalmologist. Surgery is the only existing treatment for cataracts that interfere significantly with vision. The diseased lens may be removed in one of three ways (Gale Encyclopedia of Medicine, 1999):

1. *Intracapsular surgery:* The lens and capsule are both removed.
2. *Extracapsular surgery:* The lens and the front part of the capsule are extracted.
3. *Phacoemulsification:* Ultrasonic vibration breaks the lens into extremely small pieces that are subsequently removed by aspiration.

An intraocular lens made of silicone or plastic is usually inserted into the eye during surgery to replace the diseased lens.

The risks associated with cataract surgery are minimal. Possible complications, which have been reported in only a very small percentage of patients, include endophthalmitis (infection), macular edema (retinal inflammation), retinal detachment, choroidal hemorrhage (bleeding under the retina), and onset of glaucoma (Gale Encyclopedia of Medicine, 1999). Children and adults differ in their response to cataract surgery (Magnusson, Abrahamsson, & Sjöstrand, 2000); for example, posterior capsular opacification is a postsurgical complication that occurs in 50% of adult patients but affects almost 100% of younger patients (Harding, 1999). It is suggested that diabetic patients be monitored following cataract surgery for the possible development of proliferative retinopathy (Falck & Laatikainen, 1998). Overall, however, the prognosis for cataract surgery is highly positive, with improved visual acuity normally following surgery and a lens implant (Gale Encyclopedia of Medicine).

Children presenting with cataracts may qualify for special educational services, depending upon severity and condition. Impaired vision may be addressed on an Individualized Educational Plan, and schools may need to provide specific accommodations to meet children's academic and behavioral needs. Personal counseling and prosthetic lenses may be beneficial for children who suffer low self-esteem due to anatomical defects caused by cataract surgery (Rakow, 2000). Students with diabetes and associated cataracts may need to take insulin injections at school and regulate their diet to prevent further complications. Cataracts associated with systemic disorders may require additional educational consideration, depending on the type and severity of the disorder. For example, cataracts may occur in association with chromosomal abnormalities such as Trisomy 21, a hereditary condition that is marked by moderate to severe mental retardation and that requires educational accommodations. In all cases involving genetically determined lenticular disease, genetic counseling prior to marriage and pregnancy is strongly recommended.

Additional research is needed to determine associated risk factors and prevention of cataracts. Researchers are expected to investigate the effects of smoking and alcohol consumption on cataract formation, as well as the use of anticataract drugs in the treatment and prevention of cataracts. Alternative medications for treating juvenile rheumatoid arthritis are also being investigated (Weiss, Wallace, & Sherry, 1998). Additional genetic mapping research is expected to continue in an effort to provide further insight into the genetic causes of cataracts. An increased understanding of the causes of molecular defects may lead to future therapeutic intervention for congenital cataracts.

REFERENCES

Ayala, M., Michael, R., & Söderberg, P. (2000). Influence of exposure time for UV radiation-induced cataract. *Investigative Ophthalmology and Visual Science, 41*(11), 3539–3543.

Falck, A., & Laatikainen, L. (1998). Diabetic cataract in children. *Acta Ophthalmologica Scandinavica, 76*(2), 238–240.

Francis, P. J., Berry, V., Bhattacharya, S. S., & Moore, A. T. (2000). The genetics of childhood cataract. *Journal of Medical Genetics, 37*(7), 481–488.

Gale encyclopedia of medicine. (1999). Cataracts. Detroit, MI: Author.

Harding, J. J. (1999). Can cataract be prevented? *Eye, 13,* 454–456.

Magnusson, G., Abrahamsson, M., & Sjöstrand, J. (2000). Glaucoma following congenital cataract surgery: An 18-year longitudinal follow-up. *Acta Ophthalmologica Scandinavica, 78*(1), 65–70.

National Organization for Rare Disorders, Inc. (2000). Cataracts. Retrieved from http://www.rarediseases.org

Rahi, J., & Dezateux, C. (2000). Congenital and infantile cataract in the United Kingdom: Underlying or associated factors. *Investigative Ophthalmology and Visual Science, 41*(8), 2108–2114.

Rakow, P. (2000). Making miracles with prosthetic soft lenses. *Journal of Ophthalmic Nursing and Technology, 18*(3), 120–122.

Scarpitta, A. M., Perrone, P., & Sinagra, D. (1997). The diabetic cataract: An unusual presentation in a young subject: Case report. *Journal of Diabetes and Its Complications, 11*(4), 259–260.

Weiss, A. H., Wallace, C. A., & Sherry, D. D. (1998). Methotrexate for resistant chronic uveitis in children with juvenile rheumatoid arthritis. *The Journal of Pediatrics, 133*(2), 266–268.

Retha M. Edens
Mary M. Chittooran
Saint Louis University

CENTRAL AUDITORY PROCESSING DISORDER

Central auditory processing disorder (CAPD) is the term used to describe audiological difficulties that are characterized by reduced abilities to process auditory information in individuals with normal peripheral hearing. CAPD includes difficulties in locating the source and direction of sounds, discriminating between sounds, recognizing patterns of sounds, ordering sounds that are presented in close temporal proximity, and discerning sounds in background noise (American Speech-Language-Hearing Association [ASHA], 1996).

Characteristics (ASHA, 1996)

1. Poor listening skills
2. Difficulty hearing in situations with background noise
3. Difficulty with localization of sounds
4. Difficulty following directions
5. High distractability by irrelevant noise
6. Inattention
7. History of ear infections
8. Academic difficulties, particularly in reading and spelling

The incidence of CAPD is difficult to determine but is thought to be from 3% to 5% (Chermack & Musiek, 1997). Although CAPD is estimated to be more common than hearing loss, it is diagnosed less often. Children with CAPD are a heterogeneous group; not all children with CAPD have the same difficulties and are often misdiagnosed as having unrecognized comorbidity with attention-deficit/hyperactivity disorder (ADHD) and other language disorders (Riccio, Hynd, Cohen, Hall, & Molt, 1994). There is no evidence of differences in incidence by ethnic groups. The high comorbidity with language and learning problems suggests that CAPD may be more likely to occur in males, but this has not been documented.

A preliminary screening for CAPD may include information about cognitive functioning, speech-language development, peripheral hearing status, behavioral observations, and audiological screening (Bellis, 1996). An audiologist may use a test battery to gather information about the child's dichotic listening skills (different sounds presented to both ears simultaneously), temporal ordering abilities (sequencing of sounds), and binaural interactions (a method in which ears function together). The major challenge to identification of CAPD is the lack of acceptance on measures that should be included in the battery (Schow, Seikel, Chermak, & Berent, 2000).

There are no research-supported treatments at this time for CAPD, but there are some effective management techniques. Addressing the individual needs of a child with CAPD would include modifications to the environment, remediation, and development of compensatory abilities (Bellis, 1996). Each child's auditory profile would determine the most appropriate modifications; however, there are some general recommendations. Environmental changes can include decreasing background noise, improving the room's acoustics by covering hard floors and walls, using preferential seating, monitoring understanding frequently, using several modalities for learning, using advanced organizers for new information and vocabulary, providing lecture notes to the child, and using repetition and rephrasing during presentation of material (Bellis, 1996). It may be helpful to educate the older child about their disorder so the individual can help monitor their own needs for environmental modifications.

Special education or services under Section 504 of the Americans with Disabilities Act may be appropriate for a child with CAPD. Difficulty with the recognition of phonemes due to auditory processing deficits may effect receptive language development. The child's Individual Education Plan should include appropriate environmental modifications. The disorder may qualify the child for special education services under the learning disability or specific language impairments categories to the extent that the disorder can affect the child's ability to learn (Individuals with Disabilities Education Act, 1997). Difficulty with the recognition of phonemes due to auditory processing deficits may affect receptive language development.

Current research is examining the etiology of CAPD and its relationships to other disorders. Of particular interest has been the relation with ADHD and learning disabilities (Riccio et al., 1994). Genetic factors, neurological development, brain lesions, and reoccurring episodes of otitis media are indicated as risk factors for the auditory dysfunction that affects dichotic listening, temporal processing, and binaural integration of auditory information (Bellis, 1996).

Future research may focus on etiologies of CAPD to improve our ability to prevent and treat the disorder as well as on symptom management. Greater understanding of the etiology will aid in more accurate diagnoses of CAPD and comorbidities with other disorders.

REFERENCES

American Speech-Language-Hearing Association, Report of the Task Force on Central Auditory Processing Consensus Development. (1996). *American Journal of Audiology, 5*(2), 41–54.

Bellis, T. J. (1996). *Assessment and management of central auditory processing disorders in the educational system: From science to practice.* San Diego, CA: Singular Publishing Group.

Chermack, G., & Musiek, F. (1997). *Central auditory processing disorders: New perspectives.* San Diego, CA: Singular Publishing Group.

Individuals with Disabilities Education Act. (1997). (PUB. L. No. 101–476). 20 U.S.C. Chapter 33. Amended by Pub.L. No. 105017.

Riccio, C. A., Hynd, G. W., Cohen, M. J., Hall, J., & Molt, L. (1994). Comorbidity of central auditory processing disorder and attention deficit hyperactivity disorder. *Journal of the American Academy of Child and Adolescent Psychiatry, 33,* 849–857.

Schow, R. L., Seikel, J. A., Chermak, G. D., & Berent, M. (2000). Central auditory processes and test measures: ASHA 1996 revisited. *American Journal of Audiology, 9,* 1–6.

Monica E. Wolfe
Cynthia A. Riccio
Texas A&M University

CENTRAL CORE DISEASE

Central core disease (CCD) is a relatively rare genetic disorder usually detected in infancy or early childhood. Central core disease tends to affect males and females in equal numbers. It is an autosomal dominant trait. Although less common, CCD has occurred spontaneously without a family history. This disease is characterized by abnormalities of skeletal muscles. Associated symptoms include diminished muscle tone, muscle weakness, delays in motor development, and musculoskeletal problems such as a dislocated hip at birth. In addition, CCD is associated with susceptibility to malignant hyperthermia. Malignant hyperthermia is a potentially life-threatening reaction to muscle relaxants and anesthetics. For this reason, it is essential that this risk be taken into consideration by surgeons, anesthesiologists, dentists, and other health care providers when making decisions regarding medical or dental treatments (Online Mendelian Inheritance in Man, 2000).

Typically, CCD is detected in infancy; however, some cases can go undetected until childhood, adolescence, and even adulthood. Infants diagnosed with CCD have been reported to be delivered in breech position. In addition, the infant may demonstrate limited head support and poor muscle tone. Commonly, the muscle weakness is greater in muscles closest to the trunk such as the shoulders, upper arms, hips, and thighs. Mild muscle weakness may also be evident in the facial muscles. Central core disease is a nonprogressive disorder that usually does not continue to become more severe with time. However, as previously noted, infants with CCD may demonstrate difficulty reaching developmental milestones such as crawling, standing, walking, climbing stairs, and running. For this reason, a pediatric orthopedist is essential to monitor and mediate the delays (Online Mendelian Inheritance in Man, 2000; Wyngaarden, 1992).

Characteristics

1. Abnormalities of skeletal muscles
2. Diminished muscle tone
3. Delays in motor development
4. Dislocated hip at birth

Central core disease is symptomatically treated. The treatment specialists are dependent on the symptoms presented in the affected individual. In some cases orthopedic interventions are essential to help prevent and treat different musculoskeletal abnormalities associated with this disorder. Physical and occupational services may also be useful to help with mobility and exercise. With infants experiencing severe weakness, a feeding tube may be required; thus, nutritional counseling would be recommended to ensure that the infant is getting the proper nutrients. School professionals may also be needed to help with necessary physical or learning modifications for the child depending on the limitations experienced by the child.

Because of the chronicity of this disorder, psychological services can help the affected individual as well as the family develop strategies to cope with the impacts of CCD (Wyngaarden, 1992).

REFERENCES

Online Mendelian inheritance in man. (2000). Retrieved from http://www.ncbi.nlm.nih.gov/omim/

Wyngaarden, J. B. (1992). *Cecil textbook of medicine* (19th ed.). Philadelphia: W. B. Saunders.

Lisa A. Fasnacht-Hill
Keck University of Southern California School of Medicine
University of Southern California / University Affiliated Program at Children's Hospital of Los Angeles

CENTRAL HYPOVENTILATION SYNDROME (CONGENITAL)

Congenital central hypoventilation syndrome (CCHS) is a neurological disorder typically found in infants and children. It is characterized by normal respiration during waking hours but abnormal respiration during sleep. A diagnosis of CCHS should be considered when other brainstem, lung, cardiac, or primary neuromuscular diseases have been ruled out. About 160–180 cases are identified in the world, but because it is so rare, many cases may go undiagnosed due to the physician's inability to diagnose the condition accurately (American Thoracic Society, 1999). CCHS is often mistaken for other diseases, so it is critical that the disorder be carefully diagnosed. CCHS is sometimes also known as congenital alveolar hypoventilation, congenital failure of autonomic control of respiration, idiopathic alveolar hypoventilation, Ondine's curse, primary alveolar hypoventilation, primary central hypoventilation syndrome, and idiopathic congenital central hypoventilation syndrome.

CCHS is frequently identified in newborns but may not be diagnosed until infancy. Symptoms may become manifested in the early adult years. It is characterized by ongoing difficulty with the control of breathing, particularly during sleep. As a result, the lungs do not get enough air, and tissues in the body are damaged from a lack of sufficient oxygen. CCHS may also result in feeding problems in infants. Other symptoms may be severe constipation, profuse sweating, and decreased body temperature (Hill & Goldberg, 1998). Patients with CCHS may also exhibit changes in the central nervous system (Gallina et al., 2000). If left untreated, this disorder may lead to serious complications such as organ damage and death.

In order to diagnose CCHS, it is necessary for the physician to perform a comprehensive history and physical examination. The patient should have a complete neurological evaluation, rectal biopsy, and ophthalmologic evaluation. A monitor should be used to determine patterns of spontaneous breathing while the patient is asleep and awake.

Characteristics

1. Normal respiration during waking hours, but abnormal respiration during sleep
2. May cause feeding problems in infants
3. Possibly severe constipation, profuse sweating, decreased body temperature, heart rate variability, eye irregularities, and changes in the central nervous system

Treatment of CCHS depends on the severity of the disorder. A mechanical ventilator may be used. It is critical that skilled caregivers closely monitor the patient. Parents of young children can be trained to operate the ventilator at home, but a trained nurse may also be needed. More serious cases may require a tracheostomy. In these cases, a one-way speaking valve called a Passy-Muir is used for the child to vocalize when awake (American Thoracic Society, 1999). Gozal and Simakajornboon (2000) have suggested that ventilation in children who are awake may be improved by passive motion of the feet and ankles.

Although the disorder may improve with age, CCHS is usually a lifelong diagnosis. Respiration, growth, speech, mental, and motor development should be monitored regularly. Infants and young children should be evaluated by a pediatrician and a pulmonologist every one to two months. After the age of 3 years, thorough checks should be conducted annually.

Children with CCHS must be watched closely for infections. They are not necessarily able to recognize or respond to hypoxemia (American Thoracic Society, 1999). Activity should be moderate with frequent periods of rest. Patients should participate in only noncontact sports; however, swimming is not recommended without constant supervision.

At school, children with CCHS may require special monitoring by the teacher and school nurse. They may also need to engage in limited and supervised activity. Specialized equipment may be necessary.

Tissue and organ damage may result in a variety of physical and cognitive difficulties. Depending on the individual situation, this may necessitate special education services. Some studies have found that CCHS frequently recurs in families. Ongoing research is being conducted to investigate the possibility of a genetic factor (Gozal, 1999).

If treated early and appropriately, chances of survival are good for patients with CCHS. Technological treatments can provide a good quality of life. The ultimate goal of treatment is to find the appropriate technology for each patient's lifestyle. As advances in technology occur, new methods of treatment for CCHS may be developed. Unfortunately, these types of treatments may be costly, and financial support may be inhibited by health care providers.

REFERENCES

American Thoracic Society. (1999). Idiopathic congenital central hypoventilation syndrome. *American Journal of Respiratory and Critical Care Medicine, 160*(1), 368–373.

Gallina, S., Restivo, S., Cupido, G., Speciale, R., Giammanco, A. M., & Cimino, G. (2000). Otoneurological findings in a case of congenital central hypoventilation syndrome (Ondine's curse). *Acta Otorhinolaryngologica Italica, 20*(2), 121–124.

Gozal, D. (1999). Novel insights into congenital hypoventilation syndrome. *Current Opinions in Pulmonary Medicine, 5*(6), 335–338.

Gozal, D., & Simakajornboon, N. (2000). Passive motion of the extremities modifies alveolar ventilation during sleep in patients with congenital central hypoventilation syndrome. *American Journal of Respiratory and Critical Care Medicine, 162*(2), 1747–1751.

Hill, N. S., & Goldberg, A. I. (1998). Mechanical ventilation beyond the intensive care unit: Report of a consensus conference of the American college of chest physicians. *Chest, 113*(5), 298S–344S.

Michele Wilson Kamens
Rider University

CEREBELLAR DISORDERS

The cerebellum, meaning "little brain," lies beneath the cerebral cortex and is attached to the brain stem. The cerebellum consists of three lobes, the middle (or vermis) and the outer (right and left) lobes. The cerebellum regulates muscle coordination and balance; therefore, damage to the area often leads to jerky and uncoordinated movements, as well as poor balance. Recent research also associates abnormalities in the cerebellum with cognitive and social deficits, even autistic-like behaviors. Riva and Georgi (2000), for example, demonstrated that children with right hemisphere cerebellum lesions had difficulty processing language and had poor auditory memory, whereas those with left hemisphere cerebellar lesions had visual spatial memory problems. Individuals with lesions in the middle region of the vermis showed added behavioral dysfunction, including autistic-like symptoms and postsurgical mutism.

Disorders involving the cerebellum may be present from birth or acquired later in life. Examples of congenital conditions involving the cerebellum include cerebellar arteriovenous malformations (i.e., abnormal blood vessel configuration; Griffith et al., 1998), spina bifida meningomylelocele, and Dandy-Walker syndrome (Yeates, Ris, & Taylor, 2000). Examples of acquired conditions include traumatic brain injuries (TBIs) and brain tumors. Cerebellar dysfunction can also be a cause of acquired brain injuries, especially in cases where balance is lost or distances are misjudged.

Characteristics

1. Uncoordinated muscle movements (sometimes jerky) and poor balance
2. Dysmetria, or difficulty judging distances
3. Headaches, vomiting, seizure, vision changes, drowsiness, and confusion

When tumors are the cause of cerebellar dysfunction, surgery is the treatment of choice (at times with adjunctive therapies such as radiation and chemotherapy). Surgery is also used when cerebellum problems are caused by congenital or acquired hydrocephalus or when a head injury causes a depressed skull fracture that requires evacuation of bone, blood, or fluid. In most cases of head injury, however, treatment will be limited to symptomatic relief that allows time for recovery.

Special education, if needed at all, is typically provided under the category Other Health Impairment. If a brain injury, however, is the cause of the cerebellar abnormality, a classification of TBI may be more appropriate. Regardless of the need for special education, children with cerebellar disorders are likely to need some classroom accommodations and services from a physical or occupational therapist. Speech and language services and psychological consultation (including counseling) may also be appropriate. Like the treatment, the prognosis for a child with a cerebellar disorder depends on the underlying cause and severity of symptoms and disability.

REFERENCES

Griffith, P. D., Bladser, S., Armstrong, D., Chuang, S., Humphreys, R. P., & Harwood-Nash, D. (1998). Cerebellar arteriovenous malformations in children. *Neuroradiology, 40,* 324–331.

Riva, D., & Giorgi, C. (2000). The cerebellum contributes to higher functions during development: Evidence from a series of children surgically treated for posterior fossa tumors. *Brain, 123,* 1051–1061.

Yeates, K. O., Ris, M. D., & Taylor, H. G. (2000). *Pediatric neuropsychology: Research, theory, and practice.* New York: Guilford Press.

Laura Richards
Elaine Clark
University of Utah

CEREBRAL INFARCT

Cerebral infarct refers to the sudden insufficiency of blood flow to the brain causing decreased oxygen and subsequent tissue death. A partial or complete occlusion causes the disruption of venous or arterial blood flow. Infarcts from arterial blood occlusions, however, are more common in full-term infants (than premature infants). Most infarcts to single arteries are superficial and affect both the gray and white matter (i.e., tissue closest to the blockage). Single infarcts suggest trauma (e.g., misuse of forceps for delivery or hyperextension of the infant's neck), whereas multiple infarcts suggest prenatal problems causing emboli or vasculitis (e.g., congenital heart disease and maternal use of cocaine during pregnancy; Fenichel, 1993).

Cerebral infarcts are rare in children; in fact, the rate of cerebral blood supply problems (i.e., stroke) for children under 14 years of age is estimated to be only 2 in 100,000 (Biller, Mathews, & Love, 1994). Magnetic resonance imaging (MRI) and unenhanced computerized tomography (CT) scan are commonly used to diagnose small infarcts, and ultrasound is used to detect large infarcts (e.g., in the middle cerebral artery). Imaging needs to be performed no sooner than 24 hr from the time of infarction in order for the lesion to be seen. The most common infarcts are in the internal carotid artery, lacunar, and vertebrobasilar system. Symptoms are largely determined by the age of the child and location of damage. Hemiplegia (i.e., one-sided weakness) of the face and limbs, however, is one of the most common sequelae. Speech problems (e.g., dysarthria) also occur, as does faintness and vertigo. Seizures are less common but have been associated with complications such as subarachnoid hemorrhages.

Characteristics

1. Single artery infarct seen more in full-term infants (trauma induced) and multiartery infarction seen more with congenital anomalies.
2. Symptoms depend on age of child and location of damage, but one-sided weakness is fairly common.
3. Dysarthric speech, clumsiness, unsteady gait, vertigo, and seizure can occur.
4. In some cases, no neurologic symptoms are evident, or are only temporary (i.e., less than 24 hours).

Volume replacement to increase blood flow and oxygen delivery to ischemic areas is the optimal treatment; however, most therapies are intended to treat symptoms and complications (e.g., anticonvulsants). For example, given the relatively high rate of motor problems, physical and occupational therapy is likely to be needed. Not all children with cerebral infarcts will require special education services; however, in some cases this will be critical. For infants who have infarcts, early programming will be required to ensure optimal outcome. In addition to services from the occupational and physical therapists, speech and language therapy will likely be needed as the child ages. Children who suffer significant damage may even require self-contained special education classrooms (e.g., Intellectual Disabilities). The majority will suffice with resource and related services (e.g., programs for students with Learning Disabilities and Other Health Impairments). School psychological services and counseling may also be needed to help the child adapt to the school environment and help parents better manage the child's problems and provide additional support at home. Putting parents in contact with community agencies and services may also be an invaluable service for children with infarcts.

Prognosis depends on a number of factors, not the least of which have to do with age of the child at the time of the infarct, the infarct location, and severity of damage. Although recovery begins in the first three months following the infarct, the process may take years, and even then the child may not be at his or her premorbid level. When complications take place, the chances of returning to normal baselines are even poorer. For example, children who have associated epilepsy that impacts oxygen to the brain, or cerebral edema that inhibits blood flow, thereby reducing oxygen, all have the potential negatively to impact neuronal (and neuropsychological) functioning. Research is clearly needed to find ways to prevent infarcts in children and ways to treat them when they do occur, besides symptomatic relief.

REFERENCES

Biller, J., Mathews, K., & Love, B. (1994). *Stroke in children and young adults.* Newton, MA: Butterworth-Heinemann.

Fenichel, G. (1993). *Clinical pediatric neurology* (2nd ed.). Philadelphia: W. B. Saunders.

Cristina McCarthy
Elaine Clark
University of Utah

CEREBRAL LESION, CHRONIC

Chronic cerebral lesions are the result of changes in the structure or physiological function of the brain. Cerebral lesions may occur as the result of either traumatic brain injuries (TBIs) or neurological diseases. Both TBIs and neurological diseases are associated with tissue and axonal damage. The extent and severity of damage are related to a variety of factors including the progression of the disease or length of period of unconsciousness (i.e., following a TBI).

A TBI is typically categorized as either an open or closed head injury. Open head injuries refer to injuries in which the skull or scalp is penetrated as in a gun shot or stab wound. Closed head injuries are injuries resulting in tissue damage from forceful external forces that do not penetrate the scalp (e.g., acceleration or deceleration forces from a motor vehicle accident). Common causes of childhood TBIs include motor vehicle accidents, falls, physical abuse, and to a lesser degree anoxic episodes, nutritional deficits, and exposure to toxins. TBIs are also classified as either mild, moderate, or severe based on factors such as level of consciousness, length of posttraumatic amnesia, and extent of physical damage. The prevalence of TBIs, particularly closed head injuries, is relatively high. The National Head Injury Foundation has referred to brain trauma as the "silent epidemic" that afflicts approximately 1 million children annually.

Neurological diseases, in contrast, are relatively rare in children. Neurological diseases associated with cerebral lesions in children may include intracranial neoplasms (e.g., astocytomas, medulloblastomas) and far less commonly cerebrovascular diseases. Most neurological conditions associated with cerebral lesions are rare and taken together have an incidence rate of approximately 2 per 100,000 or less in child populations (Spreen, Risser, & Edgall, 1995).

Characteristics

1. Approximately one half of the chronic cerebral lesions resulting from TBIs have concomitant motor, cognitive, communication, behavioral, and social problems.
   a. The most commonly affected cognitive domains in children with TBIs include attention, executive functions, processing speed, and learning and memory for new information.
   b. Increased fatigue is commonly associated with TBIs.
   c. Children with TBIs are 5–13 times more likely to have seizures compared to normal populations.
   d. Personality changes are observed in the majority of head injury victims.
2. The cognitive, behavioral, and social consequences of neurological diseases are less known. Localization of the pathology is strongly associated with observed functional deficits. The deficits can also involve consequences similar to those associated with TBIs.
3. The courses of recovery from either TBIs or neurological diseases also vary with most children with TBIs achieving maximal recovery within 2 years of the injuries.
   a. Factors associated with the course of recovery include severity of injury, length of posttraumatic amnesia, premorbid intellectual and behavioral status, and social support.

A variety of considerations must be made in reintegrating a child with a chronic cerebral lesion to an academic environment. Because a cerebral lesion may affect one or many functional domains (e.g., motor, social, cognitive), successful reintegration requires a multidisciplinary approach. Children may vary in the degree of services required depending on factors such as severity of the lesion. Some children may need minimal or no assistance, whereas other children may need specialized alternative school placements.

Recommendations for successful school reentry should be based on early identification, assessment, and intervention based on individualized assessment results. General recommendations for reintegration include a gradual introduction to the school program, quiet instructional settings, and methods to accommodate fatigue (e.g., reducing length of school day; Gans, Mann, & Ylvisaker, 1990).

The prognosis for children with chronic lesions also is variable depending on the severity of the lesion and environmental factors such as social support. An important consideration is the finding that school difficulties may not appear immediately after the injury. Because a common consequence of childhood chronic lesions includes impairments in learning new information, these children can initially rely on previous acquired knowledge to maintain previous levels of performance in school. As they progress through grades, they are less able to succeed based on the knowledge they acquired before the injury. Furthermore, because speed of processing and executive functions may also be impaired, children with chronic lesions also face difficulties in the transition to middle school and high school where independent learning of increased quantities of material is required.

Although substantial research exists in the field of childhood cerebral lesions, many questions remain. Cross-sectional, longitudinal studies are needed to clarify the conflicting findings of the impact of injuries across the developmental spectrum. Other areas such as brain injury rehabilitation and the nature of personality changes associated with brain injury are less researched and need far more information to facilitate treatment of this population.

REFERENCES

Gans, B., Mann, N., & Ylvisaker, M. (1990). Rehabilitation management approaches. In M. Rosenthal, E. Griffith, M. Bond, & J. D. Miller (Eds.), *Rehabilitation of the adult and child with traumatic brain injury* (2nd ed., pp. 593–615). Philadelphia: F. A. Davis.

Spreen, O., Risser, A. H., & Edgall, D. (1995). *Developmental neuropsychology.* New York: Oxford University Press.

Latha V. Soorya
Binghamton University and Institute for Child Development

CEREBRAL PALSY

Cerebral palsy (CP) is a neurological movement disorder associated with brain damage occurring before, during, or soon after birth. This disorder is not progressive, although symptoms may not be evident until a child fails to meet, or shows delays in meeting, developmental milestones. CP is divided into four subtypes: spastic, athetoid, ataxic, and mixed (WebMD, 2001). Spastic CP is characterized by severe muscle contractions in arms and legs. Athetoid CP involves writhing movements of the extremities (athetosis). Ataxic CP involves the cerebellum, and lack of balance and coordination while standing or walking predominates. Spastic CP is the most common, occurring in approximately 50% of cases; athetoid CP occurs in 20–30% of cases; and ataxic and mixed occur less often (CPIC, 2001). Severity of symptoms ranges from mild to severe.

Estimates of the prevalence of this disorder range from between 1 to 4 in 1,000 (Baron, Fennell, & Voeller, 1995; CPIC, 2001; National Organization for Rare Disorders, Inc. [NORD], 2001). CP affects males and females equally. There are many causes of CP. Basically any event that results in brain damage to a fetus, newborn, or young infant can cause CP. Etiologies include brain injury, hemorrhage, anoxia, and infection. Premature infants and low-birthweight infants appear more susceptible to CP than do full-term infants (NORD, 2001).

Characteristics

1. Motor dysfunction
2. Abnormal muscle tone (most often spasticity but sometimes hypotonia)
3. Developmental delays (especially motor and language)
4. No evidence for progressive disease or loss of previously acquired skills
5. Often vision or hearing impairment
6. Possibly seizure disorder

Diagnosis is usually made before the child is 1 year old, but children may not be diagnosed until they are several years of age. It is extremely rare that CP would not be diagnosed prior to beginning school. Diagnosis is made through brain imaging and neurological evaluation. Because damage to the brain has occurred, the goal of treatment is not to cure CP, but rather to minimize the effects of the damage. Treatment depends on symptom presentation and severity but may include medical treatments such as medicine (e.g., muscle relaxers, anticonvulsants), orthopedic surgery to release joint contractures, and surgical placement of feeding tubes. Physical therapy, occupational therapy, speech and language therapy, glasses, and hearing aids are also common forms of treatment.

Special education issues will vary widely depending on the severity of CP symptoms. These services will be available to children with CP under the handicapping condition of Other Health Impairment or Physical Disability. Some children with CP can be mainstreamed with minimal special education services, as needed, whereas others will need to utilize comprehensive services due to the severity of motor and cognitive impairments. Approximately 30–40% of children with CP have significant neurological involvement, resulting in mental retardation. These children require special education services to address limited cognitive capacity and its effect on learning. Children with CP are also at increased risk for learning disabilities, behavioral difficulty, and attentional impairments. Special education assistance may be necessary to deal with these complications of CP. Adaptations to the classroom may be necessary due to motor dysfunction. Many children with CP can participate in adapted physical education classes. Physical therapy, occupational therapy, and speech and language therapy are often necessary to meet an individual child's educational needs. A child with CP may also require assistive technology to communicate or complete academic work. Devices such as communication boards and keyboards may be useful.

When working with a child with CP, it is important to have good communication with parents and medical professionals. The child may have many absences due to surgery, medical appointments, or private therapies. He or she may have difficulty catching up with work and may require additional tutoring to keep up with these demands.

CP is a lifelong disorder. Improvement can be expected with medical and allied health intervention. There continue to be new investigational treatments to help alleviate symptoms including surgery and new medications. Many children can learn to cope with physical disabilities associated with CP and live productive lives.

REFERENCES

Baron, I. S., Fennell, E. B., & Voeller, K. K. S. (1995). *Pediatric neuropsychology in the pediatric setting.* New York: Oxford University Press.

National Organization for Rare Disorders, Inc. (2001, March 29). Cerebral palsy. Retrieved from www.rarediseases.org

WebMD. (2001, March 15). Cerebral palsy. Retrieved from http://my.webmd.com/content/asset/adam_disease_cerebral_palsy

Melissa R. Bunner
Austin Neurological Clinic

Dilip Karnik
'Specially for Children
Children's Hospital of Austin

CEREBRO-HEPATO-RENAL SYNDROME

Cerebro-hepato-renal syndrome, sometimes called Zellweger syndrome, is a rare genetically determined disorder identified as one of the leukodystrophies in which the area affected is the growth of the myelin sheath, which is the fatty covering that acts and as insulation on nerve fibers in the brain. It is characterized by the absence or reduction of cell structures that rid the body of toxic substances called peroxisomes. It has a prenatal onset and may be identified by physical characteristics such as unusual craniofacial features, enlarged liver, and a lack of muscle tone. There may also be developmental delays, jaundice, gastrointestinal bleeding, seizures, and an inability to suck (Nelson, Behrman, Kliegman, & Arvin, 1996).

Zellweger syndrome is autosomally recessive, so both parents must be carriers. It is found equally in males and females. Diagnosis is made through biochemical blood analyses to detect an accumulation of very long fatty acid chains and reduced or absent peroxisomes (Jones, 1997). It is one of the most severe forms of the leukodystrophies and is typically fatal within six months of diagnosis, which usually occurs at birth. Like most other peroxismal disorders, it can be diagnosed prenatally in the first or second trimester of pregnancy. The same techniques used postnatally to diagnosis the disorder can be used to find it prenatally (Nelson et al., 1996).

Characteristics

1. Prenatal and postnatal growth failure and failure to thrive
2. Craniofacial anomalies including low-set ears, high forehead, large fontanels, epicanthic folds in the skin extending from the root of the nose, slanted or "Mongoloid" type eyes, hypertolerism (abnormal distance between the eyes), a shallow orbital ridge, broad nasal ridge, cataracts or cloudy corneas, a redundant neck skin fold, and cleft palate
3. Limb anomalies including the lateral deviation of the forearm (cubitus valgus), campodactyly or the permanent flexation of fingers or toes, transverse palmar crease and talipes equinovarus (clubfoot)
4. Hypotonia or poor muscle tone and poor or no sucking ability
5. Enlarged liver and jaundice
6. Postnatal seizures
7. Severe mental and motor developmental delays

There is currently no cure for Zellweger syndrome, so treatment is symptomatic and supportive. Death is usually the result of gastrointestinal bleeding, liver failure, or respiratory distress.

There is no research on educational implications of this disorder, as few of its victims survive long enough to attend school.

REFERENCES

Jones, K. L. (1997). *Smith's recognizable patterns of human malformation* (5th ed.). Philadelphia: W. B. Saunders.

Nelson, W. E., Behrman, R. E., Kliegman, R. M., & Arvin, A. M. (1996). *Nelson textbook of pediatrics* (15th ed.). Philadelphia: W. B. Saunders.

Carol Schmitt
San Diego Unified School District

See also Zellweger Syndrome

CHARCOT-MARIE-TOOTH DISEASE

Charcot-Marie-Tooth disease (CMT) is a genetically heterogeneous group of neuromuscular disorders characterized by slow progressive atrophy; wasting and weakness of the distal limb muscles; sensory loss in the feet, lower legs, and hands; skeletal deformities (i.e., pes cavus); and reduced tendon reflexes (Tabaraud et al., 1999). The disease was named after three physicians who simultaneously commented on the characteristics in 1886, Howard Henry Tooth of England and Jean Martin Charcot and Pierre Marie from France. Individuals with CMT have difficulty walking and often fall and sprain their ankles. This is often the result of leg weakness. Hand weakness often results in problems with fine motor control, causing difficulty in writing, buttoning clothes, and manipulating small objects. Tendon atrophy further causes problems with foot drop and exaggerated leg lifting (i.e., to clear the ground). Pain is uncommon, but loss of sensation is frequently reported.

CMT is usually divided into two types in which the neuropathy is either demyelinating (CMT Type 1) or axonal (CMT Type 2; Birouk et al., 1998). Three major subtypes of CMT Type 1 have been identified and located on Chromosomes 1 and 17 and the X chromosome. As yet, no gene locus has been identified for CMT Type 2. Onset is typically in the first two decades of life; however, CMT Type 2 is usually diagnosed later than Type 1, and Type 1 is diagnosed in late childhood and adolescence. Severity is highly variable, and severe impairment is rare. Unlike many other neuromuscular diseases CMT has no effect on intellectual functioning and does not shorten life expectancy.

CMT is one of the most common hereditary neuromuscular disorders with an estimated frequency of 1 in 2,500. CMT Type 1 and CMT Type 2 are autosomal dominant disorders, whereas CMT Type 1 resulting from a defect in a gene located on the X chromosome is an X-linked dominant disorder (Pareyson, 1999).

Characteristics

1. Onset is typically in the first 2 decades of life.
2. Initial feature of disease is foot abnormalities such as a high arch and flexed toes.
3. Foot muscle weakness causes falls, ankle sprains, and skeletal deformity.
4. Foot drop results in a steppage gait in which the foot must be raised.
5. Hand weakness results in poor fine motor control.
6. CMT has no known effect on intellectual functioning or life span expectancy.

There is no cure for CMT, and treatment is limited to symptom relief. Physical therapy, braces, shoe inserts, and surgery are some treatment options. Physical therapy focuses on heel cord stretching exercises to prevent the Achilles tendon from shortening. Braces and shoe inserts help maintain proper foot and leg alignment and can hold the foot at a 90-degree angle in order to help keep toes from dragging when walking. If the entire lower leg is affected, braces that extend above the knee are used to give adequate support. When foot deformity is severe, surgery is used. Surgery is also an option for correcting scoliosis of the spine. Occupational therapy, like vocational therapy, may be appropriate for some individuals to maximize independent functioning.

Educational considerations for children afflicted with CMT should focus on the physical impairments of the disease. Although special education is rarely needed, classroom accommodations may be necessary to address problems with small motor coordination and mobility. Amelioration of poor small motor coordination due to weakness or tremors of the hands may be achieved through the use of assistive technology devices. Physical education would likely require monitoring and possible modification due to the high probability of injury. In the case of a severe impairment, physical education may have to be eliminated or significantly adapted.

Most individuals diagnosed with CMT live a relatively normal life; however, depending on the severity and age of onset, the disease can cause eventual disability. Long term prognosis is therefore poor due to the slow, progressive nature of the disease.

Research on the genetic transmission of the disease is ongoing, including the locus of CMT subtypes. Further information is needed to understand better the process of myelin formation and demyelination in the peripheral nervous system. Work is also being done in developing techniques for early diagnosis in order to develop drug therapies to preserve and restore structure and function of nerve fibers (and their myelin sheaths).

REFERENCES

Birouk, N., LeGuern, E., Maisonobe, T., Rouger, H., Gouider, R., Tardieu, S., Gugenheim, M., Routon, M. C., Leger, J. M., Agid, Y., Brice, A., & Bouch, P. (1998). X-linked Charcot-Marie-Tooth disease with connexin 32 mutations. *Neurology, 40*(10), 1061–1067.

Pareyson, D. (1999). Charcot-Marie-Tooth disease and related neuropathies: Molecular basis for distinction and diagnosis. *Muscle and Nerve, 22*(11), 1498–1509.

Tabaraud, F., Lagrange, E., Sindou, P., Vandenbuerghe, A., Levy, N., & Vallat, J. M. (1999). Demyelinating X-linked Charcot-Marie-Tooth disease: Unusual electrophysiological findings. *Muscle and Nerve, 22*(10), 1442–1447.

Lori Dekeyzer
Elaine Clark
University of Utah

See also Neuropathy, Hereditary Motor And Sensory, Type I; Neuropathy, Hereditary Motor And Sensory, Type II

CHILDHOOD DISINTEGRATIVE DISORDER

Childhood disintegrative disorder (CDD) is classified as a pervasive developmental disorder and is characterized by at least two years of normal early development followed by profound loss of previously acquired skills in the areas of cognition, communication, motor control, and bowel and bladder control. Once established, behaviors manifested as a result of CDD are indistinguishable from those of autism. Previously, CDD has been referred to as Heller's syndrome, dementia infantilis, and disintegrative psychosis (Filipek et al., 1999).

Etiology of the disorder is unknown; however, marked disintegration of functioning after a normal period of development suggests that the underlying mechanism is organic (e.g., neurobiological disorder or medical condition). Neurologic conditions such as tuberous sclerosis, neurolipidoses, and metachromatic leucodystrophyas have been implicated with the disorder, as have pertusis and measles (Volkmar, 1992). Children with CDD have been shown to have abnormal epileptiform electroencephalograms; however, if seizures occur, they are rarely the first sign. More often than not, seizures occur after the onset of CDD (Malhotra & Gupta, 1999).

CDD is a rare condition with prevalence rates reported to be about 1 per 100,000 children (Malhotra & Gupta, 1999). Because CDD shares a number of features with other pervasive developmental disorders, it is often indistinguishable. Children with CDD have impaired communication (verbal and nonverbal), poor social interactions, and stereotypic behaviors and interests, like children with autism. There is some indication that CDD may be more common in males than females; given how rare the disorder is, however, this remains unclear. Critical to the diagnosis of CDD is a history of normal development up to the age of 2 years followed by a marked decline. This "normal" period of development distinguishes CDD from infantile autism.

Characteristics

1. Normal early development until at least 2 years of age, followed by loss of functioning prior to age 10
2. Loss of previously acquired skills in the areas of cognitive functioning, verbal and nonverbal communication, social skills, motor skills, and bowel and bladder control
3. Intellectual functioning ranging from moderate to profound mental retardation
4. Emergence of restricted, stereotypic behavior or resistance to change (compulsive behavior)
5. Affective symptoms such as excessive fearfulness and anxiety
6. Overactivity

Treatment of CDD is typically with psychotropic medication such as antipsychotics (e.g., haloperidol), benzodiazepenes, antidepressants, lithium, and clozapine. Comorbid seizure disorders are treated with antiepileptics (e.g., carbamazepine). Behavior management is also commonly required. Children with CDD require comprehensive services, including treatment that encourages the reacquisition of cognitive and adaptive skills and speech and motor control. Most children with CDD will be served in self-contained special education classrooms. Speech and language pathology services, as well as occupational and physical therapy, will typically be required. School nurses may also be involved in the care of these children.

Prognosis is poor given that 75% of all cases have profound mental retardation. Despite treatment efforts, the course tends to be static with limited recovery of skills. The outcome, in fact, is much worse than autism, as children with CDD tend to be lower functioning and more aloof and to have higher rates of epilepsy. Life expectancy appears normal; however, due to the severe nature of the disorder, most individuals are cared for at home or in residential settings. Further research is needed to investigate the various causes of CDD and ways to prevent this unfortunate condition from occurring.

REFERENCES

Filipek, P. A., Accardo, P. J., Baranek, G. T., Cook, E. H., Jr., Dawson, G., Gordon, B., Gravel, J. S., Johnson, C. P., Kallen, R. J., Levy, S. E., Minshew, N. J., Prizant, B. M., Rapin, I., Rogers, S. J., Stone, W. L., Teplin, S., Tuchman, R. F., & Volkmar, F. R. (1999). The screening and diagnosis of autistic spectrum disorders. *Journal of Autism and Developmental Disorders, 29*(6), 439–484.

Malhotra, S., & Gupta, N. (1999). Childhood disintegrative disorder. *Journal of Autism and Developmental Disorders, 29*(6), 491–498.

Volkmar, F. R. (1992). Childhood disintegrative disorder: Issues for *DSM-IV. Journal of Autism and Developmental Disorders, 22*(4), 625–642.

Lori Dekeyzer
Elaine Clark
University of Utah

See also Pervasive Developmental Disorder

CHILDHOOD PSYCHOSIS

Childhood psychosis is a psychiatric disorder that involves disturbed thinking and poor reality testing. Psychosis in children is manifest by delusional thinking and hallucinations (i.e., auditory, visual, and tactile). It is considered rare in children younger than 6 years of age (Volkmar, 1996). Psychotic disorders are often associated with schizophrenia; however, the *Diagnostic and Statistical Manual of Mental Disorders–Fourth Edition, Text Revision* (American Psychiatric Association, 2000) lists several disorders in which psychotic processes can be observed (e.g., schizophrenia, major depression, bipolar illness, posttraumatic stress disorders, and obsessive-compulsive disorder). Prevalence rates are unclear for psychotic disorders beginning before the age of

12 (McKenna, Gordon, & Rapoport, 1994); however, childhood schizophrenia is estimated to occur in approximately .01 to .05 per 1,000 children (Eggers, Bunk, & Krause, 2000). With increasing age, the rate is much higher.

Characteristics

1. Prominent auditory (sometimes visual and tactile) hallucinations, delusions (reflecting developmental issues such as monsters), magical thinking, and thought disturbance
2. Social impairment, including trouble making and keeping friends
3. Odd, stereotypic behavior
4. Anxiety and mood disturbance (often mood-congruent with children)
5. In some adolescents, psychosis resembling adult schizophrenia

Risk factors for childhood psychosis include a family history of psychosis. Researchers have found a 9–16% increased likelihood that psychosis will develop in a child if one parent is affected, and a 40–68% increased likelihood if both parents are diagnosed with a psychotic disorder (Tolbert, 1996). Severe psychosocial stressors (e.g., death of a parent) are also associated with psychosis. Young children who are under considerable stress, for example, may experience transient hallucinations. Similarly, children who have developmental delays in language and motor skills, as well as unusual personality styles, may be predisposed to psychosis. Neurodevelopmental disorders and neurologic damage have also been implicated in the development of psychosis, including hypoxia, traumatic brain injury, and central nervous system infections (Volkmar, 1996). Psychosis is also induced by substance use (e.g., stimulants), especially in adolescents.

The assessment of psychosis is not easy, especially in very young children with immature cognitive skills and expressive language ability. After the age of 7 or 8 years, however, children are expected to think more logically and elaborate on their experiences. Understanding what a delusion is, or is not, becomes much easier during adolescence. It is also easier to determine whether psychotic symptoms are accompaning a mood disorder or are the primary problem. Although delusions are uncommon in children with unipolar depression, they are not with bipolar depressions (and hallucinations occur with both). Differentiating mood-related psychosis from schizophrenia is important for treatment. Similarly, it is important to differentiate psychotic disorders from other disorders, including pervasive developmental disorder, obsessive-compulsive disorder, and posttraumatic stress disorder. Stereotypic movement and severe communication problems also need to be ruled out (Nicolson et al., 2000).

Not all children with psychotic disorders will require special education services; many will, however, depending on the extent to which their functional skills have been impacted. In most cases, services will be provided under the category Emotional Disturbance. Regardless of eligibility for special education, these children are likely to require support and counseling services through the school (e.g., school psychologist, social worker, and counselor) as well as accommodations (e.g., reduced work load and individual tutoring to assist with missed assignments when absent from class over an extended period of time). Behavior management and social skills training may also be necessary to reduce inappropriate behaviors. In-service for school personnel may be particularly important to educate them about the features of the disorder and the importance of treatment. The most effective treatment for psychosis is medication therapy. Florid psychotic symptoms, including hallucinations, are often controlled with antipsychotics. Negative drug side effects, including sedation, however, often reduce medication compliance and treatment outcome. Behavior management, including positive behavioral supports, is also needed and can be a valuable adjunctive therapy to the psychiatrist attempting to treat the child with medications (i.e., increasing drug compliance). Parents are also likely to need help in order to find ways to increase compliance with medications, while at the same time further reducing inappropriate behaviors. School psychologists may be able to help with this and provide parents with information about community resources (e.g., alliances for people with mental illness). In some cases, family therapy, individual counseling, and social skills training are needed.

The prognosis for childhood-onset psychosis is often poor. Although partial remission occurs in approximately 25% of cases of schizophrenia, half of individuals with psychotic disorders develop a chronic course. The poorest prognosis occurs if the onset is before the age of 14 or there is a family history of psychosis (Tolbert, 1996). The risk for suicide is also high in this population given the range of functional areas affected (e.g., ability to learn, socialize with peers, and get along at home) and the propensity to have health problems (i.e., overeating and using substances such as nicotine, alcohol, and drugs). Many children and adolescents with schizophrenia end up with repeated hospitalizations for psychotic episodes or live in supervised group homes. Further research is needed to help differentiate psychosis from other conditions and developmental phenomenon in young children and to apply more effective treatments (e.g., treatments with fewer side effects than the antipsychotic drugs).

REFERENCES

American Psychiatric Association. (2000). *Diagnostic and statistical manual of mental disorders* (4th ed., Text Revision). Washington, DC: Author.

Eggers, C., Bunk, D., & Krause, D. (2000). Schizophrenia with onset before the age of eleven: Clinical characteristics of onset and course. *Journal of Autism and Developmental Disorders, 30*(1), 29–38.

McKenna, K., Gordon, C. T., & Rapoport, J. L. (1994). Childhood-onset schizophrenia: Timely neurobiological research. *Journal of the American Academy of Child and Adolescent Psychiatry, 33*(6), 771–781.

Nicolson, R., Lenane, M., Singaracharlu, S., Malaspina, D., Giedd, J. N., Hamburger, S., Gochman, P., Bedwell, J., Thaker, G. K., Fernandez, T., Wudarsky, M., Hommer, D. W., & Rapoport, J. L. (2000). Premorbid speech and language impairments in childhood-onset schizophrenia: Association with risk factors. *American Journal of Psychiatry, 157,* 794–800.

Tolbert, H. A. (1996). Psychoses in children and adolescents: A review. *Journal of Clinical Psychiatry, 57*(3), 4–8.

Volkmar, F. (1996). Childhood and adolescent psychosis: A review of the past 10 years. *Journal of the American Academy of Child Psychiatry, 37*(7), 843–851.

Lori Dekeyzer
Elaine Clark
University of Utah

CHILDHOOD SCHIZOPHRENIA

Childhood schizophrenia is a syndrome with psychotic features that may include auditory and visual hallucinations, delusions, disorganized and incoherent speech, disorganized or catatonic behavior, flat affect, and loss of interest in current activities (American Psychiatric Association [APA], 1994). The characteristics of childhood schizophrenia mimic those of adult schizophrenia in many ways; however, hallucinations are usually less organized and more likely to be visual in children (APA, 1994). Some studies suggest that hallucinations and delusions are extremely rare before the age of 7 years (Caplan, 1994). Children afflicted with this condition also may have trouble with cognitive, memory, motor, social, and language skills. Childhood schizophrenia can be divided further into several subtypes: paranoid, disorganized, catatonic, and undifferentiated. Children with paranoid schizophrenia have frequent hallucinations and delusions of a persecutory nature (APA, 1994). Those with the disorganized type have unclear and disorganized speech and behavior. They also are known to have a "flat or inappropriate affect" (APA, 1994, p. 288). Children with the catatonic type suffer from motor problems, echolalia, and rigidity of motion. Finally, those with the undifferentiated type of schizophrenia have the primary symptoms of schizophrenia, but they do not meet the criteria for the paranoid, disorganized, or catatonic types.

Childhood schizophrenia is a rare condition, but it has been found to occur more in children with a familial connection to this disorder. Children are at a greater risk to develop the disorder if a first-degree relative has schizophrenia or a schizophrenia spectrum disorder (Nicolson & Rapoport, 1999). In adults, schizophrenia is noted to occur in 1–2% of the general population, although figures involving children are less equivocal. Childhood-onset schizophrenia is more prevalent in males, but it is unclear how socioeconomic status and ethnicity affect the onset of the disorder (Rosenbaum Asarnow & Asarnow, 1996). Current research in the area supports the diathesis-stress model in the development of childhood schizophrenia. It is believed that there are multiple factors working together that lead to the early onset of the disorder (Rosenbaum Asarnow & Asarnow).

Characteristics

1. Disorganized hallucinations of a visual type (and sometimes auditory)
2. Delusions
3. Disorganized and incoherent speech (which can involve echolalia)
4. Disorganized or catatonic behavior
5. Flat affect
6. Loss of interest in current activities
7. Cognitive skills problems
8. Motor skills problems
9. Memory loss
10. Social skills deficits

Treatment for childhood schizophrenia can include antipsychotic medication. Recent research supports the use of clozapine with children who have schizophrenia (Rosenbaum Asarnow & Asarnow, 1996). Children also benefit from social and life-skills training. In addition, they may need inpatient or outpatient psychiatric care at times. Families who have children with this disorder may be in need of parent training, behavioral family treatment, or family therapy (Rosenbaum Asarnow & Asarnow, 1996). Because of the variety of ways the disorder can affect children and families, no one treatment is implemented in all cases.

Special education placement will vary with this disorder. Children who do receive services are most likely to be diagnosed with severe emotional disturbance. Unfortunately, because this condition is rare, children may be diagnosed with other conditions prior to an accurate diagnosis of childhood schizophrenia. Pervasive developmental disorder, autism, attention-deficit/hyperactivity disorder, and other disorders of speech and motor skills may be the initial diagnoses. For those in need of special education placement, services again can vary from behavioral monitoring in the classroom to residential placement. Children who remain in the public school setting often need supplementary aids and services such as speech therapy, occupational and physical therapy, counseling, and social and life-skills training. Because of the cognitive and memory skill problems that are associated with the disorder, children also may need extra academic support in the form of resource or content mastery services. Properly medicated children or those with milder forms of schizophrenia can function well with minimal support.

Childhood schizophrenia is thought to be strongly tied to adult schizophrenia (Nicolson & Rapoport, 1999). Children who receive this diagnosis are likely to continue to meet criteria as adults. Prognosis is poor once the diagnosis is made. It is believed that children who develop schizophrenia will continue to experience symptoms as they age. Future research needs to focus on diagnostic issues and genetic links in the development of the disorder.

REFERENCES

American Psychiatric Association. (1994). *Diagnostic and statistical manual of mental disorders* (4th ed.). Washington, DC: Author.

Caplan, R. (1994). Communication deficits in childhood schizophrenia spectrum disorders. *Schizophrenia Bulletin, 20,* 671–684.

Nicolson, R., & Rapoport, J. L. (1999). Childhood-onset schizophrenia: Rare but worth studying. *Biological Psychiatry, 46,* 1418–1428.

Rosenbaum Asarnow, J., & Asarnow, R. F. (1996). Childhood-onset schizophrenia. In E. J. Mash & R. A. Barkely (Eds.), *Child psychopathology.* New York: Guilford Press.

Carrie George
Texas A&M University

CHLAMYDIA TRACHOMATIS, ADOLESCENT ONSET

Chlamydia is the most common sexually transmitted bacterial infection in the United States. Its full name is chlamydia trachomatis. This kind of bacteria can infect the penis, vagina, cervix, anus, urethra, or eye (Planned Parenthood, 2000a, 2000b). Chlamydia specifically targets the mucosal membranes of these areas. In addition, the mucosal surface of the pharynx is susceptible to infection.

It is estimated that more than 4 million people are infected with chlamydia each year (National Institute of Allergy and Infectious Diseases, 2000). Chlamydia is four times as common as gonorrhea, more than 30 times as common as syphilis, and most common among women and men under age 25. For every person with herpes, there are six with chlamydia. Adolescents and young adults are at greater risk more than likely due to behavioral factors such as unprotected intercourse, multiple sex partners, and a lack of information for accurately assessing level of risk. Furthermore, chlamydia easily infects the immature cervix (specifically the tissue covering the cervix in women younger than 20 years old), making teenage girls more susceptible to infection than adult women (Kaiser Family Foundation, 1998). In some studies, up to 30–40% of sexually active teenage girls were infected (Eng & Butler, 1997).

The long-term ramifications of untreated chlamydia are serious for both women and men. In women, when transmission occurs during vaginal sex, the infection usually begins on the cervix. From the cervix it can spread to the fallopian tubes and ovaries. Untreated chlamydia can result in pelvic inflammatory disease (PID), which is a root cause of infertility in many women. At least 15% of all infertile American women are infertile because of tubal damage caused by PID (American Social Health Association, 2001). In men, when chlamydia is transmitted from an infected sexual partner to the penis, the infection can spread from the urethra to the testicles. When untreated the subsequent damage from the infection can result in a condition known as epididymitis, which can lead to sterility. Chlamydia causes more than 250,000 cases of acute epididymitis in the U.S. every year.

Characteristics

1. It is estimated that up to 75% of women and 50% of men with chlamydia have no symptoms or symptoms so mild that they do not seek medical attention (U.S. Food & Drug Administration, 1999).
2. When symptoms do occur, they usually appear between 1–3 weeks after exposure.
3. In women, signs of infection may include unusual vaginal discharge or bleeding, burning during urination, urge to urinate more frequently, abdominal pain, low-grade fever, cervical inflammation, pain during vaginal sex, inflamed rectum, or inflamed urethra.
4. In men, signs of infection may include burning and itching around the penis, unusual discharge from the penis, pain or burning during urination, pain or swelling of the testicles, inflamed rectum, or inflamed urethra.
5. The infection is transmitted primarily during anal or vaginal sex. However, transmission via oral sex is possible.
6. The infection can be transmitted even if bodily fluids are not exchanged.
7. Chlamydia can infect the eyes when discharge from an infected partner enters the eye during sex or hand-to-eye contact. If infection occurs, chlamydia may cause redness, itching, and possibly discharge.

The only accurate way to determine if chlamydial infection exists is through screening from a health center or clinic, doctor's office, or health department—most of which offer both testing and treatment. Testing is done via sending a sample of pus or discharge from the vagina or penis to a laboratory that will look for the bacteria, or a urine test that does not require a pelvic exam or swabbing of the penis. Results from the urine test are usually available within 24 hours. The following antibiotic prescriptions are most commonly given to individuals infected with chlamydia: azithromycin (taken for one day only), doxycycline (taken for seven days), erythromycin, or ofloxacin. If the symptoms do not disappear after the prescribed dosage of antibiotic, or if they return, the individual should return to her or his health care provider. In addition, any current and past sexual partners should be examined and treated if necessary.

All adolescents, whether developmentally challenged or not, need to receive accurate, sensitive, and thorough information regarding the risks of transmission for chlamydia and other sexually transmitted diseases (STDs), as well as ways and means to prevent the spread of these diseases. Although often considered asexual by many medical or social work professionals, individuals who are mentally handicapped are also at risk for chlamydial infection if they are sexually active. Additional factors to consider when assessing risk for adolescents in particular include the multitude of psychosocial issues dealt with by adolescents, creative sexual exploration that may not fall under adult definitions of sexual activity, previous sexual assault or abuse, and the practice of "serial" monogamy among many adolescents—the practice of engaging in a series of short-term monogamous relationships.

Although even "protected" sex with a condom cannot completely prevent transmission of chlamydia or other STDs, correct and consistent condom use significantly reduces the chances of getting chlamydia or other STDs. When reducing risk, latex and polyurethane condoms as well as oral barriers for vaginal, anal, and oral sex offer protection. Many doctors recommend that individuals who have more than one sex partner, and especially women less than 25 years of age, be tested for chlamydial infection regularly, even if they do not exhibit any symptoms. Furthermore, scientists are constantly seeking out better ways to diagnose, treat, and prevent chlamydial infections. Recently, the completed sequence for the chlamydia trachomatis genome was identified, thus providing scientists with invaluable information as they try to develop a safe and effective vaccine. Another area of research is in developing topical microbicides (preparations that can be inserted into the vagina to prevent infection) that are effective and easy for women to use. Left untreated, the "silent epidemic" of chlamydia threatens to cause reproductive damage and infertility in many of the individuals who contract the disease each year. In response, effective sexual health education, access to means for prevention, screening, and treatment provide the best course of action.

REFERENCES

American Social Health Association. (2001). STD statistics & "Information to live by: Chlamydia." Retrieved from http://www.asha.org

Eng, T., & William, B. (Eds.). (1997). *The hidden epidemic: Confronting sexually transmitted diseases.* National Academy Press.

Kaiser Family Foundation. (1998). *Sexually transmitted diseases in America: How many cases and at what cost?* Pittsburgh, PA: Kaiser Family Foundation and American Social Health Association.

National Institute of Allergy and Infectious Diseases, National Institutes of Health. (2000, October). Chlamydial Infection. Retrieved from http://www.niaid.nih.gov/factsheets/stdclam.htm

Planned Parenthood. (2000a, April). Chlamydia: Questions and Answers. Retrieved from http://www.plannedparenthood.org

Planned Parenthood. (2000b). Fact sheet prepared by the Katharine Dexter McCormick Library. Retrieved from http://www.plannedparenthood.org/library/STI/Chlamydia_fact.html

U.S. Food and Drug Administration. (1999). Chlamydia's Quick Cure. Retrieved from http://www.fda.gov

Leslie Burkholder
Idea Infusion Consulting and Contracting
Denver, Colorado

CHLAMYDIA TRACHOMATIS INFECTIONS

Chlamydia trachomatis infections are among the most common sexually transmitted bacterial diseases. These infections, often marked by a red and swollen area and discharge, can affect the eyes, the lungs, and the genital area. Infections can be transmitted to children either by a sexual partner or from birth by their mother. Nearly two thirds of all births to mothers with the infection result in an infected child (Bell et al., 1987). Newborns born with chlamydia trachomatis can show signs of the disease as early as three days after birth and as late as five or six weeks after birth. Antibiotic treatments can cure chlamydia trachomatis in under two weeks, although relapses can occur. If left untreated, pneumonia may develop. Pneumonia from chlamydia trachomatis may require an additional month of treatments and is often considered clinically severe (Lehmann et al., 1999).

Between 15% and 25% of infants with chlamydia trachomatis infections also develop conjunctivitis. Conjunctivitis is an inflammation that affects the eyelids and eyeball; infants who have conjunctivitis from chlamydia trachomatis do not usually have fever (Bell et al., 1987).

The presence of chlamydia trachomatis infections is often used as evidence that sexual abuse has occurred, but there is a high rate of false positives in testing children for these infections (Hammerschlag, 1997).

Characteristics

1. Infections in eyes, lungs, and genital areas
2. Infections usually red and swollen and accompanied by discharge

Most infants with chlamydia trachomatis infections should have been successfully treated by the time they reach school age. Older children who develop chlamydia trachomatis infections through sexual activities may need school counseling, but it should not affect academic performance.

Current research is focusing on new ways to test for chlamydia trachomatis infections, particularly newer noninvasive methods. Although noninvasive screenings are available for men, they are not available for women (Chernesky et al., 1990).

REFERENCES

Bell, T. A., Stamm, W. E., Kuo, C. C., Wang, S. P., Holmes, K. K., & Grayston, J. T. (1987). Delayed appearance of chlamydia trachomatis infections acquired at birth. *Pediatric Infectious Disease Journal, 6,* 928–931.

Chernesky, M., Castriciano, S., Sellors, J., Stewart, I., Cunningham, I., & Landis, S. (1990). Detection of chlamydia trachomatis antigens in urine as an alternative to swabs and cultures. *Journal of Infectious Diseases, 161,* 124–126.

Hammerschlag, M. R. (1997). Diagnosis of chlamydial infection in the pediatric population. *Immunological Investigations, 26,* 151–156.

Lehmann, D., Sanders, R. C., Marjen, B., Rongap, A., Tschappeler, H., Lamont, A. C., Hendry, G. M., Wai'in, P., Saleu, G., Namuigi, P., Kakazo, M., Lupiwa, S., Lewis, D. J., & Alpers, M. P. (1999). High rates of chlamydia trachomatis infections in young Papua New Guinean infants. *Pediatric Infectious Disease Journal, 18,* 62–69.

James C. Kaufman
Educational Testing Service
Princeton, New Jersey

CHOREA

Chorea refers to an irregular, nonrhythmic, rapid, and unsustained involuntary movement that flows from one body part to another (Fahn, Greene, Ford, & Bressman, 1998). The timing, direction, and distribution of movements stemming from chorea are unpredictable in nature. Another common feature of this disorder is motor inefficiency as evidenced by the inability to sustain muscle tone to hold or grasp objects. Several types of chorea exist and stem from five etiologies: heredity, metabolic, cerebrovascular, infectious, and structural causes (Feigin, Kieburtz, & Shoulson, 1995). The most common etiology in children is infection or coronary surgery (Fahn et al.). Sydenham's chorea is the most common type of infectious chorea in children and is associated with streptococcal infection and rheumatic fever (Feigin et al.). The second most common type of chorea involves genetic links to the disease including a history of Huntington's disease or juvenile onset of Huntington's disease.

Duration and severity of chorea depend heavily on the etiology. In Sydenham's chorea, the duration of the illness in approximately 5 to 15 weeks before full recovery. However, symptoms reoccur in approximately 20% of the cases (Feigin et al., 1995). In chorea cases associated with childhood or adolescent onset of Huntington's disease, symptoms become increasingly worse with average life expectancy not exceeding 10 years after onset (Folstein, 1989).

Characteristics

1. Irregular, involuntary movements that flow from one body part to another
2. Irregular movements in the upper and lower facial areas
3. Irregular movements in the trunk and limb areas
4. Motor inefficiency
5. Difficulty with eating or swallowing

A child presenting with chorea-like symptoms may see several doctors before an accurate diagnosis is determined (Feigin et al., 1995). Diagnosis is problematic due to the nature of the illness and the multiple etiologies. Chorea varies in duration and severity dependent on the nature of the illness. In the case of chorea as secondary symptoms of Huntington's disease, as the course of the disorder progresses, eating may become increasingly difficult due to the muscles involved with chewing and swallowing (Feigin et al.). Sydenham's chorea has been associated with obsessive-compulsive symptoms in addition to typical chorea symptoms (Asbahr et al., 1998). Chorea may increase when children are presented with a stressful stimulus or situation (Feigin et al.).

Treatment regimens consist largely of symptomatic treatment related to presenting symptoms involving medication aimed at reducing the dopaminergic neurotransmission (Feigin et al., 1995). In advanced stages of Huntington's chorea, medication may no longer be effective in controlling the muscle movements. Children may need wheelchairs, and an inability to write is common. As the disease progresses further, children may need breathing and feeding tubes (Feigin et al.).

Special education services may be available to children with chorea under the categories of Other Health Impairment or Physically Handicapped. Due to the unpredictable symptoms that arise, significant time away from the regular education classroom may be involved. If the child has significant absences (i.e., 2 to 15 weeks), homebound services may be needed. A school reentry plan including communication, social-emotional, motor skills, and academic skills may also be required to create a smooth transition back to school (Begali, 1994). It is important to work with all of the children in the classroom to help prepare them for dealing with a child with chorea. This is especially important if the disease is degenerative. Individualized one-to-one service will most likely be needed for a child to succeed. In addition, because symptoms may be exacerbated by stress, reduction of stressful situations may be necessary and depends upon the needs of the child. The vast array of symptoms associated with Huntington's chorea may require intense medical treatment. School psychology services with a focus on counseling may be necessary to deal with a chronic illness, stress, loss, and grief. If obsessive-compulsive tendencies appear comorbidly, treatment should focus on the reductions of these behaviors. Side effects from medication should be taken into account when assessing a child's abilities and needs. School psychological services should also assess the needs of the family and assist the family in accessing community resources to help the family reach goals for their child and the family as a whole.

REFERENCES

Asbahr, F. R., Negrao, A. B., Gentil, V., Zantel, D., Paz, J. A., Marques-Diaz, M. J., & Kiss, M. H. (1998). Obsessive-compulsive and related symptoms in children and adolescents with rheumatic fever with and without chorea: A prospective 6-month study. *American Journal of Psychiatry, 155,* 8.

Begali, V. (1994). The role of the school psychologist. In R. C. Savage & J. Wolcott (Eds.), *Educational dimensions of acquired brain injury.* Austin, TX: Pro-ed.

Fahn, S., Greene, P. E., Ford, B., & Bressman, S. B. (1998). *Handbook of movement disorders.* Philadelphia: Current Medicine.

Feigin, A., Kieburtz, & Shoulson, I. (1995). Treatment of Huntington's disease and other choreic disorders. In R. Kurlan (Ed.), *The treatment of movement disorders.* Philadelphia: J. B. Lippincott.

Folstein, S. (1989). *Huntington's disease: A disorder of families.* Baltimore: John Hopkins University Press.

Nicole R. Warnygora
Rik Carl D'Amato
University of Northern Colorado

CHOROIDEREMIA

Choroideremia is also known as choroidal sclerosis, progressive choroidal atrophy, progressive tapetochoroidal dystrophy, or TCD (National Organization for Rare Disorders [NORD], 2000). It is a rare inherited disorder that causes progressive loss of vision due to degeneration of the choroid and retina (*PDR Medical Dictionary,* 2000; Sebra, 1999).

Choroideremia usually affects males. Female carriers may have mild symptoms without loss of vision (NORD, 2000; *PDR Medical Dictionary,* 2000). Choroideremia is genetically passed through families by the X-linked pattern of inheritance. Females have two X chromosomes and can carry the disease gene on one of their X chromosomes. Females typically are not affected by X-linked diseases such as choroideremia because they have a healthy version of the gene on their other X chromosome. Males, however, have only one X chromosome and are therefore genetically susceptible to X-linked diseases. Males cannot be carriers of X-linked diseases. Males affected with an X-linked disease always pass the gene on the X chromosome to their daughters. Affected males never pass an X-linked disease gene to their sons because fathers pass the Y chromosome to their sons. Female carriers have a 50% chance of passing the X-linked disease gene to their daughters. They also have a 50% chance of passing the gene to their sons, who are then affected by the disease. By 1980 about 58 cases had been identified in Finland. Almost all of them came from the northern part of the country (McKusick, 2000).

Characteristics

1. Night blindness during childhood
2. Progressive constriction of visual fields
3. Complete loss of vision

Choroideremia is one the few degenerative diseases that might be detected prenatally in some cases. Female carriers are recommended to seek information about this testing from a medical geneticist. All members of affected families are encouraged to consult an ophthalmologist and genetic counselor. Recently, the exact location of the gene on the X chromosome that causes choroideremia was found. However, at present there is no effective treatment or cure. Until a treatment is discovered, help is available through low-vision aids that include optical, electronic, and computer-based devices. In addition, personal, educational, and vocational counseling, as well as adaptive training skills, job placement, and income assistance, are available through community resources (Choroideremia Research Foundation, Inc., 2000). Patients with peripheral vision loss may benefit from a rehabilitation program that combines low vision training with amorphic lenses in a bioptic configuration (Szlyk, Seiple, Laderman, Kelsch, & McMahon, 1998).

Services for this disorder range depending on the severity of the visual impairment. For mild impairments, modifications to the regular curriculum including assistive technology under the 504 Act are appropriate. For more severe impairment, the child qualifies for services as visually impaired.

Recent research on choroideremia has progressed steadily since the early 1980s. This results in a good understanding of the genetics of the disorder. This understanding may lead to a treatment for choroideremia in the coming years. Recently, a practical new test to detect choroideremia was developed. Better testing methods will help confirm the clinical suspicion of the disease. Thus, important information on the course of the disease, the likelihood of functional blindness, and the probability of maintaining useful vision can be provided to the patients and family members.

REFERENCES

Choroideremia Research Foundation, Inc. (2000, May). Choroideremia disorder. Retrieved from http://www.choroideremia.org/CHMplain.html

Foundation fighting blindness. (n.d.) Choroideremia disorder. Retrieved from http://www.blindness.org

McKusick, V. A. (2000). Choroideremia disorder. Retrieved from http://www.ncbi.nlm.nih.gov/htbin-post/Omim/dispmim?303100

National Organization for Rare Disorders. (2000). Choroideremia disorder. Retrieved from http://www.stepstn.com/cgi-win/nord.exe?proc=Redirect&type=rdb_sum&id=525.htm

PDR Medical Dictionary (2nd ed.). (2000). Montvale: Medical Economics.

Sebra, M. (1999). Molecular pathogenesis of choroideremia: Structural basis for RAB27 dysfunction. Retrieved from http://www.brps.demon.co.uk/Graphics/G_Articles_Research_9904.html

Szlyk, J. P., Seiple, W., Laderman, D. J., Kelsch, R., Ho, K., & McMahon, T. (1998). Use of bioptic amorphic lenses to expand the visual field in patients with peripheral loss. *Optom Vis Sci, 75,* 518–524.

Nina Cheng
University of Texas at Austin

CHROMOSOME 9, TRISOMY 9p (MULTIPLE VARIANTS)

In Chromosome 9, Trisomy 9p, a rare chromosomal disorder, part of Chromosome 9 appears three times (trisomy) rather than twice in body cells. Location of the trisomy varies and may be part or all of the short arm (p) or the short arm and part of the long arm (q) of the chromosome. Effects are often similar regardless of which and how much extra chromosomal material is present, although those with large amounts of extra long-arm material may be more severely affected (National Organization for Rare Disorders [NORD], 2001). Virtually all Trisomy 9p individuals show severe mental retardation, and most show growth retardation and characteristic facies. Other effects are more variable and depend in part on the amount and location of extra material. Some 5–10% die in infancy or early childhood (Jones, 1997; NORD, 2001). Cause may be a balanced translocation error in parental germ cell or a spontaneous error very early in the germinal stage (NORD, 2001). About 100 cases had been identified at the time of publication of Jones (1999).

Characteristics

1. Severe mental retardation and language deficiency
2. Growth retardation and delayed puberty
3. Facies: microcephaly, hypertelorism, deep-set eyes, down-turned palpebral fissures and corners of the mouth, large nose
4. Numerous skeletal abnormalities, including short fingers and toes, scoliosis, deformities of bones in fingers and toes
5. Occasional congenital heart disease

Initial tentative diagnosis may be on the basis of clinical signs, but confirmation will be through cytogenetic analysis. If Trisomy 9p is confirmed, the parents should also undergo cytogenetic analysis. If one is a carrier of the translocation error, risk of reoccurrence greatly increases, and genetic counseling and subsequent antenatal testing may be appropriate.

No effective treatment is currently available. Lifelong care will be needed. Special education in a separate classroom or institutionalization are likely placements. In cases where the affected individual will live at home, family counseling should be made available. A Trisomy 9 parental support group can be reached at http://www.geocities.com/Heartland/Acres/5287/.

REFERENCES

Jones, K. L. (1997). *Smith's recognizable patterns of human malformation* (5th ed.). Philadelphia: Saunders.

National Organization for Rare Disorders. (2001). Chromosome 9, Trisomy 9p (Multiple Variants). Retrieved from http://www.rarediseases.org

Robert T. Brown
University of North Carolina, Wilmington

CHROMOSOME 18p SYNDROME

18p syndrome occurs when any piece of the short arm of Chromosome 18 is missing. There are three classes of Chromosome 18 deletion syndromes; 18q, 18p, and Ring 18. Deletion syndromes of Chromosome 18 are the second most common of the autosomal deletion syndromes. Most deletions occur very early in the embryonic stage of development. There are several ways that this deletion can occur. Most children with 18p syndrome have parents who have normal chromosomes. The parent may also have a deletion on the chromosome, but the deleted piece is attached to another chromosome. As a result, the parent still has all of his or her genetic information; it is just arranged differently. This parent will not show any symptoms. Cases have also been reported in which a parent with 18p syndrome has a child with the same syndrome. Therefore, the chromosomal abnormality has been genetically passed on to the child. Because the genes that are missing vary and the content of the normal chromosome (the unaffected in the pair) can vary, the symptoms vary as well. Due to these variances, it is not possible to have a clear-cut list of symptoms. It is possible that a child might look a little different and has made it through school with Cs and Ds and actually has a chromosomal abnormality that was never diagnosed (Chromosome 18 Registry and Research Society, 1991). A belief exists that there are some people with 18p who are so mildly affected that they do not know they have a chromosomal abnormality until they have a child who is 18p and is more severely affected. There exists no evidence that this syndrome can be caused by environmental agents. It is important to note that most descriptions of this syndrome come from medical case reports. Due to the diagnostic nature of information available, very little is known about the outcomes for the affected individual (Chromosome 18 Registry and Research Society, 1991).

As of 1991, the frequency of Chromosome 18 deletion syndromes was estimated to be 1 in every 46,000. However, this included all three classes of Chromosome 18 deletion syndromes. The incidence for 18p alone is unknown. The female to male ratio of 18p is 2 to 1 (Chromosome 18 Registry and Research Society, 1991). Birth weight averages 2600 g (5 lb, 11 oz), which falls at the low end of normal. Nineteen percent of 18p newborns die from severe brain malformations.

Characteristics

1. Mental retardation occurs in 98% of patients.
2. Average IQ is around 59.
3. Other common characteristics include short stature, abnormal external ears (low set, floppy, and/or large), webbed neck, holoprosencephaly (developmental malformation of the brain that has a large range of severity and can be fatal), IgA (an infection fighting protein) deficit, which can cause upper respiratory problems, small jaw, and excessive cavities.
4. Most doctors mentioned that the patient was originally brought in for evaluation because of failure to thrive.
5. Speech is often delayed along with a dissociation between language skills and practical (nonverbal) performance (Thompson, Peters, and Smith, 1986).
6. Behavior problems such as restlessness, emotional lability, fear of strangers, poor concentration, and inability to form relationships have been reported.
7. Case studies also indicate delayed articulation (speech sound production) skills (Thompson et al., 1986).

It has been recommended that children be seen at least once by the following specialists: a pediatric neurologist, a developmental pediatrician, a dentist, and a geneticist and genetic counselor (Chromosome 18 Registry and Research Society, 1991).

Early intervention programs have been found to benefit a young child with 18p, which suggests that there is a potential for progress with remediation (Thompson et al., 1986). For children as young as 3 years old, special education programs are usually available through the public school system. Speech therapy would also likely be beneficial.

As mentioned before, reviews of literature lack outcome data of most patients. Due to the variability in symptoms, exact prognoses are difficult to determine. Although no cure exists, therapies aimed at specific problems can and will be developed (Chromosome 18 Registry and Research Society, 1991).

REFERENCES

Chromosome 18 Registry and Research Society. (1991). *Deletion syndromes of chromosome 18* [Brochure]. San Antonio, TX: Author.

Thompson, R. W., Peters, J. E., & Smith, S. D. (1986). Intellectual, behavioral, and linguistic characteristics of three children with 18p syndrome. *Journal of Developmental and Behavioral Pediatrics, 7*(1), 1–7.

Catherine M. Caldwell
University of Texas at Austin

CHROMOSOME 18q SYNDROME

18q syndrome occurs when any piece of the long arm of Chromosome 18 is missing. Deletion syndromes of Chromosome 18 are the second most common of the autosomal deletion syndromes. Most deletions occur very early in the embryonic stage of development. There are several ways that this deletion can occur. Most children with 18q syndrome have parents who have normal chromosomes. The parent may also have a deletion on the chromosome, but the deleted piece is attached to another chromosome. As a result, the parent still has all of his or her genetic information; it is just arranged differently. This parent will not show any symptoms and probably has no idea that he or she has the chromosomal abnormality. Cases have also been reported in which a parent with 18q syndrome has a child with the same syndrome. Therefore, the chromosomal abnormality has been genetically passed on to the child. Because the genes that are missing vary and the content of the normal chromosome (the unaffected in the pair) can vary, the symptoms vary as well. Moreover, the clinical picture is variable and does not always correspond to the size and site of the deletion (Miller, Mowrey, Hopper, Frankel, & Ladda, 1990). Due to these variances, it is not possible to have a clear-cut list of symptoms. There exists no evidence that this syndrome can be caused by environmental agents. It is important to note that most descriptions of this syndrome come from medical case reports. Due to the diagnostic nature of information available, very little is known about the outcomes for the affected individual (Chromosome 18 Registry and Research Society, 1991).

The frequency of Chromosome 18 deletion syndromes is estimated to be 1 in every 46,000. However, this includes all three classes of chromosome 18 deletion syndromes, including 18q, 18p, and Ring 18. Females are 1.7 times more likely than males to have this disorder (Chromosome 18 Registry and Research Society, 1991).

Characteristics

1. Mental retardation occurs in 96% of patients.
2. In one study, intelligence ranged from borderline to severely deficient (IQ, 73 to below 40; Mahr et al., 1996).
3. Other common characteristics include short stature, flat midface, hypotonia (poor muscle tone), prominent antihelix (outer curl of the ear), microcephaly (small head and brain), carp mouth (downturned corners), abnormal male genitals, abnormal female genitals, and foot deformity.
4. Impaired hearing occurs in 26% of patients.
5. In a study of a mother and son with 18q syndrome, both were found to have hearing loss, borderline cognitive functioning, and idiopathic tremor actions that progressively worsened (Miller et al., 1990).
6. Performance in specific neuropsychological functions, including attention, novel problem solving, memory, language, visuomotor integration, and fine motor dexterity, was consistently in the moderately to severely impaired range (Mahr et al., 1996).
7. Aggression, hyperactivity, and temper tantrums are common behavior problems in both males and females (Mahr et al., 1996).

It has been recommended that children be seen at least once by the following specialists: a pediatric opthalmologist, a pediatric neurologist, a developmental pediatrician, an audiologist, an otolaryngologist, and a geneticist and genetic counselor. The child's poor muscle tone will require years of occupational and physical therapy (Chromosome 18 Registry and Research Society, 1991). Special education services will also be needed due to the high incidence of mental retardation. Audiological services would also be beneficial for possible hearing impairments.

An early intervention program would likely benefit a young child with 18q. For children as young as 3 years old, special services are typically available through the public school system. For those children with hearing impairments, speech will likely be delayed, which necessitates years of speech therapy (Chromosome 18 Registry and Research Society, 1991).

As mentioned before, reviews of literature lack outcome data of most patients. One study, however, did find an IQ from 25 years prior and found that there had been no cognitive change. However, this patient did develop a progressive and debilitating tremor (Mahr et al., 1996). Due to the variability in symptoms, exact prognoses are difficult to determine. Research is currently being conducted to see the effect of growth hormone treatment. Although no cure exists, therapies aimed at specific problems can and will be developed (Chromosome 18 Registry and Research Society, 1991).

REFERENCES

Chromosome 18 Registry and Research Society. (1991). *Deletion syndromes of Chromosome 18* [Brochure]. San Antonio, TX: Author.

Mahr, R. N., Moberg, P. J., Overhauser, J., Strathdee, G., Kamholz, J., Loevner, L. A., Campbell, H., Zackai, E. H., Reber, M. E., Mozley, L. B., Turetsky, B. I., & Shapiro, R. M. (1996). Neuropsychiatry of 18q syndrome. *American Journal of Medical Genetics, 67,* 172–178.

Miller, G., Mowrey, P. N., Hopper, K. D., Frankel, C. A., & Ladda, R. L. (1990). Neurologic manifestations in 18q syndrome. *American Journal of Medical Genetics, 37,* 128–132.

Catherine M. Caldwell
University of Texas at Austin

CHRONIC FATIGUE SYNDROME

Chronic fatigue syndrome (CFS) or chronic fatigue immune dysfunction syndrome in children and adolescents is characterized by debilitating fatigue, neurological problems, and a variety of symptoms (Chronic Fatigue Immune Dysfunction Syndrome Association of America, Inc., 1996–2000). It is defined by a thorough medical examination that excludes other medical and psychiatric diagnoses and by unexplained, persistent chronic fatigue that exists for at least 6 months and is of new onset resulting in reduced occupational, educational, social, or personal activities. Second, at least four of the following symptoms co-occur: substantial impairment in short-term memory or concentration, multijoint pain without swelling or redness, headaches, sore throat, tender lymph nodes, muscle pain, unrefreshing sleep, and postexertional malaise lasting for more than 24 hours (Bell, 1995).

Etiology is unconfirmed (Swenson, 2000) but has been attributed to several theories. Persistent viral infection associated with Epstein-Barr virus, influenza-type viruses, varicella zoster, and rubella have been reported by patients; often, however, CFS patients show no laboratory evidence of these infections. Primary muscle disorder has been proposed, but no metabolic abnormality in skeletal muscle in patients has been shown. Chronic immune dysfunction has been proposed secondary to a broad range of abnormalities in the immune system by CFS patients. Often, a high association with allergies coincides with a precipitating infection. Neuroendocrine disorder has been suggested because patients with CFS have a functional abnormality of the hypothalamic-pituitary system, contributing to a secondary impairment of the adrenal system. Primary sleep disorder has also been put forth, as most CFS patients experience daytime fatigue due to a disruption in the circadian rhythm. Finally, primary depression, somatization, and stress have been cited as possible causative factors, although it is difficult to determine if these are contributing factors or results of CFS, especially in children where depression is so much a part of any chronic illness.

Prevalence rates for CFS in children and adolescents (ages 12 to 17), as indicated by physician referrals, are 8.7 cases per 100,000 (Dobbins et al., 1997). School nurse referrals, on the other hand, suggest 52.9 cases per 100,000.

Characteristics

1. Unexplained, persistent chronic fatigue for at least 6 months that is not alleviated by rest
2. Significant reduction in previous levels of occupational, educational, social, or personal activities
3. Impaired short-term memory and concentration
4. Sore throat, tender lymph nodes, muscle pain, headaches
5. Multijoint pain without joint swelling or redness
6. Unrefreshing sleep and postexertional malaise lasting more than 24 hours

Treatment for CFS is generally symptomatic, resulting in medical-oriented therapies and pharmacological enhancement of symptoms. Physical therapy is often employed to reduce pain through gentle stretching techniques, myofacial release, and heat or cold applications. Therapeutic massage can also help in pain reduction. Exercise may be an eventual goal, but it has proven controversial because it may contribute to further relapse. Initially, walking or pool therapy may be safely included. Alternative therapies have been tried with adults, but their efficacy in randomized trials has not been proven.

Physicians may prescribe medications to help manage depression and anxiety symptoms. Other medications may help musculoskeletal complaints, flu-like symptoms, and muscle aches. Antiviral and immunodulatory drugs have also been used. Cognitive behavior therapy (CBT) has been used successfully in adults to reduce depression, stress, and fatigue severity with treatment focusing on acquisition of cognitive and behavioral coping skills, identification of symptom relapse stimuli, activity modification to minimize setbacks, and stress reduction and relaxation techniques.

Special education placement under Other Health Impairment may be warranted if students are diagnosed with CFS by a physician and if it is educationally significant. Students may benefit from a modified schedule that allows for some social periods during the day at school but also accommodates their fatigue. Home-bound instruction may help minimize academic difficulties and provide ongoing tutorial support. Physical therapy services may help alleviate painful symptoms and facilitate some physical exercise to guard against negative consequences of deconditioning. Adaptive physical education (PE) may help meet PE requirements in the school. Cognitive impairments may be documented and monitored by ongoing evaluation. Occupational therapy may help with adaptations to physical roadblocks, especially related to physical output necessary for academic performance. Accommodations and adaptations may be implemented to help students be successful with state standards assessments.

Most children do recover from CFS with a mean out-of-school duration of one year. Some cycle through periods of recovery and relapse over a prolonged period of time, however, with few reports of worsening of symptoms. Future research is focusing on exact etiology and combinations of treatments, such as CBT with children combined with medical regimens.

REFERENCES

Bell, D. S. (1995). Chronic fatigue syndrome in children and adolescents. *Focus and Opinions: Pediatrics, 1,* 412–420.

Chronic Fatigue Immune Dysfunction Syndrome Association of America, Inc. (1996–2000). Chronic fatigue syndrome. Retrieved from http://www.cfids.org/youth/youth.html

Dobbins, J. G., Randall, B., Reyes, M., Steele, L., Livens, E. A., & Reeves, W. C. (1997). Prevalence of chronic fatigue illness among adolescents in the United States. *Journal of Chronic Fatigue Syndrome, 3,* 15–28.

Swenson, T. S. (2000). Chronic fatigue syndrome. *Journal of Rehabilitation, 1,* 37–42.

R. Brett Nelson
Diana L. Nebel
University of Northern Colorado

CHRONIC GRANULOMATOUS DISEASE

Chronic granulomatous disease (CGD) is a rare genetic syndrome characterized by susceptibility to recurrent severe infections and associated with immune dysfunction. It is inherited as either an X-linked or an autosomal recessive genetic disorder. At least eight subtypes are recognized, but one X-linked subtype accounts for the majority of CGD cases. Most patients present with CGD before 2 years of age. Prevalence is approximately 1 in 500,000 individuals.

Characteristics

1. Onset is usually in the first few months of life with at least one unusual or severe infection during the first year of life.
2. Eighty percent are identified with unusual susceptibility to serious infections before their second birthday.
3. Diagnosis may be delayed until adolescence or adulthood.
4. Abscess formation is the hallmark symptom and may occur in any organ of the body, including the brain.
5. Pulmonary disorders occur in nearly all children.

The primary aim of therapy for patients with CGD is prevention and cure of infection. Prophylaxis with antibiotic is standard. Steroids, and surgery in more severe cases, are required to treat granulomas affecting the gastrointestinal or genitourinary tract. Bone marrow transplantation and gene therapy have been used effectively.

CGD is a lifelong disease. Susceptibility to serious bacterial and fungal infection is a hallmark of CGD; however, the quality of life of patients has improved dramatically over the past three decades. Survival beyond the fourth decade occurs frequently. Special education services or accommodation may be required due to the long-term impact of the medical illness on school achievement. Many children with CGD qualify for services under the classification of Other Health Impairment.

REFERENCES

Nelson, W. E., Behrman, R. E., Kliegman, R. M., & Arvin, A. M. (1996). *Nelson textbook of pediatrics* (15th ed.). Bangalore, India: Prism Books.

Stiehm, E. R. (Ed.). (1996). *Immunologic disorders in infants and children* (4th ed.). Philadelphia: W. B. Saunders.

Virdette L. Brumm
Children's Hospital Los Angeles
Keck / USC School of Medicine

CHRONIC INFLAMMATORY DEMYELINATING POLYNEUROPATHY

Chronic inflammatory demyelinating polyneuropathy (CIDP) is a rare neurological disorder that results in swelling of the nerve roots and the destruction of the myelin sheath, the fatty covering that surrounds the axon of nerves in the body (National Organization for Rare Disorders, Inc. [NORD], 2001). The presentation, course, and severity of this disorder vary from case to case. To receive a diagnosis of CIDP, an individual must have been free from viral infections for at least three months prior to the presentation of symptoms (NORD, 2001). Most cases do not exhibit a family history of CIDP or related disorders (NORD, 2001).

CIDP can affect all ages, and the onset of the disorder can begin at any age. The average age of onset of CIDP is 50, with twice as many males diagnosed as females. The prevalence rate of CIDP in the United States is 1 in 100,000 individuals (NORD, 2001).

Characteristics

1. A child usually visits the doctor complaining of progressive muscle weakness or sensory dysfunction in the upper or lower extremities, usually apparent within a few months of the onset of the disease (NORD, 2001).
2. The child may also complain of a loss of sensation, abnormal sensations, or impaired motor control (NORD, 2001).
3. The course of the disease varies greatly from case to case; some individuals have symptoms that progress slowly, whereas others have symptoms that get worse, better, and then worse again (NORD, 2001).
4. Symptoms of CIDP include fatigue, numbness, burning, and tingling sensations affecting the upper and lower extremities; weak or absent reflexes in the face or upper and lower extremities; paralysis or lack of sensation of the upper and lower extremities; weakness of the torso muscles; respiratory problems; and difficulty walking (NORD, 2001).

The exact etiology of CIDP is not known. Although it has not been proven, CIDP is thought to be a disorder of the autoimmune system (NORD, 2001). Diagnosing CIDP can be difficult because of the wide range of symptoms and the differences the presentation and course of the disorder have in each individual (NORD, 2001).

Recommended treatments include glucocorticoid drugs, although side effects are common, especially at high doses. Glucocorticoid drugs are also often used in conjunction with immunosuppressive drugs (NORD, 2001). Intravenous immunoglobulin treatment, increasing immunoglobulin through intravenous injections, is also a treatment used with CIDP as a way to increase immune functioning that has been successful in some trials (Hahne, Bolton, Zochodne, Feasby, 1996: NORD, 2001). However, acute meningitis has been identified as a serious side effect of intravenous immunoglobulin treatment (King Faisal Specialist Hospital and Research Centre, Annals of Saudi Medicine, 2001). Experimental treatments include plasma transfusions and the use of alpha 2a, although the effectiveness of these treatments is currently under investigation (NORD, 2001).

Children with chronic inflammatory demyelinating polyneuropathy may need academic modifications in order to attend and function at school. If the child's symptoms are severe enough that they interfere with one or more of the major life activities, they qualify as Other Health Impairment under Section 504. Once qualified, the school is required to provide modifications, depending on the type and severity of symptoms the child is experiencing. For a child experiencing motor weakness or paralysis in the upper and lower extremities, for example, occupational therapy and wheelchair access are modifications that may be required for the child to continue in mainstream education.

REFERENCES

Hahne, A. F., Bolton, C. F., Zochodne, D., & Feasby, T. E. (1996). Intravenous immunoglobulin treatment in chronic inflammatory demyelinating polyneuropathy: A double-blind, placebo-controlled, cross-over study. *Brain, 119*(4), 1067–1077.

King Faisal Specialist Hospital and Research Centre, Annals of Saudi Medicine. (2001, March 18). Acute aseptic meningitis associated with administration of immunoglobulin in children: A case report and review of the literature. Retrieved from http://www.kfshrc.edu.sa/annals/194/98–289.html

National Organization for Rare Disorders, Inc. (2001, March 20). Chronic inflammatory demyelinating polyneuropathy. Retrieved from http://www.stepstn.com/cgi-win/nord.exe?number=903&proc=ap_fullReport

Moana Kruschwitz
Margaret Semrud-Clikeman
University of Texas at Austin

CLEFT LIP AND PALATE

Cleft lip and palate are congenital malformations affecting the jaw region. The most severe forms include disconfiguration of the lips, nose, upper jaw, teeth, and palate. These defects generally result from the palatal shelves failing to join together during the sixth to eight week of fetal development. The resulting opening, known as a cleft, may occur in the upper lip, alveolus, and palate (World Craniofacial Foundation, 1998).

Cleft lip and palate occur in approximately 1 in 700 newborns. Incidence varies across ethnic groups, with Native Americans having the highest incidence, 3.6 in 1,000 births, and African Americans the lowest, 0.3 in 1,000 births. Estimates of gender differences vary, with one source (Jones, 1997) reporting that incidence of cleft lip and palate is about twice as high in males than females, but incidence of cleft palate alone is slightly higher in females. People with clefts who do not have a family history of the malformation have only a 4% chance of passing the deformity on to their children (World Craniofacial Foundation, 1998). However, cleft lip and palate frequently occur in several genetic and prenatal syndromes (Jones, 1997) and are part of 300 craniofacial syndromes (World Craniofacial Foundation, 1998). Cleft lip and palate may be part of "a broader pattern of altered morphogenesis" in 35% of affected newborns (Jones, 1997, p. 236), suggesting the need for thorough diagnosis.

Characteristics

1. Cleft lip is identified when the two sides of the upper lip do not join together properly.
2. Cleft palate, harder to detect visually, may be first suspected when the infant regurgitates fluid from the nose during nursing.
3. Infants may have difficulty feeding because they cannot suck effectively.
4. Affected children may have hypernasal speech and articulation problems.
5. Middle ear dysfunction and resulting hearing impairment may occur.

Major treatment for both cleft lip and cleft palate is reconstructive surgery. Surgery for cleft lip is generally performed when the infant is 2 to 3 months of age because earlier surgery may not be effective and is dangerous. Before the infant is old enough for surgery, treatment may be simply to tape the two sides of the lip together. Parents likely will need training in feeding their infant both before and after surgery. Any scars resulting from this surgery usually fade away as the child develops (World Craniofacial Foundation, 1998).

Surgery for cleft palate generally occurs when the child is 6–18 months of age. Several procedures are available to repair a cleft palate, and they may be carried out in stages or in one operation. As the child gets older, other surgeries may be needed to correct problems with the lips, nose, gums, and palate. Cleft palate surgeries are 80% successful in closing the cleft in the palate and in creating normal speech. However, approximately 20% of children have remaining speech impairment, either articulation problems or nasal speech, and may need an additional operation, known as pharyngoplasty. It is performed no earlier than 3 to 4 years of age (World Craniofacial Foundation, 1998).

Owing to potential ear infections and resulting hearing impairments, surgical insertion of pressure equalizing tubes into the ear to prevent middle ear dysfunction may also be necessary. Consultations with pediatric dental specialists may also need to take place because of how the jaw and teeth are affected by the clefts (World Craniofacial Foundation, 1998).

Children with cleft palate may need special education services owing to residual hearing and articulation problems that may exist after surgery. They should receive early and frequent hearing tests and may also require speech therapy for articulation and tone (hypernasal) problems. Speech therapy is generally effective only in cases where the affected child has adequate speech mechanisms. Speech therapy programs that are highly intensive and structured appear to be most effective (Enderby & Emerson, 1996).

Prognosis with successful surgery is now very good, although some residual problems may require extended treatment, as described earlier. Because ultrasound can detect cleft lip as early as week 13 of prenatal development, intrauterine surgery repair of cleft lip is a future possibility. Recent experimental surgery on animal models has produced excellent repair outcomes but has caused premature delivery and other complications (Bender, 2000).

REFERENCES

Bender, P. L. (2000). Genetics of cleft lip and palate. *Journal of Pediatric Nursing, 15,* 242–248.

Enderby, P., & Emerson, J. (1996). Speech and language therapy: Does it work? *Student BMJ, 4,* 282–285.

Jones, K. L. (1997). *Smith's recognizable patterns of human malformation* (5th ed.). Philadelphia: Saunders.

World Craniofacial Foundation. (1998). Cleft lip and/or palate disorders. Retrieved from http://www.worldcf.org/over.html

Lucy Lewis
Robert T. Brown
University of North Carolina at Wilmington

CLUBFOOT

Clubfoot is a descriptive term for a number of congenital deformities of one or both feet that vary in severity and etiology (Clubfoot.net, 2001). Involving both the soft tissues and the bone of the leg and foot, clubfoot generally occurs in isolation with no known cause, but it may also occur with chromosomal abnormalities and neurological disorders such as cerebral palsy and spina bifida (Dietz, Rebbeck, Blake, & Mathews, 1996; Dormans & Batshaw, 1997). Milder deformations of the foot that apparently arise from the fetus's position in the womb and may correct themselves or need minimal intervention are generally not described as clubfoot (Clubfoot.net, 2001). Most cases of true clubfoot are talipes equinovarus, "a deformity in which the joints, tendons, and ligaments in the foot and ankle have developed incorrectly. The heel is drawn up such that the toes are pointed down and the bottom of the foot points straight back (thus 'talipes equines' or 'horse foot': horses walk on their toes), and the foot is twisted in toward the other foot" (Clubfoot.net, 2001). This complex disorder affects twice as many boys as girls and has an incidence of 1 in 1,000 children.

Characteristics

1. The child is born with one or both feet turned inward.
2. No pain is associated with the feet.
3. The child also has spina bifida or cerebral palsy.
4. The child is born with any deformity involving solely the feet and ankles.

Clubfoot requires treatment, and early treatment is the most successful. If uncorrected, an affected child will walk on the outside-top surface of the foot, leading to other problems (Clubfoot.net, 2001). Type and timing of treatment vary with severity of the disorder. In mild cases, the only treatment that may be needed is a regimen of regular stretching of foot muscles that parents can be taught to do at home (Clubfoot, 1994). In most cases, orthopedists use casting as the first treatment, and the cast is put on soon after birth or at a few weeks of age. In casting, the foot is twisted into the correct position and held so that the bones and muscles grow appropriately. This can be mildly painful, but the pain usually lasts only during the casting itself. Casting can take from 3–6 months, with the casts changed weekly or biweekly. A splint or special shoes may then be used to prevent regression (Clubfoot.net, 2001). In about 50% of cases, manipulation and casting alone are sufficient to correct the deformity, but regular checkups are required to ensure that the foot does not return to the deformed shape. In the remaining cases, corrective surgery, performed between 3 and 12 months of age, is needed to release all tight tendons and ligaments. The surgery is complex and difficult, with recurrences of the deformity occasionally occurring. Again, regular checkups are called for.

With early and effective treatment, prognosis is good, and those born with clubfoot can have normal or near-normal foot appearance and mobility. If untreated, the foot will continue to grow in its twisted position and cause permanent mobility problems. No further intervention is generally needed, but parents should consult with their orthopedist concerning sports and physical education activities.

REFERENCES

Clubfoot. (1994). *Pediatrics for parents* (November 2–4).

Clubfoot.net (2001, March 20). Clubfoot. Retrieved from http://www.clubfoot.net/clubfoot.php3

Dietz, F. R., Rebbeck, T. R., Blake, D. D., & Mathews, K. D. (1996). An idiopathic clubfoot family does not show linkage to the chromosome region linked to distal arthrogryposis I. *Pediatrics, 98,* 560–561.

Dormans, J. P., & Batshaw, M. L. (1997). Muscles, bones, and nerves. In M. L. Batshaw (Ed.), *Children with disabilities* (4th ed., pp. 315–332). Baltimore: Paul H. Brookes.

Robert T. Brown
Amy Morrow
University of North Carolina

COATS' DISEASE

Coats' disease, or exudative retinitis, is a rare eye disorder that is characterized by a white or yellowish matter called telangiectatic malformations in the macular area or peripheral retina. The abnormal enlargement of the retinal blood vessels results in leakage of the yellow matter into the retina. This disease usually occurs within the first 10 years of life and may result in loss of vision or detachment of the retina (National Organization for Rare Disorders, Inc. [NORD], 1999). The specific etiology of Coats' disease is unknown, but it is believed to be an anomaly in the embryologic development of retinal blood vessels (Thoene & Coker, 1995).

Coats' disease affects more males than females and usually occurs in childhood. When Coats' disease occurs in the adult population it is called hyperlipemic retinitis (NORD, 1999).

Characteristics

1. Early signs consisting of large yellowish areas in and below the retina
2. Dilated telangiectatic blood vessels in the peripheral retina
3. Usually occurs only in one eye and affects central vision or peripheral vision
4. Subretinal bleeding if retinal detachment occurs
5. May cause strabismus (squinting)

Coats' disease is sometimes treated by photocoagulation (surgery) or cyrotherapy (freezing) in order to destroy the yellowish areas or telangiectatic malformations. Removal of abnormal blood vessels will not necessarily restore vision if too much fluid leaked into the retina (Thoene & Coker, 1995). Corticosteroid drugs may also be used to alleviate symptoms.

Special education services may be available for children with Coats' disease under vision problems if the disorder results in vision loss.

Treatment that is applied early may be successful in preventing progression of Coats' disease and improving vision. Coats' disease may progress to other severe symptoms such as retinal detachment, secondary cataracts, fibrous mass in the retina, rubeosis iridis, swelling of the membrane covering the back of the eyeball (secondary uveitis), secondary glaucoma, or shrinkage of the eyeball (Thoene & Coker, 1995).

REFERENCES

National Organization for Rare Disorders, Inc. (1999). Coats' disease. Retrieved from http://www.rarediseases.org

Thoene, J. G., & Coker, N. P. (Eds.). (1995). *Physicians guide to rare diseases* (2nd ed.). Montvale, NJ: Dowden.

Jennifer Hargrave
University of Texas at Austin

COCAINE ABUSE

Cocaine is a powerfully addictive stimulant that became extremely popular and widely used in the 1980s and 1990s. It is typically sold on the street as a fine, white, crystalline powder. Cocaine can be sniffed or snorted, injected, or smoked. Street names include coke, C, snow, flake, or blow (National Institute on Drug Abuse, 2001a).

Cocaine makes the user feel instantly alert and creates a false sense of joy or a high that generally wears off within 30 min. As the effects of the drug wear off, the user may feel anxious, depressed, and tired (American Academy of Pediatrics, 2000). Cocaine appears to block the normal flow of dopamine, a neurotransmitter, in the brain. It carries messages from one nerve cell to another and is associated with awareness, motivation, body movement, judgment, and pleasure. Dopamine appears to be responsible for the addictive effects of cocaine (Swan, 1998).

Crack, the street name for the freebase form of cocaine, is made by processing powdered cocaine so that it is smokable. It is called crack because of the crackling sound heard when the substance is smoked. Crack is inexpensive both to produce and to buy. Smoking cocaine allows extremely high doses of the drug to reach the brain very rapidly, resulting in an intense and immediate high, generally within 10 s (National Institute on Drug Abuse, 2001b). As a result, crack is said to be almost instantly addictive (American Medical Association, 1999).

Research examining the extent of cocaine use among adolescents in this country indicates that approximately 4.7% of 8th graders, 7.7% of 10th graders, and 9.8% of 12th graders have used cocaine at least once in their lifetimes. Data indicate increases in this area during the 1990s, although the extent of use for high school seniors is significantly less than its peak of 17.3% in 1985 (National Institute on Drug Abuse, 2001b). Factors that appear to increase the risk for substance abuse include previous treatment with therapeutic drugs, low achievement, low self-esteem, and having an alcoholic parent (Fox & Forbing, 1991).

Short-term effects

1. Increased energy
2. Euphoria
3. Decreased appetite
4. Mental alertness
5. Increased heart rate and blood pressure
6. Constricted blood vessels
7. Increased temperature
8. Dilated pupils

Cocaine's effects appear almost immediately after taking the drug. In addition to the short-term effects, cocaine may cause anxiety, irritability, confusion, and tremors. Some users experience hallucinations including what is known as coke bugs, or a sensation of insects crawling over the skin (American Medical Association, 1999). Taking large amounts of the drug (several milligrams or more) not only intensifies the high but also can result in erratic, bizarre, and violent behavior (National Institute on Drug Abuse, 2001a).

Long-term effects

1. Addiction
2. Irritability and mood disturbances
3. Restlessness
4. Paranoia
5. Auditory hallucinations

A discernible tolerance to cocaine tends to develop with regular and continued use. Many users report that successive highs are not as pleasurable as the first one, and they increase their doses to intensify and prolong the euphoric effects. Taking the drug repeatedly and at high doses (a binge) can result in a full-blown paranoid psychosis (National Institute of Drug Abuse, 2001a).

A number of serious medical complications are also associated with cocaine use. These include abdominal pain and nausea, disturbances in heart rhythm, heart attack, chest pain, respiratory failure, and neurological problems that range from headaches to seizures and strokes. In rare instance, sudden death can occur. Other adverse effects are related to the manner in which the cocaine is used. Nosebleeds, loss of smell, problems swallowing, and a chronically inflamed, runny nose can all result from snorting cocaine. Injecting the drug can result in puncture marks and tracks, and sometimes an allergic reaction (National Institute on Drug Abuse, 2001a).

Treatment of cocaine abuse and addiction tends to be rather complex, and it must address a variety of problems because abuse and addiction involve not only biological changes in the brain but a number of social, familial, and environmental factors as well. Behavioral treatments, especially cognitive-behavioral therapy, can be effective in decreasing drug use. Generally, this approach involves helping users recognize, avoid, and cope with problems and dysfunctional behaviors associated with drug use. The use of a token economy or contingency management can also be effective with cocaine abusers and addicts. With this type of system, the user receives positive rewards for continuing treatment and remaining drug free (National Institute on Drug Abuse, 2001a). Crisis intervention may also be helpful in addressing some of the acute problems associated with abuse and addiction (Newcomb & Bentler, 1989). In addition, a number of medications are currently being evaluated in clinical trials to examine their safety and effectiveness in treating cocaine addiction (National Institute on Drug Abuse, 2001b).

Research indicates that students receiving special education services, such as those with learning disabilities and emotional or behavior disorders, may demonstrate higher rates of substance abuse and chemical dependence than do regular education students (e.g., Elmquist, Morgan, & Bolds, 1992; Karacostas & Fisher, 1993). Because of these risks, it is important that special education programs include preventive efforts such as drug education, affective skill building, and coping skills training. Research also indicates that the effects of substance abuse can result in behaviors similar to those exhibited by youth with learning problems (Fox & Forbing, 1991). Comprehensive and appropriate assessment is necessary to differentiate students with learning disorders and students abusing drugs. Future research is focusing on developing effective medications to treat addiction, as well as evaluating the efficacy of various prevention programs and therapeutic interventions.

REFERENCES

American Academy of Pediatrics. (2000). Cocaine. Retrieved from http://www.ama.org

American Medical Association. (1999). Substance abuse: Types of drugs and their effects. Retrieved from http://www.ama.org

Elmquist, D. L., Morgan, D. P., & Bolds, P. K. (1992). Alcohol and other drug abuse among adolescents with disabilities. *International Journal of the Addictions, 27*(12), 1475–1483.

Fox, C. L., & Forbing, S. E. (1991). Overlapping symptoms of substance abuse and learning handicaps: Implications for educators. *Journal of Learning Disabilities, 24*(1), 24–31.

Karacostas, D. D., & Fisher, G. L. (1993). Chemical dependency in students with and without learning disabilities. *Journal of Learning Disabilities, 26*(7), 491–195.

National Institute on Drug Abuse. (2001a). Cocaine abuse and addiction. Retrieved from http://www.nida.nih.gov/ResearchReports/Cocaine/cocaine3.html#short

National Institute on Drug Abuse. (2001b). Crack and cocaine. Retrieved from http://www.nida.nih.gov/Infofax/cocaine.html

Newcomb, M. D., & Bentler, P. M. (1989). Substance use and abuse among children and teens. *American Psychologist, 44,* 242–248.

Swan, N. (1998). Brain scans open window to view cocaine's effects on the brain. Retrieved from http://165.112.78.61/NIDA_Notes/NNVol13N2/Brain.html

M. Franci Crepeau-Hobson
University of Northern Colorado

COCKAYNE SYNDROME

Cockayne syndrome is characterized by growth retardation, microcephaly, photosensitivity, and a prematurely aged appearance. In the classical and most common form of Cockayne syndrome (Type I), growth and development generally proceed at a normal rate in infancy, with symptoms becoming apparent after 1 or 2 years of age. An early-onset or congenital form of Cockayne syndrome (Type II) is apparent at birth. This form of the syndrome generally involves more severe symptoms and earlier death. There is some recent evidence that there may be a third form, Cockayne syndrome Type III, which involves a late onset of symptoms (National Organization for Rare Disorders, Inc., 1995).

Cockayne syndrome is an inherited autosomal recessive condition. The basic fault is thought to be a defect in the enzyme or enzymes responsible for the repair of cells following exposure to ultraviolet light. The relationship between these effects and the other neurological problems observed remains unclear (Gilbert, 1993).

This progressive and debilitating disease is extremely rare: only about 150 cases of Cockayne syndrome have been reported since it was first described in the literature in 1936 (Ozdirim, Topcu, Ozon, & Aysenur, 1996). Boys and girls are equally affected with Cockayne syndrome Type I, but boys are three times more likely to be affected with Type II (Gilbert, 1993). Cockayne syndrome is typically diagnosed between the second and fourth years, although prenatal diagnosis is possible through amniocentesis (Jones, 1997).

Characteristics

1. Growth deficiency and microcephaly following a period of normal growth, with severe dwarfism as the final result. There is also a loss of subcutaneous fat and adipose tissue that results in a precociously senile appearance.
2. Mental retardation that is progressive. The decrease in mental abilities appears to be related to atrophy of brain tissue and demyelination of nerves. There are also accompanying language delays with more than 20% of cases never progressing beyond the single-word stage.
3. Severe sensitivity to sunlight. Minimal exposure generally results in a red, scaly rash that is followed by scarring, excessive pigmentation, and atrophies of the skin.
4. Cataracts and retinal atrophy are common with increasing age, and there is a risk of blindness. In addition, the eyes often have a hollow, sunken appearance, and lid closure tends to be poor.
5. Malformed or prominent ears and sensorineural deafness.
6. Decreased muscle tone and reflexes resulting in a gait disturbance.

Children with Cockayne syndrome may qualify for special education services under the handicapping conditions of Infant Disability, Preschool Disability, Significantly Limited Intellectual Capacity, or Multiple Disabilities. Because of the progressive nature of this disease, frequent assessment of cognitive functioning, language ability, and psychomotor functioning may be indicated to ensure that appropriate interventions are provided. Instruction and curriculum should be modified to be developmentally appropriate, and special education services should be multidisciplinary. Additional academic support, speech-language therapy, and occupational therapy may be indicated. In addition, most children with Cockayne syndrome will gradually lose traditional methods of communication, and assistive technology may be warranted to facilitate the use of alternative modes of communicating.

Despite their cognitive, sensory, and communicative difficulties, children with Cockayne syndrome are consis-

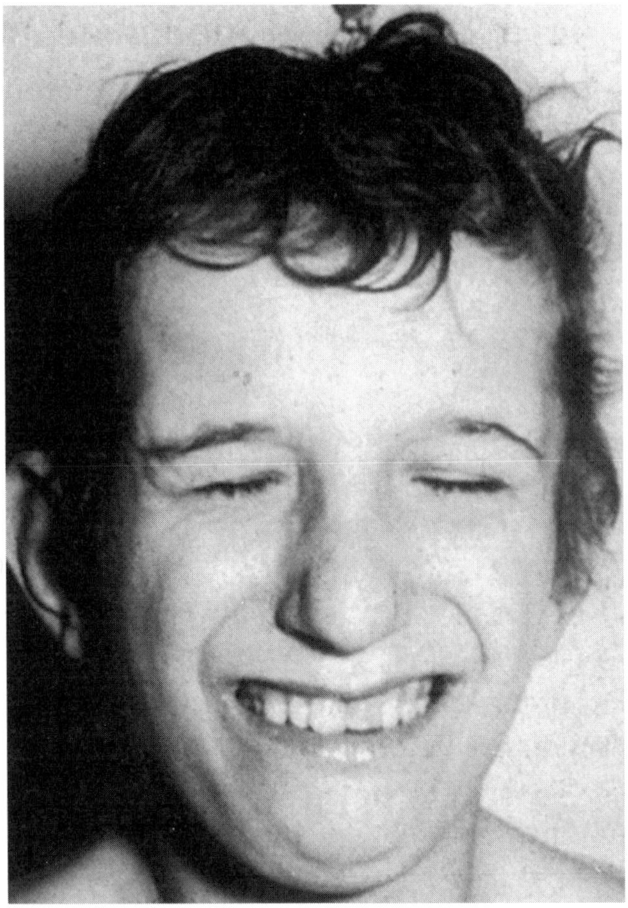

Cockayne Syndrome
Reprinted from *Clinical Syndromes,* Wiedemann and Kunze, 1997, by permission of the publisher Mosby

tently characterized in the literature as being happy, social, interactive, and friendly (Nance & Berry, 1992). However, therapeutic counseling may be indicated to help children with Cockayne syndrome cope with the progressive nature of the disease and the loss of skills. In addition, the severe and progressive nature of Cockayne syndrome can be devastating for the families of these children, and continuing psychological support and respite care should be available (Gilbert, 1993).

The symptoms of Cockayne syndrome are progressive, and most children with the disease die in early childhood, although some live into their late teens or early 20s (Gilbert, 1993). Medical treatment is limited to symptom management, as no dietary, drug, or hormonal therapy has been found to be effective in slowing or curing the disease (Nance & Berry, 1992).

REFERENCES

Gilbert, P. (1993). *The A-Z reference book of syndromes and inherited disorders: A manual for health, social and education workers.* London: Chapman and Hall.

Jones, K. L. (1997). *Smith's recognizable patterns of human malformation* (5th ed.). Philadelphia: W. B. Saunders.

Nance, M. A., & Berry, S. A. (1992). Cockayne syndrome: Review of 140 cases. *American Journal of Medical Genetics, 42,* 68–84.

National Organization for Rare Disorders, Inc. (1995). Cockayne syndrome. Retrieved from http://www.rarediseases.org

Ozdirim, E., Topcu, M., Ozon, A., & Aysenur, C. (1996). Cockayne syndrome: Review of 25 cases. *Pediatric Neurology, 15*(4), 312–316.

M. Franci Crepeau-Hobson
University of Northern Colorado

COFFIN-LOWRY SYNDROME

Coffin-Lowry syndrome is a rare genetic disorder characterized by craniofacial and skeletal abnormalities, mental retardation, short stature, characteristic hands, and hypotonia (Weidemann, Kunze, Grosse, & Dibbern, 1989). Characteristic facial features may include an underdeveloped upper jaw bone (maxillary hypoplasia), an abnormally prominent brow, downslanting eyelid folds (palpebral fissures), widely spaced eyes (hypertelorism), large ears, and unusually thick eyebrows. Skeletal abnormalities may include abnormal front-to-back and side-to-side curvature of the spine (kyphoscoliosis), unusual prominence of the breastbone (pectus carinatum), and short, tapered fingers. Additional abnormalities may also be present. Other features may include feeding and respiratory problems, developmental delay, hearing impairment, awkward gait, flat feet, and heart and kidney involvement.

The disorder affects males and females in equal numbers, but symptoms may be more severe in males. The disorder is caused by a defective gene, which was found in 1996 on the X chromosome (National Institute of Neurological Disorders and Stroke [NINDS], 2002).

Characteristics

1. Narrow, rectangular protruding forehead appearing bitemporally compressed; hypertelorism, antimongoloid slant of the palpebral fissures, thick upper eyelids, broad nasal root and short broad pug nose with a thick septum; pouting lower lip, mouth usually open; and unusual ears
2. Mental retardation; IQ usually below 50 in males.
3. Small stature, variously severe, height possibly below the third percentile
4. "Full" forearms; plumpish, lax, soft hands with tapered, hyperextensible fingers

There is no cure and no standard course of treatment for Coffin-Lowry syndrome. Treatment is symptomatic and sup-

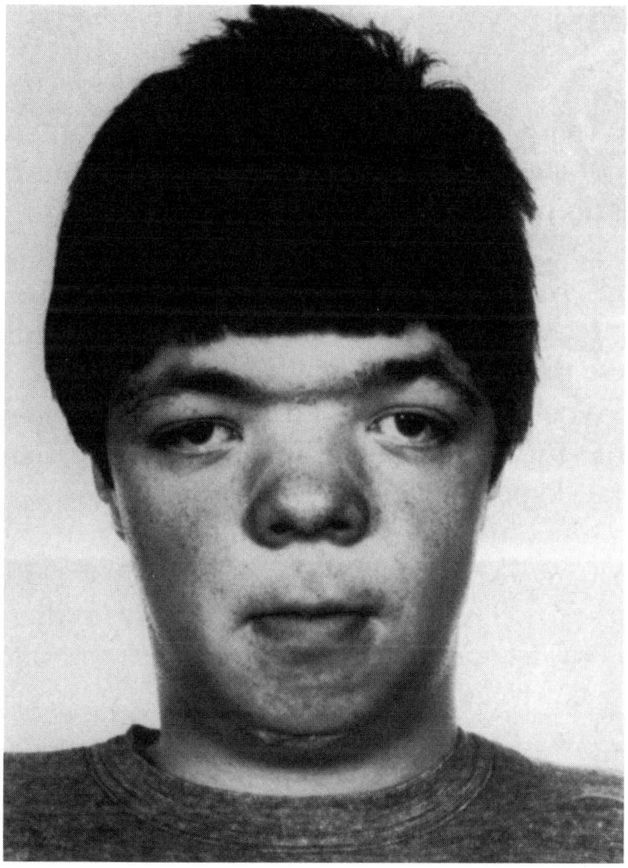

Coffin-Lowry Syndrome
Reprinted from *Clinical Syndromes,* Wiedemann and Kunze, 1997, by permission of the publisher Mosby

portive and may include physical and speech therapy and genetic counseling. Educational support from special education will most definitely be needed for these students, and placement in the least restrictive environment may be difficult to ascertain and may also change during development.

The prognosis for individuals with Coffin-Lowry syndrome varies depending on the severity of symptoms. Early intervention may improve the outlook for patients. NINDS supports and conducts research on genetic disorders, such as Coffin-Lowry syndrome, in an effort to find ways to prevent, treat, and, ultimately, cure this disorder (NINDS, 2002).

Families may obtain support and information from the Coffin-Lowry Syndrome Foundation; 3045 255th Avenue SE; Sammamish, WA 98075; e-mail, CLSFoundation@yahoo.com; Web address, http://clsfoundation.tripod.com; phone number, 425-427-0939.

REFERENCES

National Institute of Neurological Disorders and Stroke. (2002). MedlinePlus Coffin-Lowry information page. Retrieved from http://www.nlm.nih.gov/medlineplus/geneticdisorders.html.

Weidemann, H. R., Kunze, J., Grosse, F. R., & Dibbern, H. (1989). *Atlas of clinical syndromes: A visual aid to diagnosis.* St. Louis, MO: Mosby.

Elaine Fletcher-Janzen
University of Northern Colorado

COHEN SYNDROME

Cohen syndrome is characterized by truncal obesity, hypotonia, mental retardation, and ocular and craniofacial abnormalities. Characteristic craniofacial features include microcephaly, small jaw, prominent incisors, small philtrum, and high-arched palate.

Cohen syndrome is a rare disorder. Approximately 100 cases have been documented. It appears to occur with greater frequency in people of Eastern European Jewish decent. Females and males are affected equally. It is primarily an autosomal recessive genetic disorder that is present from birth. The gene responsible for the syndrome has been mapped to the long arm of Chromosome 8 (Thomaidis, Fryssira, Katsarou, & Metaxotou, 1999).

Characteristics

1. Low birth weight, delayed growth, delayed puberty, hypotonia, and obesity occurring in middle childhood
2. Prominent lips, downslant of eyelids, hyperextensible joints, narrow hands and feet, and possibly webbed feet and seizures (Jones, 1988)
3. Ocular abnormalities including diminished vision in bright light, degeneration of the retina (retina pigmentosa), optic atrophy, decreased visual acuity, and possibly total blindness
4. Mild to moderate mental retardation in 82% of cases (Gandy, 1994)

Treatment of Cohen syndrome depends on the individual's symptoms, but it may include surgery to correct abnormal facial features, visual problems, or webbed feet. Physical therapy may be necessary for children with hypotonia. Developmental delays and childhood obesity should be monitored. The child may need services from an ophthalmologist to care for visual abnormalities. Families often benefit from genetic counseling to understand better the disorder (Gandy, 1994).

The services required in school depend on the child's symptoms and needs. Children with Cohen syndrome usually qualify for special education services due to mental retardation, health problems, or visual impairments that affect learning. For children with developmental delays or hypotonia, early intervention programs are appropriate.

Individuals may require physical therapy. Periodic assessments help school personnel develop appropriate individual educational plans that maximize the student's learning potential (Plumridge, Bennett, Dinno, & Branson, 1993).

The prognosis of an individual with Cohen syndrome is variable, depending on the person's symptoms. Adults with mild mental retardation, for example, may be able to function with minimum supportive services. Future research is focused on understanding the etiology and genetics of the disorder.

REFERENCES

Gandy, A. (1994, December 4). Cohen syndrome. Retrieved from http://www.icondata.com/health/pedbase/files/cohensyn.htm

Jones, K. (1988). *Smith's recognizable patterns of human malformation.* Philadelphia: W. B. Saunders.

Plumridge, D., Bennett, R., Dinno, N., & Branson, C. (Eds.). (1993). *The student with a genetic disorder.* Springfield, IL: Charles C. Thomas.

Thomaidis, L., Fryssira, H., Katsarou, E., & Metaxotou, C. (1999). Cohen syndrome: Two new cases in siblings. *European Journal of Pediatrics, 158,* 838–841.

Susannah More
University of Texas at Austin

COLITIS, COLLAGENOUS

Collagenous colitis is a rare but treatable inflammatory disorder of the mucous membranes lining the colon. It is a poorly understood disorder that has not received much attention in the research (Microscopic/Collagenous Colitis FAQ, 1999). Collagenous colitis is often referred to as a form of microscopic colitis because it can only be detected by a pathologist using a microscope after a biopsy; with this condition during an endoscope procedure (colonoscopy or sigmoidoscopy), the colon looks normal. Collagenous colitis is also often referred to as lymphocytic colitis because it is characterized by a thickening of the subepithelial collagen layer and increased lymphocytes in the lining of the colon.

Despite controversy over the syndrome's name, the treatment and symptoms are virtually identical (Mayo Clinic Rochester, 2000). Symptoms are characterized by watery, nonbloody diarrhea that may be severe and explosive, requiring up to 30 bathroom visits per day. Episodes are extremely sudden and may be persistent or intermittent over the period of months or years. In rare cases, the diarrhea may cause dehydration; other symptoms include weakness and fatigue, difficulty eating, abdominal bloating or pain, weight loss, and nausea. Dietary factors alone do not seem to influence the sudden bouts of diarrhea although certain foods such as high fiber, fat, milk products, spices, wheat, or uncooked fruits and vegetables may exacerbate symptoms, especially diarrhea (Cleveland Clinic, 1999).

Characteristics

1. Sudden and explosive fecal incontinence up to 30 times a day
2. Watery, nonbloody diarrhea
3. Persistent or intermittent episodes that can lead to dehydration and weight loss
4. Associated with secondary symptoms of weakness and fatigue and nausea
5. Associated with secondary symptoms of abdominal bloating, pain, and poor eating abilities
6. Can be aggravated by specific foods
7. Often originates as an elusive form of arthritis

Patients sometimes seek treatment for an elusive form of arthritis as much as 10 years prior to problems controlling diarrhea (National Organization for Rare Disorders, Inc., 1998). The arthritis typically effects the back, hips, and sometimes ribs. Other associated problems with this illness may include iritis, purpura, thyroid disease, pernicious anemia, idiopathic pulmonary fibrosis, fibromyalgia, unexplained severe itching, mouth sores, fatigue, depression, mitral valve prolapse, and celiac sprue (Mayo Clinic Rochester, 2000). There does not seem to be an association with Crohn's disease, ulcerative colitis, or cancer.

The typical patient is a middle-aged woman, and the rate of onset increases after the age of 40. It is also seen in men and in children as young as 7 years, with a reoccurrence of likelihood in older individuals. Many patients diagnosed are Caucasians in Northern Europe, Canada, the United States, Australia, and New Zealand (Microscopic/Collagenous Colitis FAQ, 1999). Many patients report a close family member with the same or similar intestinal symptoms, giving the appearance of a hereditary factor. Other possible causes are unidentified chronic gastrointestinal infections such as dysentery or giardia, immune disturbances including autoimmune disease, and medications such as some nonsteriodal anti-inflammatory agents (i.e., ibuprofen, ranitidine, carbemazepine).

Diagnosis is often made through a process of elimination. There is no proven cure, but medications can arrest the syndrome (Mayo Clinic Rochester, 2000). Traditionally, treatment is started with sulfasalazine, but if patients cannot tolerate it, Asocal is typically prescribed. Antidiarrheal medications such as Imodium and Lomotil are also used for temporary relief but tend merely to delay the diarrhea. Other medications that can help are aminosalicylate, metronidazole, cholestyramine, and bismuth subsalicylate. Prednisone is also often prescribed but cannot be used long-term due to the side effects of cataract formation, high blood pressure, and increased rate of diabetes that are associated with its use. Antibiotics have shown excellent short-term results. Surgical removal of the colon by ileostomy is a radical approach that is seldom used.

Children experiencing this condition may need to engage in stress reduction activities to eliminate anxiety over illness and social stigma created from required frequent bathroom breaks. Other services may also need to be provided by the school to accommodate the child, such as conveniently located restrooms and provision of educational material when the child is unable to be in the classroom. Although special education services are typically not warranted, in rare occasions children are served under the classification of Other Health Impairment.

REFERENCES

Cleveland Clinic. (1999, September). Gastrointestinal center: Treatments for collangenous colitis. Retrieved from http://on-health.webmd.com/conditions/condctr/gasrto/item,49305.asp

Mayo Clinic Rochester. (2000). Inflammatory bowel disease interest group: Collagenous/microscopic colitis. Retrieved from http://www.mayo.edu/int-med/gi/ibd.htm

Microscopic/Collagenous Colitis FAQ. (1999, October). Retrieved from http://www.malinowski.com/faq.htm

National Organization for Rare Disorders. (1998). Colitis, collagenous. Retrieved from http://www.rarediseases.org

Walter R. Schamber
Rik Carl D'Amato
University of Northern Colorado

COLITIS, ULCERATIVE

Ulcerative colitis is an inflammatory bowel disease, often chronic, that affects the mucus of the colon. It usually begins in the rectum and sigmoid colon and spreads to the entire colon, but rarely affects the small intestine. The ulcerated areas of the large intestine become inflamed and may cause abscesses leading to episodes of bloody diarrhea, abdominal pain, urgent bowel movements, fever, weight loss, joint pain, and skin lesions (Larson, 1990). The etiology of this disease is unknown.

The epidemiology and demographic incidence of this condition is 50–150 cases per 100,000 individuals, primarily affecting women between the ages of 14 and 38 years. A second increase in incidences occurs between the ages of 55 and 70 (Ferri, 1999). It also seems more prevalent among Jewish and high socioeconomic groups (Weinstock, Andrews, & Cray, 1998). Causes are unknown but may be related to stress, alcohol use, smoking, genetic factors, and diet.

Characteristics

Early symptoms

1. Pain in the left side of the abdomen that improves after bowel movements
2. Episodes of bloody diarrhea with mucus or pus, alternating with symptom-free intervals

Acute symptoms

1. Increased bloody diarrhea of up to 10–20 bowel movements a day
2. Severe cramps and abdominal pain, especially around the rectum
3. High fever of up to 104 °F (40 °C)
4. Sweating, dehydration
5. Nausea and irritability
6. Bloated abdomen
7. Joint pain
8. Skin lesions

Treatment goals consist of controlling inflammation, replacing nutritional losses and blood volume, and preventing complications. Bed rest is necessary with intravenous fluid replacement and a clear liquid diet to reduce stool volume. Blood transfusions or iron supplements may be needed to correct anemia.

Minimal symptoms are corrected with an antidiarrheal medication prescribed by a doctor. For mild or moderate conditions, the disease can be treated orally with an aminosalicylate, usually sulfasalazine, at 500 mg twice a day until a therapeutic dose of 4 to 6 g a day is reached. In addition, medicated enemas such as hydrocortisone can be effective. For severe disease, oral, enema, or suppository corticosteroids such as prednisone (40–60 mg/day) are useful (Ferri, 1999). Approximately 20–25% of patients afflicted will require surgery if they do not respond to medication therapy. The operation most commonly performed is the ileo-anal anastomosis, in which the diseased colon and large intestine are removed but the rectum is left intact. The small intestine is then stitched to the rectum, allowing for normal passage of stool rather than a permanent use of an ileostomy bag (Larson, 1990).

Psychotherapy is useful in most patients due to the chronicity of the disease and the young age of patients. Referral to self-help groups is recommended and especially important when the illness may be related to anorexia nervosa (Ferri, 1999).

Colonoscopic surveillance and multiple biopsies should be instituted yearly after diagnosis to prevent the increased risk of colon cancer (10–20% of patients develop it after 10 years of the disease). Furthermore, 75% of patients treated medically will experience relapse and need further medical attention. Consultation for suspected cases should be brought to the attention of a gastrointestinal physician for a sigmoidoscopy or colonoscopy (Griffith, 1995).

REFERENCES

Ferri, F. (1999). *Ferri's clinical advisor: Instant diagnosis and treatment.* St. Louis, MO: Mosby.

Griffith, H. (1995). *Complete guide to symptoms: Illness and surgery* (3rd ed.). New York: Body Press/Perigee.

Larson, D. (1990). *The Mayo Clinic family health book.* New York: William Morrow.

Weinstock, D., Andrews, M., & Cray, J. (1998). *Professional guide to disease* (6th ed.). Springhouse, PA: Springhouse.

Walter R. Schamber
Rik Carl D'Amato
University of Northern Colorado

COLORADO TICK FEVER

Colorado tick fever is an acute viral infection transmitted by the bite of a tick. This disease is characterized by a sudden onset of symptoms including fever, severe muscle aches (myalgia), joint stiffness, headache, sore throat, sensitivity to light (photophobia), nausea, vomiting, fatigue, and occasionally a raised rash. More severe symptoms include sequelae such as meningoencephalitis, an inflammation of the membranes covering the brain and spinal cord. Extensive involvement of the respiratory system is rarely seen with Colorado tick fever (Byrd, Vasquez, & Roy, 1997); however, infection has been associated with vascular instability, circulatory disturbance (hemorrhagic disease), cardiac inflammation (myocarditis), and other pulmonary problems.

The prevalence of Colorado tick fever is estimated to be 200 to 300 cases annually. The infection is limited to mountainous areas in the Western United States and is most frequently reported to occur from early spring to late summer. The incubation period lasts from 3 to 6 days, and the period of illness lasts 7 to 10 days. The course of illness, however, tends to be biphasic; that is, symptoms present, remit, and then reoccur (Harrison's Principles of Internal Medicine, 1999). For example, common symptoms such as fever and muscle soreness may continue for three days and then remit, only to recur one to three days later.

Characteristics

1. This acute viral infection is transmitted by the bite of a tick in the Western United States.
2. Fever and muscle aches are the most common symptoms.
3. Full recovery is usually expected, but complications can occur (e.g., meningoencephalitis, hemorrhagic disease, myocarditis, and pulmonary involvement).
4. Permanent neurological complications can be manifest as seizures, motor abnormalities, language disturbance, and intellectual deficits.

Blood tests can be used to make the diagnosis at any stage of the disease (Attoui, Billoir, Bruey, de Micco, & de Llamballerie, 1998). Prognosis is generally good; that is, symptoms remit within the first couple of weeks. Treatment is typically focused on symptom relief after successful removal of the tick. Aspirin should not be given to infants or children who have recently had a tick bite as this treatment may exacerbate the condition (e.g., increase vascular instability).

In cases where Colorado tick fever causes the marrow cells to become infected by the virus, symptoms are likely to persist, and hospitalization may even be required. In these and other cases of complicated tick fever (e.g., encephalitis, respiratory difficulties, and hemorrhagic fevers), extended school absences may occur. It is rare, however, for children to require special education services as a result of this infection. When services are required, however, they are likely under the category of Other Health Impairment. If significant cognitive sequelae persist, it may be necessary to serve the child in classrooms for students with Intellectual Disabilities. In any case, a comprehensive psychological evaluation should be conducted before providing services. In addition, consultations should be obtained from the speech and language pathologist when language deficits are noted, and from occupational or physical therapists when motor abnormalities are observed.

Future research needs to address immune response to Colorado tick fever. It remains unclear why some individuals are affected adversely and others are not. Better understanding of the mechanism of the disease will hopefully result in greater prevention and more effective intervention (e.g., vaccines).

REFERENCES

Attoui, H., Billoir, F., Bruey, J. M., de Micco, P., & de Llamballerie, X. (1998). Serologic and molecular diagnosis of Colorado tick fever viral infections. *American Journal of Tropical Medicine and Hygiene, 59,* 763–768.

Byrd, R., Vasquez, J., & Roy, T. (1997). Respiratory manifestations of tick-borne diseases in the Southeastern United States. *Southern Medical Journal, 90,* 1–4.

Harrison's Principles of Internal Medicine. (2000). Retrieved December 2000 from http://www.harrisonsonline.com

Heather Edgel
Elaine Clark
University of Utah

CONDUCT DISORDER

Conduct disorder is a behavior pattern in which an individual violates societal norms or the basic rights of others (American Psychiatric Association [APA], 1994). Usually, it is reported in 4–9% of the population (Campbell, Gonzalez, & Silva, 1992). Conduct disorder is generally defined by age of onset as during childhood or during adolescence (Hinshaw & Anderson, 1996). Age of onset tends to be earlier for boys than for girls, and boys are diagnosed with conduct disorder four to five times more frequently (Campbell et al., 1992).

Characteristics (APA, 1994)

1. Frequent displays of temper
2. Refusal to comply or defiance of rules
3. Criminal acts (e.g., assault, rape, theft, or extortion)
4. Lying or blaming others to avoid punishment
5. Physical and emotional cruelty to animals and people
6. Truancy from school
7. Commonly described as touchy, angry, spiteful, destructive, bullying, and cruel

It is important to note that about half of the children with conduct disorder also have an internalizing disorder (e.g., depression or anxiety) and that 50–75% also have attention-deficit/hyperactivity disorder (Wood, 1996). Learning disabilities and brain injuries that predate the onset of the conduct disorder have also been extensively noted in the research literature (Tramontana & Hooper, 1997). The prognosis for improvement differs depending on the age of onset and the existence of comorbid diagnoses. Early onset is associated with problems of antisocial behavior throughout the affected individuals' lives. When the onset is during adolescence, one is less likely to maintain deviant activities and perform acts of violence (Hinshaw & Anderson, 1996).

Treatment has been addressed through various methods; it is important to note that studies comparing efficacy of the various treatments are lacking (Lavin & Rifkin, 1993). Available studies indicate that parent training has been effective for conduct disorder (McMahon, 1994). Parent management training involves the training of parents in the appropriate skills to help them alter their child's behaviors (Kazdin, 1995). This training is based on the premise that behaviors are learned or strengthened in the home and maintained inadvertently by the parents. This type of treatment is conducted primarily with the caregivers, who use what they learned from these sessions in the home (Kazdin, 1995).

The application of behavioral principles in schools by teachers has proven to be very effective in changing social behaviors in youth (Love & Kaswan, 1974). Some notable problems are that behaviors tend to reappear at the end of the program and improvements tend not to generalize well. Focusing treatment on individual behaviors does not address the constellation of behaviors making up conduct disorder, and durable changes rarely have been shown (Kazdin, 1995).

Several types of medical treatments have been used to attempt to control problems associated with conduct disorder. Generally, pharmacotherapy is considered appropriate only with aggressive and destructive behaviors accompanied by explosiveness (Campbell et al., 1992). Prior to pharmacotherapy, the level of aggressiveness has to be monitored carefully so that any change experienced with the use of the drug can be identified clearly. Drugs used for conduct disorder include lithium, stimulants, and neuroleptics.

Because children with conduct disorder often are considered disabled, they may be eligible for certain services under Section 504 of the Rehabilitation Act. Because Section 504 is civil rights legislation, schools need to be careful not to discriminate against children with this disorder (Huefner, 2000). Because conduct disorder is not a category for special education services under the Individuals with Disabilities Education Act, some states provide special education to children with conduct disorder through Other Health Impairment or Emotionally Disturbed (Huefner, 2000).

Future research should include more comprehensive evaluations of school-based techniques for working with children with conduct disorder. Teachers, both in regular education and special education, need empirically supported methods for classroom management. Given that teachers frequently use behavior management to control students, and behavior management has not been shown to be effective with these children, it is important to find out what is effective.

REFERENCES

American Psychiatric Association. (1994). *Diagnostic and statistical manual of mental disorders* (4th ed.). Washington, DC: Author.

Campbell, M., Gonzalez, N. M., & Silva, R. R. (1992). The pharmacologic treatment of conduct disorders and rage outbursts. *Pediatric Psychopharmacology, 1,* 69–85.

Hinshaw, S. P., & Anderson, C. A. (1996). Conduct and oppositional defiant disorders. In E. J. Mash & R. A. Barkely (Eds.), *Child psychopathology.* New York: Guilford Press.

Huefner, D. S. (2000). *Getting comfortable with special education law: A framework for working with children with disabilities.* Norwood, MA: Christopher-Gordon.

Kazdin, A. E. (1995). *Conduct disorders in childhood and adolescence* (2nd ed.). London: Sage.

Lavin, M. R., & Rifkin, A. (1993). Diagnosis and pharmacotherapy of conduct disorder. *Progress in Neuro-Psychopharmacology and Biological Psychiatry, 17*(6), 875–885.

Love, L. R., & Kaswan, J. W. (1974). *Troubled children: Their families, schools, and treatments.* New York: Wiley.

McMahon, R. J. (1994). Diagnosis, assessment, and treatment of externalizing problems in children: The role of longitudinal data. *Journal of Consulting and Clinical Psychology, 62*(5), 901–917.

Tramontana, M. G., & Hooper, S. R. (1997). Neuropsychology of child psychopathology. In C. R. Reynolds & E. Fletcher-Janzen (Eds.), *The handbook of clinical child neuropsychology* (pp. 120–139). New York: Plenum Press.

Wood, I. K. (1996). Conduct disorder and oppositional defiant disorder. In D. Parmelee (Ed.), *Child and adolescent psychiatry* (pp. 83–95). Baltimore: Mosby.

S. Kathleen Krach
Texas A&M University

CONDUCTIVE HEARING LOSS

Diseases or obstructions in the outer or middle ear cause conductive hearing losses. Specifically, a conductive hearing loss is the impairment of hearing due to a failure of sound pressure waves to reach the cochlea through normal air conduction channels; at the same time, the inner ear is usually normal. Etiology of a conductive hearing loss varies, including the following: (a) foreign body obstruction; (b) bacterial infections of the external ear canal (otitis externa), growths of the bony external canal (osteoma, hyperostosis, exotosis); (c) congenital atresia, middle ear infections (acute, serous, or chronic otitis media); (d) hardening of the middle ear system (otosclerosis); or (e) trauma to the outer or middle ear system that causes a blockage of sound to the inner ear. Sensitivity to sound is diminished, but clarity (interpretation of the sound) is not changed, in a person with a conductive hearing loss. Conductive losses usually affect all frequencies of hearing evenly and do not result in severe losses. A person with a conductive hearing loss usually is able to wear a hearing aid or can be helped medically or surgically. If volume is increased to compensate for the loss, hearing is usually normal.

The U.S. Department of Education reported that during the 1996–1997 school year, 68,766 students aged 6–21 years (or 1.3% of all students with disabilities) received special education services under the combined categories of hearing impairment and deafness. However, the number of children with hearing loss is undoubtedly higher because many of these students may have other disabilities as well and may be served under other categories or may not be served at all. Students who have a diagnosed conductive hearing loss specifically are thought to constitute a small percentage of the hearing impaired population, as conductive losses are usually treatable. The specific prevalence for this group alone is unknown.

Characteristics

1. The child speaks in a relatively quiet voice and is often difficult to hear.
2. The child hears loud or amplified speech well.
3. The child hears better in the presence of background noise or with noise masking.
4. Speech or language development may be delayed or may cease temporarily.
5. Speech discrimination is unimpaired.

Fortunately, patients with conductive hearing losses can undergo medical and surgical treatment, which can usually improve the hearing and frequently restore it completely. The simplest type of hearing loss to remedy is that caused by cerumen (ear wax) or a foreign object in the ear canal. Removal of the wax or foreign matter is accomplished by means of instruments and irrigation. Other nonsurgically treated losses include administration of antibiotics to control infections such as otitis media.

At times, surgery may be required for several etiologies of conductive hearing loss. In otitis media, a myringotomy may be performed to avoid rupturing of the tympanic membrane (eardrum). In this procedure, the physician makes an incision in the tympanic membrane to allow the middle ear to drain. A surgical incision is quicker to heal than a tear caused by a rupture. Another surgery available is a tympanoplasty, of which there are several types. Tympanoplasty is performed in order to restore or reconstruct damaged portions of the middle ear. The most commonly performed type, with a high incidence in the preschool population, is the placement of drainage tubes (polyethylene, or PE, tubes) in the tympanic membrane to remove fluid from the middle ear. This surgery is often performed when otitis media is recurring due to the horizontal position of the eustachian tube (the portion of the middle ear that allows for drainage of cerumen and fluid away from the tympanic membrane) during the infant and toddler years. The PE tubes may be left in place for an indefinite period of time and usually come out without medical intervention. As the child grows, the eustachian tube will become more vertical as opposed to its original horizontal direction, maximizing drainage in the middle ear and correcting drainage difficulties (Katz, 1985).

Special education services may be available to children with a conductive hearing loss under the category of Hearing Impairment. Conductive hearing loss does not affect a person's intellectual capacity or ability to learn, is often temporary, and is not accompanied by another disability. Issues that should be considered when determining special education placement for a student with a conductive hearing loss include whether the student is progressing as would be expected and whether the student is displaying characteristics not usually seen in a student without a hearing loss. Services may include regular speech, language, and auditory training from a specialist; amplification systems; favorable seating in class; assistance of a notetaker; instruction for the teacher; and counseling.

Children who are hard of hearing will find it much more difficult to learn vocabulary, grammar, word order, idiomatic expressions, and other aspects of verbal communication. A conductive hearing loss frequently affects speech and articulation development, as conductive losses are frequent in the toddler and preschool population. However, they are difficult to detect at this age because they are often fluctuating in nature. Students with conductive hearing losses usually require articulation therapy with a speech-language pathologist. It is important for the teacher, speech pathologist, and audiologist to work together to teach the child to use his or her residual hearing to the maximum extent possible.

Overall, the prognosis for a student with a conductive hearing loss is excellent, as the loss is often treatable and interventions, when necessary, are minimal. Research is being conducted on the impact of hearing loss on learning, behavior, and communication (Moores, 1987). Although some evidence suggests that hearing loss is accompanied by additional learning difficulties, hearing loss has not been determined to be the primary etiology of the learning problem. Professionals are researching and moving toward the belief that all students with hearing losses should have individualized approaches to instruction, despite their common diagnosis.

REFERENCES

Katz, J. (1985). *Handbook of clinical audiology* (3rd ed.). Baltimore: Williams & Wilkins.

Moores, D. F. (1987). *Educating the deaf: Psychology, principles, practices* (3rd ed.). Boston: Houghton Mifflin.

Jennifer Nicholls
Shelley Pelletier
Dysart Unified School District
Dysart, Arizona

CONGENITAL WORD BLINDNESS

Congenital word blindness is a term used to describe poor readers. It was first used by W. P. Morgan (1896) in the late 19th century to explain unexpected reading failures in otherwise intelligent children. Morgan assumed that the disorder was congenital rather than acquired by postnatal injury or assault. As an analogy to describe the condition, however, he used adults who demonstrated reading problems following acquired brain lesions. Congenital word blindness was first thought to be caused by a defect in the angular gyrus of the left cerebral hemisphere, an area of the brain associated with visual memory of words (Doehring, Backman, & Waters, 1983). The condition, however, was later viewed as a problem with left-right orientation and stephosymbolia (i.e., twisted word imagery) caused in part by a lack of cerebral dominance (Wallin, 1968).

The incidence of congenital word blindness was reported to be between 0.05% and 25%, but most studies reported closer to 10% (Hagger, 1968). It was generally believed that the disorder was genetic, as it was often found in first- and second-degree relatives and in 3 or 4 times more males than females (Hagger, 1968).

Characteristics

1. Specific difficulties in the area of reading despite normal vision included the following:
   a. Inability to perceive and remember the shapes of printed letters
   b. Difficulty in figure-ground discrimination in both visual and auditory fields
   c. Reversals and translocations of letters and words
   d. Mirror writing
   e. Confusion between pairs of letters (e.g., m/w; n/h; b/d)
   f. Misaligned capital letters and letters that are uneven sizes and positions
2. Spelling and writing were also frequently affected.
3. Otherwise individuals had normal intelligence.
4. The difficulty is not due to mental retardation, sensory deprivation, environmental deprivation, or emotional or social problems.

Treatment methods developed to address the visual perceptual problems believed to be inherent in congenital word blindness frequently emphasized early motor training and improving eye-hand coordination to develop learning patterns better. Specifically, materials were developed to help address the child's difficulties with figure-ground discrimination, visual closure, visual-motor speed, position in space, and form constancy. Methods that emphasized the simultaneous stimulation of several modes of sensory input (e.g., placing finger on larynx while speaking, tracing fingers over largely written words, and handling cut-out letters and words) were also popular. Although the effectiveness of these interventions in improving reading lacked support, they made an important contribution to education.

The work done by these early researchers and educators highlighted the importance of early intervention and small teacher-to-student ratio for reading remediation and increased awareness that these children were not simply unmotivated, disobedient, or lacking in intellectual prowess: They had a specific reading problem. This work also stimulated further research in the area of reading disabilities.

REFERENCES

Doehring, D. G., Backman, J., & Waters, G. (1983). Theoretical models of reading disabilities, past, present, and future. *Topics in Learning and Learning Disabilities, 3*(1), 84–94.

Hagger, T. D. (1968). Congenital word blindness or specific developmental dyslexia: A review. *The Medical Journal of Australia, 1*(19), 783–789.

Morgan, W. P. (1896). A case of congenital word blindness. *British Medical Journal, 2,* 1378–1379.

Wallin, J. E. (1968). An historical conspectus on the existence of congenital word blindness. *Journal of Special Education, 2*(2), 203–207.

Jenise Jensen
Elaine Clark
University of Utah

CONJUNCTIVITIS, LIGNEOUS

Ligneous conjunctivitis is a chronic disorder characterized by the growth of thick, wood-like lesions on mucous membranes. Lesions often begin in the eyes and later develop in other areas such as the nose, vocal cords, larynx, trachea, sinuses, and female genital tract. The etiology of this disease is unknown, but there is some evidence of an autosomal recessive inheritance (Ligneous conjunctivitis, 1990; Kanai & Polack, 1971; National Organization for Rare Disorders [NORD], 1999).

This condition begins in early childhood, during the first 3 years of life, and generally continues throughout the life course (Kanai & Polack, 1971; Schuster et al., 1997). It is a rare disorder with a prevalence rate of approximately 60 to 70 reported cases (Firat, 1974; Ligneous conjunctivitis, 1990), and it is more common in females than in males with a ratio of 3:1 (Cohen, 1990).

Characteristics

1. Recurring growth of tough, thick, wood-like lesions on mucous membranes begins in early childhood (ages 0 to 3) and continues into adulthood.
2. Chronic infections of the upper respiratory tract are common; eyes may be perforated or lost (Firat, 1974); and death from pneumonia or airway obstruction may occur (Cohen, 1990).
3. Removal of lesions causes hemorrhaging and the regrowth of thicker lesions at the removal site (Firat, 1974).

No successful treatment for ligneous conjunctivitis has been found at this time (Cohen, 1990; Ligneous conjunctivitis, 1990); however, improvement was reported for some individuals who were treated with Kinaden and chymotrypsin eye drops over a 12-month period (Firat, 1974). Antibiotics may be used to treat upper respiratory infections that are common in individuals with this disease.

Children with ligneous conjunctivitis may qualify for special education services under Other Health Impairment due to possible visual impairments and medical needs. Students with visual impairment may require an orientation and mobility instructor to help them successfully navigate their surroundings at school. It is also important for visually impaired students to learn organizational skills so that they can easily find materials needed to complete schoolwork (Bradley-Johnson, 1995).

Modifications in the classroom may be necessary as well. For example, students should be provided with materials written in Braille or large print. They should also be allowed more time to complete assignments as reading Braille or large type takes longer than reading standard print. Students may also require a Braille typewriter or a voice-activated computer. Real objects should be used for teaching math concepts and arithmetic operations (Bradley-Johnson, 1995). In addition to classroom modifications, students with ligneous conjunctivitis may require social skills training, as their social development may be delayed. In addition, the need for frequent medical attention may require children with the disorder to be absent from school often; therefore, home visits or home schooling may be necessary.

Prognosis is poor because ligneous conjunctivitis is a chronic condition with no cure (Cohen, 1990; Ligneous conjunctivitis, 1990). Individuals with the disease will continue to experience complications over the life span such as the loss of their eyes or voice, and death from pneumonia or airway obstruction may occur (Cohen, 1990; Firat, 1974). Etiology and treatment are the focus of further research.

REFERENCES

Bradley-Johnson, S. (1995). Best practices in planning effective instruction for students who are visually impaired or blind. In A. Thomas & J. Grimes (Eds.), *Best practices in school psychology* (pp. 1133–1140). Washington, DC: National Association of School Psychologists.

Cohen, S. R. (1990). Ligneous conjunctivitis: An ophthalmic disease with potentially fatal tracheobronchial obstruction. *Annals of Otology, Rhinology, and Laryngology, 99,* 509–512.

Firat, T. (1974). Ligneous conjunctivitis. *American Journal of Ophthalmology, 78*(4), 679–688.

Kanai, A., & Polack, F. M. (1971). Histologic and electron microscope studies of ligneous conjunctivitis. *American Journal of Ophthalmology, 72*(5), 909–916.

Ligneous conjunctivitis. (1990). *Lancet, 335*(8681), 84.

National Organization for Rare Disorders. (1999). Conjunctivitis, ligneous. Retrieved from http://www.rarediseases.org

Schuster, V., Mingers, A. M., Seidenspinner, S., Nussgens, Z., Pukrop, T., & Kreth, H. W. (1997). Homozygous mutations in the plasminogen gene of two unrelated girls with ligneous conjunctivitis. *Blood, 90*(3), 958–966.

Stacey L. Bates
University of Texas at Austin

CONRADI-HUNERMANN SYNDROME

This disorder is one of three clinically, genetically, and biochemically distinct forms of chondrodysplasia punctata, which is a rare hereditary bone disease. The hallmarks of Conradi-Hunermann syndrome (CHS) are mild to moderate short stature, asymmetric limb shortening, pinpoint calcifications of epiphyses (the areas of active bone growth), and large skin pores.

CHS is rare. No data are available about its incidence in the general population. The pattern of inheritance is X-linked dominant. Affected individuals are all female. The presence of the abnormal gene in the male embryo is apparently lethal.

Characteristics

1. Mild to moderate growth deficiency, failure to thrive in infancy
2. Low nasal bridge, flat face, downward slanting eyelids, cataracts
3. Asymmetric limb shortening, joint contractures of varying severity
4. Scoliosis (lateral curvature of the spine), related to abnormal mineralization of vertebrae (may be present at birth)
5. Sparse, coarse hair and patchy hair loss
6. Almost all newborns covered with a thick, yellow, scaling rash, with extremely red underlying skin
7. In older children, large skin pores resembling an orange peel; scattered areas of dry, scaly skin
8. Various degrees of mental deficiency

Treatment of children with CHS addresses their orthopedic problems. Scoliosis may require bracing, casting or surgery. Children with CHS require modifications and cognitive support through special education services based on the degree of mental deficiency. A comprehensive neuropsychological evaluation to determine cognitive strengths and weaknesses would provide the individual's educators with valuable information in developing an educational plan.

Poor weight gain and recurrent infections are common during infancy. Children who make it through this period have a favorable prognosis for continued survival. Orthopedic problems persist, however, and the incidence of cataract formation is high.

REFERENCES

Darmstadt, G. L. (2000). Disorders of keratinization. In R. E. Behrman, R. M. Kleigman, & H. B. Jenson (Eds.), *Nelson's textbook of pediatrics* (16th ed., pp. 2007–2011). Philadelphia: W. B. Saunders.

Jones, K. (1997). *Smith's recognizable patterns of human malformations* (5th ed.). Philadelphia: W. B. Saunders.

Barry H. Davison
Ennis, Texas

Joan W. Mayfield
Baylor Pediatric Specialty Services
Dallas, Texas

COPROLALIA

Coprolalia, a symptom of Tourette syndrome (TS), is the uncontrollable use of obscenities and curse words. Although popularly associated with TS, only 8–15% of affected individuals manifest coprolalia. A peak in the severity of coprolalia often occurs in adolescence, with some reduction in adulthood (Singer, 1997). A variety of basal ganglia and limbic system abnormalities have been linked to development of TS (Brown & Ivers, 1999; Singer, 1997).

Characteristics

1. Coprolalia is a complex vocal tic.
2. Obscenities and elaborate sexual and aggressive statements are uttered at inappropriate times.
3. Use of racial slurs in public situations is common.
4. Coprolalia may occur less frequently than simple motor tics, such as eye blinking or grimacing.
5. Coprolalia is more disruptive than simple motor tics.
6. When in the presence of a doctor or therapist, affected children may temporarily "lose" their tics. However, as soon as they leave, their symptoms may become more severe.
7. Coprolalia is more frequent in stressful situations.

Both pharmacological and behavioral treatments are used. More than 70% of individuals with TS are on medication. Most common medications are dopamine-blocking agents, such as haloperidol and other neuroleptics, which reduce symptoms by as much as 80%. However, adverse side effects are common.

Use of behavioral techniques has successfully decreased coprolalia (e.g., Brown & Ivers, 1999; Earles & Myles, 1994). Differential reinforcement of other behavior can be used to decrease coprolalia. This procedure involves the use of a timer, which is set to a particular interval of time. If the affected individual refrains from cursing during this interval, he or she receives a reinforcer, and the interval is reset. Over trials, the interval is increased. Thus, coprolalia may decrease if its absence is reinforced (Earles & Myles, 1994). Intermittent differential reinforcement of alternative verbal behavior is also successful: Reinforcing use of appropriate words on an intermittent reinforcement schedule, particularly during stress, decreases coprolalia (Earles & Myles, 1994).

For children with Tourette syndrome, school can be very stressful. Therefore, teachers should consider special education practices that will reduce anxiety experienced in school settings. Affected children should be allowed to take their tests in an isolated, separate location in order to reduce stress. They may also be given frequent breaks to go to the restroom or elsewhere outside of class in order to release tics and coprolalia. Allowing them to leave class a couple minutes early, thus avoiding noisy, crowded hallways, can also reduce stress.

In a recent study, delta-9-tetrahydrocannabinol, the main psychoactive ingredient in marijuana, improved both motor and vocal tics and eliminated coprolalia for a man diagnosed with TS. The subject was treated with 10 mg of delta-sup-9-THC, and drastic improvements were seen after 30 min. The improvements lasted about 7 hr. When cognitive functions were measured, improvements were seen in signal detection and sustained attention and reaction time after treatment (Mueller, Schneider, Kolbe, & Emrich, 1999). Although obviously controversial, medicinal marijuana may be an effective treatment for TS. With appropriate drug and behavioral treatment, prognosis at least for control of coprolalia is generally good.

REFERENCES

Brown, R. T., & Ivers, C. E. (1999). Gilles de la Tourette syndrome. In S. Goldstein & C. R. Reynolds (Eds.), *Handbook of neurodevelopmental and genetic disorders in children* (pp. 185–215). New York: Guilford Press.

Earles, T. L., & Myles, B. S. (1994). Using behavioral interventions to decrease coprolalia in a student with Tourette's syndrome and autism: A case study. *Focus on Autistic Behavior, 8,* 1–12.

Mueller, K. R., Schneider, U., Kolbe, H., & Emrich, H. M. (1999). Treatment of Tourette's syndrome with delta-9-tetrahydrocannabinol. *American Journal of Psychiatry, 156,* 495.

Singer, C. (1997). Coprolalia and other coprophenomena. *Neurologic-Clinics, 15,* 299–308.

Jaime Slappey
Robert T. Brown
University of North Carolina at Wilmington

COR TRIATRIUM

Cor triatrium is a birth defect in which the left atrium of the heart is doubled. The atrium is formed with a perforated membrane separating the two chambers. Severity of this condition is dependant on the degree of separation and the presence or absence of a shunt between the two sections (Dauphin et al., 1998).

Cor triatrium is often diagnosed in early childhood by echocardiography, but it has also been detected in adults who have been asymptomatic. It is a congenital heart defect, defined as being present at birth. About .8% of all children are born with some kind of heart defect, although the seriousness of the defect varies greatly.

Characteristics

1. Left atrium of the heart divided by perforated membrane
2. Infants may be born with a blue color
3. Difficulty breathing and exercising

Occasionally, children born with congenital heart defects have impaired learning. Cor triatrium is a serious defect, but it is potentially repairable. Children who have undergone corrective surgery may need to be restricted in some of their activities, especially in recess and physical education. Additionally, they may be subject to missing abnormal amounts of school due to monitoring of the heart.

REFERENCE

Dauphin, C., Lusson, J. R., Motreff, P., Lorillard, R., Justin E. P., Briand, F., Valy, Y., Lamaison, D., Chabrun, A., & Cassagnes, J. (1998). Left intra-atrial membrane without pulmonary vein obstruction: Benign condition of progressive evolution? Apropos of 7 cases. *Archives des Maladies du Coeur et des Vaisseaux, 91,* 615–621.

Allison Katz
Rutgers University

CORNEAL DYSTROPHY

The cornea is the transparent outer layer of the eye. Corneal tissue consists of five layers: the epithelium, the Bowman's layer, the stroma, the Descemet's membrane, and the endothelium. A corneal dystrophy is a condition in which one or more parts of the cornea lose their normal clarity due to the accumulation of abnormal material (Sowka, Gurwood, & Cabat, 1998). Corneal dystrophies generally affect both eyes.

There are over 20 corneal dystrophies. Most corneal dystrophies have a genetic link and are primarily autosomonal dominant; that is, only one parent needs to be a carrier of the gene in order for a child to inherit the disease (Bevan, 1997). Males and females are equally affected (National Eye Institute [NEI], 2000). With the exception of a few subtypes that predominantly affect older adults, most individuals will be diagnosed with the disease before they turn 20 years of age. However, although children may be born with a corneal dystrophy, they are more likely to be diagnosed during adolescence, and the disease usually progresses slowly throughout the patient's lifetime (Trattler & Clark, 2000).

Corneal dystrophies are classified based on the layer of the cornea that is affected. An individual is diagnosed with an anterior corneal dystrophy when the epithelium is affected. Corneal dystrophies that affect the central layer of the cornea are stromal dystrophies. These include lattice, granular, and macular dystrophies. Corneal dystrophies in the posterior layers of the cornea affect the Descemet's membrane and the endothelium (Trattler & Clark, 2000).

Characteristics

1. Some corneal dystrophies may produce no symptoms and are detected only through a routine eye exam. Other corneal dystrophies may cause repeated episodes of pain and may or may not affect vision.
2. Child may complain of eye irritation or severe eye pain.
3. Child may experience blurry vision or the sensation of a foreign object in the eye.
4. Eyes may be especially sensitive to light.
5. Although most individuals do experience some vision loss, visual impairment often does not occur until years after diagnosis.

Symptoms and prognosis vary according to the type of corneal dystrophy an individual has. Four main subtypes that would be most likely to be identified in children in their first decade are lattice-type corneal dystrophy (presents prior to age 10, and vision loss is probable by age 50; Klintworth, 1999); macular corneal dystrophy (autosomal recessive, presents prior to age 10, intense pains, visual impairment by age 30; Trattler & Clark, 2000); juvenile epithelial corneal dystrophy of Meesmann (presents by age 2, eye irritation, vision loss is not probable); and Reis-Buckler's corneal dystrophy (early childhood onset of recurrent, painful corneal erosion, rapid loss of visual acuity as child ages; National Organization for Rare Disorders, 1988).

For patients who experience pain as a result of the corneal dystrophy, doctors can prescribe ointments and eye drops (NEI, 2000) or eye patches with antibiotic ointment (Trattler & Clark, 2000). Sunglasses can help alleviate photophobia (sensitivity to light). Treatment may consist of corneal grafting to repair the cornea (Bevan, 1997). If there is a severe loss of vision, a corneal transplant may be needed. In most cases, the surgery restores sight (NEI, 2000).

Because corneal dystrophies vary greatly in their effects on vision, professionals need to evaluate each child's individual needs. In most cases, children will not experience any permanent vision loss during their school years. Nonetheless, because vision loss may be gradual, teachers need to monitor a child's responses to visual stimuli, paying careful attention to whether the child squints his or her eyes, turns his or her head to focus, or loses visual attention easily. Depending on the nature of the presenting symptoms, teachers can maximize a child's functional use of vision by incorporating visual aids that are varied in the size of the print, color contrast, and lighting and are tailored to each individual child. Teachers should also present instructional material through other sensory modalities, such as tactile and auditory. Children with vision loss may also benefit from orientation and mobility training, in which the child develops increased spatial awareness in order to move successfully around in his or her environment. Children with limited functional vision will also need instruction in Braille literacy. In rare cases where there is substantial loss of vision, it may be necessary for a child to attend programs for the visually impaired or blind (Heller, Alberto, Forney, & Schwartzman, 1996).

REFERENCES

Bevan, V. (1997). Corneal dystrophy factsheet. *Royal National Institute For the Blind.* Retrieved from http://www.rnib.org.uk

Heller, K. W., Alberto, P. A., Forney, P. E., & Schwartzman, M. N. (1996). *Understanding physical, sensory, and health impairments: Characteristics and educational implications.* Pacific Grove, CA: Brooks/Cole.

Klintworth, G. K. (1999). Perspective: Advances in molecular genetics of corneal dystrophies. *American Journal of Ophthalmology, 128*(6), 747–754.

National Eye Institute. (2000). The cornea and corneal disease. Retrieved from http://www.medhelp.org/NIHlib/GF-374.html

National Organization for Rare Disorders. (1988). Topic: Corneal dystrophy. Retrieved from http://www.healthynetwork.com/kbase/nord/nord455.htm

Sowka, J. W., Gurwood, A. S., & Cabat, A. G. (1998). Handbook of ocular disease management. *Review of Ophthalmology Online.* Retrieved from http://www.revoptom.com/handbook/hbhome.htm

Trattler, W., & Clark, W. (2000). Dystrophy, macular. *eMedicine: Ophthalmology.* Retrieved from http://www.emedicine.com

Michelle Perfect
University of Texas at Austin

CORNELIA DE LANGE SYNDROME

Cornelia de Lange syndrome (CdLS) is a rare genetic disorder that is characterized by prenatal and postnatal growth retardation, facial abnormalities, cognitive deficits or mental retardation, and developmental delays. In the United States, the disorder occurs in approximately 1 in 10,000 births and appears to affect males and females equally. Recurrence within affected families appears to be estimated at less than 1% (National Organization for Rare Disorders [NORD], 2000). Physical characteristics and symptoms vary in severity and presentation from case to case.

Characteristics

1. Cranofacial abnormalities
2. Mild to severe retardation
3. Unusually long vertical groove between the upper lip and nose, a depressed nasal bridge, anteverted nares, and a protruding upper jaw
4. Facial abnormalities such as thin down-turned lips; low-set ears; arched, well-defined eyebrows that grow together across the base of the nose; and abnormally curly long eyelashes
5. Possible limb malformations such as small hands and feet, inward deviation of the fifth fingers, or webbing of certain toes
6. For infants, possible feeding and breathing difficulties, increased respiratory problems, heart defects, a low "growling" cry, hearing deficits, or other physical abnormalities

The abnormalities characteristic of CdLS may be detected prenatally through the use of ultrasound imaging; in most cases, however, it is diagnosed at birth (Aitken et al., 1999). A diagnosis of CdLS should be considered if the child exhibits the distinctive facial characteristics listed along with the limb anomalies, mental retardation, and growth retardation. Associated abnormalities include cardiac defects, gastroesophogeal reflux, glue ear, intestinal obstruction due to gastrointestinal problems, and respiratory infection (NORD, 2000). Associated behavioral characteristics include hyperactivity, self-injury, aggression, and sleep disturbances (Berney, Ireland, & Burn, 1999).

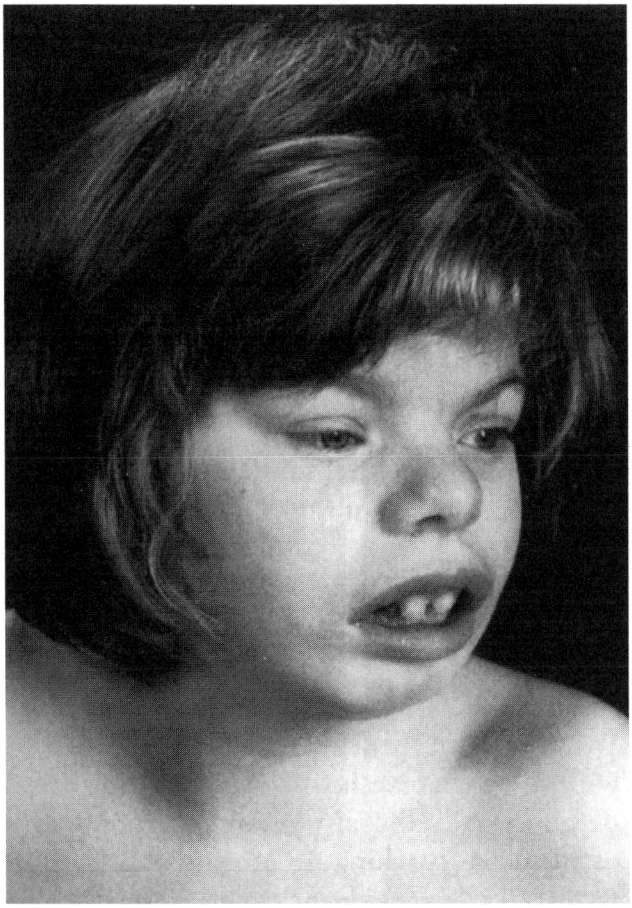

Cornelia de Lange Syndrome
Reprinted from *Clinical Syndromes,* Wiedemann and Kunze, 1997, by permission of the publisher Mosby

Treatment is directed toward the noted symptoms and may involve the collaborative efforts of numerous health care professionals including pediatricians, orthopedic surgeons, heart specialists, urologists, speech pathologists, and occupational therapists. Surgery may be performed to correct cleft palate, and orthopedic techniques may be used to treat limb deformities. Plastic surgery may also be helpful in reducing excessive hair. Antibiotic drug therapy may help fight associated respiratory infection. Anticonvulsant medication may be needed for patients who experience seizure episodes.

Early intervention is important in ensuring that children with CdLS reach their highest potentials. Special education services may be available to children with CdLS under the handicapping condition of Other Health Impairment. Services that may be beneficial include special remedial education, vocational training, speech therapy, and other medical and social services. Because of the numerous health issues associated with the disorder, children may need to spend a great deal of time in treatment and away from the classroom. Therefore, tutoring services or home-based instruction may also be required. In addition, patients may also benefit from counseling services designed to help them psychologically adjust to their illnesses. Medication side effects should be considered when formally assessing the patients' cognitive, social, or academic functionings (NORD, 2000).

Research on CdLS and its cause is ongoing. There is no known cure for CdLS, but there is hope that the Human Genome Project, sponsored by the National Institute of Health, may shed light on why genes sometimes malfunction (NORD, 2000).

REFERENCES

Aitken, D. A., Ireland, M., Crossley, B. E., Macri, J. N., Burn, J., & Conner, J. M. (1999). Second trimester pregnancy associated plasma protein-A levels are reduced in Cornelia de Lange syndrome pregnancies. *Prenatal Diagnosis, 19*(8), 706–710.

Berney, T. P., Ireland, M., & Burn, J. (1999). Behavioural phenotype of Cornelia de Lange syndrome. *Archives of Disease in Childhood, 81*(4), 333–336.

National Organization for Rare Diseases. (2000, March). Cornelia De Lange syndrome. Retrieved from http://www.rarediseases.org

Mary Corlett
University of Texas at Austin

COSTELLO SYNDROME

Costello syndrome is an extremely rare genetic disorder marked by growth delay, excessive skin, tumor growth, and mild mental retardation. There have been approximately 150 cases reported to date of Costello syndrome, and over 30 published cases. J. M. Costello first reported this syndrome and described it in 1977 (Costello, 1977, 1996). Der Kaloustian, Moroz, McIntosh, Watters, and Blaichman (1991) identified additional children with the disorder and proposed that it be called Costello syndrome.

Children with Costello syndrome tend to be of average birth weight but then experience a postnatal growth deficiency; as a result, they tend to be of very short stature. They frequently develop benign tumors in their noses or mouths. Infants may also vomit frequently and have difficulty with being fed (Kerr et al., 1998).

The distinctive facial and body appearance associated with Costello syndrome includes a large head, a coarse face, thick lips and ears, a short neck, curly hair, a depressed bridge of the nose, thick palms and soles, and excessive skin (Martin & Jones, 1993).

Costello syndrome is a genetic disorder present from birth that has been found in approximately 150 individuals (see http://www.costellokids.org.uk). Most cases are isolated cases in families, with no other family members having the disorder. Costello Syndrome is similar to both Noonan syndrome and cardiofaciocutaneous syndrome. Although most published reports focus on children with Costello syndrome, there have been published studies of adults (van Eeghen, van Gelderen, & Hennekam, 1999).

Characteristics

1. Growth delay
2. Benign tumor growth
3. Excess skin around neck and palms
4. Possible mental retardation

Children suffering from Costello syndrome are also likely to have mental retardation, and the same special education services that would be needed for mental retardation would be needed for children with Costello syndrome. In addition, children may need possible assistance for pain management or depression resulting from a serious illness.

Future research is continually being conducted on genetic disorders such as Costello syndrome; one broad example is the Human Genome Project.

REFERENCES

Costello, J. M. (1977). A new syndrome: Mental subnormality and nasal papillomata. *Australian Paediatric Journal, 13,* 114–118.

Costello, J. M. (1996). Costello syndrome: Update on the original cases and commentary. *American Journal of Medical Genetics, 62,* 199–201.

Der Kaloustian, V. M., Moroz, B., McIntosh, N., Watters, A. K., & Blaichman, S. (1991). Costello syndrome. *American Journal of Medical Genetics, 41,* 69–73.

Kerr, B., Eden, O. B., Dandamudi, R., Shannon, N., Quarrell, O., Emmerson, A., Ladusans, E., Gerrard, M., & Donnai, D. (1998). Costello syndrome: Two cases with embryonal rhabdomyosarcoma. *American Journal of Medical Genetics, 35,* 1036–1039.

Martin, R. A., & Jones, K. L. (1993). Facio-cutaneous-skeletal syndrome is the Costello syndrome. *American Journal of Medical Genetics, 47,* 169.

van Eeghen, A. M., van Gelderen, I., & Hennekam, R. C. (1999). Costello syndrome: Report and review. *American Journal of Medical Genetics, 82,* 187–193.

James C. Kaufman
Educational Testing Service
Princeton, New Jersey

CRACK, PRENATAL EXPOSURE

A child who is crack affected is one whose mother used crack or cocaine during pregnancy (Waller, 1993). The Office of the Inspector General estimates that 100,000 children are born prenatally exposed to crack in the United States each year (Berger & Waldfogel, 2000). Prenatal crack exposure significantly increases the number of children who have significant problems in learning and require special education services to be successful (Twohey, 1999).

The effects of prenatal crack exposure vary greatly, from children with severe damage to children that are apparently perfect (Humphries, 1999). Medical effects in the perinatal stage include strokes, neurological dysfunction, and hypoxia, which is low oxygenation of the brain and can result in brain damage. Infants born exposed to crack might be inconsolable and hypersensitive. They may demonstrate attachment problems, be emotionally cold, and have jerky movements or rigid bodies. As toddlers, they may be slow to crawl and walk, be easily distractible, and lack skills necessary to plan, initiate, and follow through with tasks (Hoerig & D'Amato, 1994). As children reach preschool and school age, they may demonstrate additional behavioral symptoms of prenatal crack exposure. The child might appear to be in constant motion, with a low frustration level and lack of persistence. Children may also be oversensitive to stimuli, disorganized, demonstrate limited adaptability, and have difficulties with emotional attachment. A child exposed to crack can also be clumsy in gross motor activities and experience deficits in fine motor skills. Children might have difficulty with memory, concentration, speech, and language deficits (Hoerig & D'Amato, 1994).

Characteristics

The effects of prenatal crack exposure vary from greatly damaged to seemingly perfect. These characteristics may not be present in every case.

1. Hypoxia, strokes, and neurological dysfunction
2. Delayed development of gross motor skills
3. Deficits in fine motor skill
4. Distractibility
5. Appearance of constant motion
6. Low frustration level
7. Lack of persistence
8. Oversensitivity to stimuli
9. Limited adaptability
10. Speech problems and language deficits

Most children will require the use of specific interventions. Children with severe impairments often require special education services in the classroom. For children with speech and language disorder, other health impaired, multiple handicaps, or emotional disorder, recommended interventions include allowing children to be with one teacher for more than one year; training teachers to work with and assess the behavioral symptoms of neuropsychological and neurological impairment; using multidisciplinary teams for evaluation; low teacher-child ratios; and traditional behavioral management techniques (Hoerig & D'Amato, 1994). These children learn more effectively if they are specifically taught academic and social skills rather than learning through observations (Waller, 1993). Routines are important; only one skill should be taught at a time; groups should be small; and choices and number of activities should be limited. In addition to academic instruction, appropriate facial expressions and body language should be taught (Waller, 1993). Although there can be serious consequences of prenatal crack exposure, current research is finding a greater impact on children's social development than on their medical condition, and its effects are often subtle (Twohey, 1999).

REFERENCES

Berger, L. M., & Waldfogel, J. (2000). Prenatal cocaine exposure: Long-run effects and policy implications. *Social Service Review, 74*(1), 28–62.

Hoerig, D. C., & D'Amato, R. C. (1994). Cracked but not broken: Understanding and serving crack children. *Communiqué, 23,* 33–34.

Humphries, D. (1999). *Crack mothers.* Columbus: Ohio State University Press.

Twohey, M. (1999). The crack-baby myth. *National Journal, 31*(46), 3340–3345.

Waller, M. B. (1993). *Crack affected children: A teacher's guide.* Newbury Park, CA: Corwin Press.

Jessica L. Singleton
Rik Carl D'Amato
University of Northern Colorado

CRETINISM

Cretinism is a syndrome caused by hypothyroidism (underactivity of the thyroid gland) at birth. Two types of cretinism have been distinguished. Endemic cretinism is essentially an iodine deficiency disorder. Insufficient levels of iodine cause maternal hypothyroidism, which increases the incidence of fetal hypothyroidism in the neonate (Dussault, 1997). Endemic cretinism is characterized by severe developmental delays, deaf-mutism, and spasticity of the arms and legs (Hetzel, 2000). The second form, sporadic cretinism or congenital hypothyroidism, is most commonly caused by a developmental defect of the thyroid gland, in which the thyroid gland fails to develop (aplasia) or is underdeveloped (hypoplasia; Vanderbilt University Medical

Center, 1998). Developmental delays and stunted growth are the most common complications associated with sporadic cretinism.

Endemic cretinism has been virtually eradicated in the United States and in many developed nations with the addition of iodine to table salt. In iodine-deficient areas, such as Zaire, Ecuador, India, China, and mountainous areas of the Andes and Himalayas, severe hypothyroidism can be found in 5–15% of the population. The incidence of sporadic cretinism is approximately 1 in 4,000 Caucasian infants and 1 in 30,000 African American infants. In addition, congenital hypothyroidism is twice as common in girls as in boys (Vanderbilt University Medical Center, 1998).

Characteristics

Endemic cretinism

1. Fetal hypothyroidism, which can occur as early as the fourth month of gestation
2. Severe iodine deficiency
3. Severe developmental delays and mental deficiency, particularly with marked impairment for abstract thought
4. Deafness, with up to 50% of individuals showing complete loss and subsequent mutism (those with partial hearing may or may not have intelligible speech)
5. Motor disorders characterized by proximal rigidity in both lower and upper extremities

Sporadic cretinism

1. Severe hypothyroidism
2. Markedly delayed bone maturation and short stature
3. Delayed sexual maturation
4. Mental deficiency, though often not as severe as that associated with endemic cretinism

Treatment involves a substantial preventative component. Restored maternal iodine levels prior to pregnancy, either with iodized salt or by injection of iodized oil, can eliminate maternal hypothyroidism and subsequent fetal hypothyroidism (Dussault, 1997). Screening programs in the United States (and many developed nations) test all newborn babies for congenital hypothyroidism. If hypothyroidism is detected, thyroid hormone replacement therapy with L-thyroxine can be initiated as early as 1 month of age (Dussault, 1997). Frequent clinical examination is recommended every few months through age 3, and at least yearly thereafter, to monitor growth and development.

For individuals with frank cretinism, special education placement will most likely be necessitated. Admission under the qualifying condition of multiply handicapped may be appropriate to address the hearing impairments, mutism or speech difficulties, and mental retardation that are associated with this disorder. Occupation and physical therapies may also be necessary to address coordination and gait disorders, as well as spasticity.

With early detection and intervention, the prognosis for infants with congenital hypothyroidism is good. Recent studies emphasize that early treatment is essential and have demonstrated that most optimal development is achieved if thyroid deficiencies are corrected before the third week of life (Bongers-Scholkking et al., 2000). Children who receive early treatment can achieve normal mental and psychomotor development. The World Health Organization has identified endemic cretinism as the most common preventable cause of brain damage in the world and has launched a global effort to eliminate this disorder through national iodization programs. Current research has studied the effectiveness of such iodization programs. Other trends in research focus on identifying treatment protocols to optimize outcomes in children with chronic hypothyroidism.

REFERENCES

Bongers-Scholkking, J. J., Koot, H. M., Wiersma, D., Verkerk, P. H., & de Muink Keizer-Schrama, S. M. P. F. (2000). Influence of timing and dose of thyroid hormone replacement on development in infants with congenital hypothyroidism. *Journal of Pediatrics, 136,* 292–297.

Dussault, J. H. (1997). Childhood primary hypothyroidism and endemic cretinism. *Current Therapy in Endocrinology and Metabolism, 6,* 107–109.

Hetzel, B. S. (2000). Iodine and neuropsychological development. *Journal of Nutrition, 2S,* 493S–495S.

Vanderbilt University Medical Center. (1998, June 16). Endocrinology: Congenital hypothyroidism. Retrieved from http://www.mc.vanderbilt.edu/peds/pidl/endocr/index.htm

Heidi A. McCallister
University of Texas, Austin

See also Hypothyroidism

CRI DU CHAT SYNDROME (CRY OF THE CAT SYNDROME)

Cri du chat syndrome is a congenital disorder characterized at birth by the infant's high-pitched, cat-like cry. This specific cry has been linked to a small larynx and is present immediately following birth, lasting for several weeks. Cri du chat syndrome is also known as Cat's cry or 5p- syndrome. Incidence of cri du chat syndrome in the United States is approximately 50 to 60 births per year. This syndrome is the result of the deletion of a portion of Chromosome 5 (Berkow, Beers, & Fletcher, 1997; 5p- Society, 2000; Magalini, Magalini, & de Francisci, 1990; National Organization for Rare Disorders, 2000).

Characteristics

1. Cat-like cry during the first few weeks following birth
2. Low birth weight
3. Abnormal facial features including small head, round asymmetric face, improperly closing mouth, wide-set eyes, wide nose, and low-set, abnormally shaped ears
4. Webbed fingers
5. Microcephaly
6. Poor muscle tone

There is no treatment for cri du chat syndrome (Clayman, 1989). Educational intervention should include physical therapy as well as language therapy, should be consistent, and should begin early (5p- Society, 2000). Children with the syndrome often have significant language difficulties: Some children are able to use short sentences, but others use basic words, gestures, or sign language (5p- Society, 2000). Many individuals with cri du chat syndrome also experience retarded physical and mental development, resulting in a small stature and varied levels of cognitive handicaps. It has been reported that the normal range of IQs for children with the syndrome is in the severe range of mental retardation, with levels ranging between 20 and 30 standard score points (Magalini et al., 1990). Unless stricken by more severe medical conditions, children with cri du chat syndrome have a normal life expectancy (5p- Society, 2000). Future research will focus on earlier identification of the syndrome and effective intervention strategies as well as prevention through methods such as genetic therapy.

REFERENCES

Berkow, R., Beers, M. H., & Fletcher, A. J. (Eds.). (1997). *Merck manual of medical information, home edition.* Whitehouse Station, NJ: Merck Research Laboratories.

Clayman, C. B. (Ed.). (1989). *The American Medical Association encyclopedia of medicine.* New York: Random House.

5p- Society. (2000). Overview of 5p- syndrome. Retrieved from http://www.fivepminus.org/about/ovsyn.htm

Magalini, S. I., Magalini, G., & de Francisci, G. (1990). *Dictionary of medical syndromes* (3rd ed.). Philadelphia: J. B. Lippincott.

National Organization for Rare Disorders. (2000). Cri du chat syndrome. Retrieved from http://www.rarediseases.org/lof/lof.html

Kathryn L. Guy
University of Texas

Nancy L. Nussbaum
Austin Neurological Clinic

CROHN'S DISEASE

Crohn's disease is an idiopathic, chronic inflammatory bowel disorder. The disease may be controlled through management of symptoms, but no cure is now available. Crohn's disease is very similar to ulcerative colitis, and together they belong to a category of disorders referred to as inflammatory bowel disease. Although similar, they are distinct in important ways. Crohn's disease may involve any part of the alimentary tract—mouth, esophagus, stomach, small and large intestine—but most frequently involves the small bowel and colon. Gastrointestinal involvement is transmural, meaning that all layers of the bowel wall are affected. The inflammatory process is segmental and erratic, often skipping sections of bowel with little predictability of where it will strike next (KidsHealth, 2001). On the other hand, ulcerative colitis is continuous in nature, primarily involves the large intestine and rectum with inflammation limited to the inner mucosal bowel lining, and puts individuals at high risk for developing colon cancer.

Characteristics

Presenting symptoms

1. Persistent diarrhea, abdominal pain, and rectal bleeding
2. Fever and fatigue
3. Weight loss, dehydration, and malnutrition

Later symptoms

1. Skin or eye irritations
2. Growth retardation and delay of sexual maturation
3. Malnutrition
4. Extraintestinal manifestations

The incidence of Crohn's disease is 3–4 in 100,000 and has increased over the past 10 years. In the United States, incidence in Whites and Blacks is 3–10 times greater than in Hispanics and Asians. Crohn's disease is diagnosed most often during adolescence but may also appear again at around age 40. Earlier onset is more severe and leads to more complications and involvement of other organ systems. Cause is unknown, but the disease is believed to be autoimmune in nature and to have familial tendencies. Family history is positive in 10–20% of affected individuals (Behrman, Kliegman, & Jenson, 2000).

Manifestations of Crohn's disease depend on the area of involved bowel, severity of inflammation, and presence of complications. Symptoms often resemble those of other conditions. Initially, Crohn's disease and ulcerative colitis may be hard to distinguish. Thorough history, physical exam, blood tests and radiological studies, and endoscopic exam are important for accurate diagnosis. Symptoms may not appear for years and range from mild to severe (Crohn's and Colitis Foundation of America [CCFA], 2001). Crohn's is characterized by periods of exacerbation and remission. Diagnosis may not be made until 1–2 years after onset of symptoms.

The goal of treatment in Crohn's disease is to alleviate symptoms. Owing to the complexity of this illness, treatment may involve a variety of medications and interventions. The two most commonly used categories of drugs are anti-inflammatory drugs (such as Asacol, Dipentum, Pentasa, and Balasalazide) and immunosuppressive agents (such as steroids, cyclosporin, azothioprine, and anti-TNF antibodies). Over time, the inflammatory process causes complications such as bowel strictures, fistulas, perianal disease, intra-abdominal abscess, and increased risk of cancer (CCFA, 2001). Generally, the better the inflammatory process is controlled, the longer complications are delayed. One promising focus of current study is on the role of the autoimmune process and extraintestinal complications (CCFA, 2001). In spite of good medical management, almost all those with Crohn's disease will eventually require surgery. Surgery is avoided as long as possible because the incidence of recurrence is greater than 50% at 5 years, and the risk of additional surgery increases with each operation (Behrman et al., 2000).

Aggressive nutritional therapy is beneficial as a primary treatment. Enteral feedings of elemental formula may be considered in the presence of weight loss, malnutrition, poor appetite, malabsorbtion, growth failure, and poor response to conventional therapy (Behrman et al., 2000).

Emotional stress does not cause Crohn's disease, but stress may trigger flare-ups. Use of relaxation and stress management techniques is often helpful. Although poor diet does not cause Crohn's disease, high fat and sodium foods can intensify symptoms. Thus, dietary modifications and maintenance of adequate nutrition may reduce symptoms. Frequent, small, nutritionally balanced meals are generally tolerated better than are infrequent larger meals (KidsHealth, 2001).

Children with Crohn's disease face challenges similar to all children with a chronic disease: psychosocial issues of being different, concerns over body image, restriction of activity, missed days of school, daily medications, and increased family stress. They may have further self concept and social interaction problems owing to delayed growth and puberty. Counseling may help children and adolescents deal with the consequences of the disorder. Management of diarrhea during school is of great concern to children. Crohn's is a chronic disorder with high morbidity but low mortality. Periods of remission, during which the child is symptom free, can often be achieved. Most children with Crohn's disease lead active, full lives. Special camps sponsored by CCFA are available; information is available at http://www.ccfa.org/news/camp.htm.

REFERENCES

Crohn's and Colitis Foundation of America. (2001). New insight into autoimmunity. Retrieved from http://www.ccfa.org/medcentral/library/compl/auto.htm

Behrman, R. E., Kliegman, R. M., & Jenson, H. B. (2000). *Nelson textbook of pediatrics* (16th ed.). Philadelphia: W. B. Saunders.

KidsHealth. (2001). Inflammatory bowel disease. Retrieved from http://www.kidshealth.org/parent/medical/digestive/ibd.html

Brenda Melvin
New Hanover Regional Medical Center
Wilmington, North Carolina

CROUZON SYNDROME

Crouzon syndrome, also known as craniofacial dysostosis, is characterized by premature closure of the cranial sutures between certain bones in the skull and distinctive facial abnormalities. Crouzon syndrome can be evident at birth or during infancy. Crouzon syndrome is a rare disorder that can be inherited as an autosomal dominant trait or, in some cases, results possibly from mutation, as there is no family history. Both male and female are thought to be equally affected with as many as 1 in 25,000 found at birth. Due to the variability in associated symptoms, this number may be a low estimate of the actual number of cases (Kreiborg, 1981a).

Crouzon syndrome is commonly characterized by facial features, including a flat, broad forehead, widely spaced eyes with a reversed slant, a high palate, a beak-like nose, and occasionally malformations of auditory canals. The cranial and facial malformations can vary in severity from case to case including differences seen among individuals within the same family. The degree of cranial malformation may be variable depending on the specific cranial sutures involved as well as the order and rate of progression. Limb abnormalities are rarely seen. Often, however, individuals with Crouzon syndrome experience dental abnormalities due to underdevelopment of the upper jaw. The degree of cranial malformation may be variable, depending on the specific cranial sutures involved as well as the order and rate of progression. Often there is a premature fusion of the sutures between the bones forming the forehead and the upper sides of the skull (Kreiborg, 1981a).

Studies have shown that neurological deficits include as many as 30% affected by headaches and about 12% affected by uncontrolled seizures. Mental retardation was present only in approximately 3% of the cases (Berg, 1996).

As previously stated, Crouzon syndrome can be inherited as an autosomal dominant trait; thus, the one gene from the mother or father will be expressed dominating the other normal gene and resulting in the appearance of the disease. The risk of transmitting this disease from the affected parent to the offspring is 50% for each pregnancy regardless of the sex of the child (Berg, 1996).

On rare occasions, Crouzon syndrome can occur with a skin disease known as acanthosis nigricans, which is characterized by a velvety thickening of the skin with hyperpigmentation. These skin disorders usually emerge around puberty and can occur on the neck, abdomen, chest, breasts, eyelids, and nostrils as well as under the arms and around the mouth. In addition, unlike Crouzon syndrome alone, with acanthosis nigricans individuals may suffer from hydrocephalus (impaired flow or absorption of cerebrospinal fluid potentially leading to increasing fluid pressure within the skull) and choanal atresia (bony tissue blocks the passageway between the nose and throat; Kreiborg, 1981b).

Other syndromes similar to Crouzon syndrome include Pfeiffer, Apert, Saethre-Bhotzen, and Jackson-Weiss syndromes. These disorders share the commonality of craniofacial malformations or abnormalities. Similar disorders are helpful for a differential diagnosis.

Characteristics

1. Facial abnormalities include a wide, broad forehead, beak-like nose, and widely spaced eyes.
2. Although rare, limb abnormalities can occur.
3. Neurological deficits include as many as 30% headaches and 12% uncontrolled seizures.
4. In 3% of the cases, mental retardation was present.
5. A skin disease known as acanthosis nigricans occurred in a few cases.

Early intervention is important with infants diagnosed with Crouzon syndrome. Diagnosis is often based on a variety of clinical evaluations, identification of characteristic physical findings, and specialized tests. Treatment will depend on the specific symptoms affecting the individual. A team of medical professionals including pediatricians, surgeons, orthopedists, neurologists, ophthalmologists, and other health care professions can address the defects. In addition, to help children suffering from Crouzon syndrome reach their fullest potentials, special social support, speech therapy, psychological treatment, and other vocational services may also be useful. Although only a small percentage are affected by mental retardation, special educational services may prove useful to mediate any potential learning disabilities as well as help the child maintain studies due to potential frequent absences from doctors' appointments and other medical interventions.

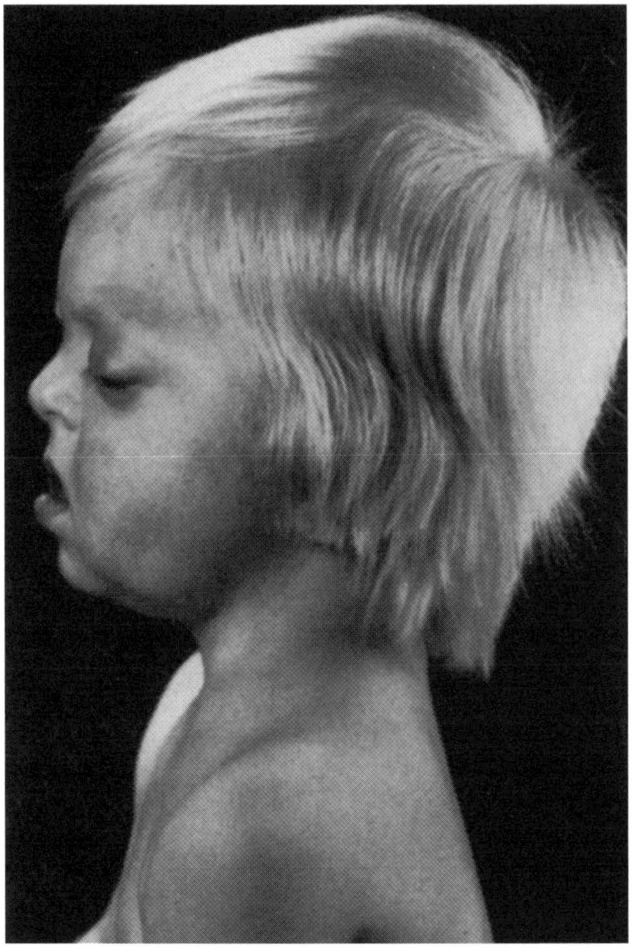

Crouzon Syndrome
Reprinted from *Clinical Syndromes,* Wiedemann and Kunze, 1997, by permission of the publisher Mosby

REFERENCES

Berg, B. (1996). *Principles of child neurology.* San Francisco: McGraw-Hill.

Kreiborg, S. (1981a). Crouzon syndrome. *Scandinavian Journal of Dental Research, 81,* 170–198.

Kreiborg, S. (1981b). Variable expressivity of Crouzon's syndrome within a family. *Scandinavian Journal of Dental Research, 85,* 175–184.

Lisa A. Fasnacht-Hill
Keck University of Southern California School of Medicine
University of Southern California / University Affiliated Program at Children's Hospital of Los Angeles

CRYPTOPHASIA

Cryptophasia was historically described as a secret language between twins that they invent themselves and that is unintelligible to others. It has been found that some words are indeed invented, but for the most part the words come from the adult language to which they are exposed. At least 90% of the vocabulary in cryptophasia can be directly related to the language of the parents (Bakker, 1987). Some research states that cryptophasia develops when twins experience a notable condition of social isolation (Levi & Bernabei, 1976).

Cryptophasia occurs in 40–47% of all twin pairs in early childhood. It is more frequent among triplets than twins, more frequent among boys than girls, and somewhat more frequent among monozygotic (identical) twins than among dizygotic (fraternal) twins (Bakker, 1987).

Characteristics

1. The words spoken lack morphology, present in a different word order, and have deviant articulation and a different syntax to the point that the language may be completely unintelligible to adult speakers.
2. Cryptophasia not only occurs in twins but also can emerge in two siblings or close friends in the same stage of language development.
3. The language is thought to stem entirely from the environment, not genetics, and is based on reinforcement from the other child or twin.
4. The unintelligible language disappears soon.
5. One source stated that nearly 5% of twins develop language difficulties (Levi & Bernabei, 1976).
6. Cryptophasia can restrain intellectual development—more specifically, language development in terms of grammatical structure and richness of vocabulary (Zazzo, 1976).
7. Children with cryptophasia tend to be slower in language acquisition than other children, particularly in articulation.

Eventually, these children adopt the proper structure in their language; it just takes longer for children who use cryptophasia. Specific treatments have not been discussed because the general consensus in the literature is that these children will outgrow this unintelligible language. It is important for parents to encourage regular language usage in their children. If the children do not begin using regular language, it would be crucial to contact a speech therapist.

Special education may need to be considered in the area of speech therapy for articulation problems. Also, it is crucial to monitor language development, as this would have effects on a child's school performance and socialization skills.

Future research needs to be conducted to determine if intelligence is, in fact, restrained due to cryptophasia. The prognosis appears to be good if language difficulties are caught early enough and the cryptophasia disappears soon.

REFERENCES

Bakker, P. (1987). Autonomous languages of twins. *Acta Geneticae Medicae et Gemellologiae, 36,* 233–238.

Levi, G., & Bernabei, P. (1976). Specific language disorders in twins during childhood. *Acta Geneticae Medicae et Gemellologiae, 25,* 366–368.

Zazzo, R. (1976). The twin condition and the couple effects on personality development. *Acta Geneticae Medicae et Gemellologiae, 25,* 343–352.

Catherine M. Caldwell
University of Texas at Austin

CUSHING'S SYNDROME

Cushing's syndrome, or hypercortisolism, is a hormonal disorder that is caused by an excess of the hormone cortisol. The syndrome is relatively rare, and its etiology has been traced to an abnormal functioning of the pituitary gland. Other causes may be as the result of high doses of cortisol or other glucocorticoid (steroid) hormones taken for prolonged periods of time for the treatment of asthma, rheumatoid arthritis, lupus, or certain allergies (Shin, 1999). The syndrome is distinguishable from Cushing's disease in that the latter involves tumors in the pituitary that cause the excessive amounts of cortisol.

This condition most commonly affects adults ages 20 to 50 (Shin, 1999). Although the condition has been found to occur up to five times more frequently in females of reproductive age, there have been reports of occurrence at all ages in both males and females (Krieger, 1982).

Characteristics

1. The child experiences obesity noticeable especially in the abdomen, face (moon face), neck, and upper back (buffalo hump) and growth retardation.
2. The child may complain of weak muscles in the upper arms and legs and has a tendency to bruise easily.
3. Other physical characteristics may include thinning of the skin and pink or purple stretch marks (striae) on the abdomen, thighs, breasts, and shoulders.
4. The child or adolescent commonly experiences increased acne, facial hair growth, and scalp hair loss in women.
5. High blood pressure and menstrual difficulties are common.

If the syndrome occurs as the result of taking hormonal steroids, withdrawing the steroids allows the body eventually to go back to normal. For Cushing's disease, in which tumors are present in the pituitary gland, surgery or radiation therapy have been found to be successful in the majority of cases. Several drugs (Mitotane, aminoglutethimide, metyrapone, and ketoconazole) help inhibit cortisol production (National Organization for Rare Disorders [NORD], 1999). Most of the clinical manifestations, and particularly growth arrest in children, are reversible with the correction of the adrenocortical hyperfunction (Binder & Hall, 1972). Treatment may last anywhere from 2 to 18 months (Shin, 1999).

Children who develop Cushing's syndrome may be eligible for special education services under the handicapping condition of Other Health Impairment or Physical Disability. Because frequent visits to the doctor are necessary during treatment, the child will most likely have many absences from school. Counseling that is sensitive to chronic illnesses should be considered, especially in light of the length of treatment and the physically undesirable characteristics associated with the disease. There is a possibility that the child will suffer from depression. Occupational therapy may also be considered for students whose symptoms include weak muscles.

The National Institutes of Health are currently researching use of the drug RU 486, a glucocorticoid antagonist, for treatment. Research is also being conducted with the drug octreotide acetate, which may shrink the tumors associated with Cushing's syndrome. Scientists are also conducting better testing methods for diagnosis. Such methods include studying fluids that have been drained from the pituitary gland to detect hormone levels that relate to the presence of pituitary tumors (NORD, 1999).

REFERENCES

Binder, C., & Hall, P. (Ed.). (1972). *Cushing's syndrome: Diagnosis and treatment.* London: William Heinemann Medical Books.

Krieger, D. (1982). *Cushing's syndrome.* New York: Springer-Verlag.

National Organization for Rare Disorders. (1999). Cushing syndrome. Retrieved July 2001 from http://rarediseases.org

Shin, L. (Ed.). (1999). *Endocrine and metabolic disorders sourcebook: Basic information for the layperson about pancreatic and insulin-related disorders.* Detroit, MI: Omnigraphics.

Christine D. Cde Baca
University of Northern Colorado

CUTIS MARMORATA TELANGIECTATICA CONGENITA

Cutis marmorata telangiectatica congenita (CMTC), also known as Van Lohuizen's syndrome, is a rare genetic skin disorder. First written about by Van Lohuizen (1922), CMTC occurs when dilated surface blood vessels result in patches of discolored skin. Often this discoloration is blue or purple and presents in a mottled pattern (Devillers, de Waard-van der Spek, & Oranje, 1999).

Cutis marmorata translates to "marbled skin," a reference to the patterns on the skin. Skin lesions and ulcers may also be present. CMTC is more likely to occur in girls than in boys. The skin discolorations usually are present only on part of an individual's body, and one side may be much more affected than the other side.

CMTC is a relatively moderate condition that usually improves by adulthood; the skin discoloration and lesions often disappear within two years. More worrisome are other congenital difficulties that sometimes are associated with CMTC, including lesions around the eyes and atrophy (Shield et al., 1990). One variant of CMTC, megalencephaly–cutis marmorata telangiectatica congenita syndrome (M-CMTC) is much more serious than CMTC. With M-CMTC, prenatal overgrowth and macrocephaly are present. Infants born with M-CMTC are at an increased risk of early death (Bottani, Chevallier, Dahoun, Cossali, & Pfister, 2000).

Characteristics

1. Discolored skin
2. Possible skin lesions and ulcers

Some infants with CMTC will be successfully treated by the time they reach school age. Others may need counseling to help with having a different appearance than other children.

Future research is continually being conducted on genetic disorders and skin disorders such as CMTC; one broad example is the Skin Federation in the Netherlands.

REFERENCES

Bottani, A., Chevallier, I., Dahoun, S., Cossali, D., & Pfister, R. (2000). Macrocephaly-cutis marmorata telangiectatica congenita (M-CMTC) syndrome can be caused by diploidy/tetraploidy skin mosaicism. *European Journal of Human Genetics, 8,* 66.

Devillers, A. C. A., de Waard-van der Spek, F. B., & Oranje, A. P. (1999). Cutis marmorata telangiectatica congenita: Clinical features in 35 cases. *Archives of Dermatology, 135,* 34–38.

Shield, J. A., Shield, C. L., Koller, H. P., Federman, J. L., Koblenzer, P., & Barbera, L. S. (1990). Cutis marmorata telangiectatica congenita associated with bilateral congenital retinal detachment. *Retina, 10,* 135–139.

Van Lohuizen, C. H. J. (1922). Ueber eine seltene angeborene Haut-anomalie (Cutis marmorata telangiectatica congenita). *Acta Dermatology Venerology, 3,* 202–211.

James C. Kaufman
Educational Testing Service
Princeton, New Jersey

CYCLIC VOMITING SYNDROME

Cyclic vomiting syndrome (CVS) is a rare childhood disorder characterized by recurrent, prolonged episodes of severe vomiting, nausea, and prostration. The etiology of this disease is unknown.

The onset of symptoms commonly occurs between 3 and 7 years of age. Males and females alike are affected without regard to family situation or geographic location (Cyclic Vomiting Syndrome Association, 1998).

Characteristics

1. Episodes almost always begin at night or when waking in the morning.
2. Symptoms include forceful, repeated vomiting, as often as 5–6 times an hour.
3. Vomiting persists from hours to several days or more and often leads to dehydration.
4. The episodes may recur several times a year to several times a month.
5. Infection, distress, and excitement are the most commonly reported triggers, but most episodes occur without an identifiable trigger.
6. There is often a family history of migraines.
7. There is no apparent cause of vomiting.
8. There are intervals of normal health between episodes.

CVS is seldom seen in clinical practice and has been difficult to diagnose because vomiting may be caused by a large number of other disorders. There are no laboratory tests, X-rays, or other technical procedures for identifying this disorder. Diagnosis is made by careful review of the patient's history, a physical examination, and tests to rule out other diseases.

Emphasis should be placed on early intervention and providing a supportive environment. It is critical to create a dark, quiet environment for sleep, and hospitalization with intravenous fluid replacement may be needed during episodes. Antimigraine agents may help prevent episodes, and HT3 blocking antiemetic agents are the most successful treatments to abort episodes (Li, 2000). Sedatives are used to attenuate symptoms during episodes. A family history of migraine headaches renders the patient more likely to respond to antimigraine therapy (Li, 2000). The value of using stress management techniques should also be recognized.

Successful management of CVS involves a responsive, collaborative doctor-patient relationship. Medical professionals must be sensitive to circumstances that may predispose the child to attacks and to stresses caused by the illness. Other important components of long-term management include the use of antiemetic agents to abort or shorten attacks, the use of prophylactic agents in patients experiencing severe and frequent episodes, and treatment of complications (Fleisher & Matar, 1993). Common complications of cyclic vomiting episodes are esophagitis, hematemesis, depletion of intracellular electrolytes, hypertension, and secretion of an inappropriate antidiuretic hormone.

Special education services may be available to children with CVS under the handicapping condition of Other Health Impairment. In severe cases, significant periods of time away from the classroom may be involved, and home visits from special educators might be necessary. Side effects of medications should be taken into account when formally assessing the cognitive, social, emotional, and academic abilities of children suffering from CVS.

CVS is a self-limited disorder, but the duration cannot be predicted. The disorder frequently diminishes during adolescence and also may begin to manifest as migraine headaches. More studies are needed to determine the long-term safety and effectiveness of treatments for CVS.

REFERENCES

Cyclic Vomiting Syndrome Association. (1998). CVS facts. Retrieved from http://www.beaker.iupui.edu/cvsa/cvsfacts.html

Fleisher, D. R., & Matar, M. (1993). The cyclic vomiting syndrome: A report of 71 cases and literature review. *Journal of Pediatric Gastroenterology and Nutrition, 17*(4), 361–369.

Li, B. U. K. (2000). Cyclic vomiting syndrome. *Current Treatment Options in Gastroenterology, 3*(5), 395–402.

Carey E. Cooper
University of Texas at Austin

CYCLOTHYMIA

Cyclothymia refers to a chronic mood disorder that involves numerous hypomanic and depressive episodes that do not meet criteria for a bipolar affective disorder (BAD). The term was first used in the late 1800s and is credited to Kahlbaum, who described the condition as cyclical insanity. It was Kraepelin, however, who described cyclothymia as a temperament that predisposed individuals to more severe (and cyclical) episodes of mania and depression. More recently, cyclothymia has been described as a chronic subsyndromal mood disorder (e.g., Lovejoy & Steuerwald, 1995; Marneros, 2001). It is distinguished from BAD in terms of duration and severity (i.e., shorter duration and less severe symptoms). Studies of individuals diagnosed with BAD, however, indicate that in about a third of the cases there was a history of cyclothymia (Howland & Thase, 1993).

Characteristics

1. Numerous periods of persistent hypomanic and depressive symptoms last 1 year if a child or adolescent and 2 if an adult.
2. During the 1- or 2-year period, the individual has not been without symptoms for more than two months at a time.
3. During the initial 1- or 2-year period, there has not been a major depressive episode or a manic episode (this can occur after the first 1 or 2 years).
4. Functioning is impaired or significant distress is caused by the condition.

Hypomanic episodes are characterized by distinct periods of abnormally expansive, elevated, or irritable mood with associated symptoms such as distractibility, increased energy, reduced need for sleep, psychomotor agitation, racing thoughts, pressured speech, grandiosity, and excessive involvement in pleasurable activities, especially those that pose risks. Depressive episodes are characterized by decreased energy, diminished interest, difficulty concentrating, problems with sleep, fatigue, problems with appetite (and sometimes weight), and loss of pleasure in previously enjoyed activities (American Psychiatric Association [APA], 2000).

Prevalence rates indicate that cyclothymia occurs in about .4–3.5% of the general population (APA, 2000). Cyclothymia is typically diagnosed during adolescence and early adulthood. The disorder is more prevalent in families with a history of BAD, with rates being particularly high in first-degree relatives (APA, 2000). There is evidence that individuals with cyclothymia may also have biological markers (e.g., endocrine problems such as hypothyroidism; Howland & Thase, 1993); however, the studies are inconclusive.

The course of cyclothymia is chronic and the prognosis unfavorable. This may be due, in part, to the fact that individuals are often diagnosed with other conditions that have poor response to treatment (e.g., borderline personality disorder). Lithium has been used for treating cyclothymia; however, the response rate has been poorer than that found among individuals diagnosed with BAD. Studies have, however, shown that lithium may have a prophylactic effect in terms of the development of major depressive episodes (Howland & Thase, 1993). Antidepressants have also been used with cyclothymia patients, and certain drugs (e.g., imipramine) have provided symptom relief. Psychological therapies may prove beneficial in helping the individual manage symptoms (e.g., cognitive-behavioral treatments). School psychologists may be an appropriate resource for this. Designing programs that help ensure maximal performance at school may also be helpful, and is a service that school psychologist can provide. Special education is not likely to be needed because marked impairment is not typically found among individuals with cyclothymia. If services through the Individuals with Disabilities Education Act are needed, however, it would likely be under the category Emotional Disturbance. In these cases, it may be necessary to refer the child for a psychiatric consultation to determine what, if any, medications are needed.

Cyclothymia has not received the same amount of attention in the literature as have other disorders from the *Diagnostic and Statistical Manual of Mental Disorders–Fourth Edition,* including BAD. There is a pressing need for information that will improve understanding about the condition, including its etiology, course, and long-term outcome. Further research is also needed to determine how best to treat cyclothymia and prevent the development of more severe symptomatology, including BAD. Drug studies that examine the efficacy of lithium, anticonvulsant medications used for BAD (e.g., carbamazepine and valproate), and antidepressants are also needed.

REFERENCES

American Psychiatric Association. (2000). *Diagnostic and statistical manual of mental disorders* (4th ed., Text Revision). Washington, DC: Author.

Howland, R., & Thase, M. (1993). A comprehensive review of cyclothymic disorder. *Journal of Nervous and Mental Disease, 181*(8), 485–493.

Lovejoy, M., & Steuerwald, B. (1995). Subsyndromal unipolar and bipolar disorders: Comparisons on positive and negative affect. *Journal of Abnormal Psychology, 104*(2), 381–384.

Marneros, A. (2001). Expanding the group of bipolar disorders. *Journal of Affective Disorders, 62*(1), 139–141.

Elaine Clark
Rex Gonzales
University of Utah

CYSTIC FIBROSIS

Cystic fibrosis (CF) is an inherited disease that causes malfunction of the exocrine system. CF primarily affects gastrointestinal and respiratory functions; however, it can also impact hepatic, pancreatic, gastrointestinal, and reproductive systems. Chronic upper respiratory infections are often the first symptom of CF, followed by frequent and severe infections involving the accumulation of mucus. This creates opportunities for bacterial infections in the mucus membranes throughout the body, which is why the disease is associated with progressive and irreversible lung damage, pancreatic insufficiency, cirrhosis of the liver, sterility, and megacolon (Davis, 2000; Wyllie, 1999).

CF affects about 1 out of 3,000 children in the general population and 1 out of 2,000 children who are Caucasian. Prevalence rates are lower for African American and Asian populations. Males and females are affected equally. The gene for CF is carried on the long arm of Chromosome 7. It is estimated that approximately 1 in 500 parents are carriers of the CF gene and 1 in 4 of their children will be affected (Grossman, 1998a, 1998b).

Characteristics

1. Genetic disorder that impacts respiratory function
2. Can also impact gastrointestinal, pancreatic, hepatic, and reproduction systems causing megacolon, liver cirrhosis, and sterility
3. Initial symptoms consisting of chronic cough and upper respiratory infection
4. Shortness of breath, decreased activity, poor appetite, and weight loss
5. Can cause progressive and irreversible lung damage and death

Diagnosis can be reliably made using the sweat chloride test. The sweat test measures the level of chloride in the body (something that is unusually high in CF populations). Other reliable methods for diagnosing CF include chest X-ray and examination of fat content in fecal material (fat content tends to be extremely high). Unfortunately, treatments for CF tend to cause physical discomfort. This includes the need to take high dosages of medication to control the imbalance of fatty acids. Drugs such as docosahexaenoic acid (DHA) have been shown to be effective in this regard (Christensen, 1999). In addition, drugs have been used to increase antioxidants in the system to prevent oxidative damage (e.g., beta-carotene, minerals, and Vitamins A, C, and E). Antibiotic nose drops have also been shown to slow the disease, and some have demonstrated that the disease can be reversed. According to Siegel-Itzkovich (2000), antibiotics have effectively "cured" the condition in 5% of all cases worldwide, and in 60% of individuals who are European Jews. Lung transplants have been used in some cases; however, there is no clear evidence that the procedure has increased survival rates (Aurora, Whitehead, & Wade, 1999).

CF is not commonly associated with learning problems, and most children with the disease will not require special education services. Problems engaging in physical exercise due to difficulties breathing (e.g., shortness of breath) and proper nutrition (e.g., poor appetite and weight loss) can, however, seriously impact learning and social interactions. Accommodations in the classroom and in physical education courses are often sufficient, but when needed, children with CF can receive special education under the category Other Health Impairment. Services from physical therapists and school nurses may be especially important to assist the child in breathing (e.g., working to clear the lungs) and accessing an education. School personnel may need to be educated about the various ways that CF can affect an individual and what needs to be done to accommodate the child in the regular classroom. Repeated absences and missed assignments will need to be addressed. In cases where this cannot be managed by the classroom teacher, the school administrator and psychologist may need to get involved to ensure an appropriate work load. School psychologists may also be needed to evaluate the child for learning problems and the need for additional services (e.g., peer and adult tutoring and reducing homework assignments). School personnel also need to work closely with the child's parents to ensure adequate assistance at home and support from the school. Because depression accompanies CF at times, in some cases an evaluation by a child psychiatrist will be necessary to determine whether psychotropic drugs are warranted.

The lifespan of individuals with CF has improved with treatment. In past years, individuals did not live much past their teens (Grossman, 1998a, 1998b). The severity of the disease itself and concomitant medical problems, however, significantly impact the quality of life. Research is needed to explore ways to prevent the disease and find less aversive ways to treat it (e.g., nutrition management and medications to reduce the production of free radicals). Studies are also needed to ensure early identification (i.e., newborns) and early treatment to improve the outcome.

REFERENCES

Aurora, P., Whitehead, B., & Wade, A. (1999). Lung transplantation of organs, tissues, etc. in children. *Lancet, 354,* 1591.

Christensen, D. (1999). Supplement could fight cystic fibrosis. *Science News, 156,* 303.

Davis, A. M. (2000). Acquired segmental megacolon in an adult patient with cystic fibrosis. *Southern Medical Journal, 93*(2), 229.

Grossman, T. (1998a). Natural protocol for cystic fibrosis. *American Journal of Natural Medicine, 5*(7), 26–29.

Grossman, T. (1998b). Natural treatment options for cystic fibrosis. *Nature's Impact, 8,* 54–56.

Siegel-Itzkovich, J. (2000). Doctors develop new treatment for cystic fibrosis. *British Medical Journal, 7237,* 734.

Wyllie, R. (1999). Gastrointestinal manifestations of cystic fibrosis. *Clinical Pediatrics, 38*(12), 735.

Cristina McCarthy
Elaine Clark
University of Utah

CYSTIC HYGROMA

Cystic hygromas are cystic lesions that are usually found in the neck. They are caused by dilated, or enlarged, lymphatic tissue that becomes malformed, resulting in a type of benign tumor. Cystic hygromas develop at approximately 40 days of gestation because of a failure of the embryonic lymphatics to connect with the venous system (PedLine, 2001). Cystic hygromas can be present at birth or can develop in early childhood. These cysts are filled with lymphatic fluid and lymph cells and may be inherited as through an autosomal recessive trait (National Organization for Rare Disorders [NORD], 2001). They are most frequently located in the posterior lower area of the neck (Tibesar, Rimell, & Michel, 1999), and they occur twice as often on the left side (NORD, 2001; PedLine, 2001).

The onset of cystic hygromas usually occurs at birth or within the first year of life. The incidence of this disorder is 1 out of every 12,000 births, and it is equally prevalent in males and females (NORD, 2001; PedLine, 2001).

Characteristics

1. The child sees the pediatrician because of the detection of a mass or masses on the base of the neck, face, mouth, tongue, or other areas of the upper torso.
2. The masses may also be identified by ultrasound, and they can be a unilocular or multilocular cyst with a thin or thick wall, filled with a clear or tan fluid, or a blood-tinged liquid if infected (PedLine, 2001).
3. Small to medium sized hygromas are often asymptomatic (PedLine, 2001).
4. Especially when located in the throat and chest area, large hygromas can cause complications such as upper airway obstruction (stridor, apneas, cyanosis), dysphagia, mandibular maldevelopment, nerve palsies, hemorrhage, and infection (PedLine, 2001).

An ultrasound of the suspected area of the child, or an ultrasound of the suspected area of the fetus, is used to detect cystic hygromas (NORD, 2001; PedLine, 2001). Testing for elevated levels of alpha-1-fetoprotein in the water sac surrounding the fetus is also a method being used to detect hygromas in vitro (NORD, 2001). Genetic testing is recommended for families with a history of hygromas (NORD, 2001). Sclerosing agents have been used with patients with cystic hygromas but have had varying results (Tibesar et al., 1999).

The recommended treatment of cystic hygromas is immediate surgical removal (NORD, 2001) or immediate removal for those that are large and symptomatic (PedLine, 2001). Multiple surgeries may be required, although some hygromas may resolve untreated (PedLine, 2001).

The prognosis of patients with cystic hygromas depends greatly on the complications that occur, which depends on the location and size of the hygromas. Recurrence of the hygromas is common (Tibesar et al., 1999), and the hygromas are often unpredictable in their growth and spread to surrounding tissue (PedLine, 2001). Patients with cystic hygromas are expected to have a normal life span and intelligence (PedLine, 2001).

Children with cystic hygromas may qualify as Other Health Impairment under Section 504, depending on the severity of their symptoms. The affected child may require home schooling during recovery time after surgeries needed to remove the hygromas. The child may also need speech and occupational therapy if the tumor interferes with these functions. Although cystic hygromas are often present without noticeable symptoms, school modifications may be necessary in specific cases.

REFERENCES

National Organization for Rare Disorders. (2001, March 20). Cystic hygroma. Retrieved from http://www.rarediseases.org

PedLine. (2001, March 8). Cystic hygroma. Retrieved from http://www.icondata.com/health/pedbase/files/CYSTICHY.HTM

Tibesar, R. J., Rimell, F. L., & Michel, E. (1999). Cystic hygroma of the skull space. *Archives of Otolaryngol Head and Neck Surgery, 125,* 1390–1393.

Moana Kruschwitz
Margaret Semrud-Clikeman
University of Texas at Austin

CYTOMEGALOVIRUS, CONGENITAL

Cytomegalovirus (CMV) is a communicable DNA virus in the herpes family that when contracted in later childhood or adulthood is generally either asymptomatic or causes a short, mild illness with a fever and other flulike symptoms. It may remain in infected individuals' systems throughout life and be excreted in their urine, saliva, breast milk, cervical secretions, and semen, even if they have never experienced symptoms (e.g., Beauchamp, 2000; Graham & Morgan, 1997). In individuals with AIDS and other patients with weakened immune systems, CMV and other viruses may cause serious and pervasive problems.

If contracted by a pregnant woman, CMV may cross the placental barrier and cause fetal death or serious deformities in her offspring. It is a member of the STORCH (syphilis, toxiplasmosis, varicella, and other infections, rubella, cytomegalovirus, and Herpes) complex, a group of maternal infections that have similar effects on offspring. It is the most common such infection, occurring in some 5–25 per 1,000 births. As with other herpes viruses, CMV exposure prior to pregnancy prevents neither recurrence nor congenital infection.

Characteristics

Symptomatic newborns

1. Petechiae (small hemorrhage spot on skin or other surface)
2. Enlargement of liver and spleen
3. Jaundice
4. Microcephaly
5. Intrauterine growth retardation

Developmental characteristics in symptomatic or asymptomatic newborns

1. Sensorineural hearing loss
2. Psychomotor retardation
3. Mental retardation
4. Dental abnormalities
5. Chorioretinitis

About 10% of fetuses infected in early prenatal development will be born with CMV and show symptoms at birth. In the rare case of severe, life-threatening CMV infection, infants may be treated with intravenous and then oral antiviral medication. Antiviral medication may be put directly into the eyes of those with CMV retinitis. However, antiviral medicines have serious side effects and are used only in extreme situations.

Of infants asymptomatic at birth, about 5–15% will develop hearing loss, low intelligence, or behavior problems during the first few years of life. Later prenatal exposure may lead to hearing loss (e.g., Graham & Morgan, 1997). Congenital CMV is more likely to occur in the offspring of women who contracted CMV for the first time during pregnancy and themselves had symptoms. Other maternal risk factors include low socioeconomic status, age over 30 years, non-White, and having been breast-fed (Roizen & Johnson, 1996).

Rarely, infants can contract CMV during or after delivery when they pass through the birth canal of, or consume breast milk from, an infected mother. Transmission through blood transfusion contaminated with CMV has been virtually eliminated through screening procedures. Most infants affected by such perinatal CMV are asymptomatic at birth but may develop lung and blood problems, poor weight gain, swollen glands, rash, and hepatitis during development. Those born prematurely are at higher risk to develop symptoms (KidsHealth, 2001).

Diagnosis must be through laboratory testing of a urine or saliva sample to identify the virus because symptoms of congenital infections are similar. Testing must be conducted early to differentiate congenital from postnatal infection, but it is often delayed in asymptomatic infants, precluding accurate diagnosis (Roizen & Johnson, 1996).

No effective treatment is available for congenital or perinatal CMV. A variety of supportive care and special education services will be required depending on the extent and variety of symptoms. Adaptive technology for sensory impairments, speech therapy, and special education may be needed. In addition, no vaccine is available, so prevention of spread of the virus is important. Common practices such as thorough hand washing, especially in day care centers where children and staff come into contact with infected children's saliva or urine, can prevent the virus from being spread from unwashed hands and shared toys.

REFERENCES

Beauchamp, G. R. (2000). Cytomegalovirus. In C. R. Reynolds & E. Fletcher-Janzen (Eds.), *Encyclopedia of special education* (2nd ed., Vol. 1, p. 528). New York: Wiley.

Graham, E. M., & Morgan, M. A. (1997). Growth before birth. In M. L. Batshaw (Ed.), *Children with disabilities* (4th ed., pp. 53–69). Baltimore: Brookes.

KidsHealth. (2001). Cytomegalovirus (CMV). Retrieved from http://www.kidshealth.org/parent/infections/bacterial_viral/cytomegalovirus.html

Roizen, N. J., & Johnson, D. (1996). Congenital infections. In A. J. Capute & P. J. Accardo (Eds.), *Developmental disabilities in infancy and childhood: Vol. 1. Neurodevelopmental diagnosis and treatment* (2nd ed., pp. 175–193). Baltimore: Brookes.

Amy Sessoms
Robert T. Brown
University of North Carolina, Wilmington

D

DARIER DISEASE

Darier disease is a skin disorder in which a red rash appears on parts of the body, particularly the forehead, ears, neck, chest, groin, and back. This rash often has a foul odor and is accompanied by weakening of the fingernails causing V-shaped indentations. The rash may also itch. Darier disease is not contagious. Darier disease has also been loosely correlated with certain neurological and psychological disorders (Cordeiro, Werebe, & Vallada, 2000).

Darier disease normally manifests itself in the teenage years, and symptoms are gradually progressive. It begins with small bumps and may lead to scaly or blistery skin. It is thought to be inherited genetically through an autosomal dominant gene.

Characteristics

1. Red rash on skin, particularly neck, forehead, ears, back, chest, and groin areas
2. Foul odor from affected areas
3. V-shaped notches in the fingernails

There is no cure for Darier disease. It can, however, be treated in several ways to help alleviate the symptoms. Doctors may prescribe Accutane, a topical gel or cream, a regimen of dry skin lotion, Vitamins A and E (Randle, Diaz-Perez, & Winkelmann, 1980), and avoidance of sunlight. Additionally, a strong antiodor soap may be helpful.

In an educational setting, it is important to be sensitive to the psychological needs of a child with Darier disease. The child will most likely be subject to more teasing from his or her peers than would unaffected children. A visit from a doctor or nurse may help to sensitize other children. Lastly, there are many online support groups that are available to individuals with this disorder.

REFERENCES

Cordeiro, Q., Jr., Werebe, D. M., & Vallada, H. (2000). Darier's disease: A new paradigm for genetic studies in psychiatric disorders. *Sao Paulo Medical Journal, 118,* 201–203.

Randle, H. W., Diaz-Perez, J. L., & Winkelmann, R. K. (1980). Toxic doses of vitamin A for pityriasis rubra pilaris. *Archives of Dermatology, 116,* 888–892.

Allison Katz
Rutgers University

DE BARSY SYNDROME

De Barsy syndrome is a heritable disorder characterized by progeria, or accelerated aging, due to loss of dermal elasticity (cutis laxa) and primarily facial features that give the individual a characteristic aged appearance. In addition to the progeroid aspect, other defining characteristics of De Barsy syndrome include involuntary movements and posturing of the arms and legs (athetosis), lax or unusually flexible small joints, marked growth retardation, and mental deficiency (Kunze et al., 1985).

De Barsy syndrome is a rare genetic abnormality inherited in an autosomal recessive manner, meaning that both parents must possess and pass on the defective gene to a child in order for the disease to manifest. Thus, occurrence is extremely rare. Only a few cases (25–30) have been reported in the medical literature, several of which have been instances of two or more siblings from one family (Kunze et al., 1985; National Organization for Rare Disorders [NORD]).

The condition is usually recognizable from birth or at a very young age, although most pregnancies and deliveries are reported to be normal (Kunze et al., 1985). Birth measurements including weight, body length, and cranial circumference are also typically normal at birth but quickly fall below normal as these infants experience slowed growth rates. The most notable symptoms in very young affected children are lax skin and an overall appearance of advanced age, as well as corneal clouding and prominent ears and forehead. The skin is usually hyperpigmented with blotches of depigmentation. A prominent nose is also a common feature. As children age, developmental deficiencies and accelerated aging become more apparent. The protruding forehead becomes replaced by microcephaly because the brain does not continue to grow at a normal rate

(Kunze et al., 1985). Thus, moderate to profound mental retardation is typically observed.

Characteristics

1. Cutis laxa (loss of skin elasticity) and excessive skin folds
2. Growth retardation
3. Skeletal abnormalities including diffuse osteoporosis with flexed rigidity of large joints and excessive flexibility of small joints, resulting in athetoid movements
4. Corneal clouding
5. Hypotonia (loss of muscle tone)
6. Sometimes only mildly affected intelligence, but usually moderate to severe mental retardation
7. Frontal bossing (protruding forehead) in small children and microcephaly developing in older children
8. Large, prominent ears with poor modeling
9. Translucent vein pattern
10. Grimacing and odd facial expressions
11. Skin atrophy with hyperpigmentation and isolated depigmentation

These children remain in the lowest percentiles for their age range in height and weight as well as in cognitive functioning. Constant grimacing is common, and affected individuals take on a gaunt appearance throughout development due to loss of muscle tone (hypotonia), lack of subcutaneous fat, and concavity of the pectoral girdle (pectus excavatum). Normal movement and gait are prevented by athetoid posturing, in which the large joints often remain flexed and rigid, whereas the small joints are abnormally flexible (Karnes, Shamban, Olsen, Fazio, & Falk, 1992). Involuntary reflex movement of both large and small joints also occurs. Thus, odd posturing and difficulty in motility are typical. De Barsy syndrome does not typically include baldness or graying hair, as do many progeroid disorders.

Individual symptoms and severity of the disease can vary widely, but progeria, growth retardation, and moderate to severe cognitive impairment remain constant. There are several associated progeroid disorders that share characteristics with De Barsy syndrome, but De Barsy is believed to encompass a specific set of symptoms and therefore is considered a distinct genetic disorder. Associated disorders include Wiedeman's syndrome, Cockayne syndrome, neonatal progeroid syndrome, Hutchinson-Gilford progeria, and the cutis laxa syndromes (NORD, 1993). All are distinguished by characteristic phenotypic differences.

The focus of treatment for individuals with De Barsy syndrome is symptom management. Treatment goals include minimizing the suffering of those affected and providing genetic counseling for the family. Of course, the goal of genetic counseling is to provide the family with information about the disease and to increase their awareness of the risks associated with future pregnancies. Treatment often centers on the health complications associated with De Barsy, most notably atherosclerosis. In some cases psychological counseling may be needed for the family, child, classroom, and school.

Most children with De Barsy syndrome require extensive special education services. Cognitive impairments including delay or absence of speech development are the norm, as is great difficulty with tasks involving fine and gross motor skills. These children therefore require comprehensive educational programs designed to facilitate the acquisition of skills in many areas. Children are typically served in the special education service areas or categories of Mental Retardation, Speech/Language, Occupational Therapy, Physical Therapy, Psychological Services, and Other Health Impairment. Because of these deficiencies, pervasive care is necessary throughout life for children with this syndrome.

Prognosis for children diagnosed with De Barsy syndrome is poor. Due to associated health complications, most of these children live only to late adolescence, with a few surviving to early adulthood. The cause of death is usually the result of myocardial infarction or heart failure due to the prevalence of atherosclerosis with this condition. There are no treatments available that significantly enhance the lives of these children during that shortened life span. Advances in our knowledge of the human genome will hopefully lead to prevention and treatment of debilitating genetic disorders like De Barsy syndrome in the future.

REFERENCES

Karnes, P., Shamban, A., Olsen, D., Fazio, M., & Falk, R. (1992). De Barsy syndrome: Report of a case, literature review, and elastin gene expression studies of the skin. *American Journal of Medical Genetics, 42*(1), 29–34.

Kunze, J., Majewski, F., Montgomery, P., Hockey, A., Karkut, I., & Riebel, T. (1985). De Barsy syndrome: An autosomal recessive, progeroid syndrome. *European Journal of Pediatrics, 144,* 348–354.

National Organization for Rare Disorders. (1993). De Barsy syndrome. Retrieved September 14, 2000, from http://www.rarediseases.org

Ryan E. McDaniel
Kerry S. Lassiter
Citadel

DEMENTIAS OF CHILDHOOD

Dementia refers to a global cognitive decline that impacts more than one component of cognitive functioning and involves a memory impairment. The term *decline* indicates deterioration in cognitive functioning from a previous higher level of functioning (American Psychiatric Association [APA], 2000). The etiology of dementia may be traced to a general medical condition, persistent effects of a substance, or multiple causes. The acquired nature of dementia suggests that it results in decreased mental functioning over time, as compared to an acute or sudden onset. Dementia describes conditions that are usually "both progressive and irreversible" (Lezak, 1995, p. 204).

Characteristics

1. Clinically significant deterioration in cognitive functioning that gets progressively worse over time.
2. Memory deficits including difficulties with registration, retention, recall, or recognition of new information.
3. Slowed reaction time.
4. Deficits in cognitive processes possibly including aphasia (language disturbance), apraxia (impaired motor functioning), agnosia (inability to recognize or identify objects), or impaired executive abilities.
5. Typically dementia presents as a gradual onset of symptoms and continued cognitive decline.
6. No evidence of impaired consciousness or awareness (not the result of delirium or amnesia).

While degenerative disorders affect less than 1% of people under 65 year of age, many conditions that occur during childhood can produce dementia (Gurland & Crass, 1986). Dementias in children can be classified similar to how they are identified in adults. They are the result of general medical conditions, persistent substance exposure, or a mixture of the two. Medical conditions that may cause dementia include brain tumors or neoplasms, which can lead to changes in cognitive functioning. The impact of a medical condition on declining mental abilities in dementia depends on the size, location, and rate of growth of the tumor or neoplasm (Lezak, 1995). Children treated with chemotherapy for acute lymphocytic leukemia or childhood leukemia have also been known to suffer from neuropsychological impairments (Teeter & Semrud-Clikeman, 1997). Dementia resulting from kidney dialysis affects less than 1% of individuals undergoing dialysis (Lezak, 1995).

Cerebrovascular disease, or strokes, can produce impairments in cognitive ability and are referred to as vascular dementia. Dementia may also be associated with traumatic brain injuries. The juvenile type of Huntington's disease can cause cognitive impairments, memory retrieval deficits, and difficulties with planning and attention (APA, 2000). Lastly, medical conditions such as brain lesions (hydrocephalus), endocrine disorders (hypothyroidism), nutritional deficiencies (Vitamin B_{12} deficiency), immune conditions, and metabolic diseases can produce symptoms of dementia (APA, 2000).

Children infected with HIV may develop symptoms of progressive neurodevelopment degeneration termed HIV encephalopathy, neuroaids, or AIDS dementia complex (Aylward, 1997). This condition initially consists of mild symptoms such as depression, forgetfulness, or difficulty sustaining attention but can develop into complete dementia (Lezak, 1995). There is no known treatment for AIDS dementia.

There is evidence that individuals with Trisomy 21, commonly referred to as Down syndrome, may experience aspects of dementia by the time they are adolescents. One possible explanation for this occurrence is an accelerated rate of aging and reduced temporal lobe functioning in this population (Miezejeski, Devenny, Krinsky-Mchale, Zigman, & Silverman, 2000). Research suggests that some individuals with Trisomy 21 experience brain atrophy and metabolic deficits similar to those associated with Alzheimer's disease (Nadel, 1999).

Acute or chronic exposure to substances can produce symptoms of dementia in children. Contact with neurotoxins, such as lead, mercury, certain insecticides, solvents, or carbon monoxide can lead to significant cognitive impairments. Ingestion of alcohol, inhalants, sedatives, hypnotics, anxiolytics, or medications such as anticonvulsants or intrathecal methotrexate can also produce indications of dementia (APA, 2000).

Although it can be difficult to assess the degree of cognitive deterioration in young children, worsening school performance, significant developmental delays, or divergence from normal development can be early signs of dementia (APA, 2000). Mental status examinations and neuropsychological assessment can be useful for identifying cognitive assets and deficits. Assessment of memory functioning including short-term memory, long-term retrieval, and recognition can also provide valuable information. Deficits in expressive and receptive language abilities and executive functioning are often present.

For special education purposes, children with dementias may be eligible to receive services under the classification Other Health Impairment. If they are eligible to receive special education services, academic support could be beneficial. Treatment typically consists of cognitive rehabilitation techniques to compensate for memory impairment (e.g., the use of visual imagery and verbal encoding strategies). External memory aids, such as tape recorders and notebooks, also can be helpful. Pharmacological interventions such as cholinergically active drugs that are known to impact memory and cognition positively may also be useful.

REFERENCES

American Psychiatric Association. (2000). *Diagnostic and statistical manual of mental disorders* (4th ed., Text Revision). Washington, DC: Author.

Aylward, G. P. (1997). *Infant and early childhood neuropsychology.* New York: Plenum Press.

Gurland, B. J., & Crass, P. S. (1986). Public health perspectives on clinical memory testing of Alzheimer's disease and related disorders. In L. W. Poon (Ed.), *Clinical memory assessment of older adults.* Washington DC: American Psychological Association.

Lezak, M. D. (1995). *Neurological assessment* (3rd ed.). New York: Oxford University Press

Miezejeski, C. M., Devenny, D. A., Krinsky-Mchale, S., Zigman, W., & Silverman, W. (2000). Aging in persons with Down syndrome and mental retardation: Receptive language, visual motor integration, and fluency [Abstract]. *Archives of Clinical Neuropsychology, 15.*

Nadel, L. (1999). Down syndrome in cognitive neuroscience perspective. In H. Tager-Flusberg (Ed.), *Neurodevelopmental disorders.* Cambridge, MA: MIT Press.

Teeter, P. A., & Semrud-Clikeman, M. (1997). *Child neuropsychology: Assessment and interventions for neurodevelopmental disorders.* Boston: Allyn & Bacon.

Bob Kirchner
University of Northern Colorado

Shawn Powell
United States Air Force Academy

DENYS-DRASH SYNDROME

Denys-Drash syndrome, also known as Drash syndrome, is the combination of Wilms tumor (a malignant cancerous tumor of the kidney), pseudohermaphroditism (unambiguous gonadal sex with ambiguous external genitalia), and nephrotic syndrome (the deterioration of the kidney's renal tubular epithelium). This syndrome is characterized as a rare genetic disorder caused by the mutation of the Wilms tumor suppressor gene (WT1; Thoene, 1995). The majority of the 150 identified cases of Denys-Drash have been male (Mueller, 1994). This syndrome is usually detected during early infancy and most commonly results in chronic renal failure (Busey, 1990).

Characteristics

Wilms Tumor

1. Abdominal pain
2. Nausea and vomiting
3. High blood pressure
4. Blood in urine

(Olendorf, Jeryan, & Boyden, 1999)

Pseudohermaphroditism

Male

1. XY karyotype
2. Male gonads
3. Female genitalia or ambiguous genitalia

Female

1. XX karyotype
2. Female gonads
3. Male genitalia or ambiguous genitalia

(Mueller, 1994)

Nephrotic Syndrome

1. Lack of appetite
2. Irritability
3. Vomiting
4. Diarrhea
5. Swelling and possible significant weight increase
6. Protein malnutrition

(Rx Med Health Resource Centre, 2001)

Genetic counseling is useful in facilitating the understanding of the diagnosis, course of syndrome, and treatment (Thoene, 1995). Individuals suffering from Denys-Drash syndrome may need to undergo surgery, chemotherapy, and radiation in order to treat the Wilms tumor (Olendorf et al., 1999). Because of the potential development of gonadal malignancy associated with pseudohermaphroditism, removal of the ovaries or testes may be necessary (Thoene, 1995). Treatment of the nephrotic syndrome is likely to include any combination of dialysis, kidney transplant, or renal transplant (Jensen, Ehrlich, Hanna, Fine, & Grunberger, 1989). The dietary requirements while undergoing dialysis, a renal transplant, or a kidney transplant are different. Therefore, nutritional counseling with a registered dietition is essential to facilitate ongoing extensive nutritional management specific to each procedure necessary to treat the nephrotic syndrome (National Kidney Foundation, 2001). Attending individual and family psychological counseling helps to promote acceptance and adjustment surrounding this serious illness and the psychosocial issues typically associated with gender ambiguity.

Individuals suffering from Denys-Drash disease may be eligible for special education services under the Other Health Impairment or Physical Disability handicapping condition. Excessive school absences due to medical treatment may warrant homebound instruction or specialized instruction within the school environment. Information gained by the family through genetic counseling should be provided to the multidisciplinary team evaluating the current level of functioning and educational needs of the student. Although it may be necessary for the student to bring lunch from home, the school's nutritional services staff should be made aware of the dietary requirements in the event that they need to provide the student with a meal. If excessive absences prove to make social integration difficult for the student, a social skills group may be helpful.

The prognosis for those suffering from Denys-Drash syndrome is variable. However, without treatment, death usually occurs during infancy (Busey, 1990). Therefore, early diagnosis and treatment are necessary for survival. Despite timely diagnosis and treatment, those cases resulting in death are most commonly due to renal failure (Mueller, 1994).

REFERENCES

Busey, M. L. (1990). *Birth defects encyclopedia.* Boston: Blackwell Scientific.

Jensen, J. C., et al. (1989). A report of 4 patients with the Drash syndrome and a review of the literature. *Journal of Urology, 141,* 1174–1176.

Mueller, R. F. (1994). The Denys-Drash syndrome. *Journal of Medical Genetics, 31,* 471–477.

National Kidney Foundation. (2001). Nutritional support for kidney disease patients. Retrieved from http://www.kidney.org/general/pubpol/renaldiet.cfm

Olendorf, D., Jeryan, C., & Boyden, K. (1999). *The Gale encyclopedia of medicine* (Vol. 5). Ann Arbor, MI: Gale Research.

Rx Med Health Resource Centre. (2001). Nephrotic syndrome. Retrieved from http://www.rxmed.com/illnesses/nephrotic_syndrome.html

Thoene, J. (1995). *Physician's guide to rare diseases* (2nd ed.). Lawrenceville, NJ: Dowden.

Juliette Cutillo
Fountain-Fort Carson School District 8
Colorado Springs

See also Wilms Tumor

DEPRESSION

Depression in childhood and adolescence encompasses a variety of specific diagnoses, including major depressive disorder, dysthymic disorder, cyclothymic disorder, and bipolar disorder. This entry focuses specifically on major depressive disorder, which is an affective disorder characterized by one or more episodes of depressed (or irritable) mood or loss of interest and pleasure in most activities for periods of at least 2 weeks (American Psychiatric Association [APA], 1994). Psychosocial stressors may precipitate the onset of an episode of major depression, and major depressive disorder may entail either a single episode or recurrent episodes. In differentiating major depressive disorder from dysthymia, the mood disturbance in major depressive disorder is typically more severe and of shorter duration.

Major depressive disorder is rare in preschool children but increases in frequency at school age and again in adolescence. The average age of onset of major depressive disorder is 11 years, and prevalence rates in the general population range from 1% in childhood to 6–8% in adolescence (Kovacs & Devlin, 1998). Episodes of major depression in youth typically last for 6 to 8 months or longer, and the risk for subsequent episodes is high. In children, males and females are equally affected, but major depressive disorder is twice as common in adolescent females as in adolescent males.

Characteristics (adapted from *DSM-IV* diagnostic criteria; APA, 1994)

1. There must be one or more periods of depressed mood (or depressed appearance in young children) for much of the day, nearly every day, or marked loss of interest and pleasure in most activities for at least 2 weeks.
2. At least five of the following symptoms must be present and occur nearly every day: (a) weight loss/gain or appetite loss/gain; (b) sleep disturbances (insomnia or hypersomnia); (c) noticeable change in psychomotor activity (agitation or retardation); (d) loss of energy or fatigue; (e) feelings of worthlessness or excessive guilt; (f) difficulty thinking, concentrating, or indecisiveness; or (g) recurrent thoughts of death, suicide ideation, specific plan for committing suicide, or suicide attempts.
3. Associated characteristics include sadness, tearfulness, social withdrawal, irritability or crankiness, and complaints of bodily aches and pains. Somatic complaints, irritability, and social withdrawal are common in children, whereas psychomotor retardation and hypersomnia are more common among adolescents.
4. Exclusionary criteria include manic episode or symptoms due primarily to substance abuse, medication, or medical condition.
5. The disorder is accompanied by significant impairment in social or academic functioning.

A variety of psychosocial treatment approaches have been documented in the literature, including psychoeducational, psychodynamic, cognitive-behavioral, and family systems interventions. Outcome data suggest that cognitive-behavioral approaches are the most thoroughly evaluated and most promising interventions in the treatment of childhood depression (Harrington, Whittaker, & Shoebridge, 1998). Clinical practice typically combines psychosocial treatment with pharmacological interventions. Although antidepressants are commonly used in the treatment of major depressive disorder in children and adolescents, to date there is a lack of well-controlled studies documenting their efficacy (Stark, Bronik, Wong, Wells, & Ostrander, 2000).

Children with major depressive disorder may qualify for special education services under the category Serious Emotional Disturbance. Due to the negative impact of episodes of major depression on academic functioning and the increased likelihood of concomitant behavior disorders, these children may also qualify for special education services under the categories Specific Learning Disability and Behavior Disorders. Impaired social interaction skills are a prominent characteristic of major depressive disorder, so social skills training may be one component of the special education services that these children require. Additionally, it is estimated that up to 15% of individuals with major depressive disorder die by suicide (APA, 1994); therefore, these youth should be appropriately monitored in school settings.

Comorbidity rates for youth diagnosed with major depressive disorder are high for disruptive behavior disorders, anxiety disorders, and attention-deficit disorders, as well as for substance abuse disorders in adolescence. Early onset of major depressive disorder is associated with an increased likelihood of recurrence into adulthood and sustained impairments in academic and social functioning. There is considerable need for further empirical research on the effective treatment of major depressive disorder and other mood disorders specific to children and adolescents as well as research highlighting the comparative efficacy of specific therapeutic and pharmacological interventions.

REFERENCES

American Psychiatric Association. (1994). *Diagnostic and statistical manual of mental disorders* (4th ed.). Washington, DC: Author.

Harrington, R., Whittaker, J., & Shoebridge, P. (1998). Psychological treatment of depression in children and adolescents: A review of treatment research. *British Journal of Psychiatry, 173,* 291–298.

Kovacs, M., & Devlin, B. (1998). Internalizing disorders in childhood. *Journal of Child Psychology and Psychiatry, 39,* 47–63.

Stark, K. D., Bronik, M. D., Wong, S., Wells, G., & Ostrander, R. (2000). Depressive disorders. In M. Hersen & R. T. Ammerman (Eds.), *Advanced abnormal child psychology* (2nd ed., pp. 291–326). Mahwah, NJ: Erlbaum.

Lora Tuesday Heathfield
University of Utah

See also Bipolar Affective Disorder

DEPRIVATION, EARLY AUDITORY

Early auditory deprivation occurs when auditory stimuli during early childhood are not sufficient for adequate development of the auditory system. Variations in quantity, quality, or timing of exposure can lead to atypical development (Ruben & Rapin, 1980). In general, the more severe or complete and early the deprivation, the more detrimental the effects (Ruben & Rapin, 1980). The implications of such deprivation are great in that early deprivation can have a long-term impact on an individual's ability to hear, produce, and understand speech sounds (Finitzo, Gunnarson, & Clark, 1990; Werner & VandenBos, 1993). In most cases, the auditory system is fully mature by age 10, so auditory deprivation that occurs before then is likely to have a greater detrimental effect (Werner & VandenBos, 1993). Premature infants are believed to be at exceptional risk for the detrimental effects of auditory deprivation because their auditory system is less developed at birth (Ruben & Rapin, 1980). A common source of early auditory deprivation is otitis media (Finitzo, 1990).

Characteristics

1. Poor differential hearing
2. Decreased sensitivity to sound in the end of the range
3. Difficulty localizing sound

Early identification of hearing loss is imperative if the aim of treatment is the prevention of long-term impairment (Rubin, 1972). The early use of hearing aids may be especially important in aiding the development of the auditory system (Ruben & Rapin, 1980). Otitis media has been associated with subsequent hearing impairment, and prompt treatment is thus likely to be critical to facilitating the normal development of hearing (Ruben & Rapin, 1980; Sak & Ruben, 1981).

Rubin (1972) suggests the use of individualized treatment to maximize the utility of any hearing present, especially regarding the generation and understanding of verbal language. The participation of caretakers in such a program is a necessity. They often need to be taught how to communicate with their children in ways that facilitate the child's developing ability to communicate. Treatment should be sensitive to the difficulty that many parents may have in accepting their child's hearing deficit. Home visits by therapists are recommended (Rubin, 1972).

Children with a hearing loss that has a negative impact on their ability to learn should qualify for special education services. If hearing is not sufficient to allow for verbal communication, American Sign Language should be taught. Educators should remember that although a child may not be able to speak, it is important for others to communicate visually as well as auditorily in order to maximize the utility of whatever level of hearing they do have (Rubin, 1972).

Whenever possible, children with hearing difficulties should be seated near the teacher so that the child can hear and see the teacher clearly (Bess, Klee, & Culbertson, 1986). Because difficulty with sound discrimination is a characteristic of those with early auditory deprivation, efforts should be made to provide a quiet setting that is free of auditory distractions.

There is some evidence that early auditory deprivation leads to difficulties with language-related cognition (Neville & Lawson, 1987; Sak & Ruben, 1981). Thus, children with hearing difficulties may struggle with tasks such as spelling and auditory decoding. Although the evidence is inconsistent, some research suggests superiority in visual skills compared to non-hearing-impaired peers (Neville & Lawson, 1987; Sak & Ruben, 1981). It should be noted that there is some indication that these differences may be due, at least in part, to the early acquisition and use of visual language rather than to the effects of auditory deprivation (Neville & Lawson, 1987). Regardless of the cause for these differences, results suggest the importance of incorporating visual modalities into instruction when working with this population.

It is believed that early auditory deprivation leads to atypical neuronal development in areas pertaining to hearing (Ruben & Rapin, 1980). Currently, there is no treatment that can repair the irregularities in development. However, the interventions just mentioned can minimize the degree of functional impairment.

A goal for future research is to continue to test the generalizability of animal studies (Rubin, 1972). In addition, future research should attempt to clarify whether the cognitive differences in those with hearing impairment are due to the effects of deprivation or the result of visual language use.

REFERENCES

Bess, F. H., Klee, T., & Culbertson, J. L. (1986). Identification, assessment, and management of children with unilateral sensorineural hearing loss. *Ear and Hearing, 7*(1), 43–51.

Finitzo, T., Gunnarson, A. D., & Clark, J. L. (1990). Auditory deprivation and early conducive hearing loss from otitis media. *Topical Language Disorders, 11*(1), 29–42.

Neville, H. H., & Lawson, D. (1987). Attention to central and peripheral visual space in a movement detection task: III. Separate effects of auditory deprivation and acquisition of a visual language. *Brain Research, 405,* 284–294.

Ruben, R. J., & Rapin, I. (1980). Plasticity of the developing auditory system. *Annals of Otology, Rhinology, and Laryngology, 89,* 303–311.

Rubin, M. (1972). Auditory deprivation in infants. *Journal of Communication Disorders, 5,* 195–204.

Sak, R. J., & Ruben, R. J. (1981). Recurrent ear effusion in childhood: Implications of temporary auditory deprivation for language and learning. *Annals of Otology, Rhinology, and Laryngology, 90,* 546–551.

Werner, L. A., & VandenBos, G. R. (1993). Developmental psychoacoustics: What infants and children hear. *Hospital and Community Psychiatry, 44*(7), 624–626.

Melanie E. Ballatore
University of Texas at Austin

DEPRIVATION, EARLY VISUAL

Early visual stimulation is critical to the normal development of the visual system. Early visual deprivation occurs when exposure to visual stimuli is limited in amount or intensity during initial stages of development (Jackson & Ellis, 1971; Perier, 2000). The outcome of early visual deprivation varies according to a variety of factors. Deprivation that is monocular and more severe and that occurs early in development generally leads to greater impairment (Boothe, Dobson, & Teller, 1985; Hyvarinen & Hyvarinen, 1982). Length of deprivation also has an impact on the amount of impairment, and longer periods of deprivation lead to more detrimental outcomes (Boothe et al., 1985). Additionally, when the previous factors are present, the duration of deprivation needed to result in negative consequences is lessened (Boothe et al., 1985).

Research indicates that specific forms of deprivation lead to differential effects on the visual pathways (Boothe et al., 1985). In cases of long-term monocular deprivation, change in ocular dominance appears to be mirrored in brain structure (Boothe et al., 1985). When early visual deprivation is long-term, it appears that other sensory modalities utilize multimodal neurons, limiting those available to the visual modality on recovery of visual input (Boothe et al., 1985; Perier, 2000). There is evidence that in cases of congenital blindness, there is some compensatory development of the auditory system (Roder, Rosler, & Neville, 1999).

Characteristics

1. Impaired spatial resolution
2. Poor visual acquity
3. In cases of monocular visual deprivation, poor binocular vision

Long-term, correctable, binocular visual deprivation is fairly rare, most commonly occurring as a result of cataracts. Some form of congenital cataracts occurs in approximately 1 out of every 250 births (Potter, 1993). In cases of short-term monocular deprivation, it is necessary not only to reinstate vision but also to allow the previously impaired eye to gain strength by temporarily limiting the use of the unaffected eye by using an eye patch. Simple reinstatement of vision in the deprived eye has little or no effect on negative symptoms. When cataracts are present, treatment generally consists of surgical removal followed by optical correction devices such as glasses or contact lenses (Boothe et al., 1985).

Children experiencing the negative effects of early visual deprivation may qualify for special education services depending on the extent of visual impairment. Possible accommodations include instruction in Braille and use of large type. In order to maximize the use of any vision present, the child should be seated near the instructor. Whenever possible, instruction should incorporate multiple sensory modalities, especially auditory.

The most common outcome of monocular deprivation is amblyopia, or lazy eye, which occurs when one eye is deprived of visual input relative to the other eye (Boothe et al., 1985). In such cases both spatial resolution and binocular function are negatively affected (Boothe et al., 1985). When deprivation is not long-term and treatment follows, prognosis is good (Boothe et al., 1985). In cases of long-term binocular deprivation, prognosis is poor, resulting in a general lack of visual responsiveness (Boothe et al., 1985).

Prognosis following treatment for cataracts is dependent on several factors (Boothe et al., 1985). For cataracts that are thick, present at birth, and cover the entire eye, prognosis is relatively poor (Boothe et al., 1985). In cases where cataracts are present at birth, immediacy of treatment is critical to maximizing vision (Boothe et al., 1985; Potter, 1993). Even when treatment is fairly successful, visual acquity is generally impaired (Boothe et al., 1985; Potter, 1993).

For ethical reasons, early visual deprivation cannot be induced in human subjects. Therefore, the bulk of research into early visual deprivation is done with animals. A goal for research is work that seeks to confirm the generalizability of such research to humans.

REFERENCES

Boothe, R. G., Dobson, V., & Teller, D. Y. (1985). Postnatal development of vision in human and nonhuman primates. *Annual Review of Neuroscience, 8,* 495–545.

Hyvarinen, J., & Hyvarinen, L. (1982). Higher functions and plasticity in visual pathways. *Acta Opthalmologica, 157*(Suppl.), 9–17.

Jackson, C. W., Jr., & Ellis, R. (1971). Sensory deprivation as a field of study. *Nursing Research, 20*(1), 46–54.

Perier, O. (2000). Deprivation, bioneural results of. In C. R. Reynolds & E. Fletcher-Janzen (Eds.), *Encyclopedia of special education: A reference for the education of the handicapped and other exceptional children and adults* (2nd ed., Vol. 1, pp. 558–559). New York: Wiley.

Potter, W. S. (1993). Pediatric cataracts. *Pediatric Opthamology, 40*(4), 841–853.

Roder, B., Rosler, F., & Neville, H. J. (1999). Effects of interstimulus interval on auditory event-related potentials in congenitally blind and normally sighted humans. *Neuroscience Letters, 264,* 53–56.

Melanie E. Ballatore
University of Texas at Austin

DERMATITIS, ATOPIC

Atopic Dermatitis is a skin disorder that occurs in adults and children. The skin is hypersensitive and reacts with inflammation. The skin can become extremely itchy, and if the condition becomes chronic, the skin may become scaly and thick.

Atopic dermatitis has a 12% prevalence rate in the United States, and 60% of the patients will show signs of this condition by the end of their first year; 90% of all the patients will show signs by the end of their fifth year (Ghidorzi, 2001). The condition occurs equally in males and females, but females do have more severe symptoms (Ghidorzi, 2001). A genetic predisposition in combination with other environmental influences seems to cause the condition. By adulthood, 70% of all patients report less severe symptoms or even disappearance of the symptoms (DermIS, 2001).

Characteristics

1. An infant is brought to the physician with a rash that seems to be resistant to over-the-counter medications.
2. The child's rash causes extreme itching but is not accompanied by fever or other symptoms.
3. The skin where the rash is present is dry and forms blisters that may ooze—leading to crusting when the ooze dries.
4. Commonly affected areas in infants and children are cheeks, trunk (diaper rash), elbows, and knees. Commonly affected areas in adults are face, neck, elbows, knees, and genital areas.
5. Skin condition is judged according to appearance:
   - *Acute.* Eczema is blistered and shows inflammation.
   - *Subacute.* Skin appears to be scaling and leathery (lichenification).
   - *Chronic.* Skin may appear lighter or darker due to pigmentation change (Ghidorzi, 2001).
6. Complications include secondary skin infections and scaring (Atopic dermatitis, 2002).

Treatment should be supervised by a physician to provide the necessary differential diagnosis as well as a treatment plan to reduce the associated symptoms of this often-chronic condition. Treatment varies according to the different stages (acute, subacute, and chronic) as well as the causes of the disorder, which can include food allergies and environmental factors such as wool and lanolin (Atopic dermatitis, 2002). To prevent irritation to the skin, bathing and the use of cosmetics and soaps should be avoided. Common treatments include anti-itch lotions as well as topical steroids under more severe circumstances. Flare-ups can be caused by change in climate, sweating, tight and irritating clothing (especially wool), exposure to tobacco smoke, and emotional stress (Ghidorzi, 2001).

To address the issues related to emotional stress and depression that often accompany a chronic condition, psychological guidance and support groups are recommended. These issues should be considered by all professionals involved in the child's daily life in school and at home. By reducing emotional stress, understanding of the condition by the patient and all involved will decrease the possibility of flare-ups and therefore enable the child to live life with the least amount of disturbances. Although atopic dermatitis cannot be cured, with appropriate treatment the causes of flare-ups can be avoided and symptoms can be managed (Greene, 2001). The majority of patients will experience a fading of their symptoms by the time they reach adulthood.

REFERENCES

Atopic dermatitis. (2002). *Mosby's medical, nursing, and allied health dictionary* (6th ed., p. 154). St. Louis, MO: Harcourt Health Sciences.

DermIS. (2001). Einleitende Informationen zur Neurodermitis. Retrieved December 12, 2001, from http://www.dermis.net/neurodermis/ueberblick/einleitung/index.htm

Ghidorzi, A. J. (2001, June 28). Atopic dermatitis. *eMedicine Journal, 2(6)*. Retrieved December 27, 2001, from http://www.emedecine.com/emerg/topic130.html

Greene, A. R. (2001). Disease—atopic dermatitis. Retrieved December 27, 2001, from http://sitemaker.medseek.com/websitefiles/drgreene/body.cfm

Monika Hannan
University of Northern Colorado

DERMATITIS, CONTACT

Contact dermatitis is an inflammation of the skin that follows contact with various irritants and allergic substances (Contact dermatitis, 2002). Contact dermatitis is differentiated according to the causes of the skin condition. The skin reacts with itching, tenderness, blistering, and swelling.

Ninety percent of all workers' compensation claims in the United States are caused by contact dermatitis (Michael, 2001). Twenty percent of all women have contact dermatitis at least once during their lifetime with the highest occurrence after childbirth. Women are twice as likely to get contact dermatitis, and 2% of the population has dermatitis affecting their hands at any given time. Children of affected individuals are 60% more likely to react positively when patch tests are administered (Michael, 2001). Overall, Caucasians tend to have a greater likelihood of developing contact dermatitis, but it might be harder to detect in other ethnic groups.

Characteristics (Greene, 2001)

1. Itching of affected areas
2. Redness or inflammation and swelling of skin
3. Skin reacting to exposure with rash or blisters, which in turn might ooze or form a crust
4. Skin reaction occurring after exposure to allergic substances

Contact dermatitis is divided into four types:

Allergic contact dermatitis is a reaction to specific allergens. Such reactions can change depending on genetic predisposition, intensity, and duration of contact. There is a wide range of possible allergens that can include plants (e.g., poison ivy), metals found in jewelry (e.g., nickel sulfate), household cleaners, medications, and other chemicals (Michael, 2001).

Irritant contact dermatitis is a reaction to mild or strong irritants. Among the irritants are acids, alkalies, solvents, and plants. The exposed area, depending on the irritant, should be thoroughly flushed with water.

Photo dermatitis is a reaction to exposure to the sun. Certain medications and foods seem to predispose some individuals to these reactions. Among the medications implicated are tetracycline and sulfa drugs, and among the foods are citrus fruits, parsnip, and celery (Michael, 2001).

Contact urticaria is an extreme reaction to different allergens. Such allergens can be found in food or in latex. Anaphylactic shock has been reported in some cases (Michael, 2001).

Treatment is dependent on the cause of the contact dermatitis. Treatment could include flushing with water, applying soothing and wet dressings, or using medication and lotions (Greene, 2001). Symptoms related to acute discomfort (anxiety, sleeplessness, lack of concentration, irritability, and mood swings) should be considered by all professionals involved in the child's daily life. The impact of the symptoms on the child's mental health depends on the severity of the dermatitis and can influence a child's ability to focus and concentrate on curricular activities. It might be necessary to examine whether the child is exposed to irritants in her or his school environment. For example, schedule changes might be necessary following a diagnosis of photo dermatitis so that the child's exposure to sun during recess is reduced.

The proper diagnosis by a physician can help the individual by identifying environmental allergens. The primary concern then must be avoidance of the allergen (Dermatitis and eczema, 1999). Following the removal of the allergen from the child's environment, the healing process may take up to three weeks.

Proper education by the physician of the child, and his or her parents, about the treatment of dermatitis is essential. This education can help the patient to avoid specific substances that have been shown to cause symptoms. Equipped with the appropriate knowledge, the child should be able to enjoy life to the fullest extent possible.

REFERENCES

Contact dermatitis. (2002). *Mosby's medical, nursing, and allied health dictionary* (6th ed., pp. 421–422). St. Louis, MO: Harcourt Health Sciences.

Dermatitis and eczema. (1999). *Harvard Medical School family health guide,* (pp. 549–550). New York: Simon & Schuster.

Greene, A. R. (2001). Disease—contact dermatitis. Retrieved December 28, 2001, from http://sitemaker.medseek.com/websitefiles/drgreene/body.cfm

Michael, J. A. (2001, November 15). Contact dermatitis. *eMedicine Journal, 2*(11). Retrieved December 27, 2001, from http://www.emedicine.com/emerg/topic131.html

Monika Hannan
University of Northern Colorado

DERMATOMYOSITIS

Dermatomyositis is a rheumatological disorder that involves multiple systems including skeletal muscle, skin, the gastrointestinal tract, and the central nervous system. Irregular skin lesions and muscle inflammation are among the most common clinical signs; however, patients may have arthralgias, arthritis, or cardiopulmonary dysfunction. Onset of dermatomyositis usually occurs in school-aged children between ages 8 and 9 and rarely occurs before the age of 2 years. Dermatomyositis malignancies occur in 20% of patients and more often in adults. However, other complications such as calcinosis occurs in approximately 20–50% of childhood cases.

Incidence of juvenile dermatomyositis has been previously estimated as 4 in 1,000,000 annually (Cawkwell, 2000). Although the etiology of dermatomyositis is unknown, involvement of cellular immune mechanisms is suspected.

Characteristics

1. Muscle weakness and tenderness, surface skin rash, and constitutional symptoms are common. Arthritis can occur, and gastrointestinal vasculitis is a potentially fatal complication.
2. Muscle atrophy and calcinosis may be severe long-term sequelae of muscle inflammation.
3. Onset usually occurs between ages 8 and 9.
4. Occlusive vasculities are the most prominent lesions found in children.
5. Twenty to 50% of childhood cases have calcinosis.
6. The disorder often involves severe muscle weakness, atrophy, contracture. Involvement of palatorespiratory muscles may lead to serious respiratory difficulties and death.
7. Cardiac complications have also been reported.

The prevalence of dermatomyositis is unknown; however, it is less common than other rheumatological diseases, such as rheumatoid arthritis, systemic lupus erythematosus, or Henoch-Schonlein purpura.

Treatment has changed dramatically in recent years with more aggressive management becoming more prevalent. However, little substantive research has been published on therapeutics (Cawkwell, 2000). Available treatments usually include systemic corticosteroids to suppress clinical symptoms with or without an immunosuppressive agent (Callen, 2000). Intravenous immunoglobulin therapy may be used to boost the immune system. Physical therapy is imperative to preserve and increase muscle strength and to prevent crippling contractures or deformities. Hygiene skin maintenance also is imperative. In cases where palatorespiratory muscles are involved, management of respiratory function is maintained with constant care and use of respiratory equipment.

Special education services may be required in the form of accommodation due to the long-term effect of chronic illness on school achievement. Many of these children will qualify for services under the classification of Other Health Impairment as a result of their medical condition.

Early treatment intervention can help modify the progression of dermatomyositis. If treated early, symptoms may subside for a number of years. The prognosis for treated children is good; however, the prognosis for untreated patients is poor, and complications may lead to death. It is estimated that approximately 40% will die from complications of dermatomyositis. Research continues to focus on outcome and disease activity markers, as well as on further delineation of the role of genetics, environment, and immunity in the pathogenesis and course of the juvenile idiopathic inflammatory myopathies (Cawkwell, 2000). New understanding of the pathobiology of the disease should lead to improved, less toxic treatments (Laxer & Feldman, 1997)

REFERENCES

Callen, J. P. (2000). Dermatomyositis. *Lancet, 355*(9197), 53–57.

Cawkwell, G. M. (2000). Inflammatory myositis in children, including differential diagnosis. *Current Opinion in Rheumatology, 12,* 430–434.

Laxer, R. M., & Feldman, B. M. (1997). General and local scleroderma in children and dermatomyositis and associated syndromes. *Current Opinion in Rheumatology, 9,* 458–464.

Virdette L. Brumm
Children's Hospital Los Angeles
Keck / USC School of Medicine

DE SANCTIS-CACCHIONE SYNDROME

De Sanctis-Cacchione (DSC) syndrome is a very rare, more severe variant of xerodosa pigmentosum (XP) that also includes mental retardation, numerous neurological abnormalities, dwarfism, and hypogonadism.

XP is itself uncommon, with an incidence of only 1 in 250,000 in the United States, and a somewhat higher rate in Japan (1 in 40,000). However, cases have been found worldwide (e.g., Lincheta, Balea, Simón, & Otano, 1998; Niederauer, Bohnert, Altmeyer, & Jung, 1992). Impaired intelligence with one or a few neurological features is seen in about 20% of the number of total XP cases (Buyse, 1990). These cases often display hyporeflexia, impaired intelligence, and progressive hearing loss. DSC patients, however, make up an even more severely affected subgroup of these, displaying intellectual impairment, numerous neurological abnormalities, and stunted physical growth and sexual development (Jones, 1997).

Characteristics

1. XP syndrome, including ultraviolet photosensitivity of exposed skin and eye tissue, leading to increased cancer risk
2. Mental retardation, including progressive cognitive deterioration
3. Progressive sensorineural hearing loss
4. Dwarfism, including microcephaly
5. Hypogonadism, leading to delayed sexual development
6. Neurological abnormalities including hyporeflexia, areflexia, ataxia, spasticity, choreoathetosis, brain atrophy, abnormal electroencephalograms (EEGs) and electromyograms (EMGs)

DSC patients belong to either Group A or D of about 10 complementation groups of XP that vary in severity (Buyse, 1990). The XP-related skin and ocular features reflect the cellular vulnerability to ultraviolet radiation due to defective DNS repair mechanisms. Photosensitivity of exposed skin leads to increased freckling, blistering, poikiloderma, and other skin anomalies, as well as a predisposition to develop neoplasia of both the skin and conjunctivas. Heightened photosensitivity as well as increased freckling can be seen in the first year of life, with most cases showing these signs by age 5. Photophobia can be seen in the neonate. As progressive damage of the eyes occurs, corneal opacities, conjunctivitis, keratitis, ectropion, and entropion may occur. In DSC the onset of these skin and ocular features may be earlier and more severe than in XP without neurological abnormalities (Buyse, 1990).

In addition to the features of XP, in DSC there are many neurological abnormalities that are typically noted in childhood, although some may have onset as late as the second decade of life. Defects include mental retardation and further progressive dementia, progressive sensorineural deafness, stunted growth (e.g., microcephaly, dwarfism), delayed sexual development (gonadal hypoplasia likely due to hypothalamic dysfunction), hyporeflexia and areflexia, spasticity, and later the onset of ataxia and choreoathetoid movements. EEGs and EMGs are often abnormal, and there may be radiological evidence of neuronal loss leading to olivopontocerebellar and cerebral atrophy, as well as signs of demyelination and neuropathy (Kanda et al., 1990).

There is no known prevention, except genetic counseling. Heterozygote carriers are thought to be clinically normal, but there may be a heightened risk of skin cancer. Prenatal screening can be done via DNA repair studies of cultured amniotic fluid cells. Life span in XP is shortened, with a 70% probability of survival attained at age 40. The survival rate of DSC patients is similar to that for XP patients without neurological compromise and depends on the degree of exposure to UV light as well as on the level of cell repair deficiency (which varies by complementation subgroup). Death is typically due to complications of associated CNS dysfunction or more commonly lethal cancers.

Treatment of the XP-related features consists primarily of avoidance of ultraviolet radiation, which in some cases may lead to a total avoidance of exposure to sunlight and indoor ultraviolet sources (e.g., fluorescent or halogen lights). For some cases, an adaptive reversal in diurnal schedule is made. These patients have sometimes been called "children of the moon" because they live their normal waking hours during the night to maximize avoidance of exposure to sunlight (Xeroderma Pigmentosum Society, Inc., 2001). Home schooling may be the only option in these cases. However, in less severe cases, accommodations (e.g., protective sunscreen and clothing, staying indoors, etc.) may allow children to attend regular school. In more serious cases, dermatome shaving or dermabrasion and corneal transplants may be indicated. Oral retinoids to prevent new neoplasms have been studied. Avoidance of additional carcinogens, including cigarette smoke and other environmental sources, is also recommended.

Treatment of the neurological abnormalities will depend on the degree and kind. Special education services are available for associated mental retardation, developmental delays, or further deterioration of cognitive function. Hearing aids and occupational and physical therapies may be warranted, and children may qualify for special services under Other Health Impairment or Physical Disability.

REFERENCES

Buyse, M. L. (1990). *Birth defects encyclopedia.* Cambridge: Blackwell Scientific.

Jones, K. L. (1997). *Smith's recognizable patterns of human malformation* (5th ed.). Philadelphia: W. B. Saunders.

Kanda, T., Oda, M., Yonezawa, M., Tamagawa, K., Isa, F., Hanakago, R., & Tsukagoshi, H. (1990). Peripheral neuropathy in xeroderma pigmentosum. *Brain, 113*(Pt. 4), 1025–1044.

Lincheta, L., Balea, A., Simón, R., & Otano, E. (1998). Xeroderma pigmentosum syndrome of De Sanctis-Cacchione: Presentation of one case. *Cuban Review of Pediatrics, 70*(2), 113–116.

Niederauer, H., Bohnert, E., Altmeyer, P., & Jung, E. (1992). De Sanctis-Cacchione syndrome: Xeroderma pigmentosum with oligophrenia, short sature and neurologic disorders. *Hautarzt, 43*(1), 25–27.

Xeroderma Pigmentosum Society, Inc. (2001, May 1). Retrieved from http://www.xps.org

Vicky Y. Spradling
Austin State Hospital

See also Xerodosa Pigmentosum

DHAT

Dhat is a culture-bound syndrome that is considered a "hypochondriacal concern associated with the discharge of semen, whitish discoloration of the urine, and feelings of weakness and exhaustion" (American Psychiatric Association, 1994, p. 849). This disorder is found primarily among males in India, Sri Lanka, Nepal, Bangladesh, and Pakistan. Other terms for this disorder are *jiryan* (India), *sukra prameba* (Sri Lanka), and *shen-k'uei* (China).

There are no known prevalence or incidence studies, such that Bhatia and Malik (1991, p. 692) observed in their study of the disorder that the "syndrome has not been studied in detail." However, according to their study, presented in the *British Journal of Psychiatry,* this disease seems to affect men exclusively, with adolescence as the earliest reported onset. The age range of Dhat onset is reportedly 16–24 years of age, with the mean age of onset 21.8 years (Bhatia & Malik, 1991). This syndrome is a commonly recognized clinical entity in Indian culture. The afflicted is typically more likely to be married or recently married and of average or low socioeconomic status (perhaps a student, laborer, or farmer by occupation) and to come from a rural area and belong to a family with conservative attitudes toward sex (Bhatia & Malik, 1991).

Characteristics

1. Weakness
2. Fatigue
3. Heart palpitations
4. Sleeplessness
5. Protein in urine

Dhat syndrome is a true culture-bound sex neurosis quite common in the natives of the Indian subcontinent. The word *dhat* is derived from the Sanskrit word *dhatu,* which means "the elixir that constitutes the body" (Bhatia & Malik, 1991, p. 691). It is a commonly held belief both culturally and within the Indian system of medicine that "disturbances in the 'Dhatus' result in an increased susceptibility to physical and mental disease" (Bhatia & Malik, 1991, p. 691).

The belief that semen is precious and life preserving is deeply ingrained in Indian culture. Practitioners of traditional systems of medicine reinforce this belief and have specific clinics to treat dhat (Bhatia & Malik, 1991). When a patient afflicted with dhat syndrome is referred to medical personnel, typical treatment is to administer antianxiety or antidepressant drugs. Some patients are also treated with a 4-week course of psychotherapy.

The likelihood of this disorder occurring in the United States is rare, and studies of affliction among emigrant Indian populations have not been formulated at this time. However, this disorder is deeply ingrained within Indian cultures, and family history as well as assimilation studies could be useful in determining dhat syndrome in afflicted students presenting dhat-like characteristics.

REFERENCES

American Psychiatric Association. (1994). *Diagnostic and statistical manual of mental disorders* (4th ed.) Washington, DC.: Author.

Bhatia, M. S., & Malik, S. C. (1991). Dhat syndrome: A useful diagnostic entity in Indian culture. *British Journal of Psychiatry, 159,* 691–695.

Kiely Ann Fletcher
Ohio State University

DIABETES INSIPIDUS

Diabetes insipidus (DI) is a syndrome that is characterized by an inability to conserve water and maintain the body's essential water homeostasis. Onset of this condition occurs when there is an insufficient level of antidiuretic hormone (ADH) or when the kidneys have a decreased sensitivity to ADH. When a deficiency in ADH occurs, the kidneys cannot reabsorb water and concentrate urine. Subsequently, an excessive volume of dilute urine is produced and excreted (Nickolaus, 1999). In response to such unregulated loss of water, individuals with diabetes insipidus experience constant thirst and must increase their fluid intake substantially to prevent dehydration.

Diabetes insipidus affects approximately 3 out of 100,000 people (Adam, 1997). Three different pathogenic mechanisms can result in DI. Neurogenic DI, the most common type, is caused by a cranial pathology that results in inadequate production or secretion of ADH. Dysfunction of, or damage to, the posterior lobe of the pituitary gland, where ADH is secreted, is typically implicated. The most common causes of neurogenic DI in children are tumor, head trauma, neurosurgery, and sequelae of meningitis. Eight percent of childhood cases are idiopathic. This type of DI affects males and females with equal frequency and can occur in all age groups (Nickolaus, 1999).

Nephrogenic DI commonly is inherited by an X-linked trait that causes a decrease in the kidneys' responsiveness to ADH. Therefore, despite normal ADH levels, abnormalities in the renal tubules that are responsible for concentrating urine lead to dilute urine output. Males are affected more frequently than females. Onset in males occurs at birth, whereas onset in females may occur at a later age and may present with milder symptoms. Nephrogenic DI can also be precipitated by medications, with lithium being the drug most commonly associated with the disorder (Adam, 1997).

The third type, dipsogenic DI, is brought on by excessive fluid intake, which inhibits ADH secretion. Two subgroups of this disorder exist and are distinguished by different causes. Primary polydipsia is caused by a lesion at the site of the thirst receptors in the brain, which causes improper stimulation of the thirst response. Psychogenic polydipsia is a mental health disorder characterized by compulsive fluid intake. Dipsogenic DI is uncommon in children (Adam, 1997).

Characteristics

1. Polyuria (passage of an excessive volume of dilute urine) with urine output in excess of 30 ml per kg per day. Nocturia and nocturnal enuresis may also be present.
2. Polydipsia (excessive drinking) with complaints of constant thirst.
3. Dehydration may occur if water balance cannot be maintained with fluid intake.

Individuals whose symptoms are mild may not require treatment. When symptoms are debilitating, treatment can greatly reduce their magnitude and substantially increase quality of life. Fluid replacement is essential regardless of type of DI and can be accomplished by always drinking enough fluids to quench thirst. Individuals with neurogenic DI are given hormone replacement therapy to restore levels of ADH. ADH replacement drugs can be given orally, by injection, or via a nasal spray. Individuals with nephrogenic DI will not benefit from hormone replacement because they are insensitive to ADH. However, prescription diuretics, along with a low-sodium diet, can be effective in reducing urine output (Baylis & Cheetham, 1998).

Many children with diabetes insipidus can be expected to participate in a regular education setting. However, classroom accommodations under Section 504 will likely be required to allow the child to have adequate access to fluids during the school day and unrestricted passes to the restroom. If nephrogenic diabetes is present at birth and is not recognized and treated at an early stage, damage to the central nervous system can occur as a result of hypertonic dehydration. As a result, children may experience neuropsychological dysfunction, which could result in learning or behavioral difficulties that may require intervention. In the most severe cases, where repeated episodes of marked dehydration occur, mental retardation may result and would warrant special education consideration. In addition, because neurogenic diabetes insipidus is often caused by some form of brain insult, some children may be eligible for services under the handicapping conditions of Other Health Impairment or Traumatic Brain Injury.

Although diabetes insipidus is a potentially serious illness, the prognosis is good because the disorder can often be treated effectively. Much of the current research in the area involves publications of case studies documenting causes of the disorder and responses to treatment protocols.

REFERENCES

Adam, P. (1997). Evaluation and management of diabetes insipidus. *American Family Physician, 55,* 2146–2152.

Baylis, P. H., & Cheetham, T. (1998). Diabetes insipidus. *Archives of Disease in Childhood, 79,* 84–89.

Nickolaus, M. J. (1999). Diabetes insipidus: A current perspective. *Critical Care Nurse, 19,* 18–30.

Heidi A. McCallister
University of Texas at Austin

DIABETES, INSULIN-DEPENDENT (TYPE I, JUVENILE DIABETES)

Insulin-dependent diabetes mellitus (IDDM), also known as Type I diabetes or juvenile diabetes, is a chronic metabolic disorder characterized by pancreatic failure and resulting inability to produce insulin and metabolize glucose. The etiology of IDDM is unknown. Genetic factors appear to be related to disease onset, but environmental and individual factors are also implicated. Although it is not known what initiates the disease course, the mechanism responsible for IDDM is considered to be an autoimmune process (Johnson, 1998). In IDDM the immune system produces antibodies that attack and destroy the insulin-producing, pancreatic beta cells, causing severe insulin deficiency.

IDDM is one of the most common chronic disorders of children in the United States. Over 120,000 individuals under the age of 19 are estimated to have IDDM, which translates to a prevalence rate in children of 1.7 per 1,000. The incidence in children is 13,000 new cases annually (La-

Porte, Matsushima, & Chang, 1995). Incidence rates show considerable variation in the United States, and approximately 40% of the variation is explained by differences in racial and ethnic composition. The highest incidence rates are seen among Caucasians and Latino populations of Puerto Rican descent, followed by African Americans and Latino populations of Mexican American descent. In Caucasians, slightly higher incidence rates are seen for males than for females, while the opposite pattern is seen in Latino and African Americans (LaPorte et al., 1995). Peak incidence is linked to puberty (LaPorte et al., 1995).

Characteristics

1. Polyuria (frequent urination) and/or glucose present in the urine
2. Polydipsia (increased thirst), excessively dry mouth, and dehydration
3. Polyphagia (increased appetite) accompanied by sudden, unexplained weight loss
4. Changes and/or blurring of vision
5. Ketonuria, or the presence of ketones in the urine
6. Fatigue or lethargy
7. Diagnosis confirmed by a positive result to any of the following three tests: a random plasma glucose level of 200 mg/dl or greater when the symptoms of diabetes are present; a fasting plasma glucose of 126 mg/dl or greater; impaired performance on an oral glucose tolerance test

Because there is no known cure for IDDM, lifelong treatment is required. Treatment focuses on keeping blood glucose levels within a target range that closely approximates the normal range of blood glucose levels found in nondiabetic individuals. This goal is achieved through an intensive daily regimen of self-care behaviors, which includes exogenous insulin replacement via multiple injections or by continuous infusion via an insulin pump; meal planning and dietary restrictions; regular exercise; and self-monitoring of blood glucose levels using a home glucose meter (Johnson, 1998). The treatment regimen must be carefully monitored and adjusted in consultation with the child's health care team. Periodic blood and urine assays are required to monitor the overall effectiveness of the regimen in controlling blood sugar metabolism and to screen for complications. Additional treatments may be required to address specific complications of IDDM (e.g., kidney failure, eye disease, etc.).

Evidence in the literature suggests that specific subgroups of children with IDDM may be at increased risk for developing neuropsychological impairments and learning disabilities, which increases the potential need for special education services in this population (Rovet, Ehrlich, Czuchta, & Akler, 1993). Children with early-onset IDDM (diagnosis prior to age 5) and children who have poor diabetes control appear to be at greatest risk. An estimated 19% of children with IDDM are in special education classes or are receiving part-time resource assistance (Rovet et al., 1993). Children with IDDM have been found to have weaknesses in visuospatial processing, verbal ability, visuomotor abilities, memory, attention, and specific learning disabilities in reading, spelling, and arithmetic. Therefore, eligibility for special education services will vary considerably depending on the specific nature and severity of neuropsychological and educational dysfunction. Children with IDDM who do not qualify for special education services may be considered for accommodations under Section 504. Because poor diabetes control can significantly interfere with learning, educational plans should include instructions for managing the child's diabetes during the school day (e.g., frequency and timing of insulin injections and blood glucose monitoring).

Although new treatments and technologies are continually improving the health outcomes of individuals with IDDM, the life expectancy is 75% of normal (Johnson, 1998). Mortality in the early years after diagnosis is typically caused by acute coma resulting from severe hyper- or hypoglycemia, whereas mortality in the middle and later years is associated primarily with kidney disease and cardiovascular disease, respectively (Portuese & Orchard, 1995). Additional serious long-term complications include blindness, stroke, amputations, and nerve disease. However, the Diabetes Control and Complications Trial Research Group (1993), a large-scale longitudinal study, showed that onset and progression of eye, kidney, and nerve damage could be significantly reduced if blood glucose levels were closely maintained in the near normal range. Current and future research efforts include development of better mechanisms for insulin delivery (e.g., inhaled insulins) and blood glucose monitoring (e.g., "bloodless" glucose meters), experimental pancreas transplants and transplants of insulin-producing pancreatic beta cells, and research on etiology and prevention.

REFERENCES

Diabetes Control and Complications Trial Research Group. (1993). The effect of intensive treatment of diabetes on the development and progression of long-term complications in insulin-dependent diabetes mellitus. *New England Journal of Medicine, 329,* 977–986.

Johnson, S. B. (1998). Juvenile diabetes. In T. H. Ollendick & M. Hersen (Eds.), *Handbook of child psychopathology* (3rd ed., pp. 417–434). New York: Plenum Press.

LaPorte, R. E., Matsushima, M., & Chang, Y. F. (1995). Prevalence and incidence of insulin-dependent diabetes. In M. Harris (Ed.), *Diabetes in America* (2nd ed., NIH Publication No. 95-1468, pp. 37–46). Bethesda, MD: U.S. Department of Health and Human Services National Institutes of Health.

Portuese, E., & Orchard, T. (1995). Mortality in insulin-dependent diabetes. In *Diabetes in America* (2nd ed., NIH Publication No. 95-1468, pp. 221–232). Bethesda, MD: U.S. Department of Health and Human Services National Institutes of Health.

Rovet, J. F., Ehrlich, R. M., Czuchta, D., & Akler, M. (1993). Psychoeducational characteristics of children and adolescents with insulin-dependent diabetes mellitus. *Journal of Learning Disabilities, 26,* 7–22.

Heidi A. McCallister
University of Texas at Austin

DIABETES, TYPE II

Diabetes is a collection of diseases that takes on different forms. All forms of diabetes involve the hormone insulin. Diabetes mellitus (diabetes means "to siphon," and mellitus means "honey") results either when the body does not produce enough insulin or when an excess of insulin is present. The latter is known as Type II diabetes, or non-insulin-dependent diabetes (Guthrie & Guthrie, 1999).

The American Diabetes Association estimated in 1999 that there were over 15 million adult Americans with diabetes. Approximately 80% of those with diabetes have Type II (Guthrie & Guthrie, 1999). Results of several research studies over the past 20 years indicate that Type II diabetes in children is perhaps growing to epidemic proportions, especially among minorities. This phenomenon coincides with the increase in obesity in young children. The male to female sex ratio from several ethnic populations varies from 1 in 6 among the First Nation Native Americans from Ontario, Canada, to 1 in 1.3 among the Mexican American population in Ventura, California. Other ethnic minorities represented in the studies were Pima Indians, African Americans, Arabs, and Japanese (Rosenbloom, Joe, Young, & Winter, 1999). Onset of Type II diabetes can occur at any age. However, onset in children has been linked to the age of puberty, possibly due to the changes in hormone levels in the body. There have been reported cases of children as young as 4 years old with Type II diabetes, but diagnosis typically occurs after age 10 and when the child is in middle to late puberty (Consensus statement, 2000).

Characteristics

1. Obesity (20% or more over desirable body weight)
2. Presence of sugar in the urine, but no ketones (chemicals that the body produces when there is not enough insulin in the blood)
3. Little or no thirst or increased urination
4. Dark, shiny patches (acanthosis nigricans) on the skin, usually found between the fingers and toes
5. Other insulin-resistant conditions present, such as high blood pressure, blood fat disorders, or polycystic ovary syndrome

Because Type II diabetes in children was previously thought to be a rare occurrence and because subtypes are still being developed (Guthrie & Guthrie, 1999), little is known about treatment. The goals of treatment are to get and keep blood sugar levels as close to normal as possible, and to prevent complications (Consensus statement, 2000). Effective treatment will likely require a team of health care professionals and include some form of oral medication, increased physical activity, meal planning, and continued education about the disease. Most patients can manage the disease by diet and exercise; however, there is a special challenge in teaching adolescents to understand the relationship between unhealthy behaviors and negative health outcomes. Additional challenges for minority youth with diabetes are the numerous cultural and socioeconomic barriers that may interfere with implementation of the necessary dietary changes (Rosenbloom et al., 1999).

Children diagnosed with Type II diabetes will most likely qualify for special education services under the category of Other Health Impairment or Physical Disability. They are also protected under Section 504 of the Rehabilitation Act. Ideally, a Diabetes Health Care Plan should be developed as a joint effort of the parent, the student's health care team, and the school. The plan should address the specific needs of the child and outline instructions and responsibilities of each party (parents, student, school personnel). Major areas of concern that need to be included in the Plan are blood glucose monitoring, medication or insulin administration, and meals and snacks (Position statement, 1999).

Although there is no cure for diabetes, with proper understanding and management of the disease, a person can look forward to a relatively normal life span. Diabetes research continues in development of newer types of insulin, better insulin-delivery systems, self-monitoring of blood glucose, success of pancreas transplantation, and a better understanding of the role of nutrition in controlling diabetes. The American Diabetes Association has funded the GENNID (Genetics of Non-Insulin-Dependent Diabetes Mellitus) study to identify genes responsible for Type II diabetes. Through the GENNID study, the association is building a national research database of genetic samples and information from families with Type II diabetes (American Diabetes Association, 2001).

REFERENCES

American Diabetes Association. (2001). Research. Retrieved from http://www.diabetes.org/main/aboutus/mission/annual_report/research3.jsp

Consensus statement. (2000). Type II diabetes in children and adolescents. *Diabetes Care, 23*(3), 381–389. Retrieved from http://www.diabetes.org/ada/Consensus/pg381.htm

Guthrie, D., & Guthrie, R. (1999). *The diabetes sourcebook.* Los Angeles: Lowell House.

Position statement. (1999). Care of children with diabetes in the school and day care setting. *Diabetes Care, 22*(1), 163–167. Retrieved from http://www.diabetes.org/clinicalrecommendations/Supplement101/S108.htm

Rosenbloom, A., Joe, J., Young, R., & Winter, W. (1999). Emerging epidemic of Type II diabetes in youth. *Diabetes Care, 22*(2), 345–352. Retrieved from http://www.diabetes.org

Christine D. Cde Baca
University of Northern Colorado

DIGEORGE SYNDROME

DiGeorge syndrome (DGS) is a set of phenotypic abnormalities including T cell–mediated immune deficits, thymic aplasia, congenital hypoparathyroidism, mild facial anomalies, developmental delay, and congenital heart defects (Thomas & Graham, 1997). The syndrome was initially described in 1965. Simultaneously, other overlapping syndromes were identified, including velocardiofacial syndrome (VCFS). Ultimately, secondary to an overlap of clinical symptoms, as well as chromosomal investigations of affected families, it was recognized that most individuals with the characteristic features of these and other syndromes have a deletion of 22q11 and that these disorders represent a set of related developmental abnormalities (Thomas & Graham, 1997) categorized under the heading of *Chromosome 22q11 deletion syndrome.*

The 22q11 deletion syndrome may be inherited in an autosomal dominant fashion or arise secondary to de novo deletions or translocations (Thomas & Graham, 1997). Individuals with similar deletions may have variable clinical presentation. Not all affected individuals have a 22q11 deletion, although 85–90% of those diagnosed with DGS do. Teratogenic exposure, maternal diabetes, or other in utero perturbation can also cause the same series of abnormalities. The syndrome is thought to be a developmental field defect occurring in about the third or fourth week of gestation (Thomas & Graham, 1997).

There are varying estimates of the incidence of a 22q11 deletion. They have ranged from 1:4,727 to 1:10,000 births (Devriendt, et al, 1999). Five percent of children with congenital heart disease are found to have this deletion.

Characteristics

1. Structural heart abnormalities (85%), with multiple anomalies, occur in a great number of identified patients.
2. A cleft palate is present in 80–85% of the patients, although this may represent an overestimation based on ascertainment bias (Graham & Thomas, 1997).
3. Infants appear normal at birth but often experience failure to thrive.
4. The typical facies become more identifiable with age. The key features include a long face with a prominent bulbar nose accompanied by a squared nasal root, minor ear abnormalities, narrow palpebral fissures, retrognathia, and abundant hair. Slender, tapered, and hyperextensible fingers are associated (58–63%).
5. Patients with DGS often have compromised immunologic function. One group with "complete" DGS has deficiency of T cell function and has increased susceptibility to infection. A second group with "incomplete" DGS has decreased immune function early in life but eventually develops adequate T cell numbers and function.
6. Learning disabilities, complicated by hearing loss associated with otitis media, are evident in 100% of those with 22q11 deletions. Mild to moderate mental retardation is evident in 40–50% of the population. Some authors identify the pattern of performance as typical of those with nonverbal learning disorders (Swillen et al., 1999).
7. Children with this syndrome are described as demonstrating impulsivity and disinhibition but also can be shy and withdrawn (Swillen et al., 1999). There is an unusual predilection for development of overt psychosis during late adolescence or early adulthood, with the prevalence of psychosis in the DGS population estimated at 10–22% (Thomas & Graham, 1997).
8. Hypocalcemia is an early problem with 10–20% of the children experiencing seizures or rigidity. The hypocalcemia most often remits with time.

Individuals with DGS require careful medical surveillance. The cardiac defect is the most pressing issue initially. If the lesion is not lethal, the abnormality is often correctable. Hypocalcemia must be managed aggressively to limit neurologic compromise. Feeding difficulties are frequent, sometimes requiring gastrostomy or nasogastric feeding (McDonald-McGinn et al., 1999). Aggressive immunotherapy is necessary. Immune function often improves after the preschool years (Thomas & Graham, 1997). There has been successful use of bone marrow transplantation in patients who have complete DGS or VCFS and lack immunologic function (Thomas & Graham, 1997).

Educational intervention is a necessary aspect of treatment. Audiologic function must be monitored. Speech therapy has been found to be more useful after surgical correction, if the patient has velopharyngeal insufficiency (>85% of these patients). Computer-assisted instruction has been found helpful. Treatment of the nonverbal learning disorder, including the social learning deficit, is required (Derynck et al., 1999).

Future research will include attempts at greater understanding of the relationship between the specific genetic abnormality and clinical presentation. An understanding of how DGS and VCFS are related to schizophrenia and other psychiatric illnesses may shed light on the neurologic abnormalities in these disorders as well.

REFERENCES

Derynck, F., Sokolowsky, M., Pech, C., Henin-Brun, F., Rufo, M., & Philip, N. (1999). Psychiatric and mother-child relational disorders in children with chromosomal deletion 22q11. *Genetic Counseling, 10*(1), 110–111.

McDonald-McGinn, D. M., La Rossa, D., Godmuntz, E., Sullivan, K., Eicher, P., Gerdes, M., Moss, E., Wang, P., Solot, C., Schultz, P., Lynch, D., Bingham, P., Keenan, G., Weinzimer, S., Mind, J. E., Driscol, D., Clarck, B. J., Markowitz, R., Cohen, A., Moshang, T., Pasqureillo, P., Randall, P., Emanual, B. S., & Zackai, E. H. (1999). The variable expression of the chromosome 22q11.2 deletion: Findings in 216 patients. *Genetic Counseling, 10*(1), 96–98.

Swillen, A., Devriendt, K., Legius, E., Prinzie, P., Vogels, A., Ghesquiere, P., & Fryns, J. P. (1999). The behavioural phenotype in velo-cardio-facial syndrome (VCFS): From infancy to adolescence. *Genetic Counseling, 10*(1), 79–88.

Thomas, J. A., & Graham, J. M. (1997). Chromosome 22q11 deletion syndrome: An update and review for the primary pediatrician. *Clinical Pediatrics, 36*(5), 253–266.

Greta N. Wilkening
University of Colorado Health Sciences Center
The Children's Hospital

DIPLEGIA (SPASTIC DIPLEGIA)

In the medical disorder cerebral palsy (CP), *diplegia* is one of the terms used to describe the extent of damage to the individual's limbs. "Plegia" means paralysis or weakness, and diplegia means that the two lower limbs are affected. In some cases of diplegia, the arms are also mildly impaired (Cerebral Palsy Institute, 2001). Hemiplegia means that one side of the body is affected, and paraplegia means that all four limbs are weak or paralyzed (Cerebral Palsy Institute, 2001). Although in many cases the cause of spastic diplegia is unknown, many cases are due to prematurity, anoxia at birth, head injury of the child, or infections, such as meningitis or encephalitis (Pediatric Orthopedic Institute, 2001).

Cerebral palsy occurs at a rate of about 2 to 4 children in 1,000, and spastic diplegia is the most common form of CP, accounting for about 80% of the cases of CP (Brainnet.org). At this time, approximately 500,000 Americans have this form of CP (Brainnet.org). Spastic diplegia, like other forms of CP, is noncontagious and is a nonprogressive disorder caused by damage to the brain. The prevalence is much greater in infants weighing less than 1,500 g (Grether & Nelson, 2000). Because of modern medical technology that allows high-risk infants to survive, there is evidence that the incidence rate has remained much the same for the last 30 years.

Characteristics

1. Symptoms lie on a continuum from very mild fine motor deficits to complete paralysis of the lower limbs and mild impairment of the arms (Brainnet.org).
2. Despite the motor difficulties, most children with spastic diplegia will be able to walk with some assistance, such as crutches (Bleck, 1987).
3. Difficulties with balance are common (Brainnet.org).
4. Although the child may have average cognitive ability, IQ is often depressed (Brainnet.org).
5. Many of the children have communication deficits related to muscle weakness and/or lower cognitive ability.
6. Visual motor and visual perceptual problems are common with these children.
7. During early infancy, the child may appear "floppy," and as the baby grows, the muscles become more spastic (Pediatric Orthopedic Institute).
8. Seizures or epilepsy occurs in as many as 50% of the children with spastic diplegia (Brainnet.org).
9. Growth problems, including failure to thrive, occur as a result of feeding problems. This is, however, much more common in children with spastic quadriplegia (Brainnet.org).
10. Some of the children will have vision problems, such as strabismus, which may impair the child's ability to judge distance, or hemianopia, which impairs the field of vision (Brainnet.org).
11. Hearing impairment is frequent among children with CP (Brainnet.org).
12. Sensory difficulties, including difficulty feeling pain, may occur (Brainnet.org).

Treatment of spastic diplegia is often aimed at improving function of the extremities and increasing the individual's independence (Pediatric Orthopedic Institute, 2001). Treatment most often includes physical and occupational therapy to improve range of motion and maintain flexibility of the muscles. Other treatments include orthotics (splints) to maintain the proper positioning of the muscles and skeleton and surgery to correct deformities (Pediatric Orthopedic Institute). Newer forms of treatment include the use of Botox (botulinum toxin), which is injected into target muscles to cause them to become paralyzed, thus decreasing spasticity. This treatment provides relief of spasticity for up to 6 month (Spasticity Management Program). Another new treatment involves surgical placement of a gamma-aminobutyric acid (GABA) pump on the spinal cord to induce control over the spasticity.

In schools, children with spastic diplegia will likely be served under the Other Health Impairment special education label because of their obvious physical disabilities. However, because of a number of possible comorbidities, other labels may be considered as well. For example, about 30% of the children may have mental retardation concomitant with the CP and may be eligible under the Multiple Disabilities criteria. They may also have communication deficits making them eligible for Speech/Language. Because several may have hearing and visual problems, they may also be eligible to receive services under the Hearing Impaired or Visually Impaired categories.

Future developments in the field of spastic diplegia will likely include improved treatments to correct muscle weakness or to correct deformities that resulted from the diplegia. For example, the GABA pump is being used more frequently, but there are unpleasant and dangerous side effects. For example, the pump requires placement of a catheter into the spine, and there is risk of infection at the site. There is also the possibility of malfunctioning of the pump, which renders the treatment useless (Pediatric Orthopedic Institute, 2001). The Botox treatment is also showing promising, though short-term, results. Perhaps an improved derivative may be developed that will provide longer term relief from the spasticity. Prevention is probably the most desirable way to improve the status of any form of CP. Learning more about the causes and educating those individuals who may have high-risk pregnancies will contribute to better prevention.

REFERENCES

Bleck, E. E. (1987). *Orthopedic management in cerebral palsy: Clinics in developmental medicine.* Philadelphia: J. B. Lippincott.

Brainnet.org. Retrieved from http://www.brainnet.org/cerebral palsy.htm

Cerebral Palsy Institute. (2001). Retrieved from http://www.cerebralpalsyinstitute.org/definitions.htm

Grether, J. K., & Nelson, K. B. (2000). Possible decrease in prevalence of cerebral palsy in premature infants. *Journal of Pediatrics, 137,* 133.

Pediatric Orthopedic Institute. (2001). Retrieved from http://www.orthoseek.com/articles/cerebral.html

DALENE MCCLOSKEY
University of Northern Colorado

DIPLOPIA (DOUBLE VISION)

Diplopia, also known as double vision, is a vision impairment in which the eye sees two images. There are two types of diplopia, monocular and binocular. In monocular, the double vision is present at all times, even when one eye is occluded or closed. Monocular diplopia is caused by defects to the front of the eye, such as cataracts or a need for glasses. In binocular, it is due to the misalignment of the images that are reflected to the brain. For example, one eye may aim higher or lower than the other so that they cannot fuse into one image. This problem can be remedied by closing one eye or occluding it. Binocular diplopia often occurs secondary to other disorders (Double vision, 2001).

In children there is a tendency to attempt unconsciously to compensate for the binocular double vision by suppressing one of the images. When this occurs, the child begins to favor one eye. Although this strategy is effective, eventually the child will have difficulty perceiving three-dimensionally. With time, it will lead to a condition known as strabismus, in which one eye turns inward or outward (Double vision, 2001). Depending on the child, both eyes can become involved, or the child can alternate eyes. If the brain continues to compensate for one eye, the unused eye loses its ability to function, and there will be a permanent vision impairment (Double vision, 2001). Strabismus occurs at a rate of 2% in children.

Diplopia has several potential causes. In children it can be the result of weakness in the eye muscles that control movement of the eye. This weakness can also occur gradually with age, which leads to diplopia in older patients. Diplopia can also occur as a result of disease or medical problems, such as thyroid deficiency, tumors, cataracts, cranial nerve paralysis, and trauma.

Characteristics

1. The child's eyes may point in different directions, especially when tired or after an illness.
2. The child blinks frequently.
3. The child may move his or her head from side to side to block double vision.
4. The child holds objects to one eye.
5. The child may have difficulty judging distance.

Treatment can take several forms. For some individuals there can be improvement by wearing specially designed eye glasses. The glasses have a special feature called a prism ground into the lens. The prism causes a realignment or compensation of the unmatched eyes and helps ease the requirements of the eye muscles. Eye exercises can be helpful for some patients, but often the results are short-term because the eye muscles continue to weaken. As a last resort, surgery can be used to provide remediation of the double vision. In surgical treatment the involved eye muscle is disabled so that the eyes can align more precisely. The disadvantage of this treatment is there are subsequent limitations in eye muscle functions (Cassell, Billig, & Randall, 1998).

Special education services for children who have educationally disabling diplopia are classified as Visually Impaired. The use of a trained vision specialist is required. There may be specialized teaching methods or materials that the child could use, including verbal instruction or books on tape. This depends on the degree of impairment. Future developments for diplopia include investigating additional treatments that may be less invasive than surgery and more effective than eye exercises.

REFERENCES

Cassell, G. H., Billig, M. D., & Randall, H. G. (1998). *The eye book: A complete guide to eye disorders and health.* Baltimore: Johns Hopkins University Press.

Double vision. (2001). Retrieved from http://vision.unco.edu/EDSE/641-00/Hadley/Lesson5/DOUBLE VISION_VISION.HTML

Dalene M. McCloskey
University of Northern Colorado

DISSOCIATIVE IDENTITY DISORDER

Dissociative identity disorder (DID), formerly known as multiple personality disorder (MPD), occurs when a child experiences more than one identity or personality state controlling the child's behavior at different times. The child may or may not be aware that he or she possesses different identities (or "alters"), and switching between alters may occur within seconds. As a result, the child often suffers lapses of memory, which represent failure to recall information that was presented, or events that occurred, when the child was in a different identity or personality state. Children with DID may experience periods of time for which they cannot account for, find items in their possession without knowing how or when they acquired them, meet people who know them but whom they do not recognize, and fail to remember material that they have learned in class. Although many individuals with DID can function well for a time, most will experience periods of decompensation marked by severe anxiety, depression, hallucinations, flashbacks, or other psychiatric symptoms.

DID is thought to be precipitated by severe abuse or trauma in childhood. Although dissociation may occur as a symptom of other disorders, genuine cases of dissociative identity disorder are thought to be very rare. The incidence is thought to be far higher in females than in males. Kluft (1991) has noted that only about 10% of individuals with MPD or DID were diagnosed prior to age 20, and only 3% were diagnosed at age 11 or younger.

Characteristics (American Psychiatric Association, 1994)

1. The presence of two or more distinct identities or personality states (each with its own relatively enduring pattern of perceiving, relating to, and thinking about the environment and self).
2. At least two of these identities of personality states recurrently take control of the person's behavior.
3. Inability to recall important personal information that is too extensive to be explained by ordinary forgetfulness.
4. The disturbance is not due to the direct physiological effects of a substance (e.g., blackouts or chaotic behavior during alcohol intoxication) or a general medical condition (e.g., complex partial seizures). In children, the symptoms are not attributable to imaginary playmates or other fantasy play.

Treatment of dissociative identity disorder may include medication, psychotherapy, or a combination of both. Medications are used to reduce the intensity of the child's reaction to external triggers and stressors and to treat psychological symptoms such as depression, anxiety, panic symptoms, attention and concentration problems, flashbacks, nightmares, sleep problems, and poor impulse control. Medications such as clonidine and propranol may be used to reduce hyperarousal, anxiety, poor impulse control, disorganized thinking, and rapid switching. Anxiety may be treated with benzodiazepines, sedative antihistamines, buspirone, beta-blockers, and small doses of neuroleptics. Depression may be treated with tricyclic antidepressants, monoamine oxidase inhibitors (MAOIs), or selective serotonin reuptake inhibitors (SSRIs; Torem, 1996).

Children suffering from severe DID resulting in behavior that is harmful to themselves or others may be psychiatrically hospitalized. Inpatient and outpatient individual psychotherapy may focus on establishing safety, teaching the child relaxation techniques to help calm anxiety, and modifying environmental stressors or desensitizing the child to them. Cognitive-behavioral techniques may focus on correcting thinking errors and erroneous beliefs, whereas experiential techniques such as play therapy with younger children, art, and movement therapy encourage expression of feeling and abreaction. Hypnosis, often used in the past to "discover" and "integrate" alter personalities, has fallen into disfavor because of the risk of creating new alters and personalities, and lawsuits have resulted. Family therapy can provide psychoeducational guidance in helping families learn to deal with the stresses of parenting a DID child and in addressing pathological family dynamics. Group therapy may be used to promote age-appropriate socialization.

Children suffering from DID may be eligible for special education services under the classification of Emotional Disturbance. Support by the school psychologist may be necessary to help the child cope with and reduce anxiety, memory, and cognitive problems caused by anxiety secondary to stimulation of traumatic memories. In extreme cases, homebound and hospitalized services may be necessary.

REFERENCES

American Psychiatric Association. (1994). *Diagnostic and statistical manual of mental disorders* (4th ed.). Washington, DC: Author.

Kluft, R. P. (1991). Clinical presentations of multiple personality disorder. *Psychiatric Clinics of North America, 3,* 605–630.

Torem, M. (1996). Medications in the treatment of dissociative identity disorder. In J. Spira & I. Yalom (Eds.), *Treating dissociative identity disorder.* San Francisco: Jossey-Bass.

Janiece Pompa
University of Utah

DISTAL ARTHROGRYPOSIS SYNDROME

Distal arthrogryposis syndrome (DAS) is a hereditary, congenital neuromuscular disorder. It is distinguished by multiple contractures of the fingers, hands, and feet. Less frequently there may be hip, knee, or shoulder involvement. Two distinct clinical forms exist.

DAS is very rare. There are fewer than 50 reported cases in the literature. DAS is transmitted in an autosomal dominant manner. There is considerable variability in the severity of the physical abnormalities in children with DAS, even among sibling groups and their affected parents. This interesting phenomenon is caused by wide swings in the abnormal gene's expressivity.

Characteristics

Type I (typical)

1. In the newborn the hand is tightly fisted. The thumb is laid flat across the palm. The index and middle fingers overlap the thumb. They are, in turn, overlapped by the ring and little fingers. This unusual finger positioning is the most distinguishing physical finding of the syndrome.
2. Positional deformities of the feet, including outward deviation and clubfoot.
3. Congenital hip dislocation and decreased hip mobility.
4. Mild flexion contractures of the knee.
5. Stiff shoulders (at birth).

Type II (atypical)

All or some of the above, in conjunction with all or some of the following:

1. Cleft lip and/or cleft palate.
2. Small tongue.
3. Droopy eyelids (ptosis).
4. Short stature.
5. Scoliosis.
6. "Borderline" intellectual functioning.

Treatment of this disorder involves rectifying the orthopedic problems, which, fortunately, are remarkably responsive to therapy. Feeding difficulties may occur with the atypical forms and require medical intervention.

Because of the rarity of the diagnosis, there is no research to indicate an educational prognosis. It is expected that children diagnosed with Type I DAS would not require special education because of the reported normal intelligence. In contrast, children with Type II DAS may require educational modifications because of borderline intellectual functioning. The amount of modification needed would be based on the intellectual functioning and academic need of the individual child. In both cases, however, children with Type I or Type II DAS may require modifications in their educational environment because of their orthopedic problems. Evaluation and treatment by an occupational and physical therapist may be warranted, as well as assistive devices or technology in the classroom to facilitate learning.

The prognosis for Type I DAS is favorable. These children have normal intelligence and orthopedic abnormalities that either improve with age or are readily correctable. However, as adults these patients may continue to have mild contractures of the fingers and outward deviation of the hands.

Patients with Type II DAS have more dysmorphic features and lower intelligence than do their Type I counterparts. Therefore, they do not fare as well.

REFERENCES

Jones, K. (1997). *Smith's recognizable patterns of human malformations* (5th ed.). Philadelphia: W. B. Saunders.

Barry H. Davison
Ennis, Texas

Joan W. Mayfield
Baylor Pediatric Specialty Services
Dallas, Texas

DISTRACTIBILITY

Distractibility refers to difficulties in sustaining attention to tasks, concentrating, tracking, and screening out interfering distractions (Lezak, 1995). A child who is distractible may appear to be daydreaming, doodling, or paying unnecessary attention to what others are doing (Children and Adults with Attention Deficit Disorders [CHADD], 2000). Children described as distractible typically display shorter attention spans than do their same-age peers, and they usually have difficulty completing assignments when multitasking is involved. Their inability to focus attention may result in uncompleted assignments and forgotten items. Distractibility negatively impacts a child's ability successfully to complete school and household tasks.

Characteristics

1. Difficulty maintaining attention to expected tasks or activities
2. Limited follow-through of required tasks
3. Slow response to directions
4. Failure to devote sufficient attention to tasks so that crucial components of the task are left out and finished products are often messy and unorganized
5. Difficulty listening and apparent inability to follow directions
6. High susceptibility to environmental distractions
7. Limitations in organizing tasks and activities; frequently loss of items needed for task completion or day-to-day items (e.g., homework or lunch money)
8. Avoidance or inability to complete assignments involving continued concentration
9. Appearance of forgetfulness with daily activities
10. Sluggish reaction time

Much of the information and research related to the topic of distractibility is derived from the inattentive subtype of Attention-deficit/hyperactivity disorder (ADHD). The term ADHD is a relatively common neurobiological disorder that affects between 3% and 7% of school-aged children, with males being between 2 to 9 times more likely to exhibit these concerns than females (American Psychiatric Association, 2000). Between 40% and 60% of children with ADHD also exhibit characteristics of other disorders including learning disabilities, emotional-behavioral disorders, mood disorders, tics or Tourette's syndrome, and anxiety disorders (CHADD, 2000). Additionally, frontal lobe injuries or deficits have been associated with limitations in focusing and shifting attention (Mirsky, 1989).

A multimodal treatment approach incorporating medical, psychological, educational, and behavior management interventions has been found to produce the best results in treating children who are distractible (Gaddes & Edgell, 1994). Psychostimulant medication is effective with 70% to 80% of children diagnosed with ADHD (CHADD, 2000); methylphenidate (Ritalin), dextroamphetamine (Dexedrine), and pemoline (Cylert) are usually prescribed. These medications are used to improve a child's ability to attend to tasks and to decrease off-task behavior. Frequently reported side effects of stimulant medication include insomnia, headaches, appetite suppression, and irritability when the dose wears off. Growth suppression can be an issue with long-term medication usage. Overall, research indicates that medication helps students with distractibility obtain maximum benefit from educational and behavioral interventions (Bohlmeyer, 1998).

Psychological interventions often include group or individual counseling. The focus of counseling interventions may include social skills development, behavioral self-monitoring, and classroom management regarding the nature of this condition. Parents are also targeted for intervention by providing them with information about distractibility and connecting them with available support groups. Parents, teachers, and others involved with the child on a daily basis can also receive training on using behavioral signals that redirect a child back to the task at hand. Behavioral contracts that outline expectations and rewards for meeting expectations are also effective in many cases (Bohlmeyer, 1998). The use of a coach who offers reminders, feedback, and encouragement may improve a child's work-completion rate and time on task (Hallowell & Ratey, 1994).

Educational techniques designed to reduce a student's level of distractibility generally involve interventions in which the child's teacher implements classroom accommodations to address the child's needs. Efficacious techniques include (a) providing brief, clear, and specific directions; (b) establishing eye contact prior to giving directions; (c) asking the child to repeat verbal directions for clarification; (d) providing the child with frequent feedback regarding performance; (e) breaking down lengthy assignments into small steps; (f) allowing students a choice of academic assignments; and (g) maintaining a consistent structure so that the child understands the expectations. Peer tutoring and self-monitoring are also school interventions that have been helpful in reducing distractibility by providing children who are distractible with exposure to a model of appropriate behavior and a source of frequent feedback (Brock, 1998).

Other alternative approaches to treating distractibility have been developed to help children stay on task. However, there is no credible scientific evidence to support the use of alternative treatments, such as dietary intervention (e.g., the Feingold diet), electroencephalogram biofeedback, applied kinesiology, optometric vision training, mineral supplements, candida yeast, or anti–motion sickness medications (CHADD, 2000).

Children who have difficulty sustaining attention are at risk for academic difficulties and emotional concerns such as lowered self-esteem. Although it once was thought that children outgrew ADHD in adolescence, it is now understood that the effects of the disability may continue into adulthood. The long-term prognosis is hopeful for those children who receive individual interventions early in life designed to meet their needs and help them succeed at home and school. Longitudinal research indicates that children who obtain appropriate interventions for ADHD exhibit fewer school, substance abuse, and interpersonal problems while demonstrating greater overall functioning than do those who do not receive individualized treatment. Although some children may continue to display distractible behaviors as adults, most can learn compensation strategies and access sources of support that help them remain on task and attain their goals.

REFERENCES

American Psychiatric Association. (2000). *Diagnostic and statistical manual of mental disorders* (4th ed., Text Revision). Washington, DC: Author.

Bohlmeyer, E. M. (1998). Attention deficit disorder: A primer for parents. In A. S. Canter & S. A. Carroll (Eds.), *Helping children at home and school: Handouts from your school psychologist* (pp. 539–541). Bethesda, MD: National Association of School Psychologists.

Brock, S. E. (1998, February). Classroom-based interventions for students with ADHD. *Communiqué,* 8–10.

Children and Adults with Attention Deficit Disorders (CHADD). (2000, November 18). Retrieved from http://www.chadd.org/facts/add_facts.htm

Gaddes, W. H., & Edgell, D. (1994). *Learning disabilities and brain function: A neuropsychological approach.* New York: Springer.

Hallowell, E. M., & Ratey, J. J. (1994). *Driven to distraction.* New York: Pantheon Books.

Lezak, M. D. (1995). *Neuropsychological assessment* (3rd ed.). New York: Oxford University Press.

Mirsky, A. S. (1989). The neuropsychology of attention: Elements of a complex behavior. In E. Perecman (Ed.), *Integrating theory and practice in clinical neuropsychology.* Hillsdale, NJ: Erlbaum.

Bob Kirchner
University of Northern Colorado
Shawn Powell
United States Air Force Academy

DOWN SYNDROME

Down syndrome is a relatively well-known genetic disorder that is strongly associated with mental retardation. It is usually identified at birth and is confirmed by a karyotype showing trisomy of Chromosome 21. Down syndrome usually is caused by an error in cell division called *nondisjunction.* However, two other types of chromosomal abnormalities, *mosaicism* and *translocation,* also are implicated in Down syndrome, although to a much lesser extent. Regardless of the type of Down syndrome that a person may have, all people with Down syndrome have an extra, critical portion of the Chromosome 21 present in all, or some, of their cells.

Down syndrome affects people of all ages, races, and economic levels. Women age 35 and older have a significantly increased risk of having a child with Down syndrome. The most frequently occurring chromosomal abnormality, Down syndrome occurs once approximately every 800 to 1,000 live births. Approximately 5,000 children with Down syndrome are born each year, and over 350,000 people have Down syndrome in the United States (National Down Syndrome Society, 2000).

Characteristics

1. Physical characteristics associated with Down syndrome include muscle hypotonia, flat facial profile, oblique palpebral fissures, dysplastic ear, a single deep crease across the center of the palm, excessive ability to extend the joints, dysplastic middle phalanx of the fifth finger, small skin folds on the inner corner of the eyes, excessive space between large and second toe, and enlargement of tongue in relationship to size of mouth.
2. There is considerable variation in medical, physical, psychological, and intellectual characteristics; for example, the IQ scores in children and adults with Down syndrome can vary over 50–60 IQ points (Carr, 1995).
3. Increased risk for congenital heart defects, increased susceptibility to infection, respiratory problems, obstructed digestive tracts and childhood leukemia occur with greater frequency.
4. Qualitative differences in cognitive development include the following (e.g., Spiker & Hopmann, 1997; Wishart, 1998):
   a. The growing use of avoidance strategies when faced with cognitive challenges
   b. The less-than-effective use of existing problem-solving skills
   c. The failure to consolidate newly acquired cognitive skills into the repertoire
   d. An increasing reluctance to take the initiative in learning
   e. Difficulty in learning contingencies and greater contentedness with noncontingent reinforcement schedule than typically developing children
5. There are greater lags and impairments in cognitive communication skills than in personal-social and adaptive behavior (Dykens, Hodapp, & Evans, 1994).

There is no genetic or pharmacological therapy available at present to cure Down syndrome. The primary methods of diminishing the effects of retardation associated with Down syndrome are psychoeducational: working directly with the individual; providing advice, support, and training to parents and others in the immediate environment; and altering the more distal social and physical environment to increase the roles and activities for which individuals with Down syndrome are suitable candidates (Spiker & Hopmann, 1997). Early intervention programs are usually individualized, systematic, and highly structured, following curricula based on developmental milestones. The emphasis in those programs is usually placed on cognitive and language development.

Under the Individuals with Disabilities Education Act, comprehensive services (e.g., family training, home visits, special instruction, medical services for diagnosis and evaluation, case management, etc.) are provided for infants, toddlers, and school-aged children with Down syndrome and their families on the basis of need as established in the individualized family service plan (IFSP) and the individualized education plan (IEP). The inclusion of students with Down syndrome in typical classrooms represents the latest effort to provide children with this disability with the best education possible in their neighborhood schools.

In spite of significant advances in the quality of life for children with Down syndrome, prognosis is not so optimistic. One of the most robust findings about cognitive development in Down syndrome is a decline in developmental rate as children get older (Wishart, 1998). Overall, mental ages of a majority of older children with Down syndrome tend to be at early school-age level in terms of academic and intelligence tests. However, there is considerable variability in later school-age children and adolescents; at least a subgroup of children with Down syndrome appears to continue their developmental growth through the adolescent years (Rynders & Horrobin, 1990). Quality educational programs, along with a stimulating home environment and good medical care, would enable children with Down syndrome to develop their full potential and become contributing members of their families and communities. Future research is required in the following areas: (a) qualitative differences in cognitive development and learning, (b) the long-term effectiveness of early intervention program, and (c) the effectiveness of different educational placement of children with Down syndrome (e.g., inclusion).

REFERENCES

Carr, J. (1995). *Down's syndrome: Children growing up.* Cambridge, England: Cambridge University Press.

Dykens, E. M., Hodapp, R. M., & Evans, D. W. (1994). Profiles and development of adaptive behavior in children with Down syndrome. *American Journal of Mental Retardation, 98,* 580–587.

National Down Syndrome Society. (2000, October 20). About Down syndrome. Retrieved from http://www.ndss.org/aboutds/aboutds.html

Rynders, J. E., & Horrobin, J. M. (1990). Always trainable? Never educable? Updating educational expectations concerning children with Down syndrome. *American Journal on Mental Retardation, 97,* 77–83.

Spiker, D., & Hopmann, M. R. (1997). The effectiveness of early intervention for children with Down syndrome. In M. J. Guralnick (Ed.), *The effectiveness of early intervention* (pp. 271–305). Baltimore: Paul H. Brookes.

Wishart, J. G. (1998). Cognitive development in young children with Down syndrome: Developmental strengths, developmental weaknesses. *Down syndrome in the 21st century: 1st biennial scientific conference on Down syndrome,* Down Syndrome Research Foundation and Resource Centre.

Donghyung Lee
Texas A&M University

See also Trisomy 21

DUANE SYNDROME

Duane syndrome is a congenital disorder that limits range of eye movement. Sometimes called Duane retraction syndrome, this disorder affects one or both eyes, causing a retraction of the eyeball when it attempts to turn in a particular direction. Eye movement is limited in one of three ways: outward toward the ear (Type 1), inward toward the nose (Type 2), and both inward and outward (Type 3). In addition, the eyes may not be aligned properly when the individual looks straight ahead (National Organization for Rare Disorders, Inc., 2000).

Duane syndrome occurs in about 0.1% of the population, is slightly more frequent in females than males, and affects only one eye (usually the left) about 80% of the time. In about 30% of cases, other anomalies of the aural, optic, neural, or skeletal systems may also be present. This necessitates a thorough physical evaluation, as well as the eye examination, to identify possible concurrent conditions.

Amblyopia (lazy eye) and possible uncorrectable vision loss may occur if Duane syndrome goes undiagnosed in children. Surgery is often recommended to reduce excessive head turning or to address cosmetic concerns, but the abnormal eye movements and the underlying nerve problem cannot be fully corrected.

Characteristics

1. Retraction of the eyeball on attempting to look in a particular direction
2. Misaligned eyes
3. May be associated with malformed bones or deafness

Alone, Duane syndrome would most likely not require any special services in the school setting, except for preferential seating, which must be individualized for each student. A consultation with a mobility and orientation specialist may be in order, particularly if visual acuity is significantly impaired. However, complications from associated anomalies, such as deafness or skeletal malformations, may indeed require significant adaptations in the child's life.

Research indicates that Duane syndrome is most likely caused by a deviation in the development of the abducens nerve (Appukuttan et al., 1999). This would occur between the 3rd and 8th weeks of pregnancy. Current research is directed at identifying more specifically which gene is responsible for the disorder.

REFERENCES

Appukuttan, B., Gillanders, E., Juo, S., Freas-Lutz, D., Ott, S., Van Auken, A., Bailey-Wilson, J., Wang, X., Patel, R. J., Robbins, C. M., Chung, M., Annett, G., Weinberg, L., Borchert, M. S., Trent, J. M., Brownstein, M. J., & Stout, J. T. (1999). Localization of a gene for Duane retraction syndrome to chromosome 2q31. *American Journal of Human Genetics, 65,* 1639–1646.

National Organization for Rare Disorders, Inc. (2000). Duane syndrome. Rerieved from http://www.stepstn.com/cgi-win/nord.exe?proc=GetDocument&rectype=0&recnum=224

Sharla Fasko
Rowan County Schools
Morehead, Kentucky

See also Wildervanck Syndrome

DUHRING DISEASE

Duhring disease, also known as dermatitis herpetiformis, is a rare and chronic skin disorder that is characterized by the presence of skin lesions that cause severe itching, burning, and stinging. The etiology of the disease, which is not fully understood, is believed to be genetic predisposition. Approximately 90% of people with Duhring disease are positive for HLA B8-DR3, a genetic marker that may predispose them to the disease (National Organization for Rare Disorders, Inc. [NORD], 1998)

Although Duhring disease can occur at any age, it is more common in middle adulthood and is very rare in childhood. In the United States about 1 in 10,000 are diagnosed with the disease, and the male/female ratio is 2:1. The disease is more common in Caucasian Americans and rare in African Americans and Asian Americans (Celiac Sprue Association [CSA], 1998)

Characteristics

1. Small blisters, fluid-filled sores, red bumps that resemble hives, and/or raised papules
2. Severe itching, burning, and stinging of affected areas
3. Lesions on both sides of body, especially the head, elbows, knees, lower back, and buttocks
4. Loss of the ability properly to digest gluten (approximately 75% of cases)

A clinical evaluation and blood tests that show the presence of certain antibodies such as reticulin and endomysium confirm a diagnosis of Duhring disease. Immunofluorescence can also be used to show the presence of IgA, a protein antibody (immunoglobulin) that usually protects the body from viral and bacterial infections (NORD, 1998).

Typically, people with Duhring disease are treated with the medication Dapsone in a dose of 25–50 mg daily. The symptoms are often relieved and the condition of the skin lesions improved 1–2 days after drug therapy is started. The dosage of Dapsone may be adjusted to maintain relief of the symptoms, and some patients take up to 100 mg daily. Dapsone can cause the destruction of red blood cells (hemolysis), so patients taking the drug must have periodic blood tests to monitor blood counts. Sulfapyridine may be used an alternative to Dapsone, especially in patients with coronary disease. A topical cortisone cream can also be used to help relieve the itching and burning associated with the disease. It is important to note that in most cases the skin lesions reappear 24–48 hr after the Dapsone therapy is discontinued (NORD, 1998).

For the percentage of the diagnosed population who also have gluten-sensitive enteropathy, following a strict gluten-free diet may relieve their symptoms. Gluten is found in all grains except rice and corn. Special gluten-free foods can be purchased commercially. It has also been shown that the gluten-free diet may benefit most patients with Duhring disease. The diet reduces the dosage of Dapsone needed, improves gastrointestinal symptoms, and focuses on the cause of the disease rather than the symptoms (CSA, 1998).

Special education for patients with Duhring disease does not seem necessary, but supportive counseling may help the child cope with the chronic and sometimes painful condition. Also, because of the social and emotional issues of the potential chronicity, it is important that the child have some form of support to use as an outlet for any problems or concerns. It might also be helpful to teach children how to dress in a manner that would minimize exposure of the rashes to help eliminate any social torment that they may experience at school or in other social settings.

The prognosis for Duhring disease is very positive if patients take their medications and follow-up with their doctor. In addition, by following the gluten-free diet, they might be able to prevent future outbreaks or minimize the severity. There is ongoing research to determine the relationship between Duhring disease and the function of the digestive system. For more information the NORD Web site recommends contacting Russell P. Hall, III, M.D., Box 3135, Duke University Medical Center, Durham, NC 27710, (919) 684-3110.

REFERENCES

Celiac Sprue Association. (1998). Dermatitis herpetiformis defined. Retrieved from http://www.csaceliacs.org/dermherp.html

National Organization for Rare Disorders, Inc. (1998). Duhring disease. Retrieved from http://www.rarediseases.org

Cynthia A. Gallo
University of Colorado

DUODENAL ATRESIA AND DUODENAL STENOSIS

Duodenal atresia (DA) is a rare congenital anomaly of the duodenum, the first section of the small intestine, which lies adjacent to and just downstream from the outlet of the stomach. In DA there is disruption and occlusion of the tubular continuity (lumen) of the gut. Duodenal stenosis refers to a narrowing of the intestinal lumen.

DA is felt to occur around the fourth or fifth week of gestation. At this time the intestine develops from a solid structure, which is normally canalized from the upper esophagus to the rectum. Intestinal atresia is caused by a failure of this process to evolve completely.

DA has many different anatomic variations, which can be classified by intrinsic and extrinsic etiologies. The intrinsic form is the most common. The usual appearance is a thin membrane across the bowel lumen.

DA occurs in about 1 in 10,000 births. It has no clear pattern of genetic transmission. It accounts for about 30–35% of all intestinal atresias. There is an equal male-to-female ratio for this disorder. About a third of infants with DA have other severe, life-threatening congenital malformations. These defects can affect other sites in the gut, as well as the heart, kidney, and anorectal area. DA is a common finding in Down syndrome, occurring in 20–30% of these babies. It is also far more frequent in premature infants than in those born at term.

Characteristics

1. Vomiting bile, usually on the first day of life, without abdominal distention. This symptom is a classic sign of upper intestinal blockage.
2. Polyhydramnios (excessive amount of amniotic fluid) is present in about 50% of pregnancies. This finding is secondary to the failure of swallowed amniotic fluid to reach the lower intestine, where it is normally absorbed.
3. X rays of the abdomen show a "double bubble sign," the result of a distended, air-filled stomach and upper segment of the duodenum.
4. Prenatal diagnosis is becoming more frequent because of the widespread use of ultrasound evaluations during pregnancy.

Treatment of DA requires surgical correction of the defect. However, that procedure is often postponed until a search for other, possibly even more serious, anomalies is concluded. Initial therapy consists of decompression of the distended stomach by nasogastric tube, intravenous fluid administration, and diagnostic studies that attempt to define other malformations.

Following operative repair of their problem, babies with DA may be unable to take oral feedings for several days, until their gut resumes normal activity. During this time they are given intravenous nutritional support composed of amino acids, glucose, fatty acids, vitamins, and minerals. This regimen promotes healing of surgical sites and, incredibly, weight gain. After gut function and continuity recover, oral feedings start, and intravenous alimentation is slowly withdrawn.

There is no research to indicate that children with DA have cognitive deficits. Problems with learning ability or developmental delay would be related to the associated anomalies present.

Prognosis for DA is largely dependent on what associated anomalies are present. Clearly, infants with Down syndrome, complex congenital heart disease, serious kidney defects, or extreme prematurity will have a much less favorable outlook than will newborns in whom DA is an isolated finding.

REFERENCES

Wylie, R. (2000). Intestinal atresia, stenosis, and malrotation. In R. E. Behrman, R. M. Kleigman, & H. B. Jenson (Eds.), *Nelson's textbook of pediatrics* (16th ed., pp. 1132–1136). Philadelphia: W. B. Saunders.

Barry H. Davison
Ennis, Texas

Joan W. Mayfield
Baylor Pediatric Specialty Services
Dallas, Texas

DWARFISM

Dwarfism is defined in terms of adult height less than or equal to 4 foot 10 inches as a result of a medical or genetic disorder (Little People of America [LPA], 2000). It is estimated that dwarfism affects over 290,000 people worldwide (LPA, 2000). Dwarfism is an umbrella term for multiple disorders; it is estimated that there are approximately 200 types of dwarfism (LPA, 2000). Of these, the most frequently occurring is achondroplasia. Whereas dwarfism of all types is associated with short stature, more specific characteristics (e.g., associated medical conditions) vary by type. Some forms of dwarfism disproportionately affect specific ethnic groups (e.g., Ellis-van Creveld syndrome, cartilage-hair hypoplasia), whereas others (e.g., achondroplasia) are prevalent at approximately the same rate across ethnic groups. Similarly, gender appears to be a factor for some forms of dwarfism, but not others.

Characteristics

1. Profound short stature (adult height less than 58 inches)
2. Overall cognitive development possibly uncompromised, but attainment of motor skills potentially delayed
3. Problems with weight control
4. High incidence of medical complications
5. Dependency or rebellion

Treatment varies depending on the nature or etiology of the dwarfism. Dwarfism due to skeletal dysplasias (e.g., achondroplasia) involves the abnormal growth and development of bone. As a result, in dwarfism that is due to skeletal dysplasias, in addition to short stature, the growth of the arms and legs is disproportionate to that of the head and trunk. Although limb-lengthening surgery is available, it is not recommended because of potential risks (LPA, 2000). Rather, treatment efforts are directed toward the potential medical and psychological complications of the dwarfism.

In contrast, for dwarfism associated with growth hormone deficiency or Turner syndrome, the individual is of short stature, but the head, trunk, and limbs develop proportionately. The administration of growth hormones can provide effective treatment after the disorder is identified (Human Growth Foundation, 1996). Similarly, dwarfism associated with other genetic disorders (e.g., thalassemia) may be responsive to growth hormones as well.

Generally, individuals with dwarfism are of average cognitive ability. Other than orthopedic or medical problems directly related to the dwarfism, their general health is usually good as well (LPA, 2000). At the same time, because of the potential need for physical accommodations, dwarfism is identified as a disability under the Americans with Disabilities Act (ADA). To the extent that children and adults of short stature may experience issues of physical access, these individuals may need specific environmental accommodations and modifications. For those children with related orthopedic or medical conditions that adversely affect educational progress, or who may have a co-occurring learning disability or other disability, additional services may be provided through special education.

Psychosocial issues associated with dwarfism may require intervention at multiple levels (Ablon, 1990; Alley & Hall, 1989). There is some evidence that adults (i.e., parents, teachers, others) behavior toward children of short stature as if they were much younger than their chronological age; this may lead to active rebellion or a failure to develop age-appropriate independent living skills. Consultation with parents and teachers to ensure that expectations and demands are appropriate for the child based on age, ability level, and any physical limitations may be needed. Helping parents and teachers define appropriate behavioral limits and foster the development of autonomy for adolescents of short stature may be beneficial as well.

Multiple support groups are available for individuals with dwarfism and their families. The Little People of America (www.lpaonline.org) and Dwarfism (www.dwarfism.org) Web sites provide general information on dwarfism and resources related to specific complications or needs that may arise in conjunction with dwarfism (e.g., proportionate furniture, bicycles, etc.). Additional support groups have been established for specific syndromes associated with dwarfism.

REFERENCES

Ablon, J. (1990). Ambiguity and difference: Families with dwarf children. *Social Sciences and Medicine, 30,* 879–887.

Alley, T. R., & Hall, D. L. (1989). Adults' responses to the physical appearance of children with growth disorders. *Child Study Journal, 19,* 117–131.

Human Growth Foundation (1996). *Achondroplasia.* Falls Church, VA: Author.

Little People of America. (October 11, 2000). Retrieved from www.lpaonline.org

Cynthia A. Riccio
Texas A & M University

DWARFISM, PITUITARY

Pituitary dwarfism (sometimes called proportionate dwarfism) is a condition of growth retardation characterized by children who are very short in stature but have normal body proportions. It is caused by a dysfunction of the pituitary gland (Tish, 1999). Pituitary dwarfism is caused by a lack of growth hormone (GH) produced by the pituitary gland, but the cause of the lack of GH can be the result of many conditions.

Children who are deficient in additional hormones secreted by the pituitary gland grow very slowly, but also have many other medical disorders. These include problems in metabolic regulation and water balance and failure to develop secondary sexual characteristics (Tish, 1999). Children who are deficient in multiple pituitary hormones may have a pituitary tumor, head injury, or brain infection or may have been subject to early abuse. Severe emotional deprivation coupled with abuse, neglect, and isolation can sometimes cause the hypothalamus to stop producing GHs. Normal growth then slows or stops, but the growth rate quickly returns to normal when the child is removed from the negative environment.

There are two main kinds of pituitary dwarfism. The first kind dominates over two thirds of all pituitary dwarfism cases and is called panhypopituitarism. It is caused by complete lack of pituitary hormones in the brain. In children, this results in a child who will not reach normal height and will not reach sexual development by adolescence. The second kind of pituitary dwarfism is found in one third of cases and is caused by an isolated insufficiency of GH. This will result in children who do not reach normal height but may mature sexually during adolescence. In both kinds of pituitary dwarfism the affected child's height will be slower in development than that of other children in his or her age group. Headaches, excessive thirst, excessive urination, and delayed sexual development (or sometimes a complete absence of sexual development) are also common symptoms for this particular disorder (drkoop.com, 2001).

Hereditary pituitary dwarfism is found in approximately 10% of all cases. An inherited recessive gene has been identified as the cause for pituitary dwarfism with sexual maturity. Differential diagnosis of this condition is difficult, as there could be many other reasons for delayed growth; therefore it is important to obtain an endochrinological evaluation to determine the reason for the slowed growth (Adam.com, 2001).

There are many tests that can be done to determine pituitary dwarfism. The most common tests are magnetic resonance imaging (MRI) and computerized axial tomography (CAT) scans. MRI is done to assist in the determination of the etiology of the condition such as size of the pituitary gland. Other useful methods of detecting the disorder are measuring the levels of growth hormone being produced in the body and using hand X rays. A hand X ray is done to compare the bone age with the child's actual chronological age. After those tests have been administered, blood and urine tests are commonly done to determine other levels of pituitary hormones in the body.

Characteristics

1. Delayed growth (beneath normal height range for age)
2. Delayed or absent sexual development
3. Headaches
4. Excessive thirst (which would result in excessive urination)

Unfortunately, at this point in time, there are few options for treatment. The most common treatment currently used (although long-term benefits are still being studied) is GH replacement therapy (Columbia Encyclopedia, 2001). If the growth hormone is replaced in pituitary dwarfism cases, the most positive result is that the child will reach normal height. Research is also underway concerning genetic replacement therapy (Tish, 1999). If an individual with pituitary dwarfism is not treated, sexual development in puberty will not occur. If the child is lacking multiple hormones, there are usually multiple medical issues, and if not treated, the individual could die. (Tish, 1999).

The lifestyle of people with pituitary dwarfism is similar to that of normal individuals in that they need to eat healthy foods, exercise regularly, obtain an education, and work as an adult. Although little people, as they prefer to be called (Arricale, 2000), are capable of doing everyday things normally, they also have to deal with some difficult adjustment issues. If an individual with pituitary dwarfism does not reach sexual maturity, he or she will be unable to have children, so adoption is a popular choice for adults with this disorder. An adaptive example that a child or adolescent with pituitary dwarfism might encounter is car safety. Airbags are potentially dangerous and should probably be removed from the car if the individual becomes a driver. The National Highway Transportation Safety Administration cites specific guidelines and tips for this subject at http://www.nhtsa.dot.gov/airbags.

Special education accommodations may not be necessary for children with this condition. However, educational and adaptive concerns will be highly individualized depending on the etiology and treatment of the disorder and medical sequelae (Arricale, 2000). Family and individual counseling will probably be necessary to assist with adjustment and developmental concerns. In addition, alignment with special organizations for little people and individuals with other growth issues will assist in positive identity formation. The Human Growth Foundation can be contacted at (800) 451-6434.

REFERENCES

Adam.com. (2001). Pituitary dwarfism. Retrieved February 28, 2001, from http://my.webmd.com/content/asset/adam_disease_dwarfism.htm

Arricale, B. (2000). Dwarfism. In C. R. Reynolds & E. Fletcher-Janzen (Eds.), *Encyclopedia of special education* (pp. 639). New York: Wiley.

Columbia encyclopedia (6th ed). (2001). Dwarfism. Retrieved August 19, 2001, from http://www.bartleby.com/65/dw/dwarfism.html

drkoop.com. (2001). *Conditions and concerns: Medical encyclopedia. Pituitary dwarfism.* Retrieved February 28, 2001, from http://phs.drkoop.com/conditions/ency/article/001176.htm

Tish, D. (1999). Pituitary dwarfism. Retrieved August 18, 1999, from http://www.mylifepath.com/article/gale/100265663

Emma Janzen
Colorado Springs, Colorado

DYSCALCULIA

Dyscalculia is a widely used term for disabilities in mathematics. Whereas the term *acalculia* is reserved for the total inability to do math, dyscalculia refers to a less severe problem performing math problems. Dyscalculia can be developmental or acquired (e.g., traumatic brain injury), and the problem can range from mild to severe. Specific math computation and comprehension difficulties include problems with counting, recognizing numbers, manipulating math symbols (mentally or in writing), sequential memory for numbers and math operations, and reversing numbers (e.g., while reading, writing, and recalling numbers).

Prevalence rates are estimated to be approximately 7% (Rourke & Conway, 1997). Unlike other learning disabilities, developmental dyscalculia affects both sexes equally. The exact cause is unknown; however, genetics are suspected to play a significant role. For example, dyscalculia has been found in 42% of persons who have first-degree relatives with a learning disability (Gross, Manor, & Shalev, 1996). Studies seeking to link dyscalculia with a particular hemisphere of the brain have had mixed results; however, the left temporoparietal lobe has had considerable support (Macaruso & Sokol, 1998). Environmental factors associated with poor math performance include failure to receive proper instruction, poorly worded textbooks, family socioeconomic status, and ethnic-racial background (Fleischner & Manheimer, 1997).

Dyscalculia often co-occurs with other learning problems including language processing deficits, poor visual-spatial organization, sequencing difficulties, and poor memory. Twenty-six percent of children with dyscalculia have been found to have attention-deficit/hyperactivity disorder (ADHD), and 17% of these children have dyslexia. Other comorbid conditions include nonverbal learning disabilities, Williams syndrome, and Gerstmann syndrome (Gross et al., 1996; Rourke & Conway, 1997).

Characteristics

1. Developmental or acquired problem that includes difficulty counting, recognizing numbers, manipulating math symbols, sequencing numbers, performing math operations, and reversing numerals
2. Prevalence rate of 7%, affecting both sexes equally
3. Cause unknown but genetics implicated and environmental factors associated (e.g., poor instruction and textbooks and family's socioeconomic status)
4. Co-occurs with other learning, attention, and neurologic conditions

Math disabilities are classified under Specific Learning Disability in the Individuals with Disabilities Education Act (IDEA) of 1997. Eligibility criteria require that a child have at least normal intelligence and that a significant discrepancy exist between math achievement and age and ability level (i.e., 2 or more years discrepant). According to the *Diagnostic and Statistical Manual of Mental Disorders–Fourth Edition* (American Psychiatric Society, 1994), children with below-average intelligence can be classified as having a Mathematics Disorder provided that there is still a significant discrepancy between achievement and the individual's age, ability, and educational level. Both classification schemes require that educational background, cultural factors, and instructional exposure be used as exclusionary criteria. If the math disability is due primarily to a sensory deficit—that is, the child cannot see or hear well enough to learn math skills—then a diagnosis is not made.

Achievement tests that are often used to diagnose math problems are included in a number of batteries (e.g., Woodcock-Johnson III Tests of Achievement, KeyMath-Revised, Kaufman Test of Educational Achievement, Peabody Individual Achievement Test–Revised, and the Wide Range Achievement Test–Third Edition). Less formal methods are also used, including error analysis (e.g., qualitative assessment of math tests and observations of math calculations and problem solving). Despite the various means to assess math ability, this disorder is often overlooked. Given the problems that can result from poor math achievement, including course failure and school dropout, it is imperative that screening be done to identify children who have math disabilities so that appropriate interventions are implemented.

When children with dyscalculia need special education assistance, it will most likely be provided under the category Specific Learning Disabilities. Not all children with dyscalculia, however, need special education and will do well with regular education classroom accommodations. Methods that have been found to be effective include teacher modeling, strategy training (e.g., learning mnemonics to remember math facts), direct instruction, and cooperative learning groups (Fleischner & Manheimer, 1997). Both the Project

Math and DISTAR Arithmetic Program have been shown to increase computational and math problem-solving skills in students with learning disabilities (Cutting & Lyon, 1998).

Factors associated with the chronicity of dyscalculia include severity math difficulty and family history of math disability (Auerbach, Gross, Manor, & Shalev, 1998). Socioeconomic status, sex, and reading disabilities have not been definitively linked to this disorder; however, dyscalculia has not received nearly the attention of researchers that reading problems have. Given the potential impact of poor math on educational and employment opportunities, further research is needed to identify causative factors and conditions that may put children at risk for dyscalculia. Research to determine what interventions work best is also needed.

REFERENCES

American Psychiatric Association. (1994). *Diagnostic and statistical manual of mental disorders* (4th ed.). Washington, DC: Author.

Auerbach, J., Gross, T. V., Manor, O., & Shalev, R. S. (1998). Persistence of developmental dyscalculia: What counts? Results from a 3-year prospective follow-up study. *Pediatrics, 133*(3), 358–362.

Cutting, L. E., & Lyon, G. R. (1998). Learning disabilities. In R. A. Barkley & E. J. Mash (Eds.), *Treatment of childhood disorders.* New York: Guilford Press.

Fleischner, J. E., & Manheimer, M. A. (1997). Math interventions for students with learning disabilities: Myths and realities. *School Psychology Review, 26*(3), 397–414.

Gross, T. V., Manor, O., & Shalev, R. S. (1996). Developmental dyscalculia: Prevalence and demographic features. *Developmental Medicine and Child Neurology, 38*(1), 25–33.

Macaruso, P., & Sokol, S. M., (1998). Cognitive neuropsychology and developmental dyscalculia. In C. Donlon (Ed.), *The development of mathematical skills* (pp. 201–225). East Sussex, England: Psychology Press.

Rourke, B. P., & Conway, J. A. (1997). Disabilities of arithmetic and mathematical reasoning: Perspectives from neurology and neuropsychology. *Journal of Learning Disabilities, 30*(1), 34–36.

Lindsey A. Phillips
Elaine Clark
University of Utah

See also Acalculia

DYSGRAPHESTHESIA

Dysgraphesthesia is the inability to recognize symbols drawn on parts of the body (Spreen, Risser, & Edgell, 1995). Often referred to as a neurological "soft sign," dysgraphesthesia is more common in children with learning disabilities or behavior disorders, although a direct causal relationship has not been found (Bigler & Clement, 1997; Spreen et al., 1995). Dysgraphesthesia has also been associated with cortical motor deficit (Spreen et al., 1995), parietal lobe dysfunction, peripheral neuropathy, vascular lesions, temporal lobe dysfunction, and inattention or confusion (Broshek & Barth, 2000; Reitan & Wolfson, 1985). There is no information available regarding prevalence or incidence.

Characteristics

1. Indicated by a significant number of errors on tactile-perception tests
2. Correlated with learning disabilities and behavior disorders

Dysgraphesthesia is assessed through the use of tests of sensory perception, specifically skin writing procedures, most often with symbols or numbers traced on the palm of the hand or on the fingertips. Fewer errors on these kinds of assessment measures are expected as children become older, and reliability of soft neurological signs such as dysgraphesthesia is greater in 8- to 11-year-olds than it is in 5- to 6-year-olds (Stevenson, 2000). Tests of dysgraphesthesia are useful for determining the lateralization of brain lesions, especially when there are no other obvious neurological signs such as aphasia (Lezak, 1995). It has been suggested that contralateral parietal lobe damage or dysfunction can be inferred when one hand is significantly more impaired than the other (Reitan & Wolfson, 1985). More pronounced deficits have been found as the lesion approaches postcentral gyrus (Spreen et al., 1995).

Clusters of low scores on sensory perception tests may be associated with apraxia, or difficulty planning nonhabitual movement (Stevenson, 2000). This may lead to problems with fine motor skills such as writing or getting dressed, necessitating the use of developmentally appropriate interventions such as occupational therapy (Broshek & Barth, 2000; Stevenson, 2000). Longitudinal studies have shown the persistence over time of soft neurological signs such as dysgraphesthesia in children who are diagnosed with learning or emotional disorders and who continue to exhibit these disorders as adults (Spreen et al., 1995).

Future research may be aimed at better defining relationships between neurological status and soft signs such as dysgraphesthesia (Spreen et al. 1995).

REFERENCES

Bigler, E. D., & Clement, P. F. (1997). *Diagnostic clinical neuropsychology* (3rd ed.). Austin: University of Texas Press.

Broshek, D. K., & Barth, J. T. (2000). The Halstead-Reitan Neuropsychological Test Battery. In G. Groth-Marnat (Ed.), *Neuropsychological assessment in clinical practice* (pp. 223–262). New York: Wiley.

Lezak, M. D. (1995). *Neuropsychological assessment* (3rd ed.). New York: Oxford University Press.

Reitan, R. M., & Wolfson, D. (1985). *The Halstead-Reitan Neuropsychological Test Battery: Theory and clinical interpretation.* Tucson, AZ: Neuropsychology Press.

Spreen, O., Risser, A. H., & Edgell, D. (1995). *Developmental neuropsychology.* New York: Oxford University Press.

Stevenson, R. J. (2000). Graphesthesia. In C. R. Reynolds & E. Fletcher-Janzen (Eds.), *Encyclopedia of special education* (p. 837). New York: Wiley.

Kathryn L. Guy
Margaret Semrud-Clikeman
University of Texas

DYSGRAPHIA

Dysgraphia is a disorder characterized by writing difficulties. More specifically, it is defined as difficulty in automatically remembering and mastering the sequence of muscle motor movements needed in writing letters or numbers. The difficulty writing is incongruent with the person's ability and is not due to poor instruction. The disorder varies in terms of severity, ranging from mild to severe.

Problems in writing and difficulty with other motor skills related to instruction are not uncommon among school-age children. Although the prevalence of dysgraphia is unknown, it is estimated that 5–20% of children demonstrate some form of deficient writing behavior (Smits-Engelman & Van Galen, 1997). Although a neurologic basis is suspected, the exact cause is unknown. What is known is that it is a problem that results from an integration failure, that is, a deficit in visual-motor integration rather than a deficit in either visual skill or motor skill alone (Bain, Bailet, & Moats, 1991). Dysgraphia is also considered to be caused by difficulty sequencing information as well as a more general auditory or language-processing problem.

Dysgraphia seldom exists in isolation but more commonly occurs with other coordination and learning problems (e.g., dyslexia, dyscalculia, and developmental coordination disorder). The problem has also been found among children who have attention problems and hyperactivity. Because fine motor coordination improves with maturation and instruction, dysgraphia is seldom recognized before the end of the first grade. In fact, the *Diagnostic and Statistical Manual of Mental Disorders-Fourth Edition's (DSM-IV)* diagnosis of Disorders of Written Expression, which dysgraphia may be a part of, stipulates that in order to be diagnosed with a disorder, the individual's writing problem must interfere with learning. In other words, children whose only problem is poor handwriting (i.e., they have no other problem with written expression) are not given a *DSM-IV* diagnosis.

Characteristics

1. Generally illegible writing despite appropriate attention and time given to the task
2. Mix of print and cursive and upper and lower case and changes in shapes, size, and slant
3. Failure to attend to writing details, unfinished words and letters, and omitted words
4. Irregular spacing between words and letters
5. Standard lines and margins not adhered to
6. Unusual grip on writing tool and unusual wrist/body/paper position
7. Excessive erasures
8. Self-talking while writing or close observation of the writing hand
9. Slow or labored writing and copying even if neat and legible

Although writing samples and behavioral observations of the child are often used to diagnose the problem, a number of standardized assessment instruments may also be helpful. This includes the Developmental Test of Visual-Motor Integration, Coding/Digit Symbol and Symbol Search subtests of the Wechsler intelligence scales (WISC-III/WAIS-III), Bender-Gestalt, and Jordan Left-Right Reversal Test. A variety of written language achievement measures may also be useful, including tests such as the Woodcock Johnson Achievement Test (WJ-3) and Test of Written Language (TOWL). In addition to assessing student characteristics, it is also important to assess the type of instruction that has been provided to the child and his or her response to the writing task. Classroom observations may be helpful in ruling out contextual variables as a significant factor in the writing problem.

Treatment of dysgraphia may include interventions to assist the child in better controlling fine motor skill. Although the classroom teacher and parent may be helpful in this regard, in some cases the child may need to be evaluated and seen by the occupational therapist to work on controlling the writing movements. Few children with dysgraphia actually qualify for special education services under the Individuals with Disabilities in Education Act (IDEA) of 1997; however, some may if the problem in writing is associated with other learning problems (e.g., written language). In the cases where dysgraphia is comorbid with other learning disabilities, children may be served under the category Specific Learning Disabilities. In most cases, children can be accommodated in the regular classroom.

Educators can employ a number of accommodations, modifications, and remediation strategies to help students with dysgraphia. Some of these include allowing the student to use a computer or typewriter to do written work, having them use special writing implements (e.g., grippers or extra-large pencils and pens), or allowing the child to write in whatever form of manuscript is easiest and most legible (e.g., print or cursive). Giving children extra time for writing assignments and allowing them to audiotape assignments, take oral tests, and do more self-correction of their written work may be beneficial. Some children, however, may need further instruction and practice in handwriting. For an excellent resource refer to the Resource Room Web site (Jones, 1998).

If untreated, the prognosis for dysgraphia is generally thought to be poor. Although some writing problems persist regardless of intervention, many children can be helped by attention paid to the problem. Not only do children need to be made aware of the problem, but also specific strategies need to be put in place to assist the child. Knowing what strategies are most effective, however, is unclear. Perhaps further studies of other associated conditions will shed light on this otherwise neglected disorder.

REFERENCES

Bain, A. M., Bailet, L. L., & Moats, L. C. (1991). *Written language disorders: Theory into practice.* Austin, TX: Pro-ed.

Jones, S. (1998). Accommodations and modifications for students with handwriting problems and/or dysgraphia. Retrieved from http://www.resourceroom.net

Smits-Engelman, B. C. M., & Van Galen, G. P. (1997). Dysgraphia in children: Lasting psychomotor deficiency or transient developmental delay? *Journal of Experimental Child Psychology, 67*(2), 164–184.

Lindsey A. Phillips
Elaine Clark
University of Utah

DYSKINESIA

Dyskinesia is a collection of movement disorders involving impairment of central nervous system motor control. It is thought to be due to damage or abnormal development of the basal ganglia, the deep subcortical nuclei in the cerebral cortex. Involuntary movement, irregular motions, or lack of coordinated voluntary movement characterizes dyskinesia (Fredericks & Saladin, 1996). Dyskinetic movement disorders include dystonia, tremor, chorea, tics, and myoclonus. Each movement disorder is uniquely characterized. For example, dystonia is characterized by involuntary, sustained posturing. Small oscillating movements at rest or with effort characterize tremor. Random, excessive, irregularly timed movements characterize chorea. Tics are brief, repetitive, involuntary movements. Involuntary movements that are rapid, shock-like, and arrhythmic (unpatterned) characterize myoclonus (Weiner & Goetz, 1999).

Each movement disorder is unique in regard to the somatic distribution and quality of movement, the age of onset, and etiology. Dyskinesia may be the primary sign or symptom or may be included with the other signs or symptoms of a syndrome. Childhood dyskinetic movement disorders include Tourette's syndrome, choreoathetoid cerebral palsy, Wilson's disease, Lesch-Nyhan syndrome, and dystonia. The etiology of a dyskinetic movement disorder is variable and may be due to genetic transmission, brain anoxia, infection, or neoplasm (Weiner & Goetz, 1999).

Prevalence and incidence of dyskinesia in childhood is not documented due to the varied nature of the etiology.

Characteristics

1. Involuntary sustained muscle contractions producing unusual postures
2. Involuntary oscillating movement at rest or during effort
3. Excessive, irregularly timed involuntary movement
4. Repetitive, brief, purposeless involuntary movement
5. Rapid, often repetitive involuntary movement

Medical intervention includes pharmacologic treatment or intramuscular injections to control the involuntary movement (Kurlan, 1995). Supportive counseling services may be helpful in educating families, peers, and school personnel regarding the nature of the dyskinesia. The school and home environment may need to be restructured or adapted to improve function depending on the severity of the dyskinesia.

In older children and adults tic disorders are a fairly common type of dyskinesia. They may include rapid repetitive facial movements such as blinking, coughing, sniffing, or lip smacking. These too are typically treated symptomatically. They may be treated through the use of relaxation techniques or antianxiety medications in an effort to reduce the stress associated with increased demonstration of this type of dyskinesia (Fredericks & Saladin, 1996). In patients treated with neuroleptic drugs, tardive dyskenesia may develop as a result of this family of drugs. This is more common in adults but may also occur in older adolescents. Unfortunately, this condition may be irreversible (NIH Health Information Index, 2000).

The impact this group of movement disorders may have on the development of children depends in part on the age at onset, the range and severity of symptoms exhibited, and the developmental level of the child. One of the key components of movement and exploration is stability and predictability of postural tone. Without this stability in the trunk, a child may be unwilling or unable to maintain a sitting position necessary to reach, grasp, and explore objects. Cognitive and perceptual motor skills exhibited in refined searching also require stability of movement. Success in this skill depends on the infant's ability to watch an item being hidden, remember where it went, and retrieve it (Piaget, 1952). Without adequate support and predictable movement patterns, this behavior may be difficult or impossible.

Moving independently in the environment, using independent self-help behaviors such as eating and fine motor skills such as stacking blocks and puzzles also requires stabile and predictable movements. A very young infant just learning to crawl may be hesitant to proceed if he or she is unable to maintain stability necessary for movement. Moving out into the environment provides opportunities to explore and increase social and language development. Without this ability, the secondary disabilities that may result include delayed cognitive, language, and social skills necessary for smooth transition to the next levels of development.

Thus, delays in development resulting from dyskinesia may not only potentially affect motor development but also impact development in social and cognitive areas as well as other areas depending on the severity of the dyskenesia. Special education placement will depend on the nature of the disability and the level of involvement for each child. A variety of special education service categories (e.g., Mental Handicap, Preschool Services, Traumatic Brain Injury, and Physical Disability) may be considered, and services provided should stem from the special needs of each child. Therefore, it is critical that intervention programs address all areas potentially impacted, such as speech, occupational, and physical therapy in addition to academic areas. The ideal program would include a transdisciplinary model in which counseling, physical, occupational, and speech therapy are incorporated into the child's daily activities.

REFERENCES

Fredericks, C. M., & Saladin, L. K. (1996). *Pathophysiology of the motor systems.* Philadelphia: F. A. Davis.

Kurlan R. (1995). *Treatment of movement disorders.* Philadelphia: J. B. Lippincott.

Piaget, J. (1952). *The origin of intelligence in children.* New York: International Universities Press.

NIH Health Information Index: National Institute of Neurological Disorders and Stroke. (2000). Dyskinesias. Retrieved from http://www.ninds.nih.gov/health_and_medical/disorder/dyskinesias_doc.htm

Weiner, W. W., & Goetz C. G. (1999). *Neurology for the non-neurologist* (4th ed.). Philadelphia: Lippincott Williams & Wilkins.

Patricia Work
Marilyn Urquhart
Lana Svien-Senne
University of South Dakota

DYSLEXIA, DEVELOPMENTAL

Dyslexia, or reading disability, is characterized by low reading achievement, as measured by an individually administered standardized test of reading accuracy or comprehension that is substantially below what would be expected given an individual's chronological age, measured intelligence (IQ), and age-appropriate education (American Psychiatric Association, 1994). It should be noted, however, that recent studies have demonstrated that the same component processes and underlying neuropsychological deficits are present in poor readers, regardless of their general cognitive potential (Pennington, Gilger, Olson, & DeFries, 1992). Thus, the application of an IQ discrepancy criterion may underdiagnose dyslexia in those individuals with lower cognitive ability.

Dyslexia is the most common learning disability, with a prevalence rate ranging from 4–10% depending on the criteria used to define the disorder. There is evidence from behavioral genetic studies that dyslexia is 50–60% heritable (DeFries et al., 1997). A child of an affected parent has approximately a 40% chance of manifesting the disorder. The male-to-female ratio approaches 4:1 among clinically ascertained populations; however, it is closer to 2:1 in population studies. Although dyslexia is likely to be a multifactorial disorder, linkage analyses have identified a number of loci (e.g., Chromosome 6) that contribute to the presence of a reading disability (Cardon et al., 1994; Grigorenko et al., 1997).

Characteristics

1. Reading achievement is age and/or IQ discrepant and is not due to a sensory deficit or general medical condition (i.e., acquired brain injury).
2. Spelling deficits are another core feature of the disorder, and difficulties with lexical retrieval and rote short-term verbal memory are variably present.
3. Young children with dyslexia (prereading age) exhibit difficulty with phoneme awareness, rhyming, and letter and sound knowledge.
4. Fifteen to 35% of children with dyslexia meet criteria for attention-deficit hyperactivity disorder (ADHD).
5. Twenty-five to 35% of children with dyslexia have had a diagnosable articulation or language deficit when younger and may continue to exhibit language difficulties in their school-age years.

Fortunately, dyslexia is one of the more treatable learning disorders, and many affected individuals learn to read and obtain high school and college degrees. However, spelling ability, reading fluency, and phonological awareness tasks (e.g., word games like "pig latin") may still pose varying degrees of difficulty for the compensated dyslexic. Theoretically sound methods of treatment acknowledge the primary deficits in phonemic awareness and phonological decoding (the ability to translate letters in words to sounds) and typically use a multisensory approach to facilitate these skills in early readers. Treatment methods also target secondary problems in comprehension, motivation, attention, and self-esteem, as necessary. The Lindamood-Bell and Orton Gillingham treatment programs are examples of interventions increasingly available in schools as well as in the community (Lindamood & Lindamood, 1975; Wise, 1991). In addition, with recent advances in technology, various text readers and speech recognition software programs are now available. This technology allows the individual with dyslexia to scan text into a computer, which then reads it out loud to him or her. Similarly, speech recognition programs are now able to interface efficiently with word processing packages so that an individual with dyslexia can dictate a letter or document directly into the computer. Spell checking programs are also ubiquitous and can be quite useful even to compensated dyslexics, whose residual deficit is likely to include a spelling deficit.

Most school districts have a category in their Individual Educational Plans (IEPs) for a specific learning disability such as dyslexia, thus allowing these children to access special education services. Due to the significant impact of dyslexia on academic performance across a number of subjects—not just reading and language arts—these children are often in need of academic tutoring as well as specific reading intervention. For example, due to the short-term memory deficits for rote information that many children with dyslexia exhibit, learning math facts is often difficult, causing them to fall behind in math. Eligibility for special education instruction in reading and other affected areas is subject to the school district's policies regarding what constitutes a reading disability (i.e., different discrepancy cutoffs are sometimes used in different districts). Fortunately, there is growing consensus and uniformity in this regard as research continues to help define the disorder and its cognitive and linguistic underpinnings.

Because dyslexia can be characterized as the lower end of the reading ability continuum, the disorder manifests with varying degrees of severity across individuals. A child with a more severe reading deficit who also has ADHD and lower IQ is likely to have a poorer prognosis than is the child with a mild reading deficit and no comorbid conditions. In general, with appropriate access to qualified reading specialists and intervention programs, children with reading disability can overcome most of the obstacles to literacy and become, at the very least, functional readers.

REFERENCES

American Psychiatric Association. (1994). *Diagnostic and statistical manual of mental disorders* (4th ed.). Washington, DC: Author.

Cardon, L. R., DeFries, J. C., Fulker, D. W., Kimberling, W. J., Pennington, B. F., & Smith, S. D. (1994). Quantitative trait locus for reading disability on chromosome 6. *Science, 265,* 276–279.

DeFries, J. C., Filipek, P. A., Fulker, D. W., Olson, R. K., Pennington, B. F., Smith, S. D., & Wise, B. W. (1997). Colorado learning disabilities research center. *Learning Disability Quarterly, 8;* 7–19.

Grigorenko, E. L., Wood, F. B., Meyer, M. S., Hart, L. A., Speed, W. C., Shuster, A., & Pauls, D. L. (1997). Susceptibility loci for distinct components of developmental dyslexia on chromosome 6 and 15. *American Journal of Human Genetics, 60,* 27–39.

Lindamood, P., & Lindamood, C. (1975). *The A.D.D. program: Auditory discrimination in depth.* Allen, TX: DLM Teaching Resources.

Pennington, B. F., Gilger, J. W., Olson, R. W., & DeFries, J. W. (1992). External validity of age- versus IQ-discrepancy definitions of reading disability: Lessons from a twin study. *Journal of Learning Disabilities, 25*(9), 562–573.

Wise, B. W. (1991). What reading disabled children need: What is known and how to talk about it. *Learning and Individual Differences, 1*(4), 307–321.

Richard Boada
University of Denver

Greta Wilkening
University of Colorado Health Sciences Center
The Children's Hospital

DYSLOGIC SYNDROME

Dyslogic syndrome, sometimes referred to as developmental or congenital aphasia, consists of the inability to express oneself through language due to a central nervous system dysfunction. Symptoms may not be the result of a sensory or cognitive deficit, nor may they occur due to loss of prior linguistic abilities (Eisenson, 1972; Nicolosi, Harryman, & Kresheck, 1983; Telzrow, 2000). The primary characteristic of dyslogia is difficulty with communication, which is likely to make learning more difficult and to cause frustration to the child. At times children with dyslogia may be misdiagnosed with mental retardation, deafness, auditory deficit, or psychological disorder due to similarities in behavioral patterns (Telzrow, 2000). True dyslogia is believed to be quite rare, although epidemiological information is not available (Eisenson, 1972).

Eisenson (1972) cited several diagnostic criteria for dyslogia that differentiate it from other language disorders. Children with dyslogia often have difficulty with integrating sensory information. This can occur across sensory modalities but in all cases includes the auditory modality. It appears that those with dyslogia have a particularly difficult time making sense of auditory information. More specifically, he suggested that they struggle to find meaningful patterns in auditory input (Chappell, 1970; Eisenson, 1972).

Characteristics

1. Perceptual dysfunction within or across sensory modalities. In nearly all cases auditory perception is impaired.
2. Auditory perceptual difficulties despite intact hearing.
3. Sequencing difficulties for auditory and sometimes visual events.
4. Child's performance on intellectual tasks below that of children of a similar age. Eisenson (1972) described this as intellectual inefficiency rather than impairment.
5. Delayed language development. Children may be effectively nonverbal until the age of 4 or 5 years. Subsequent language is lacking in vocabulary and syntax.

In addition to their struggles with language, Eisenson (1972) believes that those with dyslogia have difficulty with sequencing in general. Children with dyslogia may also exhibit symptoms of inattention and distractibility that can prevent them from working up to their cognitive ability. As these children approach ages where higher cognitive functioning is more frequently required, their difficulties with sequencing become more apparent.

It appears that with patient training, children with dyslogia may learn to recognize and understand simple words, especially nouns that can be represented by physical objects. There is less evidence for the acquisition of understanding of words that represent less concrete concepts such as feelings or actions. With some training, these children may learn to respond to specific, short directive sentences (e.g., "Come, Mary"). However, it appears that these children have a hard time generalizing their understanding, and responses may be situationally specific. Thus, a child who learns to come to the teacher may not respond to the same command when spoken at home (Chappell, 1970).

Prognosis in cases of dyslogia is varied. In some cases, the ability to communicate effectively by language may never develop. In others, the development of language will be permanently impaired, but improvement does occur (Chappell, 1970; Eisenson, 1972). It should be noted that development or recovery of language among those with dyslogia is generally less successful than is that of children with acquired aphasia (Eisenson, 1972).

The language impairment in these children may be so great that when language does begin to develop, it is likely to be impaired in its syntax and complexity. The pattern of language development is likely to be somewhat idiosyncratic and is unlikely to present as merely delayed. These children may be able to speak, but their ability to communicate verbally is likely to remain impaired (Chappell, 1970; Eisenson, 1972).

In an educational environment, care should be taken to provide these children with nonauditory cues for learning. Attempts to teach language should include simple (two to three word) sentences, extensive and patient repetition, and the pairing of vocabulary with concrete objects. It appears that these children require an optimal environment in order to reach their intellectual potentials. Eisenson (1972) suggested that factors such as irrelevant stimuli, fatigue, and frustration may be especially detrimental to children struggling with dyslogia. In such cases, common accommodations for children with attentional difficulties would likely be helpful.

REFERENCES

Chappell, G. E. (1970). Developmental aphasia revisited. *Journal of Communication Disorders, 3,* 181–197.

Eisenson, J. (1972). *Aphasia in children.* New York: Harper and Row.

Nicolosi, L., Harryman, E., & Kresheck, J. (1983). *Terminology of communication disorders.* Baltimore: Williams & Wilkins.

Telzrow, C. T. (2000). Dyslogic syndrome. In C. Reynolds & E. Fletcher-Janzen (Eds.), *Encyclopedia of special education: A reference for the education of the handicapped and other exceptional children and adults* (2nd ed., Vol. 1, pp. 636–637). New York: Wiley.

Melanie E. Ballatore
University of Texas at Austin

DYSMETRIA

Dysmetria is defined as an aspect of ataxia in which the ability to control the distance, power, and speed of an act is impaired (Stedman, 2000). The term originates from the Greek *dys,* meaning difficult or disordered, and *metron,* meaning measure. Individuals with dysmetria have problems judging the extent to which they must move their body to reach a desired goal and often have difficulty stopping their movement in a precise manner to reach the goal. Movements, therefore, undershoot (hypometria) or overshoot (hypermetria) the distance (Telzrow, 2000). Individuals with dysmetria may have difficulty raising their arms parallel to the floor (i.e., arms extended at the shoulder level). Some may also have problems moving their arms above their heads from their shoulders and back down while keeping their eyes closed.

The prevalence of dysmetria is unknown, but it has been shown to co-occur with other conditions. Some of these associated conditions include neurologic disorders (e.g., cerebellar dysfunction), learning problems (e.g., dyslexia), and psychiatric conditions (e.g., schizophrenia). Unless dysmetria is detected while evaluating for problems associated with related conditions, it is likely to remain undiagnosed. There have been cases of children with traumatic brain injury (TBI) who after being hit by a vehicle are found to have a cerebellar tumor thought to be responsible for the initial misjudgment of distance, and thus the accident. Had imaging not been done to evaluate the TBI, it is likely that the tumor would not have been detected and that the dysmetria would not have been diagnosed.

Characteristics

1. Disturbance in the ability to judge distance and control the range of movement in muscle action to reach precisely a desired goal
2. Rapid, brusque movements with more force than is typical
3. Often associated with other conditions (e.g., neurologic and psychiatric)
4. Difficult to diagnose

There is no prescribed treatment for dysmetria, and the literature is almost nonexistent. Frank and Levinson (1976) studied the effectiveness of seasick medications to treat "dysmetric dyslexia." The researchers hypothesize that dysmetric dyslexia may be due to vestibular dysfunction and respond to a specific intervention of the eyes being prevented from moving beyond printed letters and words. In the end, it may be that interventions used to correct dysmetria will be those that are designed to address related problems, including reading disabilities and other learning difficulties. Research is clearly needed to understand this condition better and to find ways to determine when dysmetria signals a more serious problem (e.g., brain tumors).

REFERENCES

Frank, J., & Levinson, H. N. (1976). Seasickness mechanisms and medications in dysmetric dyslexia and dyspraxia. *Academic Therapy, 12*(2), 133–153.

Stedman, T. L. (2000). *Stedman's medical dictionary* (27th ed., p. 553). Baltimore: Lipincott Williams & Wilkins.

Telzrow, C. F. (2000). In C. R. Reynolds & E. Fletcher-Janzen (Eds.), *Encyclopedia of special education* (2nd ed., p. 637). New York: Wiley.

Lindsey A. Phillips
Elaine Clark
University of Utah

DYSPHAGIA

Dysphagia has been defined in several different ways. For example, Buchholz (1996) offered a broad definition in which dysphagia is considered a condition resulting from some interference in eating or the maintenance of nutrition and hydration; Groher (1997) stated that dysphagia is an "abnormality in the transfer of a bolus from the mouth to the stomach" (p. 1). However, a general definition of dysphagia is having difficulty swallowing. This difficulty could be caused by a number of different conditions. The more common causes of swallowing difficulty are neurologic damage such as stroke or progressive neurologic disease such as Parkinson's disease, head and neck tumors and their treatment, medical problems such as rheumatoid arthritis, scleroderma, diabetes, and induced trauma to the esophagus, larynx, tongue, or pharynx (New York Eye and Ear Infirmary [NYEEI], 2000).

Dysphagia typically falls into one of two categories. Oropharyngeal dysphagia is the result of a stroke or neuromuscular disorder that leaves the throat muscles weakened, making it difficult to get food from the mouth into the throat. This condition is often accompanied by choking or coughing when attempting to swallow and the sensation of food going down the windpipe. The most common type of dysphagia, however, is esophageal dysphagia, which refers to the sensation of food sticking or getting caught in the base of one's throat or chest and may be accompanied by pressure or pain in the chest (Mayo Foundation for Medical Education and Research [MFMER], 1998).

A narrowing of the lower esophagus, known as peptic stricture, is a common cause of esophageal dysphagia. The resulting condition, known as gastroesophageal reflux, is a result of stomach acid bubbling up into the esophagus, causing inflammation and scarring in the esophagus. Another cause of esophageal dysphagia is a formation of a pouch in the back of the throat or esophagus, known as diverticulum.

Despite the many medically identifiable causes of dysphagia, many people experience swallowing problems that seem to have no medical basis (e.g., difficulty swallowing pills or the feeling of a lump in the throat). These problems persist in some people even though they have no other difficulty swallowing.

The incidence of dysphagia is approximately 13–14% in inpatient hospital settings, 40–50% in nursing homes, and approximately 33% in rehabilitation centers (NYEEI, 2000).

Acute forms of dysphagia are typically diagnosed by tests such as drinking a barium solution that coats the esophagus and enables an X ray to show abnormalities in the esophagus; an endoscopy, in which a tube with a special camera at the tip allows the esophagus to be viewed from the inside; or a procedure known as a manometry test, in which an instrument is inserted into the esophagus and pressure readings of esophageal muscle contractions are taken.

Characteristics

1. Pain while swallowing
2. Coughing while eating or drinking or very soon after eating or drinking
3. Wet-sounding voice during or after eating

4. Increased congestion in the chest after eating or drinking
5. Slow eating
6. Multiple swallows on a single mouthful of food
7. Obvious extra effort or difficulty while chewing or swallowing
8. Fatigue or shortness of breath while eating
9. Temperature rise 30 min to 1 hr after eating
10. Weight loss associated with increased slowness in eating
11. Frequent heartburn
12. Repetitive pneumonias

The causes of dysphagia determine the course of treatment. Pharyngeal dysphagia may be treated by a throat specialist, neurologist, or a speech pathologist for therapy. Typically, special throat exercises, liquid diets, and in severe cases a feeding tube may be recommended. Esophageal stricture may be treated by a procedure known as dilatation, in which an endoscope is inserted into the esophagus and a special balloon attached to the endoscope is inflated to expand the constricted areas of the esophagus. Acid reflux or esophageal spasms that result in dysphagia may be treated with prescription medication. In some cases, such as diverticulum or the presence of a tumor, surgery may be necessary (MFMER, 1998).

Children with dysphagia may require extra care at lunch and snack times, such as additional time to eat, adult supervision, and education of peers about the disorder.

REFERENCES

Buchholz, D. (1996). Editorial: What is dysphagia? *Dysphagia, 11,* 23.

Groher, M. E. (1997). *Dysphagia: Diagnosis and management* (3rd ed.). Boston: Butterworth-Heinemann.

Mayo Foundation for Medical Education and Research. (1998). Dysphagia: When swallowing becomes difficult. *Condition Centers.* Retrieved from http://www.mayoclinic.com/home?id=HQ00590

New York Eye and Ear Infirmary (2000). Dysphagia: What is a normal swallow? *Health Matters.* Retrieved from http://www.nyee.edu

Tracy A. Muenz
Alliant University

DYSPHONIA

Dysphonia is a general term referring to any voice disorder of phonation. Dysphonia is a deviation in pitch, intensity, and quality resulting primarily from the action of the vocal folds. Included in this definition are characteristics of the voice that consistently interfere with communication, draw unfavorable attention, adversely affect the speaker or listener, or are inappropriate to the age, sex, or perhaps the culture or class of the individual. Dysphonia is inclusive of over 30 specific types and can be organic, psychogenic, or functional in nature (Nicolosi, Harryman, & Kresheck, 1996).

The incidence of voice disorders has proved difficult to establish: Figures range from 6% (Senturia & Wilson, 1998) to 23.4% (Silverman & Zimmer, 1975) in the school age population, with the generally accepted number being closer to the 6% figure. In a study describing laryngeal disorders in children evaluated by otolaryngologists, Dobres Lee, Stempler, Kummer, & Kretchmer (1990) found the top five pathologies presented by children to be (a) subglottic stenosis, (b) vocal nodules, (c) laryngomalacia, (d) dysphonia with normal folds, and (e) vocal fold paralysis. Subglottic stenosis and laryngomalacia are considered to be congenital laryngeal pathologies. Subglottic stenosis is the maldevelopment of the cricoid cartilage causing a subglottal narrowing of the larynx. The narrowing produces an obstruction of the airway that causes the voice to be stridulous. In most cases, the cricoid cartilage continues to develop, and the problem self-corrects in infancy or early childhood (Aronson, 1990). Surgery is required in more severe cases. Laryngomalacia occurs when the epiglottis fails to develop normally, remaining very soft and pliable and causing stridor. No treatment is required for this condition, as the epiglottis will continue to grow and the condition will spontaneously clear by the third year with normal maturation (Aronson, 1990). Vocal nodules and dysphonia with normal folds are highly correlated with disorders of abuse and misuse. Vocal fold nodules are benign, callous-like growths resulting from frictional rubbing of the vocal fold edges (Nicolosi et al., 1996). Nodules can disappear following vocal rest or voice therapy, but surgical removal may be required. When the etiology of the nodules is vocal abuse or misuse, voice therapy is highly indicated to modify the behavior in order to prevent a recurrence of the condition. Disorders of phonation with normal folds result in vocal characteristics of a number of symptoms of dysphonia, which are not specific to a single etiology or dysphonia type. Vocal fold paralysis is the most common type of neurogenic voice disorder. It is typically caused by peripheral involvement of the recurrent laryngeal and the superior laryngeal nerves (Willatt & Stell, 1991). Location of the lesion along the nerve pathway will determine the type of paralysis and the resultant voice quality.

Characteristics

1. *Aphonia:* complete loss of voice, involuntary whispering
2. *Breathiness:* excessive air loss accompanying vocal tone

3. *Dipolophonia:* two tones produced simultaneously, one from the ventricular folds and one from the vocal folds
4. *Glottal attack:* extreme glottal closure prior to exhalation for speech
5. *Glottal fry:* crackling type of low-pitched phonation
6. *Harshness:* milieu of hard glottal attacks, pitch and intensity problems, and overadduction of the vocal folds
7. *Hoarseness:* low pitch with restricted pitch range, pitch breaks, and aphonic episodes
8. *Pitch break:* sudden shift of pitch during speech, usually related to an individual's speaking at an inappropriate pitch level
9. *Stridor:* tense laryngeal noise associated with respiration

Treatment for dysphonia varies with type and etiology. For disorders associated with vocal abuse and misuse, voice therapy by a speech-language pathologist is warranted. Treatment approaches are numerous and varied, but inclusion of vocal hygiene counseling is typical.

Students may receive voice therapy under the category of Speech-Language Impairment, but it is often difficult to meet the requirement of educational necessity. It should be noted that although it is not required, it is considered unethical among the speech pathology community to treat a student for a voice disorder without an examination from a physician, preferably an otolaryngologist. The responsibility for funding such an examination is often an issue.

Prognosis for recovery from dysphonia varies according to type, etiology, and student motivation and participation in a therapy program. When the dysphonia stems from vocal abuse or misuse, the lifestyles of the student and his or her family will often dictate the ease or difficulty they will have in attempting to make vocal modifications. Some students and families are not willing to modify their lifestyles for the health of their voice. A reasonable period of time and a concerted trial of therapy should always be administered.

Current research is focused on many adult dysphonias, primarily spasmodic dysphonia, and on medical management of such conditions. Research regarding children and adolescents is focused on issues of vocal hygiene, abuse, and misuse.

REFERENCES

Aronson, A. (1990). *Clinical voice disorders: An interdisciplinary approach* (3rd ed.). New York: Brian C. Decker.

Dobres, R., Lee, L., Stemple, J., Kummer, A., & Kretchmer, L. (1990). Description of laryngeal pathologies in children evaluated by otolaryngologists. *Journal of Speech and Hearing Disorders, 55,* 526–533.

Nicolosi, L., Harryman, E., & Kresheck, J. (1996). *Terminology of communication disorders: Speech-language-hearing* (4th ed.). Baltimore: Williams & Wilkins.

Senturia, B., & Wilson, F. (1998). Otorhinolaryngologic findings in children with voice deviations: Preliminary report. *Annals of Otology, Rhinology, and Laryngology, 77,* 1027–1042.

Silverman, E., & Zimmer, C. (1975). Incidence of chronic hoarseness among school-age children. *Journal of Speech and Hearing Disorders, 40,* 211–215.

Willatt, D., & Stell, P. (1991). Vocal cord paralysis. In S. Paparella & D. Shumrick (Eds.), *Otolaryngology* (3rd ed., pp. 2289–2307). Philadelphia: W. B. Saunders.

Shelley F. Pelletier
Jennifer L. Nicholls
Dysart Unified School District
El Mirage, Arizona

DYSPLASIA DISEASE, FIBROUS

Fibrous dysplasia is a skeletal disorder that affects bone growth and development within the first two decades of life; it destroys and replaces normal bone and is not usually fatal (D'Alessandro, 2001). Although classified as a benign process, local expansion can cause significant functional and aesthetic deformities (Frodel, 2000). The cause of this disease is currently unknown, although protein abnormalities have been suggested. This is a very uncommon disease, which has led to ambiguities regarding incidence; however, it is known that the male-to-female ratio is 2:1 (Papadakis et al., 2000).

This disorder is characterized by a chronic deformation of the skeletal systems that causes the expansion of bones, due to abnormal development of fibrous tissue within the bone (Mellors, 2001). A child with this disease would report bone pain, and bone deformities and fractures could occur. Fibrous dysplasia is not a disease that spreads from one bone to another, but any bone can be affected (polyostotic dysplasia). There is debate on whether more than one bone can be involved (Health on the Net Foundation, 2001). The most common sites of the disease are the weight-bearing bones such as femur, tibia, ribs, and pelvis (Methodist Health Care System, 2001). Also included are the facial bones and humerus; the skull and vertebrae of the spine are less frequently involved (National Institutes of Health, 2001). Associated with this disorder are the hormonal problems and skin pigmentation of McCune-Albright syndrome: This syndrome co-occurs with fibrous dysplasia 33% of the time (Paget Foundation, 2001). Many endocrine associations have been identified, and a possible relationship between fibrous dysplasia and hyperparathyroidism has been suggested; McCune-Albright syndrome occurs primarily in women.

When diagnosing this disorder, physicians x-ray the area of suspicion and look for a cystic lesion in the shafts of the bones (Methodist Health Care System, 2001). The lesion usually has a ground-glass appearance due to the calcification of the tumor matrix (Albracht & Mackenzie,

1996). If a physician is in doubt, he or she may take a bone sample for examination (Helzer-Julin, 2000).

Characteristics

1. Uneven bone growth, especially the weight-bearing bones
2. Fractures
3. Reports of bone pain

The child may experience surgeries to remove the affected bone, requests for bone samples, X rays, and occasionally radiation therapy.

Surgery is often used to improve mobility due to any skeletal deformities, facilitate the healing of fractures, relieve pressure on the spinal cord, and help alleviate the bone pain associated with fibrous dysplasia. Surgeries include the removal of the affected bone followed by bone grafting by another bone or pins and nails, and placement of a rod down the shaft of a bone to bridge a lesion, which helps prevent the fracture of the affected bone (NIH, 2001). Radiation therapy, although not usually recommended, could be used to treat any malignant tumors that result from the bone deformation (Paget Foundation, 2001).

A nonsurgical treatment that has observed benefits for fibrous dysplasia patients is the use of the drug Pamidronate (NIH, 2001), which controls the high blood calcium levels. Exercise is also highly recommended for maintaining skeletal health and mobility. Patients are also frequently instructed to avoid weight gain, which could stress the weight-bearing joints further; a physician should specially monitor any exercise treatment. This disorder is said to progress beyond puberty and through adulthood.

Special education services would probably be received for children with this disorder due to the amount of time away from school to administer medical monitoring and surgeries. Home-based services may provide well during emergency recovery. In addition, counseling may assist with pain management, chronic illness issues, and issues surrounding adaptive physical education and regular play with peers.

REFERENCES

Albracht, D., & Mackenzie, W. (1996). Polyostotic fibrous dysplasia, the Alfred I. duPont Institute. Retrieved from http://gait.aidi.udel.edu/res695/homepage/pd_ortho/educate/clincase/fibdysp.html

D'Alessandro, M. P. (2001). Paediapaedia: Fibrous dysplasia, Virtual Children's Hospital: The apprentice's assistant. Retrieved from http://australia.vh.org/Providers/TeachingFiles/PAP/MS Diseases/FibDysMono.html

Frodel, J. L. (2000). Management of aggressive midface and orbital fibrous dysplasia. *Journal of the American Medical Association, 284*(18), 2304–2307.

Health on the Net Foundation. (2001). Fibrous dysplasia. Retrieved from http://www.bonetumor.org/page52.html

Helzer-Julin, M. J. (2000). Dx-ray. *Physician's Assistant, 24*(2), 87–91.

Mellors, R. C. (2001). VI. Other nonneoplastic disorders of bone, the Cornell Medical Center. Retrieved from http://edcenter.med.cornell.edu/CUMC_PathNotes/Skeletal/Bone_06.html

Methodist Health Care System. (2001). What is fibrous dysplasia? Retrieved from http://www.methodisthealth.com/bone/fibrdys.htm

National Institutes of Health, Osteoporosis and Related Bone Diseases National Resource Center. (2001). Facts on fibrous dysplasia. Retrieved from http://www.osteo.org/fibdys.html

Paget Foundation. (2001). Fibrous dysplasia support online. Retrieved from http://members.aol.com/fdsupport/FAQresp1.html

Papadakis, C. E., Skoulakis, C. E., Prokopakis, E. P., Bizakis, N. J. G., Velegrakis, A., & Helidonis, E. S. (2000). Fibrous dysplasia of the temporal bone: Report of a case and a review of its characteristics. *Ear, Nose, and Throat Journal, 79*(1) 52–63.

Abbey-Robin Durkin
University of Colorado

DYSPLASTIC NEVUS SYNDROME

Dysplastic nevus syndrome is also known as B-K mole syndrome, atypical mole syndrome, or familial atypical mole-melanoma syndrome. The U.S. National Institutes of Health prefers the latter term and defines the condition in its 1992 "Melanoma: Consensus Statement" as the "(1) occurrence of melanoma in one or more first or second degree relatives, (2) large numbers of moles, often greater than 50, some of which are atypical and often vary in size, and (3) moles that demonstrate certain distinct histologic features." However, the semantics and definition of this disease are some of the most controversial and hotly debated issues in dermatology (Weber, 1997). The syndrome has been traced to an autosomal dominant allele mode of transmission (Turkington, 1996). In addition to genotypic diathesis, the actual display of the syndrome may occur during puberty under the influence of provoking conditions such as solar radiation, hormones, and altered host immunity (Ceballos, Ruiz-Maldonado, & Mihm, 1995).

In White populations the prevalence of atypical moles (dysplastic nevi) has been reported to be between 5% and 10%, and it can be assumed that people with less tolerance to light and ultraviolet radiation have a greater incidence of the disorder. Although no data are currently available to differentiate the prevalence in different ethnicities, those with the phenotypic traits of fair complexion, blond or red hair, or light-color eyes are at an increased risk (Marghoob, 1999).

Characteristics

1. More than 50 atypical moles
2. Many moles greater than 5 mm in diameter
3. Moles containing multiple and varied shades of tan, brown, black, red, and pink
4. Irregular edges of mole that blend into surrounding skin
5. Family members with the condition

The major concern for the patient with dysplastic nevus syndrome is the possibility of developing malignant melanomas with the risk of the moles developing into life-threatening melanomas 2–8 times greater than that of the general population (Weber, 1997). A patient with the condition and two or more primary family members with malignant melanomas has an almost 100% chance of developing the cancer as well because of the gene's dominance. Even if the patient does not have parents with melanomas, he or she still is at a higher risk of developing them than is the general population of developing them (Turkington, 1996). Dysplastic nevi melanoma has been documented as early as age 10, and others may manifest atypical moles by early adolescence after exhibiting an abundance of common nevi by age 5 or 6 (Ceballos et al., 1995).

Early detection and treatment of melanomas that may develop from the dysplastic nevi ensure an almost 100% cure rate, but that prognosis diminishes if the nevi are not discovered and treated before the cancer advances (Marghoob, 1999). The best method for identifying potential cancerous nevi is frequent, regular (4–6 months), total-body examinations by an experienced dermatologist beginning around puberty; baseline total body photographs; instructions for self-examinations; a thorough family history for melanomas and moles; sun-exposure reduction; and biopsy of any moles that may be suspicious for malignant melanoma. Studies have shown that sampling of melanomas by small biopsies does not spread cells into the bloodstream to any greater extent than does sampling melanomas by large-margin excisions (Weber, 1997). Patients with dysplastic nevus syndrome are reported to be at increased risk for ocular nevi and melanomas; therefore, they should ensure routine ophthalmologic examinations (Marghoob, 1999).

If the biopsy determines a diagnosis of "moderate" or "severe" atypical features, surgical removal of the mole remnant with a margin is recommended; however, if the mole is diagnosed as being "mild" atypical and is in an area the patient can readily view, the mole can be "watched" by the patient if preferred (Weber, 1997). Surgical removal of dysplastic nevi that develop into melanomas is advised, but prophylactic excision of all atypical nevi is not recommended (Marghoob, 1999).

Although dysplastic nevus syndrome may not be physically debilitating, it may cause anxiety among children. With the uncontrolled appearance of dozens of moles over the body, children may feel embarrassed in public or have social anxiety around peers. There are no reports of direct impact on intelligence, school work, or behavior.

Research is continuing to discover a more complete genetic basis for dysplastic nevus syndrome, and advances in digital imaging, scanning computers, and three-dimensional analysis show promise in creating better body maps of dysplastic nevi (Weber, 1997).

REFERENCES

Ceballos, P., Ruiz-Maldonado, R., & Mihm, M., Jr. (1995, March 9). Melanoma in children. *New England Journal of Medicine, 332*(10), 658–659.

Marghoob, A. (1999). The dangers of atypical mole (dysplastic nevus) syndrome. *Postgraduate Medicine, 105*(7). Retrieved from http://www.postgraduate.com/issues/1999/06_99/marghoob.htm

Turkington, C. (1996). *Skin deep: An A-Z of skin disorders, treatments, and health.* New York: Facts on File.

Weber, P. (1997). Atypical mole–dysplastic nevus. Retrieved from http://www.skincancerinfo.com/sectionf/atypical mole.html

Matthew Rioth
University of Colorado at Colorado Springs

DYSTHYMIA

Dysthymia is one of the predominant types of depressive disorders in children and adolescents. It is an affective disorder characterized by chronically depressed mood (or irritable mood) that occurs most of the time for at least one year (American Psychiatric Association [APA], 1994). In differentiating dysthymia from major depressive disorder, the mood disturbance in dysthymia is typically less severe, lasts longer, and may not remit (Stark, Bronik, Wong, Wells, & Ostrander, 2000). Additionally, dysthymia is thought to have an earlier onset than major depressive disorder (Kovacs, Akiskal, Gatsonis, & Parrone, 1994).

The prevalence of dysthymia in the general population of the United States is approximately 3%, and it occurs equally in males and females in childhood (APA, 1994). Average age of onset ranges from 6 to 13 years. It is reported to be more common among first-degree biological relatives with major depression.

Characteristics (adapted from APA, 1994)

1. Minimum 1-year history of chronic depressed (or irritable) mood for much of the day, more days than not. Mood disturbances are difficult to distinguish from the child's typical functioning. The child's depressed mood

is considered less severe than that characterizing major depressive disorder.

2. At least two of the following symptoms must be present: (a) poor appetite or overeating, (b) sleep disturbances (insomnia or hypersomnia), (c) low energy or fatigue, (d) low self-esteem and self-deprecation, (e) poor concentration or difficulty making decisions, (f) feelings of hopelessness or pessimism.
3. Associated characteristics include poor social skills, irritability, and anger.
4. Relief from depressive symptoms do not last longer than 2 months at a time.
5. Exclusionary criteria include major depressive episode, manic episode, hypomanic episode, or symptoms due primarily to substance abuse, medication, or medical condition.
6. Accompanied by impairment in social or academic functioning.

A variety of psychosocial treatment approaches have been documented in the literature, including psychoeducational, psychodynamic, cognitive-behavioral, and family systems interventions. Outcome data suggest that cognitive-behavioral approaches are the most thoroughly evaluated and most promising interventions in the treatment of childhood depression (Harrington, Whittaker, & Shoebridge, 1998). Clinical practice typically combines psychosocial treatment with pharmacological interventions. Although antidepressants are commonly used in the treatment of childhood depression, to date there is a lack of well-controlled studies documenting their efficacy (Stark et al., 2000).

Children with dysthymia may qualify for special education services under the category Serious Emotional Disturbance. Because dysthymia is associated with higher than average rates of academic failure (Keller, 1994), these children may also qualify for special education services under the category Specific Learning Disability. Impaired social interaction skills are a prominent characteristic of dysthymia, so social skills training may be one component of the special education services that these children require. Additionally, the presence of depression is one of the risk factors in suicide attempts among youth, so these children should be appropriately monitored in school settings.

The majority of children diagnosed with dysthymia (onset occurs before age 21) are likely to develop major depressive episodes, with a median duration of 5 years before onset (Kovacs et al., 1994). Children with dysthymia also are at greater risk for recurrent major depression, bipolar disorder, and other affective illnesses (Keller, 1994; Kovacs et al., 1994). Comorbidity rates are high for a variety of disorders, the predominant ones being anxiety disorders and disruptive behavior disorders. There is considerable need for further empirical research on the effective treatment of dysthymia and other depressive disorders specific to children and adolescents as well as research highlighting the comparative efficacy of specific therapeutic and pharmacological interventions.

REFERENCES

American Psychiatric Association. (1994). *Diagnostic and statistical manual of mental disorders* (4th ed.). Washington, DC: Author.

Harrington, R., Whittaker, J., & Shoebridge, P. (1998). Psychological treatment of depression in children and adolescents: A review of treatment research. *British Journal of Psychiatry, 173,* 291–298.

Keller, M. B. (1994). Dysthymia in clinical practice: Course, outcome and impact on the community. *Acta Psychiatrica Scandinavica, 89*(Suppl. 383), 24–34.

Kovacs, M., Akiskal, H. S., Gatsonis, C., & Parrone, P. L. (1994). Childhood-onset dysthymic disorder: Clinical features and prospective naturalistic outcome. *Archives of General Psychiatry, 51,* 365–374.

Stark, K. D., Bronik, M. D., Wong, S., Wells, G., & Ostrander, R. (2000). Depressive disorders. In M. Hersen & R. T. Ammerman (Eds.), *Advanced abnormal child psychology* (2nd ed., pp. 291–326). Mahwah, NJ: Erlbaum.

Lora Tuesday Heathfield
University of Utah

DYSTONIA

Dystonia is a neurologic movement disorder characterized by sustained muscle contractions that frequently cause twisting or repetitive movements and abnormal, sometimes painful, postures or positions. This disorder may involve any voluntary muscle in the body. Defined as a syndrome of sustained muscle contractions, dystonia encompasses motor syndromes that vary as a function of age of onset, cause, and body distribution (King, Tsui, & Calne, 1995). The symptoms of dystonia may begin during early childhood, in adolescence, or during adulthood. Dystonia may frequently be misdiagnosed or confused with other disorders. The diagnosis may be missed as the movements and resulting postures are often unusual and the condition is rare. The exact prevalence of dystonia in the general population is not known; however, an estimate of 330 cases per million has been made (King et al., 1995).

Characteristics

1. Movement is characterized by an excess of involuntary muscle activity (Rothwell, 1995).

2. Childhood dystonia often presents as abnormal foot inversions, awkward gait, and contractions of many different muscle groups and may involve one or more limbs of the proximal or distal muscle groups.
3. Dystonic movements tend to increase with fatigue, stress, and emotional states; they tend to be suppressed with relaxation, hypnosis, and sleep.
4. Dystonia is usually present continually throughout the day whenever the affected body part is in use and disappears with deep sleep.
5. Common misdiagnoses are clubfoot, scoliosis, stress, and psychogenic disorder.
6. Pain is common in some individuals.

Although dystonia has no cure, there are successful treatments that greatly reduce the symptoms and restore individuals to many daily living activities. The first step in treatment is attempting to determine the cause of the dystonia. Dystonia is classified as being primary or idiopathic, in which there is no known organic lesion, but is believed to be hereditary and to occur as the result of a faulty genes (King et al., 1995). It is also classified as being secondary, which generally arises from some insult to the basal ganglia of the central nervous system such as trauma, toxins, drugs, neoplasm, or infarction; another underlying disease process such as Wilson disease, multiple sclerosis, or stroke; or as a result of the use of certain neuroleptic or antipsychotic drugs. For secondary dystonias, treating the underlying cause may improve the dystonia. For instance, treatments for neurological conditions such as multiple sclerosis may reduce dystonic symptoms. Withdrawing or reducing neuroleptic drugs leads to slow improvement in some cases.

There are three main approaches to the treatment of primary dystonia: drug therapy, injections of therapeutic agents (botulinum toxin) directly into dystonic muscle, and surgery (Greene & Fahn, 1992). Drug therapy may include benzodiazepines, which are a class of drugs that interfere with chemical activities in the nervous system and brain, serving to reduce communication between nerve cells; baclofen, which is a drug that is used to treat individuals with spasticity; and anticholinergics, which block the action of the neurotransmitter acetylcholine, thereby deactivating muscle contractions (King et al., 1995). Surgical intervention may be considered in those individuals with severe dystonia who have not responded or have become nonresponders to drug therapy. The goal of surgery for individuals with dystonia is to attempt to rebalance movement and posture control by destroying specific regions in the brain (King et al., 1995).

Special education services may be available to children with dystonia under the handicapping condition of Other Health Impairment or Physical Disability. Movement problems usually start on the lower limbs and can progress to other parts of the body. At times they may then reach a plateau. Therefore, input from a physical therapist may be required to provide advice, monitoring, and exercises. An occupational therapist may be necessary to identify areas of concern in regard to work, play, and self-care. Speech therapy is often warranted and varies depending on the type of dystonia. A therapy program is then designed to meet individual needs, and information can be provided to the child and family about ways to promote optimal communication. Due to extensive medical intervention, school absences may require home schooling or tutoring by a special educator. Counseling services may be appropriate due to the psychosocial aspects of the physical distortions caused by muscular contractions. Finally, for the dystonic child, most all life activities take longer; this and the effect of the medication may cause fatigue. Consequently, it is important to have realistic expectations of the child's physical performance. The overall goal should be to foster a feeling of successful achievement, emphasizing the activities that children can accomplish rather than focusing on their limitations.

Research evaluating the ideology and a potential cure for dystonia has begun. Some professionals research the effects of dystonia such as the short- and long-term outcomes for afflicted children. Will the child's abilities decline over time? Will there be some psychosocial problems? What is the appropriate educational placement for children with dystonia? Reflecting on the implications of this disorder, these simple questions need further empirical study before clear answers can be provided.

REFERENCES

Greene, P. E., & Fahn, S. (1992). Baclofen in the treatment of idiopathic dystonia in children. *Movement Disorders, 7,* 48–52.

King, J., Tsui, C., & Calne, D. B. (1995). *Handbook of dystonia.* New York: Marcel Dekker.

Rothwell, J. C. (1995). *The physiology of dystonia.* New York: Marcel Dekker.

Kendra J. Bjoraker
University of Northern Colorado
The Kennedy Krieger Institute—The Johns Hopkins University School of Medicine

DYSTONIA MUSCULORUM DEFORMANS

Dystonia musculorum deformans is a disease of muscle torsion and posturing that affects children between the ages of 5 and 15. The disease first affects the feet and legs. In adolescents the symptoms tend to start in the hands and arms, sometimes resembling writer's cramp. At early onset children may gaitor prance. This is a common occurrence among children in the early stages of this disorder, and it may be one of the first signs that is noticed. Some children are more skillful at walking backward than forward during the early onset of the disease. As the symptoms progress the torsion posturing becomes more rigid and severe. Because of the nature of the torsions, the name dystonia has recently been supplanted by idiopathic torsion dystonia. Dystonic posturing may also occur in Wilson's disease, Huntington's disease, and Parkinsonism, so differential diagnosis is essential.

Idiopathic torsion dystonia is predominantly inherited in an autosomal-dominant mode. This means that the gene responsible is not a sex gene and does not influence gender dominance. The gene for dystonia is confined to a small region on Chromosome 9q32-34 (Swaiman, 1994). The population most affected is the Ashkenazi Jews: 1 in 20,000 are affected in this population. The non-Jewish community can also be affected.

Characteristics

1. Bizarre twisting movements are briefly held in an extremely unnatural posture.
2. Axial muscles are often more severely impaired than are limb muscles; however, the dystonia often first manifests in appendicular muscles.
3. There is a peculiar dancing or prancing gait.
4. The disease often progresses rapidly.
5. In some cases the disease can affect the whole body, which could result in the child's being confined to a wheelchair.
6. The disorder is generally accentuated by fatigue or emotional stress and dissipates with sleep.
7. In most cases childhood dystonia is either symptomatic or genetically determined (Swaiman, 1994).

Treatments for dystonia are limited. Drugs such as trihexyphenidyl (which works to relax the muscle tissue and the parasympathetic nervous system) are sometimes helpful. Side effects include drowsiness, dry mouth, blurred vision, dizziness, constipation, difficulty with urination, and tremor, especially in older people. Injections of botulin (a bacterial toxin that paralyzes muscles) into the overactive muscles have been the most effective treatments.

Special education services may be required for the children with the most severe cases of dystonia due to medical issues precluding school attendance, pain management, and medication side effects. Children with severe cases may be confined to a wheelchair and need special assistance in terms of accessibility, adapted physical education, and basic day-to-day tasks. For the most part these children are of average to above average intelligence and should not require special education unless their illness keeps them out of school for a period of time. Many children would benefit from counseling to help them deal with chronic illness issues and potential social side effects of the disease

Children who develop the disease early are more likely to have more severe symptoms than are those who develop it in adolescence or in later life. For early onset they could develop symptoms as severe as being confined to a wheelchair. For adolescents the prognosis is not that severe, and researchers are working on a medication called dopa-responsive dystonia to control some of the symptoms. It is thought that with dopa-responsive dystonia a new SPECT ligand binds to the presynaptic dopamine transporter (O'Sullivan, Costa, Svetislav, & Lees, 2001). This testing is still new, but so far the treatment does indicate having positive results.

REFERENCES

O'Sullivan, J. D., Costa, C. C., Svetislav, G., & Lees, A. J. (2001, January). SPECT imaging of the dopamine transporter in juvenile-onset dystonia. *Neurology, 56,* 266–267.

Swaiman, K. F. (1994). *Pediatric neurology: Principles and practice* (Vol. 2). St. Louis, MO: Mosby.

Tricia Swan
University of Colorado at Colorado Springs

E

ECHOLALIA

Echolalia is defined as the spontaneous repetition of words or phrases spoken by another person. The repetition, or echo, of verbal utterances can be either immediate or delayed. Although echolalia may occur to some degree in young children as a normal process of speech development, its presence is generally symptomatic of a functional disorder if occurring after the age of 2 1/2 to 3 years old (Roberts, 1989).

Echolalia is most commonly identified as a key feature in the language pattern of verbal children with autism; it occurs in approximately 75% of this group (Roberts, 1989; Violette & Swisher, 1992). Although echolalia can also be a symptom of schizophrenia, tic disorders such as Tourette's syndrome, mental retardation, and receptive language disorders, prevalence rates have not yet been established. Regardless of diagnosis, research suggests that echolalia is higher in stressful situations, such as exposure to unfamiliar settings and unfamiliar persons (Charlop, 1986). Additionally, the frequency of echolalic responses has been shown to decrease as an autistic child gains language skills (Howlin, 1982).

Characteristics

1. Echolalia is defined as a spontaneous repetition of words or phrases spoken by another person.
2. The repetition, or echo, can be either immediate or delayed.
3. Echolalia is commonly identified as a key feature in the language pattern of verbal children with autism.
4. Echolalia may be an element of schizophrenia, tic disorders such as Tourette's syndrome, mental retardation, and receptive language disorders.
5. Stressful situations, such as exposure to unfamiliar settings and unfamiliar persons, usually exacerbates the disorder.
6. The frequency of echolalic responses generally decreases with increased language skills.

The early literature described echolalia primarily as a meaningless repetition of words or phrases without comprehension. It was believed to interfere with the acquisition of language and social skills. Beginning in the 1970s, some researchers challenged this notion and began to explore the possible function of echolalia (Howlin, 1982; McEvoy, Loveland & Landry, 1988). The results of this research suggested that echolalia may serve as a strategy for acquiring both language and social skills (Leung, 1997; McEvoy et al., 1988). Techniques utilizing echolalia have been effective in the teaching of language skills (Huntley & Hayes, 1994). These include operant techniques, incorporation of echoic responses, and the teaching of a generalized response. For example, in using operant techniques to enhance language skills and decrease echolalia, a child's echoic responses to a trainer are initially reinforced. When a high degree of imitation is established, the trainer begins to present pictures or objects with the verbalizations. Eventually the child responds to the visual stimuli alone, and the level of echolalic responses decreases.

As echolalia is usually an aspect of pervasive developmental disorders and receptive language disorders, children with echolalia are likely to qualify for special education services under the classification of a Speech Communication/Language Disorder or Other Health Impairment. Referencing instructional style and the educational environment, research has yielded clues as to how teachers can be most effective in working with children with echolalia. Creating routines and utilizing instructional consistency appears to be important in minimizing stress and anxiety, thus eliminating an exacerbation of the echolalia. Teachers need to have the awareness and skill to adjust their instructional styles depending on the goals that are established for each individual child. Meeting the goals of some children will likely require a teacher to use a very directive verbal style, whereas it may be more effective to take a less controlled and more responsive style in meeting the needs of other children (Rydell & Mirenda, 1991).

Many questions remain as to the influence of various factors, such as environment and cognitive processing abilities, on echolalia. More research in the areas of communication, social relatedness, and cognitive processing of children with pervasive developmental disorders and receptive language disorders is necessary to understand the role echolalia plays in the acquisition of language and social skills.

REFERENCES

Charlop, M. (1986). Setting effects on the occurrence of autistic children's immediate echolalia. *Journal of Autism and Developmental Disorders, 16*(4), 273–283.

Howlin, P. (1982). Echolalic and spontaneous phrase speech in autistic children. *Journal of Child Psychology and Psychiatry, 23,* 281–293.

Huntley, K., & Hayes, L. (1994). Using a generalized verbal response to decrease unrelated verbal responses of a severely retarded adult. *Psychological Record, 44*(3), 369–382.

Leung, J. (1997). Teaching receptive naming of Chinese characters to children with autism by incorporating echolalia. *Journal of Applied Behavior Analysis, 30,* 59–68.

McEvoy, R., Loveland, K., & Landry, S. (1988). The functions of immediate echolalia in autistic children: A developmental perspective. *Journal of Autism and Developmental Disorders, 18*(4), 657–668.

Roberts, J. (1989). Echolalia and comprehension on autistic children. *Journal of Autism and Developmental Disorders, 19*(2), 271–281.

Rydell, P., & Mirenda, P. (1991). The effects of two levels of linguistic constraint on echolalia and generative language production in children with autism. *Journal of Autism and Developmental Disorders, 21*(2), 131–157.

Violette, J., & Swisher, L. (1992). Echolalic resources by a child with autism to four experimental conditions of sociolinguistic input. *Journal of Speech and Hearing Research, 35,* 139–147.

Elizabeth I. Fassig
Brian D. Johnson
University of Northern Colorado

ECHOPRAXIA

Echopraxia is defined as the involuntary and spasmodic imitation of movements made by another person (Goodwin, 1989). The imitation or repetition of body movements characteristic of echopraxia may be concomitant with a variety of disorders. Echopraxia serves as a diagnostic marker for specific developmental, psychiatric, and neurological disorders because of the frequent incidence of involuntary movement or gesture imitation associated with certain disorders. Echopraxic behavior is often a symptom of the low-incidence disorders of autism (Malvy et al., 1999), childhood schizophrenia (Schopler & Sloan, 2000), and Tourette syndrome (National Institute of Neurological Disorders and Stroke, 2000).

The imitative motor movements of a child with Tourette syndrome may represent one of the most common manifestations of echopraxia. The atypical gesture imitation of a child with autism or childhood schizophrenia with catatonic symptoms is also considered to be a type of echopraxia. Although no specific prevalence estimate is currently available for echopraxia as an isolated characteristic, the concomitant occurrence of echopraxia with childhood onset disorders underscores the importance of a clear understanding of this trait.

Characteristics

1. The child displays automatic imitation of another person's movements or gestures (e.g., scratching head or raising hand in air).
2. The imitation appears to be involuntary and occurs across a variety of settings and situations.
3. The child does not appear able to alter echopraxic behavior successfully despite frequent redirection and intervention attempts.
4. Periods of heightened anxiety and stress may result in more frequent occurrence.
5. Child may display additional behaviors and mannerisms that interfere with daily functioning (e.g., vocal tics or echolalic speech).

The neural mechanisms involved with echopraxia seem to differ from true voluntary imitation. In contrast to the involuntary and spasmodic nature of echopraxia, voluntary imitation usually represents a developmental milestone that is associated with typical growth and development (Stevenson, 1987; Rhodes, 2000). Echopraxia is also different from mirrored movements. The phenomenon of mirrored movements is observed when the simultaneous identical movement of one hand accompanies the voluntary movement of the other hand. Mirrored movements may be the result of a developmental delay in inhibition rather than a deficit in inhibition resulting in echopraxia (Stevenson, 1987; Rhodes, 2000).

A deficit in inhibition resulting in echopraxia may also be seen in individuals with frontal lobe lesions (Neurology and Neurosurgery Forum, 1997). Lesions in the frontal lobe may damage the regulatory system that assists an individual in deciding whether his or her body should move in response to stimuli or whether body movements should be inhibited. As a result, individuals with frontal lobe lesions and corresponding deficits in inhibition may move involuntarily in response to external movements or gestures.

The treatment of echopraxia is typically focused on the alleviation of symptoms through a regimen of behavioral interventions and medication. Depending on the severity of symptoms, children with Tourette syndrome, for example, may benefit from neuroleptic and antihypertensive medication in addition to biofeedback and behavioral interventions.

Special education services are typically available to children with echopraxia under the disability categories of Autism, Other Health Impairment, Physical Disability, or Emotional/Behavioral Disability. Through the child's Individualized Education Plan (IEP), a prescriptive intervention plan is established that consistently implements behavioral interventions and modifications for motor-based tasks or assignments. The unusual behaviors associated with echopraxia and resulting social considerations may also be addressed through emotional-behavioral support for the child as well as peer education and sensitivity training.

There is currently no known cure for many of the disorders with which echopraxia is associated. Increased use of biofeedback and behavioral interventions in combination with advances in medicine may further assist individuals with echopraxia to control the involuntary symptoms that they experience.

REFERENCES

Goodwin, D. M. (1989). *A dictionary of neuropsychology.* New York: Springer.

Malvy, J., Roux, S., Zakian, A., Debuly, S., Sauvage, D., & Barthelemy, C. (1999). A brief clinical scale for the early evaluation of imitation disorders in autism. *Autism, 3*(4), 357–369.

National Institute of Neurological Disorders and Stroke. (2000, August 1). Tourette syndrome. Retrieved from http://www.ninds.nih.gov/health_and_medical/disorders/tourette.htm

Neurology and Neurosurgery Forum (1997, June 9). Instantaneous dexterous reflex. Retrieved from http://medhlp.netusa.net/per16/neuro/archive/574.html

Rhodes, R. L. (2000). Echopraxia. In C. R. Reynolds & E. Fletcher-Janzen (Eds.), *Encyclopedia of special education* (2nd ed.). New York: Wiley.

Schopler, E., & Sloan, J. L. (2000). Childhood schizophrenia. In C. R. Reynolds & E. Fletcher-Janzen (Eds.), *Encyclopedia of special education* (2nd ed.). New York: Wiley.

Stevenson, R. J. (1987). Echopraxia. In C. R. Reynolds & L. Mann (Eds.), *Encyclopedia of special education.* New York: Wiley.

Robert L. Rhodes
New Mexico State University

ECSTASY ABUSE

Ecstasy (3,4-methylenedioxymethamphetamine, or MDMA) is a popular party drug that has a chemical structure similar to amphetamine and mescaline, a hallucinogen (McCann, Mertl, & Ricaurte, 1998). Ecstasy belongs to a group of drugs known collectively as "club drugs" because they are frequently used at dance clubs and all-night dance parties called raves (Stocker, 2000). Ecstasy is typically sold on the street in pill form and is ingested orally. It is also sold as a powder that can be snorted, smoked, or injected. Street names besides ecstasy include "XTC," "clarity," "essence," "Adam," and "X" (National Institute on Drug Abuse [NIDA], 1999).

Ecstasy results in a high by stimulating the release of the neurotransmitter serotonin in the neurons (NIDA, 1999). Serotonin plays a direct role in regulating mood, aggression, sleep, sexual activity, and sensitivity to pain (NIDA, 2001). Ecstasy use can result in both psychedelic and stimulant effects that can last from several minutes to an hour. Users report feelings of peacefulness, empathy, and acceptance, as well as an enhanced sense of pleasure, self-confidence, and increased energy. In addition, ecstasy can result in feelings of closeness with others and a desire to touch them. The effects related to intimacy and trust have led some clinicians to suggest that ecstasy has some potential value as a psychotherapeutic agent. However, the federal government has classified ecstasy as a drug with *no* accepted medical use (NIDA, 1999).

Research examining general drug use trends among America's youth indicates that use remained relatively stable over the last two years, except for ecstasy and steroids. For these drugs, increases were observed across grade levels. For 8th graders, past-year use of ecstasy increased from 1.7% in 1999 to 3.1% in 2000. For 10th graders, the increase was from 4.4% to 5.4%; and for 12th graders, past-year use rose from 5.6% in 1999 to 8.2% in 2000. Reported use is significantly higher among White and Hispanic students than among African Americans. Data for adolescents indicate that 7.6% of Whites and 10.6% of Hispanics reported using ecstasy in 2000, whereas only 1.3% of African Americans reported using the drug during the same year (NIDA, 2001).

Short-Term effects

1. Euphoria
2. Elevated self-confidence
3. Heightened sensory awareness
4. Increased feelings of empathy and closeness with others
5. Decreased appetite
6. Elevated anxiety and paranoia
7. Increased heart rate and blood pressure
8. Dizziness and confusion
9. Chills, sweating, faintness, and vomiting
10. Malignant hyperthermia
11. An acne-like rash

Ecstasy's rewarding and negative effects vary with the dose and purity of the drug, the environment in which it is taken, and the individual user (NIDA, 1999). Both short- and long-term use of ecstasy can result in a variety of adverse, long-lasting effects (NIDA, 2001).

Long-Term Effects

1. Panic disorder
2. Psychosis

3. Flashbacks
4. Major depressive disorder
5. Addiction
6. Brain damage

Chronic use of ecstasy has been found to harm brain neurons that release serotonin, which can result in persistent cognitive disturbances and memory problems (Mathias, 1999). Ecstasy may also cause degeneration of neurons containing the neurotransmitter dopamine. Damage to these neurons can cause motor disturbances (NIDA, 2001). A number of ecstasy-related deaths have also been reported. The stimulant effects of ecstasy can enable the user to dance for long periods, and often the end result is dehydration, hyperthermia, and heart or kidney failure (NIDA, 1999).

Most students who use ecstasy will not qualify for special education services, although psychological services may be warranted.

With the increase in the use of ecstasy and other club drugs, NIDA recently announced an increase of 40% in its funding for research on club drugs. NIDA has also joined a multimedia campaign with other national organizations to educate the public about the dangers of these drugs (NIDA, 1999). Future research is also focusing on determining more specifically the extent of long-term negative effects that result from ecstasy use, as well as evaluating the efficacy of various prevention programs and therapeutic interventions.

REFERENCES

Mathias, R. (1999). "Ecstasy" damages the brain and impairs memory in humans. Retrieved from http://165.112.78.61/NIDA_Notes/NNVol14N4/Ecstasy.html

McCann, U. D., Mertl, M., & Ricaurte, G. A. (1998). Ecstasy. In R. E. Tarter, R. T. Ammerman, & P. J. Ott (Eds.), *Handbook of substance abuse: Neurobehavioral pharmacology* (pp. 567–577). New York: Plenum Press.

National Institute on Drug Abuse. (1999). Facts about MDMA (ecstasy). Retrieved from http://165.112.78.61/NIDA_Notes/NNVol14N4/tearoff.html

National Institute on Drug Abuse. (2001). MDMA (ecstasy). Retrieved from http://www.drugabuse.gov/Infofax/ecstasy.html.

Stocker, S. (2000). Overall teen drug use stays level, use of MDMA and steroids increases. Retrieved from http://www.drugabuse.gov/NIDA_Notes/NNVol15N1/Overall.html.

M. Franci Crepeau-Hobson
University of Northern Colorado

ECTODERMAL DYSPLASIA

Ectodermal dysplasia refers to a group of genetic disorders that involve abnormalities in the layer of cells known as the ectoderm. During prenatal development, the ectoderm is the outer layer of cells in the fetus that grow into the skin, hair, nails, teeth, nerve cells, sweat glands, and parts of the ear, eye, and other organs (National Foundation for Ectodermal Dysplasias [NFED] Scientific Advisory Board, 2000). The prevalence of ectodermal dysplasias of all types is estimated to be as high as 7 of every 10,000 births (NFED Scientific Advisory Board, 2000).

Different forms of ectodermal dysplasia are evidenced by different constellations of the characteristics. Most forms of ectodermal dysplasia involve at least two of the characteristics listed here.

Characteristics

1. Fair skin, skin rashes (especially severe diaper rash in infants), extremely dry skin
2. Frequent high fevers, inability or diminished ability to sweat, very low heat tolerance
3. Absent or very sparse and fine scalp hair; absence of eyebrows, eyelashes, and other body hair
4. Thin, ridged, cracked, brittle, small, or poorly developed nails
5. Eruption of some or all teeth delayed or absent, malformed teeth, widely spaced teeth, excessive tooth decay
6. Underproduction of bodily fluids such as tears and saliva
7. Hearing or vision loss
8. Cleft lip or cleft palette

Ectodermal dysplasia is caused by a gene mutation that is inherited or a new mutation that occurs during fetal development. Some types of ectodermal dysplasias are sex-linked and occur more often in males, whereas others are transmitted on autosomal chromosomes and occur equally frequently in both genders (NFED Scientific Advisory Board, 1999).

Treatment for ectodermal dysplasia is palliative and aimed at the constellation of characteristics evident in the individual affected. Moisturizing ointments and sunscreens are used to prevent damage to the skin. Missing teeth are replaced by bridges, dentures, or implants. Avoiding excessive heat, taking cool baths, and intaking fluids is recommended for those with a decreased ability to sweat. Lubricating eyedrops and saliva substitutes should be used by those with decreased tear and saliva production. In cases of ectodermal dysplasia that result in cleft lip or palette, corrective surgery is available (NFED Scientific Advisory Board, 2000).

Ectodermal dysplasia is not associated with deficits in intelligence or developmental delays (NFED Scientific Advisory Board, 1999). Some classroom modifications may be needed for those individuals with inadequate sweat production (such as an air-conditioned classrooms or removal of physical education requirements). Children with ectodermal dysplasia are eligible for needed modifications under the Other Health Impairment handicapping condition. In those cases where cleft lip or cleft palette is involved or where hearing loss develops, children may qualify for special education services, in particular speech therapy. Children with ectodermal dysplasia differ in appearance from most other children and may suffer adjustment problems in school if they are ridiculed or ostracized by others as a result of their appearance. Teachers and school administrators should take whatever steps are necessary to prevent this behavior toward affected children.

Ectodermal dysplasia is not a progressive disorder. The life spans of affected individuals tend to be normal (NFED Scientific Advisory Board, 2000). Genetic counseling may be helpful to those with ectodermal dysplasia or with a family history of it in order to determine their risks of transmitting the disorder to their progeny. Recent research has isolated the gene for one common type of ectodermal dysplasia (NFED Scientific Advisory Board, 2000). Researchers are also working to determine what protein or enzyme deficiency is responsible for ectodermal dysplasia in order to develop treatments that address the root cause of the disorder (NFED Scientific Advisory Board, 2000).

REFERENCES

National Foundation for Ectodermal Dysplasias Scientific Advisory Board. (2000). *A family guide to the ectodermal dysplasias.* Mascoutah, IL: National Foundation for Ectodermal Dysplasias.

National Foundation for Ectodermal Dysplasias Scientific Advisory Board. (1999). *The multi-syndrome guide to the ectodermal dysplasias.* Mascoutah, IL: National Foundation for Ectodermal Dysplasias.

Nancy K. Scammacca
University of Texas at Austin

See also APECED Syndrome; Hypohidrotic Ectodermal Dysplasia; Rapp-Hodgkin Syndrome

ECTRODACTALY ECTODERMAL DYSPLASIA (EEC SYNDROME)

Ectrodactyly ectodermal dysplasia is a rare form of ectodermal dysplasia involving missing or webbed fingers and/or toes, cleft lip and/or palate, and abnormalities of the eyes and urinary tract in addition to the aberrations normally present with ectodermal dysplasia, such as usually dry hair, light colored and sparse eyebrows, dry skin, and missing teeth or teeth lacking enamel. Ectodermal dysplasias are a group of inherited syndromes derived from the ectodermal germ layer.

EEC syndrome is a rare autosomal dominant genetic trait in which symptoms vary greatly. Prevalence is unknown, and treatment is symptomatic. Surgery can be performed to correct abnormalities of the fingers and toes as well as cleft palate and lip. Families dealing with children with EEC syndrome could benefit from genetic counseling. Overall, a team of specialists is required to manage the treatment and amelioration of complications associated with this disorder. With the aid of this multidisciplinary team, children affected with ectrodactyly ectodermal dysplasia can lead long lives.

Characteristics

1. The individual has missing or irregular fingers and/or toes, commonly seen in the third digit.
2. There are abnormalities of the eyes in which the glands needed to allow tears to escape and to secrete fluid onto the back of the eyelid are absent, triggering frequent eye infections as well as vision problems.
3. Cleft palate and cleft lip are common; however, if these conditions are not present, an underdeveloped jaw, broad nose, slanted or widely spaced eyes, and a short groove in the center of the upper lip may still be present.
4. In some cases, an obstructed tube carrying urine from the kidney into the bladder causes kidney and pelvis inflammation. A deleted or duplicate kidney has been documented in some cases.

Special education issues also vary greatly among these children. Although some children present with mental retardation, many cases of normal mental functioning have been documented. However, even if mental deficits are not present, remediation may become necessary in children who present with hearing loss, speech difficulties, and visual impairment or loss, all of which are commonly found in children with EEC syndrome.

Prognosis is generally good, but symptomology varies greatly between cases. Individualized assessment on a case-by-case basis is necessary. The most serious complication of EEC syndrome is kidney difficulties, but even these can be treated effectively. Future research includes genetic mapping in an attempt to find a cure and more effective treatment.

REFERENCES

Buss, P. W., Hughes, H. E., & Clarke, A. (1995). Twenty-four cases of the EEC syndrome: Clinical presentation and management. *Journal of Medical Genetics, 32*(9), 716–723.

Jones, K. L. (Ed.). (1997). *Smith's recognizable patterns of human malformation* (5th ed.). Philadelphia: W. B. Saunders.

Miller, C. I., Hashimoto, K., Shwayder, T., el-Hoshy, K., & Horton, S. (1997). What syndrome is this? Ectrodactyly, ectodermal dysplasia, and cleft palate (EEC) syndrome. *Pediatric Dermatology, 14*(3), 239–240.

Kimberly M. Estep
University of Houston–Clear Lake

EHLERS-DANLOS SYNDROME

Ehlers-Danlos syndrome (EDS) is not a single, homogeneous disorder, but a group of nine different types of genetically inherited disorders characterized by hyperelastic skin that is fragile and bruises easily, excessive laxity (looseness) of the joints, easily damaged blood vessels, and excessive bleeding (Ainsworth & Aulicino, 2001). The syndrome is caused by abnormal formation of connective tissue due to mutations in collagen genes. Symptoms range from mild to severe within the six most prevalent types of the disorder.

There are three ways in which the various types of EDS can be inherited: The majority are autosomal dominant, but some are autosomal recessive and X-linked recessive inheritance. Carriers of one type of EDS can transmit only that specific type of gene for EDS and thus will not have a child with a type different from their own (Matsen, 2001).

EDS occurs in approximately 1 in 5,000 individuals (Ainsworth & Aulicino, 2001). EDS is most commonly found in Caucasians with European ancestry and in males, although both males and females of all races and ethnic backgrounds can be affected. There are some specific complications that can occur depending on the gender of the individual with EDS. Adolescent males are at particular risk for arterial ruptures, presumably due to defective collagen that is taxed during prepubertal growth spurts (Barabas, 2000). Pregnant females are at risk for miscarriage and premature delivery due to rupture of the uterus or fetal membrane fragility (Beers & Berkow, 1999).

Characteristics

Although nine different types of EDS have been identified, each with a distinctive set of features, the most common forms of EDS (Types I, II, and III) are characterized by phenotypic overlap:

1. Hyperelastic skin
2. Cutaneous fragility (easy to bruise, tear, and excessively scar the skin)
3. Articular hypermobility of joints (the ability to flex joints beyond the "normal" range)
4. Joint dislocation (usually occurring in the shoulders, knees, hips, collar bone, or jaw)
5. Molluscoid pseudotumors (firm, fibrous lumps that develop over elbows and knees or other pressure points)
6. Varicose veins
7. Visual difficulties (usually severe nearsightedness)

The following characteristics are usually found in the rarer forms of EDS:

1. Gum disease (Type VII)
2. Curvature of the spine (Type VI)
3. Blood clotting problems (Type IV)
4. Severe eye complications (Type VI)
5. Pulmonary difficulties (Type IV)
6. Rupture of the intestines, mitral heart valve, or uterus (from pregnancy; Type IV)

Due to the rarity of EDS and the often apparent health of individuals with this syndrome, many physicians are unaware of the symptoms of this disorder and can easily misdiagnose patients (Wilson, 2000). Doctors or other professionals who come into contact with children with EDS may also mistake bruises and torn skin for child abuse. The actual diagnosis of EDS is made based on the patient's family history and skin biopsy to determine the chemical makeup of the individual's connective tissue.

There is no specific treatment for EDS because individual problems must be evaluated and treated accordingly. Due to the extremely fragile skin and tissue of children with EDS, precautions should be taken to prevent injury. Toddlers and young children should be protected from slipping, falling, or overextending their joints by keeping hallways and doorways clear of toys and other objects and avoiding the use of stairs (Matsen, 2001).

Additional precautionary measures such as padding the legs and elbows of children will greatly lessen the chance of accidental trauma, such as scarring and bruising. Physical and occupational therapy may be beneficial in strengthening muscles and in providing information to improve daily living. Unstable joints can be treated with braces. Fragile skin should also be protected with sunscreen to prevent damage. Surgery and sutures of wounds need to be undertaken with great care, as fragile tissues may tear and excessive bleeding can occur due to ruptured blood vessels and arteries (Barabas, 2000; Beers & Berkow, 1999; Pepin, Schwarze, Superti-Furga, & Byers, 2000).

Although EDS does not affect intelligence, children may experience difficulties both emotionally and academically because of absences from school for medical problems. Due to the variety of physical disabilities that are associated with EDS, children with this syndrome can qualify for special education services. Teachers should be made aware of the nature of the illness, with its associated bruising and injuries, as well as the need for any medications that are required for the child. Children with EDS may benefit from psychological services and support groups for children with illnesses to cope with feelings of sadness and alienation. Despite the special considerations and limitations that children with EDS have, it is important that they be allowed to play with friends and be involved in activities in which they can safely participate (Matsen, 2001).

Prognosis depends on the type of EDS from which an individual suffers. People with EDS generally have normal life spans, although life expectancy can be shortened from life-threatening complications that can occur in various types of the syndrome. Examples of potentially fatal complications include failure of surgical wounds to close and rupture of major vessels and organs (Barabas, 2000; Beers & Berkow, 1999; Pepin et al., 2000; Wilson, 2000).

Genetic counseling is recommended for prospective parents with a family history for EDS. Affected parents should be made aware of the type of EDS they have and its mode of inheritance. Information about genetic counseling available in a specific area can be obtained by contacting the March of Dimes or may be determined through a knowledgeable health care provider.

REFERENCES

Ainsworth, S. R., & Aulicino, P. L. (2000, December). A survey of Ehlers-Danlos syndrome: Ehlers-Danlos National Foundation. Retrieved from http://www.ednf.org/articles/survey1.htm

Barabas, A. (2000). Correspondence: Letter to the editor. *New England Journal of Medicine, 343,* 366–368.

Beers, M. H., & Berkow, R. (Eds.), (1999). *The Merck manual of diagnosis and therapy* (17th ed.). Lawrenceville, NJ: Merck.

Matsen, F. (Ed.). (2001). Ehlers-Danlos syndrome. University of Washington: Orthopaedics & Sports Medicine. Retrieved from http://www.orthop.washington.edu/bonejoint/ezzzzzzz1_2.html

Pepin, M., Schwarze, U., Superti-Furga, A., & Byers, P. H. (2000). Clinical and genetic features of Ehlers-Danlos syndrome, type IV, the vascular type. *New England Journal of Medicine, 342,* 673–680.

Wilson, Fred. (2000). Rare Ehlers-Danlos syndrome type IV presents in common patient symptoms. *Dermatology Times.* Retrieved from http://www.findarticles.com

Andrea Holland
University of Texas at Austin

ELECTIVE MUTISM

Elective mutism (also known as selective mutism) is a psychiatric condition occurring primarily during childhood that is characterized by the refusal or failure to speak in specific situations (in school or with classmates) despite speaking in other situations (American Psychiatric Association [APA], 1994). The disorder was previously referred to as "elective mutism," but with the publication of *Diagnostic and Statistical Manual of Mental Disorders–Fourth Edition* the name was changed to emphasize that the resistance to speak is not a volitional act but a behavioral response related to environmental context (Dummit et al., 1997).

The condition is rare, affecting less than 1% of individuals in the United States, and is slightly more common in males than females. Although children with elective mutism generally have normal language skills, they occasionally have associated communication disorders or a medically based articulation problem. The diagnosis of elective mutism may be confirmed by an extensive evaluation to rule out other possible causes, such as a hearing or speech impairment. Cultural factors should also be considered. Immigrant children who may be uncomfortable with or unfamiliar with the social communication norms may be reluctant to speak in social situations, but they should not receive a diagnosis. The diagnosis of elective mutism is appropriate if the child has the *ability* to understand and speak language but does not speak in social situations (APA, 1994).

Characteristics

1. Child fails to speak in specific situations, such as in school or with classmates, although the child has age-appropriate language skills and speaks normally at home.
2. The speaking disturbance lasts at least one month, not including the first month of school, when children are often shy.
3. Associated features may include excessive shyness, controlling or oppositional behavior, fear of social embarrassment, and social isolation.
4. Child may communicate with gesturing, head nodding, or speaking in monosyllabic words.

Associated features of the disorder include fear of social embarrassment, anxiousness, withdrawal, social isolation, negativity, and oppositional or controlling behavior. Children with elective mutism may have co-occurring diagnoses of social phobia or anxiety disorder. Although the exact cause of the disorder is unknown, children with elective mutism commonly come from families who are very shy, leading researchers to suspect a genetic influence or vulnerability to this disorder. Complications of the disorder include school failure and teasing by peers (National Organization for Rare Disorders [NORD], 2000).

Special education services may be available to children with elective mutism under the condition of Emotional Disturbance. Accommodations may include counseling services designed to address social anxiety related with this disorder. Although children with selective mutism will not qualify for speech and language services, school professionals working with these children may want to consult with speech and language specialists concerning the development of social communication skills.

The duration of the disorder is highly variable, ranging from a few months to several years. Often the associated features of anxiety or social phobia may be chronic (APA, 1994). A common drug for social phobia, fluoxetine, has been shown to be beneficial in treating selective mutism, although more long-term studies are needed to determine the effectiveness and safety of this drug (Black & Uhde, 1994). Other forms of treatment include behavior management techniques such as reinforcement conditioning, counterconditioning, and shaping techniques. Family therapy is also useful to reinforce positive therapeutic changes (NORD, 2000).

REFERENCES

American Psychiatric Association. (1994). *Diagnostic and statistical manual of mental disorders* (4th ed.). Washington, DC: Author.

Black, B., & Uhde, T. W. (1994). Treatment of elective mutism with fluoxetine: A double blind, placebo-controlled study. *Journal of American Academy of Child and Adolescent Psychiatry, 33*(7), 1000–1006.

Dummit, E. S., III, Klein, R. G., Tancer, N. K., Asche, B., Martin, J., & Fairbanks, J. A. (1997). Systemic assessment of 50 children with selective mutism. *Journal of American Child and Adolescent Psychiatry, 36*(5), 653–660.

National Organization for Rare Disorderss. (2000, August 1). Selective mutism. Retrieved from http://www.rarediseases.org

Mary Corlett
University of Texas at Austin

EMOTIONAL DISTURBANCE

Emotional disturbance represents a broad category of psychological difficulties that have also been referred to as internalizing or externalizing disorders. Emotional disturbance usually includes symptoms of anxiety and depression, but it can include symptoms consistent with a psychotic disorder, such as sensory hallucinations. It is characterized by an emotional disturbance of sufficient severity to interfere significantly with a child's academic, social, and emotional functioning (PL 94-142, the Education for All Handicapped Children Act).

Prevalence estimates for the disorder depend on the definition and criteria used. The estimated prevalence of a major depressive disorder in school-age children, for example, is reported to be between 2% and 8% (Birmaher et al., 1996). Generalized anxiety disorder is estimated to occur in 3–6% (Albano, Chorpita, & Barlow, 1996); obsessive compulsive disorder occurs in 2–3% (Piacentini & Graae, 1997); and schizophrenia affects less than 0.1% of the school-age population (Remschmidt, Schulz, Martin, Warnke, & Trott, 1994). Most individuals will experience symptoms consistent with a serious emotional disturbance at some point in their lives. Consequently, evaluating the frequency, intensity, and duration of the symptoms must be considered before making a formal diagnosis. Other important factors to consider include age of onset and family history.

Characteristics (as specified by PL 94-142)

1. Inability to learn that cannot be explained by intellectual, sensory, or health factors
2. Inability to build or maintain satisfactory interpersonal relationships with others
3. Exhibits inappropriate types of behavior or feelings under normal circumstances
4. General pervasive mood of unhappiness and depression
5. A tendency to develop physical symptoms or fears associated with personal or school problems

Additional characteristics include the following:

1. Difficulty in getting mind off of things (e.g., obsessions) or excessively engaging in repetitive or useless actions (e.g., compulsions)
2. Out of touch with reality as defined by a delusional disorder or sensory hallucinations
3. Pervasive pattern of noncompliant, aggressive, or bizarre behavior that is unpredictable or exaggerated for the situation
4. Children with autism are considered to have an Other Health Impairment, *not* a serious emotional disturbance

Fifty-eight percent of children with a serious emotional disturbance (SED) fail to graduate from high school, and most drop out before the 11th grade (Mash & Wolfe, 1999). Consequently, multidisciplinary teams, including parents, should design individual education programs to meet each child's individual needs. Many children can benefit from supportive treatments and modifications within the regular classroom, but others will require at least temporary placements in special educational programs and environments. Some children will require short- or long-term stays in a residential treatment facility.

Such programs usually attempt to provide a therapeutic milieu and a structured environment where children can experience a high degree of success. Rules and routines should be stable and predictable. Contingency management plans, where children earn rewards for appropriate behavior, are most frequently employed (Kaplan & Carter, 1995). Additional types of interventions used to manage concurrent behavior problems often include token economies, behavioral contracting, and time-out. Interventions that focus on stimulus control strategies are also useful (Greene, 1998). Supportive therapies involving music, art, relaxation, and individual and group counseling are also frequently employed. Family therapy may be needed.

Prognosis for children with a SED is as varied as the conditions that constitute this category. In general, the earlier the age of onset, the more guarded the prognosis will be. Early intervention seems to be helpful in ameliorating the negative effects of many childhood disorders (Mash & Wolfe, 1999); however, other factors such as family support are extremely important as well.

REFERENCES

Albano, A. M., Chorpita, B. F., & Barlow, D. H. (1996). Childhood anxiety disorders. In E. J. Mash & R. A. Barkley (Eds.), *Child psychopathology* (pp. 282–316). New York: Guilford Press.

Birmaher, B., Ryan, N. D., Williamson, D. E., Brent, D. A., Kaufman, J., Dahl, R. E. Perel, J., & Nelson, B. (1996). Childhood and adolescent depression: A review of the past 10 years: Part I. *Journal of the American Academy of Child and Adolescent Psychiatry, 35,* 1427–1439.

Greene, R. W. (1998). *The explosive child.* New York: Harper and Collins.

Kaplan, J. S., & Carter, J. (1995). *Beyond behavior modification* (3rd ed.). Austin, TX: Pro-Ed.

Mash, E. J., & Wolfe, D. A. (1999). *Abnormal child psychology.* Belmont, CA: Brooks and Cole.

Piacentini, J., & Graae, F. (1997). In E. Hollander & D. Stein (Eds.), *Obsessive-compulsive disorders: Diagnosis, etiology, treatment* (pp. 23–46). New York: Marcel Dekker.

Remschmidt, H. E., Schulz, E., Martin, M., Warnke, A., & Trott, G. (1994). Childhood-onset schizophrenia: History of the concept and recent studies. *Schizophrenia Bulletin, 20,* 727–746.

Brian D. Johnson
Michelle Athanasiou
University of Northern Colorado

EMOTIONAL LABILITY

Emotional lability refers to a pattern of emotional changes from normal mood to states characterized by irritability, depression, anxiety, or aggression (also referred to in the psychological and psychiatric literature as emotion dysregulation, emotional incontinence, and a lack of ego control). Intense emotional and behavioral reactions to stressful events are common and may last several hours. In addition, emotionally labile individuals have greater variability in their secretion of stress hormones (i.e., cortisol and testosterone; Adler, Wedekind, Pilz, Weniger, & Huether, 1997). Rather than representing a distinct psychological diagnosis itself, emotional lability refers to a general pattern of behavior that is characteristic of a range of psychological disorders, including mood disorders, anxiety disorders, psychotic disorders, personality disorders (particularly borderline personality disorder), and the disruptive behavior disorders seen in children and adolescents.

Given that emotional lability is not recognized as a distinct psychological condition, the prevalence of this condition in the population is unknown.

Characteristics

1. Pattern of emotional changes from normal mood to states characterized by irritability, depression, anxiety, or aggression
2. Associated with a range of psychological disorders including mood, anxiety, psychotic, personality, and disruptive behavior disorders
3. Associated with higher variability in the secretion of stress hormones (i.e., cortisol and testosterone)

The presence of emotional lability in a child does not warrant diagnosis of a psychological disorder in itself but should prompt the clinician to investigate the presence of other conditions using a comprehensive, multidimensional evaluation. Emotional lability has been successfully treated as a component of several different disorders in children and adolescents using cognitive-behavioral therapy (e.g., Kendall & Braswell, 1993) and in adults using psychotropic medication (i.e., fluvoxamine; Iannaccone & Ferini-Strambi, 1996).

Emotional lability may be present in those in special education placements, particularly those with one, or more, of the aforementioned psychological conditions. Such individuals should receive a comprehensive diagnostic evaluation, and treatment should focus on cognitive-behavioral approaches aimed at reducing the emotional and behavioral outbursts and other associated symptoms.

Despite the abundance of research on emotions and emotion regulation, the field lacks a common definition of emotion and an integrative understanding of how emotions influence, and are influenced by, thoughts and behaviors. Future research is continuing to explore these areas.

REFERENCES

Adler, L., Wedekind, D., Pilz, J., Weniger, G., & Huether, G. (1997). Endocrine correlates of personality traits: A comparison between emotionally stable and emotionally labile healthy young men. *Neuropsychobiology, 35,* 205–210.

Gross, J. J. (1998). The emerging field of emotion regulation: An integrative review. *Review of General Psychology, 2,* 271–299.

Iannaccone, S., & Ferini-Strambi, L. (1996). Pharmacologic treatment of emotional lability. *Clinical Neuropharmacology, 19,* 532–535.

Kendall, P. C., & Braswell, L. (1993). *Cognitive-behavioral therapy for impulsive children* (2nd ed.). New York: Guilford Press.

Matthew K. Nock
Yale University

EMPHYSEMA, CONGENITAL LOBAR

Congenital lobar emphysema is a chronic disease involving progressive hyperinflation of one or more pulmonary lobes, resulting in the trapping of air in the affected lobes. There are two distinct types of congenital lobar emphysema: (a) an overexpansion of the normal lung lobe and (b) a polyalveolar lobe, in which there are an increased number of normally expanded alveoli. Although half of all cases have an etiology that is idiopathic, this disease can also be caused by lung obstructions or failure of the lungs to develop properly (Bhutani, 1996).

This disease has a peak incidence between birth and 6 months and is 1.5 to 3 times more prevalent in males than in females. Congenital lobar emphysema affects the left upper lobe in 41% of cases, the right middle lobe in 34% of cases, and the right upper lobe in 21% of cases (Aideyan, 2000; De Milto, 1999). No research could be found as to whether ethnicity or socioeconomic plays any role in the prevalence of congenital lobar emphysema.

Characteristics

1. Infant presents with wheezing, chronic coughing, shortness of breath, and difficulty in exhaling and may have a blue tinge to both skin and fingernail beds.
2. X ray reveals hyperinflation of the affected lobe with mediastinal shift away from the affected side.

Congenital lobar emphysema ranges in severity from severe to virtually undetectable, with many cases being mild with no need for supplemental oxygen. For those with mild or no symptoms, no treatment may be required. For those with acute or severe symptoms, surgery—either segmentectomy or lobectomy—is a common treatment (Hansen, Corbet, & Avery, 1991; Ordonez, 1997).

In most cases, whether treated medically or surgically, respiratory symptoms typically disappear by age 1. Almost all children with congenital lobar emphysema, however, show evidence of mild pulmonary obstruction by age 10, indicative of a more generalized abnormality (Hansen, Corbet, & Avery, 1991).

Congenital lobar emphysema does not often result in severe physical or cognitive disability. Like children with asthma, children with congenital lobar emphysema may require modified activities and classes. Typically, this includes allowing the child more frequent rests during strenuous physical exercise and providing alternatives for activities in which the child is unable to participate. During recess or other play periods, and in physical education classes, nonstrenuous games or tasks should be made available to the child, and the child should be allowed to choose not to participate in an activity that he or she finds difficult. Additionally, the child may have a heightened sensitivity to chemical irritants such as cleansers or other substances and should be given the same consideration when these irritants are present as he or she would be given in the case of strenuous activity. Due to the chronic nature of this illness, counseling may be required for the child and his or her family.

Congenital lobar emphysema is a chronic condition and will therefore be present throughout the child's life. In acute or severe cases, treatment results in an excellent outcome, with respiratory symptoms disappearing in most children by the end of their first year.

REFERENCES

Bhutani, V. K. (1996). *Intensive care of the fetus and neonate.* St. Louis, MO: Mosby.

De Milto, L. (1999). *Gale encyclopedia of medicine* (1st ed.). Farmington Hills, MI: Gale Research.

Hansen, T., Corbet, A., & Avery, M. E. (1991). *Diseases of the newborn* (6th ed.). Philadelphia: Harcourt Brace Jovanovich.

Ordonez, P. (1997). Congenital lobar emphysema. Retrieved from http://www.neonatology.org/syllabus/cle.html

Melissa M. Harvey
University of Colorado at Colorado Springs

ENCEPHALITIS, MYCOPLASMA PNEUMONIAE

Mycoplasma pneumoniae encephalitis is a bacterial infection that mimics a virus; that is, the bacterias lack a cell wall and receptor sites for common antibiotics. Mycoplasmas are transmitted via the respiratory route and are the smallest free-living parasites known to exist (Clyde, 1997). This type of pneumonia occurs more often in the winter months and is often accompanied by bulbous myringitis (eardrum inflammation) and otitis media (ear infections). The infection is more commonly found in school-age children and adolescents. Neurologic complications are rare: 1–7% of pneumoniae cases (Johnson, 1998), but the condition has been associated with a variety of serious problems, including lethargy, altered consciousness, agitation, psychotic behavior, seizures, aphasia, paresthesis, cranial nerve palsies, and cerebellar ataxia (Thomas, Collins, Robb, & Robinson, 1993). It has also been found in patients diagnosed with meningitis and Guillain-Barre syndrome.

The pathogenesis of mycoplasma infection is not known; however, researchers have hypothesized that the condition is due to one of three causes. The most likely explanation is that the infection results from an autoimmune response in which free-floating antibodies in the brain react with complimentary mycoplasma antibodies. Other explanations include a direct insult of the central nervous system (CNS) by bacteria crossing the blood-brain barrier and bacteria releasing a neurotoxin that damages the CNS (Thomas et al., 1993); however, few cases have been found in which bacteria has been isolated in the CNS, and the release of neurotoxins has only been shown in animals.

Characteristics

1. The bacterial infection mimics a virus and occurs more commonly in school-age children and adolescents than adults.
2. Eardrum inflammation and ear infections are common.
3. Neurologic symptoms include lethargy, agitation, seizures, and altered consciousness.
4. Prognosis is generally good, but in some cases sequelae persist such as optic atrophy, intellectual deterioration, and spastic quadriplegia.

Although respiratory infection typically precedes neurological symptoms, in some cases there is no known antecedent respiratory illness or infection. Mycoplasma pneumoniae infection, however, should be considered a possibility in all cases of acute encephalitis. The diagnosis is typically made through serologic tests that detect the antibodies (i.e., IgG and IgM). Lumbar puncture, magnetic resonance imaging, and computerized tomography scanning have all been used, but these tests are often inconclusive. Although increased levels of protein concentrations and lymphocytes are often found, bacteria in the CSF is not typically found.

The most effective treatment is that of an antibiotic, such as erythromycin and tetracycline. Penicillin and cephalosporin are not effective despite their frequent use. These antibiotics are helpful in treating bacterial infections, but there is no evidence that there is any impact on the neurologic sequelae. Further, there is no evidence that corticosteroids are effective with this infection and its aftermath (Thomas et al., 1993). Fortunately, prognosis is generally good. There are very few cases of death caused by mycoplasma pneumoniae infections; however, the seriousness of certain sequelae means that these children need to be evaluated carefully for problems such as intellectual deterioration, short-term memory impairment, seizures, optic atrophy, and movement disorders (e.g., spastic quadriplegia).

Treatment depends on the severity and the nature of the impact. For example, in cases of physical impairment, services from physical and occupational therapists are often warranted. These children may qualify for special education services under Other Health Impairment or even Section 504. In most cases, certain classroom accommodations will be needed. When cognitive impact is severe, school-age children may even warrant services for students with Intellectual Disabilities and Specific Learning Disabilities. When emotional and behavioral needs become so great as to interfere with learning and social progress, special education services for students with Emotional Disturbance may be needed. Given the impact that eardrum inflammation and ear infection can have on hearing, audiologists and speech and language pathologists should be consulted so that the child can be properly evaluated for services. Furthermore, school psychological services should be obtained to ensure that the student's educational and emotional needs are properly assessed (e.g., pre- and postencephalitis functioning and educational needs) and that interventions are appropriately designed and implemented. Children with mycoplasma pneumoniae encephalitis should also be offered counseling services to help them cope with the sudden onset of this illness (and its sequelae) and the fears and uncertainty about the future. It is critical that parents be involved in the assessment and intervention process to insure that the child with mycoplasma pneumoniae encephalitis has the benefit of state-of-the-art services.

REFERENCES

Clyde, W. A. (1997). Mycoplasmal diseases. In W. M. Scheld, R. J. Whitley, & D. T. Durack (Eds.), *Infections of the central nervous system* (2nd ed.). New York: Lippincott Raven.

Johnson, R. T. (1998). *Viral infections of the nervous system.* New York: Lippincott Raven.

Thomas, N., Collins, J., Robb, S., & Robinson, R. (1993). Mycoplasma pneumoniae infection and neurological disease. *Archives of Disease in Childhood, 69,* 573–576.

Loni Kuhn
Elaine Clark
University of Utah

ENCEPHALITIS, POSTHERPETIC

Postherpetic encephalitis, or herpes simplex encephalitis (HSVE), is caused by the herpes simplex virus–1 (HSV-1) and is characterized by inflammation of the parenchyma and the surrounding meninges. The herpes simplex virus has a predilection for certain areas of the brain, specifically, the frontotemporal region. HSVE accounts for 10% of all cases of encephalitis and is one of the most common types of fatal sporadic encephalitis (Clifton, 1991). This type of encephalitis is uncommon: It occurs annually in an estimated 1 in 250,000 individuals but is more prevalent in children than in adults. It is not entirely clear how the virus gains access to the brain, but some researchers question olfactory and orbital routes.

Symptoms of HSVE include alterations in mental status (e.g., loss of consciousness, confusion, and memory loss), headache, fever, lethargy, nausea and vomiting, generalized and focal seizures, and hemiparesis. Neurologic impairment can be permanent, including impairment in sensorimotor, language (e.g., dysnomia), intellectual skills, and behavioral functions.

Characteristics

1. HSVE is caused by the herpes simplex virus–1 and affects more children than adults.
2. Herpes simplex viruses have a predilection to the frontotemporal region of the brain and are characterized by inflammation of the parenchyma and the surrounding meninges.
3. Rapid onset of symptoms is common and can include alterations in mental status, headache, vomiting, fever, lethargy, seizures, and hemiparesis.
4. Mortality rates are as high as 70% if untreated, but drug therapies such as Acyclovir help.
5. Sensorimotor, intellectual, language, and behavioral changes are common.

HSVE is diagnosed by a number of methods, including electroencephalograms (EEGs), computed tomography (CT), tissue biopsies, and cerebral spinal fluid (CSF) evaluation. Brain biopsies have been shown to be the most reliable diagnostic tools, but examining CSF for lymphocytes, antibodies, and red blood cells has also been shown to be the most practical (Ratho, Sethi, & Singh, 1999). EEG and neuroimaging have been useful in identifying areas of the brain impacted by the virus, and they predict sequelae from the infection.

If untreated, HSVE can result in death—in some cases in 70% of all individuals infected (Clifton, 1991). The antiviral drug Acyclovir has been successful in reducing mortality rates (in some studies to 28%) and morbidity. In addition to Acyclovir, corticosteroids are occasionally given to reduce intracranial pressure. Concern has been expressed about a potential negative interaction among steroid use, the antiviral agent, and the virus itself; however, recent research in rats has failed to show an increase in herpes simplex replication using the two treatments (Blessing, Blessing, & Wesselingh, 2000).

The prognosis is improved with early diagnosis and treatment, but problems can persist long after the acute phase of illness. Educators need to be aware of potential long-term neurologic impairments caused by HSVE. This includes problems with memory and cognition, motor and language problems, and aggression, to name a few. Special education is likely to be needed, so children who have had HSVE need to be evaluated for special education—as well as regular education—needs. Speech and language therapists, as well as occupational and physical therapists, may play an important role in the child's ability to achieve.

Future research is needed to better explain the pathogenesis of the infection, in particular, where the virus is more likely to gain access. This may provide critical information for finding ways to prevent the encephalitis and facilitate early diagnosis and treatment.

REFERENCES

Blessing, K. A., Blessing, W. W., & Wesselingh, S. L. (2000). Herpes simplex replication and dissemination is not increased by corticosteroid treatment in a rat model of focal herpes encephalitis. *Journal of Neurovirology, 6*(1), 25–32.

Clifton, E. R. (1991). Herpes simplex encephalitis: An overview. *Journal of Mississippi State Medical Association, 32*(12), 437–440.

Ratho, R. K., Sethi, S., & Singh, S. (1999). Role of serology in the diagnosis of herpes simplex encephalitis. *Indian Journal of Pathological Microbiology, 42*(3), 333–337.

Loni Kuhn
Elaine Clark
University of Utah

ENCEPHALITIS, POSTINFECTIOUS MEASLES

Postinfectious measles encephalitis is an autoimmune response characterized by inflammation and demyelination that is triggered by the measles virus. The measles virus is transmitted through respiratory droplets and is thought to have impacted civilizations as early as 4000 B.C. A young Danish physician, Peter L. Panum, however, is credited with much of the information that is now known about measles, including the highly contagious nature of the disease. Panum was sent to the Faroe Islands in the mid-1800s to assist with a large-scale measles outbreak and discovered that measles have an incubation period of about 14 days (Griffin, Ward, & Esolen, 1994). In most cases, individuals begin to show signs of improvement about five days after the measles rash appears. It is not clear how the measles virus triggers the autoimmune reaction that causes encephalomyelitis. However, when this occurs there is considerable neurologic involvement, and prior to the introduction of the measles vaccine, it was the most common cause of neurological disability. Encephalitis-associated symptoms include fever, headache, seizures, and coma. It has been estimated that 50% of individuals who contract post-infectious measles encephalitis develop seizures and nearly 100% show impaired consciousness during the episode (Scheld, Whitley, & Durack, 1997). Other neurologic-related sequelae include intellectual deterioration, hemiparesis, paraplegia, and ataxia (Scheld et al., 1997).

Characteristics

1. An autoimmune response characterized by demyelinization and inflammation
2. Triggered by the measles virus, and affecting 1 per 1,000 measles cases
3. Commonly diagnosed following neurological complications from rashes
4. Mortality rate of approximately 25%
5. Neurologic sequelae including intellectual decline, hemiparesis/plegia, and ataxia

Because the measles vaccine is commonly administered in North America and Europe, measles infections are fairly infrequent. In other areas of the world, measles epidemics occur often, as does the corresponding encephalitis. Encephalitis occurs in 1 of every 1,000 cases of measles and is more commonly found among young people and the elderly (Griffin et al., 1994). There does not appear to be a sex difference as males and females are equally affected.

Most often, the diagnosis of postinfectious encephalitis is made based on clinical signs and symptoms of neurological complication (i.e., following the measles rash). In some cases, the disease is found in the urine, blood, and cerebral spinal fluid (CSF), and especially in increased levels of mononuclear cells and protein (Johnson, 1998). But these are not consistent findings, so follow-up is needed even in cases where there is no evidence of the disease in the blood or urine and the lumbar puncture is clean. Other methods to follow up on the disease include use of electroencephalograms (EEGs) and magnetic resonance imaging (MRI). In cases of postinfectious measles encephalitis, the EEG commonly displays diffuse, symmetric slowing, and the MRI often shows demyelination in the cerebellum and brain stem.

The prognosis for individuals who contract postinfectious measles encephalitis is often poor: Approximately 25% die from the disease. There are no antiviral drug treatments to treat postinfectious measles encephalitis. Although the administration of immunoglobulins following exposure has been shown to alter the course some, conflicting evidence has been found, and the overall consensus seems to be that corticosteroid treatments are not very helpful in alleviating the disease. Clearly, the most effective treatment is prevention through vaccines. In countries where the vaccine is widely used, the disease is essentially nonexistent.

For those who survive, special education services may be necessary. This includes services under the category of Other Health Impairment, Intellectual Disabilities, and Specific Learning Disabilities. Given the complexity and severity of symptoms following the contraction of the disease, regardless of special education eligibility, children will likely need some accommodations in the classroom and ancillary services such as occupational and physical therapies. Psychological services are likely to be critical to evaluate the neuropsychological consequence of the disease and determine necessary services. Home-school collaborations are likely to be necessary to ensure that the child is receiving appropriate services and making the expected progress educationally and socially. Depending on the severity of the disability caused from the disease, vocational testing and services may also be called for; therefore, children need to be evaluated early to reduce frustration and provide them with the best education possible.

REFERENCES

Griffin, D., Ward, B., & Esolen, L. (1994). Pathogenesis of measles virus infection: An hypothesis for altered immune responses. *Journal of Infectious Diseases, 170*(Suppl. 1), 24–31.

Johnson, R. T. (1998). *Viral infections of the nervous system.* New York: Lippincott Raven.

Scheld, M., Whitley, R., & Durack, D. (1997). *Infections of the central nervous system.* New York: Lippencott Raven.

Loni Kuhn
Elaine Clark
University of Utah

ENCOPRESIS

Encopresis involves the repeated passage of feces into inappropriate places (e.g., clothing or the floor), whether involuntarily or intentional. It is differentiated into either primary or secondary subtypes: the primary subtype indicates that the individual has never established fecal continence, whereas the secondary subtype indicates the disturbance developed after a period of established continence. Encopresis may stem from psychological reasons such as anxiety about defecating in a public place, a more generalized anxiety, or oppositional behavior or may be caused by physiologically induced dehydration related to hypothyroidism, a febrile illness, or a side effect of medications. Secondary encopresis may begin following a stressful event, such as the birth of a sibling, the beginning of school, or separation from a parent due to divorce or death.

Encopresis cannot be diagnosed prior to the age of 4, and there must be at least one event per month for at least three months. It is estimated that 1% of 5-year-olds have encopresis, and the disorder is five to six times more prevalent in males. Referrals for encopresis account for approximately 3% of pediatric outpatient referrals (Abrahamin & Lloyd-Still, 1984) and 5% of referrals to psychiatric clinics. A history of constipation, developmental delays in other areas, attention-deficit/hyperactivity disorder, or coercive or premature bowel training increases the risk for developing encopresis (Maxmen & Ward, 1995). Frequency of encopresis decreases with age, with a spontaneous remission rate of about 28% per year (Schaefer, 1979). Encopresis can persist intermittently for years but rarely becomes a chronic condition.

In addition to the primary and secondary distinctions of encopresis, three major categories of encopresis exist (Howe & Walker, 1992). The most common is retentive encopresis, which accounts for 80–95% of all encopretic cases (Christopherson & Rapoff, 1983). Retentive encopresis occurs when a child becomes constipated and liquid fecal mater leaks around the fecal obstruction and soils undergarments. The second type of encopresis includes chronic diarrhea and irritable bowel syndrome, most commonly associated with stress and anxiety. The third and least common form of encopresis is manipulative, intentional soiling, most commonly associated with oppositional defiance or conduct disorders.

Characteristics

1. Repeated passage of feces into inappropriate places whether involuntarily or intentionally.
2. Primary encopresis: At least one such event per month for at least 3 months.
3. Secondary encopresis: One full year of being continent prior to current episode of encopresis.
4. Chronological age is at least 4 years (or equivalent developmental level).
5. The behavior is not exclusively due to direct physiological effects of a substance (e.g., laxatives) or a general medical condition except constipation.
6. Code as either with constipation and overflow incontinence or without constipation and overflow incontinence.
7. Treatment usually includes both medical and behavioral interventions.

Treatment of encopresis usually includes both medical and behavioral interventions (Mash & Barkley, 1996). It is believed that a multifaceted approach that treats a wide range of systems (organic, behavioral, cognitive, and environmental) will achieve the most efficacious results. To avoid the retention-leakage cycle, a combination of enemas, laxatives, stool softeners, or increased dietary fiber are used to evacuate the colon. In rare cases surgical extraction of the fecal material may be required. Children are then scheduled to have regular sessions on the toilet for the purpose of muscle retraining. They are given the responsibility of cleaning both themselves and any soiled clothing or surrounding areas after bowel movements. Rewards for appropriate toileting behavior and establishing a regular time for bowel movements (usually immediately after a meal) are also helpful for treating encopresis. Shaping and fading, behavioral modification techniques, are often used to increase stimulus control as a child transitions from a diaper to the toilet (Smith, Smith, & Lee, 2000). Parents are encouraged to keep a matter-of-fact approach in helping their children in order to avoid inadvertently reinforcing attention-seeking behaviors.

The child with encopresis often feels ashamed and embarrassed, which can lead to avoidance of school and other social situations. The amount of impairment is a direct function of the effect on the child's self-esteem, social ostracism by peers at school and in the community, and rejection by the caregiver. Special education accommodations may be made if the encopresis falls under the handicapping condition of Other Health Impairment. Support and planning by the school personnel may assist the child and parent in creating a plan to decrease school absenteeism and peer isolation. Due to the nature of the disorder, children with involuntary encopresis often experience psychological problems stemming from the encopresis, rather than causing encopresis. Children with deliberate soiling behaviors may receive rewards (i.e., parental attention, school absence, etc.) that inadvertently reinforce the soiling and smearing behaviors. When incontinence is deliberate, features of oppositional defiant disorder or conduct disorder may also be present.

The frequency of encopresis decreases with age, with a spontaneous remission rate of 28% per year (Schaefer, 1979). Therefore, the initial prognosis for encopresis is good. However, the psychological impact may reach farther because the child faces the social isolation and stigmatism already created within his or her peer group. School-based interventions may decrease peer isolation and increase the child's feelings of mastery of bowel control while in social situations. School personnel may provide discrete scheduled toileting times during the school day, enhance effective toileting strategies by providing rewards for reduction of soiling, and providing a place for cleaning of clothes and self if a soiling incident occurs. The school psychologist or counselor can facilitate increased communication between school, medical personnel, and the school, encouraging consistent intervention strategies. Encopresis can persist intermittently for years, but it rarely is a chronic condition. Intervention at the school level is critical for continued social and academic success for the child experiencing encopresis.

The need for future research is evident, primarily because available studies addressing encopresis are based on case studies. Valid experimental designs to evaluate treatment effectiveness, such as random assignment of cases to experimental and control groups or to alternate treatment groups, reversal designs (ABAB), and multiple baseline design studies are needed (Schaefer, 1979) in order to rule out spontaneous remission or extraneous effects on bowel control. There is also a need for further study in identifying differential treatment for continuous versus discontinuous encopresis and for longitudinal investigations of the natural history of encopresis (Schaefer, 1979).

REFERENCES

Abrahamin, R., & Lloyd-Still, J. D. (1984). Chronic constipation in childhood: A longitudinal study of 186 patients. *Journal of Pediatric Gastroenterology and Nutrition, 3,* 460–467.

Christopherson, E. R., & Rapoff, M. A. (1983). Toileting problems in children. In C. E. Walker & M. C. Roberts (Eds.), *Handbook of clinical child psychology* (pp. 593–615). New York: Wiley.

Howe, A. C., & Walker, C. E. (1992). Behavioral management of toilet training, enuresis, and encopresis. *Pediatric Clinics of North America, 39,* 413–432.

Mash, E. J., & Barkley, R. A. (1996). *Child psychopathology.* New York: Guilford Press.

Maxmen, J., & Ward, N. (1995). *Essential psychopathology and its treatment* (2nd ed.). New York: W. W. Norton.

Schaefer, C. E. (1979). *Childhood encopresis and enuresis.* New York: Van Nostrand Reinhold.

Smith, L., Smith, P., & Lee, K. (2000). Behavioral treatment of urinary incontinence and encopresis in children with learning disabilities: Transfer of stimulus control. *Developmental Medicine and Child Neurology, 42,* 276–279.

Leslie Coyle Franklin
Brian Johnson
University of Northern Colorado

ENDOCARDIAL FIBROELASTOSIS

Characterized by an increased amount of connective tissue and elastic fibers causing a thickening in the muscular lining of the heart, endocardial fibroelastosis (EFE) is a rare condition eventually leading to congestive heart failure if it is not diagnosed early. Whereas some studies advocate that EFE may be the result of an X-linked, autosomal recessive trait, others support that EFE is caused by intrauterine viral infections, impaired lymphatic drainage of the heart, or carnitine deficiency.

Prevalence rates were once estimated at 1 in 5,000 live births; however, that number has decreased over the years, and EFE has become virtually nonexistent with the advent of vaccinations and improved neonatal health care. As expected, undiagnosed problems such as congestive hearth failure lead to problems in brain perfusion, with significant cognitive sequelae in some cases.

Treatments vary by seriousness of the condition. Drug therapies that have been found effective include diuretics used to eliminate fluid retention and cardiac glycosides that can be administered to ameliorate symptoms such as increased heart rate, myocardial contractility, and other symptoms of chronic heart failure. Anticoagulants aid in the reduction of blood clots. Heart transplants also are a viable option for some children with EFE.

Characteristics

1. Thickening of the linings of heart chambers
2. Difficulty breathing, coughing, irritability, fatigue, failure to thrive, and sometimes a bluish skin discoloration of the feet and hands
3. Unusual chest sounds, such as bubbling, rales, and murmurs, often heard with a stethoscope during routine physicians' examinations
4. Life-threatening complications, including rapid heartbeat, irregular heart rhythms, and congestive cardiomyopathy

Although the prognosis is generally poor, especially in children who present with EFE at birth, children who respond to drug therapies have been known to live healthy lives. Some children may also be caught in the middle of the spectrum and experience persistent symptoms requiring medical intervention above and beyond drug therapies. Because roughly only one third of the children survive to school age, little is known with regard to psychosocial and educational determinants. Children who respond well to drug treatments go on to live seemingly unaffected lives as long as medication is continued and the condition is monitored. Educational placement may require labeling of the child under Other Health Impairment. Future research is focusing on prevention and etiology of this lethal disorder.

REFERENCES

Keith, J. D., Rose, V., & Manning, J. A. (1978). Endocardial fibroelastosis. In J. D. Keith, R. D. Rowe, & P. Vlad (Eds.), *Heart disease in infancy and childhood* (3rd ed., pp. 941–957). New York: Macmillan.

Nelson, W. E., Behrman, R. E., Kliegmen, R. M., & Arvin, A. M. (1996). *Nelson textbook of pediatrics* (15th ed.). Bangalore, India: Prism Books.

Venugopalan, P. (2001). Endocardial fibroelastosis. *eMedicine, 2.* Retrieved June 2001, from http://www.emedicine.com/PED/topic2510.html

Kimberly M. Estep
University of Houston–Clear Lake

ENDOCRINE DISORDERS

The endocrine system consists of the pituitary, thyroid, parathyroid, adrenal, pancreas, gonads, and placenta. The general function of the endocrine system is to control growth and reproduction and to maintain chemical homeostasis in the body.

Disorders associated with the endocrine system may result from partial or total insensitivity of tissue to endogenous hormones, hypersecretion of hormones, or hyposecretion of hormones. Endocrine disorders may have a variety of etiologies including chromosomal abnormalities, prenatal deficiencies, maternal hormonal deficiencies during gestation, and a variety of environmental variables (e.g., toxins, traumatic brain injury, brain tumors, and viruses).

Endocrine disorders also vary in prevalence and in the age at which symptoms appear. Commonly, endocrine disorders in children are detected because a child's development is premature or delayed (Sandberg & Barrik, 1995). Relatively common endocrine disorders of childhood include Turner's syndrome, Klinefelter syndrome, congenital adrenal hyperplasia, hyperthyroidism, diabetes mellitus, and obesity. Rarer forms of the disorders may include hypothyroidism, which rarely appears as a birth defect, and multiple endocrine neoplasia Type 2 (MEN 2), which involves an overactivity and enlargement of the endocrine glands.

Characteristics

1. Effects of the disorders can be direct (i.e., alteration of physical state), indirect (i.e., secondary effects based on social consequences of atypical physical or hormonal development), or a combination of both direct and indirect effects.
2. Endocrine dysfunction can have direct and indirect effects on physical, sexual, behavioral, and emotional development depending on the glands involved.
3. Cognitive, motor, and speech delays are common in hypothyroidism and Klinefelter's syndrome but may appear in other disorders if appropriate treatment is not provided.
4. Behavioral, emotional, and social problems are common with many endocrine disorders and may result from the following:
    a. Hormonal imbalances
    b. Early or delayed development of secondary sexual characteristics leading to age-inappropriate sexual behavior
    c. Feelings of isolation or rejection because of physical abnormalities
5. The severity of symptoms varies widely across disorders. Some endocrine disorders such as congenital adrenal hyperplasia can be fatal. Other disorders such as diabetes are chronic conditions in which symptoms can be maintained with few functional impairments. There are also disorders such as benign tumors of the parathyroid gland in which individuals may not have noticeable symptoms. These patients may initially report feeling normal and then report improved sleep and concentration following surgical removal of the benign tumor.

Medical treatment for the hormonal imbalance is the standard defense against endocrine disorders. Hormone replacement therapy is widely used for disorders of hyposecretion or tissue insensitivity such as Turner's syndrome or hypopituitary syndromes. Estrogen replacement therapy is used to supplement the underproductive gonads of females with Turner's syndrome. In hypopituitary syndromes, growth-hormone replacement therapy is used to stimulate growth. For disorders involving hypersecretion of endocrine glands, medical treatment seeks to reduce hormone levels through the use of natural or synthetic hormones (e.g., gonadatropin-releasing hormone for overactive pituitary glands).

The psychoeducational sequelae of endocrine disorders vary as widely as do the etiology and symptoms. Disorders associated with under- or overactive pituitary glands are typically not associated with cognitive deficits. At the other extreme, global deficits in cognitive functioning can result from endocrine disorders such as hypothyroid disorders. Furthermore, domain-specific deficits may also be associated with endocrine problems. For example, chromosomal disorders such as Klinefelter syndrome and Turner's syndrome are associated with average intelligence but with specific deficits in reading and visual-spatial processing respectively.

The psychological sequelae of endocrine disorders are also important to consider in managing these conditions. Behavioral and emotional problems may result from hormonal imbalances, reactions to treatments, or reactions to looking and feeling different from peers. Future research should focus on the direct and indirect effects of the various disorders on academic and social development. The effects on school performance and behavior of the intrusive or chronic medical procedures associated with these disorders should also be evaluated.

REFERENCES

Sandberg, D. E., & Barrick, C. (1995). Endocrine disorders in childhood: A selective survey of intellectual and educational sequelae. *School Psychology Review, 24*(2), 146–170.

Latha V. Soorya
Binghamton University and The Institute for Child Development

ENGELMANN DISEASE

Engelmann disease is a rare genetic disorder characterized by progressive widening and malformation of the shafts of the long bones (diaphyseal dysplasia). This disease is also referred to as Camurati-Engelmann disease, osteoathia hyperostotica scleroticans multiplex infantalis, progressive diaphyseal dysplasia, or ribbing disease.

This disease presents in midchildhood, often before age 10, and symptoms usually resolve by age 30 (Merck Manual of Diagnosis and Therapy, 2001). All races and both sexes are affected (Online Mendelian Inheritance in Man, 2000). Engelmann disease is inherited as an autosomal dominant genetic trait.

Characteristics

1. Symptoms include muscular pain, weakness, and wasting, typically in the legs.
2. Skeletal abnormalities or weakness and underdevelopment (hyopoplasia) of various muscles are present.
3. Pain and weakness of the leg muscles may result in an unusual "waddling" walk or gait (National Organization for Rare Disorders, 1997).
4. Skeletal malformations may include abnormal side-to-side or inward curvature of the spine (scoliosis or lumbar lordosis) or hardening (sclerosis) of the bones near the base of the skull and, in rare cases, the jaw.
5. The predominant X-ray feature is marked thickening of the periosteal and medullary surfaces of the long bones' diaphyseal cortices.
6. Often, the patient has a loss of appetite (anorexia), leading to a malnourished appearance.

Treatment usually involves corticosteroids, such as cortisone or prednisone, for relief of symptoms. Eye surgery to decompress the optic nerves is most often ineffective and usually not recommended. Other treatment is symptomatic and supportive.

Children with Engelmann disease would benefit from particular special education services, such as physical and occupational therapy. Due to the various degrees of pain that may be present with the disease, pain management intervention may also be necessary.

Although the bone malformations and muscle atrophy are somewhat progressive over time, the symptoms do seem to resolve by the age of 30. Thus, although the prognosis is not optimistic for most individuals, there is some hope for at least stability of the symptoms of the disease.

REFERENCES

Merck Manual of Diagnosis and Therapy. (2001). Diaphyseal dysplasia. Retrieved from http://www.merck.com/pubs.mmanual/section19/chapter270/2701.htm

National Organization for Rare Disorders. (1997). Engelmann disease. Retrieved from http://www.rarediseases.org

Online Mendelian Inheritance in Man. (2000). Camurti-Engelmann disease. Retrieved from http://www3.ncbi.nhm.nih.gov/lltbin-post/Omim/dispmim?131300

Sarah Compton
University of Texas at Austin

ENURESIS

Enuresis is a disorder that involves accidental urination after the age of 5 years. Enuresis can more specifically be described as occurring during the day only (diurnal), the night only (nocturnal), or both (mixed). Some clinicians also differentiate between primary (no period of continence has ever been achieved) and secondary (incontinence following a period of at least 6 months of continence). Some question the clinical utility of this distinction, as treatment outcome does not differentiate type (Ondersma & Walker, 1998). Although the etiology of enuresis remains unclear, the two most strongly supported etiologic theories for nocturnal enuresis are (a) a deficiency in nocturnal secretion of antidiuretic hormone (ADH) and (b) failure to contract pelvic floor muscles during sleep (Mellon & Stern, 1998). For a minority of children, other physiological issues may be involved in enuresis. These include urinary tract infections, urinary tract anomalies, low functional bladder capacity (FBC), constipation, diabetes mellitus, and family history of enuresis. Physiological causes are more prevalent among children with diurnal enuresis. Although psychological problems have been offered as causes of enuresis, few data support this view. Children with nocturnal enuresis may have problems with anxiety or low self-esteem, but the nature of the relationship appears correlational rather than causal. Stress does appear to be a factor in some cases of secondary enuresis.

Nocturnal enuresis, or bed-wetting, is fairly common in early childhood years. Approximately 15–20% of 5-year-olds and 7–15% of 7-year-olds are enuretic at least one time per month. Furthermore, about 7% of 7-year-old boys and 3% of 7-year-old girls are enuretic weekly (Ondersma & Walker, 1998). Spontaneous remission occurs at the rate of about 16% per year, but complete continence can take several years. Fully 3% of enuretic children remain incontinent into adulthood (Mellon & Stern, 1998). Although rates of nocturnal enuresis appear to be higher for boys than for girls until 11 years of age, these rates are typically based on clinic-referred samples. In representative samples, smaller sex differences have been found. Diurnal enuresis is much less common, occurring in approximately 1% of 7- to 12-year-olds. Diurnal enuresis is more common in girls.

Characteristics

1. Enuresis involves the voiding of urine in inappropriate places.
2. The disorder can be diagnosed only in children with chronological or developmental ages of 5 years or older.
3. Enuretic episodes either occur frequently (twice per week for 3 months) or cause significant distress or impairment in important areas of functioning.
4. Enuresis is not due to general medical conditions or effects of substances.

(American Psychiatric Association, 1994)

Treatment for enuresis must always begin with a medical examination to rule out or treat physiological problems. With regard to nocturnal enuresis, the two major treatment modalities are pharmacological and behavioral interventions. Traditionally, the most common pharmacological treatment has been tricyclic antidepressants, particularly imipramine. Although the mechanism by which imipramine works is unclear, the success rate for the drug is reported to be 10–60% during treatment. A disadvantage of imipramine is concomitant side effects, which include sleep disturbances, fatigue, gastrointestinal distress, and coma or death if overdosed (Rajigah, 1996). A more recent pharmacological intervention is desmopressin (DDAVP). This drug works by stimulating the kidneys to concentrate urine so nighttime bladder capacity is not exceeded (Ondersma & Walker, 1998). Success rates for the drug are slightly better than for imipramine, and the drug produces fewer side effects, leading some to believe that it is the most viable drug treatment for enuresis (Mellon & Stern, 1998). One of the primary drawbacks to using drugs of any type to treat enuresis is the extremely high relapse rate following completion of the drug trial (i.e., up to 95%; Ondersma & Walker, 1998).

Behavioral treatments also are commonly used to treat nocturnal enuresis. Behavioral treatment commonly consists of the urine alarm, which works by sounding an alarm when urine activates the alarm's moisture sensors. Traditional alarms included a sensor pad placed on the child's bed; more recent alarms are less cumbersome, including sensors that can be worn on children's pajamas or underpants. Although progress is relatively slow with the urine alarm, success rates for the method are approximately 75%, with 41% of children experiencing relapse (Ondersma & Walker, 1998). In an effort to increase the success of the urine alarm, multicomponent behavioral interventions have been developed. One example is Full-Spectrum Home Training (Houts & Lieberman, 1984). This treatment includes the urine alarm and several other components. One is retention control training (RCT), which attempts to increase children's FBC by having them drink large amounts of fluids, and then delay urination as long as possible. The second component is overlearning, taught by having children drink increasingly larger amounts of liquid before bedtime. This procedure is intended to prevent relapse. The final component is cleanliness training, which involves instructing children to change their bedding after each wetting episode. Overall, Full-Spectrum Home Training has an 80% success rate, which is a small increase over the urine alarm alone. However, the relapse rate with Full-Spectrum Home Training is only 20% (Ondersma & Walker, 1998).

Much less research on treatments for diurnal enuresis has been conducted. As previously mentioned, diurnal enuresis may indicate a medical problem that needs to be addressed. In terms of behavioral treatment, it is often helpful to categorize children based on whether their enuresis is caused by (a) failure to perceive a distended bladder, (b) sudden urination in response to stressors, or (c) unwillingness to use the bathroom. For the first group, training in recognizing bladder sensations and controlling urination is needed. This may include RCT. Children in the second group might benefit from learning how to contract, rather than relax, sphincters in response to feared stimuli. Finally, a behavioral plan consisting of rewarding appropriate toileting behavior is warranted for children in the third group (Schmitt, 1982). Pharmacologic treatment is often used in addition to or instead of behavioral treatment.

Enuresis appears in children with and without disabilities, and in the great majority of cases no other psychological disturbance is present, and no special education services are warranted. Nevertheless, day or nighttime enuresis can cause significant embarrassment, social isolation, and anxiety, which may manifest in the school setting (Butler, 1998). Parent-child interaction problems also may surface, especially if parents punish the child for having accidents. School personnel can be helpful in several ways: (a) referring parents to a physician to rule out or treat related medical issues, (b) educating parents about the harmful effects of punishing wetting accidents, and (c) providing support for the child with enuresis. Counseling may be helpful, especially when the enuresis is secondary to a stressful life event. Finally, mental health professionals in the school might assess the problem and consult with parents to develop behavioral interventions.

The prognosis for children with enuresis is excellent. By the midteens, 99% of children are dry through the night. The high rate of spontaneous remission has led some to suggest allowing children to outgrow the disorder (Mellon & Stern, 1998). However, due to the psychosocial problems that may face children with enuresis and the relative success rate of treatments, it is preferable to treat the disorder.

Although behavioral treatments alone have been shown to be effective in treating enuresis, studies investigating the effectiveness of these treatments plus DDAVP are needed. Also, continued research into the most effective and efficient ways to deliver behavioral treatments would be helpful. Finally, research into how to promote interprofessional collaboration on enuresis treatment would help ensure a more comprehensive approach to treatment.

REFERENCES

American Psychiatric Association. (1994). *Diagnostic and statistical manual of mental disorders* (4th ed.). Washington, DC: Author.

Butler, R. J. (1998) Annotation: Night wetting in children: Psychological aspects. *Journal of Child Psychology and Psychiatry, 29,* 453–463.

Houts, A. C., & Lieberman, R. M. (1984). *Bedwetting: A guide for parents and children.* Springfield, IL: Charles C. Thomas.

Mellon, M. W., & Stern, H. P. (1998). Elimination disorders. In R. T. Ammerman & J. V. Campo (Eds.), *Handbook of pediatric psychology and psychiatry: Vol. 1: Psychological and psychiatric issues in the pediatric setting* (pp. 182–198). Boston: Allyn & Bacon.

Ondersma, S. J., & Walker, C. E. (1998). Elimination disorders. In T. H. Ollendick & M. Hersen (Eds.), *Handbook of child psychopathology* (3rd ed.; pp. 355–378). New York: Plenum Press.

Rajigah, L. S. (1996). Treatment of choice for nocturnal enuresis: Review and recommendations. *Journal of Psychological Practice, 2*(2), 33–42.

Schmitt, B. D. (1982). Daytime wetting (diurnal enuresis). *Pediatric Clinics of North America, 29,* 9–20.

Michelle S. Athanasiou
Brian D. Johnson
University of Northern Colorado

EOSINOPHILIC FASCIITIS

Eosinophilic fasciitis (Shulman's syndrome) involves inflamed fascia (layer of fibrous tissue below the skin) and muscles of the extremities due to eosinophil (a certain type of white blood cells) infiltration, which causes tenderness and swelling. It is classified as a diffuse connective tissue disease (Beers, Mark, & Berkow, 1999). The arms and forearms are affected more often than are the thighs and legs. Presence on the trunk of the body occurs in approximately 50% of the cases, but the face is usually spared (Thoene & Jess, 1995). The etiology of this disease has been linked to aberrant immune responses as well as toxic, environmental, or drug exposures (Graham & Brad, 2000). Another cause is thought to be due to sudden, strenuous physical exertion in an otherwise sedentary person (Beers et al., 1999).

This condition is very rare, and primarily affects Anglo-Americans. There is no difference in the occurrence in males versus females. Most patients are between the ages of 30 and 60 at first report, but childhood cases have been reported (Graham & Brad, 2000).

Characteristics

1. Skin appears thickened and develops a symmetric, puckered, orange-peel-like appearance, mainly over the extremities.
2. Child complains of pain in muscles and joints and may experience joint contractures (permanent tightening of the muscles, skin, and ligaments surrounding the joint) with gradual restriction of arm and leg movement.
3. The child complains that his or her hands feel weak and occasionally numb or tingly.
4. Extremities become tender and swollen.
5. Child has unusual fatigue and weight loss.

A child with eosinophilic fasciitis will endure many tests, including muscle and skin biopsies and tests of erythrocyte (a type of red blood cell) sedimentation rates (a type of blood test; Beers et al., 1999). Eosinophilic fasciitis can induce many physical limitations, such as "claw hand," and carpal tunnel-like symptoms, so the child might find himself or herself unable to engage in many of his previous activities. Fatigue and weight loss may also limit the child to low-stress activities. Arthritis and neuropathy (loss of feeling from nerve damage) are commonly present in patients with eosinophilic fasciitis.

The treatment of a patient with eosinophilic fasciitis is long and arduous. It is directed at reducing tissue inflammation. Medications such as prednisone, to which many patients respond rapidly, help alleviate the symptoms (Beers et al., 1999). Patients may need to continue low doses of these medications for 2-5 years. Glucocorticoids (which raise blood sugar and reduce inflammation), as well as oral steroids (Guttman, 1999), are common medications to prescribe to a child with eosinophilic fasciitis (Meszaros, 1995). Treatment is directed at eliminating inflammation. Although the duration of medical treatment is undetermined, most patients have a resolution of the disease within three to five years, with some recurrences being reported. Many patients have spontaneous remission, while others will see a gradual decrease in symptoms.

Eosinophilic fasciitis alters a child's physical image, and some children will find this hard to deal with. Support from family and friends will help this child with emotional difficulties associated with his or her changing physical appearances. Eosinophilic fasciitis is somewhat debilitating at its most active stages, so it is sometimes hard for a child with the disorder to function well enough to attend school daily and function better in the daily environment. At-home schooling should be considered as an option for this child. Special education services may be available under the Other Health Impairment category due to the chronic-illness nature of this disorder. The student may also need supportive counseling for pain management and hospitalization issues. Pain management will help children be able to attend school more often. Family members of a child with eosinophilic fasciitis should be encouraged to attend pain management and counseling sessions when appropriate.

REFERENCES

Beers, M. D., Mark, H., & Berkow, M. D. (Eds.). (1999). *The Merck manual of diagnosis and therapy* (17th ed.). Lawrenceville, NJ: Merck Research Laboratories.

Graham, M. D., & Brad, S. (2000, October 15). Eosinophilic fasciitis from dermatology. Retrieved from http://www.emedicine.com/derm/topic119.htm

Guttman, C. (1999, April). Unusual aspects of connective tissue diseases demand different approaches. *Dermatology Times, 20,* 34.

Meszaros, L. (1995, April). Monitor patients on glutocorticoid therapy carefully. *Dermatology Times, 16,* 65–66.

Thoene, M. D., & Jess, G. (Ed.). (1995). *Physicians' guide to rare diseases* (2nd ed.). Lawrenceville, NJ: Dowden.

Emily R. Baxter
University of Colorado–Colorado Springs

ERYTHROKERATODERMIA WITH ATAXIA

Erythrokeratodermia with Ataxia, also known as Giroux-Barbeau syndrome, was first reported in 1972. In infancy and childhood, erythrokeratodermia with ataxia presents with groups of red, hardened, scaly skin plaques developing into a neurological syndrome in early adulthood consisting of impaired muscle coordination (ataxia), dysarthria (poorly articulated speech), decreased tendon reflexes, and involuntary, rhythmic movements of the eyes (nystagmus). In childhood the plaques usually disappear in the summer months. The plaques may completely disappear in young adulthood only to reappear later in life. Normally, the neurological deficits become apparent when these plaques reappear; in rare cases, however, neurological abnormalities may be present early in life.

Characteristics

1. In infancy and childhood, red, hardened plaques appear on the skin, and these plaques may disappear during the summer months.
2. As the child reaches adulthood, a progressive neurological syndrome consisting of impaired muscle coordination, dysarthria, nystagmus, and decreased tendon reflexes replaces or accompanies the reappearance of the plaques.

Erythrokeratodermia with ataxia is a rare hereditary autosomal dominant skin disorder that equally affects males and females. Treatment is symptomatic and supportive with dermatological attention being given to the plaques early in life. When the neurological deficits appear, other support services may become needed. Special education needs may not arise because the deficits involving impaired muscle coordination, problems articulating speech, and decreased tendon reflexes occur mainly during adulthood. However, in the rare case that the neurological deficits begin during the school years, remediation requirements should be commensurate with degree and type of impairment including occupational and physical therapy, as well as speech therapy. Not much is known about erythrokeratodermia with ataxia, and research efforts are focused on learning more about the disorder and effective means of treatment.

REFERENCES

Giroux, J. M., & Barbaeu, A. (1972). Erythrokeratodermia with ataxia. *Archives of Dermatology, 106*(2), 183–188.

Magalini, S. I., & Magalini, S. C. (Eds.). (1997). *Dictionary of medical syndromes.* Philadelphia: Lippincott-Raven.

Kimberly M. Estep
University of Houston–Clear Lake

EXHIBITIONISM

Exhibitionism is defined as the deliberate exposure of one's genitals in order to elicit shock and emotional distress from an unsuspecting person for the purpose of sexual gratification. The perpetrator is usually male, and the victim is usually a woman or a child. It is considered a paraphilia—a condition in which an individual is dependent on an unusual and personally or socially unacceptable stimulus for sexual arousal—and has been termed peiodeiktophilia when the penis is exposed (Money, 1984). Although the condition is considered common, there are no exact figures with regard to incidence or prevalence (Rhoads, 1989).

Characteristics

1. Sexual gratification is achieved by arousing shock or fear in victims. This arousal satisfies the exposer's sexual drive and replaces the desire for genital intercourse.

2. Exhibitionism can occur in children as young as 10, but the average age of diagnosis is 21 years old. Most diagnosed with the disorder display exhibitionistic behavior by the age of 17 (Abel, Osborn, Twigg, 1993; Smith & Monastersky, 1986).
3. The urge to expose one's genitals is compulsive and addictive in nature.
4. The frequency, intensity, and character of the behavior vary greatly from individual to individual.
5. Individuals are often socially isolated and socially immature.
6. "Mooning," or exposing the buttocks, which is considered a prank or an act of defiance, is not considered exhibitionism if it is not sexually arousing for the exposer (Arndt, 1995).

Children often engage in exhibitionistic and voyeuristic behaviors with other children and adults at an early age. By the age of 4 years, children typically initiate or become involved in games in which there is undressing or sexual exploration (Gil & Johnson, 1993). By school age, children develop feelings of privacy, and latency-aged children (approximately 7 to 12) may engage in a range of sexual interests that may or may not involve exhibitionistic behavior.

Because there is no physical contact involved, exhibitionism has been called a hands-off sexual offense and is one of the most often-reported hands-off offenses. Sixty-five percent of people who expose themselves have committed a prior sexual offense (Fehrenbach, Smith, Monastersky, & Deisher, 1986). The recidivism rate for exhibitionism is greater than for all other sex offenses (Kelley & Byrne, 1992). Some adolescent exhibitionists will go on to commit hands-on sexual offenses such as sexual assault.

Exhibitionists often have habitual patterns of victim selection, styles of exposing, and preferred sites. Masturbatory behavior may occur before, during, or subsequent to the incident. Offenders often report antecedent fantasies as well (Ross & Loss, 1991). Hands-off adolescent offenders are typically better adjusted in school, less likely to be delinquent, less disturbed, and less likely to have a history of sexual abuse than are hands-on offenders (Saunders, Awad, & White, 1986). Exhibitionists are also more developmentally immature, have more issues of trust and shame, focus on short-term gratification, and exhibit more feelings of isolation and despair (Miner & Dwyer, 1997).

Treatment for children who expose their genitals usually includes individual and family therapy. For adolescent and adult offenders, a wide range of treatment modalities is available, including psychotherapy, cognitive therapy, and behavioral therapy. Some authors suggest that a multimodal therapeutic approach is warranted, usually initiated and backed by a court order. This approach involves behavioral management techniques for quick control of the symptoms, combined with group therapy or individual therapy that addresses personality deficits and immaturities of the patient (Rhoads, 1989). Another approach is hormone therapy with an antiandrogen concurrent with psychotherapy (Money, 1988). Moralizing, punishment, and legal threats are largely ineffective as treatments for adolescent and adult exhibitionists. Almost all interventions appear to produce only temporary reduction of the aberrant behavior (Rhoads, 1989).

Children and adolescents who expose themselves may have other behavioral or emotional problems that would come to the attention of the education system and qualify for services under a Severely Emotionally Disturbed category. If the child's behavior is disruptive in the school or day-care setting, this may warrant contact with a mental health professional. Adolescents who expose themselves compulsively and for sexual gratification may not demonstrate the behavior within the school system, and any intervention would most likely be through the legal system.

Because exhibitionists are generally poorly motivated in therapy, prognosis for recovery is difficult to predict. Research is continuing with regard to prevention, assessment, and treatment of exhibitionists, especially in the area of pharmacological treatments.

REFERENCES

Abel, G. G., Osborn, C. A., & Twigg, D. A. (1993). Sexual assault through the life span: Adult offenders with juvenile histories. In H. E. Barbaree, W. L. Marshall, & S. M. Hudson (Eds.), *The juvenile sex offender* (pp. 104–117). New York: Guilford Press.

Arndt, W. B. (1995). Deviant sexual behavior in children and adolescents. In G. A. Rekers (Ed.), *Handbook of child and adolescent sexual problems* (pp. 424–445). Lexington, MA: Lexington Books.

Fehrenbach, P. A., Smith, W., Monastersky, C., & Deisher, R. W. (1986). Adolescent sexual offenders: Offender and offense characteristics. *American Journal of Orhopsychiatry, 56*(2), 225–233.

Gil, E., & Johnson, T. E. (1993). *Sexualized children.* Rockville, MD: Launch Press.

Kelley, K., & Byrne, D. (1992). *Exploring human sexuality.* Englewood Cliffs, NJ: Prentice-Hall.

Miner, M. H., & Dwyer, S. M. (1997). The psychosocial development of sex offenders: Differences between exhibitionists, child molesters, and incest offenders. *International Journal of Offender Therapy and Comparative Criminology, 41*(1), 36–44.

Money, J. (1984). Paraphilias: Phenomenology and classification. *American Journal of Psychotherapy, 38*(2), 164–179.

Money, J. (1988). *Lovemaps: Clinical concepts of sexual/erotic health and pathology, paraphilia, and gender transposition in childhood, adolescence, and maturity.* Buffalo, NY: Prometheus Books.

Rhoads, J. M. (1989). Exhibitionism and voyeurism. In American Psychiatric Association Task Force on Treatments of Psychiatric Disorders (Ed.), *Treatments of psychiatric disorders: A task force report of the American Psychiatric Association* (Vol. 1, pp. 670–673). Washington, DC: American Psychiatric Press.

Ross, J., & Loss, P. (1991). Assessment of the juvenile sex offender. In G. D. Ryan & S. L. Lane (Eds.), *Juvenile sexual offending: Causes, consequences, and correction* (pp. 199–251). Lexington, MA: Lexington Books.

Saunders, E., Awad, G. A., & White, G. (1986). Male adolescent sexual offenders: The offender and the offense. *Canadian Journal of Psychiatry, 3,* 542–549.

Smith, W. R., & Monastersky, C. (1986). Assessing juvenile sexual offenders' risk for reoffending. *Criminal Justice and Behavior, 13,* 115–140.

Stephanie R. Forness
Brian D. Johnson
University of Northern Colorado

F

FABRY DISEASE

Fabry disease, also known as angiokeratoma corpris diffusum, is a disorder of lipid metabolism caused by an α-galactosidase-A deficiency, which leads to accumulation of glycolipid products in various muscle tissues and cells in the nervous system. Individuals inherit Fabry disease as an X-linked recessive trait (Rowland, 1995). It is caused by the gene located on the long arm of the X chromosome (Xq21.33-Xq22).

Prevalence of Fabry disease in the United States is estimated to be 2,500 individuals (Thoene & Coker, 1995). Fabry disease is most likely to affect males and individuals of Western European descent, but it can affect heterozygous females. Female carriers show signs of Fabry disease such as angiokeratomas, burning pains, and cloudiness of the cornea (Wynbrandt & Ludman, 1999).

Characteristics

1. Angiokeratomas or dark red, raised, dot-like lesions on the skin that appear during childhood and increase in size and number with age
2. Burning pain in the hands and feet triggered by exercise, fatigue, fever, emotional stress, or change in temperature; diminished ability to sweat
3. Nausea, vomiting, diarrhea, and abdominal or side pain
4. Retarded growth and delayed puberty
5. Swelling and distortion of the blood vessels in the conjunctiva and retina
6. Kidney failure or cardiovascular complications

Chronic pain in the hands and feet may be alleviated by daily doses of phenytoin (Dilantin) or low doses of diphenylhydantoin or carbamazepin (Tegretol). Other acute symptoms may be treated with Dexamethasone. Angiokeratomas may be removed with laser therapy (Thoene & Coker, 1995).

Special education services may be available for children with Fabry disease under the category of Other Health Impairment if the symptoms progress significantly. Education providers should be alerted to possible side effects of medication used to alleviate pain symptoms.

Individuals affected by Fabry disease are at risk for kidney failure or cardiovascular complications, but kidney dialysis and transplantation have improved the prognoses for these individuals. Several companies and researchers are in the process of developing drugs for enzyme replacement therapy (Schiffmann et al., 2000; Takenaka et al., 2000).

REFERENCES

Rowland, L. P. (Ed.). (1995). *Merritt's textbook of neurology* (9th ed.). Baltimore: Williams & Wilkins.

Schiffmann, R., Murray, G. J., Treco, D., Daniel, P., Sellos-Moura, M., Myers, M., Quirk, J. M., Zirzow, G. C., Borowski, M., Loveday, K., Anderson, T., Gillespie, F., Oliver, K. L., Jeffries, N. O., Doo, E., Liang, T. J., Kreps, C., Gunter, K., Frei, K., Crutchfield, K., Selden, R. F., & Brady, R. O. (2000). Infusion of α-galactosidase A reduces tissue globotriaosylceramide storage in patients with Fabry disease. *National Institute of Health, 97,* 365–370.

Takenaka, T., Murray, G. J., Qin, G., Quirk, J. M., Ohshima, T., Qasba, P., Clark, K., Kulkarni, A. B., Brady, R. O., & Medin, J. A. (2000). Long-term enzyme correction and lipid reduction in multiple organs of primary and secondary transplanted Fabry mice receiving bone marrow cells. *Proceedings of the National Academy of Sciences, 97,* 7515–7520.

Thoene, J. G., & Coker, N. P. (Eds.). (1995). *Physicians' guide to rare diseases* (2nd ed.). Montvale, NJ: Dowden.

Wynbrandt, J., & Ludman, M. D. (Eds.). (1999). *The encyclopedia of genetic disorders and birth defects.* New York: Facts on File.

Jennifer Hargrave
University of Texas at Austin

FAIRBANK DISEASE

Fairbank disease is the name for one of two traditional categories of multiple epiphyseal dysplasia, or MED. Although other variations of MED are recognized, diagnoses are still often labeled by the former names. The Fairbank variant is the more severe of the two, and the milder version is referred to as the Ribbing variant. The affected epiphyses are small, irregular, or fragmented in the Fairbank variant, whereas in the Ribbing variant the involved epiphyses are often flat (Connors, 2000).

MED is genetically caused (Curcione, 1995), and three genes responsible for the condition have been identified (Connors, 2000). MED must be differentiated from Legg-Calve-Perthes disease, hypothyroidism, psuedoacoachondroplasia (PSACH) and from other dysplasias (Burns et al., 2000). Age of onset typically ranges from 2–6 years, although problems may not occur until much later in life (Gandy, 1997). The prevalence of MED is unknown.

Characteristics

1. Commonly begins with painful or stiff legs, especially knee and hip joints.
2. May have bowing of the knees, "knock-knees," or similar hip problems.
3. Joints are affected symmetrically.
4. May have short limbs or short and stubby hands and feet.
5. May exhibit a limp or a waddling walk.
6. Young children may have delayed walking ability.

Treatment for MED varies according to the symptoms expressed and the severity of those symptoms. Frequent X rays can be expected in order to monitor the progression of the disease. Severe cases may require long spells of bed rest that will require a child to miss school and other daily activities. In milder cases, stretching exercises will be recommended as well as weight control to ensure that no additional stress is placed on the joints. High-impact sports should be avoided, and minor surgical procedures can be done to correct knee alignment when necessary (Li & Stanton, 1996).

Due to the extended absences from school that may be necessary during the initial stages of diagnosis and treatment, special education services may be available for children with MED. Home visits from educators are preferable because it is important that children remain actively involved in learning while away from the classroom (Kauffman & Hallahan, 1981).

Effects of MED persist throughout adulthood. Osteoarthritis tends to develop with advancing age (Gandy, 1997). Short stature is present but not severe. Joint replacements are usually necessary; typically hip replacements are required, but knee replacements may also be necessary (Li & Stanton, 1996).

REFERENCES

Burns, C., et al. (2000.) *Pediatric primary care: A handbook for nurse practitioners* (2nd ed.). Philadelphia, PA: W. B. Saunders.

Connors, M. (2001, April 5). Multiple epiphyseal dysplasia. Retrieved from http://www.mun.ca/biology/scarr/MED.htm

Curcione, P., & Stanton, R. (1995). Multiple epiphyseal dysplasia. Retrieved from http://gait.aidi.udel.edu/res695/homepage/pd_ortho/educate/clincase/epipdysp.htm

Gandy, A. (1997). Multiple epiphyseal dysplasia. Retrieved from http://www.pedianet.com/prof/disease/files/multiple.htm

Kauffman, J., & Hallahan, D. (Eds.). (1981). *Handbook of special education.* Englewood Cliffs, NJ: Prentice-Hall.

Li, C., & Stanton, R. (1996). Multiple epiphyseal dysplasia: Clinical case presentation. Retrieved from http://gait.aidi.udel.edu/res695/homepage/pd_ortho/educate/clincase/medyp.htm

Emily Cornforth
University of Colorado at Colorado Springs

FAMILIAL DYSAUTONOMIA (RILEY-DAY SYNDROME)

Familial dysautonomia (FD), sometimes called Riley-Day syndrome, is a hereditary sensory and autonomic neuropathy (HSAN). It stems from incomplete development of sensory and autonomic neurons and manifests in widespread sensory and variable autonomic dysfunction (New York University School of Medicine FD Center, 2001). FD is a rare autosomal-recessive disorder occurring largely in Ashkenazi Jews, in whom incidence is about .5–1 per 10,000. The FD gene is located on the long arm of Chromosome 9 (9q31q33; Meyer, 1997).

Absence of tearing is the most distinctive characteristic. Suggestive signs at birth include breech presentation, weak or absent suck, and poor tone. About 60% of cases show early difficulties with sucking and swallowing, and about 40% later react to physical or emotional stress with the dysautonomia crisis, which includes vomiting, increased heart rate and blood pressure, sweating, and behavior change. However, the disorder shows high variability in the type and severity of symptoms. Intelligence is apparently unaffected (New York University School of Medicine FD Center, 2001).

Characteristics

1. Reduced or absent ability to produce tears
2. Lack of fungiform papillae on tongue
3. Excessive sweating
4. Vasomotor instability
5. Swallowing difficulties and episodic vomiting
6. Speech and motor dysfunction
7. Reduced heat, pain, and taste perception
8. Poor growth and scoliosis

Initial diagnosis is through clinical signs. The following constellation of clinical signs strongly suggests FD: parents who are Ashkenazi Jewish in background, absence of tears and fungiform papillae on the tongue, decreased deep tendon reflexes, and lack of an axon flare following intradermal histamine. Confirmation is through genetic identification of mutations in the IKBKAP gene (New York University School of Medicine FD Center, 2001).

At present, only preventive and symptomatic treatment is available. Given the high individual differences in manifestation, treatment needs to be individualized. Common treatments include artificial tears; feeding, occupational, physical, and speech therapies; medication for autonomic manifestations; and surgery for orthopedic problems. It is important to note that in cases of reduced sensory abilities, affected individuals may need protection from accidents. Future incidence may be lowered owing to recently available antenatal diagnosis and population screening (New York University School of Medicine FD Center, 2001).

REFERENCES

Meyer, G. (1997). Syndromes and inborn errors of metabolism. In M. L. Batshaw (Ed.), *Children with disabilities* (4th ed., pp. 813–834). Baltimore: Brookes.

New York University School of Medicine FD Center. (2001). Familial dysautonomia. Retrieved from http://www.med.nyu.edu/fd/fdcenter.html#gn

Robert T. Brown
University of North Carolina, Wilmington

FAMILIAL MEDITERRANEAN FEVER

Familial Mediterranean fever (FMF) is a relatively common (in certain ethnic groups) inherited disorder of the immune system. It is classified as one of several rheumatic diseases that are characterized by an altered immune response that causes inflammation in specific organs.

The gene responsible for FMF is located on Chromosome 16. This site controls the synthesis of a protein, pyrin, which is present in neutrophils, a type of white blood cell. Although the role of pyrin in the immune response is not completely clear, it appears to function as an inhibiting agent. The underlying problem in FMF is a lack of inhibitor enzymes that can turn off the immune response and the ensuing inflammation it creates. Pleural (within the chest), peritoneal (within the abdomen), synovial (in joints) and pericardial (surrounding the heart) fluids are the most common substances affected by the inhibitor deficiency.

Several mutations of the abnormal gene in FMF cause variable severity in its symptoms. The forms with the poorest outlook and the best outlook are the most prevalent clinical types of FMF.

FMF is transmitted in an autosomal recessive manner. In certain populations, the estimation of the carrier state of the abnormal gene approaches 20%. The disorder is most common in Sephardic Jews (from Spain and Portugal), Armenians, Turks, and Arabs. Greeks, Hispanics, and Italians are less affected by FMF. It is interesting to note that FMF is rare in Ashkenazi Jews (from central and eastern Europe), Germans, and Anglo-Saxons.

Characteristics

1. Brief, acute episodes of fever and inflammation of serosal surfaces (previously mentioned) that end spontaneously and occur at irregular intervals.
2. Sixty-five percent of affected individuals will experience symptoms by 5 years of age. Ninety percent will have had at least one episode by age 20.
3. Acute attacks typically consist of fever (100%), abdominal pain (90%), arthritis and joint discomfort (85%), and chest pain (20%). Less frequent findings include pericarditis (inflammation of the membrane that encloses the heart), rash, muscle aches, splenic enlargement, and scrotal swelling.
4. Neurological complications are rare.
5. About 35–50% of untreated patients will develop amyloidosis, a condition in which an abnormal protein (amyloid) is deposited throughout the body. Unchecked amyloidosis will eventually cause kidney failure and death. This complication is most frequent among Sephardic Jews and Turks.

Treatment for FMF is prophylactic. The drug colchicine is taken daily. It not only prevents or significantly reduces the frequency of acute attacks, but also makes the development of amyloidosis much less likely. In some patients, colchicine has even caused partial reversal of amyloid deposition.

There is no research to indicate cognitive dysfunction or the need for special education services as a result of FMF.

The prognosis for FMF appears favorable, but is somewhat dependent on the clinical form (and genetic mutation) present in the individual patient. Evidence of amyloidosis is an ominous sign, but even this manifestation of FMF is responsive to therapy. For individuals with this disorder, colchicine is as close to a miracle drug as one could imagine.

REFERENCE

Gedalia, A. (2000). Familial mediterranean fever. In R. E. Behrman, R. M. Kleigman, & H. B. Jenson (Eds.), *Nelson textbook of pediatrics* (16th ed., p. 724). Philadelphia: W. B. Saunders.

Barry H. Davison
Ennis, Texas

Joan W. Mayfield
Baylor Pediatric Specialty Services
Dallas, Texas

FEEDING DISORDER OF EARLY CHILDHOOD

Feeding disorder of early childhood is characterized by an enduring failure to eat adequately that is not due to a general medical condition of lack of available food and causes the infant or child (< 6 years) to fail to gain weight or to experience significant weight loss over a period of at least 1 month.

It has been estimated that 1–5% of all pediatric hospital admissions are due to failure to gain weight (i.e., failure to thrive), and as many as one half of these admissions may be associated with feeding disorders that are not due to any predisposing medical condition (Wolraich, Felice, & Drotar, 1996; Woolston, 1991). The prevalence of feeding disorder is equal in boys and girls.

Characteristics

1. Persistent failure to eat sufficiently, causing failure to gain weight or significant weight loss over at least 1 month that is present before age 6.
2. The feeding disturbance is not due to a gastrointestinal, endocrinological, neurological, or other medical condition, or to lack of available food.
3. Infants and children with feeding disorder may be irritable, inconsolable, withdrawn or apathetic during feeding.
4. Associated problems include malnutrition, developmental delays, and growth retardation; parent-child interaction problems may also occur.

Given that the failure to gain weight or a significant loss of weight in infants and children can be due to a range of medical, psychological, and environmental conditions, a comprehensive multidimensional evaluation (integrating information from medical, nutritional, psychological, environmental, and parent-child interaction domains) is recommended in order to make a well-informed differential diagnosis and to focus treatment accordingly. After a diagnosis of feeding disorder has been made, treatment options are relatively straightforward and effective. Treatment typically involves parental education about the physiological development of eating behaviors, nutrition, child temperament, and the principles of learning and behavior change (Ramasamy & Perman, 2000; Ramsay, 1995). Effective treatments typically incorporate a behavior therapy component and include the use of a functional analysis to identify antecedents and consequences that can be manipulated in order to influence the child's eating behavior (e.g., prompting, reinforcement, and mild punishment).

Feeding disorder is more common in children with special needs due to developmental delays, chronic health conditions, communication difficulties, and physical limitations (Ramasamy & Perman, 2000). In such cases, feeding problems are most often due to an inability to manipulate or swallow certain foods, inappropriate or disruptive behavior during meals, or food selectivity. Assessment and treatment of children with special needs should employ a similar multidimensional approach and focus to that described previously (American Psychiatric Association, 1994).

If untreated, feeding disorder can lead to a range of negative outcomes such as malnutrition, growth retardation, developmental delays, susceptibility to infection and chronic illness, and possibly death; however, many children experience improved growth after some period of time. In addition, feeding disorder in infants and children is a risk factor for bulimia and anorexia nervosa later in life (Marchi & Cohen, 1990). The prognosis for feeding disorder is much more favorable if accurate diagnosis and empirically supported treatments are used early on in the course of this condition.

In an educational setting, children with feeding disorder may stand out for their lack of eating. It is necessary for a teacher to be aware of and well informed about this disorder, and special attention may be required for these children.

Although existing assessment and treatment techniques have proven effective in returning infants and children to normal eating and growth patterns, most studies have used single-case designs or small sample sizes without the use of randomization or control samples. Therefore, future research in this area should continue to explore the effectiveness of interdisciplinary assessment and treatment techniques using more complex research designs and larger and more diverse samples.

REFERENCES

American Psychiatric Association. (1994). *Diagnostic and statistical manual of mental disorders* (4th ed.). Washington, DC: Author.

Marchi, M., & Cohen, P. (1990). Early childhood eating behaviors and adolescent eating disorder. *Journal of the American Academy of Child and Adolescent Psychiatry, 29,* 112–117.

Ramasamy, M., Perman, J. A. (2000). Pediatric feeding disorders. *Journal of Clinical Gastroenterology, 30,* 34–46.

Ramsay, M. (1995). Feeding disorder and failure to thrive. *Child and Adolescent Psychiatric Clinics of North America, 4,* 605–616.

Wolraich, M., Felice, M., & Drotar, D. (1996). *The classification of child and adolescent mental diagnoses in primary care: Diagnostic and statistical manual for primary care (DSM-PC), child and adolescent version.* Elk Grove, IL: American Academy of Pediatrics.

Woolston, J. L. (1991). *Eating and growth disorders in infants and children.* Newbury Park, CA: Sage.

Matthew K. Nock
Yale University

FEEDING DISORDERS OF INFANCY

Feeding disorders are characterized by any interference in the process of deglutition. Deglutition is the semiautomatic motor function of the muscles of the respiratory and gastrointestinal tracts that are responsible for moving food from the oral cavity (mouth) to the stomach (Miller, 1986). Normal oral motor function and swallowing are integral processes in oral feeding (Arvedson & Rogers, 1993).

Feeding and swallowing disorders in children (also known as dysphagia) are often part of a larger range of medical and health problems. Current advances in the medical field have led to increased survival rates of premature, low birth weight infants; as well as children who have undergone extensive medical or surgical procedures. As a result, a number of these infants and children experience complications. In particular, damage to the central nervous system, the airway, or both can occur, which results in a disruption of the oral feeding process (Arvedson & Rogers, 1993). The prevalence of feeding and swallowing disorders is not known. Additionally, there are no known variations among these children with regard to gender or ethnicity.

Characteristics

1. Extreme prematurity and very low birth weight.
2. Uncoordinated sucking, swallowing, and breathing that continues beyond 34–37 weeks gestation.
3. A history of long-term, nonoral feedings for a variety of reasons.
4. Cerebral palsy, mental retardation, or central nervous system dysgenesis (developmental anomalies of the brain) may be present in some children.
5. Some infants have experienced brain injury.
6. Disordered parent-child interactions, behavioral problems, or both are sometimes present (Arvedson & Rogers, 1993).

There are several known etiologies of feeding disorders. Arvedson and Rogers (1993) divide these etiologies into acute and chronic. Chronic disorders can be further classified as either static or progressive. Cerebral palsy is an example of a common static cause of dysphagia. Examples of progressive causes are destructive central nervous system tumors or neurodegenerative diseases.

Feeding disorders are often complicated by other factors. Respiratory distress interferes with oral feedings, as do abnormalities of the aerodigestive tract. These children frequently cough, have tachypnea, or gasp during oral feedings. Other less common complications are severe choking, apnea, and cyanosis. Aspiration pneumonia and various forms of lung disease have also been known to occur. Gastroesophageal reflux is frequently present in these children. Because feeding disorders typically result in prolonged oral feedings and a reduction of oral intake, malnutrition and growth failure may occur (Arvedson & Rogers, 1993).

A thorough clinical evaluation of feeding and swallowing commonly includes a review of the child's medical, developmental, and feeding history. A physical examination, prefeeding evaluation, and a feeding evaluation must also be conducted. Arvedson and Lefton-Grief (1998) stated that the clinical evaluation should provide the following information: the identification of possible causes of the dysphagia, a hypothesis about the nature and severity of the condition, a baseline of oral-motor skills and respiratory function, possible therapeutic techniques and feeding options, and a determination of the need for an instrumental assessment (e.g., video fluoroscopic swallow study). This process requires the collaboration of various professionals.

Infants and children who are candidates for oral-motor and feeding therapy require individualized treatment plans. These plans should be integrated into broad-based intervention plans with functional goals. A total sensory, oral-motor, and behavioral management program is recommended, as is an interdisciplinary, team-focused approach (Arvedson, 1993; Morris & Klein, 1987). It is important to note that total oral feeding may not be the final goal for all children.

Treatment involves compensatory procedures and direct therapy services. Compensatory strategies include changes in the child's posture, sensory enhancement (taste, thermal-tactile stimulation, temperature, size of the bolus) and changes in the child's feeding pattern. Examples of direct therapy are range of motion exercises for the lips, tongue, jaw, or all three; laryngeal elevation, tongue base retraction, and swallowing maneuvers. Swallowing maneuvers are voluntary strategies the child learns in order to change the timing or strength of certain movements during swallowing. In order to be effective, treatment should be delivered several times during the day. Therefore, it is crucial that family members or other caregivers be taught the specific techniques and strategies (Logemann, 2000). Prognosis depends upon the individual child, his or her level of functioning, and any comorbid conditions (e.g. cerebral palsy) that may interfere with the normal feeding-swallowing process.

Medically based feeding and swallowing problems have increased dramatically in the public schools during the past 5 years (Logemann & O'Toole, 2000). Children with dysphagia usually meet the definition of a child with a disability because they lack the ability to successfully take in nutrition, and the risk of malnutrition can affect the child's ability to concentrate and learn (O'Toole, 2000). In addition, these children frequently have another disability, such as cerebral palsy, that further qualifies them for special education services in the public school.

Further research is needed with infants and young children, especially those with normal oral motor skills. Data-based research is needed in the area of treatment in order to prove the credibility of specific treatment approaches.

REFERENCES

Arvedson, J. C. (1993). Management of swallowing problems. In J. C. Arvedson & L. Brodsky (Eds.), *Pediatric swallowing and feeding: Assessment and management* (pp. 327–387). San Diego, CA: Singular Publishing Group.

Arvedson, J. C., & Lefton-Greif, M. A. (1998). *Pediatric videofluroscopic swallow studies: A professional manual with caregiver guidelines.* San Antonio, TX: Communication Skill Builders.

Arvedson, J. C., & Rogers, B. T. (1993). Pediatric swallowing and feeding disorders. *Journal of Medical Speech-Language Pathology, 1*(4), 203–221.

Logemann, J. A. (2000). Therapy for children with swallowing disorders in the educational setting. *Language, Speech, and Hearing Services in Schools, 31,* 50–55.

Logemann, J. A., & O'Toole, T. J. (2000). Identification and management of dysphagia in the public schools. *Language, Speech, and Hearing Services in Schools, 31,* 26–27.

Miller, A. J. (1982). Deglutition. *Physiological Reviews, 62,* 129–184.

Morris, S. E., & Klein, M. D. (1987). *Pre-feeding skills: A comprehensive resource for feeding development.* Tucson, AZ: Therapy Skill Builders.

O'Toole, T. J. (2000) Legal, ethical, and financial aspects of providing services to children with swallowing disorders in the public schools. *Language, Speech, and Hearing Services in Schools, 31,* 56–60.

Theresa T. Aguire
Texas A & M University

FEMORAL HYPOPLASIA–UNUSUAL FACIES SYNDROME

Femoral hypoplasia–unusual facies syndrome (FH-UFS) is an exceedingly rare disorder. Its main features include short stature, mildly dysmorphic facial features, and absent or underdeveloped bones of the lower extremity. Short stature is the result of severely shortened legs.

The etiology of FH-UFS is unknown. Its incidence in the general population is unclear. Thus far only six cases have been reported. Most occurrences of FH-UFS appear to be sporadic. However, there is one instance in which an affected male had a similarly affected daughter. This example suggests the possibility of an autosomal dominant mode of inheritance. Maternal diabetes is also a common finding in infants with FH-UFS.

Characteristics

1. Short stature secondary to severely shortened legs.
2. Facial features include short nose with underdeveloped sides of the lower nose, thin upper lip, small jaw, cleft palate, upward slanting of the outer corner of the eye, and malformed, low-set ears.
3. Limb deformities are bilateral (on both sides), but each extremity is not equally affected. Findings include underdeveloped (hypoplastic) or absent femur (thigh bone) and, occasionally, hypoplastic or absent tibia and fibula (bones of the lower leg, below the knee). There is usually some degree of hypoplasia of the humerus (bone of the upper arm). Fusion of the elbow joint and the adjacent radioulnar articulation is occasionally seen.
4. Other skeletal anomalies occasionally observed are underdevelopment of the pelvis, missing or deformed vertebrae, and scoliosis.
5. Associated genitourinary abnormalities have been described: undescended testicle; inguinal hernia; small penis and testes; and a variety of kidney anomalies, including complete absence of the kidney.

No treatment is available at this time for the majority of the skeletal pathology of FH-UFS. Some children are born with congenital heart defects that require surgical repair. Operative intervention may also be necessary to treat hernias, cleft palate, and esotropia (cross-eye). Although all of these patients have had normal intelligence, speech delays have been observed. These difficulties are best handled by referral to appropriate therapists.

A child with FH-UFS may require modifications in the physical environment due to physical limitations. Although referral to a speech pathologist may be needed to help with language delays, other modifications should not be required because no cognitive deficits have been reported. Because of the physical deformities, providing a positive environment that builds good self-image and education for his or her classmates will facilitate peer relationships.

Because there is such a small population of individuals with FH-UFS, prognostic discussion for the disorder is rather conjectural. However, in the absence of life-threatening cardiac or renal anomalies, there appears to be a reasonable hope for survival into adulthood.

REFERENCE

Jones, K. (1997). *Smith's recognizable patterns of human malformations* (5th ed.). Philadelphia: W. B. Saunders.

Barry H. Davison, MD
Ennis, Texas

Joan W. Mayfield
Baylor Pediatric Specialty Services
Dallas, Texas

FETAL ALCOHOL SYNDROME

Fetal alcohol syndrome (FAS) is a group of birth defects or abnormalities occurring in children who are born to women who have histories of relatively high levels of periodic or consistent alcohol consumption during pregnancy. The defects, which can include physical, mental, and behavioral problems, are irreversible (Centers for Disease Control, 2001; Mayo Clinic, 2001). FAS is not a single birth defect; rather, it is a cluster or pattern of related problems. The severity of symptoms varies, with some children experiencing problems to a far greater degree than others (Mayo Clinic, 2001).

The Centers for Disease Control estimate that anywhere from 1 in 500 to 1 in 3,000 children are born in the United States each year with FAS. This wide range is related to differences in drinking practices. A pregnant woman who drinks any amount of alcohol is at risk because a safe level of alcohol ingestion during pregnancy has not been established. However, increasing amounts appear to cause increased problems in a linear fashion. Multiple birth defects associated with classical fetal alcohol syndrome are more commonly associated with heavy alcohol use or alcoholism (MEDLINE Plus, 2002). Approximately 30–40% of children born to mothers who drink heavily during pregnancy develop FAS, and an additional 4,000 children per year display symptoms of fetal alcohol effects, which is a milder form of FAS. FAS is the leading known cause of mental retardation in children and is the only birth defect known that is completely preventable (Centers for Disease Control, 2001).

Characteristics

1. Small head circumference and brain size (microcephaly).
2. Facial malformation, such as small eyelid openings, sunken nasal bridge, thin upper lips, and smooth skin surface between the nose and upper lip.
3. Small teeth with faulty enamel.
4. Heart defects.
5. Deformities of joints, limbs, and fingers.
6. Slow physical growth before and after birth.
7. Vision difficulties, including nearsightedness (myopia).
8. Mental retardation and delayed development.
9. Behaviors may include short attention span, hyperactivity, poor impulse control, extreme nervousness, and anxiety.

Doctors cannot diagnose FAS before a baby is born, and even after birth, FAS shares many of the same physical or behavioral characteristics as other syndromes and is therefore difficult to diagnose. Doctors often rely on certain manifestations such as a growth deficiency, facial malformations, or the presence of heart defects in order to diagnose FAS. Evaluations of a child's development may also assist doctors in making a diagnosis. There is no cure for FAS, and the physical defects and mental deficiencies persist for a lifetime (Mayo Clinic, 2001).

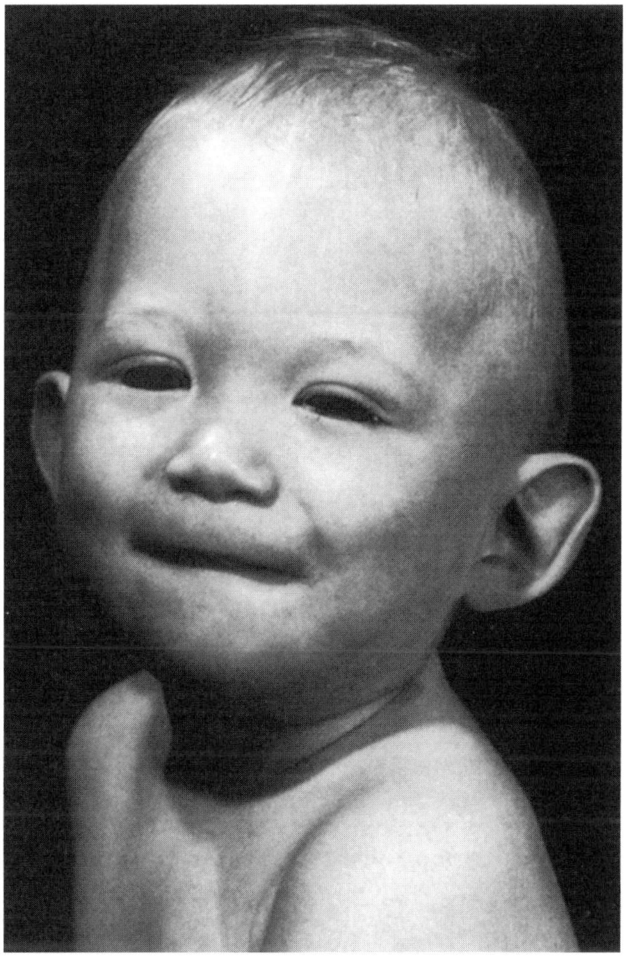

Fetal Alcohol Syndrome
Reprinted from *Clinical Syndromes,* Wiedemann and Kunze, 1997, by permission of the publisher Mosby

Depending on the severity of the symptoms, a child with FAS could qualify for special education services under several different categories, including Mental Retardation, Emotional Disturbance, Other Health Impairment, or specific Learning Disability. The school psychologist would work with the multidisciplinary team to provide appropriate services to the child with FAS that are consistent with the specified disability.

The prognosis for FAS focuses on prevention and early identification of women at risk. Educating women about the risks of alcohol consumption during pregnancy appears to be the best method of prevention.

REFERENCES

Centers for Disease Control. (2001). Fetal alcohol syndrome. Retrieved November 2001, from http://www.cdc.gov/health/diseases.htm

Mayo Clinic. (2001). Fetal alcohol syndrome. Retrieved November 2001, from http://www.mayoclinic.com/findinformation/diseasesndconditions

MEDLINE Plus Medical Encyclopedia. (2002). Fetal alcohol syndrome. Retrieved April 2002, from http://www.nlm.nih.gov/medlineplus/ency/article/000911.htm

Christine D. Cde Baca
University of Northern Colorado

FETAL AMINOPTERIN/METHOTREXATE SYNDROME

Aminopterin is a folic acid antagonist occasionally used as an abortifacient (a drug to induce an abortion) in early pregnancy; methotrexate, the methyl derivative of aminopterin and also an abortifacient, is used to treat rheumatoid arthritis and psoriasis. Offspring of mothers treated with either drug early in pregnancy may show a complex of craniofacial, growth, and limb abnormalities. An apparent critical period for adverse effects occurs at 6–8 weeks postconception. Fetal or early postnatal death may occur. In survivors, the most apparent feature are facial dysmorphologies, which result in a characteristic appearance. Surprisingly, given frequent microcephaly, intelligence and motor behavior are largely unaffected (Jones, 1997). The disorder is rare (Office of Rare Diseases, 2001), and accurate incidence figures are not available.

Characteristics

1. Craniofacial dysmorphologies (microcephaly; severe hypoplasia of frontal, parietal, temporal, and occipital bones; broad nasal ridge; wide fontanels; low-set ears; prominent eyes; epicanthal folds; and micrognathia)
2. Postnatal growth retardation
3. Limb abnormalities (shortness of arms and legs, hypo- and syndactyly)
4. Apparently normal intelligence

As with many drug-induced abnormalities, knowledge that the pregnant woman actually ingested the drug is important for accurate diagnosis. Although the morphological effects are irreversible, surgery may help to alleviate some effects. The facial dysmorphologies may lead to speech impairments that will call for therapy, but normal classroom placement would be expected. However, affected individuals may benefit from counseling to help them deal with psychological consequences of their abnormal appearance.

REFERENCES

Jones, K. L. (1997). *Smith's recognizable patterns of human malformation* (5th ed.). Philadelphia: Saunders.

Office of Rare Diseases. (2001). Rare diseases list. Retrieved from http://ord.aspensys.com/diseases.asp

Robert T. Brown
University of North Carolina, Wilmington

FETAL HYDANTOIN SYNDROME

Fetal hydantoin syndrome (FHS) is caused by the anticonvulsant drug (AED) phenytoin (Dilantin). Phenytoin is a prenatal teratogen, causing a variety of physical defects, including infant failure to thrive, dysmorphic facies and other physical abnormalities, growth deficiency, and mental retardation, usually mild. The effects, particularly craniofacial, of prenatal exposure to phenytoin are so similar to those of several other AEDs, including carbamazepine, valproic acid, mysoline, and phenobarbital, as to have led to the general descriptive term *fetal antiepileptic drug syndrome* (Jones, 1997; Zahn, Morrell, Collins, Labiner, & Yerby, 1998). As with most teratogens, major damage occurs from exposure early in prenatal development.

About 10% of infants exposed prenatally to phenytoin will manifest the full FHS, and an additional 33% will show some congenital anomalies (Buehler, Rao, & Finnell, 1994; Jones, 1997). Dose-response curve or safe levels of exposure are unknown. Risk appears to increase if the pregnant woman takes multiple anticonvulsants (Jones, 1997; Zahn et al., 1998). Fetal genotype appears to determine sensitivity to prenatal exposure to phenytoin (Jones, 1997). No clear gender differences are apparent (Zahn et al., 1998). The following are only a few of numerous characteristics described in Jones (1997), and they may appear in various combinations.

Characteristics

1. Numerous craniofacial dysmorphologies, including wide anterior fontanel; forehead ridging; ocular hypertelorism; broad, depressed nasal bridge; short nose; broad upper lip; and cleft lip and palate.
2. Mild-moderate growth deficiency, usually intrauterine growth retardation, but often continuing into early postnatal period as failure to thrive.
3. Below-average intelligence, occasionally into mild mental retardation.
4. Numerous other physical abnormalities, including hypoplastic distal phalanges with small nails, short neck, dislocation of hip, umbilical and inguinal hernias, widely spaced and small nipples, and hirsutism.

Optimal treatment for FHS—and fetal antiepileptic drug syndromes in general—is preventive. Women who are taking anticonvulsants need to be aware of the risks involved before they become pregnant. Complicating the situation is the fact that uncontrolled seizures as well as exposure to AEDs put the embryo or fetus at risk. The Epilepsy Foundation (2001) has information of value to those with epilepsy who may become pregnant. Their physician should reduce the number of anticonvulsants to one at 6 months prior to conception. Folic acid supplements during pregnancy may also be recommended (Zahn et al., 1998).

Treatment and education of children with FHD or other AED syndrome needs to be individualized, owing to wide variations in the degree and type of resulting problems. Intervention may be needed as early as infancy to deal with potential failure to thrive. The major problems in childhood that call for special services are low intelligence and mental retardation. One hopeful fact is that cognitive development in childhood may be greater than would be predicted by overall development in early infancy (Jones, 1997).

REFERENCES

Beuhler, B., Rao, V., & Finnell, R. (1994). Biochemical and molecular teratology of fetal hydantoin syndrome. *Pediatric Neurogenetics, 12,* 741–748.

Epilepsy Foundation (2001). Women and epilepsy. Retrieved from http://www.efa.org/answerplace/getsection.cfm?keyname=women

Jones, K. L. (1997). *Smith's recognizable patterns of human malformation* (5th ed.). Philadelphia: W. B. Sanders.

Zahn, C., Morrell, M., Collins, S., Labiner, D., & Yerby, M. (1998). Management issues for women with epilepsy: A review of the literature. *Neurology, 51,* 949–956.

Melanie Moore
Robert T. Brown
University of North Carolina, Wilmington

FETAL RUBELLA SYNDROME

Rubella, or German measles, is a communicable RNA virus whose effects, including rash and fever, are generally mild when contracted in later childhood or adulthood. However, if contracted by a pregnant woman, rubella may cross the placental barrier and cause fetal death or serious deformities in her offspring. A congenital maternal infection, it is a member of the STORCH complex (syphilis, toxiplasmosis, varicella and other infections, rubella, cytomegalovirus, and herpes), a group of maternal infections that have similar effects on offspring (e.g., Graham & Morgan, 1997). A complex of effects, fetal rubella syndrome (FRS) or congenital rubella syndrome affects about 85% of offspring whose mothers contracted rubella during the first 20 weeks of pregnancy. Effects are greatest in offspring exposed to rubella during the embryonic period, although visual and auditory defects may occur with exposure up to 20 weeks gestation (Centers for Disease Control and Prevention, 2001; March of Dimes, 1999).

Characteristics

1. Intrauterine growth retardation
2. Sensory defects leading to profound hearing loss or deafness, defective vision or blindness, or both
3. Mental retardation and cerebral palsy
4. Congenital heart disease and widespread damage to other internal organs
5. Delayed motor development
6. Diabetes, first appearing in childhood or adulthood

Owing to widespread vaccination of children in developed countries, both postnatal and fetal rubella have declined in recent decades—in the United States, only 12 cases of confirmed FRS occurred during 1995–1996 (Dyne, 2001). However, risk remains high in countries where childhood vaccination is not routine. FRS can cause miscarriage or stillbirth, and survivors may show serious defects. The most common problems, in order, are severe hearing impairment, congenital heart disease, and visual impairments (Roizen & Johnson, 1996; Webster, 1998).

Apparently unaffected infants whose mothers had rubella early in pregnancy should be carefully monitored because sensory, learning, autistic signs, and behavior problems may not appear until childhood (Roizen & Johnson, 1996). Transient signs, including red-purple spots on skin, low birth weight, feeding problems, diarrhea, pneumonia, meningitis, anemia, and enlarged liver and spleen apparent at birth may identify potential cases (March of Dimes, 1999).

Prognosis depends on the number and severity of organic defects: "Of those children with congenital rubella who live to adulthood, one third will be unaffected, one third will have mild to moderate defects, and one third will have severe to profound impairment" (Roizen & Johnson, 1996, p. 183). Except for transient characteristics at birth, effects of FRS are permanent, and only supportive treatment is available. As with prognosis, type and extent of assistance required depend on the variety and severity of problems. Surgery may be required for cardiac and other organic defects. Special education treatment may include adaptive technology for sensory impairments (hearing aids, computer-based reading devices), speech and language therapy, special classroom placement, or—in severe cases—institutionalization. A team approach will be needed in many cases. Parents may need long-term help with inhome care, and many affected individuals will require some degree of lifelong assistance. Clearly, the best long-term approach for FRS is prevention through childhood immunization.

REFERENCES

Centers for Disease Control and Prevention. (2001). Rubella. In *Epidemiology and prevention of vaccine-preventable diseases: The pink book.* Retrieved from http://www.cdc.gov/nip/publications/pink/rubella.pdf

Dyne, P. (2001). Pediatrics, rubella. *eMedicine Journal, 2*(6) Retrieved from http://emedicine.com/emerg/topic388.htm

Graham, E. M., & Morgan, M. A. (1997). Growth before birth. In M. L. Batshaw (Ed.), *Children with disabilities* (4th ed., pp. 53–69). Baltimore: Brookes.

March of Dimes. (1999). *Rubella.* Retrieved from

Roizen, N. J., & Johnson, D. (1996). Congenital infections. In A. J. Capute & P. J. Accardo (Eds.), *Developmental disabilities in infancy and childhood:* Vol. 1. *Neurodevelopmental diagnosis and treatment* (2nd ed.,) pp. 175–193. Baltimore: Brookes.

Webster, W. S. (1998). Teratology update: Congenital rubella. *Teratology, 58,* 13–23.

Robert T. Brown
Stephanie Anselene
University of North Carolina, Wilmington

FETAL TRIMETHADIONE SYNDROME

Trimethadione and its congener paratrimethadione are highly teratogenic. Offspring of mothers treated with either drug during pregnancy are likely to show one or more of a variety of abnormalities. According to Jones (1997), the effects are severe and predictable enough as to call for possible elective abortion if the mother is known to have used these drugs. In one review cited by Jones (1997), of pregnancies in women taking these drugs, about 25% spontaneously aborted and 83% of live births had one or more malformations, several of which were lethal. The disorder is rare (Office of Rare Diseases, 2001), and accurate incidence figures are not available.

Characteristics

1. Mental retardation
2. Intrauterine growth retardation
3. Craniofacial dysmorphologies (mild brachycephaly and midfacial hypoplasia, prominent forehead, and short upturned nose)
4. Cardiovascular defects
5. Genital deformities (ambiguous genitalia, clitoral hypertrophy)
6. Speech disorders

As with many drug-induced abnormalities, knowledge that the pregnant woman actually ingested the drug is important for accurate diagnosis. Prognosis is poor for those with severe mental retardation and cardiovascular defects. Surgery may help to alleviate the effects of some defects, but otherwise, only supportive treatment is available. Surviving children will need a variety of special education services, including special classroom placement and speech and physical therapy.

REFERENCES

Jones, K. L. (1997). *Smith's recognizable patterns of human malformation* (5th ed.). Philadelphia: Saunders.

Office of Rare Diseases. (2001). Rare diseases list. Retrieved from http://ord.aspensys.com/diseases.asp

Robert T. Brown
University of North Carolina, Wilmington

FETAL VALPROATE SYNDROME

Fetal valproate syndrome (FVS) is caused by exposure to the anticonvulsant drug (AED) valproic acid (trade name Depakene, Depakote, among others). Valproic acid is a prenatal teratogen, and a small percentage of women who take the drug in the first trimester of pregnancy will have offspring with one or more signs of the syndrome. The effects, particularly craniofacial, of prenatal exposure to valproate are so similar to those of several other AEDs, including carbamazepine, hydantoin, mysoline, and phenobarbital, as to have led to the general descriptive term *fetal antiepileptic drug syndrome* (Jones, 1997; Zahn, Morrell, Collins, Labiner, & Yerby, 1998).

Incidence estimates are based on small sample studies and thus are subject to considerable error. About 35% of infants exposed prenatally to valproic acid will manifest characteristics of FVS (Jones, 1997), and approximately 2% will have spina bifida (Epilepsy Foundation, 2001). Dose-response curve or safe levels of exposure are unknown. Risk appears to be greater than with some other AEDs (Epilepsy Foundation, 2001), and the risk tends to increase if the pregnant woman takes multiple anticonvulsants (Jones, 1997; Zahn et al., 1998). No clear gender differences are apparent (Zahn et al., 1998). The following are only a few of numerous characteristics described in Jones (1997) and Jablonski's Multiple Congenital

Anomaly/Mental Retardation (MCA/MR) Syndromes Database (1999), and they may appear in various combinations.

Characteristics

1. Numerous craniofacial dysmorphologies, including narrow bifrontal diameter, high forehead, epicanthal folds connecting to an infraorbital crease, low nasal bridge, short nose, anterverted nostrils, long philtrum, a thin upper and thick lower lip, cleft lip and palate, and low-set posteriorly rotated ears.
2. Numerous deformities of cardiovascular, respiratory, and urogenital systems
3. Skeletal deformities, including spina bifida, hand and foot polydactyly, fingerlike thumbs, and rudimentary digits.
4. Mild to moderate growth deficiency in some cases.
5. Mental and motor retardation in some cases.

Optimal treatment for FHS—an fetal antiepileptic drug syndromes in general—is preventive. Women who are taking anticonvulsants need to be aware of the risks involved before they become pregnant. Complicating the situation is the fact that uncontrolled seizures as well as exposure to AEDs put the embryo or fetus at risk. The Epilepsy Foundation (2001) has information of value to those with epilepsy who may become pregnant. Their physician should reduce the number of anticonvulsants to one at 6 months prior to conception. Folic acid supplements during pregnancy may also be recommended (Zahn et al., 1998).

Treatment and education of children with FVD or other AED syndrome need to be individualized owing to wide variations in the degree and type of resulting problems. A variety of special education services, including special classroom placement, may be necessary. Affected individuals with spina bifida will benefit from physical therapy and adaptive technology.

REFERENCES

Epilepsy Foundation (2001). *Women and epilepsy.* Retrieved from http://www.efa.org

Jablonski's Multiple Congenital Anomaly/Mental Retardation (MCA/MR) Syndromes Database. (1999). *Fetal valproate syndrome (FVS).* United States National Library of Medicine. Retrieved from http://www.nlm.nih.gov

Jones, K. L. (1997). *Smith's recognizable patterns of human malformation* (5th ed.). Philadelphia: W. B. Sanders.

Zahn, C., Morrell, M., Collins, S., Labiner, D., & Yerby, M. (1998). Management issues for women with epilepsy: A review of the literature. *Neurology, 51,* 949–956.

Robert T. Brown
University of North Carolina, Wilmington

FETAL VARICELLA SYNDROME

Varicella, or chicken pox, is an infection that if contracted by a pregnant woman may cross the placental barrier and cause serious deformities in her offspring. A congenital maternal infection, it is a member of the STORCH complex (syphilis, toxiplasmosis, varicella and other infections, rubella, cytomegalovirus, and herpes), a group of maternal infections that have similar effects on offspring (e.g., Graham & Morgan, 1997). An estimated 1–2% of offspring of mothers who contract varicella 8–20 weeks postconception show some aspects of the syndrome, and about 50% of those die in early infancy. The number and variety of defects that may be shown is large, and the range of effects is highly variable. Even basic characteristics will not appear in all cases (Jones, 1997; National Organization for Rare Disorders, 1997).

Characteristics

1. Intrauterine growth retardation
2. Mental retardation, learning disabilities, microcephaly, and cortical atrophy
3. Seizures
4. Eye deformities (including chorioretinitis, cataracts, microphthalmia)
5. Limb hypoplasia, possibly with rudimentary digits, paralysis, and limb atrophy
6. Cutaneous scars

Prevention is the best approach now that an effective vaccine is available. Approximately 50–70% of women in the Western world test immune, even if they have no memory of having had chicken pox in childhood. Women of childbearing age who test negative for immunity should receive the vaccine, but only if they are not pregnant because teratogenic effects of the vaccine are now not known (Koren, 2000).

Diagnosis is through blood and other fluid tests. Prognosis is highly variable, depending on number and severity of symptoms. Surgery may be necessary to alleviate the effects of some defects; adaptive technology may be required to help deal with the visual and limb problems, and a variety of special education services, ranging from special classroom placement to extensive physical therapy, may be needed.

REFERENCES

Graham, E. M., & Morgan, M. A. (1997). Growth before birth. In M. L. Batshaw (Ed.), *Children with disabilities* (4th ed., pp. 53–69). Baltimore: Brookes.

Jones, K. L. (1997). *Smith's recognizable patterns of human malformation* (5th ed.). Philadelphia: Saunders.

Koren, G. (2000). Varicella virus vaccine before pregnancy. *Motherisk*. Retrieved from http://www.motherisk.org/updates/oct00.php3

National Organization for Rare Disorders. (1997). Congenital varicella syndrome. Retrieved from http://www.clarian.org/kbase/nord/nord1099.jhtml

Robert T. Brown
University of North Carolina, Wilmington

FETAL WARFARIN SYNDROME

Fetal warfarin syndrome, also known as fetal anticoagulant syndrome, DiSala syndrome, fetal coumarin syndrome, or warfarin embryopathy, is the result of teratogenic effects of the anticoagulant warfarin when taken by women during pregnancy (National Library of Medicine [NLM], 1999). Warfarin is a coumarin derivative that is used to treat clotting disorders such as phlebitis and as an anticoagulant rodenticide (International Programme on Chemical Safety [Inchem], 1997). The most prescribed oral anticoagulant, it is the 11th-most prescribed drug in the United States (Horton & Bushwick, 1999).

The disorder is rare. About one third of pregnancies among women who took warfarin in Weeks 6–9 of gestation end in either spontaneous abortion or the birth of infants with congenital abnormalities. Uncertainty exists concerning the effects of ingestion later in pregnancy, but any adverse consequences apparently occur at a very low rate (Jones, 1997).

The disorder has numerous characteristics; some occur more frequently than others (Birth Disorder Information Directory, 2000; NLM, 1999). More common characteristics are listed.

Characteristics

1. Mental retardation and seizures
2. Central nervous system abnormalities (microcephaly hydrocephalus, agenesis of the corpus callosum, spina bifida)
3. Facial anomalies, including nasal hypoplasia
4. Serious visual and auditory impairments
5. Hypoplasia of fingers and toes
6. Abnormalities of cardiovascular and respiratory systems
7. Feeding difficulties and failure to thrive

Because most effects are irreversible, treatment is mainly supportive and directed at the particular complex of symptoms shown. Some skeletal anomalies may be surgically remediable. Special education services will vary with characteristics of the child. Physical therapy, speech therapy, and cognitive therapies will often be needed. Adaptive technology or special schools may be needed in cases involving serious sensory impairments. Owing to the potential number and severity of skeletal, neurological, and muscular impairments, patients may be homebound and require in-home assistance.

Although the disorder is rare, women who are on anticoagulant medication and at risk for becoming pregnant should be aware and advised on the dangers of warfarin.

REFERENCES

Birth Disorder Information Directory. (2000). Fetal warfarin syndrome. Retrieved from http://www.orpha.net

Horton, J. D., & Bushwick, B. M. (1999, Feb. 1). Warfarin therapy: Evolving strategies in anticoagulation. *American family physician.* Retrieved from http://www.aafp.org/afp/990201ap/635.html

International Programme on Chemical Safety. (1997). Warfarin. Retrieved from http://www.inchem.org/documents/pims/chemical/pim563.htm

Jones, K. L. (1997). *Smith's recognizable patterns of human malformation* (5th ed.). Philadelphia: Saunders.

National Library of Medicine. (1999). Fetal anticoagulant syndrome. Retrieved from http://www.nlm.nih.gov/mesh/jablonski/syndromes/syndrome291.html

Paula Kilpatrick
Robert T. Brown
University of North Carolina, Wilmington

FIBER TYPE DISPROPORTION, CONGENITAL

Congenital fiber type disproportion (CFTD) is a rare muscle disease, specifically Type I muscle fibers. It is characterized by scoliosis, loss of muscle tone, short stature, dislocated hips, and foot deformities, all of which are evident at birth. Although CFTD is present at birth, symptoms tend to improve with age. Some cases of CFTD are thought to occur sporadically. Familial transmission also has been evidenced, and in some cases, gene mutations have been identified in genes that encode for muscle proteins. Overall, research presents a rather heterogeneous etiology for CFTD and incidence rates are unknown.

Characteristics

1. Type I muscle fibers are abnormally small, resulting in hypertrophic Type II muscle fibers.
2. At birth, loss of muscle tone, scoliosis, high arched palate, dislocated hips, muscle weakness, and foot deformities are present.
3. Skeletal deformities such as thin face, short stature, congenital hip dislocation, clubfeet, and a hunched back (kyphoscoliosis) are common.

Treatments generally focus on correcting and preventing skeletal abnormalities with surgery; passive stretching and physical therapy to maintain muscle activity are crucial. Orthopedic aids may become necessary as the disease progresses and the child ages. Cardiomyopathy has been documented in a limited number of cases (Banwell, Laurence, Jay, Taylor, & Vajsar, 1999), and intervention will be necessary to prolong life expectancy.

Special education requirements are limited to the progression of the disorder and the degree of impairment. Prognosis is good provided that cardiac or other complications are not present. A few neonatal cases of CFTD have been fatal; however, most children with the disorder have a normal life span.

REFERENCE

Banwell, B. L., Laurence, E. B., Jay, V., Taylor, G. P., & Vajsar, J. (1999). Cardiac manifestations of congenital fiber-type disproportion myopathy. *Journal of Child Neurology, 14*(2), 83–87.

KIMBERLY M. ESTEP
University of Houston–Clear Lake

FIBRODYSPLASIA OSSIFICANS PROGRESSIVA SYNDROME

Fibrodysplasia ossificans progressiva syndrome (FOPS) is a rare hereditary connective tissue disorder. Its salient features include shortening of the big toe and swellings in tendons and other fibrous membranes in muscles of the neck, back, upper arm and upper leg (fibrodysplasia). The swellings eventually metamorphose into bony deposits within muscle and can therefore cause severe mobility deficits.

The cause of the underlying fibrous tissue defect of FOPS is unknown. The pattern of inheritance is autosomal dominant. A shortened big toe is a constant finding among these patients, but the severity of fibrodysplasia they can have is quite variable. About 90% of cases are new genetic mutations. Advanced paternal age is a factor in this patient subset. Although this condition is considered rare, about 500 cases have appeared in the medical literature since it was first described in 1692 (see Jones, 1997).

Characteristics

1. Short big toe, often with fusion of the joints. Less commonly the thumb is short.
2. Fibrous tissue swellings, sometimes painful and accompanied by fever, leading to bony deposits (ossification) in muscle. The most frequently affected areas are the neck, back, shoulder, upper parts of the extremities, and (less commonly) the jaw. Fibrodysplasia may be evident at birth or may not manifest until the third decade of life. Ossification begins within 2–8 months of onset of swelling. By age 7, 80% of patients experience restrictive ossifications. By age 15, 95% have severely limited arm mobility secondary to advanced fibrodysplasia.
3. Progressive fusion of the vertebrae in the neck.
4. Occasional findings include shortened fingers and toes (other than the thumb and big toe), inward curving of the little finger (clinodactyly), widely spaced teeth, underdeveloped genitalia, easy bruising, hearing deficits, and abnormalities of heart rhythm.

The efficacy of FOPS therapy is difficult to assess because the natural history of the disorder is characterized by numerous symptomatic exacerbations and remissions. Salicylates (aspirin) and corticosteroids may provide some pain relief. Operative removal of the bony deposits is not an option because surgical sites serve as foci for further fibrodysplasia to develop. In fact, even minor trauma and intramuscular injections can induce bony changes. These patients are also poor surgical risks because of difficulties with anesthesia administration, chronic restrictive lung disease, and cardiac rhythm disturbances.

There is no research to indicate cognitive limitations or the need for remediations academically. However, because of the physical complications, the child with FOPS may require support from physical and occupational therapists who can help with assistive and technological devices to allow the child to continue to progress academically.

No data are available regarding the life expectancy of FOPS patients. Prognosis is largely determined by the degree of fibrodysplasia that the patients develop. This finding is quite variable among affected individuals, may not begin until adulthood, and is relentlessly progressive. Therefore, it is not possible to predict in any reliable way what the future holds for a child with this disease.

For more information and parent support, please

contact International Fibrodysplasia Ossificans Progressiva Association, P.O. box 196217, Winter Springs, FL 32719-6217, (407) 365-4194, e-mail: ifopa@vol.com, home page: http://www.med.upenn.edu/ortho/fop

REFERENCES

Jones, K. (1997). *Smith's recognizable patterns of human malformations* (5th ed.). Philadelphia: W. B. Saunders.

National Organization for Rare Disorders. (1996). Fibrodysplasia ossificans progressiva (FOP). Retrieved from http://www.stepstn.com/egi-win/nord.exe?proc=GetDocument&rectype=0&recnum=366

Barry H. Davison
Ennis, Texas

Joan W. Mayfield
Baylor Pediatric Specialty Services
Dallas, Texas

FOUNTAIN SYNDROME

Fountain syndrome, which is characterized by an association between mental retardation, sensorineural deafness, coarse facies, and skeletal abnormalities, was first described in 1974 (Fountain, 1974). Fountain syndrome is an extremely rare disorder, and the prevalence is unknown (Fryns, 1989). Only seven cases have been documented at this time. The occurrence of this syndrome in siblings of normal parents indicates autosomal recessive inheritance (Fountain, 1974; Fryns, 1987, 1989).

The pathogenesis for Fountain syndrome remains unknown. Chromosomes have been found to be normal (46, XY confirmed with G- and R- banding; Fryns, 1987). Extensive biochemical and metabolic examinations (e.g., calcium, phosphorus, creatine kinase, amino acid chromatography of serum and urine, and mucopolysaccharide excretion), electroencephalography, electromyography, electrocardiography, ophthalmological examinations, and peripheral nerve and rectal biopsies revealed no specific abnormalities (Fountain, 1974; Fryns, 1987, 1989).

Characteristics

1. Mental retardation
2. Sensorineural deafness with cochlear anomalies
3. Round and coarse facies
4. Lip granuloma
5. Plump, stubby hands with broad terminal phalanges
6. Thickened calvaria

All identified individuals have been diagnosed with mental retardation, although the degree varied from mild to severe. All reported cases indicate profound sensorineural deafness that occurred between the ages of 15 and 18 months. Up to that point, hearing development appeared to be normal (Fountain, 1974; Fryns, 1987, 1989). Some rudimentary hearing at the lowest frequencies may be present. Tomography of the inner ear revealed congenital anomalies of the cochlea spirals, ranging from anomalies of the cochlear turns to the presence of a cavity. Vestibular function appears normal.

The face is round and coarse, with swelling of the subcutaneous tissue, particularly of the lips and cheeks (Fountain, 1974; Fryns, 1987, 1989). The swelling of the face has been described as progressive, gross, papular, erythematous, and granulomatous. A biopsy revealed a granulomatous infiltrate marked by large, foamy cells, which contained lipid but not stains for fat (Fountain, 1974). The pathogenesis of the swellings is unknown (Fryns, 1989). The edematous facial characteristics are similar to those seen in Melkerson-Rosenthal syndrome and Coffin-Lowry syndrome (Fountain, 1974; Fryns, 1989). Skeletal surveys using X rays show broad and short phalanges and metacarpals with thickened corticalis without ossification anomalies (Fountain, 1974; Fryns, 1987, 1989). Skull X rays show a gross thickening of the calvarium.

Fountain syndrome may also be linked with other minor and major anomalies (Fryns, 1987; Fryns, 1989). There may be marked growth retardation, psychomotor impairment, epileptic attacks, infantile seizures, and general hypotonia, which results in secondary scoliotic deformities. These associated disorders must be further delineated in additional patients.

There is no known cure or a specific treatment for Fountain syndrome. A full assessment of the child's mental or developmental age, level of adaptive behavior, and neuropsychological needs is recommended to assist with educational programming. It is important that the educational assessment evaluate the child's special education needs as to not only how they pertain to mental retardation but also how they relate to the child's hearing impairment.

REFERENCES

Fountain, R. B. (1974). Familial bone abnormalities, deaf mutism, mental retardation, and skin granuloma. *Procedures of the Royal Society of Medicine, 67*, 878–879.

Fryns, J. (1987). Mental retardation, deafness, skeletal abnormalities, and coarse face with full lips: Confirmation of the fountain syndrome. *American Journal of Medical Genetics, 26*, 551–555.

Fryns, J. (1989). Fountain's syndrome: Mental retardation, sensorineural deafness, skeletal abnormalities, and coarse face with full lips. *Journal of Medical Genetics, 26,* 722–724.

Alexandra S. Kutz
Margaret Semrud-Clikeman
University of Texas at Austin

FRAGILE X SYNDROME

Fragile X syndrome (FXS), a genetic disorder, involves a mutation of the FMR1 gene (fragile X mental retardation 1 gene), located at the bottom end of the X chromosome. A mutation in this gene lowers the production of the FMR protein. Variations in the amount of the FMR protein account for the wide range of behavioral and physical features displayed by persons with FXS. This sex-linked condition affects males more than females, because males only have one X chromosome, whereas females, with two X chromosomes, will generally have one chromosome without the mutation. FXS is the most common cause of inherited mental retardation and accounts for 30% of cases of mental retardation associated with the X chromosome (Sherman, 1996).

Prevalence studies indicate that approximately 1 in 2,500 females and 1 in 1,250 males have mental retardation attributable to FXS and that the rate of those carrying the FXS premutation is 1 in 259 for females and 1 in 700 for males (Hagerman & Lampe, 1999). FXS is a broad-spectrum disorder that can have a wide range of effects. Some children experience social and emotional problems or learning disabilities, whereas others may be mentally retarded and display autistic-like features (Hagerman, 1999).

Characteristics

1. Physical features commonly observed include long ears, prominent ears, long face, single palmar crease, cardiac murmur or click, hand calluses, flat feet, hyperextensible finger joints, double-jointed thumbs, and a high-arched palate.
2. Behavioral characteristics often seen are poor eye contact, tactile defensiveness, hand flapping, hand biting, perseveration, hyperactivity, violent outbursts, tantrums, and social anxiety.
3. Neurologic sequelae involve hypotonia, motor incoordination, sleep apnea, seizures, and sleep difficulties.
4. Typically, those who produce less of the FMR protein have the lowest IQ. Although 13% of males with FXS do not have IQs in the mentally retarded range, mean IQ scores range from 41 to 88, depending on the extent of the genetic mutation. For females with a full mutation, 50–71% earn IQs in the borderline or mentally retarded range.
5. Cognitively, deficits in processing auditory, sequential, abstract, complex information and in executive functioning (attention, planning, organization, working memory & inhibition) are observed. Relative strengths in simultaneous processing are noted.
6. Language problems involve perseveration, mumbling, cluttered speech, oral motor incoordination, poor pragmatic communication, associative word responses, and poor topic maintenance.

Sources: Hagerman & Lampe (1999), Sobesky et al. (1996), Scharfenacker et al. (1996).

Treatment for those affected by FXS emphasizes medical, developmental, educational, and behavioral concerns. Medically, interventions are aimed at treating recurrent otits media, seizures, and problems associated with loose connective tissue (i.e., gastroesophageal reflux, sinus infections, mitral valve prolapse, joint dislocations, and hernias). Medications are sometimes prescribed for the treatment of attention deficit and hyperactivity, mood lability, aggression, anxiety, and obsessive-compulsive behaviors (Hagerman, 1996).

Delays in language and motor development are best addressed through speech and language therapy and occupational therapy. Speech language interventions should address auditory processing problems, deficits in pragmatic communication, and motor dyspraxia. Speech intervention should also capitalize on language strengths that include humor, imitation, and memory skills and empathy. Occupational therapy generally emphasizes sensory integration dysfunction as well as development of fine and gross motor skills and motor planning abilities.

Children with FXS will have varying educational needs depending on the degree of involvement related to the FMR1 mutation. Some children may experience learning disabilities and will require support from a resource room. Others will be more profoundly affected and may require special education services through a program designed for students with significantly limited intellectual capacity. Special education eligibility is often through a physical disability or a multihandicapped classification. In general, because students with FXS are strong visual and imitative learners, they will benefit from inclusion in the general education classroom for some part of their school day.

Educational interventions and accommodations in the regular or special education classroom will require a multimodal approach that combines visual and auditory input. Using behavioral reinforcement, predictable routines,

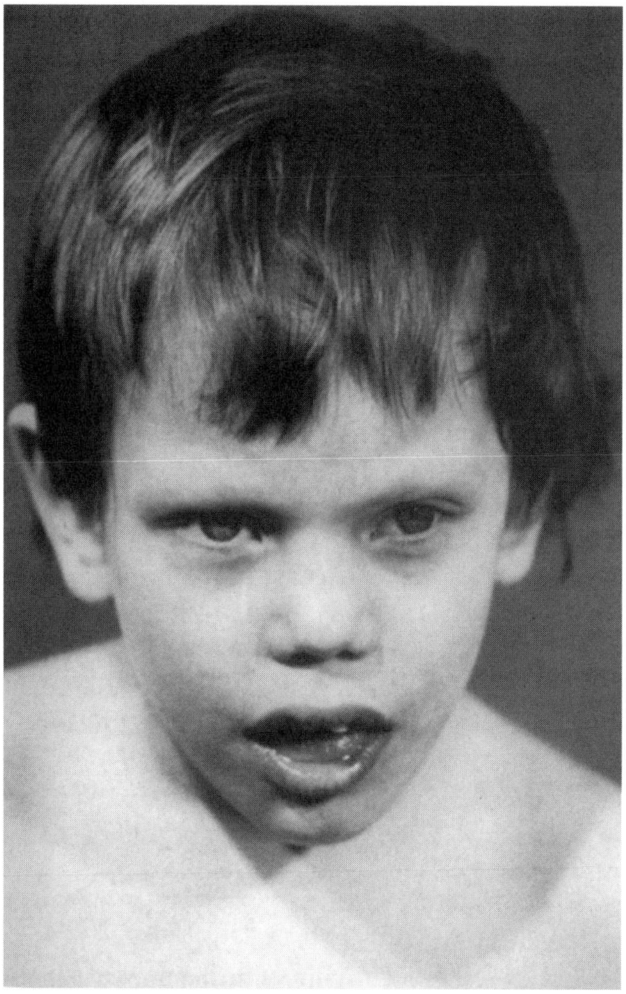

Fragile X Syndrome
Reprinted from *Clinical Syndromes,* Wiedemann and Kunze, 1997, by permission of the publisher Mosby

preparation for transitions, and calming techniques will facilitate the ability of the student with FXS to adapt to classroom demands. Issues related to poor sensory integration will require that distractions be minimized, that seat breaks are given, and that oral-motor and physical activities are integrated into the school day (e.g., allow a break to chew gum, wrap a bungee cord around the legs of the desk, etc.). Interventions useful for those with attentional problems are also appropriate; for instance, it will be helpful to provide visual, verbal, and physical prompts and to use a behavioral management approach to promote compliance with behavioral and educational goals. Computers can be used to promote learning and language skills. Adaptive peripherals may be required for students with FXS, and there are a variety of applicable computer programs such as IntelliTalk and Co-Writer (Braden, 1997; Scharfenacker et al., 1996).

In mid to late childhood, mental development and IQ scores tend to plateau. Therefore, when persons with FXS become adolescents and adults, attention to functional skills becomes increasingly important. To promote independent living, life skills involving self-care, budgeting, time management, employment, community skills, and transportation are essential. Planning for the transition from school should become a part of an individualized education plan and should incorporate the aforementioned functional areas. With adequate supports, young adults with FXS can often live in a supervised setting or perhaps independently, depending on the extent of their cognitive and adaptive development.

Advances in the field of molecular biology are making a molecular or protein treatment of FXS seem likely within the next 10 years. Protein replacement therapy may benefit those with FXS, although it is uncertain at this time what the extent of those benefits would be. Gene therapy, which would entail manipulation of genetic components, could potentially result in increased production of FMR protein and may someday lead to a cure for this disorder (Hagerman, 1999).

REFERENCES

Braden, M. L. (1997). *Fragile, handle with care: Understanding fragile X syndrome* (2nd ed.) Chapel Hill, NC: Avanta Publishing.

Hagerman, R. J. (1996). Physical and behavioral phenotype. In R. J. Hagerman & A. C. Cronister (Eds.), *Fragile X syndrome: Diagnosis, treatment, and research* (2nd ed., pp. 3–87). Baltimore: Johns Hopkins University Press.

Hagerman, R. J., & Lampe, M. E. (1999). Fragile X syndrome. In S. Goldstein & C. R. Reynolds (Eds.), *Handbook of neurodevelopmental and genetic disorders in children* (pp. 298–316).

Scharfenacker, S., O'Connor, R., Stackhouse, T., Braden, M., Hickman, L., & Gray, K. (1996). An integrated approach to intervention. In R. J. Hagerman & A. C. Cronister (Eds.), *Fragile X syndrome: Diagnosis, treatment, and research* (2nd ed., pp. 349–411). Baltimore: Johns Hopkins University Press.

Sherman, S. (1996). Epidemiology. In R. J. Hagerman & A. C. Cronister (Eds.), *Fragile X syndrome: Diagnosis, treatment, and research* (2nd ed., pp. 165–192). Baltimore: Johns Hopkins University Press.

Sobesky, W. E., Taylor, A. K., Pennington, B. F., Bennetto, I., Porter, D., Riddle, J., & Hagerman, R. J. (1996). Molecular/clinical correlations in females with fragile X. *American Journal of Medical Genetics 64*(2), 340–345.

Stacy E. McHugh
The Children's Hospital
Denver, Colorado

FREEMAN-SHELDON SYNDROME

Freeman-Sheldon syndrome, also known as craniocarpotarsal dysplasia or whistling face syndrome, is a hereditary disorder with autosomal dominant transmission. The disorder manifests at birth and is characterized with a masklike "whistling" face, hypoplastic alae nasi, ulnar deviation of the hands, flexion contractures of the fingers, and clubfeet (Wiedemann, Kunze, & Dibbern, 1992).

There are no incidence numbers available, but the condition is considered rare, with only approximately 100 being described in the literature. There is considerable overlap of symptoms with Schwartz-Jampel syndrome; therefore, differential diagnosis is important.

Characteristics

1. Round, full-cheeked face with mask-like immobility and deep-set, widely spaced eyes
2. Small nose with hypoplastic alae nasi
3. Small mouth that is difficult to open with pursed lips
4. Ulnar deviation of the hands and flexion contractures of the fingers
5. Clubfeet with contractures of the toes
6. Short neck
7. Frequent short stature
8. Occasional hearing impairment
9. Normal mental development

Treatment of Freeman-Sheldon syndrome is limited to surgical treatment of the physical anomalies and genetic counseling (Wiedemann et al., 1992). Parents and professionals should also be alert and monitor for sleep disorders that may affect daily functioning (Kohyama & Shiiki, 2000).

Special education may or may not be needed, depending on the extent of the physical anomalies and the level of interference in activities of everyday living. Psychological services may be needed for the child and the family for adjustment and life issues.

REFERENCES

Kohyama, J., & Shiiki, T. (2000). Sleep disordered breathing during REM sleep in Freeman-Sheldon syndrome. *Acta Neurologica Scandinavica, 102*(6), 395–397.

Wiedemann, H., Kunze, J., & Dibbern, H. (1992). *Atlas of clinical syndromes: A visual aid to diagnosis* (2nd ed.). St. Louis, MO: Mosby.

Elaine Fletcher-Janzen
University of Northern Colorado

FREY'S SYNDROME

Frey's syndrome is a rare neurological disorder resulting from injury or surgery near the parotid glands, damaging the facial nerve and resulting in facial flushing during mastication and possibly profuse sweating, particularly while ingesting hot, spicy, or acidic foods.

Incidence of Frey's syndrome is rare, and treatment is dependent on the severity of symptoms. Most patients have mild symptoms that can be controlled with topical creams, thus making Frey's syndrome a mild nuisance. However, in some cases of Frey's syndrome, the patient may experience excessive discomfort in which surgery on the nerves near the ear may be needed. Recent research has shown injections of botulinum toxin A (BTX) to be effective at relieving symptoms of Frey's syndrome with relatively no side effects.

Special educational needs usually are not required, except counseling to address psychosocial factors, and prognosis is good with full recovery in a majority of patients. Currently, oral medications and better topical ointments to alleviate symptoms of Frey's syndrome are topics of future research.

Characteristics

1. Excessive sweating
2. Flushing of the face
3. Possible temporary lack of sensitivity to heat, pain, or burning in the affected area

REFERENCES

Thoene, J. G., & Coker, N. P. (Eds.). (1995). *Physicians' guide to rare diseases* (2nd ed.). Montvale, NJ: Dowden Publishing Company.

von Lindern, J. J., Niederhagen, B., Berge, S., Hagler, G., & Reich, R. H. (2000). Frey syndrome: Treatment with type A botulinum toxin. *Cancer, 89,* 1659–1663.

Kimberly M. Estep
University of Houston–Clear Lake

FRONTOFACIONASAL DYSPLASIA

Frontofacionasal dysplasia (FFND) is characterized by severe abnormalities of the skull and face. Symptoms include facial asymmetry, coloboma of the iris and retina, malformation of the eyelids, narrowing of the palpebral fissures, ocular hypertelorism, telecanthus, limbic dermoid of the eye, midface hypoplasia, anomalies of the corpus callosum, cleft lip and palate, deformed nostrils, and multiple skin appendages (Al-Gazali, Dawodu, Hamada, Bakir, & Bakalinová, 1996; Temple, Brunner, Jones, Burn, & Baraitser, 1990). FFND also may be referred to as facio-frontonasal dysplasia, frontofacionasal dysostosis, or nasal-fronto-faciodysplasia; related syndromes include oculoauriculofrontonasal spectrum and frontonasal dysplasia.

FFND is thought to be an extremely rare, low-incidence condition (Temple et al., 1990). Prevalence has not been studied thoroughly, and differences regarding gender and ethnicity in the manifestation of symptoms are unknown. There is evidence for autosomal recessive inheritance of this syndrome (Gollop, Kiota, Martins, Lucchesi, & Alvarenga, 1984).

Characteristics

1. Congenital onset
2. A variety of deformities of the eyes, nose, mouth, and skull
3. Child may have poor eyesight due to eyelid malformation and folds of skin obstructing vision
4. Due to cleft lip and palate, child may experience abnormal dental development and speech difficulties

The severity of abnormalities associated with FFND is extremely variable, and it is uncertain whether some cases actually are manifesting symptoms of FFND, represent clinical variations of this condition, or represent separate conditions altogether (Al-Gazali et al., 1996). Also variable is the extent to which the eyes are involved (Gollop et al., 1984). The association between intelligence, mental retardation, and FFND is unknown (Temple et al., 1990).

Treatment commonly includes surgery to remove limbal dermoid from the eye(s) if present; this may serve to improve the child's vision. However, poor vision may persist due to coloboma (i.e., partial absence of tissue) of the iris. Cosmetic surgery may be used to remodel the nose and other facial malformations (Temple et al., 1990). Adverse effects of abnormal dental development and speech difficulties may be lessened by extensive dental care and early speech therapy, respectively. Finally, counseling may be sought in order to address self-concept issues and the emotional difficulty of being physically different.

Depending on symptom severity, children with FFND may be eligible to receive special education services under Section 504, IDEA federal regulations, or both. For example, if coloboma of the iris and retina results in partial sight that adversely affects the child's educational performance, the child would qualify for services under the Visual Impairment category of IDEA. Furthermore, if cleft lip and palate result in communication problems, such as impaired articulation or voice impairment, that adversely affect the child's educational performance, then the child would be eligible for services under the Speech or Language Impairment category of IDEA. Visual and speech impairment of children with FFND also would qualify them for services under Section 504.

There is evidence that children with FFND or similar syndromes may develop into intelligent and healthy adults (Guion-Almeida & Lopes, 1997). This likelihood may be enhanced through the surgical, dental, speech, and emotional interventions listed above. However, very little is known regarding the influence of FFND on later development, including intelligence, achievement, and employment status in adulthood. Prognosis, therefore, is difficult to determine. Future research must focus on these issues, in addition to prevalence among different ethnicities, gender differences in prevalence, differential diagnosis between FFND and similar low-incidence syndromes, and the effectiveness of psychosocial interventions in improving the emotional lives of children suffering from this disorder.

REFERENCES

Al-Gazali, L. I., Dawodu, A. H., Hamada, M., Bakir, M., & Bakalinová, D. (1996). Severe facial clefting, limbic dermoid, hypoplasia of the corpus callosum, and multiple skin appendages: Severe frontofacionasal dysplasia or newly recognized syndrome? *American Journal of Medical Genetics, 63,* 346–347.

Gollop, T. R., Kiota, M. M., Martins, R. M. M., Lucchesi, E. A., & Alvarenga, E. (1984). Frontofacionasal dysplasia: Evidence for autosomal recessive inheritance. *American Journal of Medical Genetics, 19,* 301–305.

Guion-Almeida, M. L., & Lopes, V. L. G. S. (1997). Oculoauriculofrontonasal spectrum in an adult Brazilian male. *Clinical Dysmorphology, 6,* 251–255.

Temple, I. K., Brunner, H., Jones, B., Burn, J., & Baraitser, M. (1990). Midline facial defects with ocular colobomata. *American Journal of Medical Genetics, 37,* 23–27.

Jeremy R. Sullivan
Texas A&M University

FRYNS SYNDROME

Inherited as an autosomal recessive trait, Fryns syndrome is characterized by many abnormalities present at birth. These characteristics include abnormalities of the head and face, protrusion of part of the stomach and the small intestines into the chest cavity, underdeveloped lungs, cleft palate, underdevelopment of the fingers and toes, and some degree of mental retardation.

True incidence of Fryns syndrome is unknown; however, it is estimated to be a very rare disorder affecting 0.7 children per 10,000 births. Fryns syndrome normally results in stillbirths for the children who have inherited this disorder. In the children who live with Fryns syndrome, their existence is meager with severe cognitive and physical deficits, the former the result of brain malformations. Treatment, if viable, could include surgery to correct the internal malformations. In prenatal detection, termination of pregnancy is usually offered.

Characteristics

1. Infants may exhibit a flat, broad nose; a wide mouth; cleft palate; a displaced, abnormally small jaw; underdeveloped ear lobes; and corneal clouding.
2. Many children will have short bones in the tips of their fingers, absent or undersized fingernails, or both.
3. Skeletal abnormalities, congenital cardiac defects, genital anomalies, renal defects, and brain malformation responsible for cognitive sequelae.
4. Infants may also be large for their age.

Special education issues specifically relate to multiple handicaps due to health problems and mental retardation. Prognosis is poor, and chronic management through assisted living is necessary. Future research is directed toward etiology and treatment through gene mapping.

REFERENCES

Cunniff, C., Jones, K. L., Saal, H. M., & Stern, H. J. (1990). Fryns syndrome: An autosomal recessive disorder associated with craniofacial anomalies, diaphragmatic hernia, and distal digital hypoplasia. *Pediatrics, 85*(4), 499–504.

Jones, K. L. (Ed.). (1997). *Smith's recognizable patterns of human malformation* (5th ed.). Philadelphia: W. B. Saunders.

McKusick, V. A. (1986). Online mendelian inheritance in man [Article 229850]. Retrieved June, 2001, from http://www.ncbi.nlm.nih.gov/Omim

Kimberly M. Estep
University of Houston–Clear Lake

G

GAIT DISTURBANCES

Gait disturbances are characterized by the loss of or difficulty with the ability to coordinate smooth motor movements related to gait, or locomotion. Gait disturbance can vary in severity from an almost unobservable difficulty in walking to an almost complete inability to produce independent locomotion. There are many problems and diseases that can result in gait disturbances, including an open or closed head injury, injury to the spinal cord or legs, cerebral palsy, multiple sclerosis, and other diseases. Regardless of the etiology of the disturbance, the difficulties experienced by the child can be seen in one or more of five functional categories, including deformity, muscle weakness, impaired control, pain, and spasticity.

Characteristics

1. A difficulty in or lack of an ability to produce independent, unimpaired, volitional locomotion.
2. A functional deformity may be seen when the tissues of the leg and foot do not allow the mobility required for the child to attain the normal posture and range of motion that is used in walking. The most common cause is contracture, which can result from prolonged inactivity or injury.
3. Muscle weakness could occur when the child has insufficient muscle strength to meet the demands of walking. Muscle weakness can ensue with a lower motor neuron disease or a muscular disorder, such as muscular dystrophy or muscular atrophy.
4. Sensory loss may be observed, which may take the form of the child's not being aware of the position of his hip, knee, ankle, foot, or contact with the floor. Sensory loss may occur as the result of a lesion in the brain or an open or closed injury to the spine, legs, or feet.
5. Pain may result from or be the cause of a gait disturbance. A compromise of the musculoskeletal system—usually resulting from trauma or arthritis—can introduce obstacles to effective walking.
6. Spasticity may occur as the result of a central neurological lesion to the brain or spinal cord. Spasticity is seen with limited or no control over volitional activities. Muscular control may be altered by limb position. The most common causes of a spastic gait are cerebral palsy, strokes, brain injuries, multiple sclerosis, and spinal cord injuries.

Source: Perry (1992)

Children who have gait disturbance may walk with a wide-based gait, demonstrate tremors, have difficulty maintaining an upright posture, and have difficulty hopping, skipping, and running (Gage, 1991). The incidence of gait disturbance is difficult to estimate, as there is such a wide variation in the level of disturbance in gait, based upon the cause of the problem. When gait disturbance has a cerebral implication, the basal ganglia are usually the primary site of the disturbance. Normal function of the basal ganglia is necessary for normal motor control and posture (Fahn, Greene, Ford, & Bressman, 1998).

Treatment of gait disturbances in children generally falls into one of two categories. The first area is physical and cognitive rehabilitation, and the second is the utilization of assertive devices. Physical therapy can benefit a child in the strengthening of muscles, improving flexibility, and the remediation of skills that have not been learned. Physical therapists can also create compensatory strategies to draw upon a child's motor strengths. For example, children's limbs may be placed in innate motor patterns. Hypotonia, spasticity, and dyskinesia are treated with exercises that facilitate walking, crawling, and sitting (Leonard, 1990). Assistive devices may be recommended to the child, including canes, crutches, hand railings, and walkers. These devices and ambulatory aids can help increase balance, relieve weight from one leg to another, and alleviate pain, fatigue, and muscular weakness (Olsson & Smidt, 1990).

The primary predictive factor of recovering from a gait disturbance is what type of injury or disease is responsible for the disturbance. If the cause of the gait disturbance is a pervasive condition such as cerebral palsy or multiple sclerosis, the prognosis of recovery is limited by the nature of the disease. If the gait disturbance is resulting from a neurological condition, younger children tend to have greater success in recovery than do older children, due to their increased brain plasticity. There are many predictive factors that influence a child's level of recovery. The size and type of lesion in the brain is the most critical variable. A traumatic brain injury that involves extensive damage to the basal ganglia as well as other areas of the motor cortex could produce a gait disturbance resulting in a pervasive condition from which the child would not recover.

Special education placement can be an important issue for children with gait disturbance. If the gait disturbance is as the result of a severe brain injury, the child will likely be classified as Traumatically Brain Injured. They may be served under the category of Other Health Impaired or Physically Impaired if the gait disturbance is related to a disorder such as cerebral palsy. Difficulties with gait can affect many educational, emotional, and social aspects of a child's development. The special education teacher will need to recognize the unique needs of the child. The child's social skills can also be affected because the child may have problems with positive peer interactions; this can also lead to a deficit in the development of social skills and nuances, as well as the development of appropriate behavior. Advances in research as well as assistive devices and technology will continue to offer improved rehabilitation for children with gait disturbances.

REFERENCES

Fahn, S., Greene, P., Ford, B., & Bressman, S. (1998). *Handbook of movement disorders.* Philadelphia: Current Medicine.

Gage, J. (1991). *Gait analysis in cerebral palsy.* Oxford: MacKeith Press.

Leonard, E. (1990). Early motor development and control: Foundations for independent walking. In G. L. Smidt (Ed.), *Gait in rehabilitation.* New York: Churchill Livingstone.

Olsson, E., & Smidt, G. (1990). Assistive devices. In G. L. Smidt (Ed.), *Gait in rehabilitation.* New York: Churchill Livingstone.

Perry, J. (1992). *Gait analysis: Normal and pathological function.* Lawrenceville, NJ: Slack Incorporated.

Andrew S. Davis
University of Northern Colorado

GALACTOSEMIA

Galactosemia is an inborn error of metabolism that results in an accumulation of galactose in the blood, tissue, and urine. Galactosemia is caused by an autosomal recessive gene, and heterozygotes for the trait exhibit reduced enzyme activity. Three types are known, each due to a specific enzyme deficit: (a) Classic galactosemia, the most prevalent and most severe form, occurs in approximately 1 in 70,000 births and is attributed to a marked deficiency of galactose-1-phosphate uridyl transferase; (b) Galactokinase deficiency, less severe, occurs in 1 in 155,000 births and leads to the development of cataracts; (c) A rare form, with no clear clinical abnormalities, is attributed to a deficit of EDP-glucose-4-epimerase (Hug, 1979). Classic galactosemia accounts for approximately 95% of cases.

Symptoms of classic galactosemia begin within 2 weeks after birth (Cho & Desposito, 1996). Without treatment, the disorder is usually lethal, and many affected infants die during the first few weeks of life. Surviving infants show a variety of characteristics (Desposito, 1996; Holton & Leonard, 1994). Even among treated children, mental retardation, learning disabilities, and a variety of other serious problems are common (Holton & Leonard, 1994). Biochemical changes owing to galactosemia have been reported in the liver of a second-trimester fetus, suggesting prenatal onset (Allen, Gillett, Holton, King, & Pettit, 1980).

Characteristics

1. Onset of severe symptoms in first 2 weeks of life, including jaundice, liver failure, vomiting, hypoglycemia, lethargy, and failure to thrive.
2. If the condition is untreated, death in early infancy is common.
3. If the condition is untreated, surviving infants are likely to develop cataracts, ataxia, seizures, cerebral palsy, proteinuria, aminoaciduria, mental retardation, and progressive failure.
4. Treated children are likely to show a variety of adverse characteristics (see text).

Diagnosis is determined by severity of the symptoms, previous diagnosis of galactosemia in siblings or parents, amniocentesis, and neonatal screening. The prevalent screening technique is a blood analysis for elevated galactose shortly after birth, followed—when called for—by a test for deficient enzyme activity. Although the tests are quite accurate, especially for classic galactosemia, turnaround time for the results is about 4–5 days, by which time some infants may have died owing to susceptibility to E. coli septicemia (American Liver Foundation, 1995; Cho & Desposito, 1996).

Treatment consists of elimination of galactose and lactose from the diet as early as possible. All milk products, including mother's milk, butter, cheese, and yogurt, must be avoided because galactose is mainly formed by digestion of disaccharide lactose found in animal milk. Strict adherence to diets generally based on soybeans is critical. Shortly after the beginning of dietary intervention, most physical symptoms subside. The infant gains weight; vomiting, diarrhea, and liver anomalies disappear; and cataracts regress, although any brain damage is permanent. A balanced galactose-free diet should be maintained throughout life (American Liver Foundation, 1995; Cho & Desposito, 1996). Certain carbohydrates, lipids, and proteins that eventually metabolize to galactose must also be eliminated. The diet does not cure the disorder, but it reduces the disorder's effects. Possible prenatal origin may account for the ovarian failure occasionally reported, lack of relationships between either the age at which treatment begins; and the severity of the neonatal disorder and long-term outcome (Holton & Leonard, 1994). Galactosemic women should adhere to the diet when they become pregnant to reduce levels of circulating toxins and resulting damage to the unborn fetus. Although affected women bear children, the frequency of ovarian failure in their daughters is high (Cho & Desposito, 1996). Mothers of galactosemic children should also adhere to the diet during subsequent pregnancies to lessen symptoms present at birth (American Liver Foundation, 1995).

Unfortunately, prognosis for cognitive development in treated individuals is not as good as initially thought (e.g., Holton & Leonard, 1994), and those involved in special education should be aware of the many and varied problems that treated galactosemic children may have. Even early dietary intervention generally only partially reduces the degree and severity of cognitive damage. IQs cluster in below normal to low-normal range, although variability is high and normal IQ has been reported in some cases in which treatment began before 10 days of age (Cho & Desposito, 1996). Other specific difficulties may interfere with the education of treated galactosemic children and call for additional special education services. About 50% of treated children are developmentally delayed, and learning difficulties increase with age. These effects apparently owe to progressive neurological disease or to brain damage sustained at an earlier age that becomes more apparent with age (Holton & Leonard, 1994). Treated galactosemic children may also show visual-perceptual, motor function-balance, spatial-mathematical relationship, attention, and speech-language deficits. They generally present no significant behavior problems except for occasional apathy and withdrawal that in a few severe cases is shown as a personality disorder characterized by timidity and lack of drive (Holton & Leonard, 1994). High variability in outcome calls for carefully individualized intervention programs and perhaps a team approach. Updated information is available at Herndon (2001).

REFERENCES

Allen, J. T., Gillett, M., Holton, J. B., King, G. S., & Pettit, B. R. (1980). Evidence of galactosemia in utero. *Lancet, 2,* 603.

American Liver Foundation. (1995). Galactosemia. Retrieved from http://www.gastro.com/liverpg/galactos.htm

Cho, S., & Desposito, F. (1996). Newborn screening fact sheets. *Pediatrics, 98,* 473–501.

Herndon, K. (2001). Galactosemia resources and information. Retrieved from http://www.miele-herndon.com/galactosemia/galactosemia.htm

Holton, J. B., & Leonard, J. V. (1994). Clouds still gathering over galactosemia. *Lancet, 344,* 1242–1243.

Robert T. Brown
Amy Sessoms
University of North Carolina, Wilmington

GARDNER SYNDROME

Gardner syndrome is a rare, inherited disorder of the gastrointestinal system and is a variant of familial adenomatous polyposis (Foulkes, 1995). The syndrome consists of a triad of symptoms, including colonic polyps, bone tumors, and soft tissue tumors or cysts (Pediatric Database, 2000). Often, the first symptoms to appear in childhood include osteomas of the skull and supernumerary growth of teeth, with development of intestinal (i.e., colonic) polyps more likely to be detected in young adulthood.

It is estimated that Gardner syndrome affects approximately 1 in 15,000 people in the United States (National Organization for Rare Disorders [NORD], 2000). It is a genetic disorder affecting males and females equally. Because it is autosomal dominant, children of an affected parent have a 50% chance of inheriting Gardner syndrome. Symptoms usually begin in late childhood or early adulthood, but they have been known to appear in infants and older adults. It is thought that individuals with Gardner syndrome may be at greater risk than the general population for developing certain types of cancer such as liver, thyroid, and pancreatic cancer.

Characteristics

1. Numerous intestinal polyps (up to 1,000 or more)
2. Osteomas of the skull
3. Epithelial cysts of soft tissue and skin (most often scalp, legs, and face)
4. Supernumerary dentition and other dental problems: unerupted teeth, odontomas, and absence of teeth
5. Rectal bleeding, diarrhea, constipation, abdominal pain, and weight loss (associated with intestinal polyps)
6. Congenital hypertrophy of retinal pigment epithelium (in some cases)

The main goal of treatment for Gardner syndrome is the prevention or early detection of colon cancer. Regular physical examination includes testing for occult blood in the stool, colonoscopy, or sigmoidoscopy to examine the colon walls. Children of an affected parent usually begin screening at approximately 8 years old and continue to have a colonoscopy every 2 years even if the child is asymptomatic. Surgery to remove all or part of the colon (colectomy or orileoproctostomy) is common when there is concern about the number or growth pattern of polyps. If a complete colectomy is not done, regular monitoring for the growth of new polyps is necessary. Researchers are currently studying the use of the anti-inflammatory drug, sulindac, for treatment of intestinal polyps associated with Gardner syndrome (NORD, 2000). Individuals with Gardner syndrome who develop malignant tumors in other areas of the body may be treated with surgery, radiation, or chemotherapy. Genetic counseling may also be useful when young people affected with Gardner syndrome contemplate beginning families.

Gardner syndrome does not appear to have a direct effect on neurocognitive functioning. However, if osteomas are large, malignant, and left untreated, they could invade brain area and lead to increased intracranial pressure or possibly infarction. In addition, children may experience an adjustment disorder related to changes in lifestyle associated with treatment (e.g., toileting-hygiene, effects of chemotherapy, radiation).

Special education services may be available to children with Gardner syndrome under the handicapping condition of Other Health Impaired or Physical Disability. Due to the need for frequent, specialized monitoring, particularly during early diagnostic stages, missed school for doctors' appointments will be necessary. Procedures such as colonoscopy and sigmoidoscopy may require anesthesia, thereby extending the period of time the child misses school. In addition, individuals with this syndrome often experience diarrhea. If an orileoproctostomy is done, the child will have chronic diarrhea. His parents and teachers will need to define how to handle this issue in a classroom environment, minimizing embarrassment, accidents, and adjustment time. The child who has surgery including colectomy will not be able to attend school for an extended period of time following surgery and during recuperation. He or she may need to be reintroduced to the school day slowly, starting with half days. He or she may have difficulty catching up with work and may require additional tutoring to meet these demands. Most children will be able to begin completing some schoolwork during the recuperation period. However, the child may also be learning new hygiene rituals such as taking care of (or having an adult take care of) external devices for elimination and may need additional time to adjust to this change before being reintroduced into the school. Supportive counseling may be useful at this time. As with any major surgery, it is important to consult with the child's doctor about appropriate levels of physical activity and when activity can be resumed.

Prognosis is best with early diagnosis and regular monitoring. Future research is likely to continue to investigate medications to slow or stop the growth of polyps so that less invasive monitoring and treatment procedures can be utilized.

REFERENCES

Foulkes, W. D. (1995). A tale of four syndromes: Familial adenomatous polyposis, Gardner syndrome, attenuated APC and Turcot syndrome. *Quarterly Journal of Medicine, 88,* 853–863.

National Organization for Rare Disorders. (2000, November 2). Gardner syndrome. Retrieved from http://www.stepstm.com/cgi-win/nord.exe

Pediatric Database. (2000, December 21). Gardner syndrome. Retrieved from http://icondata.com/health/pedbase/files/GARDNER%27.HTM

Melissa R. Bunner
Austin Neurological Clinic

GASTRITIS, GIANT HYPERTROPHIC

Giant hypertrophic gastritis is a chronic disorder that affects the stomach. This disorder results in the formation of ridges and folds in the inner walls of the stomach and can cause inflammation of the stomach (National Organization for Rare Disorders [NORD], 2001), and reduced acid secretion in the stomach (Griffith's Five-Minute Clinical Consult: A Reference For Clinicians, 2001). The exact etiology of this disorder is not known. It has been found to most often affect adults between the ages of 30 and 60, and it affects more males than females. A childhood variety of the disorder has also been identified (NORD, 2001).

Characteristics

1. The child may come into the physician complaining of stomach pain in the upper middle region of the torso.
2. Other symptoms that may be reported include a significant loss of appetite, nausea, vomiting and diarrhea, blood in the vomit, and ulcer-like pain after a meal.
3. Individuals with giant hypertrophic gastritis commonly have abnormally low levels of stomach acid and may have an increased risk of stomach cancer.
4. Individuals may also experience a leakage of the stomach into the abdomen causing decreases in protein absorption and the accumulation of fluids in the abdomen.
5. If leaking of the stomach into the abdomen occurs, the resulting low levels of protein in the blood may need to be treated with a high-protein diet.

Source: NORD (2001)

Recommended treatments include regular examinations by a physician and a high-protein diet to correct for the lowered protein levels in the blood; also, in some cases, a portion of the stomach may need to be surgically removed (NORD, 2001). Anticholinergic drugs can also reduce the protein loss common in the disorder. Diagnosis of the disorder is made by X ray, a gastric biopsy, or blood work, which checks for decreased levels of protein in the blood (NORD, 2001). An endoscopy, a small instrument that allows the physician to examine the inside of the intestines, may also be used in diagnosing giant hypertrophic gastritis. These various testing methods are needed to differentiate giant hypertrophic gastritis from other types of gastrointestinal disorders (NORD, 2001).

The use of the drug ostreocide to reduce the protein loss caused by the disorder is currently being researched and has demonstrated some success (NORD, 2001). Diagnostic techniques currently under investigation include new molecular biochemical and computerized morphological methods as a way to improve diagnostics of giant hypertrophic gastritis, related disorders, and early gastrointestinal cancers (Cancer Network, 2001).

Children with giant hypertrophic gastritis may need modifications at school. Homebound schooling may be necessary during times when the illness flares up and causes substantial pain that prevents the child from attending school. If the child remains in school, he or she may also require the flexibility to leave class or school after meals if he or she experiences severe pain. The child may require easy access to restrooms and the school nurse, and field trips and activities that require the child to remain away from facilities may need to be modified to accommodate the child. Depending on the severity of the symptoms, the child may need long-term support for how to manage a chronic pain illness.

REFERENCES

Griffith's Five-Minute Clinical Consult: A Reference for Clinicians. (2001, March 20). Giant hypertrophic gastritis. Retrieved from http://www.5mcc.com/SUMMARY/0366.html

National Organization for Rare Disorders. (2001, March 20). Giant hypertrophic gastritis. Retrieved from http://www.stepstn.com/cgi-win/nord.exe?number=119&proc=ap_fullReport

Cancer Network. (2001, March 20). Menetrier's disease. Retrieved from http://www.cancernetwork.com/

Moana Kruschwitz
Margaret Semrud-Clikeman
University of Texas at Austin

GASTROENTERITIS, EOSINOPHILIC

Eosinophilic gastroenteritis (EG) is composed of a group of uncommon and enigmatic disorders that affect the stomach and small intestine. Involvement of the esophagus and large intestine is occasionally seen. The salient feature of this disease is infiltration of areas of the gut with eosinophils, a type of white blood cell produced in bone marrow. Eosinophilia (increased numbers of eosinophils in the blood) is also a common finding, present in over 50% of patients. The diagnosis of EG is confirmed by biopsy of the stomach or small intestine, usually by the nasogastric route.

This condition is similar to dietary protein hypersensitivity disorders (food protein allergies) that affect the large and small intestines. The symptoms of these entities frequently overlap.

EG is quite rare. No data are available regarding its frequency in the general population. For what it is worth, this author has seen exactly one case of EG in 25 years of private pediatric practice.

Characteristics

1. Eosinophilic infiltration of the mucosa, the thin inner lining of the gut, causes all or some of the following: nausea, vomiting, diarrhea, abdominal pain, gastrointestinal (GI) blood loss, protein loss through the intestine (protein-losing enteropathy), and malabsorption (loss of the gut's ability to assimilate digested food). This mucosal variant is the most common form of EG.
2. Involvement of the muscularis (the tubular layer of muscle that forms the bowel wall) induces obstructive symptoms, particularly when the stomach outlet is affected. High GI obstructions may cause only vomiting. Blockage in the lower intestine precipitates vomiting and abdominal distention.
3. Infiltration of the serosa (the membrane that covers the outer intestinal surface) leads to ascites, an accumulation of fluid within the abdominal cavity.

Treatment options for EG are limited, may not be particularly successful, and carry the risk of serious side effects. A rare patient may respond to elimination diets if the offending food(s) can be figured out. Administration of the drug cromolyn is quite safe, but its efficacy is unpredictable and generally disappointing. Corticosteroids (prednisone) will frequently induce symptomatic improvement. However, these medications cannot be given over lengthy periods without significant and intolerable complications (cessation of growth, osteoporosis, cataracts, increased susceptibility to infection, etc.).

There is no research available to indicate cognitive or behavioral difficulties. A child with EG may meet eligibility criteria to receive support services as Other Health Impaired if an educational need is demonstrated and the child's ability to function in the classroom is affected.

The prognosis for this disorder is fairly bleak. The disease is usually chronic and runs a prolonged, debilitating course. The current lack of satisfactory therapy makes the outlook for EG patients rather poor.

REFERENCE

Ulshen, M. (2000). Eosinophilic gastroenteritis. In R. E. Behrman, R. M. Kleigman, & H. B. Jenson (Eds.), *Nelson's textbook of pediatrics* (16th ed., p. 1159). Philadelphia: W. B. Saunders.

Barry H. Davison
Ennis, Texas

Joan W. Mayfield
Baylor Pediatric Specialty Services
Dallas, Texas

GASTROESOPHAGEAL REFLUX DISEASE

Gastroesophageal reflux disease, also known as GERD, is a condition in which acidic gastric contents reflux back into the esophagus. A common concern linked with GERD is the vomiting or regurgitation of food during feedings. Extended periods of GERD can result in a child's failure to thrive.

According to Dipalma and Colon (1991), one out of every 500 children between the ages of 6 weeks and 18 months is clinically affected by GERD to a significant degree. GERD can occur in up to 70% of children with cerebral palsy (Reyes, Cash, Green, & Booth, 1993). Limited research is available concerning the etiology of GERD. It is known that reflux is a normal occurrence for infants less than 6–7 weeks of age; therefore, it is presumed that delayed development is one cause of GERD. There also appears to be a relationship between respiratory conditions and GERD in infants. It has been found that GERD is both a cause of respiratory disorders and a complication of already existing respiratory disorders (Thoyre, 1994). Morton, Wheatley, and Minford (1999) found that oral and pharyngeal motor problems and GERD in children with severe physical and learning disabilities are more likely to result in respiratory tract infections.

Characteristics

1. Child is irritable, cries constantly or suddenly, or is excessively "colicy."
2. Child may vomit or spit up frequently and does not outgrow the "spitting up" phase of infancy.
3. Child may have experienced respiratory problems.
4. Child may have difficulty sleeping.

Treatment of GERD entails various nonsurgical management techniques that focus on preventing respiratory problems and allowing time for the maturation of the lower esophageal sphincter, the mechanism that obstructs reflux (Thoyre, 1994). Postural therapy, which involves positioning a child a certain way to prevent reflux, is one technique that is frequently used. A modified feeding regimen can be suggested as well. Parents may be encouraged to feed their child small amounts of food in order to decrease gastric enlargement. Drugs also can be prescribed for the treatment of GERD. The prescription drugs help with the emptying and acidity of the stomach.

Children with GERD may receive some special education services if the condition is so severe that it is affecting their learning. If the child's illness is affecting his or her ability to learn (i.e. failure to thrive), the child may receive services under the condition of Other Health Impaired. Research has shown, however, that GERD is associated with other conditions that receive special education services, such as cerebral palsy and several other physical and learning disabilities (Reyes, Cash, Green, & Booth, 1993; Morton et al., 1999).

Infants who experience GERD before the age of 6 months have a better prognosis than do children who have a later onset. Infants experiencing GERD before 6 months usually will develop the physical mechanisms to prevent reflux; however, older children may not. Children who are under treatment for GERD may be taking some type of medication; therefore, side effects should be considered any time a formal assessment is being conducted. Future research is being conducted on various nonsurgical management techniques and the use of Ph monitoring systems is producing more reliable results to reflux research.

REFERENCES

Dipalma, J., & Colon, A. (1991). Gastroesophageal reflux in infants. *American Family Physician, 43,* 857–846.

Morton, R. E., Wheatley, R., & Minford, J. (1999). Respiratory tract infections due to direct and reflux aspiration in children with severe neurodisability. *Developmental Medicine & Child Neurology, 41,* 329–334.

Reyes, A. L., Cash, A. J., Green, S. H., & Booth, I. W. (1993). Gastroesophageal reflux in children with cerebral palsy. *Child: Care, Health and Development, 19,* 109–118.

Thyore, S. M. (1994). Mothers' internal working models with infants with gastroesophageal reflux. *Maternal-Child Nursing Journal, 22,* 39–48.

Maricela P. Gonzales
Texas A & M University

GAUCHER'S DISEASE

Gaucher's disease, or glucosyl cerebroside lipidosis, is the most common of the lipid storage diseases. It is a hereditary autosomal recessive disorder named after French physician Philippe Gaucher who first described it in 1882. The disease occurs due to a lack of the enzyme glucocerebrosidase. This deficiency results in the storage of abnormal amounts of glucocerebroside (a lipid) in specialized Gaucher cells, which are primarily located in the liver, spleen, bone marrow, and to a lesser extent in the lungs and brain. Prenatal diagnosis for Gaucher's disease can be determined through amniocentesis or use of chorionic villus sampling (CVS). Diagnosis is made by demonstrating the lack of glucocerebrosidase activity in cell cultures obtained from biopsies of the spleen, liver, or bone marrow.

The most common symptom of Gaucher's disease is the enlargement of the liver and spleen, which can also cause abdominal problems. Gaucher cells in the bone marrow that are affected can cause severe bone weakening due to loss of minerals and due to bone lesions. Blood abnormalities are also common, with easy bruising, impaired blood clotting, anemia, and sometimes death (often due to bone marrow failure).

There are three major clinical forms of Gaucher's disease that occur due to differential cellular enzyme deficiencies and are distinguished by the presence and severity of neurological complications. Type I, the adult chronic nonneuronopathic form, is the most common and is characterized primarily by hypersplenism. Type II is a fatal neurodegenerative disease that occurs in infancy and is similar to Tay-Sachs disease. Type III, the juvenile form, includes the same symptoms as Type I and less severe neurological complications.

Characteristics

Type I (adult chronic nonneuronopathic form)

1. Hypersplenism (a decrease in the numbers of red cells, white cells, and platelets in the blood resulting from destruction or pooling of these cells by an enlarged spleen)
2. Splenomegaly (enlargement of the spleen)
3. Bone lesions, swelling of joints

Type II (acute infantile neuronopathic form)

1. Splenomegaly
2. Severe neurological abnormalities
3. Neck rigidity and involuntary arching of the head, neck, and spine
4. Death, usually within the first 2 years of life

Type III (juvenile form)

1. May occur any time in childhood
2. Same symptoms as Type I
3. Also neurological symptoms, although milder than Type II

Type I of Gaucher's disease is most common among Jews of Eastern European descent, with a reported incidence of 1 out of 500 births. Approximately 1 in every 12 Eastern European Jews is a carrier for the Gaucher's gene, whereas the carrier rate for the general population is approximately 1 in 100. Although Type I symptoms usually occur in adulthood, some individuals may begin having symptoms in childhood or adolescence. Individuals of any racial or ethnic background can be affected with Type II or III Gaucher's disease.

Gaucher's disease occurs equally among males and females. Transmission of the disease requires both parents to carry the mutation of the gene. According to the National Gaucher Foundation (2000), if both parents are carriers then there is the same chance (1 in 4) that either the child has Gaucher's disease or is neither a carrier nor a victim of the disease. Likewise, there is a 1 in 2 chance that the child will be a carrier but not have Gaucher's disease.

Although there is not currently a cure for Gaucher's disease, enzyme replacement therapy is needed by the majority of individuals who suffer from Type I of this disease. Enzyme replacement therapy has produced marked clinical improvement in patients who have Type I (Beers & Berkow, 1999). It is recommended that children with Type 1 Gaucher's disease receive enzyme replacement therapy as soon as possible, before there is marked bone or organ damage. Research has indicated that the majority of symptoms can be reversed if enzyme therapy is started at an early age. However, enzyme replacement has not been shown to improve neurological symptoms from the disease (National Gaucher Foundation, 1999) Bone marrow transplants can be given if children do not respond to enzyme replacement therapy. However, such transplants are risky, with a 15% mortality rate (or a 1 in 6 chance of the bone marrow recipient's dying; Wraith, 1999). Splenectomy may be required due to patients with hypersplenia, or if the enlarged spleen is causing excessive discomfort (Beers & Berkow, 1999). Patients who suffer from pulmonary hypertension have shown improvement after receiving epoprostenol intravenously (Bakst, 1999).

It is not uncommon for two children from the same nuclear family to suffer from Gaucher's disease, which can be very stressful for the entire family seeking treatment (Wraith, 1999). Therefore, counseling for both the child with Gaucher's disease and the family may prove helpful in dealing with issues surrounding the ongoing effects of the illness.

Likewise, teachers should be made aware of the nature of the child's illness, along with any special provisions that need to be made to meet the child's health and educational needs. Schools should also be aware that children with Gaucher's disease often require frequent hospital visits for various medical needs. Children with Gaucher's disease can receive special education services after evaluation by the school for their various physiological and psychoeducational needs.

The severity and impact of Gaucher's disease varies across individuals. Some people experience chronic and severe symptoms, whereas others experience few complications. Children with Gaucher's disease usually have an early acute onset of symptoms rather than the slow progression of symptoms typically seen in adults. There is currently no effective treatment for neurological damage that occurs from Type II and Type III Gaucher's disease. The prognosis for children with Type II is poor; most die by two years of age. Patients with this disease who survive to adolescence may live for many years (Beers & Berkow, 1999). As previously mentioned, prognosis is more hopeful for patients with Gaucher's disease Type I because many have responded positively to ongoing treatment with enzyme (glucocerebrosidase) replacement therapy.

REFERENCES

Bakst, A. E. (1999). Continuous intravenous epoprostenol therapy for pulmonary hypertension in Gaucher's disease. *Chest, 116,* 1127–1129.

Beers, M. H., & Berkow, R. (Eds.). (1999). *The Merck manual of diagnosis and therapy* (17th ed.). Lawrenceville, NJ: Merck & Co.

National Gaucher Foundation. (1999, March). Gaucher disease: Prevalence and transmission. Retrieved from http://www.gaucherdisease.org/info/treatment.htm

National Gaucher Foundation. (2000, June). Gaucher disease: Prevention and treatment. Retrieved from http://www.gaucherdisease.org/info/prev.htm

National Foundation for Jewish Genetic Diseases. (2001, January). Gaucher disease. Retrieved from http://www.nfjgd.org

Wrath, Ed. (1999, July). Children with gaucher's disease. *Gaucher's news: Gaucher's association.* Retrieved from http://www.gaucher.org.uk/wraith99.htm

ANDREA HOLLAND
University of Texas at Austin

GENDER IDENTITY DISORDER

Gender identity disorder (GID) represents a profound disturbance in a child or adolescent's individual sense of identity with regard to maleness or femaleness (American Psychiatric Association, 1994). Children with GID feel as though they have been born as the wrong gender and express a strong desire to be the opposite gender. This feeling may be expressed in many ways, such as dressing as the opposite sex, discomfort with same-sex peers, and verbal statements of dissatisfaction with gender to a marked degree, accompanied by distress. Onset is usually between the ages of 2 and 4 years. Only a very small number of these children will later meet the adolescent and adult criteria for the disorder (American Psychiatric Association, 1994).

Gender identity disorder is extremely rare, is estimated to exist in less than 1% of the population, and disproportionately affects boys more than it does girls (American Psychiatric Association, 1994). However, the actual diagnosis of GID is very controversial (Bower, 2001; Cohen-Kettenis, 2001). Parents and psychologists may view GID as a normal stage that will pass with time. Others believe GID is a result of having been raised in a gender-neutral situation and is therefore beneficial. Indeed, there is some question as to whether the condition should be presented in the *DSM* (Bower, 2001; Cohen-Kettenis, 2001).

Characteristics

1. A strong and persistent cross-gender identification
2. Repeated stated desire to be (or insist that they are) the other sex
3. Intense desire to partake in games and pastimes stereotypical of the other sex
4. Strong preference for playmates of the other sex
5. Persistent discomfort with their sex or sense of inappropriateness in gender role of that sex
6. In adolescents, statements of desire to be the other sex, frequents passing as the other sex, desire to live or be treated as the other sex, or the conviction that he or she has normative reactions of the other sex

The cause of GID remains unknown. Scientists speculate that it may be due to a wide range of factors from a hormonal imbalance to psychological messages from a child's parents. GID has also been linked to depression, homosexuality, and bisexuality; therefore, many researchers believe that GID is not a disorder, but rather an expression of sexual preference. Treatment for GID is psychotherapy. In later years, some individuals may express desires for sex-reassignment surgery; however, spontaneous remission is also reported.

Because children (especially boys) with GID are often ridiculed by peers, they may be prone to school avoidance and are at especially high risk for school dropout. Hence, children with GID may require special support in the school setting in order to develop coping skills to deal with social issues. It is unlikely that special education services would be needed for these children.

The prognosis for GID of childhood is good, with an extremely small number of children diagnosed in childhood exhibiting symptoms of distress in adolescence and adulthood (Marks, Green, & Mataix-Cols, 2000).

REFERENCES

American Psychiatric Association. (1994). *Diagnostic and statistical manual of mental disorders* (4th ed.). Washington, DC: Author.

Bower, H. (2001). The gender identity disorder in the *DSM-IV* classification: A critical evaluation. *Australian & New Zealand Journal of Psychiatry, 35,* 1–8.

Cohen-Kettenis, P. T. (2001). Gender identity disorder in *DSM? Journal of the American Academy of Child & Adolescent Psychiatry, 40,* 391.

Marks, I., Green, R., & Mataix-Cols, D. (2000). Adult gender identity disorder can remit. *Comprehensive Psychiatry, 41,* 273–275.

April M. Smith
Yale University

Allison B. Katz
Rutgers University

GHOST SICKNESS

Ghost sickness is a culture-bound syndrome observed among many Native American and other indigenous tribes throughout North and South America. This disorder is that contains a "preoccupation with death and the deceased" and is often associated with witchcraft and spirit possession (American Psychiatric Association, 1994, p. 849).

This disorder is most prevalent among indigenous Indian tribes of North and South America and is sometimes associated with facial paralysis among these populations. According to ethnographic reports, facial paralysis associated with ghost sickness has been "estimated at between seventeen and twenty cases per 100,000 population per year with incidence rates increasing with age until persons over sixty experience a rate of thirty to thirty-five cases per 100,000 population per year" (Adour & Henderson, 1981, p. 196). This type of paralysis is believed to be the cause of supernatural forces among the Comanche of Oklahoma (Adour & Henderson, 1981). Rates, however, are unavailable for facial paralysis due to ghost sickness in other parts of the world such as Colombia, Puerto Rico, and Peru. According to Adour and Henderson (1981, p. 198), among the Comanche, "most victims [of ghost sickness] were males between the ages of twenty-four and forty-five." However, among the Peruvian tribes in Andean regions, ghost sickness can occur (and in some cases is prevalent) among children. In this region, ghost sickness is known as chullpa sickness, which is perceived to come from "witchcraft and malevolent spirits, which inhabit ruins" (Tschopik, 1946, p. 90).

Characteristics

1. Peripheral facial paralysis
2. Tearing
3. Pain
4. Impaired taste
5. Bad dreams
6. Weakness
7. Feelings of danger
8. Loss of appetite
9. Anxiety and hallucinations
10. Sense of suffocation

Ghost sickness is noted as "psychogenic in etiology and serves culturally relevant psychological needs of the victims" (Adour & Henderson, 1981, p. 198). Among the Comanche, this disorder is prevalent among those who have experienced a series of cultural shifts between traditional Comanche society and "white Oklahoma society" (Adour & Henderson, 1981). Typically, ghost sickness is caused by an emotional fright or some kind of emotional trauma. Research indicates that 16% of those with facial paralysis had experienced "severe emotional trauma immediately before symptoms appeared" (Adour & Henderson, 1981, p. 197).

Typically, ghost sickness is treated by traditional tribal medicine. In the case of the Comanche of Oklahoma, the therapeutic regimen to treat this disorder requires a Comanche shaman (Adour & Henderson, 1981). This step reintegrates the stresses of the marginal existence. According to ethnographic accounts, the therapeutic encounter has many components of psychotherapy. Essentially, the key aspect of ghost sickness treatment in tribal affiliation is that the afflicted is isolated from conflict, engages in prescribed ritual, and has physical rest (Adour & Henderson, 1981). The duration of treatment varied from 2 to 7 days.

The occurrence of ghost sickness among children within Native American tribes in the United States is unfortunately not known, so the likelihood of special education concerns to arise from afflicted children is unknown. However, within various tribes, this disorder is seen to arise from cultural conflict between native traditional culture and integration. Therefore, determination of the level of acculturation of the afflicted children and the degree of symptoms in terms of clinical referral would be necessary to properly treat an incidence of ghost sickness among Native American children in the United States.

REFERENCES

Adour, K., & Henderson, J. N. (1981). Comanche ghost sickness: A biocultural perspective. *Medical Anthropology, 2,* 195–205.

American Psychiatric Association. (1994). *Diagnostic and statistical manual of mental disorders* (4th ed.). Washington, DC: Author.

Tschopik, H. (1946). The aymara. Retrieved from http://ets.umdl.umich.edu/cgi/e/ehraf/harf-idx?type=html

Kiely Ann Fletcher
Ohio State University

GLAUCOMA, CHILDHOOD

Glaucoma is a disease characterized by abnormally high intraocular pressure caused by blockage or disturbance of normal fluid circulation within the eye. Glaucoma occurring in the first 3 years is commonly termed *infantile glaucoma,* and onset after the age of 3 is often referred to as *juvenile glaucoma.* The term *congenital glaucoma* suggests that the disease is present at or soon after birth, although it may be difficult to determine that the disease exists at this developmental stage. The terms *primary* and *secondary* are often used in conjunction with the terms *infantile* and *juvenile* to communicate the origin of the observed eye disease. Primary glaucoma refers to a disease associated with an embryological developmental anomaly, whereas secondary glaucoma is associated with other ocular or systemic disease. Just as is the case with adult glaucoma, elevated intraocular pressure can result in visual loss and potential blindness, so early detection and treatment are essential (Datner & Jolly, 1995; Wagner, 1993).

Primary infantile glaucoma occurs during the first 3 years of childhood and is not associated with any systemic disease or other ocular disease. Approximately 50% of infantile glaucoma is primary in type (Duke-Elder, cited in Wagner, 1993). Incidence of primary congenital glaucoma is estimated to be 1 in 10,000 live births (Duke-Elder, cited in Wagner, 1993). Incidence of all types of childhood glaucoma is believed to be approximately 1 in 2,000 (Barsoum-Homsy & Chevrette, 1986). Early diagnosis and treatment has recently resulted in cure rates of approximately 90% (Stern & Catalano, cited in Wagner, 1993). Glaucoma in the neonate and infant has four cardinal signs: corneal enlargement (an indicator of increased intraocular pressure), clouding of the cornea, tearing (epiphora), and photophobia (infants may hide their faces from light due to pain, and older children may complain that the light is "too bright").

The majority of cases of primary infantile glaucoma are bilateral in nature, involving both eyes (Wagner, 1993). The disease is more readily recognizable when it is unilateral in presentation due to the ability to compare the diseased eye with the normal eye. Ironically, children with bilateral symmetric presentation may go unrecognized for longer periods because their unusually large eyes are sometimes regarded as an attractive feature.

Characteristics

1. Enlarged corneal diameter (megalocornea). Ocular enlargement occurs due to the distensible nature of the neonate and infant eyeball.
2. Classic triad of tearing (epiphora), voluntary closure of the eyelid (blepharospasm), and light sensitivity (photophobia).
3. Excessive tearing in the absence of other signs and symptoms is an uncommon presentation.

Surgery is the usual treatment of primary infantile glaucoma, typically a goniotomy (Barkan, cited in Wagner, 1993) or trabeculotomy (Allen & Burian, cited in Wagner, 1993) and is designed to improve the outflow of aqueous fluid from the eye. Approximately 80% of cases require only a single goniotomy procedure. Approximately 30% of cases may result in a recurrence of increased intraocular pressure. Other procedures include laser treatment (Senft, Tomey, & Traverso, cited in Wagner, 1993), implantation of a Molteno implant (Billson, Thomas, & Aylward, cited in Wagner, 1993), or a variety of cytodestructive techniques. In severe cases, removal of the eye (enucleation) may be required. Pharmacological treatment prior to surgery to enhance surgical procedures or after surgery to maintain lower intraocular pressure is often indicated (see Wagner, 1993, for a more comprehensive review).

Children with glaucoma who are older than 3 years of age differ in their symptom presentation, as compared to younger children. Due to decreased elasticity, enlargement of the eye may not be a distinguishing feature. Increasing nearsightedness (myopia) is a common complaint. Less commonly, the child may complain of pain. Unfortunately, the most likely situation in an older child is a lack of symptoms, resulting in late recognition and treatment (Wagner, 1993).

Secondary glaucoma (i.e., glaucoma associated with other ocular or systemic disease) can be caused by a number of factors including but not limited to structural damage, metabolic problems, inflammatory processes, or other congenital diseases of the eye. Secondary glaucoma is responsible for approximately 50% of infantile glaucoma cases. When older children are included (i.e., juvenile glaucoma), it is estimated that approximately 78% of cases are of the secondary type (Barsoum-Homsy & Chevrette, 1986).

Glaucoma can result in a range of visual impairments depending upon the type, severity, and duration of the disease process and the efficacy of treatment interventions. Although their special education needs are often numerous, the prevalence of visually impaired students receiving special education services is very small, with approximately 0.5% of school-age children being served under the disability category of visual impairment (Heward, 2000). Standard optometric treatment (i.e., lenses, prisms) may be sufficient for some children experiencing visual impairment secondary to glaucoma; children with more severe visual impairment may require more intensive educational alternatives (National Institute of Education, 1981). Today 48% of students with visual impairments are in regular education classrooms, and only 21% attend resource classrooms for at least part of the school day. Another 17% of children with visual impairments occupy separate classrooms in U.S. public schools. Only about 9% of visually handicapped children attend residential schools (U.S. Department of Education, cited in Heward, 2000).

Prognosis for glaucoma is variable, with poorer outcomes associated with earlier onset. If present at birth, glaucoma results in blindness in over 50% of the affected eyes; later onset may result in blindness in only 20% of diseased eyes. Left untreated, the prognosis for infantile glaucoma is poor, with blindness resulting in almost all cases (Wagner, 1993).

Future research should focus on delineation of characteristics of childhood glaucoma, as well as incidence-prevalence and demographic and other information associated with identification of cases. Such research may lead to earlier detection and treatment, thus potentially limiting the degree of visual debilitation as a result of this disease.

REFERENCES

Barsoum-Homsy, M., & Chevrette, L. (1986). Incidence and prognosis of childhood glaucoma. *Ophthalmology, 93*(10), 1323–1327.

Datner, E. M., & Jolly, T. (1995). Pediatric ophthalmology. *Emergency Medicine Clinics of North America, 13*(3), 669–679.

Heward, W. L. (2000). *Exceptional children: An introduction to special education.* NJ: Prentice-Hall.

National Institute of Education. (1981). *Fact sheets from the ERIC clearinghouse on handicapped and gifted children, 1981.* Reston, VA: ERIC Clearinghouse on Handicapped and Gifted Children. (ERIC Document Reproduction Service No. ED 214320)

Wagner, R. S. (1993). Glaucoma in children. *Pediatric Clinics of North America, 40*(4), 855–867.

J. Patrick Leverett
Kerry S. Lassiter
The Citadel

GLIOBLASTOMA

A glioblastoma is a malignant astrocytoma, or brain tumor. A brain tumor is defined as a new growth of tissue in which cells multiple uncontrollably. Like all brain tumors, glioblastomas have no physiological use and are independent of surrounding tissue. One specific type of glioblastoma is a glioblastoma multiforme. These tumors are usually located in the cerebral hemisphere and grow very rapidly. Glioblastomas, regardless of the type, are always malignant and account for approximately 8–12% of all pediatric brain tumors (Robertson, 1998). Like other pediatric brain tumors, glioblastomas are usually primary site tumors—that is, they are not metastases.

The 5-year survival rate in children is approximately 35%, or about one in three children (Stewart & Cohen, 1998). Factors that improve survivability, however, are early diagnosis and treatment. If the tumor is totally resected, mortality rates decline. In cases in which the tumor cannot be entirely removed, irradiation, chemotherapy, or both can also improve a child's chance of surviving. Although radiation therapy has some drawbacks—in particular, a negative impact on a child's developing brain and thus cognitive functioning—irradiation is used more often with glioblastomas than with many other brain tumors due to the glioblastoma's highly malignant nature. Chemotherapy, although it is typically more desirable than irradiation, can also cause problems, including kidney and liver damage, cataracts, ulcers, heart and reproductive problems, slowed growth, and future cancers. Some of the short-term side effects include nausea and vomiting, diarrhea, abdominal pain, fever, chills, hair loss, jaw pain, and fluid retention.

Characteristics

1. Malignant tumor that accounts for 8–12% of all pediatric brain tumors.
2. Fast-growing tumors that cause rapid onset of symptoms such as headaches, nausea, and vomiting.
3. Other sequelae include vision problems, decreased alertness, disorientation, and personality change.
4. Due to the tumor's typical location in the cerebral hemisphere, seizures and one-sided weakness or paralysis often occurs.

More often than not, children with glioblastoma tumors will qualify for special education services under Other Health Impaired. Services are often needed to address cognitive changes, attentional difficulties, memory problems, and social-emotional concerns, including lack of interest and motivation to achieve and interact with peers. Neuropsychological evaluations may be especially important in identifying deficit areas and designing appropriate interventions. Home-school collaboration will be critical to assess both the child's needs and those of the family. A life-threatening condition such as a glioblastoma affects not only the child but also the child's parents and siblings. Families need information (e.g., what to expect and what resources are available) as well as support; therefore, it is important to put them in touch with local associations where this information can be provided and support can be found with families who are facing a similar situation.

REFERENCES

Robertson, P. L. (1998). Pediatric brain tumors. *Oncology, 25,* 323–338.

Stewart, E. S., & Cohen, D. G. (1997). Central nervous system tumors in children. *Seminars in Oncology Nursing, 14*(1), 34–42.

Laura Richards
Elaine Clark
University of Utah

See also Brain Tumor

GLYCOGEN STORAGE DISEASE Ia (VON GIERKE DISEASE)

Von Gierke disease is an inherited disorder caused by an inborn lack of the enzyme glucose-6-phosphatase (G6Pase). G6Pase is critical for its role in the liver's production of glucose, which the body uses for energy. When G6Pase is missing, glycogen accumulates in the liver, kidneys, and intestines. Von Gierke disease is one type of glycogen storage disease (GSD); there are about 11 known types altogether. Von Gierke disease may also be referred to as glycogen storage disease Ia, glycogenosis Type I, and hepatorenal glycogenosis.

In the United States, the lack of newborn screening precludes reliable incidence rate estimates. However, it is suggested that for glycogen storage disorders as a group, the incidence is around 1 case per 20,000–25,000 births. For Von Gierke disease in particular, the incidence is approximately 1 case in 100,000 births. Von Gierke disease can occur in any ethnic group but is more common in Jewish individuals.

Characteristics

Von Gierke disease presents during the first year of life. Symptoms include

1. Low blood sugar levels and liver enlargement (hepatomegaly) that may cause seizures
2. Slow growth and very short stature
3. Predispositions to bleeding episodes (e.g., nosebleeds)
4. Delayed onset of puberty
5. A characteristic "doll-like" facial appearance with full cheeks
6. Intermittent diarrhea (etiology unknown)

Long-term complications of Von Gierke disease include

1. Gout.
2. Tumors of the liver.
3. Osteoporosis.
4. Kidney stones and other kidney problems (including kidney failure).
5. Symptoms of severe hypoglycemia (low blood sugar) are likely to follow any illness that causes mild anorexia or fasting (e.g., viral gastroenteritis). This may be evidenced by the individual's feeling weak, drowsy, confused, hungry, and dizzy, with paleness, headache, irritability, trembling, sweating, rapid heartbeat, and a cold, clammy feeling. In severe cases, a person can lose consciousness and even lapse into a coma.

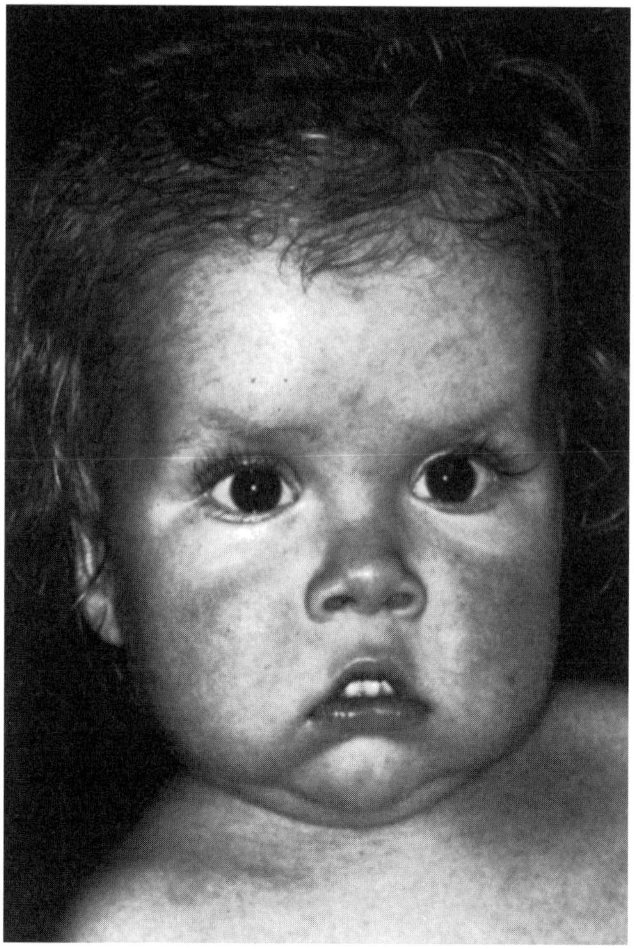

Glycogen Storage Disease Type I
Reprinted from *Clinical Syndromes,* Wiedemann and Kunze, 1997, by permission of the publisher Mosby

Treatment for Von Gierke disease is limited. It primarily consists of giving glucose drinks frequently during the day. For infants glucose drinks are also given continuously overnight through a nasogastric tube. As children get older, a treatment with cornstarch, which releases glucose slowly into the stomach may be very effective. Any illnesses that may alter glucose intake (e.g., illnesses associated with vomiting or diarrhea) may require IV glucose support until resolution to prevent hypoglycemia. The mainstay therapy for Von Gierke disease is diet; this requires close monitoring and adjustment by specialized personnel. The chief aim is to avoid excessive carbohydrates and calories while supplying adequate nutrition for growth. Close nutritional and biochemical genetic follow-up is critical, especially during initial and pubertal growth periods. Subspecialists should see patients at least every 6 months.

Students diagnosed with Von Gierke disease will probably qualify for special services under the Individuals with Disabilities Education Act (1997) within the physical disability category. This disorder may require students to be absent from school for periods of time for medical reasons. Accommodations and modifications may need to be implemented to help the student keep up with school requirements. School personnel need to be cognizant of the dietary needs and physical limitations of this disorder. These students may not be able to participate in competitive activities because of the propensity for bleeding and potential for liver damage. The student can be encouraged to engage in other physical activities up to individual limits. School personnel should also be able to recognize signs of impending hypoglycemia.

Until recently, most children with this condition died before reaching adulthood. The outlook for those who survived was dismal. Early diagnosis and effective treatment of this condition have undeniably improved the prognosis. Patients receiving proper treatment and education concerning dietary needs should have a reasonable life span. However, it remains unclear whether good control over these children's metabolic problems will reduce the incidence of long-term complications (Weinstein, Somers, & Wolfsdorf, 2001; Restaino, Kaplan, Stanley, & Baker, 1993). Individuals with Von Gierke disease and their families may benefit from contacting support groups such as Association for Glycogen Storage Disease, P.O. box 896, Durant, IA, 52747, (319) 785-6038.

REFERENCES

Restaino, I., Kaplan, B. S., Stanley, C., & Baker, L. (1993). Nephrolithiasis, hypocitraturia, and a distal renal tubular acidification defect in type 1 glycogen storage disease. *Journal of Pediatrics, 122*(3), 392–396.

Veiga-da-Cunha, M., Gerin, I., & Van Schaftingen E. (2000). How many forms of glycogen storage disease type I? *European Journal of Pediatrics, 159,* 314–318.

Weinstein, D. A., Somers, M. J., & Wolfsdorf, J. I. (2001). Decreased urinary citrate excretion in type 1a glycogen storage disease. *Journal of Pediatrics, 138*(3), 378–382.

National Organization for Rare Disorders, Inc., PO Box 8923, New Fairfax, CT 06812-8923.

Barry H. Davison
Ennis, Texas

Joan W. Mayfield
Baylor Pediatric Specialty Services
Dallas, Texas

Rachel Toplis
University of Northern Colorado

GLYCOGEN STORAGE DISEASE TYPE II (POMPE DISEASE)

Pompe disease (PD) is a rare, heritable disorder of carbohydrate metabolism. PD is typified by glycogen (a complex carbohydrate polymer) deposition in skeletal and heart muscle, which causes progressive weakness, loss of muscle mass, and failure of the heart's pumping action.

PD is associated with a deficiency of the enzyme lysosomal acid alpha 1, 4 glucosidase (acid maltase). This enzyme is normally present in lysosomes, which are cellular particles containing primarily hydrolyzing enzymes. Acid maltase is essential for the degradation of glycogen into simple sugars.

The gene for acid alpha-glucosidase production is encoded on Chromosome 17. Specific mutations of this site are believed to explain the various clinical forms of PD. The pattern of heredity for PD is autosomal recessive. Its incidence in the general population is 1:50,000 births.

Characteristics

1. PD's most severe form is infantile-onset disease. Infants appear normal at birth but soon develop hypotonia (generalized muscle weakness) and a "floppy baby" appearance, feeding problems, enlargement of the tongue, hepatomegaly (liver enlargement) and progressive cardiomegaly (heart enlargement). Death occurs prior to age 2, secondary to heart failure, respiratory failure, or both.
2. The juvenile form of PD usually manifests itself by delayed motor development and difficulty walking. Swallowing abnormalities, muscle weakness, and respiratory failure (secondary to diaphragm and chest muscle involvement) soon follow. Cardiac abnormalities are not consistently seen. Death from respiratory compromise comes before the end of the second decade.
3. The adult variant of PD is characterized by slowly progressive muscle weakness (myopathy) without associated heart involvement. Symptoms can begin as early as the second decade or as late as age 60. Myopathy is primarily proximal (affecting parts of the limbs closest to the body), with legs more severely involved than arms. Muscles of the pelvic girdle, the spine, and the diaphragm are the most seriously affected. Older children, adolescents, and adults with this disorder may initially complain of sleepiness, morning headache, and exercise-related shortness of breath as symptoms of respiratory insufficiency.

There is no available therapy for the infantile form of PD. A high-protein diet may lessen the severity of juvenile- and adult-onset disease. Nocturnal ventilatory support may be useful in adult patients, particularly during episodes of respiratory illness.

Families affected by PD should receive genetic counseling. Prenatal diagnosis is available and can usually differentiate infantile disease from the less severe types of PD.

There is no research to indicate cognitive dysfunction as a result of PD. Children with juvenile onset may benefit from evaluation and treatment from physical therapy to assist motor development. Swallowing difficulties may be addressed by a speech pathologist.

Prognosis for patients with PD is clearly dependent on the form of the disorder they have. Infantile-onset disease has the worst outlook, with death before or during the 2nd year. Juvenile-onset PD has a somewhat better course, but no patient with this variant has survived to age 20. The adult form of PD actually has a fairly good prognosis and is responsive to dietary management and supportive respiratory care.

For more information, please contact CLIMB (Children Living with Inherited Metabolic Diseases), The Quadrangle, Crewe Hall, Weston Road, Crewe, Cheshire, CW1-6UR, United Kingdom, (127) 02-50221, home page: http://www.CLIMB.org.uk

REFERENCES

Chen, Y.-T. (2000). Defects in metabolism of carbohydrates. In R. E. Behrman, R. M. Kleigman, & H. B. Jenson (Eds.), *Nelson textbook of pediatrics* (16th ed., pp. 411–412). Philadelphia: W. B. Saunders.

National Organization for Rare Disorders. (1998). Pompe disease. Retrieved from http://www.rarediseases.org

Barry H. Davison
Ennis, Texas

Joan W. Mayfield
Baylor Pediatric Specialty Services
Dallas, Texas

GLYCOGEN STORAGE DISEASE TYPE III (FORBES DISEASE)

Forbes disease is a glycogen storage disorder referred to as glycogen storage disease Type III. The disorder usually begins in infancy. Individuals with Forbes disease lack the hepatic debrancher enzyme amylo-1,6-glucosidase, which results in abnormal glycogen accumulation in the liver, muscles, and in some cases the heart. They can not convert glycogen to glucose, so they must eat frequently or they will suffer from hypoglycemia. Prominent characteristics in children with this disorder include an enlarged liver (hepatomegaly), unusual body fat distribution, hypotonia, and short stature due to retarded physical growth. After puberty, many individuals have a normal growth spurt, they experience few hypoglycemic episodes, and their liver decreases in size (Moses et al., 1986).

The overall incidence of Type III glycogen storage disease in the United States is approximately 1 in 100,000 live births, affecting males and females equally. However, in Israel the disease affects individuals of North African heritage more frequently, with 1 in 5,400 people being affected and 1 in 35 carrying the gene for the disorder (Parvari et al., 1997). The majority of individuals with the disorder have liver and muscle problems (Type IIIa). Approximately 15% of patients have only liver involvement without muscle weakness (Type IIIb), retaining enzymatic activity in muscle (McKusick, 2000). Forbes disease is inherited through autosomal recessive genes. The disorder is caused by a mutation in the glycogen-debranching enzyme gene (amylo-1,6-glucosidase), which is assigned to Chromosome 1p21 (Yang-Feng et al., 1992).

Characteristics

1. Child may have a protruding abdomen, short stature, and frequent bleeding and infections.
2. Infants may have hypotonia with muscle weakness and poor head control, hepatomegaly, failure to thrive, and possibly hypoglycemia and cardiomegaly.
3. During childhood, hepatomegaly may be present but usually disappears after puberty.
4. Hypotonia may be minimal in childhood, but progressive muscle weakness and wasting may be observed during adulthood.

The treatment of Forbes disease primarily focuses on preventing hypoglycemia. Frequent meals of carbohydrates and high-protein diets help combat hypoglycemia. Some children may receive continuous glucose or high-protein tube feedings at night to promote growth and improve muscle function (Slonim, Coleman, & Moses, 1984). The child should also be monitored for liver, heart, and muscle problems. Children with hypotonia may benefit from physical therapy to promote ambulation (Gandy, 1994).

Children with Forbes disease require dietary management during school. Communication between the school dietician, family, and medical professionals is necessary to coordinate dietary plans. Children with this disorder require frequent meals, often with cornstarch, at specific times of the day. School personnel should be able to recognize symptoms of hypoglycemia. The child should also have a health care plan so that the school knows what to do when hypoglycemia occurs. Children with poor muscle tone may benefit from physical therapy services (Plumridge, Bennett, Dinno, & Branson, 1993).

The prognosis of individuals with Forbes disease is good, especially when the disease is confined to the liver. Liver symptoms often disappear after puberty. Adults usually attain normal height and live a normal life span. Individuals with glycogen storage disease Type IIIa may experience progressive muscle weakness and wasting as adults (Gandy, 1994).

REFERENCES

Gandy, A. (1994, June 5). Forbes disease: Glycogenosis III. Retrieved from http://www.icondata.com/health/pedbase/files/Forbesdi.htm

McKusick, V. A. (Ed.). (2000, August 17). Glycogen storage disease III (Entry no. 232400). *Online mendelian inheritance in man (OMIM)*. Retrieved from http://www.ncbi.nlm.nih.gov

Moses, W. S., Gadoth, N., Bashan, N., Ben-David, E., Slonim, A. E., & Wanderman, K. L. (1986). Neuromuscular involvement in glycogen storage disease type III. *Acta Paediatrica Scandinavica, 75,* 289–296.

Parvari, R., Moses, S., Shen, J., Hershkovitz, E., Lerner, A., & Chen, Y. T. (1997). A single-base deletion in the 3-prime coding region of glycogen-debranching enzyme is prevalent in glycogen storage disease type IIIA in a population of North African Jewish patients. *European Journal of Human Genetics, 5,* 266–270.

Plumridge, D., Bennett, R., Dinno, N., & Branson, C. (Eds.). (1993). *The student with a genetic disorder.* Springfield, IL: Charles C. Thomas.

Slonim, A. E., Coleman, R. A., & Moses, W. S. (1984). Myopathy and growth failure in debrancher enzyme deficiency: Improvement with high-protein nocturnal enteral therapy. *Journal of Pediatrics, 105,* 906–911.

Yang-Feng, T. L., Zheng, K., Yu, J., Yang, B.-Z., Chen, Y.-T., & Kao, F.-T. (1992). Assignment of the human glycogen debrancher gene to chromosome 1p21. *Genomics, 13,* 931–934.

Susannah More
University of Texas at Austin

GLYCOGEN STORAGE DISEASE TYPE IV (ANDERSEN DISEASE)

Andersen disease is one of the glycogen storage diseases and is characterized by cirrhosis and liver failure. Individuals with glycogen storage diseases are unable to break glycogen down to glucose, thus causing abnormal accumulation of glycogen in the liver or muscle (Wynbrant & Ludham, 1999). Storing excess amounts of glycogen results in muscle weakness and an enlarged liver. Individuals with glycogen storage diseases are unable to convert glycogen to glucose, so they must be fed every few hours to ensure constant glucose from ingested food sources. This disease is inherited as an autosomal recessive trait and symptoms are caused by abnormal glycogen levels (Thoene & Coker, 1995).

Andersen disease is one of the rarest of the glycogen storage diseases and affects less than 5% of patients with these diseases. The glycogen storage diseases affect 1 in 40,000 people in the United States.

Characteristics

1. Infants with Andersen disease fail to thrive, develop little weight gain, lack muscle tone, and may have gastrointestinal problems.
2. The liver and spleen progressively enlarge.
3. In addition to hypotonia, neurological abnormalities include muscular atrophy and decreased tendon reflexes.

Treatment for Andersen disease generally targets treating the cirrhosis and other symptoms. Liver transplants are currently an experimental treatment for Andersen disease.

Special education services may be available for students with Andersen disease under the Other Health Impairment category, although most individuals do not survive to school age. In addition to attention to medical problems concerning the liver and spleen, these students may need services targeting motor and neurological deficits. Occupational and physical therapy may be needed to assist with development of gross and fine motor skills. Psychoeducational testing should occur to determine the presence of neurological deficits.

Andersen disease is an extremely rare form of a glycogen storage disease, and cirrhosis of the liver or scarring of muscles and heart can occur. Death usually occurs before the age of 2 years. Current research is investigating liver transplantation as a treatment.

REFERENCES

Thoene, J. G., & Coker, N. P. (Eds.). 1995. *Physicians' guide to rare diseases* (2nd ed.). Montvale, NJ: Dowden.

Wynbrandt, J., & Ludman, M. D. (1999). *The encyclopedia of genetic disorders and birth defects.* New York: Facts on File.

Jennifer Hargrave
University of Texas at Austin

GLYCOGEN STORAGE DISEASE TYPE V (McARDLE DISEASE)

McArdle disease, or glycogen storage disease Type V, is an autosomal recessive metabolic disorder that results in a defect in glycogen breakdown in skeletal muscle tissue. The breakdown of glycogen is necessary to create the energy that is especially needed during exercise. McArdle disease is characterized by a lack of the enzyme muscle glycogen phosphorylase. The primary store of glucose in the muscle tissue is in glycogen, and muscle glycogen phosphorylase acts as a catalyst in the degradation of glycogen into glucose. Without the capacity to break down glycogen, muscle tissue receives insufficient energy, resulting in fatigue and pain from only minimal activity.

The number of people diagnosed with this rare disease has been steadily growing in the past decades and is conservatively estimated at 1 in 100,000 (Haller, 2000). McArdle disease affects equal numbers of males and females (Gandy, 1994). Age of onset of McArdle disease is during childhood or in adolescence, although due to the nature of the symptoms, diagnosis of McArdle disease is often delayed until persons are in their 20s or 30s. This delay in diagnosis occurs because symptoms present in childhood are less severe and the exercise intolerance usually begins in late childhood or early adolescence (Bartram, Edwards, & Beynon, 1995). Additionally, symptoms of McArdle disease are exercise induced and are often attributed to the patient's being in poor physical condition or lacking in motivation (Haller, 2000).

Characteristics

The following symptoms are brought on by exercise: short duration, intense exercise (e.g., sprinting or lifting and carrying heavy objects) or low exertion, sustained activity (e.g., bike riding).

1. Tenderness or pain in the muscles (myalgia).
2. Severe cramps.
3. Early fatigue and muscle weakness.
4. Myoglobinuria can occur when exercise is continued after muscle pain begins. In severe cases, myoglobinuria can result in renal failure.
5. Patients report that when they rest briefly at the first sign of muscle pain, they then can continue to exercise. This is known as the "second wind" phenomenon.

These characteristics depict the typical picture of McArdle disease; there are variations, including a severe infantile presentation. Diagnosis of McArdle disease can be confirmed by histochemical staining of a muscle biopsy or by an ischemic forearm test (Gandy, 1994). Currently, there is no treatment for McArdle disease, and management focuses on symptom reduction. Symptom reduction aims to increase tolerance to exercise and is achieved by facilitating the use of energy sources other than muscle glycogen. Symptom reduction involves both exercise management and dietary management. Patients with McArdle disease should not avoid exercise. To maximize the function of muscle mitochondrial enzymes, they need to stay as active as is tolerable. Mitochondrial biogenesis reduces the dependence of the muscles on glycogen metabolism for energy. Exercise will increase circulatory capacity, which may increase mitochondrial biogenesis while also increasing delivery of blood-borne fuel to the muscle (Haller, 2000). Dietary management has also been used to reduce symptoms. Although no single diet has been determined to be the most effective for patients with McArdle disease, the diets used aim to provide alternative energy sources to the skeletal muscle. Protein, fatty acid, and carbohydrate supplementation have been used as treatments with some success (Bartram et al., 1995). Vitamin B6 supplements have been successful in some cases, although confirmation of the benefits is needed (Haller, 2000). Patients with McArdle disease must avoid excess weight because it requires more energy during activity.

Special education services may be available to children with McArdle disease under the handicapping condition of Other Health Impaired or Physical Disability, although they may not require special therapy. However, it is important that the exercise encountered in normal play is monitored so as not to cause damage to muscle or to cause episodes of myoglobinuria.

Severity of symptom expression varies for each patient. Exercise intolerance is usually lifelong because there is no cure for McArdle disease. Muscle atrophy and weakness of the muscle may begin in adolescence and become progressively worse later in life (Gandy, 1994). The earlier the diagnosis, the better the overall prognosis because muscle injury and severe episodes of myoglobinuria can be monitored or avoided. In severe cases, myoglobinuria can lead to renal failure. Current research focuses on the nutritional regimen that will best benefit patients with McArdle disease. Creatine therapy is being studied as a dietary management approach for treatment (Vorgerd et al., 2000). Gene therapy using an adenovirus to correct the enzyme deficiency is currently being researched and in the future may be a successful therapy for McArdle disease (Bartam et al., 1995).

REFERENCES

Bartram, C., Edwards, R. H. T., & Beynon, R. J. (1995). McArdle's disease: Muscle glycogen phosphorylase deficiency. *Biochimica et Biophysica Acta, 1272,* 1–13.

Gandy, A. (1994, April 13). McArdle disease: Glycogenosis V. Retrieved from http://www.icondata.com/health/pedbase/files/MCARDLED.HTM

Haller, R. G. (2000). Treatment of McArdle disease. *Archives of Neurology, 57,* 923–924.

Vorgerd, M., Grehl, T., Jager, M., Muller, K., Freitag, G., Patzold, T., et al. (2000). Creatine therapy in myophosphorylase deficiency (McArdle disease). *Archives of Neurology, 57,* 56–963.

Kellie Higgins
University of Texas at Austin

GLYCOGEN STORAGE DISEASE TYPE VI (HERS DISEASE)

Hers disease, glycogen storage disease VI, is a hereditary glycogen storage disease caused by a deficiency of the enzyme called liver phosphorylase. Typically seen in children between the ages of 1 and 5, Hers disease sometimes goes undiagnosed until adulthood. The most prominent symptom of Hers disease is an enlarged liver. This anomaly occurs as a result of low-level phosphorylase's inability to break down glycogen into glucose, thus causing the glycogen to accumulate in the liver, resulting in the enlargement of the liver.

Prevalence of Hers disease is estimated at 1 in 20,000 persons and is predominantly asymptomatic. Symptoms that are present in childhood often dissipate by puberty. Treatment often involves dietary cognizance, in that meals should be eaten on regular intervals and adjusted as needed to maintain glucose levels. Monitoring by a physician also may be helpful. Often, no special education attention is needed in patients with Hers disease and prognosis is excellent. It should be noted that rare variants of this disease do exist and are associated with fatal cardiomyopathy.

Characteristics

1. Hepatomegaly (enlargement of the liver).
2. Faintness, dizziness, hunger, and nervousness as a result of hypoglycemia.
3. Urine ketones and acetone levels may be high.
4. Growth rate may be slow and mild motor delays are present.

REFERENCES

Burwinkel, B., Bakker, H. D., Herschkovitz, E., Moses, S. W., Shin, Y. S., & Kilimann, M. W. (1998). Mutations in the liver glycogen phosphorylase gene (PYGL) underlying glycogenosis type VI (Hers disease). *American Journal of Human Genetics, 62,* 785–791.

Ierardi-Curto, L. (2001). Glycogen storage disease type IV (Hers Disease). *eMedicine, 2*(3). Retrieved June 2001 from http://www.emedicine.com/ped/topic2564.html

Kimberly M. Estep
University of Houston, Clear Lake

GLYCOGEN STORAGE DISEASE VII (TARUI DISEASE)

Glycogen storage disease Type VII, also called Tarui disease, is characterized by the accumulation of glycogen primarily in skeletal muscle resulting in exercise intolerance, muscle cramps, and fatigue after exercise.

The incidence is rare (about 20 cases worldwide), with equal occurrence in males and females, and it is the rarest of the glycogen storage diseases. The age of onset is late childhood to adolescence. This disorder appeared to be especially prevalent among people of Ashkenazi Jewish descent (McKusick, 2002). The risk factors for this disorder are genetic and are familial from autosomal recessive transmission on Chromosome 1cen-q32 phosphofructokinase (PFK) gene (muscle type). It is diagnosed by observations of decreased PFK activity in erythrocytes (50% of normal) or muscle biopsy biochemistry (< 50% of normal).

Characteristics

Musculoskeletal manifestations

1. Symptoms similar to those of McArdle disease
2. Temporary weakness and cramping of muscle after exercise
3. Exercise intolerance and fatigability
4. Normal motor development

Complications (with prolonged vigorous exercise)

1. Gross myoglobinuria due to rhabdomyolysis resulting in acute renal failure (for acute episodes)
2. Chronic renal failure (for prolonged or frequent repetitive episodes of myoglobinuria)
3. Gout
4. Recurrent jaundice
5. Normal mental development

The treatment for glycogen storage disease (GSL) is supportive and needs a multidisciplinary approach with pediatrics monitoring for exercise intolerance, for the avoidance of vigorous exercise, and for complications. Genetic counseling is also advisable.

Special education may be necessary for children with complications that require extensive medical intervention and hospitalization (i.e., renal failure). Adaptive physical education would be necessary as well as helping the child self-monitor exercise and preventing symptoms and complications. Counseling for the family and child may also be necessary to facilitate treatment compliance and home-school collaboration. The prognosis for individuals with this disorder is good with only minimal disability.

REFERENCES

McKusick, V. A. (1998). Glycogen storage disease Type VII. *Online mendelian inheritance in man.* Retrieved May 2002 from http://www.ncbi.nlm.nih.gov:80/entrez/dispomim.cgi?id=232800

Pedlynx Online Database. Tarui disease. Retrieved May 2002 from http://www.icondata.com/health/pedbase/files/TARUIDIS.HTM

Elaine Fletcher-Janzen
University of Northern Colorado

GLYCOGEN STORAGE DISEASE TYPE VIII

Glycogen storage disease Type VIII is a rare genetic metabolic disorder characterized by an accumulation of glycogen in the central nervous system and can result in substantial abnormalities and dysfunction of the central nervous system (Kornfield & LeBaron, 1984). Glycogen storage disease Type VIII affects the X chromosome and results in a deficiency of a liver enzyme called phosphorylase kinase. This deficiency eventually leads to excessive deposits of glycogen in the liver (National Organization for Rare Disorders [NORD], 2001). Because it is an X-linked, recessive genetic disorder, it is more likely to be masked in females and expressed in males (NORD, 2001).

Glycogen storage disease Type VIII is 1 of 10 identified types of glycogen storage diseases (Kornfield & LeBaron, 1984) that all together affect fewer than 1 in 40,000 persons in the United States (NORD, 2001). Glycogen storage disease Type VIII usually begins in infancy and affects more males than females. Although these symptoms can occur, liver function is usually normal, and glycogen storage disease Type VIII may remain undetected throughout life (NORD, 2001).

Characteristics

1. Child comes into the physician complaining of symptoms of hypoglycemia, including headaches, nausea, dizziness, lightheadedness, and confusion that occur several hours after eating and are relieved by food intake (NORD, 2001). Child could also be identified by blood tests indicating any of the symptoms in the following list.
2. Symptoms of glycogen storage disease may include an enlarged liver, high levels of liver glycogen, mild hypoglycemia, possible liver inflammation (NORD, 2001), possible growth retardation (Vhi Healthcare, 2001), and hypercholesterolemia (elevated levels of cholesterol in the blood; Fernandes et al., 1988).
3. Often the liver function is normal, and the disease may go undetected throughout life (NORD, 2001).

Treatment for this disease in its mild form is often not necessary because the resulting hypoglycemia is mild (Fernandes et al., 1988: NORD, 2001). During a long-term infection, fasting is not recommended, particularly when the infection is accompanied by vomiting or anorexia (Fernandes et al., 1988). Hypercholesterolaemia can be also be controlled by dietary changes, such as a diet enriched with polyunsaturated fats (Fernandes et al., 1988). Future treatment research centers on diet and genetic counseling (Fernandes et al., 1988: NORD, 2001). Severe cases of glycogen storage disease that are not responsive to dietary treatment have been treated successfully with liver transplants (Vhi Healthcare, 2001). Patients with glycogen storage disease Type VIII often go undetected, usually do not require treatment, and live normal lives (NORD, 2001).

Academic modifications are usually not necessary for children with glycogen storage disease Type VIII, although cases with severe symptoms of hypoglycemia may need to allow the child to eat small snacks throughout the school day. Special dietary accommodations by the school nutritionists may also be helpful in reducing the symptoms of hypoglycemia.

REFERENCES

Fernandes, J., Leonard, J. V., Moses, S. W., Odievre, M., di Rocco, M., Schaub, J., et al. (1988). Glycogen storage disease: Recommendations for treatment. *European Journal of Pediatrics, 147,* 226–228.

Kornfield, M., & LaBaron, M. (1984). Glycogenosis type VIII. *Journal of Neuropathology and Experimental Neurology, 43*(6), 568–579.

National Organization for Rare Disorders. (2001, March 20). Glycogen storage disease VIII. Retrieved from http:www.stepstn.com/cgi-win/nord.exe?number=400&proc=ap_fullReport

Vhi Healthcare. (2001, March 18). Glycogen storage diseases. Retrieved from http://www.vhihealthe.com/article/gale/100084628

Moana Kruschwitz
Margaret Semrud-Clikeman
University of Texas at Austin

GOLDENHAR SYNDROME

Because Goldenhar syndrome includes a wide spectrum of physical features and symptoms, a number of names have arisen. Other names for this syndrome include Goldenhar-Gorlin syndrome, the oculoauriculovertebral (OAV) spectrum, ocular-auriculo-vertebral anomaly, first and second branchial arch syndrome, facio-auriculo-vertebral (FAV) spectrum, and oculo-auriculo-vertebral dysplasia.

Goldenhar syndrome is the second most common facial birth defect after cleft lip and palate. Research suggests that late-gestation vascular disruptions may cause craniofacial anomalies (Escobar & Liechty, 1998; Poswillo, 1973; Robinson, Hoyme, Edwards, & Jones, 1987). A few rare cases with positive family histories have suggested autosomal dominant or recessive inheritance (Regenbogen, Godel, Goya, & Goodman, 1982; Summitt, 1969). The disorder is characterized by a wide spectrum of morphogenetic abnormalities derived from the region of the first and second branchial arches. Because there is no agreement on minimal diagnostic criteria, symptoms and physical features may vary greatly in range and severity from case to case. The abnormalities tend to involve the cheekbones, jaws, mouth, ears, eyes, bones of the spinal column, or any combination of these. When only ear, jaw, and cheek abnormalities are present, this problem is normally referred to as hemifacial microsomia. Heart, limb, central nervous system, and kidney abnormalities may also occur.

Abnormalities of both the external and middle ear may also be present. In some cases, the external ear may be absent or misshapen. The middle ear may be tiny or malformed, causing poor sound conduction with resultant hearing loss. There are often skin tags or pits in front of the ear or in a line between the ear and the corner of the mouth. More than half the cases have asymmetry of the face caused by underdevelopment of the muscles on the affected side. Cleft palate and a small receding chin may be present as well. Eyes may be small with yellow, pink, or milky-white growths in 33% of these cases. Skeletal abnormalities may be present, varying from malformed, absent, or fused vertebrae to abnormal forearm and thumb. Heart defects occur with greater frequency in those with this disorder than in other babies. Ventricular septal defects are one of the most common of these heart abnormalities. Five to 15% of children with this syndrome have some degree of mental retardation. Some children with very deformed faces have severe emotional problems. The phenotype overlaps many genetic and teratological syndromes.

Reported incidence is between 1 in 5,600 to 1 in 26,000 live births (Gilbert, 1993). The male-to-female and right-to-left-sided ratios are both 3:2. Although in most cases the malformations are unilateral, approximately 10–33% of affected individuals have bilateral malformations, with one side typically more affected than the other. In the majority of such cases, the right side is more severely affected than the left.

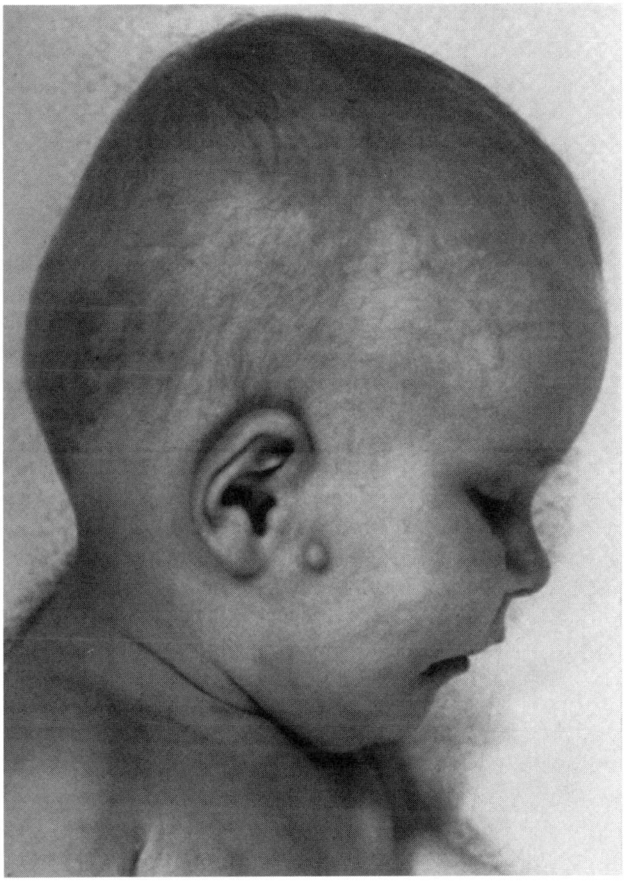

Goldenhar Syndrome
Reprinted from *Clinical Syndromes,* Wiedemann and Kunze, 1997, by permission of the publisher Mosby

Characteristics

1. A congenital disorder characterized by a wide spectrum of symptoms and physical features frequently involving the cheekbones, jaws, mouth, ears, eyes, vertebrae, or any combination of these.
2. Sixty-five to 70% of cases have some facial asymmetry. The ear may be abnormal in size or shape. Malformations of ear canal structures may lead to some degree of deafness. Thirty-five percent of cases have yellow or pink nodules in the conjunctiva at the lower outer quadrant of the eye. Cervical vertebral fusion occurs in 20–25% of cases.
3. Although most malformations are unilateral, 10–33% are bilateral but asymmetrical, with the right side more severely affected than the left.
4. Most affected individuals are of normal intelligence, although learning difficulties can occur in about 13% of cases—usually language problems as a result of deafness. In 5–15%, mild mental retardation may be present.
5. Individuals with abnormal muscle tone, bilateral involvement, and cervical vertebral anomalies are at increased risk for neurodevelopmental delay.

The complexity of this syndrome requires a multidisciplinary approach to treatment. Many special services may be required to deal with the spectrum of problems. Early intervention may be needed if the child's physical abnormalities inhibit feeding; this may occur if the lower jaw is tiny or if a cleft palate is present, with or without an associated cleft lip. There may be swallowing problems. Unusual facial features can lead to breathing difficulties. Hearing loss must be diagnosed as early in life as possible to minimize the risk of delayed speech. Early speech therapy can help these children develop speech skills that may be lost if such children do not receive help until later. Unusual facial features may prevent normal articulation of words. Orthodontic work may be needed. Cosmetic surgery is often performed in early childhood to correct external ear deformities. Plastic surgeons are also able to improve the growth of the face—particularly the jaw—through the use of bone distraction techniques. If the typical growths are present in the eye regions, they should be removed so that they do not obstruct vision. Heart defects need assessment and treatment, depending on the type. Mental abilities need to be checked by routine developmental assessment at regular intervals. Emotional problems can arise—particularly during the adolescent years—if the facial disfigurement is very marked. Sensitive counseling for the client and support from relatives and friends should reduce the impact of such problems. In a school setting, classmates may need some education about supportive responding to this child. Counseling support and education should be offered to family members.

Because Goldenhar syndrome carries a spectrum of possible abnormalities, the presence of any of them demands immediate and early assessment for the presence of hearing loss and mental retardation as well as cardiac and skeletal abnormalities. Due to delayed growth and development of the affected areas, the effects of this syndrome become more evident as the child grows. Life span is not restricted unless heart defects are severe or not amenable to treatment. Career choice may be limited if there is any substantial hearing loss. Also, facial disfigurement may be a factor precluding careers that are in the public eye.

REFERENCES

Escobar, L. F., & Liechty, E. A. (1998). Late gestational vascular disruptions inducing craniofacial anomalies: A fetal lamb model. *Journal of Craniofacial Genetic and Developmental Biology, 18,* 159–163.

Gilbert, P. (1993). *The A–Z reference book of syndromes and inherited disorders: A manual for health, social and education workers.* London: Chapman & Hill.

Poswillo, D. E. (1973). The pathogenesis of the first and second branchial arch syndrome. *Oral Surgery, Oral Medicine, and Oral Pathology, 35,* 302–328.

Regenbogen, L., Godel, V., Goya, V., & Goodman, R. M. (1982). Further evidence for an autosomal dominant form of oculoauriculovertebral dysplasia. *Clinical Genetics, 21,* 161–167.

Robinson, L. K., Hoyme, H. E., Edwards, D. K., & Jones, K. L. (1987). Vascular pathogenesis of unilateral craniofacial defects. *Journal of Pediatrics, 111,* 236–239.

Sumitt, R. L. (1969). Familial Goldenhar syndrome. *Birth Defects Original Article Series, 2,* 106–109.

Karen Bender
Rik Carl D'Amato
University of Northern Colorado

GOODPASTURE DISEASE

Goodpasture disease is a multisystem, rapidly progressive autoimmune disease that initially presents as a pulmonary-renal syndrome and—if not treated—progresses to respiratory and renal failure. Goodpasture disease in characterized by the presence of autoantibodies in the immune system that attack the lungs and kidneys and cause hemorrhaging in the basement membrane lining of the lungs and kidneys. The disease is a manifestation of human antibasement membrane diseases, but the exact cause is unknown. Smoking and inhaling hydrocarbon fumes as well as viral respiratory infections damage the basement membrane and are implicated in the promotion of Goodpasture disease (Netzer, Merkel, & Weber, 1998). In addition, there does seem to be an inherited predisposition.

The incidence of Goodpasture disease is approximately 0.1 cases per million population. It affects both genders approximately equally.

Characteristics

1. Patients in their 20s usually present with pulmonary and renal manifestations, primarily glomerulonephritis and pulmonary hemorrhage, whereas older patients usually have only nephritis.
2. Time of presentation is often the spring and summer (Savage, Pusey, Bowman, Rees, & Lockwood, 1986).
3. Other signs include coughing up blood, burning sensation while urinating, blood in the urine, flu-like symptoms, fatigue, nausea, pallor, and shortness of breath.
4. Onset is rapid and progresses to death if not treated immediately.

Treatment focuses on slowing the progression of the disease. Since the 1970s, this treatment has consisted of a combined therapy with plasmapheresis and immunosuppression. Corticosteroids are often given intravenously to control bleeding in the lungs. When the autoantibodies have ceased production and are undetectable in the body, renal transplantation is often conducted. After the autoantibodies are not detected and transplantation has occurred, patients are considered cured, although additional transplants are often needed. The recurrence rate is low (Zawada, Santella, Birch, & Jaqua, 1998).

Although presentation of Goodpasture syndrome follows a bimodal distribution with the majority of cases presenting at around ages 30 and 60, young children can also develop Goodpasture syndrome (Savage et al., 1986). Even if the disorder is detected and cured early, children with Goodpasture syndrome will miss extended amounts of school. They will need special accommodations, including but not limited to additional time on assignments, a home-school liaison to bring them assignments, and an at-home tutor. Emotional support for children with Goodpasture disease and their families is needed for coping with this often fatal disease (Avella & Walker, 1999).

Prognostic factors include percentage of crescents on biopsy and level of creatinine at the time of presentation. If left untreated, Goodpasture disease is usually fatal, but even for patients with the worst prognostic features, Goodpasture is considered curable with early diagnosis and immediate and aggressive treatment. Goodpasture disease can last from a few weeks to as long as 2 years, depending on the extent of damage and whether transplantation is necessary. It does not cause permanent lung damage, but damage to the kidney can be long-lasting. Persistent organ failure and additional renal transplantation are often the case, but patients are considered cured after surviving the acute presentation of the disease (Zawada et al., 1998).

REFERENCES

Avella, P., & Walker, M. (1999). Goodpasture's syndrome: A nursing challenge. *Dimensions of Critical Care Nursing, 18,* 2–12.

Netzer, K. O., Merkel, F., & Weber, M. (1998). Goodpasture syndrome and end-stage renal failure: To transplant or not to transplant? *Nephrology, Dialysis, Transplantation, 13,* 1346–1348.

Savage, C. O. S., Pusey, C. D., Bowman, C., Rees, A. J., & Lockwood, C. M. (1986). Antiglomerular basement membrane antibody mediated disease in the British Isles. *British Medical Journal, 292,* 301–304.

Zawada, E. T., Jr., Santella, R. N., Birch, F., & Jaqua, R. A. (1998). Cure of Goodpasture's disease. *South Dakota Journal of Medicine, 51,* 197–201.

Elizabeth Kaufmann
University of Texas at Austin

GREIG CEPHALOPOLYSYNDACTYLY SYNDROME

Greig cephalopolysyndactyly syndrome is characterized by craniofacial anomalies and polydactyly and syndactyly of the hands and feet. This syndrome is inherited as a fully penetrant autosomal dominant disorder. It has four major malformation components: postaxial polydactyly, preaxial polydactyly, syndactyly, and craniofacial anomalies (Duncan, Klein, Wilmot, & Shapiro, 1979). These four manifestations are quite variable, making the diagnosis difficult in mildly affected nonfamilial cases. In other words, they are not uniformly expressed. The origin of this syndrome may be a translocation of one or more chromosomes and may be closely linked to the region of the translocation itself (Gollop & Fontes, 1985). Development tends to be normal, except in the area of motor development, due to deformities of the hands and feet.

As of 1985, 34 patients with varying expression of this syndrome had been described (Gollop & Fontes, 1985). Current incidence rates could not be found.

Characteristics

1. The craniofacial anomalies consist of macrocephaly with broad forehead, prominent tip of the nose, and broad nasal bridge. The macrocephaly is usually benign (Chudley & Houston, 1982).
2. Postaxial polydactyly is common in the hands, and preaxial polydactyly is common in the feet. This symptom includes having an extra fingerlike appendage, often extending from the pinky finger. The big toes on the feet are often duplicated.
3. The thumbs are frequently broad, with a broad nail and misshapen distal phalanx.
4. Syndactyly is an almost constant finding in affected patients and varies from mild webbing to complete cutaneous fusion, sometimes also with nail fusion.
5. Whorl fingertip patterns on thumbs have also been reported (Duncan et al., 1979).
6. Intelligence is usually normal.

Because most literature on this syndrome consists of case studies, treatment was not often discussed. Several patients had undertaken surgery to remove extra toes and fingers.

Children with this disorder would benefit from extensive physical therapy. With or without surgery to remove the extra digits, such children will need special education assistance in the area of motor development. Other special education issues do not necessarily apply, due to normal intelligence level in children with Greig cephalopolysyndactyly. It may also be necessary to monitor the child's social and emotional well-being. It is possible that the child may encounter difficult peer issues, in which case it may be beneficial to contact a mental health professional.

Children with this disorder have a good prognosis and develop normally, according to the literature.

REFERENCES

Chudley, A. E., & Houston, C. S. (1982). The Greig cephalopolysyndactyly syndrome in a Canadian family. *American Journal of Medical Genetics, 13,* 269–276.

Duncan, P. A., Klein, R. M., Wilmot, P. L., & Shapiro, L. R. (1979). Greig cephalopolysyndactyly syndrome. *American Journal of Disorders of Children, 133,* 818–821.

Gollop, T. R., & Fontes, L. R. (1985). The Greig cephalopolysyndactyly syndrome: Report of a family and review of literature. *American Journal of Medical Genetics, 22,* 59–68.

Catherine M. Caldwell
University of Texas at Austin

GROWTH DELAY, CONSTITUTIONAL

Constitutional growth delay is a disorder that is characterized by a temporary delay in skeletal growth (National Organization for Rare Disorders [NORD], 1991). It is often a cause of parental concern about growth. This pattern occurs when a child (usually short) has a slowdown in growth just before puberty and possibly a delay in beginning puberty (Iannelli, 2000). Although children with constitutional growth delay develop slowly, they usually continue growing after other children have stopped, and many times they grow to normal adult height. There are two types of this disorder. Constitutional growth delay (familial) may be found in other individuals in the family. Constitutional growth delay (sporadic) is when the delayed pattern of growth occurs for no apparent reason (NORD, 1991).

Constitutional growth delay is sometimes called constitutional growth delay with delayed adolescence or delayed maturation. This disorder is also known as constitutional short stature, idiopathic growth delay, CDGP, sporadic short stature, or physiological delayed puberty (NORD, 1991).

Children with constitutional growth delay are usually shorter than their peers from early in their development. They grow at a slow but normal rate. The onset of puberty may occur 2–4 years later than it does in other children the same age (Rieser, 2001). Many times, after puberty, a growth spurt will occur, and the child will develop to normal height similar that of his or her parents. So-called Bone age is often 1–4 years behind the chronological age of the child (eBiocare.com, 2000). Young children with constitutional growth delay are often found to have a deficit in weight for their length (Cheng & Jacobson, 1997).

Many times, a child with constitutional growth delay is normal size at birth (Selig, 1998). In early development, usually between 6 months and 2.5 years, the child's growth slows so that height decreases to below the 5th percentile (Selig, 1998). After this point, growth is normal for the child's chronological age. The delay in skeletal growth will match the delay in height.

Constitutional growth delay is sometimes originally identified as failure to thrive (FTT) in infants and young children. These children should have a thorough evaluation to determine the cause of the growth delay. If a child has constitutional growth delay, he or she is classified as having factitious FTT; this is not considered to be a true form of FTT (Cheng & Jacobson, 1997).

Symptoms of other diseases or conditions that might affect the child's growth should be ruled out by the pediatrician through a thorough examination and family history (Cheng & Jacobson, 1997; eBiocare.com, 2000). It is also recommended that the child be evaluated and possibly treated by a pediatric endocrinologist (Iannelli, 2000).

Characteristics

1. Characterized by a temporary delay in skeletal growth.
2. Slowdown in growth just before puberty and possibly a delay in beginning puberty.
3. Most times, children eventually grow to adult height.
4. May be familial or sporadic.

Most times, this condition resolves itself and treatment is not necessary. However, a patient may undergo elective treatment with monthly hormone injections of either estrogen or testosterone. These hormone treatments can result in closure of growth plates, causing shorter height when the child reaches adulthood (Rieser, 2001). Although it has not been proven that this condition is more prevalent in males, boys are more frequently seen for treatment.

There is no direct link between constitutional growth delay and special education. However, as teenagers, these children may feel uncomfortable because they are less developed and smaller than their peers. It is possible that this condition may cause emotional stress during adolescence. Teenagers with constitutional growth delay should be observed for signs of emotional problems.

Research studies continue to be conducted to determine the physical and psychological impact of hormone treatment for constitutional growth delay.

REFERENCES

Cheng, A., & Jacobson, S. (1997). Failure to thrive: Approach to diagnosis and management. Retrieved from http://www.utmj.org/75.1/featurecontents.htm

eBiocare.com. (2000). Growth hormone deficiency. Retrieved from http://ebiocare.com/communities/ghd/faqhome.html

Iannelli, V. R. (2000). Short stature. Retrieved from http://www.keepkidshealthy.com/welcome/conditions/short_stature.html

National Organization for Rare Disorders. (1991). Constitutional growth delay. Retrieved from http://www.rarediseases.org

Rieser, P. A. (2001). *Patterns of growth.* New York: Human Growth Foundation.

Selig, S. (2000). *Constitutional growth delay.* Oak Park, IL: The Magic Foundation for Children's Growth.

Michele Wilson Kamens
Rider University

GROWTH HORMONE DEFICIENCY

Growth hormone deficiency is a condition resulting in impaired physical growth, caused by a partial or total absence of the growth hormone produced by the pituitary gland. The affected child will have normal body proportions and yet often look younger than his or her peers (Human Growth Foundation, 2000). If other pituitary hormones are lacking, the condition is called hypopituitarism; in children, the term *hypopituitarism* may be used interchangeably with *growth hormone deficiency.* The prevalence of this disorder has been estimated to be between 10,000–15,000 children in the United States and to affect 1 of every 4,000 school-aged children. The congenital form of growth hormone deficiency occurs 3 to 4 more times in boys than girls (Vanderbilt University Medical Center, 1998).

Growth hormone deficiency may be congenital (resulting from abnormal formation of the pituitary gland or hypothalamus) or acquired through damage to these glands after birth. There may be either a partial or a total lack of growth hormone production (Human Growth Foundation, 2000). In the case of a total growth hormone deficiency, height and weight are usually normal at birth. However, between 3 and 9 months, growth rate is reduced, and parents may notice additional symptoms such as delayed development of teeth and a diminished ability to gain weight (Netdoctor.co.uk, 2000). Idiopathic hypopituitarism is the most frequent mechanism causing total growth hormone deficiency. Some infants with intrauterine hypopituitarism may at birth have prolonged jaundice, hypoglycemic seizures, and if male, undescended testes and micropenis. In some children, growth hormone deficiency may also be associated with central nervous system and facial defects. These may range from severe abnormalities of brain development to cleft lip and cleft palate.

Characteristics

1. Impaired physical development, usually marked by a growth pattern of less than 2 inches per year.
2. Children often appear younger than their age, with an immature face and chubby body build. (Children may acquire a thick layer of fat under the skin that gives them a chubby body build.)
3. Children have normal body proportions.
4. Many children have heights for bone age that fall below the 3rd percentile.
5. Children may fail to undergo puberty at the appropriate age.

Growth hormone deficiency may be difficult to diagnose because the growth hormone is produced in bursts and in greatest quantities during sleep. Doctors usually first examine a child to rule out other causes (such as thyroid hormone deficiency, malnutrition, or other chronic diseases). Previous growth measurements, an X ray to determine bone age, blood samples, and measurement of growth hormone secretion also play a role in diagnosis (Levy, 1998).

Treatment consists of synthetic growth hormone therapy, usually given by injection daily or several times a week until the child stops growing (Human Growth Foundation, 2000). Although side effects are rare, the correct dosage of growth hormone must be determined exactly and child must be monitored for side effects. After treatment begins, a prompt increase in growth rate can usually be noticed in 3–4 months. Some parents have also reported an increase in appetite and loss of body fat with treatment. During the first year of therapy, children may grow 8–10 cm (Vanderbilt University Medical Center, 1998). Accurate plotting on a growth chart is important. Children who do not respond to treatment should be evaluated for hypothyroidism or the formation of antibodies to human growth hormone (Human Growth Foundation, 2000).

In the educational setting, children who are short for their age may have problems because adults and peers often treat them as younger, not just smaller. Having decreased expectations for a child may result in the child's acting younger than what is appropriate for his or her age (Human Growth Foundation, 2000). Counseling may provide emotional and social support for children. Parents may also wish to communicate with the child's educators about how any side effects of growth hormone treatment may affect learning.

Prognosis is good after a child undergoes treatment. The majority of children treated today reach normal adult height or almost their full growth potential. Early diagnosis and treatment are important for best results. If treatment does not occur before the child's bones fuse, no additional growth can occur. If growth hormone deficiency is not treated, the child's growth will be severely impaired (Levy, 1998).

Research is currently studying alternative methods of treatment, including growth hormone releasing factor (GHRF) and somatomedin. A recent study comparing once- versus twice-daily injections of growth hormone found no significant differences in growth response or bone age after 1 year (Philip et al., 1998). Other researchers have created a prediction model for growth based on the child's size and target height at start of therapy (Südfield, Kiese, Heinecke, & Brämswig, 2000). They conclude that the difference between starting height and target height is an important predictor of 1st-year growth response. The most current information on research and treatment can be found by contacting the Human Growth Foundation, a national organization of parents with affected children, at the following Web site: http://www.hgfound.org.

REFERENCES

Human Growth Foundation, Inc. (2000, November 26). Growth hormone deficiency. Retrieved from http://www.hgfound.org/growth.html

Levy, R. A. (1998). Growth hormone deficiency. Retrieved from http://www.magicfoundation.org/ghd.html

NetDoctor.co.uk. (2000, February). Growth hormone deficiency. Retrieved from http://www.netdoctor.co.uk/diseases/facts/lackofgrowthhormone.html

Philip, M., Hershkovitz, E., Belotserkovsky, O., Lieberman, E., Limoni, Y., & Zadik, Z. (1998). Once versus twice daily injections of growth hormone in children with idiopathic short stature. *Acta Paediatrica, 87,* 518–520.

Südfield, H., Kiese, K., Heinecke, A., & Brämswig, J. H. (2000). Prediction of growth response in prepubertal children treated with growth hormone for idiopathic growth hormone deficiency. *Acta Paediatrica, 89,* 34–37.

Vanderbilt University Medical Center. (1998). Endocrinology: Growth hormone deficiency. Retrieved from http://www.mc.vanderbilt.edu/peds/pidl/endocr/grohorm.html

Laura A. Guli
University of Texas at Austin

GUILLAIN-BARRE SYNDROME

Guillain-Barre syndrome is an acute inflammatory demyelinating polyneuropathy. It is an acquired neurological problem due to damage of the myelin sheath that protects the nerves. It is characterized by a rapidly progressive ascending paralysis of the extremities. It starts with parathesis of the feet, followed by weakness in the legs, arms, trunk, and face.

Guillain-Barre syndrome is the most common acquired nerve disease. It has an annual incidence of 1.5 to 2 cases per 100,000 (Johnson, 1998). In the past, it has been thought of as a winter disease but most studies show no seasonal variation. Although it can occur in all ages, it is more common in persons over 40. Some studies have shown a higher incidence rate in males.

Characteristics

1. It is an acute acquired demyelinating disorder of the peripheral nervous system that involves progressive ascending paralysis of the extremities.
2. 1.5 to 2 cases per 100,000 per year.
3. The disease has been linked to viral antecedents, but the cause is largely unknown.
4. Symptoms of disease are paresthesia, cranial nerve involvement, autonomic dysfunction, loss of reflexes, weakening of the limbs, and absence of fever in initial onset.

There is no known cause of Guillain-Barre syndrome. In the past, it was thought to be linked to surgery and childbirth. Present research, however, has shown most of these accounts to be anecdotal. In 1976, the syndrome was undoubtedly related to a swine influenza virus (Johnson, 1998). Other research has shown an increased incidence in vaccinated versus nonvaccinated individuals. Reasons explaining this increase are still completely unknown. The potential benefits of vaccines definitely outweigh the risks. Most current studies have directly linked the disease with certain antecedent viruses. One study described a case in which an individual contracted the disease following hand-foot-and-mouth disease, a type of enterovirus (Mori, Takagi, Kuwabara, Hattori, & Kojima, 2000). Other research has shown the disease to be associated with Epstein-Barre virus, herpes, influenza, hepatitis, and HIV. It is postulated that the particular upper respiratory and gastrointestinal viral infections trigger an autoimmune reaction.

Specific criteria were developed to make a differential diagnosis of Guillain-Barre. The patient must exhibit progressive motor weakness of more than one extremity, a loss or weakening of reflexes, and the cerebrospinal fluid cell counts of no more than 50 monocytes or two polymorphonuclear leukocytes (Scheld, Whitley, & Durack, 1997). A lumbar puncture must be conducted in order to extract cerebrospinal fluid. Elevated protein levels without corresponding increase in cells are commonly observed along with the aforementioned cell count criteria. Electrophysiological studies usually show slowed conduction and an absence of or prolonged F-waves. Other symptoms associated with the disease are paresthesia, cranial nerve involvement, autonomic dysfunction, and absence of fever in initial onset. The disease generally has the following progressive course: Patients reach maximum deficiency within the first 2–4 weeks and onset of recovery occurs 2–4 weeks after the cessation of progression.

Plasmapherisis and IV-IgG have been shown to be the most effective treatment modalities. Plasmapherisis is a process involving the removal of plasma from withdrawn blood with a retransfusion of formed elements into the blood. IgG is type of immunoglobin that appears to have positive effects when administered through an IV. It is also extremely important that most patients have in-hospital observation; this is so the patient's vital functions may be maintained and their muscles passively exercised. Many patients have respiratory failure and require a temporary artificial breathing machine.

Most patients slowly recover over a course of 4–6 months. The morality rate is 5–10%. Most of the deaths result from cardiac arrest due to autonomic nervous system impairment. Of the patients who recover, around 5% have a permanent disability, and 20% have some minor residual effects such as foot drop. Poorer prognosis is associated with rapid progression of the disease, older age, greater amount of neuronal damage, and the need for ventilatory assistance. There is a 5% recurrence rate in Guillain-Barre syndrome.

REFERENCES

Johnson, R. T. (1998). *Viral infections of the nervous system.* New York: Lippincott-Raven.

Mori, M., Takagi, K., Kuwabara, S., Hattori, T., & Kojima, S. (2000). Guillian-Barre syndrome following hand-foot-and-mouth disease. *Internal Medicine, 39*(6), 503–505.

Scheld, M., Whitley, R., & Durack, D. (1997). *Infections of the central nervous system.* New York: Lippincott-Raven.

Loni Kuhn
Elaine Clark
University of Utah

H

HALLERMANN-STREIFF SYNDROME

Hallermann-Streiff syndrome is a rare inherited disorder affecting an equal number of males and females. More than 150 cases have been reported in the medical literature, and no known cause has been found other than most likely a new spontaneous genetic mutation. Hallermann-Streiff syndrome is typically diagnosed shortly after birth and usually by the identification of small eyes. Characteristic facial features, premature development of teeth, or deficiency of hair on the face and on the head may also help to confirm the presence of this disorder. Other features become more apparent as the child begins to age (David, Finlon, Genecov, & Argenta, 1999).

Most typically, infants with this disorder are characterized by distinctive craniofacial abnormalities, including an abnormally small head that is usually wide with a prominent forehead; small, underdeveloped lower jaw; small mouth; and a long, narrow nose. In addition, abnormalities of the eyes, malformations of the teeth, and dwarfism (with arms and legs proportional to the body length) also occur. Abnormal widening and delayed hardening of the fibrous joints of the skull and delayed closure of the soft spot may also be evident in infants.

Craniofacial abnormalities may include underdeveloped cheekbones, small nostrils, and underdeveloped cartilage within the nose. Some cases may also include small mouth, an unusually high palate, and an abnormally large or small tongue. The presence of these abnormalities may result in narrow air passages, making it difficult for the infant to swallow, feed, and even breathe. In addition, infants may also experience recurrent respiratory infections, leading to pneumonia, obstruction of the lungs, snoring, and sleep apnea (David et al., 1999).

Ninety percent of infants born with Hallermann-Streiff syndrome experience cataracts and may experience varying degrees of vision loss and even blindness. Some infants may have small eyes, crossed eyes, rapid involuntary eye movements, and bluish discoloration of the whites of the eyes. Frequently, infants with Hallermann-Streiff syndrome experience skin and hair abnormalities, including atrophy of the skin on the scalp and in the middle of the face. The skin is usually thin and taut and may even have patches that lack any coloring. Shortly after birth, the hair commonly becomes very thin, sparse, and brittle (Cohen, 1991).

In approximately 36% of the cases, infants with Hallermann-Streiff syndrome are born prematurely and have low birth weight. Most of these children will continue to experience a deficiency in growth, resulting in a very short stature with arms and legs proportional to the body trunk. Some less common characteristics include hyperactivity, excessive sleepiness during the day, loss of consciousness associated with muscle contractions (generalized tonic-clonic seizures), and jerky movements combined with slow, writhing movements (Cohen, 1991).

Dental abnormalities that may be present include but are not limited to early development of teeth (sometimes prior to birth or shortly thereafter) severe tooth decay, extra teeth, and an underdeveloped hard outer layer.

Other disorders that are similar to Hallermann-Streiff syndrome and useful for differential diagnosis are Hutchinson-Gilford syndrome, Wiedemann Rautenstrauch syndrome, and Seckel syndrome. All of these disorders share but are not limited to symptoms of stunted growth and small facial features.

Characteristics

1. Small head
2. Small eyes
3. Wide forehead in comparison to the small head
4. Small underdeveloped lower jaw
5. Malformation of teeth
6. Beak-like nose
7. Dwarfism (with arms and legs proportion to the body length)
8. Cataract that may result in vision loss in varying degrees
9. Skin and hair abnormalities

Due to the complexity of this disorder, a multidisciplinary team is necessary in order to treat children with this disorder in a comprehensive manner. Pediatricians, surgeons, ophthalmologists, dental specialists, and mental health professionals are some of the professionals necessary for a comprehensive intervention. Other support services that may be beneficial to affected children may include special education services, physical therapy, and social and vocational specialists. Early intervention is crucial.

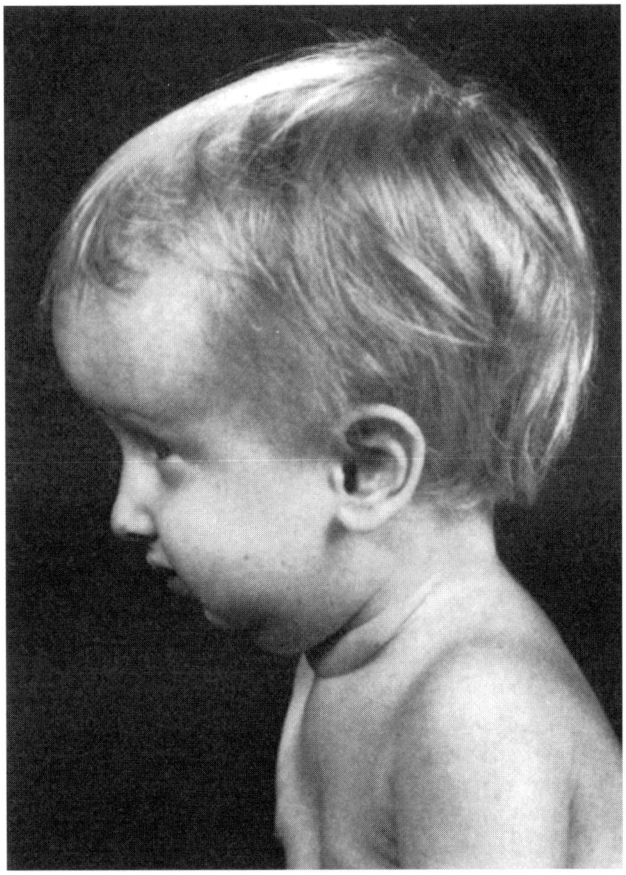

Hallermann-Streiff Syndrome
Reprinted from *Clinical Syndromes,* Wiedemann and Kunze, 1997, by permission of the publisher Mosby

REFERENCES

Cohen, M. M. (1991). Hallermann-Streiff syndrome: A review. *Journal of Medical Genetics, 41,* 488–489.

David, L. R., Finlon, M., Genecov, M., & Argenta, L. C. (1999). Hallermann-Streiff syndrome: Experience with 15 patients and review of the literature. *Journal of Craniofacial Surgery, 10*(2), 160–168.

Lisa Fasnacht-Hill
Children's Hospital, Los Angeles
University Southern California Affiliate

HALLERVORDEN-SPATZ DISEASE

Hallervorden-Spatz disease (HSD) is a rare, progressive, neurological movement disorder characterized by extrapyramidal and pyramidal motor symptoms, mental deterioration, and abnormally high deposits of iron in the brain (Sheehy, Longhurst, Pool, & Dandekar, 1999). It is an inherited autosomal recessive disorder and has been reported in both males and females (Saito et al., 2000). Incidence data was not available in the literature.

HSD is classified among the primary neuroaxonal dystrophy (NAD) diseases, including infantile, late infantile and juvenile NAD (Angelini, Nardocci, Zorzi, Strada, & Savolardo, 1992). Three subgroups of HSD have been classified, based on age at onset. The classic or postinfantile type of HSD is characterized by progressive clinical symptoms, which start between 7 and 15 years of age. The late infantile type of the disease affects children under the age of 6. The symptoms are slow but progressive and usually lead to death between the ages of 8 and 13 years. The rarest subgroup is the adult form, which starts between 22 and 64 years of age and has a fatal course within 10 years. Symptoms usually become apparent in late childhood, but HSD is often not diagnosed until postmortem inspection. In vivo brain studies using magnetic resonance imaging (MRI) have found varying features during early onset but eventual evidence of iron deposits and neuroaxonal swelling and gliosis, particularly in the globus pallidus of the basal ganglia (Ostergaard, Christensen, & Hansen, 1995).

Characteristics

1. Difficulty walking, unsteady gait, and frequent falls
2. Abnormal motor movements, such as slow writhing, distorting muscle contractions of the limbs, face, or trunk, and choreoathetosis (involuntary, purposeless, jerky muscle movements)
3. Confusion and disorientation followed by stupor and dementia as disease process progresses
4. Seizures
5. Dysphasia and dysarthria
6. Visual impairment related to retinal deterioration
7. Brain abnormalities, including MRI evidence of increasing iron deposits in the globus pallidus and substantia nigra, along with neuroaxonal swelling, neuronal loss, and gliosis on microscopy

There is no cure for HSD and no standard course of treatment. Treatment is symptomatic and supportive. Options include physical and occupational therapy, exercise physiology, and speech therapy (National Institute of Neurological Disorders and Stroke [NINDS], 2000). Sheehy et al. (1999) reported a child with HSD who presented with self-inflicted ulceration of the lip and tongue initiated during periods of intense oral-facial spasms; this behavior was eliminated by placement of upper and lower soft resin bite guards.

Special education considerations include alertness to early symptoms of HSD and referral for neurological and neuropsychological evaluation. In previously healthy young children, the warning signs of HSD include insidious walking difficulties, progressive oromandibular dystonia, and mental deterioration. In 10 cases reported by Angelini et al. (1992), neuropsychological evaluation conducted within 4 years of symptom onset revealed a general loss of intellectual ability from the early stages of the disease in all cases, with full-scale IQ scores ranging from 50 to 72 after 4 years and below 51 after 7 years. In three of these cases, only a nonverbal IQ could be computed due to severe speech impairment. In the remaining cases, verbal abilities exceeded nonverbal abilities. Although the first symptoms were typically of dystonia, in some individuals behavioral disturbance characterized by impulsivity and aggressiveness preceded motor and cognitive decline (Angelini et al., 1992). Diagnosis of HSD will result in special education classification, possibly as Other Health Impaired, Orthopedically Handicapped, or Speech Handicapped. Assistive technology in conjunction with occupational, physical, and speech therapy will be required, with eventual homebound instruction likely. Family education and counseling, with links to appropriate medical and community support, are indicated.

The prognosis for individuals with HSD is poor because of the progressive nature of the disease. Death typically occurs approximately 10 years after onset. However, there have been some reported cases of individuals with HSD surviving for several decades after onset (NINDS, 2000). Future research is needed to address issues of prevention, differential diagnosis, and effective treatment for this debilitating disorder.

REFERENCES

Angelini, L., Nardocci, N., Zorzi, C., Strada, L., & Savolardo, M. (1992). Hallervorden-Spatz disease: Clinical and MRI study of 11 cases diagnosed in life. *Journal of Neurology, 239,* 417–425.

National Institute of Neurological Disorders and Stroke. (2000). Hallervorden-Spatz disease. Retrieved from http://accessible.ninds.nih.gov/health

Ostergaard, J. R., Christensen, T., & Hansen, K. N. (1995). In vivo diagnosis of Hallervorden-Spatz disease. *Developmental Medicine and Child Neurology, 37*(9), 827–833.

Saito, Y., Kawai, M., Inoue, K., Sasaki, R., Arai, H., Nanba, E., et al. (2000). Widespread expression of alpha-synuclein and tau immunoreactivity in Hallervorden-Spatz syndrome with protracted clinical course. *Journal of Neurological Science, 177*(1), 48–59.

Sheehy, E. C., Longhurst, P., Pool, D., & Dandekar, M. (1999). Self-inflicted injury in a case of Hallervorden-Spatz disease. *International Journal of Pediatric Dentistry, 9*(4), 299–302.

Cynthia A. Plotts
Southwest Texas State University

HALLUCINOGEN ABUSE

Hallucinogens, also known as psychedelics, cause the distortion of a person's senses, emotions, perceptions, thinking, and self-awareness. These distortions are known as hallucinations. For example, vision can be perceived as sound, and smell can be perceived as vision. Pseudohallucinations are also possible; in these, the user knows that the perceptions are not reality and are due to the use of the drug (Hallucinogens: Natural and Synthetic). In general, the drugs are not considered life threatening. However, because the hallucinations may be very frightening to the user, the user may attempt to escape the perceptions; this has led to very dangerous behavior in some individuals, such as jumping from windows or running in front of moving vehicles (Hallucinogens: Natural and Synthetic).

Hallucinogens are not approved for any kind of medical use. Some hallucinogens are manufactured, such as lysergic acid diethylamide (LSD) and phencyclidine (PCP). Others are produced from natural substances, such as mescaline (peyote), dimethyltryptamine (DMT), and psilocybin (mushrooms). Substances such as LSD are usually ingested in pill, tablet, or liquid form by mouth. LSD is also sometimes produced on a "blotter" paper, which is ingested orally. It can also be injected through a hypodermic needle. Only PCP was initially used as a medication (an anesthetic) but was later discontinued because of its hallucinogenic properties (Meeks, Heit, & Page, 1996). Mescaline (peyote) can be smoked and was used by Native Americans to induce hallucinations. The high that comes from using hallucinogens can last up to 12 hours, and after prolonged use, the user may later experience flashbacks (Hallucinogens).

The highest use of hallucinogens occurred in the 1960s. The use has decreased since that time to an all-time low in the 1990s. Currently, there is a concern because of an increase in use among high school students. One survey indicated that 5.6% of all American high school seniors have tried hallucinogens (NIDA, 1991). Other research suggests that 13–17 million Americans have tried hallucinogens at least once (NIDA, 1991). The use of hallucinogens does not appear to be physically addictive (Addictions and Life Page).

Characteristics

1. Dilated pupils.
2. Heart and lung failure are possible.
3. Sleeplessness and tremors.
4. Lack of muscular coordination.
5. Decreased awareness of sensation, which can lead to self-injurious behaviors.
6. Mood and personality changes, including depression, anxiety, confusion, paranoia, or psychotic behaviors resembling schizophrenia.
7. Convulsions.

8. Violent behavior.
9. Flashbacks.

The use of hallucinogens does not in itself render a student eligible for special education services. However, a complete evaluation is warranted when a student is chronically unable to make progress in school or drug use is documented. If the etiology is solely due to a drug abuse problem, it is unlikely that the student will be eligible for special education services. However, should the student also appear to have a disability, services should be provided for the appropriate disability. Some students may be eligible for a Section 504 plan based on a drug abuse problem. In the case of hallucinogens, it is possible (but unlikely) that the student may sustain permanent emotional or psychological problems, which may suggest an emotional or behavioral disability. Treatment involves cessation of drug use. Although there are no withdrawal symptoms, it is possible for chronic users to experience unpredictable flashbacks (Strassman, 1995).

Future endeavors with the use of hallucinogens include research with human subjects in several areas (Strassman, 1995). For example, some research is being conducted with hallucinogens to attempt to identify better treatment for schizophrenia. Another study involves use of hallucinogens in the treatment of posttraumatic stress (Strassman, 1995). The use of hallucinogens in research is very controversial and will require stringent regulation. Because of statistics suggesting a recent increase in the use of hallucinogens among adolescents, preventive educational programs in schools and communities should be developed to discourage the use of these dangerous drugs in youth.

REFERENCES

Addictions and Life Page. Retrieved from http://www.addictins.com/lsd.htm

Hallucinogens. Retrieved from http://www.pinehurst.net/~apd/drug/abouthalucin.html

Hallucinogens: Natural and Synthetic. Retrieved from http://www.sayno.com/hallucin.html

Strassman, R. J. (1995). Hallucinogenic drugs in psychiatric research and treatment: Perspectives and prospects. *The Journal of Nervous and Mental Disease, 183,* 127–138. Retrieved May 13, 2001, from http://www.apa.org/journals/webref/96.html

Dalene M. McCloskey
University of Northern Colorado

HAND-FOOT-MOUTH DISEASE

Hand-foot-mouth disease is a childhood illness caused by various members of the enterovirus family. The most common cause is Coxsackie A16. Other common causes include other strains of Coxsackie A and enterovirus 71 (Ministry of Health, 2000). The virus is commonly recognized by a blister-like rash that appears most commonly on the hands, feet, and mouth. Sometimes the blisters, or vesicles, also appear on the buttocks. It is also possible to have an infection with the Coxsackie virus that causes the ulcers to form only in the mouth; this is called herpangina.

Hand-foot-mouth disease usually occurs in children younger than 6 years of age. Because it is often unreported, the number of people infected each year is unknown. It is most commonly seen in the late summer and early fall (Drkoop.com, 1998). The child is contagious when symptoms first appear, and it remains contagious until the blisters disappear. Transmission occurs directly from person to person or indirectly through contaminated articles such as toys or food utensils. The virus can be shed in the stool for several weeks. Diagnosis is usually given by symptoms; however, specific viral tests for diagnosis are available (New York City Department of Health, 2000).

Characteristics

1. A blister-like rash appears most commonly on the hands, feet, and mouth. Several blisters can be found on the palms, on the soles, and in the webs between fingers and toes.
2. The blisters are surrounded by red halos and filled with a clear fluid containing the virus. The blisters have a white or lighter colored area in the center and are approximately 1/16 to 1/8 inch in diameter. These blisters eventually burst, leaving sores.
3. Other symptoms may include low-grade fever, sore throat, headache, runny nose, and loss of appetite.
4. The incubation period is 3–6 days. The rash usually develops 1–2 days after initial symptoms.
5. The fever generally lasts 2–3 days and the blisters usually resolve in 7–10 days.

There is no specific treatment other than symptomatic relief of symptoms (Schmitt, 2000). Acetaminophen may be given to the child to treat the fever. Aspirin should *not* be given for viral illnesses in children. Because the blisters in the mouth are often painful, salt water mouth rinses may be soothing to the child, as well as a soft diet. An antacid can also be administered to alleviate mouth pain several times a day. Adequate fluids should be given to prevent dehydration and to lower fever. If child shows signs of tachycardia, severe vomiting, dehydration, stiff neck, or a severe headache, parents should contact a doctor immediately (Ministry of Health, 2000).

Because hand-foot-mouth disease is a mild communicable illness with a quick recovery, children do not usually need special education intervention. The child should stay away from school until he or she is not contagious; a good general guideline is usually 1 week after the rash appears or until the blisters resolve (Ministry of Health, 2000). Articles such as toys and eating utensils should be disinfected. If a child has neurological conditions resulting from complications of the disease, he or she may be eligible for special education services.

Hand-foot-mouth disease is generally a mild illness that resolves in 5–10 days. The child can gain immunity from a specific strain but catch the disease again from another strain of enterovirus. Prevention through hygienic practice is stressed. Complications of the disease, although they are rare, can be serious and include neurological conditions such as myocardis, meningitis, encephalitis, and acute flassid paralysis. Research is currently focusing on more serious strains of hand-foot-mouth disease causing neurological complications, such as the serious outbreaks in Taiwan in 1998 caused by enterovirus 71 (Ching-Chuan, Tseng, Wang, Wang, & Su, 2000; Huang et al., 1999). In the United States, however, such complications are rare.

REFERENCES

Ching-Chuan, L., Tseng, H., Wang, S., Wang, J., & Su, I. (2000). An outbreak of enterovirus 71 infection in Taiwan, 1998: Epidemiologic and clinical manifestations. *Journal of Clinical Virology, 17,* 23–30.

Drkoop.com: Conditions and concerns: Medical encyclopedia. (1998–2000). Hand-foot-mouth disease. Retrieved from http://www.drkoop.com/conditions/ency/article/000965.html

Huang, C. C., Liu, C. C., Chang, Y. C., Chen, C. Y., Wang, S. T., & Yeh, T. F. (1999). Neurologic complications in children with enterovirus 71 infection. *New England Journal of Medicine, 341,* 936–942.

Ministry of Health (2000, September 13). Hand-foot-mouth disease. Retrieved fromhttp://www.gov.sg/moh/mohiss/hfmd.html

New York City Department of Health (October 2000). Hand, foot, mouth disease (Coxsackie viral infection). Retrieved from http://www.ci.nyc.ny.us/html/doh/html/cd/cdcox.html

Schmitt, B. D. (2000). Parent care: Hand-foot-mouth disease. Retrieved from http://www.lebonheur.org/parentcare

Laura A. Guli
University of Texas at Austin

HARTNUP DISEASE

Hartnup disease is characterized by diminished absorption of monoamino-monocarboxylic amino acids from the intestine and from blood filtered through the kidney. This condition is presumably caused by a defect in the amino acid transporter gene located on Chromosome 2.

Hartnup disease is rare. Its incidence is 1 in 24,000 births. It is inherited in an autosomal recessive manner.

Characteristics

1. Most children with Hartnup disease are asymptomatic. Wide variability in the intestinal absorptive defect causes this phenomenon.
2. The major finding in symptomatic patients is a rough, red, occasionally itchy rash limited to sun-exposed areas of the skin. This rash may initially appear during the first few weeks of life.
3. Neurological manifestations include episodic ataxia (inability to coordinate voluntary muscle movements), irritability, and emotional lability. These symptoms can occur with or without skin abnormalities.
4. Diagnosis of Hartnup disease is made in the laboratory. Analysis of amino acid content of the patient's urine shows elevated levels of neutral amino acids but normal excretion of proline, hydroxyproline, and arginine.

In the rare symptomatic patient, treatment includes daily doses of nicotinic acid or nicotinamide and a high-protein diet. Patients with severe absorptive deficits may experience worsening symptoms of the disorder during diarrheic illness and periods of inadequate protein intake.

There is no research to indicate learning difficulties or the need for modifications in the classroom as a result of this disease.

Hartnup disease is considered a benign malady. Most children with this problem have no symptoms. Those who do have symptoms respond well to dietary modifications and daily doses of nicotinic acid. Therefore, the prognosis is excellent.

REFERENCE

Rezvani, I. (2000). Tryptophan. In R. E. Behrman, R. M. Kleigman, & H. B. Jenson (Eds.), *Nelson's textbook of pediatrics* (16th ed., pp. 353–354). Philadelphia: W. B. Saunders.

Barry H. Davison
Ennis, Texas

Joan W. Mayfield
Baylor Pediatric Specialty Services
Dallas, Texas

HAY-WELLS SYNDROME OF ECTODERMAL DYSPLASIA

Hay-Wells syndrome (H-WS) is a disorder of ectodermal dysplasia (malformation of skin, hair, nails, and teeth) in association with cleft lip, cleft palate, or both, and stringlike, fibrous band between the upper and lower eyelids (ankyloblepharon). H-WS is a congenital, hereditary condition with the previously listed abnormalities present at birth.

The mode of transmission of H-WS is autosomal dominant. There is wide variation in the physical abnormalities of individuals with this syndrome. This disorder is rare. Its actual incidence is unknown.

Characteristics

1. Oval face; broad base of the nose; cleft lip, cleft palate, or both; widely spaced, cone-shaped teeth; malformed or missing teeth; ankyloblepharon.
2. Peeling, very reddened skin in the newborn; hyperpigmentation; anhydrosis (lack of sweat glands).
3. Absent or malformed nails.
4. Sparse, wiry hair or complete absence of hair (alopecia).
5. Occasional findings include deafness, malformation of the ear, underdeveloped genitalia, and congenital heart disease.

Ankyloblepharon requires surgical correction during the 1st month of life. Cleft lip and cleft palate repair is usually done in the 1st year but may require additional operations as the child ages. Scalp infections are common, and scarring from them may necessitate skin grafting. Ear infections are frequent—probably secondary to palate anomalies—and need appropriate antibiotic treatment. Tympanostomy tube placement is indicated for recurrent middle-ear disease.

There is no research to indicate the need for special education services because the children are of normal intelligence. Because of the cleft lip and palate, the child may require early intervention from a speech pathologist to help with language development.

The prognosis for H-WS patients appears favorable after they are discharged from the surgeons' care. Intelligence is invariably normal. Heat intolerance is common secondary to a sweat gland deficiency, but hyperthermia is rarely seen. These children's eyes are also rather sensitive to bright light. However, there are no other eye anomalies associated with the rather unique and bizarre finding of ankyloblepharon.

For more information and support, please contact National Foundation for Ectodermal Dysplasias, 410 East Main Street, P.O. Box 114, Mascoutah, IL 62258-0114, (618) 566-2020, home page: http://www.nfed.org

REFERENCES

Jones, K. (1997). *Smith's recognizable patterns of human malformations* (5th ed.). Philadelphia: W. B. Saunders.

National Organization for Rare Disorders. (1998). Hay Well's syndrome. Retrieved from http://www.stepstn.com/egiwin/nord.exe?proc=GetDocument&rectype-0&recnum=880

Barry H. Davison
Ennis, Texas

Joan W. Mayfield
Baylor Pediatric Specialty Services
Dallas, Texas

HEARING IMPAIRMENT

Hearing impaired is a term used to describe individuals who have a significant hearing loss. Hearing loss can be classified into four types: conductive, sensorineural, mixed, or central. Sensorineural loss, or nerve deafness, is the most common hearing impairment (Better Hearing Institute, 1999). Hearing impairment can also be defined by severity of loss. A decibel (dB) is the unit used to measure the loudness of sound. The higher the dB, the louder the sound. *Mild loss* refers to sounds less than 40 dB; these individuals are often referred to as hard of hearing and have difficulty with quiet or distant speech. *Moderate loss* involves sounds between 41 and 70 dB; individuals with this degree of loss typically require a hearing aid but can hear when facing the speaker within 3–5 feet. *Severe loss* includes sounds between 71 and 90 dB; persons suffering this degree of loss require a hearing aid but may hear loud noises one foot from their ear. *Profound loss* refers to the sounds over 90 dB; a hearing aid and specialized training are necessary for individuals with this degree of loss. The term *deaf* refers to individuals with a loss above 70 dB.

The etiology of hearing impairments is multifaceted, and may include (a) congenital or hereditary factors; (b) obstruction or blockage of the sound pathways; (c) accidental damage to a part of the hearing mechanism; (d) otosclerosis, a spongy bony growth that immobilizes or causes malfunction of the middle-ear bones or cochlea; (e) presbycusis, or age-related hearing impairment; (f) Meniere's disease, which involves the symptoms of vertigo, tinnitus, and hearing loss; and (g) ototoxic drugs or allergies (The Better Hearing Institute, 1999). Exposure to loud noise for extended periods is also a cause of hearing impairment. The United States Department of Education (1998) reports that during the 1996–1997 school year, 1.3% of all students with disabilities received special education services under the category of Hearing Impairment. However, the number of children with hearing loss is higher because many of these students may be served under other categories. The Better Hearing Institute (1999) reports that more than 10% of the population have some degree of hearing impairment. Hearing loss is more common with increasing age. Whereas 30% of people over 65 have a hearing loss, only 14% of those 45–65 have a loss.

Characteristics

1. Strains or fails to watch speaker
2. Provides wrong answers to simple questions
3. Frequently asks for repetition of words or sentences
4. Often confuses or mispronounces speech sounds
5. Frequent earaches, colds, respiratory infections, or allergies
6. Functions below potential in school
7. Behavioral problems at home or in school
8. Withdrawn and moody behavior

Just as the etiology of hearing impairments are varied, multiple forms of treatments are also available. The preferred mode of treatment depends upon several factors, including the degree of impairment, the etiology of the impairment, and the time of onset of hearing loss. Sensorineural, mixed, and central hearing impairments are not as easily aided by amplification devices due to the extent of damage. To gain the most benefit from a hearing aid, the user needs instruction in visual communication, speech reading, and listening skills. The Better Hearing Institute (1999) reports that hearing aids can improve hearing for 95% of those with hearing impairment. Not all individuals who may benefit from a hearing aid actually utilize such a device. Treatment may also involve medical or surgical procedures.

Aural rehabilitation refers to specialized interventions aimed at reducing the degree of hearing impairments, compensating for the loss, and improving expressive and receptive communication skills. Sound and voice awareness training may be implemented to aid in the use of remaining auditory capacity. Early intervention is important to improve the outcome for young children with hearing impairments. Training designed to facilitate parental skills and improve parent-child communications is strongly encouraged (Krantz, 1985). Additionally, multiple types of assistive devices are also available. Modifications of the environment may also be beneficial (Disability Information and Resource Centre, 1999).

As the type and amount of hearing loss vary, so must the degree of educational interventions. The main goal of intervention is to teach the child to communicate. Children with hearing impairment may be eligible for special education services under the category of Hearing Impaired. The extent of special education services will vary greatly depending upon the degree of impairment and the utilization and impact of assistive devices. Training in speech and language is typically a critical component of school-based interventions. There can be profound emotional and social ramifications of hearing impairments that are left untreated.

Although some evidence suggests that hearing loss may be accompanied by additional learning deficits, hearing loss has not been identified as the primary etiology of additional learning problems. Early identification and intervention are important in the determination of prognosis. Outcome is good because multiple interventions are available. Researchers are currently investigating the impact of hearing loss on learning, behavior, and communication.

REFERENCES

Better Hearing Institute. (1999, January 3). Facts about hearing disorders. Retrieved from http://www.betterhearing.org/demograp.htm

Disability Information and Resource Centre, Inc. (1999, May 6). Hearing and hearing loss. Retrieved from http://www.dircsa.org.au/pub/docs/hear.htm

Kranz, M. (1985). Parent-infant programs for the hearing impaired. In J. Katz (Ed.), *Handbook of clinical audiology* (3rd ed.), 989–1003. Baltimore: Williams & Wilkins.

Shelley Pelletier
Jennifer Nichols
Dysart Unified School District
El Mirage, Arizona

HEART BLOCK, CONGENITAL

Congenital heart block occurs when there is an interference with the normal conduction of electrical impulses that control the heart muscle, particularly between the upper and lower heart chambers. Varying degrees of this condition exist: In first-degree heart block, the contractions of the lower chambers (ventricles) lag slightly behind the two upper chambers of the heart (atria). In second-degree heart block, one half of the atrial beats are conducted to the ventricles. In complete heart block (third degree), the ventricles and the atria beat independently.

First-degree heart block occurs primary in young adulthood with an increased prevalence in trained athletes; overall incidence is 1.3 per 1,000. Predominantly asymptomatic, first-degree heart block is generally detected by electrocardiogram (ECG) and monitored on an outpatient basis.

Mobitz I and II heart block are subgroups of second-degree heart block. Sudden occasional blocks or absences of contractions characterize Mobitz II. Mobitz II is likely to progress into complete heart block. Mobitz I type, a progressive prolongation of time between atrial and ventricle beats until one complete beat is skipped, is fairly mild with few to no symptoms. Second-degree heart block occurs in .003% of the population and requires cardiac monitoring, but again on an outpatient basis.

Characteristics

1. In first-degree heart block, the atria beat normally and the ventricles lag slightly behind. Patients may fatigue

quickly and have difficulty breathing (dyspnea); however, in most cases the child will be asymptomatic.

2. In second-degree heart block, the child may experience dyspnea, fatigue, bouts of unconsciousness (syncope), or any combination of these.
3. Children presenting with complete heart block may experience lethargy, hypotension, breathlessness, and syncope.
4. Congestive heart failure, chest pains, dizziness, cessation of the heart, and cardiomegaly are commonly seen in individuals with third-degree heart block.
5. In rare cases of complete heart block, an accumulation of fluid in body tissues will be present.

Complete heart block or third-degree heart block occurs in approximately 1 in 20,000 to 25,000 infants. Infants with complete heart block rarely live past 3 years of age, and those who do require the use of a pacemaker.

The cause of congenital heart block is not known; however, research has suggested that it could be inherited as an autosomal recessive trait, that it occurs as a secondary characteristic of underlying myocardium, and most recently that heart block occurs as a result of a maternal autoimmune disease of unknown origin (e.g., systematic lupus erythematosus). Treatment of congenital heart block varies from outpatient monitoring to implantation of a pacemaker to pharmaceuticals. Problems in cognitive realms are usually associated with poor brian perfusion responsible for neurological problems.

Prognosis ranges from poor to good depending on the degree of heart block. Future research is focused on new drug therapies to increase the atrial-ventricular conduction of the heart. Currently, the drug atropine is showing promise in achieving this goal.

REFERENCES

Brown, F. M. D. (2001). Heart block, first degree. *eMedicine, 2*(6). Retrieved June 2001, from http://www.emedicine.com/emerg/topic233.html

Brown, F. M. D. (2001). Heart block, second degree. *eMedicine, 2*(6). Retrieved June 2001, from http://www.emedicine.com/emerg/topic234.html

Brown, F. M. D. (2001). Heart block, third degree. *eMedicine, 2*(6). Retrieved June 2001, from http://www.emedicine.com/emerg/topic235.html

Klassen, L. R. (1999). Complete congenital heart block: A review and case study. *Neonatal Network, 18*(3), 33–42.

McKusick, V. A. (1997). *Online mendelian inheritance in man,* Article 234700. Retrieved June 2001, from http://www.ncbi.nlm.nih.gov/Omim

Kimberly M. Estep
University of Houston–Clear Lake

HECHT SYNDROME

Hecht syndrome (HS) is a rare, hereditary disorder of muscle development and mechanics. The first case report appeared in 1968. Subsequently, several affected individuals in an extended family group were described.

HS is inherited in an autosomal dominant manner. There is a 2:1 female-to-male occurrence, for which there is no clear explanation. No data are available regarding the rate of HS in the general population.

Characteristics

1. Small mouth with inability to open the mouth very widely.
2. Partial flexion (downward curving) of the fingers when the hand is bent upward at the wrist. This finding is secondary to shortened tendons and muscles of the forearm.
3. Occasional findings in the lower extremity are downturned toes, clubfoot, and inward curving of the forefoot (metatarsus adductus).

Surgical treatment of clubfoot may be necessary if repeated casting does not correct the deformity. Metatarsus adductus may also require orthopedic intervention. Hand and finger deformities tend to improve with age but are not particularly amenable to any type of therapy. Consequently, HS patients have difficulty performing tasks that require more than a moderate degree of manual dexterity.

There is no research to indicate cognitive difficulties; however, because of the physical limitations, children with this syndrome may require assistive devices or technology in the classroom to allow them to achieve their academic potential.

Prognosis for patients with this disorder is favorable. Feeding problems are common in infancy and childhood. Their small mouths make oral surgery, including tonsillectomy, technically difficult. Administering general anesthesia is also a challenge because of problems with intubation.

REFERENCE

Jones, K. (1997). *Smith's recognizable patterns of human malformations* (5th ed.). Philadelphia: W. B. Saunders.

Barry H. Davison
Ennis, Texas

Joan W. Mayfield
Baylor Pediatric Specialty Services
Dallas, Texas

HEMATURIA, BENIGN FAMILIAL (IDIOPATHIC HEMATURIA)

Hematuria is defined as the presence of blood in the urine. It may be further classified as gross hematuria (enough blood to make the urine look abnormal to the naked eye) or microscopic hematuria (blood can be detected only through chemical testing or microscopic examination). Gross hematuria may appear as a brown or cola-colored urine, which suggests a renal (kidney) origin of bleeding. Pink or red urine is associated with lower urinary tract blood loss. Bleeding from the bladder or urethra may also cause tiny blood clots in a urine specimen.

Benign familial hematuria (BFH) is characterized by recurrent episodes of gross hematuria that usually resolve within 1–2 weeks. Because the blood is from sites in the kidney, the urine has a brown or smoky color. The onset of hematuria is usually preceded by 1–2 days of symptoms of a viral upper respiratory infection (nasal congestion, runny nose, cough, etc.).

No data are available on the prevalence of this disorder. Because multiple individuals in the family group may be affected, the pattern of inheritance seems to be autosomal dominant.

Characteristics

1. Multiple, recurrent episodes of gross hematuria, usually associated with viral respiratory illness.
2. Microscopic hematuria may persist between the gross hematuria events. Occasionally, patients with BFH may just have constant microscopic hematuria and no gross hematuria.
3. A family history of hematuria may be found.
4. Normal blood pressure, no evidence of impaired renal function, and no proteinuria (the presence of abnormal amounts of protein in the urine.)
5. Kidney biopsy shows normal findings by the usual microscopic inspections. However, under the electron microscope, many patients will have thinning of the basement membrane. The basement membrane is the supportive structure of the glomerulus, which is the complex network of tiny blood vessels that form the kidney's filtering system.

There is no specific treatment for BFH. However, physicians caring for these children must follow them closely for abnormalities that suggest a more ominous renal disease. Persistent microscopic hematuria in conjunction with other abnormal laboratory data, as well as two or more episodes of gross hematuria, are indications for renal biopsy. This test involves passing a large bore needle into the kidney to obtain tissue for histological examination. The procedure is not without risks.

There is no research to indicate that children with BFH will have cognitive deficits or the need for modifications in the classroom.

As its name implies, BFH has an excellent prognosis. Very rarely these patients will incur progressive renal disease over a period of several decades. They do need close monitoring and may require more than one renal biopsy if hypertension, proteinuria, or deterioration in kidney function develops.

For more information and parent support, please contact National Kidney Foundation, 30 East 33rd Street, New York, NY 10016, (212) 889-2210, (800) 622-9010, home page: http//www.kidney.org

REFERENCES

Bergstein, J. M. (2000). Conditions particularly associated with hematuria. In R. E. Behrman, R. M. Kleigman, & H. B. Jenson (Eds.), *Nelson's textbook of pediatrics* (16th ed., pp. 1577–1581). Philadelphia: W. B. Saunders.

Gandy, A. (n.d.). Benign familiar hematuria. *Disease database.* Retrieved http://www.pedianet.com/news/illness/disease/files/benignfa.htm

Hematuria. (1994, January 31). *Pediatric database* (PEDBASE). Retrieved from http://icondata.com/health/pedbase/files/HEMATURI.HTM

National Organization for Rare Disorders. (1997). Hematuria, benign, familial. Retrieved from http://www.stepstn.com/cgi-win/nord.exe?proc=GetDocument&rectype=&rectype=&recnum=699

Barry H. Davison
Ennis, Texas

Joan W. Mayfield
Baylor Pediatric Specialty Services
Dallas, Texas

HEMIBALLISMUS

Hemiballismus (HB) is an abnormal hyperkinetic neuromuscular condition characterized by involuntary movement of the limbs on one side of the body, usually a result of damage to the subthalamic nucleus (STN), cerebral infarction, or hemorrhage. In the literature, hemichorea is used interchangeably with HB. Chorea is defined as involuntary jerky movements of the arms, legs, or face, and ballism can be defined by continuous, violent, coordinated, involuntary activity such that the limbs are flung about. Differential diagnosis between hemichorea and hemiballismus is sometimes difficult. HB is fairly uncommon in children and adults. HB is normally associated with an underlying pathology or lesion and will often occur in conjunction with other conditions, depending on the exact location of the insult.

Characteristics

1. Involuntary movement of the limbs on one side of the body.
2. In some cases, speech impairments may occur.
3. Stress and anxiety will intensify the movements.
4. Other neurological deficits, including mental deficiencies, muscle tone anomalies, and autonomic and sensory impairments, may be seen. However, these impairments are not necessarily due to hemiballismus but more likely related to the underlying damage of the structures surrounding the STN.

No treatment existed for this disorder in the past, and mortality rate was high. However, with medical technologies and pharmacology, individuals with HB have an increased likelihood of survival and somewhat unimpaired functioning. Special education qualifications will be Other Health Impaired, and the scope of services offered will depend on the presentation and manifestations of other organic damage. Continued research on brain lesions and methods of compensation is ongoing.

REFERENCES

Crozier, S., Lehericy, S., Verstichel, P., Masson, C., & Masson, M. (1996). Transient hemiballismus/hemichorea due to ipsilateral subthalamic nucleus infarction. *Neurology, 46,* 267–268.

Shannon, K. M. (1990). Hemiballismus. *Clinical Neuropharmacology, 13,* 413–425.

Kimberly M. Estep
University of Houston–Clear Lake

HEMIPARESIS

Hemiparesis is a condition involving a neurological deficit in which one side of the body has weakness or is partially paralyzed (Hynd & Obrzut, 1981). In hemiparesis, neurological compromise is limited to the hemisphere contralateral to the weakened or partially paralyzed side of the body. The etiology of hemiparesis has been linked to unilateral strokes, transient ischemic attacks, migraines, head injuries, diabetes mellitus, tumors, infections, demyelinating conditions, and hereditary diseases (Family Practice Notebook, 2001; Lezak, 1995). The incomplete paralysis or weakness may present as limb rigidity, spasticity, or both. Weakness and spasticity are usually the main causes of limb deformities associated with hemiparesis. This condition may involve ataxia and gait disorders.

Characteristics

1. Weakness or paralysis on one side of the body.
2. Movement or gait disorders.
3. Poorly coordinated motor skills.
4. Limb deformity.
5. Rigidity or spasticity on the involved side of the body.
6. Excess hip and knee flexion during movement.
7. Decreased weight-bearing capabilities.
8. "Drop-foot" involving limited ankle control.
9. Asymmetrical standing postures and abnormal center of gravity.
10. Decreased walking speed.
11. Becomes fatigued easily.
12. Eyes may track toward the involved hemisphere.

Cognitive deficits in individuals with hemiparesis vary depending on which hemisphere has been compromised. For individuals with left hemiparesis, the right hemisphere is implicated, and for individuals with right hemiparesis, the left hemisphere is involved. The presence of left hemiciated with the right hemisphere (e.g., sensory testing, spatial orientation, and visuospatial construction). Right hemiparesis may involve deficits in functions usually associated with the left hemisphere (e.g., speech, object naming, writing, reading, comprehension, and tactile perception).

The degree of physical and cognitive development varies greatly in children with hemiparesis. Due to the nature of this disability, it is imperative that a transdisciplinary approach to educational and treatment programming be utilized to enhance learning and maximize independent functioning. Most children with hemiparesis would benefit from special services including occupational therapy, physical therapy, speech and language therapy, adapted physical education, and special education. Intervention goals should be designed to assist children with hemiparesis to increase their ability to perform purposeful activities and follow daily routines.

Spasticity in hemiparesis ranges from mild to moderate, which can negatively influence motor control and motor planning. In locomotor movements such as running, a child with hemiparesis may ambulate with a limp and effectively pump with only the noninvolved arm. In hemiparesis, the spastic arm is typically bent and pronated while the spastic leg is noticeably smaller than the normal one. Individuals with hemiparesis generally make two types of movement—either small steps with the paretic limb or larger steps with the nonparetic limb (Jiang, McIlroy, Black, & Maki, 1998). These two motions produce asymmetrical movements that reduce functional stability. Adaptive equipment designed to improve locomotion ability in children with hemiparesis could include therapy balls to reduce spasticity and help with relaxation; rocking on a vestibular board to reduce spasticity and to develop better equilibrium reactions; wearing a shoe lift on the nonparetic limb; and scooter boards, dumbbell kickers, and adaptive tricycles to encourage the use of both hands and both legs (Aruin, Hanke, Chaudhuri, Harvey, & Rao, 2000; Sherrill, 1993).

Coordination skills and motor planning may also be problematic for children with hemiparesis and render them unable to adapt to new settings or to generalize tasks. Due to motor planning deficits, a child with hemiparesis may have difficulty executing coordinated movement patterns or sequences. Activities that may help strengthen a child's motor planning and coordination skills are beanbag activities, obstacle courses, locomotor movements using a ladder on the floor, and motor skills kits to create specific sequential patterns for motor planning skill development (Sherrill, 1993). Due to the risk of falling, when developing educational and treatment programs for children with this disorder, caution should be taken to reduce their chance of sustaining physical injury.

Children with hemiparesis often have balance problems, which can affect many areas of the child's performance not only motorically but also academically. The integration of the intersensory skills important to balance is also vital to reading and writing skills (Bailey & Wolery, 1989). In addition to balance problems, hemiparesis may result in visual perception problems. Activities to remediate visual perceptual problems include beeper or jingle balls, auditory guessing games, locomotor movements using a drumbeat, games in which the child must track using his or her eyes to follow a moving object, and exploring different ways to move body parts in a stationary position.

In addition to gross motor delays, children with hemiparesis may experience delays in the development of fine motor skills. The degree of abnormal muscle tone correlates with difficulties in the performance of fine motor tasks. Vision, head, and trunk control, upper extremity function, posture, and volitional movements all need to be carefully assessed to determine their impact on a child's fine motor development (Sherrill, 1993). Treatment programs designed to improve a child's fine motor skills must be conducted in conjunction with activities to improve muscle tone and overall movement patterns.

In the case of hemiparesis, speech and language services may be warranted, depending on which hemisphere of the brain has been damaged and the extent of the impairment. If speech services are provided, it is critical to teach functional communication skills across a variety of settings. Additionally, alternative and augmentative communication modes may need to be taught when a child has highly unintelligible speech or is nonverbal (McCormick & Schiefelbusch, 1984).

The special education teacher's role will depend on the level of cognitive involvement of the child with hemiparesis. As the severity of the cognitive disability increases, the special education teacher's involvement will typically increase. In a transdisciplinary approach, the special education teacher is usually responsible for the coordination and implementation of all services so that an optimal learning environment is provided for the child to learn new skills and to generalize these skills across different environments. In addition to being responsible for assessing and teaching cognitive skills, the special educator may also be responsible for the assessment and daily implementation of sensorimotor, play, social, communication, motor, and self-help skills. Facilitating parent-child interactions and integration issues and strategies may also be a responsibility of the special education teacher.

REFERENCES

Aruin, A. S., Hanke, T., Chaudhuri, G., Harvey, R., & Rao, N. (2000). Compelling weightbearing in persons with hemiparesis following stroke: The effect of a lift insert and goal-directed balance exercise. *Journal of Rehabilitation Research and Development, 37*(1).

Bailey, D. B., Jr., & Wolery, M. (1989). *Assessing infants and preschoolers with handicaps.* New York: Macmillan.

Family Practice Notebook.com. (2001). Hemiplegia: Hemiparesis. Retrieved from http://www.fpnotebook.com/NEU60.htm

Hynd, G. W., & Obrzut, J. E. (1981). *Neuropsychological assessment and the school-age child: Issues and procedures.* Boston: Allyn and Bacon.

Jiang, N., McIlroy, W. E., Black, S. E., & Maki, B. E. (1998, August). *Control of compensatory limb movement in chronic hemiparesis.* Paper presented at the North American Congress on Biomechanics, Waterloo, Ontario, Canada.

Lezak, M. D. (1995). *Neuropsychological assessment* (3rd ed.). New York: Oxford University Press.

McCormick, L., & Schiefelbusch, R. L. (1984). *Early language intervention.* Columbus: Charles E. Merrill.

Sherrill, C. (1993). *Adapted physical activity, recreation and sport: Crossdisciplinary and lifespan.* Dubuque, IA: WCB Brown & Benchmark.

Shawn Powell
United States Air Force Academy

Barbara Corriveau
Sharine Webber
Laramie County School District #1
Cheyenne, Wyoming

HEMIPLEGIA

Hemiplegia, or paralysis of one side of the body, usually is the result of a cerebral vascular insult or injury (Reed, 2001). This condition generally involves rupture or closure of cerebral blood flow in part of the brain (O'Sullivan, 2001). Because some parts of the nerve cells of the brain have been damaged and cannot function, the part of the body controlled by the damaged portion of the brain cannot function (Dzurenko, 1999). For example, when the left side of the brain is involved, the child's right extremities are affected; the results of this may include paralysis, sensory loss, and aphasia that may be temporary or permanent (Young, 2000). In most cases, there will be permanent neurological deficits ranging from slight neurological problems to complete loss of function in motor, sensory, or language ability (Young, 2000). Crossed hemiplegia is characterized by of muscular weakness on one side of the body. This condition is extremely rare and generally begins before the child is 18 months old (Misulis, 2000). Monoplegia refers to weakness in one limb on one side of the body (Rowland, 2000).

Pediatric strokes are the most common cause of hemiplegia in children (Gold & Cargan, 2000). The estimated annual incidence of stroke in children under the age of 14 is 2.52 per 100,000 (Gold & Cargan, 2000). Causes of strokes in children have been linked to inherited clotting disorders, congenital heart disease, and sickle cell disease (Gold & Cargan, 2000). Other causes of strokes that may lead to hemiplegia include shaking an infant, sports, and substance abuse by the mother or by a child. Hemiplegia may be caused, in some rare cases, by spinal cord damage or tumors on the spinal cord (Misulis, 2000).

In infants and children, stroke symptoms include seizures, coma, and paralysis of one side of the body (Young, 2000). Additional symptoms may involve the loss of previously acquired speech and seizures (Young, 2000). Hemiplegia is usually diagnosed by a physician using a magnetic resonance imaging (MRI) test (Young, 2000).

Characteristics

1. Paralysis of one side of the body
2. Seizures
3. Coma
4. Delay or loss of speech

Course and outcome of children with hemiplegia are variable and are dependent upon a number of factors. In the case of newborns, most continue to have seizures, motor difficulty, and some cognitive impairment (Young, 2000). In most cases, children will have persistent limb weakness. Children may experience delays in language, processing, memory, attention, and cognition, depending on the side of the brain that is involved (Reed, 2001). For example, if the left hemisphere of the brain was involved, the child may experience difficulty in language and auditory processing as well as motoric impairments. Although the child may always demonstrate residual effects, positive outcomes have been linked to return of adequate blood flow to the brain (Young, 2000).

Special education services will likely be needed to assist the child with hemiplegia. Due to the varying levels of impairment that different children experience, individualized education plans need to be tailored to the child's unique needs. The child may require assistance with many different areas, including learning, academics, self-care, motoric ability, cognitive issues, and psychosocial problems (Reed, 2001). Special education services need to focus on the building of remedial strategies, the teaching of new or lost skills, and compensatory education, the teaching of different skills to accommodate for the skills lost (D'Amato, Rothlisberg, & Work, 1999). The child may benefit from compensatory and remedial strategies in the following areas: physical therapy, occupational therapy, learning interventions, and social skills training. Physical therapy may focus on the reduction of muscle atrophy and an increase in flexion and extension. Occupational therapy could focus on grasping objects and the functional use of both the affected side of the body and compensatory strategies using the unaffected side of the body. Learning interventions may include compensatory and remedial strategies in any affected areas of academics. Social skills training may need to focus on the teaching of prosocial behaviors, increasing self-confidence, and peer relationship development (Reed, 2001). Research needs to progress in the area of intervention studies for children with hemiplegia.

REFERENCES

D'Amato, R. C., Rothlisberg, B. A., & Work, P. H. (1999). Neuropsychological assessment for intervention. In C. R. Reynolds & T. B. Gutkin (Eds.), *The handbook of school psychology.* New York: Wiley.

Dzurenko, J. (1999). Rehabilitation nursing: Educating patients toward independence. In M. G. Eisenberg, R. L. Glueckauf, & H. H. Zaretsky (Eds.), *Medical aspects of disability: A handbook for the rehabilitation professional.* New York: Springer.

Gold, A. P., & Cargan, A. L. (2000). Stroke in children. In L. P. Rowland (Ed.), *Merritt's neurology.* Philadelphia: Lippincott, Williams, & Wilkins.

Misulis, K. E. (2000). Hemiplegia and monoplegia. In W. G. Bradley, R. B. Daroff, G. M. Fenichel, & C. D. Marsden (Eds.), *Neurology in clinical practice: Practice and principles of diagnosis and management.* Woburn, MA: Butterworth-Heinemann.

O'Sullivan, S. B. (2001). Stroke. In S. B. O'Sullivan & T. J. Schmitz (Eds.), *Physical rehabilitation: Assessment and treatment.* Philadelphia: F. A. Davis.

Reed, K. L. (2001). *Quick reference to occupational therapy.* Gaithersburg, MD: Aspen.

Rowland, L. R. (1995). Head injury. In L. P. Rowland (Ed.), *Merritt's textbook of neurology.* Media, PA: William & Wilkins.

Young, R. K. (2000). Stroke in childhood. In W. G. Bradley, R. B. Daroff, G. M. Fenichel, & C. D. Marsden (Eds.), *Neurology in clinical practice: The neurological disorders.* Woburn, MA: Butterworth-Heinemann.

Nicole R. Warnygora
University of Northern Colorado

See also Alternating Hemiplegia Of Childhood

HEMISPHERECTOMY

Hemispherectomy is a surgical procedure involving the removal of "a cerebral hemisphere, including the frontal, temporal, parietal, and occipital lobes while leaving intact parts of the thalamus and basal ganglia" (Menard, Le Normand, Rigoard, & Cohen, 2000, p. 333). A hemispherectomy may be performed as a treatment for severe seizure disorders, fatal tumors, hemiplegia, and Rasmussen encephalitis. The procedure is usually reserved as a life-saving measure or may be employed to improve the life of a child with intractable seizures resulting from unilateral brain dysfunction (de Bolle & Curtiss, 200; Estes, 2000).

Characteristics

Note: These symptoms usually result in a hemispherectomy, and some may exist following this surgical procedure.

1. Intractable epileptic seizures of an ongoing severe nature
2. Hemiplegia or hemiparesis
3. Progressive declines in cognitive functioning
4. Visual neglect contralateral to the damaged hemisphere
5. Impaired expressive and receptive language functioning
6. Delayed social communication skills
7. Delayed academic achievement
8. Increased occurrence of mental illness, specifically those involving thought disorders

In cases involving a hemispherectomy, cerebral damage from atrophy, sustained seizures, disease processes, tumors, or traumatic insults may be present. The result of such damage usually involves a reduction in cognitive functioning. This reduction in cognition may be widespread or specific, depending on the etiology, course, duration, and age of occurrence when the cerebral damage initially started (Caplan, Curtiss, Chugani, & Vinters, 1996). Additionally, seizure activity may be generalized (i.e., bilateral), or focal (i.e., unilateral). In the case of bilateral seizures, the remaining hemisphere may be damaged, which prompts questions regarding its structural integrity (Boatman et al., 1999).

Depending on the age of disease onset or injury and the age when the hemispherectomy is performed, there is evidence that the remaining cerebral hemisphere may mediate functions normally associated with the removed hemisphere (Caplan et al., 1996; de Bolle & Curtiss, 2000). Thus, the right hemisphere in children with a left hemispherectomy may mediate language functions, and the left hemisphere in children with a right hemispherectomy may mediate visual-spatial functions. The age of injury and age of the hemispherectomy procedure may be more important determinants of future cognitive functions than the severity of the injury or disease process (Bradshaw & Mattingley, 1995). It has been suggested that insults that occur during at a critical period of maturation result in less opportunity for the full development of specific abilities. For example, when an insult occurs during a critical period of language development, it reduces the likelihood that a child would acquire full language skills (Menard et al., 2000).

Following a hemispherectomy, a full complement of special education services may be essential to ensure that the child has the best possible opportunity to make educational gains. These services may include speech language therapy, mobility support, occupational therapy, physical therapy, school nursing services, academic support, counseling, and case management. In addition to school-based services, frequent communication with medical care providers is necessary in order to provide the best possible educational services and to better understand the child's recovery. Seizure precautions and protocols should be established and followed because seizure disorders may persist following the hemispherectomy. General guidelines to reduce seizure activity include taking antiseizure medication as prescribed, eating three meals daily, drinking fluids, reducing or eliminating caffeine, following regular sleeping patterns, allowing rest periods, and using stress management techniques (Estes, 2000).

Parental contact should occur on a regular basis with the frequency of these contacts determined by the child's needs. Depending on the age of the child, a daily notebook between home and school may be beneficial in increasing communication. Transitional services and vocational planning with available community resources for children who have had a hemispherectomy will likely increase their ability to adapt and function as independently as possible as they mature.

REFERENCES

Boatman, D., Freeman, J., Vining, E., Pulsifer, M., Miglioretti, D, Minahan, R., et al. (1999). Language recovery after left hemispherectomy in children with late-onset seizures. *Annals of Neurology, 46*(4).

Bradshaw, J. L., & Mattingley, J. B. (1995). *Clinical neuropsychology: Behavioral and brain science.* San Diego, CA: Academic Press.

Caplan, R., Curtiss, S., Chugani, H. T., & Vinters, H. V. (1996). Pediatric Rasmussen encephalitis: Social communication, language, PET, and pathology before and after hemispherectomy. *Brain and Cognition, 32,* 45–66.

de Bolle, S., & Curtiss, S. (2000). Language after hemispherectomy. *Brain and Cognition, 43,* 135–205.

Estes, R. (2000). A closer look: Seizures. *Premier Outlook, 1*(2).

Menard, A., Le Normand, M. T., Rigoard, M. T., & Cohen, H. (2000). Language development in a child with left hemispherectomy. *Brain and Cognition, 43,* 332–340.

Shawn Powell
United States Air Force Academy

HEMOLYTIC UREMIC SYNDROME

Hemolytic urenmic syndrome (HUS) is a systemic disease marked by renal failure, hemolytic anemia, thrombocytopenia (platelet deficiency), coagulation defects, and variable neurological signs (MEDLINEPlus, 2002). This disorder is most common in children. It frequently occurs after a gastrointestinal (enteric) infection, often one caused by a strain of specific E. coli bacteria (*Escherichia coli* 0157:H7). It has also been associated with other enteric infections, including shigella and salmonella, and with some nonenteric infections (MEDLINEPlus, 2002; Rothenberg & Chapman, 1994).

HUS often begins with vomiting and diarrhea (which may be bloody). Within a week the patient develops weakness and irritability. Urine output decreases dramatically and may almost cease. Because red blood cells are being destroyed (a process called hemolysis), the patient rapidly becomes anemic and pale (MEDLINEPlus, 2002).

The incidence of HUS is 1–3 per 100,000, with the highest incidence occurring in the summer and fall. The age of onset is most common under the age of 4 years. HUS is the most common cause of acute renal failure in children (Pedlynx, 2002).

There are two forms of HUS: the typical form (idiopathic) and the atypical or sporadic form. The typical form usually affects children 3 months to 6 years of age (80% < 3 years) and is caused by an E. coli serotype 0157:H7 that can produce specific enterocytotoxins. The risk factors for E. coli acquisition are undercooked ground beef and contact with a person with diarrhea within 2 weeks prior to disease onset. One in 10 children who have E. coli 0157:H7 will go on to develop HUS (Pedlynx, 2002).

The atypical or sporadic form may be associated with an inherited autosomal recessive or dominant form and with scleroderma, radiation of kidneys, and essential or malignant hypertension. There is also a pregnancy or oral contraceptive association related to preeclampsia or postpartum renal failure (Pedlynx, 2002).

Characteristics

1. Gastroenteritis
   - Usually precedes illness by 5–10 days
   - Diarrhea, bloody stool, severe colitis
   - Fever, nausea, and vomiting
   - Rectal prolapse
2. Renal manifestations
   - Microscopic or gross hematuria
   - Proteinuria that can progress to the nephrotic level
   - Complications such as nephritic syndrome (edema, hypertension, azotemia, oliguria), nephrotic syndrome (edema, hypoalbuminemia, hyperlipidemia), and renal failure that can range from mild renal insufficiency to acute renal failure (ARF)
3. Hematological manifestations
   - Anemia
   - Sudden onset of pallor, irritability, lethargy, weakness
   - Hepatomegaly-hepatosplenomegaly
   - Thrombocytopenia (90%)
4. Complications
   - Irritability, seizures, coma
   - Colitis with melena and perforation
   - Acidosis, congestive heart failure, diabetes mellitus, fluid overload, hyperkalemia, rhabdomyolysis

Treatment usually includes transfusions of packed red cells, and platelets are given as needed. Kidney dialysis may be indicated. Medications prescribed include corticosteroids and aspirin. Plasmapheresis, also called plasma exchange (or passage of the plasma through a Protein A filter) may be performed, although its role is much less well documented than in TTP (thrombotic thrombocytopenic purpura). The blood plasma (the portion that does not contain cells, but does contain antibodies) is removed and replaced with fresh (donated) or filtered plasma to remove antibodies from the circulation (MEDLINEPlus, 2002). In addition, medical management of the complications such as nephritic syndrome, nephrotic syndrome, and chronic renal failure may include dialysis, kidney transplant, or both (Pedlynx, 2002).

Special education may or may not be needed for children with HUS. The course and outcome of the disease are highly variable, and individual educational needs will vary as well. Chronic renal problems and medications may well create the need for typical chronic illness counseling and supportive assistance.

Ninety percent of patients survive the acute phase with no renal impairment if aggressive management of acute renal failure (ARF) is instituted. A positive prognosis is associated with the age of the child, typical form, and summer months for diagnosis. A poor prognosis is associated with shock, significant renal involvement, neurological signs and symptoms, and atypical form. The prognosis for children with HUS includes a mortality rate of 7–10% and renal dysfunction of 20% (Pedlynx, 2002).

The known cause of HUS, E. coli in hamburger and ground meats, can be prevented by adequate cooking. Other unrecognized causes may not be preventable at this time.

REFERENCES

MEDLINEPlus Medine Online Encyclopedia. HUS. Retrieved from http://www.nlm.nih.gov/medlineplus/ency/article/000510.htm

Pedlynx Pedbase. Retrieved April 2002, from http://www.icondata.com/health/pedbase/files/HEMOLYTI.HTM

Rothenberg, M. A., & Chapman, C. F. (1994). *Dictionary of medical terms.* New York: Barron's.

Elaine Fletcher-Janzen
University of Northern Colorado

HEMOPHILIA A, "CLASSIC" HEMOPHILIA

Factor VIII deficiency is one of the most common forms of severe hereditary bleeding disorders. Hemophilia has been known since antiquity, as is evidenced by Talmudic scripts advising against ritual circumcision of male infants whose siblings died from bleeding caused by the procedure.

Hemophilia occurs in about 1 in 5,000 males. Eight-five percent of these individuals have Factor VIII deficiency. The remainder have Factor IX deficiency (hemophilia B). Both disorders are transmitted in an X-linked recessive manner, with females acting as carriers of the abnormal gene. This carrier state may also cause mild clotting abnormalities.

Multiple mutations of the Factor VIII gene are associated with several clinical classifications of hemophilia. Unimpaired clotting activity requires Factor VIII levels that are 35–40% of normal. Severe hemophilia is characterized by less than 1% of normal Factor VIII levels. Moderate cases range from 1–5%. Mild hemophilia is over 5%. About 5–10% of patients with hemophilia A produce abnormal, nonfunctioning Factor VIII. Forty-five to 50% of those with severe disease have an identical genetic mutation and generate no detectable Factor VIII at all.

Characteristics

1. Bleeding symptoms in the newborn are uncommon. Intracranial hemorrhage is occasionally seen. Only about 30% of affected males have excessive bleeding with circumcision.
2. Easy bruising, bleeding into muscle (intramuscular hematoma), and bleeding into joints (hemarthrosis) usually do not begin until the child starts to crawl and walk. However, 10% of hemophiliacs have no symptoms during their 1st year.
3. Hemarthrosis is the defining characteristic of this disease. It may be spontaneous or posttraumatic. The ankle is the most commonly affected joint in toddlers. Hemarthroses of the elbow and knee occur more frequently in older children and adolescents. Repeated bleeds into a joint cause scarring, severe pain, erosion of cartilage at the ends of bones forming the joint and—eventually—complete fusion.
4. Life-threatening hemorrhages are the result of bleeding into the brain, upper airway, or other vital organ. Exsanguination can occur with gastrointestinal bleeds, external blood loss, or massive intramuscular hematomas.
5. Mildly affected patients may not experience spontaneous bleeding. Their most common presenting symptoms is prolonged bleeding following dental work, surgery, or moderate trauma.

Successfully treating hemophilia requires several considerations. Prevention of trauma is important, but many bleeding events are spontaneous. Early family counseling will help parents strike a suitable compromise between overprotecting their child and permitting him reasonable freedom. Hemophiliacs should avoid aspirin and nonsteroidal anti-inflammatory drugs (e.g., ibuprofen), because such drugs may aggravate bleeding tendencies. Patients should complete the hepatitis B immunization series during infancy, and they should be screened periodically for hepatitis and abnormal liver function.

Specific therapy with Factor VIII given intravenously is needed to end bleeding events. Serious or life-threatening bleeds require Factor VIII levels to be 100% of normal. Individuals with mild hemophilia may respond to the drug DDAVP, which causes release of Factor VIII from storage sites in this particular subset of patients.

Previously, Factor VIII infusions were given only when active bleeding was evident or suspected. Prior to the introduction of purification techniques employed for about the past 15 years, repeated Factor VIII administration was associated with a high risk for infection with transmittable viral disease (hepatitis A, B, and C and HIV). The only product available until recently was derived from pooled human plasma and was therefore not totally safe. However, a recombinant factor VIII produced from genetically altered bacteria is now being marketed. Considerable interest exists for the prophylactic use of this material because it is free from any known viral contaminants. Prophylactic Factor VIII therapy prevents hemrathroses and greatly reduces the incidence of crippling joint pathology in hemophiliacs.

Education of educators and other school personnel is a integral part of keeping the child safe in the school environment. Helping them to provide play and leisure activities that will not result in compromising the health of the child with Factor VIII deficiency will be important. By providing preventive education, the school counselors can work with the other students to understand the need for safety, help the student with Factor VIII adjust to the modifications, and in turn facilitate peer relationships and self-esteem issues. Should the child with Factor VII experience bleeding in his brain, it will be important to have a comprehensive neuropsychological evaluation completed. Depending on those results, the educators will be able to develop an educational program that focuses on the child's strengths and provides ways to remediate his cognitive weaknesses.

The prognosis for newly diagnosed children with hemophilia A is generally favorable. A referral to large hemophilia comprehensive care centers is imperative for the most satisfactory outcomes. Staffed by professionals in several disciplines, these facilities employ a modern approach to factor replacement therapy (prophylactic treatment), recognize and aggressively treat initial signs of joint debilitation, and manage the complications of prolonged Factor VIII administration (hepatitis and HIV). The most realistic "cure" for this disorder is gene replacement therapy, which should become available during the lifetimes of today's patients.

For more information and parent support, please contact National Hemophilia Foundation, 116 West 32nd Street, 11th Floor, New York, NY 10001, (212) 328-3700, (800) 424-2634, e-mail: handi@hemophilia.org, home page: http://www.hemophilia.org

Word Federation of Hemophilia, 1425 Rene Levesque Boulevard West, Suite 1010, Montreal, Quebec, H3G-1T7, Canada, (514) 87-5-7944, e-mail: wfh@wfh.org, home page: http://www.wth.orgn

REFERENCES

Montgomery, R. R. (2000). Hemorrhagic and thrombotic disease. In R. E. Behrman, R. M. Kleigman, & H. B. Jenson (Eds.), *Nelson's textbook of pediatrics* (16th ed., pp. 1504–1525). Philadelphia: W. B. Saunders.

National Organization for Rare Disorders. Factor XIII deficiency. (1999). Retrieved from the http://www.stepstn.com/cgi-win/nord.exe?proc=GetDocument&rectype=0&recnum=66

Barry H. Davison
Ennis, Texas

Joan W. Mayfield
Baylor Pediatric Specialty Services
Dallas, Texas

HEMOPHILIA B

Hemophilia is a sex-linked inherited disorder in which the individual lacks the necessary blood-clotting factors to stop bleeding (Harcourt Health Sciences, 2002). The condition is transmitted via the X chromosome, but it is believed that some individuals are affected by hemophilia due to mutation of the genes on that chromosome. There are two forms of hemophilia: Type A (with the blood-clotting Factor VIII missing) and Type B (with the blood-clotting Factor IV missing; Hemophilia, 2000). Hemophilia A and B are further defined by their severity and range from mild to severe.

The condition exists in all races and ethnicities. The prevalence rate for Hemophilia A is 1 in 10,000 men and for Hemophilia B it is 1 in 40,000 men (Cutler, 2001). Fifty percent of all sons of a female carrier will be affected and 50% of the daughters will be carriers. All daughters of affected men will be carriers, but the disease affects women very rarely (Greene, 2001a). Approximately 17,000 people with hemophilia are currently living in the United States (Mayo Clinic, 2001).

Characteristics

1. The symptoms vary with the degree of the deficiency of the blood-clotting factors.
2. Often diagnosed when infants begin crawling; their injuries cause internal bleeding as in their joints and muscles, which are then visible by bruises, and their injuries bleed profusely.
3. Symptoms associated with the disorder are nosebleeds; bruising; spontaneous bleeding; bleeding into joints and associated pain and swelling; gastrointestinal tract and urinary tract hemorrhage; blood in urine or stool; prolonged bleeding from cuts, tooth extraction, and surgery; and excessive bleeding following circumcision (Greene, 2001a).

Individuals with hemophilia must be under medical care to assist with the replacement of the blood-clotting factors that are administered intravenously. The reduction or prevention of bleeding is essential during treatment because such bleeding can be life-threatening. For example, immunizations should be administered subcutaneously cutan versus intramuscularly to prevent hemorrhages. The importance of dental hygiene must be explained to the individual to prevent tooth decay and possible gum infections. Aspirin and some medications used for arthritis must be avoided because they act as blood thinners. Education of the patient regarding his or her environment and how to interact with it to avoid injury is essential for his or her well being.

Swimming and walking should be preferred over contact or high-impact sports such as boxing or football (Greene, 2001b). MedicAlert tags must be worn by the child, and emergency procedures and emergency numbers must be known by all pertinent individuals in the child's environment (Hemophilia.org, 2001b). Serious consideration must be given to any bleeding in the mouth, throat, or neck, because the patient could suffocate as a result of the bleeding. Bleeding in the joints is also a concern and—if untreated—could lead to a loss in mobility (Canadian Hemophilia Society, 2001).

To help the individual cope with the impact of the bleeding disorder, the child is best served if home, school, and medical caregivers form a strong alliance. Joining support groups with other afflicted individuals can help alleviate the stress as well. Genetic counseling for family members and afflicted individuals is also recommended (Cutler, 2001). Depending on the severity of the condition, hospitalizations and longer periods might prevent the child to participate in school on a regular basis (Hemophilia.org,

2001c). Tutoring at home and possibly at school is recommended to help the child compensate for lost school time. As precautionary measures to prevent injuries, some activities might have to be limited or avoided completely. Protective gear such as helmets and padding for elbows and knees should be available. This gear is especially important for smaller children so that the danger from hard toys and sharp edges can be minimized. To prevent the possible trauma to the child of a child abuse investigation, teachers, and care-providers must be educated about the symptoms of hemophilia. These symptoms include visible and recurring bruises and can easily be mistaken for damage resulting from child abuse (Hemophilia.org, 2001).

Due to the advances of modern medicine, individuals with hemophilia can lead happy and successful lives. Without medical attention, this condition is life threatening. There is no cure for hemophilia at this time.

REFERENCES

Canadian Hemophilia Society. The treatment of hemophilia. (2001, December 12). Retrieved December 2001, from http://www.hemophilia.ca/en/2.1.7.html

Cutler, Troy S. (2001, June 7). Hemophilia. *eMedicine Journal, 2*(6). Retrieved December 27, 2001, from http://www.emedecine.com/emerg/topic224.html

Greene, Alan R. (2001a). Disease: Hemophilia A. Retrieved December 29, 2001, from http://sitemaker.medseek.com/websitefiles/drgreene/body.cfm

Greene, Alan R. (2001a). Disease: Hemophilia B. Retrieved December 29, 2001, from http://sitemaker.medseek.com/websitefiles/drgreene/body.cfm

Harcourt Health Sciences. (2002). Hemophilia A & B. In *Mosby's medical, nursing, & allied health dictionary* (6th ed., pp. 800–801). St. Louis, MO: Author.

Hemophilia. (2000). In *Human diseases & conditions* (Vol. 2, pp. 434–438). New York: C. Scribner & Sons.

Hemophilia.org. (2001a). Child abuse issues. Retrieved December 13, 2001, from http://208.254.25.93/bdi/bdi_newly9.htm

Hemophilia.org. (2001b). Information for teachers & childcare providers. Retrieved December 13, 2001, from http://208.254.25.93/bdi/bdi_providers.htm

Hemophilia.org. (2001c). Psychological issues. Retrieved December 13, 2001, from http://208.254.25.93/bdi/bdi_newly3.htm

Mayo Clinic. (2001, September 14). Hemophilia. Retrieved December 27, 2001, from http://www.mayoclinic.com/findinformation/conditioncenters/invoke.cfm

Monika Hannan
University of Northern Colorado

HEMOPHILIA C

Hemophilia is a bleeding disorder in which there is a deficiency of selected proteins in the body's blood-clotting system. "Clotting is the process by which your blood changes from a liquid to a solid state in order to stop bleeding" (Mayo Clinic, 2001). There are three main types of hemophilia in which a different clotting factor is missing or deficient. In the most common type, Hemophilia A, clotting Factor VIII is missing or deficient. In Hemophilia B, Factor IX is missing or deficient, and in Hemophilia C, Factor XI is missing or deficient. All three types can cause prolonged bleeding.

Hemophilia is an inherited sex-linked genetic defect in which a defective X chromosome is passed from a mother to her male child. Males cannot pass along the gene that causes hemophilia to their sons because the defect is located on the X chromosome, which is inherited from the mother. In extremely rare cases, a girl may be born with hemophilia, but only if a man with hemophilia has children with a female carrier whose defective X chromosome is passed to the female child. A 1998 study estimated that one of every 5,000 boys of all races born in the United States has some form of hemophilia. The National Hemophilia Foundation estimates that more than 16,000 males in America have hemophilia, whereas in females, the incidence is only 1 in 1 million (Willett, 2001).

Characteristics

1. Abnormal bruising and bleeding.
2. Spontaneous hemorrhages into various joints—knees elbows, ankles, and hips.
3. Possible limitation of movement and swelling.
4. Internal bleeding.
5. Patient may also suffer from chronic arthritis, anemia, gastritis, and epistaxis (severe and chronic nosebleeds).

There is no cure for hemophilia—it is a lifelong condition. Treatment involves injecting the blood clotting factor that is missing into the patient's blood. Clotting factors can be injected on a regular preventive basis in an attempt to keep bleeding from occurring. Prior to the mid-1980s, it was more common for people with hemophilia to become infected with the HIV virus or with hepatitis because of contaminated blood products. The risk of infection through blood products has decreased, however, because of genetically engineered clotting products called recombinant factors, which are free of infection (Mayo Clinic, 2001). With regular injections, even persons with severe cases of hemophilia can lead near-normal lives.

Students with hemophilia could qualify for special education services under the category of Other Health Impairment. The student would most likely require a health plan so that school personnel are adequately prepared in emergencies. It is important that anyone who takes care of the child knows about the condition. The role of the school psychologist is to provide support for the student and his or her family in the form of counseling. The school psychologist could also provide education to the staff and other students about hemophilia in order to reduce the amount of misinformation that others may have about the disease.

Future research for hemophilia appears to be in the area of genetic therapy. There is also research being conducted into understanding the makeup of the factor VIII protein that is used during treatment.

REFERENCES

Katz, A. (1970). *Hemophilia: A study in hope and reality.* Springfield, IL: Charles C. Thomas.

Mayo Clinic. (2001). Hemophilia. Retrieved November 2001, from http://www.mayoclinic.com/findinformation/diseasesandconditions

Willett, E. (2001). *Hemophilia.* Berkeley Heights, NJ: Enslow Publishers.

Christine D. Cde Baca
University of Northern Colorado

HENOCH-SCHÖNLEIN PURPURA

Henoch-Schönlein (HS) purpura, also called anaphylactoid purpura, is a form of hypersensitivity vasculitis. This form of vasculitis is distinguished by erthematouricarial and purpuric rash most prominent in the lower legs and buttocks. The patient may also exhibit signs of arthralgia (pain in one or more joints), gastrointestinal difficulties, and glomerulonephritis (difficulties related to inflammation of the capillaries in or around the kidneys).

The etiology of HS purpura is unknown, although research suggests either an immune system dysfunction or allergic reaction to certain foods, drugs, bacteria, or insect bites (National Organization for Rare Disorders, Inc. [NORD], 1997). The disorder is more common in children than adults, with an incidence estimated to be as high as 18 cases per 100,000 within the pediatric age group (Henoch-Schonlein Purpura, 1996). Girls and boys appear to be equally affected. Age of onset is variable, although initial symptoms typically begin after age 2 and peak between 4 and 7 years of age. Some literature indicates that HS purpura may be a seasonal disorder because there appears to be a higher incidence in the winter months. A respiratory tract infection has preceded the onset of symptoms in approximately 50% of the cases (Szer, 1996).

Characteristics

1. Child may report sudden onset of headaches.
2. Child may have a marked loss of appetite.
3. Child may have a fever.
4. Red or purple spots (petechiae) may appear on the skin, usually in the area of the legs and buttocks.
5. Child may complain of severe cramping and abdominal pain that becomes worse at night.
6. Child may complain of joint pain, especially in the knees and ankles.
7. Other symptoms may include vomiting and diarrhea or severe constipation and dark stools.
8. Difficulty in kidney function has occurred in 23–49% of the reported cases.

The difficulty in treatment is that individual symptoms often mimic other disease processes. Therefore, symptoms are treated individually. If the HS purpura is thought to be the result of an allergic reaction, the offending substance must be avoided. If symptoms include abdominal and joint pain, glucocorticoid (steroid) drugs may be prescribed. The use of steroids in treatment is controversial, however. Although some research indicates that early steroid treatment may reduce the risk of kidney damage, other studies have shown that the steroids neither shorten the length of the illness nor reduce the frequency or recurrence of the symptoms (Causey, Woodall, Wahl, Voelker, & Pollack, 1993; Szer, 1996).

In most cases, this disorder is self-limiting with no long-term complications. The disorder may resolve and recur several times during its course, usually ending in spontaneous resolution. Only in rare cases has the disorder progressed to the point of becoming a chronic disease. Because this disorder usually does not have long-lasting or chronic results, it is unlikely that the child will be eligible for special education services.

Current research is in the area of drug therapy. As stated earlier, the effectiveness of drug therapy remains controversial and requires further research. A procedure for removing unwanted toxins from the blood (plasmapheresis) has also been recommended for severe cases of HS purpura, but this procedure also requires much more investigation and research (NORD, 1997).

REFERENCES

Causey, A., Woodall, B., Wahl, N., Voelker, C. & Pollack, E. (1993). Henoch-Schonlein purpura: Four cases and a review. *Journal of Emergency Medicine, 12*(3), 331–341.

Henoch-Schonlein Purpura. (1996). In *Cecil textbook of medicine* (20th ed., p. 576). Philadelphia, PA: W. B. Saunders.

National Organization for Rare Disorders, Inc. (1997). Purpura,

Henoch Schonlein. Retrieved July 2001, from http://rarediseases.org

Szer, I. (1996). Henoch-Schonlein purpura: When and how to treat. *Journal of Rheumatology, 23,* 1661–1665.

Christine D. Cde Baca
University of Northern Colorado

HEPATITIS

Hepatitis is an inflammation of the liver caused by different viruses, alcoholism, abuse of or side effects of medications, exposure to toxins, or an individual's lowered immune system. Hepatitis viruses are categorized and named according to various attributes, such as hepatitis A, B, C, D, E, F, and G, the first three accounting for the majority of cases and the later four being much less common. This entry focuses on the symptoms and conditions caused by hepatitis viruses A, B, and C.

Each year, 200,000 Americans and 1.4 million people worldwide become infected with hepatitis (Hepatitis Information Network [HIN], 2000a). Hepatitis A is transmitted via oral contact with fecal material. People in high-risk areas include military personnel stationed overseas, day-care employees, or individuals working in other less-than-sterile environments such as are found in some institutions and in the waste management industry. Outbreaks have been associated with raw shellfish or fruit that was contaminated with fecal bacteria through the use of unclean water or by infected food handlers (Buggs, 2001). Infections further occur after floods and earthquakes when populations may lack appropriate hygienic conditions.

Hepatitis B is estimated to affect between 1 million to 1.5 million Americans and 400 million people worldwide (HIN, 2000b). Hepatitis C is estimated to affect 4 million Americans and 170 million people worldwide. Hepatitis B and C are transmitted through the blood of the carriers. Individuals who are at a higher risk to be infected with hepatitis B and C than the general population are intravenous-drug users, health-care workers (e.g., nurses, physicians, and dentists), and prisoners ("Hepatitis," 2000). Furthermore, individuals who have sex with many partners, who have organ transplants, or who have contact with shared objects (needles or straws in the drug community), unclean instruments in tattoo and body piercing parlors, unclean hairbrushes and scissors in beauty parlors, shared razors and toothbrushes, or anything that can contain infected blood particles are at risk to contract Hepatitis B and C (Buggs, 2001; 2000). These viruses can also be transmitted from infected mothers to their infants during labor—a reason why cesarean-section births are recommended to prevent the spread of the disease if the mother is known to be infected.

Characteristics

1. Chronic hepatitis: loss of appetite, malaise, low-grade fever.
2. Acute hepatitis: nausea, vomiting, low-grade fever, loss of appetite, rash, tiredness and fatigue, jaundice, darkening of urine, abdominal pain, arthritis.
3. Symptoms for hepatitis A can take between 2 and 7 weeks to develop. These can be mild, last for a limited time, and disappear eventually on their own. In many cases (up to 70%), affected individuals do not notice any symptoms.
4. Symptoms for hepatitis B may not be noticed until 4 to 6 weeks after the infection in both children and adults. Ninety percent of children who become infected with hepatitis B in their first year of life, and 30–50% of children from 1 to 4 years of life, become chronically infected. Although this condition may go unnoticed for up to 40 years, the individual could ultimately suffer cirrhosis, which could lead to liver failure and liver cancer.
5. Symptoms for hepatitis C are similar to those for hepatitis B but may not appear until 5 to 12 weeks after the infection, and up to 80% of all infected individuals may never develop any symptoms. However, 50–60% of affected individuals may develop a chronic (lasts longer than 6 months) active infection and cirrhosis.

Home care under the supervision of a physician is the treatment of choice for hepatitis A if no severe complications such as dehydration arise. The care should include plenty of rest and a diet that consists of easy-to-digest foods, ample water, and the avoidance of alcohol. The use of over-the-counter medication should be discussed with the physician, as some medications, such as acetaminophen, can be harmful to the liver. Exercise and overexertion of the body should be avoided until the individual's health is regained (Buggs, 2001).

Treatment for hepatitis B is similar to the treatment for hepatitis A. The individual should be placed under the care of a physician as soon as possible to ensure the best possible care according to the latest medical developments. Home care is also recommended, with plenty of rest and fluids to prevent dehydration. Hospitalization may become necessary if symptoms worsen, such as when the patient becomes confused, delirious, or hard to awaken (Buggs, 2001).

The same home-care procedures apply for individuals infected with hepatitis C as discussed earlier for those with hepatitis B. Hospitalization is recommended if the symptoms worsen, such as when the patient vomits foods and fluids, his or her skin turns yellow, the patient experiences increased pain or fever, or the patient becomes disoriented and difficult to awaken. Consultation with a hepatologist is recommended to ensure that the correct medical treatment is chosen to combat the symptoms of hepatitis C because medication and treatment are constantly being researched and improved upon (Buggs, 2001). Interferon is a new medication available for the treatment of hepatitis C. This medication may be recommended by the physician for certain individuals that meet the criterion for its use. The administration of Interferon requires periodic visits (3 times weekly) and a proactive approach of the patient. Another new treatment option for some patients with chronic hepatitis C is PEG-INTRON (MayoClinic.com, 2001), which requires the patient to visit the doctor only once each week (Buggs, 2001).

Depending on the physical condition, a child might need hospitalization or home care for a longer period of time. If the physician recommends that the child can return to school and the child is chronically infected with one of the hepatitis viruses, several precautions should be taken. For the safety of others, and to prevent spreading of the viruses, children and teachers should be educated about the possible vaccinations against hepatitis A and B. Sanitary precautions such as hand washing after diaper changes or visits to the bathrooms should be implemented. To prevent the spread of hepatitis B and C, it must be understood that the virus can be spread only through infected blood. Therefore, the children and teachers can interact in a relatively carefree way with a chronically infected child without the worry of becoming infected themselves, yet they should be reminded not to share food, hairbrushes, and other objects that could contain minute blood particles. To help the infected child, teachers must understand that one of the major issues the child has to face in school is the issue of fatigue associated with the chronic condition. This could extensively hinder the child's ability to focus. Tutoring at home and school might be necessary to allow the child to focus on lesson plans or to compensate for lost school time. To help the child with the fatigue during school hours, a rest area should be made available for the child so that he or she can nap if needed. To combat the emotional stress of this disease, self-help groups and support groups should be recommended to the child and family to help alleviate the stress that can accompany a disease of this sort.

With the continued effort of vaccinating children, the spread of hepatitis A and B should eventually be able to be contained. Risks associated with hepatitis A are especially dangerous for the very young or elderly. Death from an infection with hepatitis A is rare. Risks associated with hepatitis B and C are that the diseases can become chronic and lead to liver inflammation, cirrhosis, and liver cancer (Buggs, 2001). Medical advances might be seen in more effective medications to prevent and help with the chronic aspects of the disease.

REFERENCES

Buggs, A. (2001, June 7). Hepatitis A. *eMedicine Journal, 2*(6). Retrieved December 27, 2001, from http://www.eMedicine.com/emerg/topic245.html

Human diseases and conditions. (2000). (Vol. 2, pp. 443–447). New York: Scribner & Sons.

Hepatitis Information Network. (2000a). Hepatitis A. Retrieved December 12, 2001, from http://www.hepnet.com/hepa/hepafact2000.html

Hepatitis Information Network. (2000b). Hepatitis B. Retrieved December 12, 2001, from http://www.hepnet.com/hepb.html

Mosby's medical, nursing, and allied health dictionary (6th ed., pp. 804–806). (2000). St. Louis, MO: Harcourt.

MayoClinic.com. (2001, December 6). What is Hepatitis A? Retrieved December 27, 2001, from http://www.mayoclinic.com/findinformation/conditioncenters/invoke.cfm

Monika Hannan
University of Northern Colorado

HEREDITARY SPASTIC PARAPLEGIA

Hereditary spastic paraplegia (HSP; also known as hereditary spastic paraparesis, Strümpell disease, Strümpell-Lorrain disease, hereditary Charcot disease, hereditary progressive spastic paraplegia, and French settlement disease) is a label used to represent a group of inherited degenerative spinal cord disorders characterized by a slow, gradual, progressive weakness and spasticity (stiffness) of the legs. In the late 1800s, the German neurologist Ernst Adolf von Strümpell first described this disorder. He observed two brothers and their father who had gait disorders and spasticity in their legs. After the death of the brothers, Strümpell was able, through autopsy, to show the degeneration of the motoric nerve fibers leading through the spinal cord (HSPInfo, 2002).

Symptoms may be first noticed in early childhood, or at any age through adulthood. According to some reports in the medical literature, symptom onset may occur as early as infancy or as late as the eighth or ninth decade of life: however, symptoms may most often develop during early to midadulthood. Initial findings typically include stiffness and relatively mild weakness of leg muscles, balance difficulties, unexplained tripping and falls, and an unusually clumsy manner of walking (gait). As the disorder progresses, walking may become increasingly difficult; however, complete loss of the ability to walk is relatively rare (National Organization for Rare Disorders, 2002).

The initial symptoms of HSP may include difficulty with balance, weakness and stiffness in the legs, muscle spasms, and dragging the toes when walking. In some forms of the disorder, bladder symptoms (such as incontinence) may appear, or the weakness and stiffness may spread to other parts of the body. Rate of progression and the severity of symptoms is quite variable even among members of the same family (HSPInfo, 2002).

At the present time, diagnosis of HSP is generally a process of exclusion of other disorders combined with observation of family history. There are some 15 or more gene loci associated with hereditary spastic paraplegia, of which only a few genes have been identified (HSPInfo, 2002).

In Europe the frequency of HSP has been estimated at anywhere from 1 to 9 cases per 100,000 people. HSP is rare, so it is often misdiagnosed, making the frequency rate difficult to determine. However, a reasonable estimate is approximately 3 in 100,000. This would represent less than 10,000 people in the United States. It is further estimated that about 10% of people with HSP have "complicated" HSP, which further complicates diagnosis (HSPInfo, 2002).

Characteristics

1. *Uncomplicated HSP:* Gradual weakening in the legs, urinary bladder disturbance, and sometimes impaired sensation in the feet.
2. *Complicated HSP:* Additional symptoms may include peripheral neuropathy, epilepsy, ataxia (lack of muscle control), optic neuropathy, retinopathy (disease of the retina), dementia, ichthyosis (a skin disorder causing dry, rough, scaly skin), mental retardation, deafness, or problems with speech, swallowing, or breathing.

Complicated HSP is rare, and the additional symptoms may be due to a separate disorder in addition to HSP. The patients may actually have uncomplicated HSP plus one or more other disorders. For example, a person with uncomplicated HSP may have peripheral neuropathy caused by diabetes or may have unrelated epilepsy. Additional symptoms may be present, such as impaired vibration-position sense in the toes, or corticospinal tract signs such as hyperreflexia, extensor toe sign, or ankle clonus (HSPInfo, 2002).

Currently, there is no specific treatment to prevent, retard, or reverse HSP's progressive disability. Nonetheless, treatment approaches used for chronic paraplegia from other causes are useful. The University of Michigan's HSP laboratory reports that patients in relatively early stages of the illness have obtained symptomatic improvement with oral and intrathecal baclofen and oral dantrolene. Zanaflex has also provided some reduction of spasticity. Bladder spasticity has been improved with oxybutynin (Ditropan; Fink, 2002). Regular physical therapy is important to maintain and improve range of motion and muscle strength. Furthermore, physical therapy is necessary to maintain aerobic conditioning of the cardiovascular system. Although physical therapy does not reduce the degenerative process within the spinal cord, it is considered important that HSP subjects maintain a physical therapy exercise regimen at least several times each week (Fink, 2002).

Children with HSP may well need the support of special education programming due to the chronic nature of this disorder. The obvious physiologic limitations may require extensive medical management that may take away from school attendance and attention to studies. In addition, special education services may provide physical therapy and adaptive physical education for the student. Family and individual counseling may be necessary for adjustment issues related to chronic illness.

REFERENCES

Fink, J. K. (2002). University of Michigan online hereditary spastic paraplegia homepage. Retrieved April 2002 from http://www.med.umich.edu/hsp/

HSPInfo: Hereditary Spastic Paraplegia. (2002). Retrieved April 2002 from http://www.HSPinfo.org./HSP.htm

National Organization for Rare Disorders. (2002). Hereditary spastic paraplegia. Retrieved April 2002, from http://www.rarediseases.org/cgi-bin/nord

Elaine Fletcher-Janzen
University of Northern Colorado

HERMANSKY-PUDLAK SYNDROME

Hermansky-Pudlak syndrome (HPS), which was first described in 1959 and is named after its discoverers, is characterized by a rare form of albinism that is associated with low visual acuity, bruising and prolonged bleeding, lung fibrosis, and occasionally inflammatory bowel disease and reduced kidney function (National Institute of Child Health and Development [NICHD], 2002).

HPS is seen in many countries but is quite common in northwest Puerto Rico, where 1 in every 1,800 individuals is affected, 1 in 21 is a gene carrier, and over 400 individuals have the syndrome. Several cases have also been reported in the Puerto Rican community in New York City (NICHD, 2002).

In a study conducted by the NICHD, 27 Puerto Rican patients and 22 non–Puerto Ricans were diagnosed by two symptoms characteristically seen in this syndrome: albinism and defective blood platelets. Twenty-five of the Puerto Rican patients had a specific mutation (a small region of DNA duplication) in the recently cloned gene, *HPS,* associated with the syndrome. Non–Puerto Ricans did not have this particular mutation. Several different mutations are thought to lead to HPS. Patients with and without the duplication were then compared using clinical and laboratory characteristics (NICHD, 2002).

HPS patients have a biochemical storage disorder; that

is, they accumulate a fatty product called ceroid lipofuscin. Researchers believe that this causes inflammation in tissues such as the bowel and lung. Prolonged inflammation leads to fibrosis, which in the case of the lung impairs its ability both to expel air and to exchange carbon dioxide for oxygen (NICHD, 2002).

Characteristics

1. Varying degrees of albinism (lack of skin and eye pigment), which impairs the vision of patients with albinism and often leads to involuntary rhythmic eye movements called nystagmus
2. Progressive deterioration in lung function, which is particularly prevalent in the Puerto Rican patients carrying the DNA duplication
3. Tendency to bruise easily and bleed
4. Females requiring medical intervention during their menstrual cycles or at childbirth
5. Lung dysfunction beginning with restrictive disease and then progressing inexorably to death usually in the fourth or fifth decade

In terms of treatment, HPS patients are advised to avoid blood anticoagulants, such as aspirin, and drugs can be used to prevent excessive bleeding during dental extractions and other surgical procedures. The reason HPS patients bleed easily is that their blood platelets are deficient in dense bodies. These subcellular organelles release their contents to make other platelets stick together and form a clot. Without the dense bodies, the clot forms very slowly (NICHD, 2002).

Children with HPS need to be monitored by a multidisciplinary team of professionals for the medical and adaptive monitoring of the disorder. Special education services under the physical and other health impaired handicapping conditions will serve academic and adaptive physical education needs for these children.

The cause of this inherited disease is being investigated by physicians, geneticists, and biochemists at the NICHD; the National Heart, Lung, and Blood Institute (NHLBI); and the National Eye Institute (NEI). From the gene sequence, researchers know what the protein encoded by the *HPS* gene should look like, but it is not yet known what such a protein actually does. According to William Gahl, many patients with albinism are not aware that they have HPS. They are thus at risk for hemorrhage. Anyone who has albinism and bruises easily should be checked for HPS, which is diagnosed by observing blood platelets under the electron microscope or by performing platelet aggregation studies. The NICHD has started a trial of an investigational drug, that in animal tests has been shown to prevent inflammation. With this drug, the researchers hope that they can prevent the inflammation that leads to the loss of lung function that shortens the lives of individuals with HPS.

REFERENCE

National Institute of Child Health and Development. (2002). Hermansky-Pudlak syndrome. Retrieved April 2002 from http://www.nichd.nih.gov/new/releases/hermansk.cfm

Elaine Fletcher-Janzen
University of Northern Colorado

HIRSCHSPRUNG DISEASE

Hirschsprung disease (also known as congenital intestinal aganglionosis) is characterized by an absence of nerve cells in a segment of the bowel. This disease interferes with the peristalsis action of the bowel and results in chronic bowel obstructions. For newborn infants this includes the inability to pass meconium, the infant's dark-green first bowel movement. The classic symptom for all children with this disorder is chronic constipation. For older infants, symptoms include abdominal distention and chronic diarrhea. Although usually first evident in infancy, symptoms can be manifested throughout childhood and adolescence.

Hirschsprung disease occurs in 1 out of every 5,000 live births and shows a male predominance at approximately a 4:1 ratio. Nearly 80–90% of people with Hirschsprung disease are diagnosed within the first 4 weeks of life. No ethnic or racial predispositions for the disease are noted. Hirschsprung disease results from a failure of the craniocaudal migration of ganglion (nerve) cell precursors along the gastrointestinal tract during the 5th to 12th weeks of gestation. Absence of these nerve cells interrupts the ability to relax the contracted bowel segment during peristalsis (Kirschner, 1991).

Characteristics

1. Eighty percent of cases are identified in the first 6 weeks of life.
2. The major symptom is chronic constipation that may be associated with a distended abdomen.
3. Peristalsis cannot occur in the bowel, resulting in a functional obstruction.
4. Newborn infants cannot pass meconium during the first hours of life.
5. Older children have bowel problems and constipation from birth.

Depending on the extent of the affected bowel, surgery is usually performed to remove the affected bowel. At that time the healthy bowel is brought down and connected to the anus. Many children experience a return to normal bowel functioning after surgery, but surgery does not guarantee a cure. Postoperative enterocolitis, constipation, or soiling occur in up to one third of all patients with this disorder throughout childhood, adolescence, and adulthood.

Children with Hirschsprung disease do not usually require special education intervention because many of their symptoms do not directly interfere with their learning in school. In addition, because their medical symptoms are usually not severe, many children are not even labeled with Other Health Impairment because they do not require any special intervention. There are no indications that children with Hirschsprung disease have greater school adjustment problems or emotional difficulty than do normal children. At the same time, it has been pointed out that because these children might be prone to elimination problems, teachers should be more responsive to children with Hirschsprung disease if they ask to go to the restroom. In this situation their request may reflect symptoms associated with the disease rather than a manipulation to avoid schoolwork. Children with Hirschsprung disease may need help from school personnel regarding medication management and monitoring of the child's symptoms (Frisby, 1998).

Unfortunately, there is no correlation between the amount of unhealthy bowel removed or the type of surgical procedure and eventual outcome of the disease. Symptoms are often varied and unpredictable. After surgery most children have loose and frequent stools, but as the stool becomes firmer, the frequency of defecation diminishes. Even when the child has limited sensation during defecation, most children can be adequately toilet trained. Older children sometimes have trouble with staining, but this symptom usually improves with time.

REFERENCES

Frisby, C. L. (1998). Hirschsprung's disease. In L. Phillips (Ed.), *Health-related disorders in children and adolescents: A guidebook for understanding and educating* (pp. 321–327). Washington, DC: American Psychological Association.

Kirschner, B. S. (1991). Hirschsprung's disease. In W. A. Walker, P. R. Durie, J. R. Hamilton, J. A. Walker-Smith, & John B. Watkins (Eds.), *Pediatric gastrointestinal disease* (pp. 829–832). Philadelphia: Decker.

William A. Rae
Texas A&M University

HOLT-ORAM SYNDROME

Holt-Oram syndrome, also known as heart-hand syndrome or cardiac-limb syndrome, refers to a rare genetic condition involving abnormalities of the heart and upper limbs. Those affected have malformations or abnormalities of the bones in the thumbs, wrists, and arms, but lower extremities are not affected. Bones may be missing, extra, underdeveloped, or malformed. There may also be problems with the shoulder blades and collarbones. In some children the thumb is absent (National Organization for Rare Disorders, Inc. [NORD], 2000). The severity varies greatly with the individual and may be as slight as limited range of motion or as great as complete absence of upper limbs (Jeanty & Silva, 1999).

Holt-Oram syndrome is also characterized by cardiac abnormalities. There may be structural defects such as holes in the heart or electrical impulse problems that cause the heart to beat improperly. As in the limb malformations, these may also range from mild (asymptomatic) to severe (life-threatening).

A very rare disorder, only about 100 or so cases of Holt-Oram syndrome have been documented since it was first described in 1960. A parent with Holt-Oram syndrome has about a 50% chance of passing the disorder on to each child. The condition is the result of heredity about 60% of the time; the other 40% of cases are apparently the result of a spontaneous mutation. The severity of the child's condition is unrelated to the severity of the parent's condition; a parent who is only slightly affected may produce a severely affected child.

Characteristics

1. Malformed or abnormal bones in upper body
2. May be missing bones entirely
3. Impaired range of motion
4. Normal lower body

For the children without thumbs, surgery to allow the index finger to act as a thumb has been cautiously explored, with positive results (Weber, Wenz, van Riel, Kaufmann, & Graf, 1997). In the school setting, children with orthopedic impairments that impact their learning may receive special services under the Orthopedically Impaired umbrella; such services may well include occupational therapy for fine motor skills and physical therapy for gross motor. An assistive technology system, such as a special keyboard and mouse or voice-activated software, may be appropriate for those having difficulty with handwriting. Children with serious heart complications affecting alertness, stamina, or concentration may be eligible for services under Other Health Impairment, allowing them to have adapted physical education and other modifications as needed.

REFERENCES

Jeanty, P., & Silva, S. (1999). Holt-Oram syndrome. *The fetus.* Retrieved from http://www.thefetus.net/sections/articles/musculoskeletal/Holt-Oram_syndrome.Html

National Organization for Rare Disorders, Inc. (2000). Holt-Oram syndrome. Retrieved from http://www.rarediseases.org

Weber, M., Wenz, W., van Riel, A., Kaufmann, A., & Graf, J. (1997). The Holt-Oram syndrome: Review of the literature and current orthopedic treatment concepts. *Zeitschrift für Orthopädie und thre Grenzgebiete, 135*(4), 368–375.

Sharla Fasko
Rowan County Schools
Morehead, Kentucky

HUNTER SYNDROME

Hunter syndrome (mucopolysacchridosis II, or MPS II), a progressive disorder arising from a deficiency in the enzyme iduronate sulfatase, is a sex-linked inborn error of metabolism (IEM) affecting only males. The enzyme's absence or deficiency prevents complete breakdown of the mucopolysacchrides heparen sulphate and dermatan sulfate, which then accumulate in bodily cells (National MPS Society, 2001). One of a group of lycosomal storage disorders that arise from altered mucopolysaccharide metabolism, Hunter syndrome is of two types, MPS IIA, having severe effects commonly leading to death by age 10–15 years, and MPS IIB, having milder effects and a life span of about 50 years (Flagler, 2000; Jones, 1997). Collapse of the trachea, cardiac failure, and neurological problems are usual causes of death (Jones, 1997; Pediatric Database, 1994). In both types, development is apparently normal for about the first two years of life followed by progressive deterioration. Major features of both types are presented here; Pediatric Database (1994) contains a more complete list.

Hunter syndrome is a rare disorder affecting an estimated 1 in 100,000 to 150,000 males worldwide (National MPS Society, 2001). Because females are carriers, those with family histories of Hunter syndrome may want to have genetic counseling before having children (National MPS Society, 2001).

No treatment or cure is currently available. Bone marrow transplantation has had limited effects (Meyer, 1997). The best that can be done is to provide support to these children and their families. As children with severe Hunter syndrome may have recurrent ear infections, hydrocephalus, congestive heart failure, respiratory problems, hernias, and gastrointestinal problems (Knoell, 2000; Naggs, 1999), a variety of medical interventions may be frequently needed.

Type MPS IIA Characteristics

1. Growth retardation and short terminal height
2. Progressive mental retardation and hearing and vision loss, often to severe levels
3. Hyperactivity and aggressive behavior
4. Coarse facial features, full lips, macrocephaly
5. Enlarged internal organs, leading to large abdomen
6. Progressive stiffening of joints, especially fingers
7. Severe neurologic, cardiac, and airway complications in advanced stages

Type MPS IIB Characteristics

1. Normal to mild mental retardation
2. Somatic abnormalities, including respiratory and cardiovascular, of the same type and ultimate severity as in MPS IIA but developing much more slowly
3. Carpal tunnel syndrome
4. Visual impairment owing to corneal opacities and hearing impairment

Boys with Hunter syndrome need extensive special education interventions. Having recurrent problems and a progressive disease, they need teachers who are skilled in basic medical care. These boys can have problems chewing and swallowing their food, so caretakers must ensure that they have easily managed food such as soft puddings or pureed food (Naggs, 1999). Their progressive stiffening of joints will call for physical therapy. Boys with severe Hunter syndrome may never speak or have a very small vocabulary and be prone to repetition of words or short phrases (Naggs, 1999) and will benefit from speech therapy to improve basic communication. Because their hyperactive and aggressive behavior may be disruptive (Pediatric Database, 1994), their instructors should be skilled in working with profoundly impaired students. Boys with the milder form of Hunter syndrome may be placed in a more normal school setting, although they may still need services for mild retardation and disruptive behavior disorders.

The prognosis for boys with the severe form is poor. Their progressive deterioration leads to increasing dependency, physical problems, and early death. Boys with the less severe form can be expected to live a more normal life but will still need considerable medical and educational intervention. Current research focuses on gene therapy and enzyme replacement therapy as ways of controlling Hunter syndrome (Meyer, 1997).

REFERENCES

Flagler, S. F. (2000). Hunter's syndrome (mucopoly sacchridosis II). In C. R. Reynolds & E. Fletcher-Janzen (Eds.), *Encyclopedia of special education* (2nd ed., Vol. 2, pp. 909–910). New York: Wiley.

Jones, K. L. (1997). *Smith's recognizable patterns of human malformation* (5th ed.). Philadelphia: Saunders.

Knoell, K. (2000). Denoument and discussion: Hunter syndrome (mucopolysacchardosis IIA). *Pediatrics and Adolescent Medicine, 154,* 86–89.

Meyer, G. (1997). Syndromes and inborn errors of metabolism. In M. L. Batshaw (Ed.), *Children with disabilities* (4th ed., pp. 813–834). Baltimore: Brookes.

Naggs, T. (1999). *Hunter's syndrome: Description and educational considerations* (ERIC Document Reproduction Service No. EC 307 023).

National MPS Society. (2001). MPS II Hunter Syndrome. Retrieved from http://www.mpssociety.org/mps2.htm

Pediatric Database. (1994). Hunter syndrome. Retrieved from http://www.icondata.com/health/pedbase/files/HUNTERSY.HTM

Amy Morrow
Robert T. Brown
University of North Carolina, Wilmington

HUNTINGTON'S CHOREA

Huntington's chorea (HC), also referred to as Huntington's disease, is an autosomal dominant disorder that causes deterioration of the central nervous system, in particular, the basal ganglia. HC has a 100% penetrance, and offspring have a 50–50 chance of developing the disease. Huntington's is characterized by repetitive rapid jerking of the face, trunk, and limbs. The chorea can be unilateral or bilateral and can move from one side of the body to another. The motions are involuntary but can be incorporated into voluntary movements to provide a disguise.

HC is estimated to occur in 5 to 10 individuals out of 100,000. The age of onset is typically between 35 and 55 years of age; however, in approximately 10% of cases the disease begins before the age of 20; and in 5% before the age of 14 (Fenichel, 1993). When the onset is before age 20, the disease is referred to as juvenile Huntington's chorea (JHC).

Compared to adult-onset HC, JHC has a greater paternal inheritance pattern, less prominent choreiform movements, greater rigidity, facial grimacing, and dysfluent speech. Unlike the adult who exhibits hyperkinetic movement patterns, children present more like Parkinson's patients, that is, with rigid musculature and slowed movements. With JHC there is also a propensity to develop epilepsy, often in the form of generalized myoclonic seizures. Although the disease progresses more slowly than when it begins in adulthood, the disease is often more severe in children and adolescents. Psychological problems, especially depression and paranoid ideations, are fairly common among individuals with JHC, and the disease eventually causes dementia and death.

Characteristics

1. Rigidity, epilepsy, and paternal inheritance pattern are more common in JHC.
2. Children with JHC have ataxic gait, speech dysfluency, and facial grimacing.
3. Chorea is less pronounced in children with JHC, but involuntary jerking does show.
4. There is an eventual decline in cognitive functioning and academic performance.
5. Significant psychological problems, including depression, are present.
6. The disease is more severe in JHC, and lifespan may be shorter than in adult HC.

Diagnosis is typically based on symptom presentation and family history of the disease (i.e., at least one affected parent). Magnetic resonance imaging and computerized tomography scans do, however, show a characteristic pattern of atrophy in areas of the caudate nucleus, corpus striatum, and cerebral cortex. Genetic studies can also provide information as to the likelihood that a person will develop the disease because having the HC gene predicts having the disease. Genetic testing can be done, however, when an individual is asymptomatic; testing protocols often include a minimum age of 18 and consent for follow-up counseling. Prenatal testing can also be done when parents have HC or are at 50% risk.

Children and adolescents with JHC often require special education services (e.g., as Other Health Impairment). Psychological services are also likely to be needed given the degenerative nature and severity of the disease. Supportive therapy for both the child and family should be offered, as well as help making contact with community agencies. Treatment for the disease itself consists of symptom relief, that is, drugs that improve movements by reducing the impact on the dopaminergic and cholinergic systems and drugs that treated associated problems (e.g., valproic acid, baclofen, haloperidol, and phenothiazine). Neuroleptics have the advantage of treating both abnormal movements and psychiatric symptoms.

Prognosis for HC is poor. Not only is quality of life compromised, but life span is also shortened. On average individuals with HC live 8 years from the time of onset (Fenichel, 1993). In males who have JHC with early onset of rigidity and a pattern of paternal inheritance, the duration of the disease is even shorter. Although research has made great strides in identifying the gene responsible for HC, little has been done to change the outcome. Prevention methods currently consist of genetics testing and counseling regarding pregnancy.

REFERENCE

Fenichel, G. (1993). *Clinical pediatric neurology.* Philadelphia: Saunders.

Elaine Clark
University of Utah

HURLER SYNDROME

Hurler syndrome, or gargoylism, is a type of mucopolysaccharidosis (MPS I) that produces severe mental retardation. Hurler syndrome is transmitted as an autosomal-recessive trait and is due to the lack of a specific enzyme. This enzymatic defect causes excessive buildup of mucopolysaccharides in the tissues.

Hurler syndrome is a rare condition that occurs in about 1 in 100,000 births. The onset of Hurler syndrome symptoms usually occurs within the first few months of life, until which time the infant may appear normal. Subsequent to this, mental and physical deterioration culminate in death typically by the age of 10 years.

Characteristics

1. The syndrome may be detected before birth through amniocentesis.
2. Symptoms become apparent after the first few months.
3. Subsequent to birth, the syndrome is diagnosed through urine samples, skeletal changes observed in X ray, and family history.
4. Symptoms include enlarged spleen and liver, coarse features (low forehead and enlargement of head), dwarfism, chest deformity, stiff joints, clouding of the cornea, deafness, heart murmurs, and mental deterioration.
5. The progressive syndrome leads to physical and mental retardation and severely decreased life expectancy.

(*Mosby's Medical Dictionary Revised,* 1987)

Death from Hurler syndrome is imminent and is often due to cardiac complications or pulmonary disorders. Although previously thought to be untreatable, successful treatment of infants with mutated forms of Hurler syndrome has been accomplished through bone marrow transplants (Peters, Shapiro, & Krivit, 1998). In patients treated with bone marrow transplants, quality of life ranges from restricted to near normal. Symptoms of the disorder are significantly reduced, and life span can be increased by many decades.

Because of the progressive nature of deterioration, by the time children with Hurler's syndrome reach school age, intellectual and physical functioning is severely limited. In addition, the early onset of hearing impairment produces speech and language delays and subsequent hearing loss (Clark, 1989). Children with Hurler syndrome may qualify for special education services under a number of categories including mental retardation, speech and language handicap, Other Health Impairment, and Physically Disabled. However, the progressive severity of deterioration may prevent children with Hurler syndrome from benefiting from services such as occupational or physical therapy.

Future research is focusing on bone marrow transplant, as it is the only known treatment for any form of Hurler syndrome. Generally, Hurler syndrome is considered to have no successful treatment.

REFERENCES

Clark, D. (1989). Neonates and infants at risk for hearing and speech-language disorders. *Topics in Language Disorders, 10,* 1–12.

Mosby's medical dictionary revised (2nd ed.). (1987). St. Louis, MO: Mosby.

Peters, C., Shapiro, E., & Krivit, W. (1998). Hurler syndrome: Past, present, and future. *Journal of Pediatrics, 133,* 7–9.

Kimberly D. Wilson
University of Texas at Austin

Nancy Nussbaum
Austin Neurological Clinic

See also Mucopolysaccharide Disorders

HUTCHINSON-GILFORD PROGERIA SYNDROME

Hutchinson-Gilford progeria syndrome is a very rare progressive disorder characterized by an appearance of accelerated aging in children (National Organization for Rare Disorders [NORD], 2000). Progeria is a Greek term meaning "prematurely old." The classic type is Hutchinson-Gilford progeria syndrome, first described in England in 1886 by Jonathan Hutchinson and again in 1886 and 1904 by Hastings Gilford (Brown, 2000). Signs of progeria become visible from age 6 months to 1 year, after an apparently normal early infancy. Affected individuals seldom exceed the size of a healthy 5-year-old, although they have the appearance of 60-year-old adults by the time they are 10 years of age (Encyclopaedia Britannica Online, 2001).

Hutchinson-Gilford progeria syndrome has a reported incidence of about 1 in 8 million newborns. The number of published cases since 1886 is just over 100. The disease appears to affect sexes and races equally, and cases have been reported around the world. Although the cause of progeria remains a mystery, this disorder is believed to be the result of an autosomal dominant mutation. Because neither parent carries the mutation, each case is believed to represent a sporadic new mutation that probably occurs at the time of conception (Brown, 2000; NORD, 2000).

Primary characteristics (almost always present when condition is apparent)

1. Growth failure during first year of life with diminished subcutaneous fat
2. Generalized alopecia (baldness)
3. Small face relative to head size
4. Micrognathia (small jaw)
5. Delayed tooth formation
6. Stiffness of joints and limited range of motion
7. Wide-based, shuffling gait
8. Atherosclerosis and cardiovascular problems
9. Infantile sex organs

Frequently-present characteristics

1. Dry, scaly, aged-looking skin
2. Prominent superficial veins
3. Loss of eyebrows and eyelashes
4. Open anterior fontanelle
5. Beaked nose
6. Brittle bones, with repeated nonhealing fractures

No specific tests exist for this disorder; diagnosis is based on symptoms and features found on physical examination. Diagnosis typically occurs between 1 and 2 years of age, when symptoms that resemble the regular aging process become apparent. The skin becomes wrinkled and dry; hair becomes lighter and begins to fall out; and circulatory and respiratory complications occur. Motor and cognitive development appears to be normal, although muscles may begin to atrophy (NORD, 2000).

Treatments may include injections of growth hormone and coronary bypass surgery (Dyck et al., 1987) although no effective treatment for progeria has been discovered. Special education considerations include possible heart disease, insulin-resistant diabetes, and other physical abnormalities that may require medical treatment and interfere with regular school attendance or progress. Because of quickly progressing atherosclerosis, stroke is a possible complication. A few individuals are mentally retarded; however, most have normal intelligence and may even be academically advanced. Emotional support for affected individuals and their families, including support groups, counseling, and education, is certainly warranted. School-age children with Hutchinson-Gilford progeria syndrome will likely be eligible for special education services under Other Health Impairment, and the categories of Mentally Retarded or Orthopedically Handicapped may be appropriate depending on specific symptoms and their severity. Information regarding neuropsychological or educational functioning in individuals affected with progeria is not available in the literature.

Life expectancy for patients with progeria is minimal. By age 10, extensive arteriosclerosis and heart disease have typically developed, and most patients die during adolescence. According to reviews of the literature, the age at death ranges from 7 to 27 years, with a median age of death at 13.4 (Encyclopaedia Britannica Online, 2001). Rodriguez, Perez-Alonso, Funes, and Perez-Rodriguez (1999) reported a case of a 35-week-old fetus with a severe prenatal form of progeria. Although the precise diagnosis for this fetus, who died shortly after birth, has been debated (Faivre et al., 1999), future research efforts should be directed toward prenatal identification, both for study of the development of the pathology and for possible prevention and early intervention. Treatment options should increase as a result of greater understanding of the pathology that characterizes this disorder. More information is needed about the psychosocial and educational functioning of affected individuals so that appropriate school programs and parent support can be provided.

REFERENCES

Brown, T. (2000). The progeria syndrome fact sheet, Progeria Research Foundation. Retrieved from http://www.progeriaresearch.org

Dyck, J. D., David, T. E., Burke, B., Webb, G. D., Henderson, M. A., & Fowler, R. S. (1987). Management of coronary artery disease in Hutchinson-Gilford syndrome. *Journal of Pediatrics, 111,* 407–410.

Encyclopaedia Britannica Online. (2001). Progeria. Retrieved from http://search.eb.com/bol/topic?eu=63055&sctn=1

Faivre, L., Van Kien, P. K., Madinier-Chappat, N., Nivelon-Chevallier, A., Beer, F., & LeMerrer, M. (1999). Can Hutchinson-Gilford progeria syndrome be a neonatal condition? *American Journal of Medical Genetics, 87,* 450–452.

National Organization for Rare Disorders. (2000). Hutchinson Gilford progeria syndrome. Retrieved from http://www.rarediseases.org

Rodriguez, J. I., Perez-Alonso, P., Funes, R. & Perez-Rodriguez, J. (1999). Lethal neonatal Hutchinson-Gilford progeria syndrome. *American Journal of Medical Genetics, 82,* 242–248.

Cynthia A. Plotts
Southwest Texas State University

HYDROCEPHALUS, X-LINKED

Hydrocephalus is a condition that is caused by abnormal buildup or accumulation of cerebrospinal fluid (CSF) in the ventricles or subarachnoid space of the brain. As a result, intracranial pressure is increased by overproduction of CSF, obstruction of the flow of CSF, or failure to reabsorb the fluid. Hydrocephalus can be either congenital with an early onset or acquired. The principal etiologies of congenital hydrocephalus include Dandy-Walker syndrome (DWS), neural tube defects, aqueductal stenosis, intraventricular hemorrhage (IVH), and complications from hypoxic-ischemic encephalopathy affecting premature infants (Fletcher, Dennis, & Northrup, 2000).

The prevalence rate for hydrocephalus is dependent on the specific etiology. Neural tube defects are estimated to occur in 1–2% of 1,000 births in North America, with spina bifida occurring at a rate of 0.5–1.0% in 1,000. Hydrocephalus occurs in 80–90% of children diagnosed with spina bifida and affects 70–80% of children with DWS, which has a rate of 1 in 30,000 live births. Hydrocephalus is present in 100% of cases of aqueductal stenosis, a condition that affects 0.5 in 1,000 live births. Hydrocephalus is also associated with IVH, a condition that occurs in 20% of premature infants (Fletcher et al., 2000). Acquired hydrocephalus can be caused by a number of conditions, including brain tumor, arachnoid cyst, traumatic brain injury (TBI), central nervous system infections such as meningitis, and intracranial and intraventricular hemorrhaging.

Congenital, or early-onset, hydrocephalus is identified and treated before 12 months of age. More often, however, it is diagnosed within the first few days of life. Early signs include abnormal increase in the circumference of the head in the first 8 weeks, head circumference exceeding the infant's chest, prominent veins in the scalp, and widely spaced eyes (Eaves, 2000). The pupils are often sluggish and respond unequally to light, and these infants present as lethargic and irritable. In cases of acquired hydrocephalus, the older child often complains of severe headache pain (especially on awakening) and has problems with ataxic gait.

Characteristics

1. Abnormal growth of the skull and/or ventricles as a result of accumulated CSF
2. Headaches, irritability, and lethargy
3. Poor gross and fine motor skills, including motor slowing
4. Poor visual-motor and spatial abilities

The most common treatment of hydrocephalus is the surgical placement of a shunt to divert CSF to other areas of the body (e.g., abdominal cavity). This treatment usually allows the child to have a normal life span; however, repeated shunting and complications caused by surgical interventions (e.g., shunt obstructions and infections) often reduce the quality of life. Frequent hospitalizations can also make an impact due to lengthy absences from school and interruption in academic and social activities. Nonetheless, appropriately treated hydrocephalus (i.e., surgical and medical management) gives patients the best chance to lead a normal life and have a good prognosis.

Although the cognitive abilities of a child with hydrocephalus are largely dependent on the etiology of the condition, deficits are commonly seen in nonverbal skill areas. Children with early-onset hydrocephalus have poorly developed gross and fine motor skills and have problems with visual-motor and spatial ability. Children with hydrocephalus also have high rates of behavior disorders compared to the general population (Fletcher et al., 2000). Not all children with hydrocephalus warrant special education placements. However, when serious learning and psychological problems occur, the child should be evaluated by the school psychologist and considered at an Individual Educational Plan meeting. Which category of service, if any, will depend on the severity and nature of the child's difficulty; however, possible considerations include Specific Learning Disabilities, Emotional Disturbance, Other Health Impairment, and Traumatic Brain Injury. Regardless of the need for special education, children with this condition are likely to benefit from accommodations in the regular classroom. As a result of motor slowing and poor fine motor skills, children with hydrocephalus may need extra time to take down notes from the board and complete written assignments. Tutoring may also be needed to catch the child up after lengthy absences for treatment or associated illness. Given the likelihood that the child will struggle with nonverbal skills, including math, regular monitoring and the provision of math tutoring services may be critical. Children with hydrocephalus may also need counseling to assist them with issues of self-esteem and finding better ways to cope with their problems. Collaboration with parents is also critical to ensure that children with hydrocephalus receive adequate services in the school, as well as help outside (e.g., special camp experiences and recreational activities).

Ongoing research is needed in the medical field to find ways that reduce the number of shunt revisions a child has to undergo. Further research is needed to find more effective ways to identify children who are in need of treatment before complications arise and functioning is diminished.

REFERENCES

Eaves, R. C. (2000). Hydrocephalus. In C. R. Reynolds & E. Fletcher-Janzen (Eds.), *Encyclopedia of special education* (Vol. 2, pp. 911–912). New York: Wiley.

Fletcher, J. M., Dennis, M., & Northrup, H. (2000). Hydrocephalus. In K. O. Yeates, M. D. Ris, & H. G. Taylor (Eds.), *Pediatric neuropsychology* (pp. 25–46). New York: Guilford Press.

Heidi Mathie
Elaine Clark
University of Utah

HYDROLETHALUS SYNDROME

Hydrolethalus syndrome is a recessively inherited lethal malformation syndrome involving the central nervous system. Prenatal diagnosis is most common, and the fetuses commonly present with hydrocephaly (with significant functional deficits), micrognathia (underdevelopment of the jaw), polydactyly (more than the normal number of fingers and toes), and a key-shaped defect of the occipital bone.

Incidence rates are estimated at 1 in 20,000, and hydrolethalus belongs to the Finnish disease heritage (Norio, Nevanlinna, & Perheentupa, 1973); many of the reported cases originate in Finland. There is no treatment for this lethal disorder; however, survival upwards of 5 to 8 months of age in a limited number of hydrolethalus cases has been documented (Aughton & Cassidy, 1987).

Characteristics

1. Hydrocephaly, micrognathia, polydactyly, and an absence of midline structures of the brain are present.
2. Abnormal eyes and nose, cleft lip or palate, low-set ears, defective lung lobes, clubfeet, cardiac myopathy, and abnormal genitalia have been frequently observed in hydrolethalus syndrome.
3. Most cases result in stillbirths, and those children born alive survive only minutes to a few hours at most.

REFERENCES

Aughton, D. J., & Cassidy, S. B. (1987). Hydrolethalus syndrome: Report of an apparent mild case, literature review, and differential diagnosis. *American Journal of Medical Genetics, 27,* 935–942.

Norio, R., Nevanlinna, H. R., & Perheentupa, J. (1973). Hereditary diseases in Finland: Rare flora in rare soil. *Annuals of Clinical Research, 5*(3), 109–141.

Kimberly M. Estep
University of Houston–Clear Lake

HYPERCALCEMIA

Resulting from excessive amounts of calcium in the blood, hypercalcemia most often occurs in conjunction with or as a result of other underlying endochrine conditions. Hypercalcemia commonly results from malignancy or hyperparathyroidism. In the body, calcium levels are maintained by the interplay of three major hormones: parathyroid hormone (PTH), calcitriol, and calcitonin. For hypercalcemia to develop, the normal calcium regulation system must be overwhelmed with an excess of PTH, calcitriol, or other hormones mimicking these hormones. Hyperthyroidism-related hypercalcemia is caused by increased calcium absorption in the intestines. Hypercalcemia is most commonly seen in patients with breast and lung cancer. An autosomal dominant trait has also been associated with hypercalcemia in children, and it is characterized by persistent hypercalcemia.

Hypercalcemia is a fairly common metabolic disorder affecting 10–20% of cancer patients. Hyperthyroidism is the most common cause of hypercalcemia, and 50,000 new cases occur in the United States each year. Hyperthyroidism incidence in females is much higher than in males; thus, hypercalcemia associated with this disorder is more often seen in women. Hypercalcemia associated with cancer affects males and females alike.

Characteristics

1. Calcium levels are elevated.
2. Patients with mild elevations are asymptomatic; cognitive sequelae observed in more severe cases include changes in mental status.
3. Nausea, vomiting, lethargy, constipation, depression, headache, polyuria, muscle weakness, and altered mental status are common.
4. In individuals with increased calcium, abdominal examinations may suggest pancreatitis or ulcers; however, severe hypercalcemia is associated with enlargement of the pancreas and spleen.

Hypercalcemia also may be caused by antacids, an abundance of Vitamins D or A, AIDS, advanced liver disease, milk alkali, lithium, and other syndromes (e.g., Williams syndrome). Dialysis will be necessary in patients with renal failure. Cognitive sequelae are sometimes observed leading to alterations in mental status and cognition. Mental deficiency may be observed in select cases.

Due to the medical condition of the child, special education services may be needed under Other Health Impairment. However, in cases of mild hypercalcemia, children normally do not present with any special needs. Prognosis is dependent on the underlying causes. In people with cancer, morbidity rates are high when hypercalcemia is also present. A majority of incidences of hypercalcemia occurring in conjunction with other disorders are manageable. Research is ongoing in the disorders often associated with hypercalcemia, and although hypercalcemia is manageable, often the underlying disorder results in complications for the patient.

REFERENCES

Bilezikian, J. P. (1993). Management of hypercalcemia. *Journal of Endocrinology Metabolism, 77,* 1445–1449.

Dent, D. M., Miller, J. L., Klaff, L., & Barron, J. (1987). The incidence and causes of hypercalcemia. *Postgraduate Medical Journal, 63,* 745–750.

Nelson, W. E., Behrman, R. E., Kliegmen, R. M., & Arvin, A. M. (1996). *Nelson textbook of pediatrics* (15th ed.). Bangalore, India: Prism Books.

Kimberly M. Estep
University of Houston–Clear Lake

HYPERCHOLESTEROLEMIA

Hypercholesterolemia (high cholesterol), a metabolic disorder, is characterized by high accumulations of fats in the blood. High cholesterol is the leading cause of death in the United States. In a majority of cases, symptomatology culminates as one gets older; however, rare instances of childhood onset have been documented. Particularly deadly to children is familial hypercholesterolemia (FH), which is a rare form of hypercalcemia that is believed to be an autosomal dominant trait characterized by absent or malfunctioning low-density lipoprotein (LDL) receptors. If the trait is homozygous, complications arise, and most children will not survive into young adulthood. Heterozygous FM will likely present itself in middle adulthood, and if treatment is swift, the patient can survive. Affected FM patients normally develop premature coronary artery disease (CAD) in which early detection is of the utmost importance.

As noted, hypercholesterolemia is common, occurring in about 1 in 500 persons worldwide. Men normally have earlier onset than women; however, childhood onset is rare.

Characteristics

1. Individuals have unusually high blood serum cholesterol.
2. Patients with high levels of cholesterol eventually develop coronary disease.
3. Children with the homozygous familial type will have symptoms that mimic ischemic heart disease, peripheral vascular disease, or aortic stenosis (constriction or narrowing of an opening).
4. Children with the heterozygous familial type may remain asymptomatic until adulthood.
5. Patients may have cutaneous xanthomas at birth, and planar xanthomas are most commonly seen.

Treatment includes dietary modifications and exercise. Cholesterol-lowering medications may also be needed. However, homozygous FH does not respond well to medication and requires a more aggressive approach. For instance, a liver transplant dramatically reduces low-density lipoprotein levels; however, complications then arise as a result of the transplant.

Symptomatic children qualify for special education services under Other Health Impairment, and such services vary depending on the particular child's needs. Prognosis is dependent on presentation, and if CAD is present, premature death is almost imminent. However, age of morbidity is highly varied, and early detection is the key to longevity.

REFERENCES

Citkowitz, E. (2001). Hypercholesterolemia. *eMedicine, 2*(5). Retrieved June 2001 from http://www.emedicine.com/med/topic1072.html

Granot, E., & Deckelbaum, R. J. (1989). Hypocholesterolemia in childhood. *Journal of Pediatrics, 115,* 171.

Illingworth, D. R., Duell, P. B., & Connor, W. E. (1995). Disorders of lipid metabolism. In P. Felig, J. D. Baxter, & L. A. Frohmin (Eds.), *Endocrinology and metabolism* (3rd ed., pp. 1315–1403). New York: McGraw-Hill.

Nelson, W. E., Behrman, R. E., Kliegmen, R. M., & Arvin, A. M. (1996). *Nelson textbook of pediatrics* (15th ed). Bangalore, India: Prism Books.

Kimberly M. Estep
University of Houston–Clear Lake

HYPERGLYCINEMIA, NONKETOTIC

Nonketotic hyperglycinemia (NKH) is a rare autosomal-recessive trait involving an error of glycine metabolism. Large amounts of the amino acid glycine accumulate in the body fluids, particularly in the cerebrospinal fluid. Two subtypes of this disorder exist: nonclassic NKH and neonatal NKH. The former appears later in life and presents with milder neurological deficits and varying degrees of mental retardation.

NKH is rare and the prevalence unknown; however, high occurrences of NKH have been found in Finland (von Wendt, Hirvasniemi, & Simila, 1979).

Characteristics

1. In infancy, failure to thrive, low muscle tone (hypotonia), seizures, respiratory distress, and lethargy are common.
2. Most patients die within the first year of life. Those who survive manifest severe psychomotor retardation and seizures.
3. Glycine amounts in the blood, urine, and cerebrospinal fluid are high.
4. Severe adaptive and intellectual impediments are present.

Treatment focuses on the reduction of glycine concentrations by administration of sodium benzoate; however, treatment outcomes vary greatly in the literature. Even with early diagnosis and treatment, infants who survive present with profound mental retardation and physical handicaps. Other treatment issues surround neurotransmitter activity involved in NKH. Elevated glycine levels influence two receptors in the body. The inhibitory glycine receptor, mainly in the brain stem and spinal cord, is responsible for the respiratory difficulties and the lethargy associated with NKH, and the inhibitory glycine activates the *N*-methyl-*D*-aspartate (NMDA) receptor, an excitatory receptor of glutamate. Research suggests that the latter plays the more important role in the difficulties associated with NKH; therefore, treatments aimed at protecting the NMDA receptor are advantageous. Unfortunately, this NMDA treatment is still in a preliminary phase.

Special education placement is necessary for children living with NKH. These children present with multiple health problems, developmental delays, and mental deficiencies. Most are unable to communicate with their environment.

Prognosis is not favorable, and future research is focusing on protecting the NMDA receptors and finding an antagonist to offset the effects of overstimulation. Antagonists such as dextromethorphan, ketamine, and tryptophan are currently under study.

REFERENCES

Boneh, A., Degani, Y., & Harari, M. (1996). Prognosis clues and outcome of early treatment of nonketotic hyperglycinemia. *Pediatric Neurology, 15,* 137–141.

Lu, F. L., Wang, P., Hwu, W., Yau, K., & Wang, T. (1999). Neonatal type of nonketotic hyperglycinemia. *Pediatric Neurology, 20,* 295–300.

Nissenkorn, A., Michelson, M., Ben-Zeev, B., & Lerman-Sagie, T. (2001). Inborn errors of metabolism: A cause of abnormal brain development. *Neurology, 56,* 1265–1272.

Von Wendt, L., Hirvasniemi, A., & Simila, S. (1979). Nonketotic hyperglycinemia: A genetic study of 13 Finnish families. *Clinical Genetics, 15,* 411–417.

Kimberly M. Estep
University of Houston–Clear Lake

HYPERHIDROSIS, PRIMARY

Primary hyperhidrosis is a genetic disorder of hyperactivity of the sweat glands. Sweating may occur in the hands and feet, face, underarms, groin area, and under the breasts. Patients with more severe hyperhidrosis may experience excessive sweating all over the body. More common than primary hyperhidrosis, secondary hyperhidrosis develops because of an underlying disorder.

Primary hyperhidrosis is rare, equally affecting men and women. Often, the symptoms of overactive sweat glands dissipate with age without medical intervention. However, treatment is available and consists of surgery or topical medications that have proven effective at alleviating symptomatology. Botulinum toxin A injections have also been successful in the treatment of primary hyperhidrosis.

Patients with primary hyperhidrosis do not present with any special education issues; however, due to the possible embarrassment that excessive sweating causes, psychosocial issues may arise, especially for adolescents. Prognosis is good, and future research lies in the development of effective management tools that lessen the symptoms associated with primary hyperhidrosis.

Characteristics

1. Excessive sweating is either generalized over the whole body or localized to areas such as the hands and feet, the most common areas affected.
2. Some children experience facial flushing.
3. Individuals suffering from primary hyperhidrosis may experience heightened reactions to anxiety or nervousness, exercise, and caffeine.
4. The skin may become unusually soft and smooth, scaly, or cracked, and the palms and soles of the affected individual may appear abnormally pink or bluish-white in appearance.

REFERENCES

Glasnapp, A., & Schroeder, B. J. (2001). Topical therapy for localized hyperhidrosis. *International Journal of Pharmaceutical Compounding, 5,* 28–29.

Heckman, M., Ceballos-Baumann, A. O., & Plewig, G. (2001). Botulinum toxin A for axillary hyperhidrosis (excessive sweating). *New England Journal of Medicine, 344,* 488–493.

O'Donoghue, G., Finn, D., & Brady, M. P. (1980). Palmar primary hyperhidrosis in children. *Journal of Pediatric Surgery, 15,* 172–174.

Kimberly M. Estep
University of Houston–Clear Lake

HYPERKINESIS

Hyperkinesis involves excessive involuntary movements that interfere with motor control. Both hyperkinetic and hypokinetic movement disorders are attributed to chemical and electrical imbalances that result in the malfunction of the body's motor circuit (Bogdanov, Pinchuk, Pisar'kova, Shelyakin, & Sirbiladze, 1994). Hyperkinesis is characterized by repetitive movements that may involve the face, limbs, or the entire body. Hyperkinesis was formerly the diagnosis now referred to in the *Diagnostic and Statistical Manual of Mental Disorders—Fourth Edition (DSM-IV)* as attention-deficit hyperactivity disorder. Presently, the European Diagnostic Manual ICD-10 still emphasizes the presence of abnormal levels of inattention and overactivity across multiple settings in its identification of hyperkinetic disorders (Tripp, Luk, Schaughency, & Singh, 1999).

The prevalence and severity of hyperkinesis varies according to the disorder. Hyperkinesis may manifest a variety of symptoms including tremors, dystonia, tics, chorea, athetosis, ballism, and myoclonus. Some hyperkinetic movement disorders include Huntington's disease, Tourette syndrome, and an infantile cerebral palsy classified as hyperkinetic (Bogdanov et al., 1994; Kishore & Calne, 1997). There can be instances of drug-induced hyperkinesia as well (Vitek & Giroux, 2000).

Although there is still uncertainty as to the exact neurological role played by the basal ganglia, the portion of the brain most responsible for the body's motor control, it has been implicated in the development of these movement disorders (Litvan, Paulsen, Mega, & Cummings, 1998). Decreased output from the basal ganglia reduces the level of inhibition to the thalamus and subsequently results in excessive movements. Moreover, certain drugs that stimulate dopamine neurotransmitters have also been found to induce hyperkinetic movements (Vitek & Giroux, 2000).

Characteristics

1. Involuntary movements occur at rest, while standing still, or during voluntary movement.
2. The rate of movements can range from very fast to slow.
3. The pattern of movements can be rhythmic or irregular.
4. Generally, voluntary movements of affected body parts are slow.
5. Movement is intensified in uncontrolled or stressful situations.
6. There may be a greater frequency of hyperactive behaviors such as agitation, irritation, euphoria, or anxiety.

When a child's presenting symptoms include hyperkinetic movements, physicians should first consider whether the hyperkinesis is a side effect of any medication. However, certain medical procedures have been used successfully to alleviate the hyperkinetic movements. In particular, transcranial micropolarization has been found to alleviate hyperkinesis and improve functional movements of the joints (Bogdanov et al., 1994). Biochemical therapy and motor rehabilitation therapy also have been used to treat and alleviate symptoms.

Many children with movement disorders have intelligence within the normal range. However, some may have developmental delays in several domain areas, such as motor, cognitive, socioemotional, and adaptive skills. Children with movement disorders may need adaptive physical education, alternatives to writing, and extra time to transition between locations. Physical and occupational therapists can assist children in strengthening their fine and gross motor skills as well as in learning to control their movements (Paulson & Reider, 1997).

Moreover, children may experience increased frustration at their inability to control their movements. Thus, children with movement disorders may be socially isolated due to embarrassment. As increased stress exacerbates the hyperkinetic movements, and may even limit the efficacy of physical therapy, children may benefit from counseling to address the emotional consequences of having a movement disorder (Paulson & Reider, 1997).

REFERENCES

Bogdanov, O. V., Pinchuk, D. Y., Pisar'kova, E. V., Shelyakin, A. M., & Sirbiladze, K. T. (1994). The use of the method of transcranial micropolarization to decrease the severity of hyperkinesis in patients with infantile cerebral palsy. *Neuroscience and Behavioral Physiology, 24*(5), 442–445.

Kishore, A., & Calne, D. B. (1997). Approach to the patient with a movement disorder and overview of movement disorders. In R. L. Watt & W. C. Koller (Eds.), *Movement disorders: Neurological principles and practice* (pp. 3–14). New York: McGraw-Hill.

Litvan, I., Paulsen, J. S., Mega, M. S., & Cummings, J. L. (1998). Neuropsychiatric assessment of patients with hyperkinetic and hypokinetic movement disorders. *Archives of Neurology, 55*, 1313–1319.

Paulson, G. W., & Reider, C. R. (1997). Movement disorders in childhood. In R. L. Watt & W. C. Koller (Eds.), *Movement disorders: Neurological principles and practice* (pp. 661–672). New York: McGraw-Hill.

Tripp, G., Luk, S. L., Schaughency, E. A., & Singh, R. (1999). DSM-IV and ICD-10: A comparison of the correlates of ADHD and hyperkinetic disorder. *American Academy of Child and Adolescent Psychiatry, 38*(2), 156–159.

Vitek, J. L., & Giroux, M. (2000). Physiology of hypokinetic and hyperkinetic movement disorders: Model for dyskinesia. *Annals of Neurology, 47*(1), S131–S138.

Michelle Perfect
University of Texas at Austin

HYPERLEXIA

Hyperlexia is defined as the ability of an individual to recognize words at a level superior to that predicted by their age and measured intellectual ability, which is significantly better than their reading comprehension (Aram, 1997; Nation, 1999; Rispens & Van Berckelaer, 1991). The prevalence of hyperlexia is unknown, but as with most developmental disorders, it occurs three to four times as often in males.

Hyperlexia may be regarded as a specific variant of developmental dyslexia (Nation, 1999) or as a variant of specific language impairment (Aram, 1997; Cohen, Hall, & Riccio, 1997). Although able to recognize words at an accelerated level at very early ages (e.g., 3 years of age), children with hyperlexia demonstrate significant deficits in reading comprehension. The difficulties in reading comprehension appear to be a function of core deficits in receptive and expressive language (Aram, 1997; Cohen et al., 1996).

Characteristics (Aram, 1997; Cohen et al., 1996; Nation, 1999)

1. Fluent oral reading but defective reading comprehension
2. Superior auditory memory
3. Adequate to superior visual perceptual skills
4. Decreased language ability and difficulty understanding oral communication as well as written communication
5. Impaired social relationships
6. Echolalia and scripted speech

Although the ability to decode at superior levels in the absence of comprehension is the hallmark of hyperlexia, additional characteristics include strengths in memory and visual perceptual skills. In many children with hyperlexia, decreased language abilities, echolalia, impaired social relationships, and preoccupation with numbers have been noted as well. Further, children with hyperlexia exhibit difficulty comprehending oral as well as written language. Despite their inability to comprehend what they read, children with hyperlexia may demonstrate a compulsive preoccupation with reading (Nation, 1999). The compulsive component is most likely to occur when hyperlexia co-occurs with pervasive developmental disorder.

One of the problems with the identification of children with hyperlexia is the emphasis on oral reading and decoding, as compared to comprehension, in the early grades. Beginning reading skills often are evaluated based on oral reading and decoding, skill areas in which these children excel. As a result, in the absence of other disorders, the delays in language and comprehension may not be identified until the curricular focus shifts to more abstraction and comprehension in third and fourth grades. In fact, teachers and parents may take great pride in the reading (decoding) ability of the child, not realizing that the comprehension is lacking (Kupperman, 1997).

The strong potential for the child to demonstrate receptive language problems (e.g., Cohen et al., 1997) suggests that a speech-language professional needs to be involved in the assessment and intervention planning for these children. Although articulation and language in scripted (or written) contexts may appear adequate, the difficulties in comprehending oral language as well as written language demand the involvement of speech-language pathologists in order to identify the language needs of the child and how to best address them. Special education services specific to reading comprehension (e.g., identifying main ideas, paraphrasing) may be needed as well, but interventions specific to reading comprehension must begin with basic language and vocabulary building (Aram, 1997). In addition, because of the deficits in language and communication skills, interventions in social skills areas and pragmatic communication may be needed (e.g., social skills training). For children with hyperlexia and pervasive developmental disorders, the use of the printed word may be helpful in increasing language and communication skills (Kupperman, 1997).

There is very little research available on hyperlexia and related concerns. More consistent documentation of the associated neuropsychological profile of children with hyperlexia and possible etiological factors is needed. In addition, more systematic evaluation of intervention programs to address hyperlexia, relative to both language comprehension and reading comprehension, is needed.

REFERENCES

Aram, D. M. (1997). Hyperlexia: Reading without meaning in young children. *Topics in Language Disorders, 17*(3), 1–13.

Cohen, M. J., Hall, J., & Riccio, C. A. (1997). Neuropsychological profiles of children diagnosed as specific language impaired with and without hyperlexia. *Archives of Clinical Neuropsychology, 12,* 223–229.

Kupperman, P. (1997). Precocious reading skills may signal hyperlexia. *Boston University Child and Adolescent Behavior Letter, 13*(11), 1, 3.

Nation, K. (1999). Reading skills in hyperlexia: A developmental perspective. *Psychological Bulletin, 125,* 338–355.

Rispens, J., & Van Berckelaer, I. A. (1991). Hyperlexia: Definition and criteria. In R. Joshi (Ed.), *Written language disorders: Neuropsychology and cognition* (Vol. 2, pp. 143–163). Dordrecht, The Netherlands: Kluwer Academic.

Cynthia A. Riccio
Texas A&M University

HYPEROPIA

Hyperopia, better known as farsightedness, is defined as a condition in which refracting optics of the eye are too weak given the length of the eye such that images of distant objects are focused behind the retina. This occurs in a normal sized eye when the cornea and lens power are insufficient, or in an eye that is too short when the cornea and lens power are adequate (Bullimore & Gilmartin, 1997). In other words, hyperopia is caused by an imbalance between the refractive action and the size and shape of the eye.

Bullimore and Gilmartin (1997) have described hyperopia as a regular part of the developmental process in that hyperopia is present in most newborns. Over time the natural growth cycle of the eye reduces the magnitude of the disorder. However, in cases where eye growth is halted or delayed, hyperopia becomes an ailment instead of a developmental milestone. Bullimore and Gilmartin suggested that hyperopia waxes and wanes throughout the human life span and that prevalence is a function of age. Most everyone is born hyperopic, outgrows it by adolescence, and most likely relapses in old age. Unfortunately, there is little agreement regarding prevalence rates among children and adolescents, but at the extremes of the age range there seems to be more consensus. In fact, the American Optometric Association (AOA, 1997) stated that most infants delivered full term are mildly hyperopic, whereas premature and low-birthweight infants tend to be less hyperopic. In the 6- to 8-month age range, Ingram, Arnold, Dally, and Lucas (1990) reported that approximately 6–9% of infants have hyperopia to some degree. Further, Wang, Klein, Klein, and Moss (1994) studied almost 5,000 adults and discovered that hyperopia existed in 67% of participants aged 65 to 74 years and in only 22% of participants aged 43 to 54 years.

The AOA (1997) pointed out that there are no known gender differences in the prevalence of hyperopia. However, Crawford and Haamar (1949) and Post (1962) discovered ethnic differences in prevalence rates. They reported that Native Americans, African Americans, and Pacific Islanders are among the groups with the highest reported rates of hyperopia.

Hyperopia is most commonly measured and diagnosed by retinoscopy. Static retinoscopy (measurement of the accommodation of the eye when viewing a distant object) may also be accompanied by subjective refraction and autorefraction as diagnostic techniques (AOA, 1997).

Characteristics

1. Constant to intermittent blurred vision
2. Asthenopia
3. Red, teary eyes
4. Frequent blinking
5. Decreased binocularity
6. Difficulty reading
7. Amblyopia
8. Strabismus

The most common and least invasive treatment for hyperopia is the prescription of spectacles or contact lenses. Vision therapy may also be required in some cases because lens correction alone will not be sufficient. Several other treatment options such as the use of pharmaceuticals, habit and environment modification, and refractive surgery are available. Refractive surgery has recently gained much support among professionals and popularity among the public, but as Fundingsland and Sher (1997) pointed out there are many forms of refractive surgery with no one form recognized as superior. According to Fundingsland and Sher, corneal reshaping can be achieved through incisions (hexagonal keratotomy), burns (thermokeratoplasty), laser ablations (hyperopic photorefractive keratectomy or the Excimer laser technique), lamellar cuts (keratophakia and keratomileusis), and replacement of the posterior lens.

In an educational setting, children with hyperopia may require glasses or contact lenses. While in the past such aids have been a source of teasing, hyperopia is now so common that most children find glasses or contacts to be perfectly acceptable.

REFERENCES

American Optometric Association. (1997). *Optometric clinical practice guideline: Care of the patient with hyperopia—reference guide for clinicians.* St. Louis, MO: Author.

Bullimore, M. A., & Gilmartin, B. (1997). Hyperopia and presbyopia: Etiology and epidemiology. In N. A. Sher (Ed.), *Surgery for hyperopia and presbyopia* (pp. 3–10). Baltimore: Williams & Wilkins.

Crawford, H. E., & Haamar, G. E. (1949). Racial analysis of ocular deformities in schools of Hawaii. *Hawaii Medical Journal, 9,* 90–93.

Fundlingsland, B., & Sher, N. A. (1997). Hyperopia and presbyopia: Etiology and epidemiology. In N. A. Sher (Ed.), *Surgery for hyperopia and presbyopia* (pp. 11–20). Baltimore: Williams & Wilkins.

Ingram, R., Arnold, P., Dally, S., & Lucas, J. (1990). The results of a randomized trial of treating abnormal hypermetropia from the age of 6 months. *British Journal of Ophthalmology, 74,* 158–159.

Post, R. H. (1962). Population differences in visual acuity: Review with speculative notes on selection relaxation. *Eugenics Quarterly, 9,* 189–192.

Wang, Q., Klein, B. E. K., Klein, R., & Moss, S. E. (1994). Refractive status in the Beaver Dam eye study. *Investigative Ophthalmology and Visual Science, 35,* 4344–4337.

Tracy A. Muenz
Alliant University

HYPERSOMNIA, PRIMARY

Primary hypersomnia is a disorder characterized by excessive daytime sleepiness or extremely long periods of nighttime sleep (greater than 10 hours) on a regular basis. In the recurrent form of this disorder known as Kleine-Levin syndrome, symptoms occur for at least three days at a time and reoccur several times per year for two or more years (American Psychiatric Association [APA], 1994).

The true prevalence of hypersomnia is unknown, as many who suffer from this disorder perceive their sleepiness as normal and never seek treatment. Five to ten percent of patients who seek help at sleep disorder clinics are diagnosed with primary hypersomnia, whereas in the general adult population .5–5.0% report daytime sleepiness (APA, 1994). Kleine-Levin syndrome is exceedingly rare but affects males more often than females and generally begins in adolescence (National Organization for Rare Disorders [NORD], 1997).

Characteristics

1. Excessive sleepiness for a period of one month or more (if recurrent, sleepiness may last only three days but returns several times per year
2. Long periods of sleep (10 to 20 hr)
3. Inability to remain awake during the day, especially in situations where stimulation is lacking (in class, when driving, while watching television)

In individuals with Kleine-Levin syndrome, the sleep episodes are associated with a lack of inhibition, hypersexuality, excessive eating, irritability, depression, and confusion (NORD, 1997). In diagnosing primary hypersomnia, it is important to determine whether the symptoms are caused by another disorder, such as depression or bipolar disorder, by another medical condition, by substance abuse, or by the side effects of prescribed medication (APA, 1994). Consultation with a sleep disorders specialist for assessment is often necessary (Talk About Sleep, 2000).

Treatment for the symptoms of primary hypersomnia may involve the use of stimulant medications such as methylphenidate, modafinil, or pemoline (Talk About Sleep, 2000) during periods when excessive sleepiness occurs. In some cases individuals with Kleine-Levin syndrome have responded to treatment with the anticonvulsant drug phenytoin, with lithium, or with antidepressant medication (NORD, 1997). During episodes of hypersomnia, affected individuals should not be permitted to drive or operate machinery.

Adolescents and children with primary hypersomnia are likely to need special education services under the Other Health Impairment handicapping condition. During symptomatic periods, waking in time for school and remaining awake in class is difficult. In students suffering from Kleine-Levin syndrome, school attendance may not be possible while symptoms persist. Modifications to students' class schedules and at-home study arrangements may be necessary to help those with hypersomnia maintain their academic progress.

The cause of hypersomnia is not known, but research is ongoing to discover the cause and to improve treatment. Some researchers believe that Kleine-Levin syndrome has a genetic basis and may be related to a malfunction in the hypothalamus (NORD, 1997). In most cases, symptoms of Kleine-Levin syndrome eventually dissipate by middle age (APA, 1994).

REFERENCES

American Psychiatric Association. (1994). *Diagnostic and statistical manual of mental disorders* (4th ed.). Washington, DC: Author.

National Organization for Rare Disorders. (1997). Kleine-Levin syndrome. Retrieved from http://www.rarediseases.org

Talk About Sleep. (2000). An introduction to hypersomnia. Retrieved from http://www.talkaboutsleep.com/disorders/hypersomnia/hypersomnia_index.htm

Nancy K. Scammacca
University of Texas at Austin

HYPERTELORISM

Hypertelorism refers to the physical finding of wide separation of the eyes. This diagnosis is made by measuring the inner canthal distance (ICD), which is the space between the junctions of the eyelids along either side of the bridge of the nose. When ICD equals or exceeds three standard deviations above normal for the child's age, one can be confident of the diagnosis. To confirm their clinical impression, clinicians consult genetics textbooks, which contain graphs of various facial measurements, including ICD. Hypertelorism is often associated with other eye abnormalities. The most common of these are exotropia (external deviation of the eye) and optic atrophy (underdevelopment of the optic nerve).

Hypertelorism is a frequent feature of nearly 50 syndromes and genetic disorders. It is occasionally seen in about 20 more. It can be a minor morphologic variation, such as a familiar trait. Finally, hypertelorism may be a developmental abnormality secondary to an underlying brain anomaly or the persistence of a midline cleft, which separates rapidly growing blocks of tissue that form an embryo's face and head. Physicians caring for children affected with hypertelorism should search for related findings because their presence (or absence) certainly has prognostic significance.

REFERENCES

Jones, K. (1997). *Smith's recognizable patterns of human malformations* (5th ed.). Philadelphia: W. B. Saunders.

Olitsk, S. E., & Nelson, L. B. (2000). Orbital abnormalities. In R. E. Behrman, R. M. Kleigman, & H. B. Jenson (Eds.), *Nelson's textbook of pediatrics* (16th ed., p. 1934). Philadelphia: W. B. Saunders.

Barry H. Davison
Ennis, Texas

Joan W. Mayfield
Baylor Pediatric Specialty Services
Dallas, Texas

HYPERTHYROIDISM

Hyperthyroidism, also known as thyrotoxicosis, is a metabolic imbalance caused by an overproduction of thyroid hormone. The overproduction of thyroid hormone causes an overall increase in the organism's metabolic rate, which is responsible for a host of medical problems (St. Germain, 2000). Hyperthyroidism is classified as a syndrome, and diagnosis is made based on the presence of symptoms. Two medical conditions lead to the development of hyperthyroidism. In one condition, the thyroid produces too much thyroid hormone. This can occur as a result of tumors of the thyroid gland, pituitary gland, ovaries, or testes; inflammation of the thyroid; ingestion of too much iodine; and Grave's disease (in which the immune system attacks the thyroid). In the second cause, the thyroid gland becomes damaged and leaks thyroid hormone (St. Germain, 2000).

Hyperthyroidism occurs in 1:1,000 people or about 2.5 million Americans each year. Several causative conditions are more prevalent in women, including postpartum thyroiditis and Grave's disease, leading to a greater female than male incidence rate. Grave's disease accounts for about 85% of the cases of hyperthyroidism and is much more prevalent among women, especially age 20 to 50 years. There also appears to be an increased incidence among individuals with Down syndrome.

Characteristics

1. Increased appetite with concurrent weight loss. Children and adolescents may be unusually tall and thin (Vaughan, McKay, & Behrman, 1979).
2. Changes in mood and thinking skills, including increased nervousness, restlessness, depression, fatigue, memory, and concentration problems that may impact school or job performance (Vaughan et al., 1979).
3. Heat intolerance and increased sweating.
4. Increased metabolism leading to muscle cramping, irregular heartbeat, chest pains, and perhaps heart attack (St. Germain, 2000).
6. Frequent bowel movements related to overactivity of the intestines (St. Germain, 2000).
7. Menstrual irregularities.
8. The development of goiters or enlargements of the thyroid gland (St. Germain, 2000).

The treatment of hyperthyroidism includes the use of medicine called beta-blockers, such as Inderol, to block the effect of too much thyroid hormone. This treatment is used to deter the effects of overproduction of thyroid on the heart and nervous system (St. Germain, 2000). Beta-blockers are usually the only intervention needed when there is a leakage and the condition tends to be temporary. In cases of overproduction, three types of treatments are available, including anthithyroid drug therapy (Porpylthiouracil or Methimazole) to decrease the production of thyroid hormone; use of radioiodine, which often results in hypothyroidism that persists; and surgical removal of the thyroid gland (St. Germain, 2000). Treatment of Grave's disease tends to result in short-term remediation of the symptoms, and reoccurrence is common. In children, drug therapy lasting up to 36 months is effective for permanent remediation of symptoms in 75% of the children (Vaughan et al., 1979).

Hyperthyroidism occurs in children but is more prevalent among adults. If the symptoms are significant enough to interfere with a child's academic or social functioning, it will likely be labeled under Other Health Impairment according to criteria from the Individuals with Disabilities Education Act. Down syndrome children with hyperthyroidism may receive services under the Mental Disability category or Multiple Disability category. However, hyperthyroidism is a treatable disorder that should not by itself make a child eligible for special education services.

The symptoms of hyperthyroidism tend to develop slowly and are generally not painful. As a result, there may be a lag in diagnosis. The medical field may improve diagnosis so that treatment can be initiated earlier in the course of the syndrome. It is a treatable condition, but treatments may be improved in the future. For example, radioactive iodine therapy is effective, but when using this treatment, the individual must avoid being around others, especially children. In addition, radioactive iodine therapy may induce hypothyroidism, which must then be corrected by introducing natural thyroid hormone. Surgical removal of the thyroid gland also causes hypothyroidism, which must be treated.

REFERENCES

St. Germain, D. (2000). All about hyperthyroidism. Retrieved from http://www.drkoop.com/dyncon/article.asp?id=5894

Vaughan, V. C., McKay, R. J., & Behrman, R. E. (1979). In W. E. Nelson (Ed.), *Nelson textbook of pediatrics* (11th ed., pp. 1164–1167). Philadelphia: W. B. Saunders.

Dalene M. McCloskey
University of Northern Colorado

HYPERTONIA-RD

Hypertonia is increased tension of the muscles that can make movement difficult. It can also be defined as resistance to passive movement that is not velocity dependent (Pediatric Services, n.d.). Hypertonia usually occurs in definite patterns of flexion or extension (Pedretti & Zoltan, 1990). Difficulties are most predominant in the flexor patterns for the upper extremities and in the extensor patterns of the lower extremities.

There are two main types of hypertonia—rigidity and spasticity—but both can be present in the same individual. Specifically, spasticity is an increase in resistance to sudden passive movement that is velocity dependent. It involves an imbalance between the agonist and antagonist muscle groups. The severity of spasticity is directly related to the speed of the stretch placed on the muscle. In contrast, rigidity is increased muscle tone in both agonist and antagonist muscles simultaneously (Pedretti & Zoltan, 1990). Hypertonia is the opposite of hypotonia.

Hypertonia is commonly associated with other medical disorders such as cerebral palsy (CP), multiple sclerosis (MS), amyotrophic lateral sclerosis (ALS), spina bifida, Parkinson's disease, and head injury. Although identification of the presence of hypertonia is not difficult, determination of the actual cause is significantly more problematic. Children with hypertonia may have difficulty with both fine and gross motor movements and with motor coordination depending on the severity of the condition. Prolonged hypertonicity with spasticity can lead to shortening of the muscles and subsequent contracture and deformity, resulting in severely decreased mobility.

It is not possible to estimate the prevalence of hypertonia because it is not a specific disease, and records do not necessarily specify the frequency of particular symptoms.

Characteristics

1. Resistance to passive movement that is not dependent on the velocity of the movement
2. Spasticity or rigidity of muscles

Following the identification of the presence of hypertonia, a treatment program can be developed. Although treatment will not cure the symptoms, it will aid in the prevention of future complications due to the condition. Treatment may also serve to facilitate the child's most appropriate development and teach compensatory skills. Treatment programs incorporate instruction to the child and caregivers in positioning and movement strategies. Medical and surgical interventions and drug treatments that may serve to decrease muscle tone are available.

Collaboration among parents, educators, and medical professionals is crucial to enable the most positive outcome for the child with hypertonia. Children with hypertonia are often identified at an early age through primary care medical settings. It is important for parents to be placed in contact with the local school district or state agencies that provide early intervention services for children ages 0–3 years.

Infants with hypertonia may be eligible for special education services under the provisions of Public Law 99–457 and its reauthorization in 1991 as Public Law 102–119, which mandates services for children from birth to age 3. Eligibility is dependent on associated disabilities rather than on the presence of hypertonia in and of itself. If eligible, an Individual Family Service Plan (IFSP) would be developed to identify goals and services as mandated by Part C of the Individuals with Disabilities Education Act. Preschool and elementary school children may remain eligible to receive services provided that the child falls into one of the specific eligibility classifications and meets the specific state requirements for service provision. Although a child may not be directly eligible to receive services due to the presence of hypertonia, per se, eligibility may be based on associated conditions or disorders. Specific services will be determined on an individualized basis. If educationally necessary, students with hypertonia may receive the related services of occupational, physical, and speech therapies.

The prognosis for children with hypertonia varies depending on several factors, including the root cause of the condition, the severity of the symptoms, and the provision of appropriate early interventions.

REFERENCES

Pediatric Services. (n.d.). Understanding the lingo. Retrieved from http://www.pediatricservices.com

Pedretti, L. W., & Zoltan, B. (1990). *Occupational therapy: Practice skills for physical dysfunction* (3rd ed.). St. Louis, MO: Mosby.

Shelley L. F. Pelletier
Susan Sage
Dysart Unified School District
El Mirage, Arizona

See also Myopathy, Congenital, Batten Turner Type

HYPOCHONDROPLASIA

Hypochondroplasia is a rare, hereditary type of short-limbed dwarfism. Originally described in 1913, this disorder has many similarities to achondroplasia, with which it is, and has been, often confused. Physical findings in hypochondroplasia include short stature, mildly shortened extremities, malformed vertebrae of the lower spine, and nearly normal appearance of the face and head. This last characteristic helps to distinguish hypochondroplasia from achondroplasia.

Hypochondroplasia is about one twelfth as common as achondroplasia, making its incidence 1 in 180,000 births. Like achondroplasia, it has an autosomal dominant mode of inheritance. Advanced paternal age is associated with "new" cases that appear to be fresh mutations. The abnormal gene is located on Chromosome 4, at the same site as the gene for achondroplasia. Therefore, hypochondroplasia may just represent a slightly different and clinically milder form of the mutated achondroplasia gene.

Characteristics

1. Mean birth length and weight within the low normal range
2. Growth deficiency usually apparent by age 3; adult height ranging from 46.5 to 60 inches
3. Mild, symmetric shortening of the extremities
4. Stubby hands, feet, fingers, and toes
5. Outward bowing of the legs with genu varum (bowleg deformity of the knee) that becomes more pronounced when the child starts to walk.
6. 9–25% incidence of mental retardation (IQ 50–80); mental deficiency rare in achondroplasia
7. Normal-looking head and face, although macrocephaly (abnormally large head) possible in infancy

Treatment for this disorder addresses the orthopedic problems. Although genu varum can improve during childhood, it may need surgical straightening. Exercise causes mild aching in the knees, ankles, and elbows in children. These pains usually intensify in adults, who also experience low back discomfort. Oral analgesics (acetaminophen and ibuprofen) can provide symptomatic relief for suffering patients.

Like children with achondroplasia, children with hypochondroplasia may benefit from modifications in the classroom environment, such as providing appropriate-sized desks and chairs. Evaluation and treatment by occupational and physical therapists also may be beneficial. These children should be treated in an age-appropriate manner and not according to their short statures. Because of the incidence of mental retardation in children with hypochondroplasia, educational modifications under the umbrella of special education are needed to facilitate learning. The extent of modifications is contingent on the individual child's intellectual functioning and is based on educational need.

Because of the relatively high occurrence of mental retardation in hypochondroplasia, physicians caring for affected children should be cautious when discussing their prognoses. Until formal psychological testing can be done, optimism about their outlook appears ill advised. On the other hand, early delays in psychomotor development suggest that cognitive impairment is likely.

For more information and parent support, please contact Little People of America, Inc., PO Box 745, Lubbock, TX 79408, (888) 572-2001.

REFERENCES

Gandy, A. Hypochondroplasia. *Disease Database.* Retrieved from http://www.pedianet.com/news/illness/disease/files/hypochon.htm

Horton, W. A., & Hecht, J. T. (2000). Disorders involving transmembrane receptors. In R. E. Behrman, R. M. Kleigman, & H. B. Jenson (Eds.), *Nelson's textbook of pediatrics* (16th ed., p. 2123). Philadelphia: W. B. Saunders.

National Organization for Rare Disorders, Inc. (1994). Hypochondroplasia. Retrieved from http://www.stepstn.com/cgi-win/nord.exe?proc=GetDocument&rectype=0&recnum=591

Pediatric Database (PEDBASE). (1997, November 2). Hypochondroplasia. Retrieved from http://www.icondata.com/health/pedbase/files/HYPOCHON.HTM

Jones, K. (1997). *Smith's recognizable patterns of human malformations* (5th ed.). Philadelphia: W. B. Saunders.

Barry H. Davison
Ennis, Texas

Joan W. Mayfield
Baylor Pediatric Specialty Services
Dallas, Texas

HYPOGLYCEMIA

Hypoglycemia is a clinical syndrome that results from an imbalance between glucose production and glucose utilization such that glucose levels in the bloodstream are depleted faster than they are replaced. Hypoglycemia is defined by a blood glucose concentration less than 2.2 mmol/L (Gandy, 1994). Hypoglycemia deprives the brain and nervous tissue of their primary source of energy and, as a result, may cause central nervous system dysfunction. Causes of hypoglycemia are highly varied and include numerous metabolic and endocrine disorders. Recent reviews have identified as many as 12 distinct hypoglycemic disorders (see Lteif & Shwenk, 1999) and over 30 causes of hypoglycemia (see Schwartz, 1997).

Incidence of hypoglycemia in infants is estimated at 4.4 per 1,000 live births and is more common among infants of low birth weight (15.6:1,000; Gandy, 1994). Incidence in older children is 2–3 per 1,000 (Gandy, 1994). Onset can occur at any age.

Characteristics

1. In newborn infants, symptoms of hypoglycemia are nonspecific and can include the following: hypotonia, irritability, feeding difficulties, syanosis, tachypnea, apnea, hypothermia, seizures, lethargy, and coma.
2. Older infants and children exhibit nonspecific signs consistent with autonomic nervous system arousal including sweating, hunger, tingling, heart pounding, nervousness or anxiety, and being shaky or tremulous.
3. If hypoglycemia is not treated, neuroglycopenic symptoms will emerge signaling brain glucose deprivation. These symptoms include weakness, headache, confusion, fatigue, blurred vision, dizziness, slurred speech, abnormal behavior, amnesia, seizures, and coma.
4. In addition to symptoms consistent with hypoglycemia, a low plasma-glucose concentration is present (less than 2.2 mmol/L).
5. Symptoms resolve when plasma glucose level is restored to normal levels.

Treatment of hypoglycemia is a two-step process. First, acute symptoms are treated by normalizing blood glucose concentrations through food intake, intravenous glucose infusion, or subcutaneous injection of glucagon. The next phase of treatment involves diagnosing and correcting the underlying disorder that caused the hypoglycemia. Depending on the cause, treatment may involve medication, hormone replacement therapy, or surgery (Schwartz, 1997).

The long-term effects of hypoglycemia are highly varied and depend on timing, duration, and severity of the hypoglycemic episodes. Hypoglycemia can result in structural damage or death to nerve cells. In infants who experience hypoglycemia, neurological impairment can range from none to severe. Mental retardation can occur when hypoglycemia is severe, recurrent, and prolonged. Because outcomes may include a broad range of dysfunction, special education requirements will correspondingly vary.

Infants with asymptomatic hypoglycemia without convulsions have been shown to have a better prognosis than infants who experience symptomatic hypoglycemia with convulsions (Schwartz, 1997). Frequency of hypoglycemic episodes also appears to be an important factor in determining outcomes. In a sample of preterm neonates, those experiencing frequent moderate hypoglycemia were found to have poorer neuropsychological outcomes than were those experiencing more severe but less frequent episodes (Lteif & Schwenk, 1999).

REFERENCES

Gandy, A. (1994). Hypoglycemia. *Pediatric Database.* Retrieved from http://www.icondata.com/health/pedbase/files/hypoglyc.htm

Lteif, A. N., & Schwenk, W. F. (1999). Hypoglycemia in infants and children. *Endocrinology and Metabolism Clinics of North America, 28,* 619–646.

Schwartz, R. P. (1997). Hypoglycemia in infancy and childhood. *Indian Journal of Pediatrics, 64,* 43–55.

Heidi A. McCallister
University of Texas at Austin

HYPOHIDROTIC ECTODERMAL DYSPLASIA

Hypohidrotic ectodermal dysplasia (HED) is one of a diverse group of disorders that affect the skin and skin derivatives (teeth, hair, nails, sweat glands, and sebaceous glands). Disturbances in other organ systems are common in these diseases. The hallmarks of HED are a deficiency or complete absence of sweat glands, malformed or missing teeth, and a generalized decrease in body hair.

HED is hereditary. The most common form, which is found exclusively in males, is transmitted in an X-linked recessive manner. Subtle abnormalities are usually present in carrier females. There is another clinically indistinguishable variant of HED, in which both parents are normal and their male and female offsprings are equally affected. The mode of inheritance for this subset appears to be autosomal recessive. Both types of the disorder are rare. Fewer than 150 cases of HED have been reported since its original description in 1848.

Characteristics

1. Thin skin with decreased pigmentation; considerable wrinkling around the eyes with hyperpigmentation; eczema
2. Fine, dry, light-colored hair that is sparse; complete baldness possible
3. Absent or markedly diminished number of sweat glands, which makes affected children prone to hyperthermia when they are exposed to warm environmental temperatures
4. Deficiency of mucous glands in the mouth, nose, trachea, and bronchi; chronic, foul nasal discharge, ear infections, and pneumonia possible
5. Underdeveloped and missing teeth; cone-shaped front teeth

6. Small nose; flat nasal bridge; prominent forehead; prominent bony ridge above the eyes; thick, protruding lips; large, low-set ears
7. Occasionally hoarse voice, absence of tears, obstruction of the tear duct, absence of a breast or nipple, cataracts, conductive hearing loss, varying degrees of nail malformation, and asthma

Treatment of HED requires protecting patients from heat exposure. Hyperthermia secondary to high ambient temperature not only is life-threatening but also can cause brain injury resulting in mental retardation. Dental referral is indicated early. Prostheses are provided for cosmetic reasons and to ensure that the child is able to chew food adequately. If tear glands are absent, artificial tears may be needed to prevent corneal damage. Upper and lower respiratory infections are managed with appropriate antibiotic therapy. Finally, a wig can be helpful in cases of marked hair loss.

There is no research to indicate the need for special education support services in the classroom. However, providing the child's teacher with information about HED is important to the safety of the child in the prevention of heat exposure.

The prognosis for HED is guarded. Approximately 30% of males with this disorder die before their second birthday, either from hyperthermic events or overwhelming respiratory infections.

In families where there is a concern about having a baby with HED, 90% of women carrying the defective gene can be identified by dental examination and a simple test measuring sweat gland activity. Prenatal testing is also available for detecting affected fetuses during the first trimester of pregnancy.

For more information, please contact National Foundation for Ectodermal Dysplasias, 410 East Main Street, PO Box 114, Mascoutah, IL 62258-0114; (618) 566-2020: e-mail: nfedddd1@aol.com; http://www.nfed.org.

REFERENCES

Darmstadt, G. L. (2000). Ectodermal dysplasias. In R. E. Behrman, R. M. Kleigman, & H. B. Jenson (Eds.), *Nelson's textbook of pediatrics* (16th ed., pp. 1974–1975). Philadelphia: W. B. Saunders.

Gandy, A. Hypohidrotic (anhidrotic) ectodermal dysplasis. *Disease Database.* Retrieved from http://www.pedianet.com/news/illness/disease/files/hypohidr/htm

Hypohidrotic (anhidrotic) ectodermal dysplasia. (1998, July 8). *Pediatric Database (PEDBASE).* Retrieved from http://www.icondata.com/pedbase/files/HYPOHIDR.HTM

Hypohidrotic ectodermal dysplasia. (1998). National Organization for Rare Disorders, Inc. (NORD). Retrieved from http://www.rarediseases.org

Jones, K. (1997). *Smith's recognizable patterns of human malformations* (5th ed.). Philadelphia: W. B. Saunders.

Barry H. Davison
Ennis, Texas

Joan W. Mayfield
Baylor Pediatric Specialty Services
Dallas, Texas

See also Ectodermal Dysplasia

HYPOPHOSPHATASIA

Hypophosphatasia is an uncommon disorder of bone and cartilage formation. Its salient features include poor mineralization of the skull, short ribs resulting in an underdeveloped thorax and respiratory insufficiency, and poorly formed, fragile bones. A severe deficiency of the enzyme alkaline phosphatase is present in tissue and bone.

Hypophosphatasia is hereditary and conforms to an autosomal recessive mode of transmission. There are four clinically distinct forms of the disease. Mutations of the abnormal gene are considered to be responsible for these variations. The defect has been traced to Chromosome 1. The incidence of hypophosphatasia is unknown, but since the disorder was first recognized in 1948, many cases of the uniformly lethal perinatal subset have been reported.

Characteristics

1. Short-limbed dwarfism
2. Generalized poor mineralization of bone
3. Poorly formed, globular skull
4. Bowed lower extremities
5. Short ribs with multiple fractures
6. Small thoracic cage
7. Occasionally polyhydramnios (excessive amount of amniotic fluid) and blue sclerae (the normally white part of the eyeball)

No available references for this abnormality contain therapeutic recommendations. This lack of information regarding treatment could be explained by the dismal outlook for the perinatal and infantile variants of hypophosphatasia.

There is no research to indicate cognitive dysfunction or the need for special education services.

Prognosis for hypophosphatasia depends on the clinical form affecting the child. In the perinatal group, death usually occurs in early infancy, secondary to respiratory insufficiency. In those patients who survive, poor growth, diminished muscle tone, seizures, irritability, anemia, derangements of calcium metabolism, and calcification of kidney tissue are common findings. Children with the infantile type usually develop growth failure, rickets-like skeletal changes, and increased intracranial pressure by 6 months of age. Fifty percent die during the first year. There is a milder form in children that usually presents after 6 months of age. It is characterized by premature loss of the baby teeth, ricket-like skeletal pathology, and premature fusion of the cranial sutures. Finally, the adult variant occurs later in life and therefore carries the most favorable outlook. It manifests as premature loss of teeth and recurring bone fractures.

Prenatal diagnosis of hypophosphatasia is currently available from analysis of the alkaline phosphatase content in membranes surrounding the fetus. Findings can be obtained as early as the 10th to 12th week of pregnancy. However, results require interpretation based on the history and clinical course of the disorder in each individual family.

For more information, please contact CLIMB (Children Living with Inherited Metabolic Diseases), The Quadrangle, Crewe Hall, Weston Road, Crewe, Cheshire, CW1-6UR, United Kingdom; (127) 0 2-50221; http://www.CLIMB.org.uk.

REFERENCES

Jones, K. (1997). *Smith's recognizable patterns of human malformations* (5th ed.). Philadelphia: W. B. Saunders.

National Organization for Rare Disorders, Inc. (1966). Hypophosphatasia. Retrieved from http://www.rarediseases.org

Barry H. Davison
Ennis, Texas

Joan W. Mayfield
Baylor Pediatric Specialty Services
Dallas, Texas

HYPOPLASTIC LEFT HEART SYNDROME

Hypoplastic left heart syndrome (HLHS) describes a group of complex congenital heart defects that occur in newborns. HLHS is characterized by the underdevelopment of the left atrium and ventricle of the heart. Additionally, the valve that connects these two chambers (the mitral orifice) and the aortic valve are narrowed or closed. The defects on the left side put unusual strain on the right side of the heart, causing enlargement of the chambers and the vessels on this side. When the baby is born, she or he may appear normal, but within a few days the baby will develop a bluish color to the skin (cyanosis and hypoperfusion). The infant will soon go into shock, and emergency surgery is usually required. Problems in cognition are usually the result of neurological complications associated with hypoperfusion of the brain and other structures of the central nervous system (CNS).

The cause of HLHS is unknown, and the prevalence rate is estimated to be somewhere between 0.16 and 0.36 in 1,000 live births.

Characteristics

1. Underdevelopment of the left side of the heart resulting in impaired oxygenated blood flow to the rest of the body, including the brain
2. Difficulty breathing, rales (high-pitched noise while inhaling), and a grayish blue color to the skin occurring within the first 48 hr of life
3. Hepatomegaly (an enlarged liver) in some infants
4. Symptoms such as poor feeding habits, vomiting, lethargy, and shock
5. CNS abnormalities and cognitive sequelae

Before surgical therapies were made available, mortality rates reached 100% in most cases. However, with the advent of heart transplants and multistage operations, survival rates have reached 90% or better. Staged palliation involves three operations, the first of which is the Norwood operation. The second is the bidirectional Glenn operation, and the Fontan operation is the final procedure. The Norwood is performed shortly after birth and converts the right ventricle into the main or systemic ventricle. The second procedure, performed around 6 months of age, diverts one half of the blood returning from the body to the lungs. In the Fontan procedure, all of the blood returning from the body is diverted into the lungs. This final procedure is performed around 2 years of age.

Special education issues will be nonexistent in some children because once the corrective surgeries are performed, development proceeds normally with few residual effects. In a few cases, neurological impairment may be seen, and special education and labeling (e.g., Other Health Impairment) should be commensurate with degree of impairment.

Medical intervention has transformed a once fatal disorder into a syndrome with a positive prognosis. Instances will occur in which undiagnosed children will not survive and other children will succumb to complications associated with the surgical interventions. As etiology is unknown, future research has much of its focus on designing a method of detection. Currently, this deformity of the heart is not detectable in utero, and only after life-threatening manifestations is the disorder diagnosable.

REFERENCES

Barber, G. (1998). Hypoplastic left heart syndrome. In A. Garson, Jr., J. T. Bricker, D. J. Fisher, & S. R. Neish (Eds.), *Science and practice of pediatric cardiology* (pp. 1625–1645). Baltimore: Williams & Wilkins.

Freedom, R. M., & Benson, L. N. (1995). Hypoplastic left heart syndrome. In H. D. Allen, H. D. Gutgesell, E. B. Clark, & D. J. Driscoll (Eds.), *Moss and Adams heart disease in infants, children, and adolescents* (pp. 1133–1153). Philadelphia: Lippincott Williams & Wilkins.

Kimberly M. Estep
University of Houston–Clear Lake

HYPOTHYROIDISM

Hypothyroidism results from depletion in the concentration of thyroid hormone in the body. Thyroid hormone is released by the thyroid gland situated at the base of the neck. This important hormone is fundamental for normal metabolic rates in adults and is essential for growth and maturation in children. Depletion of thyroid hormone may occur as a result of treatment for *hyperthyroidism,* damage to the thyroid gland (i.e., primary hypothyroidism), a deficiency of iodine in the diet, or by a disorder of the pituitary gland (i.e., secondary hypothyroidism). There are three major types of hypothyroidism, and these include congenital, juvenile, and adult (Noble, Leyland, & Clark, 2000; Price & Wilson, 1997).

Congenital hypothyroidism (cretinism) is noticeable at birth and is often the result of a developmental defect (Price & Wilson, 1997). Most infants with this disorder have a defective thyroid gland or no gland at all. The infant usually has prolonged jaundice and a hoarse cry. Other noteworthy physical abnormalities include a large tongue that protrudes from the mouth and an umbilical hernia. Difficulty with feeding, excessive sleep, lethargy, and mental retardation are common (Kunz & Finkel, 1987; Price & Wilson, 1997). These infants fail to meet normal developmental milestones, and their teeth are often underdeveloped. Congenital hypothyroidism is incurable. However, immediate medical treatment at birth can circumvent mental retardation and growth failure (Beckwith & Tucker, 1988; Clayman, 1989; Dallas, 2000; Price & Wilson, 1997). Permanent intellectual deficits are typical if the condition is left untreated during the first 30 months of life (Beckwith & Tucker, 1988).

Although the age of onset differentiates juvenile from adult hypothyroidism, both types share common characteristics. Juvenile hypothyroidism becomes evident around 1 or 2 years of age, whereas adult hypothyroidism (myxedema) develops during adulthood. Juveniles and adults with hypothyroidism typically present with slowing of intellectual and motor activity, cold intolerance, decreased sweating, facial puffiness, weight gain, and fatigue (Price & Wilson, 1997). Frequently, symptoms of clinical depression are also reported (Beckwith & Tucker, 1988).

About 13 million Americans have a thyroid disorder, and more than half go undiagnosed because onset is typically gradual. Women suffer from the disorder seven times more than men, and the frequency of occurrence increases with age. Indeed, adult onset is usually seen among elderly women. The disorder remains undetected in many middle-aged women because several symptoms, including fatigue, mood swings, sleep disturbances, and depression, resemble signs of menopause (Portyansky, 1999). Hypothyroidism rarely occurs in newborns (Kunz & Finkel, 1987), affecting only about 1 in every 4,000 infants (Dallas, 2000). The disorder occurs more frequently in children with Down syndrome than in the general population. However, these children often go untreated because the two disorders share common characteristics (e.g., weight gain, poor growth, and dull affect). For this reason, physicians recommend that persons with Down syndrome be routinely screened for hypothyroidism (Noble et al., 2000).

Characteristics

Congenital

1. Persistent jaundice and hoarse cry
2. Constipation, somnolence, and feeding problems
3. Short stature and coarse features
4. Protruding tongue; broad, flat nose; widely spaced eyes; and sparse hair
5. Dry skin, protuberant abdomen, and umbilical hernia
6. Hearing impairment

Juvenile and Adult

1. Fatigue and hoarseness
2. Cold intolerance and decreased sweating
3. Cool, dry skin and facial puffiness
4. Slow movements
5. Slowing of intellectual and motor activity
6. Slow relaxation of deep tendon reflexes
7. Impaired recent memory and difficulty in concentrating
8. Weight gain
9. Major depressive symptomology

Treatment for all types of hypothyroidism involves replacement therapy with the artificial thyroid hormone thyroxine (Clayman, 1989). Infants and children with hypothyroidism should take thyroid hormone as soon as possible in order to avoid irreversible damage to their nervous systems including retarded growth, delayed sexual maturity, and inhibited normal brain development (Clayman, 1989; Kunz & Finkel, 1987). Adults should feel better a few days after beginning treatment, and they should be back to normal within a few days. Biochemical tests showing either elevated (primary hypothyroidism) or lowered (secondary hypothyroidism) thyroid-stimulating hormone levels and reduced thyroxine (T4) levels make diagnosis easy (Portyansky, 1999; Price & Wilson, 1997).

The prognosis for infants who do not receive treatment is poor. Left untreated, infants will suffer irreversible brain damage and growth failure. Prognosis is good for infants who are diagnosed early, with most of the effects of hypothyroidism being reversible. Indeed, infants who are treated for hypothyroidism within the first months after birth are usually of average intelligence and grow at a normal rate.

Researchers recommend screening for congenital hypothyroidism by measuring the thyroid hormone (T4) with a blood spot test. Since the implementation of screening procedures and early childhood medical intervention, mental retardation and growth failure rarely occur (Dallas, 2000). Without early intervention, however, these children will require special education services in school and will need constant care and supervision into adulthood.

REFERENCES

Beckwith, B. E., & Tucker, D. M. (1988). Thyroid disorders. In R. E. Tarter, D. H. Van Thiel, & K. L. Edwards (Eds.), *Medical neuropsychology: The impact of disease on behavior* (pp. 197–221). New York: Plenum Press.

Clayman, C. B. (1989). *The American Medical Association home medical encyclopedia.* New York: Random House.

Dallas, J. S. (2000). Congenital hypothyroidism. The Thyroid Society. Retrieved September 16, 2000, from http://www.the-thyroid-society.org/med_letter2.html

Kunz, J. R. M., & Finkel, A. J. (1987). *The American Medical Association family medical guide.* New York: Random House.

Noble, S. E., Leyland, C. A., & Clark, C. E. (2000). School based screening for hypothyroidism in Down's syndrome by dried blood spot TSH measurement. *Archives of Disease in Childhood, 82,* 27–32.

Portyansky, E. (1999). Hard-to-diagnose subclinical hypothyroidism often undertreated. *Drug Topics, 143,* 29–31.

Price, S. A., & Wilson, L. M. (1997). *Pathophysiology clinical concepts of disease processes.* St. Louis, MO: Library of Congress.

Mellisa Beckham
Kerry S. Lassiter
The Citadel

See also Cretinism

HYPOTONIA

Hypotonia involves decreased tension of the fine muscles, making upright postures difficult to hold and independent movement difficult to produce (Pediatric Services, n.d.). It is also referred to as decreased muscle tone, flaccidity, or floppiness. Hypotonia is the opposite of hypertonia. Hypotonia is commonly associated with multiple genetic, metabolic, cerebral, spinal, or muscular disorders including muscular dystrophy, myasthenic gravis, Down syndrome, meningitis, and encephalitis. Hypotonia can also be caused by injury or trauma. Although identification of the presence of hypotonia is not difficult, determination of the actual cause of the symptom is more problematic.

Obviously, children with hypotonia are at risk for developmental delays in motor skills, poor reflexes, and limited sense of balance. Moreover, children with hypotonia are more likely to suffer from dislocations of joints, such as the hip, jaw, shoulders, and neck due to the inadequate support from the muscles to hold the joints together. Additionally, skeletal deformities are more common in children with hypotonia due to their tendency to assume abnormal positions (i.e., "W" sitting and sleeping prone in a frog-like position). Finally, other domains of functioning may be affected by hypotonia, including overall development and cognitive skill development, as the child may not be able to benefit from exploration of the environment or the child may have delayed development of language skills due to decreased muscle tone in the face and mouth.

It is difficult to estimate the actual prevalence of hypotonia, as it is not a specific disease, and records do not specify the frequency of particular symptoms.

Characteristics

1. Low tone, floppy, rag-doll appearance
2. Extreme flexibility, range of motion beyond normal
3. Delayed motor skills
4. Shallow breathing
5. Limited gag reflex, open mouth, protruding tongue
6. Abnormal posture (may cause skeletal deformities)
7. Unable to sustain movements (sucking, chewing, holding head up, sitting position, weight bearing)
8. Poor reflexes and balance reactions

Following identification of the presence of hypotonia, a treatment program can be developed. Although treatment will not cure the symptoms, it will aid in the prevention of future complications due to the condition. Treatment may also serve to facilitate the child's most appropriate development and teach compensatory skills. Treatment programs incorporate instruction to the child and caregivers in positioning and movement strategies. Hypotonic children may need extra stimulation through treatment programs that incorporate the use of sensory stimuli (i.e., touch, sound, sight, taste, smell, movement). Provision of general stimulation through swinging, rolling, and spinning activities may be beneficial (Trombly, 1989). Physical Therapy, Occupational Therapy, and Speech Services are often provided to facilitate skill development. Ankle-foot orthoses are sometimes used for weak ankle muscles.

Collaboration between parents, educators, and medical professionals is important to enable the most positive outcome for the child with hypotonia. Children with hypotonia will often be identified at an early age through primary care medical settings. It is important for parents to be placed in contact with the local school district or state agencies that provide early intervention services for children ages 0 to 3. Infants with hypotonia may be eligible for special education services. If eligible, an Individual Family Service Plan (IFSP) would be developed to identify goals and services. Preschool and elementary school students may continue to be eligible for Special Education services under provisions of the Individuals with Disabilities Education Act. Although a child may not be directly eligible to receive services due to the presence of hypotonia, per se, eligibility may be based on associated conditions or disorders. Specific services will be determined on an individualized basis. If educationally necessary, children may receive the related services of Occupational, Physical, and Speech Therapies.

The prognosis for children with hypotonia varies dependent on several factors, including the root cause of the condition, the severity of the symptoms, and the provision of appropriate early interventions.

REFERENCES

Pediatric Services (n.d.). Understanding the lingo. Retrieved from www.pediatricservices.com

Trombly, C. A. (1989). Neurophysiological and developmental treatment approaches. In C. Trombly (Ed.), *Occupational therapy for physical dysfunction* (3rd ed.). Baltimore: Williams & Wilkins.

Shelley Pelletier
Susan Sage
Dysart Unified School District
El Mirage, Arizona

HYPOXIA

Cerebral hypoxia refers to reduced oxygenation of brain tissue and is a leading cause of perinatal neurologic morbidity and encephalopathy in children (Hill & Volpe, 1994; Schwartz, Ahmann, Dykes, & Brann, 1993). In the absence of oxygen, cells switch to anaerobic glycolysis, which can sustain the brain for only a short time before cell death occurs (Brierley & Graham, 1976). In addition, hypoxia can initiate a cascade of toxic biochemical events that evolve over the course of hours to days, including glutamatergic excito-toxicity (Johnston, 1997).

Characteristics

Perinatal hypoxia is characterized by (Gross, 1990; Hill & Volpe, 1994)

1. Widespread damage to white matter, particularly in the periventricular regions and brain stem
2. Damage to the watershed regions of the cerebral cortex parasagitally
3. Focal areas of neuronal necrosis in the cerebral and cerebellar cortices, thalamus, basal ganglia, brain stem, and anterior horn cells due to concomitant ischemia or hemorrhage
4. Status marmoratus of the basal ganglia and thalamus characterized by neuronal loss, gliosis, and hypermyelination, causing a marbled appearance of these structures
5. In the preterm infant a similar pattern of white matter and brain stem damage but parasagital cortical areas less vulnerable due to anastomoses with meningeal arteries
6. The encephalopathy that ensues from perinatal hypoxia often immediately apparent and associated with loss of consciousness, hypotonia, seizures, and brain stem findings including impairments of extraocular movements, sucking response, and respiration

Hypoxia in older children is characterized by (Brierley & Graham, 1976; Taylor, Quencer, Holzman, & Naidich, 1985)

1. Brain stem and white matter become more resistant to hypoxia with age.
2. Cerebral cortex remains vulnerable, as do the hippocampus, thalamus, cerebellum, and basal ganglia.
3. Problems with attention and memory are common.
4. Less impairment with muscle tone occurs.

Perinatal hypoxia is estimated to occur in 2–4 per 1,000 live-term births. The incidence is much higher in premature births at approximately 60% due to immaturity of the lungs (Schwartz et al., 1993). Hypoxia can occur at the antepartum, intrapartum, and postpartum periods. Antepartum, the fetus is vulnerable to diseases or disorders affecting oxygen content of the mother's blood, such as cardiac arrest or hemorrhage. During the intrapartum period hypoxia may occur from abruptio placentae, uterine rupture, or traumatic delivery (Rivkin, 1997). Postpartum hypoxia can result from aspiration of meconium as well as respiratory or cardiac distress. The risk of perinatal hypoxia increases with maternal diabetes, toxemia or hypertension, delivery by cesarean section not preceded by labor, and in second twins (Gross, 1990).

In older children hypoxia can occur due to a variety of causes, including processes affecting the passage of oxygen at the alveolar level (e.g., pneumonia, asthma), inhibition of the bellows function of the chest wall (e.g., polio, spinal cord lesion), obstruction of the tracheobronchial tree (e.g., choking, hanging), and situations in which insufficient oxygen is available (e.g., drowning, high altitudes, smoke inhalation). Hypoxia can also occur secondary to ischemia, hypoglycemia, anemia, shock, cardiac disease, and histotoxic effects interfering with the cells ability to utilize oxygen (Brierley & Graham, 1976).

The newborn tends to be more resistant to the effects of hypoxia than the older child or adult. Mild perinatal hypoxia often does not result in detectable encephalopathy. The longer-term effects of moderate to severe perinatal hypoxia include mental retardation, dystonia, cerebral palsy, seizures, and death. Perinatal hypoxia has long been suspected as a causal factor in learning disabilities and ADHD. Up to 40% of infants with moderate hypoxia have been reported to have problems with school readiness at age 5 years (Hill & Volpe, 1994). In older children, dystonia and cerebral palsy are not as frequent, but cerebellar dysfunction may occur. Problems with attention, memory, and executive functions predominate. Impairment of visuospatial functions is also common.

Given the frequent motor involvement, physical and occupational therapy may be indicated. In addition, early evaluation and intervention to facilitate school readiness should be routinely considered. Special education services and specific cognitive rehabilitation therapy may be necessary with children of school age.

REFERENCES

Brierley, J. B., & Graham, D. I. (1976). Hypoxia and vascular disorders of the central nervous system. In W. Blackwood & J. A. N. Corsellis (Eds.), *Greenfield's neuropathology.* Chicago: Year Book Medical.

Gross, I. (1990). Respiratory distress syndrome. In F. Oski (Ed.), *Principles and practice of pediatrics.* Philadelphia: Lippincott.

Hill, A., & Volpe, J. J. (1994). Hypoxic-ischemic cerebral injury in the newborn. In K. F. Swaiman (Ed.), *Pediatric neurology.* St. Louis, MO: Mosby.

Johnston, M. V. (1997). Hypoxic and ischemic disorders of infants and children: Lecture for the 38th meeting of Japanese Society of Child Neurology, Tokyo, Japan, July, 1996. *Brain and Development, 19,* 235–239.

Rivkin, M. J. (1997). Hypoxic-ischemic brain injury in the term newborn: Neuropathology, clinical aspects, and neuroimaging. *Clinics in Perinatology, 24*(3), 607–625.

Schwartz, J. F., Ahmann, P. A., Dykes, F. D., & Brann, A. W. (1993). Neonatal intracranial hemorrhage and hypoxia. In J. M. Pellock & E. C. Myer (Eds.), *Neurologic emergencies in infancy and childhood.* Boston: Butterworth-Heinemann.

Taylor, S. B., Quencer, R. M., Holzman, B. H., & Naidich, T. P. (1985). Central nervous system anoxic-ischemic insult in children due to near drowning. *Radiology, 156*(3), 641–646.

David M. Tucker
Rebecca Vaurio
Austin, Texas

See also Anoxia

I

ICHTHYOSIS, CHANARIN DORFMAN SYNDROME

Chanarin Dorfman syndrome is a hereditary disorder of lipid metabolism almost always accompanied by dry, scaly skin (ichthyosis). Myopathy (degeneration of the muscles) and fat deposits appearing in the white blood cells also are commonly seen in patients with Chanarin Dorfman syndrome.

Chanarin Dorfman syndrome is believed to be a rare disorder inherited as an autosomal recessive trait. Treatment is symptomatic and generally includes skin-softening ointments and medical interventions directed toward fatty liver, ocular abnormalities, disorders of the central nervous system, and liver enlargement, which comprise part of the long list of other abnormalities occasionally seen in these patients.

Characteristics

1. Chanarin Dorfman syndrome can be detected by the presence of fat droplets in certain white blood cells in a blood smear taken from a finger, toe, heel, or ear.
2. In addition to the fat deposits, ichthyosis is present.
3. Additional symptoms include deafness, short stature, fatty liver (the liver being the most commonly affected organ), central nervous system disorders with cognitive sequelae, ocular abnormalities, myopathy, and developmental lags.

Some children will not need special education services, whereas others may require assistance. Special education issues can vary greatly from minimal intervention such as tutoring to keep a child on track to qualification of a child as handicapped due to health problems.

Prognosis is highly dependent on the affected individual. This disorder is fatal in some and merely a nuisance in others. Future research on this disorder includes gene mapping in the hopes of attainment of a cure and more definitive information regarding etiology.

REFERENCES

Pena-Penabad, C., Almagro, M., Martinez, W., Garcia-Silva, J., Del Pozo, J., Yebra, M. T., Sanchez-Manzano, C., & Fonseca, E. (2001). Dorfman-Chanarin syndrome (neutral lipid storage disease): New clinical features. *British Journal of Dermatology, 144,* 430–432.

Tullu, M. S., Muranjan, M. N., Save, S. U., Deshmukh, C. T., Khubchandani, S. R., & Bharucha, B. A. (2000). Dorfman-Chanarin syndrome: A rare neutral lipid storage disease. *Indian Pediatrics, 37,* 88–93.

Kimberly M. Estep
University of Houston–Clear Lake

ICHTHYOSIS, CHILD SYNDROME

CHILD (congenital hemidysplasia with ichthyosis erythroderma and limb defects) syndrome is an inherited disorder that is usually present at birth. It is characterized by skin anomalies and limb defects on one side of the body.

CHILD syndrome is a rare disorder transmitted through an X-linked dominant gene and thus occurs more frequently in females. Males affected by CHILD syndrome, an extremely rare occurrence, present with an XXY genetic code (Klinefelter syndrome).

Characteristics

1. The syndrome predominantly affects females at birth or in early childhood.
2. Dry, scaly, itchy, and red skin (ichthyosis erythrodermia) appears on one side of the body, although minor skin abnormalities may be seen on the opposite side of the body.
3. Children may have clawlike nails and be bald on one side of the head.
4. Pulmonary, cardiovascular, renal, and endocrine abnormalities may be present.
5. Anomalies of the central nervous system and the thyroid and adrenal glands may also occur.
6. Limb defects may be present on the same side of the body as the skin symptoms, and they may include an absence of fingers and toes or an underdevelopment of

the fingers and toes, as well as deformities of the long bones.

7. A majority of the aberrations seen in affected children are a result of underdevelopment of the affected side of the body.

Treatment of the skin disease involves the use of emollients. Surgery may become necessary to correct musculoskeletal abnormalities. Keratolytics, a category of drugs, may be administered to alleviate dry, scaly skin and help exfoliate the skin. Special education issues revolve around handicapping issues associated with health problems.

Prognosis is fatal in affected males, and in females morbidity is more often caused by anomalies not associated with the skin condition. Congenital cardiac defects are the primary cause of death among individuals with CHILD syndrome, whereas abnormalities in the lungs, skeleton, kidneys, and central nervous system pose other potential complications. Future research is focused on gene mapping to understand better the etiology and to find more effective treatments for this disorder.

REFERENCES

Fenske, N. A., & Roshdieh, B. (2001). CHILD syndrome. *eMedicine, 2.* Retrieved June 2001 from http://www.emedicine.com/derm/topic75.html

Hebert, A. A., Esterly, N. B., Holbrook, K. A., & Hall, J. C. (1987). The CHILD syndrome. *Archives of Dermatology, 123,* 503–509.

Kimberly M. Estep
University of Houston–Clear Lake

ICHTHYOSIS, CONGENITA

Ichthyosis congenita is an inherited skin disorder characterized by generalized dry and rough skin. All babies who suffer from an autosomal recessive congenita ichthyosis are collodion babies at birth. Collodion babies are born with a translucent or opaque membrane that covers the entire body and lasts for days to weeks. Congenita ichthyosis presents on a spectrum in which lamellar ichthyosis is the most severe and nonbullous congenital ichthyosis is a mild form of congenita ichthyosis. In lamellar ichthyosis the collodion membrane is replaced by dark brown platelike scales without erythroderma (abnormal redness of the skin). The nonbullous type presents with erythroderma with fine white scales.

Prevalence is estimated at 1 in 200,000 individuals in the United States. The disease affects all racial and ethnic groups and males and females alike.

Characteristics

1. Most newborns with congenita ichthyosis are collodion babies with a transparent membrane covering their body that will eventually be shed.
2. On the congenita ichthyosis spectrum is lamellar ichthyosis, which is a more severe form presenting with large dark brown and shedding scales that cover almost the entire body.
3. Children affected with the more severe form may also suffer sepsis (infection) and protein and electrolyte loss, which can lead to complications associated with death.
4. In the nonbullous cases, erythroderma and white scales are present.

Treatment involves keeping the child moist with petroleum-based ointments, and hygienic handling should be carefully followed to avoid infection. As the child ages, alpha-hydroxy acid preparations can aid in peeling and thinning of the skin. Keeping the infant hydrated is also of importance.

Given that most congenita ichthyosis resolve themselves, no long-term effects are seen except the outward signs of the ichthyosis. Therefore, no special education issues arise. However, psychological needs might surface in regard to the child's or adolescent's outward appearance. Overall, prognosis is good, and research is ongoing to find a cure for this disorder.

REFERENCES

Masashi, A. (1998). Severe congenital ichthyosis of the neonate. *International Journal of Dermatology, 37,* 722–728.

Williams, M. L., & Elias, P. M. (1987). Genetically transmitted, generalized disorders of cornification: The ichthyoses. *Clinical Dermatology, 5,* 155–178.

Kimberly M. Estep
University of Houston–Clear Lake

ICHTHYOSIS, ERYTHROKERATODERMIA PROGRESSIVA SYMMETRICA

A form of ichthyosis, erythrokeratodermia progressiva symmetrica (EPS) is a very rare hereditary skin disorder characterized by keratotic (hardened red) plaques distributed over the body and the extremities. However, the chest and abdomen area are normally void of any plaques. Cornification normally appears during the first year of life; some cases involving EPS have been documented to disappear spontaneously later in life.

Incidence rates are equal for males and females, and EPS is transmitted through autosomal dominant genes. Other than the outward manifestation of EPS, children show no other physical symptoms, and no mental deficiencies have been noted.

> Characteristics
>
> 1. Keratotic plaques cover a majority of the body, including the buttocks, head, and extremities.
> 2. In most cases, the chest and abdomen are spared cornification.
> 3. EPS appears during the first year of life and stabilizes after 1 or 2 years and in some cases even dissipates during puberty.
> 4. Lesions may also appear on the palms of the hands and the soles of the feet.

Treatment is limited to topical medications, and relief is sometimes not achieved. Prognosis is good, and future research focuses on alleviation of symptomology.

REFERENCES

Khoo, B. P., Tay, Y. K., & Tan, S. H. (2000). Generalized erythematous plaques: Progressive symmetric erythrokeratodermia (PSEK) (erythrokeratodermia progressiva symmetric). *Archives of Dermatology, 136,* 665–668.

Williams, M. L., & Elias, P. M. (1987). Genetically transmitted, generalized disorders of cornification: The ichthyoses. *Dermatology Clinics, 5,* 155–178.

Kimberly M. Estep
University of Houston–Clear Lake

ICHTHYOSIS, ERYTHROKERATODERMIA VARIABILIS

Ichthyosis erythrokeratodermia variabilis (IEV) is one of a diverse group of disorders of skin keratinization (the process in which skin cells form and are eventually shed). It is distinguished from the other members of the ichthyosis group by its unique clinical features and pattern of inheritance.

IEV is transmitted in an autosomal dominant manner. No data are available regarding its frequency in the general population. Evidence points to a genetic linkage between IEV and Rh blood type.

> Characteristics
>
> 1. Skin abnormalities usually appear early in life, progress throughout childhood, and cease during adolescence.
> 2. Distinct, thickened plaques (hyperkeratosis) with irregular borders occur in normal skin. Their appearance may be preceded by discrete patches of redness (erythema).
> 3. Patches of erythema may vary in size, shape, and location. They may migrate or remain in the same place and eventually become hyperkeratotic.
> 4. Hyperkeratosis tends to be generalized, but the face, buttocks, armpits, and outer surfaces of the extremities are most commonly involved.
> 5. Thickened skin of the palms and soles is common.
> 6. The teeth, hair, and nails are not involved.

No therapeutic recommendations for IEV can be found in the literature about this disorder. Presumably, the ichthyotic changes respond to the same treatment modalities that are effective for other diseases in this general classification of skin maladies.

There is no research to indicate that children with IEV have any specific cognitive deficits or require special education resources. The prognosis for IEV should be considered favorable. Although skin changes progress during childhood, they stabilize during adolescence. Therefore, adults with this problem can anticipate that their cutaneous abnormalities will, at least, not get any worse.

For more information, please contact the Foundation for Ichthyosis and Related Skin Types, 650 North Cannon Ave., Suite 17, Lansdale, PA 19446; (215) 631-1411 or (800) 545-3286; e-mail: ichthyosis@aol.com; http://www.libertynet.org/-ichthyos/.

REFERENCES

Darmstadt, G. L. (2000). Disorders of keratinization. In R. E. Behrman, R. M. Kleigman, & H. B. Jenson (Eds.), *Nelson's textbook of pediatrics* (16th ed., p. 2009). Philadelphia: W. B. Saunders.

National Organization for Rare Diseases, Inc. (1997). Ichthyosis, erythrokeratodermia variabilis. Retrieved from http://www.rarediseases.org

Barry H. Davison
Ennis, Texas

Joan W. Mayfield
Baylor Pediatric Specialty Services
Dallas, Texas

ICHTHYOSIS, ERYTHROKERATOLYSIS HIEMALIS

Erythrokeratolysis hiemalis (EH) or keratolytic winter erythema (KWE) is an autosomal dominant skin disorder characterized by circles of erythema (redness or inflammation of the skin) and hyperkeratosis (excessive skin lesions in which there is overgrowth and thickening of the skin). With age, the symptoms grow milder, eventually disappearing all together. This disorder is mostly seen in South Africa, where the incidence is 1 in 7,000 people.

Characteristics

1. Redness and inflammation of the skin
2. Overgrowth and thickening of the skin leading to recurrent and intermittent peeling of the palms and soles
3. Symptoms that generally subside during the summer months

The peeling and redness cause no physical discomfort, and moisturizing the affected areas or submerging them in water only exacerbates the condition. Peeling of the affected areas causes no discomfort and is done with ease. No special education issues arise as a result of EH. Future research is interested in finding the etiology of this disorder, and prognosis is good for those who are affected.

REFERENCES

Botha, M. C., & Beighton, P. (1983). Inherited disorders in the Afrikaner populations of southern Africa: Part II. Skeletal, dermal, and haematological conditions; the Afrikaners of Gamkaskloof; demographic considerations. *South African Medical Journal, 64,* 664–667.

Findaly, G. H., & Morrison, J. G. L. (1978). Erythrokeratolysis hiemalis—keratolytic winter skin or 'oudtshoorn skin.' *British Journal of Dermatology, 98,* 491–495.

Starfield, M., Hennies, H. C., Jung, M., Jenkins, T., Wienker, T., Hull, P., Spurdle, A., Kuster, W., Ramsay, M., & Reis, A. (1997). Localization of the gene causing keratolytic winter erythema to chromosome 8p22-p23, and evidence for a founder effect in South African Afrikaans-speakers. *American Journal of Human Genetics, 61,* 370–378.

Kimberly M. Estep
University of Houston–Clear Lake

ICHTHYOSIS, HARLEQUIN TYPE (HARLEQUIN FETUS)

Harlequin fetus (HF) is a rare disorder of keratinization, the process by which skin tissue forms and eventually sloughs off the body. It most likely represents several genetic mutations that have common clinical findings.

No data are available on the incidence of HF in the general population. HF is transmitted in an autosomal recessive manner. One subtype of HF has been traced to an enzyme deficiency that is encoded on Chromosome 11.

Characteristics

1. Newborns covered with extremely thick, fissured skin that obscures facial features and causes severe constriction of the digits
2. Flat nose and ears
3. Marked eversion of the eyelids with inflammation of the eyeball
4. Absent nails and hair (occasionally)
5. Eversion of the lips, gaping mouth
6. Restricted joint mobility; hands and feet are fixed, and their blood flow is impaired
7. Respiratory distress, poor suck
8. Skin infections common and potentially life-threatening

Initial therapy for affected newborns requires attention to fluid intake to replace water losses that occur through denuded skin. A warm, humid environment and application of lubricating ointments help to reduce cutaneous evaporation. Oral retinoids, drugs that correct some of the defects in the keratinization process, are also useful.

Because of the poor prognosis, there is no research available concerning cognitive deficits associated with HF.

The prognosis for HF is poor. The majority of these babies die in the first few weeks after birth. Those infants who survive the neonatal period suffer from severe ichthyosis (inflamed, scaling skin) and varying degrees of neurological damage.

Prenatal diagnosis of HF is available for individuals with a family history of this disorder. Direct visualization of the fetus (fetoscopy), biopsy of fetal skin, and culture of fetal cells found in amniotic fluid all provide valuable data for clinicians caring for concerned parents-to-be.

For more information, contact the Foundation for Ichthyosis and Related Skin Types, 650 North Cannon Ave., Suite 17, Lansdale, PA 19446; (215) 631-1411 or (800) 545-3286; e-mail: ichthyosis@aol.com; http://www.libertynet.org/-ichthyos/.

REFERENCES

Darmstadt, G. L. (2000). Disorders of keratinization. In R. E. Behrman, R. M. Kleigman, & H. B. Jenson (Eds.), *Nelson's textbook of pediatrics* (16th ed., p. 2007). Philadelphia: W. B. Saunders.

National Organization for Rare Disorders, Inc. (1997). Ichthyosis, harlequin type. Retrieved from http://www.rarediseases.org

Barry H. Davison
Ennis, Texas

Joan W. Mayfield
Baylor Pediatric Specialty Services
Dallas, Texas

ICTHYOSIS, HYSTRIX, CURTH-MACKLIN TYPE

Icthyosis is the name for a group of rare genetic disorders that causes the skin to build up and scale (Icthyosis Information, 2001). The forms of icthyosis vary and range in severity. The icthyosis disorders all involve the normal growth and shedding cycle of skin; the filament network is critical to this process. In icthyosis hystrix, Curth-Macklin type (IHCM), the filaments are rudimentary with a greater production of mucus than typically occurs (Anton-Lamprecht, 1978). IHCM is a very rare type of icthyosis. It is believed to result from an abnormality in the genes that encode proteins with resulting disruption of the keratin filament network (Curth & Macklin, 1954), possibly due to a mutation in a keratin gene (KRT1). The altered appearance of the skin in IHCM tends to be localized and may have the appearance of multiple birthmarks or nevi.

As a result of the various forms of icthyoses, the incidence rate for IHCM is very hard to establish. Two families with IHCM have been discussed extensively in the research literature (Curth & Macklin, 1954; Niemi, Virtanen, Kanerva, & Muttilainen, 1990). ICHM is genetic with autosomal dominant transmission; it also can occur through spontaneous mutation, but this is even rarer. Reliable data on the incidence of the icthyoses in general are minimal. There is no evidence of greater likelihood of occurrence of IHCM in any specific ethnic group or gender.

The disruption of the shedding process has multiple effects. The scaling that results can be painful and can restrict movement. If untreated, in the more severe forms and depending on the localization, the scaling can interfere with hearing or vision. Additionally, because skin normally is involved in the regulation of body temperature, individuals with ICHM can be very sensitive to temperature changes. Individuals with ICHM can have significant problems with overheating because the scaling may interfere with the usual cooling process of perspiration. Finally, depending on the localization and severity of the disorder, appearance can be affected negatively, and individuals with ICHM may be subjected to teasing or recurrent questions (Icthyosis Information, 2001).

Characteristics

1. Extremely dry skin
2. Buildup and scaling of skin
3. Thick, furrowed overgrowth of skin or hyperkeratosis over the joints
4. Sensitivity to temperature fluctuations
5. Problems with heat exhaustion or overheating

Treatment of icthyosis is a lifelong endeavor (Icthyosis Information, 2001) that involves frequent exfoliation and moisturizing of the affected areas of skin. Additional treatment may be needed to address itching that is associated with the scaling as well as the potential for infection. The extent of time required may vary, but skin care is needed not only to improve the appearance of the skin but also to avoid pain or restricted movement, vision, or hearing that may be associated with the scaling. Scaling can restrict range of movement, and at that level of severity, accommodations may be appropriate to compensate for the restricted motion. For children and adolescents, in-service programs on skin disorders, as well as behavior management of any teasing, may be appropriate. There is a national registry for individuals with all forms of icthyosis supported by the National Institutes for Health, as well as support groups (Icthyosis Information, 2001).

REFERENCES

Anton-Lamprecht, I. (1978). Electron microscopy in the early diagnosis of genetic disorders of the skin. *Dermatologica, 157,* 65–85.

Curth, H. O., & Macklin, M. T. (1954). The genetic basis of various types of icthyosis in a family group. *American Journal of Human Genetics, 6,* 371–381.

Icthyosis Information. (2001). Icthyosis information providing a Web-based resource for icthyosis. Retrieved March 4, 2001, from www. icthyosis.com

Niemi, K. M., Virtanen, I., Kanerva, L., & Muttilainen, M. (1990). Altered keratin expression in icthyosis hystrix Curth-Macklin. *Archives of Dermatology Research, 282,* 227–233.

Cynthia A. Riccio
Texas A&M University

ICHTHYOSIS, KERATOSIS FOLLICULARIS SPINULOSA DECALVANS

Keratosis follicularis spinulosa decalvans (KFSD) is a form of ichthyosis characterized by hardening of the skin around the hair follicles eventually leading to baldness (alopecia) and scarring. During infancy, keratosis begins on the face and moves to the extremities and trunk by childhood. Around puberty, alopecia of the scalp and eyebrows develops. KFSD is a rare X-linked disease that affects more males than females.

Characteristics

1. The skin around the hair follicles hardens, leading to scarring and alopecia.
2. Patients develop sensitivity to bright light, and corneal abnormalities may be present.
3. Eyebrows and eyelashes may be absent or thinned.

Treatment involves topical ointments to alleviate some of the discomfort associated with the dry, scaly skin.

Pharmacological advances have been made with regard to alopecia, but effectiveness varies by individual. Ophthalmologists should be consulted regarding any emerging ocular abnormalities. Special education issues revolve around any ocular anomalies that arise, and many children will suffer no deficits that require intervention other than those associated with the keratosis and hair loss. Research is ongoing in the hopes of attaining a cure for this disorder.

REFERENCES

Rand, R., & Baden, H. P. (1983). Keratosis follicularis spinulosa decalvans: Reports of two cases and literature review. *Archives of Dermatology, 119*(1), 22–26.

van Osch, L. D., Oranje, A. P., Keukens, F. M., van Voorst Vader, P. C., & Veldman, E. (1992). Keratosis follicularis spinulosa decalvans: A family study of seven male cases and six female carriers. *Journal of Medical Genetics, 29*(1), 36–40.

Kimberly M. Estep
University of Houston–Clear Lake

ICHTHYOSIS, LAMELLAR RECESSIVE (LAMELLAR ICHTHYOSIS)

Lamellar ichthyosis (LI) is one of the two major forms of hereditary, autosomal recessive, congenital disorders of keratinization, the process by which skin tissues form and are eventually shed from the body's surface. Abnormalities are present at birth or shortly thereafter. The incidence of LI has not been determined. The mode of inheritance is autosomal recessive.

Characteristics

1. Newborns with LI present either as collodion babies (these infants are covered with a thick, parchment-like membrane that sloughs off within a few days) or with generalized redness of the skin (erythroderma) and scaling.
2. Initial cutaneous findings give way to the development of generalized ichthyosis in which the body is completely covered by large, dark, quadrangular scales.
3. Marked facial involvement is common. Eversion of the eyelids (ectropion) and small, crumpled ears may be present.
4. The palms and soles have thick skin.
5. Hair is sparse and fine.
6. The teeth or mucous glands are not involved.
7. Erythroderma is not seen beyond the newborn period.
8. Blistering is not a feature of this disorder.

Treatment goals for children with LI are to relieve their intense itching, improve their appearance, and provide support and counseling for the serious psychological problems that their disease imposes. Unfortunately, the itching responds only minimally to antihistamine therapy. Prolonged bathing with moisturizing oils helps to remove scales, reduce skin dryness, and prevent bacterial colonization of dead skin. This last phenomenon causes LI patients to have a very foul body odor. High-humidity environments provide the most comfortable settings for these patients during the winter, and air conditioning during the summer is imperative. Moisturizing creams may help the scaling to some degree, but they can cause intense burning if they are applied to cracked, fissured skin. A group of medications called retinoids are given orally to reduce the severity of ichthyosis. However, they must be administered indefinitely for maximum effectiveness and are not without significant side effects (bone toxicity and severe damage to fetal tissue). Ectropion may necessitate referral to an eye specialist. Plastic surgery consultation is occasionally needed. Genetic counseling should be offered to families.

There is no current research to indicate the need for special education services due to cognitive deficits as result of the LI. Children with LI, however, will require additional psychological support to help with self-esteem as a result of the physical abnormalities. Providing educational resources to the teacher and peers in the classroom will facilitate understanding of the disease and help foster peer relationships.

Prognosis for children with LI is guarded. Their disease requires constant treatment. There is no evidence that their problems remit at all with age. In addition, their disturbing physical appearance gives rise to multiple psychological difficulties that challenge the abilities of even the most gifted and skilled therapists.

For more information and parent support, contact Foundation for Ichthyosis and Related Skin Types, 650 North Cannon Avenue, Suite 17, Lansdale, PA 19446; (215) 631-1411 or (800) 545-3286; e-mail: icthyosis@aol.com; http://www.libertynet.org/- icthyos/.

REFERENCES

Darmstadt, G. L. (2000). Disorders of keratinization. In R. E. Behrman, R. M. Kleigman, & H. B. Jenson (Eds.), *Nelson's textbook of pediatrics* (16th ed., p. 2008). Philadelphia: W. B. Saunders.

National Organization for Rare Disorders, Inc. (1997). Icthyosis, lamellar recessive. Retrieved from http://www.rarediseases.org

Barry H. Davison
Ennis, Texas

Joan W. Mayfield
Baylor Pediatric Specialty Services
Dallas, Texas

ICHTHYOSIS, NETHERTON SYNDROME

Netherton syndrome (NS) is a rare, congenital, hereditary disorder characterized by ichthyosis (an abnormality of skin development that manifests as scaling and redness), several distinct anomalies of hair, and a tendency toward a variety of allergic illnesses. Skin findings are usually evident within two weeks after birth.

NS is reportedly rare. No data are available on its incidence. The mode of inheritance is autosomal recessive. The vast majority of cases have occurred in females.

Characteristics

1. Ichthyosis is present shortly after birth. Skin around the eyes, mouth, and anus are most commonly affected. The pattern of ichthyosis has a distinctive circular shape (ichthyosis linearis circumflexa).
2. There is sparse, short scalp hair that breaks easily with minimal pressure. Eyebrow, eyelash, and body hair are also abnormal.
3. Allergic disease includes hives (urticaria), angioedema (swelling of the tissues beneath the skin or inside the respiratory or gastrointestinal tract), atopic dermatitis (skin inflammation caused by an allergic reaction), and asthma.
4. There is growth failure (failure to thrive).
5. Recurrent bacterial and yeast infections occur.
6. Mental retardation is found in some patients.

No recommendations regarding therapy can be found in the literature. Presumably, the ichthyotic skin abnormalities respond to treatments used in other disorders of this type. Infectious diseases should be managed with appropriate antibiotic or antifungal (for yeast) agents. Patients with significant allergic illness or asthma may need referral to a specialist for the best outcome.

Because some patients with NS have cognitive deficiencies, it is important to provide a comprehensive neuropsychological evaluation to determine the child's cognitive strengths and weaknesses. Based on those results, specific school recommendations, including classroom modifications, can be made to help the child reach his or her academic potential.

No data are available concerning the prognosis for NS. The rarity of this syndrome may make an understanding of its usual course impossible. Although the physical abnormalities of NS appear remedial, the possibility of mental retardation should make clinicians cautious about predicting what the future holds for an NS patient.

For more information, contact Foundation for Ichthyosis and Related Skin Types, 650 North Cannon Avenue, Suite 17, Lansdale, PA 19446; (215) 631-1411 or (800) 545-3286; e-mail: icthyosis@aol.com; http://www.libertynet.orgn/- icthyos/.

REFERENCES

Darmstadt, G. L. (2000). Diseases of keratinization. In R. E. Behrman, R. M. Kleigman, & H. B. Jenson (Eds.), *Nelson's textbook of pediatrics* (16th ed., pp. 1577–1581). Philadelphia: W. B. Saunders.

National Organization for Rare Disorders, Inc. (1999). Ichthyosis, Netherton syndrome. Retrieved from http://www.rarediseases.org

Barry H. Davison
Ennis, Texas

Joan W. Mayfield
Baylor Pediatric Specialty Services
Dallas, Texas

ICHTHYOSIS, SJOGREN-LARSSON SYNDROME

Sjoren-Larsson syndrome (SLS) is a hereditary disorder of the skin and central nervous system. It is characterized by ichthyosis (red, scaly patches of skin), mental retardation, and spasticity (increased muscle tone). A deficiency of the enzyme fatty aldehyde dehydrogenase is the primary defect in SLS.

SLS is transmitted in an autosomal recessive manner. It is rare, and no data are available regarding its actual incidence.

Characteristics

1. Lamellar ichthyosis (large, thick, dark scales) or ichthyosiform erythroderma (red skin with fine white scales); ichthyosis is distributed all over the body but is more pronounced on the arms, legs, and lower abdomen
2. Delayed motor and speech development apparent during the first year
3. Seizures
4. Mental retardation obvious by age 3
5. Spasticity of the legs or both the arms and the legs

Therapy for SLS patients is limited. The skin changes respond to measures used for ichthyosis associated with other disorders. Anticonvulsants may be needed for seizure control. Some patients may eventually become ambulatory with the use of leg braces or other orthopedic appliances. Most, however, will require a wheelchair.

Children diagnosed with SLS require occupational, physical, and speech therapy through early childhood intervention (ECI) programs to help them attain appropriate developmental milestones. As they reach school age, children with SLS continue to require additional educational support under the umbrella of special education because of their cognitive deficits. Assistive technology and devices may also be required.

The prognosis for SLS is poor. Mental retardation and other significant neurologic deficits are common. Prenatal diagnosis and detection of the carrier state of SLS are available. Families who are concerned about having a child with SLS should be counseled about the accessibility of these diagnostic procedures.

For more information and support, contact Foundation for Ichthyosis and Related Skin Types, 650 North Cannon Avenue, Suite 17, Lansdale, PA 19446; (215) 631-1411 or (800) 545-3286; e-mail: icthyosis@aol.com; http://www.libertynet.org/-icthyos/.

REFERENCES

Darmstadt, G. L. (2000). Disorders of keratinization. In R. E. Behrman, R. M. Kleigman, & H. B. Jenson (Eds.), *Nelson's textbook of pediatrics* (16th ed., p. 2009). Philadelphia: W. B. Saunders.

National Organization for Rare Disorders, Inc. (1999). Ichthyosis, Sjogren Larsson syndrome. Retrieved from http://www.rarediseases.org

Barry H. Davison
Ennis, Texas

Joan W. Mayfield
Baylor Pediatric Specialty Services
Dallas, Texas

ICHTHYOSIS, TAY SYNDROME

Tay syndrome is a hereditary disorder characterized by trichothiodystrophy (brittle, sulfur-deficient hair) and dry, scaly skin (ichthyosis). Males and females are equally affected, and Tay syndrome is believed to be an autosomal recessive trait.

Characteristics

1. Children present with ichthyosis consisting mainly of fine, dark scales covering most of the body, trichothiodystrophy, abnormal finger and toe nails, and loss of subcutaneous (beneath the skin) fat resulting in aged facial features. Reproductive organs are usually underdeveloped, and cataracts often develop in the eyes.
2. Mental retardation is evident at an early age, and physical development is slow. Some children may also be short in stature.
3. Central nervous system abnormalities include seizures, ataxia (lack of muscle control), tremors, and neurosensory deafness. Hypomyelination has also been associated with children affected with Tay syndrome.
4. Susceptibility to infection is increased, and abnormalities of the teeth and bones may be present.

Treatment is symptomatic, and medical intervention is necessary in a majority of cases. Cognitive involvement usually results in mental deficiency. Ichthyosis is treated with skin emollients. Special education qualification is handicapped due to health problems, and remediation commonly associated with mental retardation is necessary. Prognosis is poor, and future research is focusing on genetic characteristics that delineate Tay syndrome from other disorders of ichthyosis to enable researchers and health care professionals better to help the patients affected with these disorders.

REFERENCES

Happle, R. H., Taube, H., Grobe, H., & Bonsmann, G. (1984). The Tay syndrome (congenital ichthyosis with trichothiodystrophy). *European Journal of Pediatrics, 141,* 147–152.

Ostergaard, J. R., & Christensen, T. (1996). The central nervous system in Tay syndrome. *Neuropediatrics, 27,* 326–330.

Kimberly M. Estep
University of Houston–Clear Lake

ICHTHYOSIS VULGARIS

Ichthyosis vulgaris (IV) is one of a heterogeneous group of disorders of skin cornification or keratinization (the process in which skin cells are produced and eventually shed). It is typified by a specific pattern of scaling of the skin and a unique form of inheritance.

IV is the most common of abnormalities of skin keratinization. Its incidence is about 1 in 300 live births. It is transmitted in an autosomal dominant manner.

Characteristics

1. The onset of symptoms is during the first year of life. Rarely, newborns are affected with a thick, membranous covering of the skin that eventually sloughs off in large sheets during the first few days after birth (so-called collodion baby).
2. Slightly rough, scaling skin is most noticeable on the outer surfaces of the extremities (particularly the legs) and back.

3. Skin of the abdomen, neck, and face are usually normal.
4. The palms and soles are thick skinned.
5. Scaling is more severe during the winter and typically abates during the summer months.
6. Skin findings improve as patients age.
7. Disorders of the teeth, hair, mucosal surfaces, and other organs are absent.

Treatment of IV is directed toward amelioration of the scaling tendency of the skin. The use of bath oil, skin lubricants, and soaps (e.g., Dove, Caress, and Tone) that are less likely to leech out the skin's protective oils is beneficial. Patients with IV may experience considerable itching and skin irritation, particularly in low-humidity environments. Topical corticosteroids and, occasionally, oral antihistamines will improve these symptoms. Humidifiers also are helpful.

There is no research to indicate any cognitive deficiencies associated with IV.

The prognosis for IV is excellent. Usually only minimal therapeutic intervention is required to provide these patients symptomatic relief. In most cases, the problem is considered more of a nuisance than a significant illness.

For more information, contact the Foundation for Ichthyosis and Related Skin Types, 650 North Cannon Avenue, Suite 17, Lansdale, PA 19446; (215) 631-1411 or (800) 545-3286. Also contact the National Registry of Ichthyosis and Related Disorders, University of Washington, Dermatology Department, Box 356524, 1959 N.E. Pacific, Seattle, WA 98195-6524; (206) 616-3179 or (800) 595-1265; e-mail: fleck@u.washington.edu or geogg@u.washington.edu.

REFERENCES

Darmstadt, G. L. (2000). Disorders of keratinization. In R. E. Behrman, R. M. Kleigman, & H. B. Jenson (Eds.), *Nelson's textbook of pediatrics* (16th ed., pp. 2008). Philadelphia: W. B. Saunders.

National Organization for Rare Disorders, Inc. (1998). Ichthyosis vulvaris. Retrieved from http://www.rarediseases.org

Barry H. Davison
Ennis, Texas

Joan W. Mayfield
Baylor Pediatric Specialty Services
Dallas, Texas

ICHTHYOSIS, X-LINKED

X-linked ichthyosis (XLI) is a hereditary disorder of the skin that affects males almost exclusively. Female carriers of the abnormal gene may occasionally demonstrate clinical findings. Corneal opacities (clouding of the clear part of the eyeball that overlies the iris) and cryptorchism (undescended testicles) are also commonly seen in patients with XLI. Ichthyosis (reddened, scaling skin) is caused by a deficiency of the enzyme steroid sulfatase. Individuals with XLI do not possess the gene for steroid sulfatase production.

XLI is rare. Its occurrence in the general population is unclear. It is inherited in an X-linked recessive manner, in much the same way as classic hemophilia (Factor VIII deficiency).

Characteristics

1. Dry, scaly skin is occasionally present at birth. This finding usually resolves quickly but returns between 3 and 6 months of age.
2. Scaling is most severe on the neck, lower face, in front of the ears, on the front of chest and abdomen, and, particularly, on the legs.
3. Skin of the palms and soles is mildly thickened.
4. Ichthyosis worsens as patients age.
5. Corneal opacities develop in late childhood or adolescence. There is no visual impairment. Carrier females may also have this abnormality.
6. Cryptorchism occurs in 25% of patients. Testicular cancer is an occasional finding.

Treatment of the ichthyosis in patients with XLI is similar to strategies employed for the skin problems of related disorders. Liberal use of bath oils as well as skin lubricants is helpful. Cryptorchism may need surgical repair unless spontaneous descent of the testicles occurs during the first year. Because of the increased incidence of testicular malignancy, particularly in a cryptorchic organ, patients with XLI should be taught how to detect signs of a tumor through self-examination. Periodic visits to the primary care physician for screening checks for testicular cancer should be strongly encouraged.

There is no research to indicate cognitive deficits or the need for special education services for children with XLI, and the prognosis for XLI is generally favorable. Ichthyosis responds well to treatment. The ophthalmologic findings do not inhibit visual acuity and are not associated with any other eye anomalies. Testicular cancer is a worrisome problem, but it generally responds well to treatment, as long as the diagnosis is not delayed.

Families concerned about the occurrence of XLI in their children should be advised of the availability of prenatal diagnosis, as well as testing for detection of the carrier state. Gene replacement therapy may not be that far off and will result in a cure for this disorder.

For more information and support, contact the Foundation for Ichthyosis and Related Skin Types, 650 North Cannon Avenue, Suite 17, Lansdale, PA 19446; (215) 631-1411 or (800) 545-3286; e-mail: ichthyosis@aol.com; http://www.libertynet.org/-icthyos/.

REFERENCES

Darmstadt, G. L. (2000). Disorders of keratinization. In R. E. Behrman, R. M. Kleigman, & H. B. Jenson (Eds.), *Nelson's textbook of pediatrics* (16th ed., pp. 2008–2009). Philadelphia: W. B. Saunders.

National Organization for Rare Disorders, Inc. (1997). Ichthyosis, x linked. Retrieved from http://www.rarediseases.org

Barry H. Davison
Ennis, Texas

Joan W. Mayfield
Baylor Pediatric Specialty Services
Dallas, Texas

IGA NEPHROPATHY

IgA nephropathy (IgAN) is an endochrine (renal) disorder of unknown cause. IgAN occurs when deposits of the protein immunoglobulin A (IgA) enter the kidneys. The IgA protein interrupts the filtering process of the kidneys, causing blood and protein to build in the urine and resulting in swelling of the feet and hands. As this condition progresses, the filtering units of the kidneys (glomeruli) are permanently damaged, and renal failure will eventually ensue. Researchers have come to no definitive conclusions about the etiology of IgAN. Select studies claim that IgAN occurs following a flu-like viral infection of the upper respiratory tract or the gastrointestinal tract. This condition could also be the result of an autoimmune disease in which the IgA antibodies interfere with normal kidney functioning. Another possibility is that the disorder is familial. In fact, recent research has shown more definitively that IgAN may be of genetic origin and that these genetic factors may influence severity and course of IgAN.

IgAN normally occurs in adolescence or young adulthood and affects males two to three times more often than females. It is one of the leading causes of acute nephritis (inflammation and abnormal function of the kidney) in young people in the United States. Cognitive and neuropsychological sequelae may be observed as a result of chronic renal disease.

Characteristics

1. The disorder is marked by hematuria (blood in the urine) and a mild loss of protein in the urine (proteinuria) caused by acute nephritis.
2. Groin pain is common.
3. High blood pressure is seen in most patients.
4. A predominant number of cases are seen in the Native American population.
5. The course can range from benign to acute renal failure.
6. Cognitive and neuropsychological sequelae (alterations in attention, memory, etc.) may be observed as a result of prolonged renal malfunction.

Treatment is on a case-by-case basis, and much of the focus is on maintaining kidney health and longevity. When high blood pressure is present, medication and diet regulation are treatments of choice. Affected persons developing kidney failure require dialysis or possibly a kidney transplant.

Special education requirements may involve health-related difficulties, but many children presenting with IgAN lead normal lives with minimal symptomology. In that regard, prognosis is good, and serious complications develop only in rare instances. Etiology is the focus of future research in the hopes of developing better treatment and avoidance therapies.

REFERENCES

Fennell, R. S., Fennell, E. B., Carter, R. L. (1990). Association between renal function and cognition in childhood chronic renal failure. *Pediatric Nephrology, 4,* 16–20.

Floege, J., & Feehally, J. (2000). IgA nephropathy: Recent developments. *Journal of the American Society of Nephrology, 11,* 2395–2403.

Julian, B. A., Quiggins, P. A., Thompson, J. S., Woodford, S. Y., Gleason, K., & Wyatt, R. J. (1985). Familial IgA nephropathy: Evidence of an inherited mechanism of disease. *New England Journal of Medicine, 312,* 202–208.

Yoshikawa, N., Tanaka, R., & Iijima, K. (2001). Pathophysiology and treatment of IgA nephropathy in children. *Pediatric Nephrology, 16,* 446–457.

Kimberly M. Estep
University of Houston–Clear Lake

INCONTINENTIA PIGMENTI (BLOCH-SULZBERGER SYNDROME)

Incontinentia pigmenti (IP) is a rare, hereditary disorder with abnormalities in the skin, skin derivatives (hair, nails, and teeth), eyes, skeleton, and nervous system. The original cases were described in 1925 and occurred in twin sisters. Since then, several hundred affected individuals have been reported.

IP is transmitted in an X-linked dominant manner. The gene is felt to be almost uniformly lethal in males, which accounts for the observations that more than 97% of patients with IP are females. IP is reportedly rare, but its incidence has not been clearly delineated.

Characteristics

1. *Skin.* Skin findings are the most common manifestation of IP. In the newborn, groups of blisters develop in straight lines, preceded by red streaks. These lesions occur on the limbs and trunk. By about 4 months of age, these abnormalities clear, except on the legs, where the blisters evolve into scaly, wart-like plaques. Likewise, these plaques usually resolve by the end of the first year of life. Finally, the pigmentary stage, which gives this syndrome its name, may be present at birth or develop over several months. The characteristic lesion of this phase is extensive areas of increased pigmentation, more common on the trunk than on the limbs. The pattern can be whorl-like, linear, or in scattered flecks. These areas persist throughout childhood but usually fade completely by mid-adolescence.
2. *Teeth.* Missing teeth, delayed tooth eruption, cone-shaped teeth.
3. *Hair.* Patchy hair loss, especially on the back of the scalp. Hair may also be coarse, wiry, and thin.
4. *Nails.* Minor anomalies (pitting) to severe malformation.
5. *Nervous system.* One third have mental retardation, seizures, and spasticity (increased muscle tone).
6. *Eyes.* About one third of patients have poor vision, strabismus (uncoordinated eye movement), cataracts, underdevelopment of the optic nerve, and detached retina.
7. *Skeletal.* Scoliosis, vertebral anomalies, extra ribs, hemiatrophy (deficient development of one side of the body).

Treatment for patients with IP addresses problems that are unrelated to the skin pathology, which tends to resolve over time. Seizures require control with anticonvulsant medication. Eye abnormalities, particularly retinal detachment, are best handled by pediatric ophthalmologists. Significant skeletal defects should be promptly referred to pediatric orthopedic specialists.

The need for special education services for a child with IP will be variable based on the involvement of the nervous system. Because mental retardation is reported in approximately one third of the known cases, special cognitive support services are required. A comprehensive neuropsychological evaluation is helpful to determine a child's strengths and weaknesses and provide valuable recommendations to the school personnel. Vision support and physical therapy may also be required. The school counselor can provide emotional support to help the child with IP develop good self-esteem and peer relationships. Providing education to the child's teacher and classmates will facilitate understanding of this syndrome.

The prognosis for children with IP is dependent on what non-skin-related manifestations of the disorder they have. Seizures during the first month of life usually indicate a very poor outlook and significant defects in the central nervous system. However, unless this problem occurs, the vast majority of patients with IP should do well.

For more information and support, contact National Incontinentia Pigmenti Foundation, 30 East 72nd Street #16, New York, NY 10021; (212) 452-1231; e-mail: nipf@pipeline.com; http://www.medhelp.org/www/nipf.htm.

REFERENCES

Darmstadt, G. L. (2000). Hyperpigmented lesions. In R. E. Behrman, R. K. Kleigman, & H. B. Jenson (Eds.), *Nelson's textbook of pediatrics* (16th ed., pp. 1984–1985). Philadelphia: W. B. Saunders.

Gandy, A. Incontinentia pigmenti. *Disease Database.* Retrieved from http://www.pedianet.com/news/illness/disease/files/incontin.htm

Incontinentia pigmenti. *Pediatric Database (PEDBASE).* Retrieved from http://www.icondata.com/health/pedbase/files/INCONTIN.HTM

National Organization for Rare Disorders, Inc. (1999). Incontinentia pigmenti. Retrieved from http://stepstn.com/cgi-win/nord.exe?proc=GetDocument&rectype-0&recnum=409

Jones, K. (1997). *Smith's recognizable patterns of human malformations* (5th ed.). Philadelphia: W. B. Saunders.

Barry H. Davison
Ennis, Texas

Joan W. Mayfield
Baylor Pediatric Specialty Services
Dallas, Texas

INFANTILE HYPERCALCEMIA (WILLIAMS SYNDROME)

Infantile hypercalcemia, or Williams syndrome, is a congenital disorder that affects a child's cognitive, physical, and behavioral development. It has been linked to the absence of genetic material on Chromosome 7. The deletion of portions of this chromosome, where elastin is made, results in many of the physical features seen in Williams syndrome (Sundheim, Ryan, & Voeller, 1998; Williams Syndrome Association, 1997a).

Williams syndrome has been estimated to occur in anywhere from 1 out of 20,000 to 1 out of 50,000 births. It is equally common in males and females and among different racial and ethnic groups. Although Williams syndrome is extremely rare, some familial links have been found (National Organization for Rare Disorders, 2000; Sundheim et al., 1998; Williams Syndrome Association, 1997a).

> Characteristics
>
> 1. Characteristic facial features such as an upturned nose, wide mouth with full lips and long upper lip, small chin, puffiness around the eyes, and light blue or green eyes with a star-like pattern
> 2. Developmental delays in speech and language as well as other developmental milestones
> 3. Intellectual handicaps
> 4. Excessively social personality

Partial deletion of Chromosome 7 is detected in approximately 90–95% of individuals with Williams syndrome. Chromosome deletion is confirmed through the use of a DNA blood test known as fluorescent in situ hybridization (FISH). Treatment of the syndrome includes medical attention for related medical problems, which include heart and blood vessel problems as well as elevated calcium in the bloodstream. Other symptoms may be associated with Williams syndrome, such as low birth weight, slow weight gain, smaller than average stature, hernias, hyperacousis, low muscle tone, sleep difficulty, and intellectual deficiencies. Often, psychostimulants are prescribed to address co-occurring attentional and learning difficulties.

Educational implications are important given the possibility of positive outcomes from early, consistent intervention (Williams Syndrome Association, 1997a). In the school setting, mobility problems may result in a more restricted classroom placement than general education (Flagler, 2000). A thorough psychoeducational evaluation (including speech-language, occupational, and physical therapy) is needed to determine the child's educational needs. A child with Williams syndrome may qualify for special education assistance under a number of handicapping conditions (for example, Speech/Language Impairment, Mental Retardation, Physical Handicap, etc.). For physical difficulties, physical therapy helps increase muscle tone and reduce joint stiffness (Williams Syndrome Association, 1997b). Sensory integration techniques may also be helpful to alleviate some physical symptoms (Sundheim et al., 1998). To target attentional symptoms, classroom modifications are similar to those applied to children with attention-deficit/hyperactivity disorder, such as having minimal distractions, taking frequent breaks, and reinforcing attentive behaviors (Williams Syndrome Association, 1997b).

Intellectually, children with Williams syndrome have been found to have ability levels between 40 and 90 standard score points, with most falling in the mild to moderate range of mental retardation (Sundheim et al., 1998). Given the large amount of variation in IQ scores, appropriate school placement depends on the individual child. Visual-spatial skills are a significant weakness and are associated with a tendency to focus on superficial details and ignore the gestalt. Specific strengths of children with Williams syndrome include excellent musical ability, strong language skills, and high social awareness including awareness of others' emotions and the ability to express accurately their own feelings (Sundheim et al., 1998).

Individuals with Williams syndrome have an average life expectancy. It has been found that for most, placement in special education classes throughout the school career is likely. Students with Williams syndrome frequently reach an early plateau of academic skills, resulting in their need to live and work in sheltered environments as they reach adulthood. Fewer than 5% of adults with Williams syndrome live independently or are employed in the general work force (Sundheim et al., 1998).

REFERENCES

Flagler, S. L. (2000). Infantile hypercalcemia. In C. R. Reynolds & E. Fletcher-Janzen (Eds.), *Encyclopedia of special education* (p. 950). New York: Wiley.

National Organization for Rare Disorders. (2000). Williams syndrome. Retrieved from http://www.rarediseases.org/lof/lof.html

Sundheim, S. T. P. V., Ryan, R. M., & Voeller, K. K. S. (1998). Williams syndrome. In C. E. Coffey & R. A. Brumback (Eds.), *Textbook of pediatric neuropsychology* (pp. 664–668). Washington, DC: American Psychiatric Press.

Williams Syndrome Association. (1997a). Facts about Williams syndrome. Retrieved from http://www.williams-syndrome.org/facts.htm

Williams Syndrome Association. (1997b). Williams syndrome: Information for teachers. Retrieved from http://www.williams-syndrome.org/teacher.htm

Kathryn L. Guy
University of Texas

Nancy L. Nussbaum
Austin Neurological Clinic

INHALANT ABUSE

Inhalant abuse involves the voluntary inhalation of gases or fumes in an effort to achieve an intoxicated state. These substances include many household products that are legal to buy and possess, including such things as airplane glue, nail polish remover, and propellants used in certain commercial products, such as whipped cream dispensers. Generally, the vapors are inhaled through the nose or mouth, a practice referred to as huffing, but they can also be ingested or absorbed through the skin. Adolescent abusers usually choose inhalants based on availability, the desired physiological effect, and the degree of social and legal risk associated with possessing the substance (Fullwood & Ginther, 1994).

Unlike nearly all other classes of drugs, the use of inhalants is most common among younger adolescents and tends to decline as youth grow older. A recent study indicated that 19.7% of eighth graders admitted to inhalant use (Johnston, O'Malley, & Bachman, 1999), with a wide range of reported use based on gender and ethnicity. Use by African American students appears to be least prevalent, with 4.2% reporting inhalant use in the past year, compared with 13.3% of White and 11.5% of Hispanic eighth graders. Among eighth graders, females consistently have a slightly higher annual prevalence rate (11.6% in 1998 vs. 10.6% for males); however, this trend does not hold for the older grades, in which there were 7.6% of 10th-grade females using inhalants compared with 8.4% of 10th-grade males. Native American females show very high rates for lifetime use (23.9%), exceeded only by White males (28.8%; Bates, Plemons, Jumper-Thurman, & Beauvais, 1997).

Characteristics

1. Short-term memory loss or other cognitive impairments
2. Emotional instability such as irritability or anxiety
3. Slow, slurred, or incoherent speech
4. Uncoordinated movements
5. Loss of smell and taste, sometimes accompanied by loss of appetite
6. Chemical smell in clothing, hair, or breath
7. Possible sores or spots around the mouth

Most inhalant use is either one time or for a brief period of time; only 2–5% of youth report chronic use (Beauvais, 2000). Unfortunately, the consequences of even a single use can be deadly as a result of asphyxia, suffocation, or sudden sniffing death syndrome, most often from cardiac arrest. Studies have suggested that inhalant abusers respond poorly to traditional drug treatment programs (Dinwiddie, Zorumski, & Rubin, 1987), and the long-term outcomes tend to be poor for these youth: high rates of school dropout, poor social and emotional adjustment, and increased involvement in illegal activities (Beauvais, 2000; Simpson & Barrett, 1991). Programs that have focused on positively impacting the adolescents' social environment by increasing family involvement and social support for the adolescents, fostering healthy peer relationships, and maximizing client interest in and commitment to treatment have had some success (Simpson & Barrett, 1991). Additionally, treatment programs should focus on increasing users' self-efficacy and teaching adaptive coping strategies so that users are better able to deal with difficult situations in the future (Gunning & D'Amato, 1999).

Because of the associated academic and emotional difficulties reported among abusers, it is likely that many of these youth will be involved in special education programming. Although students may be enrolled in any special education program, those with learning disabilities and emotional/behavioral disturbances are especially at risk (Gunning & D'Amato, 1999). This is also the case with students that are socially maladjusted or involved with the law and the legal system. Therefore, it is especially important that special education teachers and school psychologists be aware of the signs of inhalant abuse as well as the long-term neurological damage that can occur from inhalant abuse, including poor attention and concentration and memory difficulties (Filley, Heaton, & Rosenberg, 1990). Educational professionals should be familiar with the treatment resources available in their communities in order to provide immediate referral as needed. If a student presents with a history of chronic inhalant abuse, classroom instruction should be modified to accommodate the student's concentration and memory difficulties. Schools can also help prevent inhalant use by incorporating curriculum materials that contain straightforward information on the effects of inhalant abuse on learning and its physical and emotional effects.

Specific treatment and prevention strategies for inhalant abuse must be developed and tested before successful intervention can be achieved. Future research should be directed toward longitudinal studies that help identify the predictors of solvent abuse and the outcomes of such abuse. Although research has demonstrated the relationship between poor academic performance, dropping out, and volatile solvent abuse, the direct and causal nature of those relationships remains unclear.

REFERENCES

Bates, S. C., Plemons, B. W., Jumper-Thurman, P., & Beauvais, F. (1997). Volatile solvent use: Patterns by gender and ethnicity among school attenders and dropouts. *Drugs and Society, 10*(1/2), 61–78.

Beauvais, F. (2000). Inhalant abuse: Causes, consequences, and prevention. *The Prevention Researcher, 7*(3), 3–6.

Dinwiddie, S. H., Zorumski, C. F., & Rubin, E. H. (1987). Psychiatric correlates of chronic solvent abuse. *Journal of Clinical Psychiatry, 48,* 334–337.

Filley, C. M., Heaton, R. K., & Rosenberg, N. L. (1990). White matter dementia in chronic toluene abuse. *Neurology, 40,* 532–534.

Fullwood, H., & Ginther, D. W. (1994). Inhalant abuse: The silent epidemic. *Principal 74,* 52–53.

Gunning, M. P., & D'Amato, R. C. (1999). Understanding and preventing inhalant abuse among children and adolescents in schools. *Communiqué, 25,* 31–32.

Johnston, L. D., O'Malley, P. M., & Bachman, J. G. (1999). *National survey results on drug use from the Monitoring the Future study, 1975–1998: Vol. 1. Secondary school students* (NIH Publication No. 99-4660). Bethesda, MD: National Institute on Drug Abuse.

Simpson, D. D., & Barrett, M. E. (1991). A longitudinal study of inhalant use: Overview and discussion of findings. *Hispanic Journal of Behavioral Sciences, 13,* 341–355.

Robyn S. Hess
University of Colorado at Denver

Rik Carl D'Amato
University of Northern Colorado

INSATIABLE CHILD SYNDROME

Insatiable child syndrome is characterized by a chronic inability to be satisfied (Levine, Brooks, & Schonkoff, 1980). Usually the child craves specific foods, certain activities, attention from others, or material goods. The child's insatiability may be organic or could be learned, such as when humiliating experiences leave the child feeling useless and craving for the attention of others.

The prevalence of the disorder is not well documented, and it usually appears secondary to an attention deficit disorder (Templeton, 1995). Correct diagnosis depends on ruling out the genetic disorder Prader-Willi syndrome due to similar characteristics including food insatiability. Current societal pressures and mores may increase the prevalence rates of this disorder.

Characteristics

1. Onset beginning in early infancy if the disorder is organic
2. Onset later in life if the disorder is related to environmental influences
3. An uncontrollable desire for food, activities, attention, or material goods
4. Children presenting as whiney, irritable, and unpleasant
5. Parents reporting that children are demanding and difficult to live with
6. Usually associated with a diagnosed attention deficit disorder
7. Insatiability not better accounted for by Prader-Willi syndrome, a genetic disorder characterized by overeating and gross obesity

Due to the low incidence of the disorder, treatment of insatiable child syndrome depends mostly on correct diagnosis (Reynolds, 1999). To increase the probability of an appropriate diagnosis and offer proper treatment, a functional behavior assessment should be conducted to assess the setting events, antecedents, and consequences linked to the child's insatiability.

After the data are analyzed, home and school treatment should be developed to change the behavior of the child, such as by building the child's ability to delay receiving gratification, helping the child understand that parents or other adults cannot be available all the time, and encouraging sharing with other children (Levine et al., 1980). In addition, relationship development between the child and the parents and between the child and his or her teacher should be a target of intervention. One-on-one time or special playtime with significant individuals to reinforce appropriate attention behaviors should be encouraged. The goal of special playtime is to help the child feel more secure and to decrease feelings of helplessness and deprivation (Levine et al., 1980). Another objective may be to set up specific collaborative activities with other children, such as turn-taking games, to promote sharing. Traditional family therapy may also be warranted.

School teachers should also develop special activities with the child to promote positive reinforcement (Levine et al., 1980). Teachers may use praise for completed tasks and delayed gratification to help the child feel more competent and self-sufficient. This in turn may decrease the child's insatiability.

Because insatiability is a behavior problem, prognosis is good if there is sufficient home-school collaboration on interventions. This entails school personnel and parents working together toward common goals to decrease insatiability in the home and school settings. Such collaboration increases the probability of generalization within all environments. Future research should focus on prevalence rates, etiology, and intervention strategies.

REFERENCES

Levine, M. D., Brooks, R., & Shonkoff, J. P. (1980). *A pediatric approach to learning disorders.* New York: Wiley.

Reynolds, C. R. (1999). Insatiable child syndrome. In C. R. Reynolds & E. Fletcher-Jansen (Eds.), *The encyclopedia of special education* (Vol. 2). New York: Wiley.

Templeton, R. (1995, February). ADHD: A teacher's guide. *Oregon Conference Monograph, 7.*

Sherri Lynn Gallagher
Rik Carl D'Amato
University of Northern Colorado

INTESTINAL PSEUDO-OBSTRUCTION

Intestinal pseudo-obstruction (IPO) is a congenital digestive disorder resulting from the inability of the intestines to move food through the digestive tract. The intestine may be abnormally formed, and peristalsis (involuntary wave-like contractions that propel food through the digestive system) is absent or lacking. This condition resembles a true obstruction of the intestine, but no blockage is present.

IPO is rare and is believed by some to be a X-linked recessive trait and by others to be an autosomal dominant trait.

Characteristics

1. Abdominal pain, vomiting, diarrhea, and constipation
2. Malabsorption of nutrients causing failure to thrive or weight loss in infants and children
3. Distended abdomen with accumulations of fluid or air
4. Occasionally impaired walking coordination, poor muscle sensation, abnormal dilation of the pupils, and speech disturbances

Antibiotics can be employed to treat malabsorption and diarrhea caused by bacteria accumulation when the food remains stationary in the intestines. In severe cases, food may be administered parenterally or enterally. Parenteral administration of nutrition consists of being fed in any manner that does not involve the digestive tract (e.g., intravenous, subcutaneous, or intramuscular administration). Enteral feeding involves feeding through a tube directly into the gastrointestinal tract. Surgical procedures are often necessary to implant the feeding tubes. Additional treatments are symptomatic and vary by individual.

Special education issues relate to the child's health impairments. If the child experiences speech impediments, speech pathologists should be brought in to work with the patient. Physical therapy and orthopedic assistance may also be needed if the individual presents with motor coordination difficulties.

For individuals suffering from IPO, prognosis is highly dependent on severity of symptoms and access to alternative methods of receiving nutrients. A majority of patients live out a normal life span; however, quality of life is impaired. Future research includes effectiveness of new medications that could correct the hypomotility of the small intestine, and further interest is in the genetic attributes of IPO.

REFERENCES

Scolapio, J. S., Ukleia, A., Bouras, E. P., & Romano, M. (1999). Nutritional management of chronic intestinal pseudo-obstruction. *Journal of Gastroenterology, 28,* 306–312.

Stanghellini, V., Camilleri, M., & Malagelada, J. R. (1987). Chronic idiopathic intestinal pseudo-obstruction: Clinical and intestinal manometric findings. *Gut, 28,* 5–12.

Kimberly M. Estep
University of Houston–Clear Lake

ISOVALERIC ACIDEMIA

Isovaleric acidemia is characterized by a deficiency of the enzyme isovaleryl CoA dehydrogenase. This enzyme is essential to normal metabolism of the amino acid lysine. Clinical manifestations of this disorder are caused by accumulations of large amounts of isovaleric acid and its metabolites in tissue and body fluids.

Isovaleric acidemic is rare. Its frequency in the general population is unknown. The abnormal gene is located on the long arm of Chromosome 15. Like most hereditary enzyme deficiencies, isovaleric acidemia is an autosomal recessive disorder.

Characteristics

1. The acute form causes symptoms in the first few days of life, once protein intake is established. Milder clinical forms may remain asymptomatic for a few months or even 2–3 years. The acute form accounts for 50% of cases.
2. Symptoms of the acute form include vomiting, lethargy, seizures, and a peculiar odor of sweaty feet about the baby.
3. Babies with the acute form become comatose and eventually die within a few days from the onset of illness unless prompt diagnosis is made and appropriate therapy is started.
4. Laboratory findings include severe acidosis, low white blood cell and platelet counts, low calcium, elevated ammonia, and occasionally elevated blood glucose.
5. Diagnosis is confirmed by finding elevated levels of isovaleric acid and its metabolites in body fluids, especially urine. This assay is not generally available in hospitals other than tertiary pediatric centers that specialize in the care of critically ill infants and children.

Treatment of acute attacks requires rehydration with intravenous fluids, correction of acidosis, and removal of excess isovaleric acid. Some patients may need exchange transfusions or dialysis to ensure rapid clinical and biochemical improvement. Chronic treatment of isovaleric acidemia includes a low protein diet and glycine and carnatine supplements.

The prognosis for this disorder is generally good, provided that it is promptly diagnosed and treated. Normal development can occur if these requirements are met. However, the initial symptoms of an acute attack are nonspecific and suggest many other clinical entities, such as sepsis, that are far more common than isovaleric acidemia. The astute clinician must always consider an abnormality of amino acid metabolism when confronted with an extremely ill newborn, even though it may be the only case he or she will ever encounter.

REFERENCES

Rezvani, I., & Rosenblatt, D. S. (2000). Defects in metabolism of amino acids. In R. E. Behrman, R. M. Kleigman, & H. B. Jenson (Eds.), *Nelson's textbook of pediatrics* (16th ed., pp. 344–377). Philadelphia: W. B. Saunders.

Barry H. Davison
Ennis, Texas

Joan W. Mayfield
Baylor Pediatric Specialty Services
Dallas, Texas

ITO'S HYPOMELANOSIS

Hypomelanosis of Ito (HMI) is a rare skin condition characterized by hypopigmentation (unusual lack of skin color) caused by lack of melanin. Hypopigmentation may appear on any area of the body except the palms of the hands, the soles of the feet, and the scalp. Numerous other congenital defects may be present including neurological, skeletal, hair, and dental abnormalities. Causes of HMI elude researchers, but theories point to a chromosomal mosaicism (an occurrence in an individual of two or more cell populations of different chromosomal constitutions derived from a single zygote). Sporadic mutations also may occur. Intellectual and adaptive deficits are usually present.

HMI is usually diagnosed in childhood, and genetic links have been noted with no consensus on an exact locus. HMI occurs 1.5 to 2.5 times more often in females than in males.

Characteristics

1. Hypopigmentation of the skin occurs in patches, whirls, or streaks.
2. Often the child presents with seizures, dental abnormalities such as extra cusps or incisors, deafness, and megaloencephaly (enlargement of the brain).
3. Visual problems including cataracts, a cleft along the edge of the iris of the eye, nearsightedness, and crossed eyes may be present.
4. Varying degrees of mental retardation are evident in children, as are developmental delays.
5. Affected individuals do not have the ability to sweat in the areas of hypopigmentation.

A team of specialized health care professionals is usually required to work with these children. For example, dentists are required to address dental anomalies. Orthopedists and ophthalmologists are required to assist patients with orthopedic and visual abnormalities. Psychologist are usually necessary to address cognitive limitations.

No treatment exists for the hypopigmentation, and some patients may wish to use makeup to conceal the affected areas. Medications to control seizures are usually necessary.

Affected children need special education services, and these services vary by degree of impairment, thereby making appropriate assessment vital. Children affected by HMI likely qualify for special education services as Other Health Impairment with behavior problems and speech and language delays associated with mental retardation. Occupational therapy may also be needed.

Prognosis is highly dependent on the severity of the disorders associated with HMI and is excellent for patients presenting with only cutaneous manifestations of HMI. Morbidity rates increase with the number of associated defects and complications. Anticonvulsant drugs are an area of research interest as well as research on birth defect causality and etiology.

REFERENCES

Donnai, D., Read, A. P., & Mckeown, C. (1988). Hypomelanosis of Ito: Manifestation of mosaicism or chimerism. *Journal of Medical Genetics, 25,* 809–818.

Glover, M. T., Brett, E. M., & Atherton, D. J. (1989). Hypomelanosis of Ito: Spectrum of the disease. *Journal of Pediatrics, 115,* 75–80.

Gross, N., & Ratz, J. (2000). Hypomelanosis of Ito. *eMedicine, 1*(5). Retrieved June 2001 from http://www.emedicine.com/derm/topic186.html

Pascual-Castroviejo, I., Roche, C., & Martinez-Bermejo, A. (1998). Hypomelanosis of Ito: A study of 76 infantile cases. *Brain Development, 20*(1), 36–43.

Kimberly M. Estep
University of Houston–Clear Lake

J

JOB SYNDROME

The National Organization for Rare Disorders, Inc. (NORD, 1999) states that Job syndrome (JS) is a congenital immunodeficiency disorder that is characterized by recurrent bacterial (staphylococcal) infections that focus primarily on the skin. JS is a very rare disorder that affects an equal number of males and females. Symptoms of JS are present at birth or early childhood. JS causes extremely elevated immunoglobulin E (IgE) levels. JS is also known as HIE syndrome, hyper-IgE syndrome, hyperimmunoglobulin E syndrome, hyperimmunoglobulin E staphylococcal, and Job-Buckley syndrome (NORD, 1999). Eppinger, Greenberger, White, Brown, and Cunningham-Rundles (1999) report that patients with JS have increased susceptibility of catching bacterial and fungal infections. The staphylococcal infection is the most common infection to attack patients with JS and may involve the skin, lungs, joints, and other sites. More rarely, a patient with JS will develop a potentially deadly *Aspergillus* species infection (Eppinger et al., 1999). NORD (1999) reported that JS, like other immune disorders, may impair the white blood cells (neutrophils) that destroy bacteria, cell debris, and solid particles in the blood. JS can be inherited through an autosomal dominant trait. This means that in order for a child to inherit JS, both parents must be carriers and have one normal gene and one recessive gene for JS. There is a 25% chance that a child of two carriers will receive a JS gene from both parents. A child of this couple would have a 50% chance of being a genetic carrier of JS and a 25% chance of receiving both normal genes (NORD, 1999). The minimum criteria for a diagnosis of JS can be made on the basis of the presence of elevated IgE levels, a history of staphylococcal pulmonary infections, and the presence of an eczematous skin rash (Eppinger et al., 1999).

Characteristics

1. Cold staphylococcal abscesses, which are pus-filled holes caused by bacterial infection. These abscesses are usually found on the skin but may also present on the mastoid bone behind the ear, joints, gums, bronchi (air passages in the lungs), and in the lungs.
2. Granulocyte chemotactic defect, a problem experienced by patients with JS, in which the leukocytes (the living substance of white blood cells) are unable to protectively destroy bacteria, fungi, and viruses, thereby allowing bacteria to thrive.
3. Chronic eczema, a swelling of the outer skin surface with the presence of itchy, small red blisters that become thick, scaly, and crusted.
4. Hyperimmunoglobulinemia E, a condition in which there is an excess of immunoglobulin E, one of the five fluid antibodies the human body produces, which reacts with foreign substances by releasing chemicals that redden the skin. This antibody is concentrated in the lungs, skin, and mucous membrane cells.
5. Mild eosinophilia, a mild increase in the number of leukocyte white blood cells (eosinophils), which increase when infection or allergies are present in the body.

Symptoms of JS are most effectively treated with continuous oral antibiotic prophylaxis, which serves to reduce infections from chronically recurring (Eppinger et al., 1999). Although antibiotic treatment (usually trimethoprim or sulfamethoxazole) is usually effective, patients generally experience repeated infections (NORD, 1999). NORD (1999) suggested that patients with JS and their families may be referred to genetic counseling, and other treatments may include providing relief from symptoms and a possible mental health referral for supportive therapy if needed.

In the classroom, teachers need to be aware that students with JS experience repeated health problems and may need to miss school at times. Teachers should also be aware that the student may have difficulty with peer teasing and may have self-esteem issues. In order to work with these issues, teachers can be helpful to JS students by providing makeup work or extra homework assignments as well as tutoring sessions in order to prevent a student with JS from falling behind their classmates. In addition, a teacher may want to contact the parent or refer the student to the school counselor in order to help the student deal with emotional conflicts that may result from his or her condition.

JS is a chronic disorder that usually can be managed successfully by prophylactic medication (Eppinger et al., 1999).

However, an individual with JS may be susceptible to uncommon diseases, such as aspergillus fumigatus infections, which may become deadly. Future research could focus on understanding the link between JS and granulocyte dysfunction, which leads to a possible diagnosis of aspergillus fumigatus, which has a high morbidity rate (Eppinger et al., 1999). NORD (1999) stated that the long-term safety and effectiveness of the treatment of interferon gamma for JS patients, which is designed to ameliorate excessive immunoglobulin E production, is currently being explored.

REFERENCES

Eppinger, T. M., Greenberger, P. A., White, D. A., Brown, A. E., & Cunningham-Rundles, C. (1999). Sensitization to *Aspergillus* species in the congenital neutrophil disorders chronic granulomatous diseease and hyper-Ige syndrome. *Journal of Allergy and Clinical Immunology, 104,* 1265–1272.

National Organization for Rare Disorders, Inc. (1999). Job syndrome. Retrieved from http://www.rarediseases.org

Jennie Kaufman Singer
California Department of Corrections, Region 1 Parole Outpatient Clinic
Sacramento, California

JOHANSON-BLIZZARD SYNDROME

Johanson-Blizzard syndrome is a disorder characterized by a thin, beak-like nose due to abnormalities in nostril development; coarse, thin scalp hair that grows in a distinctive upsweeping pattern; and abnormal development and functioning of the pancreas that results in a failure to grow and gain weight as expected. Approximately 60% of individuals with the disorder have a moderate developmental delay. Others may have a mild delay or normal intelligence (Moeschler & Lubinsky, 1985; National Organization for Rare Disorders [NORD], 1998). The range and severity of symptoms varies widely from case to case (Hurst & Baraitser, 1989; NORD, 1998).

Johanson-Blizzard syndrome is extremely rare, with only 22 (Hurst & Baraitser, 1989) to 26 (Gershoni-Baruch et al., 1990) reported cases. It is a genetic disorder with an autosomal recessive inheritance that is present at birth (NORD, 1998).

Characteristics

1. Thin, beak-shaped nose with absent or underdeveloped nostrils; other facial anomalies (NORD, 1998)
2. Dry, patchy scalp hair with an upsweep at the forehead (Hurst & Baraitser, 1989)
3. Pancreatic defect; malabsorption of fats and nutrients caused by enzyme deficiencies
4. Microcephaly
5. Failure to thrive; short stature
6. Developmental delay
7. Dental abnormalities including malformed primary teeth and absent permanent teeth
8. Anorectal, genitourinary, and cardiac malformations

Treatment of individuals with Johanson-Blizzard syndrome has focused on treating the pancreatic defect. Success rates have varied (Hurst & Baraister, 1989).

Children with Johanson-Blizzard syndrome may require special education services for physical weakness and psychomotor retardation, speech and hearing impairments, and medical needs. Speech and language therapy and physical and occupational therapy may be necessary. Additionally, many require placement in an educational environment that is appropriate for individuals with developmental delays. Students with the disorder may also need home-based schooling or home visits from a teacher because medical difficulties often require them to be absent from the classroom.

The prognosis for individuals with this disorder is poor. Infections and complications from malabsorption and failure to thrive often develop and lead to death in childhood (Hurst & Baraister, 1989). The focus of current and future research is on continued symptom identification and treatment.

REFERENCES

Gershoni-Baruch, R., Lerner, A., Braun, J., Katzir, Y., Iancu, T. C., & Benderly, A. (1990). Johanson-Blizzard syndrome: Clinical spectrum and further delineation of the syndrome. *American Journal of Medical Genetics, 35,* 546–551.

Hurst, J. A., & Baraitser, M. (1989). Johanson-Blizzard syndrome. *Journal of Medical Genetics, 26,* 45–48.

Moeschler, J. B., & Lubinsky, M. S. (1985). Brief clinical report: Johanson-Blizzard syndrome with normal intelligence. *American Journal of Medical Genetics, 22,* 69–73.

National Organization for Rare Disorders. (1998). Johanson-Blizzard syndrome. Retrieved from http://www.rarediseases.org

Stacey L. Bates
University of Texas at Austin

JOUBERT SYNDROME

Joubert syndrome is an autosomal-recessive disorder characterized by brain stem and cerebral malformation, as well as central nervous system deficits and motor difficulties. Children affected with this syndrome exhibit developmental delay, apnea during infancy, limited fine and gross motor coordination, and abnormal eye movement. Some neonates may have tachypnea, abnormal breathing similar to the panting of a dog. Tachypnea typically improves and disappears with age and is followed by apnea (Gitten, Dede, Fennell, Quisling, & Maria 1998).

Prenatal testing with a Level 3 ultrasound may be possible to detect the presence of Joubert syndrome. Joubert syndrome is a rare disorder, and prevalence is unknown. It has been more commonly reported in males in a 2:1 ratio.

Characteristics

1. Absence or underdevelopment of cerebellar vermis, resulting in ataxia and hypotonia
2. Malformation of brain stem and possibly the cerebral hemispheres resulting in abnormal breathing that initially presents as panting in infancy and may be followed by apnea
3. Abnormal eye and tongue movement
4. Hypotonia
5. Symptoms contributing to global developmental delay
6. Commonly mild or moderate mental retardation
7. Molar tooth sign in the mesencephalon

(Luescher, Dede, Gitten, Fennell, & Maria, 1999; Maria, Boltshauser, Palmer, & Tran, 1999)

Physical and intellectual disabilities associated with Joubert syndrome can severely impact learning and communication. Infant stimulation should be provided to address vision and motor dysfunction that may inhibit the child's ability to gather stimuli from the environment (Joubert Syndrome Foundation, n.d.). Children with Joubert syndrome are typically pleasant, easy to guide, and socially well integrated (Maria et al., 1999). Special education services may be available to children with Joubert syndrome under the handicapping condition of Other Health Impairment, Physical Disability, or Mental Retardation. Physical therapy, speech therapy, and occupational therapy should be provided to address impairment of expressive and receptive language skills, as well as motor delays.

Outcome of children with Joubert syndrome varies from death in infancy, to severe disability that may include deterioration of mental and motor functioning, to absence of symptoms at follow-up exams (Gitten et al., 1998). Severity of developmental delay is not associated with severity of central nervous system malformations, and the prognostic functioning of a child with Joubert syndrome is best determined through neuropsychological assessment rather than neurological evaluation (Gitten et al., 1998). Future research addressing the development of children with Joubert syndrome should include factors such as rehabilitation and special education received, as well as family variables (Gitten et al., 1998).

REFERENCES

Gitten, J., Dede, D., Fennell, E., Quisling, R., & Maria, B. (1998). Neurobehavioral development in Joubert syndrome. *Journal of Child Neurology, 13,* 391–397.

Joubert Syndrome Foundation. (n.d.). Homepage. Retrieved from http://users.erols.com/joubert/

Luescher, J. L., Dede, D., Gitten, J. C., Fennell, E., & Maria, B. L. (1999). Parent burden, coping, and family functioning in primary caregivers of children with Joubert syndrome. *Journal of Child Neurology, 14,* 642–648.

Maria, B. L., Boltshauser, E., Palmer, S. C., & Tran, T. X. (1999). Clinical features and revised diagnostic criteria in Joubert syndrome. *Journal of Child Neurology, 14,* 583–590.

Kimberly D. Wilson
University of Texas at Austin

JUBERG-MARSIDI SYNDROME

Juberg-Marsidi syndrome (JMS) is a rare, multisystem, congenital condition characterized by pronounced mental retardation, stunted growth, sensory deficiencies, and microgenitalism (Juberg & Marsidi, 1980). JMS is X-linked recessive; all affected cases have been males born to phenotypically normal mothers.

Although born of full-term pregnancies, infants with JMS show low birth weight, height, and head circumference (in the 5th or lower percentile), with small penis, scrotum, and impalpable testes. There are also dysmorphic facial features, such as flattened nasal bridge, dysplastic and sometimes asymmetrical ears, and high forehead. JMS children eventually show marked delays in bone maturation, hypotonia, and gross motor function (e.g., late in sitting and walking), as well as delays in speech production. In addition, JMS children show sensory deficits; most are hearing-impaired or completely deaf with some visual problems, such as retinal pigmentation and crossed eyes (Mattei, Collignon, Ayme, & Giraud, 1983). Children with JMS show severe mental retardation, manifested as disinterested gaze, poor visual tracking, and absent or limited speech production. Although the details of psychometric evaluation of JMS patients have not been reported, patients with other X-linked mental retardation syndromes typically show IQ scores well below 70.

Characteristics

1. X-linked recessive syndrome
2. Mental retardation, growth retardation, facial dysmorphisms, microgenitalism, and sensory deficiencies
3. Poor prognosis: death occurring by late childhood

Prognosis for children with JMS is poor. There is no cure, and JMS patients die by late childhood. Older JMS patients (over 5 years of age) can be incapacitated by illness or severe hypotonia.

JMS is an X-linked recessive mental retardation syndrome. There are numerous other forms of X-linked mental retardation, such as Borjeson and Lowe syndromes, that have some but not all of the characteristics of JMS (Glass, 1991). However, a recent study in which the genetic locus of JMS was isolated and a key genetic mutation in JMS-carrying families was identified that further distinguishes JMS from other X-linked syndromes (Villard et al., 1996). Such advances in understanding the genetic basis of JMS will help provide reliable genetic counseling for at-risk women. In addition, identified gene mutations will lead to an understanding of the mechanisms underlying JMS symptoms and yield new treatments.

REFERENCES

Glass, I. A. (1991). X-linked mental retardation. *Journal of Medical Genetics, 28,* 361–371.

Juberg, R. C., & Marsidi, I. (1980). A new form of X-linked mental retardation with growth retardation, deafness, and microgenitalism. *American Journal of Human Genetics, 32,* 714–722.

Mattei, J. F., Collignon, P., Ayme, S., & Giraud, F. (1983). X-linked mental retardation, growth retardation, deafness and microgenitalism: A second familial report. *Clinical Genetics, 23,* 70–74.

Villard, L., Gecz, J., Mattei, J. F., Fontes, M., Saugier-Veber P., Munnich, A., & Lyonnet, S. (1996). XNP mutation in a large family with Juberg-Marsidi syndrome. *Nature Genetics, 12,* 359–360.

Adam S. Bristol
Yale University

JUVENILE CEREBROMACULAR DEGENERATION

Juvenile cerebromacular degeneration is also called as Tay-Sachs disease (TSD). TSD is a rare, progressive, neurodegenerative, genetic disorder in which harmful quantities of a fatty substance called ganglioside GM2 accumulate in the nerve cells in the brain (McKusick, 2000; National Institute of Neurological Disorders and Stroke [NINDS], 2000; National Organization for Rare Disorders [NORD], 2000).

A baby with TSD appears normal at birth and seems to develop normally until about 6 months of age. By the time a child with TSD is 3 or 4 years old, the nervous system is very badly affected. Children with TSD usually die by age 5 (NINDS, 2000). A person's chances of being a TSD carrier are significantly higher if he or she is of eastern European (Ashkenazi) Jewish descent. Approximately one in every 27 Jews in the United States is a carrier of the TSD gene. There is also a noticeable incidence of TSD in non-Jewish French Canadians who live near the St. Lawrence River and in the Cajun community of Louisiana. In contrast, the carrier rate in the general population as well as in Jews of Sephardic origin is about 1 in 250 (NINDS, 2000).

Characteristics (NINDS, 2000; NORD, 2000; McKusick 2000)

1. Infants with TSD appear to develop normally for the first few months of life.
2. Infants' physical and mental abilities start to deteriorate relentlessly: a loss of peripheral vision, abnormal startle response to noises, decreased eye contact, listlessness, and recurrent seizures (uncontrolled electrical disturbances in the brain).
3. Infants and children with this disorder may develop cherry-red spots within the middle layer of the eyes, gradual loss of vision, deafness, uncontrolled electrical disturbances in the brain (seizures), and deterioration of cognitive processes (dementia).
4. The infant gradually increases muscle stiffness and restricted movement (spasticity). The infant loses skills and is eventually unable to crawl, turn over, sit, or reach out.
5. The infant may experience loss of coordination, inability to swallow, and breathing difficulties.
6. The child may become mentally retarded, blind, or paralyzed.

Presently there is no treatment for TSD. All the treatments are symptomatic and supportive. Even though there is no cure currently, there is a way to prevent TSD. Today, at-risk couples can choose from two available prenatal diagnostic procedures: amniocentesis and chorionic villus sampling (CVS). Amniocentesis is done at approximately the 16th week of pregnancy. CVS is a newer technique. It is performed by the 10th week, and it usually provides a test answer much sooner than does amniocentesis. Furthermore, assisted reproductive technologies are available to at-risk couples who wish to have children but who do not consider abortion as an option. One option is artificial insemination, and the other option involves in vitro fertilization. Finally, genetic counseling is also available to all carrier couples to assist them in assessing their reproductive options (NINDS, 2000).

Given the mortality rate of TSD, these children are unlikely to require special education services. At most, some of the children might receive Early Childhood service. Under Early Childhood, children could receive any type of service (speech, physical, and occupational therapy). It seems that they would be more likely to receive some kind of care such as hospice to make them comfortable and treat symptoms. If the children can attend school, they would probably qualify as multiply handicapped.

The prognosis of the TSD is very poor. Even with the best of care, children with TSD usually die by the age of 5. Studies are done to find ways to treat and prevent TSD. Currently, NINDS investigators are conducting basic biochemical and molecular genetic research studies to deliver the corrective enzyme and the normal gene to the brains of patients with TSD (NINDS, 2000).

REFERENCES

McKusick, V. A. (2000). Tay-Sachs disease. *Online Mendelian inheritance in man.* Retrieved from http://www3.ncbi.nlm.nih.gov/htbin-post/Omim/dispmim?272800

National Institute of Neurological Disorders and Stroke. (2000, June 27). Tay-Sachs disease. Retrieved from http://www.ninds.nih/health and medical/disorders/taysacks_doc.htm

National Organization for Rare Disorders (2000). Cerebromacular degeneration condition. Retrieved from http://www.rarediseases.org

Nina Cheng
University of Texas at Austin

See also Tay-Sachs Disease

K

KAISER-FLEISCHER RING

Kaiser-Fleischer ring (KFR) is an abnormality of the cornea, which is the transparent covering of the pupil and iris. KFR consists of a circular deposit of golden brown, copper-containing material of the outer edge of the cornea.

KFR is one of the hallmarks of Wilson disease (WD), a rare, autosomal-recessive disorder of copper metabolism. In addition to KFR, WD causes severe liver damage, degenerative changes in the brain, and kidney failure.

KFR may not be found in younger patients with WD. However, in previously undiagnosed individuals over 20 years old, it is invariably seen and is closely associated with neurologic complications (tremor, psychiatric disturbance, slurred speech, deterioration of academic skills, and abnormal muscle tone). Effective treatment of WD results in the disappearance of KFR, as well as in marked improvement in the patient's neurologic status.

REFERENCES

Balistreri, W. F. (2000). Metabolic diseases of the liver. In R. E. Behrman, R. K. Kleigman, & H. B. Jenson (Eds.), *Nelson's textbook of pediatrics* (16th ed., pp. 1209–1210). Philadelphia: W. B. Saunders.

Olitsky, S. E., & Nelson, L. B. (2000). Abnormalities of the cornea. In R. E. Behrman, R. K. Kleigman, & H. B. Jenson (Eds.), *Nelson's textbook of pediatrics* (16th ed., p. 1916). Philadelphia: W. B. Saunders.

Barry H. Davison
Ennis, Texas

Joan W. Mayfield
Baylor Pediatric Specialty Services
Dallas, Texas

See also Wilson Disease

KAWASAKI SYNDROME

Kawasaki syndrome, also known as mucocutaneous lymph node syndrome, is a form of acute vasculitis that occurs almost exclusively in young children. In fact, approximately 80% of cases occur in children under 5 years old. This syndrome is extremely rare in children older than age 10. Etiology of the illness is unknown, but many experts agree that an infection (viral or bacterial) is likely, although a genetic predisposition may also play a role (Burns, 1999).

It is estimated that the syndrome is seen in approximately 1 in 10,000 children less than 5 years old. Kawasaki syndrome is more common in boys than girls (1.5:1) and occurs in all parts of the world and in all ethnicities, but is most common in children of Asian decent. This syndrome is the leading cause of acquired heart disease in young children. The disease can occur in clusters of localized outbreaks, often in the winter and spring. Recurrence of the illness is rare: Recurrence rates range from < 2% (U.S.) to 4.3% (Japan). Mortality from the illness is <1% (Burns, 1999).

Characteristics

1. Fever that is unresponsive to Tylenol or aspirin for more than 5 days (often the first symptom)
2. Conjunctivitis usually without discharge (red, swollen eyes)
3. Enlarged lymph glands in the neck
4. Irritation and inflammation of the mucous membranes of the mouth and throat
5. Red rash on the hands and soles of the feet and/or groin area
6. Transverse, indented lines on fingernails and toenails
7. Risk for coronary complications related to vasculitis

The immediate effects of Kawasaki syndrome are generally not serious, but long-term coronary damage can occur, particularly if treatment is delayed. Approximately 15–20% of children affected with this disease display coronary damage, but most problems resolve in 5–6 weeks (American Heart Association [AHA], 2000). These complications include arrhythmia, myocarditis, pericarditis, and coronary artery aneurisms. Blood clots can also form, leading to myocardial infarction (heart attack). Although most of these complications resolve, some children experience long-term complications. Other potentially serious complications include arthritis and hydrops of the gall bladder.

Neurological complications are relatively rare (1–30% of cases), and most resolve within weeks. Facial nerve paralysis can occur, but it usually resolves spontaneously within 1–2 weeks. Other possible neurologic complications include asceptic meningitis, increased intercranial pressure, seizure, ataxia, hemiplegia, encephalopathy, and cerebral infarction (Vanderbilt Medical Center, 2000).

Treatment consists of gamma globulin administered intravenously to reduce inflammation and risk of coronary damage. This treatment is most effective if started within the first 10 days of the illness (incidence of coronary artery lesions decreases from 18% to 4%; Pediatric Database, 2000). In addition, high dosages of aspirin are usually administered to reduce fever and risk of blood clotting. The child is likely to be hospitalized for 1–2 days for treatment and monitoring.

As the fever resolves, rash, conjunctivitis, and inflamed lymph nodes usually disappear. Skin starts to peel around the toenails and fingernails, usually around the third week of illness. The skin may peel off in large pieces. Joint pain may continue after other symptoms resolve. The child may be followed by a cardiologist or other specialist long-term if complications arise.

Special education services may be available to children with Kawasaki syndrome under the handicapping condition of Other Health Impairment or Physical Disability. During the acute stage of the illness (first 7–10 days), the child is not able to attend school. Often, extended time away from the classroom is required during recuperation. Because the child is likely to feel weak as the illness resolves, he or she may need to be reintroduced to the school day slowly, starting with half days. He or she may have difficulty catching up with work and may require additional tutoring to keep up with these demands. For the children who experience cardiac complications, physical activity may be limited.

The effects of Kawasaki Syndrome on neurocognitive functioning are somewhat unclear at this time. King et al. (2000) found that children who had recovered from Kawasaki syndrome did not show differences from comparison children in intellectual functioning or academic achievement and that performance was generally within the average range. However, parents rated these children as having more attentional and internalizing difficulty and were more likely to have behavior problems than were comparison children (King et al., 2000). These results suggest the possibility of lingering neurocognitive and emotional effects, requiring further study.

Prognosis is best if treated early (within the first 10 days of illness). Full recovery is expected in most cases, but the possibility of increased risk for heart disease later in life even with initial recovery has yet to be fully investigated. In addition, lingering coronary problems are possible, particularly if gamma globulin treatment is delayed greater than 10 days of onset (AHA, 2000).

REFERENCES

American Heart Association. (2000, September 13). Kawasaki disease. Retrieved from http://www.amhrt.org/heartg/kawasaki.html

Burns, J. C. (1999). Kawasaki disease parent guide. Retrieved from http://www.pediatrics.ucsd.edu/research/disease/kd_pargd.htm

King, W. J., Schlieper, A., Birdi, N., Cappelli, M., Korneluk, Y., & Rowe, P. C. (2000). The effect of Kawasaki disease on cognition and behavior. *Archives of Pediatrics and Adolescent Medicine, 154* (5), 463–468.

Pediatric Database. (2000, September 18). Kawasaki's syndrome. Retrieved from http://icondata.com/health/pedbase/files/KAWASAKI.HTM

Vanderbilt Medical Center. (2000, September 18). Neurologic complications of Kawasaki disease. Retrieved from http://www.mc.vanderbilt.edu/peds/pidl/infect/kawasak2.htm

Melissa R. Bunner
Austin Neurological Clinic

KEARNS-SAYRE SYNDROME

Kearns-Sayre syndrome (KSS) is a multisystem genetic disorder caused by defects of mitochondrial DNA. KSS is one of the more frequent forms of mitochondrial respiratory chain deficiency. Most if not all cases have been sporadic. Clinical manifestations are highly variable, multisystem defects that involve abnormality of the central nervous system (CNS), skeletal muscle, heart, and kidney or a combination thereof. Cardiac conduction defects are one of the three main symptoms in KSS (Matsushita & Okadar, 2000).

Onset usually occurs before age 20 and affects both males and females. Children may have long periods with a stable neurologic picture simulating a static encephalopathy and later deteriorate either in an acute or in a slowly progressive manner (Nissenkorn et al., 2000).

Characteristics

1. Cardinal clinical features include progressive limitation of ocular movements, pigmentary degeneration of the retina, and cerebellar ataxia.
2. Progressive mental deterioration is usual, and progressive sensorineural hearing loss occurs frequently. Illness may be marked by episodes of stupor or coma.
3. There must also be at least one of the following symptoms: heart block, cerebellar syndrome, or a cerebrospinal fluid protein above 100 mg/dL.
4. Other nonspecific but common features include muscle weakness, intolerance to exercise, neuropathy, and endocrine abnormalities (e.g., short stature, diabetes mellitus, and hypoparathyroidism).

No satisfactory treatment is presently available for respiratory chain deficiency; however, coQ_{10} and carnitine have been recommended. Thus, treatment remains largely symptomatic and does not significantly alter the course of the disease. Therapy includes avoidance of drugs and procedures known to have detrimental effects. Symptomatic treatments include slow infusion of sodium bicarbonate during acute attacks of lactic acidosis, pancreatic extract administration, and repeated transfusion in cases of anemia or thrombopenia. Dietary recommendations include a high-lipid, low-carbohydrate diet and avoidance of a hypercaloric diet.

Special education needs for children with mitochondrial disorders vary considerably as they may have normal intelligence, static mental retardation, or developmental delay. Many of these children qualify for special education services under the classification of Other Health Impairment as a result of their medical conditions.

Prognosis is poor despite placement of a pacemaker. Because mitochondrial genetics differ significantly from Mendelian inheritance of chromosomes, research on the heritability and identification of mutations is a major focus of research.

REFERENCES

Matsushita, T., & Okada, S. (2000). Cardiomyopathy associated with mitochondrial disorders. *Japanese Journal of Clinical Medicine, 58,* 96–99.

Nissenkorn, A., Zeharia, A., Lev, D., Watember, N., Fattal-Valevski, A., Barash, V., Gutman, A., Harel, S., Lerman-Sagie, T. (2000). Neurologic presentations of mitochondrial disorders. *Journal of Child Neurology, 15,* 44–48.

Virdette L. Brumm
Children's Hospital Los Angeles
Keck / USC School of Medicine

KENNEDY DISEASE

Kennedy disease is one of a group of disorders referred to as spinal muscular atrophies. Kennedy disease is a progressive spinobulbar muscular atrophy (SBMA) that presents in individuals between 15 and 60 years of age. Kennedy disease involves instability of the trinucleotide repeats similar to fragile X, Huntington disease, Machado-Joseph disease, and myotonic dystrophy. In Kennedy disease it is believed that the androgen receptor gene is affected as a result of an abnormality to the X-chromosome q12-q21 (LaSpada, Wilson, Lubahn, Harding, & Fischbeck, 1991; Morrison, Mirakhur, & Patterson, 1998). As such, the presence of Kennedy disease can be determined from diagnostic DNA testing. Because it is an X-linked recessive disorder, it occurs only in males but is carried by women. It is exceptionally rare: Only about 50 families are affected worldwide. There is no evidence to suggest a higher likelihood of occurrence based on ethnic group.

Characteristics

1. Weakness of the facial and tongue muscles
2. Dysphagia (difficulty swallowing)
3. Dysarthria (speech impairment)
4. Excessive development of male mammary glands
5. Muscle fasciculation or visible, small, local contractions
6. Sexual dysfunction, reduced sperm count, testicular atrophy
7. Bulbar symptoms
8. Cramps, tremors, weakness of distal limbs

The prognosis for individuals with Kennedy disease varies, possibly in relation to the length of the trinucleotide chain (LaSpada et al., 1991); however, research is inconclusive with regard to prognosis based on the frequency of trinucleotide repeats or other neuronal markers (Karitsky et al., 1999; Morrison et al., 1998). Prognosis generally involves a progressive deterioration. In young adults, the weaknesses may be minimal, and effects may manifest through the endocrine system. The androgen insensitivity can result in changes in libido, excessive development of male mammary glands, reduced fertility, and changes to secondary sexual characteristics. Androgen insensitivity is variable, however. By 50 or 60 years of age, muscle weakness can range from simple weakness of facial muscles and muscle atrophy to loss of ambulation or respiratory problems. Muscle contractions localized to the chin or jaw may be precipitated by pursing of lips or grimacing. Although muscle deterioration is expected with age, cognitive function is generally not impaired, and life expectancy is normal.

Treatment of Kennedy disease consists predominantly of reacting to the symptoms as they present. In adolescence or early adulthood, this may include endocrinology workups and associated medical management. Supportive counseling to address the resulting emotional issues and the development of coping skills also may be appropriate. As muscle weakness increases, treatment may include respiratory therapy, physical therapy, speech therapy, and occupational therapy. For children and adolescents with a family history of Kennedy disease, genetic counseling as well as supportive counseling may be appropriate.

REFERENCES

Karitsky, J., Block, W., Mellies, J. K., Traber, F., Sperfeld, A., Schild, H. H., Haller, P., & Ludolph, A. C. (1999). Proton magnetic resonance spectroscopy in Kennedy syndrome. *Archives of Neurology, 56,* 1465–1471.

LaSpada, A. R., Wilson, E. M., Lubahn, D. B., Harding, A. E., & Fischbeck, K. H. (1991). Androgen receptor gene mutations in X-linked spinal and bulbar muscular atrophy. *Nature Genetics, 2,* 301–304.

Morrison, P. J., Mirakhur, M., & Patterson, V. H. (1998). Discordant repeat size and phenotype in Kennedy syndrome. *Clinical Genetics, 53,* 276–277.

Cynthia A. Riccio
Texas A&M University

KERNICTERUS

Kernicterus is a neurologic syndrome that results from the accumulation of bilirubin in the newborn brain. The symptoms of kernicterus begin during the first week of life and are nonspecific because they are also consistent with many other abnormalities in the neonate (infection, low blood sugar, brain hemorrhage, etc.).

Bilirubin is a yellow-orange pigment. Unconjugated bilirubin is a product of the degradation of hemoglobin, the oxygen-carrying compound in red blood cells. Normally, the liver rapidly converts unconjugated bilirubin to a conjugated form, which is removed from the body through secretion in bile. However, this process is sluggish during the first week after birth in almost 60% of otherwise normal, healthy-term infants and about 80% of prematures. The end result of this deficit is neonatal hyperbilirubinemia (elevated blood levels of bilirubin) and jaundice (a yellow or orange tone to the skin).

Increasing levels of unconjugated hyperbilirubinemia can lead to kernicterus. Prematurity, low birth weight, sepsis (infection), hemolytic anemia (secondary to accelerated destruction of red blood cells), hypoglycemia, acidosis (increased acid in body tissues), respiratory distress, and asphyxia (decreased tissue oxygenation) all enhance the likelihood that kernicterus will occur.

Kernicterus is rare in healthy-term infants. However, about a third of newborns with significant hemolytic disease and hyperbilirubinemia in the 25–30 mg/dl range develop kernicterus. Postmortem studies of premature babies who are undoubtedly exposed to multiple risk factors show that their incidence of kernicterus is 2–16%.

Characteristics

1. The syndrome precedes hyperbilirubinemia.
2. In term infants, symptoms begin at 2–5 days after birth. Lethargy, poor feeding, vomiting, and disappearance of the Moro reflex are common. Prematures may show no signs until the end of the first week of life.
3. Within a few days, more ominous symptoms occur. Babies appear extremely ill. Respiratory distress, high-pitched crying, bulging fontanel (soft spot), twitching of the face and extremities, and opisthotonus (severe muscle spasms that cause arching back of the head and lower legs, with forward bowing of the trunk) are commonly seen.
4. Neurologic manifestations of advanced kernicterus include convulsions and rigid extension of the arms, with the hands tightly fisted and rotated inward.
5. Long-term complications are opisthotonus, muscle rigidity, seizures, involuntary muscle spasms, mental deficiency, slurred speech, high-frequency hearing loss, abnormal eye movements, diminished muscle tone, and ataxia (inability to coordinate movement of muscle groups). These problems become evident by 6–36 months of age.
6. Late findings in mildly affected children are partial hearing loss, mild to moderate ataxia, and attention-deficit/hyperactivity disorder.

Kernicterus therapy is focused on aggressively preventing its happening. Although it is impossible to determine the precise risk for the development of kernicterus in the individual baby, there are specific guidelines to assist pediatricians and neonatologists in their treatment decisions. Initiation of therapy depends on the infant's gestational age, birth weight, and the presence of any complicating conditions that increase vulnerability to the problem. After all these factors are pondered, the game plan for the baby prone to kernicterus is to keep the bilirubin level lower than what is determined to make the baby susceptible to the disorder. Finally, treatment of the underlying causes of hyperbilirubinemia (sepsis, hemolytic anemia, etc.) cannot be forgotten.

Clinicians caring for jaundiced infants at risk for kernicterus employ two treatment modalities. Phototherapy is a ubiquitous, time-honored approach to managing neonatal hyperbilirubinemia. It involves exposing the infant to a bright (usually blue) light, which changes unconjugated bilirubin in the skin into a compound that is excreted in bile without the need for conjugation. Phototherapy also converts unconjugated bilirubin to lumirubin, which is readily removed by the kidneys.

The main problem with phototherapy is that it takes a while to produce any significant reduction in bilirubin levels. Hyperbilirubinemia may only decrease by 1–3 mg/dl after 12–24 hr under the light. Therefore, it is often used prophylactically in infants in whom kernicterus may result from relatively mild hyperbilirubinemia (10–12 mg/dl).

In situations of rapidly rising bilirubin levels, even intensive phototherapy may not reverse the trend. In these cases, double volume exchange transfusion is a widely employed treatment that usually prompts an acute, 50% reduction in bilirubin concentration.

Exchange transfusion requires inserting a small plastic tube (catheter) into the umbilical vein, a large vessel in the umbilical stump. The catheter tip is advanced into the abdomen until it reaches a vein in the liver or the inferior vena cava, which is the biggest vessel in the abdomen returning blood to the heart. Once the catheter is properly positioned, 15–20 cc of blood is slowly withdrawn from it (a smaller volume is removed from premature and low-birth-weight infants) and discarded. Then an equal amount of donor blood is infused into the baby. This process is repeated again and again until the amount of blood exchanged is equal to twice the patient's calculated total blood volume.

Exchange transfusion takes about 2 hr to complete. Strict sterile technique must be observed. The exchanger is gloved, gowned, and masked, just as if he or she were performing surgery. An assistant monitors the baby's status constantly and keeps track of the progress of the exchange.

Exchange transfusion has a number of complications. Five to ten percent of patients experience bradycardia (slow heart rate), apnea (cessation of breathing), and cyanosis (a blue-purple color to the skin caused by poor oxygenation). Metabolic abnormalities include hypoglycemia, acidosis, and hypocalcemia (low blood calcium). Catherization of the umbilical vein can induce bacterial infection. Viruses (hepatitis and HIV) may contaminate donor blood, although rigorous testing for their presence has greatly improved transfusion safety. The mortality rate for exchange transfusion is 0.3%.

For children who survive kernicterus, an early childhood intervention (ECI) program should be initiated to help the child reach developmental milestones. For those child who have sustained a hearing loss, speech therapy may be necessary. Continued special education services will be required as the child enters the school setting. Evaluation and treatment from occupational and physical therapy also may be needed to help with the muscle spasms and increased muscle tone.

Discussing the prognosis for infants with kernicterus is difficult because of the wide array of symptomatic severity it may cause. Infants with ominous neurological signs have a very poor outlook. There is a 75% mortality rate in this group. Of those patients who survive beyond the first few months, 80% have profound neurological sequelae (muscle spasms, mental retardation, hearing loss, and increased muscle tone in all four extremities).

For more information and support, contact March of Dimes Birth Defects Foundation, 1275 Mamaroneck Avenue, White Plains, NY 10605; (914) 428-7100 or (888) 663-4637; e-mail: resourcecenter@modines.org; http://www.modimes.org.

REFERENCES

National Organization for Rare Disorders, Inc. (1999). Kernicterus. Retrieved from http://www.rarediseases.org

Stoll, B. J., & Kliegman, R. L. (2000). Digestive system disorders. In R. E. Behrman, R. K. Kleigman, & H. B. Jenson (Eds.), *Nelson's textbook of pediatrics* (16th ed., pp. 513–519). Philadelphia: W. B. Saunders.

Barry H. Davison
Ennis, Texas

Joan W. Mayfield
Baylor Pediatric Specialty Services
Dallas, Texas

KIENBOCK DISEASE

Kienbock disease is the slow, progressive osteochondrosis (degeneration followed by recalcification) of the carpal lunate bone in the wrist. The disease causes pain, inflammation, and stiffness. It also is known as lunatomalacia, aseptic necrosis, osteochondrotitis, traumatic osteoporosis, and osteitis, and it can be classified as a type of cumulative trauma disorder (Fredricks, Fernandez, & Pirela-Cruz, 1997). Kienbock disease usually occurs when the blood supply to the lunate bone is diminished (McCarthy & Culver, 1993) and the lunate experiences either repeated or severe compressions due to extreme wrist positions (Wheeless' Textbook of Orthopaedics, 2001). However, there is still much debate with regard to determining the exact etiology of the disease (Almquist, 1986; Fredricks et al., 1997; McCarthy & Culver, 1993; Wheeless' Textbook of Orthopaedics, 2001). In its early stages, Kienbock disease may have overlapping symptoms with other disorders such as carpal tunnel syndrome and chronic wrist pain, so differential diagnosis must be made so that the proper treatment regimens may be sought (Fredricks et al., 1997; McCarthy & Culver, 1993).

Prevalence of Kienbock disease has not been determined, but it is thought to be more common than previously thought. It affects young adults from ages 15 to 40 years old (McCarthy & Culver, 1993; Wheeless' Textbook of Orthopaedics, 2001). In general, it affects the dominant hand (it is rarely bilateral), occurs twice as often in men, and often follows trauma to the wrist or hand (Fredricks et al., 1997; McCarthy & Culver, 1993).

Characteristics

1. Wrist pain radiating inward toward the forearm
2. Stiffness, tenderness, and swelling over the lunate
3. Limitation of wrist mobility
4. Weakness of grip

The literature documenting Kienbock disease in children is limited because it usually manifests after prolonged and repeated trauma. Kienbock disease predominantly is found in individuals who are employed in construction, agriculture, and factories, all of which require employees to perform similar tasks involving the arm and wrist repeatedly throughout the day (Fredricks et al., 1997; McCarthy & Culver, 1993). In addition, there may soon be an increase in the incidence of athletes, clerical aides, and children where child labor laws are poorly observed presenting with symptoms of Kienbock disease as a result of performing repetitive tasks for prolonged periods of time.

Treatment for Kienbock disease often is arduous, prolonged, and not as effective as desired. Kim, Culp, Osterman, & Bednar (1996) believed that children with Kienbock disease should be treated with immobilization before surgery is attempted to correct the problem. McCarthy and Culver (1993), however, maintained that less invasive procedures, such as immobilization, are not effective treatment methods for individuals with Kienbock disease. Surgery is the preferred and most common method of treating Kienbock disease. The first type of surgery, usually performed in earlier stages of the disease, involves the lengthening of the ulna or shortening or the radius to relieve pressure and restore blood circulation to the lunate. The second type of surgery includes replacing the lunate with a prosthesis and is usually used only in more advanced cases of the disease (Almquist, 1986).

Depending on the severity of the disorder and the functional limitations experienced by children with Kienbock disease, they may be eligible for special education services under the Individuals with Disabilities Education Act's category of Orthopedic Impairment. Given that Kienbock disease most often affects the dominant wrist, there may be extensive periods of immobility during which a student would be unable to write or perform other necessary activities. In this case, special education services may include providing voice-recognition typing programs and similar assistive technologies.

Given that a child with Kienbock disease has not incurred as much damage as has an adult with the disease, a younger child has a much better prognosis. Younger children also tend to be more resilient to the effects of Kienbock disease and heal rapidly compared with adults (Kim et al., 1996). Future research in this area should focus on early detection and differentiation from other similar wrist and hand disorders. In addition, prevalence data and etiology should be more closely examined.

REFERENCES

Almquist, E. E. (1986). Problem disorders of the wrist-symposium: Kienbock's disease. *Clinical Orthopaedics and Related Research, 202,* 68–78.

Fredricks, T. K., Fernandez, J. E., & Pirela-Cruz, M. A. (1997). Kienbock's disease: I. Anatomy and etiology. *International Journal of Occupational Medicine and Environmental Health, 10,* 11–17.

Kim, T. Y., Culp, R. W., Osterman, A. L., & Bednar, J. M. (1996, February). *Kienbock's disease in children.* Paper presented at the annual meeting of the American Academy of Orthopaedic Surgeons, Atlanta, GA.

McCarthy, J., & Culver, J. (1993, February). Grand rounds: Kienbock disease. Retrieved from http://www.visitations.com/kienbock/kienbock.htm

Wheeless' Textbook of Orthopaedics. (2001). Kienbock's disease: Lunatomalacia. Retrieved from http://www.medmedia.com/o11/209.htm

Christine L. French
Texas A&M University

See also Carpal Tunnel Syndrome

KLINEFELTER SYNDROME (XXY)

Klinefelter syndrome (KS) results from a chromosomal abnormality in which at least one extra X chromosome is present in males (i.e., XXY). Obvious signs of KS often do not appear until adolescence or adulthood, when males with KS often show hypogonadism, delayed puberty, and excessive growth of lower extremities (Klinefelter, Reifensyein, & Albright, 1942). Although the chromosomal abnormality can be diagnosed in infancy or childhood, it is most often diagnosed in adulthood when questions of fertility arise (Smyth, 1999).

Prevalence of this syndrome is approximately 1 in 500 male conceptions, making it the most common sex chromosome abnormality (Hambly & Wilson, 1999). KS cannot occur in females. This chromosomal abnormality is caused by an error in the division process in the production of gametes, where the sperm or ovum contains an extra X chromosome. The additional X chromosome results in decreased levels of testosterone. Although the cause of the chromosomal abnormality is not known, there is evidence of increased risk as maternal age increases (Nolten, 2001). In most cases (i.e., greater than two thirds of the time), the expected XXY pattern is seen. At other times, more than two X chromosomes may be present or a mosaic pattern may be present in which there is a normal XY and an abnormal XXY cell line. More variability in symptom presentation is found in people with mosaic presentation (Smyth & Bremner, 1998).

Characteristics

1. Elevated gonadotropic levels

Characteristics not usually appearing until adolescence:

1. Small testes (not growing from prepubertal size)
2. Testosterone deficiency, with production reaching a plateau at 14-years-old and not reaching normal adult levels

3. Infertility
4. Gynecomastia (swelling of breast tissue)
5. Tall stature
6. Excessive growth of lower extremities
7. Delayed puberty
8. Decreased facial and pubic hair
9. Decreased muscle and bone density

Effective treatment of KS is dependent on diagnosis. Diagnosis is made through genetic testing. An infant with KS may have a small penis, hypospadia, or undescended testes. With early diagnosis, treatment can begin when gonadotropin levels begin to rise, at 11 or 12 years old, thereby minimizing developmental problems associated with decreased testosterone levels over time (Nolten, 2001). Treatment consists of hormone replacement therapy (i.e., testosterone), usually in injection form. Even if treatment does not begin until adulthood, some benefit can be obtained including increased facial and pubic hair, increased energy and strength, and increased libido (Smyth, 1999). Positive effects on mood are also common. Testicular size, gynecomastia, and sterility are not affected.

Children with KS may qualify for special education services under Other Health Impairment or by qualifying with language impairments or learning disabilities. KS is associated with developmental delays, particularly in language and motor domains. There is also an increased incidence of learning disabilities, behavioral and social problems, and language impairments (Nolten, 2001; Smyth, 1999). For these reasons, it is important to complete a comprehensive neuropsychological and psychological evaluation with children diagnosed with KS to determine what Special Education services are necessary (if any). Although these children often show normal intellectual functioning, a decreased verbal IQ is common (Nolten, 2001). Other neuropsychological difficulties may include poor attention span, poor short-term auditory memory, and problems with memory retrieval. Special education services may be needed for the problems just mentioned. Children with KS may also require special education services due to behavioral and emotional difficulties such as impaired social skills, depression, or behavioral problems. Special education services can help remediate learning difficulties and manage behavior in the classroom. These children may also require speech and language therapy and occupational therapy. They may need specific classroom accommodations such as increased frequency of breaks and shorter assignments due to increased fatigue. In addition, accommodations to compensate for weak verbal skills are likely to be appropriate.

With appropriate treatment, children with KS can mature into healthy adults and not develop problems associated with undiagnosed KS (e.g., decreased muscle mass and bone density, lack of facial and pubic hair, and depression). Most adults with KS are infertile, but they can have productive, successful lives with minimal difficulties in adjustment.

REFERENCES

Hambly, V., & Wilson, C. (1999). What is XXY? Retrieved from http://www.47xxy.org/XXY.html

Klinefelter, H. F., Reifensyein, E. C., & Albright, F. (1942). Syndrome characterized by gynecomastia, aspermato-genesis without a leydigism and increased secretion of follicle stimulating hormone. *Journal of Clinical Endocrinological Metabolism, 2,* 615.

Nolten (2001, February). Klinefelter syndrome. Retrieved from http://www.aaksis.org/KS.html

Smyth, C. M. (1999). Diagnosis and treatment of Klinefelter syndrome. Retrieved from http://hosppract.com/issues/1999/0915/cmsmyth.htm

Smyth, C. M., & Bremner, W. (1998). Klinefelter syndrome. *Archives of Internal Medicine, 158,* 1309.

Melissa R. Bunner
Austin Neurological Clinic

KLIPPEL-TRENAUNAY SYNDROME

Klippel-Trenaunay syndrome (KTS) is a congenital, vascular condition that usually affects the extremities. It also is known as angio-osteohypertrophy, nevus varicousus osteohypertrophicus syndrome, hemangiectasia hypertrophicans, and nevus verucosus hypertrophicans (Health Encyclopedia, 2001) and is commonly confused with several other similar conditions, including Klippel-Trenaunay-Weber syndrome, and Sturge-Weber syndrome (Cohen, 2000). The most common characteristics of KTS is a port-wine stain on an extremity, although the literature does not agree with regard to which part of the body is most commonly affected (Berry et al., 1998; Cohen, 2000; Jacob et al., 1998). Although there is no clear agreement on the etiology of the disorder, it has been reasoned that the main characteristics of the syndrome are caused by diffuse capillary malformation near the surface of the skin (Berry et al., 1998; Driscoll, 2000; Jacob et al., 1998).

Prevalence data have not yet been determined, but KTS is thought to be very rare. It is usually evident at birth or early infancy. KTS has been found in individuals of all ethnicities and is evenly distributed among men and women (Berry et al., 1998; Cohen, 2000).

Characteristics

1. Congenital onset
2. Port-wine stain, usually on an extremity

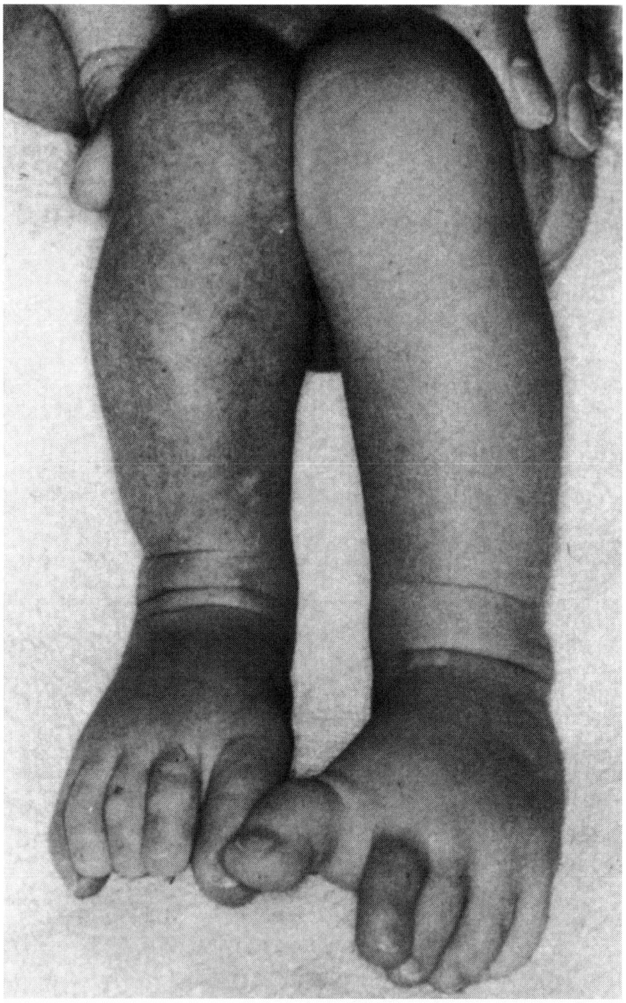

Klippel-Trenaunay Syndrome
Reprinted from *Clinical Syndromes,* Wiedemann and Kunze, 1997, by permission of the publisher Mosby

3. Soft tissue of bone hypertrophy (enlargement or overgrowth)
4. Varicose veins

There is no known cure for KTS. However, there are several documented treatments that have shown limited success. The most common treatment intervention cited in the literature consists of wearing compression garments to reduce the swelling (Berry et al., 1998; Driscoll, 2000; Jacob et al., 1998). Although compression treatment does not have an effect on the size of the limb, it may protect the limb. However, the literature does not suggest the use of compression with children because they do not tolerate the compression garments and quickly grow out of them (Berry et al., 1998; Driscoll, 2000; Jacob et al., 1998). Other nonoperative treatment techniques include the use of antibiotics and laser therapy to reduce discoloration. There are several more invasive procedures used to treat the symptoms of KTS. Removal of varicose veins is often used to relieve discomfort and improve appearance. Surgery and amputation are rare compared to the aforementioned treatment techniques. These extreme and invasive procedures are performed to ensure equal leg lengths, to improve function of an extremity, and to manage bleeding or infection that other treatments have not improved (Berry et al., 1998; Driscoll, 2000).

Children affected by KTS may be eligible for special education services under the category of Other Health Impairment or Orthopaedic Impairment, depending on the manifestation of the syndrome. The school must be sensitive to a child with KTS, particularly because the syndrome is visible to others and often is a cause of distress. Berry et al. (1998) noted "Patients with KT syndrome are best served by a multidisciplinary approach to management of their condition." It is important that parents, educators, doctors, and the affected child be active in the management of the syndrome in all settings.

Despite the visible port-wine stains, varicose veins, and inflammation, the prognosis for individuals with KTS is usually good (Cohen, 2000; Health Encyclopedia, 2001). KTS does not spread from one extremity to another (Driscoll, 2000), so the symptoms do not progress into other parts of the body. With this in mind, future research should focus on the prevalence of the syndrome, developing suitable treatments for younger children, and investigating the etiology of KTS.

REFERENCES

Berry, S. A., Peterson, C., Mize, W., Bloom, K., Zachary, C., Blasco, P., & Hunter, D. (1998). Klippel-Trenaunay syndrome. *American Journal of Medical Genetics, 79,* 319–326.

Cohen, M. M., Jr. (2000). Klippel-Trenaunay syndrome. *American Journal of Medical Genetics, 93,* 171–175.

Driscoll, D. (2000). Klippel-Trenaunay syndrome: Identifying and managing a complex condition. *Minnesota Physician, 13,* 14–15.

Health Encyclopedia. (2001). Klippel-Trenaunay syndrome. Retrieved from http://www.pittsburgh.com/shared/health/adam/ency/article/000150.html

Jacob, A., Driscoll, D., Shaugnessy, W., Stanson, A., Clay, R., Gloviczki, P. (1998). Klippel Trenaunay syndrome: Its spectrum and management. *Mayo Clinic Proceedings, 73,* 28–36.

Christine L. French
Texas A&M University

KLIPPEL-TRENAUNAY-WEBER SYNDROME

Klippel-Trenaunay-Weber syndrome (KTWS) is an uncommon disorder in which asymmetrical enlargement (hypertrophy) of a limb or limbs and hemangiomas (blood vessel malformations) are the most consistent features. Hemangiomas are found most frequently on the skin but may occur in several other areas.

KTWS is rare. Only about 700 cases have been reported since the condition was originally described in 1900. KTWS appears to be nonheritable. Its etiology is unknown. The male-to-female ratio of affected patients is 1:1. The physical abnormalities of KTWS are usually present at birth and progress in severity as patients age.

Characteristics

1. Limb hypertrophy, usually obvious at birth. Seventy-five percent of patients have one leg affected, but more than one limb may be involved. Hypertrophy may affect the entire extremity or just a portion of it (i.e., a hand, foot, or digit).
2. Hemangiomas may appear anywhere but are often restricted to the hypertrophied area. They are most common on the leg, buttocks, and abdomen. Usually only one side is affected, but involvement of both sides is not rare.
3. The color and physical characteristics of hemangiomas are quite variable. They can be pink, red, or purple. They can appear flat, roughened, or blister-like. After patients start walking, venous varicosities (dilated, tortuous veins) appear close to or within hemangiomas.
4. Mental retardation and seizures are associated with the presence of facial hemangiomas.
5. Macrocephaly (large head), which is secondary to a large brain. Hemangiomas may occur within the brain, accounting for its increased size.
6. Macrodactyly (enlarged digits), polydactyly (extra digits), syndactyly (skin fusion, bony fusion, or both of digits) and oligodactyly (missing digits).

Most patients with KTWS require little or no treatment. Elastic wraps help the discomfort of varicosities and soft-tissue swelling. Arthritis-like symptoms are common and respond to analgesic medication. Rarely, significant asymmetrical growth of an extremity may need corrective surgery (fusion of the growth plate at the end of a long bone). In very unusual cases, an appendage may become gigantic and plagued with recurrent blood clots and infection. In these situations, amputation may be necessary. Hemangiomas can also occur in virtually every organ in the body. Patients with KTWS should be investigated for these abnormalities, particularly if they develop suggestive symptoms (blood in the stool or urine, coughing up blood, enlargement of an organ, visual disturbances, etc.). Magnetic resonance imaging (MRI) is probably the most sensitive tool for detecting these defects.

Most children with KTWS will not require special education support services. In the rare cases in which facial hemangiomas are present, a comprehensive neuropsychological evaluation will be required to determine the child's cognitive status and the extent to which support services will be needed.

Except for rare patient whose conditions require surgical correction, the vast majority of children with KTWS do quite well. Mental development is normal, expect when facial hemangiomas are present. Most patients do not need treatment or respond well to very simple therapeutic interventions.

REFERENCES

Darmstadt, G. L. (2000). Hyperpigmented lesions. In R. E. Behrman, R. K. Kleigman, & H. B. Jenson (Eds.), *Nelson's textbook of pediatrics* (16th ed., pp. 1976–1978). Philadelphia: W. B. Saunders.

Jones, K. (1997). *Smith's recognizable patterns of human malformations* (5th ed.). Philadelphia: W. B. Saunders.

National Organization for Rare Disorders (1999). Klippel trenaunay syndrome. Retrieved from http://stepstn.com/cgi-win/nord.exe?proc=GetDocument&rectype=0&recnum=453.

Pediatric Database (PEDBASE). Klippel-trenaunay-weber-syndrome. (n.d.). Retrieved http://www.icondata.com/health/pedbase/files/klippel-.htm

Barry H. Davison
Ennis, Texas

Joan W. Mayfield
Baylor Pediatric Specialty Services
Dallas, Texas

KORO

Koro, or genital retraction syndrome (GRS), is a culture-bound syndrome found predominately in South and East Asia, in particular in south China, Thailand, and Malaysia (American Psychiatric Association [APA], 1994). This disorder is also known as *shuk yang, shook yang,* and *suo yang* (Chinese); *jinjinia bemar* (Assam); or *rok-joo* (Thai). Koro refers to a sudden and intense anxiety that the genitals will recede into the body and possibly cause death.

There are no known prevalence or incidence studies of koro. However, this disorder primarily affects males and is occasionally found in the West. At times, koro occurs in localized epidemics in East Asian regions (APA, 1994). According to Weber (2000, p. 1), "[t]he majority of persons with GRS are male; cases are reported to occur in women, at least in the Malaysian version, but are much more rare." This disorder is perceived to have adolescent onset, with the earliest documented case occurring in a 13-year-old male in southern China (Rosenthal & Rosenthal, 1982). The fixation of the afflicted upon penile retraction has been described as a "pathological distortion of body image" that begins with the on-set of puberty (Rosenthal & Rosenthal, 1982). In cases reported to occur in postadolescence—as was predominately the case in the koro epidemic of Singapore in 1967—there was a castration anxiety theme, as well as "immature mechanisms" that were concluded to have formed with castration anxiety during adolescence (Rosenthal & Rosenthal, 1982).

Characteristics

1. Acute anxiety
2. Loss of sleep
3. Numbness in the genital region
4. Nightmares
5. Frequent nocturnal awakenings
6. Fear of dying

In general, the literature on koro recognizes the disorder as the interaction of cultural, social, and psychodynamic factors in predisposed personalities. This syndrome has been labeled a sexual delusion and has been grouped among hypochondriac delusions in the "depressive state of manic-depressive psychosis" (Rosenthal & Rosenthal, 1982). Other cases have been associated with schizophrenic syndromes. In some extreme cases, koro—in terms of psychogenic localized depersonalization—has also been grouped with postoperative stress phenomena.

When treating koro, typically, the afflicted person is referred to medical professionals and often seeks psychiatric treatment. According to Rosenthal and Rosenthal (1982), the folk belief of so-called classical koro has heuristic value in that it facilitates an overt expression of castration anxiety, which in Occidental cultures is covert, is expressed in neurotic symptoms, or is acted out. Typically, therapy has caused symptoms to diminish—in particular, those of castration anxiety—with follow-up treatment recommended. In the case of the 13-year-old male, a neurological evaluation was done prior to psychiatric referral, including the EEG and CAT scan, neither of which showed abnormalities.

The occurrence of koro in the United States is rare; however, it is extremely important to determine the cultural factors in the development of the syndrome and particular cultural beliefs and expectations of the afflicted student. Koro is apparently an interaction of encompassing social beliefs, sexual myths, major family-induced stressors, and a critical developmental life stage. Family history is pivotal in diagnosis of koro, both in determining levels of acculturation as well as socioeconomic status and general familial environment.

REFERENCES

American Psychiatric Association. (1994). *Diagnostic and statistical manual of mental disorders* (4th ed.). Washington, DC: Author.

Rosenthal, P., & Rosenthal., S. (1982). Koro in the adolescent: Hypochrondriasis as a stress response. *Adolescent Psychiatry, 10,* 523–531.

Weber, C. (2000). Suo yang (koro): The genital retraction syndrome. Retrieved from http://weber.ucsd.edu/~thall/cbs_koro.html

Kiely Ann Fletcher
Ohio State University

KRABBE DISEASE

Krabbe disease is a rare, degenerative disorder of the central and peripheral nervous systems. It is one of a group of genetic disorders called the leukodystrophies. The disorder involves a genetic anomaly that interferes with the development of nerves in the brain, and particularly with the development of the myelin sheath that surrounds the nerve. It is identified by the presence of characteristic globoid cells in the brain tissue. Krabbe disease is inherited in an autosomal recessive pattern and occurs equally as often in boys and girls. The gene involved has been identified as 14q31. If more than one person in a family is diagnosed with Krabbe disease, they may not have the same form or express the same symptoms.

The most common form of Krabbe disease is the infantile form, accounting for 90% of incidence (Krabbe-disease.com, 2000). The onset of the infantile form generally occurs at 3–6 months of age. Krabbe disease occurs in about 1 in 100,000 births in the United States. A higher-than-expected prevalence of Krabbe disease has been found in Sicily (Fiumara et al., 1990), in North Israel and two Muslem Arab villages near Jerusalem (Zlotogora, Chakraborty, Knowlton, & Wenger, 1985), and among people of Scandinavian descent (Adam.com, 1999). There is also a late-onset form of Krabbe disease that is believed to be an allele of the infantile onset and is more common in families of European descent. The major difference between the forms is the age at onset of symptoms (Lyon et al., 1991). In addition, symptoms for the juvenile Krabbe disease form (onset age between 3 and 10 years) may last 5 years or more because the rate of deterioration is much slower than for the infantile form (Adam.com, 1999). Very rarely, symptoms can appear at age 10 to as late as age 45.

Because the nerves affected are central to the brain, Krabbe disease affects respiration, body temperature, and other involuntary (automatic) functions of the body as well as voluntary movements and muscle control. Because of the neural involvement, digestion is impaired, seizures are common, and areas within the brain atrophy.

Characteristics

1. Loss of previously attained developmental skills
2. Unexplained fevers
3. Irritability
4. Seizures
5. Blindness
6. Deafness
7. Stiffness of limbs, muscle rigidity

Development tends to be normal up to 3–6 months of age, followed by a severe and rapid deterioration of mental and motor function. For the more common infantile form, treatment for the disorder is provided for each symptom. For example, physical therapy may help maintain or increase muscle tone and circulation (National Institute of Neurological Disorders and Stroke, 2000). To avoid malnutrition, diet and possible tube feeding can be used. Drug therapy has proved useful in controlling specific symptoms, such as seizures. Gene therapy is a new method that attempts to provide working copies of genes to people with nonworking copies. Unfortunately, gene therapy cannot be used to treat Krabbe disease presently; it may offer hope for the future (Krabbe-disease.com, 2001). Surgical treatment involving bone marrow transplantation is being investigated currently (Krivit et al., 1998).

Individuals with the late onset of Krabbe disease may be learning disabled and may require special education services. Because some of the first signs of the disease are loss of vision and deterioration of fine motor movements, there may be a need for specialized services for individuals who are vision impaired and fine motor movement impaired. Services may need to be extended throughout high school because symptoms may last 20 years or more in the very rare cases of juvenile and adult forms. Whenever there is a history of Krabbe disease in a family, it is strongly recommended that nonaffected family members receive genetic counseling prior to having children because they may be carriers. There is no cure for Krabbe disease, but through genetic counseling, its incidence can be controlled.

REFERENCES

Adam.com. (1999). Krabbe disease. Retrieved from http://pcs.adam.com/ency/article/001198.htm

Fiumara, A., Pavone, L., Siciliano, L., Tine, A., Parano, E., & Innico, G. (1990). Late-onset globoid cell leukodystrophy: Report on seven new patients. *Child's Nervous System, 6,* 194–197.

Krabbe-disease.com (2001). Leukodystrohpy facts: Krabbe disease (globoid cell leukodystrophy). Retrieved from http://www.krabbe-disease.com/leukofacts.htm

Krivit, W., Shapiro, E. G., Peters, C., Wagner, J. E., Cornu, G., Kurtzberg, J., et al. (1998). Hematopoietic stem-cell transplantation in globoid cell leukodystrophy. *New England Journal of Medicine, 338,* 1119–1126.

Lyon, G., Hagberg, B., Evrard, P., Allaire, C., Pavone, L., & Vanier, M. (1991). Symptomatology of late onset Krabbe's leukodystrophy: The European experience. *Developmental Neuroscience, 13,* 240–244.

National Institute of Neurological Disorders and Stroke (2000, June 9). NINDS Krabbe disease information page. Retrieved from http://www.ninds.nih.gov/health_and_medical/disorders/krabbe_doc.htm

Zlotogora, J., Chakraborty, S., Knowlton, R. G., & Wenger, D. A. (1985). Krabbe disease locus mapped to chromosome 14 by genetic linkage. *American Journal of Human Genetics, 47,* 37–44.

Dahl A. Rollins
Texas A&M University

See also Leukodystrophy

KUFS DISEASE

Kufs disease is a late-onset variant of the neuronal ceroid lipofuscinoses (NCLs). There are four types of NCL, all of which have begun to be referred to as Batten disease. NCLs are inherited neurodegenerative storage disorders involving the accumulation of excessive abnormal lipopigments with fingerprint or granular ultrastructural patterns in the neurons and other cells throughout the central nervous system. This disease results in motor disturbances and neurological deficits that range in severity.

In the United States, all forms of NCL affect only 2–4 in 100,000 people. Although they are very rare, NCLs are more common in Newfoundland Canada, parts of northern Europe, Finland, and Sweden (Batten Disease Support and Research Foundation [BDSRA], 2000). It has been estimated that Kufs disease accounts for 10% of all the NCLs (Martin, 1991). Kufs disease usually occurs in the 30s, although the age of onset varies and can occur in the teens and 20s. Males and females are equally affected (Berkovic, Carpenter, Andermann, Andermann, & Wolfe, 1988).

Characteristics

1. Seizures.
2. Myoclonus.
3. Cognitive deficits, psychiatric abnormalities, confusion, or psychosis. When these cognitive and behavioral symptoms are the first to present and are severe in form, the patient is often misdiagnosed with a mental illness.

4. Motor disturbances including ataxia, dysarthria, dyskinesias of the face.
5. Ichthyosis.

Blindness and pigmentary retinal degeneration are absent in Kufs disease. The absence of these symptoms distinguish the adult form from the juvenile forms of NCL.

Berkovic et al. (1988) have delineated two clinical patterns often seen in the diagnosis of Kufs disease. One type is characterized by seizures, myoclonus, and neuropsychiatric symptoms in which seizures are typically the first symptom to emerge. Another type is characterized by a dominance of dementia and motor abnormalities, whereas seizures are not typically present. It should be mentioned that these two forms overlap in symptom presentation and that this classification system has yet to be universally accepted (Hinkebein & Callahan, 1997). Due to the variation and severity of presenting symptoms, diagnosis of Kufs disease is difficult. It is sometimes the case that when seizures are the primary symptom, dementia and myoclonus do not occur initially. In these cases, late-onset epilepsy is often misdiagnosed. When behavioral changes and dementia are the initial symptom, misdiagnosis of psychiatric disease may occur (Berkovic et al., 1988).

Currently, there is no cure for this progressive neurological degenerative disease. Treatment of Kufs disease focuses on management of the symptoms. Anticonvulsant drugs are used to manage the seizures. Physical therapy, occupational therapy, and nutritional approaches are supportive treatments often needed (BDSRA, 2000). As they arise, psychiatric problems also require treatment.

In the rare cases of adolescent-onset Kufs disease, these patients will qualify for special education services under Section 504 of the Rehabilitation Act of 1973 and under Individuals with Disabilities Education Act (IDEA). Educational personnel in contact with the child need to be knowledgeable of seizure disorders and of the side effects of anticonvulsant medication. Cognitive and behavioral deterioration need to be monitored, and revision of the patient's educational plan should follow the progression of the disease.

Kufs disease shortens the life span, and death typically results from progressive dementia. According to an analysis of the existing cases of Kufs disease, Berkovic et al. (1988) found that death occurred in an average of 12.5 years from age of onset, although it has been as short as 1 year. The biochemical deficits that cause Kufs disease are not known, and much research is currently focusing on all of the NCLs (BDSRA, 2000).

REFERENCES

Batten Disease Support and Research Foundation. (2000). Batten disease facts and fiction. Retrieved from http://www.bdsra.org/index.htm

Berkovic, S. F., Carpenter, S., Andermann, F., Andermann, E., & Wolfe, L. S. (1988). Kuf's disease: A critical reappraisal. *Brain, 111,* 27–62.

Hinkebein, J. H., & Callahan, C. D. (1997). The neuropsychology of Kuf's disease: A case of atypical early onset dementia. *Archives of Clinical Neuropsychology, 12*(1), 81–89.

Martin, J. J. (1991). Adult type of neuronal ceroid lipofuscinosis. *Developmental Neuroscience, 13,* 331–338.

Kellie Higgins
University of Texas at Austin

See also Batten Disease

KUGELBERG-WELANDER DISEASE

Kugelberg-Welander disease is one of a group of disorders referred to as spinal muscular atrophies (SMA); Kugelberg-Welander disease is SMA Type III. It is characterized by degeneration of the anterior horn cells of the spinal cord. It becomes evident between 2 and 17 years of age. Kugelberg-Welander disease is believed to be genetically homogeneous and associated with chromosome region 5q11.2-13.3 (Brzustowicz et al., 1990). It is an autosomal recessive disorder and is usually evident in cousins or siblings, although the parents are usually asymptomatic. There is an equal incidence in males and females; there is no evidence that Kugelberg-Welander disease is more evident in any one ethnic group. The presence of Kugelberg-Welander disease can be determined from diagnostic DNA testing (Navon et al., 1997).

Of the SMAs, Kugelberg-Welander disease is considered to be relatively mild. Muscle weakness is the major symptom and results from the premature death of the cells of the anterior horn. Proximal muscles are more involved than distal muscles; lower limbs are more affected than upper limbs. Children with Kugelberg-Welander disease may evidence delay or regression in gross motor development, but they generally are able to stand and maintain ambulation. Gower's sign may be positive (the individual with Kugelberg-Welander disease has difficulty rising to a standing position from a supine position). In addition, difficulty with walking, running, jumping, and other gross motor skills may be manifest. Tremors and other evidence of muscle weakness may be present as well. Despite the muscular difficulties, cognitive function and neural sensation remain intact. For children with Kugelberg-Welander disease, the weakness is generally static rather than progressive and more than 90% of those affected are ambulatory. In more severe cases with involvement of the intercostal muscles, respiratory problems may be evident. Unless respiratory muscles are affected, life expectancy is generally within normal limits.

Characteristics

1. Abnormal gait
2. Difficulty running
3. Difficulty climbing steps
4. Difficulty getting up from a chair
5. Tremor of hands
6. Positive Gower's sign

Treatment of Kugelberg-Welander disease predominantly consists of reacting to the weaknesses and symptoms manifested by each individual. The affected motor neurons do not show compensatory sprouting or innervation; as a result, there is no cure for Kugelberg-Welander disease (Schmalbruch & Haase, 2001). Prevention of the disorder requires genetic screening—and counseling if appropriate—of family members whenever there is a appositive history of Kugelberg-Welander disease or any other spinal muscular atrophies.

For children with Kugelberg-Welander disease, special education services may be needed, depending on severity and physical limitations. Treatment may include physical therapy, occupational therapy, or other supportive services. The extent to which children with Kugelberg-Welander disease will need special education services will vary from child to child and may include a need for adaptive physical education or other accommodations to meet the needs of the child.

REFERENCES

Brzustowicz, L. M., Lehner, T., Castilla, L. H., Penchaszadeh, G. K., Wilhemsen, K. C., Daniels, R., et al. (1990). Genetic mapping of chronic childhood onset spinal muscular atrophy to chromosome 5q11.2-13.3. *Nature, 344* (6266), 540–541.

Navon, R., Khosravi, R., Melki, J., Drucker, L., Fontaine, B., Turpin, J. C., et al. (1997). Juvenile onset spinal muscular atrophy caused by compound heterozygosity of mutations in the HEXA gene. *Annals of Neurology, 41,* 631–638.

Schmalbruch, H., & Haase, G. (2001). Spinal muscular atrophy: Present state. *Brain Pathology, 11*(2), 231–247.

Cynthia A. Riccio
Texas A&M University

See also Motor Neuron Disease

L

LABAND SYNDROME

Laband syndrome, also known as Zimmermann-Laband syndrome, is a rare genetic disorder characterized by craniofacial abnormalities, abnormalities of the hands and feet, and gingival fibromatosis.

Laband syndrome is inherited as an autosomal dominant trait, although sporadic cases have been reported suggesting recessive inheritance. Fewer than 30 cases of Laband syndrome have been reported. The majority of Laband patients are of Eastern Indian ancestry, although people of European descent have also been identified. Males and females are equally affected (National Organization for Rare Disorders [NORD], 1997).

Characteristics

1. Gingival hypertrophy or fibromatosis, usually apparent when primary teeth emerge.
2. Facial abnormalities, including bulbous, soft nose; thick, floppy ears; thick lips; large tongue; and full eyebrows.
3. Abnormalities of the hands and feet: dysplasia of or absent distal phalanges of hands and feet, deformation of the distal phalanges of the great toe and thumb, absent or dysplastic nails of both the hands and feet, and clubbed or "tree–frog–like" toes and fingers.
4. Hepatosplenomegaly can be present in infancy or develop in childhood.
5. Excessive hair growth has been observed in some children.
6. Hyperextensibility of the joints.
7. Mild to severe mental retardation is sometimes present.
8. Vertebral abnormalities, including spina bifida, kyphosis, or scoliosis.

There is not a cure for Laband syndrome, and treatment focuses on management of the symptoms. The abnormalities of the fingers and toes are usually observable at birth, and other characteristics emerge during early childhood (NORD, 1997). Gingival fibromatosis is the most common characteristic of those affected with Laband syndrome. Gingival fibromatosis becomes apparent by the time the primary teeth first emerge, but in some cases it is observable at birth. This condition is problematic because it can lead to gum disease, tooth loss, and difficulty with chewing, talking, or swallowing. Oral surgery is sometimes necessary to remove the teeth (Chodirker, Chudley, Toffler, & Reed, 1986), and surgical removal of excess gum is also performed. Enlargement of the spleen or liver requires early diagnosis and treatment (NORD, 1997). Laband patients may need to be treated with anticonvulsant drugs because seizure disorders are a secondary characteristic of Laband syndrome. Vertebral abnormalities can be severe, and orthopedic treatment may also be needed.

Children with Laband syndrome need intervention beginning in infancy and will need special education services in the school setting. These children should be eligible to receive services under the Individuals with Disabilities Education Act (IDEA), due to mental retardation, orthopedic impairments, speech or language impairments, or other health impairments, depending on the severity of symptoms. Speech therapy, physical therapy, or occupational therapy may be necessary. Diagnosis of mental retardation and proper educational placement will be needed for some children. Laband syndrome requires treatment beginning in infancy because of the risk of enlargement of the spleen and liver. Infants with Laband syndrome may qualify for early intervention services under IDEA.

The prognosis of those living with Laband syndrome will depend on severity of cognitive impairment and physical disability. Given the small number of identified patients, information on the outcome of this rare disease is limited, and the research has not included many longitudinal studies. One adult patient with severe mental retardation, seizures, and scoliosis was wheelchair bound and institutionalized (Chodirker et al., 1986), whereas another lived in supervised conditions while maintaining manual employment (Robertson, Lipp, & Bankier, 1998). A recent study found vascular and cardiac complications in a Laband patient. This was this first study to suggest that Laband syndrome may be a life-threatening disorder (Robertson et al., 1998). Genetic localization of Laband syndrome is not known and is an area for future research.

REFERENCES

Chodirker, B. N., Chudley, A. E., Toffler, M. A., & Reed, M. H. (1986). Brief clinical report: Zimmermann-Laband syndrome and profound mental retardation. *American Journal of Medical Genetics, 25,* 543–547.

National Organization for Rare Disorders. (1997). Rare disease database: Laband syndrome. Retrieved from http://www.stepstn.com/chi-win/nord.exe

Robertson, S. P., Lipp, H., & Bankier, A. (1998). Zimmermann-Laband syndrome in an adult: Long-term follow-up of a patient with vascular and cardiac complications. *American Journal of Medical Genetics, 78* (2), 160–164.

Kellie Higgins
University of Texas at Austin

LACTIC ACIDOSIS

Lactic acidosis is a common metabolic abnormality and biochemical marker for many different hereditary neurometabolic disorders associated with mitochondrial dysfunction. Excessive lactic acid production may be primary or secondary and occurs in many genetic and nongenetic associated conditions. This abnormality gives rise to acute episodes of drowsiness, stupor, and coma, as well as to neurological dysfunction. Episodes tend to be recurrent. Between attacks, children may be healthy or mildly affected or display evidence of neurological or multisystem abnormalities.

Characteristics

1. A major metabolic sign and one of the hallmarks of disease severity in mitochondrial disorders of energy metabolism.
2. Acute metabolic attacks consist of vomiting, hypotonia, lethargy, stupor or coma, respiratory irregularity, and (occasionally) seizures.
3. Ataxia (episodic or chronic).
4. Hyperlactatemia is usually due to acute or chronic multiorgan system failure or to congenital DNA mutations that compromise cellular metabolism.
5. Pulmonary hypertension.

Neither treatment of an acute crisis nor the prevention of more chronic causes of mitochondrial disease will likely be achieved by any single therapeutic intervention currently available (Stacpoole, 1997). Therapeutic recommendations include avoidance of fasting, IV glucose, and a high-carbohydrate diet (Lyon, Adams, & Kolodny, 1996).

Neurological improvement with lactic acidosis has remained elusive to date, and it remains a potentially lethal disorder. Special education is usually necessary for these children, particularly those suffering from neurological involvement.

Future research focused on interventions that improve mitochondrial function or prevent mitochondrial energy failure may have widespread therapeutic implications.

REFERENCES

Lyon, G., Adams, R. D., & Kolodny, E. H. (1996). *Neurology of hereditary metabolic diseases of children.* New York: McGraw-Hill.

Stacpoole, P. W. (1997). Lactic acidosis and other mitochondrial disorders. *Metabolism: Clinical & Experimental, 46,* 306–321.

Virdette L. Brumm
Children's Hospital, Los Angeles
Keck / USC School of Medicine

LACTOSE INTOLERANCE

Lactose intolerance is the inability of the body to digest lactose, a carbohydrate found in milk and most dairy products. It is caused by a deficiency in the enzyme lactase, which is responsible for breaking down lactose. Lactose intolerance may be classified as either primary or secondary. Primary lactose intolerance is genetic and develops around 2–3 years of age, whereas secondary lactose intolerance arises as a result of another medical condition (e.g., cystic fibrosis, chemotherapy, Whipple's disease) or unknown causes. Most often, lactose intolerance results from low lactase activity, not the complete absence of lactase. Congenital lactose intolerance, characterized by a complete absence of lactase activity, is extremely rare. Diagnosis of lactose intolerance is made by a physician either through lactose intolerance tests, breath hydrogen tests, biopsy of the small intestine, or clinical observations and interviews (Minocha, 2000; Srinivasan & Minocha, 1998; Vesa, Marteau, & Korpela, 2000).

It is estimated that as much as 70–75% of the world's population may have some form of lactose intolerance. However, it appears to be more common in African American, Hispanic, Asian, and Indian populations. According to Vesa, Marteau, and Korpela (2000), the prevalence of lactose intolerance is 50% in South America, Africa, and Asia. Within the United States, this prevalence is approximately 53% among Mexican Americans, 15% among Caucasians, and 80% among African Americans. African American and Asian children tend to develop this disorder in early childhood, whereas Caucasian children typically develop this disorder in late childhood and adolescence. Lactose intolerance is less common in Caucasian children and is often a secondary result of an infection that disappears as the infection is cured (Health Castle, 2000; Minocha, 2000; Srinivasan & Minocha, 1998; Vesa et al., 2000).

Characteristics

1. Child experiences loose stools and gassiness as a result of unabsorbed lactose.
2. Child complains of bloating, stomach pains, and nausea.

3. Evidence of flatulence and abdominal fullness.
4. Symptoms are more prevalent after consumption of milk, dairy products, or other products containing lactose.

Dietary management is one of the most common treatments for lactose intolerance. This involves restricting the amount of lactose consumed. Lactose is commonly found in dairy products that also have the most concentrated sources of calcium. As a result, it is important that children with lactose intolerance consume calcium-rich nondairy products, such as seafood, nuts, and green vegetables, or that they take a calcium supplement (Srinivasan & Minocha, 1998). In addition, lactose mixed within chocolate milk and yogurt tends to increase a child's tolerance to the carbohydrate (Health Castle, 2000; Srinivasa & Minocha, 1998). Another available treatment for lactose intolerance includes dietary aids that facilitate the digestion of lactase. These include lactase enzyme capsules or tablets, as well as many over-the-counter digestive aids.

It is important to note that lactose intolerance in typically not an absolute diagnosis; many children can consume up to 240 ml of milk each day without experiencing symptoms (Minocha, 2000). In fact, digestive aids are uncommon when lactose consumption is limited to this amount (Srinivasan & Monocha, 1998). Currently, there is no method available to determine what level of lactose will cause symptoms in a child. Some children with lactose intolerance experience problems after consumption of small amounts of lactose, whereas others have no difficulties after consuming very large amounts of lactose (Vesa et al., 2000). Parents of children with lactose intolerance should be cautious because many prescription and over-the-counter medications include lactose and may cause the symptoms to appear.

If symptoms are severe, children with lactose intolerance may qualify for special education services under Physical Disabilities or Other Health Impairments. These children may need lunch and snack modifications as well as alternative food choices with appropriate calcium and nutritional supplements. In addition, it may be necessary for these children to take a digestive aid prior to lunch and snack times to reduce the symptoms associated with lactose intolerance. After meals, these children may require frequent bathroom breaks or visits to the nurse's office if symptoms develop and persist. It is important to note lactose intolerance, especially with young children, because they may not realize how certain classroom treats, such as ice cream, could affect them.

The prognosis for children with lactose intolerance is positive. Although the symptoms are inconvenient, they are usually easily managed through dietary modifications and digestive aids (Srinivasan & Minocha, 1998). Typically, these symptoms pose no serious threat to the child's health and well-being. Secondary lactose intolerance tends to disappear as the primary medical condition is cured (Vesa et al., 2000). Moreover, some evidence suggests that exposure to lactose over time may improve symptoms of intolerance. Future research is needed to determine why some individuals with lactase deficiency are more resilient to lactose consumption than are others, as well as how age, gender, and functional bowel disorders are related to the symptoms of lactose intolerance (Vesa et al., 2000).

REFERENCES

Health Castle. (2000, November 28). Lactose intolerance. Retrieved from http://healthcastle.com/herb_lact.shtml

Minocha, A. (2000, November 28). Lactose intolerance. Retrieved from http://www.dignosishealth.com/lactose1.htm

Srinivasan, R., & Minocha, A. (1998). When to suspect lactose intolerance: Symptomatic, ethnic, and laboratory clues. *Postgraduate Medicine, 104,* 109–123.

Vesa, T. H., Marteau, P., & Korpela, R. (2000). Lactose intolerance. *Journal of the American College of Nutrition, 19,* 165S–175S.

Amy J. Dahlstrom
Rik Carl D'Amato
University of Northern Colorado

LANDAU-KLEFFNER SYNDROME

Landau-Kleffner syndrome (LKS)—also called acquired epileptiform aphasia, infantile acquired aphasia, or aphasia with convulsive disorder—is a rare, childhood neurological disorder characterized by the sudden or gradual development of aphasia (loss of language) and an abnormal electroencephalogram (EEG). This syndrome was first described in 1957 by Dr. William M. Landau and Dr. Frank R. Kleffner, who identified six children with the disorder (National Institute of Neurological Disorders and Stroke [NINDS], 2002).

LKS affects the parts of the brain that control speech and comprehension. The disorder usually occurs in children between the ages of 3 and 7. Typically, these children develop normally; then, for no apparent reason, they lose the ability to understand others and to speak. Although many of the affected individuals have seizures, some do not. The disorder is difficult to diagnose and may be misdiagnosed as autism, pervasive developmental disorder, hearing impairment, learning disability, auditory-verbal processing disorder, attention deficit disorder, mental retardation, childhood schizophrenia, or emotional-behavioral problems. The cause of LKS is unknown. Some experts think there is more than one cause for this disorder. All of the children with LKS appear to be perfectly normal until their first seizure or the start of language problems. There have been no reports of children who have a family history of LKS.

Therefore, LKS is not likely to be an inherited disorder (National Institute on Deafness and Other Communication Disorders [NIDCD], 1999).

> Characteristics
>
> 1. LKS occurs most frequently in normally developing children who are between 3 and 7 years of age.
> 2. For no apparent reason, these children begin having trouble understanding what is said to them. Doctors often refer to this problem as auditory agnosia or word deafness. The auditory agnosia may occur slowly or very quickly. Parents often think that the child is developing a hearing problem or has become suddenly deaf. Hearing tests, however, show normal hearing.
> 3. Children may also appear to be autistic or developmentally delayed.
> 4. The inability to understand language eventually affects the child's spoken language, which may progress to a complete loss of the ability to speak (mutism).
> 5. Children who have learned to read and write before the onset of auditory agnosia can often continue communicating through written language.
> 6. Some children develop a type of gestural communication or sign-like language. The communication problems may lead to behavioral or psychological problems.
> 7. Intelligence usually appears to be unaffected.
> 8. The loss of language may be preceded by an epileptic seizure that usually occurs at night. At some time, 80% of children with LKS have one or more seizures.
> 9. The seizures usually stop by the time the child becomes a teenager.
> 10. All LKS children have abnormal electrical brain activity on both the right and left sides of their brains.

Treatment of LKS usually consists of medication to control the seizures and abnormal brain wave activity (anticonvulsants) and has very little effect on language ability. Corticosteroid therapy has improved the language ability of some children. Sign language instruction has benefited others (NIDCD, 1999).

Special education programming will most likely be needed for children with LKS. Special education assessments can assist with the diagnosis and management of the condition. Speech and language therapy will also help with management and assessment. It is probable that the family and child would benefit from counseling due to the seriousness and uncertain onset of the disorder. Adjustments to chronic illness will need education and understanding on the part of the special and regular education team. School personnel can also be instrumental in the monitoring of seizure activity and sensitivity to side effects from anticonvulsant medications.

There have not been many long-term follow-up studies of children with LKS. This lack of evidence—along with the wide range of differences among affected children—makes it impossible to predict the outcome of this disorder. Complete language recovery has been reported; however, language problems usually continue into adulthood. The continued language problems can range from difficulty following simple commands to no verbal communication. If recovery takes place, it can occur within days or years. So far, no relationship has been found between the extent of the language impairment, the presence or absence of seizures, and the amount of language recovery. Generally, the earlier the disorder begins, the poorer the language recovery. Most children outgrow the seizures, and electrical brain activity on the EEG usually returns to normal by age 15. In some cases, remissions and relapse may occur. The prognosis is improved when the onset of the disorder is after age 6 and when speech therapy is started early (NINDS, 2002).

Organizations that may be helpful to families are

- Epilepsy Foundation, 4351 Garden City Drive, Suite 500, Landover, MD 20785-7223, postmaster@efa.org, http://www.epilepsyfoundation.org, (301) 459-3700, (800) EFA-1000 (332-1000), fax: (301) 577-2684
- American Speech-Language-Hearing Association (ASHA), 10801 Rockville Pike, Rockville, MD 20852, (301) 897-5700, (800) 638-8255, fax: (301) 571-0457, Internet: www.asha.org
- CANDLE (Childhood Aphasia, Neurological Disorders, Landau-Kleffner Syndrome, and Epilepsy), 4414 McCampbell Drive, Montgomery, AL 36106, (205) 271-3947

REFERENCES

National Institute on Deafness and Other Communication Disorders. (1999). Retrieved April 2002, from http://www.nlm.nih.gov/medlineplus/aphasia.html

National Institute of Neurological Disorders and Stroke. (2002). Retrieved April 2002, from http://www.ninds.nih.gov/health_and_medical/disorders/landaukleffnersyndrome_doc.htm

Elaine Fletcher-Janzen
University of Northern Colorado

LATAH

Latah occurs in female individuals who exhibit excessive verbal hostility on a sporadic basis. Outbursts of verbal insults, babbling, and shouting are often public in nature and sometimes require the individual to be removed from the situation and calmed. Latah is a psychiatric culture-bound syndrome found mostly in middle-aged Malaysian and Indonesian females (Kenny, 1978). Clinical manifestations of latah can be echopraxia, echolalia, and other trancelike behavior (American Psychiatric Association, 1994). Adolescence is the earliest that true latah appears and its occurrence at this age is uncommon (Winzeler, 1991). However, there have been documented instances of latah as early as age 6 (Kenny, 1978).

There are no known prevalence or incidence studies with regard to this culture-bound syndrome: This syndrome is self-identified, revered, and generally thought to be a learned behavior modeled by family members and the female community. Women with latah are common phenomena in various Malaysian and Indonesian cultures such that this syndrome can be somewhat defined geographically. Ethnographic documents report that latah is prevalent in the coastal and downriver villages of Indonesia, whereas incidence is absent in the interior of Sarawak (Winzleler, 1991). Other early reports demonstrate that incidence of latah is heavily concentrated in Java. This syndrome is not linguistically limited and is not exclusively associated with a particular ethnic group or grouping.

Characteristics

1. Hypersensitivity to sudden fright
2. Command obedience
3. Echopraxia
4. Echolalia
5. Dissociative or trancelike behavior
6. Parodying others' actions or other socially or morally offensive behavior

Historically, the medical and psychiatric professions have referred to women with latah as a culturally sanctioned group whose members are not only tolerated but also accepted in the community. Ethnographic studies document that women with latah may lose social prestige but can still be considered "pillars of social respectability" (Winzeler, 1991, p. 11). Indeed, women with latah are often enlisted to assist local shamans in acquiring access to the spiritual world. From ethnographic studies, latah is closely related to spiritual possession such that women with latah have a link to "witches" and the spiritual world (Kenny, 1978, p. 225).

Due to the social position of women with latah and the lack of formal neuropsychiatric research studies conducted with this group, there are no formal remedies or treatment for this syndrome.

Regarding special education concerns in the United States, clinicians need to determine the level of acculturation of the female student exhibiting latah characteristics. The need for differential diagnosis to rule out other psychological and neurological conditions (such as behavior disorder, seizure disorders, tumors, traumatic brain injury sequelae, etc.) will be dependent on the determination of the level of acculturation. Potentially, differential diagnosis may be strongly dependent on analysis of female family members exhibiting latah characteristics.

In the event of a positive diagnosis of latah, it is unlikely that special education services would be required or available; however, cultural sensitivity training for principals, teachers, and other students would be extremely important. A behavior team may well have to not only educate the school community to this condition but also develop a behavior plan with the family that reflects cultural preferences while adhering to school policies and procedures regarding appropriate verbal behavior.

REFERENCES

American Psychiatric Association. (1994). *Diagnostic and statistical manual for mental disorders* (4th ed.). Washington, DC: Author.

Kenny, M. G. (1978). Latah: the symbolism of a putative mental disorder. *Culture Medicine, and Psychiatry, 2,* 209–231.

Winzeler, R. L. (1991). Latah in sarawak, with special reference to the iban. Retrieved from http://ets.umdl.umich.edu/cgi/e/eharf/hrafidx?type=html&rgn=SECTIONS&byte=102540853

Kiely Ann Fletcher
Ohio State University

Elaine Fletcher-Janzen
University of Northern Colorado

LAURENCE-MOON SYNDROME (LAURENCE-MOON-BARDET-BIEDL SYNDROME, LMBBS)

Laurence-Moon syndrome (LMS) is a rare inherited disorder. It is thought to be inherited as an autosomal recessive genetic trait. There is some confusion regarding the difference between Laurence-Moon syndrome and Bardet-Biedl syndrome. Some researchers believe that Bardet-Biedl Syndrome is a subdivision of Laurence-Moon Syndrome, and they refer to it as Laurence-Moon-Bardet-Biedl Syndrome (LMBBS; National Organization of Rare Disorders [NORD], 2001).

Laurence-Moon syndrome is primarily characterized by rod-cone dystrophy, polydactyly, obesity, hypogonadism in males, renal anomalies, and learning disabilities. These usually occur in early to late childhood. Some of the visual difficulties include crossed eyes, night blindness, and loss of vision as a result of cataracts. Obesity usually begins at

1–2 years of age. Occasionally, obesity will not be present until puberty. Regardless of the age of onset, these children appear to have a more stocky build than do their unaffected siblings. Obesity is one of the most pronounced symptoms of this disorder (LMBBS Home Page, 2001).

Secondary features may include speech disorder, developmental delay, ataxia, diabetes mellitus, and poor coordination and clumsiness (LMBBS Home Page, 2001). Although many cases report mental retardation as a major feature, this conclusion is now considered inaccurate. Many of the early studies used IQ tests that were not appropriate for patients with visual impairments, and in general, individuals with LMS did better at performance skills than at verbal skills. More often, patients diagnosed as mentally retarded had mild to moderate learning disorders (LMBBS Home Page, 2001).

To date, there have been approximately 600 reported cases. The disease seems to affect twice as many males as females (NORD, 2001). In certain regions such as Kuwait, the incidence rate is reported as 1 in 13,500; this elevated rate is considered to be due to the high rate of interfamily marriages. In Newfoundland, the rate is reported as 1 in 17,500; in addition to interfamily marriages, founder effect is thought to be a contributing factor for this rate. The early settlers in Newfoundland came from a small number of families who emigrated from England. Other European studies estimate the incidence rate of Laurence-Moon syndrome to be anywhere from 1 in 125,000 to 1 in 160,000. Regardless, it is believed that this disease has been underdiagnosed (LMBBS Home Page, 2001).

Characteristics

1. Hypogonadism—diminished hormone production by the testes or ovaries
2. Retinitis pigmentosa—progressive loss of vision
3. Spastic paraplegia—paralysis of the legs and lower part of the body accompanied by involuntary muscle contractions
4. Obesity
5. Polydactyly and brachydactyly
6. Renal difficulties
7. Learning difficulties
8. Developmental delays
9. Speech delays
10. Diabetes
11. Short stature

Sources: LMBBS Home Page (2001), NORD (2001)

The treatment of obesity in Laurence-Moon syndrome can be a major source of stress to both the child and the parent. There is no satisfactory single treatment. A multidisciplinary approach of diet, behavioral therapy, and exercise is strongly advocated. There seem to be no proven treatments to prevent or reduce the deterioration of rod-cone dystrophy. However, much can be done to prepare one for a life with low vision. Removal of skin tags can be accomplished at birth or within the 1st year of birth. Diabetes may be controlled with diet, and in some cases, oral medications may be indicated. In cases with renal dysfunction, antibiotics have successfully been used. Dialysis has also been used with the small number of individuals who have required it. In rare cases, renal transplantation has been accomplished with good results.

Assessment of learning disabilities should be done as soon as possible before visual impairments become a factor. The Laurence-Moon-Bardet-Biedl Society publishes a booklet entitled "The LMBBS Child at School." This booklet covers educational needs and ways of meeting them. Speech therapy in the early years is strongly recommended. Parents can be taught exercises to help their children with communication skills. Regular assessment of developmental skills by a child development team can provide information necessary to help develop the child's motor skills; this is especially important during the 1st year when sitting, standing, and walking may be delayed. Genetic counseling for the family is also strongly recommended (LMBBS Home Page, 2001).

REFERENCES

Laurence-Moon-Bardet-Biedl Syndrome Home Page. (2001, March 28). Retrieved from http://www.isgrd.umds.ac.uk/laurence3htm#LEARN

National Organization for Rare Disorders. (2001, January 30). *Laurence-Moon syndrome.* Retrieved from http://www.rarediseases.org

Vedia Sherman
Austin Neurological Clinic

See also Bardet-Biedl Syndrome

LEAD POISONING

Lead is among the oldest known toxins. Because of postnatal central nervous system development and relatively weak blood-brain barrier, early exposure has the greatest effects. However, exposure at any point can have serious effects. The Center for Disease Control (CDC, 2001) estimates that in the United States, over 20% of African-American children living in pre-1946 housing and a total of 890,000 1- to-5-year-old children have elevated blood-lead levels (BLLs). Infants who tend to put things in their mouths, or children who engage in pica are at particular risk. Poverty, inner-city location, and minority status are added risk factors. Exposure is largely through deteriorated lead-based paint in older housing, dust and soil contaminated with lead-based paint, and residue from past emissions of leaded gasoline. Other sources include industrial emissions and residue from recycling of automobile batteries (Berney, 1996). In an unusual case from rural North Carolina, a 4-year-old girl suffered severe brain damage from lead emitted from plates in automobile batteries that her family burned for heat in an indoor stove.

Clinical manifestations of lead poisoning in children develop over a period of 3–6 weeks and often are misdiagnosed as colic in infants or as attention-deficit/hyperactivity disorder, behavior disorder, or mental retardation in older children. In children under the age of 2, the syndrome progresses rapidly, whereas in older children, recurrent and less severe episodes are more likely. Characteristics are shown in approximate order of appearance with increasing exposure.

Characteristics

1. Apathy and irritability
2. Anorexia, intermittent vomiting, and vague abdominal pain
3. Clumsiness and ataxia
4. Drowsiness progressing to stupor
5. Hyperirritability
6. Seizures and coma

Diagnosis is through BLL; Linakis, Anderson, & Pueschel, 1996). In children, BLL above 10 μg/dl indicate overexposure and may call for nutritional intervention. However, symptoms of lead poisoning are often not seen even at BLL of about 20, a level at which some children require pharmacological treatment. At BLL above 45, children require medical intervention. Symptoms of lead encephalopathy are generally associated with BLL above 60 mg/dl. Chronic lead exposure is sometimes measured by lead content of teeth or hair.

Lead's most serious and irreversible effects are on the nervous system. High exposure may result in lead encephalopathy, characterized by convulsions, severe mental retardation, paralysis, blindness, coma, and death. Lower exposures are associated with intellectual deficits, including lowered intelligence, hyperactivity, aggression, impulsiveness, learning disabilities, and distractibility, that may not be reversible (Pueschel, Linakis, & Anderson, 1996). Research on both humans and nonhumans indicates possible adverse effects of even low levels of exposure of lead (e.g., Brown, 2001; Needleman & Bellinger, 2001), although this conclusion is quite controversial (e.g., Stone & Reynolds, 2002). However, attribution of those effects to lead in individual cases is difficult, due to a number of generally correlated factors that produce similar effects.

Treatment involves immediate medical intervention, including chelation therapy to reduce the child's BLL and consequent brain damage. Residual damage is permanent, and only supportive treatment is available. Medication obviously will help to control seizure disorders, but a variety of special services, including adaptive therapy and potential special classroom in school or institutional placement, may be needed.

Lead poisoning is completely preventable. Education of parents and other steps are now being taken to reduce children's exposure (e.g., CDC, 2001). It is important to note that several lines of research (e.g., Dietrich, 1996) now indicate that exposure of pregnant women to low levels of lead may have adverse effects on their offspring. Information is available from the National Lead Information Center (http://www.epa.gov/lead/nlicdocs.htm#general).

REFERENCES

Berney, B. L. (1996). Epidemiology of childhood lead poisoning. In S. Pueschel, J. Linakis, & A. Anderson (Eds.), *Lead poisoning in childhood* (pp. 15–35). Baltimore: Paul H. Brookes.

Brown, R. T. (2001). Behavioral teratology/toxicology: How do we know what we know? *Archives of Clinical Neuropsychology, 16,* 389–402.

Center for Disease Control. (2001). What every parent should know about lead poisoning in children. Retrieved from http://www.cdc.gov/nceh/lead/faq/cdc97a.htm

Dietrich, K. N. (1996). Low-level exposure during pregnancy and its consequences for fetal and child development. In S. Pueschel, J. Linakis, & A. Anderson (Eds.), *Lead poisoning in childhood* (pp. 117–139). Baltimore: Paul H. Brookes.

Linakis, J. G., Anderson, A. C., & Pueschel, S. M. (1996). Screening for lead poisoning. In S. Pueschel, J. Linakis, & A. Anderson (Eds.), *Lead poisoning in childhood* (pp. 59–73). Baltimore: Paul H. Brookes.

Needleman, H. L., & Bellinger, D. (2001). Studies of lead exposure and the developing central nervous system: A reply to Kaufman. *Archives of Clinical Neuropsychology, 16,* 359–374.

Pueschel, S. M., Linakis, J. G., & Anderson, A. C. (1996). *Lead poisoning in childhood.* Baltimore: Paul H. Brookes.

Stone, B., & Reynolds, C. R. (October, 2002). *Can the NHANES-III data provide information on the relationship of low BLLs on cognitive development in children?* Paper presented at the annual meeting of the National Academy of Neuropsychology.

Lauren M. Webster
Robert T. Brown
University of North Carolina, Wilmington

LEARNING DISABILITIES

Although there has been disagreement in the field regarding a specific operational definition, the term *learning disabilities* generally refers to a group of disorders that are characterized by learning problems to the degree that academic achievement or daily functioning is significantly impaired. The three primary diagnoses include reading disorder, mathematics disorder, and disorder of written language (American Psychiatric Association [APA], 1994). A child is considered to have a specific learning disability if academic achievement in one or more of these three areas (as measured by individually administered standardized assessment tools) is substantially below that expected for the child's chronological age and assessed level of intelligence (APA, 1994). The majority of states use a discrepancy definition in the process of identifying children with learning disabilities; this discrepancy is often defined as a difference of 2 or more standard deviations between academic achievement and intelligence (Mercer, Jordan, Allsop, & Mercer, 1996). There have been continuing efforts to further delineate specific subtypes of learning disabilities such as nonverbal learning disabilities (Rourke, 1995); however, empirical support for various subtypes remains sparse (Lyon & Cutting, 1998).

Symptoms of learning disabilities may occur as early as kindergarten, but a diagnosis typically is not made before the end of first grade and may not be apparent until later grades. Learning disabilities are three to four times more common in males than in females. Prevalence rates in the general population range from 2% to 4% (APA, 1994) and account for over 50% of students receiving special education services in the schools (U.S. Department of Education, 2000). Reading disorder is estimated to affect 60–80% of students identified with learning disabilities (Lyon & Cutting, 1998). There are wide interindividual differences among children with learning disabilities, although there are some shared characteristics.

Characteristics

1. Academic achievement in reading, written language, or mathematics is not commensurate with the child's chronological age or ability level.
2. There is a severe discrepancy between the child's measured achievement and intellectual ability in the area of oral expression, listening comprehension, written expression, basic reading skill, reading comprehension, mathematics calculation, or mathematics reasoning.
3. This severe discrepancy is not primarily due to visual, hearing, or motor disability; mental retardation; emotional disturbance; cultural factors; lack of educational opportunity; or insufficient instruction.
4. Underlying cognitive processing deficits may occur, including memory, attention, linguistic processing, or visual perception.
5. Low self-esteem and deficits in social interaction skills are common.

Due to the heterogeneity of this population, treatment is typically comprised of individualized education plans that outline instructional activities specifically tailored to meet the learning needs of each individual student. The general approaches to treatment include remediation of skill deficits, as well as accommodations in instruction, assignments, and evaluation methods. Unfortunately, there is a lack of research supporting the long-term efficacy of any specific instructional method, intervention technique, or combination thereof. The majority of research has focused on reading disabilities, with findings suggesting that phonological approaches to intervention are most efficacious (Lyon & Cutting, 1998).

Children with reading disorder, mathematics disorder, or disorder of written language may qualify for special education services under the category of Specific Learning Disability, depending on a state's definition. States vary in how they calculate the discrepancy between a student's expected and actual achievement, with some states using a discrepancy formula based on standard scores and others using regression equations. Furthermore, the size of the discrepancy may not be specified by state regulations and subsequently may vary by school district (Mercer et al., 1996). Additionally, impaired social interactions are a common characteristic of learning disabilities, so social skills training may be one component of the special education services these students require.

Comorbidity rates for students with learning disabilities are high for disruptive behavior disorders, attention-deficit disorders, and depressive disorders. The school dropout rate for these students is nearly 40% and learning disorders are likely to persist into adulthood, potentially affecting employment opportunities as well as social adjustment (APA, 1994). There is a substantial need for methodologically sound research exploring the efficacy of intervention strategies for well-defined subgroups of children with learning disabilities, particularly research that examines long-term outcomes.

REFERENCES

American Psychiatric Association (1994). *Diagnostic and statistical manual of mental disorders* (4th ed.). Washington, DC: Author.

Lyon, G. R., & Cutting, L. E. (1998). Learning disabilities. In E. J. Mash & R. A. Barkley (Eds.), *Treatment of childhood disorders* (2nd ed., pp. 468–498). New York: Guilford.

Mercer, C. D., Jordan, L., Allsop, D. H., & Mercer, A. R. (1996). Learning disabilities definitions and criteria used by state education departments. *Learning Disability Quarterly, 19,* 217–232.

Rourke, B. P. (1995). *Syndrome of nonverbal learning disabilities: Neurodevelopmental manifestations.* New York: Guilford.

U.S. Department of Education (2000). *Twenty-second annual report to Congress on the implementation of the Individuals with Disabilities Education Act.* Washington, DC: Author.

Lora Tuesday Heathfield
University of Utah

LEGG-CALVE-PERTHES DISEASE

Legg-Calve-Perthes disease, or avascular necrosis of the femoral head, involves loss of blood supply to the proximal epiphysis of the femur. The etiology of this disease is unknown.

This serious condition has a peak incidence between 3 and 10 years of age, affects males 4–5 times more than it does females, and affects Anglo-American children 10 times more frequently than it does African American children (Wong, 1995).

Characteristics

1. Child is brought to the pediatrician or orthopedic surgeon because of pain in femur and limping.
2. Child complains of pain in other parts of the leg such as the groin, thigh, or inner knee.
3. When the hip is moved, pain grows more intense.
4. Rest often relieves discomfort.

The child with Legg-Calve-Perthes disease can expect to have multiple X-rays over the course of treatment (Kaniklides, Lonnerholm, & Moberg, 1994). X-ray results will show a worsening condition before a gradual improvement is observed. After a diagnosis is confirmed, the child will require careful orthopedic treatment. Legg-Calve-Perthes disease is self-limiting, but failure to properly treat this condition may lead to significant femoral head deformity and severe degenerative arthritis (Nochimson, 1998).

The treatment regime has changed over the past decade and now encompasses several therapies to enhance the healing process (Ball & Bindler, 1999; Nochimson, 1998; Wong, 1995). The initial therapy consists of rest and avoidance of weight bearing to restore motion and reduce inflammation. Traction is often used to relieve spasms, stretch out contractures, and restore hip motion. Weight bearing should be avoided on the affected limb, and the child must be contained in a non-weight-bearing device such as an abduction brace, leg casts, or harness sling. Conservative therapies are usually continued for 2–4 years. Surgical correction may speed the recovery process and allow the child to return to normal activities in 3–4 months (Wong, 1995).

Special education services may be available to children with Legg-Calve-Perthes disease under the handicapping condition of Other Health Impaired or Physical Disability. Due to extensive and ongoing medical intervention, significant periods of time away from the classroom may be involved and home visits from special educators will be necessary. The unpredictability of the disorder's scope and intensity of pain may require pain management intervention. In addition, the length of treatment and self-limiting nature of the disorder will require counseling that is sensitive to chronic illness issues. Side effects of medications for pain management should be taken into account when formally assessing the cognitive, social,, emotional, and academic abilities of these children.

Children who develop Legg-Calve-Perthes disease before the age of 6 tend to have a better prognosis and a faster recovery (Mayo Physician Group, 1997). The later the diagnosis, the more femoral damage has occurred before treatment is implemented, and the poorer the overall prognosis (Wong, 1995).

REFERENCES

Ball, J., & Bindler, R. (1999). *Pediatric nursing: Caring for children* (2nd ed.). Stamford, CT: Appleton & Lange.

Kaniklides, C., Lonnerholm, T., & Moberg, A. (1994). Legg-Calve-Perthes disease: Comparison of conventional radiography, MR Imaging, bone scintigraphy, and arthrography. *Acta Radiology, 35,* 434–439.

Mayo Physician Group (1997, February 3). Legg-Calve-Perthes (LCP) condition. Retrieved from http://www.mayohealth.org/mayo/askphys/qa970201.htm

Nochimson, G. (1998, October 29). Legg-Calve-Perthes disease. Retrieved from http://www.emedicine.com/emerg/topic294.htm

Wong, D. (1995). *Whaley & Wong's nursing care of infants and children* (5th ed.). St. Louis: Mosby.

Elaine Fletcher-Janzen
University of Northern Colorado

Kari Anderson
University of North Carolina, Wilmington

LEIGH SYNDROME

Leigh Syndrome, also termed subacute necrotizing encephalomyelopathy, presents as a progressive neurometabolic disorder and often results from mitochondrial DNA mutation. Such mutations disrupt the mitochondria's ability to produce the cellular energy. Furthermore, the central nervous system appears to be most directly affected by mitochondrial dysfunction (Wallace, 1997). The onset of Leigh syndrome is usually prior to 2 years of age, and although onset in adolescence and early adulthood is possible, it is rare (National Institute of Neurological Disorders and Stroke [NINDS], 2001).

The diagnosis of Leigh syndrome relies on pathogenic findings rather than clinical symptoms. Jellinger and Seitelberger (1970) reported degeneration in both gray and white matter. Gray-brown lesions were found in the brain stem and medulla oblongata with bilaterally symmetrical lesions appearing in the periaqueducatal region and the tegmentum. Furthermore, glial reactions and hypervasculation were evident in many of the lesion sites (as cited in van Erven et al., 1987). Degeneration of the basal ganglia in particular results in many of the motor symptoms present in this condition (Wallace, 1997). Cavanagh and Harding report symmetrical vasculonecrotic damage of variable topography across the brain stem as being the hallmark pathological finding of Leigh syndrome (1994).

In a review of 173 confirmed cases of Leigh syndrome, van Erven et al. (1987) described early clinical signs as including feeding, vision, and respiratory difficulties. Symptoms frequently displayed by infants include the following: poor sucking ability, vomiting, lack of appetite, blindness, jerky eye movements, irregular breathing, episodes of hyperventilation, and apnea. Cerebellar signs such as dysdiadochokinesia (the inability to produce rapidly alternating movements), hypermetria, and explosive speech are also common. Extrapyramidal symptoms include hypokinesis, dystonia, and involuntary movements such as atheotosis, choreoatheotosis, and ballism (van Erven et al., 1987). Leigh syndrome, then, results in motor and cognitive delay as well as elevated lactate levels in the blood, cerebrospinal fluid, or both (Rahman et al., 1996).

Although many components of the cellular energy system have been implicated, the heterogeneity of Leigh syndrome phenotypes is most likely explained by the differential levels of energy production impairment (Rahman et al., 1996). It has been suggested that higher concentrations of mutated mitochondrial DNA molecules present in the tissue may lead to lower ATP production and more severe manifestations of pathology (Wallace, 1997).

Based on a study of one geographic region, southeastern Australia, Rahman et al. (1996) determined the prevalence of strictly defined Leigh syndrome to be about 1 per 77,000. When cases presenting with similar clinical features but atypical neuropathology were included, the prevalence increased to 1 per 40,000. The probability that Leigh syndrome is underidentified suggests that the later prevalence estimate is more likely (Rahman et al., 1996). Affected males outnumber females three to two (Rahman et al., 1996); however, a review of the literature suggests that in onset after 4 years of age, males outnumber females four to one (van Erven, 1987). Several inheritance patterns have been suggested for the transmission of Leigh syndrome. Mitochondrial DNA is inherited solely through the ovum (Wallace, 1997), suggesting maternal transmission in at least some of the cases. In cases in which specific mitochondrial defects were identified, approximately half of them could be attributed to X-linked, maternal, or sporadic inheritance, whereas nuclear inheritance was implicated in other cases (Rahman et al., 1996). Furthermore, Rahman et al. (1996) suggested that autosomal recessive inheritance is suspected in only 50% or less of presenting Leigh syndrome cases.

Characteristics

1. Developmental delay and cognitive retardation, often with regression
2. Elevated lactate levels in blood, cerebrospinal fluid, or both
3. Motor disturbances such as hypotonia, involuntary movements, poor reflexes, difficulty eating and swallowing, and ataxia
4. Respiratory disturbance
5. Fatigue
6. Seizures
7. Optic atrophy

There is currently no cure for Leigh syndrome to correct the casual mechanisms (Cavanagh & Harding, 1994). Treatment usually focuses on the metabolic complications of the disorder, such as the inclusion of thiamin (vitamin B1) into the diet (NINDS, 2001) to aid in the release of energy from fats and carbohydrates. Resulting lactic acidosis may be treated with a regimen of sodium bicarbonate or sodium citrate (NINDS, 2001).

Rahman et al. (1996) depict the survival rate of patients presenting with both strictly defined Leigh syndrome and Leigh-like conditions (those subjects meeting most of the criteria but showing atypical neuropathology). Between 2 and 3 years of age, about 50% of those patients exhibiting Leigh syndrome have survived, while over 80% of those presenting with a subclinical manifestation of the disorder were still alive. The mortality rate drops at a slower pace after age 3, with less than 20% of the Leigh syndrome population surviving into their 20s. Over 60% of the Leigh-like group survive into young adulthood (Rahman et al., 1996). Later onset is generally associated with a slower-acting form of the disorder (NINDS, 2001). The most common causes of death associated with Leigh syndrome are neurogenic respiratory disturbance, sudden coma, pneumonia, cardiac difficulties, and hyperprexia. Approximately one third of case reports list the cause of death as unknown (van Erven et al., 1987).

Students with Leigh syndrome will qualify for special services under Section 504 of the Rehabilitation Act of 1973 and under the Individuals with Disabilities Education Act (IDEA). Services should focus on accommodating the student's motor disturbances, providing support for cognitive difficulties, and managing symptoms such as respiratory problems, fatigue, and seizures. Additionally, the individualized educational program planning team may consider the potential benefit of assistive technology, especially if the disorder has affected the student's vision. Educators and staff must be aware of the psychological distress associated with chronic medical disorders.

REFERENCES

Cavanagh, J. B., & Harding, B. N. (1994). Pathogenic factors underlying the lesions in Leigh's disease: Tissue response to cellular energy deprivation and their clinico-pathological consequences. *Brain, 117,* 1357–1376.

Jellinger, K., & Seitelberger, F. (1970). Subacute necrotizing encephalomyelopathy (Leigh). *Ergeb Inn Med Kinderheilkd, 29,* 155–219.

National Institute of Neurological Disorders and Stroke. (2001). NINDS Leigh's disease information page. Retrieved from http://www.ninds.nih.gov/health_and_medical/disorders/leighs disease_doc.htm

Rahman, S., Blok, R. B., Dahl, H. H. M., Danks, D. M., Kirby, D. M., Chow, C. W., et al. (1996). Leigh syndrome: Clinical features and biochemical and DNA abnormalities. *Annals of Neurology, 39* (3), 343–351.

Van Erven, P. M. M., Cillessen, J. P. M., Eekhoff, E. M. W., Gabreels, F. J. M., Doesburg, W. H., Lemmens, W. A. J. G., et al. (1987). Leigh syndrome, a mitochrondrial encephalo(myo)pathy: A review of the literature. *Clinical Neurology and Neurosurgery, 89* (4), 217–230.

Wallace, D. C. (1997, August). Mitochondrial DNA in aging and disease. *Scientific American,* 40–47.

Sarah Schnoebelen
Margaret Semrud-Clikeman
University of Texas at Austin

LENNOX-GASTAUT SYNDROME

Lennox-Gastaut syndrome (LGS) is a severe form of epilepsy. The syndrome consists of the following primary characteristics: multiple types of seizures (e.g., tonic, atonic, myoclonic, and atypical absence), a diffuse spike, or poly-spike, slow waves (< 2.0 Hz) pattern on electroencephalogram (EEG), and severe mental retardation. LGS accounts for at least 3–5% of all childhood epilepsies (Wheless & Constantinou, 1997). The age of onset is between 1 and 8 years, with a peak incidence between 3 and 5. The syndrome is slightly more common in males, with a male-to-female ratio of 1.5 to 1. More than one third of all cases involve children who had a prior history of infantile spasms. A family history of epilepsy is a risk factor, however, there is no known single cause of LGS (and about one third of all cases are idiopathic). Etiological factors related to LGS include hypoxic ischemic encephalopathy (i.e., lack of oxygen) at birth, intrauterine infections (cytomegalovirus, rubella, toxoplasmosis), traumatic brain injury, meningitis, tuberous sclerosis, brain tumors, and metabolic disorders.

About 50% of individuals with LGS have more than one seizure type. The most common seizure is that of a tonic seizure involving body stiffening, upward deviation of the eyes, dilation of the pupils, and altered respiratory patterns (Donat, 1992). Other seizure types that are frequently observed in children with LGS are atypical absence seizures (i.e., staring spells), atonic seizures (i.e., brief loss of muscle tone and consciousness, causing abrupt falls), and myoclonic seizures (i.e., sudden muscle jerks). Frequent tonic, atonic, and myoclonic seizures often result in falls that lead to further injury, including facial fractures and head injuries.

Characteristics

1. Severe form of epilepsy with onset between 1 and 8 years of age
2. Multiple seizure types requiring polydrug treatment
3. Mental retardation in 75% of all cases
4. Concomitant behavior and social skills problems (e.g., hyperactivity and aggression)

More than 75% of children with LGS develop mental retardation, and in the majority of cases the retardation is severe (Wheless & Constantinou, 1997). The earlier the age of onset, the more likely mental retardation will occur (e.g., in children under 2 years of age). Epileptic encephalopathy, or progressive loss of intellectual functioning, however, is commonly seen during the course of the syndrome. The loss of cognitive skill is attributed to hypoxia from intractable seizures and toxicity from continual medication use (i.e., anticonvulsant drugs). According to the National Institute of Neurological Disease and Stroke (NINDS, n.d.), about 25% of individuals with LGS have serious psychological problems at one point or another in their life. Many children with LGS have behavior problems, including problems with hyperactivity, aggression, and poor social skills.

Treatment of LGS is often difficult due to the number and degree of functional impairments and to the variety of seizures that are associated with the syndrome. Nonpharmacological treatments are used (e.g., ketogenic diet, vitamin B_6 supplements, and severing of the corpus callosum) but the typical regimen involves the use of multiple (and high dose) anticonvulsant drug treatment. The drug of choice for LGS is valproate (VPA), however, lamotrigine has shown some promise. Other common drugs include benzodiazepines, felbamate, topiramate, vigabatrin, adrenocorticotropic hormones, and steroids.

Special education is nearly imperative given the degree of intellectual and physical disability caused by LGS. More often than not, these children are served under the classification of Intellectual Disabilities and require a number of related services including speech and language and physical and occupational therapy. Involving the school psychologist and school nurse is also needed, given the need to consult with professionals outside the school and address psychological, health care, and medication issues. The prognosis for this syndrome is poor, given the difficulty managing seizures. Despite the common use of polydrug therapy, it is estimated that more than 80% of children with LGS will have seizures as adults. Research data from NINDS (n.d.) estimate that only 20% of individuals who have LGS will live independent lives; the remainder live with parents or in group homes.

REFERENCES

Donat, J. F. (1992). The age dependent epileptic encephalopathies. *Journal of Child Neurology, 7,* 7–18.

National Institute of Neurological Disease and Stroke. (n.d.) Retrieved from http://www.ninds.nih.gov/index.htm

Wheless, J. W., & Constantinou, J. (1997). Lennox-Gastaut syndrome. *Pediatric Neurology, 17,* 203–209.

Heidi Mathie
Elaine Clark
University of Utah

See also Seizures

LEOPARD SYNDROME

The name LEOPARD syndrome comes from the acronym of its symptoms: lentigines, electrocardiographic abnormalities, ocular hypertelorism, pulmonary stenosis, abnormalities of genitalia, retardation of growth, and deafness (sensorineural). This syndrome is associated with high prevalence of cardiac abnormalities (Shamsadini, Abazardi, & Shamsadini, 1999). Further descriptions of these symptoms are located in the characteristics box. The syndrome is inherited as an autosomal dominant trait with high penetrance and markedly variable expressivity (Gorlin, Anderson, & Moller, 1971).

As of 1990, at least 79 patients had been identified as having LEOPARD syndrome (Shamsadini et al., 1999).

Characteristics

1. Lentigines are small spots on the skin that resemble moles. In this case, they tend to be numerous and highly concentrated over the neck and upper trunk. They appear (but in smaller numbers) over the face, scalp, palms, soles, and genitalia. They are either present at birth or shortly after, and they increase with age. Large, dark café noir spots are commonly found on the trunk. These spots differ from freckles in that they appear earlier, are not related to sun exposure, and have a different microscopic makeup.
2. Electrocardiographic abnormality includes a congenital cardiac malformation. Heart murmurs are often present. This anomaly is found in patients with LEOPARD syndrome regardless of the type of cardiac malformation. In other words, it can occur both in patients with structural abnormalities of the heart and in those lacking a structural abnormality. In at least one patient, an atrioventricular block occurred (between the left atrium and ventrical in the heart), and the patient suffered a heart attack while dancing; it is the first reported case of survival from ventricular fibrillation associated with this disease (Woywodt et al., 1998).
3. Ocular hypertelorism entails ptosis of the upper eyelids, biparietal bossing, and epicanthal folds.
4. Pulmonary stenosis (valvular) is usually mild and appears to be the most common cardiac abnormality.
5. Abnormality of genitalia is different in males and females. In males, hypospadias are present in about one half of the male cases, along with cryptorchidism (or descent of only one testicle), which is also common. In females, the absence of an ovary has been found. Late menarche has also been a common finding in females.
6. Retardation of growth is common, with 85% of patients being below the 25th percentile for both height and weight, with the majority being below the 10th percentile in both categories.
7. Deafness (sensorineural) occurs in approximately 15% of cases and is therefore one of the less common facets of the syndrome.

Treatment implications for LEOPARD syndrome are unknown. Surgeries have been reported for undescended testicles, and in at least one case, a pacer-cardioverter-defibrillator device has been implanted (Woywodt et al., 1998). It is recommended that cardiologists monitor those patients with heart murmurs.

Educational implications are also uncertain. It has been reported that intelligence ranges from mental retardation to normal functioning. One case study was reported of a family with two sets of twins, in which three of them have this syndrome. In the first set of twins, the one with LEOPARD syndrome was performing at a below-average level and was considerably behind her unaffected twin sister in her schoolwork. In the other set of twins, both of whom were affected, the male twin was found to have an IQ of 77, whereas his female twin was performing at an average level. (Sommer, Contras, Caenen, & Hosier, 1971). However, how well this case study reflects the entire population of patients with LEOPARD syndrome is unknown. Thus, these children should have a full neuropsychological assessment to pinpoint their specific areas of strength and weakness.

Prognoses could not be identified through an extensive literature review. The concern with this syndrome is primarily focused around the effects of the heart. Some sources say that children with LEOPARD syndrome lead normal lives, whereas others imply the possibility of mental retardation.

REFERENCES

Gorlin, R. J., Anderson, R. C., & Moller, J. H. (1971). The Leopard (multiple lentigines) syndrome revisited. *Birth Defects: Original Article Series, 7*(4), 110–115.

Shamsadini, S., Abazardi, H., & Shamsadini, F. (1999). Leopard Syndrome. *Lancet, 354,* 1530.

Sommer, A., Contras, S. B., Caenen, J. M., & Hosier, D. M. (1971). A family study of the Leopard syndrome. *American Journal of Diseases of Children, 121,* 520–523.

Woywodt, A., Welzel, J., Haase, H., Deulholz, A., Wiegand, U., Potratz, J., et al. (1998). Cardiomyopathic lentiginosis/ LEOPARD syndrome presenting as sudden cardiac arrest. *Chest, 113*(5), 1415.

Catherine M. Caldwell
University of Texas at Austin

LEPRECHAUNISM (DONOHUE SYNDROME)

Leprechaunism (Donohue & Uchida, 1954; Imamura & Kobayashi, 1954) is caused by an autosomal recessive genetic anomaly believed to be associated with the insulin receptor gene (c.f. Psiachou et al., 1993) resulting in an endocrine disorder associated with the overdevelopment of the pancreas, insulin resistance (circulating insulin levels > 1,000 μU/ml), and excessive estrogen.

Characteristics

1. Elf-like features, including microcephaly, small face, prominent eyes, broad nostrils, prominent ears, and thick lips
2. Body and facial hirsutism (abnormal hairiness) and wrinkled skin
3. Apparent mental retardation and motor deficits
4. Genital abnormalities, including premature development of breasts and prominent nipples
5. Prenatal and postnatal growth retardation and failure to thrive
6. Reduced muscle mass and lack of adipose tissue

Leprechaunism has been postulated to be the result of abnormalities on Chromosome 19 p 13.2.

Leprechaunism is characterized by microcephaly, small face, prominent deep-set eyes, broad or wide nostrils, prominent ears, and thick lips resulting in an elf-like faces (Imamura & Kobayashi, 1954; Jones, 1997). Body and facial hirsutism (abnormal hairiness), acanthosis nigricans, and wrinkled skin also are prominent (Jones, 1997). Mental retardation and motor deficits are prominent, as are problems associated with orthopedic development. Genital abnormalities including premature development of breasts and prominent nipples, as well as reduced muscle mass and lack of adipose tissue. Prenatal and postnatal growth retardation and failure to thrive are always present. These children also suffer from hypoglycemia associated with pancreatic problems. Other endocrine problems are common. Few children with leprechaunism have been known to survive past early infancy.

Future research should focus on a better delineation of the cause of the disorder. Gene therapy also merits attention.

REFERENCES

Donohue, W. L., & Uchida, L. (1954). Leprechaunism: A euphemism for a rare familial disorder. *Journal of Pediatrics, 45,* 505.

Imamura, T., & Kobayashi, M. (1954). Donohue's syndrome. *Nippon Risho, 52,* 2643–2647.

Jones, K. L. (1997). *Smith's recognizable patterns of human malformations* (5th ed.). Philadelphia: W. B. Saunders.

Psiachou, H. (1993). Leprechaunism and homozygous nonsense mutations in the insulin receptor gene. *Lancet, 324,* 924.

Antolin M. Llorente
Baylor College of Medicine
Houston, Texas

LESCH-NYHAN SYNDROME

Lesch-Nyhan syndrome is characterized by neuromuscular difficulties such as dystonia and spasticity; speech impairment; renal disease; gout; cognitive deficits; and compulsive, self-injurious behavior. The syndrome was first reported in 1963 by Micheal Lesch and William Nyhan. Lesch-Nyhan syndrome is an X-linked recessive disorder of the enzyme hypoxanthine-guanine phosphoribosyltransferase or HPRT. There are several mutations resulting in the HPRT deficiency, making early diagnosis difficult. The disorder typically affects males because the defective gene is recessive and carried on the X chromosome. Females rarely exhibit characteristics of Lesch-Nyhan, but they may be carriers (Morales, 1999).

Characteristics

1. Severe dystonia, spasticity, and other neuromuscular difficulties
2. Speech impairment
3. Renal disease and gout
4. Difficulty swallowing and feeding
5. Cognitive impairments, including mental retardation
6. Self-injurious behaviors, including self-biting

Lesch-Nyhan syndrome is a rare disorder that occurs in about 1 in 380,000 births. It is evenly distributed among races and geographic locations (Morales, 1999). Lesch-Nyhan syndrome typically presents 10–30 days after birth, with orange crystals appearing in diapers, indicating renal failure. Other symptoms of renal failure include hyperuricemia, gout, uric acid stones, and urate nephropathy.

Neurological symptoms follow the signs of renal dysfunction and typically appear after 3 months. Severe delays in motor development are often noted at 3–6 months, suggesting significant neuromotor dysfunction. Athetosis (a slow irregular twisting movement in the upper extremities) and abnormal muscle tone (or spasticity) are seen around the same time, 3–5 months of age. Many children with Lesch-Nyhan syndrome are initially diagnosed with cerebral palsy due to the motor presentation (Morales, 1999). Between 6 and 12 months of age, children with Lesch-Nyhan syndrome become increasingly hypertonic and show spasticity, ridgidity, and flexor spasms. A characteristic movement of Lesch-Nyhan syndrome is an opisthotonic spasm involving an arching of the back, head bent back to the neck, heels bent back to the legs, and arms and hands flexing rigidly at the joints. Motor defects often become so severe that the child with Lesch-Nyhan syndrome cannot sit or stand without support.

Children with Lesch-Nyhan syndrome also manifest speech impairments (e.g., poor articulation) as a result of pseudobulbar palsy and obstructed airflow. Athetoid dysarthria and dysphagia are also seen, and children with the syndrome often lost weight as a result of dysphagia (i.e., problems swallowing and ingesting food). Cognitive impairments are present in most cases, but to varying degrees. Mental retardation has been seen as a cardinal feature of Lesch-Nyhan syndrome; however, motor and behavioral impairments probably mask some of these children's abilities. Although visual and auditory perception are considered to be intact, children with Lesch-Nyhan syndrome have such poor attentional and motor skills, scores on standardized tests are difficult to interpret. Testing is further impeded by the child's frequent self-injurious behaviors that require restraint. In many cases, self-injurious behaviors help to distinguish Lesch-Nyhan syndrome from other neurological conditions. Self-mutilating behaviors typically begin around 26 months of age (Morales, 1999). A salient features of Lesch-Nyhan syndrome is biting oneself. This begins with breaking the skin, causing lacerations on lips, fingers, and hands. As the child gets older and more physically and cognitively capable, more serious injury occurs (e.g., permanent loss of tissue, self-amputation of fingers and tongue, and loss of lip tissue). Behavioral techniques have not been successful in eliminating this self-mutilating behavior; in fact, only restraints have proved adequate. As a result, many individuals with the syndrome will have their teeth extracted to prevent mutilation of lips and tongue. According to Morales (1999), mutilation behaviors associated with Lesch-Nyhan syndrome may be due to neurotransmitter abnormalities—in particular, dysfunction in dopamine or serotonin metabolism.

Children with Lesch-Nyhan syndrome will require special education services, given the severity and chronicity of problems. More often than not, services will be provided under the category of Intellectual Disabilities. Considerable ancillary services are likely to be needed, in addition to the contained classroom setting in which these children are placed. Speech and language services, occupational and physical therapy, and school psychological services are likely to be needed so that these children's needs are properly identified and treated. Home-school collaborations will be critical to ensure that the needs of siblings are also met. Individuals with Lesch-Nyhan syndrome are unable to care for themselves or live independently; therefore, they require round-the-clock attendant care to prevent self-injury. In cases in which the child remains at home, considerable stress is placed on the family; therefore, these needs must be assessed and services provided (e.g., supportive counseling).

REFERENCES

Morales, P. C. (1999). Lesch-Nyhan syndrome. In S. Goldstein & C. R. Reynolds (Eds.), *Handbook of Neurodevelopmental and genetic disorders in children* (pp. 478–495). New York: Guilford Press.

Heidi Mathie
Elaine Clark
University of Utah

LETHAL MULTIPLE PTERYGIUM SYNDROME

Lethal multiple pterygium syndrome (LMPS) is an inherited, congenital disorder. Its distinguishing features are the presence of pterygia (tight, weblike bands of skin) in various areas of the body and death prior to (stillborn) or immediately after birth.

LMPS is rare. After its initial description in three female siblings in 1976, only about 40 cases have been reported. There are two clinically distinguishable forms of LMPS. The "early" variant is characterized by fetal death in the second trimester and hydrops (an abnormal accumulation of fluid in fetal tissue). This early form has both autosomal and X-linked recessive modes of inheritance. In the "late" form, the fetus lived into the third trimester and was not hydropic. This late subset of LMPS has a uniformly autosomal recessive pattern of inheritance. The etiology of LMPS has not been determined.

Characteristics

1. Fetal growth deficiency, polyhydramnios (excessive amniotic fluid), decreased fetal activity, breech position
2. Flat nose, small jaw, cleft palate, wide-set eyes (hypertelorism), small mouth, malformed ears
3. Contractures of the shoulders, elbows, hands, hips, knees, ankles, and feet
4. Pterygia in the following locations: chin to chest, neck, armpit, in front of the elbow, groin, behind the knee, and surrounding the ankle
5. Small chest, underdeveloped lungs, skeletal malformations

No therapy is available for this disorder. Affected individuals have either been stillborn or died shortly after delivery, probably secondary to inadequate lung development. Expectant parents who have a family history of LMPS or are otherwise concerned that their baby might have the disorder should be offered genetic counseling. No data are forthcoming regarding the availability of prenatal diagnosis of LMPS or of testing for the carrier state.

REFERENCES

Jones, K. (1997). *Smith's recognizable patterns of human malformations* (5th ed.). Philadelphia: W. B. Saunders.

Barry H. Davison
Ennis, Texas

Joan W. Mayfield
Baylor Pediatric Specialty Services
Dallas, Texas

LEUKEMIA, ACUTE LYMPHOCYTIC

Acute lymphocytic leukemia is a malignant condition in which immature white blood cells are produced in abnormally large quantities and disrupt normal blood cell growth. The blood cells, also referred to as blasts, accumulate in bone marrow, blood, and lymphatics, and they circulate throughout the blood and lymphatic system. Vital organs, including the lungs, kidney, spleen, and liver, are often damaged as a result of the condition. Leukemic cells can also affect tissue of the brain and spinal cord.

ALL is responsible for approximately 85% of leukemia in patients under the age of 21. The disease, which is more common in Caucasian males, is usually diagnosed during the preschool years. Approximately 2,000 new pediatric cases are diagnosed each year, making ALL the most common malignant condition of childhood. Prevalence rates for children between the ages of 2 and 10 is estimated to be 4.4 out of 100,000, a rate 4 times higher than that in adults (National Institute of Health [NIH], 1999). The specific etiology of ALL is unknown; however, a number of factors, including exposures to certain toxins in the environment, have been shown to increase risk for the disease. Children, for example, who have been exposed to electromagnetic radiation (even large amounts of household electrical current) and certain chemicals and drugs (e.g., benzine derivatives and alkylating agents), have been shown to have a higher incidence of ALL. Certain viral infections have also been associated with the disease, as has a positive family history. Children with an affected twin or sibling under the age of 5 have a 20% chance of developing ALL. Furthermore, children with Down syndrome have also been shown to be far more likely to develop the disease (i.e., 20 times the risk).

Characteristics

1. Excessive bleeding and bone pain
2. Frequent infection with fever, chills, and respiratory discomfort
3. Weakness, fatigue, and irritability (related to anemia)
4. Swollen lymph nodes and enlarged liver and spleen
5. Endocrine abnormalities and associated growth problems
6. Neurocognitive deficits (e.g., poor attention and memory, reduced motor and processing speed, and visual-spatial deficits)
7. Learning problems, like cognitive problems, often the result of treatment (intrathecal chemotherapy and cranial radiation)

Treatment for ALL primarily consists of cranial radiation therapy and intrathecal chemotherapy using methotrexate. These treatments have been credited with the tremendous increase in long-term survival over the past three decades, but they have also been blamed for certain medical and cognitive problems; these include growth problems associated with endocrine problems and reduced abilities and learning capacity associated with central nervous system assault. Neuropsychological problems include poor attention and memory, slowed processing speed and motor performance, and visual-spatial deficits (Waber, Bernstein, Kammerer, Tarbell, & Sallen, 1992). More recent research has suggested that females may be more sensitive to the effects of combined treatments (i.e., radiation and chemotherapy administered at the same time) and that changing the order of the drugs may alleviate certain problems (Waber & Mullenix, 2000). Males have been shown to tolerate treatment better, except for corticosteroid use. Because ALL is fatal if left untreated, there is little option other than use of these therapies. Long-term survival rates are estimated to be as high as 70% in treated cases (Waber & Mullenix, 2000). Bone marrow transplants have been used; however, the long-term benefit has yet to be determined.

Not all children with ALL require special education services; however, many will require some type of accommodation in the classroom (especially around the time of treatment). Some students may require extra time to complete missed assignments, tutoring to catch up on work, or both. In cases in which special education is needed, services under the category of Other Health Impaired may be appropriate; this includes assistance from the school nurse as well as from the school psychologist. Often, interventions include supportive counseling and education (i.e., of the school staff and peers). Schools are often a refuge for parents and children struggling to cope with a serious medical condition—especially a life-threatening disease. At times, parents have little information as to where to turn for help and are not even aware of resources in the community. School psychologists can be particularly helpful by putting parents in touch with agencies that deal with ALL (e.g., Leukemia Society of America, 600 Third Avenue, New York, NY, 10016).

There has been considerable research on the effects of treatment for ALL. The work, however, is far from complete. Further studies need to be conducted to determine more precisely the cause of ALL and to determine the treatment regimen that has the best outcome (i.e., long-term survival with the fewest physical and neurocognitive side effects).

REFERENCES

Waber, D., Bernstein, J., Kammerer, B., Tarbell, N., & Sallen, S. (1992). Neuropsychological diagnostic profiles of children who received CNS treatment for acute lymphoblastic leukemia: The systemic approach to assessment. *Developmental Neuropsychology, 8*(1), 1–28.

Waber, B., & Mullenix, P. (2000). Acute lymphoblastic leukemia. In K. O. Yeates, M. D. Ris, & H. G. Taylor (Eds.). *Pediatric neuropsychology: Research, theory and practice* (pp. 300–319). New York: Guilford Press.

Wendy Wolfe
Elaine Clark
University of Utah

LEUKODYSTROPHY

Leukodystrophy refers to a group of progressive genetic disorders that affect the brain, spinal cord, and peripheral nerves. Because each leukodystrophy affects a different chemical that makes up the myelin sheath or white matter covering nerve fibers, having one does not increase likelihood of contracting another (National Institute of Neurological Disorders and Stroke [NINDS], 2001). Leukodystrophies, described by the United Leukodystrophy Foundation (ULF, 2001), include adrenoleukodystrophy (ALD) and neonatal ALD, Aicardi-Gouthieres leukodystrophy, Alexander disease, childhood ataxia with central nervous system hypomyelination (CACH or vanishing white matter disease), cerebral autosomal dominant arteriopathy with subcortical infarcts and leukoencephalopathy (CADASIL), Canavan disease, cerebrotendinous xanthomatosis (CTX), Krabbe disease, metachromatic leukodystrophy, ovarioleukodystrophy syndrome, Pelizaeus-Merzbacher disease, Refsum disease, Van Der Knapp syndrome, and Zellweger syndrome. Each leukodystrophy has a predictable age of onset, varying from infancy to adulthood, type and severity of symptoms, and expected life span, as described by the ULF (2001), but they share several overlapping characteristics.

Characteristics

1. Progressive dementia and retarded development
2. Long-tract dysfunction manifested by spasticity, cerebral deficits and abnormalities in the visual and somatosensory afferent pathways
3. Gradual changes in infant or child who at first was thought to be well, including body tone, movements, gait, speech, ability to eat, vision, behavior and thought processes, or loss of processes later in life

Metachromatic leukodystrophy, a subgroup arising from a defect in arylsulfatase A, a major component of myelin, is the most common leukodystrophy, with an incidence of approximately 1 in 40,000 births (Menkes, 1990). Krabbe disease occurs in about 1 per 100,000 births in a year (ULF, 2001). The other disorders are extremely rare. Most occur equally across ethnic groups, except for Canavan disease, which is more frequent in Ashkenazi Jews (ULF, 2001).

Diagnosis can be difficult. Symptoms may not be recognized in the early stages of the disease because of the general gradualness of its progression. It may be suspected in an apparently normal infant or child who shows gradual deterioration in body tone, movements, gait, speech, eating, vision or hearing, behavior, memory, or thought processes (NINDS, 2001).

The following information on individual leukodystrophies is from ULF (2001). Metachromatic leukodystrophy, itself a group of disorders, is the most frequent and described in a separate entry. ALD, affecting the adrenal gland and white matter of the nervous system, has onset from childhood to adulthood and only affects boys (X-linked). However, neonatal ALD can affect males and females. The rarest leukodystrophy, Alexander disease, is a rapidly progressing neurological disorder affecting mainly males. CACH, characterized by the foamy appearance of oligodendrocytes under microscopic examination, generally has onset between 1 and 5 years of age, either spontaneously or after head trauma or febrile illness. CADASIL occurs in middle ages, is associated with cystic or necrotic lesions within the white matter, and leads to dementia and stroke. Canavan disease involves a broad breakdown of white matter; like ADL, it can develop from infancy into adulthood. Krabbe disease is an autosomal recessive disorder that results in defective myelin. Pelizaeus-Merzbacher disease is a generally nonprogressive X-linked disorder with numerous variants. Speech, mobility, and limb function may not develop in the most severe form, which has infant onset. Refsum disease is associated with retinitis pigmentosa, peripheral neuropathy, ataxia, and elevated protein in cerebrospinal fluid. Affected individuals cannot degrade phytanic acid, which comes entirely through diet; the acid accumulates and is probably responsible for all symptoms. Refsum disease can be effectively treated by a diet that avoids food containing phytanic acid. Aicardi-Gouthieres leukodystrophy, CTX, ovarioleukodystrophy syndrome, Van Der Knapp syndrome, and Zellweger syndrome are other forms of leukodystrophy.

Except for Refsum disease, no treatment that consistently alleviates symptoms is available for leukodystrophy, and prognosis is therefore usually poor. Treatment is mainly supportive and depends on the type and severity of the disorder. Experimental treatments are being tested for several of disorders. Bone marrow transplant, Lorenzo's oil, lovastatin, and 4-phenylbutyrate are being tried on ADL. Gene therapy may alleviate symptoms of Canavan disease. Bile acids help stabilize CTX. In children in whom Krabbe disease is discovered presymptomatically, hematopoietic stem cell transplantation slows progression of—and may reverse—neurological damage.

Various and generally extensive special services will be needed for those with leukodystrophy. Most leukodystrophies have early onset with readily visible and progressive symptoms, but both earlier- and later-onset types produce numerous impairments. In some cases, symptoms may not become apparent for years, and progression may be interrupted by periods of stability. Given the impact on the family, counseling and other assistance—including in-home health services—may be needed. In terms of special education, most cases will call for separate classroom placement and speech-language and physical therapy. Genetic counseling for the family may also be advisable.

Reduction of incidence of leukodystrophies may result from DNA testing. A DNA-based blood test has now become available for ALD so that would-be parents can determine whether they are carriers (ULF, 2001). Carrier testing is also available for Canavan and Krabbe diseases. Prenatal testing is available for Zellweger syndrome and Pelizaeus-Merzbacher disease. The chromosomal locus for Van Der Knapp syndrome has recently been identified, which may lead to an accurate test (ULF, 2001).

REFERENCES

Menkes, J. (1990). The leukodystrophies. *The New England Journal of Medicine 322*(1), 54–55.

National Institute of Neurological Disorders and Stroke. (2001). NINDS leukodystrophy information page. Retrieved from http://www.ninds.nih.gov/health_and_medical/disorders/leukodys_doc.htm

United Leukodystrophy Foundation. (2001). Introduction to leukodystrophy. Retrieved from http://www.ulf.org/ulf/intro/index.htm#Infl

Paula Kilpatrick
Robert T. Brown
University of North Carolina, Wilmington

See also Krabbe Disease; Zellweger Syndrome

LEUKODYSTROPHY, METACHROMATIC

Metachromatic leukodystrophy (MLD) is the most common subgroup of the leukodystrophies, a group of disorders that affects the white matter or myelin sheath. MLD is associated with the accumulation of cerebroside sulfates, a group of myelin lipids (fats); it leads to staining (metachromasia) of brain and other nervous tissue that does not occur in other leukodystrophies. MLDs are genetic and generally marked by the absence or near-absence of the enzyme arylsulfatase A.

Incidence of MLD is about 1 in 40,000 to 1 in 100,000 (Polten et al., 1991; United Leukodystrophy Foundation [ULF], 2001). Onset ranges from 6 months of age to the third or fourth decades in life. Generally, earlier ages of onset are associated with more rapid progression of symptoms. Owing to improvement in care, life expectancy has increased in recent years, from 5–10 years for infant MLD to 20 years or more for later-onset types (ULF, 2001). Characteristics are from ULF (2001) and Polten et al. (1991).

Characteristics

1. Progressive loss of physical and intellectual function, sometimes over a long duration of time
2. Neurological symptoms such as weakness, ataxia, progressive spastic tetraparesis, optic atrophy, and dementia
3. Development of seizures, tremor, contractions, abnormal posture, and loss of motor functions (if previously present)
4. Difficulties in locomotion, intellectual decline, and behavioral difficulties

The following descriptions of the MLDs are summarized from the ULF (2001):

- *Late infantile MLD.* Apparently normal development is followed by deterioration of psychomotor skills such as walking and speech. Deterioration is rapid, leading to the child's being bedridden and unable to speak or feed itself. At this point, the child may respond to parents, but further deterioration leads to blindness, nonresponsiveness, and difficulty swallowing. The child may survive for years, eventually dying from an infection such as pneumonia.
- *Juvenile MLD.* Onset is between 4–12 years and may appear as a decline in academic performance, difficulty in following directions, and behavior problems. Incontinence, gait problems, slurred speech, seizures, and other motor problems may also occur. Progression is similar to that in the late infantile form, but survival may be into adulthood.
- *Adult MLD.* Onset is after sexual maturation, from 14 to after 60 years of age. Initial symptoms involve personality change, deterioration in job performance, and emotional lability that may lead to misdiagnosis as schizophrenia or depression. Drug abuse is a common comorbid condition. Cognitive and motor functions slowly deteriorate over a period of many years.
- *Multiple sulfatase deficiency.* Onset and progression are generally similar to late infantile MLD, but it may have later onset. Because of overlapping symptoms, it may be misdiagnosed as mucopolysaccharidosis.
- *Activator deficiency.* Onset ranges from infantile to adult, but its rarity has prevented clear description.
- *Pseudodeficiency.* Clinicians should be aware of pseudodeficiency of arylsulfatase A (PD), a genetically based normal condition that leads to only about 10% of the usual arylsulfatase A enzyme activity. This level is difficult to differentiate from that in MLD patients and may lead to misdiagnosis.

Diagnosis is initially on the basis of behavioral signs. Deterioration in motor behavior, cognitive performance, and behavior generally suggest white matter disease and the need for brain imaging and biochemical evaluations. Diagnosis is generally based on severely depressed activity of arylsulfatase A in leukocytes.

Prognosis is obviously poor. Progression in metachromatic leukodystrophy is inevitable, and treatment is for the most part supportive. Drugs can regulate some symptoms but do not slow the rate of decline. Modification in diet has had no effect. Bone marrow transplant has apparently slowed or even halted the disease's progress in some cases, but it is a currently dangerous procedure and has only delayed benefits. Improvements in bone marrow transplant techniques may improve safety, but transplants will be most effective before appearance of symptoms. Reliable presymptomatic diagnostic procedures are needed. Research is ongoing on possible enzyme or functional gene replacement (ULF, 2001).

Given the cognitive deterioration associated with the disease's progression, the value of continued education needs careful consideration.

REFERENCES

Polten, M. S., Fluharty, A. L., Fluharty, C. B., Kappler, J., Figura, K., & Gieselmann, V. (1991). Molecular basis of different forms of metachromatic leukodystrophy. *New England Journal of Medicine, 324,* 18–22.

United Leukodystrophy Foundation. (2001). Metachromatic Leukodystrophy. Retrieved from http://www.ulf.org/ulf/intro/#Inf8.htm

Paula Kilpatrick
Robert T. Brown
University of North Carolina, Wilmington

LICHEN SCLEROSIS

Lichen sclerosis (LS) is an uncommon, chronic skin disorder of unknown etiology. It is characterized by fairly typical skin lesions, mild to moderate itching, and eventually atrophy (thinning) of the skin in affected areas.

The cause of LS has not been determined. Evidence suggests that it is probably an autoimmune disorder, a condition in which the body mounts an immune response against its own tissue.

No data are available regarding the incidence of LS. Its occurrence appears to be sporadic. The disorder is far more frequent in females than in males.

Characteristics

1. Onset prior to 7 years of age.
2. Vast majority of patients are female.
3. Skin lesions most frequently found in the genital, perianal, and perineal (between the vagina and anus) areas in girls. In boys, the foreskin and head of the penis are common sites.
4. Initial findings are small, pink to ivory-colored, discrete, raised bumps (papules) that eventually form large plaques. These plaques may develop into blisters or may wrinkle and atrophy, creating an hourglass configuration of thin skin in the genital and perirectal areas.
5. Spontaneous improvement may occur with the onset of menstruation. However, symptoms may also be intermittent without relationship to menstruation.
6. Long-term complications include atrophy of the inner folds (labia majora) of the external genitalia and a narrowing of the vaginal opening.

The use of potent topical steroid creams (0.05% betamethasone) generally clears the skin lesions of LS and provides relief from itching some patients have. After the condition is under control, weaker steroid preparations can be employed to prevent recurrence. Tight-fitting underwear should be avoided. Secondary bacterial infection of affected skin may require appropriate antibiotic therapy.

There is no research to indicate the need for special education services as a result of cognitive deficits.

The prognosis for LS appears favorable. Response to therapy is predictably good. Many patients will experience spontaneous improvement of their condition with the onset of menses.

For more information, please contact The National Vulvodynia Association, P.O. Box 4491, Silver Spring, MD 20914-4491, (301) 299-0775, e-mail: matenva@graphcom.com, home page: http://www.nva.org

REFERENCES

Darmstadt, G. L. (2000). Diseases of the dermis. In E. Behrman, R. M. Kleigman, & H. B. Jenson (Eds.), *Nelson's textbook of pediatrics* (16th ed., p. 2012). Philadelphia: W. B. Saunders.

National Organization for Rare Disorders. (1996). Lichen sclerosus. Retrieved from http://www.stepstn.com/cgi-win/nord.exe?proc=GetDocument&rectype=0&recnum=252

Sanfilippo, J. S. (2000). Vulvovaginitis. In R. E. Behrman, R. M. Kleigman, & H. B. Jenson (Eds.), *Nelson's textbook of pediatrics* (16th ed., p. 1662). Philadelphia: W. B. Saunders.

Barry H. Davison
Ennis, Texas

Joan W. Mayfield
Baylor Pediatric Specialty Services
Dallas, Texas

LIPODYSTROPHY

The lipodystrophies are disorders characterized by loss of body fat and other abnormalities affecting multiple bodily systems. The fat loss may be generalized, affecting extensive areas of the body, or it may be partial, affecting only limited areas of the body. The disorder can be congenital, in which fat loss is usually present at birth. It can also be acquired, often developing after an illness or infection (Foster, 1998; Garg, 2000).

Congenital generalized lipodystrophy (CGL) is a very rare autosomal recessive disorder that appears at birth. Its exact genetic cause is unknown. First described by Berardinelli (1954) and Seip (1959), its prevalence is estimated to be less than 1 case in 12 million people (Garg, 2000). The hallmark feature is loss of body fat in subcutaneous and other adipose tissues, particularly in the face, trunk, and limbs. Facial skin appears tightly drawn, and musculature appears prominent. Metabolic fat is almost completely absent, whereas supportive or cushioning fat, such as in the palms, soles and orbits, appears to be spared (Foster, 1998).

CGL presents other clinical features at infancy and early childhood. Growth is often accelerated and excessive in the first years of childhood, although final height is usually normal. Muscular hypertrophy is usually present. The skin may be dry and coarse and contain areas of gray, brown, or black pigmentation, especially in the armpits and other body folds (acanthosis nigricans). Facial features, ears, hands, and feet may appear large and prominent. Scalp hair may appear thick and curly, even in infants. Excessive hair growth (hypertrichosis) may appear on the face, neck, trunk, and limbs, even in infancy. Excessive perspiration (hyperhidrosis) is often present. Body temperature may be slightly increased, and patients may report having a feeling of heat. During infancy and childhood, skeletal abnormalities may develop, including sclerosis (Foster, 1998; Seip & Trygstad, 1996).

CGL is associated with metabolic and endocrine disturbances, often starting in infancy and appearing through childhood and puberty. Metabolic rate is overly high, even though thyroid function is normal. Hypermetabolism is associated with excessive appetite and increased caloric intake. Elevated lipids and triglycerides, disturbances in insulin and carbohydrate metabolism, insulin-resistant diabetes mellitus, and low concentrations of high-density lipoprotein (HDL) cholesterol are often seen in patients with CGL.

Other organ systems of the body are affected. Fatty infiltration and engorgement of the liver are often present, leading to protuberance of the abdomen and cirrhosis. Enlarged spleen, lymph nodes, tonsils, and adenoids may be seen, as well as enlarged heart. Kidneys are often enlarged, and renal pathology may develop over time. Pancreatitis may develop. Moderate hypertension is sometimes present. The brain is often affected, particularly the hypothalamus. Mild to moderate mental retardation is present in about 50% of cases (Foster, 1998; Seip & Trygstad, 1996).

Acquired generalized lipodystrophy (AGL) was first reported by Ziegler (1928) and later by Lawrence (1946). Whereas CGL occurs at birth, AGL usually occurs later during childhood or adolescence. AGL is more common in females than in males. Loss of body fat typically begins in childhood or adolescence rather than infancy (Garg, 2000). After fat loss has become generalized, the clinical and metabolic features of AGL are similar to those of CGL (Seip & Trygstad, 1996).

Characteristics

1. Inherited or acquired
2. Fat atrophy (generalized or partial)
3. Abnormalities in metabolism and endocrine function; accelerated growth and development; abnormalities of the liver, spleen, pancreas, heart, kidneys, genitals, skin, skeleton, and muscles; mental retardation

Treatment of patients with CGL and AGL is difficult. Because of the metabolic problems associated with this disorder, a low-fat diet is recommended for patients with elevations of lipids and triglycerides. Restriction of caloric intake is recommended for patients with voracious appetites, who are at risk of developing diabetes (Garg, 2000; Seip & Trygstad, 1996). Seip and Trygstad (1996) reported on the use of fenfluramine to control the consumption of carbohydrates. Other drugs, such as insulin, have been used with patients to control hyperglycemia. Lipid-lowering drugs have been used in patients with high triglyceride levels. Cosmetic treatments, such as facial reconstruction, have been used as a remedy for fat loss (Garg, 2000).

Because about half the cases of CGL involve mental retardation, children and adolescents with this disorder will require special education. In addition, the special dietary requirements associated with this disorder may require particular attention for children and adolescents while attending school.

CGL and AGL are serious disorders for which there is no known cure. Because these disorders adversely affect so many bodily functions and are associated with serious illness, including diabetes and liver disease, risk of mortality is elevated (Seip & Trygstad, 1996). Future research is needed to understand the genetic and other causal mechanisms underlying these disorders, which are currently not fully understood (Garg, 2000).

REFERENCES

Berardinelli, W. (1954). An undiagnosed endocrinometabolic syndrome: Report of 2 cases. *Journal of Clinical Endocrinology and Metabolism, 14,* 193–204.

Garg, A. (2000). Lipodystrophies. *The American Journal of Medicine, 108,* 143–152.

Foster, D. W. (1998). The lipodystrophies and other rare disorders of adipose tissue. In A. S. Fauci, E. Braunwald, & K. J. Isselbacher, (Eds.)., *Harrison's principles of internal medicine* (pp. 2209–2214). New York: McGraw-Hill.

Lawrence, R. D. (1946). Lipodystrophy and hepatomegaly with diabetes, lipemia, and other metabolic disturbances. *Lancet, 1,* 724–731.

Seip, M. (1959). Lipodystrophy and gigantism with associated endocrine manifestations: A new diencephalic syndrome? *Acta Paediatrica, 48,* 555–574.

Seip, M., & Trygstad, O. (1996). Generalized lipodystrophy, congenital and acquired (lipoatrophy). *Acta Paediatrica Supplement, 413,* 2–28.

Ziegler, L. H. (1928). Lipodystrophies: Report of seven cases. *Brain, 51,* 145–167.

Robert A. Chernoff
Harbor-UCLA Medical Center

LISSENCEPHALY

Lissencephaly is a disorder of brain maturation in which the brain has limited or absent gyri and sulci, resulting in a smooth brain surface. It results when early migration patterns of neurons are disrupted (Reiner & Lombroso, 1998). The cause is not certain, but both genetic and nongenetic explanations have been hypothesized, such as viral infections during the first trimester of pregnancy, insufficient blood supply to the brain during the first trimester, damage on Chromosome 17, and recessive inheritance of a recessive gene.

Several different diseases with lissencephaly exist, the three most common being isolated lissencephaly sequence (ILS), Miller-Dieker syndrome (MDS), and Walker Warburg syndrome (WWS; Reiner & Lombroso, 1998). There are several types of lissencephaly. The two most common are called Type I and Type II. Type I is associated with isolated lissencephaly sequence and Miller-Dieker syndrome.

Type II lissencephaly is found in Walker-Warburg syndrome and usually involves additional birth defects of the brain and eye and often times hydrocephalus. Characteristics, severity of symptoms, course, and prognosis differ between each type and each disease (Dobyns & Truwit, 1995). The prevalence of these syndromes and that of lissencephaly in general have not been studied.

Characteristics

1. Prenatal diagnosis is possible but rare with a detailed ultrasound. Prenatal tests can detect a missing piece of Chromosome 17.
2. Presence of minor symptoms are recognized between 2 and 6 months of age, including failure to develop visual tracking, poor feeding and weight gain, and seizures. Sometimes small head size, weak breathing, or other birth defects are present.
3. CT or magnetic resonance imaging (MRI) scan reveals smooth brain surface.
4. Patients often suffer from repeated episodes of pneumonia.

A team approach including a pediatrician, neurologist, orthopedist, occupational therapist, and physical therapist is usually involved in management of lissencephaly. Treatment of lissencephaly focuses on controlling seizures and feeding problems. ACTH shots stimulate the body to produce cortisone, thereby limiting seizures. Feeding problems include choking, gagging, refusing food, spitting up, and weight loss and are caused by aspiration and reflux. Positioning during feeding, thickening food, and medication can lessen feeding problems. If feeding problems are severe, a gastrostomy (g-tube) is often needed (Dobyns & Truwit, 1995).

There are many options for schooling, depending on the severity of the lissencephaly. All children with lissencephaly suffer from severe mental retardation and poor muscle control similar to that of children with cerebral palsy and will require special accommodations and additional aides. If the school cannot accommodate the needed medical care, home schooling may be necessary. A shortened school day or a schedule that accommodates additional therapies is often needed. In addition, transportation provided by the school is often necessary. Constant monitoring is a requirement, often with a full-time aide. Occupational therapy and life skills training are common foci of the school. Children who learn to feed themselves have twice the average life span than do those who cannot feed themselves.

The life span of children with lissencephaly is much shorter than normal, but some patients have lived until their late teens (Reiner & Lombroso, 1995). Children with isolated lissencephaly sequence have a better prognosis and longer life span than do children with Miller-Dieker syndrome or Walker-Warburg syndrome. Children with the one of the latter two syndromes often die before the age of 2, usually from aspiration and respiratory disease. Current research on neural migration patterns may lead to better understanding and treatment of lissencephaly in the future.

REFERENCES

Dobyns, W. B. & Truwit, C. L. (1995). Lissencephaly and other malformations of cortical development: 1995 update. *Neuropediatrics, 26,* 132–147.

Reiner, O., & Lombroso, P. J. (1998). Lissencephaly. *Journal of the American Academy of Child and Adolescent Psychiatry, 37,* 231–232.

Elizabeth Kaufmann
University of Texas at Austin

LOBAR EMPHYSEMA, CONGENITAL

Congenital lobar emphysema is a chronic disease involving progressive hyperinflation of one or more pulmonary lobes, resulting in the trapping of air in the affected lobe(s). There are two distinct types of congenital lobar emphysema: (a) an overexpansion of the normal lung lobe and (b) a polyalveolar lobe, in which there exist an increased number of normally expanded alveoli. Although half of all cases have an etiology that is idiopathic, this disease can also be caused by lung obstructions or failure of the lungs to develop properly (Bhutani, 1996).

This disease has a peak incidence between birth and 6 months, and is 1.5–3 times more prevalent in males than in females. Congenital lobar emphysema affects the left upper lobe in 41% of cases, the right middle lobe in 34% of cases, and the right upper lobe in 21% of cases (Aideyan, 2000; De Milto, 1999). No research could be found as to whether ethnicity or socioeconomic status plays any role in the prevalence of congenital lobar emphysema.

Characteristics

1. Infant presents with wheezing, chronic coughing, shortness of breath, difficulty in exhaling, and may have a blue tinge to both skin and fingernail beds.
2. X ray reveals hyperinflation of the affected lobe with mediastinal shift away from the affected side.

Congenital lobar emphysema ranges in severity from severe to virtually undetectable, with many cases being mild, with no need for supplemental oxygen. For those with mild or no symptoms, no treatment may be required. For those with acute or severe symptoms, surgery—either segmentectomy or lobectomy—is a common treatment (Hansen, Corbet, & Avery, 1991; Ordonez, 1997).

In most cases, whether treated medically or surgically, respiratory symptoms typically disappear by age 1. Almost all children with congenital lobar emphysema, however, show evidence of mild pulmonary obstruction by age 10, indicative of a more generalized abnormality (Hansen, Corbet, & Avery, 1991).

Congenital lobar emphysema does not often result in severe physical or cognitive disability. Like children with asthma, children with congenital lobar emphysema may require modified activities, classes, or both. Typically, such modifications include allowing the child more frequent rests during strenuous physical exercise and providing alternatives for activities in which the child is unable to participate. During recess or other play periods and in physical education classes, nonstrenuous games or tasks should be made available to the child, as well as allowing him or her to choose not to participate in an activity in which he or she finds it difficult to participate. Additionally, the child may have a heightened sensitivity to chemical irritants such as cleansers or other substances and should be given the same consideration when these irritants are present as he or she would be given in the case of strenuous activity. Due to the chronic nature of this illness, counseling may be required for the child and his or her family.

Congenital lobar emphysema is a chronic condition and will therefore be present throughout the life of the child. In acute or severe cases, treatment results in an excellent outcome, with respiratory symptoms disappearing in most children by the end of their 1st year.

REFERENCES

Avery, M. E., Corbet, A., & Hansen, T. (1991). *Diseases of the newborn* (6th ed.). Philadelphia: Harcourt Brace Jovanovich.

Bhutani, V. K. (1996). *Intensive care of the fetus and neonate.* St. Louis, MO: Mosby.

De Milto, L. (1999). *Gale encyclopedia of medicine* (1st ed.). Farmington Hills, MI: Gale Research.

Ordonez, P. (1997). Congenital lobar emphysema. Retrieved from http://www.neonatology.org/syllabus/cle.html

Melissa M. Harvey
University of Colorado at Colorado Springs

LOCURA

Locura, or ataque de locura, is a culture-bound syndrome found in Latinos in the United States and Latin America (American Psychiatric Association, 1994). This syndrome is deemed a "severe form of chronic psychosis . . . attributed to an inherited vulnerability, to the effect of life difficulties, or to a combination of both factors" (American Psychiatric Association, 1994).

There are no known prevalence or incidence studies with regard to locura. Most Western doctors and Western-trained health professionals have taken a decided stance of noninterference in areas where locura is prevalent, in particular in rural Latin American countries (Calderon, Pineros, & Rosselli, 1998). However, through ethnographic research it appears that locura is common among particular populations in rural Latin American countries. As stated by Pineros, some of the targeted populations include "young people, particularly women" (Calderon et al., 1998, p. 1427). An early case of locura was reported as afflicting a young woman, aged 13, in Embera, Colombia. This syndrome appears most prominently in lower socioeconomic strata.

> Characteristics
>
> 1. Incoherence
> 2. Agitation
> 3. Auditory and visual hallucinations
> 4. Inability to follow rules of social interaction
> 5. Unpredictability
> 6. Possible violence

Locura is also linked to conversion and dissociative disorders. Individuals with locura exhibit "repetitive episodes of what resembled a dissociative fugue disorder" (Calderon et al., 1998, p. 1427). Some symptoms include "headache, fainting, convulsive attacks and visions of people, animals or demons" (Calderon et al., 1998, p. 1427). In early stages of this disorder, such attacks are sporadic but become more frequent as the syndrome progresses.

When testing various groups, there were no significant abnormalities in the physical or neurological examinations, routine lab tests were normal, and toxicological analysis of blood and urine samples were negative. Typical treatment generally entails personal interviews detailing personal as well as family history. When Western medical and psychiatric professionals step in, generally in more severe cases in which the afflicted individual seeks medical attention, antipsychotic medications are diagnosed. However, according to Calderon et al. (1998, p. 1427), "the *DSM-IV* is, however, clear in stating that a conversion disorder should not be diagnosed if a symptom is fully explained by a culturally-sanctioned behavior or experience."

Traditional healing methods are the most common method of treatment, especially with regard to adolescent women. Both shaman and Catholic priests are utilized in treating this disorder due to the culturally held notion that locura is a "possessing spirit" (Calderon et al., 1998, p. 1427).

Further research is being conducted with regard to this syndrome, especially with regard to psychogenic expressions of cultural stress.

REFERENCES

American Psychiatric Association. (1994). *Diagnostic and statistical manual of mental disorders* (4th ed.). Washington, DC: Author.

Calderon, C., Pineros, M., & Rosselli, D. (1998). An epidemic of collective conversion and dissociation disorder in an indigenous group of Colombia: Its relation to cultural change. *Social Science and Medicine, 11,* 1425–1428.

Kiely Ann Fletcher
Ohio State University

LONG CHAIN ACYL COA DEHYDROGENASE DEFICIENCY

Long chain acyl coa dehydrogenase deficiency (LCAD) is a mitochondrial fatty acid oxidation disorder. The clinical phenotypes for this disease are hypertrophic cardiomyopathy with hypoglycemia and skeletal myopathy or hypoglycemia without cardiac manifestations.

Onset of LCAD usually occurs by 6 months of age. It is an extremely rare disorder and has been identified in approximately 15 patients. Disease course in LCAD patients has varied from death to serious mental retardation to severe psychomotor retardation, microcephaly, and cerebral atrophy. Other patients have had a less devastating course and experienced muscle cramps in adolescence or adult life.

Characteristics

1. Onset before 6 months of age
2. Repeated episodes of vomiting and coma
3. Disease course is variable often with marked muscular weakness, hepatomegaly, and cardiomyopathy
4. Major biochemical abnormalities include hypoglycemia
5. Possible microcephaly and cerebral atrophy
6. Possible mental and psychomotor retardation

Treatment involves avoidance of fasts longer than 10–12 hours, maintaining high-carbohydrate intake, frequent feeding, and treating episodes of illness with IV glucose and carnitine. Medium chain triglycerides (MCT) replacement of long chain fatty acids in the diet appears to be effective for management. Continuous intragastric feeding has appeared to be useful in some patients.

Many children with mitochondrial disorders might have normal intelligence, static mental retardation, or developmental delay. Children may have long periods with a stable neurological picture simulating a static encephalopathy and later deteriorate either in an acute or in a slowly progressive manner; thus, these children often qualify for special education services under the classification of Other Health Impaired as a result of their medical condition.

Disease course is variable. If patients survive, episodes of metabolic decompensation during fasting appear in infancy and childhood and microcephaly becomes apparent. Two of the 15 patients reported have perished; two others are seriously impaired and suffer from mental and severe psychomotor retardation, microcephaly and cerebral atrophy. Other patients have had a less devastating course and experienced muscle cramps and myloglobineria in adolescence and adult life (Lyon, Adams, & Kolodny, 1996).

REFERENCE

Lyon, G., Adams, R. D., & Kolodny, E. H. (1996). *Neurology of hereditary metabolic diseases of children.* New York: McGraw-Hill.

Virdette L. Brumm
Children's Hospital, Los Angeles
Keck / USC School of Medicine

LOW BIRTH WEIGHT/PREMATURITY

Low birth weight (LBW) infants may be born preterm (premature), at term but small for gestational age (SGA), or both preterm and SGA. LBW, very LBW (VLBW), extremely LBW (ELBW), and micropremie describe, respectively, those with birth weights of less than 2,500, 1,500, 1,000, or 800 grams (Bernbaum & Batshaw, 1997). Premature and extremely premature infants are born before week 36 or 28 of gestation, respectively. Of LBW infants, about 70% are premature. Full-term SGA infants generally have suffered from intrauterine growth retardation (IUGR), suggesting that they have not achieved their full prenatal growth potential.

Characteristic

Premature infants

1. Lanugo, or fine hair, over entire body (normally lost by 38 weeks gestational age)
2. Reddish skin color owing to thin skin and closeness of blood vessels to surface
3. Lack of breast buds and ear cartilage (normally appear at about 34 weeks gestational age)
4. Lack of skin creases in feet (normally appear at about 32 weeks gestational age)

5. Decreased muscle tone; flaccidity
6. Weak or absent neonatal reflexes, including sucking reflex
7. High-pitched aversive cries
8. Susceptibility to numerous neonatal complications
9. With increasing prematurity, mental retardation, cerebral palsy, sensory impairments, seizure disorders, and specific learning disabilities

Nonpremature SGA infants

1. Intrauterine growth retardation leading to malnourished appearance
2. Postnatal growth retardation leading to permanent short stature and low weight
3. Learning disabilities, attention-deficit/hyperactivity disorder, and behavior problems

LBW is the highest-incidence potentially handicapping condition in the United States: About 7% of births are LBW and an additional 1.3% are VLBW. For unknown reasons, incidence in African Americans is about twice that in Whites and Latinos. Advances in prenatal care and neonatal care have improved survival and development of premature and LBW infants but have not reduced their incidence. Although most affected infants develop with few sequalae, LBW is involved in about 60% of newborns' deaths and is a major cause of brain damage and developmental disabilities (March of Dimes, 2001). The degree of impairment generally is associated with the degree of low birth weight or prematurity (Bernbaum & Batshaw, 1997). Long-term effects of IUGR include decreased terminal physical growth, developmental delays, decreased IQ, cerebral palsy, learning disabilities, and perhaps cardiovascular disease as adults (Stevenson & Sunshine, 1997).

Survival rates of VLBW infants have reached 85%. Of survivors, 5–15% have spastic cerebral palsy and an additional 25–50% have cognitive disorders (Graziani, 1996). Intracranial hemorrhage and periventricular leukomalicia are major causes of neurological and developmental deficits. Although specific abnormalities are correlated with neurologic sequelae, the severity of eventual handicap is difficult to predict.

In the last decade, survival of ELBW and micropremie infants has increased to about 40%, but such infants are at great risk for serious physical, neurological, and developmental complications. Few infants born at 23 weeks gestation survive without serious neurological complications (Goldson, 1996).

Preterm infants may develop a variety of conditions. Breathing disorders include (a) apnea (irregular and nonrhythmical breathing); (b) bronchopulmonary dysplasia (BPD; damaged lungs requiring supplemental oxygen and breathing support), and (c) respiratory distress syndrome (RDS), incomplete development of the lungs and lack of surfactant, which prevents lung alveoli from sticking together during breathing. Artificial surfactant has reduced considerably adverse consequences of RDS. Retinopathy of prematurity (ROP) may result in impaired vision or blindness. ROP has many contributing factors, including the degree of prematurity, nutritional status, and exposure to light, in addition to excess oxygen (Spitzer, 1996). Intracranial hemorrhage and other forms of hypoxic brain damage can have devastating complications.

The long-term effects of prematurity, which are associated with prenatal and postnatal complications and disruption of the parent-infant attachment process, include breathing disorders, visual impairment, increased incidence of SIDS, and neurological impairment leading to sensorimotor and developmental delays. Owing to their general hyporeactivity, hyperactivity to sudden stimulation, and aversive cries, premature infants are at elevated risk for abuse, particularly by unskilled parents, although few are actually abused. Lack of attachment by the parents to the infant is more common.

Diagnosis is at or shortly after birth through physical and behavioral signs. Determination of the degree of clinical problems should be performed by an experienced neonatalogist. Clinical problems often require intensive team management providing multisystem support through incubators, ventilators, intravenous fluids, and physiological monitoring. Such care is best offered in a regional neonatal intensive care unit (NICU), which has the staff and equipment needed to deal with unpredictable and serious complications.

Infants may be LBW or premature for many reasons, although the cause in most individual cases is unknown. Causes can be categorized as fetal, maternal, placental, and environmental (Stevenson & Sunshine, 1997). Fetal factors include genetic abnormalities and differential susceptibility to drugs and congenital infections. Maternal factors, the most common cause, include maternal nutrition, chronic maternal illness, low socioeconomic status, drug use, maternal infection (congenital infections, the STORCH [syphilis, toxoplasmosis, other infections, rubella, cytomegalovirus infections, and herpes simplex] complex), and labor-intensive occupations. Abnormal placental function includes decreased placental size, poor implantation, and decreased placental blood flow. Incidence of IUGR increases with multiple gestation. Environmental factors, generally mediated by the mother, are difficult to separate from maternal factors. Although cigarette smoking is a commonly accepted cause of LBW, careful research questions its role (e.g., Ramsay & Reynolds, 2000).

Early intervention may reduce later complications. Improved infant formulas and increased support of breastfeeding have improved growth. Control of light and noise, positioning that provides support, and strategies that avoid overstimulation encourage normal growth and development. Carefully monitored physical massage improves development and reduces length of initial hospital stays (e.g., Scafidi et al., 1990). Regular developmental assessment to detect delays is important to allow for early intervention. Evidence (e.g., Guralnick, 1996) indicates that intervention beginning at discharge from hospital and continuing to at least age 3 years improves later cognitive performance, particularly of mildly LBW infants. Helping parents to deal with their infants' difficult physical and behavioral characteristics may foster attachment and reduce abuse. Many survivors will need individualized support, including physical and speech therapy, adaptive technology for sensory and motor impairments, and special education services.

REFERENCES

Bernbaum, J. C., & Batshaw, M. L. (1997). Born too soon, born too small. In M. L. Batshaw (Ed.), *Children with disabilities* (4th ed., pp. 115–139). Baltimore: Brookes.

Goldson, E. (1996). The micropremie: Infants with birthweights less than 800 grams. *Infants and Young Children, 8,* 1–10.

Graziani, L. J. (1996). Intracranial hemorrhage and leukomalacia in preterm infants. In A. R. Spitzer (Ed.). *Intensive care of the fetus and neonate* (pp. 696–703). St. Louis: Mosby.

Guralnick, M. J. (Ed.) (1996). *The effectiveness of early intervention.* Baltimore: Brookes.

March of Dimes. (2001). Low birthweight. Retrieved from http://www.modimes.org/HealthLibrary2/factsheets/Low_Birthweight.htm

Ramsay, M., & Reynolds, C. R. (2000). Does smoking by pregnant women influence birthweight, IQ, and developmental disabilities in their infants? A methodological review and multivariate analysis. *Neuropsychology Review, 10,* 1–40.

Scafidi, F. A., Field, T. M., Schanberg, S. M., Bauer, C. R., Tucci, K., Roberts, J., et al. (1990). Massage stimulates growth in preterm infants: A replication. *Infant Behavior and Development, 13,* 167–188.

Spitzer, A. R. (Ed.). (1996). *Intensive care of the fetus and neonate.* St. Louis: Mosby.

Stevenson, D. K., & Sunshine, P. (Eds.). (1997). *Fetal and neonatal brain injury: Mechanisms, management, and the risks of practice* (2nd ed.). Oxford, England: Oxford University Press.

Brenda Melvin
Robert T. Brown
University of North Carolina, Wilmington

LOW VISION

Low vision involves a severe visual impairment, after correction, with visual functioning that can be improved through the use of adaptive aids. The term *low vision* involves visual impairments that prohibit the ability to read a newspaper even with the use of eyeglasses or contacts. For special education purposes, low vision is referred to as visual impairment, which is defined by the Individuals with Disabilities Education Act (IDEA; 1997) as an impairment in vision that—even with correction—adversely affects a child's educational performance. The term includes both partial sight and blindness.

Characteristics

1. Difficulty in recognizing familiar people and objects
2. Inability to clearly see far away and or close up
3. Difficulty in copying from the board
4. Squinting when focusing on near or distant objects
5. Inability to recognize or differentiate colors, shapes, and letters of similar shape and size (e.g., *a, o; l, t; v, w*)
6. Tilting the head to one side when reading
7. Closing one eye when looking at an object
8. Skipping words when reading aloud
9. Bumping into objects or people when walking
10. Difficulties with depth perception (e.g., is unable to identify changes in surface depth, misses objects when reaching for them)
11. Involuntary rapid eye movement (e.g., eyes skip or jump and do not move smoothly)
12. Headaches, dizziness, or eye fatigue following reading

The etiology of impaired vision may be traced to genetic causes (e.g., retinoblastoma, cataract), perinatal births (e.g., births requiring oxygen resulting in retrolental fibroplasia), infections (e.g., rubella), diabetes, accidents, lesions in the visual projection fibers or visual cortex, and vascular disease (Lezak, 1995; Suran & Rizzo, 1983). Specifically, low vision may result from albinism, cataracts, corneal disorders, glaucoma, ocular hemorrhages, photophobia, retinal degeneration, scotomas, and refraction errors. Visual impairments are considered low-incidence disabilities, occurring in 12.2 of 1,000 children and adolescents under the age of 18.

When eye difficulties are suspected, the child's vision should be screened at school. If the school screening identifies visual difficulties or if questions about the child's vision remain after the school vision screening is accomplished, the child should be referred to an optometrist or ophthalmologist. It is recommended that this referral result in an examination of the child's visual acuity, visual field, and ocular motility (Beers & Berkow, 1999). Corrective lenses (glasses or contacts) may be prescribed to improve the child's vision, particularly in the case of visual refraction errors.

In evaluating students with visual impairments for special education purposes, attention should be given to several aspects of the child's vision. These aspects include visual acuity, peripheral visual field, progressive vision loss, blindness resulting from a disease process, and functional blindness. If the student's vision meets the educational handicap criteria for visual impairment, the student would be eligible to receive special education services as a result of his or her visual impairment.

In evaluation of children with visual impairments, attention should be given to the way the child uses multisensory information and how the child understands information, placing an emphasis on verbal skills, enlarging test materials, and recognizing the child's fatigue level. Educational interventions for children with visual impairments need to include improving their ability to use their present vision. Early detection and intervention are critical for children with low vision because they have less opportunity for concept development through vicarious learning. Additionally, educational programming for children with low vision should involve concrete experiences, with an emphasis placed on hands-on, haptic, learning-by-doing approaches.

Assistive technology devices that can be used to improve a child's ability to access visual information include low-vision aids (e.g., magnifying glass or magnifying screen), talking computers, large-print books, and books on tape. Increasing lighting, using proper environmental adaptations for mobility, and teaching children to read Braille may be beneficial. Braille reading is most appropriate for children with severe low vision because children with mild or moderate visual impairments can usually access visual information using low-vision aids. Training children with visual impairments to rely more on their other senses to assimilate and accommodate information is also encouraged. In addition to educationally related devices and techniques designed to improve the learning ability of a child with low vision, training in orientation and mobility is essential to the child's development and is a related service under IDEA. Orientation and mobility training is designed to assist a child with visual impairments to move safely and efficiently through the environment. Canes are frequently used to improve mobility, and several varieties of developmentally appropriate canes may be used. If a child with a visual impairment requires a guide for mobility assistance, for size compatibility and increased socialization, peers should be involved as guides. The use of sighted guide techniques is encouraged. For example, the child with the visual impairment should grasp the guide's arm above the elbow and walk slightly behind the guide.

Children with visual impairments may require counseling for emotional issues. In counseling children with visual impairments, one goal should be to increase their independence by encouraging them to advocate for themselves. One way this goal could be accomplished is through role-playing situations in which seeking assistance is appropriate, followed by a discussion of emotional aspects related to asking for help. Counseling for this population should also focus on the child's strengths, needs, emotional reactions to his or her medical condition, and similarities to other children.

The prognosis for children with low vision is very good, especially if they do not have other nonrelated medical, emotional, or educational conditions. The functioning of children with low vision can be improved by providing visual accommodations, providing necessary support services, and verifying that concept development is occurring.

REFERENCES

Beers, M. H., & Berkow, R. (1999). *The Merck manual of diagnosis and therapy* (17th ed.). Whitehouse Station, NJ: Merck Research Laboratories.

Lezak, M. D. (1995). *Neuropsychological assessment* (3rd ed.). New York: Oxford University Press.

Suran, B. G., & Rizzo, J. V. (1983). *Special children: An integrative approach* (2nd ed.). Glenview, IL: Scott, Foresman and Company.

U.S. Department of Education. (1997). *Individuals with disabilities education act: Final regulations.* Washington, DC: U.S. Government Printing Office.

Shawn Powell
United States Air Force Academy

Jill Mathis
Laramie County School District #1
Cheyenne, Wyoming

Elizabeth Ann Graf
University of Northern Colorado

LOWE SYNDROME

First described in 1952, Lowe syndrome is an X-linked recessive (chromosome location Xq26.1) disorder, of unknown etiology resulting in an ocular, cerebral, and renal syndrome. The incidence of Lowe syndrome is rare (about 50 cases worldwide), and males are at more risk than females (Pedlynx, 2002).

The age of onset is at birth, when the infant presents with hypotonia and cataracts. There are three distinct phases of syndrome: Infancy, where neurologic and ophthalmologic manifestations predominant with renal tubular dysfunction present within the first year of life; childhood, where renal tubular dysfunction continues to be present along with failure to thrive, and rickets; and late childhood, where death from inanition, pneumonia, and chronic renal failure is likely (Pedlynx, 2002).

Characteristics

1. Ophthalmologic manifestations, including superficial granulations with corneal scarring, bilateral congenital cataracts (100%), glaucoma (buphthalmos), miotic pupils, enophthalmos, and visual problems such as nystagmus and blindness
2. Neurological manifestations, including infantile hypotonia, gross motor developmental delay, reduced or absent deep tendon reflexes; muscle wasting, moderate to severe mental retardation, and speech-language-communication disabilities
3. Renal manifestations, including Fanconi syndrome: minimal expression at birth but increase in severity with age (usually present within the 1st year of life) episodes of vomiting, dehydration, weakness, and unexplained fever; anorexia and constipation; polydipsia and polyuria; failure to thrive and growth failure; and rickets
4. Other manifestations, including craniosynostosis (frontal bossing), cryptorchidism (bilateral), hyperactivity with high-pitched scream, and joint hypermobility (joint contractures)

There is no treatment for Lowe syndrome; a medical multidisciplinary approach is usually used to monitor the various conditions and provide symptom support. Genetic counseling is usually recommended (Mack, Masters, & Hockey, 1970).

Children with this disorder will most likely be in need of special education services and require considerable monitoring by the special education team for decline in functioning. As with any chronic illness, the child and family may well need supportive counseling to maximize the understanding and assessment of the least restrictive environment.

The prognosis for this disorder is poor due to significant visual problems, progressive mental retardation, and developmental delays. With no treatment, most patients with this disorder die in the first decade of life due to complications with chronic renal failure, dehydration, and infection (Pedlynx, 2002).

REFERENCES

Pedlynx. (2002). Retrieved from http://www.icondata.com/health/pedbase/pedlynx.htm

Mack, J., Masters, P., & Hockey, A. (1970). Lowe's syndrome. *Australian Journal of Mental Retardation, 1*(3), 89–93.

Elaine Fletcher-Janzen
University of Northern Colorado

LUJAN-FRYNS SYNDROME

Lujan-Fryns Syndrome (LFS) is a very low-incidence, X-linked disorder that is characterized primarily by the presence of a tall yet stooped posture, hyperextensible fingers and toes, large forehead, long yet narrow face that includes an extended nose with a high bridge, thin upper lip, arched palate, and maxillary hypoplasia (Fryns, 1991; Fryns & Buttines, 1987; Lujan, Carlis, & Lubs, 1984). A review and report of a case study by Donders, Doornik, and Toriello (2001) reports the presence of approximately 24 reported cases in the literature. Their review indicates the presence of mental retardation, significant behavioral problems, and psychotic features in the majority of cases, although exceptions do occur.

Characteristics

1. Marfanoid features
2. Craniofacial anomalies
3. Frequent occurrence of mental retardation
4. Frequent occurrence of behavioral problems
5. Frequently accompanied by psychotic symptomatology

Fryns and Van den Berghe (1991) note that the tall, stooping posture that characterizes the marfanoid features of LFS may not become fully evident until the onset of puberty, a finding also supported by Donders et al. (2001).

The physical anomalies of LFS almost always occur in conjunction with this disorder; the neuropsychological deficits that include impaired cognitive function, behavioral disinhibition, and frequently psychotic features have a more highly variable expressivity. Although mental retardation is the most frequent outcome associated with cognitive impairments, exceptions have been noted. Donders et al. (2001) reported a case in which psychiatric problems were predominantly absent and several cognitive strengths were evident. Their findings emphasize the need for comprehensive neuropsychological testing of individuals with LFS, particularly in the face of the variable expressivity of the neuropsychological deficits common to this disorder.

Children with LFS will virtually always qualify for special education services and may do so under multiple categories of the Individuals with Disabilities Education Act (IDEA). Because LFS is a genetic condition, these individuals will qualify for services as other health impaired but will also be eligible under multiple handicapping conditions that will frequently include mental retardation and emotionally disturbed. More frequent reevaluation that may be common with other special education placements is necessary due to the issues surrounding expressivity in LFS and to the fact that it is a developmentally related phenomenon as well.

REFERENCES

Donders, J., Doornik, S., & Torriello, H. (2001). Lujan-Fryns syndrome: A case study. *Newsletter 40, 19*(2), 19–21.

Fryns, J. P. (1991). X-link mental retardation with marfanoid habitus. *American Journal of Medical Genetics, 38,* 233.

Fryns, J. P., & Buttines, M. (1987). X-linked mental retardation with marfanoid habitus. *American Journal of Medical Genetics, 28,* 267–274.

Fryns, J. P., & Van den Berghe, H. (1991). X-linked mental retardation with marfanoid habitus: A changing phenotype with age? *Genetic Counseling, 2,* 241–244.

Lujan, J. E., Carlis, M. E., & Lubs, H. A. (1984). A form of X-linked mental retardation with marfanoid habitus. *American Journal of Medical Genetics, 17,* 311–322.

Cecil R. Reynolds
Texas A&M University and Bastrop Mental Health Associates

LYME DISEASE

Lyme disease (LD), the most common tick-borne disease in the United States, is transmitted mainly by the black-legged tick, often called the deer tick. The disease is a bacterial infection caused by the spirochete *Barrelia burgdorferi* (Lyme Disease Foundation, 2001). Because ticks carry numerous infectious agents, more than one disease may be transmitted by a single bite, complicating diagnosis and treatment.

LD affects all ages, but the highest rates of infection are at about 5–15 and 45–54 years. Incidence is higher in males than in females and highest in the summer. A rising incidence from 500 cases in 1982 (the 1st year records were kept) to almost 17,000 in 1998 is attributed to increases in both surveillance and actual incidence (Update On Lyme Disease, 1982–1998, 2000). Incidence varies greatly with location. It is highest in northeastern United States but occurs virtually nationwide and in Canada (Lapp, 2000). Risk is highest among those who participate in activities in wooded, bushy, or overgrown grassy areas where ticks are concentrated. Normally, the tick must be attached to the host for 24 hours for *B. burgdorferi* to be transmitted, but transmission may occur sooner if the tick either has been improperly removed or is itself systematically infected (Lyme Disease Foundation, 2001). Because no immunity develops, individuals can have the disease multiple times.

Characteristics

Early localized stage

1. Flu-like symptoms, including headache, stiff neck, fever, muscle aches, and fatigue
2. Erythema migrans (EM), an enlarging rash at the site of the bite days to weeks later

Disseminated stage

1. Profound fatigue, severe headache, fever(s), and severe muscle aches and pains
2. Serious and widespread central and peripheral neurological dysfunction
3. Mild to severe cognitive dysfunction
4. Mild to severe behavioral disorders
5. Eye disorders and deterioration in vision
6. Rash of varying size, shape, and color not at the bite site (EM)

The disease has two stages: (a) early localized, with symptoms limited to the site of the bite; and (b) Disseminated, with symptoms occurring throughout the body. Appropriate medical treatment in the early localized stage is important because effects of disseminated Lyme may be serious and permanent. Panic attacks appear to occur frequently at the onset of the disseminated stage and may be diagnostic (Panic attacks may be sign of Lyme disease, 2001). Effects at the disseminated stage are varied and widespread. Neurological complications include limb weakness or paralysis; loss of reflexes; tingling in extremities; stiff neck; meningitis; change in sensory functioning; difficulty eating or speaking; facial palsy; dizziness and fainting; stroke, abnormal brain waves, or seizures; and sleep disorders. Cognitive changes may include confusion and problems with memory, word finding, concentration, and numbers. Changes in the eyes and vision range from red eye, conjunctivitis, and inflammation to retinal damage, optic atrophy, and blindness. Disordered behavior may include panic attacks; depression; extreme agitation; impulsive, violent, manic, or obsessive behavior; paranoia, hallucinations, and other schizophrenic-like behaviors; and eating disorders. Virtually all organ systems may eventually be affected. The Lyme Disease Foundation's Web site (Lyme Disease Foundation, 2001) has a detailed description of the disease's effects.

Diagnosis of Lyme disease is difficult, and controversy exists over the appropriate stringency of diagnostic criteria (Panic attacks may be sign of Lyme disease, 2001). No current laboratory test can reliably identify presence of *B. bergdorferi,* and blood tests may produce both false positive and false negative results. Diagnosis is based on identification of appropriate clinical signs and knowledge of the patient's likely travel in tick-concentrated areas, supplemented by laboratory tests. Once diagnosed, Lyme disease is treated with a variety of antibiotics. Recently, the Infectious Diseases Society of America (IDSA) has presented empirically based guidelines for the treatment of Lyme disease (Preboth, 2001). If the disease treated in the early stage, recovery is likely to be complete (Lyme Disease Foundation, 2001).

Because of the potential serious effects of Lyme disease, prevention of infection is important. Potential vaccinations are in the final stages of testing and may become available in the future. It is clear that currently, people should reduce their exposure to tick bites. Insect repellents that contain nn-diethyl-m-toluamide (DEET) are effective but must be frequently reapplied. Individuals should wear light-colored clothing so that ticks may be seen, tuck pants legs into socks, and examine themselves or be examined after being in tick-infested areas. Appropriate and complete removal of any attached ticks is important. The tick should be grasped with tweezers as close to the skin as possible and firmly pulled straight out without twisting (Lapp, 2000).

In cases of early diagnosis and treatment, no special services should be needed. Children who have reached the dissemination stage may have a variety of serious long-lasting neurological, cognitive, behavioral, and sensory impairments. Given the varying types and degrees of outcome, treatment intervention obviously has to be individualized.

REFERENCES

Lapp, T. (2000). AAP issues recommendations on the prevention and treatment of Lyme disease. *American Family Physician, 61*(11), 3463.

Lyme Disease Foundation. (2001). Lyme disease. Retrieved from http://www.lyme.org/index2.html

Panic attacks may be sign of Lyme disease (2001). *Psychopharmacology Update, 12,* 1–4.

Preboth, M. (2001). IDSA issues guidelines on the treatment of Lyme disease. *American Family Physician, 63,* 2065–2066.

Update On Lyme Disease, 1982–1998. (2000). *Pediatric Alert, 25*(12), 69–70.

Shannon Radliff-Lee
Robert T. Brown
University of North Carolina, Wilmington

LYMPHANGIOLEIOMYOMATOSIS

Lymphangioleiomyomatosis (LAM; Ryu & Olson, 1999; Sullivan, 1998; Taylor, Ryu, Colby, & Raffin, 1990) is a very rare (although predominantly found in women of child-bearing age, childhood cases have been reported), progressive lung disease characterized by misdifferentiated unusual muscle cells that invade lung tissue and blood and lymph vessels. Leiomyomatosis, resultant from LAM, form to create bundles growing into the lung walls, blood and lymph vessels, obstructing these pathways (Naalsund, Johansen, Foerster, & Kolbenstvedt, 1996; Ryu & Olson, 1999; Sullivan, 1998; Taylor et al., 1990). Obstruction leads to symptomatology that includes shortness of breath, chest pain, and (in more advanced stages) coughing blood. Despite the fact that the unusual cells are not cancerous in nature, their growth is unregulated by the usual mechanism, and they eventually grow and cause hypoxemia.

Asymptomatic kidney tumors also may be present in patients with LAM. Although tuberous sclerosis gene mutations have been known to be associated with LAM (Carsillo, Aristotelis, & Henske, 2000), its cause remains unknown. The survival rate of LAM varies, but patients usually die within 10–20 years after the onset of the disease. The prevalence of the disease is unknown.

Cognitive sequelae associated with LAM may include those observed in patients with hypoxemia—memory deficits, reduced speed of information processing and motor skills, and in some cases, executive deficits. Reduction in psychosocial activities also are common.

Children and adolescents with this disease easily qualify under the Other Health Impaired label for special educational purposes. In addition, they should be excused from demanding and rigorous physical education. Future research should focus on determining the etiology of the disease.

Characteristics

1. Respiratory problems, including shortness of breath
2. Chest pain
3. Coughing of blood
4. Psychomotor slowing and retardation
5. Memory deficits
6. Dizziness
7. Reduction in psychosocial activities
8. Hypoxemia

REFERENCES

Carsillo, T., Aristotelis, A., & Henske, E. P. (2000). Mutations in the tuberous sclerosis complex gene TSC2 are a cause of sporadic lympyangioleiomyomatosis. *Proceedings of the National Academy of Science.*

Naalsund, A. J., Johansen, B., Foerster, A., & Kolbenstvedt, A. (1996). When to suspect and how to diagnose pulmonary lymphangioleiomyomatosis. *Respirology, 1,* 207–212.

Ryu, J. H., & Olsen, E. J. (1999). LAM: A mimic of asthma and COPD in women. *Journal of Respiratory Disorders, 20,* 488–494.

Sullivan, E. J. (1998). Lymphangioleiomyomatosis: A review. *Chest, 114,* 1689–1703.

Taylor, J. R., Ryu, J., Colby, T. V., & Raffin, T. A. (1990). Lymphangioleiomyomatosis: Clinical course in 32 patients. *New England Journal of Medicine, 323,* 1254–1260.

Antolin M. Llorente
Baylor College of Medicine
Houston, Texas

M

MACROGLOSSIA

Macroglossia is defined as enlargement of the tongue. Diagnosing macroglossia is a judgment call on the part of the examiner. Unlike the case in numerous assessments of body proportions (height, weight, head circumference, distance between the pupils of the eye, etc.), there are no charts or graphs to assist physicians in determining when the tongue is large. However, certain clinical clues may be present. The tongue may protrude from the mouth or cause symptoms of upper airway obstruction (noisy breathing, snoring, or cessation of breathing). Feeding difficulties may also be present.

Macroglossia may be acquired or congenital (present in the newborn). Examples of acquired macroglossia include tumors of the vascular and lymphatic system and increased muscle mass. Congenital macroglossia is associated with a number of syndromes and genetic disorders. Congenital hypothyroidism, Down syndrome, Beckwith-Wiedemann syndrome, and a handful of abnormalities of carbohydrate metabolism include macroglossia as a common physical trait. Therefore, the presence of a large tongue in a newborn or an infant should prompt the physician to look for other anomalies that might lead to an astute diagnosis.

REFERENCES

Jones, K. (1997). *Smith's recognizable patterns of human malformations* (5th ed.), Philadelphia: W. B. Saunders.

National Organization for Rare Disorders. (1997). Macroglossia. Retrieved from http://stepstn.com/cgi-win/nord.exe?proc=GetDocument&rectype=0&recnum=409

Stoll, B. J., & Kleigman, R. M. (2000). Hyperglycemia. In R. E. Behrman, R. K. Kleigman, & H. B. Jenson (Eds.), *Nelson's textbook of pediatrics* (16th ed., p. 534). Philadelphia: W. B. Saunders.

Barry H. Davison
Ennis, Texas

Joan W. Mayfield
Baylor Pediatric Specialty Services
Dallas, Texas

MAFFUCCI SYNDROME

Maffucci syndrome (MS) is a nonhereditary disorder of skeletal and vascular tissues. Its salient features include benign tumors of cartilage and bone (enchondromas) and blood vessel malformations (hemangiomas).

The etiology of MS is unknown. Its occurrence is apparently sporadic. NS is rare. The condition was first reported in 1881. Since it was originally described, only about 170 cases have appeared in the medical literature.

Characteristics

1. Most patients appear normal at birth. Symptoms can develop anytime during infancy, childhood, or adolescence.
2. Early bowing of the legs and arms is occasionally present, with asymmetrical growth.
3. Enchondromas primarily involve the hands, feet, and long bones of the extremities. Almost half of these tumors are unilateral.
4. Hemangiomas usually appear by age 4. They are most common in the skin and fatty tissue beneath the skin. They can occur anywhere but are usually adjacent to areas of enchondroma formation. Hemangiomas vary greatly in appearance, from a pink or red discoloration of the skin to greatly dilated veins, which have a grape-like structure and are prone to developing blood clots.
5. Occasional findings include malformation of the lymphatic system, hemangiomas of the gastrointestinal tract, and a variety of benign and malignant tumors that can appear almost anywhere in the body. Chondrosarcoma, a malignant tumor derived from cartilage, occurs in 15% of enchondromas.

Treatment available for individuals with MS is primarily orthopedic and surgical in nature. Enchondromas may not develop until adolescence. Although some cases are quite mild, most patients need multiple operations for the best outcomes. Approximately a quarter of individuals with enchondromas have fractures related to these tumors and require orthopedic referral. Chondrosarcoma often necessitates amputation of the involved extremity.

There is no research to indicate cognitive dysfunction. A child with MS, however, may require evaluation and treatment from an occupational or physical therapist due to the bowing of the arms and legs. Emotional support to help with adjustment and social relationships may be warranted.

The prognosis for MS is considered guarded. Although hemangioma formation stabilizes in adulthood, enchondromas may appear at any time and are associated with a high incidence of fracture, limb deformity, and malignant degeneration. In addition, patients with MS are at increased risk for a variety of other primary cancers (ovarian, pancreatic, brain, etc.).

REFERENCES

Darmstradt, G. L. (2000). Vascular disorders. In R. E. Behrman, R. M. Kleigman, & H. B. Jenson (Eds.), *Nelson's textbook of pediatrics* (16th ed., pp. 1302–1305). Philadelphia: W. B. Saunders.

Jones, K. (1997). *Smith's recognizable patterns of human malformation* (5th ed.). Philadelphia: W. B. Saunders.

Barry H. Davison
Ennis, Texas

Joan W. Mayfield
Baylor Pediatric Specialty Services
Dallas, Texas

MALNUTRITION

Malnutrition is defined as a condition in which the body does not obtain a sufficient supply of essential nutrients over an extended period of time (Leinwald, 1985). Others describe malnutrition as a state of altered nutrition that may occur from either too much or too little nourishment (Williams, 1997). The causes of malnutrition are numerous and include medical inability to absorb nutrients, financial constraints, refusal to eat certain foods or food groups, lack of appropriate nutritional information, illness, stress, trauma, and eating disorders.

In a study sponsored by the Tufts University Center on Hunger, Poverty, and Nutrition Policy, it was estimated that nearly 35 million Americans live in hunger or food-insecure households. Statistics from Second Harvest (2001), which is a national food assistance network, show that of the 23 million Americans who received food from food banks during 2000, 37.6% were male and 62.4% were female. Nearly 38% were age 17 or younger, 60% of food bank clients had a high school diploma, and nearly 19% had at least some college education. Williams (1997) stated that one out of every five American children lives in poverty and suffers from the ill effects of malnutrition.

Characteristics

1. Low birth weight in babies
2. Stunted growth
3. Failure to thrive
4. Iron deficiency or anemia
5. Poor dental health
6. Loss of resilience of skin
7. Puffy look, swelling of abdomen and extremities
8. Lower resistance to infection
9. Learning difficulties
10. Reduced activity level
11. Night blindness
12. Skin rashes
13. Muscle spasms

Special education implications for a student suffering from severe hunger or malnutrition are difficult to definitively determine. The child would likely have difficulty attending to tasks in school and may exhibit characteristics of a slow learner or a learning disabled child. School personnel could best provide services for these children by ensuring that such children eat nutritious breakfasts and lunches while at school. Services for the family should include resources to provide information on food stamp programs, food banks, and free meals at school.

Prognosis is different for different causes of malnutrition. Most nutritional deficiencies can be replaced. However, if the malnutrition is caused by a medical condition, that illness has to be treated in order to reverse the nutritional deficiency. There are ongoing studies and research projects in the United States regarding hunger and poverty. Despite efforts to prevent hunger in America, Second Harvest (2001) statistics indicate that even during periods of economic growth, the numbers of those seeking emergency food assistance continue to grow at alarming rates.

REFERENCES

Leinwald, G. (1985). *Hunger and malnutrition in America.* New York: Franklin Watts.

Second Harvest. (2001). Malnutrition. Retrieved December 2001 from http://www.secondharvest.org

Williams, S. (1997). *Nutrition and diet therapy* (8th ed.). St. Louis, MO: Mosby.

Christine D. Cde Baca
University of Northern Colorado

MANNOSIDOSIS

Alpha-mannosidosis is a rare metabolic disorder characterized by a deficiency of the lysosomal enzyme alpha-mannosidase. Due to this deficiency, oligosaccharides accumulate within cells of body tissues. Symptoms of the disorder vary widely, as does severity. There are two forms of alpha-mannosidosis. Type I typically develops in early childhood, with age of onset ranging from 6 months of age to 3 years. Type II develops in later childhood or adolescence, and symptoms are much less severe than those found in Type I (Autio, Louhimo, & Helenius, 1982; National Organization for Rare Disorders, n.d.). Approximately 60–80 cases of alpha-mannosidosis have been reported (Autio et al., 1982; De Jong & Petersen, 1992).

Beta-mannosidosis, in which a deficiency in the enzyme beta-mannosidase is present, has also been reported. It is extremely rare, with a prevalence of only 8–10 cases. Symptoms are similar to those found in alpha-mannosidosis but may be milder, and age of onset varies (Lavade et al., 1994; Poenaura, Akli, Rocchiccioli, Eydoux, & Zamet, 1992). Both alpha- and beta-mannosidosis have an autosomal recessive inheritance (Lavade et al., 1994; National Organization for Rare Disorders, n.d.).

Characteristics

1. Delayed development of speech, motor functions, and cognitive ability (Autio et al., 1982; National Organization for Rare Disorders, n.d.)
2. Facial and skeletal abnormalities and failure to grow (Autio et al., 1982; Wall et al., 1998)
3. Recurring ear and respiratory infections (Autio et al., 1982)
4. Deterioration with age, including hearing loss and ataxia (De Jong & Petersen, 1992; Lavade et al., 1994; Wall et al., 1998)
5. For Type I alpha-mannosidosis, death between 3 and 12 years of age (Wall et al., 1998)

There is currently no successful treatment for mannosidosis. Because this disorder is inherited, prevention measures such as genetic counseling and prenatal diagnosis have been used (De Jong & Petersen, 1992).

It is likely that children with mannosidosis will require special education services due to developmental delays, medical needs, speech and hearing impairments, and motor dysfunction. Educational placement in a classroom for developmentally delayed students may be necessary as well as speech and language therapy and physical and occupational therapy. Educational plans should match individual students' levels of cognitive ability, and due to the progressive deterioration expected with the disorder, assessment and revision of those educational plans should be frequent.

Students with mannosidosis may also require the use of assistive technology as hearing loss progresses. Due to speech and language delays, it may be beneficial for them to learn to use alternative methods of communication such as sign language. An interpreter may be necessary as well. Delays in motor development may make writing difficult; therefore, modifications such as the use of thick pencils can be made.

In addition to modifications in the classroom, home visits from teachers or tutors may be necessary for students who are unable to attend school or who are frequently absent due to medical complications. Emotional counseling may be needed as well to help the individuals and their families cope with the degenerative nature of the disorder.

The prognosis for individuals with mannosidosis is poor because they tend to regress with age (Autio et al., 1982). The focus of current research is on treatment.

REFERENCES

Autio, S., Louhimo, T., & Helenius, M. (1982). The clinical course of mannosidosis. *Annals of Clinical Research, 14,* 93–97.

De Jong, G., & Petersen, E. M. (1992). First reported case of alpha-mannosidosis in the RSA. *South African Medical Journal, 82,* 126–128.

Levade, T., Graber, D., Flurin, V., Delisle, M. B., Pieraggi, M. T., Testut, M. F., et al. (1994). Human β-mannosidase deficiency associated with peripheral neuropathy. *Annals of Neurology, 35*(1), 116–119.

National Organization of Rare Disorders. (n.d.). Mannosidosis web site. Retrieved from http://www.stepstn.com/cgi-win/ . . .tDocument&rectype=2&recnum=1996

Poenaura, L., Akli, S., Rocchiccioli, F., Eydoux, P., & Zamet, P. (1992). Human β-mannosidosis: A 3-year-old boy with speech impairment and emotional instability. *Clinical Genetics, 41*(6), 331–334.

Wall, D. A., Grange, D. K., Goulding, P., Daines, M., Luisiri, A., & Kotagal, S. (1998). Bone marrow transplantation for the treatment of a-mannosidosis. *Journal of Pediatrics, 133,* 282–285.

Stacey L. Bates
University of Texas at Austin

MAPLE SYRUP URINE DISEASE

Maple syrup urine disease (MSUD) is a progressive autosomal recessive inborn error of branched-chain amino acid (BCAA) metabolism. Leucine, isoleucine, and valine are toxic to developing brain tissue. MSUD may have four forms: classic, intermittent, intermediate, and thiamine responsive. About 75% of cases are the classic form, which if untreated has severe effects (Meyer, 1997). MSUD is rare, occurring in about 1 in 300,000 births overall. However, conservative Mennonites have a reported frequency of 1 in 176 births (Online Mendelian Inheritance in Man [OMIM], 2001).

Characteristics

Classic form

1. Opisthotonus (head and lower back bent backward and trunk arched forward from back muscle spasms) and hypertonia
2. Hypoglycemia
3. Respiratory distress
4. Generally fatal in the neonatal period if untreated
5. In untreated survivors, severe mental retardation and spasticity

Intermittent form (attacks triggered by physiological stress)

1. Ataxia
2. Behavior abnormalities
3. Drowsiness
4. Seizures

Intermediate form

1. Moderate mental retardation

Associated characteristics of all forms

1. Acidosis
2. Hypoglycemia
3. Growth retardation
4. Feeding problems

Initially, MSUD may be suspected in newborns who have poor appetite, are irritable, and whose urine smells like maple syrup. If undiagnosed and treated, they decline rapidly, initially losing their sucking reflex, becoming listless and limp with episodes of rigidity, and developing a high-pitched cry. Seizures, coma, and death follow. In some variant types, failure to thrive may be the first sign (MSUD Support Group, 2001). Confirmation is through presence of keto acids of leucine, isoleucine, and valine in the urine (OMIM, 2001). Diagnosis may be complicated among those of Mediterranean origin who use fenugreek beans as an infusion for illness. Fenugreek has a fragrant odor similar to that of maple syrup. Physicians should determine whether a distressed infant of Mediterranean origin has received fenugreek because its odor may inappropriately suggest MSUD. Further, physicians in Mediterranean areas should be aware that neurologically distressed newborns whose urine smells like fenugreek and whose mothers have not ingested fenugreek may have MSUD (OMIM, 2001).

MSUD should be diagnosed through newborn screening programs within 24 hours of birth. Because such screening may fail to detect some variant types of MSUD, any infant suspected of having MSUD should be tested. If the result is positive or suspected to be positive, treatment should be started immediately. Carriers of the Mennonite classic type of MSUD can now be identified (MSUD Support Group, 2001).

In diagnosed newborns, levels of BCAAs should be reduced immediately through IV solutions of amino acids (except BCAAs) and glucose. This procedure allows the BCAAs to be used for protein synthesis in the body, decreasing their levels. Subsequent treatment is through an artificial diet that provides essential nutrients and amino acids, omitting the BCAAs. With careful monitoring, normal food sufficient to provide appropriate levels of BCAAs is provided (MSUD Support Group, 2001). As suggested by the name, thiamine-responsive MSUD can be effectively treated with large amounts of thiamine.

Treatment appears highly successful in reducing adverse consequences; treated individuals generally lead normal lives. Individuals who did not receive early dietary restriction will need a variety of special services because only supportive treatment is then available. Institutionalization or separate classroom placement is likely for classic cases, with varied provision for the others.

REFERENCES

Meyer, G. (1997). Syndromes and inborn errors of metabolism. In M. L. Batshaw (Ed.), *Children with disabilities* (4th ed., pp. 813–834). Baltimore: Brookes.

MSUD Support Group. (2001). MSUD: Introduction and overview. Retrieved from http://www.msud-support.org/

Online Mendelian Inheritance in Man. (2001). Johns Hopkins University, Baltimore, MD. MIM No. 24860. Retrieved from http://www3.ncbi.nlm.nih.gov/htbin-post/Omim/dispmim?248600

Robert T. Brown
University of North Carolina, Wilmington

MARASMUS

Marasmus, which is sometimes referred to as protein calorie malnutrition, is a severe disorder of malnutrition. This disorder develops when an individual does not take in a sufficient amount of protein or an adequate number of calories.

Although marasmus can occur in individuals of any age,

it is generally observed in children under 1 year of age in urban areas of developing countries (Berdanier, Dattilo, & Verboeket-van de Venne, 1998). Often marasmic children were not breast-fed, or breast-feeding was discontinued when the mother stopped producing milk because of her own nutritional deficits (Berdanier et al., 1998). Other issues related to the etiology of marasmus are lack of money to obtain formula, diluted formula, contaminated bottles, and poverty (University of Iowa, 2000). The estimated incidence of severe malnutrition disorders is between 8% and 15% of newborns and between 1% and 3% of children in the first few months of life (Monckeberg, 1976).

Characteristics

1. Decreased body fat and skeletal muscle (skin-and-bones appearance)
2. Appearance of being older than chronological age
3. Wasted face
4. Low body weight
5. Low weight for height (mild 80–89% of normal, moderate 70–79% of normal, and severe < 70% of normal)
6. Decreased muscle strength and tone
7. Diarrhea
8. Good appetite
9. Lethargy, irritability

The first stage of treatment of marasmus should last 3–5 days and involves rehydration, treatment of related infections, and electrolyte regulation (Uauy, 1993). Treatment can then proceed to the second stage, which includes nutritional support with an increase in calories and a gradual increase of protein in the diet; this stage often involves the use of predigested proteins or solutions of amino acids (Berdanier et al., 1998). It may take 7–10 days for the child to reach an optimal level of caloric and protein intake (Uauy, 1993). Weight gain and growth should be monitored as recovery occurs, and 4–8 weeks after treatment begins, an infant should be of a normal weight for his or her length, and his or her appetite will naturally decrease to a normal level (Uauy, 1993). Rehabilitation is also an important part of the treatment of marasmus. Social and developmental rehabilitation are recommended. The goal of the social rehabilitation is to address the underlying issues that caused the marasmus, help the family, and prevent recurrence of malnutrition (Uauy, 1993). Developmental rehabilitation is recommended to provide appropriate psychomotor stimulation to the infant or young child (Uauy, 1993). Social intervention has been found to help counteract some of the cognitive alterations that were produced by the malnutrition, although some brain damage may remain throughout life (Uauy, 1993).

Research was done in the 1960s, 1970s, and 1980s with marasmic children and their development. Most studies of the time showed that there was permanent cognitive impairment in individuals who were malnourished during childhood (Lloyd-Still, 1976). Studies also showed that mean brain weights of malnourished children were almost 30% lower than the weights of normal children's brains (Lloyd-Still, 1976). Research has also shown that malnutrition during critical periods of brain development can lead to decreased myelinization, fewer neurons and glial cells, less dendritic branching, fewer-than-normal synaptic connections, and lower velocity of impulse conduction (D'Amato, Chittooran, & Whitten, 1992). When school-aged children were examined, they were found to have significant differences on measures of full-scale IQ and on verbal IQs (Lloyd-Still, 1976). These findings suggest the importance of the environment in which children are raised. Children who have suffered from marasmus have been found to have difficulties with language and verbal abilities and with achievement (D'Amato et al., 1992). Several studies have also discovered that the adaptive behaviors of malnourished children are also significantly different from that of controls (Lloyd-Still, 1976). These children have also been found to have impaired memory and higher rates of school failure (Barrett & Frank, 1987).

Findings suggest that assessments of cognitive abilities, achievement, memory, sensory integration, hyperactivity, attention, motor activity, and adaptive functioning are suggested for a child who has had marasmus. Assessments may need to be performed throughout development because some brain damage may not be apparent until late childhood or early adolescence (D'Amato et al., 1992). Schools should also be ready to provide social and developmental rehabilitation, special education services if needed (typically for children with mental retardation or learning disabilities), and long-term intervention for the family addressing the underlying issues related to the child's malnutrition (Uauy, 1993). Behavioral interventions may also be required while the child is recovering and could address lethargy, apathy, eating habits, and motor problems (Lloyd-Still, 1976). With younger children, delays in achieving developmental milestones may also need to be addressed.

REFERENCES

Barrett, D. E., & Frank, D. A. (1987). *The effects of undernutrition on children's behavior* (pp. 108–109, 150–161). New York: Gordon and Breach Science.

Berdanier, C. D., Dattilo, A., & Verboeket-van de Venne, W. P. H. G. (1998). Marasmus. In *CRC Desk Reference for Nutrition.* New York: CRC.

D'Amato, R. C., Chittooran, M. M., & Whitten, J. D. (1992). Neuropsychological consequences of malnutrition. In D. I. Templer, L. C. Hartlage, & W. G. Cannon (Eds.), *Preventable brain damage: Brain vulnerability and brain health* (pp. 193–213). New York: Springer.

Lloyd-Still, J. D. (1976). Clinical studies on the effects of malnutrition during infancy on subsequent physical and intellectual development. In J. D. Lloyd-Still (Ed.), *Malnutrition and intellectual development* (pp. 103–152). Littleton: Publishing Sciences Group.

Monckeberg, F. (1976). Definition of the nutrition problem: Poverty and malnutrition in mother and child. In N. S. Scrimshaw & M. Behar (Eds.), *Nutrition and agricultural development: Significance and potential for the tropics* (pp. 13–23). New York: Plenum.

Uauy, R. (1993). Marasmus. In R. Macrae, R. K. Robinson, & M. J. Sadler (Eds.), *Encyclopaedia of food science, food technology, and nutrition* (pp. 2874–2880). New York: Academic.

University of Iowa Public Health. (2001, February 20). Marasmus. Retrieved from http://www.public-health.uiowa.edu/fuortes/63260/nutrit/tsld076.htm

Elizabeth Ann Graf
Rik Carl D'Amato
University of Northern Colorado

MARDEN-WALKER SYNDROME

Marden-Walker syndrome (MWS) is an extremely rare autosomal recessive connective tissue disorder (Garcia-Alix, 1992; King & Magenis, 1978; Marden & Walker, 1966). Medical and cognitive implications associated with this syndrome have onset at birth. Although this statistic is tentative, the prevalence of MWS has been estimated at less than 1 birth per 1,000,000. With regard to gender, MWS is approximately twice as frequent in males than in females (10–11 males to 5 females).

Characteristics

1. Blepharophimosis
2. Craniofacial anomalies including facial hypoplasia, microcephaly, micrognathia, and highly arched or cleft palate
3. Multiple joint contractures
4. Fixed facial expressions
5. Mental deficiency and growth retardation
6. Reduced muscle mass and hypotonia
7. Failure to thrive
8. Possible hearing impediments

MWS is marked by fixed facial expressions, mental retardation, multiple joint contracture sometimes resulting in motor neuron disease (some resolved after the 1st birthday), microcephaly, micrognathia, blepharophimosis (tightness of eyelids), decreased mass and muscle tone, cleft or highly arched palate, growth retardation, and in some cases hearing impediments. Deaths have occurred in these children predominantly between the ages of birth to 2 years, usually associated with cardiac or respiratory failure.

In the unusual case where needed, special education for these children includes labeling as Other Health Impaired. A select number of these children also may qualify as speech impaired subsequent to palate malformations and hearing impediments affecting speech. In addition to special educational services, families with MWS children should receive genetic counseling. Their families also may benefit from such intervention as soon as the diagnosis of MWS is made.

Future research should focus in therapies designed to curtail the symptomatology of MWS and understanding the etiology of the disease.

REFERENCES

Garcia-Alix, A. (1992). Early neurological manifestations and brain anomalies in Marden-Walker syndrome. *American Journal of Medical Genetics, 44,* 41–45.

King, C. R., & Magenis, E. (1978). The Marden-Walker syndrome. *Journal of Medical Genetics, 15,* 366–369.

Marden, P. M., & Walker, W. A. (1966). A new generalized connective tissue syndrome: Association of multiple congenital anomalies. *American Journal of Diseases in Children, 112,* 225–228.

Antolin M. Llorente
Baylor College of Medicine
Houston, Texas

MARFAN SYNDROME

Marfan syndrome is a genetic autosomal dominant disorder that affects the connective tissue of the cardiovascular, musculoskeletal, and ocular systems. A gene mutation, thought to be the FBN1 gene of Chromosome 15, causes a defect in the body's production of fibrillin, an important building block of connective tissue. Marfan syndrome is found in males and females equally and affects between 1 in 5,000 and 1 in 10,000 individuals. There are no known ethnic or socioeconomic status variations (National Organization for Rare Disorders [NORD], 2000).

Characteristics

1. Unusually tall and thin with abnormally long faces and limbs, flat feet, hypotonia, protruding sternum, and curvature of the spine.
2. Reduced vision with an increased risk of ectopia lentis, myopia, cataracts, glaucoma, retinal detachment, and strabismus.
3. Emphysema is common with 5% of patients suffering a collapsed lung.

4. Bulging of the sac surrounding the spinal cord, known as dural ectasia, is also common and may be detected with magnetic resonance images at an early age in patients who may not exhibit other Marfan symptoms.
5. Cardiovascular problems are common which includes mitral valve prolapse, aortic regurgitation, aortic aneurysm and enlargement and degeneration of the aorta.

The fibrillin gene defect may present variable symptoms; therefore, Marfan syndrome is difficult to diagnose, and the symptoms may differ even within members of the same family (Eaton, 1999; NORD, 2000). There is no laboratory test for the condition and no medical treatment currently exits to prevent or reverse the fibrillin defect in Marfan syndrome (Eaton, 1999). Beta blockers are used to prevent or delay the cardiovascular problems; these medications serve to slow the heart rate and reduce blood pressure. Careful monitoring of the patient's cardiovascular status is required, and patients should avoid contact sports and strenuous exercise; instead, they should participate in activities in which they can participate at their own pace (walking, bicycling). Marfan patients should have annual eye examinations, and if eye surgery is necessary, patients should be referred to ophthalmology centers that specialize in Marfan syndrome disorder (Eaton, 1999; National Organization for Rare Disorders, 2000).

Special education services may be available to children with Marfan syndrome under the handicapping condition of Other Health Impaired. Because of the numerous health issues associated with Marfan syndrome, children may need to spend a great deal of time in treatment and away from the classroom. Therefore, tutoring services or home-based instruction may be required. In addition, patients may also benefit from counseling services designed to help them psychologically adjust to their illness. Medication side effects should be considered during formal assessment of the patients' cognitive, social, or academic functioning.

Although patients with Marfan syndrome are at higher risk for many life-threatening cardiovascular problems, the average life expectancy is approximately 70 years of age. To date, the primary treatment plan is designed to manage the cardiovascular symptoms; however, ongoing research efforts focus on the biochemistry of the connective tissue and the nature of the genetic defect that causes this disorder (National Organization of Rare Disorders, 2000).

REFERENCES

Eaton, L. M. (1999). Marfan syndrome: Identification and management. *Medsurg Nursing, 2,* 113–117.

National Organization for Rare Disorders. (2000, August 1). Marfan syndrome. Retrieved from http://www.rarediseases.org

Mary Corlett
University of Texas at Austin

MARIJUANA ABUSE

Marijuana is the term used to describe the mixture of dried, shredded leaves and flowers of *Cannabis sativa,* or hemp plant. There are many slang terms for marijuana, including *pot, grass, weed, reefer, boom,* and *gangster.* Marijuana is generally smoked in the form of loosely rolled cigarettes (joints) or hollowed-out cigars filled with marijuana (blunts). Marijuana is also smoked in pipes, often in water pipes called bongs. Some users mix it with food or brew it as a tea.

The chemical in marijuana believed to be responsible for most of the plant's psychoactive effects is delta-9-tetrahydrocannabinal, or THC. This chemical binds to nerve cell receptors, initiating cellular reactions that result in the high reported by marijuana users. This chemical suppresses the information-processing capabilities of the hippocampus, a component of the brain's limbic system that is critical for learning, memory, and integration of sensory experiences (National Institute on Drug Abuse [NIDA], 2001). The intensity of the effect marijuana has on the user depends on the manner in which the drug is ingested, the type and source of the marijuana (which affects the THC concentration), and whether the marijuana is used in conjunction with alcohol or other drugs (NIDA, 1998).

The American Academy of Pediatrics (AAP, 1999) describes marijuana as a mind-altering and addictive drug with social, academic, developmental, and legal consequences, and it states that young people who regularly use the drug may suffer adverse cardiovascular, pulmonary, reproductive, immunological, behavioral, and cognitive effects. Because marijuana impairs short-term memory, concentration, coordination, and reaction time, its use is associated with automobile accidents and risky sexual behavior. Although marijuana use does not necessarily lead to use of more dangerous drugs, it is known that most young people who use other drugs try marijuana first (NIDA, 1998).

According to the National Household Survey on Drug Abuse (Lane, Gerstein, Huang & Wright, 1997), 71 million individuals 12 or older in the United States report using marijuana in their lifetime, making it the most commonly used illicit drug in the country. Another study found that 47.1% of students nationwide had used marijuana at least once, and 26.2% of all students had used marijuana one or more times in the 30 days preceding the survey (Kann et al., 1998). Marijuana use peaked in 1996 for 8th graders and in 1997 for 10th and 12th graders, and since that time, there has been a gradual decline in use for 8th graders but little change for those in Grades 10 and 12 (Johnston, O'Malley, & Bachman, 2001).

Characteristics

1. Observable characteristics of marijuana intoxication may include poor coordination, bloodshot eyes,

increased hunger and thirst, difficulty conversing, appearing giggly or silly for no apparent reason, and sleepiness as the early effects fade (NIDA, 1998)

2. Characteristics of the subjective high reported by marijuana users include euphoria, relaxation, and disinhibition (American Academy of Pediatrics [AAP], 1999).

Adverse characteristics or effects (AAP, 1999; Pagliero & Pagliero, 1996) *include*

1. Habituation (psychological dependence)
2. Cognitive effects (altered perception, negative effect on learning, attention, short-term memory, and problem-solving skills)
3. Respiratory irritation and disease (e.g., asthma and bronchitis)
4. Amotivation syndrome (lack of motivation, inability to sustain goal-oriented behavior)
5. Psychomotor impairment and related motor vehicle crashes (slowed reaction time, decreased ability to judge speed and distance)
6. Tachycardia (abnormally rapid heartbeat)
7. Suppressed immune system
8. Reproductive effects (decreased sperm count, decreased testosterone levels, irregular ovulation; babies born to mothers who use marijuana during pregnancy are smaller and weigh less at birth)
9. Paranoia, panic reaction, toxic delirium

Pagliero and Pagliero (1996) have stated that a consistent and recurring theme in the research literature regarding drug use prevention and treatment programs for children and adolescents is the critical need for individualized approaches. Because a program that is effective for one young person may be ineffective for others, the authors recommend that professionals should be knowledgeable about a variety of treatment types so that they can select those that are most appropriate for the individual needs of their clients or patients.

Two approaches shown to be effective in reducing tobacco, alcohol, and drug use are the social influence approach (using persuasive messages from peers and the media) and an integrated social influence–competence enhancement approach (teaching social, cognitive, coping, assertiveness, and self-management strategies; Lane et al., 1997). It is recommended that school-based prevention programs should include primary grades through Grade 12, should focus on the specific needs of the school population, and should be based upon well-defined and realistic goals (Paglierio & Pagliero, 1996).

The AAP (1996) urges doctors to routinely discuss drug use as part of primary care services, as well as offering interventions and treatment options for current drug users. They note that treatment rather than punishment should be offered to youth who are dependent on marijuana. This concern was also expressed by Leone (1991), who suggested that positive alternatives to punitive and exclusionary responses to student drug and alcohol use are needed, along with increased collaboration among schools, mental health agencies, the juvenile justice system, and other community agencies that work with young people who abuse drugs.

Accidents related to drug and alcohol use may lead to head injury or orthopedic impairment that result in a student's placement in a special education program (Leone, 1991). For students already identified as having a disability, the limited data available indicate that in general, they are no more likely to abuse drugs than same age peers. However, among students who have attention-deficit/hyperactivity disorder or learning disabilities, there is conflicting evidence about prevalence of drug and alcohol use compared to their peers. It is possible that characteristics of some adolescents with disabilities (such as poorly developed interpersonal skills and school failure) may put them at higher risk for substance abuse (Leone, 1991).

Pagliaro and Paglierio (1996) call for increased focus on specific factors associated with child and adolescent substance abuse, as opposed to adult substance abuse. The authors noted the following concerns related to drug use by children and adolescents: Certain illicit substances are especially attractive to children (due to social pressure, availability, and type of psychotropic effect); children and adolescents are at risk for serious personal consequences that could have lifetime effects (e.g., automobile accidents, prostitution, sexually transmitted diseases, criminal behavior, unwanted pregnancy, suicide); and children and adolescents are a highly heterogeneous group, which makes individualized prevention and treatment approaches imperative. They go on to state that "although it is generally agreed that multimodal prevention and treatment approaches have the greatest potential for success, further research is required in order to deter or curtail substance abuse by children and adolescents" (p. 28). For students receiving special education services, attention should be given to the development of specialized prevention and treatment programs that may be necessary to meet their unique needs.

REFERENCES

American Academy of Pediatrics Committee on Substance Abuse. (1999). Marijuana: A continuing concern for pediatricians. *Pediatrics, 104*(4), 982–985. Retrieved from http://www.aap.org/policy/re9915.html

Johnston, L. D., O'Malley, P. M., & Bachman, J. G. (2001). *Monitoring the future national survey results on adolescent drug use: Overview of key findings, 2000* (NIH Publication No. 01-4923). Bethesda, MD: National Institute on Drug Abuse. Retrieved from http://monitoringthefuture.org/pubs.html

Kann, L., Kinchen, S. A., Williams, B. I., Ross, J. G., Lowry, R.,

Hill, C. V., et al. (1998). *Youth risk behavior surveillance—United States, 1997* (Morbidity and Mortality Weekly Report, Vol. 47, SS-3). Atlanta: Centers for Disease Control and Prevention. Retrieved from http://www.cdc.gov/mmwr/preview/mmwrhtml/00054432.htm

Lane, J., Gerstein, D., Huang, L., & Wright, D. (1997). *Risk and protective factors for adolescent drug use: Findings from the 1997 national household survey on drug abuse.* Retrieved from http://www.samhsa.gov/oas/nhsda/nac97/cover.htm

Leone, P. E. (1991). *Alcohol and other drug use by adolescents with disabilities.* Arlington, VA: ERIC Clearinghouse on Disabilities and Gifted Education. (ERIC EC Digest No. E506). Retrieved from http://ericed.org/digests/e506.htm

National Institute on Drug Abuse. (1998). *Marijuana: Facts parents need to know* (NIH Publication Number 98-4036). Retrieved from http://www.nida.nih.gov/MarjiBroch/Marijparentstxt.html

National Institute on Drug Abuse. (2001). *Marijuana* (Infofax No. 13551). Retrieved from http://165.112.78.61/Infofax/marijuana.html

Pagliero, A. M., & Pagliero, L. A. (1996). *Substance abuse among children and adolescents.* New York: Wiley.

Paula Perrill
University of Northern Colorado

MARINESCO-SJOGREN SYNDROME

Marinesco-Sjogren syndrome (MSS) is an hereditary neuromuscular disorder. Associated defects are common in the eye and skeleton.

The etiology of MSS is unknown. There are so few reported cases of MSS that researching its cause has proven to be a very challenging endeavor.

MSS is exceedingly rare. There are a few examples of the syndrome in sibling pairs. A larger number of affected individuals have been reported in an inbred population in southwestern Alabama. The mode of inheritance is consistent with an autosomal recessive pattern.

Characteristics

1. Cerebellar ataxia (loss of muscle coordination secondary to nerve degeneration within the cerebellum)
2. Mental retardation, microcephaly (small head and small brain)
3. Slurred (dysarthric) speech
4. Spasticity (increased muscle tone), decreased muscle tone, muscle atrophy (loss of muscle mass)
5. Eye abnormalities, including congenital cataracts (clouding of the lens of the eye that is present at birth), nystagmus (rhythmic, jerky eye movements), and strabismus (uncoordinated eye movement)
6. Growth retardation, short stature
7. Skeletal anomalies, including scoliosis (lateral curvature of the spine); kyphosis (hunched back); joint contractures; shortening of bones in the hands and feet; and long, slender extremities.

No information is available regarding treatment of this disorder.

Because of the poor prognosis and rareness of MSS, no research is available concerning educational needs. However, evaluation and treatment from occupational, physical, and speech therapy will help the child with ataxia and dysarthia. This treatment can be orchestrated through an early childhood intervention program. As the child grows, the child with MSS will require additional educational support as he or she enters school under the special educational umbrella.

Little data are published regarding the prognosis for MSS. What information there is infers that the outlook for these children is bleak. Their neuromuscular pathology, while not uniformly present at birth, is relentlessly progressive. Reports of autopsy findings suggest that massive cerebellar atrophy ultimately leads to a premature demise during childhood.

REFERENCES

Database Links. (1998). Marinesco-Sjogren syndrome: MSS. Retrieved from http://wwwe.ncbi.nlm.nih.gov/htbin-post/Omim/dispmim?24880

Farah, S., Sabry, M. A., Khuraibet, A. J., Anim, J. T., Quasrawi, B., Al-Khatam, S., et al. (1997). Marinesco-Sjogren syndrome in a Bedouin family. *Acta Neurologica Scandinavia,* 96, 387–391. Retrieved from http://www.ncbi.n.nlm.nih.gov/htbin-post/Omim/dispmim?24880

National Organization for Rare Disorders. (1995). Marinesco-Sjogren syndrome. Retrieved from http://www.stepstn.com/cgi-win/nord.exe?proc=GetDocument&rectype=0&recnum=868

Barry H. Davison
Ennis, Texas

Joan W. Mayfield
Baylor Pediatric Specialty Services
Dallas, Texas

MARSHALL-SMITH SYNDROME

Marshall-Smith syndrome (MSS) is a nonhereditary disorder of increased skeletal growth, accelerated maturation and an extensive assortment of associated defeats. MSS has its onset during fetal development. Abnormal findings are quite obvious in the newborn.

The etiology of MSS is not known. However, recent research suggests that a biochemical or distinct structural defect of bone, cartilage, and other connective tissue may be responsible for its pathology.

MSS is rare. Since its initial description in 1977, only 10 cases have been reported. All occurrences of MSS have appeared to be sporadic.

Characteristics

1. Accelerated linear growth (increased length) and markedly advanced skeletal maturation (precocious transformation of skeletal cartilage into bone) present at birth. However, newborns are very underweight for their length (failure to thrive).
2. Developmental delay, mental deficiency (mean IQ of 50), decreased muscle tone.
3. Long skull, prominent forehead, shallow eye sockets with protruding eyeballs, blue sclerae (white part of the eye), upturned nose, low nasal bridge.
4. Wide bases of the fingers and toes; tips are narrow.
5. Excessive facial and body hair.
6. Umbilical hernia (protruding navel).
7. Occasional findings include small nasal openings, anomalies of the larynx and epiglottis, deafness, brain abnormalities, defective immune system, sudden infant death (secondary to brain stem defects).

Treatment options for MSS are limited. Most children with this disorder die prior to age 2 from respiratory complications. Upper airway strictures, recurrent pneumonia, and aspiration (the entry of oral secretions and food into the lung by way of the trachea) are common. Early, aggressive management of these problems is essential for a lengthy survival of patients with MSS. Failure to thrive is a uniform finding in these individuals. It requires continual monitoring to assure proper caloric intake. Hearing loss may improve with hearing aids. Although no older children with MSS have been able to talk, alternative forms of communication (signing) should be explored. The underlying skeletal defect in MSS is not understood and therefore has no available therapy.

Because of the rarity of MSS and the poor prognosis, specific research regarding educational needs is unavailable. Because of the cognitive deficits associated with MSS, an early childhood intervention program would be important as well as speech therapy, to aid in feeding and language development. A speech pathologist would assist in nonverbal language, such as sign, and if appropriate, recommend specific assistive technology. As the child matures, continued support services in the school will be important. A comprehensive neuropsychological evaluation would be helpful to identify cognitive strengths and weaknesses.

The prognosis for MSS is fairly dismal. It carries a mortality rate of over 50% during infancy and early childhood. Mental retardation is common among older patients, although two individuals (ages 7 and 8) with this syndrome are considered to have a low normal IQ. Vigorous treatment of the respiratory complications associated with this disorder may ensure a relatively prolonged survival for these patients and provide a more complete picture of their long-term outlook.

REFERENCES

Jones, K. (1997). *Smith's recognizable patterns of human malformation* (5th ed.). Philadelphia: W. B. Saunders.

National Organization for Rare Disorders. (1999). Marshall Smith syndrome. Retrieved from http://www.stepstn.com/cgi-win/nord.exe?proc=GetDocument&rectype=0&recnum=820

Barry H. Davison
Ennis, Texas

Joan W. Mayfield
Baylor Pediatric Specialty Services
Dallas, Texas

MASA SYNDROME

MASA syndrome is a rare hereditary, X-linked recessive disorder that has specific, progressively appearing neurological and clinical signs (Fryns, Schrander-Stumpel, Die-Smulders, Borghgraef, & Van Den Berghe, 1992; Rietschel et al., 1991). MASA is the acronym for the four main characteristics that delineate the syndrome (mental retardation, aphasia, shuffling gait, and adducted thumbs). MASA syndrome is often used interchangeably with CRASH syndrome (also named for its characteristics), which are corpus callosum hypoplasia (underdevelopment), mental retardation, adducted thumbs, spastic paraplegia, and hydrocephalus (Fransen, Van Camp, D'Hooge, Vits, & Willems, 1998). Without genetic assay, MASA syndrome is difficult to diagnose in infants and young children because the characteristic symptoms are not apparent until a later age (Fryns et al., 1992; Winter, Davies, Bell, Huson, & Patterson, 1989).

Adducted thumbs is the only one of the main characteristics that is usually identifiable at birth. It may range from completely adducted thumbs to only dimpling at the base of the thumbs (Winter et al., 1989). If a child had MASA syndrome but did not present with adducted thumbs or a family history of the syndrome, clinical diagnosis of MASA would be nearly impossible (Rietschel et al., 1991). In addition, symptom manifestation and clinical severity are widely variable (Kaepernick, Legius, Higgins, & Kapur, 1991).

The etiology of MASA syndrome is unknown at this time. It has been associated with several other X-linked disorders—namely, X-linked hydrocephalus (hydrocephalus due to the stenosis of the aqueduct of Sylvius [HSAS]), complicated spastic paraplegia, and X-linked agenesis of the corpus callosum (ACC; Kaepernick et al., 1994; Fransen et al., 1998). It is interesting to note that like fragile X syndrome, MASA syndrome can only be transmitted by females (Rietschel et al., 1991) and is generally expressed very mildly in females compared to their male counterparts (Kaepernick et al., 1994). Studies investigating the familial expression of MASA syndrome found that although mothers and female relatives might exhibit some signs of the syndrome, they were generally not as severely afflicted as their male relatives, nor did they exhibit all of the diagnostic signs (mental retardation, aphasia, shuffling gait, and adducted thumbs; Fryns et al., 1992; Kaepernick et al., 1994). With this in mind, MASA syndrome is expressed more frequently in males than females, although exact data is not available. Similarly, there are no prevalence or incidence data reported in the literature, but the syndrome is thought to be very rare (Rietschel et al., 1991).

Characteristics

1. Congenital onset
2. Mental retardation
3. Aphasia or delay in speech acquisition
4. Shuffling gait
5. Adducted thumbs (drawn toward the palm)
6. Scoliosis and lordosis (swayback) of the back
7. Clinodactyly (deviation or deflection) of the index finger
8. Progressive neurological signs in the lower limbs

There is no cure for MASA syndrome at the present time. Treatment regimens usually focus on the characteristics expressed by those affected with the syndrome. For instance, surgery is often required to correct severely adducted thumbs, clinodactyly of the index finger, or other problems in the lower extremities that impede walking (Rietschel et al., 1991). Treatment may include speech and occupational therapy because of speech impairments and gait impairments, respectively. Genetic counseling with parents may be a viable prevention technique.

Children presenting with MASA syndrome may be eligible for special education services under several categories of IDEA. Depending on the degree of involvement, a child with MASA syndrome may meet the criteria as a student with mental retardation, speech impediment, or orthopedic impairment and may be labeled as such or using a combination of these labels.

There are few data with regard to the prognosis of children with MASA syndrome. Future research should focus on finding a means of early diagnosis (Fryns et al., 1992), determining prevalence and incidence data, developing viable treatment options, and investigating the benefits of prevention and genetic counseling.

REFERENCES

Fransen, E., Van Camp, G., D'Hooge, R., Vits, L., & Willems, P. J. (1998). Genotype-phenotype correlation in L1 associated diseases. *Journal of Medical Genetics, 35,* 399–404.

Fryns, J. P., Schrander-Stumpel, C., Die-Smulders, C., Borghgraef, M., & Van Den Berghe, H. (1992). MASA syndrome: Delineation of the clinical spectrum at prepubertal age. *American Journal of Medical Genetics, 43,* 402–407.

Kaepernick, L., Legius, E., Higgins, J., & Kapur, S. (1994). Clinical aspects of the MASA syndrome in a large family, including expressing females. *Clinical Genetics, 45,* 181–185.

Rietschel, M., Friedl, W., Uhlhaas, S., Neugebauer, M., Heimann, D., & Zerres, K. (1991). MASA syndrome: Clinical variability and linkage analysis. *American Journal of Medical Genetics, 41,* 10–14.

Winter, R. M., Davies, K. E., Bell, M. V., Huson, S. M., & Patterson, M. N. (1989). MASA syndrome: Further clinical delineation and chromosomal localisation. *Human Genetics, 82,* 367–370.

Christine L. French
Texas A&M University

MASTOCYTOSIS

Mast cells, connective tissue cells, play an eminent role in defending tissue, including the skin and select organ tissue, from disease. Mastocytosis is a relatively rare disorder affecting approximately less than 1% of births in the United States. Mastocytosis is caused by the proliferation or presence of too many mast cells in children and adults. There are two types of mastocytosis. Cutaneous mastocytosis, also referred to as urticaria pigmentosa, first described circa 1869, occurs when mast cells enter or get into the skin and begin proliferation. Systemic mastocytosis, described circa 1933, refers to the proliferation of mast cells in organ tissue. Systemic mastocytosis may affect organs, including the liver, small intestine, and spleen.

With regard to symptomatology, cutaneous mastocytosis may lead to allergic responses, including hives and itching, and in severe cases may lead to skin lesions, and shock. In the case of more severe cutaneous mastocytosis, but particularly in systemic mastocytosis, the patient also may experience abdominal discomfort. Individuals with systemic mastocytosis additionally may experience diarrhea, nausea, vomiting, bone pain, and intestinal ulcers. Systemic shock and hypotension also may occur.

Treatments for mastocytosis usually focus on symptom

abatement. More aggressive chemical therapy may be necessary if mastocytosis becomes malignant.

With regard to special education, these children may be labeled under the Other Health Impaired label. Special attention should be given to social and psychosocial aspects of the disease through the use of therapy, particularly in the case of observable cutaneous mastocytosis. Future research should continue to focus on early identification of mast cells and the etiology responsible for mast cell proliferation. Future research also should continue to develop cost-effective treatments capable of reducing mast cell proliferation.

Characteristics

1. High concentrations of mast cells in the skills (cutaneous) (by observation) or in select organs (systemic) (through biopsy)
2. Allergic responses including hives
3. Itching, nausea, vomiting, and skin lesions
4. Shock in severe mastocytosis cases
5. Abdominal cramping or discomfort and hypotension in severe cases
6. Pain in bone in severe cases
7. Ulcers and diarrhea in severe cases

REFERENCES

Nelson, W. E., Behrman, R. E., Kliegmen, R. M., & Arvin, A. M. (1996). *Nelson's textbook of pediatrics* (15th ed.). Bangalore, India: Prism Books PVT LTD.

National Institute of Allergy and Infectious Diseases. (2000, June). *Mastocytosis fact sheet.* Washington, DC: U.S. Department of Health and Human Services.

Antolin M. Llorente
Baylor College of Medicine
Houston, Texas

MASTURBATION, COMPULSIVE

Bodily exploration and genital stimulation are part of normal child development. It is common for children under 24 months of age to explore and fondle their genitals, and for children from 3–5 years to engage in masturbation for pleasure and even to experience orgasm (Gordon & Schroeder, 2001). Indeed, there remains no evidence to support the centuries of proclamations that self-stimulation is harmful. However, compulsive masturbation refers to self-stimulation of the genitals that is excessive (compared to same-age peers) and interferes with other age-appropriate activities or causes impairment in functioning or physical harm.

It has been estimated that 5% of the U.S. general population engage in compulsive sexual behavior (Coleman, 1992); however, only a small portion of these involve childhood compulsive masturbation. Thus, the precise prevalence of compulsive masturbation in children is not known. Although gender differences in the rates of childhood compulsive masturbation have not been demonstrated empirically, clinical observation suggests that boys engage in earlier and more frequent masturbation than do girls.

Characteristics

1. Self-stimulation of the genitals that is excessive and interferes with other age-appropriate activities or that causes impairment in functioning or physical harm.
2. The function of the compulsive behavior may be either to produce pleasure or to provide escape from internal discomfort (e.g., anxiety, tension).

Treatments for compulsive masturbation that have empirical support in the research literature include behavior therapy and medication management. Several studies have demonstrated the effectiveness of behavioral contracting and operant conditioning procedures for eliminating childhood compulsive masturbation for up to 9 months of follow-up (e.g., Janzen & Peacock, 1978). In addition, selective serotonin reuptake inhibitors (e.g., Prozac) have been successful in reducing compulsive masturbation in adults (e.g., Kornreich, Den Dulk, Verbanck, & Pelc, 1995); however, the effectiveness of these medications for such behaviors has not been investigated in children. More traditional forms of psychotherapy (e.g., play therapy) have not demonstrated a reduction in compulsive masturbation.

Children with impaired cognitive functioning, poor social judgment, and difficulties with impulse control may be more likely to engage in compulsive masturbation in the presence of others. While no studies have reported on the effectiveness of psychotropic medications with this population (as mentioned above), the use of behavior therapy has been successful with this population and is recommended.

The main difficulties associated with childhood compulsive masturbation are typically impaired functioning at home and at school and the experience of interpersonal difficulties. Physical injury can occur but is likely to be quite rare and minor in nature. No large-scale studies are reported; however, existing studies using primarily behavior therapy suggest that the prognosis with treatment is quite favorable.

Considering the relatively small amount of systematic research on children with compulsive masturbation and other inappropriate sexual behaviors, future work in this area will focus on the further development of effective methods for identifying, assessing, and treating children with these conditions.

REFERENCES

Coleman, E. (1992). Is your patient suffering from compulsive sexual behavior? *Psychiatric Annals, 22,* 320–325.

Gordon, B. N., & Schroeder, C. S. (2001). Sexual problems of children. In C. E. Walker & M. C. Roberts (Eds.), *Handbook of clinical child psychology* (3rd ed., pp. 495–522). New York: Wiley.

Janzen, W. B., & Peacock, R. (1978). Treatment of public masturbation by behavioral management. *American Journal of Psychotherapy, 32,* 300–306.

Kornreich, C., Den Dulk, A., Verbanck, P., & Pelc, I. (1995). Fluoxetine treatment of compulsive masturbation in a schizophrenic patient. *Journal of Clinical Psychiatry, 56,* 334.

Matthew K. Nock
Yale University

MCCUNE-ALBRIGHT SYNDROME

McCune-Albright syndrome (MAS) is a nonhereditary condition characterized by multiple thickened areas of bone (polyostotic fibrous dysplasia), irregularly shaped splotches of increased skin pigmentation, and extremely early onset of puberty (precocious puberty). The skin findings are usually present at birth or appear within the first few months of life. Bony abnormalities become evident during childhood and are usually progressive. Pubertal changes may occur as early as 4 months of age, but the average age of their appearance is 3 years.

The etiology of MAS has been tracked to a mutation in the gene responsible for the production of G-proteins. These substances control the activity of several endocrine systems (gonadal, adrenal, thyroid, pituitary, etc.). They also govern the rate of bone growth and the proliferation of melanocytes, the skin's pigment-producing cells. Unregulated amounts of G-proteins circulating throughout the body cause the physical abnormalities found in MAS, which are secondary to glandular hyperfunction.

MAS is rare. Since the first case reports appeared in the 1930s, only about 100 additional affected individuals have been described. The occurrence of MAS is sporadic. There is a 3:2 female-to-male ratio in patients with this disorder.

Characteristics

1. Fibrous dysplasia occurs in many areas. The most commonly affected bones are in the legs, arms, and pelvis. Facial bones, ribs, and the skull may also be involved. These changes can cause deformity, asymmetry, and thickening of bone. If the base of the skull is affected, constriction of cranial nerves may result in blindness, deafness, or both.
2. Irregular, patchy brown pigmentation, most common over the lower back, buttocks, and upper spine.
3. Endocrine abnormalities include precocious puberty, hyperthyroidism, growth hormone–secreting pituitary tumors, Cushing's syndrome (secondary to adrenal gland hyperactivity) and acromegaly (enlargement of the face, hands, and feet caused by excessive growth hormone).
4. Accelerated growth during childhood, with early skeletal maturation and relatively short adult height.
5. Enlarged ovary, ovarian cyst, ovarian tumor (often estrogen secreting) and, testicular enlargement.

Several therapeutic modalities are available for patients with MAS. Girls who have high estrogen production may respond to drugs that inhibit estrogen synthesis and limit the hormone's effects on sexual development and skeletal maturation. Cushing syndrome necessitates removal of the adrenal glands. Octreotide, a drug that blocks growth hormone activity, may also be useful. Hyperthyroidism may respond to medication, irradiation, or surgical excision of part of the gland.

There is no research to indicate cognitive dysfunction or the need for special support services as a result of this syndrome.

The prognosis for patients with MAS is generally favorable. The disorder has no effect on life expectancy. However, fibrous dysplasia predisposes bones to easy fracture, may cause severe deformities and can engender the loss of significant sensory functions (sight and hearing), if cranial nerve compression develops.

REFERENCES

Garibaldi, L. (2000). Disorders of pubertal development. In R. E. Behrman, R. M. Kleigman, & H. B. Jenson (Eds.), *Nelson's textbook of pediatrics* (16th ed., pp. 1692–1693). Philadelphia: W. B. Saunders.

Jones, K. (1997). *Smith's recognizable patterns of human malformation* (5th ed.). Philadelphia: W. B. Saunders.

National Organization for Rare Disorders. (1999). McCune-Albright syndrome. Retrieved from http://www.stepstn.com/cgi-win/nord.exe?proc=GetDocument&rectype=0&recnum=183

Barry H. Davison
Ennis, Texas

Joan W. Mayfield
Baylor Pediatric Specialty Services
Dallas, Texas

MECKEL-GRUBER SYNDROME

Meckel-Gruber syndrome (MGS) is a genetically transmitted disorder that affects the central nervous system and kidneys. Associated defects commonly involve the eyes, face, mouth, heart, lungs, genitalia, and extremities.

The etiology of MGS has been traced to an abnormality in Chromosome 17. There is great variation in the clinical features of MGS among affected neonates. Cystic changes in the kidney occur in virtually all cases, but almost 20% have no brain anomalies.

MGS is rare. The first case was described in 1822. Since then only about 200 more examples of the syndrome have appeared in the medical literature. The pattern of inheritance is autosomal recessive. There are no apparent abnormalities in carriers of the gene.

Characteristics

1. Variable prenatal growth deficiency.
2. Occipital encephalocoele (a defect in the back of the skull through which the tough, outer covering of the brain and brain tissue protrude). Other nervous system anomalies include microcephaly (small head), underdevelopment of the brain, anencephaly (complete absence of the brain and skull) and hydrocephaly (accumulation of fluid within the cavities of the brain, causing enlargement of the head).
3. Small eyes, cleft palate, small jaw, malformed ears.
4. Polydactyly (extra toes, fingers, or both).
5. Kidney malformation with variable cystic changes.
6. Undescended testicle and malformation of external and internal sex organs.
7. Congenital cardiac malformations.
8. Underdeveloped lungs.

No treatment is presently available for this disorder. Prenatal diagnosis may be possible through analysis of amniotic fluid or ultrasonography, which can demonstrate the presence of encephalocoele and kidney enlargement. Genetic counseling should be offered to families who have had a pregnancy affected by MGS.

Prognosis for MGS is poor. Patients rarely survive longer than a few days or weeks after birth. Death is usually secondary to severe central nervous system defects or kidney pathology and subsequent renal failure.

REFERENCES

Haslam, R. H. A. (2000). Congenital anomalies of the central nervous system. In R. E. Behrman, R. M. Kleigman, & H. B. Jenson (Eds.), *Nelson textbook of pediatrics* (16th ed., p. 1806). Philadelphia: W. B. Saunders.

Jones, K. (1997). *Smith's recognizable patterns of human malformation* (5th ed.). Philadelphia: W. B. Saunders.

Pediatric Database (PEDBASE). (1997). Meckel-Gruber syndrome. Retrieved from http://www.icondata.com/health/pedbase/files/MECKEL-G.HTM

Barry H. Davison
Ennis, Texas

Joan W. Mayfield
Baylor Pediatric Specialty Services
Dallas, Texas

MEDIUM-CHAIN ACYL-COA DEHYDROGENASE DEFICIENCY

Medium-chain acyl-CoA dehydrogenase (MCAD) is an enzyme that is active in the liver, white blood cells (leukocytes), and connective tissue cells (fibroblasts). This enzyme is necessary for the breakdown of fatty acids in the body. A deficiency in MCAD may lead to an accumulation of fatty acids in the liver and the brain (National Organization for Rare Disorders, 1998).

It is estimated that MCAD deficiency occurs in up to 1 in 50,000 live births within the general population. In Anglo American children, the disorder can occur in up to 1 in 23,000 live births (Menkes, 1995). The sex ratio is even, with the disorder affecting males and females equally in over 200 cases reported in the medical literature to date. The etiology of this disorder is that it is inherited as an autosomal recessive genetic trait; this means that the child inherited the same defective gene for the same trait from each parent. Onset occurs usually between the ages of 3 to 15 months, but prenatal diagnosis is possible through amniocentesis. The disorder is potentially fatal if unrecognized and patients generally have no symptoms at birth—that is, they are healthy until clinical onset (Iafolla, Thompson, & Roe, 1994).

Characteristics

1. Child may have recurrent episodes of hypoglycemia (low levels of sugar in the blood).
2. Child may become lethargic and unenergetic.
3. Child may have liver malfunction.
4. Vomiting is a common characteristic.
5. Some children may suffer from seizures during a clinical episode.
6. Symptoms are usually triggered when the child does not eat for an extended period of time or if the child has an infection.

Preventive measures should be included as part of treatment. Awakening the child at night for feeding will possibly prevent onset, which can be triggered by the child's going for long periods of time without eating. Those diagnosed with MCAD deficiency may benefit by following a low-fat diet. If the child is diagnosed early and treatment is initiated, the chances that the child will experience developmental disabilities decreases significantly. The families may benefit from genetic counseling (National Organization for Rare Disorders, 1998).

Research literature indicates that a significant number of patients diagnosed with MCAD deficiency during infancy later experienced developmental and behavioral disabilities, attention deficit disorder, and speech delays (Menkes, 1995; Iafolla et al., 1994). A student might qualify for special education services under the Individuals with Disabilities Education Act (IDEA, 1997) or modifications under Section 504 of the Rehabilitation Act of 1973 as a result of one of these disabilities.

Ongoing research is being conducted in the area of enzyme replacement therapy. Because newborns are generally healthy until clinical episodes and because such episodes place the child at risk for sudden death, several organizations are now lobbying for newborn screening for MCAD deficiency to prevent clinical episodes from occurring (Iafolla et al., 1994).

REFERENCES

Iafolla, A. K., Thompson, R., Jr., & Roe, C. (1994). Medium-chain acyl-coenzyme A dehydrogenase deficiency: Clinical course in 120 affected children. *The Journal of Pediatrics, 124*(3), 409–415.

Menkes, J. (1995). *Textbook of child neurology* (5th ed.). Philadelphia: Williams & Wilkins.

National Organization for Rare Disorders. (1998). Medium chain acyl coA dehydrogenase deficiency. Retrieved July 2001, from http://www.rarediseases.org

Christine D. Cde Baca
University of Northern Colorado

MEDULLARY CYSTIC KIDNEY DISORDER

Medullary cystic kidney disorder is a familial disorder that is progressive in nature and results in renal failure. Historically believed to be the same disorder, nephrophthisis (NPH), the autosomal recessive form of medullary cystic disease, is more likely to become evident in late adolescence, and therefore males and females are affected equally. There is also a form of medullary cystic disease that is autosomal dominant (Scolari et al., 1999). Medullary cystic kidney disorder occurs in 2 in 100,000 individuals and usually is not evident until adulthood (Wise, Hartman, Hardesty, & Mosher, 1998). There is considerable genetic variability of gene loci (Hildebrandt & Otto, 2000), and recent research suggests that NPH and medullary cystic disorder may involve different genetic loci (Gusmano, Ghiggeri, & Caridi, 1998). Despite the differences, NPH and medullary cyctic disease are often grouped together and share similar presentation. Both forms are evident across ethnic groups.

Manifestations of the disorder occur predominantly in association with renal function. The cause of the renal failure is related to the presence of tubular atrophy within the kidneys, which are generally smaller than normal (Gusmano et al., 1998). The onset is insidious, with polyuria (frequent need for urination) as one of the earliest symptoms. Associated with the polyuria and impaired renal concentration, individuals may experience polydipsia (frequent thirst) as well. Children may also experience anemia, bone disease, and short stature. Growth retardation and bone disease may develop at a slow rate and not be detected or identified until uremic problems are manifested. In addition, there may be other secondary effects, including pigment changes to the retina as found in retinal-renal dysplasia syndrome (Gusmano et al., 1998).

Characteristics

1. Polyuria
2. Polydipsia
3. Nocturia
4. Anemia that is proportional to the degree of renal failure
5. Bone disease
6. Short stature

Treatment is usually medical in nature and responsive to the progression of the disorder. Medical interventions include dietary restrictions (fluid monitoring, dietary control of salt), use of diuretics, albumin transfusions, prednisone, and other medications. As progression continues, treatment is similar to that used with other renal diseases and may include dialysis and kidney transplant. Special education services for children and youth with medullary cystic disease may be appropriate depending on the progression of the disease and the individual needs of the child. Supportive counseling for the individual and the family as well as school staff to address issues associated with progressive disorders may be needed over time. Genetic counseling is a critical factor in the prevention of medullary cystic kidney disease.

REFERENCES

Gusmano, R., Ghiggeri, G. M., & Caridi, G. (1998). Nephronophthisis-medullary cystic disease: Clinical and genetic aspects. *Journal of Nephrology, 11*(5), 224–228.

Hildebrandt, F., & Otto, E. (2000). Molecular genetics of nephronophthisis and medullary cystic kidney disease. *Journal of the American Society of Neurology, 11,* 1753–1761.

Scolari, F., Puzzer, D., Amoroso, A., Caridi, G., Ghiggeri, G. M., Maiorca, R., et al. (1999). Identification of a new locus for medullary cystic disease on chromosome 16p12. *American Journal of Human Genetics, 64*(6), 1655–1660.

Wise, S. W., Hartman, D. S., Hardesty, L. A., & Mosher, T. J. (1998). Renal medullary cystic disease: Assessment by MRI. *Abdominal Imaging, 3,* 649–651.

Cynthia A. Riccio
Texas A&M University

MEDULLARY SPONGE KIDNEY DISORDER

Medullary sponge kidney disorder is a familial disorder that has autosomal dominant transmission. In some cases, however, the occurrence of medullary sponge kidney disorder can be sporadic (Appel, 1998; Klemme et al., 1998). It is estimated that 1 in 100 to 200 individuals have some form of medullary sponge kidney, but many may be asymptomatic. The true incidence may be closer to 1 in 5000 who evidence the disorder. In medullary sponge kidney disorder, the tubules of the kidneys that hold urine are irregular in diameter, forming small cysts of urine in the dilated portions. The dilation and cysts result in a spongey appearance to the kidneys. Associated with the dilation of the tubules is an increased likelihood of calcium deposits forming in the kidneys and subsequent kidney stones. Medullary sponge kidney may not be symptomatic unless calcium deposits are formed. As such, manifestation and identification of the disorder may be associated more with diet than with gender or ethnicity (Thomsen et al., 1997).

Characteristics

1. Back pain associated with the presence of kidney stones
2. Blood in the urine
3. Cloudy urine
4. Burning on urination
5. Kidney infections

Prognosis for individuals with medullary sponge kidney disorder is good; medullary sponge kidney disorder is not likely to result in renal failure unless symptoms are ignored and infections are not treated in a timely manner. Treatment is usually medical in nature and responsive to the symptoms of the disorder. Medical interventions include dietary restrictions (fluid monitoring, low-calcium diet) and the use of diuretics. Treatment of infection at the first symptoms provides the best long-term prognosis; kidney infection is treated with antibiotics. When kidney stones are present, these can be treated with lithotripsy, which breaks the stones into smaller particles. Should the urinary tract become obstructed or the stones become too large, surgery may be necessary (Thomsen et al., 1997).

REFERENCES

Appel, G. B. (1998). Nephrology: VIII. Tubulointerstitial diseases. *Scientific American, 3,* 1–12.

Klemme, L., Fish, A. J., Rich, S., Greenberg, B., Senske, B., & Segall, M. (1998). Familial ureteral abnormalities syndrome: Genomic mapping, clinical findings. *Pediatric Nephrology, 12,* 349–356.

Thomsen, H. S., Levine, E., Meilstrup, J. W., van Slyke, M. A., Edgar, K. A., Barth, J. C., et al. (1997). Renal cystic diseases. *European Radiology, 7,* 1267–1275.

Cynthia A. Riccio
Texas A&M University

MEDULLOBLASTOMA

Medulloblastomas are malignant neoplasms of the central nervous system and account for 30% of all pediatric brain tumors (Cohen & Garvin, 1996; Jallo & Jallo, 2001). In children, the cerebellum is most commonly affected, and tumor infiltration is usually midline (Jallo & Jallo, 2001). Medulloblastomas arise from the cerebellar vermis and are usually solid (Hanieh, 2001). The mass lesion is pinkish-gray in color, and cysts, necrosis, and calcification are uncommon. Histologically, cells are small and have scant cytoplasm and few stroma. Frequent mitotic figures are found, and pseudorosettes have been noted. Differentiation is generally poor. Originally classified as a glioma, medulloblastoma is now considered a primitive neuroectodermal tumor (PNET; Brett & Harding, 1997; Jallo & Jallo, 2001).

The median age of diagnosis is 9 years, with 75% of all medulloblastomas occurring in children (Jallo & Jallo, 2001). Medulloblastomas are rare in adolescence (Brett & Harding, 1997). However, patients of any age can be affected. Incidence of medulloblastoma is 1.5–2 cases per 100,000 population, with 350 new cases in the United States each year. Males are affected more often than females, with a ratio of 1.5 to 1. Hereditary conditions are associated with this tumor, including Gorlin syndrome (nevoid basal cell carcinoma syndrome), blue rubber-bleb nevus syndrome, Turcot Syndrome (glioma polyposis syndrome), and Rubenstein-Taybi syndrome (Jallo & Jallo, 2001).

Characteristics

1. Patients with medulloblastoma most commonly have symptoms related to increased intracranial pressure, especially headache or vomiting upon awakening (Brett & Harding, 1997; Cohen & Garvin, 1996; Jallo & Jallo, 2001). Decreased mental status, papilledema (in up to 90% of patients), diplopia (double vision), lateral gaze paresis, nystagmus, listlessness, irritability, and decreased social interactions are also found. In infants, the only presenting symptoms may be increased head circumference or behavioral change (Jallo & Jallo, 2001).
2. Specific cerebellar symptoms, most commonly found in children, include gait ataxia in up to 60% of patients (Brett & Harding, 1997). Torticollis and neck stiffness are also noted (Jallo & Jallo, 2001).
3. Severe weakness may be a sign of leptomeningeal dissemination (Jallo & Jallo, 2001).

Diagnosis usually begins with a noncontrast head CT scan, due to the presenting problem of headache. With enhancement, the hyperdense medulloblastoma shows marked contrast, with surrounding vasogenic edema appearing hypodense. Compression of the fourth ventricle and marked hydrocephalus is the rule. Diagnosis using magnetic resonance imaging (MRI) with gadolinium enhancement is preferred. Tumors appear hypointense on T-1 weighted imaging, with T-2 weighted imaging showing a hyperintense mass with surrounding edema. MRI of the spine can detect metastatic lesions. When MRI is contraindicated, myelography is utilized with CT. Skeletal imaging can identify lytic or sclerotic lesions in a child with bone pain (Jallo & Jallo, 2001).

In most cases, gross total resection of the medulloblastoma is possible (Hanieh, 2001). In one third of cases, the tumor adheres to the ventricular floor, precluding gross total resection (Hanieh, 2001; Jallo & Jallo, 2001). Staging of the medulloblastoma is accomplished via cytology of cerebrospinal fluid (CSF) obtained through lumbar puncture, through ventricular drain, or at the time of surgery. Ventriculostomy relieves hydrocephalus, with 15% of patients with preoperative intracranial pressure requiring long-term placement of a ventricular shunt (Jallo & Jallo, 2001).

Adjuvant therapy is standard, especially in cases in which gross total resection is not possible (Hanieh, 2001; Jallo & Jallo, 2001). Most common is radiation therapy of the entire neuroaxis, with local boost to the primary tumor site (Brett & Harding, 1997; Cohen & Garvin, 1996; Jallo & Jallo, 2001). Chemotherapy has been effective in reducing or postponing irradiation, especially in young children. Acutely, glucocorticoids can aid in decreasing vasogenic edema. Diuretics can be useful acutely to prevent further increases in intracranial pressure (Jallo & Jallo, 2001).

One of the most common complications of surgical resection is cerebellar mutism, usually occurring in children under 15 years of age. This syndrome involves apathy, minimal-to-absent speech, emotional lability and irritability, refusal to initiate movement, swallowing apraxia, and hemiparesis in the absence of an identifiable etiology. Consciousness commonly remains unimpaired. Classically, onset is delayed postoperatively, and the symptoms typically resolve after several weeks (Vandeinse & Hornyak, 1997; see also Jallo & Jallo, 2001).

Long-term complications resulting from radiation therapy can include mental retardation, radiation necrosis of the white matter, behavioral abnormalities, small stature, endocrine dysfunction, and secondary neoplasms (Hoppe-Hirsch et al., 1990; Jallo & Jallo, 2001). In a longitudinal study (Hoppe-Hirsch et al., 1990), cognitive sequelae were significant and worsened over the years for children with medulloblastoma. The younger the child at the time of radiotherapy, the lower the IQ at 10 years after treatment (see also Chapman et al., 1994). Special education services may be available under the Other Health Impaired or Physical Disability handicapping conditions. A Section 504 plan is another alternative, allowing for classroom and learning modifications. Ongoing medical intervention will necessitate multiple absences from school.

Prognosis is most favorable with gross total resection and radiotherapy. Adjuvant chemotherapy resulted in 20% improvement in 5-year survival rates (Cohen & Garvin, 1996). Subsets of pediatric patients have 70% survival at 5 years, although fewer than 50% of children with medulloblastoma survive to adulthood (Sagar & Israel, 1998). Even after a positive response to treatment, recurrence within 2 years is common. Systemic metastases in the absence of a CSF shunting system occur in 10–20% of patients. Increasing age at diagnosis has been associated with a better prognosis, and females have a longer recurrence-free interval (Jallo & Jallo, 2001).

REFERENCES

Brett, E., & Harding, B. (1997). Intracranial and spinal cord tumors. In E. M. Brett (Ed.), *Paediatric neurology* (3rd ed., 537–553). New York: Churchill Livingstone.

Chapman, C. A., Waber, D. P., Bernstein, J. H., Pomeroy, S. L., LaVally, B., Sallan, S. E., et al. (1994). Neurobehavioral and neurologic outcome in long-term survivors of posterior fossa brain tumors: Role of age and perioperative factors. *Journal of Child Neurology, 10*(3), 209–212.

Cohen, B., & Garvin, J. (1996). Tumors of the central nervous system. In A. M. Rudolph, J. E. Hoffman, & C. D. Rudolph (Eds.), *Rudolph's pediatrics* (20th ed., pp. 1900–1920). Stamford, CT: Appleton & Lange.

Hanieh, A. (2001, November). Neoplasm: Pediatric brain tumors. Retrieved from http://www.health.adelaide.edu.au/paed-neuro/neoplasm.html

Hoppe-Hirsch, E., Renier, D., Lellouch-Tubiana, A., Sainte-Rose, C., Pierre-Kahn, A., & Hirsch, J. F. (1990). Medulloblastoma in childhood: Progressive intellectual deterioration. *Child's Nervous System, 6,* 60–65.

Jallo, G., & Jallo, G. (2001, March). Pediatric Neurology: Medulloblastoma. In R. D. Sheth, F. Talavera, K. J. Mack, M. J. Baker, & N. Y. Lorenzo (Eds.), *eMedicine Journal, 2,*(3) Retrieved from http://www.emedicine.com/neuro/topic624.htm

Sagar, S., & Israel, M. (1998). Tumors of the nervous system. In A. S. Fauci, J. B. Martin, E. Braunwald, D. L. Kasper, K. J. Isselbacher, S. L. Hauser et al. (Eds.), *Harrison's principles of internal medicine* (14th ed., pp. 2398–2409). New York: McGraw-Hill.

Vandeinse, D., & Hornyak, J. E. (1997). Linguistic and cognitive deficits associated with cerebellar mutism. *Pediatric Rehabilitation, 1*(1), 41–44.

Laurie L. Ferguson
The Wright Institute
Berkeley, California

Greta N. Wilkening
University of Colorado Health Sciences Center
The Children's Hospital

MEGALOCORNEA MENTAL RETARDATION SYNDROME

Megalocornea mental retardation (MMR) syndrome is characterized by distinctive abnormalities of the eyes and varying degrees of mental retardation (Antinolo, Rufo, Borrego, & Morales, 1994). MMR syndrome is an extremely rare, recessively inherited genetic disorder. The range and severity of symptoms may differ from child to child.

A hallmark characteristic of the MMR syndrome is megalocornea, which occurs when the corneas in both eyes are abnormally large. Children with MMR syndrome may experience visual impairments resulting from eye abnormalities, such as an underdeveloped iris (hypoplasia) and other ocular anomalies. As the name of the syndrome suggests, most children also have mild to severe mental retardation. Other developmental abnormalities are sometimes associated with the MMR syndrome. These abnormalities may include diminished muscle tone, or hypotonia, present at birth, delayed motor development, and minor facial anomalies. Some children may also experience seizures (Neuhauser, Kaveggia, France, & Opitz, 1975).

Characteristics

1. Megalocornea (enlargement of the cornea in both eyes)
2. Mental retardation
3. Developmental anomalies, including short stature, hypoplasia, and hypotonia
4. Seizures

Because mental retardation is a major symptom of MMR, afflicted children will require special education services. A full psychological and educational evaluation is suggested in addition to the child's medical examinations in order to determine the type and range of educational services the child may need.

A recurring issue of debate is the diagnostic criteria for MMR syndrome. The MMR spectrum is not clearly defined, making differential diagnosis of the disorder difficult (Frydman, Berkenstadt, Raas-Rothschild, & Goodman, 1990). Many investigators believe that the MMR syndrome diagnosis is too broad and needs more specificity (Frydman et al., 1990; Raas-Rothschild, Berkenstadt, & Goodman, 1988). However, Del Giudice and Andria (1988) stated that the only symptoms required for a diagnosis of MMR are megalocornea and mental retardation presenting together.

Future research will seek to identify the genetic basis of MMR so that genetic counseling may be given to parents who are carriers. Due to the high degree of clinical variability of MMR, delineating the MMR spectrum will also be an important part of future research (Antinolo et al., 1994).

REFERENCES

Antinolo, G., Rufo, M., Borrego, S., & Morales, C. (1994). Megalocornea-mental retardation syndrome. *American Journal of Medical Genetics, 52,* 196–197.

Del Guidice, E., & Andria, G. (1988). Megalocornea and mental retardation syndrome. *American Journal of Medical Genetics, 29,* 223.

Frydman, M., Berkenstadt, M., Raas-Rothschild, A., & Goodman, R. (1990). Megalocornea, macrocephaly, mental and motor retardation (MMMM). *Clinical Genetics, 38,* 149–154.

Neuhauser, G., Kaveggia, E. G., France, T. D., & Opitz, J. M. (1975). Syndrome of mental retardation, seizures, hypotonic cerebral palsy and megalocorneae, recessively inherited. *Zeitschnift feur Kinderheilkunde, 120,* 1–18.

Raas-Rothschild, A., Berkenstadt, M., & Goodman, R. (1988). Megalocornea and mental retardation syndrome. *American Journal of Medical Genetics, 29,* 221–223.

Jennifer M. Gillis
University of California, Irvine

MEIGE SYNDROME

Meige syndrome or blepharospasm-oromandibular dystonia is a syndrome that is characterized by dyskinesia or the impairment of voluntary movement of muscles of the eyelids and lower jaw. Movement is impaired such that there may be fragmentary or incomplete movements as well as uncontrolled or involuntary movements. With Meige syndrome, the muscles of the face and eyelids are most likely to be affected; in some individuals, muscles of the tongue and throat may be affected as well. There is some evidence to suggest that Meige syndrome is associated with dysfunction of the basal ganglia (Casey, 1980). Other evidence suggests involvement of the lymphatic system (Rubegni et al., 2000).

Meige syndrome is most likely to present when the individual is in his or her 50s (Sharma, Behari, & Ahuja, 1996). However, eye blinking and facial grimacing symptoms have been known to start in childhood (Elston, Granje, & Lees, 1989). The ratio of males to females affected is generally equal. Symptom presentation and severity vary across individuals.

Characteristics

1. Jaw grinding
2. Grimacing
3. Blephoraspasm or tonic spasm of the muscles of the eyelid (orbisularis oculi) such that there is almost complete closure of the eyelids and pressure is put on the cornea; this may appear as frequent eye-blinking
4. Oromandibular dystonia or drooping of the lower jaw

A number of possible risk factors for Meige syndrome have been identified (Behari, Sharma, Changakoti, Sharma, & Pandey, 2000). These factors include various medications, caffeine, tobacco use, and betel nut chewing. Meige syndrome can be precipitated by the administration of specific classes of medication, including antidepressants, antimania, antihistamine, antipsychotic, neuroleptic, or antiparkinsonian drugs (Sachdev, 1998). The onset of symptoms can be as soon as 2 months after initial administration of the drugs up to 35 years later (Mauriello, Carbonaro, Dhillon, Leone, & Franklin, 1998; Sachdev, 1998). In those instances in which the symptoms do not remit with cessation or decreased dosage of medication, botulinum toxin A has been used successfully. Based on their sample, Behari et al. (2000) concluded that betel nut chewing and tobacco use were significant predictors of Meige syndrome.

The symptoms of Meige syndrome tend to last for about 3–4 years unless treated effectively (Sharma et al., 1996). If the individual is on any medications that may trigger Meige syndrome and the medications can be discontinued, this is often the first line of treatment. When that is not possible or when discontinuing medication does not result in remission of symptoms, botulinum toxin A has been used to treat Meige syndrome (Maurellio et al., 1998).

REFERENCES

Behari, M., Sharma, A. K., Changkakoti, S., Sharma, N., & Pandey, R. M. (2000). Case-control study of Meige's syndrome: Result of a pilot study. *Neuroepidemiology, 19,* 275–280.

Casey, D. E. (1980). Pharmacology of belpharospasm-oromandibular dystonia syndrome. *Neurology, 30,* 690–695.

Elston, J. S., Granje, F. C., & Lees, A. J. (1989). The relationship between eye-winking, frequent eye-blinking and blepharospasm. *Journal of Neurology, Neurosurgery, and Psychiatry, 52*(4), 477–480.

Maurellio, J. A., Jr., Carbonaro, P., Dhillon, S., Leone, T., & Franklin, M. (1998). Drug-associated facial dyskineseas: A study of 238 patients. *Journal of NeuroOphthalmology, 18,* 153–157.

Rubegni, P., Fimiani, M., Tosi, G. M., DeAloe, G., Miracco, C., & Andreassi, L. (2000). Conjunctival edema and alopecia of the external third of the eyebrows in a patient with Meige syndrome. *Gravefes Archive for Clinical and Experimental Ophthalmology, 238,* 98–100.

Sachdev, P. (1998). Tardive blepharospasm. *Movement Disorders, 13,* 947–951.

Sharma, A. K., Behari, M., & Ahuja, G. K. (1996). Clinical and demographic features of Meige's syndrome. *Journal of the Association of Physicians of India, 44,* 645–647.

Cynthia A. Riccio
Texas A&M University

MELKERSSON-ROSENTHAL SYNDROME

Melkersson-Rosenthal syndrome (MRS) is a disease that generally begins late in childhood and is characterized by swelling of facial features, most frequently the lips. The areas of swelling may include the eyelids (Cockerham et al., 2000). MRS is most likely to become evident in childhood or adolescence. The swelling and facial palsy are believed to be due to lymphatic stasis and the resulting buildup of protein. The swelling may be accompanied by inflammation. The swelling and paralysis may be unilateral or bilateral. Facial swelling may involve both lips, only one lip, or only one side of the lip. MRS flare-ups may be triggered by bacterial infections.

Characteristics

1. Chronic swelling of the face, often confined to the swelling of the lips
2. Peripheral facial palsy that may or may not be bilateral
3. Loss of taste in the anterior part of the tongue and swelling of the tongue
4. Swelling of the eyelids
5. Fissured or grooved tongue

MRS is a rare genetic disorder, believed to be autosomal dominant with incomplete penetrance (Smeets, Fryns, & Van den Berghe, 1994). Other evidence suggests involvement of the gene located at 9p11 (Smeets et al., 1994). All of the characteristics of MRS do not manifest in all who inherit. The mechanism of the syndrome is not fully understood, but it has been suggested that MRS is an autoimmune disorder. Others believe that MRS is associated with the occurrence of Bell's palsy (e.g., Kunstadter, 1965). The actual incidence of MRS is not known; however, females are more likely to be affected than are males. MRS initially was identified in Europe, and most of the available case studies are specific to individuals of European descent (National Organization for Rare Disorders, 2001).

In most cases, the symptoms of MRS resolve spontaneously within days, weeks, or months. Use of steroid medications (e.g., prednisone) may facilitate the remission. Other medications are being field-tested for their use in the treatment of MRS (National Organization for Rare Disorders, 2001). During the attack, however, the swelling of the lips and tongue may impair speech intelligibility as well as create possible feeding problems. Swelling of the eyelids can impair vision. In severe cases, the swelling and facial palsy recur, and it may be necessary for the facial nerve to be decompressed surgically (Dutt, Mirza, Irving, & Donaldson, 2000). The swelling and paralysis tend to recur; however, there may be lengthy periods during which the individual is asymptomatic and the swelling and paralysis may not occur at the same time. In rare cases, the facial palsy may not remit (National Organization for Rare Disorders, 2001).

Cognitive impairment is not specifically associated with MRS, so its impact on the child will most likely be in the area of social and emotional functioning. For children and youth affected by MRS, supportive counseling may be necessary during the acute phases of MRS in addition to the medical management. Additional accommodations, depending on the extent to which speech becomes impaired, may be needed as well in order to limit any negative impacts on education. In-service programs on MRS and other related disorders may be appropriate to increase understanding of the disorder and intermittent nature of the symptoms.

REFERENCES

Cockerham, K. P., Hidayat, A. A., Cockerham, G. C., Depper, M. H., Sorensen, S., Cytryn, A. S., et al. (2000). Melkersson-Rosenthal syndrome: New clinicopathologic findings in four cases. *Archives of Ophthalmology, 118,* 227–232.

Dutt, S. N., Mirza, S., Irving, R. M., & Donaldson, I. (2000). Total decompression of facial nerve for Melkersson-Rosenthal syndrome. *Journal of Laryngology and Otology, 114,* 870–873.

Kundstadter, R. H. (1965). Melkersson's syndrome: A case report of multiple recurrences of Bell's palsy and episodic facial edema. *American Journal of Diseases of Childhood, 110,* 559–561.

National Organization for Rare Disorders. (2001). Retrieved May 22, 2001, from http://www.rarediseases.org

Smeets, E., Fryns, J. P., & Van den Berghe, H. (1994). Melkersson-Rosenthal syndrome and de novo autosomal t(9;21) (p11; p11) translocation. *Clinical Genetics, 45,* 323–324.

Cynthia A. Riccio
Texas A&M University

MEMORY DISORDERS

Memory processes are thought to be inseparable from other cognitive or learning processes, but memory is often conceptualized as the ability to encode, store, and retrieve information (Krener, 1996). Disorders of memory are often referred to as amnesia and typically involve impairment in the ability to learn new information or to recall previously learned information or events.

It is unclear whether congenital amnesia exists, but acquired causes of amnesia do occur in childhood and adolescence (Mauer, 1992). Because of multiple etiologies and difficulty assessing memory deficits distinct from other cognitive deficits, true prevalence rates of memory disorders are unknown. The two primary etiologies for memory disorders in children and adolescents are closed head injuries and seizure disorders (Pennington, 1991). Approximately 1 million children in the United States (1.6%) suffer closed head injuries yearly, of which 90% survive. Closed head injuries are approximately two to three times more common in males than in females. Seizure disorders occur in approximately 1–2% of the population with a ratio of 1.5 to 2 times greater frequency in males than in females (Pennington, 1991). Of these, children with temporal lobe epilepsy are at the greatest risk for memory disorders. Other conditions that can affect memory in children and adolescents include brain tumors affecting the temporal lobe, infections (e.g., herpes simplex, Reye syndrome), encephalitis, meningitis, perinatal anoxia, toxic exposure (e.g., carbon monoxide poisoning), and strokes, as well as side effects of some medications (Mauer, 1992; Pennington, 1991).

Characteristics

1. Difficulty learning new information, inability to recall previously learned information or events, or both.
2. Difficulty remembering everyday information.
3. Word-finding problems.
4. Deficits may be more evident with either visual-spatial or verbal stimuli.
5. Child may remember remote past events better than more recent events.
6. May include confusion and disorientation to place and time.
7. Corresponding cognitive deficits may be present.

There has been some research supporting the cognitive rehabilitation of memory disorders, but the primary focus of intervention has been on environmental compensation (Pennington, 1991). Treatment strategies aimed at enhancing the encoding, storage, and retrieval of information have included use of mnemonic strategies, rehearsal and repetition strategies, and multimodal cuing, whereas environmental compensations focus on the use of daily planners, event calendars, and charts (Baron, 2000).

Because disorders of memory significantly affect learning as well as other cognitive processes, children with memory disorders are likely to qualify for special education services under the category of Specific Learning Disability. These children may also qualify for special education services as Other Health Impaired due to the multitude of medical conditions that can affect memory function.

Due to variations in etiology, age of onset, and resulting impairments of multiple memory functions, prognosis for improvement is not easily determined. There has been some evidence of memory gains using specific rehabilitation strategies, although it is unclear whether these improvements result in functional gains for individuals (Pennington, 1991). There is considerable need for further research examining the efficacy of specific intervention strategies on various memory functions of children and adolescents.

REFERENCES

Baron, I. S. (2000). Clinical implications and practical applications of child neuropsychological evaluations. In K. O. Yeates, M. D. Ris, & H. G. Taylor (Eds.), *Pediatric neuropsychology: Research, theory, and practice* (pp. 439–456). New York: Guilford.

Krener, P. (1996). Acquired disorders of memory in childhood. In J. H. Beitchman, & N. J. Cohen (Eds.), *Language, learning, and behavior disorders: Developmental, biological, and clinical perspectives* (pp. 338–366). New York: Cambridge University Press.

Mauer, R. G. (1992). Disorders of memory and learning. In S. J. Segalowitz & I. Rapin (Eds.), *Handbook of neuropsychology: Vol. 7. Child neuropsychology* (pp. 241–260). Amsterdam, Netherlands: Elsevier Science.

Pennington, B. F. (1991). *Diagnosing learning disorders: A neuropsychological framework.* New York: Guilford.

Lora Tuesday Heathfield
University of Utah

See also Amnesia

MENINGIOMA

A meningioma is a type of tumor that arises from the meninges, a membrane that covers the brain and spinal column. Meningiomas occur most often in the brain but can also occur along the spinal column. Meningiomas are rare in children; in fact, they account for only 2% of the 2,000 new cases of pediatric brain tumors diagnosed each year (Yoon et al., 1999); this is in contrast to the relatively high rate in adults. Meningiomas that develop during childhood also differ from those that occur in adults in that pediatric meningiomas are more common in males, tend to be larger and more cyst-like, occur more often in unusual sites, and are more aggressive and malignant. Further, these tumors have been strongly associated with neurofibromatosis. It is estimated that 13–41% of children with meningiomas have neurofibromatosis (Erdincler, Lena, Sarioglu, Kuday, & Choux, 1998).

The onset of symptoms is typically slow but progressive. Common signs of a meningioma include headaches, nausea, and vomiting, or symptoms associated with intracranial pressure (ICP). The tumors often occur along the optic pathway; therefore, these children will often show changes in their vision. Other common symptoms of meningiomas include drowsiness, seizures, hemiparesis (i.e., one-sided weakness) and paralysis.

Characteristics

1. Localized swelling and cranial enlargement may be noted as the first and only symptom found in younger children (Erdincler et al., 1998).
2. Other symptoms include drowsiness, seizures, hemiparesis, vision change, and signs of intracranial pressure (e.g., headaches and vomiting).
3. Rare in children, but in contrast to the form found in adults, tends to be more aggressive and malignant and occur more often in males and in more unusual sites.
4. Found often in children with neurofibromatosis.

Surgery is the treatment of choice for a meningioma because the majority of meningiomas can be entirely resected surgically. Studies have found rates of total resection to range from 54–86% (Erdincler et al., 1998). In cases in which the meningioma cannot be totally removed (e.g., cases in which the tumor is located near vital blood vessels and neural structures) irradiation, chemotherapy, or both are used. It is not clear, however, how effective irradiation and chemotherapy are in treating childhood meningiomas. Some prefer even partial surgery or repeated surgeries to irradiation of these types of tumors in order to increase survival and the quality of the child's life (Erdincler et al., 1998).

The prognosis for a child with a meningioma is much better if it is not accompanied by neurofibromatosis (NF). One study reports no deaths for children with meningiomas without NF, compared to 5 deaths out of 12 children with meningioma accompanied by NF. After surgery, the majority of children without NF remained neurologically intact after more than 5 years, although approximately one fourth of the children showed moderate disabilities. The disability rate as well as the death rate was higher for children with both meningioma and NF (Erdincler et al., 1998).

A serious condition such as a meningioma can cause tremendous stress on the entire family, and the nature of family life can have an abrupt change. The quality of life for children with a meningioma can change suddenly. They may experience lengthy hospitalizations, pain, and physical discomfort from the tumor itself and the treatments. These children are often forced to miss school, and upon return they have difficulty with catching up on missed assignments. The neurological changes that accompany the tumor and its treatment also make schoolwork more difficult for some children than previously experienced.

Children with a meningioma are likely to qualify for services under the category of Other Health Impaired if they need special education. Not all children with a meningioma require special education; however, many will need accommodations in the regular classroom setting. Neuro-ophthalmological evaluation and psychological testing may also help to ensure that the child is being adequately served in the classroom setting. Because emotional and social needs often arise for children with any type of brain tumor (especially one that is so rare and has a high malignancy rate) individual and family counseling is likely to be needed. It is important to keep in contact with the child's parents to communicate the school's support and willingness to help the child do as well as possible. Putting parents in contact with community resources and agencies is also recommended.

REFERENCES

Erdincler, P., Lena, G., Sarioglu, A. D., Kuday, C., & Choux, M. (1998). Intracranial meningiomas in children: Review of 29 cases. *Surgical Neurology, 49,* 136–141.

Yoon, H. K., Kim, S. S., Kim, I. O., Na, D. G., Byun, H. S., Shin, H. J. et al. (1999). MRI of primary meningeal tumors in children. *Pediatric Neuroradiology, 41,* 512–516.

Laura Richards
Elaine Clark
University of Utah

MENINGITIS

Meningitis is a bacterial or viral infection of the brain. This disease causes inflammation of the membranes that cover the brain and spinal cord, and it frequently causes damage to the brain. The infection is caused by bacteria or a virus, including *Enterobacter, Escherichia coli, Haemophilus influenzae* Type b, *Klebsiella, Neisseria meningitidis, Listeria monocytogenes,* and *Streptococcus pneumoniae* (Beers & Berkow, 1999).

Characteristics

1. Poor feeding or vomiting
2. Lethargy, listlessness, or apathy
3. Fever or hypothermia
4. Seizure or convulsions
5. Jaundice, paleness, or cyanosis (bluish discoloration of the lips)
6. Bulging fontanelle (enlarging head size)
7. Hypotonia (decreased muscle tone)
8. Shrill cry, paradoxic irritability (quiet when still and cries when held), or irritability
9. Respiratory distress or apnea

There are approximately 3,000 cases of meningitis per year in the United States (Centers for Disease Control and Prevention, 2000). Seventy percent of bacterial meningitis cases occur in children 2 years old or younger. In the first 23 months of life, 1 per 25,000 children contract *Neisseria meningitidis,* and *Streptococcus pneumoniae* causes 1 per 15,400 cases. Neonatal bacterial meningitis is present in 1 per 400 to 1 per 1,000 live births, 1 per 6,600 full-term births and 1 per 400 premature births. Mortality is high with neonates, and survivors frequently have long-term difficulties resulting from meningitis. Mortality is highest during the first year of life and in the elderly; it is lower during midlife. *Streptococcus pneumoniae* occurs in 1 per 90,900 individuals, and *Neisseria meningitidis* occurs in 1 per 166,600 individuals. *Listeria monocytogenes* occurs in 1 per 500,000 individuals and is especially common in newborns, elderly individuals, and those who are immunocompromised. *Haemophilus influenzae* Type b occurs in 1 per 500,000 unvaccinated individuals. Generally African Americans and male neonates are two groups that are at the greatest risk of contracting meningitis. The overall mortality rate for meningitis is approximately 20% of those who contract the disease (Carson-DeWitt, 1999).

Characteristics for infants and children

1. Nuchal rigidity (stiff neck), bulging fontanelle (enlarging head size), or opisthotonos (abnormal posturing with rigidity and severe arching of the back, with the head thrown backwards)
2. Convulsions or seizures
3. Photophobia (sensitivity to light)
4. Alterations of the sensorium or changes in consciousness (irritability, confusion, drowsiness, stupor, coma)

5. Anorexia, nausea, vomiting, or dehydration
6. Fever or hypothermia
7. Upper respiratory infection symptoms, headache, sore throat, or stiff neck

Several strains of meningitis are preventable with a vaccination. Although the use of a vaccination is not currently required, it is generally recommended for those who are traveling abroad to areas that have meningitis epidemics and is suggested for college freshmen due to the recent onset of meningitis epidemics at colleges.

Preferred treatment includes antimicrobial therapy within 30 min of emergency room presentation. The virus or bacteria should also be treated with common antibiotics. All individuals diagnosed with meningitis should be isolated during the first 24 hours of treatment to prevent the possible spreading of the disease (Beers & Berkow, 1999).

When returning to school after recovering from meningitis, children may have some adjustment difficulties. Physical and emotional difficulties can include problems sleeping, enuresis (inappropriate urination), fatigue, headaches, giddiness, balance difficulties, depression, and mood swings (Meningitis Foundation of America, 2000). Behavioral and educational difficulties can include attention-seeking behavior, temper tantrums, regressive behavior, not remembering recently learned skills, difficulty concentrating, clumsiness, and learning difficulties (these can be generalized or can occur in specific areas; Meningitis Foundation of America, 2000). Problems may also include deafness, tinnitus (ringing in the ears), joint soreness, vision problems, seizures, epilepsy, or brain impairment (Meningitis Foundation of America, 2000). There are continuing medical concerns with individuals who have recently had meningitis, such as blood poisoning, seizure disorders, or an obstruction of the normal flow of the cerebrospinal fluid. In some rare instances, the medical recovery process may also include scarring or painful medical procedures such as skin grafts and amputation.

Long-term deficits occur in approximately 30% of the children who have had meningitis. Long-term deficits can include nerve deafness, cortical blindness, hemiparesis, quadriparesis, muscular hypertonia, ataxia, complex seizure disorders, mental motor retardation, learning disabilities, obstructive hydrocephalus, and cerebral atrophy. Mild to severe hearing impairment occurs in 20–30% of children who have had meningitis. Hearing impairments can interfere with normal oral language development, and children should be assessed to determine whether speech-language therapy or instruction in sign language is required. Other children who have recovered from meningitis have motor difficulties, and these children should be evaluated and physical therapy, occupational therapy, or rehabilitation services may be recommended to help such children adjust and improve their functioning. With some children, behavioral difficulties can be a complication after meningitis. These changes can be permanent, and these children may require medication, counseling, or a behavior management plan. With the wide variety of special educational issues that can occur with an individual who has had meningitis, a full assessment (cognitive, neuropsychological, and behavioral-emotional) is recommended if the child presents with educational, emotional, social, or physical difficulties.

Prognosis varies with cause of meningitis, severity of illness, age, and general medical condition prior to illness. When the illness progresses very rapidly or the patient presents with marked neurological impairment, the mortality (50–90%) and morbidity rates are greatly increased (Lazoff, 2001). Detection and prevention of meningitis are ongoing areas of concern and exploration.

REFERENCES

Carson-DeWitt, R. S. (1999). In D. Olendorf, C. Jeryan, & K. Boyden (Eds.), *The gale encyclopedia of medicine* (pp. 1900–1903). Detroit, MI: Gale.

Centers for Disease Control and Prevention (2000, September 29). ACIP modifies recommendations for meningitis vaccination and the ABC's of safe and healthy child care. Retrieved from http://www.cdc.gov/od/oc/media/pressrel/r991021.htm

Beers, M. H., & Berkow, R. (Eds.). (1999). Acute bacterial meningitis, acute viral encephalitis and aseptic meningitis, subacute and chronic meningitis, & neonatal meningitis. In *The merck manual of diagnosis and therapy* (17th ed., pp. 1431–1440). Whitehouse Station, NJ: Merck.

Meningitis Foundation of America (2000, September 29). Statistics, recovery, treatment, prevention. Retrieved from http://www.musa.org

Elizabeth Ann Graf
Rik Carl D'Amato
University of Northern Colorado

MENINGOMYELOCELE

Meningomyelocele is a neural tube defect resulting in the herniation of the meninges and spinal cord through a vertebral defect. Neural tube defects (NTDs) refer to a group of malformations of the spinal cord, brain, and vertebrae, the most common being spina bifida, which is characterized by a split of a section of the vertebral arches. When spina bifida is associated with both a meningeal sac and a malformed spinal cord, the condition is called meningomyelocele (or myelomeningocele). Most meningomyeloceles are open, meaning that a portion of the spinal cord is visible at birth as an open sac overlying part of the vertebral column (Liptak, 1997; Pediatric Database [PEDBASE], 1994).

The incidence of meningomyelocele is approximately 60 in 100,000 births. Females are affected three to seven times as frequently as males. The incidence also increases with lower socioeconomic status and increasing maternal age. The age of onset for meningomyelocele is less than 26 days gestational age, when the neural tube has folded over to become the spinal cord and vertebral arches. If a portion of the neural tube does not completely close, an NTD results. Although the specific etiology is unknown, meningomyelocele may result from a biochemical abnormality of hyoluronate metabolism (related to development of connective tissue that holds cells together and acts as a protective agent). Genetic abnormalities involving a multifactorial inheritance pattern are also associated with the development of NTDs (PEDBASE, 1994). Other conditions that have been linked to NTDs include maternal exposure to the antiepileptic drugs valproic acid and carbamazepine and the acne medication isotretinoin, excessive maternal use of alcohol, maternal hyperthermia resulting from use of saunas during pregnancy, and maternal diabetes. Seventy-five percent of meningomyeloceles affect the lumbosacral region; the remaining 25% affect all other regions along the neuroaxis. The extent and degree of neurological deficit depends upon the location of the meningomyelocele (Liptak, 1997).

Characteristics

1. Paralysis and loss of sensation below the site of the lesion
2. Arnold-Chiari malformation of the brain, associated with hydrocephalus
3. Abnormalities of the corpus callosum
4. Decreased mobility as a function of the height of the lesion and associated muscle weakness
5. Cognitive impairments
6. Seizure disorders
7. Visual impairments, particularly strabismus
8. Musculoskeletal deformities, such as clubfoot and hip deformities
9. Spinal curvatures (scoliosis) and humps
10. Urinary, bowel, and sexual dysfunction

Treatment of meningomyelocele depends upon the site of the lesion and the associated symptoms. Prevention is the primary goal and is possible because of the strong link between NTDs and folic acid deficiency. Daily supplemental doses of folic acid can reduce the incidence of new NTD cases by at least 50% in the general population. Prenatal diagnosis at 16–20 weeks gestation is possible through maternal serum alpha-fetoprotein (AFP) screening followed by high-resolution ultrasound or amniocentesis (Pediatric Neurosurgery, 2001). Within the first few days following birth, the defect can be surgically closed to prevent infection and to protect exposed nerves. In addition, a shunt procedure is often required to prevent hydrocephalus (Fletcher, Dennis, & Northrup, 2000). Mobility aids, such as crutches, braces, walkers, and wheelchairs are often required. Treatment with antiepileptic medication will be necessary in the approximately 15% of individuals who develop a seizure disorder. Strabismus is present in about 20% of these children and often requires surgical correction. Musculoskeletal deformities and spinal curvatures may also necessitate orthopedic supports or corrective surgery. A catheterization program is often used to address urinary dysfunction. Surgical procedures are also available to address both urinary and bowel dysfunction. When precocious puberty results from hypothalamic involvement, leuprolide (Lupron), a synthetic sex hormone, is an effective treatment (Liptak, 1997).

For individuals and families affected by meningomyelocele, special education and psychosocial support are essential. A multidisciplinary approach involving the child's medical doctors, physical and occupational therapists, and regular and special education school personnel is needed to maximize profit from services. Referral to an early intervention program should occur by 6 months of age, and a full psychoeducational evaluation should be completed before school entry. Approximately 75% of children with meningomyelocele have intelligence within the low average range; the remaining 25% are mentally retarded. Affected children may have significant impairments of perception, attention, memory, processing speed, and eye-hand coordination, along with possible learning disabilities (Liptak, 1997). Specific special education eligibility categories will vary, but typically will include Other Health Impaired and Orthopedically Handicapped.

In the 1990s, about 85% of children with meningomyelocele survived to adulthood. Most deaths from this disorder occur before age 4. The adult population is quite heterogeneous with varying degrees of independence and mobility (Liptak, 1997; Pediatric Neurosurgery, 2001). Fletcher et al. (2000) recommend that large-scale studies be undertaken to begin to map out the relationship between outcomes and the numerous sources of variability in this group of children. Meningomyelocele is considered a nonprogressive condition; therefore, any deterioration in function should lead to a search for a treatable cause.

REFERENCES

Fletcher, J. M., Dennis, M., & Northrup, H. (2000). Hydrocephalus. In K. O. Yeates, M. D. Ris, & H. G. Taylor (Eds.), *Pediatric neuropsychology: Theory, research, and practice* (pp. 25–46). New York: Guilford Press.

Liptak, G. S. (1997). Neural tube defects. In M. L. Batshaw (Ed.), *Children with disabilities* (4th ed., pp. 529–552). Baltimore: Paul H. Brookes.

Pediatric Database. (1994). Myelomeningocele. Retrieved from http://www.icondata.com/health/pedbase/files/MYELOMEN.HTM

Pediatric neurosurgery. (February 12, 2001). Myelomeningocele. Retrieved from http://nyneurosurgery.org/child/myelomeningocele/spina/bifida.htm

Cynthia A. Plotts
Southwest Texas State University

MENKES SYNDROME (KINKY HAIR DISEASE)

Menkes syndrome is inherited as an X-linked recessive disorder. It primarily affects males. It is characterized by severe mental degeneration, kinked or twisted brittle hair, skeletal changes, and the body's inability to absorb copper.

Affected infants are often born prematurely. Hypothermia and excess bilirubin levels in the blood may occur, causing jaundice. Normal or slightly slowed developmental delay, loss of early developmental skills, and convulsions may occur. Brain abnormalities such as a blood clot at the base of the brain and/or rupture or thrombosis of arteries in the brain may occur. Spastic dementia and seizures may eventually arise. (National Organization for Rare Disorders, Inc. [NORD], 2000).

An Australian study of cases of Menkes syndrome conducted from 1966 to 1977 suggested an incidence of 1 in 35,500 live births. In 1980 this figure was modified to 1 in 90,000 live births, and other scientists put the number of cases between 1 in 50,000 to 1 in 100,000 (NORD, 2000).

Characteristics

1. Pudgy, rosy cheeks
2. Floppy baby (hypotonia)
3. Brittle, kinky hair
4. Seizures
5. Low body temperature
6. Bone spurs

(LYCOS Health with WebMD, 2000)

With Menkes syndrome there is usually a family history of the disease. Tests for the syndrome include X rays of the skull and skeleton that may show abnormal bone appearances, as well as tests for serum copper levels and serum ceruloplasmin levels.

Although there is no truly effective treatment for Menkes syndrome, copper histidinate appears to have been effective in increasing the life expectancy in some patients from 3 to 13 years of age (National Center for Biotechnology Information, 2000). Other treatments include copper acetate administered intravenously. Genetic counseling is strongly recommended for parents with a family history of Menkes syndrome, as most treatments are symptomatic and supportive.

Some research is being conducted on diseases that are similar to Menkes syndrome, and a similar syndrome has been identified in mice. It is hoped that work on these diseases will help to develop an effective treatment to fight Menkes syndrome in humans.

Special education services are available under the handicapping of Other Health Impairment or Mental Retardation. Because it is unlikely that the child might survive past the age of 4, support services may include physical therapy or contractures and speech-language consultation for feeding assistance along with consultations to the pediatric neurologist and urologist.

REFERENCES

LYCOS Health with WebMD. (2000, September 22). Retrieved from http://webmd.lycos.com/content/asset/adam_disease_menkes_syndrome

National Center for Biotechnology Information. (2000, September 26). Retrieved from http://www.ncbi.nlm.nih.gov/disease/menkes.html

National Organization for Rare Disorders, Inc. (2000, October 10). Menkes disease. Retrieved from http://www.rarediseases.org

Vedia Sherman
Austin Neurological Clinic

MENTAL RETARDATION, MILD TO MODERATE

Mental retardation is defined as a disorder in which the overall intellectual functioning of a person is well below average, he or she has a significantly impaired ability to cope with common life demands, and he or she lacks the daily living skills required of others within their same age group. Mental retardation is a particular state of functioning that begins in childhood and may interfere with one's ability to learn, communicate, provide self-care, live independently, have meaningful social interactions, and be aware of one's own safety (ARC, 2001). Mental retardation is neither a medical nor a mental disorder, but rather is a disorder defined by society that is based on a statistical concept and not on the qualities inherent in those who have the disorder (Barlow & Durand, 1999). The *Diagnostic and Statistical Manual of Mental Disorders–Fourth Edition* (American Psychiatric Association [APA], 1997) lists four degrees of severity of mental retardation: mild, moderate, severe, and profound.

Characteristics

1. Significantly subaverage intellectual functioning: mild, 35–40 to 70 needing intermittent supports; moderate, 35–40 to 50–55 needing limited supports
2. Concurrent deficits or impairments in adaptive functioning
3. Onset before age 18

An estimated 6.2 to 7.5 million individuals have mental retardation, based on figures from the 1990 U.S. Census (ARC, 2001). Approximately 85% of those with the disorder fall within the mild range; 10% fall within the moderate range; 3–4% fall within the severe range; and 1–2% fall within the profound range (APA, 1997).

Mental retardation affects more males than females, and a disproportionate number of minority children are identified as mildly retarded (Boyd-Wright, 2000). The three major known causes of mental retardation are Down syndrome, fetal alcohol syndrome, and fragile X, but in approximately one third of cases the cause is unknown.

Although mental retardation is a lifelong, irreversible disorder, treatment is related to the system of supports one will require in order to overcome limits in adaptive skills. The support required falls into four levels of intensity. Intermittent support refers to support on an as-needed basis and does not necessarily require continuous or daily support. Limited support occurs over a limited time span, such as during transition from school to work. Extensive support provides for assistance on a daily basis and may be required at home and at school or work. Pervasive support is constant support across all environments and may include life-sustaining measures (ARC, 2001).

Mental retardation is one of the 14 categories of disabilities outlined in the Individuals with Disabilities Education Act of 1997. As such, members of the special education team will likely need to assess, identify, and provide services for those students in the school with mental retardation. It is important for the team to keep in mind that the label should not prevent school personnel from viewing the child as an individual, just like any other child (Sattler, 2002). Although assessment may be difficult, the focus should be on the child's strengths and abilities, rather than on the child's limitations.

During the past 30 years, significant advances in research in the areas of newborn screening for phenylketonuria, congenital hypothyroidism, Rh disease, and other screenings have prevented many cases of mental retardation (ARC, 2001). Research is also being conducted on the development and function of the nervous system and on gene therapy to correct defective genes that may cause mental retardation (ARC, 2001).

REFERENCES

American Psychiatric Association. (1997). *Diagnostic and statistical manual of mental disorders* (4th ed.). Washington, DC: Author.

ARC. (2001). Introduction to mental retardation. Retrieved December 2001 from http://thearc.org/faqs/mrqa.html

Barlow, D., & Durand, V. M. (1999). *Abnormal psychology.* Pacific Grove, CA: Brooks/Cole.

Boyd-Wright, E. (2000). Mental retardation. In C. R. Reynolds and E. Fletcher-Janzen (Eds.), *Encyclopedia of special education* (2nd ed.). New York: Wiley.

Sattler, J. (2002). *Assessment of children: Behavior and clinical applications* (4th ed.). San Diego: Jerome M. Sattler.

Christine D. Cde Baca
University of Northern Colorado

MENTAL RETARDATION, SEVERE TO PROFOUND

Severe and profound mental retardation (SMR, PMR) are characterized by a below-average level of intellectual functioning that affects 3–4% of individuals diagnosed with mental retardation. According to the *Diagnostic and Statistical Manual of Mental Disorders–Fourth Edition, Text Revision* (*DSM-IV-TR*), (DSM-IV), an IQ range of below 20–25 and 20–40 respectively generally typifies individuals with SMR and PMR (American Psychiatric Association [APA], 2000). Corresponding severe impairments in adaptive functioning are also apparent in these individuals. Both the APA and the American Association on Mental Retardation (AAMR, 1992) stress the importance of impaired adaptive functioning in the classification process. The AAMR classifies mental retardation according to the level of support that the individual requires. APA's criteria for SMR is roughly equivalent to the AAMR's individual who requires "extensive" levels of support, and for PMR the individual who requires "pervasive" levels of support.

During early childhood years, individuals with SMR and PMR often fail to acquire normal speech and are slow to develop motor skills. They are usually diagnosed in infancy due to the significant impairment in early development (Zeanah, 2000). During school-age years individuals with SMR and PMR may learn to talk and can be trained in elementary self-care skills. Communicative abilities, however, remain limited throughout their lives.

Assessment of mental retardation is similar across most classification systems (e.g., *DSM-IV-TR*). A two-pronged approach assessing IQ and adaptive behavior is typically used (Zeanah, 2000). For assessing IQ, a variety of standardized measures may be used. Selecting the appropriate instrument depends, however, on the estimate level of functioning, as well as the presence of physical and sensory deficits and cultural background. For children functioning at lower levels of mental retardation (i.e., severe to profound), clinicians are often forced to use instruments that may be less sound psychometrically (e.g., tests with poorer reliability and more limited normative data). For this reason, it is critical that the child be assessed with a number of measures and tasks and be observed in a variety of settings. Informants familiar with the child, including biological parents and childcare workers (e.g., social workers), should be interviewed to obtain information regarding development and functional abilities. In most cases, a multidisciplinary team approach needs to be taken to ensure adequate assessment (e.g., teams consisting of a special education teacher who works with severe intellectual disabilities, a school psychologist, a speech and language pathologist, and an administrator).

There is no specific etiology for mental retardation. Genetic causes, however, make up the largest portion of severe cases (Murphy, Boyle, Schendel, Decoufle, Yeargin-Allsop, 1998). More than 500 genetic disorders, in fact, have been linked to mental retardation. Prenatal events have been found to be more prevalent in SMR than other types of mental retardation; in fact, researchers estimate the rate to be as high as 25–55% (Zeanah, 2000). Some of the more common genetic and prenatal etiologies include chromosomal abnormalities, brain malformation, and maternal substance abuse (e.g., fetal alcohol syndrome). Another 7–10% of individuals with SMR and PMR are believed to have a postnatal etiology, including intractable seizure disorders, central nervous system infections (e.g., encephalitis), lead and chemical exposure, malnutrition, and traumatic brain injury (TBI). As a general rule, however, the more severe the retardation, the more likely is a genetic cause.

Characteristics

1. IQ, as measured by a standardized test, is in the range of below 20 (PMR) and 20–40 (SMR)
2. Significant comorbid disabilities, including self-care
3. Poor motor development and physical coordination
4. Limited language ability and failure to acquire expected milestones at expected ages
5. Need for close or constant monitoring and supervision, often provided in residential placements
6. Intellectual and adaptive deficits apparent before the age of 18

Most children with SMR are served in special education programs under the Individuals with Disabilities Education Act's classification of Intellectual Disabilities, whereas individuals with PMR may need residential placement. Educational services can begin as early as birth and continue until young adulthood. Home-based services are often provided until the child is of school age. These include speech and language services and physical therapy. School services are typically provided in self-contained classrooms with inclusion in certain nonacademic regular education activities. It is not uncommon for these children to receive assistance from a number of related services personnel. Children with cerebral palsy, for example, often require the services of the speech and language pathologist as well as the occupational and physical therapist. School nurses may also be necessary to attend to the medical needs of children with critical medical needs. Although direct services by the school psychologist and school counselor may be less frequent, consultations with teachers and parents regarding behavior management and transition issues (e.g., post–high school) are often needed. Guidance personnel may also be in the best position to provide support to the family and information about community agencies and resources (e.g., respite care, financial assistance, and long-term life planning).

Interventions with the child tend to be intensive and behavioral. Approximately 20–35% of individuals with SMR have significant behavior problems or psychiatric diagnoses (Mash & Barkley, 1998). For children in residential settings the rate may be as high as 60%. There are some behavior problems that do appear to be specific to mental retardation, including self-injurious behaviors such as hair pulling, hitting, biting, and head banging. Medication is often used to control behaviors (e.g., mood stabilizers and anticonvulsants). Single drugs, however, are often ineffective, and a polydrug approach is often needed. Unfortunately, this has its own unwanted side effects, including sedation and reduced singular drug potency.

The prognosis for individuals with SMR and PMR is poor. Not only is the life span shortened by the various concomitant medical problems (e.g., coronary disease and respiratory conditions), but quality of life is also limited by these and other conditions (e.g., sensory handicaps that limit exposure to the environment).

REFERENCES

American Association on Mental Retardation. (1992). *Definition, classification, and system of supports* (9th ed.) Washington, DC: Author.

American Psychiatric Association. (2000). *Diagnostic and statistical manual of mental disorders* (4th ed., Text Revision). Washington, DC: Author.

Mash, E. J., & Barkley, R. A. (1998). Treatment of childhood disorders (2nd ed.). New York: Guilford Press.

Murphy, C. C., Boyle, C., Schendel, D., Decoufle, P., & Yeargin-Allsop, M. (1998). Epidemiology of mental retardation in children. *Mental Retardation and Developmental Disabilities Research Reviews, 4,* 6–13.

Zeanah, C. H. (2000). *The handbook of infant mental health* (2nd ed.). New York: Guilford Press.

Rex Gonzales
Elaine Clark
University of Utah

MERRF SYNDROME, MYOCLONUS EPILEPSY WITH RAGGED RED FIBERS

MERRF syndrome belongs to a group of neuromuscular disorders called mitochondrial myopathies. These disorders stem from a mitochondrial dysfunction that cause damage to muscles and nerve cells in the brain by impairing energy metabolism. Characteristic of MERRF syndrome are mitochondrial function and abnormal mitochondrial morphology resulting in ragged red fibers that can be seen in the muscle tissue after Gomori staining.

MERRF syndrome is caused by a maternally inherited mitochondrial DNA mutation with a base substitution at Nucleotide 8344 (Shoffner et al., 1990). The age of onset of MERRF syndrome varies, and it affects equal numbers of males and females (National Organization for Rare Disorders [NORD], 2000).

Characteristics

1. Myoclonic seizures affecting the whole body or just the limbs
2. Ataxia
3. Progressive muscular weakness with exercise intolerance occurring by the patients 20s
4. Lactic acidosis sometimes present
5. Difficulty speaking
6. Optic atrophy
7. Short stature
8. Hearing loss
9. Dementia
10. Nystagmus
11. Lipomas
12. Progressive mental deterioration
13. Nausea, headache, and breathlessness (sometimes)

There is no cure or specific treatment for MERRF syndrome or any of the mitochondrial myopathies. Treatment regimens focus on symptom reduction, although symptom presentation varies greatly with each patient. Symptoms of MERRF syndrome usually begin to emerge in childhood or early adulthood. The disorders range in severity from progressive weakness to death (National Institute of Neurological Disorders and Stroke [NINDS], 2000). MERRF is a heterogeneous disorder, and many systems of the body can be affected, explaining why symptom presentation and severity vary. The heterogeneity of MERRF syndrome is due to the distribution of the mutant mitochondria throughout the body and the different sensitivities of various affected tissues and cells to the consequences of mitochondrial dysfunction (Howell, 1999). Simply stated, tissues have different thresholds for tolerable amounts of defective mitochondria above which symptoms will emerge. Standard treatments for seizures are used, and physical therapy can address muscular weakness and exercise intolerance. Coenzyme Q, caritine, and other vitamin therapies have been found to be effective in alleviating symptoms in some patients with mitochondrial myopathies (NINDS, 2000).

Children with MERRF syndrome may be eligible for services under the Individuals with Disabilities Education Act as having multiple disabilities or as Other Health Impairment. Due to the progressive mental deterioration, these children need to have periodic psychoeducational testing to determine the need for the development of or modification to the child's individual educational plan. Physical therapy is necessary to address the muscle weakness characteristic in MERRF syndrome. In the severe cases of MERRF syndrome, communication between parents, school, and medical professionals is important because of the rapid deterioration that is possible in MERRF syndrome.

Despite the heterogeneity of MERRF syndrome, it has been documented that when the onset occurs in childhood, the course of the disease is markedly more rapid and can result in death within a few years. In general, the earlier the age of onset of MERRF syndrome, the greater is the severity of symptom presentation (Sanger & Jain, 1996). A long-term evaluation of patients and their families with mitochondrial DNA mutations has begun, and future results should yield information regarding treatment, prognosis, and pathophysiology of MERRF syndrome (Clinical Research Mitochondrial Disorders at Columbia University, 2000).

REFERENCES

Clinical Research Mitochondrial Disorders at Columbia University. (2000, August 25). Retrieved from http://www.hnrc.cpmc.Columbia.edu/melas-1.html

Howell, N. (1999). Human mitochondrial diseases: Answering questions and questioning answers. In K. W. Jeon (Ed.), *International review of cytology: Vol. 186. A survey of cell biology* (pp. 49–116). San Diego, CA: Academic Press.

National Institute of Neurological Disorders and Stroke. (2000, June 27). NINDS mitochondrial myopathies information page. Retrieved from http://www.ninds.nih.gov/health_and_medical/disorders/mitochon_doc.htm

National Organization for Rare Disorders. (2000, November). Rare Disease Database: MERRF syndrome. Retrieved from http://www.rarediseases.org

Sanger, T. D., & Jain, K. D. (1996). MERRF syndrome with overwhelming lactic acidosis. *Pediatric Neurology, 14*(1), 57–61.

Shoffner, J. M, Lott, M. T., Lezza, A. M. S., Seibal, P., Ballinger, S. W., & Wallace, D. C. (1990). Myoclonic epilepsy and ragged-red fiber disease (MERRF) is associated with a mitochondrial DAN $tRNA^{Lys}$ mutation. *Cell, 61,* 931–937.

Kellie Higgins
University of Texas at Austin

METAPHYSEAL DYSPLASIA, JANSEN TYPE

Jansen type metaphyseal dysplasia (JTMD) is an extremely rare, heritable disorder of bone and cartilage formation. Its distinguishing characteristics include severely short stature; short limbs; and wide, irregularly shaped ends (metaphyses) of the long bones.

JTMD is exceedingly uncommon. Only 14 case reports have appeared in the medical literature. It is transmitted in an autosomal dominant manner. Fresh genetic mutations account for the majority of affected individuals.

Characteristics

1. Severe growth retardation that is postnatal in onset; average adult height only about 49 inches; short arms and legs
2. Small face, prominent eyes, slightly enlarged forehead and nose, small jaw
3. Irregular cysts in the ends of long bones (metaphyseal dysplasia) caused by faulty bone formation; pelvic bones may be similarly affected; bowing of the legs is common
4. Flexion deformations of joints, particularly the hip and knee; these abnormalities cause a characteristic squatting stance and a peculiar, duck-like, "waddling" gait
5. Short, clubbed fingers; thickened bone at the base of the skull; occasional deafness

Unfortunately, very few therapeutic modalities are available for patients with JTMD. Hearing loss, which is secondary to dense bone formation at the base of the skull, may or may not respond to treatment (hearing aids, etc.).

There is no research to indicate the need for special education services as a result of cognitive deficits. However, children with JTMD will require emotional support to help with self-esteem problems and appropriate peer interaction. Because of their short stature, appropriate-sized furniture (desks and chairs) will be necessary.

The prognosis for children with JTMD is not favorable. Although the skeletal and joint pathology may not be apparent at birth, it is progressive and, in adult patients, rather severe. In addition, the dysmorphic features of JTMD become more pronounced with age and can create major psychosocial problems for these individuals and their families.

For more information and parent support, contact Little People of America, Inc., PO Box 745, Lubbock, TX 79408; (888) 572-2001; e-mail: Ipadatabasse@juno.com; http://www.Ipaonline.org.

REFERENCES

Jones, K. (1997). *Smith's recognizable patterns of human malformations* (5th ed.). Philadelphia: W. B. Saunders.

National Organization for Rare Disorders, Inc. (1998). Jansen type metaphyseal chondrodysplasia. Retrieved from http://stepstn.com/cgi-win/nord.exe?proc=GetDocument&rectype=0&recnum=894

Barry H. Davison
Ennis, Texas

Joan W. Mayfield
Baylor Pediatric Specialty Services
Dallas, Texas

METAPHYSEAL DYSPLASIA, MCKUSICK TYPE

Metaphyseal dysplasia, McKusick type (MDMT), is an uncommon genetic disorder of bone and cartilage formation (osteochondrodysplasia). Associated findings include short stature, abnormalities of hair, and a variety of immunologic and hematologic (blood cell) defects. MDMT is heritable, and its etiology has been traced to a defective gene on Chromosome 9.

MDMT is considered rare. However, its incidence is most prevalent in the Amish, perhaps secondary to inbreeding. There is also a higher occurrence than usual of the syndrome in individuals of Finnish descent. The pattern of heredity is autosomal recessive.

Characteristics

1. Short limbs and short stature are apparent in 75% of newborns. Ninety-eight percent of affected children have these findings by age 1. Final adult height ranges from 40.5 to 58.2 inches.
2. Hair is fine, light, and sparse and breaks easily. Eyelash, eyebrow, and body hair are also deficient.
3. Short limbs; mildly bowed legs; flat feet; short hands, fingernails, and toenails; loose joints of the hands and

feet; scoliosis (lateral curvature of the spine); and lordosis (sway back) are common.

4. The ends of long bones about the knee and ankle are flared. These defects are best seen on X rays.
5. Diminished cellular immune response, low lymphocyte count (a type of white blood cell), low neutrophil count (another type of white blood cell), and anemia also characterize the disorder.
6. Individuals are vulnerable to chickenpox and live virus vaccines, secondary to immune deficiency.
7. Intestinal pathology includes malabsorption (inability to absorb digested food), Hirschsprung disease (deficient development of nerve tissue in the colon), and celiac disease (malabsorption and chronic diarrhea caused by an intolerance to gluten, a protein found in several grains).
8. The incidence of malignancy in adults is 6–10%. Tumors occur most commonly in the skin and lymphatic system.

Scant material is available concerning therapy for MDMT. Skeletal changes of the syndrome are not treatable. Intestinal malabsorption tends to improve with age. Celiac disease responds to the avoidance of wheat, rye, and barley products. Hirschsprung disease necessitates removal of the affected portions of the large intestine. Congenital anemia can be fatal but often resolves without treatment. Patients with immunodeficiency and impaired T-cell function should not receive live virus vaccines (MMR and Varivax). Their response to inactivated immunizations (DaPT, IPV, Hib and hepatitis B) may be insufficient to provide full protection from these infectious illnesses. Administration of varicella zoster immune globulin, which contains high titers of antibodies against the chickenpox (varicella) virus, should be considered for all children with MDMT who have had recent exposure to varicella. Finally, genetic counseling should be provided to all families who have a child with this disorder.

A child with MDMT may require modifications in the physical environment due to physical limitations. Because of the physical deformities, providing a positive environment that builds good self-image and education for the child's classmates will facilitate peer relationships. There is no research to indicate cognitive dysfunction or the need for academic support services.

The prognosis for this syndrome is guarded. Although the gastrointestinal and hematologic problems of MDMT usually abate with age, affected individuals remain vulnerable to infection, and particularly varicella, which may be life threatening. In addition, once these patients become adults, their risk of developing malignant disease is much greater than that of the general population.

For more information and support, contact Little People of America, Inc., PO Box 745, Lubbock, TX 79408; (888) 572-2001; e-mail: 1padatabase@juno.com.

REFERENCES

Horton, W. A., & Hecht, J. T. (2000). Disorders for which defects are unknown. In R. E. Behrman, R. M. Kleigman, & H. B. Jenson (Eds.), *Nelson textbook of pediatrics* (16th ed., pp. 1302–1305). Philadelphia: W. B. Saunders.

Jones, K. (1997). *Smith's recognizable patterns of human malformation* (5th ed.). Philadelphia: W. B. Saunders.

National Organization for Rare Disorders, Inc. (1999). McKusick type metaphyseal chondrodysplasia. Retrieved from http://www.stepstn.com/cgi-win/nord.exe?proc=GetDocument&rectype=0&recnum=636

Barry H. Davison
Ennis, Texas

Joan W. Mayfield
Baylor Pediatric Specialty Services
Dallas, Texas

MICROCEPHALY

Microcephaly refers to a smaller than normal head circumference with the presumption that the smaller size reflects a smaller-sized brain (Cowie, 1987; Dorman, 1991). Rather than a disorder or disease entity, microcephaly is viewed as a sign of cerebral malformation. Microcephaly does not have a single cause, but rather can result from a number of different factors. Microcephaly can occur as a result of genetics, both in autosomal recessive form and in autosomal dominant form. The autosomal recessive form is more likely to occur if parents are cousins. A third form of genetic transmission of microcephaly is X-linked: The mother is a carrier for the disorder, but only sons are affected. Other genetic causes of microcephaly are directly related to other disorders that result from chromosomal defects (e.g., Trisomy 21). Syndromes that include microcephaly as a marker are continuously being identified (e.g., Martinez-Frias, Martin, Pardo, Fernandez de las Heras, & Frias, 1995; Partington & Anderson, 1994).

Microcephaly can result from nongenetic causes as well. Prenatal infections (e.g., rubella, cytomegalovirus, toxoplasmosis), maternal illness (e.g., phenylketonuria, active genital herpes), and maternal alcohol or substance abuse are associated with the occurrence of microcephaly in infants. Additional causes of microcephaly include fetal stroke, anoxia at birth, and meningitis in early infancy. Because microcephaly is associated with autosomal dominant and recessive disorders and various other disorders, incidence is not known. Available research does not address differences in incidence of microcephaly by gender or ethnicity.

Microcephaly can occur by itself or in conjunction with other disorders; the delays associated with microcephaly can range from mild to severe. Effects of microcephaly vary from individual to individual and become known only as the child matures. Severely affected children are more likely to have cerebral palsy, epilepsy, visual impairment, mental retardation, or other problems. In other cases, there may be only minor intellectual impairment (Cowie, 1987; Dorman, 1991).

Characteristics

1. Circumference of head is less than that of 97–99% of the population
2. Large face relative to head
3. Loose scalp
4. Receding forehead
5. Overall physical growth may be below average as well

There is no treatment for the microcephaly; treatment is directed to the deficit areas identified for the individual child. In schools, children with microcephaly may need only support services or more intensive and extensive services due to mental retardation. A comprehensive evaluation to identify the needs and most appropriate services for each child affected is necessary due to the variability of disorders or conditions that result in microcephaly. The range of symptoms will be affected by any associated syndromes that the individual child may have as well. Prognosis is generally poor: A relatively shorter life expectancy is associated with microcephaly (Dorman, 1991). Investigation of the causative factor of the microcephaly is important in order to assess the need for genetic counseling with other family members.

REFERENCES

Cowie, V. (1987). Microcephaly: A review of genetic implications in the causation. *Journal of Mental Deficiency Research, 31,* 229–233.

Dorman, C. (1991). Microcephaly and intelligence. *Developmental Medicine and Child Neurology, 33,* 267–269.

Martinez-Frias, M. L., Martin, M., Pardo, M., Fernandez de las Heras, F., & Frias, J. L. (1995). *American Journal of Medical Genetics, 55*(2), 213–216.

Partington, M., & Anderson, D. (1994). Mild growth retardation and developmental delay, microcephaly, and distinctive facial appearance. *American Journal of Medical Genetics, 49*(2), 247–250.

Cynthia A. Riccio
Texas A&M University

MICROCEPHALY, GENETIC

Microcephaly is an anomaly of the central nervous system where head circumference is significantly (3 standard deviations) smaller than average given the age and gender of the infant or child (National Institute of Neurological Disorders and Stroke [NINDS], 2000). This reduced head size usually occurs as a result of diminished brain mass (micrencephaly) but can also reflect poor skull growth (Pediatric Database, 1994).

Microcephaly can arise from genetic and nongenetic causes. Conditions associated with primary or genetic microcephaly include the chromosomal disorders of Trisomy 21, 18, and 13 and cri du chat syndrome. Also associated with genetic microcephaly are those disorders (e.g., Dubowitz syndrome and Cornelia De Lange syndrome) that are attributed to the presence of an autosomal recessive gene. Microcephaly is also often present in syndromes such as Rubinstein-Taybi syndrome in which there are multiple congenital anomalies.

Because microcephaly is heterogeneous in causation, prevalence rates vary significantly and are related to the prevalence rate of the specific syndrome or causative agent. For example, the prevalence rate of Trisomy 21 is reported to be 1:800 (National Institute of Child Health and Human Development, 2000), whereas the prevalence rate for cri du chat syndrome is estimated to be 1:50,000 (Pediatric Database, 1994).

Characteristics

1. A small, conical head is the predominant feature of microcephaly, although some infants are born with normal head size that subsequently fails to keep pace with facial development. These children have small heads, large faces with receding foreheads, and loose wrinkled scalps (Disability Dictionary, 2000). Individuals with microcephaly are also often small in stature and are underweight.
2. Intellectual deficit and microcephaly co-occur very frequently with smaller head size related to more severe cognitive impairment. However, not all microcephalic individuals have reduced intellectual functioning. For example, individuals with Bloom syndrome often have normal intelligence, as do children whose reduced head size is due to a malabsorption disease (Neonatology on the Web, 1998). Milder decreases in head size have been associated with learning disabilities and language disorders (Baroff & Olley, 1999).
3. Motor difficulties are also often present, although the degree of impairment can vary markedly from mild clumsiness to spastic quadriplegia (Disability Dictionary, 2000).

There is no treatment designed specifically for microcephaly, but a complete medical evaluation that may include genetic testing is recommended to determine causation. Treatment efforts are usually supportive and focus on associated symptomatology related to specific syndromes or causative agents.

The majority of children with microcephaly require special education accommodations and services. However, as the degree of intellectual and physical impairment associated with microcephaly varies, a comprehensive evaluation, including a detailed medical and development history, is very important to provide educational services adequately. Individuals who evidence severe cognitive impairment can receive services under the special education category of mental deficiency. Special education accommodations also need to be provided to individuals who present with learning difficulties. Both groups of individuals may also require adjunctive services such as speech and physical therapy.

In the vast majority of cases of microcephaly, prognosis for normal brain functioning is poor. Life expectancy is often low as well, with overall prognosis depending on associated difficulties (Disability Dictionary, 2000). The National Institute of Neurological Disorders and Stroke supports research that examines brain development. This research has a long-term goal that includes the prevention and treatment of microcephaly (NINDS, 2000). Included on the NINDS microcephaly information Web page is a list of support organizations.

REFERENCES

Baroff, G. S., & Olley, J. G. (1999). *Mental retardation: Nature, cause, and management* (3rd ed.). Philadelphia: Brunner/Mazel.

Disability Dictionary. (2000, July). Microcephaly. Retrieved from http://www.geocities.com/dol911

National Institute of Neurological Disorders and Stroke. (2000, July). Microcephaly information page. Retrieved from http://www.ninds.nih.gov/health_and_medical/disorders/microcephaly.htm

National Institute of Child Health and Human Development. (2000, June). Facts about Down syndrome. Retrieved from http://www.nicnd.nih.gov/publications/pubs/downsyndrome.down.htm

Neonatalogy on the Web. (1998). Division of Neonatology, Cedars-Sinai Medical Center. Microcephaly. Retrieved from http://www.neonatology.org/syllabus/microcephaly.html

Pediatric Database. (1994). Microcephaly. Retrieved from http://www.icondata.com/health/pedbase/files/microcep.htm

Louise O'Donnell
University of Texas Health Science Center–San Antonio

MIKULICZ DISEASE

Mikulicz disease is one of the autoimmune disorders with Sjögren syndrome and systemic lupus erythematosis. With Mikulicz disease there is chronic bilateral enlargement of glands in the neck area (e.g., lacrimal, parotid, and salivary glands) similar to what might be expected with the mumps. Other glands in the area of face and neck may be involved as well. Although originally believed to be relatively benign, it is associated with decreased or absent production of tears (lacrimation) and dryness of the mouth (xerostomia). Mikulicz disease may be accompanied by chronic lymphyocytic infection (National Organization of Rare Diseases, Inc. [NORD], 1994).

Characteristics

1. Recurring fevers
2. Swollen eyes
3. Diminished production of tears
4. Inflammation of parts of the eyes
5. Extreme dryness of the mouth
6. Difficulty swallowing

The cause of Mikulicz disease is unknown, but it is believed to be associated with the autoimmune system. Males and females are equally likely to be affected. However, Mikulicz disease does not occur in isolation. It always occurs in association with another disorder such as tuberculosis, leukemia, syphilis, Hodgkin's disease, lymphosarcoma, Sjögren syndrome, or lupus. Mikulicz disease differs from Sjögren syndrome in that lacrimal gland acinar cells maintain their function (Tsubota, Fujita, Tsuzaka, & Takeuchi, 2000). In addition, there were few changes to the ocular surface associated with Mikulicz disease.

Swelling of the glands may remit and recur, or it may remain for a long period of time. Symptom presentation will follow a similar pattern. Treatment is dependent on the severity and presentation of the disease. Symptoms are addressed as they present. For the lack of tearing, artificial tears can be used to keep the eyes from drying out. Artificial saliva can be used to relieve the dry mouth and facilitate swallowing. Because of the glandular dysfunction, individuals affected may develop dental problems and regular dental checkups are needed for prevention. A soft diet may be recommended depending on the extent of pain and difficulty associated with chewing and swallowing (NORD, 1994).

Because Mikulicz disease never occurs in isolation, additional interventions will be needed to address the cooccurring disorder. These will vary based on the cooccurring disorder and the severity of that disorder. Supportive counseling to deal with health issues may be appropriate.

REFERENCES

National Organization of Rare Disorders, Inc. (1994). Mikulicz syndrome (#205). Retrieved May 26, 2001, from http://www.rarediseases.org

Tsubota, K., Fujita, H., Tsuzaka, K., & Takeuchi, T. (2000). Mikulicz's disease and Sjögren's syndrome. *Investigations in Ophthalmology and Visual Science, 41,* 1666–1673.

Cynthia A. Riccio
Texas A&M University

MILLER-DIEKER SYNDROME

Miller-Dieker syndrome (MDS) is a congenital, genetic disorder of brain development. Associated anomalies involve the face, genitalia, extremities, heart, and kidney.

Ninety percent of children with MDS demonstrate a deletion (absence) of genetic material on Chromosome 17. This finding can be caused by subtle chromosomal abnormalities in the parents (carriers), but some cases appear to be spontaneous mutations. The literature suggests that the defect may be difficult to detect on chromosome analysis, but the distinction between an inherited or mutational etiology in the individual patient is extremely important when counseling families about the risk of recurrence. No data are available on the frequency of MDS. It is considered rare.

Characteristics

1. Lissencephaly, meaning "smooth brain," refers to the fact that the convolutions normally present on the brain's surface are completely absent. Unless a postmortem exam is done, this diagnosis is made by computerized tomography or magnetic resonance imaging, which also show enlarged ventricles.
2. Severe mental deficiency, initial hypotonia (decreased muscle tone), spasticity later, seizures, and growth failure.
3. Microcephaly (small head), prominent forehead, vertical furrows in the middle of the forehead (especially with crying), small nose with upturned nostrils, protruding upper lip, small jaw, and low-set ears.
4. Undescended testicle, incurving of the little finger, congenital heart defects, and cystic kidney malformations.

Very little in the way of therapy is available for infants with MDS. Anticonvulsants may help with seizure control. Gastrostomy (an opening into the stomach through the abdominal wall) may be necessary for feeding because of inadequate oral intake, repeated aspiration (the passage of food and oral secretions into the lung), and malnutrition. Genetic counseling, including advice about prenatal diagnosis, should be offered to affected families.

Because of the severe mental deficiency and motor development, children with MDS require special education support. However, the number of children who survive into school age is small; therefore, there is no specific research to document specific educational strategies or behavioral problems.

The prognosis for MDS is very poor. Motor development rarely progresses beyond the 2–4 month level. Most patients die within the first two years. One child with the disorder survived to age 9.

REFERENCES

Haslam, R. H. A. (2000). Congenital anomalies of the central nervous system. In R. E. Behrman, R. M. Kleigman, & H. B. Jenson (Eds.), *Nelson textbook of pediatrics* (16th ed., p. 1087). Philadelphia: W. B. Saunders.

Jones, K. (1997). *Smith's recognizable patterns of human malformation* (5th ed.). Philadelphia: W. B. Saunders.

Barry H. Davison
Ennis, Texas

Joan W. Mayfield
Baylor Pediatric Specialty Services
Dallas, Texas

MIXED CONNECTIVE TISSUE DISORDER

Mixed connective tissue disorder (MCTD) is one of many rheumatic diseases. Although it shares some similarities with lupus erythematosus and systemic sclerosis, MCTD differs in regard to the autoimmune factors (IgG autoantibodies) implicated (Maddison, 2000). Age of onset ranges from 5 to 80 years. Juvenile MCTD is rare; early identification and treatment can improve the prognosis. Based on current findings, 80% of those affected with MCTD are female (Robinson, 1999). Recent research suggests a particular genetic susceptibility for Mexicans as well as for African Americans (Weckmann et al., 1999).

Individuals affected with MCTD exhibit features similar to systemic lupus erythematosus (SLE) or polymyositis but do not meet the diagnostic criteria for either of these disorders. Characteristics associated with MCTD include inflammation of the tissues, loss of joint function or stiffness, intermittent bilateral interference in the blood flow to the fingers or toes (Raynaud's phenomenon), insufficient movement of the esophagus, and pulmonary hypertension. Although changes in kidneys have been found, renal disease is not commonly associated with MCTD. Arthralgias and swelling of the hands may be present. In some cases, individuals may present with rashes similar to those found with SLE. The extent to which these symptoms occur is dependent on the connective tissue involved. In severe cases, MCTD can result in multiple organ damage due to the constriction of blood vessels and impaired blood flow associated with the inflammation. Diagnosis may be facilitated by various laboratory tests; however, only about 50% of individuals with MCTD will be positive for rheumatoid factor (Robinson, 1999). Tests for antinuclear antibodies (ANA) are considered the most helpful in making the diagnosis.

Characteristics

1. Inflammation
2. Swelling of hands and fingers
3. Raynaud's phenomenon
4. Esophageal dysfunction
5. Pulmonary hypertension

The course and prognosis for MCTS is variable. Generally, the prognosis is good with treatment. Treatment may include the use of low-dose immunosuppressants and nonsteroid anti-inflammatory drugs or NSAIDs (Scheja, Elborgh, & Wildt, 1999). Corticosteroid treatment has been successful as well (Robinson, 1999). For some individuals, the prognosis is not as good. Remission is likely in up to 27% of those affected (Michels, 1999), and complications can occur. Complications may include renal involvement, loss of joint junction, pulmonary dysfunction, and cardiovascular problems; severity is variable. Cognitive impairment is rare but if present is moderate to severe. For children with MCTD, the need for special education services under Other Health Impairment need to be determined based on the individual needs of the child.

REFERENCES

Maddison, P. J. (2000). Mixed connective tissue disease: Overlap syndromes. *Best Practice and Research in Clinical Rheumatology, 14,* 111–124.

Michels, H. (1999). Course of mixed connective tissue disease in children. *Annals of Medicine, 29,* 359–364.

Robinson, D. R. (1999). Systemic lupus erythematosus. *Scientific American, 3*(15), 1–11.

Scheja, A., Elborgh, R., & Wildt, M. (1999). Decreased capillary density in juvenile dermatomyositis and in mixed connective tissue disease. *Journal of Rheumatology, 26,* 1377–1381.

Weckmann, A. L., Granados, J., Cardiel, M. H., Adnrade, F., Vargas-Alarcon, G., Alcocer-Varela, J., & Alarcon-Segovia, D. (1999). Immunogenetics of mixed connective tissue disease in a Mexican Mestizo population. *Clinical and Experimental Rheumatology, 17,* 91–94.

Cynthia A. Riccio
Texas A&M University

MOEBIUS SYNDROME

Moebius syndrome is characterized by paralysis of the facial muscles (diplegia), resulting in an inability to produce facial expressions corresponding to common emotions. This paralysis leaves the child with an unchanging, mask-like face. Cranial nerves VI and VII specifically are affected; involvement of these nerves is a primary criterion for diagnosis of Moebius syndrome. In addition to facial diplegia, characteristics include tongue hypogenesis, high nasal bridge, inability to close eyelids, ear deformities, and limb anomalies including clubfoot (Meyerson & Foushee, 1978).

Prevalence has not been determined, but the condition is thought to be rare. Differential prevalence rates by gender and ethnicity are unknown. Although most cases of Moebius syndrome are sporadic, a genetic link has been hypothesized (Calder, Keane, Cole, Campbell, & Young, 2000).

Characteristics

1. Congenital onset
2. Feeding problems and impaired ability to suck
3. Turning of head to follow moving objects due to inability to follow objects with the eyes
4. Lack of facial expression, including inability to smile
5. Speech impairment due to tongue hypogenesis

The majority of people with Moebius syndrome appear to have average or above-average intelligence. Mental retardation has been noted in about 10% of cases; however, children may be mislabeled as mentally retarded due to their speech delays (Meyerson & Foushee, 1978). Feeding problems in infancy (due to paralysis of the facial muscles and limited movement of the tongue) may lead to poor growth, failure to thrive, and small stature. Limb anomalies may limit mobility, depending on the extent of the deformity.

In infancy, the inability to express emotions facially may make it difficult for the infant to form attachments with parents; attachment may be enhanced, however, as the child begins to speak (Szajnberg, 1994). Given their inability to express themselves facially, children with Moebius syndrome also may have difficulties with social interaction. In fact, they may even grow to avoid social interactions and communication because their lack of facial expression is often misinterpreted as lack of feeling or emotion (Meyerson & Foushee, 1978). Indeed, it is difficult to discern how others feel if their facial expressions cannot be relied upon when navigating the intricacies of nonverbal communication and social cues. It has been suggested that children with Moebius syndrome have difficulty interpreting the facial cues and expressions of others because of their inability to express their own emotions facially. Some evidence lends support to this hypothesis (Giannini, Tamulonis, Giannini, Loiselle, & Spirtos, 1984); other evidence does not

(Calder et al., 2000). Interpersonal communication problems are compounded by difficulties in speech production and intelligibility that children with Moebius syndrome often exhibit due to hypogenesis of the tongue.

Treatment may consist of surgery to correct limb anomalies and facial deformities. Surgery on facial muscles and nerves also may be attempted in order to improve facial expression. Intensive physical and speech therapy is recommended for problems with feeding and speaking; this therapy should be initiated as early as possible (Meyerson & Foushee, 1978). Children with Moebius syndrome also may benefit from education in interpreting the facial cues and expressions of others (Giannini et al., 1984), in addition to coping skills training for dealing with the teasing that they may experience. Finally, long-term electromyographic biofeedback treatment has shown positive effects on facial movement and emotional expression (Gallegos, Medina, Espinoza, & Bustamante, 1992).

Given the multiple avenues for treatment, many children with Moebius syndrome can be adequately served in the regular classroom. They are most likely to receive services under the Speech or Language Impairment category of the Individuals with Disabilities Education Act (IDEA) due to articulation impairment. Depending on the severity of limb anomalies, children with Moebius syndrome also may be eligible for services under the Orthopedic Impairment category of IDEA. These children also could receive services for these impairments under Section 504.

Despite the numerous challenges posed by Moebius syndrome, the literature contains multiple success stories of individuals with this condition who have been able to compensate for and overcome limitations, live effective lives, and become highly successful professionals (e.g., Cole, 1998; Giannini et al., 1984). Thus, given adequate and early intervention efforts (such as those just described), in conjunction with appropriate and effective special education services, the prognosis would appear to be positive. Future research on Moebius syndrome must focus on the prevalence of this disorder, further exploration of the hypothesized genetic link, development of additional treatments, and the refinement of established interventions.

REFERENCES

Calder, A. J., Keane, J., Cole, J., Campbell, R., & Young, A. W. (2000). Facial expression recognition by people with Möbius syndrome. *Cognitive Neuropsychology, 17,* 73–87.

Cole, J. (1998). *About face.* Cambridge, MA: MIT Press.

Gallegos, X., Medina, R., Espinoza, E., & Bustamante, A. (1992). Electromyographic feedback in the treatment of bilateral facial paralysis: A case study. *Journal of Behavioral Medicine, 15,* 533–539.

Giannini, A. J., Tamulonis, D., Giannini, M. C., Loiselle, R. H., & Spirtos, G. (1984). Defective response to social cues in Möbius' syndrome. *Journal of Nervous and Mental Disease, 172,* 174–175.

Meyerson, M. D., & Foushee, D. R. (1978). Speech, language and hearing in Moebius syndrome: A study of 22 patients. *Developmental Medicine and Child Neurology, 20,* 357–365.

Szajnberg, N. M. (1994). Möbius syndrome: Alternatives in affective communication. *Developmental Medicine and Child Neurology, 36,* 459–462.

Jeremy R. Sullivan
Texas A&M University

MONILETHRIX

Monilethrix is a rare genetic disorder of the hair; it is one of the keratin disorders. Hair keratins have two forms, one acidic and one basic; in monilethrix, one or both of the keratin genes have mutated. The effect of the disorder on the individual's hair is variable. In most cases the hair is thin and brittle. The hair shaft is sufficiently fragile that the hair breaks before it is able to get very long. The affected hair may be confined to one region of the head, or it may not be localized. Even within a localized, affected section of the head, not all hairs may be affected (Healey et al., 1995). The area around the hair follicles may be enlarged or covered with scales. Because keratin is also involved with fingernails and toenails, these may be affected as well. Finally, monilethrix may combine with other ectodermal disorders.

Characteristics

1. Moniliform hair or beading of the hair (presence of nodes evident on microscopic evaluation only)
2. Enlargement of the hair follicles and surrounding cells (perifollicular hyperkeratosis)
3. Patches of hair loss, baldness (alopecia)
4. Narrowing of hair shaft
5. Hair fragility and brittleness

Monilethrix is believed to be inherited through autosomal dominant transmission. Linkage studies have mapped monilethrix to Chromosome 12 (Birch-Machlin et al., 1997). Although the majority of reported cases are of European descent, there have been cases from other ethnic groups. Heterozygous individuals have variable degrees of involvement; homozygous individuals are more severely affected (Horev et al., 2000). Males and females are equally likely to be affected. Although not evident at birth, normal hair at birth is replaced by abnormal hair within the first few months to 2 years of age. The symptoms usually begin at the nape of the neck and the occipital region. Most frequently, only the scalp hair is affected, but any or all body hair (e.g., eyebrows) can be affected. There are cases of individuals who virtually lacked scalp hair as well as body hair from the age of 2 months old (Zlotogorski, Horev, & Glaser, 1998). The dystrophia may be lifelong or may disappear in adolescence or during pregnancy with regrowth of normal hair.

Medical treatments for monilethrix include the use of various drugs and the hormone progesterone. Treatments have not had lasting success, however. The biggest issue that children affected with monilethrix will face in school settings is the potential for being victims of teasing and developing a negative self-image related to body image. Supportive counseling as well as directed therapy specific to best ways to deal with teasing may be appropriate. At the same time, increased teacher vigilance with regard to teasing may be needed. Depending on severity and feasibility, cosmetic solutions (e.g., hair braiding, wigs, hats, or scarves) may be useful for older children and adolescents. Genetic counseling is recommended for all family members of an affected individual.

REFERENCES

Birch-Machin, M. A., Healy, E., Turner, R., Haldane, F., Belgaid, C. E., Darlington, S., Stephenson, A. M., Munro, C., Messenger, A. G., & Rees, J. L. (1997). *British Journal of Dermatology, 137,* 339–343.

Healy, E., Holmes, S. C., Belgaid, C. E., Stephenson, A. M., McLean, W. H. I., Rees, J. L., & Munroe, C. S. (1995). A gene for monilethrix is closely linked to the type II keratin gene cluster at 12q13. *Human Molecular Genetics, 4,* 2399–2402.

Horev, L., Glaser, B., Metzker, A., Ben-Amitai, D., Vardy, D., & Zlotogorski, A. (2000). Monilethrix: Mutational hotspot in the helix termination motif of the human hair basic keratin 6. *Human Heredity, 50,* 325–330.

Zlotogorski, A., Horev, L., & Glaser, B. (1998). Monilethrix: A keratin hHb6 mutation is co-dominant with variable expression. *Experimental Dermatology, 7,* 268–272.

Cynthia A. Riccio
Texas A&M University

See also Alopecia Areata

MOTOR NEURON DISEASE

Motor neuron disease is a term used to refer to a group of diseases, all of which are characterized by degeneration of motor neurons. Motor neurons are nerve cells that control the behavior of muscles. Motor neuron disease may affect motor neurons in the spinal cord (lower motor neurons) and in the brain stem (upper motor neurons). Motor neuron disease is characterized in general by muscle weakness and atrophy of varying degrees. Intellectual functioning is normal.

Forms of motor neuron disease affecting children or young adults are inherited, primarily by means of an autosomal recessive trait. Some believe that separate forms of the disease do not actually exist; rather, symptoms occur on a continuum without specific, distinct subtypes (Prior & Russman, 2000). However, motor neuron diseases are usually categorized according to symptoms and age of onset, even though there may be a blending of symptoms. Childhood and adolescent classifications of motor neuron disease are as follows: *Werdnig-Hoffman disease,* also known as infantile spinal muscular atrophy, spinal muscular atrophy I, or acute spinal muscular atrophy; *Dubowitz disease,* also known as chronic spinal muscular atrophy or spinal muscular atrophy II; *Kugelberg-Welander syndrome* (or disease), also known as juvenile spinal muscular atrophy or spinal muscular atrophy III; and *Fazio-Londe syndrome* (or disease), also known as progressive bulbar palsy. It should be noted that classification of all these forms varies depending on the source.

Incidence of motor neuron disease is variable, depending on the type. The National Organization for Rare Disorders, Inc. (2000), considers the disease to be generally rare.

Characteristics

As noted, classifications are not always distinct, and there may be a blending of symptoms between different forms. Some likely characteristics of each subtype are shown here.

Werdnig-Hoffman Disease

1. Generalized, severe muscle weakness, twitching and wasting
2. Can progress rapidly to include respiratory, excretory, and swallowing difficulties
3. Very early onset, usually diagnosed before 6 months of age

Dubowitz Disease

1. Varying degrees of muscle weakness and wasting, but not as severe as with the earlier onset form
2. Tremors of outstretched fingers
3. Onset usually between the ages of 6 and 12 months

Kugelberg-Welander Syndrome

1. Variable muscle weakness and wasting, may also show muscle twitching and slowed reflexes
2. Depending on muscles affected, can include loss of bowel control, breathing difficulties, vision problems, and irregular heartbeat
3. Onset after 1 year of age, up to late adolescence

Fazio-Londe Syndrome

1. Weakness and wasting of muscles of the tongue, lips, and throat causing difficulties in chewing, swallowing, talking, and breathing
2. Age of onset ranging from childhood to late adolescence

Treatment of all forms of motor neuron disease is directed toward alleviating symptoms. Certain drugs may be used to help control muscle symptoms, and physical and occupational therapy can enhance gross and fine motor skills. Patients can be supported in physical activities by braces, splints, use of a wheelchair, and so on. If scoliosis (curvature of the spine) develops, corrective surgery may be an option. Respiratory aids can be used with patients who have trouble breathing. For swallowing difficulties, softer foods and the use of specific assistive devices may be necessary. Pacemakers can be implanted in patients with impaired cardiac function. Genetic counseling can benefit individuals and families affected by motor neuron disease and assist them in making informed choices regarding prevention and treatment.

Special education services for children with motor neuron disease are focused on providing programs and treatments that are specific to each child's needs. For students who require medical assistive technology (e.g., mechanical ventilation, cardiorespiratory monitors, feeding tubes, etc.), specialized nursing care may be needed. Nonmedical assistive technology, such as wheelchairs, seating and positioning equipment, communication devices, and so on, may be necessary. School staff and parents may need to act as advocates to ensure that services are provided by adequately trained personnel. Information about medical needs and specialized support must be provided to school staff as necessary. The need for adaptive devices and their functions should be explained to classmates as well, in a way that honors the preferences and dignity of the student.

Individual manifestations of disease symptoms and the level of technology dependence will have an effect on how a child is able to learn and to function socially. Educational programs for children with motor neuron disease should be designed to capitalize on their unique strengths and should include consideration of the child's physical, academic, social, and emotional needs. Counseling, social skills training, friendship groups, and so on may be necessary to help alleviate feelings the student may have about being different. A school and classroom climate that fosters acceptance of students with disabilities will enhance the likelihood of positive peer relationships.

Families who are dealing with the financial, emotional, and physical strain of caring for a child with severe physical disabilities will require understanding and support. Professionals should be considerate of each family's unique situation, treat parents as equal partners, and empower parents to advocate for their child.

Prognosis for children with motor neuron disease depends on the age of onset and the symptoms. Werdnig-Hoffman disease and Fazio-Londe syndrome have the shortest life expectancy, often less than two years from onset. For other forms, one study found that 68% of patients with Dubowitz disease were alive at 25 years of age and that the life expectancy of patients with Kugelberg-Welander syndrome was similar to that of the general population (Prior & Russman, 2000). If a child with motor neuron disease who attends school were to die, counseling support should be provided for students and staff at the school.

Ongoing research into genetic defects, nerve and muscle metabolism, and the molecular and cellular mechanisms of motor neuron loss may eventually lead to better prevention and treatment options. Several pharmaceutical studies are investigating the possibility that certain drugs may slow the progression of motor neuron disease.

REFERENCES

Adams, R. D., Victor, M., & Ropper, A. H. (1997). *Principles of neurology* (6th ed.). New York: McGraw-Hill.

Levy, S. E., & Pilmer, S. L. (1992). The technology assisted child. In M. L. Batshaw & C. Perret (Eds.), *Children with disabilities: A medical primer* (3rd ed., pp. 137–157). Baltimore: Paul H. Brooks.

National Organization for Rare Disorders, Inc. (2000). Motor neuron disease, Werdnig-Hoffman disease, Kugelberg-Welander syndrome. Retrieval from https://www.stepstn.com/cgi-win/nord.exe

Prior, T., & Russman, B. (2000, February 23). Spinal muscular atrophy. Geneclinics: Medical Genetics Knowledge Base. Retrieved October 30, 2000, http://www.geneclinics.org/profiles/sma/details.html Accessed 30 Oct., 2000.

Paula Perrill
Rik Carl D'Amato
University of Northern Colorado

See also Kugelberg-Welander Disease

MOTOR SPEECH DISORDERS

Developmental motor speech disorders are a class of disorders that include several forms of dysarthria and apraxia of speech (Crary, 1995). The dysarthrias were categorized by Darley, Aronson, and Brown (1975) as flaccid, spastic, hyperkinetic, hypokinetic, ataxic, and mixed. The hallmark of a motor speech disorder is mild to severe speech production problems. These problems may include disturbances in the speed, strength, steadiness, coordination, precision, tone, and range of movement in the speech musculature

(Love, 1992). All childhood dysarthrias are considered secondary to neurological disease or conditions (Love, 1992). Cerebral palsy accounts for nearly 50% of the cases of dysarthrias in children. Other causes include Duchenne's muscular dystrophy and closed head injury (Love, 1992).

Characteristics

Ataxic

1. Has dragging and blurred quality of speech, sounds like drunken speech.
2. Occurs as a result of damage to the cerebellum.

Hyperkinetic

1. Includes involuntary and bizarre jerks, tics, tremors, writhing, slow movements, or stoppages of movement.
2. Damage is believed to be in the extrapyramidal system, including the basal ganglia and corpus striatum.

Hypokinetic

1. A reduction in the mobility of movement for speech production.
2. Speech may have a monopitch and loudness with imprecise articulation.
3. Lesions are in the basal ganglia, including the substantia nigra.

Spastic

1. Slow and labored speech because of paralysis or paresis of involved speech musculature.
2. Damage to the upper motor neuron.

Flaccid

1. All speech systems possibly affected, including respiration, phonation, resonance, and articulation.
2. Damage occurring in the cranial or peripheral nerves.

Mixed

1. Results from damage in any of the mentioned areas, and speech reflects the type and severity of damage.

Treatment is directed toward supporting improvement in speech production or developing compensatory strategies to facilitate communication, depending on the severity and course of the underlying medical condition (Strang, 1995). Particularly with children, the treatment will likely include strengthening the articulatory system to improve the child's speech intelligibility (Strang, 1995). Compensatory articulation, through such means as palatal lift, may help improve intelligibility for some. For individuals with the most severe dysarthrias, an augmentative communication system may provide the best treatment so that the person can interact.

Dysarthric speech can occur as a result of many congenital or acquired medical conditions and can be identified under several labels in special education, depending on the nature of the disorder. For children who have a congenital (i.e., cerebral palsy, muscular dystrophy) or health-related (i.e., tumor, disease) disorder, the Physical and Other Health Impairment labels may be considered. For acquired conditions that result from trauma, a Traumatic Brain Injury label may be appropriate. When speech is the only area that is affected (slow, labored speech), the Speech and Language label may be used. The major complicating factor is that motor speech disorders do not occur in isolation. They occur in the context of a child's developmental stage. As a result, language acquisition also needs to be considered and perhaps addressed. It may be difficult to address all of the child's health and communication needs through a school-based program depending on the etiology of the motor speech disorder. Depending on the nature of the underlying medical condition, the child's educational plans may need to be reviewed more frequently than on an annual basis.

At this time, there is an acute need in the literature for efficacy studies to document treatment in the schools. There are also questions regarding the possibility of subtypes of the various types of dysarthrias.

REFERENCES

Crary, M. A. (1995). Clinical evaluation of developmental motor speech disorders. *Seminar in Speech and Language, 16,* 110–124.

Darley, J. L., Aronson, A. E., & Brown, J. R. (1975). *Motor speech disorders.* Philadelphia, PA: W. B. Saunders.

Love, R. J. (1992). *Childhood motor speech disability.* New York: MacMillan.

Strang, E. A. (1995). Treatment of motor speech disorders in children. *Seminars in Speech and Language, 16,* 126–139.

Dalene M. McCloskey
University of Northern Colorado

MOYAMOYA DISEASE

Moyamoya disease (MD) is a rare, heritable neurologic disorder characterized by narrowing and occlusion (blockage) of arteries in the neck and brain. Moyamoya is a Japanese term meaning "hazy, like a puff of smoke drifting in the wind." This nomenclature originates from the appearance of cerebral angiograms (X rays of the brain done after injecting dye into arteries in the neck), which demonstrate an abnormal cloudiness in basal ganglia (structures on the underside of the brain). This finding is secondary to dilation of small arteries and capillaries (telangiectasia).

The etiology of MD is controversial and possibly multifactorial. Studies in familial MD have revealed abnormal genes on Chromosome 3. However, familial MD accounts for only about 10% of patients with the disorder. Most of the cases have been reported in siblings, but about 25% have involved a parent and his or her child. Another analysis of 32 unrelated Japanese patients with MD showed a high association with HLA-B51, a marker on a type of white blood cell (lymphocyte) that is associated with autoimmune disorders (Behçet's disease), Kawasaki disease, and childhood stroke of unknown etiology. Finally, a few cases of MD have occurred in children with other neurologic problems (neurofibromatosis, tuberous sclerosis, Sturge-Weber syndrome).

MD is rather rare. Its highest incidence is in Asians, particularly the Japanese. A small number of cases have been found in North America. These individuals were siblings and the offspring of consanguineous parents. MD is more common in females. The female-to-male ratio of patients is 3:2. Although the mode of heredity is not completely clear, many familial cases of MD are consistent with an autosomal recessive pattern.

Characteristics

1. Most individuals develop symptoms prior to age 10 but may be affected as young as 3 years old.
2. Initial complaints are headache, transient muscle paralysis, or weakness and disturbances in vision. These phenomena are secondary to poor cerebral blood flow (ischemia).
3. Chorea (irregular, involuntary muscle spasms affecting the limbs and face) is a less frequent presenting sign.
4. Late findings include progressive neurologic deterioration, severe motor dysfunction and disability, mental retardation, and psychosis.
5. Noninvasive studies of the cerebral vasculature (computerized tomography and magnetic resonance imaging) of individuals in families with MD have revealed that some cases of MD are asymptomatic.

Treatment strategies for MD are limited and produce unpredictable results. Various surgical procedures to enhance blood flow to the brain have been attempted, but consistent benefit from them has not been demonstrated. One paper, which reported a child and maternal grandmother with MD, showed that drugs that prevent aggregation of platelets (cell fragments that are present in blood and important in clotting) were able to halt further ischemic events. Genetic counseling is indicated in familial cases.

Children with MD require educational modifications and support services under the special education umbrella. The amount of services is dependent on the degree of neurologic impairment. Because the disease is progressive, continued monitoring of the child's cognitive status is imperative.

Review of the available literature suggests that MD has a poor prognosis. The disorder usually runs a relentless, progressive course and ultimately causes severe neurologic impairment. The lack of satisfactory therapy makes it foolish to be optimistic about the long-range outlook for children with this disorder.

For more information and parent support, contact Families with Moyamoya Support Network, 4900 McGowan Street SE, Cedar Rapids, IA 52403.

REFERENCES

Haslam, R. H. A. (2000). Acute stroke syndromes. In R. E. Behrman, R. M. Kleigman, & H. B. Jenson (Eds.), *Nelson textbook of pediatrics* (16th ed., pp. 1855–1856). Philadelphia: W. B. Saunders.

Moyamoya. Database links. Retrieved from http://www3.nchi.nlm.gov/htbin-post/Omim/dispmim?252350

National Organization for Rare Disorders, Inc. (1996). Moyamoya disease. (NORD). Retrieved from http://www.stepstn.com/cgi.win/nord.exe?proc=GetDocument&rectype=0&recnum=617

Barry H. Davison
Ennis, Texas

Joan W. Mayfield
Baylor Pediatric Specialty Services
Dallas, Texas

MUCHA HABERMANN DISEASE

Mucha Habermann disease or Habermann disease is one of a subgroup of parapsoriasis and pityriasis. Habermann disease also is known as pityriasis lichenoides. Habermann can occur in an acute form or in a chronic form. As with other diseases within the pityriasis group, it is characterized by skin eruptions. In the acute form, the disease manifests as a recurring and generalized, reddish-brown, maculopapular eruption or rash. The lesions may be red and elevated with a blister-like appearance; there may be hemorrhage beneath the skin. The eruptions or sores become scaly and crusted and can ulcerate. Often the lesions result in a scar and have the appearance of being pigment depressed. The acute form may or may not progress to the chronic form. The chronic form is somewhat milder but still is characterized by sores and eventual skin death and scarring (National Organization for Rare Disorders [NORD], 1995).

Characteristics

1. Skin eruptions or necrosis that itch and burn
2. Scarring with depressed pigmentation
3. Headache, chills
4. Joint pain

The cause of Habermann disease is unknown, but there are some indications that it involves the autoimmune system. In at least one case, the eruptions were precipitated by administration of a medication, Tegafur, supporting some autoimmune involvement in the etiology of Habermann (Kawamura, Tsuji, & Kuwabara, 1999). The mechanism, if any, for genetic transmission has not been established. Habermann disease is most likely to occur in young adults, but it can manifest in children and youth. Males and females are equally likely to be affected; there is no indication that members of one ethnic race are more likely to develop Habermann than any other (NORD, 1995).

Treatment of Habermann is with standard administration of antibiotics (e.g., tetracycline). Other cytotoxic or corticosteroids (e.g., prednisone) may be prescribed to provide temporary relief from the itching and burning. Additional support (e.g., counseling, analgesics) may be needed as well. Habermann is generally benign, but there are cases where Habermann disease has cloned into malignant T cell lymphoma (Niemczyk, Zollner, Wolter, Staib, & Kaufmann, 1999). Continual monitoring of the status of skin lesions is recommended in order to ensure early identification of any transformed cells.

REFERENCES

Kawamura, K., Tsuji, T., & Kuwabara, Y. (1999). Mucha-Habermann disease-like eruptions due to Tegafur. *Journal of Dermatology, 26,* 164–167.

National Organization for Rare Disorders. (1995). Mucha Habermann disease (Article No. 752). Retrieved May 25, 2001, from www.rarediseases.org

Niemczyk, U. M., Zollner, T. M., Wolter, M., Staib, G., & Kaufmann, R. (1999). The transformation of pityriasis lichenoides chronica into parakeratosis variegata in an 11-year-old girl. *British Journal of Dermatology, 137,* 983–987.

Cynthia A. Riccio
Texas A&M University

MUCOPOLYSACCHARIDE DISORDERS

Mucopolysaccharide disorders are rare inborn errors of metabolism (IEM) resulting from a failure in mucopolysaccharide metabolism. They are among a larger group of disorders, all of which involve disordered lysosomal (complex carbohydrate) storage. Each has a specific enzymatic defect and genetic transmission (National MPS Society, 2001). Seven groups of syndromes with overlapping features are currently recognized, several of which have subtypes: Type I: Hurler (MPS IH), Hurler-Scheie (MPS IH/S), and Scheie (MPS IS), ranging from severe to mild, respectively; Type II: Hunter Severe and Mild (MPS IIA and IIB, respectively); Type III: Sanfilippo A–D (MPS IIIA–D, respectively); Type IV: Morquio A and B (MPS IVA and IVB, respectively); Type VI: Maroteaux-Lamy Classic Severe, Intermediate, and Mild (MPS VI), Sly (MPS VII), and Diferrante (MPS VIII). Scheie syndrome, previously MPSV, is now classified Type I, leaving the MPSV category empty at this time (Murphy, 1999). Except for Hunter syndrome, which is sex-linked recessive, all MPS disorders are autosomal recessive. All are rare, having individual incidences of about 1 in 100,000 or lower, but overall MPS incidence is about 1 in 25,000 (National MPS Society, 2001).

Characteristics

1. Growth retardation leading in some cases to dwarfism
2. Mental retardation (most, but not all)
3. Macrocephaly
4. Coarse facies (mild to severe)
5. Corneal opacities (most, but not all) and hearing loss
6. Respiratory and cardiac abnormalities
7. Joint stiffness and claw hand
8. Inguinal and umbilical hernias
9. Skeletal abnormalities

Each type and subtype has numerous and wide-ranging characteristics; a few generally common ones are listed. The four types of Sanfilippo are distinguishable biochemically, but not clinically. Exceptions to the common features are that intelligence is generally in the normal range in Hunter Mild (MPS IIB), Morquio (MPS IV), and Maroteaux-Lamy (MPS VI); height is normal in Sanfilippo (MPS III). Early death owing to a variety of complications is common in the more severe forms of each type or subtype. Assessment is generally by biochemical assay for deficiency of particular substances in white cells and other areas and presence of substances in the urine. Antenatal diagnosis is possible for most. Detailed descriptions of assessment procedures, genetic, biochemical, and clinical characteristics, and outcomes are in individual entries in *Online Mendelian Inheritance in Man* (2000). Owing to the varying characteristics and rate of progress among the disorders, accurate diagnosis is important.

Because little effective treatment is currently available for MPS disorders, appropriate management is critical. A team approach will generally be needed, with the particular specialists varying with the condition. Physical and speech therapy will often be necessary, as will provision of a variety of special education services. Teachers and others will need to be skilled in dealing with behavior management problems. The abnormal appearance of those with normal or near-normal intelligence may call for counseling to help deal with social interaction problems.

Enzyme replacement therapy has not generally been effective. Retroviral gene transfer into human bone marrow shows promise. Perhaps the most promising line of current research involves the use of embryonic stem cells in the development of treatments (National MPS Society, 2001).

REFERENCES

National MPS Society. (2001). The MPS disorders. Retrieved from http://www.mpssociety.org/

Murphy, P. (1999). Index of the lysosomal diseases. *Rare genetic diseases in children: An Internet resource gateway.* Retrieved from http://mcrcr2.med.nyu.edu/murphp01/lysosome/dischart.htm#mps

Online Mendelian Inheritance in Man. (2000). McKusick-Nathans Institute for Genetic Medicine, Johns Hopkins University and National Center for Biotechnology Information, National Library of Medicine. Retrieved from http://www.ncbi.nlm.nih.gov/omim

Robert T. Brown
University of North Carolina, Wilmington

See also Hurler Syndrome

MULIBREY NANISM SYNDROME

Mulibrey nanism syndrome (MNS), also known as Perheentupa syndrome, is a hereditary form of dwarfism first described in 1970. The word *mulibrey* derives from an acronym for the organs most affected in this syndrome: (mu)scle, (li)ver, (br)ain, and (ey)es. Nanism is a synonym for dwarfism.

The etiology of MNS is unclear. It is a rare disorder. About 40 cases have been reported. Seventy-five percent of these individuals have been Finnish. The pattern of inheritance is autosomal recessive.

Characteristics

1. Prenatal growth deficiency; average birth weight is 5.3 pounds; average birth length is 17.5 inches; these measurements are slightly less than the lower limits of the normal range for term infants; mean adult height is 58 inches for males and 54 inches for females
2. Relatively large hands and feet
3. Dolichocephaly (narrow, elongated skull), triangular face, prominent forehead, small tongue, overlapping teeth
4. Decreased retinal pigmentation and yellow dots in the retina; visual deficits may occur
5. Progressive thickening of the pericardium (the fibrous sack that surrounds the heart); the pericardium adheres to the heart and interferes to some extent with its normal pumping action; the net result of this abnormality is sluggish blood return to the right side of the heart, which causes distended neck veins and liver enlargement (hepatomegaly)
6. Decreased muscle tone, high-pitched voice
7. Occasional growth hormone deficiency and immunodeficiency
8. Normal intelligence

No data are available regarding treatment for MNS. Problems secondary to pericardial constriction appear anytime from infancy to late childhood. It is unclear if symptoms become severe enough to warrant intervention (e.g., surgery) or significantly impact life expectancy. Laboratory confirmation of growth hormone deficiency might prompt replacement therapy, but the short stature associated with MNS is not generally caused by an inadequacy of growth hormone. Because there is a significant risk (25%) of recurrence of MNS with subsequent pregnancies, genetic counseling should be made available to couples with an affected child.

Children with MNS may benefit from modifications in the classroom, such as providing an appropriate-sized desk and chair. Evaluation and treatment by occupational and physical therapists may be needed to address decreased muscle tone. These children should be treated in an age-appropriate manner and not according to their short stature.

There are no data in the literature on prognosis for MNS. It is unclear whether patients eventually succumb to the pericardial pathology and failure of the heart to function as a pump. It is equally unclear whether the cardiac problems they incur respond to any treatment that is currently available.

For additional information and support, contact Little People of America, Inc., PO Box 745, Lubbock, TX 79408; (888) 572-2001; e-mail: 1padatabase@juno.com.

REFERENCE

Jones, K. (1997). *Smith's recognizable patterns of human malformation* (5th ed.). Philadelphia: W. B. Saunders.

Barry H. Davison
Ennis, Texas

Joan W. Mayfield
Baylor Pediatric Specialty Services
Dallas, Texas

MULTIPLE SCLEROSIS

Multiple sclerosis (MS) is a demyelinating disease of the central nervous system (CNS). The disease was first described by Jean Martin Charcot, a 19th-century neurologist. Early in the disease, inflammation and edema occur. In the later stages, scarring occurs, and plaques are formed, especially around the lateral ventricles. The multiple patchy lesions destroy the myelin sheath surrounding nerve cells, thereby disrupting neural transmission.

MS typically occurs by the age of 30 and is found twice as often in females as in males. The prevalence rate in the U.S. is 60 out of 100,000; however, rates vary significantly according to geographic region. MS is rare in tropical and subtropical areas but increases dramatically the further away from the equator. One of the highest rates, for example, is found in the Orkney Islands northeast of Scotland. Even individuals who migrate to the Orkneys are three times more likely to develop MS as are those in their country of origin. The prevalence rate in the Orkneys is estimated to be 309 per 100,000 (Hogancamp, Rodriguez, & Weinshenker, 1997). Unusually high rates are also found in certain cities in the United States (e.g., Key West, Florida, and Los Alamos, New Mexico) and in regions where military troops were stationed during World War II. Just a couple years after troops arrived in Iceland and the Faroe Islands, these regions experienced epidemic proportions of MS. Although infectious agents have been implicated as a cause, there is reason to suspect a defective immune system as well as genetic susceptibility. Individuals who have a close relative with MS are eight times more likely to develop the disease (NINDS, 2000), and children of sufferers are at 30 to 50 times the risk. Furthermore, monozygotic twins have been shown to have a 26% rate of co-occurrence, whereas dizygotic twins have a 2.4% rate.

Characteristics

1. Muscle weakness, unsteady gait, and poor fine motor coordination
2. Numbness and paresthesias
3. Visual disturbance (sudden loss of acuity, blurred or double)
4. Slurred speech
5. Weakness and extreme fatigue
6. Possible incontinence and cognitive impairment (e.g., poor attention and memory)

Individuals with MS often experience visual disturbance as an initial symptom. This includes loss of acuity (e.g., blurred vision and blindness), double vision, and color distortion. Paresthesias (e.g., tingling and feelings of pins and needles), vertigo, muscle weakness, and problems with motor control (e.g., clumsiness and unsteady gait) also occur. In some cases, speech is slurred, and cognitive problems are reported in nearly half of the cases (e.g., impaired attention and concentration, diminished memory, and poor problem-solving skills). These individuals also have significant psychological problems, including depression (Arnett, 1999). In fact, the rates for emotional problems severe enough to warrant treatment are higher than are those for many other groups suffering from physically disabling diseases (e.g., rheumatoid arthritis, spinal cord injury, muscular dystrophy, and amyotrophic lateral sclerosis). Depression, however, is not the only psychological symptoms, some individuals with MS have euphoria (e.g., extreme optimism and cheerfulness) and symptoms of prefrontal lobe dysfunction (e.g., indifference, lack of self-awareness, and low motivation and initiation).

The diagnosis of MS is often delayed; in fact, on average it takes four years. Although age, clinical history of symptom onset and presentation, neurologic exam findings, and magnetic resonance imaging (MRI) results are useful in diagnosing MS, the variable, and sometimes unpredictable, course of the disease makes it difficult to diagnose. The fact that it also mimics other neurologic conditions, including stroke and CNS tumors, also complicates matters. Concomitant psychiatric problems can also interfere with accurate diagnosis, making it imperative that careful follow-up examinations be conducted. In addition to MRI (and computerized tomography scans), vision examinations by neuro-opthalmologists familiar with MS and lumbar puncture can assist with diagnosis.

The prognosis for MS varies depending on the different pattern. Some individuals have a relapsing remitting course, whereas others have a slow downward progression. In the former case, the course of the disease is fairly stable, at least for the majority of people. In this case, the individual suffers periods of symptom exacerbation followed by remission, but no real deterioration in functioning. It is possible, however, for these individuals to have gradual progressive decline. Overall, it is estimated that in 10–20% of cases, the disease is severe with chronic, progressive physical deterioration (NINDS, 2000). MS has not been shown to shorten the life span appreciably, but it has been found to affect the quality of life significantly.

Drugs such as ACTH and prednisone have helped to reduce exacerbations of the disease (including mood-related symptoms); however, these drugs have not been shown to alter its course. These drugs can also negatively impact the person's functional ability, including cognitive functioning. For individuals who are studying at college or working jobs that require certain cognitive skills that are impacted by the disease, or its treatment, accommodations may be needed (e.g., extra time for exams and assignments, audiotaped books and tests). It is more likely that accommodations through the Americans with Disabilities Act will be needed to address various physical and psychological disabilities associated with the disease. Counseling and psychotropic drugs (e.g., antidepressants) may be especially helpful. Providing support and assistance to family members also needs to be considered, including education about the disease and helping to put them in contact with community agencies.

Research is needed to define better the role of potential etiological factors, including the autoimmune system, infection, and genes. Drug studies are also needed to ensure maximal benefit from treatment and minimum side effects.

REFERENCES

Arnett, P. A. (1999). Depressed mood in multiple sclerosis: Relationship to capacity demanding memory and attentional functioning. *Neuropsychology, 13*(3), 434–446.

Hogancamp, W., Rodriguez, M., & Weinshenker, B. (1997). The epidemiology of multiple sclerosis. *Mayo Clinical Proceedings, 72*, 871–878.

NINDS. (2000). NINDS multiple sclerosis Web site. Retrieved from www.ninds.nih.gov/health

Elaine Clark
University of Utah

MUMPS

Mumps is a viral infection that causes swelling in one or both salivary glands inside of the mouth. This virus is spread through the air by infected individuals and has an incubation period of 14 to 24 days. One third of infected individuals do not display symptoms (Human Diseases & Conditions, 2000).

Mumps can be prevented with a vaccination. The mumps vaccination is usually administered during the second year of life in combination with vaccinations against measles and rubella. Before the introduction of the mumps vaccination in 1967, between 150,000 and 185,000 cases of mumps were reported in the United States every year. After the vaccination was introduced, the number of reported cases dropped to 1,500 to 1,600 per year (Felter, 2001). Internationally, the numbers vary accordingly depending on the vaccination status of the population in each country.

Characteristics

1. Swelling of salivary glands is common (Mosby's 2002).
2. During the beginning of the infection, symptoms include anorexia, headache, malaise, low-grade fever (which can be accompanied by earaches), and swelling of the salivary glands (which causes pain when swallowing; (Mosby's 2002).
3. Body temperature increases to 101–104°F (38–40°C; Mosby's 2002).
4. 25% of infected adult men develop epididymoorchitis, which is expressed by swelling and tenderness of the testes (Mosby's 2002).
5. 10% of infected individuals develop meningitis; the risk for males is 3 to 5 times higher than in females (Felter, 2001).

The mumps virus is diagnosed through laboratory testing of the blood, urine, or saliva (Human Diseases & Conditions, 2000). The patient should be isolated to prevent the spread of the infection to others who may not be vaccinated against the virus. Bed rest and medication to alleviate the symptoms are recommended. Mortality rate for infected individuals, who also develop meningoencephalitis, is about 1.4%. The usual course of a case of mumps in most children is unproblematic and resolves in about 9 days, with an incubation period of 14 to 21 days. The child can infect others two to three days before any symptoms appear (Felter, 2001). School personnel should be alerted to the diagnosis of mumps to help contain the spread.

REFERENCES

Felter, R. (2001, July 3). Mumps. *eMedicine Journal, 2*(7). Retrieved December 28, 2001, from http://www.emedecine.com/emerg/topic324.html

Human diseases and conditions (2000). (Vol. 2, pp. 602–604). New York: Scribner & Sons.

Mosby's medical, nursing, and allied health dictionary (2002). (6th ed., pp. 1131–1132). St. Louis, MO: Harcourt Health Sciences.

Monika Hannan
University of Northern Colorado

MUNCHAUSEN SYNDROME BY PROXY

Munchausen syndrome by proxy (MSBP), a member of the family of factitious disorders, shares certain features with Munchausen syndrome and is considered a special form of child abuse. The most common element is the tendency for people to fabricate or produce physical or psychological symptoms in order to assume the patient role and gain the attention, care, and special grace that may come with this role. The name itself derives from Baron von Münchausen, a notorious 18th-century teller of tall tales.

Most case reports of MSBP identify the mother as the primary perpetrator (90–95%), although some rare cases may involve the father, babysitter, or other relative. The victim is typically a toddler or infant, although elderly adults and animals have also suffered the abuse. Although there is no established profile of perpetrators of MSBP, there is the underlying motivation to gain primary attention from the medical or mental health community. The parent is driven to gratify his or her own needs at the expense of the child. Doctor shopping may be a hallmark sign of possible MSBP, and with basic medical information readily available on the Internet, many perpetrators can develop a great deal of knowledge about specific symptoms sufficient to fabricate convincingly or induce a diagnosis in their offspring.

Feldman and Lasher (1999) offered several warning signs that may help with the detection of MSBP. These include the following: (a) Episodes of illness begin when the mother has recently been alone with the child; (b) the child's illness abates when separated from the mother; (c) the child has been to numerous caregivers without cure or clear diagnosis; (d) symptoms do not appear to respond to appropriate treatment; (e) the suspected disease or disease pattern is very rare; (f) the mother has a history or diagnosis of factitious or somatoform disorder; (g) the mother is unusually eager to have the child undergo extensive testing or surgery; (h) the mother is less anxious than the medical staff about the diagnostic difficulty; (i) the mother is suspected of providing false information or fabrication of problem; and (j) physiologic or lab tests are consistent with induced illness.

MSBP is relatively rare, although it is becoming more common as parents access detailed medical information through the Internet (Feldman, 2000). Hundreds of case studies appear in the literature, and several recent books are dedicated to this topic (i.e., Adshead & Brooke, 1999).

There is virtually no physical or mental condition that cannot be fabricated or produced in MSBP abuse, and some perpetrators use several forms of dissimulation across time (Feldman & Lasher, 1999). These abusive acts are done to mislead health professionals into offering treatment to the child and thereby gratify the parent's need to have the vicarious benefits of the care and attention of the health care system. In the case of false allegations of abuse, the parent may gain specific custody benefits or increase his or her enmeshed relationship with the dependent child. Some mothers may set out consciously and deliberately to create the appearance of illness in their child, whereas others may even develop their own quasi-delusional thinking and believe that the illness is real.

Although MSBP is considered a reportable form of child abuse, it is rarely diagnosed or even considered by most pediatricians or mental health providers, including those who work in child protective service agencies. Few professionals have even heard of it, perhaps due to its relative recency on the diagnostic scene. It does not appear in the *Diagnostic and Statistical Manual of Mental Disorders–Fourth Edition,* although other factitious disorders and Munchausen syndrome are included. Because medical and psychiatric examination relies heavily on the self-report of the parent or caretaker to establish symptom patterns, there is ample opportunity for the perpetrator to offer misleading reports to the physician. At a minimum, such acts as just outlined constitute a form of emotional abuse, often accompanied with physical abuse or neglect. It is estimated that the mortality rate for MSBP is nearly 10% because the victims may die as a result of symptom fabrication or exaggeration taken beyond the limits of what the child can withstand (Rosenberg, 1987). Death may also be the result of false history information provided to the doctor, leading to iatrogenic morbidity and eventual death.

Characteristics

1. The child has extensive history of illness, particularly rare illness, with few specific diagnoses.
2. The child has experienced multiple hospitalizations and multiple exploratory surgeries.
3. The child has symptoms that do not respond to typical treatment.

Treatment typically includes some form of litigation or involvement with child protective services, dependency court, and family counselors who seek to address the underlying unmet dependency needs of the perpetrator parent while easing the complications of abuse and enmeshment that the child has experienced. Individual and family counseling may require extended periods of treatment and monitoring by the legal authorities.

There are no known special education concerns, although teachers may become aware of recurrent medical conditions that suggest this form of abuse. As a special form of child abuse, teachers may become required to report their suspicions to child protective services. Prognosis remains guarded at best. Case studies are common, although empirical research remains sparse at best concerning characteristics of the victims or perpetrators or addressing treatment outcomes.

REFERENCES

Adshead, G., & Brooke, D. (Eds.). (1999). *Munchausen's syndrome by proxy: Current issues in assessment, treatment, and research.* London: Imperial College Press.

Feldman, M. D. (2000). Munchausen by Internet: Detecting factitious illness and crisis on the Internet. *Southern Medical Journal, 93*(7), 669–672.

Feldman, M. D., & Lasher, L. J. (1999). Munchausen by proxy: A misunderstood form of maltreatment. *Forensic Examiner, 8* (9–10), 25–29.

Rosenberg, D. A. (1987). Web of deceit: A literature review of Munchausen syndrome by proxy. *Child Abuse and Neglect, 11,* 547–563.

Daniel J. Rybicki
ForenPsych Services
Agoura Hills, California

MUSCULAR DYSTROPHY, DUCHENNE

Duchenne muscular dystrophy is a degenerative disorder in which there is progressive symmetrical weakness of skeletal muscles with proximal muscles affected more than distal and lower limbs affected first (Jennekens, ten Kate, de Visser, & Wintzen, 1998). The etiology is genetic, with an X-linked recessive transmission, usually familial, but with a relatively high occurrence (15–30%) of transmission via mutation (Adams & Victor, 1993; Tsao & Mendell, 1999). The specific genetic mechanism has been identified as deletions, and occasionally duplications or point mutations, in the dystrophin gene that result in dystrophin deficiency, which in turn causes a cascade of events ending in muscle fiber breakdown (Tsao & Mendell, 1999; Tiller et al., 2000).

This ultimately lethal disease has an incidence rate of approximately 13–33 per 100,000 per annum; approximately 1 in 3,500 live born males is afflicted (Adams & Victor, 1993). Rarely, females who have Turner's syndrome or other XX genotype abnormalities have been affected (Adams & Victor, 1993).

Characteristics

1. Rapidly progressing weakness involving selective but widespread muscles with onset usually noted between 2 and 6 years of age due to falls, swayback posture, waddling gait, and difficulty rising, climbing, and ambulating
2. Elevated creatine kinase (CK), which is an enzyme that leaks out of damaged muscle
3. Pseudohypertrophy of the calves (enlargement due to an accumulation of fat and connective tissues in the muscle)
4. Possible involvement of the smooth muscles of the gastrointestinal tract, causing symptoms such as potentially life-threatening intestinal pseudo-obstruction or constipation
5. Normal extraocular muscles
6. Wheelchair bound by age 12
7. Nonprogressive mental retardation in a small but significant portion of patients, with the average IQ of affected individuals falling one standard deviation below the normal population mean and some indication of a relative weakness in verbal intellectual abilities and verbal memory
8. Cardiac involvement including fibrosis in the posterobasal portion of the left ventricular wall, which rarely results in overt signs of congestive heart failure or cardiac failure until the late stages, when congestive heart failure and arrhythmias occur, especially during times of stress from intercurrent infections
9. Death around age 20 due to complications of respiratory insufficiency

(See Adams & Victor, 1993; Hinton, De Vivo, Nereo, Goldstein, & Stern, 2000; Shield, 1998; Tiller et al., 2000; Tsao & Mendell, 1999)

Treatment is generally supportive and palliative. Physical therapy, orthoses, and corrective orthopedic surgery can improve quality of life by helping to prevent contractures and delaying the progression of scoliosis (National Institute of Neurological Disorders and Stroke [NINDS], 2000; Tiller et al., 2000; Tsao & Mendell, 1999). Corticosteroids have been shown to increase muscle strength, pulmonary function, and functional ability, although side effects are significant (see Tsao & Mendell, 1999). Gene therapies are currently being investigated.

Special education services are available under the handicapping condition of Other Health Impairment. The presence of mental retardation also qualifies a student for special education services. Patients require assistance and accommodations for tasks dependent on normal motor functioning, including ambulation, writing, and other graphomotor tasks.

Porter, Hall, and Williams (n.d.) outlined several issues and accommodations in their booklet for teachers. For instance, potential obstacles in school include difficulty in taking notes quickly or for a long period of time; slowness or inability to get ready for class (lifting a book and opening it to the correct page, getting out a pencil and paper, etc.); need for assistance with toileting; and inability to rise from a seated position on the floor or in a chair to a standing position. Heavy doors, steps, and long distances become obstacles.

Porter et al. (n.d.) further described several helpful environmental adaptations, including raised toilet seats, special desktops, ramps instead of steps, and handrails. For the child who uses a wheelchair, doorways must be wide enough for the wheelchair, privacy for toileting needs should be provided, water fountains must be at wheelchair level, and going through the lunch line in a cafeteria should be facilitated. Assigning a buddy to assist with toileting, feeding, getting to classes, and completing class work may be an option if acceptable to the student. The student may need extra time to take tests and may need to leave classes a few minutes early to get to the next class. Adaptive equipment may include items such as feeding utensils and special cups, a foam rubber cylinder that fits over a small pen or pencil to make it easier to grasp, tape recorders for note taking when writing becomes too difficult, jar openers, and devices to aid in buttoning and zipping.

In their booklet for teachers, Porter et al. (n.d.) also pointed out that affected children need to be kept out of school during cold and flu epidemics due to the respiratory problems. They may additionally miss school for therapies and surgeries and thus will benefit from extra support in the form of temporary home schooling or tutoring during long absences. Porter et al. (n.d.) additionally highlighted the importance of counseling and emotional support, particularly in light of the student's probable increasing awareness of their impairments as well as their shortened life expectancies.

Patients with Duchenne muscular dystrophy are generally wheelchair bound by age 12 or so (Tsao & Mendell, 1999; Shield, 1998). Sadly, this disease usually results in death by the late teens to early 20s due to complications of respiratory insufficiency (NINDS, 2000; Tsao & Mendell, 1999; Shield, 1998). A small number of patients live to more than 30 years of age (Shield, 1998). As noted, gene therapies are currently being investigated as potential means to halt the disease's progression.

REFERENCES

Adams, R., & Victor, M. (1993). *Principles of neurology* (5th ed.). New York: McGraw-Hill.

Hinton, V., De Vivo, D., Nereo, N., Goldstein, E., & Stern, Y. (2000). Poor verbal working memory across intellectual level in boys with Duchenne dystrophy. *Neurology, 54,* 2127–2132.

Jennekens, F., ten Kate, L., de Visser, M., & Wintzen, A. (1998). Diagnostic criteria for neuromuscular disorders. European Neuromuscular Centre. Retrieved from http://enmc.spc.ox.ac.uk

National Institute of Neurological Disorders and Stroke. (2000). Muscular dystrophy. Retrieved from http://www.ninds.nih.gov/health_and_medical/disorders.md.htm

Porter, P., Hall, C., & Williams, F. (n.d.). A teacher's guide to Duchenne muscular dystrophy. MDA Publications. Retrieved September 6, 2000, from http://www.mdausa.org:80/publications/tchrdmd/index.html

Shield, L. (1998). Fact sheet: Muscular dystrophies: Duchenne and Becker. Muscular Dystrophy Association. Retrieved from http://www.mda.org.au/specific/mdadmd.html

Tiller, G., Hamosh, A., McKusick, V., Brennan, P., Smith, M., Antonarakis, S., & Hurko, O. (2000). 310200 Muscular Dystrophy, Pseudohypertrophic Progressive, Duchenne and Becker Types. Online Mendelian Inheritance in Man (OMIM). Retrieved from http://www.ncbi.nlm.nih.gov:80/entrez/dispomim.cgi?id=310200.

Tsao, C., & Mendell, J. (1999). The childhood muscular dystrophies: Making order out of chaos. *Seminars in Neurology, 19,* 9–23.

LESLIE D. ROSENSTEIN
Neuropsychology Clinic, P.C.
Austin, Texas

MUSCULAR DYSTROPHY, EMERY-DREIFUSS

Emery-Dreifuss muscular dystrophy is a degenerative myopathy in which there is slow, progressive, symmetrical weakness of skeletal and cardiac muscles. There are early contractures of the neck, elbows, and ankles (Achilles tendons), often predating the muscle weakness of the shoulder girdle (scapular), upper arms (humeral), and lower legs (peroneal; Emery, 2000; Muscular Dystrophy Association [MDA], n.d.-b). There is cardiomyopathy and/or conduction defect (Adams & Victor, 1993; Emery, 2000), even in a portion (i.e., 10–20%) of female carriers (Lopate, 2000). The etiology is genetic, usually with an X-linked recessive transmission, although there are rarer autosomal dominant (Emery, 2000; Lopate, 2000) and autosomal recessive (McKusick, 2000) forms. In the X-linked recessive form, the gene has been mapped to the tip of the long arm of the X chromosome (Yates, n.d.). There is a deficiency, usually a complete absence, of the nuclear membrane protein, emerin, in the affected muscles, as well as skin and other tissues in that form (Emery, 2000; Lopate, 2000; Smith, McKusick, & Lo, 2000). In the autosomal dominant form, there is an abnormality in lamin A/C, another inner nuclear membrane protein (Emery, 2000; Lopate, 2000; Tiller & McKusick, 2000).

This rare disease has an incidence rate estimated at 1 in 100,000 for the X-linked recessive form; the autosomal dominant form is much rarer (Lopate, 2000). Onset of the more common X-linked recessive form is usually noted in childhood, and rarely after age 20 (Yates, n.d.). Onset of the autosomal dominant form is usually in the late teens to early 40s (Tiller & McKusick, 2000).

Characteristics

1. Slow progression
2. Onset usually noted in childhood in the X-linked recessive form; late teens to early forties in the autosomal dominant form
3. Triad of early contractures (especially of the elbows and ankles, sometimes also in the wrist and fingers), scapulo-humero-peroneal (i.e., shoulder girdle, upper arms, and lower legs) muscle weakness, and cardiac conduction defects (only in the recessive form)
4. Contractures resulting in a tendency to toe walk and hold the arms flexed; neck characterized as stiff due to limited flexion
5. Increased lumbar lordosis, scoliosis, pes cavus, and Achilles tendon shortening
6. Pectus excavatum
7. No pseudohypertrophy of the calf muscles
8. Elevated serum creatine phosphokinase in the majority of cases

(See Emery, 2000; Lopate, 2000; MDA, n.d.-a, n.d.-b; Smith et al., 2000; Tiller & McKusick, 2000; Yates, n.d.)

Treatment is generally supportive and palliative. Physical therapy is beneficial in minimizing contractures, which may be more debilitating than the weakness, and pacemakers may be required to treat the cardiac problems (Emery, 2000; Lopate, 2000; National Institute of Neurological Disorders and Stroke, 2000). Treatment is also aimed at preventing and correcting skeletal abnormalities such as scoliosis. Orthopedic surgery, such as tendon release, as well as bracing and passive stretching, are important in maintaining independent functioning as long as possible (Emery, 2000; Lopate, 2000).

Special education services are available under the handicapping condition of Other Health Impairment. Patients will require assistance and accommodations for tasks dependent on normal motor functioning, including ambulation, writing, and other graphomotor tasks. Many of the considerations and accommodations outlined by Porter, Hall, and Williams (n.d.) apply to students with Emery-Dreifuss muscular dystrophy as well.

The progression of Emery-Dreifuss muscular dystrophy is characteristically slow (Emery, 2000; Lopate, 2000; Smith et al., 2000). Risk of sudden death due to the cardiac conduction defects is significant and is the major cause of mortality and morbity (Lopate, 2000). Research has evolved from individual case studies to clinical trials comparing diagnostic procedures and measurements to evaluate treatments (e.g., MDA, n.d.-a). Studies of potential gene therapies may be possible once an animal model for emerin deficiency has been found (Emery, 2000).

REFERENCES

Adams, R., & Victor, M. (1993). *Principles of neurology* (5th ed.). New York: McGraw-Hill.

Emery, A. (2000). Emery-Dreifuss muscular dystrophy: A 40 year retrospective. *Neuromuscular Disorders, 10,* 228–232.

Lopate, G. (2000). Emery-Dreifuss muscular dystrophy. *eMedicine.* Retrieved from http://www.emedicine.com/neuro/topic513.htm

McKusick, V. (2000). #604929 Emery-Dreifuss muscular dystrophy, autosomal recessive. *National Center for Biotechnology Information's Online Mendelian Inheritance in Man.* Retrieved from http://www.ncbi.nlm.nih.gov:80/entrez/dispomim?604929.

Muscular Dystrophy Association. (2000a). Emery-Dreifuss Muscular Dystrophy: A guide to related materials on MDA's Web site. Retrieved from http://www.mdausa.org/disease/edmd.html

Muscular Dystrophy Association. (2000b). Major characteristics of the nine (9) muscular dystrophies. *Facts about Muscular Dystrophy.* Retrieved from http://www.mdausa.org/publications/fa-md-9.html

National Institute of Neurological Disorders and Stroke. (2000). *Muscular dystrophy.* Retrieved from http://www.ninds.nih.gov/health_and_medical/disorders/md.htm

Porter, P., Hall, C., & Williams, F. (2000). A teacher's guide to Duchenne muscular dystrophy. *MDA Publications.* Retrieved from http://www.mdausa.org:80/publications/tchrdmd/index.html

Smith, M., McKusick, V., & Lo, W. (2000). 310300 Emery-Dreifuss muscular dystrophy. *National Center for Biotechnology Information's Online Mendelian Inheritance in Man.* Retrieved from http://www.ncbi.nlm.nih.gov:80/entrez/dispomim.cgi?id=310300

Tiller, G., & McKusick, V. (2000). 181350 Emery-Dreifuss muscular dystrophy, autosomal dominant: EDMD2. *National Center for Biotechnology Information's Online Mendelian Inheritance in Man.* Retrieved from http://www.ncbi.nlm.nih.gov:80/entrez/dispomim.cgi?id=181350

Yates, J. (2000). Emery-Dreifuss muscular dystrophy. *European Neuromuscular Centre.* Retrieved from http://enmc.spc.ox.ac.uk/DC/EDMDcrit

Leslie D. Rosenstein
Neuropsychology Clinic
Austin, Texas

MUSCULAR DYSTROPHY, FACIOSCAPULOHUMERAL

Facioscalpulohumeral muscular dystrophy is a neuromuscular disease also referred to as FSHD, FSH, FMD, and Landouzy-Dejerine muscular dystrophy. FSHD involves a wasting of the muscles that move the face (facio), shoulders (scapula), and upper arm bone (humerus). FSHD is autosomal dominant in males and females; however, there are instances (10–30% of affected individuals) of FSHD with no genetic link. There is no known cure for FSHD (Muscular Dystrophy Association, 2001).

FSHD is the third most common form of muscular dystrophy diagnosed in clinics, with a prevalence of approximately 1 in 20,000, and it appears to affect males and females in almost equal numbers (Kissel, 1999).

Progression of FSHD is usually slow with long periods of stability interspersed with shorter periods of rapid muscle deterioration and increased weakness. Age of onset is teens to early adulthood (Muscular Dystrophy Association, 2001). Initial complaints of individuals with FSHD are weakness and muscle fatigue. Difficulties that can occur but often are considered to be medically insignificant include being unable to whistle or drink through a straw because of facial weakness or having been described in childhood as having a "funny smile." Patients with FSHD recall the inability to perform activities involving the shoulder muscles such as climbing trees, swinging golf clubs, and throwing baseballs. Many FSHD patients are asymptomatic with diagnosis being established on the basis of a physical examination (Kissel, 1999).

Characteristics

1. Child or adolescent experiences muscle weakness in the face and shoulders that spreads to the abdomen, feet, upper arms, pelvic area, and lower arms.

2. Child or adolescent may experience hearing loss, retinal abnormalities, and in rare instances, mental retardation.
3. Early signs of FSHD are forward-sloping shoulders with difficulty raising arms over head and closing of the eyes.
4. In severe cases of FSHD, the child or adolescent may experience impairment of walking, chewing, swallowing, and speaking.

No specific treatment is currently available for FSHD. The child with FSHD can expect to undergo physical therapy to help maintain muscle flexibility and prevent contracture development. There are physical and adaptive aids that may be helpful in performing certain activities. Severe cases of FSHD may require use of wheelchairs. Speech therapy, assistive devices, or supportive techniques may be utilized to improve speech and communication problems associated with hearing impairment and facial weakness. In some cases surgery may be necessary to attach the shoulder blades to the chest wall to stabilize the scapulae and improve mobility of the upper arms (National Organization for Rare Disorders, Inc., 2001).

Research toward prevention and treatment of FSHD is ongoing. FSHD patients have been found to be capable of responding to movement therapy, which suggests that motor learning therapy may be a useful treatment modality (Bakhtiary, Phoenix, Edwards, & Frostick, 2000). Studies involving the effects of albuterol as an aid in improving muscle mass and strength are currently under way through two randomized controlled trials (Kissel, 1999).

Children with FSHD may qualify for special education services under the handicapping condition of Other Health Impairment or Physical Disability. Students with FSHD may require occupational therapy and speech-language services. FSHD is a degenerative disease, and affected children have a unique set of problems that need to be investigated and understood by school personnel.

The school experience for children with physical disabilities is very important. Because the disability can limit their employment possibilities, children with FSHD need to rely on cognitive abilities to have a chance at gainful employment and independence as adults. Additionally, school allows for the social contact that is important to their emotional development and well-being. School can provide a valuable social arena outside of the family. Children with FSHD will encounter loss of motor activity, and it is important for teachers and peers to understand that this loss of activity is not synonymous with loss of cognitive ability (Charash, Wolf, Kutscher, Lovelace, & Hale, 1983).

REFERENCES

Bakhtiary, A., Phoenix, J., Edwards, R., & Frostick, S. (2000). The effect of motor learning in facioscapulohumeral muscular dystrophy patients. *European Journal of Applied Physiology, 83*(6), 551–558.

Charash, L., Wolf, G., Kutscher, A., Lovelace, R., & Hale, M. (1983). *Psychosocial aspects of muscular dystrophy.* Springfield, IL: Charles C. Thomas.

Kissel, J. (1999). Facioscapulohumeral dystrophy. *Seminars in Neurology, 9*(1), 35–43.

Muscular Dystrophy Association. (2001). Facts about muscular dystrophy. Retrieved April 2001 from http://www.mdausa.org

National Organization for Rare Disorders, Inc. (2000). Facioscapulo-humeral dystrophy. Retrieved April 2001 from http://www.rarediseases.org

Carla Cde Baca
University of Northern Colorado

MUSCULAR DYSTROPHY, FUKUYAMA

Fukuyama muscular dystrophy is a degenerative disorder in which there is generalized muscle weakness, hypotonia, and mental retardation from early infancy (Leyton, Gabreëls, Renier, & ter Laak, 1996; McKusick, Hurko, & Smith, 2000; Toda & Kobayashi, 1999; Toda, Kobayashi, Kondo-Iida, Sasaki, & Nakamura, 2000). The etiology is genetic, with an autosomal recessive transmission (McKusick et al., 2000; Toda & Kobayashi, 1999; Toda et al., 2000; Tsao & Mendell, 1999). The specific genetic mechanism has been identified as probably being a loss of function of the gene fukitin, which is an extracellular protein (McKusick et al., 2000; Toda et al., 2000; Tsao & Mendell, 1999).

Estimates of the incidence of this disease range from rates of approximately 2–12 per 100,000 in Japan (Toda et al., 2000; Tsao & Mendell, 1999), and the disease is rarely found in Western populations (Leyton et al., 1996). It is considered to be the second most common form of childhood muscular dystrophy, and one of the most common autosomal recessive disorders, in the Japanese population (Toda et al., 2000). Males and females are affected almost equally (Leyton et al., 1996).

Characteristics

1. Hypotonia and generalized muscle weakness from infancy, with the face, proximal muscles of the upper body, and distal muscles of the lower body being most affected.
2. Brain malformations including mild cobblestone lissencephaly.
3. Mental retardation, often severe.
4. Pseudohypertrophy of the calves and forearms by early childhood in many cases.
5. Pseudohypertrophy of the cheeks in infancy and weakness of the facial muscles resulting in characteristic

changes in appearance with aging; the mouth is usually held partially open and assumes an inverted V shape.

6. Joint contractures, not evident at birth, but by the end of the first year, affecting the hips, knees, and elbows; the tendon reflexes are decreased or absent.
7. Seizures occur in about half the cases.
8. There can be eye involvement including myopia, cataracts, abnormal eye movements, pale optic discs, and retinal detachment.
9. Elevated creatine kinase (CK).
10. Most patients never ambulate, with maximal function being a sliding crawl while in a sitting position.
11. Most patients are bedridden by age 10 and die by age 20.

(See Dubowitz, 2000; Leyton et al., 1996; McKusick et al., 2000; Muscular Dystrophy Association, 2000; Toda & Kobayashi, 1999; Toda et al., 2000; Tsao & Mendell, 1999)

Treatment is generally supportive and palliative. Physical therapy is needed to minimize the contractures, and medications are prescribed for the seizures (Muscular Dystrophy Association, 2000).

Special education services will be available under the handicapping condition of Other Health Impairment. The mental retardation will also qualify a student for special education services. Patients will require assistance and accommodations for tasks dependent on normal motor functioning, including ambulation, writing, and other graphomotor tasks. Many of the considerations and accommodations outlined by Porter, Hall, and Williams (2000) apply to students with Fukuyama muscular dystrophy as well. Those considerations are reviewed in this manual in the Duchenne muscular dystrophy entry.

Patients with Fukuyama muscular dystrophy are usually bedridden by age 10 due to the contractures and generalized muscle atrophy, and they usually die by the age of 20 (Toda et al., 2000; Tsao & Mendell, 1999). Research continues to focus on the genetic etiology.

REFERENCES

Dubowitz, V. (2000). Congenital muscular dystrophy. *European Neuromuscular Centre.* Retrieved October 5, 2000, from http://enmc.spc.ox.ac.uk

Leyton, Q., Gabreëls, F., Renier, W., & ter Laak, H. (1996). Congenital muscular dystrophy: A review of the literature. *Clinical Neurology and Neurosurgery, 98,* 267–280.

McKusick, V., Hurko, O., & Smith, M. (2000). Fukuyama muscular dystrophy: FCMD. *National Center for Biotechnology Information's Online Mendelian Inheritance in Man (OMIM).* Retrieved from http://www.ncbi.nlm.nih.gov:80/entrez/dispomim.cgi?id=253800

Muscular Dystrophy Association. (2000). Major characteristics of the nine (9) muscular dystrophies. *Facts about Muscular Dystrophy.* Retrieved August 27, 2000, from http://www.mdausa.org/publications/fa-md-9.html

Porter, P., Hall, C., & Williams, F. (2000). A teacher's guide to Duchenne muscular dystrophy. *MDA Publications.* Retrieved September 6, 2000, from http://www.mdausa.org:80/publications/tchrdmd/index.html

Toda, T., & Kobayashi, K. (1999). Fukuyama-type congenital muscular dystrophy: The first *human* disease to be caused by an ancient retrotransposal integration. *Journal of Molecular Medicine, 77,* 816–823.

Toda, T., Kobayashi, K., Kondo-Iida, E., Sasaki, J., & Nakamura, Y. (2000). Review article: The Fukuyama congenital muscular dystrophy story. *Neuromuscular Disorders, 10,* 153–159.

Tsao, C., & Mendell, J. (1999). The childhood muscular dystrophies: Making order out of chaos. *Seminars in Neurology, 19,* 9–23.

Leslie D. Rosenstein
Neuropsychology Clinic
Austin, Texas

MUSCULAR DYSTROPHY, LIMB GIRDLE

The limb girdle muscular dystrophies are a heterogenous group of progressive myopathies or dystrophies in which the shoulder or pelvic girdle musculature is affected first or to a greater degree than other symptoms (see Bushby, 1999, 2000; Muscular Dystrophy Association [MDA], 2000b; Tsao & Mendell, 1999). The mode of transmission is genetic, and there are several different forms, including at least three autosomal dominant and eight autosomal recessive forms (see Bushby, 1999, 2000; Tsao & Mendell, 1999).

Incidence rates are difficult to ascertain given the heterogeneity, rarity, and ever-changing diagnostic precision of the limb girdle muscular dystrophies. Males and females are affected (Adams & Victor, 1993). Onset varies widely from early childhood through the fourth decade. Progression also varies widely from very slow to very rapid. These variances in onset and progression are both between and within the different forms.

Characteristics

Autosomal Dominant (designated LGMD1A, LGMD1B, LGMD1C/caveolin deficient, and LGMD1D

1. Progressive weakness primarily or predominantly in the shoulder and/or pelvic girdle musculature with sparing of the facial, extraocular, and pharyngeal muscles.
2. Onset varies from early childhood to late 30s, except among those with caveolin deficiency, whose onset is usually around age 5.

3. Slow progression in LGMD1A and B, variable in caveolin deficiency, usually with a relatively benign course, except among those with cardiomyopathy (LGMB1B).
4. Cardiomyopathy (e.g., conduction defects) common among one group (LGMB1B).
5. Dysarthria among a pedigree with LGMD1A.
6. Normal mentation.
7. Serum creatine kinase elevated among those with caveolin deficiency (LGMD1C) or LGMD1D.

Autosomal Recessive (sarcoglycanopathies, calpainopathy, dysferlinopathy, and LGMD2G and 2H):

1. Progressive weakness primarily or predominantly in the shoulder and/or pelvic girdle musculature with sparing of the face, except among those with Hutterite type, who progress to have a flat smile along with waddling gait due to involvement of the guadriceps. Those with dysferlinopathy may have initial weakness in distal muscles.
2. Slow progression and onset in childhood to the 20s, except among those with SCARMD, severe forms of the sarcoglycanopathies, whose onset is between 3 and 5 years, with rapid progression, loss of ambulation, and then death by the 20s.
3. Longevity may be normal among the milder forms.
4. Calf hypertrophy is common, but not invariable across the recessive forms.
5. Calf contractures with tip-toe walking among the calpain-3-deficient patients; inability to walk on toes among others.
6. Elevated serum creatine kinase in calpainopathy, dysferlinopathy, and SCARMD.
7. Normal mentation.

(See Adams & Victor, 1993; Bushby, 1999, 2000; McKusick, 1997, 1998, 1999; McKusick & Hamosh, 1999; McKusick, Hurko, Smith, & Wright, 2000; McKusick & Tiller, 2000; Tsao & Mendell, 1999)

Current treatment is generally supportive and palliative. Treatments include physical therapy such as stretching to minimize contractures, bracing and surgery for scoliosis, and pacemaker insertion or heart transplant for some with cardiac problems (see Tsao & Mendell, 1999).

Special education services are available under the handicapping condition of Other Health Impairment. Patients will require assistance and accommodations for tasks dependent on motor functioning, particularly ambulation. Many of the considerations and accommodations outlined by Porter, Hall, and Williams (2000) apply to students with limb girdle muscular dystrophy as well. Those considerations are reviewed in this manual in the Duchenne muscular dystrophy entry.

The progression of limb girdle muscular dystrophy varies (Bushby, 1999). There is risk of sudden death due to cardiac conduction defects, particularly among those with one of the autosomal dominant forms (Tsao & Mendell, 1999), and respiratory complications are notable among some of the recessive forms (Bushby, 1999). Life expectancy may be nearly normal in the milder forms (McKusick, 1997), or shortened into late adolescence or the early 20s in more severe forms (McKusick, 1986). Investigations into gene therapies are ongoing, having moved from the lab out into the field with human studies (see MDA, 2000a; Tsao & Mendell, 1999).

REFERENCES

Adams, R., & Victor, M. (1993). *Principles of neurology* (5th ed.). New York: McGraw-Hill.

Bushby, K. (1999). Invited review: Making sense of the limb-girdle muscular dystrophies. *Brain, 122,* 1403–1420.

Bushby, K. (2000). Limb-girdle muscular dystrophy. *European Neuromuscular Centre.* Retrieved August 27, 2000, from http://enmc.spc.ox.ac.uk.DC/LGMDcrit

McKusick, V. (1986). No. 254110 Muscular dystrophy, limb-girdle, Type 2H; LGMD2H; Muscular dystrophy, Hutterite type. *National Center for Biotechnology Information's Online Mendelian Inheritance in Man.* Retrieved from http://www.ncbi.nlm.nih.gov/htbin-post/Omim/dispmim?254110

McKusick, V. (1997). No. 601173 Muscular dystrophy, limb-girdle, autosomal recessive. *National Center for Biotechnology Information's Online Mendelian Inheritance in Man.* Retrieved from http://www.ncbi.nlm.nih.gov/htbin-post/Omim/dispmim?601173

McKusick, V. (1998). No. 254110 Muscular dystrophy, limb-girdle, Type 2H; LGMD2H: Muscular dystrophy, Hutterite type. *National Center for Biotechnology Information's Online Mendelian Inheritance in Man.* Retrieved from http://www.ncbi.nlm.nih.gov/htbin-post/Omim/dispmim?254110

McKusick, V. (1999). No. 603511 Muscular dystrophy, limb-girdle, Type 1D; LGMD1D. *National Center for Biotechnology Information's Online Mendelian Inheritance in Man.* Retrieved from http://www.ncbi.nlm.nih.gov/htbin-post/Omim/dispmim?603511

McKusick, V., & Hamosh, A. (1999). No. 253601 Muscular dystrophy, limb-girdle, Type 2B; LGMD2B. *National Center for Biotechnology Information's Online Mendelian Inheritance in Man.* Retrieved from http://www.ncbi.nlm.nih.gov/htbin-post/Omim/dispmim?253601

McKusick, V., Hurko, O., Smith, M., & Wright, M. (2000). No. 253700 Muscular dystrophy, limb-girdle, Type 2C; LGMD2. *National Center for Biotechnology Information's Online Mendelian Inheritance in Man.* Retrieved from http://www.ncbi.nlm.nih.gov/htbin-post/Omim/dispmim?253700

McKusick, V., & Tiller, G. (2000). No. 159001 Muscular dystrophy, limb-girdle, Type 1B; LGMD1B. *National Center for Biotechnology Information's Online Mendelian Inheritance in Man.* Retrieved from http://www.ncbi.nlm.nih.gov/htbin-post/Omim/dispmim?159001

Muscular Dystrophy Association. (2000a). Active neuromuscular clinical trials and studies selective listing. *MDA Research*. Retrieved from http://www.mdausa.org/research/ctrials.html

Muscular Dystrophy Association. (2000b). Major characteristics of the nine (9) muscular dystrophies. *Facts about muscular dystrophy*. Retrieved from http://www.mdausa.org/publications/fa-md-9.html

Porter, P., Hall, C., & Williams, F. (2000). A teacher's guide to Duchenne muscular dystrophy. *MDA Publications*. Retrieved from http://www.mdausa.org:80/publications/tchrdmd/index.html

Tsao, C., & Mendell, J. (1999). The childhood muscular dystrophies: Making order out of chaos. *Seminars in Neurology, 19,* 9–23.

Leslie D. Rosenstein
Neuropsychology Clinic
Austin, Texas

MUTISM, SELECTIVE

According to the fourth edition of the *Diagnostic and Statistical Manual of Mental Disorders* (American Psychiatric Association, 1994), selective mutism is the "persistent failure to speak in specific social situations (e.g., school, with playmates) where speaking is expected, despite speaking in other situations" (p. 114). This disturbance interferes with educational or occupational achievement and must be evident for at least 1 month, specifically not the first month of school. In the case of selective mutism, failure to speak is not better explained by a communication disorder (e.g., stuttering) or lack of familiarity with the language.

In general, selective mutism is a relatively rare disorder occurring in less than 1% of individuals treated in mental health clinics, and slightly more females than males are given this diagnosis. No cultural variables have been indicated; hesitance to speak in certain settings by immigrant children should not be considered selective mutism. Typically, the disorder lasts a few months, but in some cases it continues for years.

Characteristics

1. Persistent failure to speak in specific social situations when speaking is expected, despite speaking in other situations.
2. Individual may be willing to speak in some situations but not others and with some people but not others. It is common for children with selective mutism to speak with other children in the classroom when adults are out of hearing range, but not in the presence of the teacher or other adults.
3. Excessive shyness, fear of social embarrassment, social isolation and withdrawal, clinging, compulsive traits, oppositional behavior, temper tantrums, and negativism are associated features.
4. Typically begins before age 5, but is noticed when the child enters school.

Selective mutism has been conceptualized as a manifestation of a child's anxiety (Cunningham, Cataldo, Mallion, & Keyes, 1983). Thus, the formulation of an intervention for a child with selective mutism often involves anxiety-reducing techniques such as stimulus and situation fading. It also has been conceptualized as a means of obtaining attention from adults. That is, a child with selective mutism may gain attention both from teachers who are working to elicit the child's speech and from peers who may begin speaking on behalf of the child. The attention may provide positive reinforcement for the child to avoid speaking.

Many techniques have been employed to treat selective mutism. These methods include positive prompts (Kazdin, 1994), peer modeling (Kazdin, 1994), self-modeling (Kehle et al., 1998), family therapy (Tatem & DelCampo, 1995), stimulus fading (Cunningham et al., 1983; Kehle et al., 1998), shaping (Cunningham et al., 1983; Porjes, 1992), reinforcement techniques (Cunningham et al., 1983; Kehle et al., 1998), self-reinforcement (Kehle et al., 1998), contingency management (Cunningham et al., 1983; Porjes, 1992), escape-avoidance techniques (Cunningham et al., 1983; Porjes, 1992), aversive contingency (Cunningham et al., 1983), reinforcement sampling (Labbe & Williamson, 1984), pharmacological therapy (Kehle et al., 1998), and mystery motivators (Kehle et al., 1998). Several researchers proposed employing a combination of multiple methods executed in concert. For instance, Kehle et al. used a combination of self-modeling, positive reinforcement, stimulus fading, and mystery motivators.

Treatment may be implemented in the regular education classroom. Barring additional comorbid disorders, special education services generally are not necessary for individuals with selective mutism. Intervention typically requires the aid of a school psychologist working in consultation with the teacher and parents. Treatment of selective mutism relies on the assistance of persons with whom the target child interacts. Cooperation of parents, teachers, and peers increases the likelihood of a successful intervention for the disorder.

Selective mutism is particularly resistant to treatment (Kehle et al., 1998). Research emphasizes the importance of quickly implementing a multimethod intervention for selective mutism. That is, research indicates that the disorder becomes more resistant to change as the duration of the intervention (and the disorder) increases. Outcomes reported in recent studies, however, suggest that multimethod approaches to treatment are effective both immediately and in follow-up examination.

REFERENCES

American Psychiatric Association. (1994). *Diagnostic and statistical manual of mental disorders* (4th ed.). Washington, DC: Author.

Cunningham, C. E., Cataldo, M. F., Mallion, C., & Keyes, J. B. (1983). A review and controlled single case evaluation of behavioral approaches to the management of elective mutism. *Child and Family Behavior Therapy, 5,* 25–49.

Kazdin, A. E. (1994). *Behavior modification in applied settings.* Pacific Grove: Brooks/Cole.

Kehle, T. J., Madaus, M. R., Baratta, V. S., & Bray, M. A. (1998). Augmented self-modeling as a treatment for children with selective mutism. *Journal of School Psychology, 36,* 247–260.

Labbe, E. E., & Williamson, D. A. (1984). Behavioral treatment of elective mutism: A review of the literature. *Clinical Psychology Review, 4,* 273–292.

Porjes, M. D. (1992). Intervention with the selectively mute child. *Psychology in the Schools, 29,* 367–376.

Tatem, D. W., & DelCampo, R. L. (1995). Selective mutism in children: A structural family therapy approach to treatment. *Contemporary Family Therapy, 17,* 177–194.

Renée M. Tobin
Texas A&M University

MYALGIC ENCEPHALOYELITIS (NEURASTHENIA)

The term *neurasthenia* (from the Greek *neur,* "nerve" and *asthenia,* "weak") is attributed to the 19th-century American neurologist George M. Beard, who coined it in 1869. Beard and other physicians began to notice patients who suffered from a constellation of symptoms that included fatigue, muscle soreness, insomnia, difficulty concentrating, general malaise, weakness of extremities, and an occasional fever-like delirium. These symptoms were typically observed after a period of prolonged physical or mental stress. Sometimes an infection preceded the onset of symptoms, but, more often, no prior infection was observed. Reports of contagion (e.g., affliction among family members, associates, or health care workers exposed to the patient) were rare. The condition also appeared to be chronic: Symptoms recurred at times of emotional stress or minimal physical exertion. This presentation caused physicians of the late-19th and early-20th century to propose that neurasthenia resulted when the body was pushed, by overwork or excessive emotional strain, beyond its limits. In medical writings of the time, the condition was also referred to as "nervous exhaustion." The recommended treatment was bed rest, improved nutrition, mild exercise, hydrotherapy (medicinal baths), massage, and avoidance of "mental and emotional excitement" (Musser & Kelly, 1912; for reviews, see Sichherman, 1977; Wessley, 1999).

Before World War I, the diagnosis carried no particular stigma and in fact conferred a certain status to the sufferer, as it was seen as afflicting persons of the middle and upper classes. However, Freud's recasting of neurasthenia as a manifestation of hysteria and its association with "battle neurosis" during the war caused persons with the diagnosis to be considered "mentally ill" and, especially in a military context, simultaneously cast them under suspicion of malingering.

Currently in the United States, the mental health professions have adopted the taxonomy of the American Psychiatric Association's *Diagnostic and Statistical Manual of Mental Disorders,* now in its fourth edition (*DSM-IV*), which does not include neurasthenia as a diagnostic category. Professionals who use the *DSM-IV* tend to attribute components of neurasthenia to other psychiatric diagnoses (e.g., mood and anxiety disorders, posttraumatic stress disorder). Also, as medical knowledge has grown, the diagnoses of ailments with similar symptoms but of known infectious origin, such as Lyme disease, have thinned the ranks of persons who would have been viewed as neurasthenic. Hence, in the United States the term *neurasthenia* has fallen out of use. There are, however, patients who present with the central features of neurasthenia and do not fit neatly into other current diagnostic categories. This has fueled a growing popular and professional interest in chronic fatigue syndrome (CFS) and its British counterpart, myalgic encephaloyelitis (ME)—syndrome that have many of the core features of neurasthenia.

Neurasthenia is frequently diagnosed in other parts of the world, particularly Eastern Europe and Asia. The term appears in the most current version of the International Classification of Diseases–10th Revision (ICD-10, 1992), published by the World Health Organization for use in classifying and collecting data on medical and psychological illnesses worldwide. Further research will tell whether neurasthenia is best understood as a collection of separate psychological and medical syndromes or whether it stands on its own as a distinct diagnostic entity.

Characteristics (adapted from ICD-10 criteria):

1. Persistent and distressing complaints of increased fatigue after mental effort

OR

2. Persistent and distressing complaints of bodily weakness and exhaustion after minimal effort
3. At least two of the following: Feelings of muscular aches and pains; dizziness; tension headaches; sleep disturbance; inability to relax; irritability; dyspepsia
4. Depressive or autonomic symptoms not sufficiently persistent and severe to fulfill the criteria for any of the more specific mental disorders

The educational implications of neurasthenia are similar to those for other chronic, intermittent, debilitating diseases (such as multiple sclerosis). The fatigue, weakness, muscle pain, and impairments in concentration and memory reported in neurasthenia could create substantial challenges for the sufferer in adapting to the demands of a standard learning environment (i.e., a school, college, etc.). For elementary and secondary education students, flexibility in testing and assignment deadlines could be useful, and lapses in attendance could be offset by increased teacher-parent contact and home assignments. For difficult cases, home schooling might be indicated.

In the United States, postsecondary students (i.e., students in college, graduate-level, or certification programs) suffering from neurasthenia-like symptoms may, depending on the nature and severity of their impairments, obtain assistance under the Americans with Disabilities Act of 1990. The law states that postsecondary institutions must make reasonable accommodations (i.e., procedural changes) for students with verified disabilities to help them compete equally with nondisabled students. There are limits: Institutions are not required to make changes that affect the core elements of their curricula or that incur an undue administrative or financial burden. Persons dealing with neurasthenia-like symptoms would be well advised to contact their school's disability office and discuss their needs. In cases where impairment is severe or drastically unpredictable, distance learning and Internet-based educational options may be more appropriate choices.

REFERENCES

Musser, J. H., & Kelly, O. A. (Eds.). (1912). A handbook of practical treatment. Retrieved from http://pages.prodigy.com/Meridian Institute/neurasth.htm

Sichherman, B. (1977). The uses of a diagnosis: Doctors, patients and neurasthenia. *Journal of the History of Medicine, 32,* 33–54.

Wessley, S. (1999). Chronic fatigue syndrome: A 20th century illness? *Scandinavian Journal of Work and Environmental Health, 23,* 17–34.

ICD-10 classification of mental and behavioral disorders: Clinical descriptions and diagnostic guidelines. (1992). Geneva: World Health Organization.

Donald A. Kirson
Counseling Center, University of San Diego

MYELITIS

Myelitis is the label describing a category of diseases marked by inflammation of the spinal cord. Adams and Victor (1993) summarized the adjectives commonly used to describe the course of myelitis. *Acute* refers to the development of symptoms within a few days, whereas *subacute* indicates that the clinical signs onset over a period of two to six weeks. Furthermore, *poliomyelitis* describes gray matter inflammation, whereas *leukomyelitis* is reserved for those cases presenting with only white matter complications.

The common etiologies of myelitis often serve to form subclassifications under this broad diagnostic category (Adams & Victor, 1993). Viral agents may cause spinal cord inflammation associated with poliomyelitis, rabies, herpes, and AIDS. Myelitis as a reaction to bacterial, fungal, or parasitic disease is relatively easier to diagnose than is that resulting from a virus because of indications in the cerebrospinal fluid (CSF), although the contraction of myelitis as a result of fungus or parasites is rare in the United States. In a severe presentation, however, both the spinal cord and the surrounding meninges may be affected (Adams & Victor, 1993). Myelitis has also been reported to occur after infections or immunizations. Although rare, spinal cord inflammation and damage resulting from cancerous tissue, paraneoplastic myelitis, has been observed (Lynn, 2001).

Another differentiating feature among the types of myelitis involves the distinction between the transverse and diffuse nature of the disorder (Adams & Victor, 1993). The term *transverse* indicates a cross-sectional focus of inflammation at one level of the spinal cord, with normal presentation of functioning above the disturbance and compromised functioning below it (Johns Hopkins Transverse Myelopathy Center [JHTMC], 2000a). Much of the research on myelopathy has focused on transverse myelitis, which is associated with several diseases, including multiple sclerosis, systemic lupus erythematosus, syphilis, and Lyme disease (JHTMC, 2000b). Multiple sclerosis, however, is diagnosed only after at least two episodes of demyelination. Therefore, it is possible that patients with transverse myelitis may later receive a diagnosis of multiple sclerosis; furthermore, those patients who are shown to have an abnormal MRI at the time of the first onset of myelitis are more likely to be later diagnosed with multiple sclerosis (Lynn, 2001). Additionally, transverse myelitis linked to vascular causes, such as ischemia or bleeding in the spinal cord, is more common among older patients and those with a history of cardiac disease (JHTMC, 2000b). Transverse myelitis is relatively rare, with reported prevalence rates ranging from approximately 1 per million (Berman, Feldman, Alter, Zilber, & Kahana, 1981, as cited in Lynn, 2001) to nearly 5 per million (Jeffery, Mandler, & Davis, 1993).

Transverse myelitis is often of idiopathic origin. Researchers, however, suggest that autoimmune processes are involved, causing an attack on the spinal cord and subsequent inflammation (Lynn, 2001). Furthermore, the abnormal immune response to the infection is implicated, rather than the agent itself (Adams & Victor, 1993). The diagnostic process must rule out lesions compressing the spinal cord, and this is generally done through MRI or myelography (a series of X rays conducted after dye is inserted into the sac surrounding the spinal cord). If both blood work and lumbar puncture fail to reveal the cause of the inflammation, the diagnosis would be idiopathic or parainfectious transverse myelitis (Lynn, 2001). Although most individuals do not suffer from a second case of transverse myelitis (Lynn, 2001), the prognosis for these patients is variable. Recovery generally starts two weeks to several months after onset, and patients rarely achieve full recovery (National Institute of Neurological Disorders and Stroke [NINDS], 2001). Furthermore, many individuals with this disorder suffer from long-term disability, including sensory, motor, and bowel complications. No cure exists for this disorder, and treatment efforts focus on minimizing symptoms (NINDS, 2001).

Characteristics

1. Inflammation of the spinal cord
2. Damage to neural tissue
3. Motor and sensory disturbance
4. Bowel and bladder complications and radicular pain common in transverse myelitis

Students with myelitis qualify for special services under Section 504 of the Rehabilitation Act of 1973 and under the Individuals with Disabilities Act. Specifically, children and adolescents presenting with this disorder would be offered accommodations under the disability categories of Orthopedic Impairment or Other Health Impairment. Motoric functioning may be severely compromised for many of these students, requiring adaptations of the school environment for their physical impairment. Additionally, the individualized educational program planning team may consider the potential benefit of assistive technology. Educators should also be aware of any bladder or bowel control difficulties the student exhibits, in addition to the psychological effects of a medical illness.

REFERENCES

Adams, R. D., & Victor, M. (1993). Diseases of the spinal cord. In *Principles of neurology* (5th ed., pp. 1078–1116). New York: McGraw-Hill.

Berman, M., Feldman, S., Alter, M., Zilber, N., & Kahana, E. (1981). Acute transverse myelitis: Incidence and etiological considerations. *Neurology, 31*(8), 966–971.

Jeffery, D. R., Mandler, R. N., & Davis, L. E. (1993). Transverse myelitis: Retrospective analysis of 33 cases, with differentiation of cases associated with multiple sclerosis and parainfectious events. *Archives of Neurology, 50,* 532–535.

Johns Hopkins Transverse Myelopathy Center. (2000a). Definitions and anatomy. Retrieved from http://www.med.jhu.edu/jhtmc/JHTMC_denfandanat_nf.htm

Johns Hopkins Transverse Myelopathy Center. (2000b). Diseases associated with TM. Retrieved from http://www.med.jhu.edu.jhtmc/JHTMC_diseases_nf.htm

Lynn, J. (2001). Transverse myelitis: Symptoms, causes and diagnosis. Retrieved from http://www.myelitis.org/tm.htm

National Institute of Neurological Disorders and Stroke. (2001). NINDS transverse myelitis information page. Retrieved from http://www.ninds.nih.gov/health_and_medical/disorders/transversemyelitis_doc.htm

Sarah Schnoebelen
Margaret Semrud-Clikeman
University of Texas at Austin

MYELOFIBROSIS, IDIOPATHIC

Myelofibrosis is said to occur when there is a formation of fibrous tissue or fibrosis within the bone marrow. Idiopathic myelofibrosis is the term used when the cause of the fibrosis within the bone marrow is unknown. Myelofibrosis may be a reaction to injury that results in the death of bone marrow tissue. In some instances, it is associated with metastasis or the spread of cancer to the bone marrow, metabolic disorders, or chronic myeloid leukemia. Idiopathic myelofibrosis affects both men and women equally with onset usually in adulthood. Myelofibrosis rarely occurs in children; when it does, it is most likely in connection with Albers-Schönberg disease, which affects bone (National Organization for Rare Disorders [NORD], 2000). In two cases, idiopathic myelofibrosis was found to be familial with presentation in two sisters who were 4 years and 7 months at age of onset respectively (Bonduel, Sciuccati, Torres, Pierini, & Galla, 1998). There are no indications that idiopathic myelofibrosis occurs in one ethnic group more frequently than in any other groups.

As a result of the fibrosis, the bone marrow's ability to produce red blood cells may be affected, and anemia can result (Manoharan, 1998). Also related to the bone marrow and red blood cell production, the individual may develop an abnormally large spleen (splenomegaly); the liver may be similarly enlarged (hepatomegaly). Additional problems may include abdominal pain, weight loss, weakness, and fatigue. The progression of the disorder is generally slow. It can be difficult to differentiate idiopathic myelofibrosis from other disorders due to the variability of clinical and morphological findings among individuals affected (Thiele, Kvasnicka, Zankovich, & Diehl, 2001).

Characteristics

1. Weight loss
2. Fatigue, dizziness, and generalized weakness associated with anemia

3. Splenomegaly or hepatomegaly
4. Jaundice
5. Fever
6. Headache
7. Severe pain in bones, joints, and abdomen

Treatment is symptomatic and supportive depending on the individual and the presence of any other disorders. For anemia and decreased production of red blood cells, blood transfusions may be required. Additional treatments may include the use of corticosteroids, androgens, and myelosuppressive agents have been used as well (Cervantes, Hernandez-Boluda, Alvarez, Nadal, & Montserrat, 2000; Manorharan, 1998). Radiation or surgery to reduce the size of an enlarged spleen or liver may be necessary. A number of additional treatments are being investigated, including the use of allogeneic or autologous stem-cell transplantation. Stem cells are involved in the production of red blood cells, and transplanted cells may be health cells from the affected individual (autologous) or from a family member (allogeneic). Two new drugs being researched are interferon-alpha and pirdenidone, but these require additional study (NORD, 2000).

Depending on the level of impaired mobility associated with the weakness and fatigue, as well as the bone and joint pain, accommodations may be needed for individuals affected. In those rare instances when children may be affected by idiopathic myelofibrosis, accommodations in school may be needed for medical complications (e.g., surgery due to splenomegaly, fatigue) under Other Health Impairment to the extent that the child's education may be impacted. There is no indication that idiopathic myelofibrosis has a direct impact on cognition or learning.

REFERENCES

Bonduel, M., Sciuccati, G., Torres, A. F., Pierini, A., & Galla, G. (1998). Familial idiopathic myelofibrosis and multiple hemangiomas. *American Journal of Hematology, 59,* 175–177.

Cervantes, F., Hernandez-Boluda, J. C., Alvarez, A., Nadal, E., & Montserrat, E. (2000). Danazol treatment of idiopathic myelofibrosis with severe anemia. *Haematologica, 85,* 595–599.

Manoharan, A. (1998). Idiopathic myelofibrosis: A clinical review. *International Journal of Hematology, 68,* 355–362.

National Organization for Rare Disorders. (2000). Myelofibrosis, idiopathic. Retrieved June 3, 2001, from www.rarediseases.org

Thiele, J., Kvasnicka, H. M., Zankovich, R., & Diehl, V. (2001). Clinical and morphological criteria for the diagnosis of prefibrotic idiopathic (primary) myelofibrosis. *Annals of Hematology, 80*(3), 160–165.

Cynthia A. Riccio
Texas A&M University

See also Albers-Schönberg Disease

MYHRE SYNDROME

Myhre syndrome, or growth-mental deficiency syndrome of myhre, is an extremely rare disorder. It is an inherited disorder believed to be autosomal dominant and a result of mutation of paternal origin (Garcia-Cruz et al., 1993). All six cases reported in the literature have been males, born to parents in their late thirties (Garcia-Cruz et al., 1993; Myhre, Ruvalcaba, & Graham, 1981; Soljak, Aftimos, & Gluckman, 1983; Whiteford, Doig, Raine, Hollman, & Tolmie, 2001). The disorder is exceptionally rare (only six cases reported), and no information is available on its relative incidence across ethnic groups.

Characteristics

1. Mental retardation
2. Short stature
3. Unusual facial features including narrow skin folds between the upper and lower eyelids, underdevelopment of the upper jaw bone, and an unusually prominent lower jaw
4. Various skeletal abnormalities
5. Hearing impairment
6. Abnormal enlargement of the muscles
7. Joint stiffness
8. In boys, failure of the testes to descend

At the time of birth, the infants may be smaller than expected, but in some cases the child's development is otherwise initially typical (Soljak et al., 1983). When the growth deficiency is manifest prenatally, the infant may be identified as being of low birth weight. In addition to shorter stature (growth deficiency) and other physical signs (e.g., unusual facial features), individuals with Myhre syndrome tend to have generalized muscle hypertrophy leading to stiffness and decreased joint movement. Mental retardation and early-onset hearing loss are also characteristic of the syndrome (Myhre et al., 1981; Soljak et al., 1983).

Once the disorder is fully manifest in early childhood, the individual affected will be in need of special education services due to cognitive deficits and deafness or hearing impairment. Although the mental retardation will not be the most obvious problem and is usually in the mild range, clinical evaluation should be conducted prior to school entry to ensure appropriate early intervention programming. Physical accommodations may also be needed depending on the limitations of the child as a result of the stiffness and lack of joint motility, as well as the child's short stature. Medical complications, including cardiac problems, may hinder the child's progress as well. Skeletal abnormalities may require surgical intervention. With the multiple challenges facing individuals with Myhre disorder, it is important that treatment efforts be coordinated across various professional staff including physicians, psychologists, physical therapists, audiologists, and teachers. Parents likely will need supportive counseling, especially if the child had previously seemed to be developing typically. All unaffected family members should participate in genetic counseling given the familial risk.

REFERENCES

Garcia-Cruz, D., Figuera, L. E., Ferio-Velazco, A., Sanchez-Corona, J., Garcia-Cruz, M. O., Ramirez-Duenas, R. M., Hernandez-Cordova, A., Ruiz, M. X., Bitar-Alatorre, W. E., Ramirez-Duenas, M. L., & Cantu, J. M. (1993). The Myhre syndrome: Report of two cases. *Clinical Genetics, 44,* 203–207.

Myhre, S. A., Ruvalcaba, R. H. A., & Graham, C. B. (1981). A new growth deficiency syndrome. *Clinical Genetics, 20,* 1–5.

Soljak, M. A., Aftimos, S., & Gluckman, P. D. (1983). A new syndrome of short stature, joint limitation, and muscle hypertrophy. *Clinical Genetics, 23,* 441–446.

Whiteford, M. L., Doig, W. B., Raine, P. A., Hollman, A. S., & Tolmie, J. L. (2001). *Clinical Dysmorphology, 10*(2), 135–140.

Cynthia A. Riccio
Texas A&M University

MYOCLONUS

Myoclonus is a symptom and not a diagnosable disease (National Institute of Neurological Disorders and Stroke [NINDS], 2000). It is defined as a sudden, brief, jerky, shock-like, and usually irregular, involuntary movement emanating from the central nervous system. Five distinguishing traits characterize myoclonus: positivity or negativity, distribution, regularity, its relation to motor activity, and synchronization (Fahn, Marsden, & Van Woert, 1986).

When the myoclonic jerk is the result of a muscular contraction, it is called positive myoclonus, but if it is the result of a temporary suspension in muscular activity, it is called negative myoclonus (Tassinari, Rubboli, & Shibasaki, 1998). Myoclonic jerks can be distributed across one area (focal), two or more adjacent areas (segmental), or in various areas of the body (generalized). The regularity with which these myoclonic jerks present themselves allows clinicians to classify them as rhythmic (very regular), arrhythmic (irregular), or oscillatory (in the presence of a sudden stimulus). Moreover, the rate at which these involuntary movements occur can range anywhere from many times in 1 min to random or isolated events (Fahn et al., 1986). Voluntary or intentional movements, such as when a person is asked to reach for a target, can produce myoclonic jerks. However, myoclonic jerks can also be present during a restful state. Synchronicity is another important feature of myoclonus. Synchronous myoclonus involves sudden, involuntary movements that take place within milliseconds of each other, as opposed to asynchronous myoclonic movements (Fahn et al., 1986).

Prevalence of myoclonus has not been studied thoroughly, and differences regarding gender and ethnicity in the manifestation of the symptoms are unknown. The multifarious nature of myoclonus has made this task difficult to carry out. Myoclonus seems to emerge as a consequence of chemical or drug poisoning, brain tumors, head or spinal cord injury, lipid storage disease, oxygen deprivation to the brain (hypoxia), liver or kidney failure, stroke, infection, or other medical conditions. Myoclonus is also usually one of many symptoms associated with diverse disorders of the nervous system, but it can also be found unaccompanied by another disorder (NINDS, 2000).

Characteristics

1. Sudden, involuntary jerking of a muscle or group of muscles is caused by muscle contractions or muscle relaxation.
2. Duration of the jerks ranges from multiple times in 1 min to random occurrences.
3. Regularity of jerks can be very regular (rhythmic), irregular (arrhythmic), or oscillatory (in the presence of a sudden stimulus).
4. Jerks can occur while in a restful state or during voluntary movements.
5. The distribution of the jerks can involve one area (focal), two or more areas (segmental), or in various areas of the body (generalized).
6. Jerks can be synchronous or asynchronous.

Medications such as clonazepam, valproate, primidone, piracetam, acetazolamide, baclofen, fluoxetine, propranolol, and 5-hydroxytryptophan (5-HTTP) have proven to be effective in the reduction of myoclonic symptoms (Myoclonus Research Foundation, 2000). However, the cluster of symptoms in which myoclonus is found may call for the use of various drugs in order for the treatment to be effective (NINDS, 2000).

Special education services may be available to children with myoclonus under the handicapping condition of Other Health Impairment, Specific Learning Disorder, or Traumatic Brain Injury. Depending on the degree of the disability and on individual characteristics, these children may be educated in regular classes with the assistance of special education teachers, in separate classes, or in residential classes. These children may also need the services of a speech pathologist, psychologist, or social worker. Side effects of medications for myoclonus should be considered when conducting academic, social, emotional, and cognitive assessments.

Prognosis for myoclonus will vary for each individual

because symptom reduction is contingent on the medical condition of that individual and any other disorders that may be present. Scientists are currently investigating the role that neurotransmitters and receptors play in myoclonus. Any findings linking neurotransmitters and receptors to the cause of myoclonus will allow future researchers to identify the nature and extent of those genetic alterations, allowing diagnostic tests and specific drug treatments to be developed (NINDS, 2000).

REFERENCE

Fahn, S., Marsden, C. D., & Van Woert, M. H. (1986). Definition and classification of myoclonus. *Advances in Neurology, 43,* 1–5.

Myoclonus Research Foundation. (2000, June 10). How is myoclonus treated? Retrieved from http://www.myoclonus.com/howis.htm

National Institute of Neurological Disorders and Stroke. (2000, June 23). NINDS myoclonus information page. Retrieved from http://www.ninds.nih.gov/health_and_medical/disorders/myoclonu_doc.htm

Tassinari, C. A., Rubboli, G., & Shibasaki, H. (1998). Neurophysiology of positive and negative myoclonus. *Electroencephalography and Clinical Neurophysiology, 107,* 181–195.

Roman Garcia de Alba
Texas A&M University

MYOPATHY, CONGENITAL, BATTEN TURNER TYPE

Batten Turner type congenital myopathy is a very rare muscular disorder that is progressive in nature. Initially evident by the lack of muscle tone at birth, Batten Turner type congenital myopathy is similar to congenital hypotonia. Also similar to Werdnig-Hoffman, in Batten Turner type the symptoms continue to progress through childhood before stabilizing in adolescence or early adulthood (National Organization for Rare Disorders [NORD], 1994).

Batten Turner type congenital myopathy is a genetic disorder with autosomal recessive transmission. Males and females are equally as likely to be affected. The incidence is exceptionally rare with only nine cases reported in the medical literature, and six of these were within the same family (NORD, 1994). Due to its rarity, no conclusions as to likelihood of occurrence based on ethnic group can be made.

Characteristics

1. Lack of muscle tone, "floppiness"
2. Delayed gross and fine motor development
3. Prone to falling or stumbling

Treatment is specific to a regular regimen of exercise and diet to avoid obesity (NORD, 1994). Although adults affected with Batten Turner type continue to demonstrate muscular weakness and decreased tone, they are able to be ambulatory and rarely need physical accommodations.

REFERENCE

National Organization for Rare Disorders. (1994). Myopathy, congenital, Batten Turner type (#139). Retrieved June 3, 2001, from www.rarediseases.org

Cynthia A. Riccio
Texas A&M University

See also Hypertonia-Rd

MYOPATHY, DESMIN STORAGE

Desmin storage myopathy is a muscle disorder that is so named based on the findings of accumulations of desmin in affected individuals. Desmin is a necessary protein that is involved in skeletal and cardiac muscle; desmin storage myopathy occurs when there are excessive amounts of desmin resulting in impaired muscle development or function (Goebel, 1995).

There are three forms of desmin storage myopathy, each of which manifests at different ages and with differing symptoms (Goebel, 1995). When desmin storage myopathy presents at birth (congenital), there is typically muscle weakness in the face and torso (shoulders and pelvic area) with proximal muscles affected. In addition, there is deformity to the spine such that it is curved (kyphoscoliosis). Heart disease may be present with desmin storage myopathy (cardiomyopathy). Desmin storage myopathy characterized by cardiomyopathy can present at any age level and may be life-threatening. Research suggests that desmin storage myopathy is caused by a mutation of the desmin gene (Goldfarb et al., 1998). For the congenital proximal and the cardiomyopathy desmin storage myopathy, the etiology of the mutation of the gene is unknown.

Characteristics

1. Muscle weakness of proximal muscles (congenital)
2. Cardiomyopathy as primary muscle affected (cardiomyopathy)
3. Muscle weakness of distal muscles (late onset)

The third form (late onset) presents in adulthood, usually after age 40. Primary symptoms include weakness of muscles in the hand and feet (Barohn, Amato, & Griggs, 1998). The late-onset distal form of desmin storage myopathy is progressive and familial with autosomal dominant transmission. The variability of causes, severity, and age of symptom onset preclude any accurate estimation of incidence; however, males and females appear to be affected at equal rates. No research has been done to investigate any differences based on ethnic group membership.

Treatment may include physical therapy or occupational therapy to address problems with muscle weakness. For children affected with desmin storage myopathy, early intervention and appropriate physiotherapy to facilitate gross and fine motor development may be appropriate. Depending on the extent of weakness, the use of assistive equipment (e.g., computer) may be needed as an alternative to written completion of assignments. The extent and nature of special education services should be based on the needs of the individual child. In addition to educational modifications, the possibility of cardiomyopathy will require medical monitoring, and if cardiomyopathy develops, medical management will need to be implemented. If there is a familial history of desmin storage myopathy, genetic counseling for the individual as well as unaffected family members is appropriate.

REFERENCES

Barohn, R. J., Amato, J. J., & Griggs, R. C. (1998). Overview of the distal myopathies: From the clinical to the molecular. *Neuromuscular Disorders, 8,* 309–316.

Goebel, H. H. (1995). Desmin-related neuromuscular disorders. *Muscle and Nerve, 18,* 1306–1320.

Goldfarb, L. G., Park, K.-Y., Cervenakova, L., Gorokhova, S., Lee, H.-S., Vasconcelos, O., Nagle, J. W., Semino-Mora, C., Sivakumar, K., & Dalakas, M. C. (1998). Missense mutations in desmin associated with familial cardiac and skeletal myopathy. *Nature Genetics, 19,* 402–403.

Cynthia A. Riccio
Texas A&M University

MYOPATHY, MYOTUBULAR

Myotubular myopathy is one of many neuromuscular diseases. It manifests as a cessation or arrest of muscle development at the myotubular stage of development or at about 8–15 weeks gestational age. Diagnosis is possible prenatally due to the characteristic decrease in movement of the fetus. The arrest is related to the failure of vimentin and desmin to decrease in amount and results in a flaw in the structure of the muscles. Myotubular myopathy also is referred to as centronuclear myopathy. The most common form of myotubular myopathy is X-linked and therefore manifests only in boys; other forms of transmission are believed to exist, but less is known about these forms (Myotubular Myopathy Resource Group, 2001). Even for the X-linked form, there is evidence of some heterogeneity in the transmission and penetrance with a range of gene mutations (Laporte et al., 2000). There is no research to suggest that myotubular myopathy is more likely to occur in any one ethnic group.

Characteristics

1. Decreased movement of fetus
2. Generalized decreased muscle tone and muscle weakness
3. Drooping of eyelids
4. Foot drop
5. Respiratory distress
6. Absence of deep tendon reflexes
7. Undescended testicles
8. High, arched palate and thin tongue
9. Difficulty sucking, swallowing, and coughing

Respiratory complications often occur with myotubular myopathy and may be critical, requiring respiratory support such as tracheostomy, assisted ventilation, and chest percussion therapy. Feeding problems, particularly esophageal reflux, are not uncommon and may require the use of gastrostomy tubes. Difficulty swallowing may be a contributing factor to both feeding and speech problems (Myotubular Myopathy Resource Group, 2001). Because of these problems, there is a high neonatal mortality associated with myotubular myopathy (Barth & Dubowitz, 1998).

Recent research suggests that of those children with myotubular myopathy who survive the first year of life, the vast majority of them are partially or totally dependent on a ventilator. Even children who are not severe enough to warrant continuous medical management of respiration are at significant risk of respiratory problems if they become sick. Children who survive can evidence additional medical problems. Diminished blinking and failure of the eyes to close completely at night can result in dryness of the eyes and discomfort. Due to weakness of the abdominal muscles, testicles may not descend. In some instances, the testicles gradually descend over time; in other cases, surgery may be required. Scoliosis is a significant problem for individuals with myotubular myopathy, and therapies include the use of various forms of braces or surgery or some combination. Additional medical issues related to anemia and liver problems have been linked to myotubular myopathy in some individuals.

Children generally are never able to become ambulatory. For those children who survive the medical complications, the muscle disorder appears to be nonprogressive and cognitive abilities do not appear to be impaired. Vision problems (e.g., strabismus) may exist in addition to other problems (Myotubular Myopathy Resource Group, 2001).

Treatment requires a multidisciplinary approach in order to address the medical complications and needs of the child, the educational needs of the child, and the social-emotional needs of the child. These children may require physical accommodations as well as the availability of medically trained personnel (e.g., if using feeding tubes or if other medical issues warrant). Physical limitations have social repercussions, and it is important to identify activities such that the child can participate successfully with peers in a social milieu. Depending on educational needs, the child with myotubular myopathy may require academic assistance; for more medically involved students, home-based programming may be necessary. Support services, including genetic counseling, is appropriate for all family members.

REFERENCES

Barth, P. G., & Dubowitz, V. (1998). X-linked myotubular myopathy: A long term follow-up study. *European Journal of Paediatric Neurology, 2*(1), 49–56.

Laporte, J., Biancalana, V., Tanner, S. M., Kress, W., Schneider, V., Wallgren-Pettersson, C., Herger, F., Buj-Bello, A., Blondeau, F., Liechti-Gallati, S., & Mandel, J. L. (2000). MTM1 mutations in X-linked myotubular myopathy. *Human Mutation, 15,* 393–409.

Myotubular Myopathy Resource Group. (2001). Retrieved May 29, 2001, from www.mtmrg.org

Cynthia A. Riccio
Texas A&M University

MYOPATHY, NEMALINE

All of the myopathies are associated with muscle weakness and lack of muscle tone (dystonia). Nemaline myopathy is differentiated from other myopathies by the presence of rod-shaped inclusion bodies or nemaline rods in the skeletal muscles; there is also a higher than normal preponderance of slow muscle tissue. Nemaline myopathy is evident from birth or infancy and therefore is considered to be congenital. Large muscles groups (e.g., thighs) may be very weak or thin; due to the lack of muscle tone these infants may be described as "floppy" (McKusick, 1999).

Characteristics

1. Generalized hypotonia or decreased muscle tone
2. Muscle weakness
3. Delayed development of gross motor skills
4. High, arched palate and prominent jaw
5. Nemaline rods evident on muscle biopsy

In most cases, nemaline myopathy is familial. Genetic transmission is believed to be autosomal dominant with incomplete penetrance, involving Chromosome 1q21-q23 and the gene responsible for encoding nebulin (Laing et al., 1992). There is some indication that in more severe cases, more than one chromosome and mechanism may be implicated (Wallgren-Pettersson et al., 1999). For the autosomal dominant form of the disorder, the actual risk that the disorder will be transmitted from an affected parent to a child is 50% regardless of the gender of the child. Another form of nemaline myopathy follows an autosomal recessive pattern with involvement of Chromosome 19; as with the autosomal dominant form, there is an equal likelihood for males and females to be affected or to be carriers. Despite the equal likelihood of transmission, more females have been identified with nemaline myopathy than males (Wallgren-Pettersson et al., 1999). One form of the autosomal recessive nemaline myopathy has only been found among the Amish; this form is referred to as Amish nemaline myopathy (Johnston et al., 2000). No other ethnic group differences were identified. There is some evidence that nemaline rod accumulation also may occur as a rare reaction to muscle injury with adult onset.

Severity ranges from mild to severe. In the mildest form, the myopathy does not progress beyond the muscle weakness evident at birth. In other mild forms, the myopathy has a slow progression; in the severe form, the myopathy is rapidly progressive and fatal. Nemaline myopathy is most likely to be mild with onset in infancy evidenced by hypotonia and weakness. Gross motor development is generally delayed for these children. The more severe form is marked by more severe muscular weakness including muscles involved in respiration with recurrent pneumonias and death. The Amish nemaline myopathy differs somewhat from the other nemaline myopathies in that there are associated tremors and contractions of the muscles as well as progressive muscle atrophy and weakness associated with the contractions (Johnston et al., 2000).

Treatment requires a multidisciplinary approach to address any medical problems as a result of involvement of intercostal muscles, to foster and monitor ambulatory skills through physical therapy, and genetic as well as supportive counseling. Dysphagia or difficulty swallowing is common and may necessitate intervention to prevent aspiration. As with many other myopathies, a high arched palate is one characteristic seen in children with this disorder; this may impact speech production and necessitate provision of speech therapy. There is also significant risk for the development of scoliosis. Diagnosis can be made prenatally or at birth, thus triggering early intervention services and supports for the family. The family service plan needs to address communication between physicians and therapists in order to monitor progress or status of the disorder as well as to deal with any complications that may arise. Depending on the status of the child's motor skills, additional services may be needed through the local education agency once the child attains age 3 years. The most frequent specialized service is that of physical therapy in order to address maintenance of muscle strength and range of motion as well as to address mobility and functional daily living skills.

REFERENCES

Johnston, J. J., Kelley, R. I., Crawford, T. O., Morton, D. H., Agarwala, R., Koch, T., Schaffer, A. A., Francomano, C. A., & Biesecker, L. G. (2000). A novel nemaline myopathy in the Amish caused by a mutation in troponin T1. *American Journal of Human Genetics, 67,* 814–821.

McKusick, V. A. (1999). Nemaline myopathy. *Mendelian Inheritance in Man: Catalogs of human genes and genetic disorders.* Retrieved May 24, 2001, from www3.ncbi.nlm.nih.gov/Omim

Wallgren-Pettersson, C., Pelin, K., Hilpela, P., Donner, K., Porfirio, B., Graziano, C., Swoboda, K. J., Fardeau, M., Urtizberea, J. A., Muntoni, F., Sewry, C., Dubowitz, V., Iannoccone, S., Minetti, C., Pedemonte, M., Seri, M., Cusano, R., Lammens, M., Castagna-Sloane, A., Beggs, A. H., Laing, N. G., & de la Chapelle, A. (1999). Clinical and genetic heterogeneity in autosomal recessive nemaline myopathy. *Neuromuscular Disorders, 9,* 564–572.

Cynthia A. Riccio
Texas A&M University

MYOPATHY, SCAPULOPERONEAL

Scapuloperoneal myopathy is a form of myopathy so named because of the involvement of the muscles in the shoulder girdle (Pal, Bedekovics, & Gati, 1999). Scapuloperoneal myopathy usually presents in young adulthood but may present in early adolescence. Muscle weakness is due to atrophy of the affected musculature. The atrophy raises the question of whether this is truly a myopathy or whether it is actually one of the spinal muscular atrophies. Muscle biopsy reveals dead tissue as well as generating fibers and increased connective tissue; atrophy tends to be focal rather than diffuse (Wilhelmsen et al., 1996).

Autosomal dominant inheritance linked to Chromosome 12 has been suggested for scapuloperoneal myopathy (Tawil, Myers, Weiffenbach, & Griggs, 1995; Wilhelmsen et al., 1996). However, autosomal recessive inheritance also has been documented (Tandan, Verma, & Mohue, 1989). Additionally, sporadic cases of scapuloperoneal myopathy have been reported (Yee, Hahn, & Gilbert, 1988).

Characteristics

1. Muscle weakness of shoulder girdle
2. Progression of weakness to lower extremities
3. Possible weakness of facial and pelvic muscles as well

Scapuloperoneal myopathy follows a slow progression beginning at the shoulder girdle. It spreads to the lower extremities over time. Facial muscles may or may not be involved; similarly, pelvic muscles are sometimes, but not always, affected. Progression may be slow and relatively benign, or it may be rapid and debilitating (Pal et al., 1999).

Treatment is supportive and depends on the severity and symptom presentation. In more severe cases, accommodations to increase mobility and ensure access may be needed. Supportive counseling as well as genetic counseling may be appropriate.

REFERENCES

Pal, E., Bedekovics, T., & Gati, I. (1999). Familial scapuloperoneal myopathy and mitochondrial DNA defect. *European Neurology, 42,* 211–216.

Tandan, R., Verma, A., & Mohue, M. (1989). Adult onset autosomal recessive neurogenic scapuloperoneal syndrome. *Journal of Neurological Science, 94*(1–3), 201–209.

Tawil, R., Myers, G. J., Weiffenbach, B., & Griggs, R. C. (1995). Scapuloperoneal myopathy: Absence of linkage of the 4135 FSHD locus. *Archives of Neurology, 52,* 1069–1072.

Wilhelmsen, K. C., Blake, D. M., Lynch, T., Mabutas, J., DeVera, M., Nyestat, M., Bernstein, M., Hirano, M., Gilliam, T. C., Murphy, P. L., Sola, M. D., Bonilla, E., Schotland, D. L., Hays, A. P., & Rowland, L. P. (1996). Chromosome 12-linked autosomal dominant scapuloperoneal muscular dystrophy. *Annals of Neurology, 39,* 507–520.

Yee, W. C., Hahn, A. F., & Gilbert, J. J. (1988). Adult onset scapuloperoneal myopathy: Diagnostic value of nerve morphometry and multiple muscle biopsies. *Journal of Neurology, Neurosurgery, and Psychiatry, 51,* 808–813.

Cynthia A. Riccio
Texas A&M University

MYOSITIS

Myositis is a rare disease that comes in multiple forms and is one of the inflammatory muscle myopathies (Myositis Association of America, 1999). As with other inflammatory myopathies, myositis is believed to be an autoimmune disorder in which inflammatory cells surround, invade, and destroy muscle fibers resulting in muscle weakness or rash. Myositis is estimated to affect about 1 in 100,000 individuals. Although there are gender differences depending on the type of myositis, clear ethnic differences have not been identified. Recently, there is some indication that the incidence rate for myositis is increasing faster among the African American population as compared to other groups (Olsen, 2000). Myositis has multiple possible causes including previous or current infection or virus, as well as certain medications. In some instances, there appears to be a familial link.

Characteristics (Myositis Association of America, 1999)

1. Skin lesions
2. Difficulty getting up from a chair, climbing stairs, and raising arms
3. Muscle weakness or pain
4. Fatigue
5. Difficulty in swallowing or breathing
6. Inflammation including fever
7. Positive tests for specific antibodies
8. Nondestructive arthritis or arthralgias

There are multiple types of myositis. The type of myositis that is characterized by skin lesions, often in the facial area, is dermatomyositis. The rash precedes the muscle weakness. Dermatomyositis can occur at any age from childhood to adulthood; in children complaints of muscle pain and tenderness are more likely. Dermatomyositis is more common in females than in males (Myositis Association of America, 1999) with a female to male ratio of 2:1 (Olsen, 2000).

Polymyositis does not start with a rash, and the muscle inflammation and weakness are generally slower than with dermatomyositis. Polymyositis is more common after age 20, but it has been identified in children and infants. As with dermatomyositis, women are twice as likely as men to be affected with polymyositis. Polymyositis can be confused with mixed connective tissue disorder due to the inflammation (Myositis Association of America, 1999).

Inclusion body myositis is similar to polymyositis with gradual muscle weakness in both proximal and distal muscles and atrophy of the forearms and legs evident. Inclusion body myositis is not usually identified until after age 50 and occurs more frequently in men than in women. Although dermatomyositis and polymyositis do not appear to be hereditary, about 10% of the cases of inclusion body myositis are hereditary (Myositis Association of America, 1999).

Another form of myositis is juvenile idiopathic inflammatory myopathy, or juvenile myositis. Juvenile myositis may be preceded by a rash as in dermomyositis with muscle weakness developing over a period of days, weeks, or months. The muscles impacted tend to be those closer to the trunk, including the neck, hip, trunk, and shoulder muscles. Abdominal pain, hoarseness, and difficulty swallowing may be associated with juvenile myositis as well. As suggested by the name, this type of myositis occurs most frequently in children. Unlike adult forms of myositis, soft tissue calcifications are much more common. Long-term outcome of juvenile myositis is variable (Myositis Association of America, 2001).

Treatment of all forms of myositis include the administration of corticosteroids (e.g., prednisone) or intravenous immune globulin infusions. In many cases, if treated early and the individual is responsive, the myositis will go into remission. For those individuals who experience pain with the myositis, additional medication management may be appropriate. In some cases, additional rehabilitation to address residual muscle weakness may be necessary. This may mean provision of physical therapy or occupational therapy through special education. Depending on the residual problems and the child's responsiveness to medication management, the child may need to have accommodations (e.g., decreased movement, assistance with moving from place to place, adaptive physical education). In addition, the family of the child with myositis may need help in coping and dealing with their child's illness (Myositis Association of America, 2001).

REFERENCES

Myositis Association of America. (1999). Retrieved from www.myositis.org/about-im2

Myositis Association of America. (2001). Retrieved from www.myositis.org/

Olsen, N. J. (2000). Idiopathic inflammatory myopathies. *Scientific American, 15,* 1–4.

Cynthia A. Riccio
Texas A&M University

See also Polymyositis

MYOSITIS, INCLUSION BODY

Myositis is a rare disease that comes in multiple forms and is one of the inflammatory muscle myopathies (Myositis Association of America, 1999). As with other inflammatory myopathies, myositis is believed to be an autoimmune disorder in which inflammatory cells surround, invade, and destroy muscle fibers resulting in muscle weakness or rash. Inclusion body myositis or myopathy is similar to other myopathies in that gradual muscle weakness is evident in both proximal and distal muscles with atrophy of the forearms and legs evident. Unlike other myopathies, inclusion body myopathy is not usually identified until after age 50 and occurs more frequently in men than women. Inclusion body myopathy gets its name from the presence of rimmed vacuoles evident in laboratory analysis. About 10% of the cases of inclusion body myopathies are hereditary (Myositis Association of America, 1999). When genetic transmission has been indicated, the transmission was most often autosomal dominant with male to male transmission (Patel, Berry, MacLeod, & Dunn, 1983).

There is also some evidence of an autosomal recessive form of inclusion body myopathy (Mitriani-Rosenbaum, Argov, Blumenfield, Seidman, & Seidman, 1996). This form of inclusion body myositis also has its onset in adulthood, but it usually becomes evident prior to the mid-40s (Argov & Yarom, 1984). Notably, the autosomal recessive form of the disorder has been documented only among Persian and Iranian Jewish families (Argov & Yarom, 1984; Mitrani-Rosenbaum et al., 1996; Zlotogora, 1995). Genetic studies indicate linkage of 9p1-q1 for the autosomal recessive form. This same gene has been indicated in Nonaka myopathy, an inflammatory myopathy that is specific to the Japanese (Ikeuchi et al., 1997).

Characteristics (Myositis Association of America, 1999)

1. Pelvic and shoulder weakness
2. Difficulty getting up from a chair, climbing stairs, or raising arms
3. Falling and tripping
4. Difficulty swallowing
5. Muscle weakness or pain
6. Fatigue
7. Respiratory problems

Treatment of all forms of inflammatory myopathy include the administration of corticosteroids (e.g., prednisone) or intravenous immune globulin infusions. In some cases, if treated early and the individual is responsive, the myositis may go into remission. With inclusion body myositis, there is increased likelihood that the progressive weakness will be resistant to treatment. Additional medication management may be appropriate for those individuals who experience pain. In some cases, additional rehabilitation to address residual muscle weakness may be necessary (Delakas, 1994). Because about half of the individuals with inclusion body myositis evidence difficulty with swallowing or dysphagia, alternative methods of feeding may be necessary. The most significant complication is often respiratory distress as a result of the weakening of the intercostal muscles. The family members of the individual with inclusion body myositis may need help in coping and dealing with the illness (Myositis Association of America, 2001). Given the potential for genetic transmission, particularly among certain groups, genetic counseling may be appropriate.

REFERENCES

Argov, A., & Yarom, R. (1984). "Rimmed vacuole myopathy" spating the quadriceps: A unique disorder in Iranian Jews. *Journal of Neurological Science, 64,* 33–43.

Delakas, M. (1994). Current treatment of the inflammatory myopathies. *Current Opinion in Rheumatology, 6,* 595–601.

Ikeuchi, T., Asaka, T., Saito, M., Tanaka, H., Higuchi, S., Tanaka, K., Saida, K., Uyama, E., Mizusawa, H., Fukuhara, N., Nonaka, I., Takamori, M., & Tsuji, S. (1997). Gene locus for autosomal recessive distal myopathy with rimmed vacuole maps chromosome 9. *Annals of Neurology, 41,* 432–437.

Mitriani-Rosenbaum, S., Argov, Z., Blumenfield, A., Seidman, C. E., & Seidman, J. G. (1996). Hereditary inclusion body myopathy maps to chromosome 9p1-q1. *Human Molecular Genetics, 5,* 159–163.

Myositis Association of America. (1999). Retrieved from www.myositis.org/about-im2

Myositis Association of America. (2001). Retrieved from www.myositis.org/

Patel, H., Berry, K., MacLeod, P., & Dunn, H. G. (1983). Cytoplasmic body myopathy: Report on a family and review of the literature. *Journal of Neurological Science, 60,* 281–292.

Zlotogora, J. (1995). Hereditary disorders among Iranian Jews. *American Journal of Medical Genetics, 58,* 32–37.

Cynthia A. Riccio
Texas A&M University

MYOTONIA CONGENITA

Myotonia congenita is a hereditary muscle disease that belongs to a group of myotonic disorders seen in children. Myotonia congenita comes in two forms; autosomal dominant form (DMC), also known as Thomsen's disease, and autosomal recessive form, or recessive generalized myotonia (RGM). The autosomal dominant myotonia congenita is slightly less severe, although both forms are nondystrophic and nonprogressive disorders with the main characteristic of myotonic stiffness. This stiffness occurs when after a period of rest sudden movement is performed. The myotonia congenitas result from a gene defect in Chromosome 7 that results in a chloride channel mutation affecting the skeletal muscle tissue.

Symptoms of DMC begin in infancy to early childhood, whereas RGM has a slightly later onset during childhood and sometimes begins in the second decade (Moxley, 1996). Both forms of myotonia congenita affect between 0.2 and 7.3 per 100,000 (Weinberg, Curl, Kuncl, & McFarland, 1999). Males and females are equally affected (Gandy, 2000).

Characteristics

1. Myotonia; temporary muscle stiffness or the inability of the muscles to relax after contraction. This occurs when movement is initiated after a period of rest or when the same position has been maintained for as short as 5 min. The stiffness can also occur when the patient has been active for a longer duration.

2. "Warm up" phenomenon; the myotonic stiffness improves after repeated muscle use.
3. Muscle groups affected by the myotonia vary, although leg muscles are typically affected.
4. Hypertrophy of the muscles is frequent in both dominant and recessive forms, and the children often appear very well developed.
5. Myotonia of the eyes; after forceful closing of the lids, reopening can be difficult. The same difficulty in reopening occurs in the hands after having made a tight fist.
6. Laryngeal and pharyngeal muscles can be affected resulting in difficulties with speech, chewing, or swallowing.
7. Percussion myotonia.
8. Sudden exposure to cold can trigger myotonic stiffness.
9. Transient weakness after relaxation and when first initiating movement is characteristic of RGM.

The muscles affected by myotonia congenita vary, as does symptom severity. Although symptoms are present from childhood, diagnosis of myotonia congenita often does not occur until later in life because symptom severity can be mild and easily managed (Gutmann & Phillips, 1991). Diagnosis of myotonia congenita can be made from an EMG or muscle biopsy (Gandy, 2000).

Abatement of myotonic stiffness by means of antimyotonia drugs is the therapy most often prescribed for patients with myotonia congenita, as there is no cure for the disorder. Mexiletine, an antagonist of voltage-dependent sodium channels, is most often used in antimyotonia therapy (Moxley, 1996). In some cases, the myotonia is not severe enough to require pharmacological treatment. For those with RGM, avoidance of prolonged periods of rest is advised because of the associated muscle weakness (Moxley, 1996). Exercise is an important component to treatment of myotonia congenita, and pharmacological therapy minimizes the symptoms that occur surrounding exercise and activity so that activity can continue. While participating in sports and other activities, patients should stay active (warmed up) to avoid onset of myotonic stiffness. In general, long periods of rest should be avoided. There are no adverse consequences to continued exercise, and it should be encouraged (Weinberg et al., 1999).

Myotonia congenita has a minimal impact on a child's educational performance. As previously mentioned, myotonia congenita often goes undiagnosed for long periods of time because it can be easily managed. It is possible, in severe cases, that children might require time to move their bodies around so as not to develop weakness or excessive stiffness.

The prognosis is good for both the dominant and recessive forms of myotonia congenita because there are no manifestations other than manageable muscular disturbances. Life span is not shortened, and there are no mental deterioration, cardiomyopathy, or conduction defects in these patients (Gutmann & Phillips, 1991). They are still able to be physically active, and their lifestyles are usually not inhibited from the disease. Those with RGM are sometimes more affected because of the progressive muscle weakness and muscle wasting that can occur with this form.

REFERENCES

Gandy, A. (2000). Thomsen's disease (myotonia congenita). Retrieved from http://www.pedianet.com/news/illness/disease/disease.htm

Gutmann, L., & Phillips, L. H. (1991). Myotonia congenita. *Seminars in Neurology, 11*(3), 244–248.

Moxley, R. T. (1996). The myotonias: Their diagnosis and treatment. *Comprehensive Therapy, 22*(1), 8–21.

Weinberg, J., Curl, L. A., Kuncl, R. W., & McFarland, E. G. (1999). Occult presentation of myotonia congenita in a 15-year-old athlete. *American Journal of Sports Medicine, 27*(4), 529–531.

Kellie Higgins
University of Texas at Austin

N

NAIL-PATELLA SYNDROME (HEREDITARY OSTEO-ONYCHODYSPLASIA)

Nail-patella syndrome (NPS) is a rare genetic disorder of connective tissue. The most frequently affected organs are nails, bone, eye, and kidney.

Individuals with NPS have a gene abnormality on Chromosome 9. Although its etiology is not completely clear, NPS appears to be caused by defective collagen synthesis and/or degradation. Collagen is the principal protein substance from which all connective tissue, bone, and cartilage are formed.

NPS is rare. Its frequency is 2 in 100,000 births. Since the condition was first described in 1897, about 400 cases have been reported. The pattern of heredity is autosomal dominant. Among patients with NPS there is tremendous variability in gene expression and, consequently, in clinical severity of the disorder.

Characteristics

1. Underdeveloped (hypoplastic), discolored, or split nails. Poorly formed or triangular lunulae (the white semicircle at the base of the nail). The thumbnail is most commonly involved. Fingernails are more frequently abnormal than toenails.
2. Hypoplastic or absent patella (knee cap). The ends of the femur (thigh bone) and tibia (shin bone) that create the knee joint may also be hypoplastic. Recurrent patellar dislocation.
3. Elbows cannot be fully extended. Hypoplasia of the lower end of the humerus (the bone in the upper arm). Poorly developed upper end (head) of the radius (the bone located on the thumb side of the forearm). Recurrent dislocation of the head of the radius is common.
4. Bony spurs of the ilium (the wing-like bone that forms the rear of the pelvis). These structures can usually be felt by pressing around the lower back and upper buttocks.
5. Dark pigmentation around the inner circle of the iris. This change has a cloverleaf shape.
6. Nephropathy (kidney disease). Manifestations are quite varied. They include proteinuria (protein in the urine), edema (fluid accumulation in tissues), and hypertension. Almost 50% of patients have some degree of kidney involvement. Of this group, 30% experience progressive disease and chronic renal failure.
7. Other common features include absence of the distal phalangeal joint (between the middle and last bones of the fingers and toes), "knock-knee" deformity, osteoarthritis (particularly of the knees and elbows), and a wide range of anomalies of the feet.
8. Mental deficiency, cleft lip or palate, hearing loss, and several kinds of eye anomalies are occasional findings.

No treatment is available for the underlying defect in NPS. Referral to an orthopedic surgeon is indicated for chronic dislocations and joint pathology that limits mobility. Children should be examined at regular intervals for scoliosis, particularly as puberty begins to rear its ugly head. Patients with nephropathy do best in the care of a nephrologist (kidney specialist). This medical discipline has the expertise to manage hypertension, electrolyte imbalances, edema, and protein losses that are associated with kidney failure. Fluid restriction, limitation of salt intake, diuretic drugs, and prednisone are in their therapeutic bag of tricks. End-stage renal disease, which occurs in about 10% of patients with NPS, necessitates chronic hemodialysis and, eventually, kidney transplantation. Kidney biopsy is indicated in all patients who develop renal abnormalities.

Because children with NPS may have cognitive difficulties, screening from an early childhood intervention program is recommended to help ensure that the child is meeting developmental milestones. A comprehensive neuropsychological evaluation may be required at a later date if deficits become evident. The child with NPS may also profit from evaluation and treatment from a speech pathologist if the cleft lip or palate and/or hearing loss have affected language development.

NPS is considered a relatively benign condition. However, this rosy outlook is dependent on either no renal involvement or kidney disease that responds to medical management. Progressive renal pathology can lead to kidney failure as early as late adolescence, but this ominous development does not usually show up until patients are in their 30s.

For more information or support, please contact

National Kidney Foundation, 30 East 33rd Street, New York, NY 10016; (212) 889-2210 or (800) 622-9010; http://www.kidney.org.

REFERENCES

Jones, K. (1997). *Smith's recognizable patterns of human malformation* (5th ed.). Philadelphia: W. B. Saunders.

National Organization for Rare Disorders, Inc. (1999). Nail patella syndrome. Retrieved from http://www.stepstn.com/cgi-win/nord.exe?proc=GetDocument&rectype=0&recnum=567

Pediatric Database (PEDBASE). (1994). Nail-patella syndrome. Retrieved from http://www.icondata.com/health/pedbase/files/NAIL-PAT.HTM

Barry H. Davison
Ennis, Texas

Joan W. Mayfield
Baylor Pediatric Specialty Services
Dallas, Texas

NARCISSISTIC PERSONALITY DISORDER

Narcissistic personality disorder (NPD) is characterized by a pervasive pattern of grandiosity, need for admiration, and lack of empathy that begins by early adulthood and is present in a variety of contexts. Individuals with NPD display an unusually obvious sense of entitlement and right to be served (Millon, 1996). It is estimated that less than 1% of the general population may have this personality disorder, and clinical populations are thought to range from 2% to 16% (American Psychiatric Association [APA], 2000). Approximately 50–75% of cases diagnosed with NPD are male. Like other personality disorders, NPD is usually not diagnosed until late adolescence or early adulthood.

Characteristics

1. Grandiose sense of self-importance (e.g., exaggerates achievements and talents).
2. Preoccupied with fantasies of unlimited power, brilliance, and beauty, to name a few.
3. Propensity to engage in interpersonally exploitative relationships in which others are taken advantage of to achieve personal goals and meet personal needs.
4. Lack of empathy for others and an unwillingness to recognize or identify with others' feelings and needs.
5. Intense need for attention and admiration.
6. Display of arrogant and haughty behaviors.
7. Potential for angry outbursts (e.g., verbal and physical assault, and property destruction) and depression when self-image is wounded.

Diagnosing NPD before adulthood is difficult given that narcissistic attitudes and behaviors are common during adolescence. Delaying diagnosis until adulthood is therefore recommended. Obtaining further developmental, and relationship, histories also helps to rule out other personality disorders that overlap with NPD (e.g., borderline and antisocial personality disorders). One trait that helps to differentiate NPD from other personality disorders, however, is the grandiosity displayed by the individual (APA, 2000). Individuals with NPD tend to be overly sensitive to criticism, and their self-image is easily wounded by negative comments, even constructive feedback. Although the sensitivity is often well disguised, perceived threats can lead to verbal rage and physical assault. In addition, these individuals often experience feelings of worthlessness and depression and have suicidal ideation. Interpersonal relationships are often strained as a result of the person's excessive self-focus (e.g., extreme need for admiration), feelings of entitlement, and insensitivity to others' feelings and needs (APA, 2000).

Despite interpersonal problems, individuals with narcissistic personalities are often successful in what they do. Typically, schoolwork and jobs are unaffected, and special assistance is not warranted. It is feasible, however, that some adolescents with NPD may require special education services under the Emotional Disturbance label of the Individuals with Disabilities Education Act. For example, in cases where narcissistic traits are so maladaptive and significant functional impairments and subjective distress arise, special programming may be necessary. More often than not, counseling will suffice as far as school services. The counselor, however, needs to be familiar with the therapeutic issues and the most appropriate strategies for NPD. Treatment of individuals with narcissism can be frustrating, and even counterproductive, if the therapist has not had much experience treating personality disorders. Confrontation of narcissistic behaviors is often perceived as criticism and can lead to early termination of therapy. The novice therapists may not know to "go with the resistance" and work slowly to understand better the function (e.g., defense) that the narcissism serves. Treatment also needs to address any concurrent clinical syndromes. Individuals with NPD often experience depression and anxiety as a result of their excessive self-focus and the lack of attention and admiration received from others. In some cases, threats or attacks to a person's self-esteem can result in acting-out behaviors. Johnson et al. (2001) found that among individuals with NPD there was an increased risk for involvement in arson and vandalism, as well as physical threats and assaults (even in cases where no antisocial personality disorder was coexistent).

The etiology of NPD is likely to be developmental and environmental (e.g., interactional) in nature. Birth order and parental overvaluation, for example, have been speculated to be causal factors of NPD (Millon, 1996), and there does not appear to be any more definitive information about cause. Research may help better understand the dynamics involved and whether there is any genetic predisposition toward this personality disorder. Well-controlled studies examining the effectiveness of various therapies would also be helpful in understanding how best to approach treatment in order to get the desired outcome.

REFERENCES

American Psychiatric Association. (2000). *Diagnostic and statistical manual of mental disorders* (4th ed., Text Revision). Washington, DC: Author.

Johnson, J. G., Cohen, P., Smailes, E., Kasen, S., Oldham, J. M., Skodol, A. E., & Brook, J. S. (2001). Adolescent personality disorders associated with violence and criminal behavior during adolescence and adulthood. *American Journal of Psychiatry, 157*(9), 1406–1412.

Millon, T. (1996). *Disorders of personality: DSM-IV and beyond* (2nd Ed.). New York: Wiley.

Rex Gonzales
Elaine Clark
University of Utah

NARCOLEPSY

Narcolepsy is a form of hypersomnia associated with a tetrad of symptoms: (a) uncontrollable episodes of daytime sleep, (b) sudden loss of muscle tone (cataplexy), (c) sleep paralysis, and (d) hypnagogic hallucinations. Only about 10% of affected individuals show all four symptoms (Merck Manual of Diagnosis and Therapy [Merck], 2001). Of major concerns are sleep attacks, which often occur several times a day without warning at inappropriate places and times. Affected individuals may fall asleep during class, business meetings, conversations, or meals. Because they are usually unaware of their disorder, they are often undiagnosed and untreated. Parents, teachers, spouses, and employers often mistakenly attribute patients' sleepiness to disinterest, laziness, hostility, or rejection. Fewer than 10% of patients have narcoleptic sleep episodes longer than 8 min, but some episodes last longer than 60 min (Sleepchannel, 2001). Of interest, the disorder was first diagnosed in a poodle at the Stanford University sleep laboratory by Mitler and Dement in 1974; animal models are used in much current research and are responsible for the recent discovery of the disorder's basis (Sleepyheads.org, 2001).

Narcolepsy can occur at any age, including childhood, but onset is usually between about 10 and 25 years of age. Symptoms generally are initially mild and perhaps difficult to see, but they gradually become more severe over time. Narcolepsy appears equal in both sexes and affects about 1–2 in 1,000 in the United States, Japan, and Israel (Center for Narcolepsy, 2001).

Characteristics

1. Uncontrollable episodes of daytime sleep
2. Cataplexy (sudden loss of muscle function)
3. Hypnagogic or hypnopompic hallucinations (vivid experiences while falling asleep or awakening)
4. Sleep paralysis (temporary inability to talk or move when falling asleep)
5. Disturbed nighttime sleep
6. Automatic behavior (irrelevant speech or inappropriate actions)

Symptoms other than uncontrollable daytime sleep include the following: (a) Cataplexy, unique to narcolepsy, involves unpredictable episodes of loss of skeletal muscle function ranging from limpness at the neck or knees to complete body collapse. Ranging in length from a few seconds to several minutes, attacks may be triggered by sudden reactions such as laughter, anger, or fear. The person remains conscious. It affects approximately 60% of cases. (b) Hypnagogic or hypnopompic hallucinations occur frequently in most individuals with narcolepsy and occasionally in many other people as they are falling asleep or waking up. They are dreamlike experiences that may be multimodal (visual, auditory, and tactile) and so vivid as to be difficult to differentiate from reality. (c) Sleep paralysis, affecting about 60% of cases, is a brief and unpredictable inability to talk or move while falling asleep. When accompanying a hypnagogic or hypnopompic hallucination, it may be very frightening. (d) Disturbed nighttime sleep is frequently experienced as tossing and turning, awakening, restlessness, or leg jerking. (e) Automatic behaviors, usually accompanied by amnesia and occurring during monotonous activities, affect 80% of cases. Individuals may make inappropriate comments or do inappropriate things for periods ranging from a few seconds to several minutes (Sleepyheads.org, 2001).

Diagnosis is generally on the basis of clinical signs supplemented when necessary by testing in a sleep clinic. Differential diagnosis is important because of overlapping symptoms with other sleep disorders such as sleep apnea and with psychological and physical disorders ranging from depression to brain tumors, cardiac conditions, and anemia. Two commonly used sleep clinic tests are polysomnography and the multiple sleep latency test (MSLT). A polysomnogram continuously records brain waves and muscle functions during nighttime sleep. A two-week withdrawal period from any drugs that disrupt sleep precedes testing. When tested, people with narcolepsy fall asleep quickly, enter REM sleep early, and awaken often during the night. A polysomnogram helps to differentiate between narcolepsy and other possible sleep disorders. The MSLT, performed after a normal night's sleep and often after the polysomnography, measures EEG, EOG, heart rate, and chin EMG. The patient tries to take several 20-min naps, one every 2 hr. Individuals with narcolepsy generally show short sleep latencies that vary widely instead of becoming progressively longer. In addition, REM sleep during the first 15 min of sleep (sleep-onset REM, or SOREM) after a normal night's sleep is indicative of narcolepsy (Sleepchannel, 2001).

The biochemical basis for most narcolepsy has recently been discovered as an outgrowth of animal research. Mignon's research has shown that narcoleptic dogs have a gene mutation that causes defects in receptors for hypocretins, a group of neuropeptides produced in the hypothalamus. Subsequently, humans with narcolepsy have been found to lack hypocretins, although they have normal receptors. Because narcolepsy in humans is rarely familial, even showing low concordance in monozygotic twins, inheritance is an unlikely mechanism for hypocretin deficiency. One suggestion is that an autoimmune disorder leads those who develop narcolepsy to produce antibodies against their own hypocretin nerve cells. Research to specify further the physiological links underlying the disorder may lead to both a better understanding of the mechanisms of normal sleep and a more effective treatment for narcolepsy (Sleepyheads.org, 2001).

Narcolepsy at this time cannot be cured; it is treated symptomatically with sleep hygiene and drug medication. Sleep hygiene, combining a consistent sleep schedule with avoidance of shift work and alcohol, may help reduce not only daytime sleeping but also cataplexy. Rotating shift work and operation of dangerous machinery should be avoided. Two or three programmed daily naps reduce excessive daytime sleepiness and provide temporary alertness. Stimulants, including methylphenidate (Ritalin), modafinil, dextroamphetamine, and pemoline help reduce excessive daytime sleepiness and sleep attacks. Because these medications can have serious adverse side effects, they must be titrated and monitored carefully. Tricyclic and selective serotonin reuptake inhibitor (SSRI) antidepressants are used to reduce the common co-occurring symptoms of cataplexy, hallucinations, and sleep paralysis. The trycyclics are the most widely used and may result in improvement in cataplexy, hallucinations, and sleep paralysis within a few days. Side effects may include blurred vision, dry mouth, and sweating. SSRIs such as Prozac often reduce cataplexy and occasionally even sleep attacks (Sleepchannel, 2001). Prognosis for reduction, if not elimination, of symptoms with appropriate treatment is good.

Ongoing research on the effects of injected hypocretin on narcoleptic dogs may eventually lead to the development of a drug that will replace the deficiency in affected humans.

REFERENCES

Center for Narcolepsy. (2001). More on narcolepsy. Retrieved from http://www-med.stanford.edu/school/Psychiatry/narcolepsy/

Merck Manual of Diagnosis and Therapy. (2001). Narcolepsy. Lawrenceville, NJ: Merck.

Sleepchannel. (2001). Narcolepsy. Retrieved from http://www.sleepdisorderchannel.com/narcolepsy/index.shtml

Sleepyheads.org. (2001). Narcolepsy. Retrieved from http://www.sleepyheads.org

Robert T. Brown
Amy Sessoms
University of North Carolina, Wilmington

NEU-LAXOVA SYNDROME

Neu-Laxova syndrome (NLS) is a rare, hereditable disorder of brain formation. Associated anomalies of the face, skin, extremities, and eyes are also common.

The etiology of NLS is unclear. It is a rare disorder. Only about 30 cases have been described since the initial reports surfaced in 1971 and 1972. The pattern of heredity is autosomal recessive. Consanguinity is apparently a factor in half of affected families.

Characteristics

1. Prenatal growth deficiency present in virtually all affected fetuses
2. Microcephaly (small head and small brain), lissencephaly (absence of convolutions on the brain's surface), underdevelopment (hypoplasia) of the cerebral hemispheres and cerebellum, absence of internal structures within the brain
3. Sloping forehead; widely spaced, bulging eyes; absent eyelids; gaping mouth with thick lips; flattened nose; small jaw; prominent ears
4. Yellow tissue under the skin; the skin itself is thick, transparent, and scaly
5. Short limbs, syndactyly (fingers and toes are webbed), puffiness of the hands and feet, clubfoot, contractures of large joints with pterygia (web-like bands of skin)
6. Cataracts, microphthalmia (underdeveloped eyeball)
7. Occasionally underdeveloped genitalia, polyhydramnios (excessive amount of amniotic fluid), short umbilical cord, and small placenta

No treatment is currently available for NLS. Genetic counseling should be offered to affected couples. Many of the syndrome's developmental anomalies are detectable on fetal ultrasonography. Therefore, an abnormal sonogram should alert the clinician at least to the possibility of NLS, particularly when there is a history of previously affected newborns.

NLS has a uniformly grim prognosis. Most patients with the disorder have been stillborn or died within a few hours after birth. The oldest survivor lived seven weeks.

REFERENCES

Jones, K. (1997). *Smith's recognizable patterns of human malformation* (5th ed.). Philadelphia: W. B. Saunders.

National Organization for Rare Disorders, Inc. (2000). Neu-Laxova syndrome. Retrieved from www.stepstncom/cgi=win/nord.exe?proc=GetDocument&rectype-0&recnum=980

Barry H. Davison
Ennis, Texas

Joan W. Mayfield
Baylor Pediatric Specialty Services

NEUROACANTHOCYTOSIS

Neuroacanthocytosis (NA), also known as Levine-Critchley syndrome, is a rare neurological disease associated with malformed red blood cells (also known as acanthocytes). Historically, NA has also been referred to as familial amyotrophic chorea with acanthocytosis or chorea-acanthocytosis, each referring to the common motor symptoms: chorea of the limbs, mouth, and tongue as well as hypo- or areflexia. Psychiatric symptoms can include behavior disturbances, personality change, and cognitive impairments (Kartsounis & Hardie, 1996).

Typically, NA is diagnosed in early or middle adulthood, but affliction during childhood (8–12 years) has been found to occur. NA appears to have an autosomal recessive inheritance, but dominant forms may also exist (Rubio et al., 1997). Because the symptoms of NA (unbalanced gait, exaggerated facial expressions, and other motor tics) and the neurolopathology (degeneration of the striatum) are very similar to those of Huntington's disease, misdiagnoses often occur. Diagnosis of NA involves screening the blood for the presence and prevalence of acanthocytes, in conjunction with computerized tomography (CT) scans, standard motor assessments, and neuropsychologic tests (Moskowitz, 1994).

The clinical course is usually progressive but can vary considerably. Of the 19 cases of neuroacanthocytosis studied by Hardie et al. (1991), three had developed the disorder during childhood. Two of the three child cases presented initially with mild motor impairments such as facial tics and limb dystonia. All three showed progressive worsening of various motor capacities, particularly in speech production and gait. Psychologically, two of the cases showed similar behavior problems, including childish compulsivity and emotional lability, that persisted into adolescence. Also, two were determined to be dyslexic. Educational performance varied across the three cases; one case maintained average school performance requiring no remedial teaching, whereas the two dyslexic cases either achieved only below-average performance or required special schooling because of learning difficulties. With their disease states having progressed considerably, none worked as adults.

Characteristics

1. Onset is typically in the third to fifth decade. Childhood cases are rare.
2. Movement disorders consist of orofacial dyskinesia, chorea of limbs, and dysarthric speech.
3. The disease is characterized by neuropathology and presence of acanthocytes in blood films.
4. Treatment is symptomatic.

Treatment of NA is symptomatic, focusing mainly on alleviating the most troublesome symptoms (Moskowitz, 1994). In adults, typical interventions include pharmacological agents to lessen chorea and motor tics, although these often have undesirable side effects.

REFERENCES

Hardie, R. J., Pullon, H. W. H., Harding, A. E., Owen, J. S., Pires, M., Daniels, G. L., Imai, Y., Misra, V. P., King, R. H. M., Jacobs, J. M., Tippett, P., Duchen, L. W., Thomas, P. K., & Marsden, C. D. (1991). Neuroacanthocytosis: A clinical, haematological, and pathological study of 19 cases. *Brain, 114,* 13–49.

Kartsounis, L. D., & Hardie, R. J. (1996). The pattern of cognitive impairments in neuroacanthocystosis: A frontosubcortical dementia. *Archives of Neurology, 53,* 77–80.

Moskowitz, C. (1994). Movement disorders. In E. M. Barker (Ed.), *Neuroscience Nursing* (pp. 536–558). St. Louis, MO: Mosby.

Rubio, J. P., Danek, A., Stone, C., Chalmers, R., Wood, N., Verellen, C., Ferrer, X., Malandrini, A., Fabrizi, G. M., Manfredi, M., Vance, J., Pericak-Vance, M., Brown, R., Rudolf, G., Picard, F., Alonso, E., Brin, M., Nemeth, A. H., Farrall, M., & Monaco, A. P. (1997). Chorea-acanthocytosis: Genetic linkage to chromosome 9q21. *American Journal of Human Genetics, 61,* 899–908.

Adam S. Bristol
Yale University

NEUROCUTANEOUS MELANOSIS

Neurocutaneous melanosis (NM) is a rare congenital syndrome characterized by the presence of multiple or large melanocytic nevi (moles or birthmarks) in association with benign or malignant pigment cell tumors of the leptomeninges (pia mater and arachnoid mater).

Present at birth, the cutaneous nevi presented in NM, which are usually brown, hirsute, lumpy, or folded in appearance, are histologically similar to pigmented nevi of other skin conditions (Mark, Mihm, Liteplo, Reed, & Clark, 1973). They are unusually large (greater than 20 cm in diameter) and numerous (more than three), usually located around the head and neck, shoulders, and lower back and buttocks (DeDavid et al., 1996). The important diagnostic criterion for NM, however, is the presence of melanosis or melanoma of the leptomeninges, which may be diffuse or localized. Neurologic manifestations of NM, which often present within the first two years of life, typically result from the excess cell mass obstructing the circulation of cerebrospinal fluid (hydrocephalus). Accordingly, the major symptoms include increased head circumference, lethargy, recurrent vomiting, generalized seizures, photophobia, neck stiffness, and occasionally palsies indicative of damage to cranial nerves VI and VII, all of which are associated with increases in intracranial pressure (Kadonaga & Frieden, 1991). A small percentage of NM cases initially present in adolescence with additional symptoms indicative of spinal cord compression. As the disease progresses, patients develop psychiatric symptoms, language disorders, and problems with motor coordination and bowel control.

Incidence of NM is sporadic, as a family history of NM has rarely been reported. Male and females are afflicted equally often. Some investigators have hypothesized a greater prevalence of NM among Whites than Blacks, but no large-scale epidemiological data exist to evaluate this claim. Diagnosis of provisional NM begins with dermatological evaluation of the melanocytic nevi and onset of neurologic symptoms, notably hydrocephalus. Confirmation of definite NM can involve laboratory analysis of cerebrospinal fluid composition, EEG, or neuroimaging assays, such as CT scans or MRI, to identify the central melanosis (Kinsler, Aylett, Coley, Chong, & Atherton, 2001).

Characteristics

1. Multiple large congenital melanocytic nevi about the head, neck, shoulders, and lower back
2. Neurologic manifestations due to tumors of the leptomeninges
3. Onset before age 2, usually terminal by age 10

Treatment for NM is limited. The central and cutaneous melanocytosis put NM patients at an increased risk of developing malignant tumors. Kadonaga and Frieden (1991) stated an estimate of nearly 50% of NM patients developing leptomeningeal melanoma. Surgical removal of the cutaneous nevi can be used for cosmetic improvements, but its benefit in reducing cancer risks are doubted (Lawrence, 2000). Restrictions on sun exposure are also recommended. In patients with meningeal melanoma, treatment with radiation or chemotherapy has little effect on the symptoms or the pathological course of NM. Palliative surgical measures, such as shunt placement to relieve intracranial pressure, offer symptomatic treatment and transient improvement. Prognosis for NM patients is poor as nearly 70% die before the age of 10. However, recent advances in understanding the genetic basis of NM and other pigmentary skin syndromes may soon yield therapeutic or curative interventions.

Young children with NM may or may not be able to attend school. If they are able, they will need special care for medical symptoms and emotional-psychological problems. Peers will also need to be educated due to the outward appearance of the disease if teasing is to be minimized. Support groups should be very helpful to effected children.

REFERENCES

DeDavid, M., Orlow, S. J., Provost, N., Marghoob, A. A., Rao, B. K., Wasti, Q., Huang, C. L., Kopf, A. W., & Bart, R. S. (1996). Neurocutaneous melanosis: Clinical features of large congenital melanocytic nevi in patients with manifest central nervous system melanosis. *Journal of the American Academy of Dermatology, 35,* 529–538.

Kadonaga, J. N., & Frieden, I. J. (1991). Neurocutaneous melanosis: Definition and review of the literature. *Journal of American Academy of Dermatology, 24,* 747–755.

Kinsler, V. A., Aylett, S. E., Coley, S. C., Chong, W. K., & Atherton, D. J. (2001). Central nervous system imaging and congenital melanocytic naevi. *Archives of Disease in Childhood, 84,* 152–155.

Lawrence, C. M. (2000). Treatment options for giant congenital naevi. *Clinical and Experimental Dermatology, 25,* 7–11.

Mark, G. J., Mihm, M. C., Liteplo, M. G., Reed, R. J., & Clark, W. H. (1973). Congenital melanocytic nevi of the small and garment type: Clinical, histologic, and ultrastructural studies. *Human Pathology, 4,* 395–418.

Adam S. Bristol
Yale University

NEUROFIBROMATOSIS, TYPE 1

Neurofibromatosis is one of a series of disorders described as neurocutaneous syndromes (phakomatoses). Neurofibromatosis is an autosomal dominant genetic disorder that affects the development and growth of ectodermal tissues. There are two distinctive forms of NF, Type 1 (NF-1) and Type 2 (NF-2). NF-1 is characterized by multiple hyper-

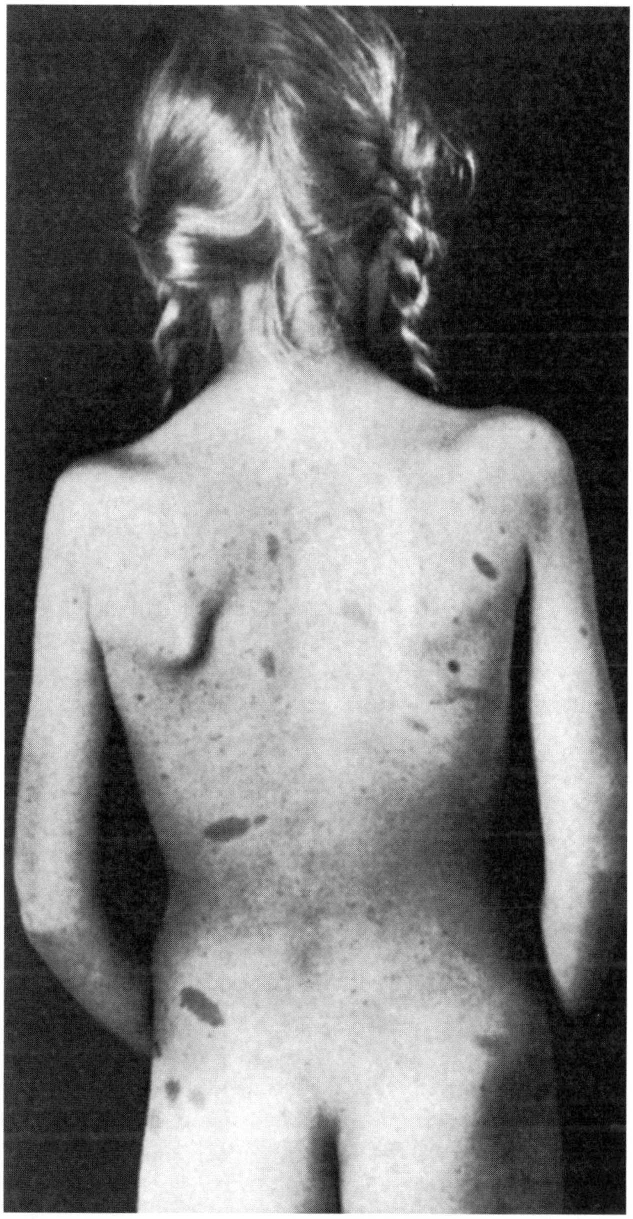

Neurofibromatosis, Type 1
Reprinted from *Clinical Syndromes*, Wiedemann and Kunze, 1997, by permission of the publisher Mosby

pigmented areas and peripheral neurofibromas. NF-2 is characterized by the development of acoustic (8th cranial nerve) neuromas and other intracranial and/or intraspinal tumors. NF is associated with variable medical and neurologic conditions, and different individuals with the same diagnosis experience variable symptoms and severity of symptoms. Although some affected individuals have minimal involvement that has no substantial impact on their lives, others encounter disfigurement secondary to multiple neurofibromas, life-threatening tumors (Moore, Ater, Meedle, Slopis, & Copeland, 1994). Neurofibromatosis occurs in about 1 in 3,000 to 1 in 400 individuals (Berg, 1999; Seashore et al., 1995). NF affects both sexes and occurs in all races and ethnic groups. The NF-1 gene has been localized to Chromosome 17. NF-2 has been linked to Chromosome 22 (Berg, 1999). About half the cases of neurofibromatosis represent spontaneous mutations.

Characteristics

The diagnosis of neurofibromatosis Type 1 (NF-1) is based on a National Institutes of Health (NIH) Consensus Development Conference Statement (1988). Diagnosis requires two or more of the following criteria to firmly establish the diagnosis.

1. Six or more cafe-au-lait spots (areas of increased skin pigmentation) ≥ 5mm in diameter in prepubertal patients and ≥ 15mm in postpubertal patients
2. Two or more neurofibroma of any type, or one plexiform neurofibroma (tumors that grow on a nerve or nerve tissue, under the skin) or one plexiform neurofibroma (involving multiple nerves)
3. Freckling in the axillary or inguinal region
4. Optic glioma (a tumor of the optic nerve)
5. Two or more Lisch nodules (a benign growth on the iris of the eye)
6. A distinctive bone lesion, such as sphenoid dysplasia, or cortical thinning of long bones, with or without pseudoarthrosis
7. A first-degree relative with NF-1 based on the preceding criteria

(Seashore et al., 1995)

Diagnostic criteria for NF-2:

1. Bilateral 8th nerve masses seen on appropriate imaging
2. A first-degree relative with NF-2 and either unilateral 8th nerve mass, and two of the following: neurofibroma, meningioma, glima, schwannoma, and juvenile posterior subcapsular lenticular opacity

(Berg, 1999)

The complications of NF are multisystem. Individuals with NF have an increased risk for malignancy, particularly of the skin and nervous system, although these patients are also at increased risk for developing leukemia (Berg, 1999). Hypertension, kyphosis, and scoliosis, contributing to pulmonary compromise, gastrointestinal bleeding secondary to gastrointestinal neurofibromata, and neurologic abnormalities occur. Learning difficulties, speech problems, attentional disorders, and seizures are common.

The learning needs of children with NF-1 have been extensively evaluated. Intellectual ability is generally in the normal range, although the curve is shifted to the left, with mean reported IQs generally in the low 90s (Moore et al., 1994; North et al., 1994). There is a disproportionate requirement for special education with as many as 73% of those children with NF-1 evaluated requiring special services (Duffner, Cohen, Seidel, & Shuccard, 1989). There has been some suggestion of a specific pattern of learning disorder, a nonverbal learning disability, associated with NF-1 (Eldridge et al., 1989), though this has not been consistently replicated (Moore et al., 1994). Attentional issues are common (North et al., 1994). Many children with NF-1 will have abnormalities on MRI (72%; Duffner et al., 1989), although these abnormalities may be transient and are of questionable significance. The relationship between these structural abnormalities and academic performance remains inconclusive (North et al., 1994).

Treatment of patients with NF is symptomatic (Berg, 1999). Neurofibromas of the peripheral nerves are generally not a problem unless they are regularly irritated or present a cosmetic impediment. Intracranial tumors are managed with neurosurgical and oncologic intervention. The treatment of optic gliomas is controversial and generally expectant (Berg, 1999). Anticipatory counseling to deal with psychosocial and educational issues is important, and parent support groups may be helpful (Seashore et al., 1995). Educational intervention is the most pressing need for many children with NF. Children with a diagnosis of NF should be carefully monitored and their educational needs met in an expeditious and energetic fashion.

Much research is directed toward the understanding and treatment of this relatively frequent and often debilitating disease. Future work will focus on understanding and perhaps correcting the function of the NF genes (NINDS Workshop, 2000). The relationship between the NF-1 protein and learning is being investigated with the hope that if the pathway could be described and understood, medications could be developed to mitigate the learning issues associated with NF-1. The association between NF and malignancy suggested that understanding NF may allow for the development of new forms of treatment for cancer.

REFERENCES

Berg, B. (1999). Neurocutaneous syndromes: Phakomatoses and allied conditions. In K. F. Swaiman & S. Aswal (Eds.), *Pediatric neurology: Principles and practice* (3rd ed.). St. Louis, MO: Mosby.

Duffner, P. K., Cohen, M. E., Seidel, F. G., & Shuccard, D. W. (1989). The significance of MRI abnormalities in children with neurofibromatosis. *Neurology, 39,* 373–378.

Eldridge, R., Denckla, M. B., Bien, E., Myer, S., Kaiser-Kupfer, M. J., Pikus, An, Schlesinger, S. L., Parry, D. M., Dambrosia, J. M., Zasloff, M. A., & Mulvihill, J. J. (1989). Neurofibromatosis Type 1 (Recklinghausen's disease): Neurologic and cognitive assessment with sibling controls. *Archives of Diseases in Children, 143,* 833–837.

Moore, B. D., Ater, J. L., Meedle, M. N., Slopis, J., & Copeland, D. R. (1994). Neuropsychological profile of children with neurofibromatosis, brain tumor or both. *Journal of Child Neurology, 9,* 368–377.

North, K., Joy, P., Yuille, D., Cocks, N., Mobbs, E., Hutchins, P., McHugh, E., & de Silva, M. (1994). Specific learning disability in children with neurofibromatosis type 1: significance of MRI abnormalities. *Neurology, 44,* 878–883.

Seashore, M., Cho, S., Despiosita, F., Sherman, J., Wappner, R. S., & Wilson, M. G. (1995). Health supervision for children with neurofibromatosis. *Pediatrics, 96,* 368–372.

Greta N. Wilkening
University of Colorado Health Sciences Center
The Children's Hospital

NEUROFIBROMATOSIS, TYPE 2

Neurofibromatosis Type 2 (NF-2) is a less common type of neurofibromatosis. Neurofibromatoses are genetically transmitted disorders of the nervous system that often have an autosomal dominant pattern of transmission. These disorders may cause tumor growth on nerves and other abnormalities, such as multiple skin changes (e.g., café au lait spots) and bone deformities (National Institute of Neurological Disorders and Strokes [NINDS], 2001; Spreen, Risser, & Edgell, 1995). Neurofibromatosis Type 1 (NF-1) is the more common type of neurofibromatosis.

NF-2 is characterized by bilateral tumors on the 8th cranial nerve. It was thought to be primarily associated with tumors on a branch of the 8th cranial nerve associated with hearing and formerly was known as bilateral acoustic neurofibromatosis or central bilateral acoustic NF. These names are no longer technically correct because tumors also are known to occur on the vestibular nerve branch of the 8th cranial nerve in NF-2 (NINDS, 2001).

Characteristics

1. Bilateral 8th cranial nerve tumors
2. First-degree relative (parent, sibling, offspring) with NF-2 and a unilateral 8th nerve tumor
3. First-degree relative with NF-2 and any two of the following: glioma, meningioma, neurofibroma, schannoma, or cataract at an early age
4. Possible early symptoms: hearing loss, ringing in the ears (tinnitus), balance problems

NF-2 occurs in approximately 1 in 40,000 individuals worldwide. Individuals may inherit the disorder from a parent; however, approximately 50% of new cases occur spontaneously through change in the individual's genes. This mutation then can be transmitted to the individual's offspring. NF-2 is found in both genders and in all racial and ethnic groups (NINDS, 2001).

The following diagnostic workup for individuals suspected of having NF-1 is recommended: personal medical and family history with particular attention to NF-2 features, comprehensive examination and imaging studies of the brain and spine, audiometric testing, and opthamological evaluation (National Neurofibromatosis Foundation [NNF], 2001). In addition, children of parents with NF-2 may be diagnosed by a blood test before any symptoms are apparent (Neurogenetics Clinic, 2001).

Although tumors on the 8th cranial nerve are most common, many individuals with NF-2 also develop tumors (schwannomas) on other nerves (NNF 2001; Riccardi, 1992). The symptoms of these tumors depend on their location. For example, tumors that grow on spinal cord nerves may cause numbness of a part of the body, or if they grow large enough to press on the spinal cord, they may cause weakness and numbness in the legs. In addition, individuals with NF-2 frequently develop other types of tumors, which grow on the coverings of the brain and spinal cord (e.g., meningiomas). It is important that persons with NF-2 have an annual neurological examination to assist in the early detection of tumors. Finally, some persons with NF-2 develop a particular type of cataract (juvenile posterior sublenticular opacity) or have other vision problems.

Currently, the treatment of NF-2 involves management of the symptoms of the disorder. Neuroimaging technologies such as MRI can detect tumors as small as a few millimeters in diameter, and thus allow for early treatment (NINDS, 2001). The only treatment available for tumors of NF-2 is surgery and radiation therapy. Most individuals with NF-2 will require at least one surgery during their lifetime (NNF, 2001). Recently, the House Ear Institute in conjunction with the Cochlear Corporation developed a device that allows some individuals with deafness due to NF-2 to perceive sound. This device (an auditory brainstem implant, or ABI) is now undergoing research trials worldwide (NNF, 2001).

Most individuals with NF-2 do not become symptomatic until they are teenagers (Neurogenetics Clinic, 2001). If they are still in school, they may qualify for special education assistance under the categories of Hearing Impaired or Visually Handicapped. Depending on the severity of these sensory impairments, the student may require certain classroom accommodations. The child with vision problems may require large-print text or extended time in order to meet their individual needs. Similarly, the child with hearing impairment may need preferential seating or classroom amplification.

Individuals and families with NF-2 may find it helpful to obtain advice and treatment at a multidisciplinary NF clinic. Also, support groups and information from Web sites, such as the NNF's (neurofibromatosis.org), may be helpful and informative.

There is ongoing research into many aspects of NF-2. Research teams with information from the National Institutes of Health Clinical Center located the exact position of the NF-2 gene on Chromosome 22. Research continues regarding genetics, diagnosis, and treatment of NF-2 (NINDS, 2001).

REFERENCES

National Institute of Neurological Disorders and Stroke. (2001). Neurofibromatosis Type 2. Retrieved from http://www.ninds.nih.gov

National Neurofibromatosis Foundation. (2001). Neurofibromatosis Type 2. Retrieved from http://www.neurofibromatosis.org

Neurogenetics Clinic. (2001). Neurofibromatosis Type 2. Retrieved from http://www.neurosurgery.mgh.harvard.edu/NF2.htm

Riccardi, V. M. (1992). *Neurofibromatosis: Phenotype, natural history, and pathogenesis* (2nd ed.). Baltimore: Johns Hopkins University Press.

Spreen, S., Risser, A. T., & Edgell, D. (1995). *Developmental neuropsychology.* New York: Oxford University Press.

Vedia Sherman
Nancy L. Nussbaum
Austin Neurological Clinic

NEURONAL MIGRATION DISORDERS

Neuronal migration disorders (NMDs) are a group of disorders caused by the abnormal migration of nerve cells (neurons) very early in the development of the fetal nervous system. Neuronal migration is the process in which neurons move from their place of origin to their permanent location. When this process is disrupted, the result is a structurally abnormal brain involving the cerebral hemispheres, cerebellum, brainstem, and/or hippocampus (NINDS, 2002).

NMDs may include schizencephaly, porencephaly, lissencephaly, agyria, macrogyria, pachygyria, microgyria, micropolygyria, neuronal heterotopias (including band heterotopia), agenesis of the corpus callosum, and agenesis of the cranial nerves. These disorders may be associated with other abnormalities, including other NMDs. NMDs may be associated with early death. Most individuals with NMDs have a normal physical appearance, but there may be variations in facial appearance that can be noticed by trained professionals (NINDS, 2002).

NMDs may be caused by genetic or biochemical abnormalities (e.g., Zellweger syndrome). Several genetic abnormalities have been identified, including a deletion of a gene on Chromosome 17p13.3, which causes lissencephaly, and a mutation of a gene on Chromosome Xq22.3, which causes lissencephaly in males and band heterotopia in females. The Reelin gene on Chromosome 7q22 causes microcephaly, lissencephaly, cerebellar hypoplasia (small cerebellum), and lymphedema. Abnormalities on a number of other genes have been identified as the cause of NMDs, yet their roles in neuronal migration are not well understood (NINDS, 2002).

Characteristics
Symptoms vary and may include

1. Hypotonia (reduced muscle tone)
2. Seizures
3. Developmental delay
4. Mental retardation
5. Growth failure
6. Feeding difficulties
7. Lymphedema (puffiness of the extremities due to poor fluid drainage)
8. Microcephaly
9. Motor dysfunction

Treatment is symptomatic and may include antiseizure medication and special or supplemental education consisting of physical, occupational, and speech therapies. The prognoses for individuals with NMDs vary depending on the specific disorder and the degree of neurological deficit and brain malformation. The NINDS conducts and supports a wide range of studies that explore the complex systems of normal brain development, including neuronal migration. The knowledge gained from these studies provides the foundation for understanding how this process can go awry and thus offers hope for new means to treat and prevent NMDs (NINDS, 2002).

Individuals needing support or further information should contact the following organizations: March of Dimes Birth Defects Foundation, 1275 Mamaroneck Avenue, White Plains, NY 10605; resourcecenter@modimes.org; http://www.modimes.org; 914-428-7100 or 888-MODIMES (663-4637); fax, 914-428-8203; or the Lissencephaly Network, 10408 Bitterroot Court, Ft. Wayne, IN 46804; lissnet @lissencephaly.org; http://www.lissencephaly.org; 219-432-4310; fax, 219-432-4310.

REFERENCE

NINDS. (2002). National Institute of Neurological Disorders and Stroke Online Database. Neuronal migration disorders. Retrieved April 2002 from http://www.ninds.nih.gov/health_and_medical/disorders/neuronal_migration.htm

Elaine Fletcher-Janzen
University of Northern Colorado

NEUROPATHY, GIANT AXONAL

Giant axonal neuropathy (GAN) is a rare neurologic disorder characterized by slowly progressive peripheral neuropathy and signs of central impairment. Common symptoms include muscle weakness and wasting, visual impairments, ataxia, and, at later stages, mental decline and dementia.

Onset usually occurs before the age of 2 or 3, but always before age 7 (Ouvrier, McLeod, & Pollard, 1990). GAN appears to affect males and females equally often. Early clinical symptoms, such as delayed motor development, symmetrical muscle weakness in limbs, hyporeflexia, and gait disturbances, are largely attributable to malfunction of the peripheral nervous system, whereas later presenting symptoms, such as nystagmus, dysarthria, and heart and respiratory problems, are more indicative of central involvement (Kretzschmar, Berg, & Davis, 1987; Tandan et al., 1987). Scoliosis is often present by age 10. Many individuals with GAN possess very tightly curled, kinky hair. Children with GAN die by the end of their late teens or early 20s.

As the name suggests, pathological analyses of peripheral nerves reveal numerous enlarged axon fibers containing an overabundance of intermediate neurofilaments, woven proteins that provide cells with structural support. Although exposure to environmental toxins such as hexacarbon solvents can lead to similar neuropathy ("glue sniffer's" neuropathy; Schmidt, Schnoy, Altenkirch, & Wagner, 1984), it is not considered a cause of GAN. GAN shows an autosomal recessive pattern of inheritance. Recently, Bomont et al. (2000) identified a gene encoding a cytoskeletal protein called gigaxonin that is mutated in patients with GAN, thus providing an important step in understanding the etiology and finding a treatment for GAN.

In general, children with GAN show deterioration of mental aptitude as the disease progresses. At early stages, cases commonly show normal intelligence. At later stages, however, GAN patients exhibit mild mental retardation or below-average intelligence as measured by standard scales (e.g., full-scale IQ of approximately 70 on the Wechsler Intelligence Scale for Adults–Revised; Ouvrier, Prineas, Walsh, Reye, & McLeod, 1974) eventually leading to signs of dementia (e.g., Guazzi, Malandrini, Geril, & Federico, 1991). Moreover, affliction with GAN typically results in requiring wheelchair use rather early with eventual loss of independent mobility entirely.

At present, there is no cure for GAN. Treatment consists of active exercise physiotherapy with occasional care of immediate dangers, such as pulmonary and respiratory complications, when necessary (Ouvrier et al., 1990). Recently, penicillamine, an inhibitor of vimentin filament aggregation, has been used to treat GAN successfully (Mahadevan et al., 2000; Tandan, Bradley, & Fillyaw, 1990). The existence of a canine GAN that bears striking resemblance to the human GAN (e.g., hereditary, peripheral neuropathy, kinky hair; King et al., 1993) affords the opportunity to study an animal model of GAN.

Characteristics

1. Onset between infancy and age 7
2. Symptoms such as progressive multisystem deterioration of motor and cognitive capacities
3. Characterized by peripheral and central neuropathy

REFERENCES

Bomont, P., Cavalier, L., Blondeau, F., Hamida, C. B., Belal, S., Tazir, M., Demir, E., Topaloglu, H., Korinthenberg, R., Tuysuz, B., Landrieu, P., Hentati, F., & Koenig, M. (2000). The gene encoding gigaxonin, a new member of the cytoskeletal BTB/kelch repeat family, is mutated in giant axonal neuropathy. *Nature Genetics, 26,* 370–374.

Guazzi, G. C., Malandrini, A., Geril, R., & Federico, A. (1991). Giant axonal neuropathy in 2 siblings: A generalized disorder of intermediate filaments. *European Neurology, 31,* 50–56.

King, R. H., Sarsilmaz, M., Thomas, P. K., Jacobs, J. M., Muddle, J. R., & Duncan, I. D. (1993). Axonal neurofilamentous accumulations: A comparison between human and canine giant axonal neuropathy and 2,5-HD neuropathy. *Neuropathology and Applied Neurobiology, 19,* 224–232.

Kretzschmar, H. A., Berg, B. O., & Davis, R. L. (1987). Giant axonal neuropathy. *Acta Neuropathologica, 73,* 138–144.

Mahadevan, A., Santosh, V., Gayatri, N., Ratnavalli, E., NandaGopal, R., Vasanth, A., Roy, A. K., & Shankar, S. K. (2000). Infantile neuroaxonal dystrophy and giant axonal neuropathy: Overlap of diseases of neuronal cytoskeletal elements in childhood? *Clinical Neuropathology, 19,* 221–229.

Ouvrier, R. A., McLeod, J. G., & Pollard, J. (1990). *Peripheral neuropathy in childhood.* New York: Raven Press.

Ouvrier, R. A., Prineas, J., Walsh, J. C., Reye, R. D. K., & McLeod, J. G. (1974). Giant axonal neuropathy: A third case. *Proceedings of the Australian Association of Neurologists, 11,* 137–144.

Schmidt, R., Schnoy, N., Altenkirch, H., & Wagner, H. M. (1984). Ultrastructural alterations of intrapulmonary nerves after exposure to organic solvents: A contribution to "sniffer's disease." *Respiration, 46,* 362–369.

Tandan, R., Bradley, W. J., & Fillyaw, M. J. (1990). Giant axonal neuropathy: Studies with sulphydryl donor compounds. *Journal of Neurological Sciences, 95,* 153–162.

Tandan, R., Little, B. W., Emery, E. S., Good, P. S., Pendlebury, W. W., & Bradley, W. G. (1987). Childhood giant axonal neuropathy: Case report and review of the literature. *Journal of the Neurological Sciences, 82,* 205–228.

Adam S. Bristol
Yale University

NEUROPATHY, HEREDITARY MOTOR AND SENSORY, TYPE I

Hereditary motor and sensory neuropathy Type I (HMSN1) is also known as Charcot-Marie-Tooth disease (CMT1). It is characterized by demyelination and markedly reduced nerve conduction velocities (Sghirlanzoni, Pareyson, Scaiolio, Marazzi, & Pacini, 1990). It is typically inherited as an autosomal dominant trait but can also be inherited as an X-linked or an autosomal recessive inheritance (MacMillan & Harper, 1994). The disease is characterized by upper and lower distal limb muscle weakness and wasting, impaired reflexes, foot deformity, and distal sensory loss (MacMillan & Harper, 1994). HMSN1 cannot be differentiated from HMSN Type II (HMSN2) on the basis of clinical features alone, although some signs occur more frequently in Type I. However, because HMSN1 involves demyelination and therefore slowed conduction velocities, accurate diagnosis can typically be made through nerve conduction studies (Sghirlanzoni et al., 1990).

HMSN1 is the most common of the hereditary sensory and motor neuropathies and occurs at a rate of about 9–11 per 100,000 (MacMillan & Harper, 1994). The average age of onset is difficult to estimate due to the variability in severity of clinical signs and the often subtle disease progression. However, 81% of symptomatic individuals report an onset before age 10 (MacMillan & Harper, 1994). The mean age of onset is 12.6 years of age (Sghirlanzoni et al., 1990). There is no difference in prevalence or severity of the disease between males and females (MacMillan & Harper, 1994).

Children at risk for the disorder (i.e., children with one parent with HMSN1) can be assessed and reliably diagnosed in the absence of overt clinical symptoms. Affected children show signs of slowed motor conduction velocities as young as 1 year or less even in the absence of overt clinical signs (Feasby, Hahn, Bolton, Brown, & Koopman, 1992). Early clinical signs may include foot abnormality, mild foot wasting, ankle weakness, and impaired reflexes (Feasby et al., 1992).

Characteristics

1. Decreased median nerve conduction velocity
2. Progressive weakness and muscular atrophy in upper and lower limbs
3. Foot deformity (e.g., pes cavus)
4. Impaired reflexes
5. Distal sensory loss

In an educational setting this may mean that an affected child will need to be excused from physical education classes. It also may be necessary for the child's peers to be educated to reduce teasing of the child.

There is no known treatment for the disease itself.

Supportive treatment for complications resulting from leg weakness is typically used. Most patients will require orthopedic footware or braces (Gabreels-Festen, Joosten, Gabreels, Jennekens, and Janssen-van Kempen, 1992). Because the disease is transmitted genetically, genetic counseling is recommended for affected individuals. There is no known method of prevention.

Although motor and sensory disability increases with age, the disorder does not lead to a shortened life span (MacMillan & Harper, 1994). Progression of the neuropathy tends to be slow, and many patients experience minimal progress after adolescence (Gabreels-Festen et al., 1992). In adults, common symptoms include sensory dysfunction in lower limbs, cold extremities, discolored skin, and scoliosis (Gabreels-Festen et al., 1992).

REFERENCES

Feasby, T., Hahn, A., Bolton, C., Brown, W., & Koopman, W. (1992). Detection of hereditary motor sensory neuropathy type I in childhood. *Journal of Neurology, Neurosurgery, and Psychiatry, 55,* 895–897.

Gabreels-Festen, A., Joosten, E., Gabreels, F., Jennekens, F., & Janssen-van Kempen, T. (1992). Early morphological features in dominantly inherited demyelinating motor and sensory neuropathy (HMSN type 1). *Journal of the Neurological Sciences, 107,* 145–154.

MacMillan, J., & Harper, P. (1994). The Charcot-Marie-Tooth syndrome: Clinical aspects from a population study in South Wales, UK. *Clinical Genetics, 45,* 128–134.

Sghirlanzoni, A., Pareyson, D., Scaiolio, V., Marazzi, R., & Pacini, L. (1990). Hereditary motor and sensory neuropathy type I and type II. *Italian Journal of Neurological Science, 11,* 471–479.

Laura Arnstein
State University of New York at Binghamton

See also Charcot-Marie-Tooth Disease

NEUROPATHY, HERDITARY MOTOR AND SENSORY, TYPE II

Hereditary motor and sensory neuropathy Type II (HMSN2) is a form of Charcot-Marie-Tooth disease (CMT2). It is characterized by axonal degeneration with normal or near-normal nerve conduction velocities (Emeryk-Szajewska, Badurska, & Kostera-Pruszczyk, 1998). It is inherited as an autosomal dominant trait (MacMillan & Harper, 1994).

Individuals suffering from HMSN2 show clinical signs such as foot deformity, muscular atrophy and weakness in the upper and lower limbs, moderate reflex depression, and mild sensory loss.

The average age of onset is difficult to estimate due to the variability in severity of clinical signs and the often-subtle disease progression. The peak of onset is during the first and second decades of life, although onset can range from early childhood to the sixth or seventh decade of life (Sghirlanzoni, Pareyson, Scaiolio, Marazzi, & Pacini, 1990). The mean age of onset is 17.35 years of age, slightly later than HMSN Type I, which tends to begin in early childhood (Sghirlanzoni et al., 1990). The estimated prevalence of HMSN2 is 2.7 per 100,000 (MacMillan & Harper, 1994).

Characteristics

1. Inherited as an autosomal dominant trait and characterized by axonal degeneration
2. Muscular atrophy and distal weakness in upper and lower limbs
3. Foot deformity (e.g., pes cavus)
4. Moderate depression in tendon reflexes
5. Mild sensory loss

There is no known treatment for the disease itself. Supportive treatment for complications resulting from leg weakness is typically used. Because the disease is transmitted genetically, genetic counseling is recommended for affected individuals. There is no known method of prevention.

The progression of the disease tends to be very slow, but there is a significant correlation between age and disease severity (MacMillan & Harper, 1994).

In schools, children with HSMN2 may need to be excused from physical education classes. They may also be susceptible to teasing from their peers, which may be alleviated by a visit from a parent or doctor to explain the disorder.

REFERENCES

Emeryk-Szajewska, B., Badurska, B., Kostera-Pruszczyk, A. (1998). Electrophysiological findings in hereditary motor and sensory neuropathy type I and II: A conduction velocity study. *Electromyography and Clinical Neurophysiology, 38,* 95–101.

MacMillan, J., & Harper, P. (1994). The Charcot-Marie-Tooth syndrome: Clinical aspects from a population study in South Wales, UK. *Clinical Genetics, 45,* 128–134.

Sghirlanzoni, A., Pareyson, D., Scaiolio, V., Marazzi, R., & Pacini, L. (1990). Hereditary motor and sensory neuropathy type I and type II. *Italian Journal of Neurological Science, 11,* 471–479.

Laura Arnstein
State University of New York at Binghamton

See also Charcot-Marie-Tooth Disease

NEUROPATHY, PERIPHERAL

Peripheral neuropathy refers to a large and diverse class of peripheral nerve disorders. The signs and symptoms associated with these disorders are often complex and require careful assessment. The neuropathies affecting infants and children can vary in course and severity. The exact causes of these disorders are not always well understood. Many of the disorders are hereditary, with a prevalence of about 1 case per 3,000 to 6,000. Symptoms may have motor, sensory, and autonomic features (Asbury, 1998).

Hereditary motor neuronopathy (HMN) represents a heterogeneous group of disorders involving neuronal atrophy and degeneration of predominantly lower motor neurons (Harding, 1993). Werdnig-Hoffmann disease is the acute infantile form of the disorder. The chronic childhood form (Type II) of the disorder is an autosomal recessive condition that usually develops in the first or second year of infancy. Symptoms may include muscle weakness, wasting, paralysis, skeletal deformities, calf hypertrophy, facial weakness, wasting of the tongue, difficulty with speech articulation (dysarthria), weakening of the intercostal muscles affecting respiration, and mental retardation (Harding, 1993).

Autosomal dominant proximal HMN of juvenile onset (Type III) is less debilitating than Type II and progresses slowly. In 90% of cases, onset occurs before age 5. In infancy, skeletal muscle tone is diminished (hypotonia), and motor milestones are often delayed. Other symptoms include muscle weakness, depressed or absent tendon reflexes, forward curvature of the lumbar spine (lordosis), and mild joint contractures (Harding, 1993).

A severe infantile form of distal HMN can result in widespread muscle weakness and diaphragmatic paralysis, leading to respiratory failure. Death usually occurs before age 1. Fazio-Londe disease, a type of bulbar HMN, often begins in the second or third year of childhood but can have onset as late as age 12. Symptoms include excessive drooling, repeated respiratory infections, difficulty swallowing (dysphagia), facial and generalized weakness, wasting, and loss of muscle tone and reflexes. Death due to respiratory failure often occurs within 18 months of onset (Harding, 1993).

Hereditary sensory and autonomic neuropathy (HSAN) consists of a group of heterogeneous inherited disorders in which primary sensory and autonomic neurons fail to develop or undergo systemic atrophy and degeneration (Dyck, 1993). HSAN types I and II are described elsewhere in this volume. HSAN Type III, also known as familial dysautonomia, is an inherited disorder seen predominantly in Ashkenazi Jewish infants and children. Symptoms include poor sucking, failure to thrive, unexplained fever, repeated episodes of pneumonia, difficulty feeding and swallowing, defective lacrimation, blotching of skin, poor gag reflex, absence of fungiform papillae of the tongue, vomiting, defective temperature control, excessive perspiration, decreased visual acuity, and insensitivity to pain (Dyck, 1993).

Refsum's disease is an inherited disorder of lipid metabolism. Clinical onset is gradual, beginning in childhood. Lower limbs are typically affected, with widespread muscle atrophy and weakness in the limbs and trunk, foot drop, and loss of tendon reflexes. Sensory disturbances include reduced sensitivity to stimulation (hypoesthesia, stocking type), impairment in the sense of touch (dysesthesia), and spontaneous pain (Skjeldal, Stokke, & Refsum, 1993).

Peripheral neuropathy often accompanies diphtheria, a disease that is rare in the United States and Western Europe but is still common in the developing world. The incidence of diphtheritic neuropathy is variable but appears to be about 20%. Generalized peripheral neuropathy appears in the 8th to 12th week of the illness. Sensory and motor disturbances may include abnormal sensations (paresthesias), impairment of vibration and joint position sense, aching and tenderness in the limbs, impaired tendon reflexes, and reduced muscular coordination (ataxia). Other symptoms may include weakness, wasting, and rapid heart rate (tachycardia; McDonald & Kocen, 1993).

Characteristics

1. The disorders are inherited or acquired.
2. Symptoms can be varied and complex, with sensory, motor, and autonomic features.

Treatment of peripheral neuropathy is variable, depending on the exact nature of the disability. Treatment may include the use of orthotic appliances and rehabilitative procedures, surgery to prevent or delay progressive skeletal deformities, the use of assisted ventilation, medication for the control of neuropathic pain, genetic counseling, and supportive care for chronically disabled children (Harding, 1993). Special education may be required to meet the needs of children with chronic physical or mental disabilities. Future research is needed to better understand the pathogenesis underlying these disorders.

REFERENCES

Asbury, A. K. (1998). Diseases of the peripheral nervous system. In A. S. Fauci, E. Braunwald, & K. J. Isselbacher, (Eds.), *Harrison's principles of internal medicine* (pp. 2457–2469). New York: McGraw-Hill.

Dyck, P. J. (1993). Neuronal atrophy and degeneration predominantly affecting peripheral sensory and autonomic neurons. In P. J. Dyck, P. K. Thomas, J. W. Griffin, P. A. Low, & J. F. Poduslo (Eds.), *Peripheral neuropathy* (3rd ed., pp. 1065–1093). Philadelphia: W. B. Saunders.

Harding, A. E. (1993). Inherited neuronal atrophy and degeneration predominantly of lower motor neurons. In P. J. Dyck, P. K. Thomas, J. W. Griffin, P. A. Low, & J. F. Poduslo (Eds.), *Pe-*

ripheral neuropathy (3rd ed., pp. 1051–1093). Philadelphia: W. B. Saunders.

McDonald, W. I., & Kocen, R. S. (1993). Diphtheritic neuropathy. In P. J. Dyck, P. K. Thomas, J. W. Griffin, P. A. Low, & J. F. Poduslo (Eds.), *Peripheral neuropathy* (3rd ed., pp. 1412–1417). Philadelphia: W. B. Saunders.

Skjeldal, O. H., Stokke, O., & Refsum, S. (1993). Phytanic acid storage disease. In P. J. Dyck, P. K. Thomas, J. W. Griffin, P. A. Low, & J. F. Poduslo (Eds.), *Peripheral neuropathy* (3rd ed., pp. 1149–1160). Philadelphia: W. B. Saunders.

Robert A. Chernoff
Harbor-UCLA Medical Center

See also Werdnig-Hoffman Disease

NEUTROPENIA, CYCLIC

Cyclic neutropenia (CN) is a congenital, inherited disorder of white blood cell production. Its most characteristic feature is regular, periodic decreases in the numbers of circulating neutrophils (neutropenia). Neutrophils are a type of white blood cells produced in bone marrow. They are major players in combating infections caused by invading bacteria, viruses, and fungi.

The precise etiology of SN is unclear. Patients with this disorder suffer from malfunctioning regulation of blood-forming precursor cells.

Although it is considered rare, no data are available on the prevalence of CN. Many cases conform to an autosomal dominant pattern of inheritance. In some patients, however, the mode of heredity is uncertain.

Characteristics

1. Regular, oscillating decrease in the number of circulating neutrophils. Values drop from normal to below normal. Changes occur every 21 (±3) days.
2. Periods of neutropenia give rise to oral ulcers, fever, stomatitis (inflammation of the mucous lining of the mouth), pharyngitis (inflammation of the throat), and lymph gland enlargement.
3. More serious consequences of neutropenia include pneumonia and recurrent ulcerations of the mouth, vagina, and rectum. Some patients die from overwhelming infection. They are particularly vulnerable to the bacterium that causes gas gangrene.
4. Periodontitis (inflammation of the gums, with subsequent loss of the supporting structures of the teeth).

No known therapy exists for the underlying defect (neutropenia) of CN. Bacterial infections usually respond to aggressive antibiotic therapy, but in the face of profoundly low neutrophil counts, no antibiotic is very effective. Periodontal disease necessitates good dental hygiene and, possibly, referral to dental specialists who treat gum disorders.

No data are available concerning cognitive deficits as a result of CN.

Patients with CN who survive into adulthood have a favorable prognosis. Some of them will experience an improvement in their symptoms as they age, with less pronounced swings in their neutrophil counts. However, others will go on to develop chronic neutropenia and must contend with a prolonged inability to handle a variety of potentially serious infectious processes.

For more information and support, contact the National Neutropenia Network, PO Box 205, 6348 North Milwaukee Avenue, Chicago, IL 60646; (800) 638-8768; Bolyard@U.Washington.edu; or Neutropenia Support Association, Inc., PO Box 243, 905 Corydon Avenue, Winnepeg, Manitoba, R3M-3S7, Canada; (204) 489-8454 or (800) 663-8876; stevensl@neutropenia.ca; http://www.neutropenia.ca.

REFERENCES

Boxer, L. A. (2000). Leukopenia. In R. E. Behrman, R. M. Kleigman, & H. B. Jenson (Eds.), *Nelson textbook of pediatrics* (16th ed., pp. 623–624). Philadelphia: W. B. Saunders.

National Organization for Rare Disorders, Inc. (1998). Neutropenia, cyclic. Retrieved from http://www.stepstn.com/cgi-win/nord.exe?proc=GetDocument&rectype=0&recnum=663

Barry H. Davison
Ennis, Texas

Joan W. Mayfield
Baylor Pediatric Specialty Services
Dallas, Texas

NEUTROPENIA, SEVERE CHRONIC

Severe chronic neutropenia is a blood disorder. It is characterized by abnormally low levels of the white blood cells that play an integral role in fighting infection. These bacteria-fighting white cells are called neutrophils. Neutrophils are produced within the bone cavities; any disorder, drug, or injury that affects bone marrow can result in a failure to produce sufficient neutrophils and give rise to severe chronic neutropenia.

Neutropenia comes in three forms based on etiology and manifestation pattern: congenital, idiopathic, and cyclic neutropenia (National Organization for Rare Disorders, 1998). Severe chronic neutropenia may be inherited, acquired, or of unknown etiology (idiopathic). If genetic, transmission can be either autosomal dominant or autosomal recessive. In the United States, it is estimated that 2,000–5,000 individuals have this disorder. Neutropenia can also be acquired secondary to treatment for other disorders or in conjunction with other disorders (e.g., leukemia). Neutropenia can also result from infections or exposure to specific poisons that affect production of neutrophils. Children and adults can be affected; males and females are affected equally (National Organization for Rare Disorders, 1998). There is no indication of differences in incidence based on ethnicity. Diagnosis is made based on blood testing, with results indicating a lower-than-normal level of neutrophils (Welte & Dale, 1996).

Characteristics

1. Recurring fevers
2. Periodontal problems with inflammation of the gums (gingivitis)
3. Mouth sores or ulcers
4. Recurring infections, including pneumonia

Symptoms may last for years or remit in a shorter period of time. The congenital forms tend to be the most severe and become evident during early childhood. Complications to severe chronic neutropenia originate from the individual's inability to fight infection. With the congenital form of severe chronic neutropenia, it is not uncommon for the child with this disorder to develop pneumonia or other problems. The most severe form of congenital neutropenia is referred to as Kostmann disease. Individuals with severe chronic neutropenia of unknown origin (idiopathic) tend to have the least severe symptom presentation; however, infection is still a problem and can become life threatening. With the cyclic form, the manifestation of symptoms follows a cyclical pattern, with recurrence of symptoms (e.g., oral ulcers) every 3 weeks and lasting a few days each occurrence (Welte & Dale, 1996).

Treatment is symptomatic and supportive. Infections are treated with antibiotics. In some cases, treatment may include the use of anti-inflammatory drugs that suppress the immune system or with infusions of antibodies (Welte & Dale, 1996). Bone marrow transplantation is another option of treatment. Finally, synthetic drugs and orphan drugs to stimulate the production of neutrophils have been used to elevate the neutrophil level with positive results (e.g., Dunn & Goa, 2000). There is no indication of any effects on the central nervous system in particular or on cognitive ability. Modification of attendance rules and allowances or precautions to address the risk for recurrent infections may be appropriate to the extent feasible in the school setting. If the child's absences or health issues are seen as severely impairing educational benefit, consideration of eligibility for special education services as other health impaired (OHI) may be appropriate. If the severe chronic neutropenia is familial in origin, genetic counseling for individuals affected and family members will be needed.

REFERENCES

Dunn, C. J., & Goa, K. L. (2000). Lenograstim: An update of its pharmacological properties and use in chemotherapy induced neutropenia and related clinical settings. *Drugs, 59,* 681–717.

National Organization for Rare Disorders. (1998). Neutropenia, severe chronic (#857). Retrieved May 25, 2001, from http://www.rarediseases.org

Welte, K., & Dale, D. (1996). Pathophysiology and treatment of severe chronic neutropenia. *Annals of Hematology, 72,* 158–165.

Cynthia A. Riccio
Texas A&M University

NEZELOF SYNDROME

Nezelof syndrome is one of many immunodeficiency disorders. Other names for Nezelof syndrome include Nezelof thymic aplasia, thymic dysplasia with normal immunoglobulins, combined immunodeficiency with immunoglobulins, pure alymphocytosis, Nezelof-type severe combined immunodeficiency, and immune defect due to the absence of the thymus (National Organization for Rare Disorders, 1999). As with other immunodeficiency disorders, Nezelof syndrome is characterized by decreased ability of the individual to fight infections. Immunodeficiency in Nezelof syndrome is attributed to the absence of the thymus gland. The thymus gland, when present, is located in the neck and is critical to the function of the lymphatic system. Because T-lymphocytes are matured in the thymus gland, although immune factors (immunoglobulin) are present in the blood, there is an absence of T-cell function in Nezelof syndrome, and immune response is not present.

Characteristics

1. Frequent and severe infections
2. Delayed growth
3. General loss of muscle
4. Potentially fatal reactions to immunization that uses live vaccines
5. High incidence of malignant tumors

The cause of Nezelof syndrome is unknown, but it is believed to be an autosomal recessive or X-linked trait; consistent with these possibilities, Nezelof syndrome is more likely to affect males than to affect females. There are, however, only 50 cases reported in the medical research literature, and this paucity of research limits the extent to which the genetic transmission can be studied (National Organization for Rare Disorders, 1999). The form of Nezelof syndrome with purine nucleoside phosphorylase (PNP) deficiency has been linked to the long arm of Chromosome 14; only 34 cases of the PNP form of Nezelof were reported in the medical research as of 1991 (Markert, 1991).

Nezelof syndrome becomes evident from birth with frequent and severe infections that include skin infections, oral thrush or candidiasis, diarrhea, infections of the blood (septicemia), pneumonia or other infections of the lungs, and cytomegalovirus. The specific immunity defect in Nezelof syndrome results in an absence of immune reaction and can result in potentially fatal reactions to immunizations that use live vaccines as a result. Individuals with Nezelof syndrome are susceptible to graft-versus-host disease. In some cases, Nezelof syndrome is due to the absence of one enzyme, PNP, that is needed for the production of antibodies to fight infection. In those cases in which the PNP enzyme is absent, progressive paralysis and uncontrolled muscle contractions occur.

Treatment is geared at addressing the infections as they occur with various antifungal, antibiotic, and related medications; some infections, however, are difficult to treat. Bone marrow transplant from a compatible donor is an option if a donor is available. For those individuals with the PNP type of Nezelof syndrome, blood transfusions to decrease the excess purine have been used. Prior to blood transfusion, the blood to be transfused must be washed of all live lymphocytes that might cause a problem such as graft-versus-host disease. Some drugs have been used to treat the PNP form but without success (National Organization for Rare Disorders, 1999).

Prevention of infection is key to the health and well-being of individuals with Nezelof syndrome in any form. This means that individuals with Nezelof syndrome need to be protected to the extent feasible from infectious agents, including other individuals who may be ill with infectious diseases, as well as vaccines that use live viruses. Use of corticosteroids or surgeries that suppress the immune system further also need to be avoided. Given the findings of a genetic link for Nezelof syndrome, individuals with the disorder as well as family members should obtain genetic counseling.

REFERENCES

Markert, M. L. (1991). Purine nucleoside phosphorylase deficiency. *Immunodeficiency Review, 3,* 45–81.

National Organization for Rare Disorders. (1999). Nezelof's syndrome (#75). Retrieved June 3, 2001, from http://www.rarediseases.org

Cynthia A. Riccio
Texas A&M University

NIEMANN-PICK DISEASE

Niemann-Pick disease (NPD) is a member of the lipidoses disease group. Lipidoses are disorders of lipid (fat) storage that affect several organ systems. Multiple clinical forms of NPD have been identified. Types A, B, C and D are the most prevalent.

NPD Types A and B are caused by a deficiency of the enzyme sphingomyelinase. This enzyme is necessary for the degradation of sphingolipids, which are complex molecules integral to the formation of cell membranes everywhere in the body. Defective sphingomyelinase activity creates an accumulation of sphingomyelin, a type of sphingolipid, in the monocyte-macrophage system (liver, spleen, and lymphatics), as well as the central nervous system. These sites are locations of the pathology observed in NPD Types A and B. A specific gene mutation on Chromosome 11 is responsible for decreased production of sphingomyelinase.

NPD Types C and D are characterized by defects in cholesterol transport and metabolism. Some reduction in sphingomyelinase activity may occur. These two NPD variants have clinical similarities and may be secondary to a common genetic mutation.

All forms of NPD are very rare. No data are available regarding the incidence of the disorder in the general population. Like most diseases caused by enzyme deficiencies, NPD is inherited in an autosomal recessive manner.

Characteristics

1. Type A NPD was the first form of the disorder to be described. Infants appear normal at birth, but prolonged jaundice during the newborn period is occasionally seen. Symptoms develop by the age of 6 months. They include psychomotor retardation, enlargement of the liver and spleen (hepatosplenomegaly) and generalized lymph node enlargement (lymphadenopathy). The clinical course is rapidly downhill, with neurodegeneration, spasticity, loss of intellectual ability, and (finally) death by 2–3 years old.
2. In contrast, NPD Type B causes very little neurologic symptomatology. Most patients with this form of the illness have a normal IQ. The clinical course of the illness is extremely variable. Initial abnormal findings are often spleen or liver enlargement, which is picked up on routine physical exam. At the time of diagnosis, pulmonary pathology in the form of nodular deposits of sphingomyelin throughout the lung may be present on X rays. However, most patients do not experience significant pulmonary disease until adulthood. Although mildly affected individuals may not show any abnormalities until late adolescence or adulthood, those with severe illness can experience significant deterioration of lung function by 15–20 years of age and can also experience life-threatening cirrhosis (diffuse scarring of the liver).

3. Patients with NPD Type C may have prolonged neonatal jaundice but often appear normal during the first year or two of life. After that point, slow neurological deterioration occurs. Hepatosplenomegaly is less commonly seen than it is in the NPD Types A and B.
4. NPD Type D usually does not have onset of neurological symptoms until the latter part of childhood. The course, however, is slowly progressive and ultimately leads to overwhelming neurological malfunction and death.

No treatment is currently available for patients with NPD. Liver transplant in Type A disease and amniotic cell transplant for Type B illness have been ineffective. Bone marrow transplant in one individual with NPD Type B did result in a partial improvement in hepatosplenomegaly and sphingomyelin deposition in the lung. However, this child died 3 months after the procedure; therefore, this case did not produce enough data to draw any meaningful conclusions about the efficacy of this therapeutic approach.

Families who have children affected by NPD should have genetic counseling. The disease carries a 25% risk of recurrence in subsequent offspring. Every effort should be made to delineate the type of NPD in question because this information has a profound effect on the disorder's clinical course. Finally, parents should be advised of the availability of prenatal diagnosis, as well as testing for the carrier state of NPD through DNA analysis.

The type of NPD the child has will affect the type of intervention required in the school setting. There is no research indicating the specific educational modifications needed. A comprehensive neuropsychological evaluation would be helpful in defining cognitive strengths and weaknesses and in providing recommendations for remediation.

The lack of effective treatment for NPD's underlying cause makes the disorder's prognosis poor. Patients with Type B disease have the greatest variability in disease severity and minimal or no neurological involvement. Of this subset, patients with mild illness have the best outlook and may survive well into adulthood.

REFERENCE

McGovern, M. M., & Desnick, R. J. (2000). Defects in metabolism of lipids. In R. E. Behrman, R. M. Kleigman, & H. B. Jenson (Eds.), *Nelson textbook of pediatrics* (16th ed., pp. 398–402). Philadelphia: W. B. Saunders.

Barry H. Davison
Ennis, Texas

Joan W. Mayfield
Baylor Pediatric Specialty Services
Dallas, Texas

NONVERBAL LEARNING DISABILITIES

Nonverbal learning disability (NVLD) is defined as a discrepancy between good or average verbal skills and poor nonverbal skills (Little, 1993). More specifically, NVLD is characterized by difficulty with nonverbal skills such as social perception, visual-spatial organization and perception, problem solving, arithmetic, abstract thinking, and psychomotor integration (Johnson, 1987; Little, 1993). There is some research to suggest that NVLD is associated with right-hemisphere dysfunction (Semrud-Clikeman & Hynd, 1990).

The social difficulties associated with NVLD are commonly considered to be the most distinguishing and debilitating aspect of the disorder. Children with NVLD have great difficulty dealing with novel situations due to their inability to accurately read social cues and to express appropriate affect. Social difficulty and peer rejection are commonly associated with NVLD during childhood and predict later emotional and interpersonal difficulties (Little, 1993; Semrud-Clikeman & Hynd, 1990).

Characteristics

1. Disturbances in visual-spatial organization
2. Poor psychomotor coordination
3. Disturbed social perception, judgement, and skills
4. Difficulty with abstract thinking and concept formation
5. Lower math achievement relative to reading ability

The degree of impairment associated with NVLD varies across individuals. Likewise, the pattern of specific symptoms exhibited may vary from case to case (Johnson, 1987). Current estimates of the prevalence of NVLD vary according to selection criteria, making an accurate estimate difficult (Little, 1993; Myklebust, 1975).

Effective treatment of NVLD symptoms has not been adequately researched. The most common form of treatment consists of social skills training; however, empirical support for their efficacy is inconclusive. Teachers, parents, and mental health professionals should be aware of the possibility that these youngsters are at increased risk for both internalizing and externalizing socioemotional problems (Little, 1993). However, Johnson (1987) cautioned that more traditional psychotherapy might not be useful to practitioners with NVLD clients. Such clients' primary need is to resolve immediate and practical problems associated with their learning disability rather than to work to resolve emotional symptomotology.

Children diagnosed with NVLD qualify for special education services. Often the impairments characteristic of NVLD will affect academic performance. Typically, individuals with NVLD will have significantly higher verbal scores than performance scores on the Wechsler Intelligence Scale for Children. More specific areas of academic difficulty include handwriting, arithmetic, and geometry (Johnson,

1987). These children will likely require detailed lessons on concepts of time and direction (Myklebust, 1975). In addition, due to difficulties in visual-spatial perception and psychomotor coordination, they often struggle in courses such as physical education and art (Johnson, 1987).

Educators and parents may have to provide lessons that are beyond those of a traditional academic curriculum. Children with NVLD are likely to benefit from direct instruction on basic self-care and social skills (Myklebust, 1975). Because these children are frequently on the receiving end of negative social feedback, it is important that such instruction be presented in a warm and patient manner. Whenever possible, lessons should mimic and include real-life situations. Educators should keep in mind that because children with NVLD often have strong verbal skills, they may be capable of providing verbal solutions that they are unable to put into practice (Johnson, 1987). Therefore, it may be necessary to actively encourage and facilitate social interaction.

Educators are encouraged to provide routine and consistency for children with NVLD because organizational and problem solving skills are likely to be poor. Because these children have difficulty interpreting the actions and emotions of others, clear explanation of discipline and reinforcement is necessary. Without explanation, traditional forms of consequences may be meaningless to the child (Johnson, 1987; Myklebust, 1975).

Current research indicates that the difficulties associated with NVLD remain throughout the lifetime. Over time, however, many individuals learn to adapt to their disability, and symptoms may lessen. However, despite these gains the effects of this disorder continue to be a source of great frustration, often leading to difficulties interpersonally and professionally.

Currently there is a need for further investigation into differential diagnostic criteria for NVLD. Many researchers call for research into forms of effective treatment for NVLD (Semrud-Clikeman & Hynd, 1990; Little, 1993).

REFERENCES

Johnson, D. J. (1987). Nonverbal learning disabilities. *Pediatric Annals, 16*(2), 133–141.

Little, S. S. (1993). Nonverbal learning disabilities and socioemotional functioning: A review of recent literature. *Journal of Learning Disabilities, 26* (10), 653–665.

Myklebust, H. R. (1975). Nonverbal learning disabilities: Assessment and intervention. In H. R. Myklebust (Ed.), *Progress in learning disabilities* (Vol. 3), pp. 85–121. New York: Gruene Stratton.

Semrud-Clikeman, M., & Hynd, G. W. (1990). Right hemispheric dysfunction in nonverbal learning disabilities: Social, academic, and adaptive functioning in adults and children. *Psychological Bulletin, 107*,(2), 196–209.

Melanie E. Ballatore
University of Texas at Austin

NOONAN SYNDROME

Noonan syndrome is a rare genetic disorder that causes a wide range of clinical features of varying severity, most commonly involving distinctive facial features, cardiac abnormality, chest deformity, and short stature. The condition was originally reported in 1883 but described more thoroughly by Noonan and Ehmke (1963). It is named for Jacqueline A. Noonan, a pediatric cardiologist, who identified the clinical and genetic characteristics of the syndrome (Noonan, 1995). The syndrome is transmitted as an autosomal dominant trait, with some cases attributed to spontaneous mutation. As with many other autosomal dominant disorders, there is widely variable expressivity, which can make mildly affected individuals difficult to recognize. Noonan syndrome is genetically heterogeneous, with research indicating association with multiple gene locations (Online Mendelian Inheritance in Man, 2001). It is identified by clinical characteristics, and there is currently no diagnostic test for it. Chromosome studies are normal. Several other conditions have symptoms similar to those of Noonan syndrome, including cardiofaciocutaneous syndromes, Turner syndrome, Costello syndrome, Noonan-like multiple giant cell lesion syndrome, neurofibromatosis-Noonan syndrome, Watson syndrome, and LEOPARD syndrome (National Organization for Rare Disorders, 2001).

Noonan syndrome is usually apparent at birth. Birth weight is usually normal but may be increased due to subcutaneous edema or peripheral lymphedema. The head appears large, long, narrow, and pointed at the top (turricephalic). Eye abnormalities are common, including ocular hyperteliorism, ptosis, strabismus, epicanthal folds, an antimongoloid slant, and amblyopia. Feeding problems in early infancy and failure to thrive are also common. Facial features frequently follow predictable changes over time (Allanson, Hall, Hughes, Preus, & Witt, 1985): In later childhood, the face appears more triangular, the neck lengthens such that pterygium colli appears more pronounced, trapezii appear more prominent, and wispy scalp hair becomes wooly or curly. In adolescence, the nasal bridge becomes higher and thinner, the eyes become less prominent, and development of secondary sexual characteristics may be delayed or reduced. Some males are infertile; most females have normal fertility. In later adulthood, there are high forehead hairline, wrinkled and unusually transparent skin, and prominent nasolabial folds.

The incidence of Noonan syndrome is approximately 1 in 1,000–2,500 newborns. There is speculation that the true incidence may be higher because wide variability in expressivity may result in mild cases being seen as a normal variant. Males and females are equally affected. No variability has been found related to race or geographic location.

Characteristics

1. Wide range of symptoms and physical features of varying severity, usually including distinctive facial features and cardiac and skeletal abnormalities.
2. Craniofacial features: ocular hyperteliorism, epicanthal folds, ptosis, strabismus, amblyopia, light blue or light green irides, deep philtrum, prominent protruding upper lip, high arched palate, malocclusion, micrognathia, low nasal bridge, webbed neck, low posterior hairline, and low-set, prominent, abnormally rotated ears.
3. Skeletal malformations: chest deformities (over 90%) including pectus carinatum, pectus excavatum, or both; short stature, with growth rate normal before puberty, but adolescent growth spurt decreased or absent; kyphosis, scoliosis, or both; and cubitus valgus (outward deviation of the elbows).
4. Cardiac abnormalities (in about 50% of cases): Pulmonary valvular stenosis is most common; other cardiac abnormalities include atrial septal defect and hypertrophic cardiomyopathy.
5. Circulatory abnormalities: Malformation of some blood and lymph vessels, coagulation factor deficiencies, thrombocytopenia (low platelet levels), and platelet function deficiencies.
6. Mental retardation, usually mild, or learning disability in at least one third of cases; mild motor delay, conductive hearing loss, and language delay are common.
7. Other features include cryptorchidism (failure of testicles to descend by age 1 year, in over half of males), delay in puberty, neurological problems, skin discolorations, and prominent fetal pads on the fingers and toes.

Special education services are likely to be needed for a child with Noonan syndrome to remediate possible cognitive, language, and motor developmental delays. Specific services required depend on the individual case. Interventions for learning disabilities and mental retardation, as well as physical and occupational therapy services, psychological and vocational counseling, and genetic counseling for the patient and family may be necessary. Early detection is important due to the range and severity of symptoms that may require treatment and is medically essential due to the large number of potential health problems and unusual risks that may be present. For example, some individuals with Noonan syndrome show unusual anesthetic and medication sensitivities, requiring special care. Awareness of blood abnormalities is important to reduce the risk of excessive bleeding.

Prognosis in Noonan syndrome depends on the severity of the condition and availability of treatment. A team of specialists is often required, including those specializing in cardiology, hematology, pediatrics, and others. Current research includes exploration of recombinant human growth hormone as a treatment for short stature. Future genetic research may lead to the discovery of the causes of Noonan syndrome, from which methods of earlier detection, prevention, and treatment may be possible.

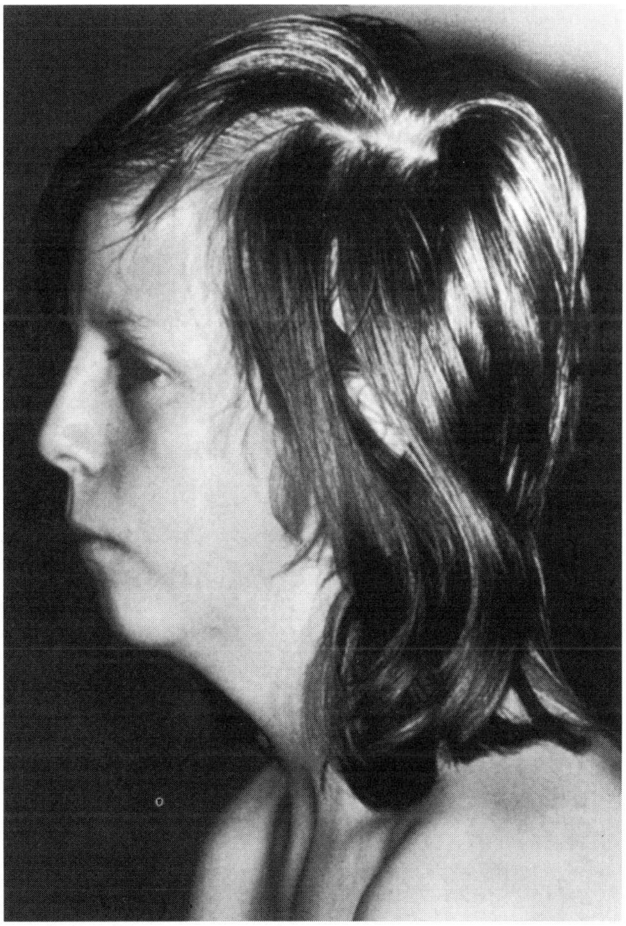

Noonan Syndrome
Reprinted from *Clinical Syndromes,* Wiedemann and Kunze, 1997, by permission of the publisher Mosby

REFERENCES

Allanson, J. E., Hall, J. G., Hughes, H. E., Preus, M., & Witt, R. D. (1985). Noonan syndrome: The changing phenotype. *American Journal of Medical Genetics, 21,* 507–514.

National Organization for Rare Disorders. (2001). Noonan syndrome. Retrieved from http://www.rarediseases.org/

Noonan, J. A. (1995). Noonan syndrome: An update and review for the primary physician. *Clinical Pediatrics, 33,* 548–555.

Noonan, J. A., & Ehmke, D. A. (1963). Associated noncardiac malformations in children with congenital heart disease. *Journal of Pediatrics, 21,* 515–518.

Online Mendelian Inheritance in Man. (2001). Entry *163590: Noonan syndrome 1; NS1. Retrieved from http://www3.ncbi.nlm.nih.gov/htbin-post/Omim/dispmim?163950

David R. Steinman
Austin Neurological Clinic and Department of Psychology, University of Texas at Austin

NORRIE DISEASE

Norrie disease is a syndrome of retinal malformation characterized by dysplasia of retina and associated with mental retardation and deafness.

The incidence of this disease is extremely rare, with approximately 100 cases reported to date (Pediatric Database, 1994). The disease occurs at birth and is a familial X-linked recessive trait, which makes it more commonly found in males.

Characteristics

1. The affected child experiences blindness in both eyes (bilateral) at birth.
2. The lens of the eyes may become cloudy (cataracts) during early infancy, and the eyeballs may shrink (phthisis bulbi) (National Organization for Rare Disorders, 1996).
3. In some forms of the syndrome, there are brain abnormalities, particularly microcephaly, resulting in mental retardation in 25% or less of the cases (Pediatric Database, 1994).
4. Besides blindness, sensorineural deafness may occur in 25–35% of cases (Pediatric Database, 1994).

Treatment often involves a multidisciplinary approach including pediatricians and ophthalmologists. Hearing aids may provide support for some patients. Early surgical intervention can aid in cataract extraction, vitrectomy, and retinal detachment repair. Also, surgery may prevent phthisis bulbi but does not improve vision. Routine follow-up with an ophthalmologist is recommended in all individuals with Norrie disease even when vision is severely reduced. Given that most individuals with the disease are blind, it is critical that hearing be monitored routinely so that hearing loss can be detected early and managed appropriately. Cochlear implantation should be considered when hearing-assisted audiological function is significantly impaired.

Behavioral issues are a lifelong challenge to many patients with Norrie disease and to their guardians-caretakers, regardless of whether mental retardation or cognitive impairment is present. Intervention and therapy are supportive and aimed at maximizing educational opportunities. An empirical trial of psychotropic medications may be warranted, although no studies have addressed or supported the use of specific medications in Norrie disease.

The prognosis is that the affected person will be irreversibly blind from birth. Life span may be shortened by general risks associated with mental retardation, blindness, and hearing loss, such as increased risk of trauma, aspiration pneumonia, and complications of seizure disorder (Geneclinics, 1999).

REFERENCES

Geneclinics. (1999). Norrie disease. Retrieved from http://www.geneclinics.org/profiles/home/details.html

National Organization for Rare Disorders. (1996). Norrie syndrome. Retrieved from http://www.stepstn.com/cgi-win/nord.exe?proc=getdocument&rectype=0&recnum=568

Pediatric Database. (1994). Norrie disease. Retrieved from http://www.icondata.com/health/pedbase/files/NORRIEDI.HTM

Sarah Compton
University of Texas at Austin

O

OBESITY

A person is considered obese when adipose (fat) tissue makes up a greater than normal percentage of his or her body weight—that is, when body weight is in excess of biological needs (Lemberg, 1999). This excess in body fat often results in a significant impairment of health. Obesity occurs as a result of a complex interaction between one's genes and the environment.

According to the National Institutes of Health (2001), approximately 97 million adults in the United States are overweight or obese. Between 1960 and 1994, obesity increased from 12.8% to 22.5% in adults between the ages of 20 and 74. Of greater concern is the increase in obesity among American youth and minority populations. Results from the Third National Health and Nutrition Survey estimated that 13.7% of children and 11.5% of adolescents who responded were overweight. Other studies suggest that as many as 40% of children from minority populations in the United States are obese (National Institutes of Health, 2001).

Characteristics

1. Body mass index (an individual's weight in kilograms divided by the square of his or her height in meters) of 25–29 indicates mild obesity, 30–39 indicates moderate obesity, and over 40 indicates severe obesity.
2. For women, greater than 30% of total body weight consists of fat tissue.
3. For men, greater than 25% of total body weight consists of fat tissue.
4. Central obesity occurs more commonly in males and results in a large proportion of the excess fat's being stored in the abdominal area.
5. Peripheral obesity occurs more commonly in females and results in the excess body fat's being stored in the hip and thigh areas.

A person who is obese is also at a higher risk for other health impairments, such as Type 2 diabetes, stroke, sleep apnea, respiratory problems, some cancers, and possibly even morbidity from hypertension (National Institutes of Health, 2001). Treatment methods range from modifications in diet, which result in slow but steady weight reduction, to surgical intervention in the form of gastric bypass for severe obesity. Those who incorporate exercise into their lifestyle are usually more successful at keeping weight off.

A student with a medical diagnosis of obesity would possible qualify for special education services under the category of Other Health Impairments. The school psychologist, as part of the multidisciplinary team, would probably provide direct services in the form of counseling to explore with the student the issues surrounding the development or maintenance of obesity. Group therapy may also be provided through the school if there is a need.

Future research appears to be in the areas of drug therapy. Medications currently under investigation are serotonin reuptake inhibitors and lipase inhibitors, which increase energy expenditure and inhibit the absorption of fat from the gastrointestinal tract.

REFERENCES

Lemberg, R. (Ed.). (1999). *Eating disorders: A reference sourcebook.* Phoenix, AZ: Oryx Press.

The National Institutes of Health. (2001). Obesity. Retrieved October 2001, from http://nih.org

Christine D. Cde Baca
University of Northern Colorado

OBSESSIVE-COMPULSIVE DISORDER

Obsessive-compulsive disorder (OCD) is an anxiety disorder that includes excessive, persistent thoughts or behavioral impulses that interfere with everyday functioning (American Psychiatric Association, 1994). Children must experience obsessions or compulsions, but most often both are present. Themes of obsessions for children and adolescents often involve fears of contamination, physical injury, religiosity, and topics such as sex or violence. Compulsions involve uncontrollable urges to complete acts such as washing rituals, counting, organizing, hoarding, or checking. The child is usually aware that his or her behavior is unreasonable, but this is not a requirement for diagnosis.

The mean age of onset of OCD is 10 years of age (Swedo, Rapaport, Leonard, Lenane, & Cheslow, 1989). In childhood, there tend to be more males diagnosed than females. The discrepancy is probably due to the tendency of earlier onset for males; however, an equal proportion is identified by adolescence. Prevalence appears to be around .8% of the general population (Swedo et al., 1989).

Characteristics

1. Excessive thoughts or impulses that interfere with everyday functioning (American Psychiatric Association, 1994).
2. Behaviors or thoughts that are performed repeatedly in order to obtain relief from anxiety (Leonard, Swedo, Allen, & Rapoport, 1994).
3. OCD is often a lifetime disorder, even after treatment (Leonard et al., 1993).

More research on the etiology of OCD is needed. Development of OCD may be related in some cases to streptococcus infections, termed pediatric autoimmune neuropsychiatric disorders associated with streptococcus (PANDAS; National Institute of Mental Health, 1998) or to parental diagnosis (Lenane et al., 1990). Identification of risk factors such as a genetic predisposition may enable the development of intervention plans to avoid onset of OCD or at least minimize the effects. Comorbidity is quite common, with only 26% of 70 children studied receiving a diagnosis of only OCD (Swedo et al., 1989). OCD appeared to be comorbid most often with tic disorders (30%) and major depression (26%).

Treatment for OCD usually includes cognitive-behavioral therapy (CBT), psychopharmacology, or a combination of the two. CBT works well with children and usually involves exposure treatment (March, Mulle, & Herbel, 1994) coupled with cognitive restructuring, teaching the child to cease obsessive thoughts, and relaxation techniques (Kendall, 1991). Psychopharmacological treatment of OCD involves the use of selective seratonin reuptake inhibitors (e.g., clomiprimine, fluvoxamine, fluoxetine, and sertraline) or benzodiazepines. The most commonly studied, clomiprimine, has been found to be superior to placebo for children in several studies (e.g., Flament et al., 1985).

Children with OCD do not qualify for special education services unless they have a comorbid condition or their behaviors significantly affect their ability to establish and maintain social relationships (i.e., demonstrating a severe emotional disturbance). Some children may require accommodations such as extra time to finish assignments due to constantly checking and rechecking answers or concern with neatness. In addition, teachers may consider modifying tests to create formats that a child finds least distressing (e.g., some children may find multiple choice to be overwhelming due to persistent second-guessing).

Prognosis is usually chronic and poor, especially when confounded with treatment noncompliance (Leonard et al., 1993). Difficulties involve social and academic impairment, as well as stress on the child's family. When treating children for OCD, one must be alert to newly developing rituals or obsessions as existing impulses are often modified and replaced. Treating comorbid conditions often provides relief, although OCD usually remains an issue to be addressed.

Longitudinal studies of children with OCD are needed to better identify manifestation of the illness across the life span.

REFERENCES

American Psychiatric Association. (1994). *Diagnostic and statistical manual of mental disorders* (4th ed.). Washington, DC: Author.

Flament, M., Rapoport, J. L., Berg, C. J., Sceery, W., Kilts, C., Mellstrom, B., et al. (1985). Clomipramine treatment of childhood obsessive compulsive disorder: A double-blind controlled study. *Archives of General Psychiatry, 42,* 977–983.

Kendall, P. C. (1991). *Child and adolescent therapy.* New York: Guilford.

Lenane, M. C., Swedo, S. E., Leonard, H. L., Pauls, D. L., Sceery, W., & Rapoport, J. L. (1990). Psychiatric disorders in first degree relatives of children and adolescents with obsessive-compulsive disorder. *Journal of the American Academy of Child and Adolescent Psychiatry, 29*(3), 407–412.

Leonard, H. L., Swedo, S. E., Lenane, M. C., Rettew, D. C., Hamburger, S. D., Bartko, J. J. et al. (1993). A two to seven year follow-up study of 54 obsessive compulsive children and adolescents. *Archives of General Psychiatry, 50,* 429–439.

Leonard, H. L., Swedo, S. E., Allen, A. J., & Rapoport, J. L. (1994). Obsessive-compulsive disorder. In T. H. Ollendick, N. J. King, & W. Yule, *International handbook of phobic and anxiety disorders in children and adolescents* (pp. 207–221). New York: Plenum Press.

March, J., Mulle, K., & Herbel, B. (1994). Behavioral psychotherapy for children and adolescents with obsessive-compulsive disorder: An open trial of a new protocol driven treatment package. *Journal of the American Academy of Child and Adolescent Psychiatry, 33*(3), 333–341.

National Institute of Mental Health (1986). Current NIMH research. Retrieved from http://intramural.nimh.nih.gov

Swedo, S. E., Rapoport, J. L., Leonard, H., Lenane, M., & Cheslow, D. (1989). Obsessive-compulsive disorder in children and adolescents: Clinical phenomenology of 70 consecutive cases. *Archives of General Psychiatry, 46*(4), 335–341.

Elizabeth A. Bubonic
Texas A&M University

OCULOCEREBRAL SYNDROME WITH HYPOPIGMENTATION

Oculocerebral syndrome with hypopigmentation is a rare disorder in which the skin and hair lack normal color or have characteristics of albinism. This syndrome also is referred to as Cross syndrome, Cross-McKusick-Breen syndrome, or Kramer syndrome. In addition, central nervous system (CNS) involvement specific to the eyes and oculocerebral areas is present. Vision problems associated with clouding (opacities) of the cornea, involuntary eye movements or nystagmus, or decreased size of one or both eyes may be present (National Organization for Rare Disorders, 1996). As with other forms of albinism, sensitivity to light is a frequent problem as well.

Oculocerebral syndrome with hypopigmentation is transmitted as an autosomal recessive trait. It is equally likely to affect males and females. It is an extremely rare disorder with approximately 15 cases reported in the literature (Lerone et al., 1992; National Organization of Rare Disorders, 1996; Tezcan et al., 1997). With such small numbers, there have been no studies of incidence differences across ethnic groups.

Characteristics

1. Light skin color
2. Silvery hair
3. Abnormalities of the eyes that may include small size, clouding of the cornea, involuntary eye movements
4. Involuntary muscle contractions
5. Loss of muscle function (spastic paraplegia)
6. Developmental delays
7. Mental retardation
8. Light sensitivity (photosensitivity)
9. High, arched palate

Source: National Organization for Rare Disorders (1996)

Oculocerebral syndrome with hypopigmentation initially is identified at birth due to the light skin color and silvery hair color. As the infant matures, the associated vision problems become apparent. Additional problems with movement become more evident as well. Movement can be affected in that the child may have slow involuntary movements, spastic contractions, impaired ability to control voluntary movement, hyperextension or increased range of motion of the head, or increased rigidity of specific muscle groups. The muscle groups and the severity differ across individuals; however, the legs, arms, shoulders, and hips are most commonly the areas affected. With motor skills and vision affected, developmental delays are not uncommon. Physical development may be slowed (growth retardation). In some children, there will be enlargement of the gums (gingival fibromatosis) that—if not corrected—can result in problems with breathing, swallowing, or speech production (National Organization for Rare Disorders, 1996; Tezcan et al., 1997).

Treatment is specific to the presentation of symptoms and complications for the individual child. Because of the range of needs that a child might have, a team approach that includes physicians, ophthalmologists, physical therapists, occupational therapists, speech therapists, and dentists is recommended. With identification possible at birth, early intervention services can be initiated in a timely manner and the appropriate services determined as problems occur or are addressed effectively. For the vision problems, corrective lenses or surgery may be required; in some cases, the child may qualify for specialized services due to vision impairment. Special services to address developmental delays, cognitive delays (i.e., mental retardation), and speech delays may be needed as well. Family members may benefit from supportive services as well as genetic counseling.

REFERENCES

Lerone, M. Pessagno, A., Taccone, A., Poggi, G., Romeo, G., & Silengo, M. C. (1992). Oculocerebral syndrome with hypopigmentation (Cross syndrome): Report of a new case. *Clinical Genetics, 41,* 87–89.

National Organization for Rare Disorders (1996). Oculocerebral syndrome with hypopigmentation (#1061). Retrieved June 3, 2001, from http://www.rarediseases.org

Tezcan, I., Demir, E., Asan, E., Kale, G., Muftuoglu, S. F., & Kotiloglu, E. (1997). A new case of oculocerebral hypopigmentation syndrome (Cross syndrome) with additional findings. *Clinical Genetics, 51,* 118–121

Cynthia A. Riccio
Texas A&M University

OLIVOPONTOCEREBELLAR ATROPHY

Olivopontocerebellar atrophy (OPCA) is a rare progressive heterogeneous neurological condition characterized by neuronal loss in the inferior olives, ventral pons, and cerebellar cortex brain regions. Several subclassifications of OPCA exist based on differences in inheritance patterns (familial and sporadic) and age of onset (infantile, juvenile, and adult onset), a variety that suggests multiple underlying etiologies resulting in similar clinical presentation and neuropathology.

The majority of OPCA cases are of the familial (autosomal dominant), adult-onset type (approximate onset in third decade of life). A small percentage of adult-onset OPCA are autosomal recessive forms, although in cases in which family history is insufficient, these cases are often considered sporadic. All of these disorders affect the cerebellum and its pathways, with cases first presenting with progressive ataxia manifested by unsteadiness of gait, uncoordinated limb movements, impaired skilled movements such as handwriting, and dysarthria. Some OPCA cases have oculomotor disturbances and retinal degeneration. The corticospinal pathway, basal ganglia, and autonomic nuclei of the brain stem and spinal cord may also be affected in these disorders, resulting in parkinsonism, hyperreflexia, and—in late stages—dementia (Weiner & Lang, 1989). Diagnosis of adult-onset OPCA also involves neuroimaging and electrophysiological measures. Adult-onset OPCA is fatal, usually within 10–15 years of onset.

Infantile and juvenile forms of OPCA are extremely rare in populations with low parental consanguinity. Dyken and Krawiecki (1983) noted only one case in the previous 20 years at two major American medical institutions. Whereas the adult-onset form of OPCA progresses slowly, juvenile and infantile forms progress rapidly, with death occurring within months to a few years. The juvenile form initially presents in middle to late childhood with symptoms similar to the adult-onset form, such as progressive cerebellar ataxia and other motor delays and speech impairments (Colan, Snead, & Ceballos, 1981). Juvenile OPCA may also result in chronic seizures and progressive visual impairments. Usually, children who eventually present with OPCA symptoms have had seemingly normal development previously. Intellectual decline often accompanies motor decline, with social regression and dementia present at later stages.

Indicators of infantile OPCA may be present in utero or present within months after birth. The most common symptoms include failure to thrive, weight loss, and motor regression (Enevoldson, Sanders, & Harding, 1994). Additionally, apneic episodes and dysmorphic features may also be present.

Diagnosis of OPCA involves clinical evaluation combined with CT scans or magnetic resonance imaging (ultrasounds in the case of prenatal diagnosis) and genetic background analysis. Juvenile OPCA can be sporadic or hereditary, usually indicating an autosomal dominant pattern (Pratap Chand, Tharakan, Koul, & Dilip Kumar, 1996). In contrast, most cases of infantile OPCA have been reported to follow an autosomal recessive pattern of inheritance (Bawle, Kupsky, Damato, Becker, & Hicks, 1995), although at least one case of known prenatal exposure to teratogens has been described. The inconsistent genetic data and the unknown etiology of OPCA underscore the possibility that it is not a single disease entity but rather the result of several possible genetic or biochemical conditions.

Characteristics

1. Adult, juvenile, and infantile forms.
2. Marked cell loss in the inferior olives, ventral pons, and cerebellar cortex.
3. Symptoms include progressive multisystem deterioration of motor capacities—notably, cerebellar ataxia, with possible autonomic and cognitive disturbances.
4. Prognosis is poor; death occurs within months to a few years in juvenile and infantile forms.

Treatment for OPCA is limited and symptomatic. Pharmacological interventions, such as the antiparkinsonian L-dopa, and other drugs targeting different neurotransmitter systems have produced no consistent therapeutic benefits and only short-term benefits at best when used on adults. Future research will investigate certain biochemical deficiencies identified in patients with OPCA with the goal of identifying curative interventions (Probst-Cousin, 1997).

Children diagnosed with OPCA as infants rarely live to an age at which schooling is a concern. Children diagnosed as juveniles will be able to attend school until mental degeneration interferes. It will also be especially important to provide support groups and therapy to children and their friends when a child is diagnosed as a juvenile.

REFERENCES

Bawle, E. V., Kupsky, W. J., Damato, C. J., Becker, C. J., & Hicks, S. (1995). Familial infantile olivopontocerebellar atrophy. *Pediatric Neurology, 13,* 14–18.

Colan, R. V., Snead, O. C., & Ceballos, R. (1981). Olivopontocerebellar trophy in children: A report of seven cases in two families. *Annals of Neurology, 10,* 355–363.

Dyken, P., & Krawiecki, N. (1983). Neurodegenerative diseases of infancy and childhood. *Annals of Neurology, 13,* 351–364.

Enevoldson, T. P., Sanders, M. D., & Harding, A. E. (1994). Autosomal dominant cerebellar ataxia with pigmentary macular dystrophy: A clinical and genetic study of eight families. *Brain, 177,* 445–460.

Pratap Chand, R., Tharakan, J. K. J., Koul, R. L., & Dilip Kumar, S. (1996). Clinical and radiological features of juvenile onset olivopontocerebellar atrophy. *Clinical Neurology and Neurosurgery, 98,* 152–156.

Probst-Cousin, S. (1997). Olivopontocerebellar atrophy: A heterogeneous morphologic syndrome. *Fortschritte der Neurologie Psychiatrie, 65,* 562–577.

Weiner, W. J., & Lang, A. E. (1989). *Movement disorders: A comprehensive survey.* Mount Kisco, NY: Futura.

Adam S. Bristol
Yale University

OLLIER DISEASE (OSTEOCHONDROMATOSIS SYNDROME)

Ollier disease (OD) is a disorder of bone and cartilage formation. Findings may be present at birth but generally are not obvious until 1–4 years of age.

The etiology of OD is unknown. It is considered rare. Since the initial case was described in 1899, about 100 individuals with the disorder have been reported. Its occurrence appears to be sporadic. However, infrequent examples of OD in family members have been seen. This observation points to the possibility of a genetic basis for the disorder.

Characteristics

1. Cylindrical masses of cartilage (enchondromas) appear in the ends (metaphyses) and, later, the midsections (diaphyses) of long, tubular bones.
2. Enchondromas are usually bilateral (occur on both sides) but asymmetrically affect the growth of long bones.
3. Pelvic bones are occasionally affected. Skull and rib involvement is rare.
4. Long bone growth deficiency may be present at birth but usually does not become obvious until 1–4 years of age.
5. Enchondroma sites are prone to repeated fractures. Asymmetrical limb growth and deformity are common. A small but significant risk exists for chondrosarcoma (malignancy) occurrence within enchondromas.
6. Rarely, ovarian (granulose cell) tumors have been associated with OD.

Orthopedic surgeons are trained and experienced in handling the majority of problems that patients with OD encounter. They treat fractures, limb deformities, restricted joint mobility, scoliosis (curvature of the spine), and short stature caused by enchondromas. Prompt referral to this specialty assures the most favorable outcome for individuals with this disorder.

There is no research to indicate the need for educational support services as a result of this disease.

The prognosis for OD is generally favorable. However, patients with this syndrome may require several operative procedures to assure optimal cosmetic results. Enchondroma growth ceases in adulthood. Expansion of a bony lesion in the adult patient is an ominous sign and suggests the existence of cancerous degeneration.

For more information and support, please contact Ollier/Maffucci Self-Help Group, 1824 Millwood Road, Sumter, SC 29150, (803) 775-1757, e-mail: Olliers@aol.com, home page: http://uhsweb.edu/olliers/olliers.htm

REFERENCES

Shanghnessy, W. J., & Arnot, C. A. S. (2000). Benign tumors. In R. E. Behrman, R. M. Kleigman, & H. B. Jenson (Eds.), *Nelson textbook of pediatrics* (16th ed., pp. 1302–1305). Philadelphia: W. B. Saunders.

Jones, K. (1997). *Smith's recognizable patterns of human malformation* (5th ed.). Philadelphia: W. B. Saunders.

National Organization for Rare Disorders. (1998). Ollier disease. Retrieved from http://www.stepstn.com/cgi-win/nord.exe?proc=GetDocument&rectype=0&recnum=337

Barry H. Davison
Ennis, Texas

Joan W. Mayfield
Baylor Pediatric Specialty Services
Dallas, Texas

OPPOSITIONAL DEFIANT DISORDER

Children with oppositional defiant disorder (ODD) exhibit noncompliant behaviors in excess of what is normal for similarly aged children. Symptoms often include temper tantrums, irritability, and difficulty controlling anger. In order to distinguish clinical behavior from normal limit-testing, behaviors must markedly interfere with social and academic functioning (American Psychiatric Association [APA], 1994). Several researchers proposed a developmental model of ODD, suggesting that the disorder may be a predecessor of conduct disorder (CD) for some children, particularly for those with earlier onset, attention problems, and a lack of familial harmony (Lahey & Loeber, 1994).

Prevalence of ODD is estimated to be 2–16% of the population (APA, 1994). The mean age of onset is around 6 (Loeber, Green, Lahey, Christ, & Frick, 1992) to 8 years of age (APA, 1994), with some researchers reporting median onset of ODD behaviors as early as 4–5 years of age (Loeber, Lahey, & Thomas, 1991). Onset tends to be earlier for boys than for girls, with differences in prevalence disappearing by 15 years of age (McGee, Feehan, Williams, & Anderson, 1992). There is little known evidence supporting ethnic or socioeconomic status differences.

Characteristics

1. Excessive defiant behaviors that interfere with everyday functioning (APA, 1994).
2. ODD tends to peak around age 14–16 and then decreases (Cohen, Cohen, & Kasen, 1993).
3. Younger onset is indicative of greater severity and persistence (Loeber, Green, Lahey, Christ, & Frick, 1992).
4. ODD is often comorbid with attention-deficit/hyperactivity disorder (ADHD; Biederman, Newcorn, & Sprich, 1991).

5. Academic problems (Hinshaw & Anderson, 1996).
6. Poor peer relations (Hinshaw & Anderson, 1996).
7. Distorted arousal and reactivity patterns (Hinshaw & Anderson, 1996).

Treatment of ODD often include parent training (e.g., Forehand & McMahon, 1981) and social skills training (Kazdin, 1993). Parent training involves teaching parents to give effective commands, reward compliance, deal with noncompliance, and improve parenting skills. Social skills training addresses cognitive distortions (e.g., assuming negative intentions by others) and cognitive deficiencies (e.g., not knowing how to approach others). Researchers also have been studying pharmacological treatments such as anticonvulsants, nontricyclic antidepressants such as buproprion, and tricyclic antidepressants (Shreeram & Kruesi, 1999); however, further research must be conducted before conclusive recommendations can be made.

ODD is not a special education category as defined by the Individuals with Disabilities Education Act. However, if a student meets requirements in his or her state under the definition of emotional disturbance or has a comorbid disability, he or she may receive special education services. Although services and placement must be individualized for each child, the most restrictive placement is usually a classroom for children exhibiting behavior problems. Services dependent on comorbid conditions as well. For instance, many children with ODD also have ADHD. Therefore, these children may require services that address attention and hyperactivity as well.

Prognosis for children with early-onset ODD often includes academic problems, poor peer relations, risk of head injury due to violent behavior, distorted arousal and reactivity patterns (Hinshaw & Anderson, 1996), and for some, development of conduct disorder (Lahey & Loeber, 1994). Children exhibiting late-onset ODD and resiliency factors such as a positive home environment usually have a better prognosis.

Future research should focus on effective prevention as well as treatment for children with ODD and comorbid conditions. In addition, longitudinal studies must be conducted to determine developmental implications.

REFERENCES

American Psychiatric Association (1994). *Diagnostic and statistical manual of mental disorders* (4th ed.). Washington, DC: Author.

Biederman, J., Newcorn, J., & Sprich, S. E. (1991). Comorbidity of attention deficit hyperactivity disorder with conduct, depressive, anxiety, and other disorders. *American Journal of Psychiatry, 148,* 564–577.

Cohen, P., Cohen, J., & Kasen, S. (1993). An epidemiological study of disorders in late childhood and adolescence:I. Age- and gender-specific prevalence. *Journal of Child Psychological Psychiatry, 34,* 851–867.

Forehand, R., & McMahon, R. J. (1981). *Helping the noncompliant child: A clinician's guide to parent training.* New York: Guilford.

Hinshaw, S. P., & Anderson, C. A. (1996). Conduct and oppositional defiant disorders. In E. J. Mash & R. A. Barkley, *Child psychopathology* (pp. 113–149). New York: Guilford.

Kazdin, A. E. (1993). Treatment of conduct disorder: Progress and directions in psychotherapy research. *Development and Psychopathology, 5,* 277–310.

Lahey, B. B., & Loeber, R. (1994). Framework for a developmental model of oppositional defiant disorder and conduct disorder. In D. K. Routh (Ed.), *Disruptive behavior disorders in children.* New York: Plenum Press.

Loeber, R., Lahey, B. B., & Thomas, C. (1991). The diagnostic conundrum of oppositional defiant disorder and conduct disorder. *Journal of Abnormal Psychology, 100,* 379–390.

Loeber, R., Green, S. M., Lahey, B. B., Christ, M. A. G., & Frick, P. J. (1992). Developmental sequences in the age of onset of disruptive child behaviors. *Journal of Child and Family Studies, 1,* 21–41.

McGee, R., Feehan, M., Williams, S., & Anderson, J. (1992). *DSM-III* disorders from age 11 to age 15 years. *Journal of the American Academy of Child and Adolescent Psychiatry, 31,* 50–59.

Shreeram, S. S., & Kruesi, M. J. P. (1999). Pharmocologic treatment of behavior disorders in adolescents. *Annals of the American Society for Adolescent Psychiatry, 24,* 179–211.

Elizabeth A. Bubonic
Texas A&M University

ORAL-FACIAL-DIGITAL SYNDROME

Oral-facial-digital syndrome (OFDS) is an heritable disorder characterized by anomalies of the mouth, face, toes, and fingers. Associated abnormalities of teeth, hair, brain, and kidney are occasionally seen. OFDS has nine subsets that are distinguished from each other by clinical findings and patterns of heredity. This discussion concerns OFDS Type 1 (OFDS 1).

OFDS 1 is felt to be caused by a defective gene on the X chromosome. The syndrome is rare. Since its initial description in 1954, about 160 cases have been reported. The mode of transmission is X-linked dominant. Virtually all patients are female, suggesting that the gene's presence in the male embryo usually causes fetal demise.

Characteristics

1. Folds of mucous membrane (the moist lining of the mouth) extending from the inside of the cheek (buccal mucosa) to the ridges of bone that surround the tooth

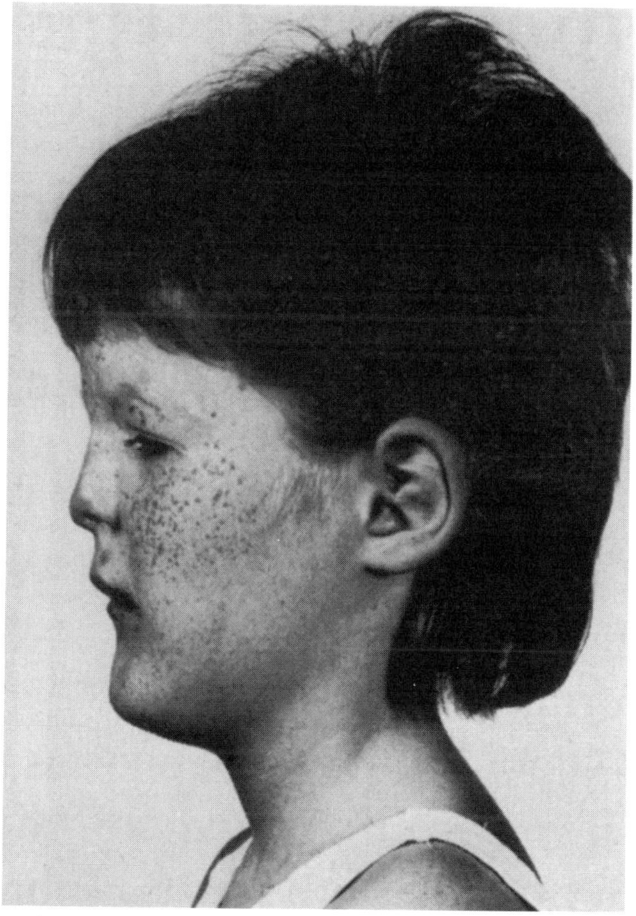

Oral-Facial-Digital Syndrome
Reprinted from *Clinical Syndromes*, Wiedemann and Kunze, 1997, by permission of the publisher Mosby

sockets. Additional oral anomalies include cleft lip, cleft palate, missing or malformed teeth, dental decay, and bifid (forked) tongue.

2. Underdevelopment (hypoplasia) of cartilage that forms the sides of the nose, wide separation of the inner corners of the eyes.
3. Shortening of digits that is asymmetrical, short hands, syndactyly (webbing of the fingers), and polydactyly of the feet (extra toes).
4. Dry, sparse hair and scalp.
5. Variable mental retardation (60%). Mean IQ is 70. Brain anomalies, including agenesis of the corpus callosum and defective gray matter formation.
6. Adult-onset polycystic kidney disease.
7. Infrequent findings include extra teeth, tumors of the tongue, narrowing of the nasal openings, prominent forehead, developmental anomalies of the lower jawbone (mandible), tremor, hydrocephalus, seizure disorder, and alopecia (absence of hair).

Treatment of OFDS 1 involves surgical repair of the oral defects and usually extensive dental work. Dentures are occasionally necessary when a significant number of teeth are absent. The high incidence of mental deficiency requires early psychometric testing, particularly when psychomotor delays are obvious. The increased frequency of polycystic kidney disease mandates periodic assessment of renal function.

For the children who survive past infancy, cognitive deficits are reported. A comprehensive neuropsychological evaluation will be necessary to determine cognitive strengths and weaknesses and help the educators and parents develop strategies to optimize learning. Additional support from an early childhood intervention program would help the child in attaining developmental milestones. Continued support under the special education umbrella will be needed.

Overall, the prognosis of OFDS 1 is not favorable. About a third of children with the disorder die during infancy, although the reason for this high mortality rate is not explained in the medical literature. The incidence of mental retardation is over 50% in those who survive past the first few months. Finally, the specter of chronic renal pathology hangs over those patients who make the trek into adulthood.

For parent support, please contact NIH/National Oral Health Information Clearinghouse, 1 NOHIC Way, Bethesda, MD 20892-3500, (301) 402-7364, e-mail: nihic@nider.nih.gov, home page: http://www.nohic.nidcr.nih.gov

REFERENCES

Jones, K. (1997). *Smith's recognizable patterns of human malformation* (5th ed.). Philadelphia: W. B. Saunders.

National Organization for Rare Disorders. (1999). Oral facial digital syndrome. Retrieved from http://www.stepstn.com/cgi-win/nord.exe?proc=GetDocument&rectype=0&recnum=531

Barry H. Davison
Ennis, Texas

Joan W. Mayfield
Baylor Pediatric Specialty Services
Dallas, Texas

ORNITHINE TRANSCARBAMYLASE DEFICIENCY

Ornithine transcarbamylase (OTC) deficiency is a rare, genetically transmitted error of protein metabolism. OTC is one of several enzymes essential to the urea cycle, a series of related chemical reactions by which ammonia, a by-product of protein breakdown, is converted to urea and rapidly removed by the kidney. An absence or inadequacy of OTC causes accumulations of ammonia in tissue and blood (hyperammonemia). This hyperammonemic state is extremely toxic to nerve cells and is responsible for the symptoms and lingering sequelae of this disorder.

OTC deficiency is associated with a genetic mutation of the X chromosome. The abnormal gene is known to have about 20 distinct variations. Males with this genetic defect have early onset and severe illness. Females with OTC deficiency may be asymptomatic or have mild disease that does not manifest until sometime in childhood. The more benign symptomatology in female patients is explained by the presence of paired X chromosomes. The normal gene on the unaffected X chromosome is believed to have an ameliorating effect on OTC production.

OTC deficiency is rare. It occurs in only 1 in 30,000 births. Its incidence is higher in males than in females.

Characteristics

1. Affected male infants are normal at birth. Symptoms develop within 1–3 days, after significant protein intake is established. They include poor feeding, vomiting, lethargy, convulsions, hypotonia (poor muscle tone), tachypnea (rapid breathing), and hypothermia. Within a few days (or less), coma occurs, followed rapidly by death. Other than abnormal neurological findings, physical exam may only reveal hepatomegaly (liver enlargement).
2. Abnormal laboratory values in ill newborns include elevated blood ammonia (at least five times the normal value) and elevated amounts of orotic acid in the urine.
3. Ten percent of heterozygous (having one normal and one mutated X chromosome) females are symptomatic. They usually present during infancy or early childhood with problems related to episodes of hyperammonemia. Complaints include vomiting, migraine-like headaches, confusion, hyperactivity, combativeness, and ataxia (uncoordinated muscle movement). These attacks are separated by periods of normal behavior. Acute episodes may be preceded by infection, stress, or high-protein intake. Hyperammonemic coma and even death may occur during these events.
4. In surviving patients, mild to moderate mental retardation is a common finding. An increased incidence of gallstones has also been noted. The etiology of this abnormality is unclear.

Treating infants and children with OTC deficiency has both immediate and long-range objectives. In the critically ill newborn, prompt correction of hyperammonemia is imperative because the severity of neurological damage is directly proportional to the duration of high ammonia levels. Prolonged therapy of the disorder demands a multidisciplinary approach to assure the best outcome, with pediatricians, metabolic specialists, neurologists, geneticists, dieticians, and so forth all working together.

The goals of hyperammonemia therapy are prompt removal of ammonia and prevention of its production. Oral feedings are discontinued. Calories are provided by IV infusions of glucose and lipid (fat) solutions. Essential amino acids in IV fluids stop further protein breakdown within the body and therefore halt ammonia formation. Ammonia is poorly removed by the kidney, but the drugs sodium benzoate and sodium phenylacetate react with ammonia to form compounds that are readily filtered by the kidney. Another medication, citrulline, is helpful by functioning as receptor for the ammonia molecule. The essential amino acid, arginine, may also prove beneficial.

If the preceding measures fail to decrease blood ammonia significantly within a few hours the next course of action is hemodialysis. This procedure is not without risks, however, and may be technically impossible in a newborn or infant. When hemodialysis is impractical, peritoneal dialysis is a reasonable alternative. This procedure involves inserting a plastic tube through the abdominal wall into the cavity surrounding the abdominal contents. Dialysing fluid passes through this tube, filling the abdomen. Toxins diffuse through membranes covering the abdominal organs and cavity into the dialysis material, which is withdrawn and then replaced by fresh fluid. Dialysis usually results in a drastic drop in blood ammonia and near-normal levels within 48 hours.

After biochemical improvement in the patient's condition is assured, feedings are resumed with special low-protein formulas. Neurological recovery usually lags far behind normalization of ammonia levels. It may take several days for a convalescing infant to become completely alert.

Long-term therapy of OTC deficiency necessitates some protein restriction and chronic administration of benzoate phenylacetate, arginine, citrulline, or a combination of these. Blood levels of these medications as well as ammonia levels require periodic monitoring. Avoidance of situations that trigger hyperammonemia (infection, stress, high-protein diet) should be encouraged.

Finally, genetic counseling should be provided to all families who have a child with this disorder. Prenatal diagnosis is available. Asymptomatic females can be detected by checking blood ammonia levels following a large-protein meal. The diagnosis can also be verified by measuring OTC activity in liver, intestinal, or rectal tissue samples. Heterozygous females have a 50% chance of passing on the abnormal gene.

Because mild to moderate mental retardation is associated with children with OTC deficiency, special education support services will be important. A neuropsychological evaluation will be helpful to determine cognitive strengths and weaknesses and provide educational recommendations.

Prenatal diagnosis of OTC deficiency and prospective treatment from birth assure a reasonably good prognosis. Prolonged hyperammonemia has a 100% mortality rate. Even if repeated bouts are successfully treated, patients are undoubtedly left with some neurological damage. Strict compliance with therapy, which requires dietary restrictions and taking several medications daily, is difficult for children and their families. Mild to moderate mental retardation is frequently seen in OTC deficiency survivors. Even so-called asymptomatic females have mild neurological deficits when compared to their unaffected siblings. Although liver transplantation has provided a "cure" for some patients, it is associated with high rates of mortality and morbidity. In the future, gene replacement therapy offers the best hope for definitive treatment of this disorder.

REFERENCES

Batshaw, M. L. (1996). Urea cycle disorders. In F. D. Burg, J. A. Inglefinger, R. A. Polin, & E. R. Wald (Eds.), *Gellis and Kagan's current pediatric therapy* (15th ed., pp. 380–383). Philadelphia: W. B. Saunders.

Gandy, A. (n.d.). Ornithine transcarbamylase (OTC) deficiency. Retrieved from http://www.pedianet.com/news/illness/disease/files/ornithin.htm

National Organization for Rare Disorders. (1996). Ornithine transcarbamylase deficiency. Retrieved from http://www.stepstn.com/cgi-win/nord.exe?proc=GetDocument&rectype=0&recnum=309

Rezvani, I. (2000). Defects in metabolism of amino acids. In R. E. Behrman, R. M. Kleigman, & H. B. Jenson (Eds.), *Nelson textbook of pediatrics* (16th ed., pp. 367–371). Philadelphia: W. B. Saunders.

Barry H. Davison
Ennis, Texas

Joan W. Mayfield
Baylor Pediatric Specialty Services
Dallas, Texas

OSTEOGENESIS IMPERFECTA

Osteogenesis imperfecta is a genetic disorder characterized by bone fragility, which is caused by defective synthesis of Type I collagen. There are primarily four types of osteogenesis imperfecta that vary in their clinical presentation. The disorder's clinical manifestations generally include bone fractures, short stature, blue sclerae, hyperextensible joints, dentinogenesis imperfecta, osteoporosis, and hearing loss. The severity of the disorder can range from perinatal death to mild cases that are difficult to diagnose (Plumridge, Bennett, Dinno, & Branson, 1993).

The estimated prevalence of osteogenesis imperfecta is 1 in 20,000 births, affecting males and females equally. The disorder is usually inherited as an autosomal dominant gene, but a recessive pattern has been identified in a few patients. Mutations in one of two genes COL1A1 and COL1A2 that encode Type I collagen synthesis is the primary cause of the disorder (Kuurila, Grenman, Johansson, & Kaitila, 2000). Type 1 is the most common form of osteogenesis imperfecta, occurring in 1 in 28,000 births. Type II is lethal at birth, occurring once in every 60,000 births. Types III and IV occur in about 1 in 70,000 births (Sillence & Barlow, 1992).

Characteristics

1. Type I is characterized by blue sclerae, hearing loss, spinal curvature, and hyperelasticity of joints and ligaments. An average of 20–40 fractures occur before puberty (Matsen, 2000).
2. Infants with Type II have multiple fractures and die before or shortly after birth.
3. Type III individuals have an average height of 3–4 feet, scoliosis, barrel-shaped rib cage, early-onset hearing loss, and fragile teeth.
4. Type III children tend to have 20 or more fractures before age 3 and 100 or more fractures during their lifetime that result in progressively deformed limbs (Plumridge et al., 1993).
5. Type IV have fractures, short stature, spinal curvature, deformed rib cage that can cause lung problems, fragile teeth, and hearing loss.
6. Children with Types I and IV are often ambulatory or can walk with crutches. Type II individuals are usually wheelchair dependent.

Treatment of osteogenesis imperfecta can vary depending on the severity of symptoms. However, all individuals benefit from therapies that increase bone density and minimize bone loss. Physical activity, calcium and fluoride supplements, and growth hormone treatment help reduce bone loss. Surgery is utilized to straighten deformed bones and promote walking, and rods may be placed in bones to provide stability. Surgical treatment of the spine may be necessary in children with progressive spinal deformity (Engelbert, Pruijis, Beemer, & Helders, 1998).

Children with osteogenesis imperfecta have normal intelligence. However, their academic performance may be lower than that of their peers due to chronic illness and absences from school, which interfere with academic achievement. Children and adolescents with this disorder may experience low self-esteem and feel isolated from their peers as a result of their disability. It is important for school personnel to understand the disorder so that they do not unnecessarily exclude the child from activities and interactions with peers (Cole, 1993). Learning about the disorder

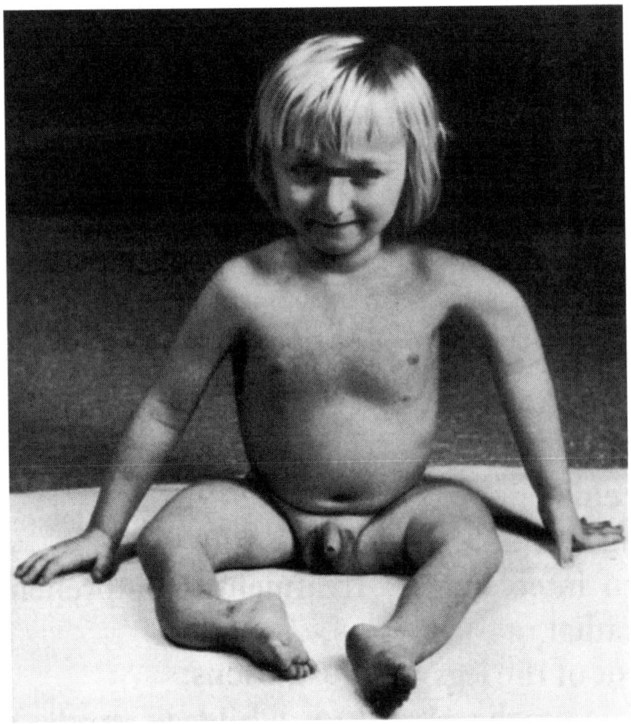

Osteogenesis Imperfecta
Reprinted from *Clinical Syndromes*, Wiedemann and Kunze, 1997, by permission of the publisher Mosby

can help protect parents from being falsely accused of child abuse. The school should be barrier free. For example, the school should be equipped to accommodate wheelchairs. Children often require physical therapy and occupational therapy to maximize physical activity and independence. Hearing and speech services may be necessary for children with hearing impairments. A school should have a plan of action that can be used when an accident occurs so that personnel know what course of action to take and who to contact in emergency situations (Plumridge et al., 1993).

The prognosis of individuals with osteogenesis imperfecta is very good. Most people with the disorder live fulfilling and productive lives. Research is primarily focused on the cure, prevention, and diagnosis of osteogenesis imperfecta. Researchers are also investigating the effects of growth hormone on bone quality and are looking at ways in which physical therapy can minimize bone loss and prevent loss of muscle strength. Genetic studies are being conducted to discover how mutations in Type I collagen genes result in bone brittleness (Matsen, 2000).

REFERENCES

Cole, D. E. (1993). Psychosocial aspects of osteogenesis imperfecta: An update. *American Journal of Medical Genetics, 45,* 207–211.

Engelbert, R. H., Pruijs, H. E., Beemer, F. A., & Helders, P. J. (1998). Osteogenesis imperfecta in childhood: Treatment strategies. *Archives of Physical Medicine and Rehabilitation, 79,* 1590–1594.

Kuurila, K., Grenman, R., Johansson, R., & Kaitila, I. (2000). Hearing loss in children with osteogenesis imperfecta. *European Journal of Pediatrics, 159,* 515–519.

Matsen, F. (2000, October 2). Osteogenesis imperfecta. Retrieved from http://www.orthop.washington.edu

Plumridge, D., Bennett, R., Dinno, N., & Branson, C. (Eds.). (1993). *The student with a genetic disorder.* Springfield, IL: Charles C. Thomas.

Sillence, D. O., & Barlow, K. K. (1992). *Osteogenesis imperfecta: A handbook for medical practitioners and health care professionals.* Rydalmere, Australia: Osteogenesis Imperfecta Society.

Susannah More
University of Texas at Austin

OSTEONECROSIS

Osteonecrosis is a bone disorder that results from the loss of blood supply to the bones. The lack of blood supply causes the bone to collapse and generally leads to the collapse of articulating joints such as the hip joint. Osteonecrosis is most likely to occur at the ends of long bones such as the femur or in the knee. Osteonecrosis may affect only a single bone, or it may affect multiple bones. Osteonecrosis usually occurs in early adulthood through midlife (20s–40s) but can occur in younger and older individuals. This disorder affects both men and women equally. In the United States alone, osteonecrosis is estimated to affect 10,000 to 20,000 new people each year. There is no indication that osteonecrosis occurs in one ethnic group more frequently than in any other.

Characteristics

1. Joint pain when weight bearing and then at rest
2. Limited range of motion in the joint

The causes of osteonecrosis vary. The blood supply to the bone can be blocked as a result of injury, by increased pressure within the bone that causes the blood vessels, by some medications (e.g., steroids), or by excessive alcohol use. Osteonecrosis also is associated with systemic lupus erythematosus (Mont, et al., 1997). Osteonecrosis of the knee is associated with steroid treatment in individuals with autoimmune disorders. In other individuals, fatty substances also may block or reduce the blood supply to bones. Other risk factors for osteonecrosis include blood disorders (e.g., sickle cell disease), radiation treatments, chemotherapy, pancreatitis, and Gaucher's disease (Mont, Pacheco, & Hungerford, 1996).

Osteonecrosis is asymptomatic in the early stages. As it progresses, there is gradually increased pain in the joint or bone involved. Magnetic resonance imaging or bone scans may provide the best diagnostic tools for identification of symptomatic or asymptomatic osteonecrosis. If untreated, the individual will suffer severe pain and limitation in movement within 2 years from the onset of the disorder (Mont et al., 1996). The prognosis for osteonecrosis depends on the extent to which the bone effectively rebuilds itself, the part of a bone that is affected, and how much of the bone or bones is affected. In many cases, with osteonecrosis, the collapse of bone is faster than the rebuilding process.

If osteonecrosis is identified early in the disease process, the prognosis is better. Treatments include decreased weight bearing, pain medication, surgical decompression of the bone, surgical reshaping of the affected bone or osteotomy, bone grafting, and arthroplasty or total joint replacement. Other treatments are being investigated, including the use of electrical stimulation and medications to increase the growth of bone and blood vessels (Mont et al., 1997). Youth and young adults who are affected by osteonecrosis may benefit from supportive counseling throughout their rehabilitation. Educational supports may be needed if medical management results in absence from school in order to maintain educational progress.

REFERENCES

Mont, M. A., Glueck, C. J., Wang, P., Pacheco, I. H., Hungerford, D. S., & Petri, M. (1997). Risk factors for progression to osteonecrosis in patients with systemic lupus erythematosus. *Rheumatism, 24,* 654–662.

Mont, M. A., Pacheco, I. H., & Hungerford, D. S. (1996). Nontraumatic osteonecrosis of the femoral head: Part I. Demographics, pathogenesis, diagnosis, and staging. *Bombay Hospital Journal, 38,* 546–553.

Cynthia A. Riccio
Texas A&M University

OSTEOPETROSIS

Osteopetrosis is a rare hereditary disorder that is caused by a deficit in bone resorption and results in abnormally dense bones that are nonetheless fragile and brittle. The primary underlying mechanism involved in osteopetrosis is due to defects in osteoclasts, which are specialized cells that are necessary for forming bone marrow. Due to the lack of bone marrow (which is responsible for the production of blood cells), several clinical problems can manifest, such as anemia, excessive bleeding (due to inability of blood to clot), and increased infection (due to impairment of white blood cells).

There are three major types of osteopetrosis that have been identified in humans: (a) osteopetrosis congenita (with precocious manifestations, or malignant infantile form), (b) marble bone disease (or intermediate form), and (c) osteopetrosis tarda (Albers-Schönberg disease, or benign osteopetrosis; see characteristics box for subtype characteristics).

Osteopetrosis congenita is extremely rare, whereas osteopetrosis tarda is relatively common, with a wide variety of ethnic and geographic occurrences (Beers & Berkow, 1999). Males and females are equally affected by this disease (National Institute of Health [NIH], 1997).

Characteristics

Osteopetrosis congenita (malignant infantile form)

1. Autosomal recessive disorder (both parents must be carriers of the gene for the disease for it to be expressed in the child)
2. Presents in infancy
3. Is considered the most severe form of the disease
4. Growth retardation (failure to thrive)
5. Excessive thickening of the bones
6. Proptosis (forward displacement of organs)
7. Blindness, deafness, and hydrocephalus (enlarged ventricles due to excessive cerebral spinal fluid); is associated with compression from bone overgrowth
8. Bone marrow failure
9. Pancytopenia (simultaneous decrease of red cells, white cells, and platelets in the blood)
10. Spontaneous bruising, anemia, and hemorrhaging
11. Enlargement of the spleen and liver
12. Facial palsies

Marble bone disease (intermediate form)

1. Autosomal recessive disorder
2. Also presents in infancy
3. Excessive weakness
4. Growth retardation; shortened stature
5. Intracranial calcifications
6. Hearing loss
7. Psychomotor retardation
8. Renal tubular acidosis (kidneys lose the ability to acidify urine properly)

Osteopetrosis tarda (Albers-Schönberg, or benign form with delayed manifestations)

1. Autosomal dominant disorder (only one parent is necessary as a carrier for the disease to be expressed in the child)

2. Can present at any age, but typically manifests in adulthood
3. 50% of cases asymptomatic (Carolino, Perez, & Popa, 1998)
4. Mild craniofacial disproportion
5. "Rugger jersey" spine (horizontal banding appearance of the vertebral end plates due to sclerosis)
6. Brittle bones, with frequent bone fractures, degenerative joints, osteomyelitis (inflammation and infection of the bone marrow), osteitis (inflammation of the bone, usually in the mandible)
7. Occasional facial palsies or deafness
8. Mild anemia

Diagnosis of osteopetrosis is usually made when dense bones are revealed on X rays. Bone biopsies confirm the diagnosis and are accompanied by additional tests to evaluate other complications associated with the disease (i.e., anemia). Confirmation as to the subtype of osteopetrosis that a patient has is important for receiving appropriate treatment (NIH, 1997).

The most effective treatment to date for osteopetrosis congenita is bone marrow transplantation because it has been shown to offer a cure for bone marrow failure and metabolic disturbances (Beers & Berkow, 1999; Carolino et al., 1998). Nutritional therapy has also resulted in improved growth and enhanced response to other treatment modalities in children with osteopetrosis (Carolino et al., 1998). Patients with renal tubular acidosis are typically treated with alkaline medications. Patients with osteopetrosis tarda may need surgery to repair degenerative joints or bones. In some cases they may also need treatment with splenectomy or transfusions for anemia. Control of infection is also required for the different variations of this disease.

Children with osteopetrosis tarda often will not need special accommodations in the schools because over half of patients with this form of the disease are asymptomatic. Also, these children are generally of normal intelligence (Beers & Berkow, 1999). However, for those children who are experiencing difficulties with fractures due to weakened bones, special considerations should be made (e.g., partial participation) for sports and physical activities to avoid injuries.

Children with the more life-threatening forms of osteopetrosis are in need of attention and contact from their parents and family despite long-term hospitalization. Parents are encouraged to stay with their children in the hospital and limit separations as much as possible because children may feel scared and confused. It is also recommended that parents talk to children about their illnesses in a matter-of-fact, age-appropriate manner (Potter, 1998).

Prognosis is poor for children with osteopetrosis congenita because they usually succumb to anemia, hemorrhage, or severe infection within the first 2 years of life (Beers & Berkow, 1999; Carolino et al., 1998). Children with this type of osteopetrosis rarely reach adulthood, but in cases in which life is prolonged, a variety of health complications must be faced, such as anemia, recurrent fractures, blindness, and deafness (Carolino et al., 1998). Children with marble bone disease have a similar prognosis to that for those with osteopetrosis congenita, although they have a somewhat longer life span expectancy. However, prognosis is good for patients with osteopetrosis tarda, and patients with this form of the disease typically live a normal life span.

Because there is currently not a cure for osteopetrosis, research is focusing on a search for a new drug in correcting the defect in osteoclasts, which would allow the bone marrow cavity to form correctly. There is also experimental research involving treatments with vitamin D and interferon-gamma drugs that have shown promise in increasing bone resorption (Carolino et al., 1998; Key et al., 1995, NIH, 1997; St. Jude's, 1996). Treatment with corticosteroids (i.e., prednisone) is also showing promise in treating anemia and thrombocytopenia in patients with osteopetrosis congenita (Carolino et al., 1998; NIH, 1997). Gene research is also attempting to identify the gene or genes that cause osteopetrosis.

REFERENCES

Beers, M. H., & Berkow, R. (Eds.). (1999). *The merck manual of diagnosis and therapy* (17th ed.). Lawrenceville, New Jersey: Merck.

Carolino, J., Perez, J. A., Popa, A. (1998). Osteopetrosis. *American Family Physician, 57*(6), 1293–1296.

Key, L. L., Rodriguez, R. M., Willi, S. M., Wright, N. M., Hatcher, H. C., Eyre, D. R., et al. (1995). Long-term treatment of osteopetrosis with recombinant human interferon gamma. *New England Journal of Medicine, 332*(24), 1594–1599.

National Institutes of Health Osteoporosis and Related Bone Diseases National Resource Center (1997). *Understanding osteopetrosis, 3*(7). Retrieved from http://www.osteo.org/understand.html

Potter, M. L. (1998). Chronically ill children. In A. Canter & S. A. Carroll (Eds.), *Helping children at home and school: Handouts from your school psychologist.* Bethesda, MD: National Association of School Psychologists.

St. Jude's Children's Research Hospital (last updated in May, 1996). Osteopetrosis. Retrieved from http://www.stjude.org/Medical/osteopetrosis.htm

Andrea Holland
University of Texas at Austin

See also Albers-Schönberg Disease

OTITUS MEDIA

Otitis Media (OM) is characterized by an inflammation of the middle ear and is typically associated with an accumulation of fluid. This fluid may or may not be infected. Infection is usually a bacterial or viral infection secondary to a cold, sore throat, or other respiratory problem. When the fluid is not infected, it results in a condition called otitis media with effusion (OME). Another name for this condition is Serous otitis media. If the fluid in the middle ear becomes infected, then the condition is referred to as acute otitis media (AOM). In both cases, there is fluctuating loss in hearing, which returns to normal. Rarely can a permanent hearing loss occur (Roberts & Medley, 1995).

Children between the ages of 6 and 13 months have the highest risk of developing OM. At least 50% of children have had at least one episode by 1 year of age. The incidence remains high throughout the preschool years. An estimated 35% of children between 1 and 3 years of age will have recurrent episodes of OM (American Speech-Language-Hearing Association [ASHA], 2000). Young children run the highest risk of developing OM because their eustachian tubes are more horizontal, shorter, and wider than those in adults. When a child has a cold, allergy, or some type of upper respiratory infection, the eustachian tube can become blocked, preventing the fluid from draining out of the middle ear (ASHA, 2000; Roberts & Medley, 1995).

Boys seem to have OM more frequently than do girls (ASHA, 2000). Native American, Eskimo, or Hispanic children have the highest prevalence rates for developing OM. Caucasian and then African American children have the next-highest incidence rates (Bluestone & Klein, 1990). Children who are at risk for OM include those with craniofacial anomalies such as cleft palate and those with various syndromes (e.g., Down Syndrome). There are other risk factors that include family history of OM, day care attendance, passive smoke exposure, poor hygiene, and low socioeconomic status (Roberts & Medley, 1995).

Characteristics

1. Unusual irritability
2. Difficulty sleeping
3. Tugging or pulling at ears
4. Fever
5. Loss of balance
6. Difficulty hearing quiet sounds
7. Sitting too close to the television or increasing the volume
8. Fluid drainage from the ear (National Institute on Deafness and Other Communication Disorders [NIDCD], 1997)
9. Inattentiveness
10. Earache or pain
11. Misunderstanding directions (AHSA, 2000)

Treatment usually consists of use of antibiotics. If the fluid does not diminish, persists for more than 3 months, and a hearing loss is associated, the physician may recommend a myringotomy (insertion of a pressure equalization tube in the affected ear). The tube allows for ventilation in the middle ear and aids in keeping the air pressure in the middle ear near equal to that of the environment. The tube normally stays in the ear for 6–12 months and is typically expelled spontaneously (NIDCD, 1997).

Because of associated hearing loss, language and learning difficulties may result, especially in cases of recurrent OM. The ability to receive information via the auditory channel is compromised, causing the child to receive a partial or inconsistent auditory signal. This results in the child's encoding information imprecisely and may put the child at a disadvantage for acquiring speech and language. Consequently, later academic achievement—specifically in the area of reading and related language-based areas—may be affected. Inattentiveness may result from an inconsistent auditory signal; this may manifest as distractibility and problems working independently (Roberts & Medley, 1995).

Teachers and caregivers can provide an optimal listening environment for the child by using face-to-face interaction, seating the child near the person who is speaking, attaining the child's attention before speaking, speaking clearly, and using natural intonation. The environment can be modified to reduce background noise (Roberts & Medley, 1995).

Consultation or evaluation by an audiologist and speech-language pathologist should be sought to further define the scope of the effects of recurrent OM. In some cases, delays in articulation and language development are sufficient enough to warrant speech-language therapy services in the school setting. These services generally produce positive results.

Research linking recurrent OM to later developmental difficulties is controversial. Further research is needed to clarify this relationship. Until then, medical management combined with collaboration with other allied health care professionals, caregivers, and teachers can minimize the effects of OM (Roberts & Medley, 1995).

REFERENCES

American Speech-Language-Hearing Association. (2000). Otitis media hearing & language development. Retrieved October 5, 2000, from http://www.asha.org/consumers/brochures/otitis_media.htm

Bluestone, C. D.,, & Klein, J. O. (1990). Otitis media, atelectasis and eustachian tube dysfunction. In C. D. Bluestone, S. E. Stool, & M. D. Scheetz (Eds.), *Pediatric otolaryngology,* (pp. 320–486). Philadelphia: W. B. Saunders.

National Institute on Deafness and Other Communication Disorders. (1997). Otitis media (ear infection). Retrieved October 5, 2000, from http://www.nih.gov/nidcd/health/pubs_hb/otitism.htm

Roberts, J. E., & Medley, L. P. (1995). Otitis media and speech-language sequelae in young children: Current issues in management. *American Journal of Speech-Language Pathology, 4,* 15–24.

Theresa T. Aguire
Texas A&M University

P

PACHYDERMOPERIOSTOSIS

Pachydermoperiostosis (PDP) is a rare, heritable disorder that affects skin, skin derivatives (hair and sebaceous glands), and skeletal tissues. Originally described in 1868, the syndrome was more thoroughly delineated in 1935.

The etiology of PDP is unknown. Its occurrence in the general population is uncertain. The presence of PDP in parent-child pairings suggests an autosomal dominant mode of transmission. Clinical findings are quite variable. However, males are usually more severely affected than are females.

Characteristics

1. Usually normal appearance at birth. Most children with PDP show signs of the disorder by age 3. Findings become accentuated at puberty and may progress for up to a decade.
2. Coarse, elongated facial features (acromegaly).
3. Deep furrows and folds in the scalp and occasionally in the forehead (cutis verticus gyrata).
4. Clubbing (broadened, thickened ends of the fingers).
5. Thickening of the lower ends of long bones (periostosis).
6. Oily skin on the face and forehead.
7. Enlarged pores that become plugged with material produced by sebaceous glands (seborrheic hyperplasia).
8. Hirsutism (increased body and facial hair).
9. Joint and muscle discomfort.
10. Hyperhidrosis (excessive sweating) of the hands and feet.
11. Ptosis (drooping) of the eyelids.

No data are available regarding treatment strategies for PDP. The condition may be so mild that specific therapy is unnecessary.

There is no research to indicate cognitive deficits or the need for special education support services based on this disorder.

PDP appears to be a benign malady in most cases. Males are (in general) more severely affected than are females. Worsening of the characteristics of the disorder can be anticipated during puberty and through early adulthood.

For more information, please contact NIH/National Arthritis and Musculoskeletal and Skin Diseases Information Clearinghouse, 1 AMS Circle, Bethesda, MD 20892-3675

REFERENCES

Jones, K. (1997). *Smith's recognizable patterns of human malformation* (5th ed.). Philadelphia: W. B. Saunders.

National Organization for Rare Disorders. (1998). Pachydermoperiostosis. Retrieved from http://www.stepstn.com/cgi-win/nord.exe?proc=GetDocument&rectype=0&recnum=927

Barry H. Davison
Ennis, Texas

Joan W. Mayfield
Baylor Pediatric Specialty Services
Dallas, Texas

PALLISTER-HALL SYNDROME

Pallister-Hall syndrome (PHS) is a rare disorder of brain development affecting the hypothalamus and pituitary gland. Associated anomalies of the face, respiratory tract, limbs, anus, and heart are also common.

The etiology of PHS is unclear. Its incidence in the general population is not known. Five parent-child examples of PHS suggest an autosomal dominant mode of transmission. Passage of the trait from the father appears more frequently than from the mother (parent-of-origin effect). Sporadic cases have also been observed and are believed to be caused by fresh genetic mutations.

Characteristics

1. Mild prenatal growth deficiency.
2. Hypothalamic hamartoblastoma. This lesion is a usually malignant tumor that completely replaces the hypothalamus, which is located on the underside of the brain above the pituitary gland. Developmental defects of the pituitary gland are also common, resulting in a deficiency of pituitary hormones (panhypopituitarism).

3. Flattened, short nose; malformed ear, absent ear openings; small jaw.
4. Underdeveloped epiglottis and trachea; absent or abnormally formed lung.
5. Malformed nails; webbing of fingers and toes; extra digits (polydactyly); missing digits (oligodactyly); shortened bones of the hands and feet.
6. Imperforate anus (no anal orifice); rectal atresia (narrowing of the rectum).
7. Congenital heart malformations.
8. Poorly developed adrenal glands.

Patients with PHS demonstrate extensive variability in disease severity. However, therapeutic options for profoundly affected individuals are limited. Hypothalamic hamartoblastoma is generally inoperable. Surgical correction of certain anomalies (heart and anus) is possible. Neonatal hypoglycemia (secondary to endocrine abnormalities) requires intravenous glucose infusion. Infants and children have needed thyroid and growth hormone replacement as well as corticosteroid therapy secondary to adrenal hypofunction. Familial cases of PHS have a 50% chance of recurrence. Therefore, genetic counseling should be made available to affected couples.

The need for special education support services will be dependent on whether the child with PHS has central nervous system involvement. A neuropsychological evaluation to determine cognitive strengths and weaknesses can offer valuable information to his or her parents and teachers on ways to optimize the child's learning.

The prognosis for PHS in general is fairly bleak. The majority of patients with the disorder have died prior to their 3rd birthday. However, as more cases have been reported, it is now obvious that hypothalamic hamartoblastoma is not a consistent feature of the syndrome. Affected children who were free from central nervous system involvement have had normal intelligence and survival into adulthood.

For more information and support, please contact Pallister-Hall Foundation, Ross, 8 Heather Dr. #E, White River Junct, VT 05001-9302, e-mail: messer@sover.net.

REFERENCES

Jones, K. (1997). *Smith's recognizable patterns of human malformation* (5th ed.). Philadelphia: W. B. Saunders.

National Organization for Rare Disorders. (1998). Pallister-Hall syndrome. Retrieved from http://www.stepstn.com/cgi-win/nord.exe?proc=GetDocument&rectype=0&recnum=1016

Barry H. Davison
Ennis, Texas

Joan W. Mayfield
Baylor Pediatric Specialty Services
Dallas, Texas

PANDAS (PEDIATRIC AUTOIMMUNE NEUROPSYCHIATRIC DISORDER ASSOCIATED WITH STREPTOCOCCI)

PANDAS, or pediatric autoimmune neuropsychiatric disorder associated with streptococci, has been used to describe a group of disorders—in particular, obsessive-compulsive disorder (OCD) and tic disorder or Tourette syndrome (American Psychiatric Association [APA], 2000). PANDAS has been associated with Group A beta-hemolytic streptococcus (GABHS), as well as Sydenham chorea, a condition that results from rheumatic fever following strep infection. Although PANDAS shared certain features of Sydenham—in particular, OCD and tics—it is not clear whether PANDAS represents acute rheumatic fever (i.e., a subset of Sydenham chorea; Murphy, Goodman, Ayoub, & Voeller, 2000).

Swedo and her colleagues at the National Institute of Mental Health (NIMH; Swedo et al., 1998) have established criteria for PANDAS. These criteria include an abrupt onset during childhood, usually between the ages of 3 and puberty. There must be a temporal association with the GABHS infection during symptom exacerbation. The relationship between PANDAS and GABHS, however, is not as strong as the relationship between GABHS and Sydenham chorea (SC). The onset of PANDAS tends to occur about 6–9 months after infection; later recurrences, however, are not necessarily associated with the GABHS infection. The child must meet the *Diagnostic and Statistical Manual of Mental Disorders–Fourth Edition* (*DSM-IV*) criteria for OCD or tic disorder (APA, 2000). Other psychiatric problems and neurological abnormalities accompany periods of symptom exacerbation. For example, individuals with PANDAS have been found to be emotionally labile, to be anxious (i.e., separation anxiety, nighttime fears, and bedtime rituals), and to show oppositional behaviors (Swedo et al., 1998). There is also evidence of hyperactivity (motor) and choreiform movements (i.e., piano-playing finger movements) during relapses. There is no evidence, however, that frank chorea is a part of the condition, and if chorea is present, Sydenham chorea is typically diagnosed.

Characteristics

1. Abrupt onset during childhood (between 3 years and puberty)
2. Temporal association of symptom exacerbation with GABHS infection
3. Meet *DSM-IV* criteria for obsessive-compulsive disorder, tic disorder, or both
4. Episodic course with periods of exacerbation interspersed with remission
5. Neurological symptoms during exacerbations

The course of PANDAS is episodic—that is, periods of partial or complete remission are interspersed between periods of exacerbated symptoms. It is not clear whether the condition is chronic or if total remission can be achieved (Murphy et al., 2000). There is no indication, however, that prophylactic treatments to prevent recurrences of the GABHS infection is indicated as it is with Sydenham chorea. Symptoms of PANDAS can, however, be improved with therapy—specifically, plasmapheresis and intravenous immunoglobulin.

There is no indication that children who have PANDAS require special education services. Some children, however, may benefit from assistance and classroom accommodations during periods of symptom exacerbation. School psychological services may be particularly important in order to identify what the child's needs are and what intervention would be most appropriate to address these needs. Given the abrupt onset of the condition and its episodic nature, it is likely that the child and his or her family will need supportive therapy. Parents may be especially open to suggestions about ways to manage the variety of psychiatric and neurological problems that accompany PANDAS. A psychiatric evaluation is therefore critical to determine whether medications will benefit the child and reduce associated problems (e.g., tics, obsessions and compulsions, anxiety, lability, and hyperactivity).

Research is still needed to clarify the relationship between PANDAS and other conditions—in particular, Tourette syndrome, OCD, and Sydenham chorea. A better understanding of this relationship and of the etiology of the disorder will probably lead to more effective treatments. Further studies may also provide critical information about who is at risk for developing the condition and ways to prevent PANDAS in the first place or alter its course (i.e., prevent relapses). At the present time, long-term outcomes are poorly understood.

REFERENCES

American Psychiatric Association . (2000). *Diagnostic and statistical manual of mental disorders* (4th ed., text revision). Washington, DC: Author.

Murphy, T., Goodman, W., Ayoub, E., & Voeller, K. (2000). On defining Sydenham's chorea: Where do we draw the line? *Biological Psychiatry, 47,* 851–857.

Swedo, S., Leonard, H. Garvey, M., Mittleman, B., Allen, A., Perlmutter, S., et al. (1998). Pediatric autoimmune neuropsychiatric disorders associated with streptococcal infections: Clinical description of the first 50 cases. *American Journal of Psychiatry, 155*(2), 264–271.

Elaine Clark
Jenise Jensen
University of Utah

PANIC DISORDER

A panic disorder is characterized by recurrent, unexpected panic attacks. A panic attack is a discrete period of intense fear or terror that has a sudden onset and reaches a peak within 10 minutes or less. Panic attacks fall within three general categories defined by the presence or absence of triggers. Uncued panic attacks occur unexpectedly and out of the blue, with no apparent situational context. In contrast, both cued or situationally bound panic attacks occur whenever a person encounters or anticipates encountering a feared object or situation. At least one of the aforementioned panic attacks must be followed by at least a month of one or more of the following consequences: persistent concern about additional attacks, worry about the meaning of the attacks, and an appreciable change in behavior related to the attacks. Panic disorder often occurs along with agoraphobia. The child or adolescent may refuse to leave his or her home or may refuse to go to school. Although agoraphobia may develop at any point in conjunction with a panic disorder, it usually occurs within 1 year of recurrent panic attacks.

Lifetime prevalence rates for panic disorders are thought to be between .6% and 3.5%, with higher rates of up to 15% found in clinic-referred populations. Panic attacks occur more frequently in adolescents, with some studies reporting 16% of teens ages 12–17 experiencing at least one discrete panic attack (King, Ollendick, Mattis, Yang, & Tonge, 1997). Panic disorder is rare in young children and tends to occur more frequently in young adults and adolescents. There may be a bimodal distribution of the disorder, with one peak in late adolescence and a later smaller peak in the mid-30s. More cases are reported for girls than for boys. A small number of cases have been reported in childhood.

Characteristics

1. Recurrent unexpected panic attacks.
2. At least one attack has been followed by persistent worry about additional attacks, concern about the implications of the attacks, and a significant change in behavior related to the attack.
3. Attacks are not due to direct physiological effects of an ingested substance or general medical condition.

Source: Adapted from American Psychiatric Association (1994).

The most efficacious treatments for childhood anxiety disorders include behavior therapy, cognitive-behavioral treatments, and pharmacological treatments. Behavioral treatments include contingency management, response prevention, systematic desensitization involving graduated exposure to feared stimuli, modeling (using self or live or symbolic models) and self-control strategies. Empirical validation of the effectiveness of traditional psychotherapy for this disorder has been inadequate (Ollendick & King, 1998).

Pharmacological interventions for anxiety-based disorders include the use of serotonin reuptake inhibitors (SRIs) such as Prozac, Paxil, Zoloft, Luvox, or Celexa with initial dosages lower than recommended and slowly adjusted for maximum therapeutic effect. Benzodiazepines such as Xanax and Ativan as well as trycyclic antidepressants have shown minimal to modest benefit and in some cases have been no more effective than placebo in children (Bernstein et al., 1998). These treatments are usually provided as an adjunct to psychological treatments.

Special education services may be available to children or adolescents diagnosed with panic disorder under specific categories of Other Health Impaired, Emotional Disturbance, or Behavior Disorder; this may be particularly important if the disorder is chronic in nature. Accommodations may also be requested and provided under Section 504 of the Rehabilitation Act of 1973. Due to the nature and scope of the disorder, school attendance may become problematic. Families can benefit from additional counseling and support to effectively implement a treatment plan across both school and home settings.

Adolescents who present with panic disorders are likely to have a family history of panic attacks or related anxiety symptoms. These children or adolescents also tend to exhibit other problems and may meet diagnostic criteria for depression or other types of internalizing disorders. Some individuals may experience episodic outbreaks with several years of remission between panic episodes. The high proportion of children diagnosed with panic disorder who also report a history of separation anxiety problems has led to speculation that separation anxiety is a precursor to the development of a panic disorder. A developmental model of panic has been proposed (Mattis & Ollendick, 1997) whereby the stress associated with repeated separations, vulnerability to temperament factors (i.e., overreactive response to stress), and insecure-ambivalent attachment lead to expression of the disorder.

REFERENCES

American Psychiatric Association. (1994). *Diagnostic and statistical manual of mental disorders* (4th ed.). Washington, DC: Author.

Bernstein, G. A., Bourchard, C., Perwein, A., Crosby, R., Kushner, M., & Thuras, P. (1998). *Treatment of school refusal with imipramine.* Poster session presented at annual meeting of American Academy of Child and Adolescent Psychiatry, Anaheim, CA.

King, N. J., Ollendick, T. H., Mattis, S. G., Yang, B., & Tonge, B. (1997). Nonclinical panic attacks in adolescents: Prevalence, symptomatology and associated features. *Behavior Change, 13,* 171–183.

Mattis, S. G., & Ollendick, T. H. (1997). Panic disorder in children and young adults: A developmental analysis. In T. H. Ollendick & R. S. Prinz (Eds.) *Advances in clinical child psychology* (Vol. 20). New York: Plenum Press.

Ollendick, T. H., & King, N. J. (1998). Empirically validated treatments for children with phobic and anxiety disorders: Status. *Journal of Clinical Child Psychology, 27,* 156–167.

Daniel Olympia
University of Utah

See also Posttraumatic Stress Disorder; Trauma, Psychological

PAPILLITIS

The optic papilla is part of the optic nerve; it enters the eye and connects to the membrane lining the retina. The optic papilla is also referred to as the blind spot. In papillitis, the optic disk (papilla) becomes inflamed. When an individual develops papillitis, the individual experiences loss of vision in the eye affected within hours.

Papillitis may occur by itself (e.g., as a result of a virus) or in conjunction with another disorder (National Organization for Rare Disorders, 1997). Specific causes that have been identified include inflammation of the temporal artery, toxins or chemicals, syphilis, or a tumor. Related disorders include multiple sclerosis and systemic lupus erythromatosus. In some cases, individuals with papillitis have been subsequently diagnosed with multiple sclerosis; this is less likely when papillitis occurs in childhood (Morales, Siatkowski, Howard, & Warman, 2000). With a myriad of causes, papillitis is equally likely to occur in males and females, it can occur at any age, and it is equally likely to occur across ethnic groups.

Characteristics

1. Vision impairment in affected eye(s)
2. Decreased color perception

Severity of visual problems can range from a slight deficiency to complete loss of light perception. Color perception can be impaired as well. In some individuals, recovery will be spontaneous; in other cases, permanent visual impairment may result. In children, there is more likely to be bilateral occurrence with associated greater severity of visual impairment (Morales et al., 2000). The severity, treatment, and outcome depend on the underlying cause of the papillitis. When recovery is not spontaneous, use of corticosteroids such as prednisone or methylprednisone may be prescribed (National Organization for Rare Disorders, 1997). Supportive therapy may be appropriate as well. In the event of permanent visual impairment, appropriate corrective lenses or other accommodations may be needed.

REFERENCES

Morales, D. S., Siatkowski, R. M., Howard, C. W., & Warman, R. (2000). Optic neuritis in children. *Journal of Pediatric Ophthalmology & Strabismus, 37,* 254–259.

National Organization for Rare Disorders. (1997). Papillitis (No. 744). Retrieved June 3, 2001, from http://www.rarediseases.org

Cynthia A. Riccio
Texas A&M University

PARENTAL ALIENATION SYNDROME

Parental alienation syndrome (PAS) is a process label proposed by Gardner (1998) for describing how children in contested divorce situations can become hostile and distant from one of their parents. Parental alienation creates a singular, enmeshed relationship between a child and one parent. The fully alienated child does not wish to have any contact whatsoever with one parent and expresses only negative feelings for that parent and only positive feelings for the other parent. There are varying degrees to which this problem may manifest. Incidence rates remain largely unknown, although custody evaluators and family attorneys find repeated instances of this phenomenon in their caseloads.

Dunne and Hedrick (1994) report that cases of parental alienation syndrome appeared to be primarily a function of the pathology of the alienating parent and that parent's relationship with the children. In more severe cases, the alienating parent demonstrates marked personality disturbance. Professional focus has been on viewing this problem as a dysfunctional family system dynamic that may serve to maintain the alienating parent's symbiotic dependence on the child, assist in managing the anger and revenge felt by the child or alienated parent, protect the alienating parent's self-esteem, or avenge the alienated parent's abandonment of the family. When PAS occurs, the relationship with the alienated parent is damaged or destroyed, and there is increased risk for maladjustment in the child (Cartwright, 1994). Passive and dependent children are at greater risk (Stahl, 1999).

Characteristics

1. Child engages in denigration of alienated parent, with weak and absurd rationale.
2. Child has lack of ambivalence toward alienated parent and no guilt over cruelty or exploitation of alienated parent.
3. Child borrows scenarios from and reflexively supports alienating parent.
4. Child spreads animosity to the friends and family of the alienated parent.

Treatment and intervention by the court may vary according to the level of severity of the alienation process. Minor intervention may involve psychotherapy for parent and child, up to the point of removing the child through hospitalization or temporarily changing physical custody. Although these problems are not unique to special education children, teachers may become cognizant of the symptoms and help refer the family for further evaluation. Prognosis depends on the level of severity and the immediacy of detection. There is an emerging body of literature on this topic (see http://www.rgardner.com), but more empirical research is needed.

REFERENCES

Cartwright, G. F. (1994). Expanding the parameters of parental alienation syndrome. *American Journal of Family Therapy, 21*(3), 205–215.

Dunne, J., & Hedrick, M. (1994). The parental alienation syndrome: An analysis of sixteen selected cases. *Journal of Divorce and Remarriage, 21*(3–4), 21–38.

Gardner, R. A. (1998). *The parental alienation syndrome* (2nd ed.). Cresskill, NJ: Creative Therapeutics.

Stahl, P. (1999). *Complex issues in child custody evaluations.* Thousand Oaks, CA: Sage.

Daniel J. Rybicki
ForenPsych Services
Agoura Hills, California

PARKINSON'S DISEASE

Parkinson's disease is a degenerative motor disease caused by changes in the pigmented cells of the substantia nigra and nuclei in the brainstem. Symptoms of the disease are primarily associated with dopamine deficiency in the frontal cortex and basal ganglia. Decreased levels of serotonin, however, also contribute to Parkinson's. The disease was first described by James Parkinson in the early 1800s as a "shaking palsy" (due to the presentation of tremors and immobility).

Onset of the disease is typically after the age of 60. In most cases, the initial symptom is a one-sided hand tremor (appearing as if the person is rolling a pill). In cases in which the disease begins early—that is, before the age of 40—the first symptom is often dystonia (i.e., tightening of muscles and limbs). As the disease progresses, the individual has increased difficulty initiating and executing movements, moves quite slowly (i.e., bradykinesia), and in some cases loses the ability for voluntary motion (i.e., akinesia). The individual may walk stooped over and may have a shuffling gait. Limb rigidity is also observed during walking because the person with Parkinson's may not have a normal arm swing. Furthermore, on examination, cogwheel rigidity may be observed. These individuals often have a significant reduction in eye blinks, causing the face to appear masklike. Micrographia and soft speech may be noted.

It is estimated that more than 1 million Americans have Parkinson's disease, with 60,000 new cases diagnosed each year. The disease primarily affects older adults—that is, an estimated 1 in 100 (Koller & Hubble, 2000). Only 40% of cases are under the age of 60, and only 5% are younger than 40. Parkinson's disease affects both females and males; however, males tend to have more severe parkinsonian symptoms, and females tend to have more L-dopa-induced dyskinesias. The disease has been shown to affect more Caucasians than it does African Americans; however, the difference appears to be related more to geographic region than to protection from higher melanin pigmentation (e.g., Eastham, Lacro, & Jeste, 1996).

Characteristics

1. Tremor (often one-sided and nonintentional)
2. Limb rigidity (limited arm swinging while walking)
3. Extremely slow movements, problems initiating voluntary motion, stooped posture, and shuffled gait
4. Soft voice and masklike facial expression

The etiology of Parkinson's is unclear; however, both environment and genetics have been linked with the disease. An abnormality on Chromosome 4, a gene involved in protein production, has been implicated in the disease and found in some family members with Parkinson's. The gene, however, does not account for all cases, and infection (e.g., viral) and toxic exposure appear to be associated. It may be that certain individuals have an inherited tendency to develop Parkinson's but that repeated exposure to environmental conditions may be needed to trigger its onset.

There are no medical tests to confirm a diagnosis of Parkinson's disease. Even autopsies showing high levels of Lewy bodies have failed to provide conclusive evidence. In elderly patients, however, the disease can be rather easily identified based on symptom presentation and course. It is critical, however, that conditions mimicking certain parkinsonian symptoms be differentially diagnosed. Such conditions include Wilson disease and carbon monoxide poisoning, in which tremors and dystonic movements are present. In some of these cases, neuroimaging with magnetic resonance imaging (MRI) may be useful to rule out Parkinson's and rule in another condition. A history of drug usage, however, needs to be considered, including prescribed and illegal drugs that affect the dopamine system (e.g., neroleptics to treat schizophrenia and heroin).

The prognosis for Parkinson's is poor in that there is no known cure. There are, however, a number of treatment options, including drugs and surgical treatments to reduce symptoms of the disease. During the initial stages, no treatment may be necessary, but as the disease progresses some form of therapy is typically required. The treatment of choice is L-dopa, a drug used to replace depleted dopamine. The drug has been helpful in reducing tremors and rigidity but has not been shown to be as effective in improving the execution of movement. Furthermore, L-dopa has been found to have a number of side effects, especially in females and young-onset Parkinson's patients (e.g., muscle tightening, body jerks, and chorea). Surgical interventions include implantation of electrical stimulators and tissue transplant. Whereas tissue transplants replace dopamine, stimulators alter cells that receive inaccurate signals from the substantia nigra (i.e., cells in the basal ganglia).

Approximately 40–50% of patients with Parkinson's evidence signs of depression, and 20–35% of cases display psychotic symptoms (e.g., visual hallucinations, delusions, and mania; Rao, Huber, & Bornstein, 1992). Treatment is therefore needed to address these associated problems. This treatment may include drug treatment as well as counseling to help patients cope more effectively with the debilitating nature of the disease. Because Parkinson's is a disease that primarily affects older adults, educational assistance is not likely to be needed; however, for adults who are still working, accommodations through the Americans with Disabilities Act may be necessary. Such accommodations may include additional time to complete work and adaptive equipment to aid them in the process. Neuropsychological assessments may help to identify what some of these needs are and to determine whether the individual has any related cognitive problems. Although depression has been implicated as a causative factor in cognitive problems of Parkinsonian patients, the problems are still significant (e.g., slowed speed of information processing, poor delayed recall, and problems with executive function; Rao et al., 1992). Educating the individual and family may be critical to understanding the various aspects of the disease, and putting affected individuals in contact with community agencies who work with persons who have Parkinson's may be the most efficient way to achieve this goal (e.g., National Parkinson Foundation Web site: http://www.parkinson.org).

REFERENCES

Eastham, J., Lacro, J., & Jeste, D. (1996). Ethnicity and movement disorders. *Mount Sinai Journal of Medicine, 63*(5), 314–319.

Koller, W., & Hubble, J. (2000). *Young Parkinson's handbook: Parkinson's web.* http://www.neuro-chief-e.mgh.harvard.e . . . /main/YOPD_Handbook/Chapter_2.html

Rao, S., Huber, S., & Bornstein, R. (1992). Emotional changes with multiple sclerosis and Parkinson's disease. *Journal of Consulting and Clinical Psychology, 60*(3), 369–378.

Elaine Clark
University of Utah

PARRY ROMBERG SYNDROME

Parry Romberg or Romberg syndrome is characterized by hemifacial atrophy or atrophy of the soft tissues of one side of the face, usually the left side (National Organization for Rare Disorders, 1996). It is a rare, progressive disorder usually evident by the time the individual reaches age 20. The atrophy progresses over a period of 3–5 years before stabilizing. As the atrophy progresses, there are changes to the eyes and hair. Neurological effects including seizures may also present but less frequently. There may be bouts of severe pain to the areas of the mouth, tongue, cheek, nose, or other parts of the face associated with the trigeminal nerve (fifth cranial nerve). Dental problems may be present; changes to hair, including alopecia (baldness), may be present as well.

The cause of Parry Romberg syndrome is unknown, although in some reported cases, there is a familial pattern, suggesting autosomal dominant transmission (Larner & Bennison, 1993). In other cases, there is a high frequency (25%) of a previous injury to the affected side of the face. Others have suggested that Parry Romberg syndrome is a specialized case of connective tissue disorder called scleroderma or that the autoimmune system is involved. In one case, the facial hemiatrophy occurred following the onset of epileptic seizures in a young child rather than following the typical sequence of hemiatrophy presenting prior to the seizures (Yano, Sawaishi, Toyono, Takaku, & Takada, 2000). Additional research is needed regarding the syndrome's etiology. Parry Romberg syndrome is more likely to affect females than to affect males (3:2 ratio); the incidence of Parry Romberg syndrome by ethnic group is unknown.

Characteristics

1. Facial changes that progress from the upper lip to the mouth, nose, eye, and ear or neck
2. Dark pigmentation or depigmentation of the skin covering affected tissue
3. Seizures
4. Severe headaches
5. Facial pain
6. Vision problems
7. Delayed dental eruption or dental malocclusion

The range and severity of symptoms vary from individual to individual, necessitating differing treatment options (National Organization for Rare Disorders, 1996). In addition to cosmetic issues, vision (ocular) problems may occur as well, including the inability to fully close the eye, drooping eye, problems with lens accommodation for focusing, abnormal pupil constriction, nystagmus, or inability to move the eye at all. Surgical correction or reconstruction after the atrophy has become inactive can be undertaken to address cosmetic as well as functional problems. Seizure control and pain during the active phase of the disorder generally are treated medically.

There are no indications of cognitive impairment or learning disability associated with Parry Romberg syndrome; however, when the syndrome is evident at birth, atrophy of the same hemisphere as that with the facial hemiatrophy has been found (Chang et al., 1999) and may be evidenced in cognitive, academic, or motor problems. Severity of symptoms will vary, and interventions should be tailored to individual needs. In addition to medical and educational management, however, given the developmental issues of adolescence (when the disorder is most likely to present), supportive counseling through the reconstructive process may be appropriate. Although research is not conclusive, genetic counseling may be appropriate for the individual affected as well as for other family members.

REFERENCES

Chang, S. E., Huh, J., Choi, J. H., Sung, K. J., Moon, K. C., & Koh, J. K. (1999). Parry Romberg syndrome with ipsilateral cerebral atrophy of neonatal onset. *Pediatric Dermatology, 16,* 487–488.

Larner, A. J., & Bennison, D. P. (1993). Some observations on the aetiology of progressive hemifacial atrophy ("Parry Romberg syndrome"). *Journal of Neurology, Neurosurgery, and Psychiatry, 56,* 1035–1039.

National Organization for Rare Disorders. (1996). Parry Romberg syndrome. Retrieved June 3, 2001, from http://www.rarediseases.org

Yano, T., Sawaishi, Y., Toyono, M., Takaku, I., & Takada, G. (2000). Progressive facial hemiatrophy after epileptic seizures. *Pediatric Neurology, 23,* 164–166.

CYNTHIA A. RICCIO
Texas A&M University

PEELING SKIN SYNDROME

Peeling skin syndrome is an extremely rare congenital condition characterized by continuous and spontaneous skin peeling. It has also been referred to as skin shedding (keratolysis exfoliativa congenita), deciduous skin, idiopathic deciduous skin, familial continual skin peeling, and continual skin peeling syndrome. The term *peeling skin syndrome* was first coined in 1982 by the researchers Levy and Goldsmith, who reported two patients with a universal ichthyosiform dermatosis since birth (Mevorah, Frenk, Saurat, & Siegenthaler, 1987). Since then, only 22 cases (14 males, 8 females) have been reported. In the majority of these cases, skin lesions appeared either at birth or early in life. However, similar sporadic cases have been reported in the literature since the 1920s (Tastan, Akar, Gür, & Deveci, 1999). It is believed to be an inherited autosomal recessive disease, but little else is known about its etiology. Ultrastructural studies and differences among patients suggest that there may be different pathogenic mechanisms behind diagnosis (Causeret et al., 2000). Specifically, the peeling is due to the separation of the stratum corneum layer just above the stratum granulosum layer of skin (Tastan et al., 1999).

Characteristics

1. Widespread discrete peeling skin patches of variable size.
2. Peeling skin is produced easily by rubbing or stroking skin without bleeding. In some cases, individuals have been able to manually remove sheets of skin.
3. Other findings include itching (pruritis), inflammation, burning sensation, and newly formed hairs that can be plucked easily.
4. Seasonal changes may be reported.
5. Generally there is an absence of spared areas.
6. In some cases, there have been associated anomalies of appendages and short stature, as well as blood amino level abnormalities.

In a case study, the skin peeling was observed to follow a pattern: A reddish spot spreads out peripherally with a thin horny collarette at the border. This spot forms into a patch. The surface at first is smooth and then becomes covered with large greyish scales of skin that flake off, leaving regenerated background skin. When grasped with the fingers, the skin can easily be peeled back. Rubbing the skin produces the whole sequence of changes; otherwise, the process takes 6–8 days (Mevorah et al., 1987).

There is currently little information on the treatment of this disease. No effective treatment has been reported (Tastan et al., 1999). Some patients have reported improvement with the passage of time. Resistance to treatment, including administration of oral isotretinoin and oral etretinate, has also been reported (Mevorah et al., 1987). Special education may be available to children with peeling skin syndrome under the handicapping condition of Other Health Impaired. Most individuals with peeling skin syndrome have reported otherwise good health; however, the physical and emotional discomfort associated with the chronic condition may require special educational provisions, resources, and emotional support for the child with this condition. Counseling sensitive to chronic illness issues and the social difficulties this illness may present should also be considered. Side effects of medication given for symptom management should be taken into consideration in assessments of a child's progress.

There is currently no cure for this lifelong disease. Current research is focusing on the etiology of peeling skin syndrome because it is still not well understood and there is an absence of a single biological marker for the disease. Research on the disorder is scarce. A keratohyalin abnormality was found in through ultrastructural studies of the skin in one individual with peeling skin syndrome; this finding has been supported through other research with case studies (Mevorah et al., 1987; Tastan et al., 1999).

REFERENCES

Causeret, A. S., Grezard, P., Hafteck, M., Roth, B., Forestier, J. Y., & Perrot, H. (2000). Acquired peeling skin syndrome in an adult. *Annals de Dermatologie et de Venereologie, 127,* 194–197.

Mevorah, B., Frenk, E., Saurat, J. H., & Siegenthaler, G. (1987). Peeling skin syndrome: A clinical, ultrastructural and biochemical study. *British Journal of Dermatology, 116,* 117–125.

Tastan, H. B., Akar, A., Gür, A. R., & Deveci, S. (1999). Peeling skin syndrome. *International Journal of Dermatology, 38,* 207–216.

Laura A. Guli
University of Texas at Austin

PELIZAEUS-MERZBACHER DISEASE

Pelizaeus-Merzbacher disease is a rare disorder of the central nervous system. It is progressive, with coordination, motor abilities, and intellectual functioning gradually deteriorating over time (Menkes, 1990). These effects occur because Pelizaeus-Merzbacher disease is associated with the leukodystrophies that involve the myelin sheath of nerves in the brain and results in deterioration of the white matter of the brain.

As with other leukodystrophies, Pelizaeus-Merzbacher disease is genetically determined and X-linked. There are four forms of Pelizaeus-Merzbacher. Classical Pelizaeus-Merzbacher follows the typical manifestation for an X-linked trait. Because it is X-linked, boys are more likely to have this disorder than are girls. Classical acute Pelizaeus-Merzbacher can be identified prenatally. Infantile Pelizaeus-Merzbacher, however, is autosomal recessive and affects boys and girls equally. In contrast, the adult onset Pelizaeus-Merzbacher is autosomal dominant. Males and females are affected by the adult onset form with equal frequency. The fourth form occurs when the presence of Pelizaeus-Merzbacher is not hereditary and the cause is unknown; this is referred to as sporadic Pelizaeus-Merzbacher (Menkes, 1990). There are no indications that incidence varies by ethnic group.

Characteristics

1. Slowed growth
2. Failure to develop control of head movements or delay in development of control

3. Jerky eye movements or nystagmus
4. Tremors and spasticity
5. Unsteady gait and lack of coordination of movement (ataxia)
6. Repeated episodes of vomiting

Three of the four forms of Pelizaeus-Merzbacher have an onset in early infancy with delayed or slowed growth, difficulty with control of head movements, and problems with eye movement. The fourth form of Pelizaeus-Merzbacher has an adult onset, with tremor, involuntary movements or spasms, and unsteady gait. The symptoms of adult onset generally manifest after age 30 and before age 50 (Menkes, 1990).

Regardless of the form of Pelizaeus-Merzbacher, the prognosis for individuals with Pelizaeus-Merzbacher is not good; progressive deterioration occurs over time. Treatment is limited to addressing symptoms and providing needed supports to the individual with Pelizaeus-Merzbacher and his or her family. Because three of the four forms have a genetic etiology, genetic counseling for family members is recommended.

REFERENCES

Menkes, J. (1990). The leukodystrophies. *The New England Journal of Medicine, 322,* 54–55.

Cynthia A. Riccio
Texas A&M University

PEMPHIGOID, BENIGN MUCOSAL

Benign mucosal pemphigoid is a rare disorder that affects the mucous membranes lining various body cavities, particularly the mouth and the eyelids (conjunctiva). Gums may be selectively affected with the appearance of gingivitis (Roche & Field, 1997). There are multiple subtypes of benign mucosal pemphigoid disorder based on the location of the blisters as well as on the severity; some forms are chronic, whereas others remit and recur (Mantich, Craig, & Glass, 1987).

Benign mucosal pemphigoid is believed to be an autoimmune disorder, with the blisters evidencing the attack of healthy tissue by the individual's body. Benign mucosal pemphigoid rarely occurs in children (Roche & Field, 1997); it is more common in middle-aged and older individuals. Males and females are affected in equal numbers; there is no indication of differences in incidence across ethnic groups (National Organization for Rare Disorders, 1996). In addition to genetic transmission, there is some research to suggest that ocular benign mucosal pemphigoid may be precipitated by topical medications for glaucoma (Fiore, Jacobs, & Goldberg, 1987).

Characteristics

1. Blisters of mucous membranes in mouth
2. Inflammation of the conjunctiva and red eyes
3. Blistering of the pharynx and esophagus, nose, vulva, or urethra

The blistering eventually results in scarring; there may be a reoccurrence of the blisters after a period of remission. During the active phase of the disorder, corticosteroid drugs (e.g., prednisone) are prescribed for symptomatic relief. Corticosteroids aid in suppression of the immune system and treatment is usually effective (Mantich et al., 1987). Topical antibiotics may be needed to relieve inflammation or infection. Assuming infection is dealt with before any permanent tissue damage has occurred, individuals with benign mucosal pemphigoid usually do not require special accommodations. If accommodations are needed, these should be supportive and address the individual's needs.

REFERENCES

Fiore, P. M., Jacobs, I. W., & Goldberg, D. B. (1987). Drug-induced pemphigoid: A spectrum of diseases. *Archives of Ophthalmology, 105*(12), 1660–1663.

Mantich, N. M., Craig, R. M., & Glass, B. J. (1987). Red, blistering, and erosive lesions of the oral mucosa. *Journal of the American Dental Association, 115,* 457–458.

National Organization for Rare Disorders. (1996). Phemigoid, benign mucosal (No. 652). Retrieved June 3, 2001, from http://www.rarediseases.org

Roche, C., & Field, E. A. (1997). Benign mucous membrane pemphigoid presenting as desquamitive gingivitis in a 14-year-old child. *International Journal of Paediatric Dentistry, 7*(1), 31–34.

Cynthia A. Riccio
Texas A&M University

PENA-SHOKEIR PHENOTYPE

Pena Shokeir is a primary motor neuropathy associated with the absence of anterior horn cells in the spinal cord and diffuse muscle atrophy. Muscles involved include those of the respiratory system, and underdevelopment of the lungs is evident. There are at least two forms of Pena-Shokeir; however, some researchers have identified five subtypes (Hall, 1986). Due to the variations, Hagerman, Willemse, van Ketel, Barth, and Lindhout (1987) suggested that Pena-Shokeir syndrome not be considered as a unique syndrome but rather a phenotype of fetal akinesia.

The characteristic developmental pattern associated with Pena-Shokeir is evident in the lack of movement or decreased movement of the fetus in the womb (fetal akinesia or hypokinesia) and can be detected by sonography. Lack of activity or akinesia may initially be limited to the upper body, with the lower part of the body evidencing normal movement and growth (Tongsong, Chanprapaph, & Khunamornpong, 2000). It is believed that with lack of movement of muscles, there is a lack of development or developmental arrest. With no or insufficient muscle movement, including those involved in respiration, Pena Shokeir is fatal; some fetuses do not progress through full gestation (Tongsong et al., 2000). Only five individuals with Pena Shokeir are known to have survived beyond 1 month of age.

Characteristics

1. Fetal akinesia or hypokinesia and associated muscle atrophy
2. Swelling of the scalp
3. Lung hypoplasia
4. Rocker-bottom feet
5. Hypertelorism
6. Cleft or high arched palate

There are some indications that Pena Shokeir may be inherited following an autosomal recessive pattern, with an estimated 10–15% risk of recurrence within a family with one individual affected (Hall, 1986). Risk of recurrence is higher when the mother has a diagnosis of myasthenia gravis, even if the mother is asymptomatic (Brueton et al., 1994; Brueton et al., 2000). These findings suggest involvement of specific antibodies (anti-AchR) in Pena Shokeir phenotype. In some cases, however, there is no indication of a family history of Pena Shokeir or maternal myasthenia gravis and etiology is unknown.

There is no treatment for Pena Shokeir phenotype; in the event of a live birth, the life expectancy is exceedingly short. Postnatally, interventions should try to decrease any distress and ensure that the infant is as comfortable as possible. Additional interventions should be directed at helping the family deal with their loss as well as genetic counseling.

REFERENCES

Brueton, L., Huson, S., Thompson, E., Vincent, A., Haawke, S., Price, J., et al. (1994). Myasthenia gravis: an important cause of the Pena-Shokeir phenotype. *Journal of Medical Genetics, 31,* 167.

Brueton, L., Huson, S. M., Cox, P. M., Shirley, I., Thompson, M. E., Barnes, P. R. J., et al. (2000). Asymptomatic maternal myasthenia as a cause of the Pena-Shokeir phenotype. *American Journal of Medical Genetics, 92,* 1–6.

Hagerman, G., Willemse, J., van Ketel, B. A., Barth, P. G., & Lindhout, D. (1987). The heterogeneity of the Pena-Shokeir syndrome. *Neuropediatrics, 18,* 45–50.

Hall, J. G. (1986). Analysis of Pena-Shokeir phenotype. *American Journal of Medical Genetics, 25,* 99–117.

Tongsong, T., Chanprapaph, P., & Khunamornpong, S. (2000). Prenatal ultrasound or regional akinesia with Pena-Shokeir phenotype. *Prenatal Diagnosis, 20,* 422–425.

Cynthia A. Riccio
Texas A&M University

PEPCK DEFICIENCY

Mitochondrial PEPCK deficiency is a disorder of carbohydrate metabolism inherited as an autosomal recessive genetic trait. PEPCK is believed to be related to a deficiency of the enzyme phosphoenolpyruvate carboxykinase, a key enzyme in the conversion of proteins and fat to glucose. This enzyme is essential for the functioning of many organs and systems in the body, especially the central nervous system.

Mitochondrial PEPCK deficiency affects males and females in equal numbers. This disorder is extremely rare and very few cases have been reported.

Characteristics

1. Excess acid in the circulating blood (lactic acidemia)
2. Low blood sugar (hypoglycemia)
3. Loss of muscle tone (hypotonia)
4. Abnormal enlargement of the liver (hepatomegaly)
5. Inability to gain weight and grow normally (failure to thrive)
6. Potential developmental delays
7. Possible learning disabilities and visual and hearing impediments
8. Possible mental retardation
9. Progressive dementia observed in some cases

Treatments may involve ketogenic diet, thiamine, and carnitine. Treatment of severe lactic acidosis with dichloroacetate appears to improve certain laboratory tests but does not result in improvement of symptoms. Genetic counseling is recommended and can be quite complex.

Children and adults who have mitochondrial disease experience a vast array of symptoms and special education needs. Although a few may have only mild symptoms such as learning disabilities, others may face more severe problems such as developmental delay, mental retardation, progressive dementia, visual problems, hearing problems, and motor problems associated with poor growth, loss of motor control, or muscle weakness.

With regard to prognosis, among the few reported cases, one patient died during infancy and one patient survived to age 10 with persistent muscular weakness (Lyon, 1996). Research on inborn errors of metabolism in PEPCK deficiency is focused on the cause of the disorder and enzyme replacement therapies that will return missing enzyme(s) to the body and thereby correct the metabolic defect.

REFERENCES

Lyon, G., Adams, R. D., & Kolodny, E. H. (1996). *Neurology of hereditary metabolic diseases of children.* New York: McGraw-Hill.

VIRDETTE L. BRUMM
Children's Hospital, Los Angeles
Keck / USC School of Medicine

PERSEVERATION

Perseveration is defined as the involuntary and pathological persistence of the same verbal response or motor activity regardless of the stimulus or its duration (Mosby, 1998). A child exhibiting perseverative behavior will often continue a task beyond the normal end point and may have difficulty making the transition to another task (Cuneo & Welsch, 1992).

Perseveration is typically considered a subtle indicator or soft sign of neurological abnormalities and is often associated with brain damage or organic mental disorders (Goodwin, 1989). Within the school-age population, this condition is thought to be most common among children who have a learning disability or brain injury (Reynolds, 2000). Perseveration may also be present in schizophrenia as an association disorder (Crider, 1997).

Characteristics

1. Child displays persistent repetition of words, ideas, or activities.
2. Child continues self-initiated or assigned activities beyond a reasonable period and has difficulty making the transition to another activity.
3. Changes in normal routine or schedule may be met with extreme resistance.
4. Perseveration is most often observed during motor activities but may also be present across verbal activities and problem-solving tasks.

The treatment of perseverative behaviors is dependent upon the etiology of the concern. Although perseveration occurs in a small number of normally developing individuals (Ramage, Bayles, Helm-Estabrooks, & Cruz, 1999), it is most often the result of neurological abnormalities resulting in one of three areas of deficit: impaired attention, memory dysfunction, or disordered motor patterns (Hotz & Helm-Estabrooks, 1995). In addition to neurological difficulties, perseveration is also thought to occur as the result of a fear of failure or feeling of anxiety related to a particular task (Reynolds, 2000). Perseveration may also be the result of the repetitive application of a previously rewarding or successful behavior (Painting, 1979).

Treatment for perseveration within the classroom typically begins with a discussion with the student to make the student aware of his or her current behavior and to explain expected or desired behaviors. If such a task is developmentally appropriate, the student should be asked to monitor his or her own behavior along with the teacher or other education professional. This increased self-awareness may help minimize repetitive actions and behavior. Because of the habitual nature of perseveration, a private signal may be worked out between the teacher and student to alert the student when repetitive behavior occurs without drawing unnecessary attention from peers. The student may be reinforced for incremental progress in monitoring and reducing perseverative behavior. In addition to behavioral intervention strategies, it is important to allow a transition period between activities and evaluate the difficulty level of assignments and tasks.

Special education services are typically available to children who exhibit perseverative behavior because of neurological or emotional difficulties; such services are usually available under the disability categories of Specific Learning Disability, Other Health Impaired, Traumatic Brain Injury, Physical Disability, and Emotional Disturbance. For example, a child who continues to print the letter *A* on a writing assignment rather than moving on to other assigned letters or a child who develops the same response patterns to questions regardless of the nature of the question may have a specific intervention strategy developed for him or her as part of an overall individualized education plan.

The severity of neuropsychological abnormalities and emotional difficulties will mediate the effectiveness of intervention efforts. Early intervention and the use of multiple strategies appear to be important factors in the alleviation of perseverative behaviors.

REFERENCES

Crider, A. (1997). Perseveration in schizophrenia. *Schizophrenia Bulletin, 23*(1), 63–74.

Cuneo, K., & Welsch, C. (1992). Perseveration in young children: Developmental and neuropsychological perspectives. *Child Study Journal, 22*(2), 73–92.

Goodwin, D. M. (1989). *A dictionary of neuropsychology.* New York: Springer.

Hotz, G., & Helm-Estabrooks, N. (1995). Perseveration: A review. *Brain Injury, 9*(2), 151–159.

Mosby's Medical, Nursing, and Allied Health Dictionary. (1998). Perseveration. Retrieved from http://web5.infotrac.galegroup.com/itw

Painting, D. H. (1979). Cognitive assessment of children with SLD. In W. Adamson & K. Adamson (Eds.), *A handbook for specific learning disabilities.* New York: Halsted.

Ramage, A., Bayles, K., Helm-Estabrooks, N., & Cruz, R. (1999). Frequency of perseveration in normal subjects. *Brain and Language, 66*(3), 329–340.

Reynolds, C. R. (2000). Perseveration. In C. R. Reynolds & E. Fletcher-Janzen (Eds.), *Encyclopedia of special education* (2nd ed.). New York: Wiley.

Robert L. Rhodes
New Mexico State University

PERVASIVE DEVELOPMENTAL DISORDER

The category of pervasive developmental disorders (PDD) includes autistic disorder, Rett syndrome, Childhood disintegrative disorder (CDD), Asperger's disorder, and pervasive developmental disorder–not otherwise specified (PDDNOS; American Psychiatric Association [APA], 1994). PDD is characterized by impairment during the first few years of life in social, affective, communicative, and cognitive development. It is difficult to estimate an overall prevalence rate for the five disorders due to disagreement regarding different diagnosis. For example, there is some research to suggest that autism and PDDNOS are different points on a continuum (Tsai, 1998).

Prevalence rates for disorders in the PDD category are as follows: Autism and Aspergers together occur in 1 per 1,000 children, Rett syndrome occurs in approximately 1 in 10,000–15,000 (primarily females), and CDD is extremely rare (Tanguay, 2000). The increasing incidence of PDD disorders is due in part to greater knowledge regarding diagnosis and broader diagnostic categories. Social class was thought to affect the occurrence of PDD; however, research indicates that PDD occurs across all social classes (Klinger & Dawson, 1999). PDD is three to four times greater in males than in females and is found all over the world, with similar incidence and prevalence rates regarding gender, social class, and cognitive abilities. Rett syndrome is primarily found in females; few male cases have been documented. Differential diagnosis is needed for disorders within the PDD category as well as several other disorders, including developmental language delay, childhood schizophrenia, a degenerative central nervous system disorder, and Landau-Kleffner syndrome.

Characteristics

1. Deficits in social skills vary in severity depending on the disorder and child characteristics but may include
   - Avoidance of eye contact or contact with other children.
   - Atypical attachment patterns to caregivers.
   - Dampened facial expression and difficulty recognizing emotions from facial expressions of others.
2. Ritualistic or compulsive behaviors such as repetitive behaviors (self-stimulation), unusual persistent interests and activities, or irrational fears.
3. Under- or overresponsiveness to sensory input (noise, taste, texture, visual).
4. Difficulties in speech or language.
   - May include difficulty with prosody.
   - Pronoun reversal.
   - Delayed or immediate echolalia.
   - Difficulties with language pragmatics or social meaning.
   - Language use may be concrete and literal only.
5. Cognitive deficits (IQ < 70) have a comorbidity rate as high as 89%.

Source: APA (1994); Klinger & Dawson (1999).

In conjunction with the need for differential diagnosis, several disorders may be comorbid with the PDD, such as mental retardation, ADHD, obsessive-compulsive disorder, anxiety disorders, and Tourette syndrome (Bernet & Dulcan, 1999). The need for additional diagnosis for children with PDD is debated.

PDD describes a set of neurological disorders, but the exact nature of the disorders is unknown at this time (Tanguay, 2000). Treatments for PDD are designed to address deficits and improve symptoms, but there is no known cure. Treatment plans are multidimensional, often including behavior modification, medications, speech therapy, occupational therapy, counseling, and structured education programs. Many children have problems generalizing information across settings and may need assistance with generalizing skills.

In 1990, the Individuals with Disabilities Education Act (IDEA) recognized autism and a distinct entity defined as "a disorder characterized by extreme withdrawal, self-stimulation, cognitive deficits, language disorders, and onset before the age of thirty months" (IDEA, 1997). Children with PDD need consistent, structured classes that present information verbally and visually. Visual (i.e., pictorial) class schedules can be helpful. Typically developing peers often can model appropriate social interaction and language. Modifications to curriculum should be based on the child's individual strengths and weaknesses.

Individual prognosis varies greatly depending on severity and the specific diagnosis. A child with autism or Aspergers who has few cognitive deficits may live independently as an adult with few noticeable symptoms. In contrast, a child who develops Rett syndrome will need long-term care, and 26% die prematurely (Tanguay, 2000).

Future research may improve assessment techniques, refine diagnosis, and investigate possible causal factors. Increased understanding of genetic, biological, and environmental factors that contribute to these disorders will improve treatment options available to children diagnosed with a PDD and to their families.

REFERENCES

American Psychiatric Association. (1994). *Diagnostic and statistical manual of mental disorders.* (4th ed.), Washington, DC: Author.

Bernet, W. D., & Dulcan, M. K. (1999). Practice parameters for the assessment and treatment of children, adolescents, and adults with autism and other pervasive developmental disorders. *Journal of American Academy of Child & Adolescent Psychiatry, 38*(12), 32S–54S.

Individuals with Disabilities Education Act, 20 U.S.C. § 33 (1997).

Klinger, L. G., & Dawson, G. (1999). Childhood disorders. In E. J. Mash & R. A. Barkley (Eds.), *Child psychopathology* (pp. 196–241). New York: Guilford Press.

Tanguay, P. E. (2000). Pervasive developmental disorders: A 10-year review. *Journal of the American Academy of Child & Adolescent Psychiatry, 39*(9), 1079–1095.

Tsai, L. Y. (2001, May 15). Pervasive developmental disorders: National information center for children and youth with disabilities. Retrieved from http://www.nichy.org/pubs/factshe/fs20txt.htm

Monica E. Wolfe
Texas A&M University

See also Aspergers Syndrome; Childhood Disintegrative Disorder; Rett Syndrome

PETERS'-PLUS SYNDROME

Peters'-plus syndrome, also known as Peter's syndrome, is widely believed to be an autosomal recessively inherited disorder (Camera, Pozzolo, Carta, & Righi, 1994; Hennekam et al., 1993) and thus occurs infrequently. Currently there appears to be some consensus that Peters'-plus syndrome and Krause-Kivlin Syndrome (or Kivlin syndrome) are the same disorder (Frydman, Weinstock, Cohen, Savir, & Varsano, 1991; Thompson, Winter, & Baraitser, 1993). Peters'-Plus Syndrome is characterized by a typical face, short limb dwarfism, Peter's anomaly (a corneal abnormality), and growth retardation. In many cases, cleft lip and palate, visceral anomalies, and mental retardation are also present (Camera et al., 1994; Hennekan et al., 1993). Increased incidence of fetal loss in families in which Peters'-plus syndrome is present suggests the intrauterine death of some fetuses affected by Peters'-plus syndrome (Hennekan et al., 1993).

Characteristics

1. Typical face: round face in childhood, hypertelorism, short palepebral fissures, long philtrum, "cupid's bow" upper lip with thin vermilion border.
2. Peters' anomaly or anterior chamber cleavage—often results in clouded vision or blindness. This condition is sometimes improved by surgery.
3. Short-limb dwarfism.
4. Growth retardation.
5. Visceral abnormalities, mental retardation, and cleft palate are often present.

Peters'-Plus Syndrome is rare, but prevalence is unclear. Attempts at estimation based upon clinical literature are unreliable because the syndrome has been described under a variety of names. In addition, the possibility of increased incidence of fetal death suggests that many cases may go unrecognized. There is no evidence that this syndrome is more common among specific ethnicities, although no cases of African origin were reported in the literature. Although Hennekan et al. (1993) cite an increased incidence of fetal loss and increased infant mortality in those with visceral anomalies, the mortality rate among those who live past early infancy does not appear to be significant. Despite consensus that Peters'-plus syndrome is an autosomal recessive disorder, chromosomal location is yet to be determined and cause is unknown (Hennekan et al., 1993).

Currently, there is no treatment that targets the syndrome in total; instead, treatment focuses on amelioration of the individual symptoms of the syndrome. For example, those children born with Peters' anomaly often undergo surgery to optimize vision. Thompson notes the importance of regular vision screening for this population because eye abnormalities often worsen with age. Treatment is also likely to target cleft palate and visceral abnormalities when they are present.

Many children with Peters'-plus syndrome may qualify for special education services under the 504 provision for the handicapping conditions of Other Health Impaired or Physical Disability. As with medical treatment, special education accommodations will vary according to the child's symptomatology. For many children with Peters'-plus syndrome, extensive medical treatment will result in frequent absences from school. Because visual abnormalities are a characteristic of this syndrome, accommodations should be made accordingly. There have been no behavioral difficulties

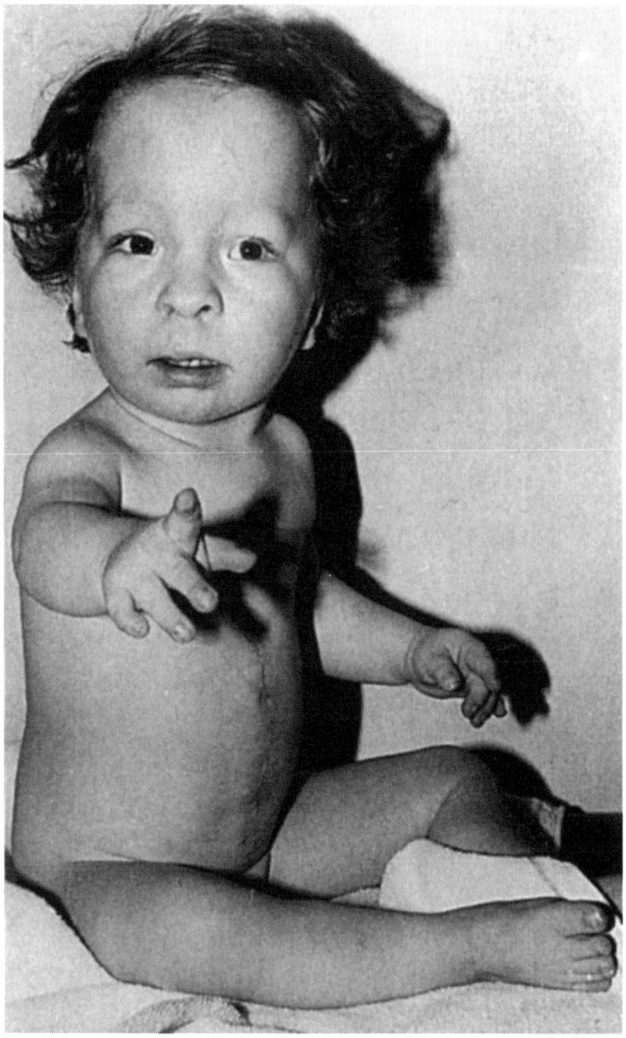

Peters'-Plus Syndrome
Reprinted from *Clinical Syndromes*, Wiedemann and Kunze, 1997, by permission of the publisher Mosby

associated with Peters'-plus syndrome; in fact, several cases were reported to be friendly and pleasant in personality.

REFERENCES

Camera, G., Pozzolo, S., Carta, M., & Righi, E. (1994). Peters'-plus syndrome: Report on an unusual case. *Pathologica, 86,* 637–675.

Frydman, M., Weinstock, A. L., Cohen, H. A., Savir, H., & Varsano, I. (1991). Autosomal recessive peters anomaly, typical facial appearance, failure to thrive, hydrocephalus, and other anomalies: Further delineation of the Krause-Klivin syndrome. *American Journal of Medical Genetics, 40,* 34–40.

Hennekan, R. C. M., Van Schooneveld, M. J., Ardinger, H. H., Van Den Boogaard, M.-J. H., Friedburg, D., Rudnik-Schoneborn, S., et al. (1993). The peters'-plus syndrome: Description of 16 patients and review of the literature. *Clinical Dysmorphology, 2,* 283–300.

Thompson, E. M., Winter, R. M., & Baraitser, M. (1993). Klivin syndrome and peters'-plus syndrome: Are they the same disorder? *Clinical Dysmorphology, 2,* 301–316.

Melanie E. Ballatore
University of Texas at Austin

PEUTZ-JEGHERS SYNDROME

Peutz-Jeghers syndrome (PJS) is a rare, heritable condition typified by abnormal pigmentation (freckling) around and inside the mouth and hamartomatous polyps of the gastrointestinal (GI) tract. Hamartomas are benign tumors of embryonic origin and are caused by anomalous development of organ tissues.

PJS is associated with a defective gene responsible for the production of the enzyme serine-threonine kinase. Patients with PJS have an unusual predisposition to malignant disease. This clinical manifestation of the disorder is felt to be linked to the protein kinase deficiency.

PJS is rare. No data are available regarding its precise incidence in the general population. The mode of transmission is autosomal dominant. Fresh genetic mutations have accounted for almost half of the reported cases of PJS.

Characteristics

1. Blue-gray or brownish spots on the lips, around the mouth, and on the buccal mucosa (the moist tissue that covers the inside of the cheeks). The palate, gums, and tongue are less commonly involved. Abnormal pigmentary changes may also appear on the nose, hands, fingers, feet, perianal areas, and genital areas. Buccal mucosal findings are most suggestive of the syndrome. Freckling appears in infancy or early childhood and resolves during puberty.
2. Polyps occur (in order of decreasing frequency) in the small intestine, colon, and stomach. Solitary or multiple lesions may be present. These tumors are *not* premalignant. Polyps may occasionally appear in the nose, urinary bladder, bile duct, and bronchus. 70% of patients with GI polyps will have symptoms by age 20. Colicky abdominal pain and bleeding into the GI tract are the most common findings. Iron deficiency anemia may develop secondary to chronic blood loss.
3. 50% of patients with PJS will have to deal with a malignancy. 25% of them will develop cancer before age 30. The sites most commonly involved are the GI tract, lung, thyroid gland, gallbladder, breast, pancreas, cervix, ovary, and testicle. The majority of cancers are in middle-aged individuals.
4. Clubbing (broadening and thickening of the ends of the fingers).

GI polyps that are symptomatic need removal. Surgical excision of these tumors is indicated if they cause significant bleeding, obstruction, or severe and recurrent abdominal pain. Screening for malignant disease is essential. Endoscopy (looking into the upper and lower GI tract with a flexible fiber-optic scope) and barium studies are the procedures of choice for monitoring gut status. In female patients, pelvic ultrasound can detect ovarian abnormalities. Periodic screening of males for testicular cancer and education regarding self examination are important. Women should also be taught how to check themselves for breast tumors. Malignant lesions may require surgery, irradiation, chemotherapy, or a combined therapeutic approach for the best outcome. Finally, because PJS has such a high incidence of severe clinical manifestations and affected individuals a 50% likelihood of passing the abnormal gene on to offspring, genetic counseling should be arranged for affected families.

There is no research to indicate cognitive deficits are associated with PJS.

Although an occasional patient with PJS may have pigmentary changes as the only sign of the disorder, most must go through life with the black cloud of cancer hanging over them. Therefore, the prognosis for this syndrome should be considered guarded.

REFERENCES

Darmstadt, G. L. (2000). Hyperpigmented lesions. In R. E. Behrman, R. M. Kleigman, & H. B. Jenson (Eds.), *Nelson textbook of pediatrics* (16th ed., p. 1984). Philadelphia: W. B. Saunders.

Gandy, A. Peutz-Jeghers syndrome: Disease database. Retrieved from http://www.pedianet.com/news/illness/disease/files/peutzje.htm

Jones, K. (1997). *Smith's recognizable patterns of human malformation* (5th ed.). Philadelphia: W. B. Saunders.

National Organization for Rare Disorders. (1999). Peutz-Jeghers syndrome. Retrieved from http://www.stepstn.com/cgi-win/nord.exe?proc=GetDocument&rectype=0&recnum=149

Ulshen, M. (2000). Tumors of the digestive tract. In R. E. Behrman, R. M. Kleigman, & H. B. Jenson (Eds.), *Nelson textbook of pediatrics* (16th ed., pp. 1183–1184). Philadelphia: W. B. Saunders.

Barry H. Davison
Ennis, Texas

Joan W. Mayfield
Baylor Pediatric Specialty Services
Dallas, Texas

PFEIFFER SYNDROME

Pfeiffer syndrome is one of the acrocephalosyndactyly syndromes (Apert syndrome, Apert-Crouzon syndrome, Chotzen syndrome) characterized by craniosynostosis, mild syndactyly of the hands and feet, and newborn dysmorphic facial features. Pfeiffer syndrome was first described in 1964 by R. A. Pfeiffer (Pedlynx, 2002).

The incidence of this disorder is not known, but there have been 30 cases published. Males and females are equally affected. The etiology is due to an autosomal dominant inheritance as well as to sporadic incidence due to fresh gene mutation (Jones, 1997).

The major diagnostic criteria in Pfeiffer syndrome are craniosynostosis and syndactyly, plus malformations of the thumb and great toe (coarse, broad, short, and usually deviated medially); there is a wide range of expressivity of phenotypes (Weideman, Kunze, & Dibben, 1992).

Characteristics

1. Acrocephaly (cone-shaped head)
2. Brachycephaly (shortened A-P diameter)
3. High prominent forehead
4. Mild soft tissue syndactyly usually involving the second and third digits of the hands and feet
5. Flattened face with maxillary hypoplasia
6. Low-set ears
7. Hearing loss (mild)
8. Down-slanting palpebral fissures
9. Prominent eyes
10. Hypertelorism
11. Strabismus
12. Depressed nasal bridge
13. Beaked nose
14. High-arched palate
15. Crowded teeth
16. Short, broad thumbs and great toes that are often malformed (rudimentary, duplicated, absent) and deviated medially (hallux varus)
17. Normal intelligence in a majority of cases
18. Complications may include hydrocephalus, seizures, or both

There is essentially no treatment for the underlying disorder, and treatments such as craniotomy, corrective surgery, and cosmetic surgery are obviously individualized. Genetic counseling is recommended because the recurrence risk is not elevated with unaffected parents but is 50% with one affected parent (Pedlynx, 2002).

Special education programming may be required due to occasional incidence of seizures and mental retardation with certain subtypes of Pfeiffer syndrome. An individualized assessment and individual education plan would address the sequelae of these conditions. The craniofacial appearance tends to improve with age with this syndrome;

however, supportive counseling with the child and family would assist in adjustments to the demands of everyday living. The prognosis for children with Pfeiffer syndrome depends on the severity of the condition but on the whole is favorable (Jones, 1997).

REFERENCES

Jones, K. L. (1997). *Smith's recognizable patterns of human malformation* (5th ed.). pp. 78–79.

Pedlynx. (2002). XXX syndrome. Retrieved from http://www.iconodata.com/health/pedbase/files/XXXSYNDR.HTM

Wiedemann, H., Kunze, J., & Dibben, H. (1992). *Atlas of clinical syndromes: A visual aid to diagnosis* (2nd ed.). St. Louis, MO: Mosby.

Elaine Fletcher-Janzen
University of Northern Colorado

PHENCYCLIDINE (PCP) ABUSE

Phencyclidine (PCP) was originally developed as an intravenous surgical anesthetic in the 1950s. It was used routinely in veterinary medicine, but clinical trials with humans were discontinued in 1965 due to a number of adverse side effects, including agitation, delirium, and irrational behavior (National Institute on Drug Abuse, 2001b). It is classified as a dissociative anesthetic because users experience a trancelike, out-of-body feeling as well as a detachment from their environment (National Institute on Drug Abuse, 2001a).

First introduced as a street drug in the 1960s (Brust, 1993), PCP was initially widely abused in pill form. However, because of the delay in feeling the effects of the drug after ingesting it, illicit use of this form of PCP receded (National Institute on Drug Abuse, 2001a). Since the 1970s, PCP has typically been sold on the streets as a white crystalline powder, although it is sometimes colored with water-soluable dyes. Phencyclidine can be snorted, smoked, or eaten. When smoked, PCP is mixed with a leafy material such as marijuana, oregano, parsley, or tobacco. Street names for PCP include angel dust, ozone, wack, and rocket fuel. When combined with marijuana, PCP is referred to as crystal supergrass and killer joints (National Institute on Drug Abuse, 2001b).

The chemical PCP produces its mind-altering and dissociative effects by altering the distribution of a neurotransmitter, glutamate, in the brain. Glutamate carries messages from one nerve cell to another and is involved in the perception of pain, learning and memory, emotions, and responses to the environment. Phencyclidine also appears to alter the actions of dopamine, another neurotransmitter responsible for the high associated with many abused drugs (National Institute on Drug Abuse, 2001a). Phencyclidine is highly addictive and its use can lead to craving and compulsive PCP-seeking behavior (National Institute on Drug Abuse, 2001b).

Since the early 1980s, illicit use of PCP has declined substantially (National Institute on Drug Abuse, 1990), in part due to its unpredictable and potentially negative effects. Research evaluating trends in PCP use indicate that past year use among high school seniors has decreased from 7.0% in 1979 to 2.3% in 1997 (National Institute on Drug Abuse, 2001b). Data related to lifetime use indicate that 1.2% of youth between the ages of 12 and 17 have used PCP at least once.

The effects of PCP are both complex and dose-dependent. PCP use can result in tranquilizing and anesthetic effects similar to those produced by heroin use, hallucinogenic effects similar to those produced by LSD, amphetamine- or cocaine-like arousal, or any combination of these effects (Giannini, 1998).

Characteristics

Short-term effects (low to moderate doses):

1. Euphoria
2. Increased breathing rate
3. Pronounced rise in blood pressure and heart rate
4. Generalized numbness of the extremities
5. Flushing and profuse sweating
6. Muscular incoordination
7. Agitation, anxiety, and excitation
8. Distinct changes in body awareness
9. Disinhibition

Short-term effects (high doses):

1. Pronounced drop in blood pressure, heart rate, and respiration
2. Nausea and vomiting
3. Blurred vision, dizziness, and loss of balance
4. Decreased awareness of pain
5. Detachment from reality
6. Hallucinations and delusions
7. Violent or suicidal behavior
8. Seizures, coma, and death

Smoking or snorting PCP allows the drug to pass rapidly into the brain so that the effects are felt within a few minutes. These effects typically last for a few hours, although some users report feeling the effects for days (National Institute on Drug Abuse, 2001a).

Characteristics

Long-term effects:

1. Addiction
2. Memory loss
3. Depression and other mood disorders
4. Difficulties with speech and thinking
5. Weight loss

In addition to the aforementioned effects, PCP use can produce psychoses very similar to schizophrenia. This PCP-induced psychosis can last for weeks despite abstinence (see Stenpreis, 1996, for a review). In adolescents, PCP use may interfere with hormones related to normal growth and development as well as with the learning process (National Institute on Drug Abuse, 2001a).

A tolerance to PCP develops with repeated or prolonged use. Withdrawal symptoms generally include craving the drug, cold sweats, tremor, anxiousness, and gastrointestinal upset (Brust, 1993). Treatment of acute PCP intoxication is generally aimed at decreasing the intensity and duration of specific negative symptoms. A calm, darkened room can be helpful in alleviating agitation and some psychotic symptoms. Antipsychotic medications can also be helpful. Gastric suctioning and activated charcoal are used for gastrointestinal problems that may result from PCP use. Restraints may be necessary to prevent the PCP user from hurting him- or herself and others (Brust, 1993).

Current research is focused on developing medications that blunt the effects of PCP use. Developing a drug that could detoxify PCP abusers quickly and efficiently would reduce the harm that the abuser could inflict on him- or herself and others. In addition, decreasing the pleasurable effects of the drug is hoped to reduce the incentive to use it again. In addition, researchers are attempting to develop comprehensive treatment programs that include both behavioral approaches and medications (Mathias, 2000).

REFERENCES

Brust, J. (1993). Other agents: Phencyclidine, marijuana, hallucinogens, inhalants, and anticholinergics. *Neurologic Clinics, 11*(3), 555–561.

Giannini, A. J. (1998). Phencyclidine. In R. E. Tarter, R. T. Ammerman, and P. J. Ott (Eds.), *Handbook of substance abuse: Neurobehavioral pharmacology* (pp. 579–587). New York: Plenum Press.

Mathias, R. (2000). Antibody may treat PCP overdose and abuse, also block prenatal harm. Retrieved from http://165.112.78.61/NIDA_Notes/NNVol15N2/Antibody.html

National Institute on Drug Abuse (1990). *Semi-annual report: Emergency room data January 1997–December 1989, medical examiner data July 1986–June 1989.* Rockville, MD: US Department of Health and Human Services.

National Institute on Drug Abuse. (2001a). Hallucinogens and dissociative drugs. Retrieved from http://www.nida.nih.gov/ResearchReports/Hallucinogens/Hallucinogens.html

National Institute on Drug Abuse. (2001b). PCP (Phencyclidine). Retrieved from http://www.drugabuse.gov/Infofax/pcp.html

Stenpreis, R. E. (1996). The behavioral and neurochemical effects of phencyclidine in humans and animals: Some implications for modeling psychosis. *Behavioural Brain Research, 74,* 45–55.

M. Franci Crepeau-Hobson
University of Northern Colorado

PHENYLKETONURIA

Phenylketonuria (PKU) is the most common of all aminoacidopathies and is caused by autosomal recessive deficiency of the hepatic phenylalanine hydroxylase system (DeFreitas, Izumi, Lara, & Greene, 1999). This metabolic abnormality results from a markedly reduced activity (< 2% of normal) of phenylalanine hydroxylase, the hepatic enzyme that converts phenylalanine to tyrosine (Hsia, 1966). The deficiency of this enzyme results in toxic levels of phenylalanine in the blood and a potential deficiency of the amino acid tyrosine. If treatment is not begun in the early days following birth, mental retardation, microcephaly, epilepsy, tremors, hypopigmentation of skin, and hyperactivity can occur (DeFreitas et al., 1999).

PKU is an autosomal recessive inborn error of metabolism that occurs in approximately 1 in 10,000 births each year in Anglo-Americans and Asian Americans, but its incidence is much lower in African Americans (Batshaw, 1997). Neonatal screening for blood phenylalanine levels continues to be the primary strategy for the diagnosis of PKU. An individualized diagnosis that characterizes the severity of the disease in each patient provides objective and effective criteria for the dietary treatment of each particular case (DeFreitas et al., 1999). When dietary treatment with phenylalanine restriction is started early, the child can achieve close-to-normal development (DeFreitas et al., 1999). It has long been recommended that individuals with PKU follow dietary restrictions during the first 5–6 years of life, when brain growth is most rapid (Sheard, 2000). Continuation of the diet after this time also appears to be beneficial because loss of IQ, behavioral changes, or both have been reported in older children and adolescents who did not adhere to the diet (Sheard, 2000).

Characteristics

1. Disorder manifestation between the 3rd and 6th month of age
2. Microcephaly

3. Abnormal electroencephalogram
4. Eczema
5. Varying degrees of mental retardation
6. Hyperactivity
7. Neuropsychological deficits similar to those found in children with brain injury such as frontal-lobe syndrome and deficits in executive functions
8. Perceptual-motor deficits
9. Arithmetic deficits
10. Visuospatial skill deficits

In most PKU cases, the control of phenylalanine ingestion is sufficient to avert mental retardation. Some patients, however, do not respond to dietary treatment. Such cases have led to the discovery of other types of PKU (DeFreitas et al., 1999). It is important to distinguish among types of PKU because a correct diagnosis will determine the most appropriate treatment for each case (DeFreitas et al., 1999). The identification of Types 4 and 5 is particularly important because these variants do not respond to treatment with dietary phenylalanine restriction and therefore require other therapies.

Dietary phenylalanine restriction requires restriction of protein-rich foods, especially those of animal origin. It is important to note that phenylalanine is an essential amino acid and therefore should be present in the diet, albeit in controlled amounts. The recommended amount of phenylalanine depends on the characteristics of each patient. Monitoring blood phenylalanine levels is very important in planning the diet for each patient (DeFreitas et al., 1999).

In terms of adolescent females and maternal phenylketonuria, early diagnosis together with treatment and follow-up has resulted in a growing number of women with PKU who have a normal life during their fertile years. It has been well established that lack of treatment of pregnant women with PKU will lead to fetal microcephaly, congenital heart disease, and retarded growth. It is important to achieve early metabolic control during pregnancy in women with PKU because as metabolic control improves and delays in achieving control are reduced, cognitive and behavioral outcomes improve in their offspring.

Rigorous dietary control beginning before conception and continuing throughout pregnancy is recommended. The treatment of maternal PKU consists mainly of dietary phenylalanine restriction, although it has been suggested that additional educational and social support lead to more successful changes in behavior and attitudes, with subsequent better treatment compliance. In addition to phenylalanine restriction, supplementation with tyrosine has been proposed because a low plasma concentration of tyrosine may be a determinant factor in terms of injury to the fetus in maternal PKU (DeFreitas et al., 1999).

Special education may not be necessary in well-controlled cases. However, school personnel may have to support dietary restrictions because recent research now supports lifelong dietary restrictions as opposed to former practice that discontinued the diet at around age 8. Special education programming will be necessary for those children who have been identified late or children whose diets may have been less than adequate.

Future research should address the following issues: From a practical point of view, DNA studies should permit the development of easy and accessible diagnostic methods and genetic engineering (DeFreitas et al., 1999). Enzymatic treatment is one alternative treatment that is being investigated. It is difficult, however, to obtain this enzyme in stable form and in large amounts in purified form. An important unresolved issue, however, is how to motivate and support women with PKU to make the necessary dietary changes that will result in the best developmental outcome in their children.

REFERENCES

Batshaw, M. L. (1997). PKU and other inborn errors of metabolism. In M. L. Batshaw (Ed.), *Children with disabilities* (4th ed., pp. 389–404). Baltimore: Brookes.

DeFreitas, O., Izumi, C., Lara, G. L., & Greene, L. J. (1999). New approaches to the treatment of phenylketonuria. *Nutrition Reviews, 57,* 65–70.

Hsia, D. Y. Phenylketonuria: A study of human biochemical genetics. *Pediatrics, 38,* 173–184.

Sheard, N. F. (2000). Importance of diet in maternal phenylketonuria. *Nutritional Reviews, 58,* 236–239.

Michael La Conte
District 11 Public Schools
Colorado Springs, Colorado

PHENYLKETONURIA, MATERNAL

Phenylketonuria (PKU) is an autosomal recessive inborn error of metabolism in which a person cannot metabolize phenylalanine (Phe) into tyrosine and its constituent components. As a result, Phe accumulates in the blood, causing widespread brain damage, consequent severe mental retardation, and other organic problems. Before birth, nutrients are metabolized by the mother and transmitted through the umbilical cord, so damage begins only when the newborn begins to feed. In the 1960s, national screening of newborns for PKU and treatment of affected individuals with a synthetic diet low in Phe prevented much damage associated with this disorder. The initial protocol called for affected individuals to stay on the diet until late childhood or early adolescence, after which they could eat normal food because brain development was thought to be complete. However, the diet did not cure the disorder, and Phe then began to accumulate in their blood. Most treated adults have low average intelligence and live near-normal lives.

Characteristics

1. Microcephaly
2. Mental retardation
3. Intrauterine growth retardation
4. Congenital heart defects
5. Craniofacial dysmorphologies

Maternal PKU (MPKU) is an iatrogenic aspect of the treatment of PKU. Because of the success of the identification and treatment programs, about 3,000 childbearing-age women in the United States have treated PKU (Maternal PKU Collaborative, 1997). Because most have gone off the special diet, during pregnancy they transmit high levels of Phe through the umbilical cord to the embryo and fetus. The likelihood that an offspring of a PKU mother will have PKU itself is relatively low (about 1 in 120), but nutrients (including unmetabolized Phe) enter the embryo's bloodstream antenatally. Phe is teratogenic, and offspring are at high risk for severe defects. Percentages of newborns in a collaborative MPKU study of various defects were the following: spontaneous miscarriage, 24%; intrauterine growth retardation, 40%; microcephaly, 73%; mental retardation, 92%; and congenital heart defects, 10%. Survivors were also at risk for growth retardation, neurological disorders, and minor craniofacial dysmorphologies. Frequency and severity of abnormalities were apparently correlated with the degree of maternal Phe levels during pregnancy (American Academy of Pediatrics Committee on Genetics, 2001). Furthermore, even women with PKU whose Phe levels have been partially controlled during pregnancy are at risk for having offspring with serious problems. In a collaborative study, maternal levels of phenylalanine during Weeks 4–8 of gestation were controlled at an average level well below the uncontrolled levels. Of the offspring, 7.5% had congenital heart defects, and of those, 55% also had microcephaly. Of those without congenital heart disease, 31% had microcephaly. Again, degree of offspring defects was correlated with maternal level of Phe during pregnancy. To reduce defects further, women with PKU who could become pregnant need to have Phe levels maintained at an even lower level (Rouse et al., 2000).

Children with MPKU effects who also test positive for PKU should be placed on the special diet immediately to reduce further damage. Because effects of MPKU are irreversible, prognosis depends on the degree of early impairment. After impairment occurs, only supportive treatment is available. Many affected individuals will need various types of special education. Inclusion will be appropriate in many cases, but others will require separate classroom placement.

Currently the best treatment is prevention. Women with PKU who have been treated with the special diet must be informed of the risk of high levels of Phe to their offspring and urged to seek medical and nutritional advice before becoming pregnant. Unfortunately, prenatal control of Phe levels is difficult, and women with treated PKU are at risk for unplanned and uncontrolled pregnancy: "Unplanned pregnancies, avoidance of birth control, failure to begin treatment before pregnancy, and inadequately controlled metabolic levels were distressingly frequent among the women with phenylketonuria in our study" (Waisbren, Hamilton, St. James, Shiloh, & Levy, 1995, p. 1641).

REFERENCES

American Academy of Pediatrics Committee on Genetics. (2001). Maternal phenylketonuria. *Pediatrics, 107,* 427–428.

Rouse, B., Matalon, R., Koch, R., Azen, C., Levy, H., Hanley, W., et al. (2000). Maternal phenylketonuria syndrome: Congenital heart defects, microcephaly, and developmental outcomes. *Pediatrics, 136,* 57–61.

Waisbren, S. E., Hamilton, B. D., St. James, P. J., Shiloh, S., & Levy, H. L. (1995). Psychosocial factors in maternal phenylketonuria: Women's adherence to medical recommendations. *American Journal of Public Health, 85,* 1636–1642.

Amy Morrow
Robert T. Brown
University of North Carolina, Wilmington

PHOBIAS

Specific phobias are persistent fears of clearly identified circumscribed objects or situations, usually leading to an immediate anxiety response and avoidance of the stimulus. Common specific phobias in children include fears of the dark; weather-related phenomena such as thunder and lightning; doctors, dentists, or medical procedures requiring physical contact; and animals or insects. The focus of the fear may be some expected harm from the object or situation (e.g., fear of dogs associated with a fear of being bitten). The diagnosis is not warranted unless the child's fears reflect clinically significant impairment—for example, school refusal or excessive fear of going out to play because an encounter with an animal may occur. To differentiate between specific phobias and other anxiety disorders in children, the child's fear may not be related to other fears such as panic attacks, social humiliation-embarrassment, or separation from a parent. Specific phobias may also vary as a function of beliefs associated with different cultures and ethnic groups. Fears of supernatural phenomena (i.e., spirits, etc.) should only be considered a specific phobia only if they are obviously in excess of cultural norms and cause significant impairment. Specific phobias may provoke panic attacks, especially if the person perceives that there is no escape. Anxiety is invariably experienced immediately when encountering the feared stimulus and may be expressed by crying, tantrums, or freezing or clinging behavior. Children often do not recognize that the fears are excessive or unreasonable and typically do not verbally express distress about the phobias.

The combined prevalence rates for anxiety disorders in children is higher than that for virtually all other mental disorders of childhood and adolescence (Surgeon Generals Report, 2000). A 1-year prevalence rate for specific phobias of 9% has been reported, with lifetime rates varying from 10–11.3%. Age of onset tends to be bimodal, with a peak in childhood for phobias associated with heights, animals, and possible sighting of blood or contact with doctors. Whereas children normally exhibit a surprisingly large number of fears, the prevalence rates of intense fears range from under 1–5% across the general population. Ratio of males to females varies by specific phobia type; 75–90% of animal phobias are reported by females, whereas males report 25–45% of medically related phobias.

Characteristics

1. Marked and persistent fear of a specific object or situation that is excessive or unreasonable. The fear is cued by the actual presence or the anticipation of the feared object or situation.
2. Exposure to the stimulus provokes an immediate anxiety response expressed in children by crying, clinging, or tantrums.
3. In adolescent and older individuals, the individual must recognize that the response is excessive, although children may not achieve that insight.
4. Avoiding the phobic situation or enduring the stimulus under extreme duress.
5. Children must experience symptoms for at least 6 months.
6. Specific phobias are further classified under animal, blood injection or injury, natural environment, situational, and other stimuli.

Source: Adapted from American Psychiatric Association (1994).

Although initial descriptions and proposed treatments originated from Freud's psychodynamic theory, most successful treatment of specific phobias has largely occurred from within the behavioral and cognitive-behavioral perspectives. One of the most successful treatments for a specific phobia is systematic desensitization (Ollendick & King, 1998). Variants of systematic desensitization include imaginal desensitization, in vivo desensitization, and emotive imagery. Modeling treatments based on social learning theory require that the child visually observe a peer interacting adaptively with the feared object and gradually participating with the peer in making gradual contact with the feared object or situation. Contingency management with reinforced practice introduces a positive consequence following interaction with the feared stimulus and no positive consequences for avoidance of the same stimulus. Cognitive-behavioral treatments for specific phobias have been most recently represented by the work of Kendall (1997) and Dadds (1997). Kendall documented the effectiveness of a 16- to 20-week program using a combination of self-talk strategies, recognition of symptoms, challenging self-talk, and previously described behavioral treatments. Dadds has included a family component with a specific parent-training program. Pharmacological treatments for specific phobias follow the general pattern of use for other anxiety disorders but are often relegated to a secondary role in treatment.

Special education support services may be available to children diagnosed with a specific phobia under specific categories of Other Health Impaired, Severe Emotional Disturbance, or Behavior Disorder if an impact on the child's education can be established. Such services may be particularly important if the disorder is chronic in nature. Accommodations may also be requested and provided under Section 504 of the Rehabilitation Act of 1973. Families can benefit from additional counseling and support to effectively implement a treatment plan across both school and home settings.

Information on the natural course of specific phobias is limited. The general impressions that specific phobias in children are relatively harmless and that improvement will occur over time with or without treatment have been modified on the basis of retrospective reports from adults with the disorder. With the exception of claustrophobia, specific phobias have the earliest age of onset and occurrence during childhood, and for some individuals, they persist over time. Most of the available literature deals with fears and phobias of mild to moderate levels of intensity; treatment of specific phobias of a severe nature is underrepresented. There is some evidence to suggest that aggregate groups of first-degree biological family members report similar patterns of specific phobias.

REFERENCES

American Psychiatric Association. (1994). *Diagnostic and Statistical Manual of Mental Disorders.* (4th ed.). Washington, DC: Author.

Ollendick, T. H., & King, N. J. (1998). Empirically supported treatments for children with phobic and anxiety disorders: Current status. *Journal of Clinical Child Psychology, 27,* 156–167.

Daniel Olympia
University of Utah

PICA

The word *pica* originates from the Latin word for magpie, a bird known for ingesting a wide variety of food and nonfood items (Danford & Huber, 1982). Pica as a disorder is characterized by habitual ingestion of inedible substances (Kerwin & Berkowitz, 1996). Frequently associated with mental retardation (Danford & Huber, 1982), it also occurs in normal young children (younger than age 3) and in pregnant women in certain cultural groups. For example, in infancy and early childhood, children often chew on their cribs, wood, sand, and grass as a method of early exploration (Erickson, 1998). Pica sometimes continues into adolescence and adulthood (Diamond & Stermer, 1998).

Prevalence is not known, but pica may be both underdiagnosed and undertreated (Katsiyannis, Torrey, & Bond, 1998). In the United States, it occurs more often in individuals from low socioeconomic backgrounds. Eating of nonnutritive material may meet nutritional or cultural needs. In the United States, it may occur in cases of iron-deficiency anemia and deficiencies in nutrients such as zinc (Rose, Porcerelli, & Neale, 2000). The practice of eating soil is termed *geophagy* and may relieve hunger, provide grit for grinding food, provide nutritional value, cure diarrhea, buffer stomach contents, or protect against toxins. In the southeastern United States, pregnant women may eat clay or laundry starch because of a superstitious belief that the practice prevents fetal curses and reduces the side effects of pregnancy (see Webster & Brown, 2000, for a summary).

Characteristics

1. Persistent eating of nonnutritive substances.
2. Eating of nonnutritive substances is inappropriate for the individual's developmental level and culture.
3. Eating of nonnutritive substances is not associated with normal hunger or avoidance of food.

Diagnosis may be difficult because it often rests on self-reports of pica behavior, and affected individuals may be reluctant or unable to report the behavior. Frequently, diagnosis occurs only after the individual presents with medical complications. Although medical assessment may strongly suggest pica, confirmation rests upon reports by the affected individual, parents, or a caregiver (Rose et al., 2000). The first two characteristics listed are diagnostic criteria of the *Diagnostic and Statistical Manual of Mental Disorders–Fourth Edition* (*DSM-IV;* American Psychiatric Association [APA], 1994). The *DSM-IV* also states that if pica behavior occurs with another mental disorder (e.g., mental retardation, pervasive developmental disorder, schizophrenia), it should be sufficiently severe to warrant independent clinical attention to justify a separate diagnosis.

Pica can be life threatening or can contribute to the development of other disorders, depending on the items eaten, and its risks should not be underestimated. Paint chips, dirt and sand, paper, fabric, feces, cigarette stubs, and bugs are among materials commonly eaten. Of particular concern is eating of dirt or paint that contains lead—pica is the major route for exposure to lead (Farber, Yanni, & Batshaw, 1997). Pica can lead to severe nutritional deficits, intestinal obstruction or perforation, parasitic infections such as toxoplasmosis (through eating of cat feces), and even death (Katsiyannis et al., 1998; Kerwin & Berkowitz, 1996). In a case known to the first author, a retarded boy ate large parts of mops to the point that his stomach was blocked, and the materials had to be surgically removed.

The cause of pica remains unknown, even after hundreds of years of study (Rose et al., 2000). Pica is a learned behavior that may be initially acquired through normal exploration of the environment or imitation. Its maintenance may owe to a number of factors. The first consideration is a nutritional inadequacy, so medical and nutritional analyses should precede any behavioral treatment (Katsiyannis et al., 1998). If it is associated with a nutritional inadequacy, pica may be successfully treated through dietary change or mineral supplements targeted at the deficiency. In cases in which no nutritional problem is found, a functional analysis of behavior should be conducted. Several types of behavioral interventions have been used successfully, ranging from less intrusive (e.g., differential reinforcement for nonpica behavior) to more aversive (e.g., overcorrection or brief physical restraint contingent upon pica). Obviously, any treatment program should begin with the least restrictive interventions unless the child's behavior presents an immediate risk. One interesting treatment uses a pica box, a small box containing edible items for a child. When a child attempts to eat a nonedible item, he or she is stopped; after a brief time-out, the child is reinforced by being allowed to get a treat out of the pica box. This method has been especially effective with mildly retarded and autistic children (Hirsch & Myles, 1996). Particularly good sources for those in special education are Katsiyannis et al. (1998), who not only describe several programs in detail but also provide useful case studies; and Rose et al. (2000), who provide a thorough review of the literature. The latter resource has the additional advantage of being available on-line.

Those in special education may have to implement treatment programs for developmentally disabled children with pica. All those who work with young children should be alert to pica behavior and make appropriate referrals.

REFERENCES

American Psychiatric Association. (1994). *Diagnostic and statistical manual of mental disorders* (4th ed.). Washington, DC: Author.

Danford, D., & Huber, A. (1982). Pica among mentally retarded adults. *American Journal of Mental Deficiency, 87,* 141–146.

Diamond, J., & Stermer, D. (1998). Eat dirt. *Discover, 19*(2), 70–76.

Erickson, M. T. (1998). *Behavior disorders of children and adolescents.* Upper Saddle River, NJ: Prentice Hall.

Farber, A. F., Yanni, C. C., & Batshaw, M. L. (1997). Nutrition: Good and bad. In M. L. Batshaw (Ed.), *Children with disabilities* (4th ed., pp. 183–208). Baltimore: Brookes.

Hirsch, N., & Myles, B. (1996). The use of a pica box in reducing pica behavior in a student with autism. *Focus on Autism and Other Developmental Disabilities, 11,* 222.

Katsiyannis, A., Torrey, G., & Bond, V. (1998). Current considerations in treating pica. *Teaching Exceptional Children, 30*(4), 50–53.

Kerwin, M. E., & Berkowitz, R. I. (1996). Feeding and eating disorders: Ingestive problems of infancy, childhood, and adolescence. *School Psychology Review, 25,* 316–329.

Rose, E. A., Porcerelli, J. H., & Neale, A. V. (2000). Pica: Common but commonly missed. *Journal of the American Board of Family Practice, 13,* 353–358. Retrieved from http://www.medscape.com/ABFP/JABFP/2000/v13.n05/fp1305.5.rose/pnt-fp1305.05.rose.html

Webster, L. M., & Brown, R. T. (2000). Pica. In C. R. Reynolds & E. Fletcher-Janzen (Eds.), *Encyclopedia of special education* (2nd ed., Vol. 3, pp. 1385–1386). New York: Wiley.

Robert T. Brown
Amy Sessoms
University of North Carolina, Wilmington

PITYRIASIS, RUBRA PILARIS

Pityriasis rubra pilaris is one of many forms of pityriasis, a group of skin diseases characterized by the presence of fine scales on the skin. It is a chronic, inflammatory condition characterized by eruptions or lesions of the skin that tend to be pointy with the appearance of a horn, are a reddish-brown color, and are embedded with hair (National Organization for Rare Disorders, 1999). The eruptions form yellowish-pink scaling patches. There are two forms of pityriasis rubra pilaris, differentiated by the age of onset. Type I usually occurs in older adulthood; Type II generally presents within the first 5 years of life.

Pityriasis is believed to be caused by a genetic metabolic defect, possibly involving vitamin A; however, this research is still preliminary. Type II (juvenile onset) is an autosomal dominant trait and occurs with equal frequency in males and females. Type I (adult onset) is not believed to be familial (National Organization for Rare Disorders, 1999).

Characteristics

1. Reddish-brown eruptions with embedded hair
2. Chronic itchiness
3. Reddening and thickening (hyperkeratosis) of the palms and soles
4. Fingernails may be dull, rough, thickened, brittle, or striated

Treatment consists of the use of various skin emollients. The symptoms of pityriasis rubra pilaris become more severe at times and decrease in severity at other times. Although the hereditary form is generally less severe than the idiopathic form, prognosis for remission is better for Type I than for Type II (National Organization for Rare Disorders, 1999). Depending on the severity and extent to which the individual's appearance is affected by the disorder, supportive counseling may be appropriate. In addition, because pityriasis rubra pilaris is believed to have a genetic etiology, genetic counseling may be appropriate as well.

REFERENCE

National Organization for Rare Disorders. (1999). Pityriasis rubra pilaris (No. 475). Retrieved June 3, 2001, from http://www.rarediseases.org

Cynthia A. Riccio
Texas A&M University

PLANTAR REFLEX

The plantar reflex (PR) is a neurological finding characterized by involuntary contraction of groups of muscles in the foot and lower leg, in response to a mildly noxious stimulus applied to the sole of the foot. The usual noxious stimulus is provided by the examiner's firmly grasping the patient's heel and dragging his or her thumbnail along the outer edge of the foot from the heel to the base of the little toe. This maneuver produces flexion (downward deviation) of all the toes.

PR is an example of a spinal reflex. Both sensory and motor phases of a spinal reflex are processed within a small section of the spinal cord. However, upper motor neurons (nerve cells inside the brain) exert influence over the nature and vigor of muscle contraction in PR. Therefore, any disease, traumatic injury, or immaturity of upper motor neurons or their nerve tracts within the spinal cord can produce an abnormal PR, which is also known as a Babinski reflex. Extension (upward movement) *or* flexion of the lesser toes and extension of the big toe following stroking of the sole constitute the Babinski reflex.

An abnormal PR can identify infants and toddlers with neurological deficits. Asymmetry of the Babinski response can determine which side of the brain is the likely site of the pathology. Extension of the big toe in PR is occasionally seen in neonates. However, by 4–6 months of age, a flexor response occurs in over 90% of normally developing babies. Persistence of a Babinski reflex in a 9-month-old child is strong evidence of significant central nervous system defects.

REFERENCES

Haslam, R. H. A. (2000). Neurologic evaluation. In R. E. Behrman, R. M. Kleigman, & H. B. Jenson (Eds.), *Nelson textbook of pediatrics* (16th ed., p. 1799). Philadelphia: W. B. Saunders.

Notes from readers: On the Babinski. (1999). *Pediatric Notes, 23*(6), 22.

The rise and fall of the plantar response in infancy. (1998). *Pediatric Notes, 22*(45), 180.

Barry H. Davison
Ennis, Texas

Joan W. Mayfield
Baylor Pediatric Specialty Services
Dallas, Texas

POLYCYSTIC KIDNEY DISEASES

Polycystic kidney diseases are genetic disorders characterized by the presence of multiple fluid-filled cysts in both kidneys. The number of cysts present can vary from few to many, depending on the individual. The cysts range in size and become larger as the disease progresses.

There are several different types of polycystic kidney disease (PKD), which can be divided into two main categories. The first type, autosomal recessive polycystic kidney disease (ARPKD), is caused by a recessive gene located on Chromosome 6 (6p21.1-12; National Organization for Rare Disorders, 2000). The second main type, autosomal dominant polycystic kidney disease (ADPKD), is caused by the transmission of the dominant genetic trait. However, in some cases the disorder is caused by a sporadic mutation in the gene. Researchers have identified at least three causal genes for ADPKD.

The two types of PKD affect adults and children differentially. ADPKD generally affects adults and is rare in children. ARPKD, however, affects children of all ages, and four classifications for the disorder are identified; they are based primarily on the age of onset. The four subtypes for ARPKD are perinatal, neonatal, infantile, and juvenile. Generally, individuals who are younger at time of onset experience a more rapidly progressing and severe form of the disorder.

The prevalence of PKD is distributed equally between males and females. Overall, approximately 50,000 people in the United States and 12 million people worldwide are affected by some type of PKD, with the majority of individuals affected by the adult form of the disorder, ADPKD (National Organization for Rare Disorders, 2000). The prevalence for ARPKD in infants in the United States is 1 in 10,000 (PKD Foundation, 2001).

Characteristics

1. Fatigue
2. Frequent urination and dehydration
3. Back pain
4. Enlarged abdomen
5. Unusual craniofacial features, including small jawbones, a broad and flat nose, and large and low-set ears
6. Nausea and vomiting
7. Swelling (edema) in the arms and legs
8. Failure to thrive

Many children with ARPKD are symptomatic at birth or shortly after birth in the neonatal period. Other children may not develop symptoms associated with ARPKD until they are infants or after the age of 1 year; in some cases, symptoms do not develop until adulthood. The symptoms for ARPKD vary depending on the stage of the disorder and the age of the individual. Physically, children with ARPKD have unusual craniofacial features, including small jawbones, a broad and flat nose, and large and low-set ears; the child's face may look like it is being pushed against a window. These characteristics collectively are referred to as Potter's face. With PKD, the kidneys usually become enlarged and harden; this symptom is particularly evident in young infants. In severe cases, children with ARPKD may have underdeveloped arms, legs, and lungs, as well as congenital heart defects. ARPKD may affect other organs in the body, such as the spleen and the liver. Ultimately, children with ARPKD may develop hypertension, difficulty with kidney functioning resulting in uremia (i.e., accumulation of waste products in the blood), and end-stage renal failure. In ADPKD, symptoms usually develop in the third through fifth decades of life. Often, ADPKD results in the formation of cysts in the liver as well as the kidneys. Symptoms associated with ADPKD are similar to those associated with ARPKD, with the exception of effects on physical development and facial characteristics. Individuals with ADPKD often experience painful, excessive, or frequent urination, or they may have blood in the urine. As with ARPKD, individuals with ADPKD also may develop further problems in the liver or spleen as the disease progresses. Usually, diagnosis of PKD is completed with the assistance of imaging techniques such as ultrasonography (US); a clinical evaluation that includes genetic testing, patient and family histories, and observation of physical characteristics associated with the disorder can aid in diagnosis.

Treatment for individuals with PKD can vary depending on the age of the individual and the severity of the disorder. In all cases, however, the primary goal of treatment is to slow the progression of kidney disease and maintain normal renal functioning for as long as possible. Generally, interventions for the symptoms of PKD include treatment for hypertension and urinary tract infections through medication and antibiotics. In some cases it may be necessary to treat problems that become present in the liver through surgery or the implantation of a portacaval shunt. Individuals whose PKD progresses to end-stage renal failure may need to utilize standard therapies associated with this condition, including dialysis, transplantation, or both.

It is desirable for an interdisciplinary team of specialists to work together when treating individuals with PKD. Supportive therapy and genetic counseling may prove beneficial to individuals with PKD and their families, and early interventions including positive medical and socioemotional supports for children with ARPKD should be utilized. In addition, individuals with PKD may benefit from avoiding anti-inflammatory drugs as well as foods and beverages containing caffeine and those that are high in sodium.

REFERENCES

National Organization for Rare Disorders. (1998). Polycystic kidney diseases. Retrieved June 3, 2001, from http://www.stepstn.com/cgi-win

Polycystic Kidney Disease Foundation. (2001). Learning about polycystic kidney disease. Retrieved June 12, 2001, from http://www.pkdcure.org/aboutPkd.htm

Brigitte N. Frederick
Texas A&M University

POLYCYSTIC LIVER DISEASE

Polycystic liver disease (PCLD) is a genetic disorder characterized by an overgrowth of biliary epithelium and supportive connective tissue, resulting in the presence of multiple cysts in the liver. The cysts are fluid filled, and the number of cysts present can vary from few to many, depending on the individual. The cysts can range in size from a few millimeters to more than 15 centimeters.

In most cases, the tendency to form the cysts in the liver is present at birth and is believed to be caused by an autosomal dominant gene. With this form of the disorder, the actual risk of the disorder's being transmitted from affected parent to child, regardless of gender, is 50%. According to Reynolds et al. (2000), the causative gene for PCLD is mapped to 19p13.2-p13.1. Although most cases of PCLD are of the aforementioned form, in some cases the disorder is caused by a random genetic mutation.

The prevalence of PCLD is distributed equally between males and females. However, females with the disorder are more likely to have more and larger cysts than are males with the disorder. In addition, females who have been pregnant or have taken estrogen are more likely to develop cysts (Reynolds et al., 2000). Although PCLD has been diagnosed in individuals from all age groups, the formation of cysts is less frequent in children than in adults.

Characteristics

1. Abdominal swelling and discomfort
2. Enlargement of the liver
3. Fever
4. Jaundice
5. High blood pressure

Autosomal dominant PCLD commonly occurs in association with autosomal dominant polycystic kidney disease (ADPKD) Types 1 and 2. However, PCLD also may exist as a separate entity that is genetically distinct from ADPKD Types 1 and 2; recent data support the theory that PCLD and ADPKD may be located on separate chromosomes (Iglesias et al., 1999; McKusick, 2000; Pirson et al., 1996). Although the two disorders are distinct entities, approximately 50% of individuals with PCLD also have cysts in their kidneys (National Organization for Rare Disorders, 1998). The frequency of comorbidity increases with age; approximately 20% of individuals with ADPKD in their 30s and 75% of individuals with ADPKD in their 70s have PCLD. However, some individuals and possibly some families with ADPKD never develop liver cysts (Reynolds et al., 2000).

Generally, liver functioning is unaffected if the individual with PCLD has only a few cysts or the cysts are small in size, because the noncystic tissue in the liver remains essentially normal. Individuals with PCLD may be asymptomatic, or they may have some minor symptoms associated with the disorder. Symptom presentation varies by individual and may include abdominal swelling and discomfort and enlargement of the liver. Although there are no medical issues related to the cysts themselves, fever may occur if the cysts break or if there is bleeding into the cyst. Rarely, a yellowing of the skin (i.e., jaundice) may occur in individuals with PCLD if a cyst compresses the bile ducts. Finally, high blood pressure in the blood flow from the intestines to the liver may occur if a cyst condenses these veins.

If PCLD is present, often no treatment is necessary. However, if treatment is needed, the type of treatment largely depends on the number, size, and distribution of the cysts. If cysts are large or if the individual with PCLD experiences symptoms related to the cysts, then aspiration or draining of the fluid in large cysts may be necessary; this usually is accompanied by an antibiotic treatment. In severe cases of PCLD, some investigational therapies have been used. Some of these therapies include removal of the membrane of the cyst and sometimes draining the fluid from the cyst (unroofing), creation of an opening in the cyst (fenestration), or removal of a portion of the liver (hepatectomy). Hepatectomy is used only in the most severe cases of PCLD.

In all individuals with PCLD, it may be desirable to offer genetic counseling for patients and their families. Otherwise, treatment for most individuals with PCLD will consist of the treatment of any symptoms that may be associated with the disorder. Supportive therapy also may prove beneficial to individuals with PCLD. Individuals with a severe form of PCLD may benefit from avoiding estrogens and excessive consumption of alcohol as well as other hepatic toxins.

REFERENCES

Iglesias, D. M., Palmitano, J. A., Arrizurieta, E., Kornblihtt, A. R., Herrera, M., Bernath, V., et al. (1999). Isolated polycystic liver disease not linked to polycystic kidney disease 1 and 2. *Digestive Diseases and Sciences, 44,* 385–388.

McKusick, V. A. (2000). Polycystic liver disease: PCLD. *Mendelian inheritance in man: Catalogs of human genes and genetic disorders.* Retrieved March 24, 2001, from http://www3.ncbi.nlm.nih.gov/htbin-post/Omim

National Organization for Rare Disorders. (1998). Polycystic liver disease. Retrieved June 3, 2001, http://www.stepstn.com/cgi-win

Pirson, Y., Lannoy, N., Peters, D., Geubel, A., Gigot, J. F., Breuning, M., et al. (1996). Isolated polycystic liver disease as a distinct genetic disease, unlinked to polycystic kidney disease 1 and polycystic kidney disease 2. *Hepatology, 23,* 249–252.

Reynolds, D. M., Falk, C. T., Li, A., King, B. F., Kamath, P. S., Huston, III, J., et al. (2000). Identification of a locus for autosomal dominant polycystic liver disease, on chromosome 19p13.2-13.1. *American Journal of Human Genetics, 67,* 1598–1604.

Brigitte N. Frederick
Texas A&M University

POLYDIPSIA

Polydipsia is a disorder marked by excessive ingestion of water beyond the amount necessary to maintain fluid balance in the body (often defined as consumption in excess of 3 l per day). Polydipsia is associated with extreme thirst and with polyuria, excessive production of urine. Because a common symptom of diabetes is extreme thirst, careful evaluation is necessary to distinguish primary polydipsia from excessive water intake associated with diabetes. Evidence from both animal and human research suggests that dopamine activity may be involved in polydipsia (Mittleman, Posner, & Schaub, 1994).

The disorder is typically seen in chronic psychiatric patients. Prevalence estimates in this population range from 6.6% to more than 20% for primary polydipsia (de Leon, Verghese, Tracy, Joiassen, & Simpson, 1994). However, excessive water drinking is also seen in individuals with developmental disabilities and in infants. The prevalence of polydipsia in individuals with autism is thought to be about 16.3% (Terai, Munesue, & Hiratani, 1998). It is not known how common polydipsia is in infants and young children. However, it can be diagnosed in infants as young as 5–6 weeks of age (Joshi et al., 1987). Polydipsia associated with illness (e.g., diabetes) is treated by treating the primary disease or disorder. Primary polydipsia can be treated by restricting water intake to invisible loss plus 25–30% of normally expected urine output according to the caloric system (Joshi et al., 1987). It is necessary to monitor the child for signs of weight loss and dehydration during this process. Additionally, parents should be educated about the potential negative effects of excessive water consumption (Horev & Cohen, 1994). Improvement is expected to occur quickly (within 1 week).

A serious complication associated with polydipsia is water intoxication, a syndrome in which the kidneys fail to excrete all excess fluid, resulting in brain edema. This edema can cause neurological and psychiatric symptoms, and—in severe cases—death (de Leon et al., 1994). Excessive consumption of fluoridated water can also cause developmental defects of tooth enamel in which the enamel becomes opaque, pitted, and stained (Sowe & Tomsett, 1994).

Characteristics

1. Excessive ingestion of water beyond the amount necessary to maintain normal fluid balance. This amount is often defined as ingestion in excess of 3 l per day.
2. Typically associated with polyuria (increased production of urine).
3. Can occur as a result of excessive thirst associated with a disease (e.g., diabetes or kidney hypercalciuria) or can occur in the absence of physical abnormality (known as primary polydipsia).
4. Can cause water intoxication, in which the kidneys fail to excrete all excess fluid, resulting in brain edema.

Children with this disorder will stand out in the classroom for their abnormally frequent trips to the water fountain and bathroom. Special help in the form of water at a child's desk or access to a bathroom without having to obtain permission may be warranted during treatment. Affected children may also miss excess school for monitoring during treatment. Because behavior associated with this disorder is fairly obvious, it may be wise to educate the child's peers to minimize teasing.

REFERENCES

DeLeon, J., Verghese, Cherian, Tracy, J. I., Josiassen, R. C., Simpson, G. M. (1994). Polydispia and water intoxication in psychiatric patients: A review of the epidemiological literature. *Biological Psychiatry, 35,* 408–419.

Horev, Z., & Cohen, A. H. (1994). Compulsive water drinking in infants and young children. *Clinical Pediatrics, 24*(2), 169–172.

Joshi, R. M., Vulur, C. T., Abhyankar, S. H., Vidvauns, A. S., Kamat, J. R., Joshi, M. K., et al. (1987). Primary polydipsia in infancy. *Indian Pediatrics, 24*(2), 169–172.

Mittleman, G., Posner, A. L., Schaub, C. L. (1994). Polydipsia and dopamine: Behavioral effects of dopamine D1 and D2 receptor agonists and antagonists. *Journal of Pharmacology and Experimental Therapeutics, 271*(2), 638–650.

Seow, W. K., & Tomsett, (1994). Dental fluorisis as a complication of hereditary diabetes insipidus: Studies of six affected patients. *Pediatric Dentistry, 16*(2), 128–132.

Terai, K., Munesue, T., & Hiratani, M. (1999). Excessive water drinking behavior in autism. *Brain and Development, 21*(2), 103–106.

Laura Arnstein
State University of New York at Binghamton

POLYMYOSITIS

Myositis is a rare disease that comes in multiple forms and is one group of the inflammatory muscle myopathies (Myositis Association of America, 1999). As with other inflammatory myopathies, myositis is believed to be an autoimmune disorder in which inflammatory cells surround, invade, and destroy muscle fibers, resulting in muscle weakness or rash. Unlike other forms of myositis, polymyositis does not start with a rash, and the muscle inflammation and weakness are more gradual. Polymyositis is more common after age 20, but it has been identified in children and infants. Women are twice as likely as men to be affected with polymyositis; this is particularly true for women between the ages of 40 and 60 years old. Polymyositis can be confused with mixed connective tissue disorder due to the inflammation (Myositis Association of America, 1999). There is no indication of incidence differences based on ethnic group membership for polymyositis. The cause or trigger of the inflammation is not known.

Characteristics

1. Difficulty getting up from a chair, climbing stairs, raising arms
2. Muscle weakness or pain specific to upper or lower extremities and trunk
3. Fatigue, aches, cramping, and tenderness
4. Inflammation, including fever
5. Nondestructive arthritis or arthralgias
6. Loss of appetite

Source: Myositis Association of America (2001a, 2000b)

Polymyositis is characterized by muscle inflammation and weakness. Although the inflammation may not be painful, the attacks can be quite intense. The muscle weakness, aches, and arthralgia may be intermittent over a number of weeks or months. Individuals with polymyositis may complain of general feelings of fatigue and loss of appetite (Myositis Association of America, 2001).

Treatment of all forms of myositis include the administration of corticosteroids (e.g., prednisone) or intravenous immunoglobulin infusions. Research suggests that short but intense administration of corticosteroids may be less toxic and more effective than traditional dosing (Myositis Association of America, 2001). In many cases, if the condition is treated early and the individual is responsive, the myositis will go into remission. For those individuals who experience pain with the myositis, additional medication management may be appropriate. In some cases, additional rehabilitation to address residual muscle weakness may be necessary. This treatment may mean provision of physical therapy or occupational therapy. In addition, the family of the child with myositis may need help in coping and dealing with their child's illness (Myositis Association of America, 2001).

REFERENCES

Myositis Association of America. (1999). Retrieved from http://www.myositis.org/about-im2

Myositis Association of America. (2001a). Retrieved May 29, 2001, from http://www.myositis.org/2001_neurology_conference/

Myositis Association of America. (2001b). Retrieved May 29, 2001, from http://www.myositis.org/criteria

Cynthia A. Riccio
Texas A&M University

See also Myositis

POPLITEAL PTERIGIUM SYNDROME (FACIO-GENITO-POPLITEAL SYNDROME)

Popliteal pterigium syndrome (PPS) is a heritable, congenital disorder composed of associated oral, extremity, and genital malformations. Skeletal anomalies are occasionally seen with this disorder.

The etiology of PPS is not known. Clinical severity of

the syndrome is quite variable. No clinical feature of PPS is a consistent finding in all patients.

PPS is considered rare. Since the first case report in 1869, about 80 additional individuals with the disorder have been described. The pattern of inheritance appears to be autosomal dominant.

Characteristics

1. Cleft palate with cleft lip (90%), pits in the lower lip (on the inner surface), and fibrous bands between the upper and lower jaw.
2. Popliteal web (pterigium). In extreme cases, a fibrous band of tissue may extend all the way down the back of the leg from the lower buttock to the heel. Malformed toenails and syndactyly (webbing of the toes) are also common.
3. More than 50% of patients have genital anomalies that include underdeveloped labia majora (the outer lips of the vagina), malformation of the scrotum, and undescended testicles.
4. Occasional findings are missing teeth, webbing of the eyelids, pterygia in the groin area, syndactyly of the fingers, underdeveloped or missing fingers or toes, valgus (outward deviation) deformity of the feet, vertebral anomalies, scoliosis (lateral curvature of the spine), rib anomalies, abnormal positioning of the penis or testes, and underdevelopment of the vagina or uterus.

Treatments of the anomalies associated with PPS are cosmetic and orthopedic in nature. Popliteal pterygia requires careful surgical repair because these cord-like structures may contain both nerves and blood vessels essential to normal function of the lower leg. After the pterygia are fixed, there may be additional muscle defects in the lower extremity that need the orthopedist's attention. Genital distortions are usually secondary to webbing between the inner thigh and the base of the penis and respond well to surgical correction. A number of operations may be necessary for the best functional results, but the majority of patients with PPS can anticipate being able to move about normally.

There is no cognitive dysfunction associated with PPS. Therefore, based on this diagnosis, the need for special education services is not warranted.

The prognosis for PPS is good. Although several operative procedures may be necessary to treat the syndrome's defects, these children usually have normal intelligence and can look forward to satisfactory mobility after they have been discharged from the orthopedic surgeon's care.

REFERENCES

Jones, K. (1997). *Smith's recognizable patterns of human malformation* (5th ed.). Philadelphia: W. B. Saunders.

National Organization for Rare Disorders. (1998). Popliteal pterygium syndrome. Retrieved from http://www.stepstn.com/cgi-win/nord.exe?proc=GetDocument&rectype=0&recnum=1069

Barry H. Davison
Ennis, Texas

Joan W. Mayfield
Baylor Pediatric Specialty Services
Dallas, Texas

PORPHYRIAS

Porphyria is not a single disorder; rather, it is a group of inherited disorders in which there is only one normal gene to produce a key enzyme in the biosynthesis of chelated iron or heme. With only one normal gene, there is a reduced level of normal enzyme activity, resulting in a buildup of the precursors behind the deficient enzyme. This buildup accumulates in body fluids and tissues and results in toxicity.

Although no prevalence rate is reported, porphyria is relatively rare and may be underdiagnosed unless it is symptomatic (Downey, 2001; Moore, 1999). It may be inherited or it can be acquired. When the porphyria is inherited, there is an equal chance that males and females will inherit. Some forms are dominant and one parent will be symptomatic; one form (congenital porphyria) is recessive and both parents are asymptomatic but are carriers of the disorder. Autosomal dominant porphyrias are termed acute porphyrias. In acquired porphyria, the porphyria is secondary to another condition (e.g., kidney disease being treated with hemodialysis) or the use of alcohol or certain drugs (e.g., estrogen). Multiple causes and conditions have been postulated (Downey, 2001). Inherited forms of porphyria are usually identified between the ages of 2 and 20 based on critical levels of specific porphyria precursors in the urine, blood, or feces. When a parent is symptomatic, children are tested on a regular basis to determine whether they have the disorder.

Depending on the enzyme involved, the clinical manifestations of porphyria differ. In some forms, individuals with porphyria are subject to acute attacks that can be dangerous. Acute attacks can be associated with specific drugs (e.g., alcohol), infection, changes in diet, and smoking (Moore, 1999). Exposure to sunlight can aggravate any skin sensitivity, and skin abrasions can be common.

Characteristics

1. Cutaneous lesions, blisters, and open sores
2. Abdominal pain
3. Hepatic disease

4. Increased erythrocytes
5. Acute attacks of abdominal pain, cramps, constipation, or vomiting
6. Marked anxiety
7. Profuse sweating, pallor, hypertension, pyrexia
8. Seizures

Many individuals with porphyrias lead perfectly normal lives. Management and treatment of porphyrias are prominently achieved through avoidance of situations that are associated with the specific deficient enzyme (e.g., alcohol, specific foods). Individuals with a porphyria need to be careful of any medications that may increase toxicity, including over-the-counter medications. For those individuals with skin sensitivity, appropriate preventive steps need to be taken, including avoidance of sun exposure and use of gloves when working on machinery or with sharp elements. In a school setting, it may be necessary to ensure that dietary restrictions are respected and that students who need to dress differently to avoid sun exposure are not ridiculed in any way. Medications may be prescribed to address the acute manifestations of porphyria (Moore, 1999). In more severe cases, hempheresis or bone marrow transplants may be considered (Kauffman, Evans, Stevens, & Weinkove, 1991). In some cases, it is necessary for the individuals to be monitored for hepatic complications as they age.

Neurological dysfunction is usually only associated with acute attacks and may take the form of confusion or inappropriate behavior, including agitation, mania, depression, hallucinations, and schizophrenic types of behaviors. Teachers and parents should be aware that the presence of these behaviors may be an indication of toxicity that requires follow-up by a physician. In-service programming with teachers to ensure that the behaviors are responded to appropriately may be needed. There is no indication of any learning problems associated directly with the porphyrias, but evaluation of learning problems should be undertaken if there are any questions about the child's ability to progress.

In more severe cases in which the child may be absent due to frequent acute attacks, modification of attendance requirements and provision of homebound instruction may be a consideration. In those cases in which the porphyria results in neuropathy, however, the student may meet eligibility criteria under the category of other health impaired or physical disability. With variable presentation and severity, the individual needs of the child will have to determine the services provided.

REFERENCES

Downey, D. (2001). Porphyria: The road not traveled. *Medical Hypotheses, 56,* 73–76.

Kaufmann, L., Evans, D. I. K., Stevens, R. F., & Weinkove, C. (1991). Bone-marrow transplantation for congenital erythropoietic porphyria. *Lancet, 337* (8756), 1510–1511.

Moore, M. R. (1999). Porphyria: A patient's guide. Retrieved from http://www.uq.edu.au/porphyria/porhpg.htm

Cynthia A. Riccio
Texas A&M University

PORPHYRIA, CONGENITAL ERYTHROPOIETIC

The porphyrias are a group of inherited disorders in which there is only one normal gene to produce a key enzyme in the biosynthesis of chelated iron or heme. With only one normal gene, there is a reduced level of normal enzyme activity, resulting in a buildup of the precursors behind the deficient enzyme. This buildup accumulates in body fluids and tissues and results in toxicity. Each type of porphyria involves different enzymes. Depending on the enzyme involved, the clinical manifestations of porphyria differ. In congenital erythropoietic porphyria or Gunther's disease, the enzyme involved is uroporphyrinogen III cosynthase (UROS). Although no prevalence rate is reported, congenital porphyria is relatively rare and may be underdiagnosed unless it is symptomatic (Downey, 2001).

When the porphyria is inherited, there is an equal chance that males and females will inherit. Congenital porphyria is autosomal recessive; both parents are asymptomatic but are carriers of the disorder. It is very rare, with only 20 cases reported in the literature as of 1992. Congenital porphyria is usually identified between the ages of 2 and 20, and diagnosis is based on critical levels of specific porphyria precursors in the urine, blood, or feces. When a parent is symptomatic, children are tested on a regular basis to determine whether they have the disorder. Prenatal diagnosis is possible (Deybach, de Verneuil, Boulechfar, Grandchamp, & Nordmann, 1980).

Characteristics

1. Cutaneous lesions, blisters, and open sores that eventually scar
2. Reddish urine
3. Enlarged spleen (splenomegaly)
4. Increased hair growth
5. Sun and light sensitivity

Many individuals with porphyria lead perfectly normal lives. Management and treatment of congenital porphyria are predominantly achieved through prevention and avoidance of situations that are associated with the specific deficient enzyme. For those individuals with congenital porphyria, appropriate preventive steps need to be taken, including avoidance of sun exposure and use of gloves when working on machinery or with sharp elements. In a school setting, it may be necessary to ensure that students who need to dress differently to avoid sun exposure are not ridiculed in any way. In more severe cases, hempheresis or bone marrow transplants may be considered (Kaufmann, Evans, Stevens, & Weinkove, 1991; Tezcan et al., 1998).

There is no indication of any learning problems associated directly with the porphyrias, but evaluation of learning problems should be undertaken if there are any questions about the child's ability to progress. Because of the disorder's variable presentation and severity, the individual needs of the child will have to determine the services provided. Supportive and genetic counseling may be indicated.

REFERENCES

Deybach, J. C., deVerneuil, H., Boulechfar, S., Grandchamp, B., & Nordmann, Y. (1990). Point mutations in the uroporphyrinogen III synthase gene in congenital erythropoietic porphyria (Gunther's disease). *Blood, 75,* 1763–1765.

Kaufmann, L., Evans, D. I. K., Stevens, R. F., & Weinkove, C. (1991). Bone-marrow transplantation for congenital erythropoietic porphyria. *Lancet, 337*(8756), 1510–1511.

Tezcan, I., Xu, W., Gurgey, A., Tuncer, M., Cetin, M., Oner, C., et al. (1998). Congenital erythropoietic porphyria successfully treated by allogeneic bone marrow transplantation. *Blood, 92,* 4053–4058.

Cynthia A. Riccio
Texas A&M University

POSTCONCUSSION SYNDROME

Postconcussion syndrome is an acquired disorder of the brain, most commonly caused by mild to moderate head trauma. It is defined by a constellation of somatic complaints, cognitive difficulties, and emotional changes beginning after significant cerebral concussion and persisting for a minimum of 3 months (American Psychiatric Association, 1994). Approximately 200,000 children are hospitalized with head injuries each year, and of these children between 30% and 40% meet criteria for diagnosis of post-concussion syndrome 3 months following their head trauma (Tomkins et al., 1990). Follow-up studies indicate that approximately 10% meet full criteria for diagnosis 1 year following their injury (Ingebrigtsen, Waterloo, Marup-Jensen, Attner, & Romner, 1998).

Characteristics

1. Concussion with or without loss of consciousness
2. Three or more symptoms from the following domains, lasting at least 3 months:
   - Somatic complaints, including headache, dizziness-vertigo, fatigue, blurry or double vision, light sensitivity, and noise intolerance
   - Cognitive difficulties, including difficulty concentrating, diminished attention, difficulty shifting attention, difficulty attending to multiple cognitive tasks, slow cognitive processing, memory impairment, and intellectual impairment
   - Emotional changes, including irritability, anxiety, depression, or affective lability

Effective treatment of post-concussion syndrome is dependent on accurate diagnosis. Compared to adults, children are less likely to be able to understand the cognitive and emotional changes they are experiencing following a head injury. They also often lack the vocabulary to accurately describe these changes to parents or physicians. As a result, they may be misdiagnosed as having attention-deficit/hyperactivity disorder or oppositional defiant disorder based on outward behavioral changes (Mittenberg, Wittner, & Miller, 1997). It is therefore recommended that children treated for head injury undergo cognitive or neuropsychological testing in the first 3 months following injury to assess for memory or attentional difficulties. Attentional deficits may be helped with stimulant medications and with standard ADHD educational modifications. Children with post-concussion syndrome are more likely to show highly variable functioning on intellectual tests; their scores on tests tapping memory, attention, and speed of processing are generally significantly poorer than their scores on other tests (Fuld & Fisher, 1977). Follow-up testing is also recommended in the year following the injury to track improvement.

Research indicates that post-concussion syndrome may be caused by a combination of the physical effects of the brain injury as well as anxiety about the symptoms caused by the injury (Mittenberg et al., 1997). Environmental stressors such as family changes (e.g., moves or divorce) or difficulty with peers are also likely to exacerbate the symptoms of post-concussion syndrome (Fuld & Fisher, 1977). Consequently, it is important to minimize stress in the months following a head injury—particularly in younger children, who appear to be more sensitive to the effect of environmental stressors (Tompkins et al., 1990). Psychological treatment for anxiety or stress management may help children adjust to cognitive changes and develop coping skills to minimize emotional regulation problems. Anxiolytic medication may also help to minimize post-concussion symptoms (Mittenberg et al., 1997).

Research also indicates that subsequent head injuries are more likely to worsen symptoms of post-concussion syndrome and may in some cases lead to more serious cognitive deficits or even death (Bijur, Haslum, & Golding, 1996). Children who have sustained a head injury should therefore avoid athletic activity that puts them at risk for further head trauma for a minimum of 1 week and for at least 1 month if they lost consciousness as a result of the head injury (Genuardi & King, 1995).

It has been suggested that children who experience a mild to moderate head injury may be more likely to be aware of changes in their cognitive and emotional functioning than are children who experience a more severe injury. Similarly, they may be more likely to be distressed by these changes. This increased awareness-distress has in turn been hypothesized to explain why children with mild to moderate head injury are more likely to develop post-concussion syndrome than are more severely injured children (Mittenberg et al., 1997). These same children are also likely to be rapidly returned to a regular academic and social schedule because they display few outward signs of their injury. This rapid return to normal activities may be overwhelming due to changes in cognitive and emotional functioning. Consequently, children's academic and social progress should be closely monitored in the first months following a concussion, and academic modifications should be considered for children and adolescents in the 1st year after injury. These modifications may include a quiet work area, extended time for tests and assignments, reduced class load, tutoring, or special education placement (Fuld & Fisher, 1977).

The prognosis for children with post-concussion syndrome is generally good. Most children make a full recovery following a concussion; however, approximately 33% of children will meet criteria for post-concussion syndrome 3 months after the injury, and 10% will continue to meet criteria for diagnosis 1 year after their injury. For those with symptoms enduring for more than 1 year, the prognosis is more mixed. These children are likely to do more poorly academically, limiting their employment possibilities. The emotional and somatic difficulties they experience may lead them to miss school and work and seek medical attention more often than do their peers. In addition, a retrospective study of adults sustaining head injury in childhood indicates that this group seeks disability benefits at an earlier age and at a higher rate than do their peers (Enberg & Teasdale, 1998).

REFERENCES

American Psychiatric Association. (1994). *Diagnostic and statistical manual of mental disorders* (4th ed.). Washington, DC: Author.

Bijur, P. E., Haslum, M., & Golding, J. (1996). Cognitive outcomes of multiple mild head injuries in children. *Developmental and Behavioral Pediatrics, 17*(3), 143–148.

Engberg, A., & Teasdale, T. W. (1998). Traumatic brain injury in children in Denmark: A national 15-year study. *European Journal of Epidemiology, 14,* 165–173.

Fuld, P. A., & Fisher, P. (1977). Recovery of intellectual ability after closed-head injury. *Developmental Medicine and Child Neurology, 19,* 495–502.

Genuardi, F. J., & King, W. D. (1995). Inappropriate discharge instructions for youth athletes hospitalized for concussion. *Pediatrics, 95*(2), 216–218.

Ingebrigtsen, T., Waterloo, K., Marup-Jensen, S., Attner, E., & Romner, B. (1998). Quantification of post-concussion symptoms 3 months after minor head injury in 100 consecutive patients. *Journal of Neurology, 245,* 609–612.

Mittenberg, W., Wittner, M. S., & Miller, L. J. (1997). Postconcussion syndrome occurs in children. *Neuropsychology, 11*(3), 447–452.

Tompkins, C. A., Holland, A. L., Ratcliff, G., Costello, A., Leahy, L. F., & Cowell, V. (1990). Predicting cognitive recovery from closed head-injury in children and adolescents. *Brain and Cognition, 13,* 86–97.

Rebecca Vaurio
David M. Tucker
Austin, Texas

POSTTRAUMATIC STRESS DISORDER

Posttraumatic stress disorder (PTSD) is a constellation of symptoms resulting from severe anxiety following exposure to a catastrophic event. The child may have either witnessed or directly experienced an event that involved actual or potential death or serious injury to him- or herself or others (American Psychiatric Association [APA], 1994). Such events may include physical assault, domestic violence, sexual abuse, natural disaster, automobile accidents, and so on. The child reexperiences the traumatic event in nightmares and flashbacks or may engage in repetitive play regarding the event. Intense psychological distress, physiological responses, or both when the child is exposed to an event resembling or symbolizing the traumatic event is common. Increased arousal and symptoms of severe anxiety are characteristic, as are avoidance of reminders and emotional numbing.

Fletcher (1994) estimates that the prevalence of PTSD among children who are exposed to trauma is 36%. There are no clear indications in the literature as to how common PTSD is among children; however, in one study of young urban adults, 39% reported having exposure to at least one traumatic event during their first 25 years (Breslau, Davis, Andreski, & Peterson, 1991). In order to diagnose PTSD, symptoms must last for at least 1 month and cause significant distress or impairment in important areas of functioning (e.g., school and social interactions). PTSD may occur immediately following a traumatic event or after a delay. Children who have been exposed to trauma, regardless of when they manifest the problems, are at risk for the development of serious psychological problems, including dissociative symptoms and identity disorder, depression, drug abuse, conduct disorder, anxiety disorders, and personality disorders (e.g., borderline personality disorder).

Characteristics

The child has experienced or witnessed a traumatic event involving both of the following:

1. Possible or actual death, serious injury, or physical harm to self or others
2. Feelings of fear, helplessness, or horror (often expressed by disorganized or agitated behavior)

The child reexperiences the traumatic event in at least one of the following ways:

1. Recurrent and distressing memories (young children may manifest trauma in repetitive play)
2. Recurrent distressing dreams of the event or frightening dreams without identified content
3. Flashbacks in which the child acts or feels as if the traumatic event is recurring
4. Intense psychological distress when exposed to stimuli symbolizing or resembling the trauma
5. Physiological reactions when exposed to stimuli symbolizing or resembling the trauma

The child persistently avoids stimuli associated with the trauma and experiences emotional numbing in three or more of the following ways:

1. Efforts to avoid thoughts, feelings, or conversations associated with the trauma
2. Efforts to avoid activities, places, or people that stimulate memories of the trauma
3. Inability to remember an important part of the trauma
4. Markedly diminished interest or participation in significant activities
5. Feeling of detachment or estrangement from others
6. Restriction in range of affect (e.g., unable to feel loving feelings)
7. Sense of foreshortened future (e.g., not expect to graduate high school or get married)

The child experiences persistent symptoms of arousal as indicated by at least two of the following: difficulty with sleep, irritability and anger outbursts, problems concentrating, hypervigilance, exaggerated startle response.

Source: APA (1994)

There are few studies examining the efficacy of psychological treatment for children with PTSD, which is an area that deserves future research. Cognitive-behavioral individual and family therapy, play therapy, gradual exposure to feared stimuli, modeling, coping skills, parent training, relaxation, group therapy, and pharmacotherapy may be used to treat PTSD symptoms in children (Wolfe, 1998). Eye movement desensitization retraining (EMDR) has also been employed to reduce reactivity to traumatic memories in children (Shapiro, 1995). Children with PTSD may be eligible for special education services under the classification of Emotional Disturbance. Support by the school psychologist may be necessary to help the child cope with and reduce anxiety as well as memory and cognitive problems caused by anxiety secondary to stimulation of traumatic memories. In some cases, hospitalization may be needed.

Children who are exposed to one traumatic event that does not involve abuse are less likely to suffer long-term psychological symptoms. However, when a child is exposed to repeated, abusive, or multiple traumas, psychological symptoms are likely to persist into adulthood (Fletcher, 1996).

REFERENCES

American Psychiatric Association. (1994). *Diagnostic and statistical manual of mental disorders* (4th ed.). Washington, DC: Author.

Breslau, N., Davis, G. C., Andreski, P., & Peterson, E. (1991). Traumatic events and posttraumatic stress disorder in an urban population of young adults. *Archives of General Psychiatry, 48,* 216–222.

Fletcher, K. (1994). *What we know about children's post-traumatic stress responses: A metal-analysis of the empirical literature.* Unpublished manuscript, University of Massachusetts Medical Center, Worcester.

Fletcher, K. (1996). Childhood posttraumatic stress disorder. In E. Mash & R. Barkley (Eds.), *Child psychopathology.* New York: Guilford Press.

Shapiro, F. (1995). *Eye movement desensitization and reprocessing: Basic principles, protocols and procedures.* New York: Guilford Press.

Wolfe, V. (1998). Child sexual abuse. In E. Mash & R. Barkley, *Treatment of childhood disorders* (2nd ed.). New York: Guilford Press.

Janiece Pompa
Elaine Clark
University of Utah

PRADER-WILLI SYNDROME

Prader-Willi Syndrome is a multisystem disorder characterized by neonatal hypotonia, onset of obesity in later childhood, hyperphagia, small hands and feet, short stature, and mental retardation (Butler, Weaver, & Meaney, 1982; Couper, 1999). Although it arises from a genetic defect, it is not inherited and is instead a rare birth defect. It is caused by the partial deletion of the paternal Chromo-

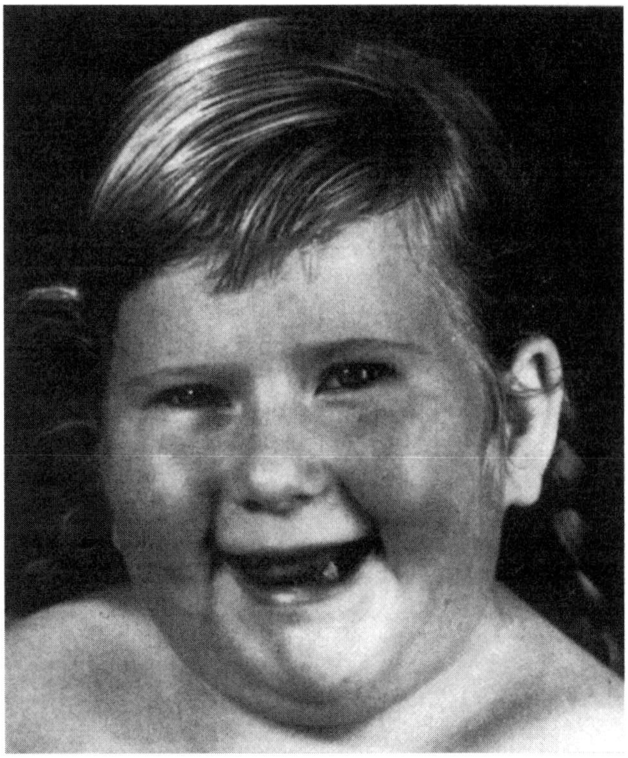

Prader-Willi Syndrome
Reprinted from *Clinical Syndromes*, Wiedemann and Kunze, 1997, by permission of the publisher Mosby

some 15 in 70% of patients or by the inheritance of two copies from one parent (usually termed maternal disomy) in the remaining patients (Barrett, 1999; Couper, 1999). The exact gene that causes Prader-Willi syndrome has not been discovered (Smith, 1999).

Prader-Willi syndrome is a rare birth defect that occurs in about 1 in 15,000 births (Smith, 1999). It affects both genders and all races (Barrett, 1999). However, there is a paucity of cases reported among African Americans (Butler et al., 1982).

Characteristics

1. Nonprogressive infant hypotonia
2. Onset of excessive food seeking and obesity in early childhood
3. Mental deficiency (IQ = 20–80, with a mean of 60)
4. Short stature, small hands and feet
5. Hypogonadism
6. Delayed motor, language, and sexual development
7. High pain threshold, obsessive-compulsive behavior, conduct problems

Source: Couper (1999)

Obesity and related problems (which can lead to death) are treated through strict monitoring of food intake and regular exercise (Barrett, 1999; Couper, 1999). Medication such as selective serotonin reuptake inhibitors have been found to improve behavioral problems (Couper, 1999). Psychotropic medication has also been found to be helpful in treating psychological problems.

Patients with Prader-Willi syndrome are infertile. Hormones can be used to treat sexual development; however, side effects such as increased weight gain and exacerbated oppositional behavior may occur, and treatment should be monitored on an individual basis.

If possible, children with Prader-Willi Syndrome should be incorporated into the normal classroom. Food may be used cautiously as a reinforcer for good behavior and learning. It is important to provide clear and consistent messages as well as structure to control temper tantrums as well as eating habits. Children with Prader-Willi may require occupational therapists, speech pathologists, orthopedic surgeons, dietitians, and exercise therapists in addition to other pediatric medical professionals (Couper, 1999). Special education services may be available to children with Prader-Willi syndrome under the handicapping condition of Other Health Impaired, Speech Impaired, or Mental Retardation. There is no known cure for Prader-Willi syndrome (Barrett, 1999). With weight control, life expectancy can be normal.

REFERENCES

Barrett, J. (1999). Prader-Willi syndrome. *Gale Encyclopedia of Medicine,* 2333.

Butler, M. G., Weaver, D. D., & Meaney, F. J. (1982). Prader-Willi syndrome: Are there population differences? *Clinical Genetics, 22,* 292–294.

Couper, R. T. L. (1999). Prader-Willi syndrome. *Journal of Pediatric Child Health, 35,* 331–334.

Smith, A. (1999). The diagnosis of Prader-Willi syndrome. *Journal of Pediatric Child Health, 35,* 335–337.

Kimberly D. Wilson
University of Texas at Austin

PREMENSTRUAL DYSPHORIC DISORDER

Premenstrual dysphoric disorder (PMDD) is a transient mood disorder (Man, MacMillan, Scott, & Young, 1999) and is a severe form of premenstrual syndrome (PMS). Previously known as late luteal phase dysphoric disorder, it is currently listed as PMDD in the *Diagnostic and Statistical Manual of Mental Disorders–Fourth Edition* (*DSM-IV;* American Psychiatric Association, 1994), in an appendix of diagnoses needing further study. According to Muzina and Gonsalves (1998), diagnostic criteria for PMDD include the presence of symptoms during most of the menstrual cycles in the past year, and five or more symptoms must be present during the last week of the luteal phase. The symptoms must begin to lessen and go away a few days after the onset of menses and be absent a week after menses is discontinued. The symptoms must interfere noticeably with activities such as school, work, social events, and relationships. To be diagnosed with PMDD, the symptoms cannot be an exacerbation of symptoms of another disorder, such as major depressive disorder. A diagnosis of PMS, in contrast with PMDD, does not require the symptom severity to cause a significant level of functional impairment (Steiner, 1997).

Muzina and Gonsalves (1998) report that as many as 75% of menstruating women have been reported to have some symptoms of PMS. PMDD is much less frequent and has been reported to affect 2.5–5% of regularly menstruating women between the ages of 20 and 44. Studies have found symptoms of PMDD to be most severe in women in their late 20s through mid-30s. Additionally, Muzina and Gonsalves (1998) report that depression is a main risk factor linked with PMDD: Approximately 80% of women diagnosed with PMDD have suffered from depression or a related mood disorder at some point in their lives. Before giving a patient a diagnosis of PMDD, organic causes of symptoms, such as thyroid disorders, perimenopause, and menopause should be considered.

Steiner (1997) suggests that the main etiological trigger for PMDD is ovarian functioning. PMDD may be caused by the normal endocrine events of the ovarian cycle. Serotonin, the chemical most associated with mood and anxiety disorders, is proposed to be the most important neurotransmitter involved in the pathogenesis of PMDD. Steiner (1997) suggests that reduced serotonin may be involved with the characteristic symptoms of PMDD.

Characteristics

1. Depression, anxiety, irritability, and mood lability
2. Reduced interest in usual activities, difficulty concentrating, and fatigue
3. Appetite changes (including binge eating and craving)
4. Insomnia
5. Breast tenderness or swelling, headaches, and bloating

There are three tiers of treatment of PMDD (Muzina & Gonsalves, 1998; Steiner, 1997). First-step treatment for PMDD includes education and lifestyle modifications, including stress management, dietary changes, exercise, and vitamin and mineral supplements. If lifestyle improvements do not alleviate symptoms, second-step treatment for PMDD would include hormonal therapies aimed at modifying the menstrual cycle with oral contraceptives, estradiol with progestins, or GnRH agonists and danazol. If adding hormones does not mollify PMDD symptoms, more permanent action such as a surgical ovariectomy may be considered. Although an ovariectomy may eradicate PMDD symptoms, it may also cause other symptoms and other unwanted effects. If symptoms persist through first- and second-tier treatment, psychotherapy is recommended as the third-step strategy. Psychologists and psychiatrists are qualified to treat difficult or treatment-resistant cases of PMDD (Muzina & Gonsalves, 1998).

In the classroom, high school teachers may be aware of emotional symptoms of PMS or PMDD. Although PMDD is more common to women in their early 20s, postmenarche adolescent females may also be at risk for this disorder. Studies have shown that women have impaired short-term working memory skills during the late luteal phase of their menstrual cycle (Man et al., 1999). However, women with PMDD have not been shown to differ from regularly menstruating women in this area. A teacher of high-school-age girls would need to be aware that any female might have impaired performance in short-term working memory during this stage of the menstrual cycle. More concerning issues might be a student's difficulty concentrating on her schoolwork and potential interpersonal problems that might interfere with learning and school performance. Teachers may want to refer possibly distressed female students to a school counselor if necessary.

The etiology of PMDD is still unclear, although theory postulates that the normal cycle of the ovary and the neurotransmitter serotonin might be involved in this disorder (Muzina & Gonsalves, 1998; Steiner, 1997). Future research will help resolve the true etiology of PMDD and further investigate the role of serotonin in PMDD. Steiner (1997) reports that serotonin is linked logically to the causation of late luteal phase dysphoric mood symptoms because reduced platelet uptake of serotonin has been shown to occur during the week before menstruation in women with PMS. Women with PMS have also been shown to have a lowered level of platelet serotonin content. Finally, serotonin is indicated as a related factor to PMDD because of the successful treatment of PMDD with selective serotonin reuptake inhibitors.

REFERENCES

American Psychiatric Association. (1994). *Diagnostic and statistical manual of mental disorders* (4th ed.). Washington, DC: Author.

Man, M. S., MacMillan, I., Scott, J., & Young, A. & H. (1999). Mood, neuropsychological function and cognitions in premenstrual dysphoric disorder. *Psychological Medicine, 29*, 727–733.

Muzina, K. S. & Gonsalves, L. (1998). Commonly asked questions about premenstrual dysphoric disorder. *Cleveland Clinic Journal of Medicine, 65*(3), 142–149.

Steiner, M. (1997). Premenstrual syndromes. *Annual Review of Medicine, 48*, 447–455.

Jennie Kaufman Singer
California Department of Corrections, Region 1 Parole Outpatient Clinic
Sacramento, California

PRIMARY IMMUNE DEFICIENCY

The primary immunodeficiency diseases are a group of disorders in which the primary defect appears to be intrinsic to one or more components of the immune system. The immune system is conveniently divided into four necessary compartments: the B-lymphocyte system, the T-lymphocyte system, the phagocytic system, and the complement system (Winkelstein, 1992).

Each of these necessary compartments of the immune system plays a precise role in host defense against infection and inflammation. Although each system has specific roles in the normal function of the immune system, each works best when functioning in agreement with the others.

One of the most useful ways of classifying the primary immunodeficiency diseases is according to which functional portion of the immune system is damaged. Thus, there are disorders that affect the B-lymphocyte system, the T-lymphocyte system, both the B-lymphocyte and T-lymphocyte systems, the phagocytic system, and the complement system.

The primary immunodeficiency diseases were originally thought to be quite rare. In fact, however, some of the primary immunodeficiency diseases are relatively common. For example, selective immunoglobulin A (IgA) deficiency occurs in as many as 1 in 500 to 1 in 1,000 individuals. Other primary immunodeficiency diseases are much less common and occur with a frequency of between 1 in 1,000 and 1 in 100,000. However, because there are so many primary immunodeficiency diseases, when taken together as a group of disorders, they become a significant health problem, occurring with a frequency equal to that of leukemia and lymphoma in children and four times as frequently as cystic fibrosis (Winkelstein et al., 1992).

Although the initial description of patients with primary immunodeficiency diseases focused on their increased susceptibility to infections, these patients may also exhibit a variety of other clinical manifestations. In fact, in some patients, the noninfectious manifestations such as autoimmune disease, gastrointestinal disease, or both may be the predominant clinical expression of their underlying immunodeficiency (Winkelstein et al., 1992).

Characteristics

1. An increased susceptibility to infection.
2. In most children, this susceptibility is manifested by recurrent infections. Often, individual infections are not more severe than those that occur in a normal host. Rather, the striking clinical feature is the recurring, chronic nature of the infections.
3. Typically, the infections do not occur only in a single anatomic site; rather, they usually involve multiple organs or multiple sites within the same organ. For example, some children will have recurrent otitis media in association with recurrent sinusitis or pneumonia, whereas other children may have recurrent pneumonia, with episodes occurring in different lobes. Recurrent sinopulmonary infections such as otitis, sinusitis, bronchitis, and pneumonia are the most common.

There are a number of specific medical therapies available to patients with primary immunodeficiency diseases. Two of the most common of these therapies are gamma globulin therapy and bone marrow transplantation. Their specific indications and the disorders for which they may be of benefit should be discussed with a physician (Immune Deficiency Foundation).

In the case of B-cell disease, a near-normal life may be expected if the diagnosis is made early and treatment is begun before serious infections develop. In any event, he or she will require some form of gamma globulin replacement therapy throughout life.

In the case of T-cell deficiency diseases, therapy tends to be more difficult. In many instances, bone marrow transplantation is the preferred therapy.

Due to the chronic nature of these disorders and the aftereffects of the disease, many of those affected alter their lifestyles to preserve their health. The most common obstacles to overcome are those associated with absences from school. Absences may frequently occur due to illnesses or the need for doctor visits and therapy. Homebound programs and dual enrollment options provide the flexibility needed to adapt to these unusual situations. Often, the school setting provides the opportunity for affected children to become more responsible for their own health care. Public education, although it results in increased infection exposure, is usually well tolerated by children whose immune systems are being reconstituted.

Other special needs may be required on an individual basis, not as a direct result of the immune disorders but due to the aftereffects of repeated infections. Some examples include special diets, frequent meals or special restroom privileges due to intestinal malabsorption, hall passes or scheduled nursing visits for medication administration, or assignment of classes to minimize absences (Reynolds & Fletcher-Janzen, 2000).

The study of primary immune deficiencies has resulted in several major advances in medicine. These advances include the first bone marrow transplants in 1968, the first use of enzyme replacement therapy (injection of the missing gene product) in 1985, and the first use of human gene therapy in 1990 (Immune Deficiency Foundation).

Intensive research continues into the cause, diagnosis, treatment, and cure of primary immune deficiency diseases. The recent identification of several of the specific genetic causes of primary immune deficiency will allow better diagnosis and therapy. Further research is needed to completely understand the intricate coordination of the various parts of the immune system and how to strengthen a person's immunity. As in the past, continued investigations into the cause and treatment of primary immune deficiency diseases will lead to new hope not only for those who have primary immunodeficiency disease, but also for individuals with the more than 4,000 other known genetic disorders.

REFERENCES

Immune Deficiency Foundation. *Immune deficiency diseases: An overview.* Ellicott City, MD:

Immune Deficiency Foundation. *Patient and family handbook.* Ellicott City, MD:

Reynolds, C., & Fletcher-Janzen, E. (2000). *Encyclopedia of special education* (2nd ed.). New York: Wiley.

Winkelstein, J. (1992). *Diseases: A primer for physicians, 1992.* Ellicott City, MD:

Susie Whitman
Immune Deficiency Foundation
Odessa, Texas

PROGEROID SYNDROMES (PROGERIA)

Progeria is a rare genetic disorder characterized by an appearance of accelerated aging. Its name is derived from the Greek, meaning *prematurely old.* The classic type is the Hutchinson-Gilford Progeria syndrome, which was first described in England in 1886 by Dr. Jonathan Hutchinson and again in 1886 and 1904 by Dr. Hastings Gilford. Some progeroid syndromes manifest symptoms of premature aging at birth, such as Bamatter-Francescetti syndrome, Berardinelli-Seip syndrome, De Barsy syndrome, Hallerman-Streiff syndrome, Von Lohuizen syndrome, and Wiedemann-Rautenstrauch syndrome. Others become clinically apparent later in life, such as Cockayne syndrome, Hutchinson-Gilford progeria syndrome, and Werner syndrome. Progeroid syndromes occur in about 1 per 4 million births. They affect both sexes in equal proportion and have been observed in all races (Brown, 2000).

Characteristics

1. A distinct physical appearance, including characteristics generally associated with old age—for example, aged-looking skin, baldness, loss of subcutaneous fat, loss of teeth, and dwarfism
2. The presence of secondary disorders typical of older individuals, such as atherosclerosis, joint stiffness, and cardiovascular problems
3. Normal intellectual development
4. Premature mortality, which varies depending on the specific syndrome

There is no specific treatment or cure for progeria. However, there are progeria support groups, as well as a foundation devoted to progeria research accessible via the Internet, which may be useful to children and their families, both in monitoring medical developments and in increasing social support (Brown, 2000).

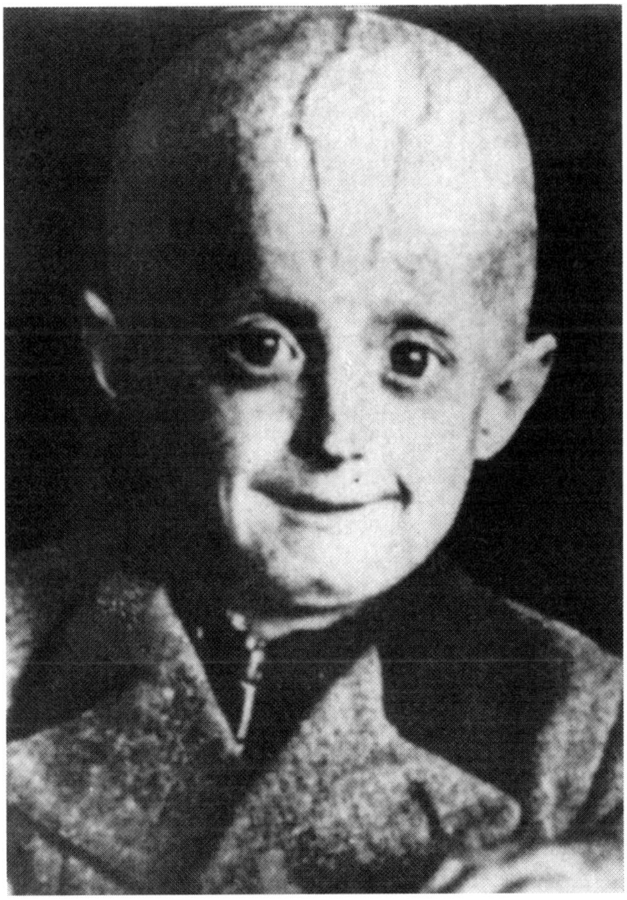

Progeria
Reprinted from *Clinical Syndromes,* Wiedemann and Kunze, 1997, by permission of the publisher Mosby

Although children with progeria have normal intellectual functioning, their medical condition may present challenges in an educational context. Frequent medical attention may be needed by children with progeria, resulting in loss of school time. Moreover, their unusual appearance may be a source of unwanted attention from others who are not familiar with the disorder. This attention sometimes takes the form of stares, teasing, or intrusive questions. A sense of isolation has also been reported among individuals with progeria and their families, due to the extreme rareness of the illness. If these issues are addressed, however, there is no reason that children with progeria cannot function in a mainstream educational context.

REFERENCE

Brown, W. T. (2000). *The progeria syndrome fact sheet.* Peabody, MA: Progeria Research Foundation.

Derek D. Satre
University of California

PROGRESSIVE OSSEOUS HETEROPLASIA

Progressive osseous heteroplasia (POH), which is characterized by patches of dermal ossification during infancy and progressive heterotopic ossification of superficial and deep connective tissues such as muscles, tendons, and ligaments during childhood, was first described in 1994 (Kaplan, Glaser, Gannon, & Shore, 1998; National Organization for Rare Disorders [NORD], 1996). POH is an extremely rare disorder; Kaplan et al. (1998) report 13 classic cases, and the International Fibrodysplasia Ossificans Progressiva Association (IFOPA, 1999) reports fewer than 36 known patients.

Although it has been found that POH is transmitted in an autosomal dominant Mendelian fashion, the etiology and pathogenesis of POH remain unknown. Researchers investigating genetic explanations have reported several key developments. The role of a promising candidate gene, which has been linked to bone formation, in regulating the expression of the phenotype is being investigated (Kaplan et al., 1998). A recent report from IFOPA (1999) may have identified a gene for POH that encodes a protein found in nearly every cell of the body. This protein functions as a relay switch to instruct the cell's nucleus what the cell should become. More research is necessary to determine how the protein triggers ectopic bone formation, but at present, it is hypothesized that the protein normally inhibits the activity of other genes involved in bone formation.

Characteristics

1. Congenital papular rash
2. Cutaneous ossification
3. Muscle ossification
4. Superficial to deep progression
5. Severe limitation of mobility
6. May have ectopic ossification after trauma (e.g., a fall)

Source: Kaplan et al.(1998)

Plaques of bone formation on the skin can be identified soon after birth (Kaplan et al., 1998; NORD, 1996). Eventually, deeper connective tissues are invaded, which can result in the severe restriction of movement in the affected joints, restrain growth in an affected limb, or both. The primary pathway for heterotopic ossification is intramembranous. Also, it is possible for marrow elements to be present in the ectopic bone (Kaplan et al., 1998). No congenital skeletal malformations or predictable regional patterns of progression are evident (Kaplan et al., 1998; NORD, 1996). Patients with POH have been documented to have normal intelligence, normal developmental milestones, and normal sustained biochemical and endocrine functioning (Kaplan et al., 1998).

There is no known cure or specific treatment for POH (Kaplan et al., 1998; NORD, 1996). Long-term prognosis for patients with POH is also uncertain at this time. Medications can be prescribed to manage associated symptoms such as pain and inflammation (IFOPA, 1999). Children with POH may be eligible to receive services under the Individuals with Disabilities Act (IDEA) due to physical disability. Because of the progressive nature of POH and the increasing restriction of movement, teaching and classroom accommodations such as the use of assisted technologies may become increasingly necessary.

REFERENCES

International Fibrodysplasia Ossificans Progressiva Association. (1999). POH gene found. Retrieved September 2001, from http://earth.vol.com/~skant//research/report/poh.htm

Kaplan, F. S., Glaser, D. M., Gannon, F. H., & Shore, E. M. (1998, Spring). The molecules of immobility: Searching for the skeleton key. *University of Pennsylvania Orthopaedic Journal, 11.* Retrieved September 2001, from http://health.upenn.edu/ortho/oj/oj11sp98p59.html

National Organization for Rare Disorders. (1996). NORD Rare Disease Database: Progressive Osseous Heteroplasia. Retrieved September 2001, from http://www.rarediseases.org/cgi-bin/nord/abstrfly?id=s45X22Nb&mv_arg=RDB%2d1046&mv_pc=143

Alexandra S. Kutz
Margaret Semrud-Clikeman
University of Texas at Austin

PROTEUS SYNDROME

Described clearly as a syndrome only as recently as 1983, Proteus syndrome, named for the Greek god, Proteus the polymorphous, is a progressive disorder associated with characteristic abnormalities in growth, skin and subcutaneous tissue, and the skeletal system. Current evidence suggests that Joseph Merrick (known as the Elephant Man) probably had Proteus syndrome, not neurofibromatosis as had been long thought. The name indicates the wide variability in expression of the disorder: Abnormalities of various degree may develop in virtually all bodily systems. Indeed, too many abnormalities occur occasionally to list here. The disorder does not appear to be familial, and its specific cause is unknown. As might be expected considering the variability of bodily areas affected, somatic mosaicism is a likely basis (Jones, 1997). The disorder is rare, with only 90 confirmed cases worldwide (Proteus Foundation, 2001).

Characteristics

1. Overgrowth that may be general, unilateral, limited to one limb, or even one digit; increased height and macrocephaly

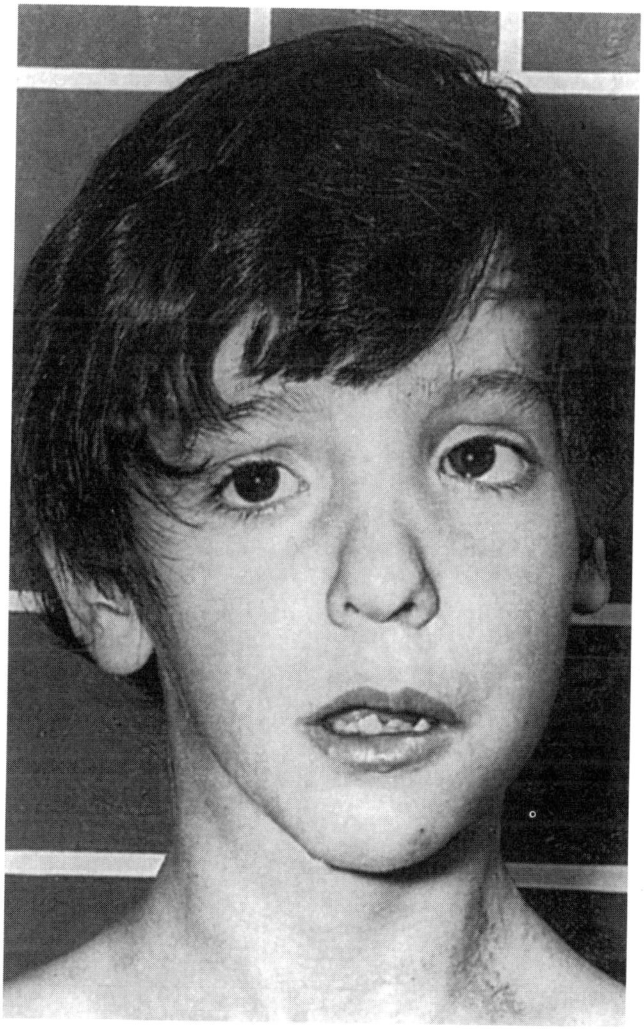

Proteus Syndrome
Reprinted from *Clinical Syndromes,* Wiedemann and Kunze, 1997, by permission of the publisher Mosby

2. Overall thickening of the skin and subcutaneous tissue, with numerous specific abnormalities largely limited to the thorax and upper abdomen
3. Variety of skeletal defects, including hemihypertrophy, prominent bony areas in skull, knee deformities, scoliosis and kyphosis, hip dislocation, clinodactyly, and macrodactyly

Newborns are generally normal in appearance except for increased body weight, although a few have shown classic signs shortly after birth. Features appear during the 1st year of life and progress through childhood. After puberty, general overgrowth diminishes or stops. Depending on the location and degree of abnormalities, spinal stenosis and various neurological problems may develop. Mental retardation occurs in about 20% of cases. Early death because of a variety of complications is common, and careful medical monitoring is necessary.

Diagnosis is on the basis of clinical signs, which may include one or more of the following: partial and usually asymmetrical enlargement of the hands, feet, or both; pigmented nevi (patches of darkened, raised, and rough skin); subcutaneous tumors similar to lymphangionas and lipomas); skull anomalies such as macrocephaly or hemihypertrophy; and plantar hyperplasia (Proteus Foundation, 2001).

No treatment that stops the progress of the disorder is available. Surgery may be necessary to reduce the extent of skeletal and skin-subcutaneous deformities. A variety of special services, particularly physical therapy, may be needed. Counseling to help affected individuals and their families deal with the abnormal appearance and functioning associated with the disorder may also be useful.

REFERENCES

Jones, K. L. (1997). *Smith's recognizable patterns of human malformation* (5th ed.). Philadelphia: W. B. Saunders.

Proteus Foundation. (2001). About Proteus syndrome. Retrieved from http://www.proteus-syndrome.org/

Robert T. Brown
University of North Carolina, Wilmington

PRUNE BELLY SYNDROME

Children born with prune belly syndrome (PBS) share three main characteristics (a) insufficient abdominal musculature, (b) urinary anomalies, and (c) undescended testes in males. Prune belly syndrome may also be called Eagle-Barrett syndrome and occasionally abdominal muscle deficiency syndrome, congenital absence of the abdominal muscles, Obrinsky syndrome, or mesenchymal dysplasia (Furness, Cheng, Franco, & Firlit, 1998; National Organization for Rare Disorders, 2000; Sutherland, Mevorach, & Kogan, 1995).

Incidence of PBS ranges from 1 in 35,000–50,000. Although the cause is unknown, PBS may be a sex-linked recessive disorder because only 3–5% of cases occur in females. Researchers have also found associations with malnutrition, maternal cocaine use, other sex-linked disorders, autosomal recessive disorders, and chromosomal anomalies such as trisomy 18 (Sutherland et al., 1995).

Characteristics

1. Child is born with a distended abdomen and has prune-like wrinkled skin on stomach.
2. High serum creatine levels in the first few days after birth indicate renal insufficiency.

3. A variety of urethral, bladder, and renal anomalies become apparent.
4. In males, the testes are undescended.

Diagnosis of PBS usually occurs at birth. When a newborn has a distended abdomen and wrinkled skin on the belly (and undescended testes in males), PBS should be suspected and immediate action taken to test the newborn's urinary activity and renal function to identify characteristic anomalies. An ultrasound can be used to determine problem areas such as renal failure or urinary obstructions (Sutherland et al., 1995).

Treatment consists of one or more surgeries to reduce functional and aesthetic problems in the child with PBS: (a) urinary tract reconstruction rectifies the reflux problem and helps alleviate voiding problems; (b) abdominal wall reconstruction tightens the abdominal muscles and removes excess skin, creating a more aesthetically pleasing appearance and alleviating some of the pressure on internal organs; and (c) orchidopexy brings the testes down into the scrotum (Pediatric Urology Associates, 2001). All three surgeries are not necessary in every case, but they can be done simultaneously if needed. Orchidopexy should be performed in infancy to increase chances of fertility (Sutherland et al., 1995).

The infant with PBS may experience delays in motor development, including sitting up and walking, due to the lack of abdominal muscles. The main problem for children with PBS is abnormal bladder drainage. These children may experience renal deterioration or urinary infection, so they must be monitored closely so that preventive antibiotics can be administered. Self-catheterization may be possible after the child is old enough to perform the task (Sutherland et al., 1995).

Of those with PBS, 20% will be stillborn and 50% will die within 2 years after birth (Magalini & Scrascia, 1981). For those who survive infancy, prognosis is good. These children can be expected to live long lives with relatively minor complications such as lifelong catheterization. Aside from the effects of possible multiple surgeries, children with PBS can be expected to develop normally in other physical aspects (Sutherland et al., 1995).

Incidence of PBS is so low that very few follow-up cases have been studied for special needs in emotional and mental development. Little is known about special education needs for such children. At one time, before technological advances in reconstructive surgery, the child with PBS could be expected to suffer from severe low self-esteem due to poor self-image. At present, the child with PBS is most likely to suffer the psychological sequelae associated with multiple surgeries and hospital stays and later with the continued catheterization.

Current research on the diagnosis of PBS allows for prenatal ultrasonographic detection of abnormal urinary tract dilation. In the past, termination of the fetus was the only preventive option, but technological advances now allow prenatal intervention. In particular, antenatal decompression of the dilated bladder can improve the postnatal functioning of the lungs, improving chances for survival (Sutherland et al., 1995). Other areas of research focus on improvements in reconstructive surgery, both in urinary tract reconstruction and abdominal wall reconstruction (Furness et al., 1998).

REFERENCES

Furness, P., Cheng, E., Franco, I., & Firlit, C. (1998). The prune-belly syndrome: a new and simplified technique of abdominal wall reconstruction. *Journal of Urology, 160,* 1195–1197.

Magalini, S., & Scrascia, E. (1981). *Dictionary of medical syndromes* (2nd ed.). Philadelphia: J. B. Lippincott.

National Organization for Rare Disorders. (2000). Prune belly syndrome. Retrieved from http://www.rarediseases.org/

Pediatric Urology Associates. (2001). Prune belly syndrome. Retrieved from http://www.pedsurology.com/prune.htm

Sutherland, R., Mevorach, R., & Kogan, B. (1995). The prune-belly syndrome: Current insights. *Pediatric Neurology, 9,* 770–778.

Melanie Moore
Robert T. Brown
University of North Carolina, Wilmington

PSEUDO-HURLER POLYDYSTROPHY

Pseudo-Hurler polydystrophy or mucolipidosis III is one of many disorders involving the mucopolysaccharides (complex carbohydrates) and mucolipids (fatty substances). In particular, multiple lysosomal enzymes and glycoproteins are implicated in pseudo-Hurler polydystrophy, with a resulting accumulation of mucopolysaccharides and glycolipids.

Pseudo-Hurler is transmitted in an autosomal recessive pattern, with multiple enzymes implicated. There are equal numbers of males and females affected (National Organization for Rare Disorders, 1998). There is no indication of a greater likelihood of pseudo-Hurler polydystrophy in any particular ethnic group(s).

Characteristics

1. Acne
2. Joint stiffness
3. Dwarfism
4. Mild mental retardation
5. Hearing loss
6. Enlarged tongue

The severity with which the polydystrophy is manifested ranges from mild to more severe (Ward et al., 1993), possibly due to heterozygosity or homozygosity. Symptoms generally manifest in childhood but may manifest in adulthood. Often the initial symptoms include progressive stiffness of the joints of the hands and may be misinterpreted as a rheumatological disorder (Brik et al., 1993). Pseudo-Hurler can be distinguished from rheumatological disorders by the elevated levels of plasma alpha-L-fucosidase. Additional characteristics of pseudo-Hurler polydystrophy include decreased mobility or restricted range of motion, short stature, defective bone formations, and cardiac complications, including aortic valve disease.

Individuals with pseudo-Hurler polydystrophy are not likely to experience pain, swelling, or tenderness in association with the joint stiffness. Although they are initially progressive in nature, limitations to movement as a result of joint stiffness generally stabilize with no further deterioration at puberty. With age, it is not uncommon for there to be an increased likelihood of cardiac and circulation problems; medical conditions will require monitoring.

Mild mental retardation frequently occurs in conjunction with pseudo-Hurler polydystrophy. As a result, children affected will require special education intervention when they begin school. Additional supports may be necessary (e.g., orthopedic care or physical therapy, accommodations for physical limitations or fatigue), depending on the severity of the disease presentation. Genetic counseling of family members may be beneficial as well.

REFERENCES

Brik, R., Mandel, H., Aizin, A., Goldsher, D., Ziegler, M., Bialik, V., et al. (1993). Mucolipidosis III presenting as a rheumatological disorder. *Journal of Rheumatology, 20,* 133–136.

National Association for Rare Disorders. (1998). Pseudo Hurler Polydystrophy (Report 303). Retrieved May 25, 2001, from www.rarediseases.org

Ward, C., Singh, R., Slade, C., Fensom, A. H., Fahmy, A., Semrin, A., et al. (1993). A mild form of mucolipidosis type III in four Baluch siblings. *Clinical Genetics, 44,* 313–319.

Cynthia A. Riccio
Texas A&M University

PSEUDOHYPOPARATHYROIDISM

Pseudohypoparathyroidism is a rare hereditary disorder that affects bone growth and the metabolism of minerals (Williams, 1974). It is one of a group of diseases resulting from hypocalcemia due to the body's inadequate response to the parathyroid hormone. Pseudohypoparathyroidism is sometimes also known as Martin-Albright syndrome (National Organization for Rare Disorders, 1999). It may also be found when Turner syndrome exists (Williams, 1974).

Parathyroid hormone is produced by the four parathyroid glands, which surround the thyroid gland in the neck. These glands produce more parathyroid hormone when there is a decrease in the calcium concentration in the blood. This parathyroid hormone stimulates the kidneys to activate vitamin D, which in turn improves the ability of the gastrointestinal tract to absorb calcium. Parathyroid hormone also stimulates the bones to release calcium into the blood and causes the kidneys to excrete less calcium into the urine (Berkow, Beers, Bogin, & Fletcher, 1997). A patient with pseudohypoparathyroidism will have normal to elevated levels of parathyroid hormone in the body, but the bones and kidneys will not have a normal response to this hormone (Berkow et al., 1997).

An individual with pseudohypoparathyroidism will exhibit poor bone growth, which results in short stature. The disorder is often accompanied by headaches, weakness, unusual sensations, lack of energy, fatigue, blurred vision, and abnormal sensitivity to light. Some patients may have convulsions (Williams, 1974). A round face, obesity, abnormally short fourth fingers, defective nails and teeth, cataracts, and brain calcification are also symptoms of pseudohypoparathyroidism. Some patients have also complained of stiffness or cramps in the arms or legs, abdominal pain, and palpitations (National Organization for Rare Disorders, 1999; Tierney, McPhee, & Papadakis, 2001).

Typically, patients are diagnosed at between 5 and 10 years of age (Williams, 1974). Symptoms can be very similar to those exhibited from hypoparathyroidism. The difference can be determined by analyzing the body's chemical reaction to treatment with parathyroid hormone.

Characteristics

1. Poor bone growth, resulting in short stature.
2. Rare hereditary disorder that affects bone growth and the metabolism of minerals.
3. Round face, obesity, abnormally short fourth fingers, defective nails and teeth, cataracts, and brain calcification.
4. Often accompanied by headaches, weakness, unusual sensations, lack of energy, fatigue, blurred vision, and abnormal sensitivity to light.
5. Some patients may have convulsions, stiffness, or cramps in the arms or legs, abdominal pain, and palpitations.
6. Frequently identified in newborns.
7. May also exhibit changes in the central nervous system.
8. Other symptoms may be severe constipation, profuse sweating, decreased body temperature, heart rate variability, and eye irregularities.

Parathyroid hormone, calcium replacement, and sometimes vitamin D therapy have been shown to help patients with pseudohypoparathyroidism (National Organization for Rare Disorders, 1999). However, this treatment may not inhibit the lack of growth. The prognosis for this disorder can be positive with early diagnosis and treatment. However, dental changes, cataracts, and brain calcification are permanent (Tierney et al., 2001). It is important to periodically check the calcium levels in the blood to modify treatment accordingly.

Pseudohypoparathyroidism may result in mental retardation (National Organization for Rare Disorders, 1999). Children affected in this way may require special education services. A study by Megson (2000) suggests that children with one parent with pseudohypoparathyroidism may be genetically at risk for a protein defect that could possibly result in autism.

Ongoing research is being conducted to identify the gene mutations that cause pseudohypoparathyroidism (Spiegel, 2001). This research may result in additional methods of treatment for the disorder.

REFERENCES

Berkow, R., Beers, M. H., Bogin, R. M., & Fletcher, A. J. (Eds.). (1997). *The Merck manual of medical information.* Whitehouse Station, NJ: Merck Research Laboratories.

Megson, M. H. (2000). Is autism a G-alpha protein defect reversible with natural vitamin A? *Medical Hypotheses, 54*(6), 979–983.

National Organization for Rare Disorders. (1999). Pseudohypoparathyroidism. Retrieved from http://www.stepstn.com/cgi-win/NationalOrganizationforRareDisorders.exe?proc=GetDocument&rectype0&recnum=625

Spiegel, A. M. (2001). Senior scientists' projects. Retrieved from http://www.niddk.nih.gov/intram/people/aspiegel.htm

Tierney, L. M., Jr., McPhee, S. J., & Papadakis, M. A. (Eds.). (2001). *Current medical diagnosis and treatment* (40th ed.). New York: Lange Medical Books, McGraw-Hill.

Williams, R. H. (Ed.). (1974). *Textbook of endocrinology.* Philadelphia: Saunders.

Michele Wilson Kamens
Rider University

PSEUDOSEIZURES

Pseudoseizures, also known as psychogenic seizures, are episodes of altered movement or behavior that resemble epileptic seizures but have no associated electroencephalogram (EEG) findings and no identifiable physiological cause. The episode lacks certain characteristic features of a true seizure but simulates a generalized tonic-clonic seizure. Less often, pseudoseizures mimic complex partial, atonic, myoclonic, or absence seizures. Unlike what occurs in a true tonic-clonic seizure, individuals report a marked degree of awareness during the seizure. The motor behaviors are also unusual, consisting of brief irregular clonic movements (e.g., thrashing and jerking). Unusual flapping, arching of the back, and pelvic thrusting can also be observed.

Pseudoseizures occur during childhood but are more common during adolescence and adulthood. The diagnosis of a psychogenic seizure is made in 5–9% of individuals referred to epilepsy centers and is made more often in females than in males by a ratio of 3:1 (Lancman, Asconape, Graves, & Gibson, 1994). Observation of the actual event can distinguish a pseudoseizure from a true seizure in most cases; however, diagnosis can be difficult at times. It is therefore important to do simultaneous EEG-video monitoring in order to observe behaviors while recording electrical activity. Obtaining a complete history of the seizure beforehand, however, can alert clinicians to the likelihood of a pseudoseizure. Certain descriptions that suggest seizure-like activity is not due to epileptiform abnormalities found in true seizures include reports of memory for seizure activity, predominant daytime seizures, combativeness (when not being restrained), and vulgarities. Unlike true seizures, psychoseizures have rare incidence of urinary incontinence and self-injury (e.g., tongue biting).

Characteristics

1. Absence of epileptiform EEG activity.
2. Aura is absent or consists of palpitation, malaise, or choking sensation.
3. Periods of unresponsiveness.
4. Movements consist of brief and irregular clonic movements, or thrashing, jerking movements (including flapping and pelvic thrusting).
5. Different types of movements may occur simultaneously.
6. Urinary incontinence and tongue biting are rare.
7. Episode terminates suddenly, and former activities are resumed with no postictal confusion.
8. Distress is expressed followed by nonstereotyped but semipurposeless behaviors.

Many children who experience pseudoseizures have witnessed a real seizure at some point, and a significant percentage of children with pseudoseizures also have true epilepsy, usually in the form of complex partial or generalized motor seizures (Holmes & Stafstrom, 1998). Often the pseudoseizures begin after the actual seizures have come under control and the secondary gain of the epilepsy is lost (Fenichel, 1997). Emotional stress may be a precursor to the onset of symptoms. There is some evidence that histories of PTSD and trauma, including physical and sexual abuse, are more common in those who have psychogenic nonepileptic seizures than in patients with true epileptic seizures (Rosenberg, Rosenberg, Williamson, & Wolford, 2000).

Pseudoseizures reflect underlying psychopathology that necessitates proper diagnosis and psychological treatment. Prior to the onset of treatment, a functional behavioral assessment should be conducted to determine what function(s) the pseudoseizure serves, and what potential triggering events may be. Special education services may be needed in rare cases in which the child's learning is affected by the disorder. In these cases, services are likely to be provided under Emotional Disturbance. Psychological therapy is more likely needed to provide alternative coping mechanisms and reduce stress (e.g., teaching stress management and relaxation techniques, biofeedback, etc.).

The prognosis for pseudoseizures depends on a number of factors, including the age at which the disorder is diagnosed and treated. Younger children who fail to get proper treatment often have worse outcomes; however, in general, younger people tend to have a better prognosis than do adults. In fact, between 78% and 81% of children and adolescents have been found to be free of pseudoseizures 3 years after diagnosis (Holmes & Stafstrom, 1998). Research, however, is needed to determine risk factors. Information about effective treatments is also needed—in particular, behavioral treatments.

REFERENCES

Fenichel, G. M. (1997). *Clinical pediatric neurology: A signs and symptoms approach* (3rd ed.). Philadelphia: W. B. Saunders.

Holmes, G. L., & Stafstrom, C. E. (1998). The epilepsies. In R. B. David (Ed.), *Child and adolescent neurology* (pp. 183–234). St. Louis, MO: Mosby Year-Book.

Lancman, M. E., Asconape, J. J., Graves, S., & Gibson, P. A. (1994). Psychogenic seizures in children: Long-term analysis of 43 cases. *Journal of Child Neurology, 9,* 404–407.

Rosenberg, H. J., Rosenberg, S. D., Williamson, P. D., & Wolford, G. L. (2000). A comparative study of trauma and posttraumatic stress disorder prevalence in epilepsy patients and psychogenic nonepileptic seizure patients. *Epilepsia, 41,* 447–452.

Elizabeth Christiansen
Elaine Clark
University of Utah

PSEUDOXANTHOMA ELASTICUM

Pseudoxanthoma elasticum (PXE) is an inherited disorder in which elastic fibers in three organ systems (the skin, retina of the eyes, and cardiovascular system) become slowly calcified.

PXE is reported to occur in approximately 100,000 individuals. It is believed by those who study this disorder, however, that this estimate is conservative and that there are probably many undiagnosed individuals.

Characteristics

1. The first manifestation of PXE is the appearance of highly characteristic, slightly thickened, cobblestone-like patches of skin. These patches first appear on the neck and later on other folds of skin (e.g., underarms, groins, and behind knees).
2. Changes generally appear around 13 years of age, but they can appear from as early as 2 years and as late as 20 years.
3. By age 20–25, most patients have angioid streaks (thin cracks in the retina).
4. Angioid streaks do not cause visual defects but are sites for future retinal hemorrhages that occur with increasing frequency after age 45.
5. Retinal hemorrhages often occur in the macula (area of central sharp vision) and result in central vision loss.
6. Cardiovascular involvement, usually in the peripheral arteries in the legs and arms, occurs after skin and retina lesions, commonly in the form of intermittent claudication (pain or aching in the legs after walking or vigorous exercise).
7. Heart attacks and strokes can happen, but the occurrence is not more prevalent than in the general population.
8. Bleeding from the stomach occurs in 10% of people with PXE. It usually begins suddenly and may require hospitalization.

There is no cure at this time. The following have been found to reduce the frequency and severity of PXE: a regular exercise program; sports such as track, swimming, or bicycling (however, sports that include heavy strain or the possibility of head injury should be avoided, e.g., boxing, soccer, weightlifting); maintenance of normal weight; regular checkups of blood pressure and cholesterol levels; maintenance of a calcium intake at or slightly lower than the recommended daily allowance (800 mg per day); avoidance of anti-inflammatory drugs (e.g., aspirin) because they thin the blood and make bleeding easier. There are prescription medicines that can help the intermittent claudication. Any slight vomiting of blood or black, tarry stools require immediate medical attention. Individuals with the disorder should have regular eye exams, preferably with someone who understands PXE; some ophthalmologists recommend a vitamin supplement (vitamins A, C, and E, plus zinc and selenium). This measure may be helpful in preventing retinal hemorrhages.

A child with PXE may be eligible for special education

services under IDEA if he or she meets the criteria for Physical Disability. To qualify for that category, a letter from the student's physician may be needed to identify the student's medical diagnosis and how the disease affects educational functioning. Alternatively, such children may benefit from some accommodations under Section 504. Children with PXE will need continued medical and visual monitoring to examine the progression of the disorder. No cure or medical intervention is known at present; this may be a cause for concern for the family and for the student. Therefore, counseling to address this issue and to address questions of self-esteem and body image may be necessary. New coping skills for living with the everyday challenges of PXE must be learned. Children with PXE should avoid activities that may result in injuries to the head; various sporting activities should therefore be avoided. However, students should be encouraged to maintain regular exercise and diet to help relieve some of the effects of PXE.

In December 1996, Chromosome 16 was identified as carrying the defective gene. Therefore, current research is attempting to identify the location of the defective gene upon Chromosome 16. In the meantime, clinical studies indicate that control of the environmental risk factors mentioned previously can manage the effects of PXE.

REFERENCE

Hacker, S. M., Ramos-Caro, F. A., Beers, B. B., & Flowers, F. P. (1993). Juvenile pseudoxanthoma elasticum: Recognition and management. *Pediatric Dermatology 10*(1), 19–25.

Rachel Toplis
University of Northern Colorado

PSYCHOSIS, AMPHETAMINE

Amphetamines are stimulants to the central nervous system. Their effect is similar to that of the body's own adrenaline. Even though amphetamines mimic the effects of adrenaline, they act for a much longer time in the body. Illicit synthesis and use of methamphetamine is the chief type of amphetamine abuse in North America. Although they are available by prescription, amphetamines are no longer used as appetite suppressants and infrequently used for other conditions. An amphetamine psychosis is similar to paranoid schizophrenia. It occurs when the person misinterprets others' actions, hallucinates, and becomes unrealistically suspicious. After the stimulation phase, individuals experience intense fatigue, a need for sleep, and a prolonged depression, during which suicide is possible. The psychosis results from long-term use of high IV doses but can result from high oral doses.

Characteristics

1. Characteristics similar to those of paranoid schizophrenia
2. Delusions of persecution and feelings of omnipotence
3. Paranoid delusions, including auditory and visual hallucinations
4. Increased alertness, talkativeness, and aggression
5. Reduced appetite
6. Increased heart rate, breathing rate, and blood pressure
7. Rise in body temperature

Additional effects include the following:

1. Fever and sweating
2. Impaired speech
3. Loss of coordination
4. Insomnia

Prolonged use of amphetamines can lead to the following:

1. Malnutrition
2. Skin disorders
3. Ulcers
4. Weight loss
5. Depression with a risk of suicide

The acute agitated psychotic state responds very well to medications such as phenothiazines (e.g., chlorpromazine). Ammonium chloride may be given to acidify the urine and hasten amphetamine excretion. Antidepressants and sedatives may be prescribed on a short-term basis. Individuals will also require reassurance and a quiet, nonthreatening environment to aid recovery. In addition, treatment should include group counseling and peer pressure because these forms of therapy have been found to be effective with this population. The psychotic state usually dissipates in about a week after treatment.

A student experiencing amphetamine psychosis requires immediate medical attention. School personnel should follow crisis intervention guidelines to provide effective service for the student, family, and peers. Follow-up interventions should include referrals to local drug treatment agencies, rehabilitation, and counseling.

Research into the use of amphetamine psychosis includes looking into treatment effects (e.g., Srisurapanont, Kittiratanapaiboon, & Jarusuraisin, 2001) and the function of neuropsychological factors (e.g., dopamine receptors) on amphetamine sensitivity (Richtand, Woods, Berger, & Strkowski, 2001). For more information on amphetamine psychosis and support groups, contact National Institute on Drug Abuse, 6001 Executive Boulevard,

Bethesda, MD 20892-9561, (301)443-1124, http://www.drugabuse.gov

REFERENCES

Bartosik, V. (2000). Amphetamine psychosis. In C. R. Reynolds & E. Fletcher-Janzen (Eds.), *Encyclopedia of special education* (2nd ed.). Wiley.

Richtand, N. M., Woods, S. C., Berger, S. P., & Strkowski, S. M., (2001). D3 dopamine receptor, behavioral sensitization, and psychosis. *Neuroscience Biobehavioral Review, 25*(5), 427–443.

Srisurapanont, M., Kittiratanapaiboon, P., & Jarusuraisin, N. (2001). Treatment for amphetamine psychosis (Cochrane Review). *Cochrane Database Systems Review, 4, CD003026.*

Rachel Toplis
University of Northern Colorado

PSYCHOSIS, STEROID

Steroid psychosis (SP) is a syndrome caused by an acute response to treatment with corticosteroids, such as prednisone. SP may persist even if corticosteroid treatment is discontinued. Treatment with steroids such as prednisone is common for individuals with respiratory conditions, such as asthma, or systemic conditions, such as lupus nephritis. SP is a rare and variable side effect of corticosteroid treatment (Davis, Leach, Merk, & Janicak, 1992).

It has been difficult to assess the exact incidence of SP because studies have generally used a narrow definition of SP and because the amount and length of steroid use have varied widely in patient groups researched (Wolkowitz, Reus, Canick, Bronson, & Lupien, 1997). In general, Wolkowitz et al. (1997) suggest that the higher the dose of corticosteroids ingested, the greater the risk of side effects such as SP. Reported incidence is 1.3% at less than a 40-mg dose of a prednisone equivalent to up to 18.4% at prednisone doses of greater than 80 mg. Wolkowitz et al. (1997) authors also suggest that although dose is a predictor of some SP symptoms, dose does not predict onset, severity, or type of SP symptoms observed. In addition, prior psychiatric history of mental illness and even history of having had a prior SP response do not reliably predict whether an individual is more at risk for experiencing SP (Wolkowitz et al., 1997). However, female gender may be associated with a higher risk of SP with corticosteroid use.

Characteristics

1. Affective symptoms include insomnia, mixed mood disturbance (hypomania, mania, depression, suicidal thinking), paranoia, and anxiety.
2. Psychotic symptoms include prominent hallucinations or delusions that are judged to be the direct physiological effects of corticosteroids.

If a person with SP is taken off corticosteroids, 79% of affected individuals will experience few if any symptoms after a few days (Davis et al., 1992; Wolkowitz et al., 1997). However, sometimes patients have additional withdrawal symptoms such as depression, irritability, labile affect, apathy, a sense of emptiness, fatigue, sleep and appetite disturbances, somatic complaints (i.e., "band-like" sensations in the head), depersonalization, and decreased concentration and memory (Wolkowitz et al., 1997). Withdrawal symptoms generally disappear in 6–8 weeks, although in certain rare cases, symptoms have persisted for up to several months. In some cases of SP, if the patient has a life-threatening medical need for corticosteroid treatment, treatment for SP would be initiated without ending corticosteroid treatment.

Aside from removing a patient with SP from corticosteroid treatment, lowering his or her dose of corticosteroids, or taking a respite from this treatment, there are other ways of dealing with SP symptoms. Successful remedies include treatment with a low dose of neuroleptic or antipsychotic medication, which Davis and colleagues (1992) report an 82% positive response rate. In addition, electroconvulsive therapy (ECT) has been helpful in the rapid remission of medication-resistant affective steroid psychosis, resulting in the amelioration of symptoms in almost all cases (Davis et al., 1992). Less conclusively researched but utilized in the treatment of SP are antimanic agents such as lithium and carbamazepine. Tricyclic antidepressants have been found to exacerbate symptoms of SP and are contraindicated (Davis et al., 1992).

Teachers may have students involved with continued corticosteroid treatment for common illnesses such as asthma and less common illnesses such as lupus. If a student who normally presents as calm and mentally stable begins to exhibit symptoms typical of SP, the teacher should immediately refer his or her student to the school counselor or school psychologist. Any student experiencing SP symptoms such as hallucinations, delusions, mood disturbance, or anxiety will need to leave school premises until the symptoms are under control. SP symptoms are severe enough to warrant concern about the afflicted student's safety as well as the safety of other students. The counselor would need to notify the student's parents of the severity of the situation and should recommend that the parents take the student to a hospital emergency room as soon as possible for evaluation. The teacher and counselor have no way of knowing whether the student is exhibiting signs of a psychotic break that will be a long term mental health issue or whether the student is experiencing the more transient symptoms of SP. A trained doctor familiar with the student will help to diagnose and treat the affected student.

Davis and colleagues (1992) report that although most cases of SP respond quickly to treatment, the presence of a psychosis can be an imminent danger to the patient. Psychotic symptoms, even if they are temporary, are associated with higher morbidity and mortality rates. Future research regarding SP could focus on a variety of areas, such as more effective medication treatment and prophylactic treatment. Research in this area has been scant because SP occurs too infrequently to use random assignment and double-blind approaches, therefore lessening the scientific impact of each study's findings (Davis et al., 1992). However, these authors recommend that more researchers study SP because quantity of results can compensate for less-than-ideal research designs.

REFERENCES

Davis, J. M., Leach, A., Merk, B., & Janicak, P. G. (1992). Treatment of steroid psychosis. *Psychiatric Annals, 22,* 487–491.

Wolkowitz, O. M., Reus, V. I., Canick, J., Bronson, L., & Lupien, S. (1997). Glucocorticoid medication, memory and steroid psychosis in medical illness. *Annals of the New York Academy of Sciences, 823,* 81–96.

Jennie Kaufman Singer
California Department of Corrections, Region 1 Parole Outpatient Clinic
Sacramento, California

PUBERTY, PRECOCIOUS

Precocious puberty, also known as pubertas praecox, is an endocrine system disorder that results in the early maturation of children prior to the normal age of puberty. Precocious puberty is defined differently for each sex because of different maturational rates of girls and boys. For girls, precocious puberty occurs when sexual maturation occurs prior to the age of 8, and for boys, precocious puberty occurs when sexual maturation occurs prior to the age of 9 (InteliHealth, 1996). Alternative definitions of precocious puberty define the disorder as the appearance of secondary sexual characteristics, such as the appearance of pubic hair, early breast development, and so on, more than 2 standard deviations earlier than the population average (Pathomvanich, Merke, & Chrousos, 2000).

There are several known causes of precocious puberty. Among the most common are genetic predispositions, development of tumors, abnormal levels of normal hormones, and dysfunction of the adrenal gland (Sandberg & Barrick, 1995). Different medical tests such as pelvic ultrasound and CAT scans are sometimes recommended to rule out brain, ovarian, or adrenal tumors as causes of this disorder (Turkington, 1999).

The major concern with precocious puberty relates to the abnormal pattern of growth that it causes. Specifically, the increase in physical height that is caused by early pubertal development ultimately produces stunted bone growth (Sandberg & Barrick, 1995). Specifically, accelerated bone growth can result in fusion of the normal bone growth plates, causing short stature during adolescence and adulthood (Sandberg & Barrick, 1995).

Several studies have examined a possible link between precocious puberty and cognitive development as well as precocious sexual activity. It is interesting to note that research has revealed that no difference exists between the cognitive performance of children with precocious puberty and children with normal pubertal development (e.g., Meyer-Bahlburg et al., 1985). Additionally, recent research indicates that early sexual activity among children is not strongly associated with precocious puberty (Sandberg & Barrick, 1995; also see Mourisden & Larsen, 1992). Thus, precocious puberty does not appear to have a deleterious effect on social development and cognition.

Precocious puberty occurs infrequently, with estimates ranging from 1 case per 20,000–100,000 individuals (Rosenberg, Crowner, Thomas, & Gourash, 1992) to 1 case per 5,000–10,000 children (Turkington, 1999). The disorder is also 4–8 times more common among girls compared to boys (Turkington, 1999). The onset of this disorder is often first diagnosed by the observance of a pubertal growth spurt that occurs outside the normal time frame for pubertal maturation (Sandberg & Barrick, 1995). Other early indications are the appearance of pubic hair growth and (for girls) early breast development (Turkington, 1999).

Characteristics

1. Onset of sexual or pubertal development prior to age 8 in girls
2. Onset of sexual or pubertal development prior to age 9 in boys
3. Growth spurt prior to the normal age range for puberty
4. More common in girls than in boys
5. Early appearance of secondary sexual characteristics (e.g., breast development, appearance of pubic hair, penis growth, testicular development) prior to the normal age of pubertal onset
6. Can result in stunted bone growth if left untreated
7. Appears to have no deleterious effect on cognitive development
8. Has been linked with occurrence of earlier sexual behavior, but little research supports this conclusion

Treatment of precocious puberty varies as a function of etiology (e.g., tumor, early activation of the pituitary, etc.).

Most treatments are designed to slow the abnormal growth patterns that characterize this disorder. In order to slow down the abnormal bone growth, gonadotrophin-releasing hormone agonists (GnRH) are administered to patients (Blondell, Foster, & Dave, 1999; Pace, Miller, & Rose, 1991; Walvoord & Pescovitz, 1999). If the disorder has a threatening medical cause like a tumor, then more extensive medical procedures may be required. It also should be noted that in some instances no apparent underlying cause is pinpointed for early-onset puberty, other than early entry into pubertal maturation (Blondell et al., 1999).

Regarding the psychosocial effects of puberty, several possible courses of action have been recommended. For example, family counseling may be recommended to aid the family in understanding the effects of this disorder. Furthermore, some researchers have suggested that the affected child be placed in a classroom with older students who more closely approximate his or her physical age. School psychology services with an emphasis on social development and therapy may be needed. Such services may be especially beneficial for children who are intellectually gifted (Sandberg & Barrick, 1995). Special education services are not typically related to this disorder.

REFERENCES

Blondell, R. D., Foster, M. B., & Dave, K. C. (1999). Disorders of puberty. *American Family Physician, 60*(1). Retrieved November 28, 2000, from DISCUS/InfoTrac Search-Bank: Health Reference Center-Academic/A55419332 at http://web4.infotrac.galegroup.com/itw/session/

InteliHealth. (1996). Precocious puberty. Retrieved November 24, 2000, from http://www.intelihealth.com

Meyer-Bahlburg, H. F. L., Bruder, G. E., Feldman, J. F., Ehrhardt, A. A., Healy, J. M., & Bell, J. (1985). Cognitive abilities and hemispheric lateralization in females following idiopathic precocious puberty. *Developmental Psychology, 21*(5), 878–887.

Mourisden, S. E., & Larsen, F. W. (1992). Psychological aspects of precocious puberty: An overview. *Acta-Paedopsychiatrica: International Journal of Child and Adolescent Psychiatry, 55*(1), 45–49.

Pace, J. N., Miller, J. L., & Rose, L. I. (1991). GnRH agonists: Gonadorelin, leuprolide and nafarelin. *American Family Physician, 44*(5). Retrieved November 28, 2000, from DISCUS/InfoTrac Search Bank: Expanded Academic ASAP/A11666516 at http://web6.infotrac.galegroup.com/itw/session/

Pathomvanich, A., Merke, D. P., & Chrousos, G. P. (2000). Early puberty: A cautionary tale. *Pediatrics, 105*(1). Retrieved November 28, 2000, from DISCUS/InfoTrac Search Bank: Health Reference Center-Academic/A59034694 at http://web4.infotrac.galegroup.com/itw/session/

Rosenberg, D. R., Crowner, S., Thomas, C., & Gourash, L. (1992). Psychosis and idiopathic precocious puberty in two 7-year-old boys. *Child Psychiatry and Human Development, 22*(4), 287–292.

Sandberg, D. E., & Barrick, C. (1995). Endocrine disorders in childhood: A selective survey of intellectual and educational sequelae. *School Psychology Review, 24*(2), 146–170.

Turkington, C. A. (1999). Precocious puberty. *Gale encyclopedia of medicine, 1.* Retrieved November 28, 2000, from DISCUS/InfoTrac Search Bank: Health Reference Center-Academic/A54823542 at http://web4.infotrac.galegroup.com/itw/session/

Walvoord, E. C., & Pescovitz, O. H. (1999). Combined use of growth hormone and gonadotrophin-releasing hormone analogues in precocious puberty: Theoretic and practical considerations. *Pediatrics, 104,* 1010–1014.

T. Darin Matthews
Kerry S. Lassiter
The Citadel

PURPURA, IDIOPATHIC THROMBOCYTOPENIA

Idiopathic thrombocytopenia purpura (ITP) is an acquired disorder of platelets, which are cellular fragments that circulate in blood. Platelets play several important roles in the clotting of blood (hemostasis). ITP causes platelet counts to fall below normal levels (thrombocytopenia), resulting in hemostatic abnormalities typified by bruising (purpura) and bleeding from the gums and mucous membranes (inside the mouth, nose, gut, etc.).

Although the term *idiopathic* usually implies an undetermined etiology, ITP is felt to be caused by antibodies directed toward the platelet. Antibody-coated platelets are recognized by the spleen as abnormal and removed from circulation. As a consequence, platelet counts drop from a normal 150–450 × 10^9/L to as low as 10 × 10^9/L or less.

Why some children produce these antiplatelet antibodies is unclear. However, more than 50% of patients with ITP have a history of viral infection preceding their illness by 1–4 weeks. In addition, ITP has been closely linked to specific viral diseases such as infectious mononucleosis and HIV. It is possible that there are antigenic similarities between viral particles and the platelet surface that are the source of this autoimmune response.

The incidence of ITP is unknown. It is, however, not an unusually rare disorder. During the course of a career in general practice, most pediatricians will see at least a few cases.

Characteristics

1. History of a viral illness 1–4 weeks prior to onset of symptoms.
2. Sudden development of a generalized petechiae (tiny purple dots) and purpura in an otherwise well child, typically 1–4 years old.
3. Occasional bleeding from gums and other mucous membranes, usually associated with platelet numbers

less than 10×10^9/L. Severe nosebleeds and excessive menstrual blood loss may also be seen with profound thrombocytopenia.

4. Except for skin findings, physical exam is essentially normal. Spleen enlargement is rare. Enlargement of the spleen and liver or prominent lymph nodes indicate another cause for thrombocytopenia.
5. Complete blood count (CBC) shows platelet numbers below normal (150×10^9/L). Excessive blood loss may cause anemia. White blood cell indexes are normal.
6. Spontaneous resolution of ITP within 6 months of onset of symptoms is usual in 70–80% of patients.
7. Ten to 20% of patients will go on to develop chronic ITP (thrombocytopenia lasting > 6 months).

It is interesting that there is no consensus on how to manage acute ITP. Platelet counts $< 20 \times 10^9$/L are considered unsafe because of the small risk (1%) of intracranial hemorrhage (bleeding into the brain). Although there is no convincing evidence that currently available therapy reduces the likelihood of intracranial bleeding, treatment modalities are employed when thrombocytopenia plummets below the 20×10^9/L mark.

Intravenous immunoglobulin (IVIG) infusion given over 1–2 days induces a rapid increase in platelet counts in 95% of patients with ITP. This approach is quite expensive, time-consuming, and associated with a high frequency of side effects (headaches and vomiting).

Oral prednisone, a corticosteroid, has been used for many years to treat ITP. Data show that patients given prednisone experience a more rapid increase in platelets than do control subjects. Treatment courses usually last 2–3 weeks or until platelet counts rise significantly. Some authorities believe that before corticosteroids are started in a patient, a bone marrow examination should be done. This procedure rules out more ominous causes of thrombocytopenia (leukemia or other malignancy) that might be modified but not entirely controlled by steroid therapy. Splenectomy (removal of the spleen) is an option in ITP therapy for two specific clinical scenarios. It is a viable tactic in older children (older than 4 years of age) who have severe thrombocytopenia unresponsive to medical management and disease that has lasted longer than 6 months. The other situation in which it should be considered is in the child who experiences intracranial hemorrhage and thrombocytopenia refractory to drug treatment or platelet transfusions. Splenectomy, however, is not a benign procedure. It is associated with a lifelong risk of overwhelming infection with specific (encapsulated) bacteria.

About 10–20% of children with ITP will develop chronic disease, which is defined as illness lasting over 6 months. At this point, patients should be reevaluated. Other disorders commonly causing thrombocytopenia (malignancy, HIV, lupus, X-linked thrombocytopenia, Wiskott-Aldrich syndrome) should be definitely ruled out. Management is directed toward controlling clinically important blood loss and symptoms. Splenectomy produces permanent remission in about 75% of patients with chronic ITP. However, the risks of this procedure must be considered against the complications and inconvenience of long-term medical therapy.

If there should be bleeding in the brain (intracranial hemorrhage) as a result of ITP, the child may require additional educational support through special education. A neuropsychological evaluation will be necessary to determine cognitive strengths and weaknesses and to recommend appropriate modifications.

ITP is generally a benign malady. In the overwhelming majority of patients, it runs its course in 6 months or less. Ten to 20% of affected children go on to experience chronic disease. They require prolonged medical therapy and possibly splenectomy. The latter leaves patients vulnerable to life-threatening bacterial infections. Vaccines and daily oral penicillin give postsplenectomy patients some protection from this serious complication, but these treatments only partially eliminate the risk.

REFERENCES

Montgomery, R. R., & Scott, J. P. (2000). Disorders of the platelets and blood vessels. In R. E. Behrman, R. M. Kleigman, & H. B. Jenson (Eds.), *Nelson textbook of pediatrics* (16th ed., pp. 1520–1522). Philadelphia: W. B. Saunders.

National Organization for Rare Disorders. (1999). Purpura, idiopathic thrombocytopenic. Retrieved from http://www.stepstn.com/cgi-win/nord.exe?proc=GetDocument&rectype=0&renum=258

Barry H. Davison
Ennis, Texas

Joan W. Mayfield
Baylor Pediatric Specialty Services
Dallas, Texas

PYODERMA GANGRENOSUM

Pyoderma gangrenosum is an ulcerative skin disorder. It may occur alone or as a complication of another syndrome—for example, ulcerative colitis and Crohn's disease. The cause is not known, but it is suspected to have an autoimmune etiology. Pyoderma gangrenosum is a diagnosis of exclusion because biopsies of the skin lesions reveal nonspecific inflammation.

Males and females are equally affected. However, the disease is less common in children and more common in middle-aged women.

Characteristics

1. Pyoderma gangrenosum begins as small bumps or blisters on the skin, which progress to form ulcers.
2. Ulcers most frequently develop on the legs but may appear anywhere on the body.
3. Ulcers are extremely painful, purplish skin lesions that may grow to 20 cm in size.
4. Ulcers can appear at sites of trauma.

At present, treatment for pyoderma gangrenosum is not satisfactory, and other options are being investigated. Treatment is aimed at relieving symptoms—for example, surgical removal of lacerated skin or the use of a medicine such as zinc sulfate, an astringent and weak antiseptic. In severe cases, systemic steroids and antibiotics may be prescribed. Pyoderma gangrenosum is often associated with other underlying disorders (e.g., inflammatory bowel disease); therefore, the course of the skin disorder may parallel the course of the bowel disorder. Thus, treatment of the bowel disorder may alleviate the symptoms of pyoderma gangrenosum. Additionally, nutritional deficiencies associated with disorders such as ulcerative colitis and Crohn's disease must be treated.

A student diagnosed as having pyoderma gangrenosum may qualify for services under IDEA (1997) within the physical disability category if the disorder is prolonged, abnormal, and requires continual monitoring. Students with this disorder may need specialized pain management counseling in addition to counseling designed to help the student come to terms with certain limitations the disorder may place upon his or her ability to function in every day living. Physical activity may be restricted and transportation may be necessary depending on the severity of the case. School personnel should be informed of the limitations of the disorder; for example, students must avoid trauma because it can trigger pyoderma gangrenosum lesions.

Other treatments for pyoderma gangrenosum are being investigated, including thalidomide. However, this drug is especially dangerous in certain populations (e.g., pregnant women) due to its teratogenic properties and must be thoroughly examined (Thoene, 1995; Moraes & Russo, 2001).

More information on pyoderma gangrenosum can be found by contacting the National Institutes of Health National Arthritis and Musculoskeletal and Skin Diseases Information Clearinghouse, 1 AMS Circle, Bethesda, MD 20892, (301) 495-4484.

REFERENCES

Moraes, M., & Russo, G. (2001). Thalidomide and its dermatological uses. *American Journal of Medical Sciences, 321*(5), 321–326.

Thoene, J. G. (Ed.). (1995). *Physicians guide to rare diseases* (2nd ed.). Dowden.

Rachel Toplis
University of Northern Colorado

PYRUVATE CARBOXYLASE DEFICIENCY

Pyruvate carboxylase deficiency is a rare progressive neurological disorder resulting from the absence or decreased activity level of pyruvate carboxylase, an enzyme that aids in the formation of energy for the body. The disorder is associated with rapid neurological and intellectual deterioration.

The disorder is transmitted in an autosomal recessive pattern and has a relatively low incidence estimated at 1 in 250,000 (Wallace, Jitrapakdee, & Chapman-Smith, 1998). Pyruvate carboxylase deficiency is more prevalent in particular ethnic groups including Native American populations, particularly Algonkian-speaking nations (Robinson, 1989). In addition, the disorder is also more common in individuals of Arab descent (Robinson, 1995).

Characteristics

1. Lactic acidemia (the accumulation of lactic acid in the blood stream at a faster rate than it can be eliminated)
2. May exhibit symptoms of failure to thrive, including poor feeding, vomiting, apathy, and irritability
3. Progressive neurological symptoms, including poor muscle tone (hypotonia), abnormal eye movements, seizures, and inability to coordinate muscular movements
4. Mental, psychomotor, and growth retardation

The disorder has classically been divided into two groups—one characterized by a moderate form of the disease and the second by a more severe form (Robinson et al., 1984). The former presents several months after birth, with moderate lactic acidemia as well as delays in development. In the more severe form, the patient presents with severe lactic acidemia right after birth, with death usually occurring by 3 months of age. The difference between these two types is related to the degree of residual enzyme activity. More recently, a mild form of pyruvate carboxylase deficiency has been described that is associated with lactic acidemia and minimal side effects (Van Coster, Fernhoff, & De Vivo, 1991).

Treatments of the disorder have focused on providing the individual with pharmacological doses of cofactors involved in pyruvate metabolism and the substitution of missing end products. However, although these treatments can reverse some of the biochemical abnormalities, the neurological outcome remains very poor (Ahmad et al., 1999). Medical treatment also involves a close monitoring of the child's lactate levels. The diet of children with pyruvate carboxylase deficiency should be monitored closely to prevent activation of gluconeogenesis. Treatment of the mild form of pyruvate carboxylase deficiency, which is found in those patients actually with a defect in biotin metabolism (rather than having a direct absence of the pyruvate carboxylase enzyme) has been met with greater success. Biotin supplements have been found to lead to an almost full symptom recovery in individuals with the mildest form of the disorder (Wallace et al., 1998).

Due to the severity of the neurological deterioration and profound mental retardation associated with pyruvate carboxylase deficiency, children with the disorder will qualify for special education services. Services provided by a multidisciplinary team involving a physical therapist, occupational therapist, nurse, and a speech therapist will be necessary in most cases. Because of the severity of the deterioration associated with the disorder, death often occurs during the teen years. Therefore, significant attention should be given to working with the family in dealing with the emotional distress associated with a terminal illness. In addition, respite care may be needed in helping provide the family with extra support.

Research on treatments of pyruvate carboxylase deficiency have run into problems in the past due to the blood-brain barrier. The blood-brain barrier has contributed to why treatment of the disorder can result in maintaining metabolic control but cannot stop the neurological deterioration (Ahmad et al., 1999). Efforts in future research will attempt to deal with this issue.

REFERENCES

Ahmad, A., Kahler, S. G., Kishnani, P. S., Artigas-Lopez, M., Pappu, A. S., Steiner, R., et al. (1999). Treatment of pyruvate carboxylase deficiency with high doses of citrate and aspartate. *American Journal of Medical Genetics, 87,* 331–338.

Robinson, B. H. (1989). Lactic acidemia: Biochemical, clinical, and genetic considerations. In H. Harris & K. Hirschhorn (Eds.), *Advances in human genetics* (pp. 151–179). New York: Plenum Press.

Robinson, B. H. (1995). Lactic acidemia: Disorders of pyruvate carboxylase, pyruvate dehydrogenase. In C. R. Scriver, A. L. Beaudet, W. S. Sly, & D. Valle (Eds.), *The metabolic and molecular basis of inherited disease* (7th ed., pp. 1479–1499). New York: McGraw-Hill.

Robinson, B. H., Oei, J., Sherwood, W. G., Applegarth, D., Wong, L., Haworth, J., et al. (1984). The molecular basis for two different clinical presentations of classical pyruvate carboxylase deficiency. *American Journal of Human Genetics, 36,* 283–294.

Van Coster, R. N., Fernhoff, P. M., & De Vivo, D. C. (1991). Pyruvate carboxylase deficiency: A benign variant with normal development. *Pediatric Research, 30,* 1–4.

Wallace, J. C., Jitrapakdee, S., & Chapman-Smith, A. (1998). Pyruvate carboxylase. *The International Journal of Biochemistry and Cell Biology, 30*(1), 1–5.

Cassandra Burns Romine
Texas A&M University

R

RAPP-HODGKIN SYNDROME

Rapp-Hodgkin syndrome (RHS) belongs to a group of genetic disorders known as ectodermal dysplasia syndromes. In general, ectodermal dysplasia syndromes are caused by defects in the formation of the ectoderm (the outermost layer of embryonic tissue) during gestation. Ectodermal dysplasia syndromes are multisystem disorders that are characterized by the deficient function or absence of at least two of the following ectodermal structures: skin, teeth, hair, nails, and glands (National Foundation for Ectodermal Dysplasias [NFED], 2001). More than 200 clinically or genetically distinct forms of ectodermal dysplasia have been identified, with classification based on the following considerations: extent, nature, and severity of ectodermal involvement; the presence of associated malformations; and the mode of inheritance (Walpole & Goldblatt, 1991).

Although ectodermal dysplasia syndromes occur in approximately 7 in 10,000 births (NFED, 2001), Rapp-Hodgkin syndrome is an extremely rare condition. Only a few dozen cases have been reported in the medical literature and have included both familial and sporadic cases (National Organization for Rare Disorders [NORD], 1999). Rapp-Hodgkin syndrome, which affects males and females in equal numbers, is inherited as an autosomal dominant genetic trait (NORD, 1999). Features of the disorder may be present at birth in some cases but may not manifest until late infancy in others. The symptoms and physical features of Rapp-Hodgkin syndrome vary widely from case to case (NORD, 1999).

Characteristics

1. Reduced number of sweat glands, pores of the skin, or both, which results in impaired ability (hypohidrosis) or inability (anhidrosis) to sweat. Increased body temperatures (hyperthermia) and heat intolerance may be noted.
2. Cleft palate (incomplete closure of the roof of mouth), cleft lip (abnormal groove in upper lip), or both.
3. Missing or malformed teeth. Teeth may be abnormally small and may have underdeveloped enamel.
4. Abnormally sparse, coarse, and wiry scalp hair in children, with premature hair loss frequently occurring during adulthood.
5. Slow-growing and poorly developed nails on fingers and toes.
6. Other common facial features include abnormally high forehead; narrow nose; high, arched palate; small mouth; and underdeveloped upper jawbone.

Rapp-Hodgkin syndrome has no cure. Treatment is directed toward specific symptoms and is therefore highly individualized. A comprehensive treatment plan requires multidisciplinary coordination across medical specialties (e.g., craniofacial surgeons, dermatologists, dentists). Reconstructive surgery may be warranted to repair cleft palate and cleft lip. Oral surgery, corrective devices, or dentures may be required to provide adequate dentition. During episodes of extended exercise and during summer months (or other periods of high temperatures), monitoring of body temperature is required to avoid hyperthermia.

Intellectual and psychomotor development are typically within normal limits in children with Rapp-Hodgkin syndrome. Special education placement for speech therapy may be required if speech difficulties associated with cleft palate are noted. If the child is susceptible to heat intolerance, air conditioning in the school environment may be necessary, and participation in physical education classes will need to be closely monitored.

Prognosis for children with Rapp-Hodgkin syndrome is good in that general health and life span are within normal expectations (NFED Scientific Advisory Board, 2001). Because Rapp-Hodgkin syndrome is rare, current research is limited primarily to case-study analysis, which serves to document the variability in the clinical expression of this disorder and helps to establish the natural history of the disease.

REFERENCES

National Foundation for Ectodermal Dysplasias. (2001). What is ectodermal dysplasia? Retrieved from http://www.nfed.org/ectoderm.htm

National Foundation for Ectodermal Dysplasias Scientific Advisory Board. (2001). Rapp-Hodgkin syndrome. Retrieved from http://www.nfed.org/multisyndrome.htm#Rapp

National Organization for Rare Disorders. (1999). Rapp-Hodgkin syndrome. Retrieved from http://www.stepstn.com/cgi-win/nord.exe?number=715&proc=ap_fullReport

Walpole, I. R., & Goldblatt, J. (1991). Rapp-Hodgkin hypohidrotic ectodermal dysplasia syndrome. *Clinical Genetics, 39,* 114–120.

Heidi A. McCallister
University of Texas at Austin

RASMUSSEN ENCEPHALITIS

Rasmussen encephalitis is a relatively rare disorder defined by chronic inflammation of the brain (unilateral cerebral pathology) that results in progressive deterioration of function in one hemisphere, often followed by gradual partial recovery of function associated with reorganization. Etiology is generally unknown with no indications of viral pathogenesis (e.g., cytomegalovirus) or genetic determination. Rasmussen encephalitis is generally identified following the onset of intractable seizures (Geller et al., 1998; Topcu et al., 1999), but it may not be diagnosed until surgery to address seizure frequency. Actual prevalence of the disorder is unknown.

Characteristics

1. Intractable epilepsy
2. Progressive hemiparesis
3. Progressive cognitive decline
4. Progressive decline of motor abilities on one side of body
5. Difficulty with problem solving in social situations
6. Precocious puberty
7. Impaired academic performance
8. Lack of behavioral inhibition

Source: Caplan, Curtiss, Chugani, & Vinters (1996); Topcu et al. (1999)

Although Rasmussen encephalitis is usually identified in children, cases have been reported in adolescence and adulthood (McLachlan, Girvin, Blume, & Reichman, 1993). With later onset, there appears to be less of an impact on overall cognitive ability. However, later onset has been associated with increased motor and sensory impairment (McLachlan et al., 1993).

Treatment usually involves resective surgery with electrocorticography. Following surgery, prognosis for seizure control is fairly good (Caplan et al., 1996; McLachlan et al., 1993; Topcu et al., 1999). Improvements have been reported in social relations and language in some individuals as well (Caplan et al., 1996). Alternative treatment involves the use of immunoactive drugs (Geller et al., 1998; Topcu et al., 1999).

Due to the presence of both behavioral and academic concerns, children with Rasmussen encephalitis will be eligible for special education services and will require interventions that address multiple areas. Because of the lack of inhibition and precocious puberty associated with progressive deterioration of the frontal cortex, the priorities for intervention (i.e., behavioral control) might suggest identification as severely emotionally disturbed (SED); however, given the underlying cause of the behavioral problems as well as the accompanying cognitive and motor impairments, identification as Other Health Impaired would be most appropriate. The individual educational plan for a child with Rasmussen encephalitis should include goals specific to academic and functional skills, social skills, and increased behavioral control regardless of categorization or placement.

Because of the rarity of the disorder, long-term prognosis in children with Rasmussen chronic encephalitis has not been studied extensively. Multisite studies that control for the extent and location of resection, that control for neuropsychological status prior to and immediately following surgery, and that use long-term follow-up are needed.

REFERENCES

Caplan, R., Curtiss, S., Chugani, H. T., & Vinters, H. V. (1996). Pediatric Rasmussen encephalitis: Social communication, language, PET, and pathology before and after hemispherectomy. *Brain & Cognition, 32,* 45–66.

Geller, E., Faerber, E. N., Legido, A., Melvin, J. J., Hunter, J. V., Wang, Z., et al. (1998). Rasmussen encephalitis: Complementary role of multitechnique neuroimaging. *American Journal of Neuroradiology, 19,* 445–449.

McLachlan, R. S., Girvin, J. P., Blume, W. T., & Reichman, H. (1993). Rasmussen's chronic encephalitis in adults. *Archives of Neurology, 50,* 269–274.

Topcu, M., Turanli, G., Aynaci, F. M., Yalnizoglu, D., Saatci, I., Yigit, A., et al. (1999). Rasmussen encephalitis in childhood. *Childs Nervous System, 15,* 395–402, 403.

Cynthia A. Riccio
Texas A&M University

REACTIVE ATTACHMENT DISORDER

Reactive attachment disorder (RAD) is characterized by a pervasive disturbance in social relatedness and associated with a history of inadequate care, in which a child's physical and emotional needs are often neglected, attachment is disrupted by repeated change in the primary caregiver, or both. Not all children who experience neglect or abuse develop RAD, however; many of the children who are spared have formed stable relationships with other significant adults.

According to the *Diagnostic and Statistical Manual of Mental Disorders–Fourth Edition* (*DSM-IV*), there are two subtypes of RAD: inhibited and disinhibited (American Psychiatric Association, 1994). The inhibited child may be withdrawn, hypervigilant, or both and may seek physical proximity to caregivers in an ambivalent or unusual way (e.g., approach caregiver and fall to the ground crying). The disinhibited child may indiscriminately seek proximity to any caregiver, even strangers. For both groups, delays in emotional, language, communication, and cognitive development are often found, but in some cases regression occurs following a period of normal development.

Onset of symptoms must occur before the age of 5 years. The disorder, however, can be diagnosed as early as 1 month. The course is often continuous if interventions are not made early or are inadequate to meet the child's basic needs. There are no reliable prevalence rate data (Zeanah, 2000); however, some researchers estimate the occurrence to be about 1% (Richters & Volkmar, 1994).

Characteristics

1. Marked disturbance and delay in age-appropriate social relatedness must be observed before the age of 5 years.
2. Seen as withdrawn and inhibited or as indiscriminant and disinhibited (e.g., ranging from excessive clinginess to aggressiveness).
3. Emotional delays (e.g., mood lability and low frustration tolerance), as well as delays in language, communication, and cognition not due to MR or PDD.
4. Regression does occur in some cases after a period of normal development.
5. Evidence of pathological care (e.g., persistent neglect of basic needs).

A positive response to therapeutic intervention helps distinguish RAD from other developmental disorders (e.g., pervasive developmental delay, PDD; and mental retardation, MR). Treatment for RAD needs to be multimodal and focus on the interaction between caregiver and child; therefore, parent training and parent education are likely to be key factors in treatment outcome.

Early educational interventions may reduce the negative impact on emotional, cognitive, communication, and language skill development. Interventions that address the marked deficits in social relatedness may in fact help to prevent other difficulties in social and emotional development and later learning. Programs such as Head Start may be of particular benefit for children with RAD. Prognosis, however, is dependent on a number of factors, including the presence of other developmental problems and the ongoing quality of the relationship between the child and significant adults (e.g., parents, relatives, and teachers).

Further research is needed to address problems having to do with the reliability and validity of the diagnostic criteria (Boris, Zeanah, Larrieu, Scheeringa, & Heller, 1998). Not only have the *DSM* criteria changed since the disorder's first inclusion in 1980, but it is also still difficult to differentiate RAD from other pervasive developmental disorders (Mukaddes, Bilge, Alyanah, & Kora, 2000). Developmental researchers also believe there is a need to distinguish between the consequences of so-called pathogenic care and disorders of attachment. To help in this regard, additional criteria have been developed for attachment disorder subtypes, including self-endangering, inhibited, vigilant-hypercompliant, role-reversed, and disrupted attachment disorder (see Zeanah, 2000).

REFERENCES

American Psychiatric Association. (1994). *Diagnostic and statistical manual of mental disorders* (4th ed.). Washington, DC: Author.

Boris, N. W., Zeanah, C. H., Jr., Larrieu, J. A., Scheeringa, M. S., & Heller, S. S. (1998). Attachment disorders in infancy and early childhood: A preliminary investigation of diagnostic criteria. *American Journal of Psychiatry, 155*(2), 295–297.

Hayes, S. H. (1997). Reactive attachment disorder: Recommendations for school counselors. *The School Counselor, 44,* 353–361.

Mukaddes, N. M., Bilge, S., Alyanak, B., & Kora, M. E. (2000). Clinical characteristics and treatment responses in cases diagnosed as reactive attachment disorder. *Child Psychiatry and Human Development, 30*(4), 273–287.

Richters, M. M., & Volkmar, F. R. (1994). Reactive attachment disorder of infancy or early childhood. *Journal of American Academy of Child and Adolescent Psychiatry, 33*(3), 328–332.

Zeanah, C. H., Jr. (2000). *Handbook of infant mental health* (2nd ed.). New York: Guilford Press.

Lori Dekeyzer
Elaine Clark
University of Utah

REIFENSTEIN SYNDROME

Reifenstein syndrome (partial androgen insensitivity) is an inherited condition caused by a mutation of the androgen receptor gene in which testes are present but both male and female sexual characteristics exist (Marcelli, Zoppi, Wilson, Griffin, & McPhaul, 1994). In approximately two thirds of the cases, the syndrome is inherited from the mother; in the other third, a mutation occurs. Outward genitalia can range from female (Grade 7), to mixed male and female, to male (Grade 1). Although they possess the chromosomal makeup of males, babies with Reifenstein syndrome may be raised as either males or females, depending on the severity of the syndrome. The approximate prevalence is approximately 1 in every 20,000 births (Gottlieb, Pinsky, Beitel, & Trifiro, 1999). Symptoms of Reifenstein syndrome include sterility, a lack of testosterone, breast development, and the failure of one or both testes to descend into the scrotum. Reifenstein syndrome is present at birth. Other names for Reifenstein syndrome include androgen resistance syndrome, feminizing testes syndrome, Gilbert-Dreyfus syndrome, Goldberg-Maxwell syndrome, incomplete testicular feminization, Lubs syndrome, male pseudohermaphroditism, Morris's syndrome, Rosewater syndrome, testicular feminization syndrome, and Type I familial incomplete male pseudohermaphroditism. A more severe form of Reifenstein syndrome is complete androgen insensitivity (Sinnecker, Nitsche, Holterhus, & Kruse, 1997).

Reifenstein syndrome can be diagnosed prenatally with sequence analysis of the androgen receptor gene (Lumbroso et al., 1994). It is unlikely that specific special education services would be needed for this disorder, other than possible psychological counseling for such issues as gender identity. Although most children with Reifenstein syndrome would have had any needed surgery at a young age, some children may require later surgery; as a result, they may need to miss several days of school.

Characteristics

1. Sterility.
2. Failure of one or both testes to descend into scrotum.
3. Lack of testosterone development.
4. Development of breasts.
5. Tubules in testes become hardened.
6. Urethra present on underside of penis.
7. Gynecomastia upon puberty.

Treatment for Reifenstein syndrome depends on the severity and nature of the disorder. If the external genitalia are mostly female, then the usual procedure is removal of the testes and estrogen replacement therapy; the child is then raised as a female. If the external genitalia are less determined, then the decision is left up to the parents and the health care officials as to which gender the child will be. If a child is raised as a male, then androgen replacement therapy will be needed. In both cases, reconstructive surgery and subsequent psychological counseling are usually required (Price et al., 1984).

Future research is continually being conducted on genetic disorders such as Reifenstein syndrome for a wide variety of possible outcomes, included better prenatal screening and more surgical outcomes. This research ranges from the Human Genome Project to more specific genetic studies on all androgen insensitivity disorders.

REFERENCES

Gottlieb, B., Pinsky, L., Beitel, L. K., & Trifiro, M. (1999). Androgen insensitivity. *American Journal of Medical Genetics, 89*(4), 210–217.

Lumbroso, S., Lobaccaro, J. M., Belon, C., Amram, S., Bachelard, B., Garandeau, P., et al. (1994). Molecular prenatal exclusion of familial partial androgen insensitivity (Reifenstein syndrome). *European Journal of Endocrinology, 130*(4), 327–332.

Marcelli, M., Zoppi, S., Wilson, C. M., Griffin, J. E., & McPhaul, M. J. (1994). Amino acid substitutions in the hormone-binding domain of the human androgen receptor alter the stability of the hormone receptor complex. *Journal of Clinical Investigation, 94*(4), 1642–1650.

Price, P., Wass, J. A., Griffin, J. E., Leshin, M., Savage, M. O., Large, D. M., et al. (1984). High dose androgen therapy in male pseudohermaphroditism due to 5 alpha-reductase deficiency and disorders of the androgen receptor. *Journal of Clinical Investigation, 74*, 1496–1508.

Sinnecker, G. H., Nitsche, E. M., Holterhus, P. M., & Kruse, K. (1997). Functional assessment and clinical classification of androgen sensitivity in patients with mutations of the androgen receptor gene: German Collaborative Intersex Study Group. *European Journal of Pediatrics, 156*, 7–14.

James C. Kaufman
Educational Testing Service
Princeton, New Jersey

RESPIRATORY DISTRESS SYNDROME, ADULT

Adult (or acute) respiratory distress syndrome is an inflammatory disease of the lung characterized by the sudden onset of pulmonary edema and respiratory failure. The disorder is also known as wet lung, shock lung, stiff lung, and posttraumatic pulmonary insufficiency (O'Toole, 1992).

The incidence of adult respiratory distress syndrome has been difficult to determine, in part because there are a variety of causes. Published estimates range from 1.5–71 cases per 100,000 (American Lung Association, 2001). Early signs of adult respiratory distress syndrome are generally subtle and nonspecific, making an accurate diagnosis difficult (Loeb, 1991). Although adult respiratory distress syndrome is more often observed in adults, it is a well-recognized cause of respiratory failure in children (Walker, 1999) and is associated with a variety of acute diseases in youth who are critically ill (Moloney-Harmon, 1999).

The typical patient with adult respiratory distress syndrome is generally young and otherwise healthy, with no previous lung disease (Loeb, 1991). Adult respiratory distress syndrome occurs as a result of direct injury to the lungs or acute illness (National Organization for Rare Disorders, 1999). The numerous etiological factors associated with adult respiratory distress syndrome include fluid aspiration, septic shock, drug overdose, near drowning, smoke inhalation, pancreatitis, transfusion reaction, and massive trauma or burns (O'Toole, 1992). Adult respiratory distress syndrome usually develops within 24–48 hours after the initial injury or illness. As the disease evolves, a number of respiratory abnormalities develop. These symptoms include hypoxemia (decreased arterial oxygenation), hypoxia (decreased tissue oxygenation), diminished lung compliance, and reduced lung volume (Loeb, 1991).

Characteristics

1. Breathing difficulties
2. Rapid, shallow breathing
3. Hyperventilation
4. Tachycardia (abnormally rapid heart rate)
5. Insufficient levels of oxygen in the circulating blood
6. The appearance of cyanotic (bluish-colored) or mottled skin

The progression of adult respiratory distress syndrome is characterized by four phases. Phase I occurs immediately after the initial injury, infection, or illness. During this phase, the individual is generally alert but may begin to hyperventilate. During Phase II, signs of subclinical respiratory distress, such as tachycardia, and rapid and shallow breathing become apparent. The individual also begins to appear fairly anxious during this phase. It is during the third phase that the person with adult respiratory distress syndrome begins to appear gravely ill, exhibiting numerous and severe symptoms of the disease. Acute respiratory failure occurs during Phase IV, and the individual lapses into a coma. Complications that may result from the late phases of adult respiratory distress syndrome include fatal pulmonary damage, secondary pulmonary infection, and cardiac dysfunction (Loeb, 1991).

Treatment of adult respiratory distress syndrome must begin at the first signs of hyperventilation and decreasing levels of oxygen in the blood if progression of the disease is to be slowed or stopped (O'Toole, 1992). Treatment for adult respiratory distress syndrome typically includes continuous positive airway pressure or mechanical ventilation, fluid management, drug therapy that includes antibiotics for any infection, and nutritional support therapy. Adult respiratory distress syndrome is also frequently treated with steroids (Loeb, 1991).

Special education services may be available to children who have suffered from permanent lung damage related to adult respiratory distress syndrome. Generally, these children will qualify for services with the handicapping conditions of Other Health Impaired or Physical Disability.

The overall mortality rate of patients, including children, with adult respiratory distress syndrome is greater than 50% (WEBMD, 1999). Most survivors of adult respiratory distress syndrome recover normal lung function and lead normal or near-normal lives (Soubani & Pieroni, 1999). However, some individuals may suffer permanent lung damage, which can range from mild to severe (WEBMD, 1999).

REFERENCES

American Lung Association. (2001). Fact sheet: Adult (acute) respiratory distress syndrome. Retrieved from http://www.lungusa.org/diseases/ARDSfactsheet.html

Loeb, S. (Ed.). (1991). *Cardiopulmonary emergencies.* Springhouse, PA: Springhouse Corporation.

Moloney-Harmon, P. A. (1999). When the lung fails: Acute respiratory distress syndrome in children. *Critical Care Nursing Clinic of North America, 11*(4), 519–528.

National Organization for Rare Disorders. (1999). Acute respiratory distress syndrome. Retrieved from http://www.stepstn.com/cgi-win/nord.exe?proc=Redirect&type=rdbsum&id=611.htm

O'Toole, M. (Ed.). (1992). *Miller-Keane encyclopedia and dictionary of medicine, nursing, and allied health* (5th ed.). Philadelphia: W. B. Saunders.

Soubani, A. O., & Pieroni, R. (1999). Acute respiratory distress syndrome: A clinical update. *Southern Medical Journal, 92*(5), 450–457.

Walker, T. A. (1999). The acute respiratory distress syndrome in children: Recent UMMC experience. *Journal of Mississippi State Medical Association, 40*(11), 371–375.

M. Franci Crepeau-Hobson
University of Northern Colorado

RESPIRATORY DISTRESS SYNDROME, INFANT

Respiratory distress syndrome is a pulmonary disorder that occurs primarily in infants born prematurely. The disorder is a result of incomplete lung development. Respiratory distress syndrome is due to insufficiency of a foamy fluid known as surfactant, a substance essential to expansion of the alveoli, or air sacs of the lungs. Because of their immaturity, premature infants tend to lack surfactant, and their lungs are unable to inflate (American Lung Association, 2000).

Respiratory distress syndrome occurs in 1% of newborns and is the most common lung disease of premature infants (Blackman, 1990). The majority of babies born before 32 weeks of pregnancy will have respiratory distress syndrome (University of Maryland Medicine, 2000). The incidence of the disorder declines with gestational age at birth. Approximately 60% of infants born at less than 28 weeks gestation, 30% of those born at 28–34 weeks, and less than

5% of those born after 34 weeks will have respiratory distress syndrome (American Lung Association, 1999).

> Characteristics
>
> 1. Audible grunting noise with each breath
> 2. Rapid breathing
> 3. Flaring of the nostrils and retracting of the muscles between the ribs and under the rib cage
> 4. Cyanosis (bluish coloring) around the lips and nail beds
> 5. Lethargy
> 6. Apneic (cessation of breathing) episodes

In anticipation of respiratory distress syndrome in premature infants, neonatal intensive care units routinely monitor the child's pulse and respiration, along with the amount of oxygen in the blood. Treatment is begun at the first clinical sign of respiratory distress syndrome (Blackman, 1990). High oxygen and humidity concentrations are given initially. Intravenous fluids may also be administered. Further treatment depends on the severity of the respiratory distress syndrome. Infants with mild symptoms are given supplementary oxygen whereas those with more severe symptoms may be intubated and managed on a mechanical respirator to prevent the alveoli from collapsing (University of Maryland Medicine, 2000). Special oxygenated liquid may also be instilled in the lungs of infants with severe cases (American Lung Association, 1999). In addition, artificial surfactant may be infused into the lungs of infants who are of high risk for respiratory distress syndrome immediately after birth to prevent or improve the course of the syndrome (University of Maryland Medicine, 2000). Treatment of respiratory distress syndrome without complications generally lasts 5–7 days, with the infant gradually needing less added oxygen. The condition usually improves as the infant begins producing adequate amounts of surfactant (Blackman, 1990).

The vast majority of infants with respiratory distress syndrome survive, with recent estimates around 90%. The majority of these infants will develop normally and do well in regular education classes (Blackman, 1990). However, sometimes long-term complications may develop. Complications can be the result of oxygen toxicity, high pressures delivered to the lungs, or the severity of the disease. These complications during the early days of life may affect cognitive development, physical development, and the child's future health status (Blackman, 1990). Longitudinal research has indicated that children with respiratory distress syndrome generally score significantly lower on measures of cognitive and motor functioning than do children without a history of respiratory distress syndrome. It should be noted, however, that in spite of these differences, most of the respiratory distress syndrome samples still scored within the average range by their 1st birthday (see Creasey, Jarvis, Myers, Markowitz, & Kerkering, 1993, for a review). Research has also indicated that school-age children with a history of respiratory distress syndrome—especially when it is severe—are more likely to have poorer memory skills than do children who did not have respiratory distress syndrome (Rose & Feldman, 1996).

Depending on the presence and severity of complications and on any resulting developmental impact, children who had respiratory distress syndrome as infants may qualify for special education services under a number of handicapping conditions. These conditions include Infant Disability, Preschool Disability, Learning Disability, Mental Retardation, or Other Health Impaired.

The prognosis for infants with respiratory distress syndrome generally is dependent on gestational age and birth weight, which are related to the severity of the disorder (Myers et al., 1992). Complications develop in 10–20% of infants with respiratory distress syndrome overall, and approximately 10% will die (Blackman, 1990). Potential complications include cardiac arrest while being intubated; hemorrhage into the brain or the lung; respiratory illness, including bronchopulmonary dysplasia; retrolental fibroplasia and blindness; and delayed mental development and mental retardation associated with anoxic brain damage or hemorrhage (University of Maryland Medicine, 1999).

Other, more minor problems may also develop. Children with respiratory distress syndrome are more likely to have severe colds and other respiratory infections and are more likely to be hospitalized during the first 2 years of life. These children are also more likely to have an increased sensitivity to lung irritants such as smoke and pollution and to suffer from wheezing and other asthma-like problems in childhood (University of Maryland Medicine, 1999). Early and effective treatment is critical to preventing and decreasing complications related to respiratory distress syndrome.

REFERENCES

American Lung Association. (2000). Fact sheet: Respiratory distress syndrome. Retrieved from http://www.lungusa.org/diseases/Respiratory Distress Syndromefac.html

Blackman, J. A. (1990). *Medical aspects of developmental disabilities in children birth to three* (2nd ed.). Rockville, MD: Aspen.

Creasey, G. L., Jarvis, P. A., Myers, B. J., Markowitz, P. I., & Kerkering, K. W. (1993). Mental and motor development for three groups of premature infants. *Infant Behavior and Development, 16,* 365–372.

Myers, B. J., Jarvis, P. A., Creasey, G. L., Kerkering, K. W., Markowitz, L., & Best, A. M., III. (1992). Prematurity and respiratory illness: Brazelton Scale (NBAS) performance of preterm infants with broncho-pulmonary dysplasia (BPD), respiratory distress syndrome (RDS) or no respiratory illness. *Infant Behavior and Development, 15,* 27–41.

Rose, S. A., & Feldman, J. F. (1996). Memory and processing

speed in preterm children at eleven years: A comparison with full-terms. *Child Development, 67,* 2005–2021.

University of Maryland Medicine. (2000). Respiratory distress syndrome (infants). Retrieved from http://umm.drkoop.com/conditions/ency/article/001563.htm

M. Franci Crepeau-Hobson
University of Northern Colorado

RESTRICTIVE DERMOPATHY

Restrictive dermopathy is a rare, fatal skin disease. The skin of infants with restrictive dermopathy is bright red, tight, and inflexible. In infants who survive for more than 2 weeks, the skin becomes progressively more rigid. These infants are generally born with opened mouths and fixed joints. These infants have few creases and furrows on their skin. Most of these infants are born prematurely at about 31 weeks of gestation, and premature rupture of membranes are characteristic. These infants typically have underdeveloped lungs and generally die from respiratory failure or septicemia.

This condition is rare and is inherited in an autosomal recessive pattern. There have been multiple cases of recurrence with siblings.

Characteristics

1. Tight, rigid shiny red skin
2. Scaling and erosion of the skin
3. Minimal crease and skin furrows
4. Small open mouth at birth
5. Small pinched nose
6. Crumpled, flattened, or low set ears
7. 50% of the infants are born with natal teeth
8. Fixed joints
9. Small jaw

There is no known effective treatment for this condition, and to date there have been no long-term survivors.

Because there have been no long-term survivors of this condition, there are no implications for special education at this time.

Current research focuses on trying to determine what the primary genetic defect may be. Another area of research is examining the biochemistry involved with the keratin proteins and with the failure of the keratinocytes.

REFERENCES

Sybert, V. (1997). *Genetic skin disorders.* New York: Oxford University Press.

Urdang, L., & Swallow, H. (1983). *Mosby's medical and nursing dictionary.* Mosby.

Witt, D., & Hayden, M. (1986). Restrictive dermopathy: A newly recognized autosomal recessive skin dysplasia. *American Journal of Medical Genetics, 24,* 631–648.

Tammy Branan
University of Northern Colorado

RETINITIS PIGMENTOSA

Retinitis pigmentosa (RP) or "more appropriately named rod-cone generalized dystrophy, is a varied group of disorders characterized by . . . [progressive] retinal rod and cone degeneration" (Reynolds, 2001, p. 1). No single classification system has been generally accepted; one version is the following: "1) Congenital RP or Leber's Congenital Amaurosis. 2) Autosomal Recessive RP. 3) Autosomal Dominant RP. 4) X-linked or Sex-linked Recessive RP. 5) Sporadic RP. 6) RP Associated with Systemic Diseases" (Reynolds, 2001, p. 1). Types 1 and 6 are rare; Type 5 is not familial. About 22% and 9% of RP cases are autosomal dominant and sex-linked, respectively. Most of the remaining cases appear to have an autosomal recessive basis, but RP cases do not always follow Mendelian patterns of inheritance, leading to uncertainty about their genetic basis (Baumgartner, 2000). Overall incidence is about 1 in 4,000. Generally, rods are affected first and more severely, leading initially to loss of night and peripheral vision, although cones may become involved in advanced cases (MEDLINEplus Health Information, 2001).

The type of RP influences severity, time of onset, speed of progression, and order of appearance of symptoms. Congenital RP is present at birth and associated with persistent visual loss. Recessive RP (Types 2 and 4) usually have childhood or early adolescent onset and poor prognosis. Dominant RP (Type 3) tends to be milder. Sporadic RP has variable outcome. The systemic illnesses with which Type 6 is associated are rare and often fatal; severe RP symptoms often occur early and involve central vision loss (Reynolds, 2001).

Characteristics

1. Night blindness
2. Tunnel vision
3. Vision loss
4. Splotchy pigmentation on the retina

Frequently, RP is not diagnosed until an affected individual begins to lose night or peripheral vision. An ophthalmologist's exam will show splotchy pigmentation on the retina. Vision continues to decline, although total blindness is rare. Because RP is associated with a number of other conditions and disorders, differential diagnosis is important (Beauchamp, 2000).

The symptoms of RP are progressive and often follow a predictable course in which the first symptom is night blindness. Some RP patients may not realize that they have night blindness, although they have noticed difficulty seeing at dusk or nighttime. The next symptom of RP is tunnel vision: The RP patient loses peripheral vision, but central vision is still intact. When RP is in the advanced stages, central vision is compromised and blindness is a possibility. Rate of progression is highly variable from patient to patient and may be correlated with type of RP (Baumgartner, 2000).

No effective treatment to stop the progression of RP is available. Sunglasses may help preserve sight by protecting the retina from ultraviolet light. Some recent but controversial studies suggest that treatment with antioxidant agents such as vitamin A palmitate may delay progression. Treatment consists of vision aids such as corrective glasses or contact lenses, although prescriptions need to be updated in order to keep up with the disorder's progression. More sophisticated aids to vision may be needed depending on the disorder's progression. Counseling is also recommended to help the patient deal with the psychological aspects of vision loss, and a low-vision specialist may help to maintain patient independence (MEDLINEplus Health Information, 2001).

REFERENCES

Baumgartner, W. (2000). Etiology, pathogenesis, and experimental treatment of retinitis pigmentosa. *Medical Hypotheses, 54,* 814–824.

Beauchamp, G. R. (2000). Retinitis pigmentosa (RP). In C. R. Reynolds & E. Fletcher-Janzen (Eds.), *Encyclopedia of special education* (2nd ed., Vol. 3, pp. 1546–1547). New York: Wiley.

MEDLINEplus Health Information. (2001). Retinitis pigmentosa. Retrieved from http://www.nlm.nih.gov/medlineplus/ency/article/001029.htm

Reynolds, J. D. (2001). Retinitis pigmentosa: Med Help International. Retrieved from http://medhlp.netusa.net/lib/retinit.htm

Melanie Moore
Robert T. Brown
University of North Carolina at Wilmington

RETINOBLASTOMA

Retinoblastoma is a rare form of childhood cancer in which malignant tumor(s) originate in the retina of the eye. The majority (75%) of cases are unilateral retinoblastoma, in which tumors develop in one eye. Tumors that are found in both eyes are referred to as bilateral retinoblastoma (Abramson & Servodidio, 1997).

Retinoblastoma affects one in every 15,000–30,000 children who are born in the United States (Abramson & Servodidio, 1997). There are approximately 300 newly diagnosed cases each year in this country (Abramson & Servodidio, 1997; Demirci, Finger, Cocker, & McCormick, 1999). It affects children of both genders and of all races equally (Abramson & Servodidio, 1997; Margo, Harman, & Mulla, 1998).

Although there are still many unanswered questions as to why retinoblastoma occurs, it is known that in all cases there is an abnormality in Chromosome 13, the chromosome responsible for controlling retinal cell division. In retinoblastoma, a piece of the chromosome is either deleted or mutated, causing retinal cell division to proceed and the tumor(s) to develop (Abramson & Servodidio, 1997; Finger, 2000; Margo et al., 1998). Most patients (90%) have no family history of the disease. However, when it is inherited, the prevalence rate of retinoblastoma is more common in children whose parents have the bilateral form of the disease (45%) than in children whose parents have the unilateral form (7–15%; Abramson & Servodidio, 1997).

Characteristics

1. Initial signs of retinoblastoma usually include pupils that have an abnormal white appearance (leukocoria) or crossed eyes (strabismus).
2. Possible redness in eye, pain, poor vision, or inflammation of tissue surrounding the eye.
3. Small tumors appear as translucent, off-white patches, or well-defined nodular lesions of retinal vessels.
4. Large tumors often produce retinal detachment; some portions of the detached retina appear creamy-white, with newly formed blood vessels extending over the surface and dividing into the substance of a tumor.
5. Other indications include failure to thrive (trouble eating or drinking), extra fingers or toes, malformed ears, or mental retardation.

Retinoblastoma can be diagnosed through retinal dilation. An ultrasound examination and a CAT scan may also be performed. Treatment of retinoblastoma varies according to the extent of the disease within and outside of the eye. The current methods for treating retinoblastoma include enucleation, external beam radiation, radioactive plaques, laser therapy, cryotherapy, and chemoreduction. Enucleation involves the surgical removal of the eye and fitting the socket with a synthetic implant at the time of surgery (Abramson & Servodidio, 1997).

Retinoblastoma is a progressive disease. Therefore,

most children have vision through at least their 1st year of life (Warren, 1994). In fact, the majority of children retain vision in at least one eye (Abramson & Servodidio, 1997). Because children with this disorder usually are able to adapt quite well, they are able to lead a normal life and to attend a regular education classroom (Heller, Alberto, Forney, & Schwartzman, 1996). However, it is very important that they wear protective eyewear when engaging in sports and other hazardous activities. There are some instances in which normal vision is sufficiently impaired so as to necessitate the assistance of visual aids and supports systems in order for these children to attend mainstream classes. Some educational components might include using assistive technology, adapting written material, coordinating orientation and mobility services, fostering the development of appropriate play with toys, and promoting peer interactions (Heller et al., 1996). In cases of more serious loss of vision, it may be necessary for some children to attend programs for individuals who are visually impaired or blind (Rosser & Kingston, 1997). There also seems to be a bimodal distribution of intelligence scores among children with retinoblastoma; some children's performance falls in the low-average range, whereas other children perform in the well-above-average range (Warren, 1994).

Prognosis is generally successful, especially if the diagnosis occurs early. However, children who inherit retinoblastoma from a parent who has had the bilateral form of the disease may also be at risk for developing other cancers, such as bone tumors (osteogenic sarcoma), skin cancers (cutaneous melanoma), muscle and connective tissue tumors (soft tissue sarcoma), and brain tumors (pineoblastomas; Finger, 2000). Thus, those with a genetic form of the disorder have a less favorable prognosis (Margo et al., 1998). Current research is focused on genetic testing as well as on combating secondary cancers (Rosser & Kingston, 1997).

REFERENCES

Abramson, D. H., & Servodidio, C. (1997). A parent's guide to understanding retinoblastoma. Retrieved from http://www.retinoblastoma.com/guide

Demirci, H., Finger, P. T., Cocker, R., & McCormick, S. A. (1999). Interactive case challenge: A 7-week-old female with a "White Pupil" in the left eye. *Medscape Oncology, 2*(5).

Finger, P. T. (2000). Retinoblastoma. Retrieved from http://www.eyecancer.com/conditions/Retinal%20Tumors/retino.html

Heller, K. W., Alberto, P. A., Forney, P. E., & Schwartzman, M. N. (1996). *Understanding physical, sensory, and health impairments: Characteristics and educational implications.* Pacific Grove, CA: Brooks/Cole.

Margo, C. E., Harman, L. E., & Mulla, Z. D. (1998). Retinoblastoma. *Cancer Control: Journal of the Moffitt Cancer Center, 5*(4), 310–316.

Rosser, E., & Kingston, J. (1997). Retinoblastoma: Fighting eye cancer in children. Retrieved from http://ds.dial.pipex.com/rbinfo/information.html

Warren, D. H. (1994). *Blindness and children: An individual differences approach.* New York: Cambridge University Press.

Michelle Perfect
University of Texas at Austin

RETINOPATHY OF PREMATURITY

Retinopathy of prematurity (ROP) is the most common cause of retinal damage in infancy. Incidence has recently been stable, but prevalence is increasing because of the increased survival of infants with very low birth weight—about 67% of infants who weigh less than 3 pounds (1,251 g) and about 80% of infants who weigh less than 2.2 pounds (1,000 g) at birth will manifest some degree of ROP (Menacker & Batshaw, 1997; Merck Manual of Diagnosis and Therapy [Merck], 2001). Exposure to excessive or prolonged oxygen is the major risk for ROP, but presence of other medical complications also increases risk. Unfortunately, threshold safe levels or durations of oxygen are not known (Merck, 2001).

Characteristics

1. Abnormal proliferation of blood vessels in the retina.
2. Progressively, the vascular tissue invades the vitreous and sometimes engorges the entire vasculature of the eye.
3. Abnormal vessels stop growing and may subside spontaneously.
4. In severe cases, scarring from abnormal vessels contract, leading to retinal detachments and vision loss in early infancy.

Development of the inner retinal blood vessels occurs across the second half of pregnancy. Thus, their growth is incomplete in premature infants. If they continue growth abnormally, ROP results. Incidence and severity of ROP vary with the proportion of retina that is avascular at birth (Merck, 2001).

Vision loss ranges from myopia (correctible with glasses) to strabismus, glaucoma, and blindness (Menacker & Batshaw, 1997). Children with moderate, healed ROP but who have cicatrices (dragged retina or retinal folds) have increased risk for retinal detachments later in life.

Diagnosis is through ophthalmological examination by a specialist in examination of premature infants. Premature infants should have regular examinations over the 1st year of life because early detection can often lead to effective treatment. ROP is defined by both the stage or degree of the disorder and the area in which it occurs. The American Academy of Pediatrics Section on Ophthalmology

(2001) has recently provided detailed recommendations for screening for and intervening in cases of ROP. Appropriately managed premature infants with birth weights of more than 1,500 grams (3 lb 5 oz) rarely develop ROP, so differential diagnosis of other disorders such as familial exudative retinopathy or Norrie disease should be considered.

Prevention of premature birth when possible is the best approach to avoiding ROP (Menacker & Batshaw, 1997; Merck, 2001). Where prematurity does occur, levels of oxygen should be at the lowest safe levels and surfactant should be provided to reduce respiratory distress. Recent developments in treatment of ROP with cryotherapy and laser therapy have reduced the incidence of posterior retinal traction folds or detachments by more than 40% and of blindness by about 24% (American Academy of Pediatrics Section on Ophthalmology, 2001). Affected individuals with residual scarring should be examined at least annually for life. Later retinal detachments resulting from such scarring can often be treated effectively if they are detected early. For cases with residual visual loss, special education and adaptive technology may be needed.

REFERENCES

American Academy of Pediatrics Section on Ophthalmology. (2001). Screening examination of premature infants for retinopathy of prematurity. *Pediatrics, 108,* 809–811.

Menacker, S. J., & Batshaw, M. L. (1997). Vision: Our window to the world. In M. L. Batshaw (Ed.), *Children with disabilities* (4th ed., pp. 211–239). Baltimore: Brookes.

Merck Manual of Diagnosis and Therapy. (2001). Retinopathy of prematurity (retrolental fibroplasia). Retrieved from http://www.merck.com/pubs/mmanual/section19/chapter260/2601.htm

Robert T. Brown
Brenda Melvin
University of Northern Carolina, Wilmington

RETT SYNDROME

Rett syndrome (RS) is a pervasive neurodevelopmental disorder that affects almost solely females. It is marked by a period of apparently normal development for 6–18 months, followed by rapid physical and mental deterioration (Brown & Hoadley, 1999). The discovery in 1999 of the X-linked methyl-CpG-binding protein 2 gene (MeCP2) mutation confirmed RS's long-inferred genetic basis (Van den Veyver & Zoghbi, 2000).

Although estimates vary, RS occurs in about 1 in every 15,000 female births. RS is apparently lethal prenatally to males because of the absence of an unaffected X chromosome. RS occurs worldwide, affecting all racial and ethnic groups. Occurrence of RS appears to be random; recurrence rates within the same family are less than .4% (International Rett Syndrome Association [IRSA], 2001).

RS has necessary, supportive, and exclusionary criteria. Necessary characteristics are listed.

Characteristics

1. Apparently normal pre-, peri-, and early postnatal development
2. Deceleration of head growth beginning from 3 months to 3 years of age
3. Loss of acquired skills (voluntary hand skills, verbal and nonverbal communication skills) beginning from 3 months to 3 years of age
4. Appearance of obvious mental retardation in early childhood
5. Appearance of intense and persistent hand stereotypies, including hand wringing, squeezing, washing, patting, rubbing; mouthing, tongue pulling
6. Gait abnormalities in ambulatory cases

Supportive criteria include breathing dysfunctions, bloating and marked air swallowing, electroencephalogram (EEG) abnormalities, seizures, spasticity, muscle wasting, peripheral vasomotor disturbances, scoliosis, hypotrophic small and cold feet, and growth retardation. Exclusionary criteria include signs of storage disease, retinopathy or optic atrophy, microcephaly at birth, existence of metabolic or other hereditary degenerative disorder, neurological disorder from severe infection or head trauma, intrauterine growth retardation, and peri- or postnatal brain damage.

Classic RS generally develops through a four-stage sequence of behavioral and physical changes first described by Hagberg and Witt-Engerström (1986). However, not all RS children show all the features of each stage, and the age of onset, duration of transition from one stage to another, and the duration of each stage is highly variable. The stages can be summarized as follows:

1. *Early-onset stagnation* (begins around 6–18 months; duration of months): Developmental stagnation, deceleration of head growth, hyptonia; diminished eye contact, communication, hand-use ability; diminished interest in play and the environment; development of random movements.
2. *Rapid developmental regression* (begins around 12–36 months; duration of weeks to months): Appearance of hand stereotypies, including hand wringing, washing, and mouthing; onset of sleep disturbances, breathing irregularities, and seizure-like spells; deterioration of cognitive functioning, hand use, and

expressive language; behavior may resemble and be diagnosed as autism.

3. *Pseudostationary* (begins around preschool age; duration until about 10 years of age): Decrease in autistic-like features; gait and stance become fixed; increased severity of mental retardation, breathing irregularities, bruxism, body rigidity, and seizures; development of scoliosis.
4. *Late motor deterioration* (begins around 10 years of age; duration lifelong): Loss or decrease in expressive or receptive language and any remaining motor function, including chewing, swallowing, and walking; apparent communication through "eye pointing"; increase in rigidity, scoliosis, and muscle wasting.

No cure or effective treatment for RS is available, although some symptoms can be managed. Treatment is specific to the individual and the severity of symptoms at any particular time. A multidisciplinary approach is necessary, typically beginning with treatment from a neurologist, developmental pediatrician, or both. Lifelong physical, occupational, and speech therapy are often necessary, as are academic, social, vocational, and supportive services. Each symptom needs a specific treatment for alleviation, such as medication for seizures and agitation and braces, surgery, and physical therapy for scoliosis (WE MOVE, 2001). Behavior modification has had limited effectiveness in treating RS (e.g., Brown & Hoadley, 1999).

Patients with RS may benefit from special education. A thorough communication evaluation is crucial in guiding special education efforts. Exposure to enriching environments and situations that are strongly motivating and allowing adequate time for processing and responding can be helpful. Alternative communication techniques (e.g., augmentative communication) should be employed specifically to individual strengths and weaknesses (IRSA, 2001).

A child diagnosed with RS will live well into her 40s, but quality of life is at best severely compromised. Some functioning may show brief spontaneous recovery, but prognosis is poor and the progressive course of the disorder is currently irreversible. Affected girls will require lifelong close care and supervision, placing a heavy burden on their caretakers. Families may benefit from early and maintained counseling (Brown & Hoadley, 1999).

The recent discovery of the genetic basis for this disorder and advances in biotechnology have led to several promising avenues of research. These topics include discovering the mechanisms by which the mutated MeCP2 gene manifests itself, determining how to silence the effects of the mutation, and developing treatment such as stem cell transplants that may halt or reverse the course of the disorder (National Institutes of Health, 2001; Rett Syndrome Research Foundation, 2001).

REFERENCES

Brown, R. T., & Hoadley, S. L. (1999). Rett syndrome. In S. Goldstein & C. R. Reynolds (Eds.), *Handbook of neurodevelopmental and genetic disorders in children* (pp. 459–477). New York: Guilford Press.

Hagberg, B., & Witt-Engerström, I. (1986). Rett syndrome: A suggested staging system for describing impairment profile with increasing age toward adolescence. *American Journal of Medical Genetics, 24*(Suppl. 1), 47–59.

National Institutes of Health. (2001). Rett syndrome fact sheet. Retrieved from http://www.ninds.nih.gov/health_and_medical/pubs/rett.htm

Rett Syndrome Research Foundation. (2001). Research update. Retrieved from http://www.rsrf.org/research_update.htm

Van den Veyver, I. B., & Zoghbi, H. Y. (2000). Methyl-CpG-binding protein 2 mutations in Rett syndrome. *Current Opinion in Genetics & Development, 10,* 275–279.

WE MOVE. (2001). Rett syndrome. Retrieved from http://www.wemove.org/rett.html

Sarah L. Hoadley
Robert T. Brown
University of North Carolina, Wilmington

See Also Pervasive Developmental Disorder

REYE SYNDROME

Reye syndrome is a condition of unknown origin that is characterized by encephalopathy and fatty degeneration of the liver (National Reye's Syndrome Foundation, 2001). Reye syndrome is acute, rapidly progressive, and typically occurs following a viral illness in children and adolescents treated with aspirin, but rare cases have been found in adults (Ward, 1997). Just as the child appears to be recovering from the viral infection (frequently influenza), protracted, recurring vomiting occurs, followed by neurological and behavioral changes such as listlessness or aggression (National Reye's Syndrome Foundation, 2001; Ward, 1997).

At its peak in 1980, 555 cases of Reye syndrome were reported in the United States. After its association with aspirin was reported in the early 1980s, no more than 36 cases per year have been reported since 1987 (Belay et al., 1999).

Characteristics

1. Prodromal viral-like illnesses
2. Protracted, recurrent vomiting (in infants, vomiting is replaced by diarrhea)

3. Altered mental status such as lethargy, confusion, agitation, and irrational behavior
4. Coma and death likely in undiagnosed cases
5. Biopsy of the liver needed to truly detect the syndrome

Source: National Reye's Syndrome Foundation (2001); University of Michigan Health Systems (2001)

Chances of recovery from Reye syndrome are excellent when the condition is diagnosed and treated in the early stages. However, the degree of recovery is related to damage incurred from brain swelling. There is no cure for Reye syndrome; it should be treated as a medical emergency because of its rapid progression. Treatment is typically directed at reducing brain swelling and returning the body chemistry to normal (University of Michigan Health Systems, 2001).

Because a range from slight to severe brain damage may occur subsequent to recovery from Reye syndrome, psychological and neuropsychological evaluations should be conducted to determine level of functioning. Children who are affected by Reye syndrome may qualify for special education services under a number of categories, including Mental Retardation and Other Health Impaired. In addition, mandates such as the Individuals With Disabilities Education Act and Section 504 should be consulted as resources to better understand services available to the Reye syndrome survivor in the public education system.

Progress has been made in differentiating Reye syndrome from other metabolic disorders. Reye syndrome is not contagious, and incidence has been greatly reduced by public awareness campaigns regarding the dangers associated with medicating children with aspirin (National Reye's Syndrome Foundation, 2001; Ward, 1997). In addition, increased health providers' awareness of symptoms can aid in early detection and greatly reduce the effects of the progression of Reye syndrome.

REFERENCES

Belay, E. D., Bresee, J. S., Holman, R. C., Khan, A. S., Shahriari, A., & Schonberger, L. B. (1999). Reye's syndrome in the United States from 1981 through 1997. *New England Journal of Medicine, 340*(18), 1423–1424.

National Reye's Syndrome Foundation. (2001). Retrieved from http://reyessyndrome.org

University of Michigan Health Systems. (2001). Retrieved from http://med.umich.edu/1libr/child/child46.htm

Ward, M. R. (1997). Reye's syndrome: An update. *Nurse Practitioner, 22,* 45–46.

Kimberly D. Wilson
University of Texas at Austin

Dilip Karnik
'Specially for Children Children's Hospital
Austin, Texas

RHYTHMIC MOVEMENT DISORDER

Rhythmic movement disorder (RMD), also known as stereotypic movement disorder (SMD; American Psychiatric Association, 1994), *jactatio captis nocturna* and *rythmie de sommeil,* refers to a group of stereotypical, rhythmic, repetitive movements or vocalizations (Gillberg, 1995). RMD is diagnosed if it occurs in children—particularly preschool-age children—during drowsy or sleep periods or during the sleep-wake period of the sleep cycle, unlike other types of movement disorders, including SMD.

RMD may include head banging, head rolling, or body rocking, or a combination thereof, involving large muscles of the body. If self-injurious behaviors are included, they usually have poor prognostic outcome.

Characteristics

1. Rhythmic body movements occurring during drowsy or sleep states
2. Stereotyped, repetitive movements involving large muscles
3. Usually involves head and neck
4. Unusual vocalizations
5. Continued humming
6. Head banging
7. Head rolling
8. Body rocking

The prevalence of RMD, or some form of movement disorder associated with the sleep-wake cycle, has been estimated to occur in two thirds of all infants age 9 months and less than 8% of children 4 years of age or older. The disorder is more common in boys than in girls with an approximate ratio of 3:1. The etiology of these conditions is unknown.

With regard to developmental typology, body rocking appears more common in the 1st year and other types of RMD tend to be found in older children. A select group of these children go on to develop more serious problems of attention, including attention-deficit/hyperactivity disorder (Gillberg, 1995). Treatment usually involves reasurance of the parents and behavioral interventions (in more severe cases) until RMD disappears as the child matures.

Because most children outgrow this condition, special education is usually not necessary.

REFERENCES

American Psychiatric Association. (1994). *Diagnostic and statistical manual of mental disorders* (4th ed.). Washington, DC: Author.

Gillberg, C. (1995). *Clinical child neuropsychiatry.* Cambridge, England: Cambridge University Press.

Antolin M. Llorente
Baylor College of Medicine
Houston, Texas

RICKETS, HYPOPHOSPHATEMIC

Hypophosphatemic rickets is a disorder that affects the normal growth and repair process of bones. The disorder was previously called *vitamin D resistant* because rickets persisted despite sufficient intake of vitamin D. However, the term was limiting because there also appears to be a disruption in the mineralization of calcium, phosphorus, and alkaline phosphatase. Most forms of hypophosphatemia are X-linked dominant; however, there are also autosomal recessive and sporadic forms of the disease (Carpenter, 1997; Winger, Steeksma, & Jacobson, 2000).

Estimates on the incidence of those born with the disorder have ranged from 1–10 out of a million to 1 in 20,000 (Carpenter, 1997). Although most individuals are born with the disorder, symptoms can appear in early infancy (Carpenter, 1997) up through adulthood (Arnold & Bibb, 2000). In the most common form, X-linked hypophosphatemia (XLH), girls are more likely to inherit the disorder than are males because it can never be passed on from a father to a son (Whyte, Schranck, & Armamento-Villareal, 1996). However, there is evidence to suggest that males have more pronounced symptoms than do females (Carpenter, 1997; Whyte et al., 1996).

Although much still remains not understood about this disorder, it is known that symptoms manifest because the body has difficulty converting vitamin D into its active form, which is needed to regulate calcium and phosphate levels in the bloodstream (National Organization for Rare Disorders [NORD], 2000). Moreover, there appears to be a genetic defect on the kidney; this defect interferes with the proximal renal tubular reabsorption of phosphate (Verge et al., 1991). Consequently, the kidneys leak phosphate into the urine (Winger et al., 2000), and there is excess urinary excretion of the mineral. Because phosphorus is needed for calcium metabolism to stimulate bone growth, the weakened bones become thin and bend (NORD, 2000). There can also be problems pertaining to the parathyroid (Carpenter, 1997).

Characteristics

1. Child may experience damage to the skeletal system, such as bowed legs (genu varum), a waddling gait, short stature, narrow head (dolichocephaly), and knees that are too close together (knock-knee or genu valgum).
2. Child may experience pain in his or her bones.
3. Child may have weakened or painful muscles.
4. Child's teeth may also be affected, including tooth decay, abscesses, enlargement of pulp cavity, intraglobular dentin irregularities, occasional enamel defects, or periapical infections.
5. Child may experience frequent vomiting or constipation.
6. Child may experience respiratory or myocardial difficulties.
7. There may be alterations in the child's mental state, in which the child becomes irritable, becomes confused, or lapses into a coma.

Blood samples can be drawn in order to determine a child's level of phosphorus, calcium, and alkaline phosphatase. Urine samples should also be taken in order to determine an individual's renal phosphate handling. A skeletal examination including radiographic testing is also indicated (Carpenter, 1997).

Currently, there is no cure for the disorder. Individuals with hypophosphatemia are generally treated according to their age as well as the severity of the symptoms (Carpenter, 1997). A common biochemical intervention includes a combination of calcitrol (a form of vitamin D) and phosphate supplements. Because of possible medical complications, it is important to monitor the calcium and phosphate levels in the child's blood and urine (Carpenter, 1997; Verge et al., 1991). Treatment with oral phosphate and vitamin D has been shown to be effective in improving the growth rate and controlling the progression of bowleg deformity (Verge et al., 1991; Winger et al., 2000). However, a child might need surgery to correct severe bone deformities (Verge et al., 1991).

Because phosphate deficiency often causes muscles to be weak, individuals diagnosed with hypophosphatemia should have an examination in order to assess their motor strength. Children may need assistance in developing their gross motor skills and strengthening their muscles. Consequently, it is likely that children with more severe forms of hypophosphatemia will require physical and occupational therapy. Little is known of the cognitive implications; however, just as the physical treatment is contingent upon the presenting symptoms, attention should be given to any manifestations of emotional or cognitive difficulties that call for psychological interventions. The prognosis of hypophosphatemia varies according to the severity of the disease. With the proper medical treatment, most individuals are able to live a normal life span (Verge et al., 1991).

REFERENCES

Arnold, J. L., & Bibb, J. (2000). Hypophosphatemia. Retrieved from http://www.emedicine.com/cgi-bin/foxweb.exe/showsection@d:/em/ga?book=oph&topicid=92

Carpenter, T. O. (1997). New perspectives on the biology and treatment of X-linked hypophosphatemic rickets. *Pediatric Clinics of North America, 44*(2), 443–466.

National Organization for Rare Disorders. (2000). Familial hypophosphatemia. Retrieved from http://www.rarediseases.org

Verge, C. F., Lam, A., Simpson, J. M., Cowell, C. T., Neville, J. H., & Silink, M. (1991). Effects of therapy in X-linked hypophosphatemic rickets. *The New England Journal of Medicine, 325*(26), 1843–1848.

Whyte, M. P., Schranck, F. W., & Armamento-Villareal, R. (1996). X-Linked hypophosphatemia: A search for gender, race, anticipation, or parent of origin effects on disease expression in children. *Journal of Clinical Endocrinology and Metabolism, 81*(11), 4075–4080.

Winger, L., Steeksma, C., & Jacobson, E. (2000). XLH network flyer: XLH network. Retrieved from http://georgia.ncl.ac.uk/VitaminD/vitaminD.html

Michelle Perfect
University of Texas at Austin

RICKETS, VITAMIN D DEFICIENCY

Vitamin D deficiency rickets is a bone disorder caused by an insufficient intake of vitamin D in a person's diet or inadequate exposure to ultraviolet rays in sunlight. Inadequate phosphorus or calcium in a child's diet can also lead to the development of rickets. The diagnosis of rickets dates back to the mid-17th century, when nearly half of all children born had rickets (Welch, Bergstrom, & Tsang, 2000). Today, incidents of rickets in the United States are extremely low due to the availability of foods that are either naturally rich in vitamin D or fortified with vitamin D. For instance, unless an infant is exposed to a vegetarian diet that does not include milk, most children consume vitamin D in their formulas (Winger, 2000). There are also vitamin D supplements that can be given to children born prematurely or on vegan diets. Nonetheless, in recent years, reports of rickets have increased slightly, especially among African American infants (Kreiter et al., 2000; Welch et al., 2000).

Rickets is most common among children between the ages of 4 months and 2 years. Environmental conditions, such as smog and pollution in cities, can prevent adequate exposure to sunlight. Moreover, rickets may also occur when children wear protective clothing or sunscreen that shields them from the sun's rays (Welch et al., 2000). Additionally, children with dark skin are at an increased risk for rickets because their pigmentation may reduce the production of vitamin D that is derived from exposure to light (Kreiter et al., 2000).

Characteristics

1. Child may have bowlegs, raised bony bumps along the ribs (rachitic rosaries), and other bone deformities.
2. Mild forms may cause only bone and muscle weakness.
3. Enlargement of wrists and ankles is an early sign of rickets.
4. The baby's soft spot may be enlarged, and its closure may be delayed.
5. Shape of the head may become boxlike due to the thickening of skull bones.
6. Delayed formation of teeth, dental deformities, increased sensitivity in the teeth, or damaged tooth enamel may occur.
7. There may be excessive sweating, especially around the head.
8. Child may exhibit restlessness, irritability, restless sleep, muscle weakness, and delays in learning to walk.

Because the body needs vitamin D in order to properly absorb calcium, the bones may become deformed. Initially, the weakened bones begin to bend in response to the child's sitting and progressively become more bowed when the child begins to use the weight-bearing limbs (e.g., the arms and legs; Palfrey, Katz, Schulman, & New, 1995). A physical screening to measure a child's levels of alkaline phosphatase, calcium, and phosphorus can be performed (Winger, 2000). Such tests would include X rays and blood tests (Palfrey et al., 1995). These tests may not be able to identify the condition if a child has a mild case of rickets; however, in these cases a normal diet should be effective in strengthening bones and muscles (Aronson, 1998).

The severity of rickets depends upon how long a child was deprived of vitamin D either from foods or from exposure to light. Treatment of rickets includes a diet rich in vitamin D, which includes food and beverages such as fish, liver (Palfrey et al., 1995; Winger, 2000), milk, soy products fortified with calcium and vitamin D, and formula that is fortified with vitamin D (Aronson, 1998; Palfrey et al., 1995). Many times these foods are not sufficient, and doctors must prescribe vitamin D supplements. Higher doses of vitamin D may be necessary for children with more severe rickets. Additionally, children also need to be exposed to both natural and artificial light (Aronson, 1998).

Vitamin D deficiency rickets can usually be treated successfully, and its harmful effects can usually be reversed. However, if the disease is not identified and treated immediately or if the case is more severe, symptoms such as bone deformities may not be reversible (Aronson, 1998). Treatment may include wearing supportive shoes or leg braces (Palfrey et al., 1995; Winger, 2000). Children will most likely also need assistance in developing their gross motor skills. In particular, these children may need supports with learning to crawl, stand, and walk. Additionally, rickets may result in children's having poorly developed or decreased muscle tone. Such children may need support in increasing their muscle strength, flexibility, and stamina. As a result, some children may require services from a physical or occupational therapist.

Prognosis is generally favorable after children are put on a diet nutritionally rich in vitamin D. Therefore, the primary mode of intervention is ensuring that the child receives the proper nutritional supplements. The family may need assistance with monitoring the child's diet, especially if the family is living in poverty. Children who have had rickets may also need to be referred to a dentist because tooth eruption may be delayed or the enamel may be damaged. Future research is focused on preventing the disease in rural or economically disadvantaged areas. In particular, heavy emphasis is being placed on preventing vitamin D deficiency in children in orphanages in China and in Easter European nations, where there continues to be a high occurrence (Aronson, 1998).

REFERENCES

Aronson, J. (1998). Rickets in Chinese children. Retrieved from http://members.aol.com/jaronmink/rickets.htm

Kreiter, S. R., Schwartz, R. P., Kirkman, H. N., Charlton, P. A., Calikoglu, A. S., & Davenport, M. L. (2000). Nutritional rickets in African American breast-fed infants. *Journal of Pediatrics, 137,* 153–157.

Palfrey, J., Katz, A. K., Schulman, I., & New, M. I. (Eds.). (1995). *The Disney encyclopedia of baby and child care.* New York: Hyperion.

Welch, T. R., Bergstrom, W. H., & Tsang, R. C. (2000). Vitamin D-deficient rickets: The reemergence of a once-conquered disease. *The Journal of Pediatrics, 137*(2), 143–145.

Winger, L. (2000). Vitamin D metabolism and rickets: XLH network. Retrieved from http://georgia.ncl.ac.uk/VitaminD/vitaminD.html

Michelle Perfect
University of Texas at Austin

RIEGER SYNDROME

Rieger syndrome is an autosomal dominant gene disorder characterized by eye anomalies associated with glaucoma, mild craniofacial abnormalities, and absence or malformation of teeth.

This rare disorder of wide expression is estimated to affect fewer than 1 in 200,000 children in the United States (Moody & Moody, 2000).

Characteristics

1. Hypoplasia and malformation of the iris, anterior displacement and thickening of Schwalbe space and adhesion of the iris to Schwalbe space are predominant characteristics.
2. Microdontia, hypodontia, and anodontia are common.
3. Maxillary hypoplasia, cleft palate, and protruding lower lip.
4. Umbilical abnormalities and anal stenosis are occasional.
5. Conducive deafness, blindness, mental retardation, and psychomotor retardation occur in some cases.

Glaucoma develops in 50% of people with Rieger syndrome, making it of primary concern in treatment. Medical therapy is initially implemented. Medications such as beta-blockers, alpha agonists, and carbonic anhydrase inhibitors that decrease aqueous output are more effective than are medications affecting outflow such as pilocarpine (Economou & Simmons, 1999). If medication is no longer effective, surgical interventions such as goniotomy and trabeculectomy are used (Economou & Simmons, 1999). Craniofacial, dental, and orthodontic surgeries are treatments for craniofacial and dental abnormalities. Cleft palate can be surgically corrected as early as 6 months of age, and other procedures may be needed as the face matures and changes (Craniofacial Foundation of Arizona, 1999).

Children with Rieger syndrome may need special education services for their visual impairment. Services may also be required for mental and psychomotor retardation as well as for hearing impairment.

Early glaucoma testing and interventions as well as routine monitoring of intraocular pressure and optic nerve head changes are measures for better prognosis.

REFERENCES

Craniofacial Foundation of Arizona. (1999). Craniofacial conditions. Retrieved from http://www.azcranio.com/conditions.html

Economou, A., & Simmons, S. T. (1999). Axenfeld-Rieger syndrome. In M. Yanoff & J. S. Duker (Eds.), *Yanoff: Ophthalmology* (1st ed., pp. 12.21.2–12.21.3). London: Mosby.

Moody, J., & Moody, K. (2000, November). Rieger syndrome. Retrieved from http://rarelinks4parents.homestead.com/RiegSynInfo.html

Iman Teresa Lahroud
University of Texas at Austin

ROBINOW SYNDROME

Robinow syndrome is a genetic disorder that is often called fetal face syndrome due to the characteristic facial appearance resembling that of a fetus of about 8 weeks gestation. Mesomelic dwarfism, hypoplastic genitalia, and dental abnormalities also characterize the disorder.

Robinow syndrome is a rare condition, but exact prevalence is not known. The cases of at least 84 patients have been reported (Aksit et al., 1997). The incidence of the disorder appears to be relatively higher in Turkish populations. One quarter of the reported cases in the literature are Turkish children (Aksit et al., 1997).

Characteristics

1. Craniofacial features—eyes wide apart (hypertelorism), short upturned nose, broad nasal bridge, boxlike forehead (frontal bossing), down-slanting eyes, and wide eye openings (wide palpebral fissures)
2. Dental abnormalities—crowded, crooked, missing teeth
3. Short stature and mesomelic shortening of the forearms
4. Hypoplastic (underdeveloped) genitalia
5. Normal intelligence in most cases, mildly impaired in some
6. Skeletal abnormalities—vertebral anomalies, rib defects, shortening of the ulna and radius, bifid phalanges, and scoliosis

The rare combination of anomalies associated with Robinow syndrome has both autosomal dominant and recessive inheritance patterns (Wilcox, Quinn, Ng, Dicks-Mireaux, & Mouriquand, 1997). The recessive type is the rarer of the two and also the more severe. Children born with the recessive version of Robinow syndrome have more marked dwarfism, multiple rib abnormalities, shorter limbs, and shorter fingers and toes (Kantaputra, Gorlin, Ukarapol, Unachak, & Sudasna, 1999).

Reconstructive surgery is often necessary in individuals with Robinow syndrome, particularly in patients with severe scoliosis. Treatment with recombinant human growth hormone has been shown to result in a significant increase in the growth rate of children with Robinow syndrome (Castells, Chakurkar, Zazi, & Bastian, 1999).

There are a number of special educational considerations regarding a child with Robinow syndrome. Developmental delays and mental retardation have been associated with 18% of individuals with the disorder (Butler & Wadlington, 1987). Therefore, psychoeducational testing and the implementation of individualized educational plans may be necessary. Because of the presence of a number of physical deformities, a child with Robinow syndrome is considerably at risk for such psychosocial difficulties as decreased self-esteem, depression, and social maladjustment. However, a child with Robinow syndrome has few physical limitations or health problems and is able to participate in regular activities, including athletics.

The prognosis for children with Robinow syndrome is quite good. Most individuals with the disorder live full lives with normal life expectancy and good health (Butler & Wadlington, 1987). Future research on the disorder will focus on the identification of the gene involved in this disorder and will try to build an understanding of this gene's role in both endocrine function and skeletal development.

REFERENCES

Aksit, S., Aydinlioglu, H., Dizdarer, G., Caglayan, S., Bektaslar, D., & Cin, A. (1997). Is the frequency of Robinow syndrome relatively high in Turkey? Four more case reports. *Clinical Genetics, 52,* 226–230.

Butler, M. G., & Wadlington, W. B. (1987). Robinow syndrome: Report of two patients and review of literature. *Clinical Genetics, 31,* 77–85.

Castells, S., Chakurkar, A., Qazi, Q., & Bastian, W. (1999). Robinow syndrome with growth hormone deficiency: Treatment with growth hormone. *Journal of Pediatric Endocrinology and Metabolism, 12*(4), 565–571.

Kantaputra, P. N., Gorlin, R. J., Ukarapol, N., Unachak, K., & Sudasna, J. (1999). Robinow (fetal face) syndrome: Report of a boy with dominant type and an infant with recessive type. *American Journal of Medical Genetics, 84,* 1–7.

Wilcox, D. T., Quinn, F. M. J., Ng, C. S., Dicks-Mireaux, C., & Mouriquand, P. D. E. (1997). Redefining the genital abnormality in the Robinow syndrome. *The Journal of Urology, 157,* 2312–2314.

Cassandra Burns Romine
Texas A&M University

ROMANO WARD SYNDROME

Romano Ward syndrome is one variety in a group of genetic heart disorders known as long QT syndrome. Romano Ward syndrome is the most common form of long QT syndrome (it accounts for approximately 60%). The QT interval refers to a quantity measured on the electrocardiogram (ECG). The duration of the QT interval is a measure of the time needed for repolarization or recharging of the electrical system after each heartbeat. The prolongation of the QT interval renders people vulnerable to very fast, abnormal heart rhythm (arrhythmia) known as torsade de pointes; when this occurs, no blood is pumped out of the heart and the brain quickly becomes deprived, resulting in loss of consciousness and sudden death. Long QT syndrome is caused by dysfunction of protein structures in the heart cells called ion channels. These ion channels produce the electrical activity in the heart. Abnormality of these channels is usually inherited, although it can be acquired.

The inherited syndrome is transmitted by autosomal dominant inheritance. The individual receives one abnormal and one normal gene; therefore, each child born to an affected parent has a 50% chance of receiving an abnormal copy and a 50% chance of receiving the normal copy. Acquired long QT syndrome can also be drug induced or associated with stroke or other neurological disorders.

It is estimated that long QT syndrome is present in 1 in every 5,000 people (approximately 50,000 people in the United States) and may cause as many as 3,000 deaths per year, mostly in children and young adults. It is present in all ethnic groups.

Characteristics

1. Symptoms may begin as early as the first few days or weeks of life or as late as middle life. Most commonly symptoms occur during preteen and teenage years.
2. Symptoms start earlier in males (average 8 years) than in females (average 14 years).
3. Common symptoms are sudden loss of consciousness (syncope) and sudden death.
4. Loss of consciousness and death can be brought on by physical exertion or emotional excitement (e.g., fear, anger, or startle). It can also occur during sleep or arousal from sleep.
5. After loss of consciousness occurs, the torsade de pointes rhythm reverts to normal and the person regains consciousness. If the torsade de pointes rhythm continues, ventricular fibrillation occurs, and the outcome is usually death.
6. One third of gene carriers never develop symptoms; however, at present it is not possible to predict who will subsequently have symptoms.

Romano Ward syndrome is diagnosed from a prolonged QT interval on the ECG, usually following the occurrence of syncope or cardiac arrest. Treatment is usually beta-blocker drug therapy, or in extreme cases, patients may be implanted with a defibrillator. Young adults and children usually respond well to beta-blockers. The risk of developing symptoms later in life (40–45 years and older) is quite low. Patients need to avoid low blood potassium (e.g., caused by diuretic drug use, vomiting, and diarrhea) and the many drugs that lengthen QT interval. Romano Ward is treatable but not curable. After treatment has begun, medications should be taken daily because the protective effects are gone within 1–2 days after stopping the medication.

Students diagnosed with Romano Ward syndrome will be eligible for special education services under the physical disability category of the Individuals with Disabilities Education Act (1997). Because the symptoms of Romano Ward can be brought on by physical exercise, it is advisable that these students do not participate in competitive sports. If these students are in compliance with daily treatment, it is possible that they can be involved in recreational sports. However, all personnel involved with the student need to be informed about the condition and the potential for syncope. It is advisable that family members and school personnel learn cardiopulmonary resuscitation (CPR). Special education students with serious emotional disturbance such as depression and anxiety disorders that are often treated with antidepressants who also have Romano Ward are complicated to treat because many common antidepressant medications, anxiolytics, and some neuroleptics are contraindicated in any form of QT prolongation syndrome. Many such drugs can induce cardiac arrythmias of various forms that can become fatal in the presence of QT delays. Although research is not yet definitive on this point, there is some recent evidence that Romano Ward syndrome and prolonged QT interval may be associated with sudden infant death syndrome (Schwartz et al., 1998). Other research continues to attempt to identify the specific genes involved in this disorder. The prognosis for someone diagnosed with Romano Ward syndrome is positive. This disorder is treatable, and as long as patients are aware of the effects of Romano Ward, these individuals can live a productive life. For more information on this disorder, contact International Long QT Syndrome Registry, P.O. Box 653, University of Rochester Medical Center, Rochester, NY 14642-8653, (716) 275-5391.

REFERENCE

Schwartz, P. J., Stramba-Badiale, M., Segantini, A., Austoni, P., Bosi, G., Giorgetti, R., et al. (1998). Prolongation of the QT interval and the sudden infant death syndrome. *New England Journal of Medicine, 338,* 1709–1714.

Rachel Toplis
University of Northern Colorado

ROTHMUND-THOMSON SYNDROME (POIKILODERMA CONGENITALE SYNDROME)

Rothmund-Thomson syndrome (RTS) is a rare, heritable disorder of the skin and skin derivatives (hair and nails). Approximately 50% of affected individuals will also develop cataracts during the first decade of life.

The etiology of RTS is unknown. There are no data regarding its frequency in the general population. The syndrome was first described in 1868 by a German ophthalmologist (Rothmund), who reported several cases in an inbred population near Munich. More than 200 examples of RTS have appeared in the medical literature.

The pattern of inheritance in RTS is autosomal recessive. The disease appears to be far more common in females than it is in males.

Characteristics

1. Wide variation in clinical manifestations of the disorder.
2. Short stature with prenatal growth deficiency.
3. Splotchy redness of the skin, rarely present at birth, that usually begins by 3–12 months of age. Within a

few years, these changes progress to poikiloderma. This term encompasses a variety of dermal abnormalities, including dilation of blood vessels (telangiectasia), scarring, depigmentation, irregular hyperpigmentation, and atrophy (thinning). These findings give the skin a peculiar and characteristic marbled appearance. Sun-exposed skin is most commonly affected, but the buttocks are also frequently involved. About one third of patients have wart-like lesions. 20% experience blistering prior to the appearance of poikiloderma. Photosensitivity (exaggerated response to sunlight) appears in 35% of patients.

4. Sparse hair that grays early. Thinning of scalp, facial, eyebrow, eyelash, and pubic hair is common. Most patients are bald by age 20–30.
5. Fifty percent of patients develop cataracts in both eyes between 2 and 7 years of age.
6. Small hands and feet, underdeveloped or absent thumbs, syndactyly (webbing or fusion of digits), absent kneecap, clubfoot, and cystic bone changes. Increased incidence of osteoporosis and osteosarcoma (bone cancer).
7. Prominent forehead; small, "saddle" nose.
8. Underdeveloped or absent teeth, dental decay.
9. Small, malformed nails.
10. Skin cancer (basal and squamous cell carcinoma).
11. Five to 13% incidence of mental deficiency.

RTS may engender skin disfigurement severe enough to require plastic surgery. Cataracts causing significant visual impairment should be removed. Hair, nail, and tooth deformities may demand considerable cosmetic attention to improve appearance. Growth deficiency secondary to growth hormone inadequacy may respond to replacement therapy.

Because 5–13% of children with RTS have some degree of mental deficiency, a neuropsychological evaluation will be helpful to evaluate cognitive strengths and weaknesses. Based on those results, modifications can be implemented if they are needed. Vision support services are available under the special education umbrella for children who develop cataracts and require assistance.

Most patients with RTS have normal mental development and can anticipate normal life expectancy. However, they are at increased risk for developing skin cancer and other types of noncutaneous malignancies. Frequent screening for these problems combined with prompt treatment assures the best prognosis.

For more information, please contact National Institutes of Health/National Arthritis and Musculoskeletal and Skin Diseases Information Clearinghouse, 1 AMS Circle, Bethesda, MD 20892-3675, (301) 495-4484.

REFERENCES

Darmstadt, G. L. (2000). Photosensitivity. In R. E. Behrman, R. M. Kleigman, & H. B. Jenson (Eds.), *Nelson textbook of pediatrics* (16th ed., p. 2001). Philadelphia: W. B. Saunders.

Jones, K. (1997). *Smith's recognizable patterns of human malformation* (5th ed.). Philadelphia: W. B. Saunders.

National Organization for Rare Disorders. (1997). Rothmund-Thomson syndrome. Retrieved from http://www.stepstn.com/cgi-win/nord.exe?proc=GetDocument&rectype=0&recnum=694

Barry H. Davison
Ennis, Texas

Joan W. Mayfield
Baylor Pediatric Specialty Services
Dallas, Texas

ROUSSY-LEVY SYNDROME

Roussy-Levy syndrome (RSL) is a movement disorder with onset in early childhood. The disorder was first identified in 1926. It is an autosomal dominant inherited degenerative disease of the central nervous system characterized predominantly by ataxia, high arched feet, and areflexia; it is eventually associated with distal muscle atrophy, postural tremor, and minor sensory loss. Slow nerve conduction and demyelination of nerve fibers led to consideration of RLS as a variant of demyelinating Charcot-Marie-Tooth disease (Plante-Bordeneuve, Guiochon-Mantel, Lacrois, Lapresle, & Said, 1999).

Characteristics

1. Onset in early childhood.
2. Slowly progressive, degenerative disease of the central nervous system.
3. Prominent features include delayed motor milestones (i.e., delayed walking and maintaining balance) and an unsteady gait during early childhood, with foot deformities and areflexia.
4. Associated with distal muscle atrophy and weakness, clumsiness, postural tremor, and distal sensory loss.
5. Atrophy of the muscles of the lower extremities, with a pattern of wasting similar to that observed in Charcot-Marie-Tooth disease.

The course of RLS tends to be homogeneous. In most cases, the disease progresses very slowly and remains benign, with only mild to moderate functional handicap and normal life expectancy (Lyon, Adams, & Kolodny, 1996). However, prognosis may be poor due to hypertrophic cardiomyopathy with progression to intractable congestive heart failure, which is the cause of death for many patients. Research is needed to determine the cause of gait ataxia and essential tremor, which distinguish this syndrome from Charcot-Marie-Tooth syndrome.

REFERENCES

Lyon, G., Adams, R. D., & Kolodny, E. H. (1996). *Neurology of hereditary metabolic diseases of children.* New York: McGraw-Hill.

Plante-Bordeneuve, V., Guiochon-Mantel, A., Lacrois, C., Lapresle, J., & Said, G. (1999). The Roussy-Levy family: From the original description to the gene. *Annals of Neurology, 46,* 770–773.

VIRDETTE L. BRUMM
Children's Hospital, Los Angeles
Keck / USC School of Medicine

RUBELLA

Rubella, commonly known as German measles, is a viral infection that primarily affects the skin and lymph glands (March of Dimes, 1999). Although the infection is usually benign in children and adults, it poses a significant threat to pregnant women and their fetuses. Approximately 25% of infants whose mothers contract rubella during the first trimester of pregnancy have one or more birth defects, known collectively as congenital rubella syndrome (CRS); however, infants whose mothers are infected after the 20th week of pregnancy are largely unaffected (Lee & Bowden, 2000). Congenital rubella syndrome has been associated with multiple organ and system malformations, including cardiac, ocular, central nervous system, and skeletal abnormalities (March of Dimes, 1999), and more recently with the onset of schizophrenia in adulthood (Brown et al., 2001).

The pathophysiology of rubella has been confirmed as a single-stranded RNA togavirus that is transmitted through respiratory droplets (Dyne, 2001); replicates in the nasopharyngeal area and lymph nodes; and subsequently spreads to the skin, central nervous system, synovial fluid, and (through the placenta) the developing fetus. Although the specific link between the rubella virus and teratogenecity in the fetus has not been clearly established, it is thought that cell growth inhibition is somehow implicated (Lee & Bowden, 2000). Rubella is known to be highly contagious; about 10% of young adults and 20% of women of childbearing age are susceptible to the virus (National Coalition for Adult Immunization, 2000). The incidence of rubella in the United States was reported to be 20,000 cases in 1964; however, the introduction of large-scale vaccination programs in 1969 has resulted in a significant reduction in the number of new cases. Despite comprehensive efforts by health care professionals, outbreaks of rubella continue to occur in the United States—most recently in upstate New York in 1998 (among young adult Hispanic males; Danovaro-Holliday et al., 2000) and in Nebraska in 1999 (Dyne, 2001). Rubella is endemic throughout the world (Lee & Bowden, 2000) but is more common in countries such as Ethiopia and Greece where a vaccination program is not consistently used (King, 1999).

Characteristics

1. Rubella in childhood may begin with 1 or 2 days of low-grade fever (99–100 °F) and swollen glands in the neck or behind the ears. On the 2nd or 3rd day, a rash appears at the hairline and spreads downward to the rest of the body. The rash does not itch and generally lasts up to 5 days.
2. Other symptoms such as headache, joint pain, loss of appetite, and sore throat are more common in infected adults and teenagers than in children.
3. All symptoms of rubella appear within 12–23 days after infection. Rubella is contagious from 7 days before to 5–7 days after the appearance of the rash.
4. Characteristics of CRS may include visual defects, hearing loss (Niedzielska, Katska, & Szymula, 2000), heart defects, mental retardation, and (rarely) cerebral palsy.
5. Infants with CRS may be of low birth weight and may experience temporary problems with feeding, liver and spleen enlargement, diarrhea, pneumonia, meningitis, or anemia. Occasionally, reddish-purple spots that bleed easily may appear on the face or body (March of Dimes, 1999).

Rubella is initially diagnosed upon clinical examination; however, it is confirmed by a positive serological test for rubella immunoglobulin M (IgM) antibody, a substantial increase in titers in serum rubella immunoglobulin G (IgG) antibody levels, or isolation of rubella virus (Dyne, 2001). The most effective approach to eradicating rubella is a three-pronged, preventive regimen that includes (a) vaccination of all children, (b) screening of women of childbearing age for rubella immunity, and (c) vaccination of those susceptible to rubella. Immunization is successful in 97% of patients, with vaccine-induced antibodies persisting for at least 10 years (King, 1999). The American Academy of Pediatrics (1998) recommends that children be immunized beginning at 12–15 months of age and again at school entry, at 4–6 years of age; however, high coverage with the first dose remains critical (Paulo, Gomes, Casinhas, Horta, & Dominguez, 2001). There is some controversy regarding the relative merits of monovalent (Birchard, 2000) versus multivalent vaccines (Samoilovich et al., 2000); however, the combined measles-mumps-rubella (MMR) vaccine is used most frequently in the United States. Although adverse reactions to the vaccine are uncommon after age 6, mild reactions such as fever (Virtanen, Peltola, Paunio, & Heinonen, 2000) and temporary cerebellar ataxia (Plesner et al., 2000) have been reported in children under the age of 6. Use of the MMR vaccine has recently been linked with autism and has caused a public outcry (Birchard, 2000); however, extensive studies by Dales, Hammer, and Smith (2001) have failed to corroborate this risk. Overall, the benefits of vaccination far outweigh the risks associated with lack of immunity against rubella.

Treatment of rubella in children and adults is symptomatic, with medications containing acetaminophen, NSAIDS, or antihistamines often prescribed for temporary relief. Children with congenital rubella syndrome may qualify for special educational services under the categories of physical or multiple disabilities and must have their needs addressed through a comprehensive individualized educational program (IEP). Surgical intervention with follow-up care may be necessary for children with cardiac and visual defects, and infants with hearing or vision losses may benefit from special education programs that provide early intervention and build communication and learning skills. Psychoeducational interventions for children with congenital rubella syndrome vary with degree of involvement. Children with cognitive delays will benefit from early intervention and will benefit later from placement in inclusive classrooms, depending on their level of functioning. Children with physical disabilities may need assistance in the school environment; others with multiple disabilities may require early intervention from a team of professionals. Prognosis for rubella in children and adults is positive, with the infection taking a mild, limited course. Prognosis for children with congenital rubella syndrome is variable and depends on severity.

Future research efforts must be directed toward studying the seroepidemiology of rubella, the teratogenecity of the rubella virus, and the links between prenatal exposure to the virus and subsequent problems in adulthood. Additional studies are needed to study the effectiveness of single versus combined vaccines as well as ways to reduce the incidence of rubella in at-risk populations.

REFERENCES

American Academy of Pediatrics. (1998). *Policy statement: Age for routine administration of the second dose of measles-mumps-rubella vaccine.* (RE9802). *Pediatrics, 101*(1), 129–133.

Birchard, K. (2000). Ireland holds hearing on merits of measles, mumps, and rubella vaccine. *Lancet, 356*(9242), 1665.

Brown, A. S., Cohen, P., Harkavy-Friedman, J., Babulas, V., Malaspina, D., Gorman, J. M., et al. (2001). Prenatal rubella, premorbid abnormalities, and adult schizophrenia. *Biological Psychiatry, 49*(6), 473–486.

Dales, L., Hammer, S. J., & Smith, N. J. (2001). Time trends in autism and in MMR immunization coverage in California. *Journal of the American Medical Association, 285*(9), 1183–1185.

Danovaro-Holliday, M. C., LeBaron, C. W., Allensworth, C., Raymond, R., Borden, T. G., Murray, A. B., et al. (2000). A large rubella outbreak with spread from the workplace to the community. *Journal of the American Medical Association, 284*(21), 2733–2739.

Dyne, P. (2001). Rubella. Retrieved from http://www.emedicine.com/emerg/topic388.htm

King, S. (1999). Vaccination policies: Individual rights (upsilon) community health. *British Medical Journal, 319*(7223), 1448–1449.

Lee, J. Y., & Bowden, D. S. (2000). Rubella virus replication and links to teratogenicity. *Clinical Microbiological Reviews, 13*(4), 571–587.

March of Dimes. (1999). Rubella: Public health education information sheet. Retrieved from http://www.noahhealth.org/english/pregnancy/march_of_dimes/pregnancy.illness/rubella.html

National Coalition for Adult Immunization. (2000). Facts about rubella for adults. Retrieved from http://www.nfid.org/factsheets/rubellaadult.html

Niedzielska, G., Katska, E., & Szymula, D. (2000). Hearing defects in children born of mothers suffering from rubella in the first trimester of pregnancy. *International Journal of Pediatric Otorhinolaryngology, 54*(1), 1–5.

Paulo, A. C., Gomes, M. C., Casinhas, A. C., Horta, A., & Dominguez, T. (2000). Multiple dose vaccination against childhood diseases: High coverage with the first dose remains crucial for eradication. *The IMA Journal of Mathematics Applied in Medicine and Biology, 17*(3), 201–212.

Plesner, A. M., Hansen, F. J., Taudorf, K., Nielsen, L. H., Larsen, C. B., & Pedersen, E. (2000). Gait disturbance interpreted as cerebellar ataxia after MMR vaccination at 15 months of age: A follow-up study. *Acta Paediatrica, 89*(1), 58–63.

Samoilovich, E. O., Kapustik, L. A., Feldman, E. V., Yermolovich, M. A., Svirchevskaya, A. J., Zakharenko, D. E., et al. (2000). The immunogenicity and reactogenicity of the trivalent vaccine, Trimovax, indicated for prevention of measles, mumps, and rubella, in 12-month-old children in Belarus. *Central European Journal of Public Health, 8*(3), 160–163.

Virtanen, M., Peltola, H., Paunio, M., & Heinonen, O. P. (2000). Day-to-day reactogenicity and the healthy vaccine effect of measles-mumps-rubella vaccination. *Pediatrics, 106*(5), E62.

Mary M. Chittooran
Jill E. Crowley
Saint Louis University

RUMINATION DISORDER

Rumination disorder is mainly an eating disorder of infancy and childhood. After a period of normal development, an infant or child begins repeatedly and voluntarily to regurgitate and either spit out or (more commonly) rechew food. The food is regurgitated shortly after feeding. Retching or nausea associated with normal regurgitation is not usually seen.

The disorder is uncommon but generally occurs in members of two different groups at different ages. In developmentally normal children, onset is usually at about 3–12 months of age, whereas in those with mental retardation, onset is not until about 5–6 years of age (Kerwin & Berkowitz, 1996). Onset has also been observed in adults. Mortality rate, reported as high as 25% (American Psychiatric Association [APA], 1994), appears to be declining in infants, perhaps because of medical advances (Kerwin & Berkowitz, 1996).

Affected infants and children may adopt a stance with the back arched and head held back while straining and may thrust their tongue or abdomen during regurgitation (Kerwin & Berkowitz, 1996). Children may show some signs of satisfaction or enjoyment after regurgitating but also be irritable between episodes. Malnutrition may occur even in cases in which children eat unusually large amounts of food (APA, 1994).

Characteristics

1. Repeated voluntary regurgitation and spitting out or rechewing of food.
2. Weight loss, malnutrition, dehydration, growth retardation, or failure to meet expected weight gains secondary to regurgitation.

Main criterion for diagnosis of rumination disorder is repeated regurgitation and rechewing of food for at least 1 month following normal functioning. It needs to be differentiated from gastrointestinal or other medical conditions in which regurgitation also occurs and should not be diagnosed if anorexia nervosa, bulimia, or any general medical condition is primarily involved. Differentiation from organic bases for regurgitation may be particularly important in individuals with mental retardation because undiagnosed gastrointestinal and oropharyngeal problems are common in this population (Kerwin & Berkowitz, 1996). If the child has mental retardation or a pervasive developmental disorder, rumination disorder should be separately diagnosed only if it is severe enough to call for clinical attention itself (APA, 1994).

Rumination disorder in developmentally normal infants may go into spontaneous remission (Health Central, 1998). Several behavioral treatments are available for other cases. The most common treatment is mild aversive training, but oral hygiene, differential reinforcement, or food satiation may also be used (Kerwin & Berkowitz, 1996). Special education is ordinarily not an issue with this disorder, but other services may be available through provisions of the Education of the Handicapped Act Amendment of 1986 (Kerwin & Berkowitz, 1996). Because lack of stimulation, neglect, stress, and problems in parent-child relationships may be predisposing factors (APA, 1994), family therapy and intervention may be useful.

REFERENCES

American Psychiatric Association. (1994). *Diagnostic and statistical manual of mental disorders* (4th ed.). Washington, DC: Author.

Health Central. (1998). Rumination disorder. Retrieved from http://www.healthcentral.com/mhc/top/001539.cfm

Kerwin, M. E., & Berkowitz, R. I. (1996). Feeding and eating disorders: Ingestive problems of infancy, childhood, and adolescence. *School Psychology Review, 25,* 316–328.

Robert T. Brown
Paula Kilpatrick
University of North Carolina, Wilmington

RUSSELL-SILVER SYNDROME

Russell-Silver syndrome is a rare disorder characterized by retarded growth, asymmetry of the body and face, and a triangular face.

There is no known etiology for this disorder; most cases occur from sporadic gene changes. This very rare genetic disorder has a wide variation of characteristics.

Characteristics

1. Low weight and abnormally short length at birth.
2. Delayed closure of anterior fontanel.
3. Face with a triangular shape that decreases with age and downturned corners of mouth.
4. Growth retardation, delayed bone age, weak muscle tone, and poor appetite.
5. Fifth-finger clinodactyly.
6. Asymmetry of the body.
7. Rarer traits include hydrocephalus, frequent ear infections, café au lait spots, high energy, migraine headaches, passing-out spells, and attention-deficit/hyperactivity disorder.

Treatment is symptomatic. A diet high in calories, hypoglycemia treatment, periactin used as an appetite stimulant, a feeding pump, recombinant growth hormone, and gastrostomy may be used to enhance appetite and growth (Cowger, 1998).

Shoe lifts, limb-lengthening surgery, and corrective

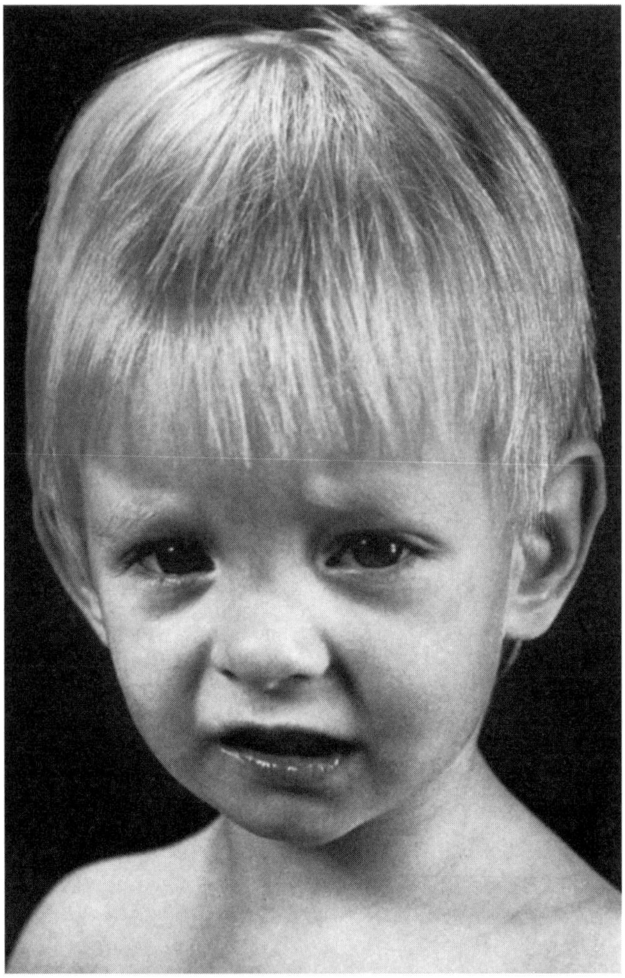

Russell-Silver Syndrome
Reprinted from *Clinical Syndromes,* Wiedemann and Kunze, 1997, by permission of the publisher Mosby

surgery are methods used to correct asymmetry and other physical abnormalities (Cowger, 1998).

Children with Russell-Silver syndrome may qualify for special education services for physical therapy for the physical disabilities associated with asymmetry and growth retardation. Speech therapy may be needed for speech difficulties due to a hypoplastic mandible. The developmental delays can result in learning disabilities that merit special education services as well. Low self-esteem and emotional problems may arise with appearance, requiring psychological assessment and services.

Prognosis for Russell-Silver syndrome is good because most of the characteristics minimize with time. Research has found some possible locations of a chromosome linked to the syndrome, but none have been confirmed (Cowger, 1998).

REFERENCE

Cowger, M. (1998). Russell-Silver syndrome. Retrieved from http://magicfoundation.org/rss.html

Iman Teresa Lahroud
University of Texas at Austin

S

SAETHRE-CHOTZEN SYNDROME

Saethre-Chotzen syndrome is one variant in a group of rare disorders known as acrocephalosyndactyly. Saethre-Chotzen syndrome is a relatively mild form of acrocephalosyndactyly with a variable pattern of craniofacial, digital, and bone abnormalities. It is also known as acrocephalosyndactyly Type III (ACS III), Chotzen syndrome, and dysostosis craniofacialis with hypertelorism. Saethre-Chotzen syndrome is usually found in several generations of a family (Niemann-Seyde, Eber, & Zoll, 1991). It is an inherited disorder; however, the features can be minor, and the syndrome therefore may remain undiagnosed. It is an autosomal disorder caused by a change or mutation in only one copy of a gene from one biological parent. Therefore, a parent with Saethre-Chotzen syndrome has a 50% chance of passing it on to a child. The altered gene is located on Chromosome 7.

Saethre-Chotzen syndrome affects between 1 and 2 people in every 50,000.

Characteristics

1. Due to early closure of the cranial sutures, the infant may have a misshapen head and facial asymmetry (craniofacial asymmetry).
2. Additional malformation of the skull and facial region may also include widely spaced eyes (ocular hypertelorism), shallow eye cavities, drooping of the upper eyelids (ptosis), and abnormal deviation of one eye in relation to another (strabismus).
3. Other symptoms sometimes include a beaked nose, small low set malformed ears, and an underdeveloped upper jaw (hypoplastic maxilla).
4. This disorder is also associated with malformations of the hands and feet. Certain fingers and toes may be partly fused together (webbed). Short digits (brachydactyly) and great broad toes are also associated with this disorder.
5. Although intelligence is usually normal, some individuals may have mild to moderate mental retardation.

With Saethre-Chotzen syndrome, the facial appearance tends to improve as the child grows. However, surgery may be necessary in infancy to correct the fusion of cranial structures and the webbing of fingers. Reconstructive surgery may be needed for the eyelids and nose.

Students with Saethre-Chotzen syndrome may not qualify for special services under the Individuals with Disabilities Education Act (1997) if they appear to be benefiting from general education. If mild or moderate mental retardation is present, they may qualify under the mental retardation or significant limited intellectual capacity category. However, students may be able to receive some accommodations under Section 504 of the Rehabilitation Act of 1974. Major plastic surgery should have been carried out during infancy. However, if craniofacial features are a concern to the student, he or she may benefit from individual counseling, especially during identity formation and if the student expresses preadolescent and adolescent concern with body image.

Research investigating Saethre-Chotzen syndrome appears to be making advances in locating the abnormal genetic structure on Chromosome 7 (e.g., Reardon, McManus, Summers, & Winter, 1993). Further research is addressing the possible improvement of physical symptoms. For example, Clauser, Galie, Hassanipour, and Calabrese (2000) had success with surgical remodeling to correct craniofacial deformities in a 13-year-old girl.

The prognosis for someone with Saethre-Chotzen syndrome depends on the severity of the symptoms. Severity runs along a continuum; some individuals have mild symptoms that are never diagnosed, whereas other individuals have severe craniofacial, digital, and bone abnormalities. Plastic surgery can help mediate the effects of some of these symptoms. A few individuals may have mild to moderate mental retardation as a result of this disorder. It is likely that these individuals will need some kind of support throughout school and life.

REFERENCES

Clauser, L., Galie, M., Hassanipour, A., & Calabrese, O. (2000). Saethre-Chotzen Syndrome: Review of the literature and report of a case. *Journal of Craniofacial Surgery, 11*(5), 480–486.

Niemann-Seyde, S. C., Eber, S. W., & Zoll, B. (1991). Saethre-Chozen syndrome (ACS III) in four generations. *Clinical Genetics, 40*(4), 271–276.

Reardon, W., McManus, S. P., Summers, D., & Winter, R. M. (1993). Cytogenetic evidence that the Saethre-Chotzen gene maps to 7p21.2 *American Journal of Medical Genetics, 47*(5), 633–636.

Rachel Toplis
University of Northern Colorado

SANDHOFF DISEASE

Sandhoff disease is a rare, genetic, lipid storage disorder that results in the progressive deterioration of the central nervous system. It is caused by a deficiency of the enzyme hexosaminidase that results in the accumulation of certain fats (lipids) in the brain and other organs of the body (National Institute of Neurological Disorders and Stroke [NINDS], 2002).

Although Sandhoff disease is a severe form of Tay-Sachs disease, which is prevalent primarily in people of European Jewish descent, it is not limited to any ethnic group. Onset of the disorder usually occurs at 6 months of age (NINDS, 2002).

Characteristics

1. Motor weakness
2. Startle reaction to sound
3. Early blindness, progressive
4. Mental and motor deterioration
5. Frequent respiratory infections
6. Macrocephaly (an abnormally enlarged head)
7. Doll-like facial appearance
8. Cherry-red spots in the back of the eyes
9. Myoclonus (shock-like contractions of a muscle) and seizures

There is no specific treatment for Sandhoff disease. Treatment is symptomatic and supportive. The prognosis for individuals with Sandhoff disease is poor. Death usually occurs by age 3 and is generally caused by respiratory infections (NINDS, 2002).

Research scientists have had some limited success in studies using the mouse model of this disorder by inhibiting the formation of the accumulating lipid. The animals fare better, but the treatment is still far from lifesaving (NINDS, 2002).

Individuals interested in gaining support and further information should contact National Tay-Sachs and Allied Diseases Association, 2001 Beacon Street, Suite 204, Boston, MA 02135, NTSAD-boston@worldnet.att.net, http://www.ntsad.org, (617) 277-4463 or (800) 90-NTSAD (906-8723), Fax: (617) 277-0134.

REFERENCE

National Institute of Neurological Disorders and Stroke. (2002). Sandhoff disease. Retrieved April 2002 from http://www.ninds.nih.gov/health_and_medical/disorders/sandhoff.htm

Elaine Fletcher-Janzen
University of Northern Colorado

SCHILDER DISEASE (ADRENOLEUKODYSTROPHY)

Schilder disease is a very serious progressive disorder characterized by the breakdown or loss of the myelin sheath surrounding nerve cells in the brain and nervous system in addition to the dysfunction of the adrenal gland. There are three forms of this rare genetic disorder: childhood adrenoleukodystrophy (ALD) in 35% of cases, adrenomyeloneuropathy (AMN) occurring in adolescent males and adult men in 40–45% of cases, and Addison's disease in 10% of cases (Moser, Moser, & Boehm, 1999).

Schilder disease is inherited as an X-linked recessive trait, affecting males with females as the carriers. The prevalence approximates between 1 in 20,000 and 1 in 50,000 equally across races and ethnic groups (Moser, Moser, & Boehm, 1999). The childhood form and Addison's disease are discussed as they both pertain to childhood disorders.

Characteristics

1. Onset between 4 and 10 years of age.
2. Initially behavioral and attentional deficits, resulting in ADD diagnosis until underlying problems arise such as memory loss, perceptual difficulties, deterioration of handwriting skills and school performance, visual impairment, reading difficulties, and difficulty understanding speech.
3. Child also develops coordination disturbance and displays aggressive behavior.
4. Seizures may occur.
5. Between 2 years of age and adulthood, adrenal malfunction (Addison's disease) may cause bronze pigmentation of the skin along with unexplained vomiting and weakness or coma (Moser, Moser, & Boehm, 1999).

Treatment for Schilder disease is experimental. Bone marrow transplantation may be effective, especially for boys and adolescents who are early in the course of childhood onset, who show magnetic resonance imaging (MRI) evidence of brain involvement, and who have a performance IQ above 80 (Moser, Moser, & Boehm, 1999). Adrenal impairment can be treated with corticosteroid replacement therapy.

Another possible treatment consists of dietary supplements with glycerol trioleate and glycerol trierucate (Lorenzo's oil diet), which improves the body's composition of fatty acids but fails to stop the progression of neurological impairment (Apatoff, 1997).

Various special education implications arise with this serious disorder. Physical therapy will be needed to help coordination, gross motor skills, and fine motor skills. Services for learning disabilities in reading, spatial ability, and understanding speech as well as services for mental retardation may also be required. Services should also be provided for visual impairment. Psychological therapy or counseling should be sought for alleviating aggression and other behavioral and personality changes that result from the disease as well as for alleviating the psychological impact of a progressive condition. School staff should be able to effectively handle seizures, should the child experience them.

The severe childhood form becomes fatal in 1–10 years. The effectiveness of new therapies such as lovastatin and 4-phenylbutyrate are to be tested in future research.

REFERENCES

Apatoff, B. R. (1997). Adrenoleukodystrophy. In R. Berkow, M. H. Beers, R. M. Bogin, & A. J. Fletcher (Eds.), *The Merck manual of medical information: Home edition* (p. 321). New York: Pocket Books.

Moser, H. W., Moser, A. B., & Boehm, C. D. (1999, March 9). X-linked adrenoleukodystrophy. Retrieved from http://www.geneclinics.org/profiles/x-ald/details.html?

Iman Teresa Lahroud
University of Texas at Austin

See also Balo Disease

SCHINZEL-GIEDION SYNDROME

Schinzel-Giedion syndrome is thought to be inherited as an autosomal recessive trait. It is a terminal form of infantile epilepsy, and infants with Schinzel-Giedion syndrome rarely live beyond 2 years of age. It is characterized by midface retraction and anomalies of the skeleton, kidney, hair, and brain.

Schinzel-Giedion syndrome appears to affect equal numbers of males and females; however, very few cases have been reported. Thoene (1995) stated that only 10 cases had been identified.

Characteristics

1. Schinzel-Giedion syndrome is evident at birth. Infants have short necks with excessive skin; low-set ears; a short, low-set nose; short lower arms and legs; and ocular hypertelorism (excessive width between eyes).
2. A major symptom is obstruction of the tube that carries urine from the kidney into the bladder, causing the pelvis and kidney duct to become swollen (hydronephrosis).
3. Growth delays are apparent at an early age.
4. Bones are not fused, and fontanels are widely open.
5. Hypertrichosis (excessive growth of hair).
6. Atrial septal defects, other heart disorders, and other internal abnormalities are present.
7. Epilepsy and seizures.
8. Vision and hearing problems.
9. Sleep apnea.
10. Those children who live beyond 2 years are likely to be severely mentally retarded.
11. Less common features include
    - High, protruding forehead.
    - Delayed growth of teeth.
    - Enlargement of the tongue (macroglossia).
    - Underdeveloped nipples, short penis, and undescended or abnormally descended testes.
    - Abnormal nails of the fingers and toes and/or polydactyly (more than normal number of fingers or toes).
    - Clubfoot.

Treatment for Schinzel-Giedion syndrome includes temporary drainage of the ureter to alleviate hydroephorsis. Surgery may be necessary if kidney function is compromised or if pain or infection occurs. Surgery may also be necessary to repair heart defects. The success rate for septal defect surgery is quite high. Anticonvulsant drugs may be helpful in controlling the seizures.

If an individual who has been diagnosed with Schinzel-Giedion syndrome lives to school age, it is likely that the student will be diagnosed with moderate to severe mental retardation. Therefore, these students will qualify for special services under the Individuals with Disabilities Education Act (IDEA, 1997) either under the significant limited intellectual capacity category or the physical disability category. It is likely that these students will need a lot of support in school and in the classroom. School personnel need to be cognizant of the possibility of seizures and how to respond to if seizures do occur. Specialized nonteaching staff will probably be needed to work with the student, and transportation may be necessary. Close liaison with medical personnel outside of the school will probably be necessary. Students, peers, and family members may benefit from counseling.

Research appears to be focusing on identifying all the symptoms associated with Schinzel-Giedion syndrome in order to make a differential diagnosis (e.g., Verloes et al., 1993) as well as to attempt to understand the underlying etiology of the syndrome (e.g., Shah, Smith, Griffiths, & Oarrel, 1999). For further information regarding this syndrome, contact the Arc (a national organization on mental retardation), 1010 Wayne Ave, Suite 650, Silver Spring, MD 20910, (301) 565-3842.

REFERENCES

Shah, A. M., Smith, M. F., Griffiths, P. D., & Ouarrel, O. W. (1999). Schinzel-Giedion syndrome: Evidence for a neurodegenerative process. *American Journal of Medical Genetics, 82*(4), 344–347.

Thoene, J. G. (Ed). 1995. *Physicians guide to rare diseases* (2nd ed.). Dowden.

Verloes, A., Moes, D., Palumbo, L., Elmer, C., Francois, A., & Bricteux, G. (1993). Schinzel-Giedion Syndrome. *Eur J Pediatr, 152*(5), 421–423.

Rachel Toplis
University of Northern Colorado

SCHMIDT SYNDROME

Schmidt syndrome is an endocrine disorder that is diagnosed when there are several different malfunctions in the endocrine glands, which are responsible for the production of hormones. Hypothyroidism and Addison's disease are the main characteristics of Schmidt syndrome, although problems with the functioning of other endocrine glands such as the gonads, parathyroids, and pancreas; insulin-dependant diabetes; and autoimmune disorders are common in those with Schmidt syndrome.

Addison's disease specifically refers to the malfunction of the adrenal glands and in most cases a diminished amount of cortisol in the body. This deficiency in turn leads to weakness, fatigue, low blood pressure, and weight loss.

Schmidt syndrome is thought to be inherited by some method, and it seems as if relatives of individuals with Schmidt syndrome are more likely to develop serious endocrine disorders (Anderson, Fein, & Frey, 1980).

Characteristics

1. Addison's disease
2. Hypothyroidism
3. Insulin-dependant diabetes
4. Failure of one or more endocrine glands
5. Autoimmune disorders

Children with Schmidt syndrome are at risk for several different health problems. Addison's disease will cause children to be especially weak and fatigued, and they may not have the energy to attend a full day of school or to keep up with peers at play. Hypothyroidism may lead to problems with weight gain and may make the child susceptible to teasing. Diabetes must be monitored closely—including while the child is in school—and proper instructions for care must be available at all times. Other glandular failure may cause a decrease in the production of various hormones, which may lead to delayed development and other associated health risks, depending on the particular hormones that are lacking. Finally, autoimmune disorders make the child more susceptible to catching colds and more serious diseases from his or her peers.

REFERENCE

Anderson, P. B., Fein, S. H., & Frey, W. G., III. (1980). Familial Schmidt's syndrome. *Journal of the American Medical Association, 244,* 2068–2070.

Allison Katz
Rutgers University

SCHWACHMAN SYNDROME (SCHWACHMAN-DIAMOND SYNDROME)

Schwachman syndrome (SS) is a rare, heritable disorder consisting of pancreatic insufficiency (inadequate amounts of pancreatic digestive enzymes), neutropenia (decreased number of neutrophils, a type of white blood cell), defects in neutrophil function, anomalous bone formation, postnatal growth retardation with poor weight gain (failure to thrive), and short stature. Patients are usually normal at birth but soon develop steatorrhea (greasy, foul-smelling stools secondary to fat malabsorption caused by pancreatic enzyme deficiency) and growth failure.

The etiology of SS is unknown. Its incidence is 1 in 20,000 births. The disorder is found more frequently in males than in females (M:F = 1.8:1). The mode of inheritance is autosomal recessive.

Characteristics

1. Normal appearance at birth
2. Streatorrhea and failure to thrive begin in infancy. Average age of onset is 7–9 months.

3. Neutropenia occurs in more than 95% of patients. Symptoms become evident during infancy or early childhood. Neutropenia predisposes these children to recurrent bacterial infections of skin and mucous membranes (ear infections, pneumonia, dermatitis). Osteomyelitis (bone infection) and sepsis (bacteria in the blood) may also occur and can be fatal.
4. Along with neutropenia, 70% of patients have thrombocytopenia (low platelet counts) and 50% are anemic. A decrease in all three cell lines is called pancytopenia. Thrombocytopenia may lead to spontaneous bruising and bleeding from mucous membranes. Anemia can cause lethargy and (in severe cases) congestive heart failure.
5. Metaphyseal dysostosis (malformed ends of long bones). This characteristic occurs in about 40% of patients.
6. Short stature, syndactyly (webbing and fusion of digits).
7. Ptosis (droopy eyelids) and strabismus (incoordination of eye movement).
8. Dry, scaly skin (ichthyosis), increased skin pigmentation.
9. Increased incidence of lymphoreticular malignancy (lymphoma, leukemia).
10. Cleft palate, dental anomalies.

The initial findings in SS (streatorrhea, failure to thrive, recurrent phenumonias) are also seen in infants with cystic fibrosis, which is a far more common disorder. Thus, SS patients may be initially misdiagnosed. However, these two disorders can be differentiated by a relatively simple laboratory test (sweat chloride analysis) and determination of the presence of the cystic fibrosis gene.

Pancreatic insufficiency is managed by giving enzyme replacement orally. Although this strategy results in improved steatorrhea and fat malabsorption, infants with SS may continue to grow poorly. By age 4, pancreatic abnormalities frequently resolve, and replacement therapy is no longer necessary.

Neutropenia is frequently cyclic. It may require antibiotic therapy when it is accompanied by fever. Packed red blood cell infusions are indicated when hemoglobin levels fall below 80g/L. Platelet transfusions are given when counts are less than 30,000 or for clinically significant bleeding secondary to thrombocytopenia. Some cases of pancytopenia may respond to corticosteroids with or without androgen augmentation. The drugs cyclosporin A and G-CSF are presently undergoing clinical trials for the treatment of pancytopenia.

This disorder has a 25% chance of recurrence in subsequent progeny. Therefore, genetic counseling should be provided for affected families.

There are no specific cognitive deficits associated with SS. Therefore, a child would not require special support services as a result of having SS. If, however, the child's ability to function in the classroom is impaired by his or her illness, he or she would meet eligibility criteria to receive support services as Other Health Impaired.

The average life expectancy of a patient with SS is about 35 years. Individuals with pancytopenia live slightly less than 15 years. These grim statistics indicate a rather poor prognosis for this disorder.

REFERENCES

Gandy, A. Shwachman-Diamond syndrome. Retrieved from http://www.pedianet.com/news/illness/disease/files/shwachman.htm

National Organization for Rare Disorders. (1999). *Shwachman syndrome.* Retrieved from http://www.stepstn.com/cgi-win/nord.exe?proc=Getdocument&rectype=0&recnum=371

Werlin, S. L. (2000). Disorders of the exocrine pancreas. *Nelson textbook of pediatrics* (16th ed., p. 1190). Philadelphia: W. B. Saunders.

Barry H. Davison
Ennis, Texas

Joan W. Mayfield
Baylor Pediatric Specialty Services
Dallas, Texas

SCHWARTZ-JAMPEL SYNDROME

Schwartz-Jampel syndrome (SJS) is an autosomal recessive condition. It is characterized by muscle stiffness, mild muscle weakness, and a number of minor morphological abnormalities. This disorder is caused by a genetic abnormality linked to one or more regions of the first chromosome. This disorder is known by several other names: myotonic myopathy, dwarfism, chondrodystrophy, ocular and facial anomalies, Schwartz-Jampel-Aberfeld syndrome (SJA syndrome), and chondrodystrophic myotonia. Generally, authorities now recognize subtypes of Schwartz-Jampel syndrome. Type 1 is the classic type, usually apparent at birth. Type 1A is often not diagnosed until later in childhood and tends to be less severe. Type 1B is apparent at birth and is more clinically severe. Type 2 is noticeable at birth; however, it does not map onto the same chromosome as Type 1 does and is probably a disorder known as Stuve-Wiedermann (Sigaudy et al., 1998; Superti-Furga et al., 1998), which is more often discussed in the rheumatological and orthopedic literature.

In the United States, Schwartz-Jampel is considered a very rare disease; there is no significant information available on its distribution between ethnic groups. It has been described in both males and females; however, gender prevalence information is not available.

Characteristics

1. Depending upon the subtype of the disorder, symptoms are apparent at birth (Types 1, 1B, 2) or in later childhood (Type 1A).
2. Symptoms include abnormalities of the skeletal muscles, including weakness and stiffness (myotonic myopathy); abnormal bone development (bone dysplasia); joint contractures (bending or extension of joint in a fixed position); and growth delay resulting in short stature (dwarfism).
3. Individuals may also have small, fixed facial features characterized by a puckered facial appearance.
4. Abnormalities of the eyes, such as hypertrichosis of the eyelids (excessive hair growth on and pigmentation of the eyelids).
5. A subset of individuals (20%) may also have mental retardation.

In treating this disorder, the aim is to reduce muscle stiffness and cramping. Nonpharmacological methods such as massage, gradual warming up before exercise, and gradual stretching can help. Some medications (e.g., anticonvulsants and antiarrhythmics) have been found to be useful in other myotonic disorders; however, because this disorder is so rare, at present there are no controlled trials assessing the effectiveness of these drugs with Schwartz-Jampel symptoms. Patients with the characteristic physical appearance of Schwartz-Jampel syndrome may need additionally psychosocial support.

Students diagnosed with Schwartz-Jampel syndrome may benefit from general education without special services. However, each case needs to be assessed on an individual basis. Some individuals may qualify for services under the Individuals with Disabilities Education Act (IDEA, 1997) if they have some level of mental retardation. Others may qualify for services due to psychological morbidity caused by the physical deformities (e.g., if the student becomes depressed). Services may be allocated either under IDEA within the category of Emotional Disturbance or under Section 504 of the Rehabilitation Act of 1974. Students with Schwartz-Jampel syndrome may benefit from counseling during their school career, especially if physical abnormalities are present or if physical limitations caused by muscle weakness or stiffness are frustrating. School personnel should be informed of the effects of Schwartz-Jampel syndrome and support and monitor the use of nonpharmacological (and if necessary, pharmacological) interventions used to reduce muscle stiffness especially before and after physical exercise, but also during the school day if necessary.

Muscle stiffness or weakness may gradually worsen or remain relatively stable. However, except for patients with Stuve-Wiedemann syndrome (Schwartz-Jampel Type 2),

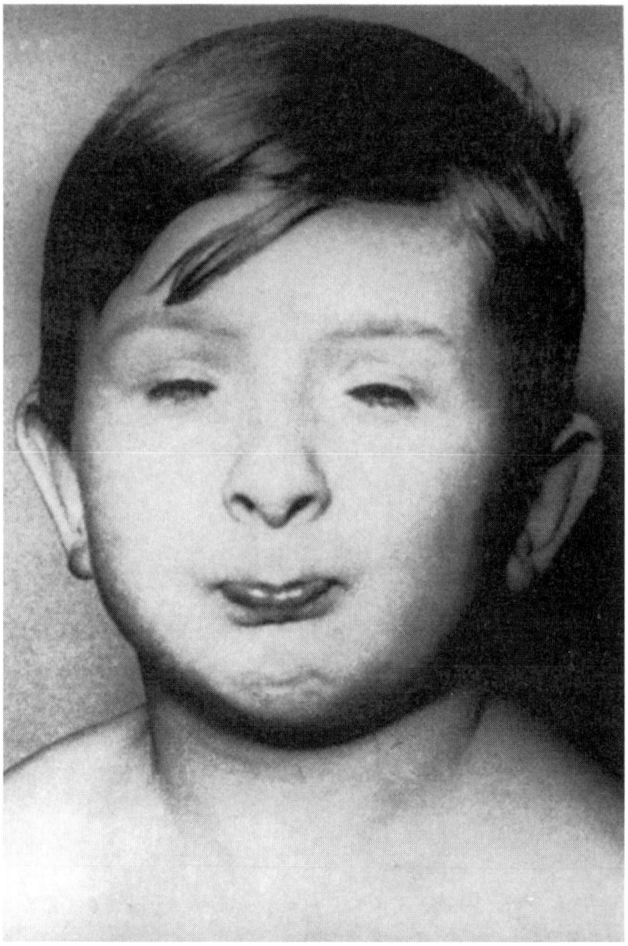

Schwartz-Jampel Syndrome
Reprinted from *Clinical Syndromes,* Wiedemann and Kunze, 1997, by permission of the publisher Mosby

which is fundamentally a different disorder, most patients have a reasonably good prognosis. The muscle weakness can be a factor in delayed motor milestones, such as walking. However, in most cases children do learn to walk and become self-sufficient.

Research continues to investigate the differences and similarities between Schwartz-Jampel syndrome and Stuve-Wiedemann syndrome to clarify this issue. Some researchers suspect that a muscle ion-channel abnormality or a muscle enzyme defect (causes underlying other myotonic disorders) may also underlie this condition.

REFERENCES

Sigaudy, S., Moncla, A., Fredouille, C., Bourliere, B., Lampert, J. C., & Philip, N. (1998). Congenital bowing of the long bones in two fetuses presenting features of Stuve-Wiedemann syndrome and Schwartz-Jampel syndrome type 2. *Clinical Dysmorphology,* 7(4), 257–262.

Superti-Furga, A., Tenconi, R., Clementi, M., Eich, G., Steinmann,

B., Boltshauser, E., et al. (1998). Schwartz-Jampel syndrome type 2 and Stuve-Wiedemann syndrome: A case for "lumping." *American Journal of Medical Genetics, 78*(2), 150–154.

Rachel Toplis
University of Northern Colorado

SCLERODERMA

Scleroderma is an autoimmune disorder that can affect the skin or the internal organs. In individuals with scleroderma, the immune system causes cells to overproduce collagen. The excess collagen causes normal tissue in the skin or internal organs to be replaced with dense, thick tissue (Cleveland Clinic, 1999). Scleroderma that affects only the skin or muscles is known as localized scleroderma. Localized scleroderma is far more common in children than is systemic sclerosis, the type of scleroderma where the internal organs are involved (Scleroderma Foundation, 2000). However, systemic sclerosis is much more serious and life-threatening. Scleroderma is not contagious and does not appear to be inherited (Cleveland Clinic, 1999).

Overall, approximately 300,000 Americans currently have some form of scleroderma (Scleroderma Foundation, 2000). Of these, 5,000 to 7,000 are children (Cleveland Clinic, 1999). Scleroderma affects females twice as often as it does males, but there are no racial or ethnic group differences in prevalence (Cleveland Clinic, 1999).

Characteristics

1. A patch of skin appears lighter or darker in color than normal.
2. Thickened area of skin, ridges, or small pits in skin.
3. Lack of flexibility in skin in affected area.
4. Pain or stiffness due to joint inflammation.
5. Extreme sensitivity to cold, usually in the hands and experienced as tingling, discomfort, or color changes in hands.
6. Heartburn and trouble swallowing.
7. Fatigue and muscle weakness.
8. Itching.

Initially, scleroderma causes little pain; therefore, parents and children may not seek treatment until the disorder has been present for some time. Treatment cannot commence until the type of scleroderma involved is diagnosed. For localized scleroderma, some medications have been shown to slow the spread of the disease, and some physicians recommend oral vitamins D and E as a treatment (Scleroderma Foundation, 1998). Steroids are used to treat inflammation and fatigue (Cleveland Clinic, 1999). Individuals with localized scleroderma are advised to avoid sun exposure and use moisturizing lotions on the affected areas (Scleroderma Foundation, 2000). Physical therapy also is recommended to maintain range of motion and flexibility and to increase muscle strength and blood flow to the affected areas (Cleveland Clinic, 1999). Orthopedic surgery to correct joint contractures in the hand is needed only in very severe cases (Cleveland Clinic, 1999).

The systemic sclerosis form of scleroderma is more difficult to treat effectively. In addition to the treatments mentioned previously for localized scleroderma, some recommend the drugs d-penicillamine, cyclosporine, and methotrexate (Lehman, 2000). However, these drugs have potentially serious side effects, and patients must be closely monitored while taking them.

There are no reported cognitive effects of any type of scleroderma. Children with joint inflammation as a result of localized scleroderma may need modifications in physical education requirements and would qualify under the Other Health Impaired handicapping condition. Those with systemic sclerosis may require at-home study arrangements as their disease progresses.

Localized scleroderma generally is not life-threatening and in almost all cases does not progress into systemic sclerosis. With physical therapy, most children with this type of scleroderma can maintain their joint mobility and the effects of the disease on the child's growth can be limited (Scleroderma Foundation, 1999). Systemic sclerosis can cause serious and life-threatening damage to the internal organs, including the heart, lungs, and kidneys (Lehman, 2000). The long-term prognosis for survival in these severe cases is poor.

REFERENCES

Cleveland Clinic. (1999). Scleroderma in children. Retrieved from http://onhealth.webmd.com/conditions/condctr/arthritis/item, 52762.asp

Lehman, T. (2000). Scleroderma. Retrieved from http://www.goldscout.com/sclero.html

Scleroderma Foundation. (1999). *Localized scleroderma.* Danvers, MA: Author.

Scleroderma Foundation. (2000). Scleroderma fact sheet. Retrieved from http://www.scleroderma.org/fact.html

Nancy K. Scammacca
University of Texas at Austin

SCOLIOSIS

Scoliosis is a side-to-side (lateral) curvature of the spine that can be caused by congenital, developmental, degenerative, or idiopathic (unknown) causes. The curvature of the spine from scoliosis may develop as a single curve (shaped like the letter *C*) or as two curves (shaped like the letter *S*). Scoliosis may occur in the upper back (thoracic) or lower back (lumbar), but most commonly it develops in the area between the thoracic and lumbar areas (thoracolumbar area). Idiopathic scoliosis (unknown causes) is the most common form of scoliosis, occurring in approximately one half million adolescents in the United States. Family members of children diagnosed with scoliosis often have the same condition, which indicates a genetic predisposition.

It has been estimated that 3 out of every 100 people have this disorder to some degree (Izenberg, 2000). About 10 percent of all adolescents have some degree of scoliosis. Less than 1 percent, however, require medical attention other than careful observation of the problem. Mild curvature occurs about equally in girls and boys, but serious scoliosis is five times more prevalent in girls. Scoliosis appears most often in adolescents between the age of ten and thirteen, when a growth spurt is occurring (Newton, Olendorf, Jeryan, & Boyden, 2000).

The cause of scoliosis is known in only about 20% of the cases (Newton et al., 2000). These cases are classified as follows: Congenital scoliosis is caused by defects in the spine that are present at birth; neuromuscular scoliosis is caused by problems with the nerves or muscles, which are too weak to support the spine (cerebral palsy, muscular dystrophy, and polio); and degenerative scoliosis is caused by deterioration of the disks that separate the vertebrae in the spine.

Characteristics

1. Most often develops in adolescents and progresses during the adolescent growth spurt.
2. In severe cases (curvature exceeding 70°) can cause the ribs to press against the lungs, restrict breathing, and reduce oxygen levels. If the curve exceeds 100°, both the lungs and heart can be injured.
3. Back pain is not common during adolescence
4. Abnormal posture that includes a tilted head, protruding shoulder blade, tilted pelvis, and one hip or shoulder that is higher than the other, causing an uneven hem or shirt line.
5. The child may lean more to one side than to another.
6. The child may become fatigued from sitting or standing too long.

The treatment is determined by the cause of the scoliosis, the size and location of the curve, and the stage of bone growth (how near the growth centers are to closure). Most cases of adolescent idiopathic scoliosis require no treatment (less than 20°) but should be followed at regular intervals (often every 6 months). The treatment of scoliosis is to consider treating curves greater than 25° or those that progress by 10° while being monitored. Braces are recommended for moderate curves (curves of 25–40°), and surgery is recommended for more severe curves.

The prognosis depends on the cause, location, and severity of the curve. The greater the curve, the greater the chance of progression after growth has stopped. Mild cases of scoliosis are often successfully treated with bracing. People with surgically corrected idiopathic scoliosis also do very well and can lead active, healthy lives (Roye, 2001).

Genetic research is being done to determine which genes cause idiopathic scoliosis. Research is also being done on enzymes known as matrix metalloproteinase, which is involved in repair and remodeling of collagen, the critical structural protein found in muscles and bones. High levels of this enzyme can cause abnormalities in components in the spinal discs, contributing to disc degeneration (Health With Web MD, 2001).

REFERENCES

Health With Web MD. (2001, Dec. 17). Scoliosis. Retrieved from http://content.health.msn.com/content/dmk/dmk_article_40074

Izenberg, N. (2000). *Human diseases and conditions.* New York: Charles Scribner & Sons.

Newton, D., Olendorf, D., Jeryan, C., & Boyden, K. (2000). *SICK! Diseases and disorders, injuries and infections.* Detroit: U-X-L.

Roye, B. (2001).Retrieved from http://www.nlm.nih.gov/medlineplus/ency/article/001241.htm

Karen Wiley
University of Northern Colorado

SEITELBERGER DISEASE (INFANTILE NEUROAXONAL DYSTROPHY)

Seitelberger disease is an inherited central nervous system condition that is characterized by progressive degeneration of muscular and coordination ability. The disease is inherited as an autosomal recessive trait. The symptoms and physical characteristics of Seitelberger disease occur due to swelling and degeneration of nerve endings (dystrophic axonal swellings) in areas of the brain and in the central and peripheral nerves. This disease may be referred to as prenatal or connatal neuroaxonal dystrophy. There is also some evidence that this disease is an infantile form of Hallervorden-Spatz syndrome.

Although it is extremely rare, Seitelberger disease appears to be slightly more common towards females.

Characteristics

1. The onset of Seitelberger disease is usually before 2 years of age. Many children and infants appear to develop normally until approximately 14–18 months.
2. Often, a progressive decrease in walking ability is evident, or children may experience delays or an arrest in the acquisition of other skills requiring coordination.
3. Children may begin to lose previously acquired skills—for example, sitting or standing.
4. General muscle weakness and muscle tone (hypotonia) may be evident.
5. Involuntary movements of the hands and face (e.g., jerking of the head).
6. Spasticity of the lower arms and legs (sudden involuntary muscle spasms).
7. Progressive paralysis of the lower part of the body (paraplegia).
8. Children with Seitelberger disease also experience vision defects such as involuntary rapid side-to-side movement of the eyes, strabismus (crossing of the eyes), and deterioration of the nerves of the eyes.
9. As neurological impairment progresses, children may experience disorientation, loss of intellectual functioning, and progressive brain abnormalities.
10. Susceptibility to respiratory tract infections increases.
11. Progressive mental retardation occurs.
12. Serious, potentially life-threatening complications may develop.
13. Most affected children die before age 6.

At present, there is no cure for this disease. Genetic counseling is available for individuals who carry the abnormal gene and are considering starting a family. The standard treatment for Seitelberger disease is supportive and addresses the symptoms of the disease—for example, respiratory infections can be treated. However, affected individuals and their families may benefit from services for the visually and physically impaired.

The majority of affected children with this disease do not live beyond 6 years of age. If a child with this diagnosis enters school, it is highly likely that the child will be mentally retarded and have physical disabilities. Therefore, such children will qualify for special services under the Individuals with Disabilities Education Act (1997) within the mental retardation or physical disability category. Students with Seitelberger disease will probably need a variety of services, from specialized nonteaching aides and transportation to physical therapist and speech-language therapists. These students may need assistive devices to communicate and participate in school life as fully as possible. Students with Seitelberger disease may require intensive medical interventions. For example, repeated respiratory tract infections and other serious, potentially life-threatening complications may require these students to be away from school for extended periods of time. School personnel need to be informed of the restrictions of this disorder and work closely with medical personnel, the student, and his or her family. Because the disease is degenerative, accommodations and modifications necessary for students with Seitelberger disease will change over time. School personnel need to be conscientious of the terminal nature of this disease and attempt to prepare the student, his or her peers, and others working with the child. Grief counseling may be necessary.

The prognosis for Seitelberger disease is that it is terminal, with the majority of affected children dying before the age of 6. More information is needed to understand this disease. At present, research investigating Seitelberger disease appears to be aimed at understanding the disorder, investigating its etiology, and developing reliable diagnostic criteria (Nardocci et al., 1999). Some studies suggest that this disease may be related to another neuroaxonal diseases (e.g., giant axonal neuropathy; Begeer et al., 1979); Mahadevan et al., 2000).

REFERENCES

Begeer, J. H., Houthoff, H. J., van Weerden, T. W., de Groot, C. J., Blaauw, E. H., & le Coultre, R. (1979). Infantile neuroaxonal dystrophy and giant axonal neuropathy: Are they related? *Annals of Neurology, 6*(6), 540–548.

Mahadevan, A., Santosh, V., Gayatri, N., Ratnavalli, E., NandaGopal, R., Vasanth, A., et al. (2000). Infantile neuroaxonal dystrophy and giant axonal neuropathy: Overlap diseases of neuronal cytoskeletal elements in childhood? *Clinical Neuropathology, 19*(5), 221–229.

Nardocci, N., Zorzi, G., Farina, L., Binelli, S., Scaioli, W., Ciano, C., et al. (1999). Infantile neuroaxonal dystrophy: Clinical spectrum and diagnostic criteria. *Neurology, 52*(7), 1472–1478.

Rachel Toplis
University of Northern Colorado

SEIZURES, ABSENCE

An absence seizure, formerly known as a petit mal, is defined as a sudden, involuntary, transient alteration in cerebral function due to abnormal discharge of neurons in the central nervous system (CNS; Thiele, Gonzalez-Heydrich, & Riviello, 1999). Absence seizures fall in the category of generalized seizures, of which there are two types: primary and secondary. Primary generalized seizures are characterized by synchronous bilateral epileptic discharges. The first sign of seizure appears simultaneously in both hemispheres. A secondary generalized seizure is one that begins in one hemisphere and then spreads throughout the brain. In some cases, generalized tonic-clonic seizures develop; in fact, approximately 50% of children with absence seizures have at least one generalized tonic-clonic seizure during their lifetimes (Fenichel, 1997).

Approximately 150,000 children in the United States are diagnosed each year with a seizure disorder, and fewer than 10% of these seizures are reported to be absence (Hauser, 1994; Holmes, 1999). Absence seizures occur more often in females than in males. The onset is between the ages of 3 and 12 but peaks between the ages of 4 and 8 (Fenichel, 1997). These seizures often remit in adolescence but may persist into adulthood.

Most absence seizures are characterized by frequent episodes of staring and brief loss of consciousness (i.e., 5–30). The episodes often occur 20 or more times a day and have an abrupt onset and cessation. Most absence seizures involve staring without prominent motor features but some do involve motor phenomena. Atypical absence occurs less frequently but lasts longer. Children with seizure disorders can however go for several days without a seizure. When seizures do occur, the period in which consciousness is altered is also longer, and the onset and cessation are slower. With atypical absence seizures, the child may also have automatisms (i.e., semipurposeful behaviors in which the child is unaware and has no recall), reduced postural tone, and tonic-clonic movements (i.e., symmetrical and rhythmical jerking). The atypical absence seizure tends to occur more often with other syndromes (e.g., see entry on Lennox-Gastaut syndrome) and is more likely caused by a CNS insult. Children with atypical absence seizures are also more likely to have developmental delay (Menkes & Sankar, 2000).

Characteristics

1. Seizures may be mistaken for daydreaming or inattention.
2. Characterized by an abrupt cessation of activity and brief episodes of staring with a blank face, rolling eyes, and fluttering eyelids.
3. Consciousness can be impaired for up to 30 s, and amnesia can occur afterward.
4. Onset is abrupt and without aura or postictal fatigue; activity resumes immediately after the seizure.
5. Seizure activity may occur frequently throughout the day (e.g., 20 or more times).
6. In cases of complex absence, rhythmical and symmetrical jerking can occur, along with changes in postural tone and brief automatisms.

Antiepileptic drug therapy is the recommended treatment for absence seizures—in particular, valproate, clonazepam, and ethosuximide. With antiepileptic drug treatment, prognosis for absence seizures is highly favorable, with complete remission in 70–80% of cases (Holmes, 1999). Although prognosis for absence seizures is good, many children who have this type of seizure will need to be seen for psychological assessments to determine service needs.

Special education services are not necessarily indicated. Regular classroom accommodations and disability services, however, may be needed to ensure that the child has access to the educational environment (e.g., tutoring by a peer or classroom aide to catch up on work that was missed and allowance for extra time to complete assignments). When special education services are needed, they are likely to be provided for associated conditions rather than for the absence seizure itself (e.g., genetic syndromes and CNS insults causing seizure activity). Educators still need to be aware that untreated recurrent seizures put children at risk for cognitive impairments and psychological disturbance. Depression, anxiety, and behavior problems are not that uncommon. These problems may be explained in part by the fact that the child is the recipient of negative reactions from peers as well as from teachers who mistake the seizure for daydreaming or inattention. Educating school staff and peers may be as critical as any other treatment—that is, aside from medication therapy. Information about seizure types and some of the potential side effects of drug treatment (e.g., decreased motor speed and memory impairment) may be particularly important for the child in the classroom.

Research is still needed to investigate ways in which children with absence seizures can be treated most effectively, including nondrug therapies.

REFERENCES

Fenichel, G. M. (1997). *Clinical pediatric neurology: A signs and symptoms approach* (3rd ed.). Philadelphia: W. B. Saunders.

Hauser, W. A. (1994). The Prevalence and incidence of convulsive disorders in children. *Epilepsia, 35*(2), S1–S6.

Holmes, G. L. (1999). Generalized seizures. In K. Swaimann & L. Ashwall (Eds.), *Pediatric neurology: Principles and practice* (pp. 634–645). St. Louis, MO: Mosby.

Menkes, J. H., & Sankar, R. (2000). Paroxysmal disorders. In J. H. Menkes & H. B. Sarnat (Eds.), *Child neurology* (pp. 919–1026). Philadelphia: Lippincott Williams & Wilkins.

Thiele, E. A., Gonzalez-Heydrich, & Riviello, J. J. (1999). Epilepsy in children and adolescents. *Child and Adolescent Psychiatric Clinics of North America, 8*(4), 671–694.

Elizabeth Christiansen
Elaine Clark
University of Utah

SEIZURES, ATONIC

Atonic seizures are also referred to as drop attacks and epileptic fall. Hughlings Jackson first described "sudden epileptic falls" in 1886. Unlike most epileptic seizures that involve either positive motor behavior (e.g., tonic, clonic, and myoclonic) or the absence of motor behavior (e.g., absence seizures), atonic seizures involve negative motor phenomena (Andermann & Tenembaum, 1995). The primary characteristic of an atonic seizure is a sudden loss of muscle tone that lasts 1–2 s. In a small number of cases, myoclonic jerks precede the loss of muscle tone; however, in most cases there is no warning (or aura). As a result, falls and injuries are common. The seizure is accompanied by a brief period of unconsciousness lasting 300 ms to 3 s and has an electroencephalogram (EEG) pattern of bilateral synchronous polyspike wave and spike wave (Holmes, 1999).

The atonic seizure typically occurs shortly after awakening and continues throughout the day.

Characteristics

1. Onset is between 2 and 5 years of age.
2. Loss of muscle tone and postural control causes falls and limb-jaw drops.
3. Referred to as drop attacks and epileptic fall.
4. Momentary loss of consciousness during the fall (but rapid recovery).
5. Typically start shortly after awakening but occur frequently during the day.
6. The majority of children with atonic seizures also have myoclonic jerks or tonic seizures.
7. Often seen in children with Lennox-Gastaut syndrome.

The seizures begin between the ages of 2 and 5 but are considered rare in children. The prevalence rate is largely unknown because atonic seizures have been associated with a number of seizure types (both generalized and partial, as well as tonic, clonic, and myoclonic). The condition is often associated with Lennox-Gastaut syndrome (LGS) or with a myoclonic-astatic seizure type. In LGS, seizures occur at an early age, involve multiple seizure types, and have a generalized slow-spike and wave EEG pattern. Accompanying the syndrome is impairment in developmental skills, including intellectual ability.

Children who have atonic seizures with associated conditions such as LGS will likely receive special education services in the schools (e.g., self-contained classrooms for students with intellectual disabilities). For children without LGS or other similar syndromes (e.g., Doose syndrome), Other Health Impaired services may be needed—in particular, services provided by the school nurse (e.g., medication management and consultation with treating physicians) and therapists (e.g., occupational or physical therapists if falls have resulted in injuries that prevent the child from accessing an education). Given the frequency of atonic seizures (i.e., sometimes 100 or more episodes a day) and the attentional problems that some of these children have, the resource teaching staff may be needed to ensure adequate exposure to learning material and adequate help completing assignments. Tutoring may also help; such tutoring could be provided by peer tutors or by paraprofessionals in the classroom. Children with atonic seizures should also be provided with counseling to help them to develop mechanisms to cope with their condition. The unexpected nature of the seizures and the safety risks seriously limit some of the activities in which these children can engage, including recreational and social activities.

Unfortunately, antiepileptic drugs have not been found to be particularly helpful in treating atonic seizures. Some of the drugs that are effective in treating associated seizures have in fact been shown to exacerbate atonic seizures (e.g., valproate and clonazepam, both of which have been shown to improve myoclonic seizures). Other drugs have also been found to increase falling, including carbamazepine (Bourgeois, 1995). Felbamate has shown some promise with children who have LGS; however, the drug is indicated more for partial or generalized seizures associated with LGS, not the atonic seizure.

Treatment of atonic seizures remains a challenge and further research is needed to determine what will provide the best control, including both drugs and alternative treatment methods (e.g., the ketogenic diet).

REFERENCES

Andermann, F., & Tenembaum, S. (1995). Negative motor phenomena in generalized epilepsies: A study of atonic seizures. In S. Fahn, M. Hallett, H. Luders, & C. Marsden (Eds.), *Advances in neurology* (Vol. 67, pp. 9–28). Philadelphia: Lippincott-Raven.

Bourgeois, B. (1995). Clinical use of drugs useful in the treatment of atonic seizures. In S. Fahn, M. Halett, H. Luders, & C. Marsden (Eds.), *Advances in neurology* (Vol. 67, pp. 361–367). Philadelphia: Lippincott-Raven.

Holmes, G. L. (1999). Generalized seizures. In K. Swaimann & L. Ashwall (Eds.), *Pediatric neurology: Principles and practice* (pp. 634–645). St. Louis, MO: Mosby.

Elizabeth Christiansen
Elaine Clark
University of Utah

SEIZURES, GENERALIZED TONIC-CLONIC

Generalized tonic-clonic seizures are one of the most common childhood neurological disorders. The seizure involves synchronous bilateral electrical epileptical discharges; therefore, the first signs reflect involvement of both hemispheres of the brain. The seizure, however, can begin in a focal area of the brain (or one hemisphere) as a partial seizure and spread to other areas and become a generalized seizure. Seizures are defined as a sudden, involuntary, transient alteration in neurological function resulting from excessive electrical discharge of neurons. Generalized tonic-clonic seizures, formerly known as grand mal seizures, are the most common and dramatic of childhood seizure manifestations.

Characteristic features include loss of consciousness followed by repetitive rapid (but rhythmic) jerking of the limbs. These movements are followed by slower irregular movements, eyes rolling back, rapid breathing causing saliva to froth, and sometimes incontinence (urinary and bowel). Following the seizure is a postictal sleep phase in which the individual is difficult to awaken. These seizures are often considered to be idiopathic; however, fever, central nervous system infections, and genetic transmission are possible causes. According to Fenichel (1997), the seizure typically occurs during adolescence if there are no associated absence seizures. If absence seizures, however, accompany the generalized seizure, onset tends to be earlier—that is, in the first decade.

The incidence of epilepsy (recurrent unprovoked seizures) in children between birth and 16 years of age is approximately 40 in 100,000 annually. The highest incidence occurs in the 1st year of life, with 120 in 100,000 cases (Hauser, 1994).

Characteristics

Tonic phase (10–30 s in length)

1. Eyes roll upward or deviate to one side.
2. Immediate loss of consciousness.
3. Falls to ground.
4. Stiffens.
5. Symmetrical tonic contraction of entire body musculature.
6. Rigid extension of arms and legs.
7. Mouth forcibly closed.
8. May utter cry sound as abdomen and vocal chords contract.
9. Increased salivation.
10. Arrest of ventilation or apnea.
11. Pallor or cyanosis is common.

Clonic phase (generally 30–60 s but can last up to 30 min)

1. Rigidity replaced by violent jerking movements.
2. Rhythmic contraction and relaxation of trunk and extremities.
3. Movements rapid and rhythmic initially, then become slower and more irregular as seizure ends (decrescendo in frequency but not strength of movements).
4. Urinary or bowel incontinence.

Postictal phase (immediately follows clonic phase and varies in duration)

1. Sleep or sleepiness, difficulty in arousal.
2. Confusion or agitation.
3. Headache, nausea, vomiting.
4. Slurred speech.
5. Visual disturbances.

Anticonvulsant drug therapy is the recommended form of treatment for children with generalized tonic-clonic seizures. Drugs used for tonic-clonic seizures include phenobarbital, phenytoin, carbamazepine, and primidone, to name a few. Treatment of generalized seizures with partial onset is the same as that for primary generalized seizures. If the child does not respond to antiepileptic drug therapy, however, surgery may be used to remove damaged tissue.

Approximately 70–90% of children with epilepsy of unknown causes become seizure free. Prognosis for continued remission is particularly good if the onset of seizure occurred after 2 years of age, the seizures were a primary generalized type, and the child has normal intelligence. Children who require polydrug treatment for seizure management, however, are more likely to relapse following discontinuance of treatment. Children with recurrent seizures tend to have a greater risk of developing psychological problems than do healthy children or children with other chronic illnesses (Austin, Risinger, & Beckett, 1992).

Depression and anxiety as well as behavior problems are common among children with tonic-clonic seizures. These children are subject to peer rejection and teasing, and some even receive negative reactions from adults. These situations serve only to exacerbate the problems these children have adjusting to their seizure condition and functioning in daily life (e.g., academically and socially). School nurses can help to educate peers and teachers alike about seizures. The child may also need this information as well as information as to how best handle others' reactions. In some cases, it will be necessary to provide psychological therapy for the child. Such therapy may include supportive-insight-oriented treatments, as well as assertiveness training and social skills tips. Including parents is critical, not only to keep them and the child's physician informed about the response to treatment, but also to ensure ample social opportunities outside of school and adequate assistance with homework. Special education services are probably not needed; however, in some cases services for students with other health impairments will be necessary to ensure adequate learning. Section 504 plans are likely to suffice in providing adequate accommodations in the classroom, including reduced workload and peer tutoring to help the child catch up on material missed (e.g., school absences or postictal sleep).

REFERENCES

Austin, J. K., Risinger, M. W., Beckett, L. A. (1992) Correlates of behavior problems in children with epilepsy. *Epilepsia, 33,* 1115–1122.

Fenichel, G. M. (1997). *Clinical pediatric neurology: A signs and symptoms approach* (3rd ed.). Philadelphia: W. B. Saunders.

Hauser, W. A. (1994). The prevalence and incidence of convulsive disorders in children. *Epilepsia, 35*(2), S1–S6.

Elizabeth Christiansen
Elaine Clark
University of Utah

SEIZURES, MYOCLONIC

Myoclonic seizures, formerly called minor motor seizures, are characterized by brief, involuntary muscle contractions and may affect one or many muscles bilaterally, although not necessarily symmetrically. A hand may suddenly fling out, a shoulder may shrug, a foot may kick, or the entire body may jerk. It can occur as a single event or as a series of jerks. The abrupt jerking may affect the legs, causing the child to fall, or it may cause the child to drop or spill what he or she is holding. Myoclonic seizures should not be confused with tics, tremors, chorea, or startle responses. Tics can usually be suppressed—at least temporarily—by an effort of will, whereas myoclonus cannot; and myoclonus does not have the characteristic continuous flow of movements as in chorea or the smooth to-and-from movements of tremors.

Characteristics

1. Sudden, brief, involuntary contractures of a muscle or group of muscles
2. Sudden onset without aura or postictal state
3. May or may not experience loss of consciousness
4. May or may not be symmetrical
5. Often occurs early in the morning
6. May occur in association with other seizure forms
7. Often associated with severe central nervous system (CNS) disorders

The multiple seizure types of Lennox-Gastaut syndrome often include myoclonic seizures (see entry on Lennox-Gastaut); however, they are a minor part of the syndrome. The most common types of myoclonic seizure syndromes in children include the syndromes of infantile spasms (see West syndrome) and juvenile myoclonic epilepsy. Benign myoclonic epilepsy and severe myoclonic epilepsy are the rarest types of myoclonic seizures.

Benign myoclonic epilepsy, which has an onset between 4 months and 2 years of age, is characterized by brief myoclonic attacks, which may include merely nodding of the head or may be severe enough to throw the child to the floor (Fenichel, 1997). Symptoms include head dropped to the chest, eyes rolled back, arms thrown outward, and legs flexed. Affected infants remain neurologically normal but may develop tonic-clonic seizures in adolescence. Complete seizure control can be obtained through the use of valproate.

On the other hand, a healthy infant who develops severe myoclonic epilepsy will experience progressive neurological deterioration that often results in severe brain damage. Onset is usually around 1 year of age and often occurs in conjunction with other seizure types such as generalized tonic-clonic or partial complex seizures. These seizures are resistant to anticonvulsant drugs, and following the onset of these myoclonic seizures, development slows while ataxia and hyperreflexia gradually become evident (Fenichel, 1997).

Juvenile myoclonic epilepsy (JME), also known as Janz syndrome, often occurs upon awakening and is often mistaken for nervousness (Baram, 1999). Onset, which typically occurs at the time of puberty, ranges from 12 to 18 years of age. Juvenile myoclonic epilepsy accounts for between 5.4% and 10.2% of epilepsy types (Grunewald, Chroni, & Panayiotopoulos, 1992). Many children (up to 90%) who experience Janz syndrome also have generalized tonic-clonic seizures and one third experience absence seizures (Fenichel, 1997; Holmes & Stafstrom, 1998). Tonic-clonic seizures may precede myoclonic seizures, or they may be the culminating effect following a series of myoclonic seizures.

Myoclonic seizures are often precipitated by sleep deprivation, alcohol ingestion, or awakening from nocturnal or daytime sleep. Hormonal changes due to menstruation are also a significant precipitant in adolescent females. The drugs of choice in treating juvenile myoclonic epilepsy (JME) include benzodiazepines and valproate. Although valproate has been used more for absence seizures, it has been shown to be effective in 85–90% of cases of JME, and lamotrigine and clonazepam have been considered as potential alternative drug treatments (Baram, 1999). Adrenal steroids and adrenocorticotropic hormone (ACTH) have been used to treat myoclonic seizures that are refractory to other drugs. Relapse occurs in 75–100% of individuals with juvenile myoclonic epilepsy when medication is withdrawn. Medication is generally needed for life to maintain seizure control.

Special education services or classroom accommodations may be needed for children whose seizures are concomitant with CNS disorders or whose cognitive functioning has been diminished as a result of the seizures (e.g., severe myoclonic epilepsy). Educators need to be aware that untreated seizures put children at risk for cognitive impairments and psychosocial or psychological maladjustment. Social isolation and poor peer relationships are particularly problematic for school-aged children and adolescents with epilepsy. Depression and anxiety as well as behavior problems are common. Social skills and assertiveness training may be helpful for some children and adolescents (Mitchell, 1999). Peer relations may also be improved by providing information about seizures to the child and to his or her classmates. School staff need to be educated about the seizure type, how to respond if a seizure occurs at school, and the potential side effects of drug treatment (e.g., confusion). This training will allow them to communicate more effectively with parents about seizure activity occurring at school and about the child's progress in school, as well as to provide physicians with critical feedback regarding drug effectiveness.

REFERENCES

Baram, T. Z. (1999). Myoclonus and myoclonic seizures. In K. Swaimann & L. Ashwall (Eds.), *Pediatric neurology: Principles and practice* (pp. 668–675). St. Louis, MO: Mosby.

Fenichel, G. M. (1997). *Clinical pediatric neurology: A signs and symptoms approach* (3rd ed.). Philadelphia: W. B. Saunders.

Grunewald, R. A., Chroni, E., & Panayiotopoulos, C. P. (1992). Delayed diagnosis of juvenile myoclonic epilepsy. *Journal of Neurology, Neurosurgery, and Psychiatry, 55*(6), 497–479.

Holmes, G. L., & Stafstrom, C. E. (1998). The epilepsies. In R. B. David (Ed.), *Child and adolescent neurology* (pp. 183–234). St. Louis, MO: Mosby-Year Book.

Mitchell, W. G. (1999). Behavioral, cognitive, and social difficulties in childhood epilepsy. In K. Swaimann & L. Ashwall (Eds.), *Pediatric neurology: Principles and practice* (pp. 742–746). St. Louis, MO: Mosby.

Elizabeth Christiansen
Elaine Clark
University of Utah

SEIZURES, PARTIAL

Partial seizures, like all other seizures, result from excessive synchronous discharge of neuronal activity. This activity denotes abnormal cortical functioning. Seizures are fairly common—in fact, 1% of the population have chronic, recurrent episodes, or what is referred to as epilepsy (Thiele, Gonzalez-Heydrich, & Riviello, 1999). Individuals who are predisposed to epilepsy experience seizures when their basal level of neuronal excitability exceeds a critical level or threshold. In 70–80% of children with epilepsy, however, remission eventually occurs (Wolf, Ochoa, & Conway, 1998). Among children with epilepsy, 40% have partial seizures, which include temporal lobe seizures and seizures that have specific foci of abnormal electrical discharge (e.g., focal motor seizures).

The etiology of partial seizures varies, but they are often associated with an underlying disease or trauma. Possible causes include cerebral scars, central nervous system infection (i.e., meningitis), vascular lesions, porencephalic cysts, neoplasms, developmental cerebral anomalies, and traumatic brain injury. Clinical manifestations of a partial seizure vary depending on the foci of the abnormal electrical activity (e.g., posturing and jerky movements with motor strip foci), including the degree to which the seizure spread and affects other areas of the brain. As a result, partial seizures are classified as one of three categories: simple partial, complex partial, and partial seizure with secondary generalization.

Children who have simple partial seizures will not have impairment of consciousness or an aura. The seizure is more likely to manifest as a motor and sensory response. For example, the child may complain of numbness and tingling, have a bad taste sensation, and experience changes in auditory and visual perception (e.g., distortions of sound and seeing objects as being larger or smaller than they actually are). With complex partial seizures, there is an impairment of consciousness as well as an aura that precedes the seizure. This aura can include fear, déjà vu, abdominal pain, and unusual taste or odor. Automatisms, or repeated purposeless activities, often occur after a brief period of staring (e.g., playing with buttons on clothing, facial grimacing, lip smacking, and making irregular hand movements). Mental confusion and lethargy are also common, as is temporary aphasia (or difficulty communicating). In some cases, partial seizures develop into generalized seizures, in which the electrical activity spreads throughout the brain, causing tonic-clonic and myoclonic movements and brief episodes of staring and loss of consciousness (see entries on generalized tonic-clonic, myoclonic, and absence seizures).

Characteristics

Simple partial seizures

1. No impairment of consciousness or aura
2. Motor responses involving one side of body (e.g., jerking, posturing, and hypertonia)
3. Sensations such as parasthesias, numbness, tingling, auditory experiences, or visual experiences
4. Macropsia or micropsia (i.e., perceiving objects to be larger or smaller than real)

Complex partial seizures

1. Impairment of consciousness
2. Aura that includes complex sensory experiences (e.g., anxiety, fear, déjà vu, unreal feelings, abdominal pain, and unusual taste or odor)
3. Staring into space followed by automatisms (i.e., repeated purposeless activities such as facial grimacing, hand fumbling, lip smacking and chewing, sucking, and walking)
4. Posturing, stiffness, and flaccidity
5. Mental confusion (or disorientation) and transitory aphasia
6. Lethargy

Partial seizures with secondary generalization

1. Begins as a partial seizure and then spreads throughout the brain, resulting in generalized tonic-clonic, myoclonic, and absence seizure

Treatment of choice for seizures is drug therapy. Anticonvulsant drugs are used to keep the level of neuronal excitability below seizure threshold. Although it is preferred, single-drug use is often ineffective, resulting in polydrug use. Drug treatment for partial seizures includes carbamazepine, phenytoin, and primidone, to name a few. Felbamate is also used for children who have partial seizures associated with Lennox-Gaustaut syndrome. Complete control of partial seizures is achieved only 75% of the time (Wong, 1999), and in some cases surgery is needed to remove abnormal tissue or treat the underlying cause (e.g., a brain tumor).

Many of the medications used to prevent seizures can negatively affect learning. Phenobarbital, for example, depresses psychomotor speed and diminishes cognitive speed in memory tasks. Often children treated with this drug develop hyperactivity, motor slowing, and impairment in memory, concentration, and cognitive processing. As a result of negative side effects of antiepileptic medications, some have tried alternative treatments such as the ketogenic diet. Despite some data showing effectiveness in 70% of children with refractory seizures, the ketogenic diet remains controversial (Thiele et al., 1999).

Many children with seizures are absent from school several days a year, thereby missing instructional opportunities and time to complete assignments. It is difficult for these children to compete with unaffected peers. Given the long-term risk of learning problems (Bailet & Turk, 2000), special education services may be needed to help the child with seizures learn the expected amount of information. Services for this population are often provided under the category of Other Health Impaired; however, depending on the specific deficits, services may be more appropriately provided under Specific Learning Disabilities or Emotional Disturbance. Regardless of category, children with partial seizures need to be closely followed to ensure that adequate assistance is provided. School nursing and psychological services will be important to monitor progress and identify areas where services are needed (e.g., speech and language and occupational therapy). Counseling may also be important to help the child cope with this medical problem and deal with the frustration that is often experienced. Working with families, especially educating parents and siblings, will also be important and may be an important area on which school psychologists can focus their attention.

The prognosis for children with seizures depends on several factors; however, some of the best predictors of remission include seizure onset under 12 years of age, no history of neonatal seizures and fewer than 21 seizures before treatment, and normal intelligence (Wong, 1999). Like all other seizures, research is needed to determine the treatment that is most effective and has the fewest side effects.

REFERENCES

Bailet, L. L., & Turk, W. R. (2000). The impact of childhood epilepsy on neurocognitive and behavioral performance: A prospective longitudinal study. *Epilepsia, 41*(4), 426–431.

Thiele, E. A., Gonzalez-Heydrich, D., & Riviello, J. J. (1999). Epilepsy in children and adolescents. *Child and Adolescent Psychiatric Clinics of North America, 8*(4), 671–694.

Wolf, S. M., Ochoa, J. G., & Conway, E. E. (1998). Seizure management in pediatric patients for the nineties. *Pediatric Annals, 27*(10), 653–664.

Wong, D. (1999). *Whaley & Wong's nursing care of infants and children* (6th ed.). St. Louis, MO: Mosby.

Elizabeth Christiansen
Elaine Clark
University of Utah

SEPARATION ANXIETY DISORDER

Childhood anxiety centered on the child's attachment figure(s) or home that is not developmentally appropriate, is excessively frequent and persistent, and interferes with a child's normal daily routine is characteristic of separation anxiety disorder (American Psychiatric Association [APA], 1994). Separation anxiety is developmentally appropriate for children between 7 months and 6 years of age; however, most children resolve their fears about separation by 24 months of age (U.S. Public Health Services, 2000). Intense fear of separation may lead to attendance problems at school. Younger children may cling to caregivers, whereas older youth are more likely to refuse outings with peers and have a preoccupation with the caregiver's schedule to avoid separations (Albano, Chorpita, & Barlow, 1999). Differential diagnoses for social phobia or school phobia should be considered. Separation anxiety revolves around fears of separations or excessive concern about the caregivers' safety and is not a fear of school or social interactions (APA, 1994).

Approximately 4% of children and youth meet the diagnostic criteria for separation anxiety disorder (U.S. Public Health Services, 2000). The disorder is more common in girls than it is in boys. Risk factors for developing this disorder include living in an emotionally dependent or close-knit family, experiencing stress from a family member's death or illness, or experiencing other traumatic events (Albano et al., 1999). Family characteristics such as low socioeconomic status, parents' level of education, and level of parental anxiety also have been linked to greater risk for separation anxiety disorder. One third of the children diagnosed with separation anxiety disorder had comorbid overanxious disorder, and one third developed depression within several months of the onset of separation anxiety (Last, Strauss, & Francis, 1987).

Characteristics

1. Intense anxiety when separating from attachment figure(s) and/or home.
2. Intense, pervasive worries about the loss or harm of attachment figure(s).
3. May experience reluctance or refusal to attend school.
4. Fearful of sleeping away from home and parent.
5. Repeated somatic complaints (i.e., headaches, nausea, and stomachaches).
6. Anxiety substantially affecting social or academic functioning.
7. Marked anxiety for at least 4 weeks.
8. Occurs before age 18.
9. Early onset can occur before age 6.

Separation anxiety disorder has been effectively treated with cognitive-behavioral therapies, including relaxation techniques, systematic desensitization, increased problem-solving skills, imagery, and modification of self-talk to correct cognitive distortions (e.g., Kendall et al., 1997). Because children with this disorder tend to have cognitive distortions overestimating the likelihood of negative events or outcomes, role-playing exercises or in vivo experiences are recommended to reinforce the children's use of coping skills such as deep breathing, imagery, and positive self-talk (Kendall, 1993). Enmeshed or overly protective parents may need assistance in recognizing their contributions to the disorder. They can reinforce their children's irrational fears and avoidance behaviors. Parents may need techniques for coping with their own anxiety to avoid communicating it to their children (Albano et al., 1999).

Special education or services under Section 504 of the American Disabilities Act may be appropriate for a child with separation anxiety disorder. The disorder may qualify the child for special education services under the seriously emotionally disturbed category to the extent that the disorder can affect the child's attendance, academic performance, relationships with teachers and peers, and ability to learn (Individuals with Disabilities Education Act, 1997). School refusal and somatic complaints may interfere with school attendance and class participation. Academic performance and ability to learn can be affected by the child's anxiety, causing difficulty with attention, preoccupation with safety, and a desire to be close to an attachment figure. A child may not interact with peers and teachers or may refuse to participate because of excess worry and anxiety over separations. If a child is taking medication for anxiety, side effects should be considered when evaluating academic, behavioral, and emotional status.

Current findings indicate that children with separation anxiety do improve with psychological interventions but can relapse during periods of stress, great developmental change, and absences from school such as vacations and summer breaks (Albano et al., 1999). There is a growing body of research to support that some children with anxiety disorders may develop anxiety disorders and depression into adulthood (Albano et al., 1999; U.S. Public Health Services, 2000). These findings underscore the importance of early diagnosis and the use of empirically supported interventions with separation anxiety disorder.

REFERENCES

Albano, A. M., Chorpita, B. F., & Barlow, D. H. (1999). Childhood disorders. In E. J. Mash & R. A. Barkley (Eds.), *Child psychopathology* (pp. 196–241). New York: Guilford Press.

American Psychiatric Association. (1994). *Diagnostic and statistical manual of mental disorders* (4th ed.). Washington, DC: Author.

Individuals with Disabilities Education Act, 20 U.S.C. §33. (1997).

Kendall, P. C. (1993). Cognitive-behavioral therapies with youth: Guiding theory, current status, and emerging developments. *Journal of Consulting and Clinical Psychology, 61,* 235–247.

Kendall, P. C., Flannery-Schroeder, E., Panichelli-Mindel, S. M., Southam-Gerow, M., Henin, A., & Warman, M. (1997). Therapy for youths with anxiety disorders: A second randomized clinical trial. *Journal of Consulting and Clinical Psychology, 65,* 366–380.

Last, C. G., Strauss, C. C., & Francis, G. (1987). Comorbidity among childhood anxiety disorders. *Journal of Nervous and Mental Disease, 175,* 726–730.

U.S. Public Health Services. (2000, September 29). Mental health:

A report of the Surgeon General. Retrieved from http://www.surgeongeneral.gov/library/mentalhealth

Monica E. Wolfe
Texas A&M University

SEPTO-OPTIC DYSPLASIA (DE MORSIER SYNDROME)

Septo-optic dysplasia (SOD) is a birth defect characterized by a malformed optic disk and nerve, pituitary deficiencies, and often the absence of the septum pellucidum, which is a layer of nerve tissue that separates the two lateral ventricles of the brain. Without the septum pellucidum, communication between the ventricles of the midbrain is impaired (Stirnweis, 2001).

Septo-optic dysplasia is a rare disorder that affects males and females in equal numbers. It occurs during the first trimester of gestation. Symptoms are present at birth and the cause is unknown. Affected children are often the firstborn offspring of young mothers (Thoene, 1995).

Characteristics

1. Visual impairment—decreased or no vision, involuntary movement of the eyeballs (nystagmus), variable pupil dilation, and deviation of the eyes.
2. Hormonal deficiencies—primarily growth hormone (hypopituitarism).
3. Learning disabilities or mental retardation.
4. Hypotonia (low muscle tone).
5. Jaundice occasionally occurs at birth.
6. Seizures may occur.
7. Sensorimotor delays.
8. If the hypothalamus is damaged, regulatory functions of body temperature, heart rate, breathing rate, and blood pressure may be affected.

Typically people with SOD have abnormalities of the brain that can be detected by MRI (magnetic resonance imaging) or CT (computerized tomography). Treatment for SOD is symptomatic and supportive. Hormone deficiencies may be treated with hormone replacement therapy. If SOD is diagnosed early and pituitary hormone deficiencies are identified, growth retardation and other manifestations of the pituitary hormone deficiency (such as symptoms of thyroid and adrenal deficiency) can be prevented.

In addition to the characteristics listed, many of these children can also have hypoglycemia, hypothyroidism, cortisone deficiency, central (neurogenic), diabetes insipidus (DI), a malfunctioning thirst center, language delays, and other difficulties.

Special education placement for these children needs to include a program for children who are visually impaired. Although some children with SOD have normal intelligence, others have learning disabilities and mental retardation. Most of these children, however, are developmentally delayed because of vision impairment or neurological problems (National Institute of Neurological Disorders and Stroke, 2001).

The prognosis for individuals with SOD varies according to the presence and severity of symptoms. Neurogenetic research, which focuses on identifying and studying the genes involved in normal brain development, is being done and may eventually give some understanding of this disorder. SOD patients with variable phenotypes are being screened to determine whether interactions with other proteins, the environment, or both may be crucial factors in the manifestation of a phenotype (Woods, McNay, Turton, & Dattani, 2001).

REFERENCES

National Institute of Neurological Disorders and Stroke. (2001, July 1). NINDS septo-optic dysplasia information page. Retrieved from http://www.ninds.nih.gov/health_and_medical/disorders/septo-optic.htm

Stirnweis, S. D. (2001). Septo optic dysplasia, diabetes insipidus in children with septo-optic dysplasia. Retrieved from http://diabetesinsipidus.maxinter.net/septo.htm

Thoene, J. C. (1995). *Physicians' guide to rare disease* (2nd ed.). Montvale, NJ: Dowden.

Woods, K. S., McNay, D., Turton, J. P. G., & Dattani, M. T. (2001, October). SOD: A multigenic disorder? *American Journal of Human Genetics, 69*(4), 628.

Karen Wiley
University of Northern Colorado

SEXUAL ALLEGATIONS IN DIVORCE (SAID) SYNDROME

As the name suggests, the SAID diagnosis applies to false allegations of sexual abuse in the context of contested divorces (Blush & Ross, 1987). Divorce cases that have been prolonged in the court system or have unresolved custody and visitation issues are more likely to generate false accusations. The critical element in diagnosis is considering the contextual issues indicating ulterior motives for the accusing parent.

There are no known data concerning prevalence rates, although some estimates suggest that 20–55% of custody disputes may require investigation for allegations of sexual abuse. Estimates suggest that nearly 1 million children annually are involved with the divorce of their parents.

> Characteristics
>
> 1. Child is typically female, under age of 8, and has been involved with contentious divorce proceedings.
> 2. Child is with custodial parent with histrionic or borderline personality.
> 3. Allegations of child's abuse surface through custodial parent.

Treatment begins with investigations by the child protective service workers, who generally have little training in recognizing the contextual factors that would define SAID and may hold unfounded beliefs about children (e.g., children don't lie, children cannot talk about things they haven't experienced). The remedy requires a properly trained multidisciplinary team to better evaluate the context of the allegations, including critiquing the failings in the initial investigation and seeking a more comprehensive study. Contextual issues and personality of the accuser are as important to study as the alleged perpetrator and the alleged victim. The child must be interviewed in a fashion that decreases bias and suggestibility. Multiple data sources and contextual factors are given high priority in evaluating the allegations prior to taking legal actions that may have unintended effects (e.g., Daly, 1992).

Because teachers are mandated reporters of alleged abuse, they may have occasion to initialize the protective service investigation. It is critical that they maintain objectivity and create clear records of their observations and sources of information for any subsequent review of the case. There are no customary special education issues, although children with special needs are more likely to be involved in divorce situations due to added family stress. The added demands for special services and more costly care with such children may also increase the likelihood that SAID allegations will surface in this population. Prognosis improves with early detection and intervention by the courts, with continued court supervision over the 1st year of treatment. Additional empirical research on detection and treatment outcome is needed.

REFERENCES

Blush, G. J., & Ross, K. L. (1987). Sexual allegations in divorce: The SAID syndrome. *Conciliation Courts Review, 25*(1), 1–12.

Daly, L. W. (1992). Child sexual abuse allegations: Investigative approaches and identifying alternative hypotheses. *Issues in Child Abuse Accusations, 4*(3), 111–117.

Daniel J. Rybicki
ForenPsych Services

SHAKEN BABY SYNDROME

Shaken baby syndrome (SBS) is a type of child abuse in which a child is violently shaken while being held by the extremities or shoulders (National Center on Shaken Baby Syndrome [NCSBS], 2000; Wyszynski, 1999). The shaking, which results in a whiplash-like acceleration and deceleration of the head, causes the brain to strike the inner surface of the skull and may have severe—even fatal—consequences. The trauma may lead to the classic triad of SBS: subdural hematoma, brain swelling, and retinal hemorrhages. Bruises of the part of the body held during shaking and fractures of the long bones and of the ribs may also be seen. Crying often triggers the caretaker or guardian's severe shaking (NCSBS, 2000).

Difficult to diagnose because symptoms are often internal, SBS is the leading cause of infant mortality and morbidity in the United States (NCSBS, 2000). Number of deaths and serious injuries has fluctuated in recent years between 750 and 3,750, and many cases remain undiagnosed, so incidence is unknown (Wyszynski, 1999).

Both presenting and outcome characteristics are highly variable, depending on the number and severity of shaking incidents and on the length of time between incidents. According to NCSBS (2000, paragraph 2): "Approximately 20% of cases are fatal in the first few days after injury and the survivors suffer from handicaps ranging from mild—learning disorders, behavioral changes—to moderate and severe, such as profound mental and developmental retardation, paralysis, blindness, inability to eat or a permanent vegetative state."

Parents or caretakers may call for assistance or bring the infant to the emergency room claiming that it has accidentally fallen from a sofa, bed, or other relatively low object. However, although falls are common in young children, damage of the degree seen in SBS is virtually unknown in such falls. Some presenting characteristics—particularly intraocular hemorrhage—may be symptomatic and helpful in initiating evaluation (NCSBS, 2000). In many states, suspicion of child abuse mandates notification of appropriate authorities. Outcome characteristics of survivors are highly variable and may be seen in virtually any combination (Wyszynski, 1999).

> Characteristics
>
> *Presenting*
>
> 1. Range from minor to severe: irritability, lethargy, tremors, vomiting, bradycardia, hypothermia, poor feeding, failure to thrive, seizures, bulging or full fontanels, stupor, or coma
> 2. Highly symptomatic: subdural hematoma, brain swelling, or retinal hemorrhages

Outcome

1. Mental retardation
2. Motor disorders, including seizure disorders, paralysis, spasticity, and inability to eat
3. Visual and auditory impairments
4. Learning disabilities, behavior disorders, and personality change

Treatment of a child with SBS obviously depends on the type and degree of neurological damage and the length of time since the shaking occurred. Often a team approach following a protocol calling for the same interventions used in other types of traumatic brain injuries should immediately follow diagnosis (Wyszynski, 1999). Social service agencies are invariably called to assess the risk to the child in the home. Immediate action should be taken to stabilize the victim's condition. Because brain damage cannot be reversed, much treatment is supportive. According to the Shaken Baby Alliance (1999), a child may need up to seven different therapies, including cognitive rehabilitation and occupational, physical, and speech therapies. Adaptive technology may help reduce the impact of sensory and motor impairments. In some instances the child will need full-time assistance. Appropriate classroom setting will need to be individually determined.

Clearly the best approach to SBS is prevention through education or perhaps direct training of parents, guardians, and other child care providers. Parents should inform all who care for their infant of the dangers of shaking (NCSBS, 2000). Stress management classes may be helpful in some situations. Clearly, at least hypothetically, SBS is 100% preventable.

REFERENCES

National Center on Shaken Baby Syndrome. (2000). SBS questions. Retrieved from http://www.dontshake.com

The Shaken Baby Alliance. (1999). Impact on the family. Retrieved from http://www.shakenbaby.com

Wyszynski, M. E. (1999). Shaken baby syndrome: Identification, intervention, and prevention. *Clinical Excellence for Nurse Practitioners, 3,* 262–267.

Paula Kilpatrick
Robert T. Brown
University of North Carolina, Wilmington

SHENJING SHUAIRUO

Shenjing shuairuo, or neurasthenia, is a culture-bound syndrome found predominately in China, and other East Asian cultures, such as Hong Kong and Korea. In many cases, this syndrome meets the criteria for *Diagnostic and Statistical Manual of Mental Disorders–Fourth Edition* (*DMS-IV*) mood or anxiety disorder and is commonly referred to as "weakness of nerves" (American Psychiatric Association, 1994, p. 849). This disorder is also included in the *Chinese Classification of Mental Disorders.*

Shenjing shuairuo is the second most common diagnosis in Chinese psychiatric hospitals, and one of the most common neuropsychological diagnoses in general (Weber, 2000). This disorder is also known by a number of indigenous terms: *shen-ch'ing, shuai-jo,* or *huo-ch'ta.* According to Chan et al. (2000, p. 2), shenjing shuairuo is closely related to chronic fatigue syndrome in Western cultures such that "clinical similarity . . . has led to the contention that chronic fatigue syndrome and [shenjing shuairuo] are equivalent disorders cloaked in disparate terminology." According to studies by Chan et al. (2000), pure shenjing shuairuo, or neurasthenia, had a 12-month prevalence rate of 3.66% among Chinese Americans. This rate was higher than the rate of depressive or anxiety disorders. This study thus concluded that "subthreshold anxiety-depression with a symptom profile remarkably similar to that of 'weakness of nerves' has been shown to be the most common form of primary care psychiatric morbidity in the United States" (Chan et al., 2000 p. 2). This disorder apparently has little prevalence among children and affects men and women at similar rates.

Characteristics

1. Physical and mental fatigue
2. Dizziness
3. Headaches
4. Difficulties with concentration
5. Sleep disturbance
6. Memory loss

As stated by Chan et al. (2000, p. 8), "weakness of nerves is flexibly defined by the presence of any three symptoms out of five non-hierarchical groups of fatigue, pain, dysphoria, mental agitation, and sleep symptoms."

This illness is quite prevalent in China and other Asian cultures such that treatment is traditionally referred to medical professionals, especially when the illness presents in somatoform symptoms. It is very important to construct a medical history of the individual with the disorder as well as determine the level of acculturation. Typically, patients take the following assessments to determine levels of acculturation and also to determine whether diagnosis and subsequent medical referral are necessary: Explanatory Interview Catalogue, Structured Clinical Interview for *DSM-III-R* (SCID), Hamilton Range Scale for Depression, and the Hamilton Rating Scale for Anxiety (Chan et al., 2000).

The likelihood of this disorder's occurring in adolescence or other school-age children is not known and would probably be determined by level of acculturation for high school students. Special education services would probably be unavailable for this condition due to the difficulty of diagnosis and comorbidity with other medical conditions.

REFERENCES

American Psychiatric Association. (1994). *Diagnostic and statistical manual of mental disorders* (4th ed.). Washington, DC: Author.

Chan, C., Chen, C., Lee, D., Lee, S., Weiss, M., & Wing, Y. (2000). Psychiatric morbidity and illness experience of primary care patients with chronic fatigue in Hong Kong. Retrieved from http://ajp.psychiatryonline.org/cgi/content/full/157/3/380

Weber, C. (2000). Shenjing shuairuo: The case of neurasthenia. Retrieved from http://weber.ucsd.edu/~thall/cbs_neu.html

Kiely Ann Fletcher
Ohio State University

SHORT-CHAIN ACYL COA DEHYDROGENASE DEFICIENCY (SCAD)

Short-chain acyl coa dehydrogenase (SCAD) deficiency is an extremely rare inherited mitochondrial fatty acid oxidation disorder first reported in 1987. SCAD has been identified in only a few patients with highly variable clinical features, including (a) a lethal neonatal syndrome; (b) psychomotor retardation, muscle weakness, microcephaly, and poor feeding, all appearing during infancy; and (c) a myopathy in adulthood. Diagnosis may be based on the specific metabolite profile in blood and urine.

> Characteristics
>
> 1. A lethal neonatal syndrome with failure to thrive, developmental delay, microcephaly, feeding difficulties, vomiting, lethargy, hypertonia, chronic acidosis, seizures, and myopathy
> 2. A myopathy in adulthood

Treatment involves limitation of fasting stress and dietary fat. Many children with mitochondrial disorders might have normal intelligence, static mental retardation, or developmental delay. Children may have long periods with a stable neurological picture simulating a static encephalopathy and later deteriorate either in an acute or in a slowly progressive manner (Nissenkorn, 1999). Many of these children will qualify for services under the classification of Other Health Impaired as a result of their medical complications.

This disorder has been reported in two neonates. One patient died in the neonatal period with hepatic disease and brain edema. Another patient survived with apparently normal development to the age of 2 years. Current research is focused on pathogenesis of the variations and natural history of children with SCAD. Clinical studies are necessary to establish the incidence of SCAD deficiency and to define the spectrum of its clinical manifestations (Corydon et al., 2001).

REFERENCES

Corydon, M. J., Vockley, J., Rinaldo, P., Rhead, W. J., Kjeldsen, M., Winter, V., et al. (2001). Role of common gene variations in the molecular pathogenesis of short-chain acyl coa dehydrogenase (SCAD). *Pediatric Research, 49,* 18–23.

Virdette L. Brumm
Children's Hospital, Los Angeles
Keck / USC School of Medicine

SICKLE CELL DISEASE

Sickle cell disease is a chronic hemolytic anemia occurring almost exclusively in those of African American descent, characterized by sickle-shaped red blood cells (RBCs) due to homozygous inheritance of hemoglobin S (HbS). In HbS, valine is substituted for glutamic acid in the sixth amino acid of the β-chain. Due to this molecular change, this form of hemoglobin is less soluble and can form rodlike tactoids that cause red blood cells to sickle at sites of low oxygen pressure. Distorted, inflexible RBCs plug small arterioles and capillaries, which leads to occlusion and infarction. Because sickled RBCs are too fragile to withstand the mechanical trauma of circulation, hemolysis occurs after they enter the circulation (Powars, Wilson, Imbus, Pegelow, & Allen, 1978).

Homozygotes for HbS have sickle cell anemia. This condition afflicts approximately 0.3% of the African American population in the United States. Heterozygotes for HbS are not anemic, although the sickling trait can be demonstrated in vitro. Approximately 8–13% of African Americans in the United States are heterozygotes for HbS.

> Characteristics
>
> 1. Anemia and vaso-occlusive events resulting in tissue ischemia and infarction.

2. Aplastic crises in both children and adults, occurring when marrow RBC production slows during acute infections.
3. Painful crises, characterized by some or all of the following: long bone pain, severe pain in hands and feet in children, abdominal pain with vomiting, back and joint pain, and arthralgia with fever.
4. Hemiplegia, cranial nerve palsies, and other neurological and cognitive disturbances may result from occlusion of major intracranial vessels. Clinical and subclinical strokes occur in approximately 11–28% of those with sickle cell disease.
5. Morphological changes can include relatively shorter trunk with long extremities and tower-shaped skull. Bone changes due to chronic marrow hyperactivity can be observed on X ray.
6. Hepatosplenomegaly is common in children.

Therapy is symptomatic because no effective in vivo anti-sickling agent exists. Partial blood transfusions are used, particularly when the anemia is severe (Russell et al., 1984). Recent studies also suggest that prophylactic transfusions of those individuals who have suffered a clinical stroke may reduce the risk of recurrent stroke, especially in children under 18 years of age (Adams, 2000). Crises are often managed with oral and IV hydration and analgesics, including narcotics, for pain. Prophylactic antibiotics, the pneumococcal vaccine, and early identification and treatment of serious bacterial infection have reduced mortality, particularly in childhood.

Due to the increased risk and prevalence of clinical and silent strokes in this population, many children with sickle cell disease manifest a number of neurological and cognitive deficits that may make them eligible for special education services (Portney & Herion, 1978). Children with clinically evident strokes are generally more impaired, with the potential of having motoric as well as cognitive sequelae. Those children with silent strokes (those not clinically evident on neurological exam) have also been shown to perform more poorly than children with sickle cell disease who have not had any central nervous system (CNS) pathology (Brown et al., 2000). Due to the pathophysiology involved, strokes occur most frequently in the frontal lobe regions of the brain. Thus, the most robust neuropsychological findings for both groups of children (overt and silent strokes) are symptoms of inattention, distractibility, impulsivity, and executive functioning. In the recent study by Brown and colleagues (2000), the majority of children (>70%) with brain scan evidence of CNS pathology were receiving special education services. Additionally, a full third of the children with sickle cell disease who did not have CNS pathology also were receiving specialized instruction in a number of areas, including language, reading, and math. It is likely that a number of factors may be contributing to poorer performance of these children in academic areas, including the effects of living with a chronic illness, CNS pathology, and socioeconomic factors of this population.

A number of prophylactic and symptomatic interventions have decreased the morbidity of this disorder. The life span of homozygous sickle cell patients has steadily increased to over 40 years of age. More recent advances include increasingly sensitive methods for the detection of silent strokes (Wang et al., 2000), medical treatments for the reduction of pain, and interventions to reduce the effects of vaso-occlusive events. With the increased understanding of genetics and gene therapy techniques, treatments at the molecular level for this disorder may be also forthcoming.

REFERENCES

Brown, R. T., Davis, P. C., Lambert, R., Hsu, L., Hopkins, K., & Eckman, J. (2000). Neurocognitive functioning and magnetic resonance imaging in children with sickle cell disease. *Journal of Pediatric Psychology, 25,* 503–513.

Portney, B. A., & Herion, J. C. (1978). Neurologic manifestations in sickle cell disease. *Annals of Internal Medicine, 76,* 643–652.

Powars, D., Wilson, B., Imbus, C., Pegelow, C., & Allen, J. (1978). The natural history of stroke in sickle cell disease. *American Journal of Medicine, 65,* 461–471.

Russell, M. O., Goldberg, H. I., & Hodson, A. (1984). Effect of transfusion therapy on ateriographic abnormalities and on recurrence of stroke in sickle cell disease. *Blood, 63,* 162–169.

Wang, C. W., Gallagher, D. M., Pegelow, C. H., Wright, E. C., Vichinsky, E. P., Abboud, M. R., et al. (2000). Multicenter comparison of magnetic resonance imaging and transcranial doppler ultrasonography in the evaluation of the central nervous system in children with sickle cell disease. *Journal of Pediatric Hematology / Oncology, 22*(4), 335–339.

Richard Boada
University of Denver

Greta N. Wilkening
University of Colorado Health Sciences Center
The Children's Hospital

SINGLETON-MERTEN SYNDROME

Singleton-Merten syndrome is defined by Edward B. Singleton and David F. Merten (1973) as a syndrome of widened medullary cavities of the metacarpals and phalanges, aortic calcification and abnormal definition. It involves the unusual clinical features of abnormalities in, loss of, or absences of permanent teeth; calcium deposits on the aorta; and progressive diminution of bone density (Gay & Kuhn, 1976). The disorder appears to occur randomly, and its etiology is unknown. There is a possibility of autosomal dominant inheritance, which means that a single copy of the disease gene dominates the normal gene (The National Organization for Rare Disorders [NORD], 1997). Age of onset is between 4 and 24 months, and most cases reported a history of fever of unknown origin prior to onset (Gay & Kuhn, 1976; Singleton & Merten, 1973).

Cases reported in the literature identify females as being affected with this disorder more frequently than are males at a 3:1 ratio (NORD, 1997). No race predilection is noted.

Characteristics

1. Child may suffer from moderate to severe muscle weakness.
2. Child will experience generalized osteoporosis, particularly in the small bones of the hands and feet.
3. Severe dental dysplasia is present in most cases.
4. After age 4, child may experience progressive calcification of the proximal aorta.
5. Calcific aortic stenosis, which is a narrowing of the aortic outflow tract, may develop in mid- or late childhood.
6. Child may suffer from certain forms of psoriasis in later childhood.
7. Other symptoms may include small stature and poor physical development, eye abnormalities, and soft-tissue calcification.

Because this disorder affects many different areas of the body, treatment is individualized and is directed toward specific symptoms. Treatment may include input from a variety of specialists, including pediatricians, surgeons, heart specialists, dentists, physical therapists, and dermatologists. The initial complaint of the child will likely be muscle weakness. Treatment should therefore be directed toward the muscular weakness, including orthopedic deformities ("Singleton-Merten Syndrome," 1990). Genetic counseling is recommended as part of treatment and prevention.

Through the Individuals with Disabilities Education Act (1997), the child may be eligible for special education services under the handicapping condition of Other Health Impaired or Physical Disability. Because the child will probably be under the care of more than one medical specialist, close monitoring of the child's physical condition is recommended. The child may require social support, occupational therapy, and other medical, social, or vocational services (NORD, 1997).

In the four original research cases and the only published cases, patients died before age 18. The prognosis, therefore, is that death will most likely occur from cardiac failure at any time from 4–16 years after onset ("Singleton-Merten Syndrome," 1990). Mental development of the patients appears to be normal in the four published cases, and no cases have been published since the late 1970s. Although there is apparently no research currently underway specifically for Singleton-Merten syndrome, the National Institute of Health is attempting to map every gene in the human body to learn why genes malfunction. It is hoped that this Human Genome Project will lead to new knowledge surrounding treatment and prevention of genetic disorders (NORD, 1997).

REFERENCES

Gay, B., Jr., & Kuhn, J. (1976). A syndrome of widened medullary cavities of bone, aortic calcification, abnormal dentition, and muscular weakness (the Singleton-Merten syndrome). *Radiology, 118,* 389–395.

National Organization for Rare Disorders. (1997). Singleton Merten syndrome. Retrieved July 2001, from http://www.rarediseases.org

Singleton, E., & Merten, D. (1973). An unusual syndrome of widened medullary cavities of the metacarpals and phalanges, aortic calcification and abnormal dentition. *Pediatric Radiology, 1,* 2–7.

Singleton-Merten syndrome. (1990). In *Birth defects encyclopedia* (p. 1540). Dover, MA: Blackwell Scientific Publications.

Christine Cde Baca
University of Northern Colorado

SLEEP APNEA

Sleep apnea is characterized by recurrent apneas (breathing cessations) during sleep, which can result in a temporary cessation or reduced flow of oxygen to the brain, as well as regular interruptions of the normal sleep pattern (Bedard, Montplaisir, Malo, Richer, & Rouleau, 1993). At the termination of this apneic event, the patient will awaken and then resume breathing. For children with this disorder, this process is often repeated hundreds of times each night (Valencia-Flores, Bliwise, Guilleminault, Cilveti, & Clark, 1996). Individuals with this disorder usually present with complaints of snoring, restlessness, lethargy, and headaches. Symptoms may be transient or more permanent, depending upon the degree of oxygen reduction and the chronicity (Kelly, Claypoole, & Coppel, 1990). The incidence of sleep apnea in children can be estimated to be at between .5% and 3% of the population.

Characteristics

1. Characterized by a temporary cessation of oxygen flow to the brain, resulting in an interruption of the regular sleeping pattern.

2. Common nighttime symptoms include snoring, restlessness, sleepwalking, and enuresis.
3. Daytime symptoms include noisy breathing, morning headaches, and a chronic runny nose.
4. Children with this disorder may exhibit signs and symptoms of diffuse neurological impairment, including a decrease in the ability to learn new information, impaired motor ability, concentration and attention problems, and visual-spatial deficits.
5. Neuropsychological problems may include difficulties with memory, abstract reasoning, cognitive flexibility, and executive tasks (Bedard et al., 1993).
6. Daytime sleepiness can be seen in children with sleep apnea. This can result in vigilance impairments, behavior problems, agitation and mood disturbance.

The most successful treatment in children is the removal of the child's tonsils and adenoids. Continuous positive airway pressure (CPAP) can also be used with children, especially if children are symptomatic after an adenotonsillectomy. CPAP consists of small (5–20 cm H20) positive pressure, which is introduced through the use of a lightweight mask that the patient wears while he or she sleeps. This treatment does not involve the administration of nocturnal oxygen; rather, CPAP is effective because it splints open the airway and prevents occlusion from occurring (Valencia-Flores et al., 1996). This treatment can be a cumbersome procedure that involves sleeping with a mask over one's face. Compliance from children for this treatment may be problematic. Another surgical technique that has been found to be effective is called a tracheostomy. During this procedure the trachea is entered by vertical incision of the second and third tracheal rings. A tracheostomy tube is used to keep the airway open.

Children who are suffering from sleep apnea can have many special education issues. In addition to the behavior problems that may arise from sleepiness, children with sleep apnea may exhibit difficulty with concentration, attention, and memory; impaired motor ability; impaired planning and reasoning ability; and emotional and behavioral problems.

The symptoms of sleep apnea may be mistaken for attention deficit disorder or an attention-deficit/hyperactivity disorder. Teachers will need to be aware that the child may have trouble attending to or following simple directions. The child may have trouble differentiating between relevant and irrelevant stimuli. The regular education or special education teacher will have to make adjustments such as frequently reviewing the daily schedule with the child or employing multiple teaching modalities such as auditory, tactile, and visual techniques. It is likely that children with sleep apnea who are exhibiting severe symptomology may be served as children classified as Other Health Impaired. If the child's problems are mostly focused in the academic areas, they may be served with children who are diagnosed with learning disabilities.

Children with sleep apnea may also demonstrate difficulty with executive functions. These problems could manifest in limited planning, shifting, and abstraction abilities. These problems may be further complicated by deficits in visual-spatial difficulties. Examples of these problems include having difficulty finding their way around the school, difficulty learning and understanding abstract concepts such as units of measurements, and problems learning how to read and do math. It is important for regular and special education teachers to employ patience and target the individual symptoms of sleep apnea and not just focus on the child's troubled behavior.

The prognosis for children with sleep apnea is varied. Factors that affect recovery include the child's weight and comorbidity with other psychological and physiological disorders. In some cases, irreversible anoxic brain damage may have occurred, which can significantly lower the chances of recovery. Because research is currently being conducted about childhood brain impairment, we can expect to see continuing improvements in our ability to treat and understand sleep apnea.

REFERENCES

Bedard, M., Montplaisir, J., Malo, J., Richer, F., & Rouleau, I. (1993). Persistent neuropsychological deficits and vigilance impairment in sleep apnea syndrome after treatment with continuous positive airway pressure (CPAP). *Journal of Clinical and Experimental Neuropsychology, 15,* 330–341.

Kelly, D., Claypoole, K., & Coppel, D. (1990). Sleep apnea syndrome: Symptomology, associated features, and neurocognitive correlates. *Neuropsychology Review, 1,* 323–341.

Valencia-Flores, M., Bliwise, D., Guilleminault, C., Cilveti, R., & Clark, A. (1996). Cognitive function in patients with sleep apnea after acute nocturnal nasal continuous positive airway pressure (CPAP) treatment: Sleepiness and hypoxia effects. *Journal of Clinical and Experimental Neuropsychology, 18,* 197–210.

Andrew S. Davis
University of Northern Colorado

SLEEP TERROR

Sleep terror, also referred to as night terror, is an episode of sudden extreme fright and panic during the night. The individual is abruptly awakened from sleep and emits a piercing scream. Yelling and incoherent verbalizations are common, but the individual is amnestic for the event. Sleep terrors usually occur during the first hour of sleep—that is, during the first non-REM stage of sleep. The longer into the non-REM phase, however, the more severe the episode. The episodes last for no more than 10 or 15 min, at which time heart rate is in excess of 160 beats per min (Murray, 1991).

Sleep terror occurs in about 1—5% of children under the age of 10. The problem is sometimes difficult to distinguish from nightmares; however, in the case of nightmares, there is less vocalization and panic. Sleep terrors, unlike nightmares, are also more common in children than in adults, and about half of the cases resolve spontaneously by the age of 8. Although adolescents experience sleep terrors, it is quite rare to find these persist into adulthood. When sleep terrors do persist, however, or begin at a later stage than normal (i.e., after age 10), the problem occurs more frequently and appears related to stress. Most cases of sleep terror, however, do not even meet the *Diagnostic and Statistical Manual of Mental Disorders–Fourth Edition* (*DSM-IV*) criteria for sleep terror disorder (American Psychiatric Association, 2000) because the diagnosis requires that a person's functioning be impaired in a relevant area of daily life (e.g., school, work, and social interactions).

Characteristics

1. Sudden arousal from sleep with intense panic and terror.
2. Episode occurs about an hour into sleep and lasts only a few minutes.
3. Autonomic arousal, including rapid heartbeat and breathing, and sweating.
4. Person remains asleep despite appearance of being awake.
5. Frequency is about once a week (in children).
6. Typically begins before age 10 and is outgrown by adolescence.

Sleep terrors are rarely dangerous; however, objects from around the bed that pose a safety risk should be removed. Some individuals do attempt to leave the bed, and when the sleep terror is accompanied by sleepwalking, they will get up. These episodes are extremely frightening for the observer; however, efforts to awaken the person should be avoided (the observer should instead talk to the person in a reassuring voice). Other interventions are rarely needed. In cases in which sleep terror occurs frequently or is associated with other problems (e.g., sleepwalking and daytime functional problems), a physician should be consulted. In some cases, medical conditions may be contributing to the problem (e.g., seizures), and with treatment, the sleep terrors could be resolved. Furthermore, in cases in which individuals are using certain substances or taking medications that exacerbate the problem, this too can be evaluated (e.g., sedatives, including hypnagogic drugs and alcohol). Certain medications are useful to reduce sleep terrors; these medications include diazepam and imipramine, drugs that suppress slow-wave sleep (Murray, 1991). Adults may also benefit from a psychological consult to help identify potential stressors that might be triggering the problem and ways to manage stress more effectively (e.g., stress management training and relaxation therapy). Medical consults may also be important in order to rule out conditions that share certain characteristics, especially those that are treatable (e.g., epilepsy).

Rarely would a child with sleep terror require treatment or even come to the attention of a psychologist. If counseling or any special services (i.e., special education services and classroom accommodations) were needed, they would more likely be unrelated to sleep terror (e.g., learning disabilities).

REFERENCES

American Psychiatric Association. (2000). *Diagnostic and statistical manual of mental disorders* (4th ed., text revision). Washington, DC: Author.

Murray, J. (1991). Psychophysiological aspects of nightmares, night terrors, and sleepwalking. *Journal of General Psychology, 118*(2), 113–128.

Wendy Wolfe
Elaine Clark
University of Utah

SLEEPWALKING

Sleepwalking, also referred to as somnambulism, is a fairly common problem among children. It involves sitting, walking, or performing other routine behaviors while asleep. Although the individual who sleepwalks typically has his or her eyes open and avoids bumping into objects, there is no indication of awareness. Sleepwalking episodes, which last from 5 to 30 min, typically occur 2 hours after the onset of sleep (i.e., during slow-wave, non-REM sleep). It is estimated to occur in 10–30% of children, most often between the ages of 4 and 8 (American Psychiatric Association [APA], 2000). Sleepwalking typically occurs over several years, but more often than not it remits spontaneously by the age of 15.

Sleepwalkers usually have their eyes open, but they show no recognition except avoidance of objects at times. Sleep talking can be observed; however, communications are often unintelligible (e.g., words and phrases are mumbled). Other behaviors that can occur during sleepwalking include eating and urinating, most often in the bathroom. Individuals may also engage in more complex behaviors, including unlocking doors and using appliances. At times, sleep terror is observed, and individuals may appear to be fleeing harm. Awakening someone during a sleepwalking episode is ill-advised because it can lead to disorientation.

Confusion does, however, clear in minutes, and the sleepwalker has no recollection of the sleepwalking event.

Conditions that have been associated with sleepwalking include respiratory-related sleep disorders (e.g., obstructive sleep apnea), a family history of sleepwalking, and psychological stress. Children who are anxious, have experienced traumas, or are under a great deal of stress may be particularly vulnerable to sleepwalking behaviors (DeFrancesco, 1998; Laberge, Tremblay, Vitaro, & Montplaisir, 2000). Furthermore, taking certain drugs, including drugs that reduce REM sleep, are likely to increase sleepwalking.

Characteristics

1. Repeated episodes of walking in sleep, usually starting 2 hours into sleep.
2. Episodes typically last between 5 and 30 min.
3. Eyes are open and the person may talk, but he or she is unresponsive to others and difficult to awaken (forced awakening during sleepwalking is ill-advised).
4. Amnesia for the event upon awakening.
5. Functional status quickly returns to normal after the person is awake.
6. Drugs that reduce REM sleep and stress can increase sleepwalking.

Treatments that have been found to be effective in reducing sleepwalking behavior include relaxation therapies, biofeedback, and hypnosis (DeFrancesco, 1998). In most cases, however, treatment consists of preventing injury during the sleepwalking episode. This treatment may be done using an alarm that alerts parents that the child is out of his or her bedroom or is in certain areas of the house. Other safety measures include removing dangerous objects and protecting the child from falling down stairs or leaving the house. When sleepwalkers are found wandering around, they should be assisted to bed rather than awakened suddenly. In cases in which sleepwalking cannot be reduced or eliminated so that safety is ensured, medications may be necessary (e.g., benzodiazepines, diazepam, and alprazolom). Children and adolescents who take certain medications (e.g., antidepressants and antipsychotic drugs) may also be more prone to walk in their sleep. A physician consult will therefore be critical to determine whether prescribed drugs are reducing the child's REM sleep and increasing sleepwalking.

Educators need to be aware of sleepwalking primarily for the purpose of accommodating the often-sleepy child in the classroom. When special services are needed, they are usually intended to treat contributing factors, not the sleepwalking behavior itself. For example, counseling may be necessary to help the child learn better coping strategies (e.g., stress management techniques and relaxation exercises). In cases in which sleepwalking causes significant distress or impairment in learning and social functioning, a *Diagnostic and Statistical Manual of Mental Disorders–Fourth Edition* (*DSM-IV*) diagnosis of sleepwalking disorder (APA, 2000) may be warranted and appropriate services should be provided. If learning is significantly impaired, children may be eligible to receive special education service under the category of Emotional Disorder. Services from the school psychologist may be in order in these cases to not only evaluate the child but also consult with parents and teachers to ensure that everything possible is being done to reduce the child's stress and increase learning and opportunities. A referral to a sleep clinic also needs to be considered in extreme cases.

The prognosis for sleepwalking is good. In fact, it frequently remits spontaneously during adolescence, typically by age 15 (APA, 2000). In some cases episodes may recur, but when the onset is during childhood, this is uncommon. If sleepwalking disorders begin in adults or recur at that time, symptoms are more persistent and the course is one of repeated episodes.

Further research that examines the effectiveness of various treatments is needed—in particular, therapies that are intended to improve REM sleep and consequently prevent sleepwalking (e.g., relaxation therapies and biofeedback). Drug studies are also critical to evaluate new-line drugs that are being prescribed to children and adolescents (e.g., anxiolytic drugs). Finally, research that examines the relationship between sleepwalking and night terrors is needed, given the features that are shared by these two conditions. It is hoped that this research will provide further insights into successful treatment of both.

REFERENCES

American Psychiatric Association. (2000). *Diagnostic and statistical manual of mental disorders* (4th ed., text revision). Washington, DC: Author.

DeFrancesco, J. (1998). Sleepwalking in children. In A. S. Canter & S. A. Carroll (Eds.), *Helping children at home and school: Handouts from your school psychologist.* Bethesda, MD: National Association of School Psychologists.

Laberge, L., Tremblay, R. E., Vitaro, F., & Montplaisir, J. (2000). Development of parasomnias from childhood to early adolescence. *Pediatrics, 106*(1), 67–74.

Cristina McCarthy
Elaine Clark
University of Utah

SLY SYNDROME

Sly syndrome (mucopolysaccharidosis Type VII [MPS VII]), is the rarest mucopolysaccharidoses lysosomal storage diseases (National Organization for Rare Disorders [NORD],

2000), but has the widest effects. Types I (neonatal) and II (early onset) have severe effects, whereas Type III (late onset) has milder ones. In all types, deficiency of the enzyme beta-glucuronidase leads to an accumulation of complex carbohydrates in the brain. Type I is one of the few mucopolysaccharidoses that is present at birth (Pediatric Database, 1994).

Sly syndrome is a very rare (about 20 known cases have been reported worldwide) inherited autosomal recessive metabolic disorder (Pediatric Database, 1994). Characteristics are highly variable across type (Online Mendelian Inheritance in Man [OMIM], 2000).

Characteristics

1. Postnatal growth deficiency and short stature
2. Macrocephaly, skull deformities, hydrocephaly, coarse facies, hearing loss, and corneal opacities
3. Mental retardation and neurodegeneration
4. Multiple skeletal deformities
5. Hirsutism
6. Cardiovascular and other internal organ abnormalities
7. Hydrops fetalis

Because no cure or remedial treatment for the underlying disease is available, treatment is usually supportive. The variety of symptoms call for a team approach involving pediatric, neurological, orthopedic, and ophthalmological specialists and perhaps genetic counseling for the parents (Pediatric Database, 1994). The severity of the early forms necessitate extensive support. Children with the later form will probably be able to attend either special or normal classrooms.

Research on several species of animal models—particularly mice—may lead to experimental treatments. Gene therapy has successfully prevented the disease, and transplants of healthy cells have led to production of beta-glucuronidase in affected mice. The gene for Sly syndrome is now known, and its discovery may lead to further treatments (OMIM, 2000).

REFERENCES

National Organization for Rare Disorders. (2000). Sly syndrome. Retrieved from http://www.stepstn.com/cgi-win/nord.exe?proc=Redirect&type=rdb_sum&id=291.htm

Online Mendelian Inheritance in Man. (2000). Mucopolysaccharidosis type VII. Retrieved from http://www.ncbi.nlm.nih.gov/htbin-post/Omim/dispmim?253220#TEXT

Pediatric Database. (1994). Sly syndrome. Retrieved from http://www.icondata.com/health/pedbase/files/SLYSYNDR.HTM

Paula Kilpatrick
Robert T. Brown
University of North Carolina, Wilmington

SMITH-LEMLI-OPITZ SYNDROME

Smith-Lemli-Opitz syndrome (SLOS) is a rare, heritable disorder characterized by growth deficiency, facial abnormalities, genital malformations (ambiguous genitalia in males) and severe mental retardation. Two distinct clinical forms of SLOS have been described.

The etiology of SLOS has been linked to an abnormality in cholesterol production. Cholesterol is essential to the synthesis of cell membranes, vitamin metabolism, production of steroids and sex hormones, and formation of the nervous system. Many of the clinical features of SLOS are manifestations of a relative cholesterol deficiency. Despite these observations, there is no correlation between the degree of cholesterol inadequacy and the severity of disease.

Chromosome analysis in some patients with this disorder has shown an abnormal gene on chromosome 7. The incidence of SLOS is 1 in 20,000 births. It is transmitted in an autosomal recessive manner.

Characteristics

1. Moderate prenatal growth deficiency with persisting growth failure after birth (failure to thrive).
2. Moderate to severe mental retardation; extreme irritability and shrill cry during infancy; and hypotonia (decreased muscle tone) initially, later giving way to hypertonia (increased muscle tone).
3. Microcephaly (small head); low-set ears; droopy eyelids (ptosis), uncoordinated eye movement (strabismus); upturned nostrils and broad nasal tip; and small jaw.
4. Syndactyly (webbing with or without fusion) of the second and third toes.
5. Seventy percent of patients (males) have genital malformations. These include hypospadius (abnormal positioning of the urethral opening), undescended testis, micropenis, and underdeveloped scrotum and urethra.
6. Sixty percent of affected individuals have internal urinary tract anomalies.
7. Occasional findings include seizure disorder, cataract, flexion deformity of the fingers, congenital hip dislocation, cleft palate, congenital heart disease, inguinal hernia, and Hirschsprung disease (failure of nerve development in the large bowel).

Most authorities agree that two clinical forms of SLOS exist. Type I (classic form) has most of the features described previously. The majority of Type I males have ambiguous genitalia, but female patients do not demonstrate this anomaly. Type II disease (acrodysgenital syndrome) is associated with more severe anomalies than is Type I—polydactyly (extra digits), extremely abnormal external genitalia, and death during the 1st year. Cleft palate and skeletal abnormalities are also seen more commonly in patients with Type II disease.

No treatment is available for the underlying disorder of cholesterol metabolism associated with SLOS. Some of the syndrome's anatomic malformations may respond to surgical intervention (congenital heart disease, Hirschsprung disease, etc.). Affected families should receive genetic counseling, because the risk for recurrence for this disorder in subsequent offspring is 25%. Prenatal diagnosis is possible through biochemical analysis of amniotic fluid early in the second trimester of pregnancy.

Because of the poor prognosis, few children survive long enough to benefit from support services. However, for the few who have survived, special education support services are a necessity due to the severe cognitive deficits associated with the disorder.

The prognosis for SLOS is very poor. Stillbirth and death in early infancy are common. Twenty percent of patients who survived beyond the first few months did not live to their 1st birthday. Two patients with the disorder lived into adulthood but had IQs in the 20–30 range. As the cause of the cholesterol deficiencies and genetic basis of SLOS become clearer, better therapeutic options for treating these children may be discovered.

For more information and support, please contact Smith-Lemli-Opitz/RSH Advocacy and Exchange, 32 Ivy Lane, Glen Mills, PA 19342, (610) 361-9663, e-mail: bhook@erols.com, home page: http://members.aol.com/slo97/index.html

REFERENCES

Jones, K. (1997). *Smith's recognizable patterns of human malformations* (5th ed.). Philadelphia: W. B. Saunders.

National Organization for Rare Disorders. (1998). Smith-Lemli-Opitz syndrome. Retrieved from http://www.stepstn.com/cgi-win/nord.exe?proc=GetDocument&rectype=0&recnum=292

Rapaport, R. (2000). Hermaphroditism (intersexuality). In R. E. Behrman, R. M. Kleigman, & H. B. Jenson (Eds.), *Nelson textbook of pediatrics* (16th ed., p. 1765). Philadelphia: W. B. Saunders.

Barry H. Davison
Ennis, Texas

Joan W. Mayfield
Baylor Pediatric Specialty Services
Dallas, Texas

SMITH-MAGENIS SYNDROME

Smith-Magenis Syndrome (SMS; Greenberg et al., 1991; Magenis, Brown, Allen, & Reiss, 1986; Smith et al., 1986) is a multiple congenital anomaly chromosomal disorder associated with deletion in the proximal arm of Chromosome 17 [(17)(p11.2)]. Albeit underdiagnosed, SMS is considered a rare genetic disorder when compared to other genetic abnormalities with an approximate incidence of 1 in 25,000. The clinical phenotype of SMS is marked by brachycephaly, midface hypoplesia, prognatism, hoarse voice, speech delay with or without hearing loss, sleep disturbances, psychomotor and growth retardation, intellectual impairment, and behavior problems including hyperactivity, aggression, onychotillomania, self-hugging, and inappropriate insertion of foreign objects into body orifices. In some cases, children with a complete deletion of arm 17p11.2 are more severely afflicted with facial malformations, cleft palate, and major congenital malformations of the heart, skeletal, and genitourinary systems (Smith et al., 1986; Potocki, 2000). The overall intellectual level of these children has been reported to be within the deficient range. Within this range, most investigations have revealed intellectual skills in the moderate range of mental deficiency (Dykens, Finucayne, & Gayley, 1997; Llorente, Voigt, Potocki, & Lupinski, 2001; Smith et al., 1986). With regard to adaptation, the adaptive level of children with SMS is usually in the impaired range (low) across all domains (communicative, daily living skills, and social; Dykens et al., 1987; Llorente et al., 2001).

Characteristics

1. Mental retardation
2. Developmental and speech delay with or without hearing loss
3. Behavioral difficulties
4. Dysmorphic head and facial features possible (brachycephaly, midface hypoplesia, prognatism, cleft palate)
5. Possible congenital malformations of the heart, skeletal, and genitourinary systems
6. Hoarse voice and psychomotor and growth retardation
7. Insertion of foreign objects in body orifices

Based on the broad spectrum of clinical severity that children with SMS may experience, and despite the fact that there is no current cure for this genetic disorder, it is important to be flexible in designing any treatment regimen including medication and behavior analytic interventions targeting the behavioral alterations observed in these children. Because there is significant variability of symptom prevalence and manifestation, children diagnosed with SMS may be eligible for special education services under several categories of the Individuals with Disabilities Education Act. Depending on the level of intellectual functioning, a child with SMS may meet the criteria as a student with mental retardation. In addition, if a child has significant speech delays, he or she would be eligible for services under the Speech or Language Impairment category. A child with SMS, particularly one suffering from a congenital abnormality or other severe medical condition (e.g., congenital heart disease), may be eligible for services also under the Other Health Impairment category. Therefore, it is essential that doctors, parents, teachers, and others involved in the care of the child participate in devising the most appropriate educational plan and goals for the child.

Future research should continue to emphasize the determination of more exact cognitive and adaptive profiles, further genetic delineation of the syndrome through genetic research, and potential genetic therapies.

REFERENCES

Dykens, E. M., Finucane, B. M., & Gayley, C. (1997). Brief report: Cognitive and behavioral profiles of persons with Smith-Magenis syndrome. *Journal of Autism and Developmental Disorders, 27,* 203–210.

Greenberg, F., Guzzetta, V., Oca-Luna, R. M., Magenis, R. E., Smith, A. C. M., Richter, S. F., Kondo, I., Dobyns, W. B., Patel, P. I., & Lupski, J. R. (1991). Molecular analysis of the Smith-Magenis syndrome: A possible contiguous-gene syndrome associated with del(17)(p11.2). *American Journal of Human Genetics, 49,* 1207–1218.

Llorente, A. M., Voigt, R. G., Potocki, L., & Lupski, J. R. (2001, May). Cognitive and adaptive profiles of children with Smith-Magenis syndrome. *Proceedings from the 2001 Pediatric Academic Societies Annual Meeting,* 184A (Abstract 1043).

Magenis, R. E., Brown, M. G., Allen, L., & Reiss, J. (1986). De novo partial duplication of 17p[dup(17)(p12 B>p11.2]: Clinical report. *American Journal of Medical Genetics, 24,* 415–420.

Potocki, L. (2000). Circadian rhythm abnormalities of melatonin in Smith-Magenis syndrome. *Journal of Medical Genetics, 37,* 428–433.

Smith, A. C. M., McGavran, L., Robinson, J., Waldstein, G., Macfarlane, J., Zonona, J., Reiss, J., Lahr, M., Allen, L., & Magenis, E. (1986). Interstitial deletion of (17)(p11.2p11.2) in nine patients. *American Journal of Medical Genetics, 24,* 393–414.

Antolin M. Llorente
Baylor College of Medicine
Houston, Texas

SMITH-OPITZ SYNDROME

Smith-Opitz syndrome, better known as Smith-Lemli-Opitz syndrome (SLOS), is an autosomal recessive syndrome characterized by multiple congenital anomalies, mental retardation, behavioral difficulties, and characteristic dysmorphic facial features (Irons et al., 1997). SLOS is a relatively common inborn error of metabolism caused by deficient activity of the enzyme needed to catalyze cholesterol (Nowaczyk, Whelan, Heshka, & Hill, 1999).

Following phenylketonuria (PKU), SLOS is the second most common recessive hereditary syndrome that causes mental retardation (Nowaczyk et al., 1999). The gene for the enzyme in which individuals with SLOS are deficient has recently been found on Chromosome 11 (Nowaczyk et al., 1999). Incidence information seems to suggest that individuals of Northern European ancestry are more likely to have SLOS in comparison with very low incidence or nonexistent findings of SLOS in individuals of African or Asian descent. Current estimates of the incidence of SLOS state that it occurs in approximately 1 in 20,000 to 40,000 births, although this might be an underestimate considering the lack of research regarding diagnostic issues (Kelley, 1997; Nowaczyk et al., 1999). Furthermore, specific prevalence data regarding SLOS in the general population are as yet unknown.

Based on the wide spectrum of clinical severity that children with SLOS may experience, it is important to be flexible in designing any treatment regimen. Successful outcomes in the areas of growth, behavior, and overall health have been found by implementing dietary therapy with high cholesterol intake (Kelley, 1997; Nowaczyk et al., 1999), although a feeding tube is often necessitated for infants and very young children with feeding problems.

Characteristics

1. Microcephaly
2. Mental retardation
3. Developmental and speech delay
4. Feeding difficulties
5. Behavioral difficulties
6. Genital malformations
7. Dysmorphic facial features
8. Syndactyly (webbing) of second and third toes
9. Failure to thrive

For women who are carrying a SLOS-affected fetus, cholesterol supplementation has been suggested as well (Nowaczyk et al., 1999). Similarly, bile acid supplementation has been successful with some children (Irons et al., 1997; Nwokoro & Mulvihill, 1997).

Because there is a wide variability of symptom prevalence and manifestation, children diagnosed with SLOS may be eligible for special education services under several categories of the Individuals with Disabilities Education Act. Depending on the level of intellectual functioning, children with SLOS may meet criteria for Mental Retardation or Speech or Language Impairment, or the Other Health Impairment category. As noted, children with SLOS may be affected in many ways. Therefore, it is essential that doctors, parents, teachers, and others participate in providing care and devising the educational plan and goals for the child (Nowaczyk et al., 1999).

The prognosis for children with SLOS is variable. Severe cases have a very high neonatal mortality rate (Kelley, 1997; Nowaczyk et al., 1999). Children with SLOS have benefited from cholesterol replacement therapy. The dietary therapy has restored normal growth patterns and reduced behavioral difficulties in many children and adults with SLOS (Nowaczyk et al., 1999). With this in mind, future research should continue to measure the effect of current treatments and determine more exact prevalence and incidence data.

REFERENCES

Irons, M., Elias, E. R., Abuelo, D., Bull, M. J., Greene, C. L., Johnson, V. P., Keppen, L., Schanen, C., Tint, G. S., & Salen, G. (1997). Treatment of Smith-Lemli-Opitz syndrome: Results of a multicenter trial. *American Journal of Medical Genetics, 68,* 311–314.

Kelley, R. I. (1997). Editorial: A new face for an old syndrome. *American Journal of Medical Genetics, 65,* 251–256.

Nowaczyk, M. J. M., Whelan, D. T., Heshka, T. W., & Hill, R. E. (1999). Smith-Lemli-Opitz syndrome: A treatable inherited error of metabolism causing mental retardation. *Canadian Medical Association Journal, 161,* 165–170.

Nwokoro, N. A., & Mulvihill, J. J. (1997). Cholesterol and bile acid replacement therapy in children and adults with Smith-Lemli-Opitz (SLO/RSH) syndrome. *American Journal of Medical Genetics, 68,* 315–321.

Christine L. French
Texas A&M University

SOCIAL PHOBIA

Social phobia is a class of anxiety disorder characterized by a persistent fear of situations in which the person is exposed to possible scrutiny by others. The individual fears that he or she may act in a way that will be humiliating and embarrassing. The key feature of social phobia is the fear of being judged by others. In a school setting, this might occur in situations where a child avoids giving speeches in class or entering the school cafeteria or fears asking questions in a classroom. In other settings the child might refuse to eat, drink, or write in public or to attend social activities such as birthday or graduation parties, scout meetings, or church activities. Social phobias can be very selective in that a child may have an intense fear of a single situation, such as speaking in front of a class, but be perfectly comfortable in other situations (Rabian & Silverman, 2000). In applying the criteria to children, it must be demonstrated that the individual has the capacity to engage in socially appropriate behavior with familiar people and that the difficulties are not due to impaired social skills. The social anxiety must also occur in peer settings, not just with adults. Clinical presentation of symptoms may vary across cultures subject to unique social demands. For example, in Japanese and Korean cultures, social phobias may be expressed in terms of fears of giving offense (via excessive blushing, eye contact, or body odor) to others in social situations rather than personal behavior.

Social phobia is estimated to occur in 1% of children and adolescents. Age of onset typically occurs around puberty and peaks after the age of 30. It can occur at younger ages but is rarely diagnosed in children under age 10. The lifetime prevalence rates for social phobia ranges from 3–13%. Although a general fear of public speaking is estimated to be as high as 20% in the general population, only 2% experience an intense fear sufficient to warrant the diagnosis.

Characteristics (Adapted from American Psychiatric Association, 1994)

1. Marked and persistent fear of social-performance situations in which the child is subject to scrutiny.
2. Must have evidence of capacity for age-appropriate social relationships with familiar people, and the anxiety must also occur in peer settings.
3. Under age 18, symptoms must be present for at least 6 months.
4. Recognition that the fear is unreasonable, but preadolescent children may not demonstrate this feature.
5. Exposure to the feared situation almost always provokes anxiety and avoidance.
6. Anxiety must interfere with school or academic performance and social relationships or produce marked distress about the feared situation.

Although anxiety disorders comprise the most common disorder in childhood, very little research is available supporting the effectiveness of traditional psychotherapy or psychodynamic approaches (Kendall et al., 1997; Rabian & Silverman, 2000). For the management and treatment of childhood phobias, contingency management has been the only treatment considered to be well established (Ollendick & King, 1998). Using criteria established by the American Psychological Association, the following treatments are also considered probably efficacious for treating phobias: systematic desensitization, modeling using the observational learning approach, and several cognitive-behavioral therapy (CBT) approaches. CBT has four major components: recognizing anxious feelings, clarifying cognitions in anxiety-provoking situations, identifying a plan for coping with those situations, and evaluating the success of the coping strategies. In vivo graduated exposure coupled with CBT treatments has also proven effective. Pharmacological interventions for anxiety-based disorders include the use of selective serotonin reuptake inhibitors (SSRIs) such as Prozac, Paxil, Zoloft, Luvox, or Celexa with initial dosages lower than recommended and slowly adjusted for maximum therapeutic effect. Benzodiazepines such as Xanax and Ativan as well as trycyclic antidepressants have shown minimal to modest benefit and in some cases have been no more effective than placebo in children. These treatments are usually provided as an adjunct to psychological treatments.

Children with social phobia may experience declines in classroom performance, school refusal, or avoidance of age-appropriate activities such as going out on dates or socializing with peers. Special education support services may be available to children diagnosed with social phobia under specific categories of Other Health Impairment or Severe Emotional Disturbance or Behavior Disorder if an impact on the child's education can be established. This may be particularly important if the disorder is chronic in nature. Accommodations may also be requested and provided under Section 504 of the Rehabilitation Act of 1973. Families can benefit from additional counseling and support to implement effectively a treatment plan across both school and home settings.

Social phobia tends to fluctuate throughout the life span, subject to life stressors and situational demands experienced in different settings. Children and adults may experience a remission or decrease in the severity of the symptoms when life circumstances change. The disorder tends to occur in families where there is evidence of anxiety or phobic-based disorders. Rather than a specific anxiety disorder, there tends to be a predisposition in families to some variant within the range of anxiety disorders.

REFERENCES

American Psychiatric Association. (1994). *Diagnostic and statistical manual of mental disorders* (4th ed.). Washington, DC: Author.

Kendall, P. C., Flannery-Schroeder, E., Panicelli-Mindel, S. M., Southam-Gerow, M., Henin, A., & Warman, M. (1997). Therapy for youths with anxiety disorders: A second randomized clinical trial. *Journal of Consulting and Clinical Psychology, 65,* 366–380.

Ollendick, T. H., & King, N. J. (1998). Empirically supported treatments for children with phobic and anxiety disorders: Current status. *Journal of Clinical Child Psychology, 27,* 156–167.

Rabian, B., & Silverman, W. (2000). Anxiety disorders. In M. Hersen & R. Ammerman (Eds.), *Advanced abnormal child psychology* (pp. 271–289) Mahwah, NJ: Erlbaum.

Daniel Olympia
University of Utah

SOTOS SYNDROME (CEREBRAL GIGANTISM)

Sotos syndrome is characterized by prenatal onset of excessive size that persists through at least the first 4 years of life with macrocrania, a high forehead (dolichocephalic), hypertelorism, prominent jaw, premature eruption of teeth, and a narrow palate with prominent, lateral palatine ridges.

Sotos syndrome is believed to be a rare condition, but prevalence is unknown and has not been studied in detail. It is suspected to be an autosomal dominant disorder in familial cases but is most often sporadic, with occurrence increasing with the age of the parents; however, true and confirmed etiology remains unknown (Gillberg, 1995).

Characteristics

1. Prenatal onset of excessive growth persisting until at least age 4 and sometimes into puberty.
2. Macrocephaly, dolichoencephaly, hypotonia, hyperreflexia, and delayed development of gross motor function.
3. Variable levels of intellectual development with reported IQs of 18 to 119, with a mean of 72, and 67% of cases with IQs between 50 and 70 and 75% of the remainder between 71 and 90.
4. Behavior problems are common but highly variable ranging from ADHD-like symptoms to full blown cases of comorbid autism (e.g., Zappella, 1990).
5. Speech problems and delayed language acquisition are common.

Treatment of Sotos syndrome is entirely symptomatic, and in addition to the previous characteristics, there are more than 40 other occasional abnormalities that occur on an occasional basis in Sotos syndrome. These may require special treatment consideration and may include various seizure disorders, complete to partial callosal agenesis, hypoplasia of the septum pellucidum, septum interpositum, and the cerebellar vermin, glucose dysregulation, increased incidence of at least nine cancers, and multiple orthopedic abnormalities.

Special education placement will approach 100% in cases of Sotos syndrome, but learning and academic skills vary greatly. Individual psychoeducational testing and revisions of educational plans should both occur at least annually between the ages of 4 years and one year postpuberty. Qualification for special education services is most often as multiply handicapped due to health problems, behavioral problems, and speech and language delays that are often accompanied by mental retardation. (However, as many as 10% of these children may have IQs within the normal range.) Occupational therapy services are often required due to coordination deficits.

Behavior problems evident in Sotos syndrome include very poor overall social adjustment, increased aggressiveness, temper tantrums, and related difficulties with the self-regulatory systems of the brain producing attention, concentration, and impulse control problems. Social adjustment and emotional problems characterized as emotional immaturity persist into adulthood (Jones, 1997). Prognosis is poor, and some form of supervised living throughout the individual's life along with chronic management via psychopharmacotherapy occurs in nearly all cases. Future research is focusing on etiology and prevention of this serious and pervasive disorder.

REFERENCES

Gillberg, C. (1995). *Clinical child neuropsychiatry.* Cambridge, England: Cambridge University Press.

Jones, K. L. (1997). *Smith's recognizable patterns of human malformation* (5th ed.). Philadelphia: W. B. Saunders.

Zappella, M. (1990). Autistic features in children affected by cerebral gigantism. *Brain Dysfunction, 3,* 241–244.

Cecil R. Reynolds
Texas A&M University and Bastrop Mental Health Associates

SPASTICITY

Spasticity, a type of muscle hyperactivity, is a disorder associated with a lesion of the central nervous system. Most commonly the lesion is in the sensorimotor area of the cerebral cortex or associated pathways. Spasticity is a diagnostic sign of an upper motor neuron syndrome such as cerebral palsy. It is defined as a velocity-dependent increase in muscle tone (hypertonia) with hyperactive deep tendon reflexes (DTRs). Clinically, spasticity is manifested by an increase in resistance to passive movement (i.e., muscle stiffness). Conversely, the presence of spasticity may impair voluntary motor control, thereby impacting specific functions such as gait, upper extremity tasks such as reaching, and self-help skills. Spasticity may be rated as mild, moderate, or severe. Prolonged spasticity may lead to muscle and joint contractures, bone deformities, and muscle atrophy (Fredericks & Saladin, 1996).

The degree and distribution of the hypertonia may fluctuate depending on the position of the body. In general, spasticity predominates in the antigravity musculature (i.e., the flexor muscles of the upper extremities and the extensor muscles of the lower extremities). The somatic distribution of the spasticity varies depending on the location of the lesion in the brain. For example, spasticity may affect all four extremities, only the lower extremities, or either the right or left upper and lower extremity. The exact pathophysiology of spasticity is not entirely understood. It is thought to be due to increased motor neuron excitability. In all probability, there are multiple mechanisms that interact to produce spasticity (Fredericks & Saladin, 1996). The prevalence and incidence of spasticity is not available, as it is a sign or symptom of a number of upper motor neuron syndromes.

Characteristics

1. Resistance to passive stretch of muscles (i.e., muscle stiffness)
2. Increased deep tendon reflexes
3. Impaired muscle selectivity during volitional movement

Treatment is aimed at reducing the hypertonus, preventing or reducing deformity, and enhancing function. One or more of the following may be used to reduce or minimize the effects of spasticity: muscle relaxants, neurosurgery, orthopedic surgery, orthotics, and physical and occupational therapy. Involvement of the family is critical in the success of the treatment (Campbell, 1999).

The etiology of spasticity commonly occurs as a result of infection or injury. Typically, onset in children occurs during the prenatal period or in early infancy. The characteristics of spasticity may not be initially apparent. However, risk may be determined based on the prenatal or birth history. Factors such as prematurity, maternal infection, anoxia, meningitis, tumors, stroke, and brain injury are known risk factors that may lead to brain damage that results in spasticity (Blackman, 1997). The impact that spasticity may have on the development of children depends in part on the severity of symptoms exhibited and the regions of the body affected. Also important are the current stage of development, the age at onset, and any previously acquired skills. Not surprisingly, the earlier the onset of spasticity that seriously limits mobility, the greater is the likelihood that many or all developmental areas will be negatively impacted (Blackman, 1997).

Often it is when one or more major developmental milestones have been missed that concerns are raised in young children. A baby may not roll over at the expected time or reach and grasp objects, or these behaviors may be present but the quality of movement is suspect. For example, rather than rolling over with a segmental head and trunk movement, the baby may arch the back and attempt to flip over. Movements may be rigid and limited to primitive patterns rather than smooth and fluid rolling. A baby who is at the developmental age but is unable to maintain sitting may attempt to use compensatory patterns (i.e., keeping both hands on the floor for balance, arching backward to get to a more secure position) to avoid this situation. Other observable patterns may include extension and increased stiffening patterns when excited or when trying to move. When these compensatory behaviors occur, they present challenges for transitioning to the next developmental stage. For example, if the only way that a baby can maintain sitting posture is to use both hands on the floor, the next level of exploration—exploring objects with both hands, moving from sitting to crawling, and moving out into the environment—may not occur.

One of the major milestones in development is independent locomotion. When the spasticity is evident during the first year of life, such skills as crawling, sitting, walking, and balancing may be inhibited. Because spasticity may inhibit or compromise movement, babies may be unwilling or unable to attempt exploratory activities. If the spasticity is severe and mobility is restricted, learning becomes restricted to what the environment presents rather than to what is gained through independent exploration. This also prohibits the baby's moving out into the environment to explore and gain perceptual motor, social, language, and cognitive skills. These barriers impact progress across all developmental domains and may cause the secondary disabilities that include decreased awareness of means-ends and causality issues (how things work and why), social interactions (turn-taking, waving bye-bye), and further exploration of the environment.

In older children and adults the presence of spasticity is also made apparent by muscle hyperactivity that results in a limited range of motion and reduced quality of movement. As stated previously, joint development and structure may be compromised due to the limited use of limbs and constant hyperactivity of impacted muscles remaining flexed. Because both gross and fine motor movement may be compromised by spasticity, devices are commonly used to assist students in movement skills such as walking, writing, typing, or moving. Braces, use of a walker, or a mouth stick to aid in typing are only a few examples of aides that might be utilized (Bowe, 2000).

When working with a child or adult, fatigue is a factor that must be addressed. Short breaks or naps may be needed for children and adults with spasticity due to fatigue that results from muscles being constantly flexed. In classroom settings an area of floor space or an apparatus on which a child may be positioned to reduce muscle hyperactivity may assist in reducing fatigue.

Teachers, parents, and other caregivers typically work under the direction of a physical therapist to address impacted muscle groups to maintain flexibility and range of motion. A regime of exercise and positioning may need to be practiced across all areas of a child's life several times a day to ameliorate the spasticity. Thus, all participants may need to be trained and become proficient in the use of several devices (Bowe, 2000).

Thus, the motor challenges that a child may have as a result of spasticity not only affect movement but also may compromise development across domains. Although special education may be delivered under the category of Other Health Impairment, services are likely to be needed in a variety of areas. Special education placement will depend on the nature of the disability and the level of involvement for each child. The ideal program would include a transdisciplinary model in which psychology and physical, occupational, and speech therapy activities are incorporated into the child's daily activities. Therefore, it is critical that intervention programs address all areas of development. The prognosis for children who have spasticity depends on the etiology, specific diagnosis, course of the disorder, and severity of the characteristics.

REFERENCES

Blackman, J. A. (1997). *Medical aspects of developmental disabilities in children birth to three* (3rd ed.). Rockville, MD: Aspen.

Bowe, F. (2000). *Physical, sensory, and health disabilities: An introduction.* Upper Saddle River, NJ: Merrill.

Campbell, S. (1999). *Decision making in pediatric neurologic physical therapy.* New York: Churchill Livingstone.

Fredericks, C. M., & Saladin, L. K. (1996). *Pathophysiology of the motor systems.* Philadelphia: F. A. Davis.

Patricia Work
Lana Svien-Senne
Marilyn Urquhart
University of South Dakota

SPIELMEYER-VOGT DISEASE

Spielmeyer-Vogt disease is the juvenile form of a group of progressive neurological diseases known as neuronal ceroid lipofuscinoses (NCL). Also known as Speilmeyer-Vogt-Sjogren-Batten disease or Batten disease after a British pediatrician who first described it in 1903. Spielmeyer-Vogt disease is an autosomal recessive disorder. Therefore, when both parents carry the gene, their children have a 25% chance of developing the disease. Symptoms of Spielmeyer-Vogt disease are linked to the buildup of lipopigments in the body's tissues. These lipopigments are made up of fats and proteins and build up in the cells of the brain and eyes as well as the skin, muscles, and other tissues.

Spielmeyer-Vogt disease is relatively rare, occurring in an estimated 2 to 4 out of every 100,000 births in the United States. This disorder appears to be more common in Northern Europe, Scandinavia, and Newfoundland, Canada. This disease often strikes more than one person in families who carry the defective gene.

Characteristics

1. Vision loss (optic atrophy) is often an early sign, so Spielmeyer-Vogt disease may first be suspected during an eye exam.
2. It is usually diagnosed between 5 and 8 years of age.
3. Individuals may suffer from seizures, ataxia, or clumsiness.
4. This form of NCL progresses less rapidly than do other forms.
5. Although some individuals may live into their 30s, this disease usually ends in death in the late teens or early 20s.

As yet no treatment is known that can halt or reverse the symptoms of Spielmeyer-Vogt disease or other NCLs. However, some of the symptoms can be controlled. Seizures may respond well to anticonvulsant drugs, and other medical problems can be treated as they arise. Some research has reported a slowing of the disease when patients are treated with vitamins C and E and diets low in vitamin A. However, these treatments did not prevent the fatal outcome of the disease.

Children diagnosed with Spielmeyer-Vogt disease will be eligible for special services under the Individuals with Disabilities Education Act of 1997 within the physical disability category. The accommodations and modifications necessary will change with the progression of the illness. Psychosocial support will be necessary for the child and his or her family as they come to terms, and live with this illness, but also in preparation for death. Teachers and those working with the student need to be well informed about the illness and its symptoms. School staff will need to be able to deal with the manifestation of the illness as it presents itself in class. For example, the student may be able to complete work one day and find it hard to complete any assignments the next day. Additionally, the student may need time away from the classroom to talk about feeling and express anger and concerns. Depending on their medical and psychological needs, students may miss long periods of school.

Research appears to be focusing on identifying the genetic cause of Spielmeyer-Vogt disease. The genes involved may be located on Chromosomes 13 and 15. Identification of specific genes can lead to the development of DNA diagnostics and carrier and prenatal tests. Other research is investigating the theory that Spielmeyer-Vogt disease may be related to a shortage of a key body enzyme called phospholipase A1. Identifying the faulty enzyme may make it possible to treat affected children with natural or synthetic enzymes to counteract the effect and clear away the storage of lipopigments. Other investigators are working to understand the role that lipopigments play in Spielmeyer-Vogt disease and other NCLs. Recently, scientists have identified large portions of the built-up material characteristic to Spielmeyer-Vogt disease as a protein called subunit C. This protein is usually found inside a cell's mitochondria. Scientists are now working to understand why this protein ends up in the wrong location and accumulates inside diseased cells. Another approach taken by researchers has been to test the usefulness of bone marrow transplantations in sheep and mice with NCLs. Using an animal model such as this will make it easier for scientists to study the genetics of these diseases and improve the overall understanding and treatment of these disorders.

REFERENCES

DeStefano, N., Lubke, U., Martin, J. J., Guazzi, G. C., & Federico, A. (1999). Detection of beta-A4 amyloid and its precursor protein in the muscle of a patient with juvenile neuronal ceroid lipofuscinosis (Spielmeyer-Vogt-Sjogren). *Acta Neuropathology, 98*(1), 78–84.

Eksandh, L. B., Ponjavic, V. B., Eiberg, H. E., Uvebrant, P. E., Ehinger, B. E., Mole, S. E., & Andreasson, S. (2000). Full-field ERG in patients with Batten/Spielmeyer-Vogt disease caused by mutations in the CLN3 gene. *Ophthalmic Genetics, 21*(2), 69–77.

RACHEL TOPLIS
University of Northern Colorado

SPINA BIFIDA

Spina bifida is a neural tube defect that results from the spine's failure to close during the first month of pregnancy. This disorder can range from generally asymptomatic (occulta) with a very small spinal opening to a completely open spinal column (rachischisis) with severe neurological damage (Beers & Berkow, 1999). The partially exposed spinal cord is susceptible to both infection and direct injury, resulting in loss of function.

Spina bifida is the most common neural tube defect, occurring in approximately 0.5–1 in 1,000 births in the United States (National Organization for Rare Disorders [NORD], 2001; Spina Bifida Association of America [SBAA], 2001). The causes of spina bifida appear to be multifactorial including heredity, nutrition, and other factors. Research has shown that adequate levels of folic acid (.4 mg/day) immediately prior to pregnancy and during the first trimester decrease risk of neural tube defects including spina bifida up to 75% (Centers for Disease Control, 1992).

Most children born with spina bifida have no family history. However, risk for spina bifida increases dramatically if a family history is present. If one parent is affected, the child has a 1–5% probability of being born with spina bifida, whereas if both parents are affected, the risk increases to 15% (SBAA, 2001). Siblings of children with spina bifida also have an increased risk of being affected (1–5%: SBAA, 2001).

Characteristics

1. Failure of spinal column to close during the first month of pregnancy
2. Difficulty with mobility, ranging from mild to complete paralysis
3. Meningocele (protrusion of the meninges through the gap in the spine) or myelomeningocele (exposure of spinal cord and roots) may protrude from the back

4. Abnormal development of lower trunk and extremities
5. Muscle contractures and abnormal posture
6. Problems with bowel and bladder control (incontinence)
7. Often accompanied by hydrocephalus
8. Often extreme sensitivity to latex products

Diagnosis is usually made at birth or prenatally. A common way to diagnose neural tube defects prenatally is through a blood test for maternal alpha-fetoprotein (AFP) at 16 to 18 weeks gestation. The AFP test has been in use since the early 1980s to diagnose neural tube defects (Kurtzweil, 1999).

The mildest cases may not require medical treatment, but surgery to close any openings in the spinal cord may be performed during infancy (often during the first 24 hr following birth). Early intervention may help to prevent further damage to the spinal cord and limit the risk of infection. When hydrocephalus is present, a shunt is placed to drain excess cerebrospinal fluid (CSF). Physical and occupational therapy are often necessary to improve mobility, flexibility, and adaptive functioning. People with spina bifida may require assistive devices such as crutches, walkers, wheelchairs, and braces.

Special education issues will differ among children depending on the severity of symptoms. These services will be available to children with spina bifida under the handicapping condition of Other Health Impairment or Physical Disability. Children with spina bifida are likely to require assistance to cope with physical limitations. The type of assistance may include occupational therapy, physical therapy, and adapted physical education. Children with spina bifida are at increased risk for learning disabilities, language impairment, and attentional difficulties (SBAA, 2001). In fact, about 30% have slight to severe mental retardation (Kurtzweil, 1999). The SBAA (2001) recommends a complete neuropsychological evaluation for children with spina bifida prior to entering school to determine cognitive functioning and decide what special education services are appropriate for an individual child. Children with spina bifida are also at risk for emotional and social difficulties and may require intervention to learn coping strategies and social skills.

Research continues to investigate the causes, prevention, and treatment of this disorder. It is likely that the incidence of spina bifida and other neural tube defects will decrease as more is learned about the causes and function of nutrition in fetal development. With proper intervention, many children with spina bifida are successful in school and learn to cope with their physical challenges. However, due to the severity of the spina bifida, some children may require chronic management or supervision and medical care into adulthood.

REFERENCES

Beers, M. H., & Berkow, R. (Eds.). (1999). *The Merck manual* (17th ed.). Whitehouse Station, NJ: Merck Research Laboratories.

Centers for Disease Control. (1992). Recommendations for the use of folic acid to reduce the number of cases of spina bifida and other neural tube defects. *Morbidity and Mortality Weekly Report, 41,* 1–7.

Kurtzweil, P. (1999). How folate can help prevent birth defects. Retrieved from www.fda.gov/fdac/features/796_fol.html

National Organization for Rare Disorders, Inc. (2001, March 29). Spina bifida. Retrieved from https://www.stepstm.com/cgi-win/nord.exe

Spina Bifida Association of America. (2001, May 5). Facts about spina bifida. Retrieved from http://sbaa.org

Melissa R. Bunner
Austin Neurological Clinic

SPINAL CORD INJURIES

Pediatric spinal cord injuries involve severe damage to the spinal cord in children from birth to 15 years. The injury can result in a loss of both mobility and feeling. It is estimated that there are approximately 8,000 to 10,000 new cases of spinal cord injuries each year. These injuries tend to be less common in the pediatric population, with approximately 1–10% of the new cases involving this group (Apple, Anson, Hunter, & Bell, 1995; National Spinal Cord Injury Association [NSCIA], 2000). Males are four times more likely to suffer a spinal cord injury than are females. The most common cause of a spinal cord injury is a motor vehicle accident. Acts of violence are the second leading cause, followed by falls, sports-related injuries, and other injuries (NSCIA, 2000; Spinal Cord Injury Information Network, 2000).

Spinal cord injuries can be classified as complete or incomplete. With complete injuries, there is no mobility below the level of injury, and there is equal damage to both sides of the body. There may be some functioning below the level of injury with the incomplete type. Persons with an incomplete injury may also have more functioning on one side of the body or be able to feel body parts that they cannot move (NSCIA, 2000).

Persons with spinal cord injuries can also be classified as paraplegics or quadriplegics, depending on the degree and place of injury. Higher injuries (as with quadriplegics) tend to cause more loss of functioning because more body parts are affected. The proportion of these two types of injuries are approximately 50–50, although more individuals with quadriplegia also have incomplete functioning (NSCIA, 2000; Spinal Cord Injury Information Network, 2000).

Characteristics

Complete Quadriplegia

1. Child sustains injury to one of eight cervical segments of the spinal cord.
2. There is no functioning or feeling below the level of injury.

Incomplete Quadriplegia

1. Child sustains injury to one of eight cervical segments of the spinal cord.
2. Child may have some functioning or sensation below level of injury, use one side of the body more than the other, or feel parts of the body that cannot move.

Complete Paraplegia

1. Child sustains injury to thoracic, lumbar, or sacral regions of spinal cord.
2. Child has no functioning or sensation below the level of injury.

Incomplete Paraplegia

1. Child sustains injury to thoracic, lumbar, or sacral regions of spinal cord.
2. Child may have some functioning or feeling below level of injury, use one side of the body more than the other, or feel parts of the body that cannot move.

Overall, the pediatric population appears more resistant to spinal cord injuries due to the developing nature of the spine (Jarosz, 1999). However, when injuries do occur, they tend to be more severe. Children and youth have more high spinal cord injuries, as well as more complete injuries. This is likely due to the elasticity of the immature spine, which protects it from mild traumas but leads to severe neurological injuries in higher force traumas (Jarosz, 1999).

Initially, surgery may be required to relieve pressure and swelling on the spinal cord, and hospitalization will be necessary until the spine is stabilized. Treatment often involves comprehensive rehabilitation programs, which focus on helping persons develop the necessary skills to return home, to school, and into the community (NSCIA, 2000). The psychosocial aspects of rehabilitation are critical if the individual is to achieve success. This includes strengthening remaining muscles, learning to use any equipment (wheelchairs, crutches, etc.), and relearning basic living skills (dressing, traveling, cooking, etc.). The goal is for these individuals to maintain both physical and emotional health over time (Vogel, Klaas, Lubicky, & Anderson, 1998). Alternative therapies are also available, such as drug treatments and electrical stimulation. These are more controversial, and none provide a cure for the injuries (NSCIA, 2000).

Children with spinal cord injuries may qualify for special education services under Physical Disabilities or Other Health Impairments. Extensive absences from school for rehabilitation may follow an injury. The school must be handicap accessible, and ample space within the classroom must be provided so these children can move about using equipment needed for mobility. Children with limited use of their limbs will require modifications for written activities and exams, including note takers and special computers. Adaptations will be needed in physical education classes and other activities requiring physical activity, and special transportation to and from school may be required. These children may benefit from psychological services, including individual and family counseling to help them cope and adjust to their injuries.

There is no cure for spinal cord injuries, although all individuals may improve as swelling decreases. Although less than 1% of injured individuals fully recover, persons with incomplete injuries can see increases in functioning as long as 18 months after injury (NSCIA, 2000). The prognosis for most injured individuals is good. Most rehabilitated individuals live in a private residence, and more than half go on to hold jobs and marry (NSCIA, 2000; Spinal Cord Injury Information Network, 2000). Treatment that focuses on psychosocial factors is the best predictor for adult life satisfaction among individuals who have suffered a pediatric spinal cord injury (Vogel et al., 1998). Current research is focusing on spinal cord regeneration and nerve cell replacement through surgery, drug treatments, and alternative therapies (NSCIA, 2000).

REFERENCES

Apple, D. F., Anson, C. A., Hunter, B. A., & Bell, R. B. (1995). Spinal cord injury in youth. *Clinical Pediatrics, 34,* 90–95.

Jarosz, D. A. (1999). Pediatric spinal cord injuries: A case presentation. *Critical Care Nursing Quarterly, 22,* 8–13.

National Spinal Cord Injury Association. (2000, September 26). Retrieved from www.spinalcord.org

Spinal Cord Injury Information Network. (2000, September 26). Retrieved from www.spinalcord.uab.edu

Vogel, L. C., Klaas, S. J., Lubicky, J. P., & Anderson, C. J. (1998). Long-term outcomes and life satisfaction of adults who had pediatric spinal cord injuries. *Archives of Physical Medicine and Rehabilitation, 79,* 1496–1503.

Amy J. Dahlstrom
Rik Carl D'Amato
University of Northern Colorado

SPONDYLOEPIPHYSEAL DYSPLASIA, CONGENITA

Congenital spondyloepiphyseal dysplasia (SED) is a rare inherited disorder transmitted in an autosomal dominant manner. This disorder is typified by a growth deficiency before birth; it is associated with spinal malformations and abnormalities of the eyes. As the individual ages, the growth deficiency usually results in short stature (dwarfism). SED congenita may also be referred to as pseudo-achondroplasia.

SED occurs approximately once in every 100,000 births, making it one of the most common forms of dwarfism along with achondroplasia and diastophic dysplasia. This disorder affects males and females in equal numbers.

Characteristics

1. This disorder is apparent at birth.
2. Symptoms include curved spine, cervical spinal compression, and short neck. Instability of the spine at C1 and C2 may be present.
3. Individuals may have clubfoot and poorly formed femur heads.
4. Cleft palate is present.
5. Myopia (nearsightedness) is present in 40% of cases. Retinal detachment can occur.
6. As the individual ages, a characteristic appearance develops: The chest is often broad and barrel-like, and the neck is short and gives the appearance of the head resting directly on the shoulders. The extremities are short but long in proportion to the trunk. Hands and feet are normal.
7. A waddling, wide-based gait is evident in early childhood.
8. Motor development may be delayed in infants and children.
9. SED children are susceptible to ear infections.
10. In late childhood, the lumbar spine becomes lordotic (swaybacked). Kyphoscoliosis (spinal deformity) can also occur.
11. Intelligence is usually normal.
12. Adult height ranges from 36″ to 67″ (90 cm to 167.5 cm).

At present there is no cure for this disorder. Although the gene for SED has been located, there is variability in the location of the gene among persons with SED. Prenatal tests are available, but expensive. Medical care focuses on management of complications and orthopedic issues. An evaluation of the cervical spine at C1 and C2 may be performed to assess whether a spinal fusion is needed. Lax ligaments in the neck could lead to spinal injury during contact sports and car accidents. This disorder may result in chest constriction, which can decrease lung capacity. Due to risks related to lung capacity, small airways, and spine instability, caution should be taken during anesthesia. It is important for individuals with SED to have their cervical or neck vertebrae monitored with careful neurological exams, X rays of the neck flexion and extension, and magnetic resonance images if needed. Orthopedic care may be needed to evaluate hip, spinal, and knee complications. Hip replacements are sometimes warranted in adults. Regular eye exams should be done to evaluate for nearsightedness and detached retinas. Hearing should be checked, and ear infections should be closely monitored. Tubes may need to be placed in the ear. Symptoms such as clubfoot or cleft palate may need to be surgically corrected.

As individuals with SED usually have normal intelligence, it is quite likely that they will benefit academically from regular education and may not need special services under the Individuals with Disabilities Education Act (IDEA) of 1997. This will depend on the psychosocial effects of the disorder on the individual. If students are found to be struggling academically because of social-emotional issues, they may be eligible for services under the Emotional Disturbance category of IDEA 1997. Additionally, these individuals may be able to access services under Section 504 of the Rehabilitation Act of 1974 if it is deemed necessary. Students with SED may benefit from counseling to address the social-emotional components of this disorder. For example, they may need support to build self-esteem and confidence and to accept (or accommodate) their bodily image within their self-concept and identity. School personnel should be cognizant of the limitations of this disorder. For example, SED students may require time away from school for a variety of medical reasons. Additionally, due to neck instability, individuals with SED should exercise caution and avoid activities and sports that could result in trauma to the neck or head.

The prognosis for this disorder is that it is nonlethal but associated with many complications. Research continues to assess ways to remediate some of the complications of SED, such as correcting the instability of the spine (Ledoux, Naftalis, & Aronin, 1991) and retinal detachments (Ikegawa, Iwaya, Taniguchi, & Kimizuka, 1993). Additionally, research is attempting to investigate possible ways to identify SED prenatally (Kirk & Comstock, 1990).

REFERENCES

Ikegawa, S., Iwaya, T., Taniguchi, K., & Kimizuka, M. (1993). Retinal detachment in spondyloepiphyseal dysplasia congenita. *Journal of Pediatric Orthopedics, 13*(6), 791–792.

Kirk, J. S., & Comstock, C. H. (1990). Antenatal sonographic appearance of spondyloepiphyseal dysplasia congenita. *Journal of Ultrasound Medicine, 9*(3), 173–175.

LeDoux, M. S., Naftalis, R. C., & Aronin, P. A. (1991). Stabilization of the cervical spine in spondyloepiphyseal dysplasia congenita. *Neurosurgery, 28*(4), 580–583.

Rachel Toplis
University of Northern Colorado

ST. VITUS DANCE

St. Vitus Dance, also referred to as Sydenham chorea, is a transitory movement disorder of childhood that is characterized by purposeless, arrhythmic, involuntary movements of the arms, legs, and face; muscle weakness; and emotional lability (May & Koch, 1999). Movement difficulties may occur on one side of the body (hemichorea) or may be generalized (Goldenberg, Ferraz, Fonseca, Hilario, Bastos, & Sachetti, 1992).

The term *chorea* was first used in 1686 by British physician Thomas Sydenham to refer to the frenzied movements of religious fanatics who traveled to the shrine of St. Vitus during the Middle Ages. Although its etiology and pathophysiology are unconfirmed, Sydenham chorea appears to be a delayed complication of Lancefield Group A beta-hemolytic streptococcal infections (Merck Manual, 2001). It also occurs in about 10% of children following an episode of acute rheumatic fever, with reduced incidence over the last 50 years (Merck Manual, 2001). Sydenham chorea is thought to be associated with excessive dopamine activity in the basal ganglia (Shannon & Fenichel, 1990) and with immunological response factors, such as the production of antineuronal antibodies (Swedo et al., 1993). Sydenham chorea may serve as a precursor to other choreas in adulthood; for example, Cardoso et al. (1999), studied 129 adults with chorea gravidarum, many of whom had a history of Syndenham chorea or rheumatic fever during childhood. Sydenham chorea has also been linked with other disorders, such as obsessive-compulsive behaviors (Mercadante et al., 2000; Swedo et al., 1993) and attention-deficit/hyperactivity disorder (ADHD); in fact, Mercadante et al. (2000) concluded that ADHD appears to be a risk factor for Sydenham chorea in children with rheumatic fever.

Initial suspicions of Sydenham chorea may occur following parent reports of unusual clumsiness in their children or teacher reports of suddenly illegible handwriting. There is some controversy in the literature regarding its onset, with some sources claiming that symptoms appear gradually and others describing a more abrupt onset. At present, Sydenham chorea is diagnosed primarily on clinical presentation, as laboratory tests may be negative for infection and the electrocardiogram and neurological exam may be normal. Differential diagnosis must consider familial chorea, mass lesion in the central nervous system, effects of other drugs or toxins, collagen vascular diseases, repetitive spasms, and uncontrolled movements associated with cerebral palsy and attention-deficit/hyperactivity disorder (Merck Manual, 2001).

Characteristics

1. Sydenham chorea often follows streptococcal infection or rheumatic fever, with up to a 12-month delay before the first symptoms appear. It occurs most often in temperate climates during the summer and early fall.
2. It occurs primarily in prepubescent girls, with peak incidence between 7 and 14 years; occurrence after age 20 is rare.
3. Generally, onset is gradual, and the course is variable, beginning with nervousness, fine motor difficulties, and occasional grimacing. Speech may become indistinct, and characteristic choreic movements may develop.
4. Choreic movements are often aggravated by stress or efforts at control but disappear during sleep.
5. Other signs include a clucking sound during speech production due to tongue contractions, difficulty with tongue control when it is protruded, flexion of the wrists and hyperextension of the joints in the hands and arms when the arms are extended, and spasmodic contractions of the hands during intentional grasping of objects.
6. Associated problems may include hypotonia, emotional lability, obsessive-compulsive behaviors, hyperactivity, and distractibility (Swedo et al., 1993).

Treatment of Sydenham chorea is symptomatic and may include mild sedatives, tranquilizers, or muscle relaxants to control involuntary movements and to prevent self-injury from flailing arms and legs. Antibiotics such as penicillin and erythromycin are often prescribed until adulthood to minimize complications and prevent recurrence of symptoms (National Institute of Neurological Disorders and Stroke, 2000). Drug treatment has been attempted with varying degrees of success as well as risk. For example, antipsychotics such as haloperidol and risperidone have been found effective, but the former is associated with side effects such as tardive dyskinesia, and the latter is not approved for use in children. Anecdotal evidence suggests that severe forms of Sydenham chorea that do not respond to antipsychotics may be treated effectively with corticosteroids. In addition, neuroleptics such as pimozide have been found successful in some cases (e.g., Shannon & Fenichel, 1990) but unsuccessful in others (e.g., May & Koch, 1999). Finally, the presence of neuronal antibodies in more than 90% of affected children (Swedo et al., 1993) has suggested the use of intravenous immunoglobulin therapy as an alternative to other forms of treatment; in fact, May and Koch (1999) reported rapid improvement in two young girls who had not responded to more conventional therapies. The prognosis for Sydenham chorea is generally favorable, with spontaneous recovery in 3 to 6 months without lasting effects on muscle control, intelligence, personality, or emotions. However, relapses are not uncommon, and mild signs of chorea may appear intermittently during the year following an acute episode.

Children with Sydenham chorea may not qualify for special educational services, primarily because of the brief duration of symptoms. They may, however, be eligible for temporary accommodations, depending on the severity of symptoms and the degree to which they interfere with normal functioning in the classroom. Children may need help with handwriting, managing school items, dressing, and feeding. Instruction in self-care skills may allow the child to maintain independence, and an emphasis on safety skills may minimize the possibility of harm to self and others. Older children with Sydenham chorea may be particularly susceptible to feelings of embarrassment and shame about their inability to control their movements and the reaction that their behaviors elicit from uninformed peers and adults. Such children will need education about their condition, emotional support, and, if necessary, psychotherapy or counseling, both for themselves and their families. Many individuals who come into contact with affected children may be frightened by the nature of Sydenham chorea; it is essential that they be educated about its possible manifestations, reminded about its temporary nature, and reassured that it is not contagious. Finally, although affected children may need to stay home during the acute phase of the condition, they should be encouraged to return to school as soon as possible.

Additional research that confirms the etiology and pathophysiology of Sydenham chorea may lead to improved efforts at prevention and treatment. Preferred drug therapies with minimal side effects must be identified. Finally, controlled research studies that focus on the issue of differential diagnosis may help improve management of this condition.

REFERENCES

Cardoso, F., Vargas, A. P., Cunningham, M. C. Q., Amaral, S. V., Guerra, A. A., & Horizonte, A. (1999). Chorea gravidarum: New lessons from an old disease. *Neurology, 52*(Suppl. 2), A121.

Goldenberg, J., Ferraz, M. B., Fonseca, A. S., Hilario, M. O., Bastos, W., & Sachetti, S. (1992). Sydenham chorea: Clinical and laboratory findings: Analysis of 187 cases (abstract only). *Revista de Paulista Medicina, 110*(4), 152–157.

May, A. C., & Koch, T. (1999). Successful treatment of Sydenham's chorea with intravenous immunoglobulin: Two cases. *Neurology, 52*(Suppl. 2), A42.

Mercadante, M. G. T., Busatto, G. F., Lombroso, P. J., Prado, L., Rosario-Campos, M. C., do Valle, R., Marques-Dias, M. J., Kiss, M. H., Leckman, J. F., & Miguel, E. C. (2000). The psychiatric symptoms of rheumatic fever. *American Journal of Psychiatry, 157*(12), 2036–2038.

National Institute of Neurological Disorders and Stroke. (2000). NINDS Sydenham chorea information page. Retrieved from http://www.ninds.hih/giv/health_and_medical/disorders/sydenham.html

Merck Manual. (2001). *Sydenham's chorea.* Whitehouse Station, NJ: Merck.

Shannon, K. M., & Fenichel, G. M. (1990). Pimozide treatment of Sydenham's chorea. *Neurology, 50,* 186.

Swedo, S. E., Leonard, H. L., Schapiro, M. B., Casey, B. J., Mannheim, G. B., Lenane, M. C., & Rettew, D. C. (1993). Sydenham's chorea: Physical and psychological symptoms of St. Vitus Dance. *Pediatrics, 91*(4), 706–713.

Mary M. Chittooran
Saint Louis University

See also Chorea

STEINERT MYOTONIC DYSTROPHY SYNDROME

Steinert myotonic dystrophy is also known as myotonic dystrophy. It is transmitted via an autosomal dominant inheritance and is the most common form of muscle disease. It is a multisystem disease typically affecting other tissues as well as skeletal and smooth muscles. This disorder can affect the eyes, heart, endocrine system, and central nervous system. Steinert myotonic dystrophy can affect people at any age, but the majority of people are diagnosed by their early 20s.

Steinert myotonic dystrophy has three subtypes. Congenital myotonic dystrophy is the most severe form of the disorder. It is present at birth, and individuals with the congenital form are born to mothers who have myotonic dystrophy (children of fathers who have the disorder are less likely to develop the more severe form of the disorder). Juvenile/adult myotonic dystrophy (also known as classical myotonic dystrophy) generally appears between the ages of 10 and 30 years. Minimal myotonic dystrophy appears at 50 years and above. The symptoms of myotonic dystrophy appear to get more severe, and appear at a younger age, with each successive generation. Steinert myotonic dystrophy affects approximately 1 person in 8,000 worldwide and can be passed on to children of either sex. Thus, males and females can be equally affected.

At the moment there is no cure for Steinert myotonic dystrophy. Problems associated with the disorder are treated individually. For example, surgery is available for cataracts; medication can help counter the effects of myotonia; a specialist can treat heart problems; and ankle and leg braces can help to support muscles as weakness progresses. Remaining active is recommended for everyone with Steinert myotonic dystrophy.

Characteristics

1. Individuals with minimal myotonic dystrophy may have
   - Cataracts, mild myotonia (difficulty relaxing the muscles after they have been contracted), and diabetes mellitus
   - Fully active lives and a normal or minimally shortened life span
2. Classical myotonic dystrophy is evidenced by
   - Myotonia and muscle weakness of the voluntary muscles, starting gradually and progressing slowly (the first muscles to be affected are those of the face, neck, hands, forearms, and feet); muscle stiffness
   - Drooping eyelids and long, expressionless face; difficulty raising head when lying, holding objects firmly, and climbing stairs or getting up from a seated position; shuffling gait
   - Unclear pronunciation of words
   - Cataracts that develop early—as young as 30 years
   - Dysfunction of the heart muscles, causing the individual to experience palpitations or dizzy spells
   - Difficulty swallowing; cold foods may cause some individuals to choke; other digestive problems may include constipation.
   - Premature balding possible in males and thinning of the hair in females
   - Possibly respiratory problems such as infections and shortness of breath
3. Congenital Myotonic Dystrophy is associated with the symptoms of the classical form plus
   - Stillbirth
   - Difficulty breathing, sucking, and/or feeding
   - Weakness in virtually all muscles
   - Slowness and difficulty developing language and motor skills (affected children are usually able to walk, but a progressive myopathy occurs eventually)
   - Mental retardation in 50–60% of the population
   - Potential fatality, especially in the early weeks of life, but a child who lives beyond his or her first birthday is likely to live to become an adult

Students diagnosed with Steinert myotonic dystrophy are eligible for special services under the physical category of the Individuals with Disabilities Education Act of 1997. The extent of modifications will change according to the progression of the disorder. Students with Steinert myotonic dystrophy may benefit from assistive technology (especially as the muscle weakness progresses) and may need to be assigned a nonteaching assistant. Children with developmental delays may require speech therapy. Physiotherapy and occupational therapy are very important ways of improving or maintaining a child's physical condition, as is a program of regular exercise (e.g., swimming). School personnel need to be informed of the disabilities and their effects to be able to accommodate the student in the school. A student with Steinert myotonic dystrophy may need additional psychosocial support to manage the effects of the disorder and live a full life.

Having found the location of the defective gene (Chromosome 19), researchers are now trying to determine the role of the gene. Ultimately, knowledge of the defective gene will allow accurate diagnostic tests and will allow early antenatal diagnosis as well as the possibility for an effective treatment. Other research continues to investigate the problems associated with the disorder and how they can be addressed (e.g., Mammarella et al., 2000).

Help and support for the student, family, friends, and school personnel can be found through support groups such as the Muscular Dystrophy Association, Sunrise Drive, Tucson, AZ 85718; (800) 572-1717.

REFERENCE

Mammarella, A., Paradiso, M., Antonini, G., Paoletti, V., De Matteis, A., Basili, S., Donnarumma, L., Labbadia, G., Di Franco, M., & Musca, A. (2000). Natural history of cardiac involvement in myotonic dystrophy (Steinert's disease): A thirteen year follow-up study. *Advanced Therapeutics, 17*(5), 238–251.

Rachel Toplis
University of Northern Colorado

STEREOTYPY

Stereotypy is a constellation of motor behaviors that can be categorized as a disorder or as a symptom of a disorder. When stereotypic behaviors are severe, a diagnosis of stereotypic movement disorder is appropriate (American Psychiatric Association [APA], 1994). Stereotypic behaviors also are observed as symptoms in autism, mental retardation, and other developmental disorders. Stereotypic behaviors include recurrent and repetitive rocking, hand flapping, eye blinking, head banging, face slapping, biting or sucking body parts, and/or other self injurious behaviors (APA, 1994; Edelson, 1995; Kerr & Nelson, 1998). Theories vary regarding the cause of stereotypic behaviors. One set of theories states that the individual is hyposensitive and requires more sensory input and stimulation. Another set of theories states that the individual is hypersensitive and needs sensory input as a calming device (Edelson, 1995). In this view, the stereotypic behavior helps the person "block-out the overstimulating environment" and focus his or her attention inwardly (Edelson, 1995, p. 1).

Stereotypic behavior is typical in development (Wehmeyer, 1994). Infants display a variety of repetitive motor behaviors such as "foot kicking, body rocking, head rolling, and banging" (Wehmeyer, 1994, p. 34). In usual development, stereotypies peak between 6 and 10 months of age. In developmentally delayed individuals, stereotypies may peak at a later date and occur for a longer duration (Wehmeyer, 1991). Operant learning theory suggests that these behaviors continue atypically due to reinforcement and contingencies in the environment. For atypical stereotypic behaviors, prevalence information is limited. According to the *DSM-IV*, 2–3% of children with mental retardation have stereotypic behaviors (APA, 1994).

Characteristics

1. Recurrent motor behavior
2. Motor behavior with no apparent function
3. Motor behavior that causes bodily injury
4. Motor behavior that interferes with daily routine
5. Symptoms such as rocking, hand flapping, hitting or biting self, mouthing objects, sniffing people, staring at objects, tapping fingers, etc.

(APA, 1994; Edelson, 1995; Kerr and Nelson, 1998)

Treatment for stereotypy can include behavioral interventions. A functional analysis of the child's behavior is the first step to understanding the stereotypic behavior. Research supports the use of differential reinforcement of other activities (DRO) and overcorrection techniques. DRO involves teaching the child alternate behaviors that are incompatible with the stereotypic behavior. While it is helpful in teaching other behaviors, research does not support its use in eliminating stereotypic behaviors (Kerr & Nelson, 1998). In overcorrection the child receives a consequence for engaging in stereotypic behaviors. Overcorrection techniques can involve restitution in which the child corrects "the environmental effects of the inappropriate behavior" (Kazdin, 1994, p. 185) or positive practice in which the appropriate behavior is practiced repeatedly. Overcorrection has been shown to be successful in eliminating stereotypic behaviors (Kerr & Nelson, 1998). Because of the variety of ways the stereotypy can affect children, no one treatment is implemented in all cases.

Special education placement will vary with this disorder. In schools, children who receive services are most likely to be diagnosed with autism, pervasive developmental disorder, mental retardation, or emotional disturbance. Because stereotypy is often a feature of other disorders, it will not typically be the primary diagnosis. For those in need of special education placement, services can vary from behavioral monitoring in the classroom to residential placement. Children who remain in the public school setting often need supplementary aids and services such as speech therapy, occupational and physical therapy, and social–life skills training for the motor abnormalities. Those with milder forms of stereotypy can function well with minimal support.

Stereotypy has no typical age of onset, although some evidence suggests that the behaviors may follow a "stressful environmental event . . . [or] a painful medical condition" (APA, 1994, p. 120). Once stereotypies occur, prognosis is mixed. For some individuals, the behaviors may subside by the end of adolescence. For others, especially those with severe mental retardation, the behaviors may persist (APA, 1994). Future research will need to focus on prognosis as well as the genetic and environmental influences in the onset of the disorder.

REFERENCES

American Psychiatric Association. (1994). *Diagnostic and statistical manual of mental disorders* (4th ed.). Washington, DC: Author.

Edelson, S. M. (1995). Stereotypic (self-stimulatory) behavior. Available from www.autism.org/stim.html

Kazdin, A. E. (1994). *Behavior modification in applied settings* (5th ed.). Pacific Grove, CA: Brooks/Cole Publishing.

Kerr, M. M., & Nelson, C. M. (1998). *Strategies for managing behavior problems in the classroom* (3rd ed.). Upper Saddle River, NJ: Prentice Hall.

Wehmeyer, M. L. (1991). Typical and atypical repetitive motor behaviors of young children at risk for severe mental retardation. *American Journal of Mental Retardation, 96,* 53–63.

Wehmeyer, M. L. (1994). Factors related to the expression of typical and atypical repetitive movements of young children with intellectual disability. *International Journal of Disability, Development, and Education, 41*(1), 33–49.

Carrie George
Texas A&M University

STEROID ABUSE

Anabolic-androgenic steroids, better known as simply anabolic steroids, are artificial or synthetic drugs that mimic the effects of testosterone, the male sex hormone. Anabolic steroids are used medicinally to help rebuild tissues that have become weak because of serious injury, illness, or continuing infections. They are also used to treat some types of anemia, to treat certain kinds of breast cancer, and to treat hereditary angiodema, a disorder that causes swelling in the arms, legs, face, windpipe, or sexual organs (WebMD Health, 2000).

In addition to medicinal uses, anabolic steroids have been taken by athletes to build muscle size and boost athletic performance since the 1950s. Increasingly, other segments of the population, including adolescents, have also begun using anabolic steroids (National Institute on Drug

Abuse, 2001b). Some youths use steroids in an attempt to reduce body fat or build muscles, whereas others abuse them as part of a pattern of high-risk behaviors (National Institute on Drug Abuse, 2001a).

Steroids are used in several ways. Some are taken orally; others are injected intramuscularly; and a few are contained in creams and gels that are rubbed into the skin (National Institute on Drug Abuse, 2001a). Most users use a combination of oral and injectable forms, a practice known as stacking. Users stack the drugs because it is widely believed that this practice results in a greater effect than when the drugs are used individually, a theory without scientific support. Another common practice is pyramiding. This involves taking the drugs in 6- to 12-week cycles and slowly increasing doses over the course of the cycle. Drugs are taken in this fashion in an effort to allow the body to adjust to the drug and to decrease toxic side effects. As with stacking, these benefits have not been substantiated scientifically (American Academy of Pediatrics, 1997).

Anabolic steroid abuse is increasing among adolescents, and most rapidly among females, although use is still much more common in males. Rate of lifetime use among high school students in this country varies between 4% and 12% for males and 0.5% and 2% for females, depending on grade level (Bahrke, Yesalis, & Brower, 1998). Since 1991, steroid use has increased by 50% among 8th and 10th graders and by 38% among 12th graders (National Institute on Drug Abuse, 2001b).

Research indicates that there are generally few significant side effects associated with the low-dose, intermittent-use patterns typical of most adolescents (Rogol & Tesalis, 1992). However, there are a number of adverse side effects that result from higher doses and more prolonged use of anabolic steroids.

Characteristics

Short-Term Effects

1. Euphoria
2. Acne and other skin changes
3. Increased energy and diminished fatigue
4. Irritability
5. Increased aggressiveness
6. Changes in libido
7. Impotence
8. Distractibility and confusion
9. Mood swings

Long-Term Effects

1. Liver damage and dysfunction
2. Potentially permanent damage to the heart and kidneys
3. Premature closing of the epiphyseal growth plate in children and adolescents, resulting in shorter adult height
4. Hypertension
5. Extremely aggressive and violent behavior known as "roid rage"
6. Male pattern baldness in both sexes
7. Reduced sperm production, shrinking of the testicles, and irreversible breast enlargement in males
8. Masculine characteristics such as deepening of the voice and excessive body hair, as well as decreased breast size and menstrual irregularities in females

In addition to the adverse effects associated with steroid use, there are also a number of deleterious consequences that can result when anabolic steroid use is discontinued. These include fatigue, restlessness, mood swings, insomnia, headache, muscle and joint pain, and depressed mood and suicidal ideation (National Institute on Drug Abuse, 2001b).

Research evaluating the effectiveness of anabolic steroids in producing desired effects such as increases in muscle mass and strength have yielded mixed results. Factors such as previous strength training, continued strength training, and adequate dietary protein intake appear to impact steroid efficacy (see Hough, 1990, for a review).

Very few studies examining treatment for anabolic steroid abuse have been conducted. Thus, much of the current knowledge in this area is based on anecdotal evidence from physicians working with individual abusers experiencing withdrawal. For many users, medications designed to restore the hormonal system can be helpful, as can medications that target specific withdrawal symptoms, such as antidepressants and analgesics. In some cases, supportive therapy is sufficient. For severe or prolonged withdrawal symptoms, medications or hospitalization may be necessary (National Institute on Drug Abuse, 2001a).

The key to addressing steroid use and abuse lies in preventive efforts. Historically, efforts have focused on drug testing and educating students about the adverse effects of taking steroids. Research suggests that simply teaching youth about the negative side effects does not result in the internalization of the information, nor does it discourage future use. Presenting both the risks and benefits of steroid use to young people tends to be perceived as more credible, but still does not discourage use. More comprehensive approaches to prevention show greater promise. Effective programs include information related to potential effects of steroids, training on how to refuse offers of drugs, instruction regarding building muscle with strength training and proper nutrition, and proper weight training (National Institute on Drug Abuse, 2001b). Future research efforts are focusing on developing more effective treatment and intervention programs.

REFERENCES

American Academy of Pediatrics. (1997). Adolescents and anabolic steroids: A subjective review. Retrieved from www.medem.com/MedLB/article_detaillb.cfm?article_ID=ZZZPJP4M08C&sub_cat=23

Bahrke, M. S., Yesalis, C. E., & Brower, K. J. (1998). Anabolic-androgenic steroid abuse and performance enhancing drugs among adolescents. *Child and Adolescent Clinics of North America, 7,* 821–838.

Hough, D. O. (1990). Anabolic steroids andergogenic aids. *American Family Physician, 41*(4), 1157–1164.

National Institute on Drug Abuse. (2001a). Anabolic steroid abuse. Retrieved from http://www.nida.nih.gov/ResearchReports/Steroids/anabolicsteroids3.html#why

National Institute on Drug Abuse. (2001b). Anabolic steroids: Community drug alert bulletin. Retrieved from http://www.nida.nih.gov/SteroidAlert/SteroidAlert.html

Rogol, A. D., & Tesalis, C. E., III. (1992). Anabolic-androgenic steroids and the adolescent. *Pediatric Annals, 21*(3), 175–188.

WebMD Health. (2000). Anabolic steroids (systemic). Retrieved from http://mywebmd.com/content/asset/uspdi.202035

M. Franci Crepeau-Hobson
University of Northern Colorado

STICKLER SYNDROME (HEREDITARY ARTHRO-OPHTHALMOPATHY)

Stickler syndrome is a connective tissue disorder that affects vision, hearing, joints, craniofacies, and the heart. This progressive condition is inherited as an autosomal dominant trait and is estimated to affect 1 in 10,000 people, although it is one of the rarest to be diagnosed (B. Houchin, 1994).

Characteristics

1. Sight problems including retinal detachment, myopia, cataracts, and glaucoma
2. Hearing loss and deafness in extreme cases
3. Bone and joint problems such as early-onset arthritis, joint pain and hyperextensibility, spine curvature, and abnormality to the ends of long bones
4. Flat face, cleft palate, submucous or high arched palate, and micrognathia
5. Occasional mitral valve prolapse (MVP)

Treatment of Stickler syndrome involves a multidisciplinary approach. Eye examinations should be held regularly with an eye doctor familiar with the syndrome because treatment for cataracts, detached retinas, and glaucoma is more effective with early identification (B. Houchin, 1994). Baseline hearing should also be assessed regularly to monitor hearing loss.

Rheumatological assessment and follow-up is advised for older patients who may benefit from physiotherapy for arthropathy. Presently, no prophylactic therapies exist to lessen joint damage. Treatment for mild spondyloepiphyseal dysplasia includes over-the-counter anti-inflammatory medications both before and after physical activity (Robin & Warman, 2000). Support of the joints is also recommended.

For cleft palate and craniofacial abnormality, otolaryngology, plastic surgery, oral and maxillofacial surgery, pediatric dentistry, and orthodontics are possible treatments (Robin & Warman, 2000).

Screenings for mitral valve prolapse should also be implemented, especially with complaints of chest pain or episodic tachycardia.

Although children with Stickler syndrome are typically of normal intelligence, hearing and visual impairments may lead to learning disabilities (Stickler Syndrome Support Group, 2000). Special education services under Learning Disabled or Other Health Impairment may be needed for the child. Another educational consideration is the removal of the child from contact sports or rigorous physical activity that may displace the retina or damage the joints (Robin & Warman, 2000).

The diagnostic criteria for Stickler syndrome are soon to be published. Longevity is not affected, and prognosis depends on which gene is mutated and on preventative medical care that can properly diagnose this syndrome (P. Houchin, 2000).

REFERENCES

Houchin, B. (1994). Stickler syndrome. Retrieved from http://www.stickler.org/sip/def.html

Houchin, P. (2000). Stickler syndrome. Retrieved from sip@sticklers.org

Robin, N. H., & Warman, M. L. (2000, June 8). Stickler syndrome. Retrieved from http://www.geneclinics.org/profiles/stickler/details.html

Stickler Syndrome Support Group. (2000). About Stickler syndrome. Retrieved from http://www.stickler.org.uk/info.htm

Teresa M. Lyle
University of Texas at Austin

STIMULANT ABUSE

Stimulant abuse can include a broad category of substances from amphetamines to caffeine that are taken to increase mental activity, offset drowsiness and fatigue, improve athletic performance, curb appetite, and reduce symptoms of depression (A. M. Pagliaro & Pagliaro, 1996). Amphetamines and their derivatives are chemically produced central nervous system (CNS) stimulants that are also commonly used for the treatment of ADHD (e.g., Ritalin; L. A. Pagliaro, 1992). Other forms of stimulants include cocaine, crack (a chemically produced form of cocaine), and crystal meth or "ice," as well as legal substances such as caffeine and nicotine (for persons 18 and older). Of recent concern is the increase among adolescents abusing Ritalin (street named Vitamin R, R-ball, or smart drug). Stimulants can be ingested in tablet or liquid form, smoked, inhaled (snorted), or injected into the blood stream.

As with many other illicit drugs, amphetamines made a comeback in the early 1990s. Use peaked for 8th- and 10th-grade students by 1996 and has gradually continued to decline in these two age groups (Johnston, O'Malley, & Bachman, 1999). The lifetime prevalence use of amphetamines for 12th-grade students continues to hover around 16%. The rates for other forms of stimulants such as cocaine and crack has continued to rise slightly, with a 1999 lifetime prevalence rate for 12th-grade students at 9.8% and 4.6%, respectively. These data do not include nicotine or prescribed drugs such as Ritalin. The *Monitoring the Future* study (Johnston et al., 1999) suggests that Ritalin abuse has risen from 1% to 2.8% in the last five years. Approximately 3 million children and adolescents in the United States regularly use nicotine (Accessibility of cigarettes, 1992).

Characteristics (listed in order from low to high doses; adapted from A. M. Pagliaro & Pagliaro, 1996)

1. Dilation of pupils; decreased appetite; increased blood pressure, heart rate, and respiratory rate
2. Increased mood, sociability, and initiative; improved concentration and "clearer" thinking; increased wakefulness and alertness; decreased boredom
3. Heart palpitation, chest pain, tremor, nausea, headache, dizziness, insomnia, blurred vision, constipation or diarrhea, urinary retention
4. Depersonalization, restlessness, anxiety, confusion, irritation, inability to concentrate
5. Automatic jerking movements; stereotyped, repetitive acts
6. Severe paranoid psychosis, fear, hallucinations, delusions, self-consciousness

Prevention programs that address social influences and teach children and adolescents to resist societal pressures have demonstrated the most effectiveness in preventing or decreasing use of selected substances, although no program has demonstrated widespread, long-lasting effectiveness (A. M. Pagliaro & Pagliaro, 1996). Cognitive therapy directed at modifying irrational belief systems and deficient coping skills is the most commonly used form of psychotherapy in the treatment of problematic patterns of substance abuse among children and adolescents (A. M. Pagliaro & Pagliaro, 1996). Recovery support groups also appear to be effective adjuncts to behavioral interventions that can lead to long-term recovery. Unfortunately, the rate of relapse following successful treatment is quite high (A. M. Pagliaro & Pagliaro, 1996).

Other than the transdermal nicotine patches and chewing gum widely used as adjuncts to smoking cessation programs (A. M. Pagliaro & Pagliaro, 1996), there are currently no pharmacological treatments for dependence on stimulants. However, medications are sometimes used to treat the side effects of overdose or withdrawal (e.g., antidepressants to combat depressive symptoms sometimes found in those who stop using). The research literature consistently supports the need to use a variety of treatment approaches that are tailored to meet the individual needs of young substance abusers (A. M. Pagliaro & Pagliaro, 1996).

From an educational perspective, substance abuse is clearly associated with decreased academic performance, higher absenteeism, and lower school completion rates (A. M. Pagliaro & Pagliaro, 1996). In addition to these concerns, studies have reported significant residual memory impairment among former cocaine users (e.g., Mittenberg & Motta, 1993). Furthermore, learning among students with ADHD may be adversely affected by the medication commonly prescribed for the treatment of the disorder (Swanson, Cantwell, Lerner, McBurnett, & Hanna, 1991).

To develop the most effective treatment strategies for treating substance abuse in younger populations, further research outlining those approaches that have succeeded with particular groups as well as those that have failed is needed (A. M. Pagliaro & Pagliaro, 1996). Given recent trends in Ritalin abuse, it is important for teachers and schools to be on alert for students selling their medication to others, and it is recommended that schools adopt and enforce policies regarding the use and dispensing of medication (Musser et al., 1998).

REFERENCES

Accessibility of cigarettes to youths aged 12–17 years—U.S., 1989. (1992). *Annals of Pharmacotherapy, 26,* 133–148.

Johnston, L. D., O'Malley, P. M., & Bachman, J. G. (1999). *National survey results on drug use from the Monitoring the Future study, 1975–1998: Vol.. 1. Secondary school students* (NIH Publication No. 99-4660). Bethesda, MD: National Institute on Drug Abuse.

Mittenburg, W., & Motta, S. (1993). Effects of chronic cocaine abuse on memory and learning. *Archives of Clinical Neuropsychology, 8,* 477–483.

Musser, C. J., Ahman, P. A., Theye, F. W., Mundt, P., Broste, S. K., & Mueller-Rizner, N. (1998). Stimulant use and the potential for abuse in Wisconsin as reported by school administrators and longitudinally followed children. *Journal of Developmental and Behavioral Pediatrics, 19*(3), 187–192.

Pagliaro, A. M., & Pagliaro, L. B. (1996). *Substance use among children and adolescents.* New York: Wiley.

Pagliaro, L. A. (1992). The straight dope: Focus on learning—Interpreting the interpretations. *Psychopsis, 14*(2), 8.

Swanson, J., Cantwell, D., Lerner, M., McBurnett, K., & Hanna, G. (1991). Effects of stimulant medication on learning in children with ADHD. *Journal of Learning Disabilities, 24,* 219–230.

Robyn S. Hess
University of Colorado at Denver

STURGE-WEBER SYNDROME

Sturge-Weber syndrome is a rare, congenital, and progressive condition that affects the blood vessels in the skin and the brain. Characteristically, a large pink to purple hemangioma (a birthmark caused by abnormal distribution of blood vessels) extends over one side of the face, including the eye and neck, and is often disfiguring when there is a growth of connective tissue. The facial angioma is usually unilateral but may extend to the other side and conforms largely but not strictly to trigeminal nerve subdivisions (Wyngaarden & Smith, 1988). A similar malformation of blood vessels in the brain may cause some degree of weakness on the opposite side of the body, glaucoma, and epilepsy. This condition develops during embryonic development.

The cause of Sturge-Weber syndrome is unknown, and risk factors have not yet been recognized. The incidence is about 5 in 100,000 births (Wyngaarden & Smith, 1988), and it occurs equally in both sexes. The incidence of Sturge-Weber syndrome is thought to be 8–15% in live births with an associated port-wine stain. Neurologic disorders are also prominent in patients with Sturge-Weber syndrome, and up to 89% of these patients will have seizures that are controllable with medical therapy in only 50% of cases. A smaller proportion of children with Sturge-Weber syndrome (6%) will develop hemiparesis and hemiplegia.

Characteristics

1. Facial port-wine stain
2. Convulsions (seizure disorder) beginning during the first year and worsening with age
3. Visual problems (hemianopsia)
4. Paralysis (hemiparesis-paralysis on one side)
5. Learning disabilities
6. Developmental delays of motor skills

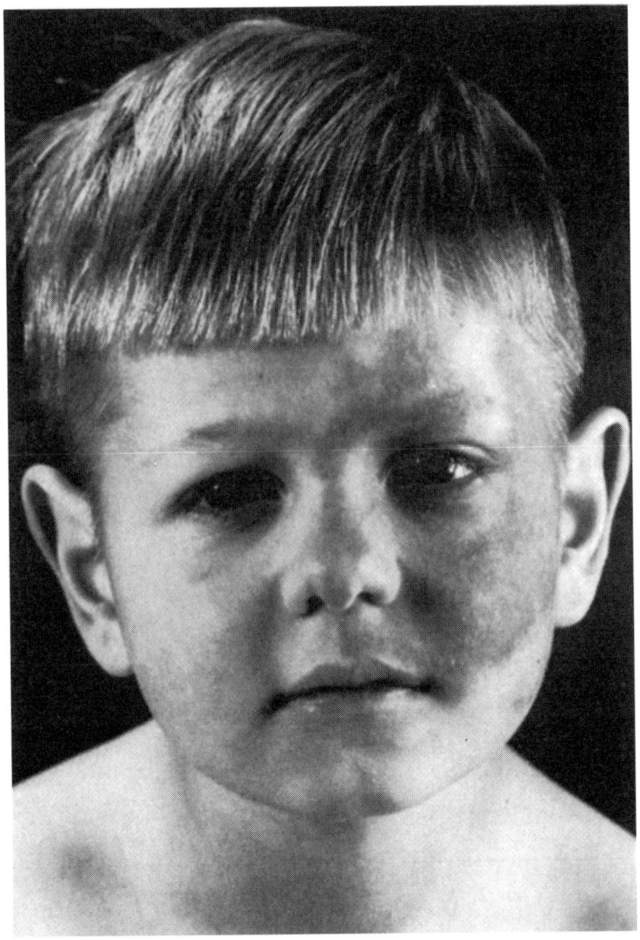

Sturge-Weber Syndrome
Reprinted from *Clinical Syndromes,* Wiedemann and Kunze, 1997, by permission of the publisher Mosby

Treatment for Sturge-Weber syndrome is symptomatic. Laser treatment is available to lighten or remove port-wine stains. Anticonvulsant medications may be used to control seizures. Paralysis or weakness is treated with appropriate physical therapy. Surgery or eyedrops may be prescribed to control glaucoma. Regular ophthalmologic examinations at 6- to 12-month intervals are recommended. Skull X rays taken after the first 2 years of life usually reveal gyriform ("tramline") intracranial calcification, especially in the occipitoparietal region, due to mineral deposition in the cortex beneath the intracranial angioma (Tierney, McPhee, Papadakis, 1997). Surgical treatment of the intracranial lesion is sometimes successful in reducing seizures.

Special education services, genetic counseling, and physical therapy may benefit patients and their families because progressive mental retardation occurs in 50% of cases, along with learning disabilities—both of which require appropriate school intervention.

Although Sturge-Weber-related seizures can sometimes

place patients in potentially life-threatening situations, the disease itself is not fatal. Most cases of Sturge-Weber are mild, and life expectancy is normal.

REFERENCES

Tierney, L. M., Jr., McPhee, S. J., & Papadakis, M. A. (1998). *Current medical diagnosis and treatment* (37th ed.). Stamford, CT: Appleton & Lange.

Wyngaarden, J. B., & Smith, L. H., Jr. (1988). *Cecil textbook of medicine* (18th ed.). Philadelphia: W. B. Saunders.

Karen Wiley
University of Northern Colorado

STUTTERING

Stuttering is a speech fluency disorder characterized by disruption of the normal flow of speech with frequent repetitions or prolongations of speech sounds, syllables, or words, or by an individual's inability to start a word (National Institute on Deafness and Other Communication Disorders [NIDCD], 1997). Other facial tremors or movements may also be present as the individual attempts to speak. Stuttering may be exacerbated by specific situations such as speaking on the telephone or in front of the group of people. In contrast, speech fluency may improve when singing or speaking aloud. The onset of the disorder may be sudden or gradual.

Stuttering is a disorder distinct from two other speech fluency disorders, cluttering and spasmodic dysphonia. Cluttering is characterized by excessive interruptions of the flow of speech due to disorganized speech planning, talking too fast, or a lack of awareness of what one wants to say. The voice disorder, spasmodic dysphonia, involves interruption of phonation due to overadduction of the vocal folds. Other speech problems, such as cluttering and disordered phonology, may occur with stuttering and should be evaluated.

The etiology of stuttering may be genetic, although the specific cause is unknown; nor has a specific gene for stuttering been identified (NIDCD, 1997). It is known that stuttering may run in families as a heritable disorder. Three types of stuttering have been identified: developmental, neurogenic, and psychogenic. Stuttering may be a developmental process that reflects the inability of the child's speech and language skills to meet the verbal demands. Specifically, the individual may be trying to access the word that he or she wants to speak. Stuttering may also be an exacerbation of the dysfluency that is a normal part of speech development.

Neurogenic stuttering reflects miscommunications between the brain and nerves or muscles. Components of the speech process are not effectively coordinated. This type of problem may be related to a brain injury, such as an accident or stroke.

The final type of stuttering reflects only a small percentage of those who stutter and involves psychogenic causes. This type of stuttering may be present in individuals with mental illness for those suffering severe stress. Most individuals who stutter do not have greater emotional pathology than those who do not stutter (Dejoy, 1998).

According to the NIDCD (1997), over 3 million Americans stutter. Although individuals of all ages may be affected, the disorder is more common in children between the ages of 2 and 6, as well as in boys. Fewer than 1% of adults are believed to stutter.

Characteristics

1. Frequent sound or syllable repetition
2. Prolongations of sounds
3. Tremors around the mouth or jaw during speech
4. Rise in pitch or loudness during the prolongation of sounds
5. Tension and struggle or look of fear while speaking
6. Avoidance or delay in speaking

There is no formal cure for stuttering, but a variety of treatments are available to improve speech fluency. Evaluation and possible intervention by a speech therapist are suggested for children who stutter for more than six months. When stuttering is determined to be developmental in nature, recommendations are often aimed at assisting parents and modifying the environment and interactions relating to communication. Programs have been developed to assist individuals in relearning speaking skills and addressing emotional factors that may arise from the stuttering problem.

Interventions are also available in the form of medication or electronic devices. However, the usefulness of such interventions has not been clearly demonstrated (NIDCD, 1999). The majority of children who stutter (75%) will improve by young adulthood. Many children improve spontaneously within the first year of onset.

Children may stutter for a period of time and then outgrow the problem. Special education services are unlikely to be provided when stuttering is a transient problem. Conversely, for children whose stuttering persists for more than six months, an evaluation by a speech-language therapist and consideration of possible treatment may be warranted. Children whose stuttering negatively impacts their educational performance may be eligible to receive special education services under the category of Speech and Language Impairment (SLI). School psychologists sometimes help with relaxation training, social skill development, and self-esteem building.

The prognosis for a child who stutters is generally quite good. As noted, many children develop fluent speech spontaneously without treatment, and others show improvement following direct or indirect interventions developed by a speech-language therapist (Stuttering Foundation of America [SFA], n.d.). For the few individuals who continue to stutter into adulthood, speech therapists may offer continued assistance in improving functional communication skills, although they will not cure the problem (SFA, n.d.).

Researchers are investigating the causes of stuttering, as well as new interventions. Geneticists are searching for the specific gene that causes hereditary stuttering. Brain imaging studies are underway to examine the functional organization of the brains of individuals who stutter.

REFERENCES

Dejoy, D. A. (1998). Current facts and myths about stuttering. In A. De Fao (Ed.), *Parent articles II: More articles to enhance parent involvement* (pp. 61–62). San Antonio, TX: Communication Skill Builders.

National Institute on Deafness and Other Communication Disorders. (1997, August). Health information, voice, speech, and language: Stuttering. Retrieved from http://www.nidcd.nih.gov/health/pubs_vdi/stutter.htm

Stuttering Foundation of America. (n.d.). Turning onto therapy (Publication No. 22). Retrieved from http://www.stuttersfa.org

Shelley F. Pelletler
Jennifer L. Nicholls
Dysart Unified School District
El Mirage, Arizona

SUBACUTE SCLEROSING PANENCEPHALITIS

Subacute sclerosing panencephalitis (SSPE), or Dawson encephalitis, is a progressive, usually fatal neurological disorder typically affecting only children and adolescents. SSPE causes intellectual deterioration, convulsive seizures, and motor abnormalities.

SSPE tends to occur several years after contracting the measles (rubella) virus. Often, the victims and their families are unaware of the dangers of SSPE, as the child has the appearance of completely recovering from the measles infection. Initial symptoms are subtle and insidious (Pediatric Database, 2000). Parents often will not recognize that a child is suffering from this neurological disorder because the physical symptoms of SSPE are few until the disease is advanced.

Characteristics

Initial Stage

1. Diminished performance in schoolwork (often due to forgetfulness, distractibility, and sleeplessness)
2. Bizarre behavior (aggression, changes in speech, hallucinations
3. Myoclonic jerking (muscle spasms)

Intermediate Stage

1. Seizures
2. Dementia
3. Difficulty swallowing
4. Optic changes including papilledema (swelling of the optic nerve), cortical atrophy, and retinopathy (blindness)
5. Rigidity of body musculature

Final Phase

1. Hypothalamic complications such as hyperthermia (elevated temperature), diaphoresis (excessive sweating), and irregular pulse
2. Coma
3. Death

The diagnosis of SSPE is confirmed by electroencephalogram (EEG), elevated globulin levels, and excessive quantity of measles virus antibody in the serum and spinal fluid (Beers & Berkow, 1999). Brain imaging studies have been conducted of patients with SSPE through computerized tomography (CT) and magnetic resonance imaging (MRI). These studies have revealed cortical atrophy and ventricular enlargement in the brain as a result of SSPE (Pediatric Database, 2000; Sawaishi, Abe, Yano, Ishikawa, & Takada, 1999).

SSPE occurs worldwide, and especially in impoverished regions where immunizations are not readily available. However, the incidence of this disease has dramatically decreased in the United States and Western Europe following the implementation of widespread measles immunization programs. It is estimated that SSPE occurs in about 6–22 per million cases of measles infections and is lower in vaccinated individuals, at about 1 case per million (Beers & Berkow, 1999). SSPE tends to affect more males than females (2:1) and generally occurs in children and adolescents.

A risk factor for developing SSPE is the contraction of the measles infection before 1 year of age. The risk of SSPE is 16 times greater for children who are 1 year or younger than for children over 5 years old due to increased susceptibility to viral infection, immaturity of the brain, and increased danger of contracting another concurrent viral infection (Sawaishi et al., 1999).

Fatality is usually the end result of SSPE, often because of terminal bronchial pneumonia that is contracted due to the patient's weakened immune system. Affected individuals generally succumb 1 to 3 years after diagnosis, but some may survive for longer periods. There have been rare incidents of some patients having remission of SSPE (Beers & Berkow, 1999).

No specific therapy currently exists for SSPE. Supportive therapy is indicated as symptoms appear. Treatment with inosiplex (an antiviral drug) has been tried, but results are pending. Generally, only symptomatic treatment with anticonvulsants and supportive measures can be offered (Beers & Berkow, 1999).

Immunization against measles is the only known prevention for SSPE. Children are recommended to have received immunization for measles, mumps, and rubella by 15 months of age (Harrington, 1998). Caretakers are urged to contact their healthcare provider or local health clinic if their child has not completed his or her scheduled immunizations. Children who are experiencing symptoms of SSPE and who have been infected with measles or who have not been immunized against measles should be brought to medical attention immediately due to the danger of contracting SSPE.

REFERENCES

Beers, M. H., & Berkow, R. (Eds.). (1999). *Merck manual of diagnosis and therapy* (17th ed.). Whitehouse Station, NJ: Merck.

Harrington, R. G. (1998). Communicable disease in childhood: A guide for parents. In A. Canter & S. A. Carroll (Eds.), *Helping children at home and school: Handouts from your school psychologist.* Bethesda, MD: National Association of School Psychologists.

Pediatric Database. (2000, December 21). Subacute sclerosing panencephalitis: Retrieved from http://www.icondata.com/health/pedbase/files/subacute.htm

Sawaishi, Y., Abe, T., Yano, T., Ishikawa, K., & Takada, G. (1999). SSPE following neonatal measles infection. *Pediatric Neurology, 20*(1), 63–65.

ANDREA HOLLAND
University of Texas at Austin

SUDDEN INFANT DEATH SYNDROME

Sudden infant death syndrome (SIDS) is defined as the sudden death of an infant under 1 year of age that remains unexplained after a thorough investigation, which includes performance of an autopsy, examination of the death scene, and a review of the victim and family case history (National Institute of Child Health and Human Development [NICHD], 1997).

SIDS is the leading cause of death in infants between 1 month and 1 year of age. The majority of deaths due to SIDS occur by the end of the 6th month, with a peak incidence between 2 and 4 months of age (SIDS Network, 1993). The prevalence of SIDS in the United States has progressively declined from 1.2 per 1,000 live births in 1992 to 0.74 in 1,000 live births in 1996 (Burnett, 2000). SIDS occurs in all ethnicities and at all socioeconomic levels. However, Native American infants are approximately three times more likely to die of SIDS than are Caucasian infants, and African American infants are two to three times more susceptible to SIDS than Caucasian infants (NICHD, 1997). There also is a higher incidence of SIDS for low birth weight and premature infants (NICHD, 1997). Additionally, 60–70% of SIDS victims are males, and 65% of SIDS deaths occur in autumn and winter (Burnett, 2000).

Characteristics

1. Occurs between 1 month and 1 year of age
2. Has no known cause and is currently unpredictable
3. Infant appears to be healthy prior to death
4. Death occurs very quickly, usually during sleep and with no signs of suffering
5. Causes intense grief for parents and families

(Based on information cited in SIDS Network, 1993)

Because of the currently unpredictable and unpreventable nature of SIDS, the focus has turned to risk-factor intervention. Numerous environmental and behavioral influences appear to place an infant at higher risk of dying from SIDS. For example, studies have revealed that infants who were placed to sleep on their stomachs were at a greater risk for SIDS. Therefore, caregivers can eliminate this risk factor by placing infants on their backs or sides when they go to sleep (NICHD, 1997). Other recommendations include good prenatal care; avoiding exposure of the baby to smoke, drugs, or alcohol both during pregnancy and after the birth; using firm bedding materials; avoiding overdressing the baby; taking the infant to regular well baby checkups; and breast-feeding the baby (NICHD, 1997). However, following these recommendations does not necessarily prevent death from SIDS.

When an infant dies from SIDS, this can elicit intense emotional reactions from the parents and family. The inability to explain the infant's death may provoke self-questioning and self-blaming by parents and other caregivers (Carroll & Siska, 1998). Normal reactions include guilt, anger, and grief. In addition, high rates of anxiety and depression have been found in mothers of SIDS victims (Boyle, 1997), and low income and less education have been linked to more prolonged distress (Murray & Terry, 1999). Given the detrimental effects of losing a child or a family member to SIDS, it is imperative that emphasis be placed on providing these families with information, counseling, and support. To illustrate, parent support groups are widely available, and early participation may help promote effective communication and decrease the isolation that these families feel (DeFrain, Taylor, & Ernst, 1982). Additionally, the family may benefit from individual, marital, or family counseling.

The siblings of the SIDS victim also will be significantly affected by the death of the infant. Care should be taken when informing children of the baby's death. It is recommended that parents explain the death as a result of a physical failure in the infant's body and reassure their children that this will not happen to them (DeFrain et al., 1982). Children may feel guilty and upset about their sibling's death but may not show their feelings in obvious ways (NICHD, 1997). If the child is disturbed by the death, he or she may have academic or social difficulties in school. Early identification of the child's maladjustment may be aided by considering other signs, such as bed wetting, nightmares, misbehaving, and clinging to parents (NICHD, 1997).

Future research should explore the effects of support groups and counseling on the recovery of families who have lost a baby to SIDS. Additionally, subsequent studies should examine how families of SIDS victims might be affected when they do not seek social support. Future research should focus also on the etiology and prevention of SIDS.

REFERENCES

Boyle, F. M. (1997). *Mothers bereaved by stillbirth, neonatal death or sudden infant death syndrome.* Aldershot, England: Ashgate.

Burnett, L. B. (2000, September 8). Pediatrics, sudden infant death syndrome. Retrieved September 27, 2000, from http://www.emedicine.com/emerg/topic407.htm

Carroll, J. L., & Siska, E. S. (1998, April 1). SIDS: Counseling parents to reduce the risk. Retrieved September 19, 2000, from http://www.aafp.org/afp/980401ap/carroll.html

DeFrain, J., Taylor, J., & Ernst, L. (1982). *Coping with sudden infant death.* Lexington, MA: Lexington Books.

Murray, J. A., & Terry, D. J. (1999). Parental reactions to infant death: The effects of resources and coping strategies. *Journal of Social and Clinical Psychology, 18,* 341–369.

National Institute of Child Health and Human Development. (1997, April). Fact sheet: Sudden infant death syndrome. Retrieved September 27, 2000, from http://www.nichd.nih.gov/sids/sids_fact.htm

SIDS Network. (1993). What is SIDS? Retrieved September 19, 2000, from http://www.sids-network.org/sidsfact.htm

Eve N. Rosenthal
Karla Anhalt
Texas A&M University

SUICIDAL IDEATION

Suicidal ideation describes destructive thoughts and plans about dying. All people may occasionally experience such thoughts, but in a suicidal person they are uncontrollable and chronic. Suicide can be seen as the final step on a path that begins with suicide ideation and proceeds to planning, threatening, attempting, and completing suicide (Barrios, Everett, Simon, & Brener, 2000). Some young people make suicide attempts impulsively but more initially have suicidal thoughts. Although many more youth engage in suicide ideation than actually commit suicide, suicide is a leading cause of death in that age group. The 1999 national Youth Risk Behavior Surveillance System (YRBSS) survey (Kann et al., 2000) found that in the United States, approximately 75% of all deaths among those 10–24 years of age owed to motor-vehicle accidents, other accidents, homicide, and suicide. Of the respondents, 7.8% reported at least one suicide attempt during the 12 preceding months.

Characteristics

1. Chronic feelings of sadness and hopelessness that interfere with daily activities
2. Chronic and uncontrollable thoughts about one's own death
3. Has made specific suicide plan

Overall, during the 12 months preceding the YRBSS survey, (a) 28.3% of students felt so sad or hopeless for two or more consecutive weeks that they stopped some usual activities; (b) 19.3% seriously considered suicide; (c) 14.5% made a specific suicide plan; (d) 8.3% attempted suicide at least once; and (e) 2.6% made a suicide attempt that had to be treated medically. Generally, incidence in all categories except for the last was higher in female students than in male students across racial-ethnic and grade subpopulations. Racial-ethnic differences also appeared, with incidence higher in Hispanic students than in Blacks, and higher in Black students than Whites (Kann et al., 2000).

Suicidal ideation predicts not only suicide attempts in both high school and college students, but also other risk-taking behaviors including not using seat belts as driver or passenger, driving after drinking alcohol, carrying weapons, and engaging in physical fights. Additionally, suggestive relationships exist between suicide ideation and playing with firecrackers, pointing a gun at someone, accepting dares, and behaving in a way that leads police to shoot at them. Suicide ideation may also be related to using drugs (tobacco, alcohol, and others) and engaging in unprotected sex (Barrios et al., 2000).

Across age, risk conditions for suicide attempts include depression (particularly with signs of hopelessness), substance abuse (particularly alcohol), schizophrenia, panic disorder, and borderline personality disorder. Additional risk conditions in adolescents are impulsive, aggressive, and antisocial behavior and history of family violence and disruption. Probability of an attempt increases with the number of conditions shown and with occurrence of a stressful event (Gliatto & Rai, 1999).

Treatment for individuals either directly manifesting suicidal ideology or a number of the above conditions initially involves detailed interviews, initially directed toward determining whether suicidal ideology has occurred, and if so, in what detail. The following is summarized from Gliatto and Rai (1999), who presented detailed information on steps in diagnosis and treatment options for potentially suicidal patients. A patient who has a specific plan, has access to the means to carry out the plan, and has suffered recent stressors should be hospitalized immediately—involuntarily if necessary. Confidentiality can be legally breached if a patient at serious risk for harming himself or herself refuses permission for the therapist to contact anyone, and family members should be informed of hospitalization. The patient should not be left alone until placed in a secure environment. Depending on the seriousness of the suicidal ideation and the number of accompanying conditions, either inpatient or outpatient treatment may be appropriate. For patients who show minimal levels of ideation, have no specific plan, are not intoxicated or showing pathological behavior, and have not previously attempted suicide, signing a "no-harm contract" may be sufficient. In the contract, the patient agrees not to harm himself or herself for a specific and brief time, generally one or two days, and to contact the therapist if anything changes. Frequent direct or telephone follow-up is necessary, as is renewal of the contract as it expires.

The National Center for Injury Prevention and Control is focusing on science-based prevention strategies to reduce injuries and deaths from suicide. Suicide prevention programs are available for adolescents and young adults (Centers for Disease Control and Prevention, 1994). School and community gatekeeper training helps school staff, community members, and clinical health care providers to identify and refer students at risk for suicide. Suicide education teaches students about suicide, warning signs, and how to seek help. Screening programs use questionnaires to identify those at high risk. Crisis centers and hotlines provide telephone counseling for suicidal persons. Intervention after a suicide focuses on friends and relatives of persons who have committed suicide in part to help to prevent suicide contagion.

REFERENCES

Barrios, L. C., Everett, S. A., Simon, T. R., & Brener, N. D. (2000). Suicide ideation among US college students. *Journal of American College Health, 48,* 229–234.

Centers for Disease Control and Prevention. (1994). Programs for the prevention of suicide among adolescents and young adults; and suicide contagion and the reporting of suicide: Recommendations from a national workshop. *Morbidity and Mortality Weekly Report (MMWR). 43*(No. RR-6), 1–23.

Gliatto, M. F., & Rai, A. K. (1999). Evaluation and treatment of patients with suicidal ideation. *American Family Physician, 59,* 1500–1507.

Kann, L., Kinchen, S. A., Williams, B. I., Ross, J. G., Lowry, R., Grunbaum, J. A., Kolbe, L. J., & State and Local YRBSS Coordinators. (2000, June 9). Youth Risk Behavior Surveillance—United States, 1999. *Morbidity and Mortality Weekly Report, 49/SS05,* 1–96. Retrieved from http://www.cdc.gov

Amy Sessoms
Robert T. Brown
University of North Carolina

SUSTO

Susto, or "soul loss," is a folk illness attributed to a frightening or traumatic event. It is said that the event causes the soul to leave the body and results in unhappiness and sickness (American Psychiatric Association [APA], 1994). Other terms for this culture-bound syndrome include espanteo, pasmo, tripa ida, perida del alma, and chilbih (APA, 1994). This disorder can also be classified as a culture-specific idiom of disease and distress such that symptoms are extremely variable and may occur months or years after the supposedly precipitating event (Weber, 2000).

Behavioral manifestations of susto are similar to childhood depression and many other simple childhood illnesses. In some cases it has been postulated that susto is "equivalent to ailments characterized by modern medicine such as hypoglycemia" (Castro & Eroza, 1998, p. 204). According to ethnographic case studies, this disorder can be measured in terms of "degree of social stress" present in symptomatic cases, and explained as a result of "the lack of adjustment present in relation to social expectations" (Castro & Eroza, 1998, p. 204).

Typically, susto is related to psychological experiences associated with situations involving loss or grief. However, susto in children is more likely related to a frightening or traumatic event (Castro & Eroza, 1998). According to Castro and Eroza (1998), there are two stages to the susto process in children. First, they might simply be frightened, in which they will cry continuously during the night and cannot sleep. Second, if the susto symptoms persist, they begin to exhibit the same characteristics of adults, such as lack of appetite and fatigue. Thus, a child with susto can exhibit the previous characteristics at various stages of the syndrome.

There are no known prevalence or incidence studies with regard to susto, but there are ethnographic case studies of this disorder. Susto is primarily prevalent among Mexican, Central American, and South American populations. According to ethnographic reports, susto impacts high percentages of women and children. Men can also exhibit susto and report similar symptoms but at a lower concentration (Castro & Eroza, 1998).

Characteristics

1. Physical weakness
2. Somnolence
3. Loss of appetite
4. Fever and diarrhea
5. Depression
6. Hesitancy

By most ethnographic accounts, susto is treated by both traditional healers and medical professionals. However, within some Latin cultures there is a correlation between doctors and pain; therefore, many susto sufferers, termed *asustados,* do not seek medical attention for their ailments. Traditional healers use the basic measure of "sensing the sick person's pulse" to begin treatment. According to ethnographic reports, after finding the pulse, the healer "throws a little red corn into a container of blessed water and then prays, 'Shadow, come back to your center'" (Castro & Eroza, 1998, p. 215). With three complete sessions, the patient is deemed cured of susto. If symptoms persist after traditional treatment, the *asustado* will be referred to a *doctura* by the traditional healer (Castro & Eroza, 1998, p. 215).

It is unlikely that instances of susto would be identified in the United States in terms of referral for special education assessment for services. However, if the duration of the symptoms are long-term or chronic, academic achievement may be affected, and personnel may be brought in for child studies.

Differential diagnosis of this syndrome hinges on an acculturation assessment of the child and family. A family history of this condition should be noted as well as an analysis of current cultural practices and beliefs of the immediate and extended family. Differential diagnosis may also be dependent on ruling out common childhood illnesses that present with similar symptoms, and therefore a multidisciplinary approach with medical professionals would be very helpful.

A positive instance of Susto will require a culturally sensitive treatment plan that includes significant educational personnel and support and input from the family. Relevant school personnel and students may need to be educated as to the nature of the student's condition with recommendations for support.

REFERENCES

American Psychiatric Association. (1994). *Diagnostic and statistical manual of mental disorders* (4th ed.). Washington, DC: Author.

Castro, R., & Eroza, E. (1998). Research notes on social order and subjectivity: Individuals' experience of susto and fallen fontanelle in rural community in central Mexico. *Culture, Medicine, and Psychiatry, 22,* 203–230.

Weber, C. (2000). Culture-specific idioms of distress and disease. Retrieved from http://weber.ucsd.ecu/~thall/cbs_glos.html

Kiely Ann Fletcher
Ohio State University

SYPHILIS, CONGENITAL

Congenital syphilis is a form of syphilis diagnosed in children who are born with the disease. It is caused by the same spirochete, *Treponema pallidum,* that causes syphilis in adults. The disease is passed to the fetus from the infected mother before birth. Children with congenital syphilis may have symptoms immediately upon birth or may have none for several years (Syphilis, congenital, n.d.).

The incidences of syphilis are rising in the United States, from 691 cases diagnosed and reported in infants under 1 year of age in 1988 to 3,209 cases diagnosed and reported for the same age group in 1993. The risk of transmission from an infected mother to her fetus is 70–100% if the mother is untreated (Bennett, Lynn, Klein, & Balkowiec, 1997). Because it is transmitted to unborn fetuses, males and females are affected equally by the disease.

Characteristics

1. Prenatal characteristics of the disorder include inflammation of the umbilical chord, reduction in the mother's estrogen level, and an increase in serum progesterone levels in the mother.
2. Early symptoms in the infant include high cholesterol levels; anemia; fever; jaundice; shedding of skin or blisters on palms and soles; bloody discharge from nose-called "snuffles"; failure to thrive; rash near the mouth,

genitalia, or anus; impaired hearing; and an abnormal nose with no bridge, known as "saddle nose."

3. Later symptoms include enlarged liver and/or spleen; bone pain; lower leg bone abnormality called "saber shins"; joint swelling; Hutchinson teeth, which are notched and peg-shaped; vision loss; gray areas on the anus and vulva; convulsions; and mental retardation.

(Bennett et al., 1997; Congenital syphilis, n.d.; Syphilis congenital, n.d.)

The treatment for congenital syphilis is penicillin. If the mother is diagnosed with syphilis while pregnant, she may also take penicillin, which can prevent the child from being born with the infection (Syphilis, congenital, n.d.). Blood tests or analysis of cerebrospinal fluid can be used to diagnose the mother or newborn child with syphilis. However, serum tests at times give false negatives and make it more difficult to diagnose infants with syphilis when it may be present (Bennett et al., 1997).

Some children born with congenital syphilis may be in need of special education services due to mental retardation and hearing loss. Speech therapy may be indicated in some cases. Other issues facing education professionals are related to diagnosis of the disorder in young children and reporting of possible sexual abuse. If symptoms of syphilis are not visible or reported until the child is older, it is then difficult to determine whether the child actually has congenital syphilis or syphilis secondary to sexual abuse. Medical and education professionals may be in the difficult position of determining whether a report of possible child sexual abuse should be made (Christian, Lavelle, & Bell, 1999).

The best prognosis for congenital syphilis can be given if the mother is diagnosed and treated during her pregnancy, thus not passing the disease on to her fetus. There is a high infant mortality rate (30–40%) of children born with syphilis. For those who live, if syphilis is suspected, the child should be tested and treated as soon as possible. The child should also continue to be tested for syphilis, in case another round of treatment is necessary. Although syphilis can be treated, the effects cannot be reversed. Some (i.e., Glasser, 1996) argue that infants with no symptoms at birth, but whose mothers had syphilis while the child was in utero, should be treated with penicillin. The Centers for Disease Control have also established guidelines for medical professionals to follow when an infant is at risk for having syphilis (Glasser, 1996).

REFERENCES

Bennett, M. L., Lynn, A. W., Klein, L. E., & Balkowiec, K. S. (1997). Congenital syphilis: Subtle presentation of fulminant disease. *Journal of the American Academy of Dermatology, 36,* 351–354.

Christian, C. W., Lavelle, J., & Bell, L. M. (1999). Preschoolers with syphilis. *Pediatrics, 103,* e4.

Congenital syphilis. (n.d.). Retrieved August 1, 2001, from http://www.nlm.nih.gov.medlineplus/ency/article/001344.htm

Glasser, J. H. (1996). Centers for Disease Control and Prevention guidelines for congenital syphilis. *Journal of Pediatrics, 129,* 488–490.

Syphilis, congenital. (n.d.). Retrieved August 1, 2001 from http://www.stepstn.com/cgi-win/nord.exe

Mary Helen Snider
Devereux Cleo Wallace

SYRINGOBULBIA

Syringobulbia is closely associated with syringomyelia. Both are forms of brain stem neurological disorders that are characterized by a cavity or cyst (syrinx) in the spinal cord. Syringomyelia, which is the more common form, is characterized by cavitation of the central spinal cord and often extends downward along the entire length of the spinal cord. Syringobulbia is characterized by cavitation that appears in the brain stem. These disorders are slowly progressive disorders that are congenital, although there is evidence that syringomyelia and syringobulbia may also be a result of trauma (Kettaneh, Biousse, & Bousser, 2000; Thoene, 1995). These disorders are often associated with craniovertebral anomalies (e.g., Arnold-Chiari syndrome).

Syringobulbia is very rare (fewer than 1 in 100,000 births) and can affect either gender, although there appears to be a slight predilection towards males.

Characteristics

1. Although the defect may be congenital, for unknown reasons the cavity does not increase in size until teenage years or young adulthood. Therefore, symptoms may not be present until this time.
2. Symptoms often begin with loss of peripheral sensory functioning. For example, the deficit often begins with a lack of pain or temperature sensation in the fingers.
3. Syringobulbia may include vocal chord paralysis.
4. Atrophy and fibrillation of the tongue muscles (muscle twitching involving individual muscle fibers acting without coordination).
5. Difficulty in articulating words (Dysarthria).
6. Vertigo.
7. Rapid involuntary oscillation of eyeballs (nystagmus).
8. Abnormal deficiency or absence of sweating.

9. Bilateral facial sensory impairment.
10. Distal sensory or motor dysfunction due to medullary compression.

To treat syringobulbia, possible underlying problems, such as anomalies of the spine or base of the brain, should be corrected. Surgical drainage of the cavity may be necessary, and shunts may be implanted. This type of surgery has been found to be successful in alleviating the symptoms of syringobulbia, but severe neurological deterioration may not be surgically reversible.

Because the disorder does not usually become apparent until the teens or early adulthood, it is likely that students with a diagnosis of syringobulbia will already be in junior high or high school. These students will be eligible for special services under IDEA (1997) within the Other Physical Disability category. The type of services needed will depend on the symptoms and progression of the disorder. If the disorder is diagnosed before severe neurological damage has taken place and the individual responds to surgery well, school-based services may not be as intense and encompassing as for a student who experiences severe neurological impairment.

Students may need speech and language assistance if they have experienced vocal chord paralysis and dysarthria. Services may include counseling to understand and accommodate the necessary changes in their lives due to the disorder. For example, students with spinal cord disorders may have to limit their physical activities to reduce the possibility of damage and trauma to the spine. Syringobulbia may be associated with moderate to severe back pain. Therefore, students may need to be educated in pain management techniques. These students may require close observation and monitoring of medication, so school personnel need to be cognizant of the limitations of the disorder and to work closely with medical personnel. Students with syringobulbia may require extended time away from school for medical reasons. For example, students diagnosed during their school years will probably require spinal surgery, which is often associated with long recovery periods. Therefore, the school will need to make accommodations to help the student keep up with schoolwork and eventually reintegrate the student back into the school.

Present research is addressing the need for a comprehensible differential diagnosis for syringobulbia and syringomyelia (e.g., Penarrocha, Okeson, Penarrocha, & Angeles Cervello, 2001). Additionally, research is addressing the possibility of trauma to the head and neck as a cause for these disorders (e.g., Kettaneh et al., 2000).

REFERENCES

Kettaneh, A., Biousse, V., & Bousser, M. G. (2000). Neurological complications after roller coaster rides: An emerging new risk? *Presse Med, 29*(4), 175–180.

Penarrocha, M., Okeson, J. P., Penarrocha, M. S., & Angeles Cervello, M. (2001). Orofacial pain as the sole manifestation of syringobulbia-syringomyelia associated with Arnold-Chiari malformation. *Journal of Orofacial Pain, 15*(2), 170–173.

Thoene, J. G. (Ed.). (1995). *Physicians guide to rare diseases* (2nd ed.). Dowden.

Rachel Toplis
University of Northern Colorado

T

TAIJIN KYOFUSHO

Taijin Kyofusho syndrome (TKS) is a culture-bound psychiatric syndrome distinctive to Japan that in some ways resembles social phobia defined in the *DSM-IV* (American Psychiatric Association [APA], 1994). This disorder resembles social anxiety reaction. TKS is a cultural variation of social anxiety and is a function of how given cultures shape the way in which its members define and construe the self as the object of social threat (Dinnel, Kleinknecht, & Kleinknecht, 1997). This syndrome is included in the official Japanese diagnostic system for mental disorders.

There are no known incidence or prevalence studies on TKS, and according to Dinnel et al. (1997) epidemiological data are not available. However, according to APA (1994), this disorder is distinctive to Japan. As with social phobias in Western cultures, "the typical age of TKS onset in Japan is in adolescence and early adulthood" (Dinnel et al., 1997, p. 160). TKS is conceptualized as running a wide range of severity from "the highly prevalent but mild social concerns of adolescence, through social phobia, to inordinate concern with bodily features in which the person obsesses on some imagined or exaggerated physical defect" (Dinnel et al., 1997, p. 161). There are also clinical data that indicate that inversely to Western social phobias, more males than females exhibit the TKS condition (Dinnel et al., 1997).

Taijin kyofusho literally means symptoms (*sho*) of fear (*kyofu*) experienced when people have face-to-face contact. TKS is described as an "obsession of shame, manifest by morbid fear of embarrassing or offending others by blushing, emitting offensive odors or flatulence, staring inappropriately, improper facial expressions, a blemish or physical deformity" (Dinnel et al., 1997, p. 161). The key factor in this type of social avoidance is the fear of disrupting group cohesiveness by making others uncomfortable. The essential feature of social phobia is marked fear in social or performance situations in which one might be embarrassed or in which others might judge one to be odd or different. The same conceptual fear is present in TKS, except that the fear is not for oneself but for one's familial or social group.

Characteristics

1. Obsession with shame
2. Morbid fear of embarrassment
3. Social avoidance
4. Extreme fear of social interaction

In terms of treatment, it is extremely important to discern the cultural background and level of assimilation of the person exhibiting TKS characteristics. A particular scale is utilized to assess both the characteristics of TKS and the level of acculturation of the afflicted student: the Suinn-Lew Asian Self-Identify Acculturation Scale. This scale was developed by Suinn, Rickland-Figueroa, Lew, and Vigil in 1987 and is available in both the United States and Japan. In East Asian cultures, largely one's familial or social group defines the self, such that the self is an extension of that group. According to Dinnel et al. (1997, p. 161), "individualism, self-aggrandization, or deviation from the group is not tolerated: 'the nail that stands out gets pounded.'" Therefore, determining the level of acculturation to Western standards and perceptions about group-self identification is necessary with these individuals.

It is doubtful that special education services would be available for students exhibiting TKS. However, referrals to culturally appropriate and competent mental health service providers would be essential.

REFERENCES

American Psychiatric Association. (1994). *Diagnostic and statistical manual of mental disorders* (4th ed.). Washington, DC: Author.

Dinnel, D. L., Kleinknecht, E. E., & Kleinknecht, R. A. (1997). Cultural factors in social anxiety: A comparison of social phobia symptoms and taijin kyofusho. *Journal of Anxiety Disorders, 11,* 157–177.

Kiely Ann Fletcher
Ohio State University

TANGIER DISEASE

Tangier disease is an extremely rare autosomal recessive metabolic disorder. The disease is characterized by decreased levels or even a complete absence of high-density lipoproteins (HDL) concentrations in one's plasma and increased cholesteryl esters in the tonsils, spleen, liver, skin, and lymph nodes.

The reported cases of Tangier disease range from 40 to 50 cases worldwide (Smith & Villagomez, 2000). The majority of the cases tend to be localized in one single area of the United States (Tangier Island, Virginia). The original settlers to the island came in 1686, and it is possible that one or two of them were carriers of the disease and passed it down through their bloodline.

Characteristics

1. Very large, orange tonsils that have a characteristic gross and histological appearance, as well as enlarged liver, spleen, and lymph nodes.
2. Hypocholesterolemia, abnormal chylomicron remnants, and markedly reduces HDLs in the plasma also characterize Tangier Disease.
3. An increased incidence of atherosclerosis is also common.
4. A small number of patients have also been diagnosed with coronary artery disease and ocular abnormalities (Online Mendelian Inheritance in Man, 2000; Smith & Villagomez, 2000).
5. Patients with the disease have a defect in cellular cholesterol and lipid removal, which results in near-zero plasma levels of HDL and in massive tissue deposition of cholesterol esters.

Currently, the treatment for Tangier patients is dependent on the various symptoms, ranging from heart surgery to removal of organs. Also, some of the disease's affects may be controlled by some dietary changes, for example, less dietary intake (Smith & Villagomez, 2000). Gene therapy has been proposed as a possible treatment but is difficult because there is nothing specifically wrong with the gene involved in HDL conversion. The problem is in the cellular transportation (Newman, 1997). Many of the specific processes within the cell are still not known, so any extensive treatment is still investigational.

Due to the nature of the symptoms in Tangier disease, it is not likely that special education services would be necessary. The exception would be if the child is experiencing ocular abnormalities, in which case the child may require assistance through vision impairment services.

Prognosis depends mostly on the symptoms exhibited by the patient. If complications such as heart disease and atherosclerosis go undetected, the eventual outcome may be an early death. The recent discovery of the link between the ABC1 transporter and Tangier disease genes and a better understanding of its mechanism might shed new light on a new treatment for this disease (Smith & Villagomez, 2000).

REFERENCES

Newman, J. (1997). Tangier disease. Retrieved from http://www-personal.umd.umich.edu/~jcthomas/JCTHOMAS/1997%20case%20studies/J.%20Newman1.htm

Online Mendelian Inheritance in Man. (2000). Tangier disease. Retrieved from http://www3.ncbi.nhm.nih.gov/lltbin-post/Omim/dispmim?203400

Smith, A., & Villagomez, S. (2000). Tangier disease. Retrieved from http://endeavor.med.nyu.edu/student-org/ama/docs/mgb1999-2000/ab14.htm

Sarah Compton
University of Texas at Austin

TARDIVE DYSKINESIA

Tardive dyskinesia (TD), which means late abnormal movement, is an iatrogenic effect of long-term use of neuroleptic or antipsychotic medications. Individuals who have been on chronic antipsychotic medications may develop uncontrollable movements, ranging from mild tongue movements to chorea, that impair their daily life. They may have problems with manual dexterity, eating, speaking, and even breathing. Symptoms may (a) increase under stress, during voluntary motor activity, and during attempts to inhibit the movements; (b) decrease under sedation; and (c) disappear during sleep (Alexander & Lund, 1999). After medication is discontinued, TD may gradually diminish in severity or persist and become permanent. Therefore, prevention is crucial (Healthnotes Online, 2000).

Characteristics

1. Orofacial dyskinesia (most characteristic feature): slow onset of mild tongue movements and lip smacking followed by bulging of the cheeks, chewing movements, grimacing, and arching of the eyebrows.
2. Movements of extremities and trunk including choreoathetoid-like movements of fingers, hands, arms, and feet.
3. Rocking and swaying and rotational pelvic movements.

Prevalence estimates for TD vary widely, owing in part to variation across study in type and length of medication, age and gender of patients, and diagnostic criteria used. One estimate is 14% among all those on neuroleptic medications. The strongest correlate of both incidence and severity of TD is increasing age. Some studies report higher rates in women and those who smoke (Alexander & Lund, 1999).

Early differential diagnosis is important for prevention of TD. L-DOPA, taken by patients with Parkinson's disease, is the only nonneuroleptic drug that consistently produces dyskinesia, but it may actually improve neuroleptic-induced TD. TD-like conditions have occasionally been reported in patients using a variety of medications to treat a variety of disorders. These medications include reserpine, tetrabenazine, metoclopramide, tricyclic antidepressants, benztropine, phenytoin, and amphetamines. Information on the onset of symptoms is important for differential diagnosis. TD may need to be differentiated from Sydenham and Huntington chorea, congenital torsion dystonia, somatoform disorders, and stereotyped behaviors that frequently accompany schizophrenia itself.

No effective treatment is available for TD. Either discontinuing or reducing the dosage of patients' current medication or switching them to an atypical antipsychotic medication such as clozapine or olanzapine may decrease the symptoms. On the theory that TD stems from dopamine hypersensitivity, most pharmacological treatments have used drugs that reduce dopamine activity or enhance CNS cholinergic effect. However, none of the numerous drugs tried have had consistently positive results. Clinicians have reported effectiveness of a variety of vitamin and mineral supplements (Healthnotes Online, 2000), but positive effects in some cases have decreased as quality of evaluation research increased. Perhaps the most and best research has been on vitamin E, but its effects vary widely across study, even among those using double-blind designs (Alexander & Lund, 1999). Much of the research is limited by small samples, variations in subject population, and supplement regimen, making overall interpretation difficult. Other alternative treatments continue to be tried, with mixed results at best (Healthnotes Online, 2000).

Despite the lack of effective treatment, prognosis is better than traditionally thought. Spontaneous recovery occurs much more frequently than early reports suggested, particularly in younger patients. Overall, about 60% of TD patients show decreased symptoms within 2–3 years after stopping taking neuroleptics, with an inverse relationship between improvement and patients' age.

REFERENCES

Alexander, B., & Lund, B. C. (1999). Clinical psychopharmacology seminar: Tardive dyskinesia. *Virtual Hospital: The Apprentice's Assistant,* 1–20. Retrieved from http://www.vh.org/Providers/Conferences/CPS/08.html

Healthnotes Online. (2000). Tardive dyskinesia. Retrieved from http://www.healthwell.com/healthnotes/Concern/Tardive_Dyskinesia.cfm

Shannon Radliff-Lee
Robert T. Brown
University of North Carolina, Wilmington

TAY-SACHS DISEASE

Tay-Sachs disease is a degenerative disease of the nervous system. It is due to a deficiency of the enzyme B-hexosaminidase. The absence of this enzyme causes a lack of lipid metabolism that results in an accumulation on the brain (Mosby's Medical Dictionary, 1987). It is inherited as an autosomal recessive trait. Tay-Sachs disease is found predominately in Ashkenazi Jewish people of Eastern and Central European ancestry. Prevalence for Tay-Sachs disease in Ashkenazi Jewish infants is 1 in 2,500. However, for non-Jewish babies the disorder is very rare and occurs in 1 in about 360,000 (Lipsitz, Anderson, O'Brien, & Desnick, 1986).

Characteristics

1. Developmental delays first apparent at four to eight months
2. Developmental skills and mental functioning deteriorate, loss of peripheral vision, unusual startle response
3. By 2 years, toddler has severe seizures and difficulty sitting and in general is weak and debilitated
4. Swelling of the head due to fatty deposits in the brain
5. By 5 years, the child has difficulty breathing and swallowing; blindness, paralysis, and death ensue

(Gelbart, 1998; Lipsitz et al., 1986).

The Tay-Sachs infant appears normal until about 8 months, at which point mental and physical deterioration occur until an early death, usually by the age of 5 (Gelbart, 1998; Lipsitz et al., 1986). There is no treatment for Tay-Sachs disease. Focus has remained on prevention of the disease through parental screening and in utero diagnosis via amniocentesis. Subsequent to infant detection, treatment focuses on symptom management and familial emotional support.

Because of the progressive nature of Tay-Sachs disease, the child does not live to attend school. However, the rarer form, juvenile Tay-Sachs disease, has an onset of 3 to 5 years and has a slower but similar progression. Some children with juvenile onset live to be 15 (Gelbart, 1998). Because of the progressive nature of deterioration, by the time children with juvenile Tay-Sachs disease reach school age, intellectual and physical functioning is severely limited. Children with Tay-Sachs disease may qualify for special education services under a number of categories including Mental Retardation, Other Health Impairment, or Physically Disabled.

Future research for Tay-Sachs disease will focus on gene therapy to address the defective gene or on supplying the missing enzyme (Hecht, Anatole, & Szucs, 1984). At present, efforts have been made to increase screening for Jewish Americans, the majority of which are Ashkenazi.

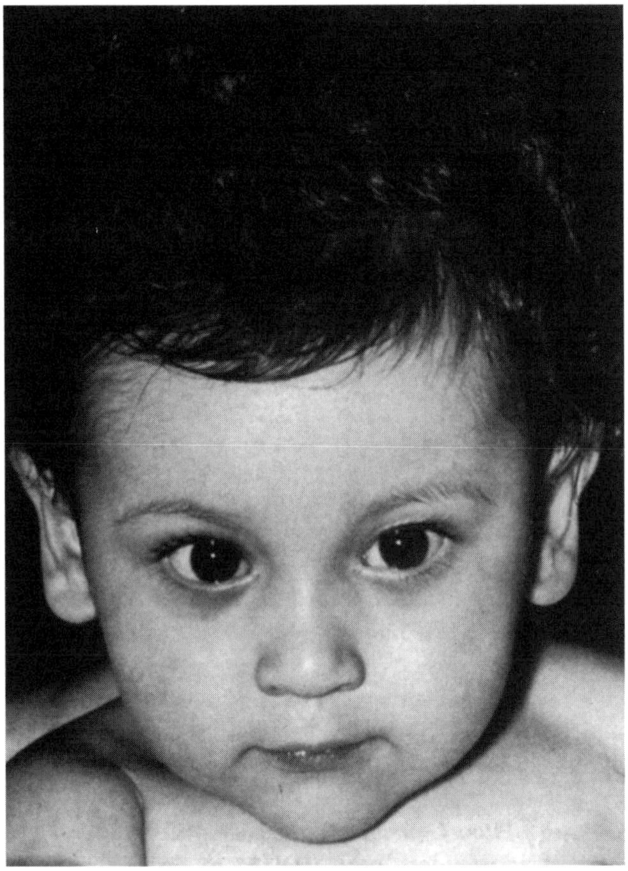

Tay-Sachs Disease
Reprinted from *Clinical Syndromes,* Wiedemann and Kunze, 1997, by permission of the publisher Mosby

REFERENCES

Gelbart, M. (1998). In our parent's shadow: Tay-Sachs disease. *Nursing Times, 94,* 39.

Hecht, F., Anatole, P., & Szucs, S. (1984). Tay-Sachs disease: Part 2. Model of a fatal, preventable, metabolic, genetic disorder. *Arizona Medicine, 10,* 661–664.

Lipsitz, D., Anderson, V., O'Brien, J., & Desnick, R. (1986). Tay-Sachs disease prevention in Minnesota. *Minnesota Medicine, 69,* 272–275.

Mosby's Medical Dictionary Revised (2nd ed.). (1987). St. Louis, MO: Mosby.

Kimberly D. Wilson
University of Texas at Austin

See also Juvenile Cerebromacular Degeneration

TETHERED SPINAL CORD SYNDROME

Tethered spinal cord syndrome occurs when the spinal cord does not hang freely in the spinal canal but instead is attached at the coccyx (Nelson, Behrman, Kliegman, & Arvin, 1996). It has a variety of identifying characteristics, including external manifestations such as lipomas or fatty tumors, skin tags, sacral dimple, benign tumors composed of blood vessels, excessive growth of hair in the middle of the lumbar and thoracic region, a lesion resembling a cigarette burn, or asymmetrical buttock creases. There may also be orthopedic deformities, such as scoliosis or muscle atrophy in feet and legs, urological difficulties, and neurological manifestations such as decreased sensation and reflexes in the lower extremities (Cartwright, 2000).

The external cutaneous manifestations are often present and can be useful in diagnosing tethered spinal cord syndrome. There may also be evidence of degenerative motor weakness, which will delay development of walking or cause gait difficulties in children who have already learned to walk. Symptoms usually become noticeable at times of rapid growth spurts and are typically reported before 5 years of age. Most cases are identified before age 21, and the syndrome is more prevalent in females with a two to one ratio. Magnetic resonance imaging (MRI) may be used in diagnosis.

Characteristics

External spinal physical manifestations

1. Lipoma or fatty tumors at the base of the spine
2. Meningocele manque, which is a lesion resembling a cigarette burn
3. Dermal sinus tract or sacral dimple
4. Asymmetrical buttock crease
5. Hemangioma, which is a benign tumor comprised of blood vessels
6. Skin tags
7. Hypertrichosis, or the appearance of an excessive growth of hair, in the midline region

Urological physical manifestations

1. In infants an absence of dry periods between diaper changes
2. A lack of success in toilet training, increased toileting urgency, and/or incontinence

Orthopedic physical manifestations

1. Back pain and/or scoliosis
2. Foot deformities such as an exaggerated height of the arch or discrepancies in foot or leg length
3. Muscle atrophy of the lower extremities

Neurological physical manifestations

1. Decreased or absent reflexes
2. Decreased sensation to touch and temperature in the lower extremities
3. Lower extremity weakness

Surgery may be considered to free the spinal cord to prevent further damage, but usually the patient will not regain motor control that has already been lost (Greif & Stalmasek, 1989). If unrepaired, a reported 90% of patients will develop irreversible deficits. There is a 50% chance of returning to baseline mobility. Orthopedic anomalies and bladder dysfunctions have lower probabilities of correction (Cartwright, 2000). Early diagnosis and treatment are important in curbing the permanent effects.

A patient with tethered spinal cord syndrome may have many special needs. With bladder dysfunction, catheterization may be necessary. Because of loss of feeling in the lower extremities, care should be taken in examining for bruising, cuts, and blistering, as the patient may not realize they are present. If scoliosis is present, it may need to be surgically corrected. The muscle atrophy may produce a need for walking assistance through the use of a cane, crutches, or wheel chair in extreme situations. Modifications may need to be made in an educational setting to accommodate children with this syndrome.

REFERENCES

Cartwright, C. (2000). Primary tethered cord syndrome: Diagnosis and treatment of an insidious defect. *Journal of Neuroscience and Nursing, 32,* 210–215.

Greif, L., & Stalmasek, V. (1989). Tethered cord syndrome: A pediatric case study. *Journal of Neuroscience Nursing, 21,* 86–91.

Nelson, W. E., Behrman, R. E., Kliegman, R. M., & Arvin, A. (1996). *Nelson textbook of pediatrics* (15th ed.). Philadelphia: W. B. Saunders.

Carol Schmitt
San Diego Unified School District

TETRAHYDROBIOPTERIN DEFICIENCY (BH_4)

Deficiency in tetrahydrobiopterin (BH_4) is a rare genetic disorder due to a defect in metabolism of amino acids. BH_4 impairs the metabolism of enzymes resulting in hyperphenylalanimia and a defect of neurotransmitter synthesis. Clinical manifestations are similar and usually indistinguishable from classic phenylketonuria (PKU). In most cases of BH_4, progressive neurological symptoms appear between the ages of 2 and 12 months despite excellent dietary control. The syndrome may involve mental deterioration, intractable seizures, arrest in motor development, microcephaly, and occasionally abnormal movements.

Characteristics

1. Hyperphenylalaninemia
2. Progressive neurological symptoms between the ages of 2 and 12 months despite excellent dietary control
3. Neurological and neurocognitive manifestations: mental deterioration, loss of head control, hypertonia, drooling
4. Swallowing difficulties and myoclonic seizures despite adequate dietary therapy
5. Plasma phenylalanine levels as high as those in classic PKU or in the range of benign hyperphenylalaninemia

The incidence of BH_4 deficiency is approximately 1 to 2 per million live births, compared to 150 per million in the hyperphenylalaninemias. Incidence is about 2% of infants with hyperphenylalaninemia.

Long-term efficacy of various therapies is unknown and includes the following:

1. *Low phenylalanine diet.* If a restricted diet is given early, ideally in the first months of life, the adverse consequences of persistent hyperphenylalanimia are mostly avoided. When such treatment is started later, results are less favorable. Diet in conjunction with additional therapies is recommended for at least the first two years of life.
2. *Neurotransmitter precursors.* Administration of 1-dopa and 5-hypdroxytryptophan may prevent neurological damage if started early in life. Treatment started after 6 months of age, although resulting in some improvement, has not reversed existing neurological damage.
3. All patients with hyperphenylalanine should be tested for BH_4 deficiency as early as possible because it gives rise to devastating neurological illness. BH_4 replacement via oral administration of the cofactor in small daily doses is necessary to normalize serum levels of phe.

The duration of treatment, as well as the development of novel treatments, continues to be a focus of BH_4 research.

Children suffering from BH_4 should be evaluated for special education services and may be eligible under the classification of Other Health Impairment as a result of their medical condition.

REFERENCES

Lyon, G., Adams, R. D., & Kolodny, E. H. (1996). *Neurology of hereditary metabolic diseases of children.* New York: McGraw-Hill.

Nelson, W. E., Behrman, R. E., Kliegman, R. M., & Arvin, A. M. (1996). *Nelson textbook of pediatrics* (15th ed.). Bangalore, India: Prism Books.

Scriver, C. R. (Ed.). (1995). *The metabolic and molecular basis of inherited disease* (7th ed.). New York: McGraw-Hill.

VIRDETTE L. BRUMM
Children's Hospital Los Angeles
Keck / USC School of Medicine

THALASSEMIA MAJOR

Thalassemia is a blood disorder of genetic origin that results from the interaction of thalassemia genes and those genes associated with abnormal hemoglobins. Heterozygous thalassemia or thalassemia minor is the less serious form of the disorder and is generally without symptoms. Homozygous thalassemia or thalassemia major is the more serious form of the disorder and if untreated can lead to massive splenomegaly and death by 5 years of age. Thalassemia major also is referred to as Cooley's anemia or Mediterranean anemia due to its high prevalence in Mediterranean and Middle Eastern countries (e.g., Cyprus, Greece, Turkey, and Italy) and descendants from these areas. Other regions where thalassemia major may be found include Southeast Asia and Africa. With increased mobility and marriage between ethnic groups, the prevalence of thalassemia major has decreased considerably over time; with geographic differences in prevalence, no single prevalence rate is cited. Although prevalence of the major form is of increasing rarity, individuals with thalassemia minor are carriers for the major form and should engage in genetic counseling prior to having children.

Characteristics

1. Anemia characterized by slowed production of red blood cells and decreased life of red blood cells
2. Medical complications associated with iron overload caused by recurrent transfusions
3. Impaired growth due to the enlargement of the spleen (splenomegaly)
4. Jaundice
5. Skeletal changes and osteopenia
6. Growth retardation
7. Possible cognitive impairment

If untreated, thalassemia major will result in death prior to school age. Treatment options for thalassemia major include regular blood transfusions, use of iron chelation therapy, splenectomy, and bone marrow transplant (Al-Salem, 1999; Muretto & Angelucci, 1999). Continual follow-up care is needed, and medical complications, including iron overload in the case of transfusions, may arise from the treatment. It is important for communication to be kept open among parents, physicians, and school personnel to ensure that all persons working with the child are kept up to date on the child's medical status.

Cognitive impairment can be associated with thalassemia major (Monastero, Monastero, Ciaccio, Padovani, & Carmarda, 2000). The extent of cognitive decline was found to be associated with the duration of transfusional therapy and the delay between beginning transfusion therapy and the onset of chelation therapy (Monastero et al., 2000). If this is the case, or if the child's progress in school is affected by medical issues, the child may be eligible for special education services, including homebound tutoring during medical crises.

Psychosocial issues for children and adolescents with thalassemia are similar to those for children with chronic illness in general (Nash, 1990; Tsiantis, 1990). Parents often tend to be overprotective, and this can result in child behaviors associated with learned helplessness and dependence. This overprotection can be enhanced by the "delayed" growth (dwarfism) associated with the disorder. At the same time, there is increased stress on the child and the family, including siblings. Psychological interventions need to be ecological in nature and build on the strengths of the family (Nash, 1990). Across cultures, having a child with thalassemia often has a unifying effect on the family (Tsiantis, Dragonas, Richardson, & Anastopoulos, 1996). Factors associated with less positive response to the child's illness include father's educational level and the extent of major medical complications. Because of the genetic component to thalassemia major, the possibility exists for more than one child in a family to have the disorder, and this would further complicate the impact on the family.

Although aggressive medical treatment can offset the major problems associated with thalassemia major, the frequent transfusions and resulting iron overload can bring on additional complications. Combined with other medical treatments including bone marrow transplants and splenectomy, and with the introduction of iron chelation therapy, it is estimated that 80% of individuals with thalassemia major reach a median age between 23 and 31 years. This is a significant increase in life expectancy from 30 years ago; medical advances may increase this even further in the future. With the increased life expectancy, however, additional issues regarding family status, genetic counseling, and employment issues that were not previously of concern are in need of research (DiPalma, Viello, Zani, & Facchini, 1998).

REFERENCES

Al-Salem, A. H. (1999). Is splenectomy for massive splenomegaly safe in children? *American Journal of Surgery, 178,* 42–45.

DiPalma, A., Viello, C., Zani, R., & Facchini, A. (1998). Psychosocial integration of adolescents and young adults with thalassemia major. *Annals of the New York Academy of Sciences, 850,* 355–360.

Monastero, R, Monastero, G., Ciaccio, C., Padovani, A., & Carmarda, R. (2000). Cognitive deficits in beta-thalassemia major. *Acta Neurologica Scandinavia, 102,* 162–168.

Muretto, P., & Angelucci, E. (1999). Successful treatment of severe thalassemia. *New England Journal of Medicine, 341,* 92.

Nash, K. B. (1990). A psychosocial perspective: Growing up with thalassemia, a chronic disorder. *Annals of the New York Academy of Sciences, 612,* 442–449.

Tsiantis, J. (1990). Family reactions and relationships in thalassemia. *Annals of the New York Academy of Sciences, 612,* 451–461.

Tsiantis, J., Dragonas, T., Richardson, C., & Anastopoulos, D. (1996). Psychosocial problems and adjustment of children with beta-thalassemia and their families. *European Child and Adolescent Psychiatry, 5,* 193–203.

Cynthia A. Riccio
Texas A&M University

THALIDOMIDE AND THALIDOMIDE SYNDROME

Thalidomide was among the first drugs identified as a teratogen, a chemical agent that can cross the placenta and cause congenital malformations to the developing embryo and fetus. Effective as a sedative and a tranquilizer, thalidomide had positive effects on the mother but devastating consequences for the embryo (e.g., Stephens & Brynner, 2001).

Teratogenicity became suspected with the birth of numbers of babies with phocomelia (seal-flipper limbs) and other deformities in Europe in the late 1950s and early 1960s. Phocomelia is a condition in which the arms or legs are drastically shortened or absent and fingers and toes extend from the foreshortened limbs or the trunk. Thalidomide was widely distributed in Europe, where it affected over 7,000 individuals, but it was never approved by the Food and Drug Administration for use in the United States (Moore, 1982). Teratogenicity was unusually high; over 90% of women who took thalidomide during a particular period in pregnancy had infants with some type of defect (Holmes, 1983). Thalidomide syndrome is now only of historical interest.

Characteristics

1. Phocomelia ("seal-flipper" limbs, fingers, and toes extending from trunk)
2. Absence or malformation of external ear
3. Malformation of the thumbs
4. Dislocation of the hip
5. Complete absence of arms and/or legs

Thalidomide is the only drug whose timing of harmful effects has been well established, causing defects only if taken by the mother when the embryo was 34 to 50 days old; earlier or later consumption had few if any adverse effects (Holmes, 1983). Phocomelia was the most common and pronounced sign, but absent or deformed ears and digits were common, and malformations of forehead, heart, and digestive system occasionally occurred. Generally, overall intelligence was unaffected, but some language deficits were reported (e.g., Moore, 1982). Because thalidomide has teratogenic but not mutagenic qualities, thalidomide-syndrome individuals would be expected to have normal children.

Despite the severe consequences of prenatal exposure to thalidomide, research on other potential benefits of the drug began shortly after withdrawal from the market. Initially found to be a highly effective treatment for leprosy, thalidomide has since been used experimentally to treat many other diseases. It appears effective in treating a number of types of cancer, including brain and prostate, inflammatory disease, and autoimmune disorders, perhaps even AIDS (e.g., Cancer Weekly Editors, 2000). Thalidomide is now the subject of hundreds of reports in both the professional and popular presses (e.g., Bethune, 2001).

However beneficial, thalidomide remains a major human teratogen, and therefore its use must be carefully monitored. If recurrences of thalidomide syndrome are to be avoided, women should never take the drug, particularly early in pregnancy.

REFERENCES

Bethune, B. (2001). Hope and despair. *Maclean's, 114*(22), 37–38.

Cancer Weekly Editors. (2000, July 16). Thalidomide appears to be effective treatment in variety of cancers. *Cancer Weekly,* 16–17.

Holmes, L. B. (1983). Congenital malformations. In R. E. Behrman & V. C. Vaughn (Eds.), *Nelson textbook of pediatrics* (12th ed., pp. 311–317). Philadelphia: W. B. Saunders.

Moore, K. L. (1982). *The developing human* (3rd ed.). Philadelphia: W. B. Saunders.

Stephens, T., & Brynner, R. (2001). *Dark remedy: The impact of thalidomide and its revival as a vital medicine.* Cambridge, MA: Perseus.

Robert T. Brown
University of North Carolina, Wilmington

TIC DISORDER

Tics are sudden, repetitive, stereotyped motor movements or phonic productions that can be distinguished by their anatomical location, number, frequency, duration, and complexity (Leckman, King, & Cohen, 1999). Tics are often described as being simple (i.e., involving one muscle group) or complex (i.e., involving multiple muscle groups in a sequential movement; Hagerman, 1999).

According to the *DSM-IV-TR* (American Psychiatric Association, 2000), tics are classified under Tourette disorder, chronic motor or vocal tic disorder, transient tic disorder, or tic disorder not otherwise specified (NOS). Differential diagnosis among the tic disorders is made on the basis of the type of tics, duration, and age of onset. For example, Tourette disorder requires that at least two motor tics and one vocal tic be present for one year, and that no period longer than three months be tic-free. Chronic motor or vocal tic disorder requires the presence of either motor or vocal tics, but not both, for at least one year. Transient tic disorder includes motor and/or vocal tics lasting for at least four weeks but no longer than 12 consecutive months. All three diagnoses require that the age of tic onset is before 18 years. In cases where the tic begins after that time, or not all criteria are met (e.g., tics present for less than 4 weeks), a diagnosis of tic disorder NOS is given.

The median age of onset for tics is 6 to 7 years. In 75% of children with tic disorders the tics begin by age 11 (Hagerman, 1999). The only prevalence data found consistently in the literature is for Tourette Disorder with rates of 4–5 per 10,000. The prevalence of other tic disorders is thought to be much higher given the transient and mild nature of many cases of tics. Some believe that up to 12% of children display some type of tic symptom (Popper & Steingard, 1994). Tic disorders have been reported worldwide and are believed to affect 3–4 times more males than females (Hagerman, 1999).

Characteristics

1. The first tic is usually motor and involves facial muscles.
2. Vocal tics typically begin one or more years after the motor tic and more often involve sounds instead of words (e.g., sniffing and throat clearing).
3. Sensory urges are often reported to precede the tic with increasing inner tension until the tic is performed.
4. Tics tend to wax and wane and can be aggravated by stress (e.g., fatigue, heat, and boredom).

Tic disorders may present with a variety of associated problems including inattention, learning difficulties, and physical injury (e.g., neck strain). Children with tics may also have emotional and behavioral problems, all of which may require intervention. Psychopharmacologic management is not always used; in fact, in many cases medications are only given if the tic is so severe it interferes with learning or social-recreational activities. A variety of medications are used, including Haloperidol and Pimozide. According to some, the best treatment is patience and tolerance on behalf of others (Hagerman, 1999). This may require education of the child's parents, teachers, and peers about tic disorders. The child with the tic may also benefit from information about the disorder, as well as psychological counseling and social skills training.

If special education services are required, most often it is for comorbid learning and behavior problems (e.g., Specific Learning Disabilities and Emotional Disturbance). In some cases, however, these children may require services under the category of Other Health Impairment (e.g., children whose attentional or motor problems warrant specialized interventions). In most cases, modifications in the regular education classroom will be sufficient to facilitate learning and adequate social adjustment. Tics are often exacerbated by stress, so allowing extra time to take tests and complete other written assignments can be beneficial. Reducing the workload may also help children whose tics are so severe that written work puts undue stress on them. Allowing them to leave the classroom in order to discharge tics in a private location may also be helpful to relieve the stress of having to repress a tic or being embarrassed by it. Handwriting problems that are commonly found among children with tics may also warrant intervention. For example, allowing children to take oral exams and dictate their assignments may be helpful. In cases where considerable lecture information is given, the teacher may consider providing the child with a copy of his or her notes.

Although the frequency and duration of tics are usually the worst in early adolescence, prognosis is generally good, as nearly two thirds of patients experience remission or significant improvement by late adolescence or adulthood. Current and future research is focusing on understanding the genetic linkage and transmission of tics and other related disorders, including attention-deficit/hyperactivity disorder and obsessive-compulsive disorder.

REFERENCES

American Psychiatric Association. (2000). *Diagnostic and statistical manual of mental disorders* (4th ed., Text Revision). Washington, DC: Author.

Hagerman, R. J. (1999). Tourette syndrome. In *Neurodevelopmental disorders: Diagnosis and treatment* (pp. 133–172). New York: Oxford University Press.

Leckman, J. F., King, R. A., & Cohen, D. J. (1999). Tics and tic disorders. In J. F. Leckman & D. J. Cohen (Eds.), *Tourette's syndrome—Tics, obsessions, compulsions: Developmental psychopathology and clinical care* (pp. 23–42). New York: Wiley.

Popper, C. W., & Steingard, R. J. (1994). Disorders usually first diagnosed in infancy, childhood, or adolescence. In J. A. Talbott, R. E. Hales, & S. C. Yudofsky (Eds.), *The American Psychiatric*

Press textbook of psychiatry (2nd ed., pp. 729–832). Washington, DC: American Psychiatric Press.

Jenise Jensen
Elaine Clark
University of Utah

TONGUE, GEOGRAPHIC

Geographic tongue is a term applied to a map-like appearance of the tongue resulting from irregular bare patches on its surface. This patchy form of glossitis (loss of papillae causing the tongue to appear smooth) changes location and appearance from day to day. It is a benign condition but can be persistent. This disorder is often self-limiting and does not require treatment. The causes of geographic tongue are unknown, although allergies or local irritants such as hot, spicy food may be involved. It is also possible that this condition may be a reaction to stress. Geographic tongue may also be known as benign migratory glossitis.

Geographic tongue is a relatively common tongue problem that affects males and females alike.

> Characteristics
>
> 1. Red, "bald" patches accentuated by white rings found on the upper surface of the tongue (the dorsum).
> 2. In some cases individuals may feel sore or burning pain.
> 3. The location changes from day to day (migration).

Once diagnosed, frequently no treatment is applied. This condition is often self-limiting. If treatment is required, it responds well to topical steroids, which can be prescribed by a dentist (e.g., Lidex gel applied 4 times a day). Treatment may provide significant improvement but does not permanently cure the condition. If the condition is reoccurring and persistent, the affected individual may need to avoid local irritants (e.g., hot and spicy food, alcohol, tobacco, etc.), or an allergy assessment may be needed. Alternatively, stress may be involved, and addressing the cause of the stress may be necessary.

A student with this diagnosis may be experiencing mild to moderate discomfort. Therefore, a student experiencing intermittent mouth pain may be seen by the school nurse frequently. In most cases, however, the condition is self-limiting, and no treatment is prescribed. Symptoms should diminish within approximately 10 days. If the condition persists, the student may need further medical consultation and treatment. School personnel may be involved in monitoring the student and administering medication. If it is determined that the condition is due to an allergic reaction to food or another allergen, it may be necessary for the school to provide an alternative diet for this student. In certain cases, stressors may exacerbate the condition. In this case, the student may benefit from counseling to alleviate stress or find ways to deal with the stress more effectively.

The prognosis for geographic tongue is excellent. The condition is often self-limiting. Research continues to explore treatment approaches for geographic tongue (Flaitz & Baker, 2000) and etiological factors (Gonzaga, Torres, Alchorne, & Gerbase-Delima, 1996).

REFERENCES

Flaitz, C. M., & Baker, K. A. (2000). Treatment approaches to common symptomatic oral lesions in children. *Dent Clin North Am, 44*(3), 671–696.

Gonzaga, H. F., Torres, E. A., Alchorne, M. M., & Gerbase-Delima, M. (1996). Both psoriasis and benign migratory glossitis are associate with HLW-Cw6. *British Journal of Dermatology, 135*(3), 368–370.

Rachel Toplis
University of Northern Colorado

TOURETTE SYNDROME

Tourette syndrome (TS) is a neurological disorder that is characterized by motor and vocal tics. The tics are repetitive, rapid, involuntary movements that vary in the age of onset, severity, and complexity but must be present before age 18. The tics often wax and wane over time (American Psychiatric Association [APA], 2000).

> Characteristics
>
> 1. Presence of both motor and vocal tics, although they do not have to occur concurrently.
>   - Vocal tics can have unusual rhythms, tone, accents, loudness, and repetition of one's own words or words of others. In rare cases vocal tics can contain obscene or aggressive speech.
>   - Motor tics may include eye blinking, shrugging, jerking movements, hopping, facial expressions, and imitation of others movements.
> 2. Tics occur frequently, often in bouts, for more than a year with no more than three months that are tic-free.
> 3. Causes marked distress or impairment in social, occupational, academic, or other areas.
> 4. The disturbance cannot be attributed to other medical conditions or substance use.

5. Often secondary problems may develop, including depression, antisocial behaviors, and anxiety.

TS occurs in 1 in 2,500 children (Bruun, Cohen, & Leckman, 2000). TS is primarily a genetic disorder, but 10–15% of persons with TS do not have a genetic link to TS. There is a 50% chance of passing the TS gene to children if it is present. There is a 70% chance of gene expression in girls and 99% chance in boys. This gender difference in the gene expression accounts for the greater prevalence of the disorder in males. Although males are twice as likely to be diagnosed with TS than females, there are no differences indicated in the incidence rates of TS across social class, ethnicity, or culture.

TS needs to be differentiated from other disorders such as Huntington disease, stroke, Lesch-Nyhan syndrome, Wilson's disease, multiple sclerosis, head injury, Syndenham chorea, postviral encephalitis, obsessive-compulsive disorder, attention-deficit/hyperactivity disorder (ADHD), mental retardation, autism, and effects from medications (APA, 2000). Neuroimaging and blood tests may be used to rule out other disorders. In addition to the need for differential diagnoses, several disorders frequently cooccur with TS, including ADHD (as high as 50%), obsessive-compulsive disorder, and learning disorders. There is a complex and controversial relationship between TS and ADHD, with a high rate of comorbidity and a correlation between stimulant use and the onset of tics. It is currently thought that a genetic predisposition to TS may be triggered by some stimulants used to treat ADHD.

There is no known cure for TS. The disorder often improves with age, and the majority of children cope without medication (Kurlan, 2000). Neuroleptics such as Haldol are sometimes prescribed to reduce symptoms; however, careful monitoring of side effects is needed. Side effects may include excessive fatigue, weight gain, intellectual dulling, memory problems, and school or social phobia. Phobias would generally appear in the first few weeks of treatment with medication. Secondary problems including depression, anxiety, and antisocial behaviors may worsen with age and require treatment. Educating families, schools, and fellow students and providing counseling may prevent or reduce the need for medication and the development of secondary problems associated with TS.

Given the variety in the severity of symptoms and comorbid disorders, education programs need to be designed to best meet the individual's needs. Consideration of tic frequency, attention problems, social adjustment, learning disabilities, and other problems related to TS should be addressed. Although there is great variability in TS severity, most children fall into the mild to moderate range of symptoms, and often students with TS function well in regular education settings.

Modifications can include breaking assignments into shorter tasks, numbering sequential tasks, providing models, giving written and verbal directions with visual cues, preferential seating, and reducing distraction in the environment. The student may benefit from assistance with organizational and time management skills. In addition, the teacher and child may locate a designated private place such as a study carrel where a student can go if tics become severe (Gaffney, 2001). Promoting understanding in the schools regarding the nature of TS also may reduce the social problems associated with TS.

Future research will continue to investigate the genetic and environmental components and possible treatment of TS. New medications are being examined to reduce the symptoms of TS.

REFERENCES

American Psychiatric Association. (2000). *Diagnostic and statistical manual of mental disorders* (4th ed., Text Revision). Washington, DC: Author.

Bruun, R. D., Cohen, D. J., & Leckman, J. F. (2000, November 8). Guide to the diagnosis and treatment of tourette syndrome. Retrieved from http://www.mentalhealth.com/book/p40-gtor.html

Gaffney, G. R. (2001, March 4). Modifications for students with Tourette syndrome, attention-deficit disorder and obsessive-compulsive disorder. Retrieved from http://www.vh.org/Patients/IHB/Psych/Tourette/Modifications/html

Kurlan, R. (2000, October 1). Current pharmacology of Tourette syndrome. Retrieved from http://tas.mgh.Harvard.edu/medsci/medicationsanddosages.html

Monica E. Wolfe
Texas A&M University

TOXIC SHOCK SYNDROME

Toxic shock syndrome is a very rare disease that is associated with strains of *Staphylococcus aureus,* which is a bacterium that is a common inhabitant of the skin, oral cavity, and vagina. The staph bacterium can, under certain conditions, produce a toxin that attacks the immune system through the bloodstream (Toxic shock syndrome, 2000). This potentially life-threatening bacterial infection has been most often associated with the use of tampons during a woman's menstrual cycle.

Annual incidence in the United States in 1987, according to the Centers for Disease Control, was 1–2 out of 100,000 women ages 15–44. During that period, there was a small epidemic of toxic shock syndrome, reportedly caused by use of superabsorbent tampons. Since that time, reported cases have fallen to fewer than 10 per year since 1995. In some cases, use of barrier contraceptive devices has also been associated with toxic shock syndrome. Approximately 5% of all reported cases are fatal.

Characteristics

1. Sudden fever of 102 degrees or higher
2. Vomiting or diarrhea
3. Dizziness or feeling of weakness, fainting, or disorientation
4. Rash resembling a sunburn that appears on palms of hands and soles of feet
5. Headache
6. Sore throat
7. Aching muscles
8. Bloodshot eyes

Treatment involves providing blood and urine samples for detection of an infection. Hospitalization for a short period of time is likely, with a flood of antibiotics in order to clear the infection. There is a slight chance that the toxins produced by the staph bacteria could result in kidney failure (Toxic shock syndrome, n.d.).

It is unlikely that a student who has had toxic shock syndrome would qualify for special education services. Because the syndrome is completely curable with antibiotics and there are no severe or long-term effects in the majority of the cases, it is not a handicapping condition as outlined in IDEA 1997.

Following the outbreak of toxic shock syndrome in the early 1980s that was associated with the use of superabsorbent tampons, manufacturers began to print warning labels on tampon boxes about the possible dangers of prolonged use. Once women became aware of the dangers and began either to use tampons intermittently or to use tampons that were less absorbent, the outbreak subsided. There have been no extensive research studies on toxic shock syndrome since that time.

REFERENCES

Toxic shock syndrome. (n.d.). The Mayo Clinic. Retrieved December 2001 from http://mayoclinic.com/findinformation/diseasesandconditions

Toxic shock syndrome. (2000). Microsoft Encarta Online Encyclopedia 2000. Retrieved December 2001 from http://encarta.msn.com

Christine D. Cde Baca
University of Northern Colorado

TOXOCARIASIS (VISCERAL LARVA MIGRANS)

Toxocariasis is an infection that results from the invasion of parasites found in the intestines of dogs and cats. About 10,000 people are affected annually with toxocariasis in the United States.

Characteristics

1. Child ingests vegetation, dirt, or feces contaminated with the toxocara parasite eggs.
2. The eggs hatch in the child's intestine, and the larvae burrow into the intestinal wall.
3. The larvae migrate to the brain, eye, liver, lung, heart, and other organs, causing inflammation and tissue damage.
4. The child may develop a fever, cough, wheezing, an enlarged liver, and seizures.
5. Rashes and pneumonia may also occur.
6. Ocular larva migrans (larva entering the eye) may cause inflammation and formation of a scar on the retina, decreasing visual acuity and possibly causing crossed eyes.

Usually symptoms are so mild that treatment is not used, however, for more severe symptoms there is no current proven effective treatment. Mebendazole may be the most successful treatment. Diethylcarbamazine may also be beneficial, and prednisone may be taken to alleviate symptoms (Piessens, 1997). Eye treatment is more difficult and may entail measures designed to prevent further eye damage.

Children who experience visual impairment from the ocular larva migrans may need special education services to support their handicap.

The infection usually comprises mild symptoms that go away without treatment in 6 to 18 months (Piessens, 1997). However, each year more than 700 people infected with ocular larva migrans have permanent partial loss of vision (Division of Parasitic Diseases, 1999).

REFERENCES

Division of Parasitic Diseases. (1999, August 15). Toxocariasis. Retrieved from http://www.cdc.gov/ncidod/dpd/parasites/toxocara/factsht_toxocara.htm

Piessens, W. F. (1997). Toxocariasis. In R. Berkow, M. H. Beers, R. M. Bogin, & A. J. Fletcher (Eds.), *Merck Manual of medical information–Home edition* (pp. 904–905). New York: Pocket Books.

Teresa M. Lyle
University of Texas at Austin

TOXOPLASMOSIS

Toxoplasmosis is caused by an intracellular protozoan parasite called *Toxoplasma gondii* (also called a coccidian). The parasite affects both humans and warm-blooded animals. Toxoplasmosis is characterized by tissue cysts that form in the host after infection. Cysts are found primarily in the brain and skeletal and heart muscles but may also be found in other tissue. Toxoplasmosis may be transmitted by consumption of undercooked meat, exposure to cat feces, and congenital infection (Gilstrap & Faro, 1997). If congenital, symptoms of toxoplasmosis include chorioretinitis (i.e., ocular lesions), hydrocephalus, microcephalus, cerebral calcifications, and other neurologic signs. Even if the infection occurs later (e.g., adulthood), there are a number of physical signs and symptoms (e.g., fever, swollen lymph nodes, stiff neck, fatigue, and confusion).

The pathogen exists in three forms: the oocyst, a resistant form; the trophozoite, a proliferative form; and the cystozoite or bradyzoite, which is intracystic (Couvreur, Thulliez, & Dafos, 1993). The host becomes infected by ingesting meat containing tissue cysts. Gardening in infected soil, eating infected fruits or vegetables, and drinking water with the parasite can cause toxoplasmosis. Once the pathogen gains entrance to the host cell, it reproduces and proliferates.

Toxoplasmosis is one of the most common infections in humans. One third of adults have serologic evidence of previous exposure to *T. gondii*. In the United States, approximately 3.7 million infants acquire the infection in utero (Gilstrap & Faro, 1997). If the mother is infected during pregnancy, she has a 40% chance of transmitting the infection to her neonate. Prevalence between sexes is evenly distributed. There are, however, differences among various geographic regions. For example, areas with colder temperatures have fewer human infections than warmer areas, and urban areas have lower infection rates than rural.

Whereas adults tend to develop immunities to infections and therefore show fewer or no symptoms, neonates and children are often seriously impacted by the parasite. Many children who have been exposed prenatally will have retinal damage, and some will be blind as a result of this. Most infants, however, will be asymptomatic at birth, with symptoms becoming more apparent as they get older. The severity of sequelae varies from mild to severe, but 40% of infected neonates will manifest some degree of impairment, and some quite severe (e.g., prematurity, intrauterine growth retardation, and intellectual disabilities). Seizures are also common and will be the first sign in 50% of infants with toxoplasmosis.

Characteristics

1. Parasite is transmitted congenitally or by infection (e.g., cat feces and meat).
2. Congenital exposure causes visual and intellectual impairments and other neurologic involvement (e.g., hydro/microcephaly). Later exposure produces more transient symptoms (stiff neck, headache, and confusion).
3. Infection most likely is transmitted in the third trimester (the outcome is worse if transmitted in the first). Toxoplasmosis is deadly in individuals with compromised immune system.

Diagnosis is achieved through serologic methods that detect and isolate the parasite (i.e., *T. gondii*). Confirmatory testing can be done during pregnancy for both the mother and the fetus. Treatment with an antiparasitic agent reduces the risk of infection, whereas an antibiotic impacts only the sequelae (i.e., the rate and severity of symptoms), not the transmission of the infection (Foulon et al., 1999). Early diagnosis and treatment are the most effective methods to ameliorate the impact from toxoplasmosis; however, prevention requires early education of women, especially those who are pregnant. This education includes awareness of the more subtle symptoms of infection (e.g., unexplained stiff neck and fatigue).

Prognosis for congenital exposure and infection varies depending on the time of infection. For example, the worst outcome occurs when the fetus is infected during the first trimester (e.g., blindness and severe intellectual impairment). Fortunately, most neonates (about 60%) are infected in the third trimester when the impact is less severe, and far fewer infants are infected in the first and second trimesters (i.e., 15% and 25%, respectively).

Special education placement is often necessary for children infected by *T. gondii,* especially those infected in utero or as neonates. In some cases, services for children with intellectual disabilities and visual impairments are needed. For others, accommodations through regular education programs and itinerant staff will suffice (e.g., vision and reading specialists).

Long-term follow-up studies of children congenitally infected with toxoplasmosis would be highly useful. Cognitive and behavioral profiles based on the time of infection and type of treatment would allow educators and parents to develop more effective strategies to address the complex problems that these children face.

REFERENCES

Couvreur, J., Thulliez, P., & Dafos, F. (1993). Toxoplasmosis. In D. Charles (Ed.), *Obstetric and perinatal infections* (pp. 158–180). St. Louis, MO: Mosby Year Book.

Foulon, W., Villena, I., Stray, P., Decoster, A., Lappalainen, M., Pinion, J. M., Jenum, P. A., Hedman, K., & Naessens, A. (1999). Treatment of toxoplasmosis during pregnancy: A multicenter study of impact on fetal transmission and children's sequelae at age 1 year. *American Journal of Obstetric Gynecology, 180*(2, Pt. 1), 410–415.

Gilstrap, L., & Faro, S. (1997). *Infections in pregnancy* (2nd ed.). New York: Wiley-Liss.

Heather Edgel
Elaine Clark
University of Utah

TRAUMA, PSYCHOLOGICAL

Traumatic incidents, which are usually unexpected and uncontrollable, create psychological trauma. They are events where the individual's life or another person's life is in danger, or their safety is severely compromised. Examples would include serious injury, natural disaster, school violence, childhood sexual or physical abuse, torture, rape, or watching a parent experience violence. Individuals who experience a traumatic incident tend to feel insecure and vulnerable (Lerner & Shelton, 2001; Volpe, 1996).

Survivors of trauma experience the "imprint of horror": the sights, sounds, and smells recorded in the victim's mind during the traumatic event. Traumatic stress can cause victims to experience emotional, cognitive, behavioral, and physiological effects that overwhelm their coping and problem-solving abilities (Lerner & Shelton, 2001). The longevity and severity of the trauma impact the intensity of the resultant symptoms. For example, a single, short-term event such as a severe beating will typically result in less impact on an individual's level of functioning than chronic victimization, such as ongoing child sexual or physical abuse. However, any traumatic event has the potential to cause psychological damage (Lerner & Shelton, 2001; Volpe, 1996).

Studies of the prevalence of childhood trauma indicate that it is a public health problem (Volpe, 1996). Several hundred thousand cases of child sexual and physical abuse are reported yearly, and this number generally reflects an underestimate. More and more children are at risk for violence as incidents increase in schools. Over half of school-age children in domestic violence shelters show clinical levels of anxiety and posttraumatic stress (Volpe, 1996).

Characteristics

Acute responses to trauma can include shock, denial, dissociation, panic, fear, hopelessness, horror, grief, irritability, confusion, hypervigilance, perseverative thoughts, aimless pacing, erratic behavior, and physiological symptoms such as elevated heart rate, elevated blood pressure, muscle tension, dizziness, headaches, and gastrointestinal upset.

Less acute symptoms include the following:

1. *Preschool Children* (ages 1–5): Engaging in behaviors that are immature and that have been abandoned in the past, such as thumb sucking, bed wetting, fear of the dark, loss of bladder control, speech difficulties, decreases or increases in appetite, clinging and whining, and separation difficulties.
2. *Childhood* (ages 5–11): Sadness and crying, school avoidance, poor concentration, physical complaints (e.g., headaches), fear of personal harm, regressive behavior (clinging, whining), nightmares, aggressive behavior at home or school, bed wetting, confusion, eating difficulty, irritability, attention-seeking behavior, anxiety and fears, and withdrawal-social isolation.
3. *Early Adolescence* (ages 11–14): Sleep disturbance, increase or decrease in appetite, withdrawal or isolation from peers, loss of interest in activities, rebelliousness, generalized anxiety, school difficulties, including fighting, fear of personal harm, physical ailments (e.g., bowel problems), poor school performance, depression, concentration difficulties.

Treatment for psychological trauma can be provided by either school personnel or outside therapists. Counseling techniques would include giving the client a chance to "tell their story" about the event, which would include talking about the facts about the experience, what they were doing at the time of the event, physical reactions, and their thoughts and feelings at the time of the event. Counseling would also help to support clients, educate them about the effects of trauma and what symptoms they can expect, and help them normalize responses to an abnormal situation so that they know they are not alone. Longer term psychological treatment would include individual or group therapy focused on helping the child to understand that their current dysfunctional behaviors and symptoms may have helped them cope with the trauma they experienced. In addition, therapy would help the child develop necessary skills not previously learned because of the arrest in emotional development after a severe trauma. Finally, therapy would help the child to establish boundaries, help them with communication and relationship skills, and help them to feel more empowered and able to advocate for themselves (Harris, 1998).

There are many ways that schools can help children cope with traumatic events that have taken place in both the home and the school. Traumatized children are at risk for delinquency, other acting-out behaviors, and regressive behavior in the classroom. School-based programs can aid these children in their recovery. Children who have experienced violence in the home should be referred to the school psychologist, guidance counselor, or social worker. However, when the school is the location of the trauma, more global measures should be taken. Classrooms can provide curricular materials about traumatizing events, symptoms of stress-related disorders, and healthy responses to stress that can help create discussions in a supportive atmosphere. Other interventions can include small-group activities and projective techniques such as artwork, play, writing in a journal, and storytelling. The school can also teach coping skills, relaxation techniques, and encourage normalization and recovery as well as correcting misperceptions and fears (Pfefferbaum et al., 1996; Volpe, Lerner, & Lindell, 1998). Pfefferbaum et al. (1996) also point out that the school environment is not a place to discuss revenge fantasies and that the school must be sensitive to when it is prudent to refer an at-risk child to an outside clinician for more intensive individual work.

Individuals can respond to a trauma in myriad ways, depending on whether they have a history of trauma, personality variables, severity and proximity of the event, level of social support, genetic predisposition to mental health disorders, and availability of immediate treatment (Volpe, Lerner, & Lindell, 1998).

If treatment for traumatized children is administered promptly and effectively, future problems generally associated with childhood trauma such as increased suicide risk, increased mental health disorders such as depression and PTSD, increased health problems due to higher level of risk taking behaviors, and substance abuse can be ameliorated (Lerner & Shelton, 2001; Read et al., 2001). However, without treatment, children are at a significant risk for delinquency, substance abuse, school dropout, and problems in their relationships with others (Volpe, 1996).

REFERENCES

Harris, M. (1998). *Trauma recovery and empowerment: A clinicians guide for working with women in groups* (pp. xiii–xiv). New York: Free Press.

Lerner, M. D., & Shelton, R. D. (2001). *Acute traumatic stress management (ATSM): Addressing emergent psychological needs during traumatic events.* New York: American Academy of Experts in Traumatic Stress.

Pfefferbaum, B., Jonas, P., Jonas, R., Moore, V. L., Sconzo, G. M., Gurwitch, R. H., & Messenbaugh, A. K. (1996). The Oklahoma City bombing: The Oklahoma City public school response. *Trauma Response, 2,* 15–17.

Read, J., Agar, K., Barker-Collo, S., Davies, E., & Moskowitz, A. (2001). Assessing suicidality in adults: Integrating childhood trauma as a major risk factor. *Professional Psychology: Research and Practice, 32,* 367–372.

Volpe, J. S. (1996). Effects of domestic violence on children and adolescents: An overview. *Trauma Response, 2,* 12–13.

Volpe, J. S., Lerner, M. D., & Lindell, B. (1998). *A practical guide for crisis response in our schools.* Commack, NY: American Academy of Experts in Traumatic Stress.

Jennie Kaufman Singer
California Department of Corrections
Parole Outpatient Clinic

April M. Smith
Yale University

See also Panic Disorder; Posttraumatic Stress Disorder

TRAUMATIC BRAIN INJURY

Traumatic brain injury (TBI) refers to any class of mechanical injury to the brain. Approximately 100,000 children and adolescents are hospitalized annually for TBI (Kraus, Fife, & Conroy, 1987). It is estimated that an additional 100,000 children sustain TBI annually but either do not seek medical treatment or are treated and released by emergency facilities. TBI is one of the leading causes of hospitalization and mortality throughout childhood and adolescence, with the incidence peaking sharply between the ages of 15 and 24 years. Males are two to four times more likely than females to sustain a head injury, particularly during adolescence (Goldstein & Levin, 1990).

Characteristics

1. Immediate loss of consciousness (LOC) of variable duration may occur from the initial trauma. Later onset LOC may occur secondary to hematoma or other causes of increased intracranial pressure.
2. Posttraumatic amnesia (dense anterograde amnesia of variable duration) may occur following regaining consciousness or following the injury in the absence of LOC. Retrograde amnesia for events preceding the TBI is also common.
3. The pattern of neuropsychological dysfunction can vary widely. Often there is focal neurological injury resulting from contusion, hemorrhage, and laceration, along with more diffuse injury resulting from diffuse axonal injury, excitotoxicity, edema, or other causes of mass effect.
4. The neuropsychological outcome of TBI is largely dependent on the age of the individual at the time of injury and on the nature, location, and severity of the injury involved. Longer term sequelae often include declines in intellectual-executive functioning, attention, and memory.
5. Personality change following TBI is common, particularly problems with temper modulation, initiation, motivation, and affective lability.
6. The majority of children have Glasgow Coma Scale (GCS) scores less than or equal to 4, and 65% of children with GCS of 5–8 have outcomes associated with mortality, persistent vegetative state, or severe neurological disability.
7. The majority of children with GCS of 13–15 have good outcomes with little or no neurological deficits.

Head injuries are classified as either closed, in which the skull and dura are not compromised, or open, in which these structures are penetrated. The mechanisms of injury in TBI are multifactorial. First, as the head undergoes rapid acceleration or deceleration, injury occurs as the brain strikes the interior surface of the skull. This can result in focal contusion or laceration. The frontal and temporal poles are particularly vulnerable due to frictional abrasion with bony protuberances of the anterior and middle cranial fossae (Bigler, 1990). In addition, because the brain and skull are of different densities and accelerate and decelerate at different velocities, repeated oscillations of these collision-abrasive forces occur. Hence, in addition to damage at the point of initial impact (coup), damage at the opposite pole (contracoup) and other sites is common. Angular, or shearing, forces also result in diffuse axonal injury, particularly at the gray-white matter junction, corpus callosum, and brain stem. Biochemical perturbations also contribute to neuronal damage through excitotoxicity. Specifically, mechanical trauma to the brain can cause the indiscriminate release of neurotransmitters (particularly glutamate), eventually leading to necrosis (Povlishock & Christman, 1995). A variety of other secondary factors can cause injury and affect outcome including hemorrhage into the dural spaces, ventricles, or parenchyma, as well as cerebral edema, hydrocephalus, increased intracranial pressure, hypotension, ischemia, and failure of other bodily systems.

The typical etiology of head injury and associated pathological findings vary over the course of childhood (Goldstein & Levin, 1990). Children aged 5 years or younger are most likely to sustain TBI in accidents and falls. Because children's skulls are not fully fused and the physical force in this type of injury is more focal, younger children are more likely to sustain skull fracture and delayed intracranial hematoma than are older children. School-aged children are more likely to be injured in pedestrian-motor vehicle accidents, bicycle accidents, and sports activities. These injuries are most often associated with concussion. Older children and adolescents, aged 10–19, most often sustain TBI in motor vehicle accidents.

Neuropsychological assessment is recommended to assist in treatment planning. Speech, occupational, and physical therapies are often necessary early in rehabilitation. Psychotherapy for the child and his or her family is also recommended to assist them in adjusting to the effects of TBI (Telzrow, 1990). Specific behavioral therapy may be necessary to help with problems with temper modulation, frustration tolerance, and task persistence. Formal social skills training may also be indicated. Academic accommodations are usually necessary in cases of moderate to severe TBI. Special education programs for these children should include an environment designed to minimize stress, with a low pupil-to-teacher ratio. Academic programs should utilize intensive, repetitive instruction with an emphasis on integrating classroom instruction with real-life situations by including parents and physicians in the academic process (Telzrow, 1990).

REFERENCES

Bigler, E. D. (1990). Neuropathology of traumatic brain injury. In E. D. Bigler (Ed.), *Traumatic brain injury: Mechanisms of damage, assessment, intervention, and outcome.* Austin, TX: Pro-Ed.

Goldstein, F. C., & Levin, H. S. (1990). Epidemiology of traumatic brain injury: Incidence, clinical characteristics, and risk factors. In E. D. Bigler (Ed.), *Traumatic brain injury: Mechanisms of damage, assessment, intervention, and outcome.* Austin, TX: Pro-Ed.

Kraus, J. F., Fife, D., & Conroy, C. (1987). Pediatric brain injuries: The nature, clinical course, and early outcomes in a defined United States population. *Pediatrics, 79*(4), 501–507.

Povlishock, J. T., & Christman, C. W. (1995). Diffuse axonal injury. In S. G. Waxman, J. D. Kocsis, & P. K. Stys (Eds.), *The axon: Structure, function and pathophysiology.* New York: Oxford University Press.

Telzrow, C. F. (1990). Management of academic and educational problems in traumatic brain injury. In E. D. Bigler (Ed.), *Traumatic brain injury: Mechanisms of damage, assessment, intervention, and outcome.* Austin, TX: Pro-Ed.

Rebecca Vaurio
David M. Tucker
Austin, Texas

TRAUMATIC BRAIN INJURY, MILD

A mild traumatic brain injury results from a change in brain functioning due to physical trauma with possible permanent sequelae. There are open head injuries, when the skull is penetrated, and closed head injuries, when the skull is not penetrated. After one head injury, the risk of a second injury is tripled; and after a second head injury, the risk of a third injury is eight times greater (Brain Injury Association, 1995). The severity of brain injury is determined through the utilization of a number of standardized scales. The most commonly used scale is the 15-point Glasgow Coma Scale (GCS), which evaluates the stimulus required for the child to induce eye opening, motor response, and verbal response. A mild injury is classified as a score of 13 or more. A second means of measuring brain injury severity is the length of posttraumatic amnesia, which is the time between the injury and the return of ongoing memory. A mild injury involves amnesia of 1 hr or less.

The reason for numerous measures lies with the lack of consensus relating to the definition of traumatic head injury and how to measure it. For example, it is common knowledge that a person does not have to lose consciousness to have a head injury (Bigler, 1990). Furthermore, children can sustain a more serious injury than an adult without losing consciousness, which leaves in question the appropriateness of using the same scales for all ages (Ewing-Cobbs, Fletcher, Levin, Francis, Davidson, & Miner, 1997). Finally, medical staff do not evaluate all injuries at the time of the accident, so measures required are not recorded at requisite times if at all.

It is estimated that 56,000 Americans die annually from brain injuries (Brain Injury Association, 1995). Further, 373,000 Americans are hospitalized annually as a result of head injuries, and 99,000 of those injuries result in moderate to severe lifelong disabilities (Brain Injury Association, 1995). Males are reported as incurring more head injuries than females. For example, Bigler (1990) reported that the ratio of male to female injuries was 2:1 in his information search. Traumatic brain injury (TBI) has become a major medical issue (Hilton, 1994), and "the economic cost of brain injuries in the United States is estimated to be $48.3 billion annually" (Brain Injury Association, 1995, p. 1).

Characteristics

1. Cognitive deficits.
2. Cognitive profiles are varied; no two head injuries are exactly alike.
3. Fatigue.
4. Language deficits, particularly social language.
5. Behavior problems.
6. Premorbid behavior problems are exacerbated.
7. Behavioral deficits and adaptive skills are found in longitudinal studies to adulthood.
8. The earlier in life the injury, the worse the developmental outcome is.
9. The more severe the injury, the worse the outcome is.
10. Developmental course may be changed. A skill may be delayed or not develop, and the structure of the skill may be changed.
11. Recovery may take up to five years for children versus three years for adults. Some advocate that for every year younger the child is, the longer is the recovery process.
12. Deficits become more apparent as time goes on. Children often do not keep up with their peers, and developmental skills often are not accomplished or lag behind.

Treatment of mild TBI starts with medical providers in case of a concussion, a hemorrhage, or other physical sequelae. Once the child is medically stable, school and social activities may resume except for contact sports, and care should be taken not to incur another injury (e.g., wearing a helmet for biking). If all symptoms are not resolved by three months, an evaluation is recommended. The most thorough assessment is a neuropsychological evaluation, which focuses on brain-behavior relationships. The assessment should include cognitive, academic, emotional, social, adaptive, and behavioral functioning. The assessment will be the basis for further treatment and a baseline so that developmental progress can be monitored. Many interventions require changes in the environment such as a structured routine and a reduced level of stimulation. The child needs to learn to pace him- or herself and recognize limits. If adjustment problems develop, counseling with a therapist knowledgeable about mild TBI is warranted. Unfortunately, mild injuries are often not diagnosed, or once the initial trauma is over, the child is thought to have fully recovered. As development unfolds and later skills are affected, no one connects a previous TBI with deficit.

Traumatic brain injury is recognized as a specific diagnostic category as of the reauthorization of P.L. 94-142 (now P.L. 101-476, or IDEA, 1990). Therefore, school staff may complete or participate in the assessment of the child for special education services. Specialized training is required before providing needed services for students with TBI; therefore, a school district may need to consult with providers in the community successfully to fulfill educational obligations for the child (D'Amato, & Rothlisberg, 1996). A positive and collaborative relationship between school staff and parents is particularly important as the family has a moderator effect on the recovery of the child. The higher functioning the family is, the better the prognosis for outcome (Taylor, Yeates, Wade, Drotar, Klein & Stancin, 1999).

Prognosis is positive for the majority of children incurring a mild brain injury. A small portion of children have permanent sequelae that will require special education classes, and compensatory strategies for a life time. Researchers are involved with longitudinal studies, deficits and developmental intertwine (Ewing-Cobbs et al., 1997), and moderator factors in recovery (Taylor et al., 1999). These lines of research are needed for a long-term understanding.

REFERENCES

Bigler, E. D. (Ed.). (1990). *Traumatic brain injury.* Austin, TX: Pro-Ed.

Brain Injury Association. (1995). *Fact sheet: Traumatic brain injury.* Washington, DC: Author.

D'Amato, R. C., & Rothlisberg, B. A. (1996). How education should respond to students with traumatic brain injury. *Journal of Learning Disabilities, 29*(6), 670–683.

Ewing-Cobbs, L., Fletcher, J. M., Levin, H. S., Francis, D. J., Davidson, K., & Miner, M. E. (1997). Longitudinal neuropsychological outcome in infants and preschoolers with traumatic brain injury. *Journal of the International Neuropsychological Society, 3,* 581–591.

Hilton, G. (1994). Behavioral and cognitive sequelae of head trauma. *Orthopedic Nursing, 13*(4), 25–32.

Taylor, H. G., Yeates, K. O., Wade, S. L., Drotar, D., Klein, S. K., &

Stancin, T. (1999). Influences on first-year recovery from traumatic brain injury in children. *Neuropsychology, 13*(1), 76–89.

Theresa M. Gisi
Colorado Neuropsychological Associates, P.C.
Denver and Colorado Springs, Colorado

TRICHO-RHINO-PHALANGEAL SYNDROME

Tricho-rhino-phalangeal syndrome (TRP) is a genetic ectodermal dysplastic disorder affecting multiple systems. Three types have been distinguished (Buyse, 1990). All three types, however, share a common set of characteristic physical anomalies.

Characteristics

All TRPS Types

1. *Craniofacial abnormalities,* including thin sparse hair; bulbous, pear-shaped nose; large prominent ears; flattened or elongated philtrum.
2. *Skeletal deformities,* including brachydactyly, epiphyseal coning, micrognathia, and winged scapulae.
3. *Decelerating growth,* resulting in short stature.

TRPS Type I

1. Normal intellectual range.

TRPS Type II (Langer-Giedion Syndrome; TRPS with Exostoses)

1. Mild to severe mental retardation (in 70% of cases); disproportionate delays in speech development; hearing deficit.
2. Multiple cartilaginous exostoses; redundant or excess skin in infancy, regressing with age; microcephaly; maculopapular nevi; lax joints.
3. Frequent respiratory infections early in life.

TRPS Type III (Sugio-Kajii Syndrome)

1. More severe brachydactyly and stunted growth than in Type I.
2. Normal intelligence and absence of exostoses (in contrast to Type II).

The craniofacial features typically include fine sparse hair, flattened or elongated philtrum, large or prominent ears, broad nose with bulbous tip (pear-shaped nose), an abnormally small jaw (micrognathia), and dental anomalies. Other characteristic physical anomalies include abnormally short fingers and toes (brachydactyly), cone-shaped malformation of the growing ends of certain bones, especially the phalanges (epiphyseal coning), winged scapulae, and decelerating growth resulting in short stature.

In TRPS Type I there is a mutation in the TRPS1 gene on Chromosome 8, and inheritance is primarily autosomal dominant, although recessive forms and sporadic cases have been reported. Males and females appear equally affected. There have been over a dozen kindred families reported, including several of Japanese descent. The phenotype is variable across as well as within families, and as such the range and severity of symptoms may vary from case to case. Nevertheless, with Type I the prognosis is rather good, with expectations for normal-range intelligence and normal life span. Primary treatment concerns focus on the cosmetic appearance and repercussions of the skeletal deformities (e.g., possible treatment of hip, osteonecrosis, and capital femoral epiphysis; development of related arthritic changes). No special education is expected to be necessary, although patients may benefit from physical and occupational therapies to address growth deficits and adaptations.

TRPS Type II, which is also known as Langer-Giedion Syndrome and TRPS With Exostoses, includes the features of TRPS Type I but is additionally associated with a very distinctive pattern of multiple bony growth projections on the surfaces of various bones (*exostoses*). Often, there is also altered growth pattern in the lower extremities and deformity due to marked ligamentous laxity. Because of this pattern of obvious osteochondromata, patients often first come to the attention of orthopedic surgeons (Bauermeister & Letts, 1992). In contrast to TRSP Type I, patients with TRSP Type II often have microcephaly (60%), mild to severe mental retardation (70%), and disproportionate speech delays in the majority of cases. There may also be redundant or excess skin at birth that improves with age, neonatal hypotonia ("floppy infant"), recurrent upper respiratory infections, hearing loss, and discolored elevated spots on the skin (maculopapular nevi). TRSP Type II involves the genetic mutation of the TRSP1 gene as well as mutation of the EXT1 gene. All of the approximately 50 cases reported in the literature of Type II have been sporadic and the majority of cases are males (3:1). The prognosis for these cases depends heavily on the degree of mental retardation. Treatment includes special education, especially regarding speech delays, as well as surgical excision of impinging exostoses as needed.

TRSP Type III, also known as Sugio-Kajii syndrome, is caused by a mutation in the same TRSP1 gene, again with an autosomal dominant inheritance pattern. However, TRSP Type III is thought to represent the severe end of the TRPS spectrum. It is distinguished by a more severe form of brachydactyly that involves shortness in all phalanges, metacarpals, and metatarsals. There is typically more severe short stature than is observed with TRPS Type I. In contrast to TRPS Type II, there is a lack of mental deficiency and absence of exostoses (Nagai et al., 1994).

Approximately twice as many affected females than males have been identified. Fewer than 10 cases have been reported, most within one Japanese family, but cases have been identified in a variety of ethnicities (Buyse, 1990; Vilain, Sznajer, Rypens, Desir, & Abramowicz, 1999). As with Type I, intelligence and life span are normal, and patients can be expected to participate in regular education classes with appropriate accommodations for their physical limitations. Treatment is focused on the physical anomalies for both cosmetic concerns and adaptation to stunted growth, as well as addressing discomfort from the skeletal deformities.

REFERENCES

Bauermeister, S., & Letts, M. (1992). The orthopaedic manifestations of the Langer-Giedion syndrome. *Orthopaedic Review, 21*(1), 31–35.

Buyse, M. L. (1990). *Birth defects encyclopedia.* Oxford, England: Blackwell Scientific.

Nagai, T., Nishimura, G., Kasai, H., Hasegawa, T., Kato, R., Ohashi, H., & Fukushima, Y. (1994). Another family with tricho-rhino-phalangeal syndrome type III (Sugio-Kajii syndrome). *American Journal of Medical Genetics, 49*(3), 278–280.

Vilain, C., Sznajer, Y., Rypens, F., Desir, D., & Abramowicz, M. (1999). Sporadic case of trichorhinophalangeal syndrome type III in a European patient. *American Journal of Medical Genetics, 85*(5), 495–497.

Vicky Y. Spradling
Austin State Hospital

TRICHOTILLOMANIA

Trichotillomania is an impulse disorder characterized by recurrent pulling of hair. Sufferers can pull hair from any part of the body, including the scalp, eyebrows, eyelashes, and pubic region. However, in children, the most common areas affected are the scalp and eyelash-eyebrow areas (Reeve, Bernstein, & Christenson, 1992).

Trichotillomania is believed to be a rare condition, affecting less than 1% of the population. Childhood onset involves an equal number of males and females. The most common age of onset is 12–13 years, but many cases begin at younger or older ages than this.

Characteristics

1. Recurrent pulling out of one's hair resulting in noticeable hair loss
2. An increasing sense of tension immediately before pulling out the hair or when attempting to resist the behavior
3. Pleasure, gratification, or relief when pulling out the hair
4. The disturbance is not better accounted for by another mental disorder and is not due to a general medical condition (e.g., a dermatological condition)

The cause of trichotillomania is currently unknown. It has been linked to inheritance, diet, hormonal changes, and stress. Trichotillomania is sometimes informally classified in the same family of disorders as obsessive-compulsive disorder, although it is actually classified with compulsive disorders such as compulsive gambling or stealing.

Treatment of trichotillomania usually consists of cognitive behavior therapy, drug treatment with a family of drugs called selective serotonin reuptake inhibitors (SSRIs), or a combination of the two (Seedat, Stein, & Harvey, 2001). Additionally, some relief of symptoms may be found with changes in diet, increased skin care, support groups, and hypnosis.

Children diagnosed with trichotillomania will usually require extra assistance in school to alleviate the hair-pulling behaviors. Additionally, these children may experience very low self-esteem and may develop issues with body image and sexuality. Peer education may be needed in classes where a student has trichotillomania, as it can be very visually apparent.

The prognosis for early-onset trichotillomania is good, with most children making a full recovery. However, there are few longitudinal studies of childhood-onset trichotillomania. This question is an area to be addressed by future research.

REFERENCES

Reeve, E. A., Bernstein, G. A., & Christenson, G. A. (1992). Clinical characteristics and psychiatric comorbidity in children with trichotillomania. *Journal of American Academy of Child and Adolescent Psychiatry, 31,* 132–138.

Seedat, S., Stein, D. J., & Harvey, B. H. (2001). Inositol in the treatment of trichotillomania and compulsive skin picking. *Journal of Clinical Psychiatry, 62,* 60–61.

April M. Smith
Yale University

Allison B. Katz
Rutgers University

TRISOMY 13: 13+ SYNDROME (PATAU SYNDROME)

Patau syndrome, now more commonly called Trisomy 13, is a severe disorder in which the child has an extra Chromosome 13 in every cell. Some 95% of affected individuals die in infancy, most shortly after birth. The few survivors will have severe mental retardation, sensory impairments, and probably seizures and failure to thrive. The disorder has several variants. Trisomy 13 mosaicism leads to mixed chromosomal makeup: Some of the individual's cells have the normal two 13 chromosomes, and others have three. Outcome depends on the number of abnormal cells and may vary from near fully impaired to near normal. Partial trisomies on either the proximal or distal segment of Chromosome 13 lead to craniofacial abnormalities and severe mental retardation. Partial trisomy on the distal segment generally has more severe effects (Jones, 1997).

Incidence is about 1 in 5,000–10,000 births and increases with mothers' age. No gender difference is known (Jones, 1997; Pediatric Database, 1993).

Characteristics

1. Severe brain damage, with incomplete development of forebrain and optic and olfactory nerves; spina bifida in many cases
2. Microcephaly with sloping forehead
3. Sensory defects, including apparent deafness and visual impairments (microphthalmia, numerous other eye defects)
4. Cleft palate or lip
5. Numerous skeletal deformities, including polydactyly of hands, flexion of fingers, thin or missing ribs
6. Cardiac abnormalities
7. Abnormal genitalia

Diagnosis is on the basis of chromosomal analysis. Either amniocentesis or chorionic villus sampling may provide prenatal diagnosis. Prognosis for the full Trisomy 13 is poor, and provision of extreme measures to prolong life is questionable (Jones, 1997). Treatment is supportive. The few cases of full Trisomy 13 that survive infancy will need a wide range of medical services including surgery to repair the most serious physical impairments. The even fewer cases that survive to childhood will need a range of interventions, including separate classroom placement and services for severe visual and auditory impairments. Outcomes of the variants range from near normal to near fully impaired and call for case-by-case determination of needs. Parents may be referred to the Support Organization for Trisomy 18, 13, and other Related Disorders (SOFT) Web site for assistance: http://www.trisomy.org/info/Default.htm.

REFERENCES

Jones, K. L. (1997). *Smith's recognizable patterns of human malformation* (5th ed.). Philadelphia: Saunders.

Pediatric Database. (1993). Trisomy 13 syndrome. Retrieved from http://www.icondata.com/health/pedbase/files/TRISOMY1.HTM

Robert T. Brown
University of North Carolina, Wilmington

TRISOMY 18

Trisomy 18 or Edwards syndrome, named for the researcher who first identified it (Edwards, Hamden, Cameron, Crosse, & Wolff, 1960), is an autosomal dominant chromosome abnormality. The autosomes are the 22 pairs of nonsex chromosomes. A dominant gene is a gene that overrides the normal copy from the partner and has a 50% chance of being passed on. There are three types of Trisomy 18. In the full form, every cell in the body has three number 18 chromosomes instead of the normal pair. With the mosaic form, there is a mixture of abnormal cells (three number 18 chromosomes) and normal cells (pairs of number 18 chromosomes). In the third condition (partial form), either the long arm (18q+) or the short arm (18p+) of Chromosome 18 is duplicated (Young, 1994).

Trisomy 18 follows Trisomy 21 (Down syndrome) as the second most common autosomal disorder, with estimated prevalence rates of 1 out of every 3,000 (Pueschel & Thurline, 1983) to 1 out of every 8,000 live births (Smith, 1982). The full form type accounts for 80% of the trisomy cases, and the mosaic and partial forms account for 10% of the cases each (Pueschel & Thurline, 1983). The disorder occurs in females three times more frequently than in males, although of the infants with the full-form type, females live an average of 10 months compared with males, who on average live 2 months (Pueschel & Thurline, 1983). An 11-year epidemiological study conducted in Hawaii found that the racial-ethnic group with the highest prevalence of Trisomy 18 anomalies was Far East Asians (Forrester & Merz, 1999). However, the authors attributed this trend to differences in maternal age; mothers with Trisomy 18 tended to be older, and increased prenatal diagnosis of the disorder.

Characteristics

1. *Trisomy 18 full form:* The mortality rate of affected infants is around 90% during the first year of life. Phenotypic anomalies can include congenital malformations of the heart, lung, diaphragm, kidneys, and ureters.

Other physical characteristics that may be present include cleft palate; low-set, malformed ears; epicanthal folds; narrow palpebral fissures; ptosis of the eyelids; microcephaly (small head) with a prominent back of the head; rocker-bottom feet; and webbed fingers and toes (Pueschel & Thurline, 1983). At birth, these infants are small for gestational age with very low Apgar ratings. They may need to be resuscitated. Feeding difficulties can develop as a result of poor sucking reflexes, and apneic episodes are often present. Surviving children have significant language and motor delays with communication limited to single words or gestures (Udwin, 1994).

2. *Trisomy 18 mosaic form:* The ratio of normal to abnormal cells determines the severity of this form of the syndrome (Young, 1994). Consequently, the degree of impairment can vary markedly. Children with a high ratio of abnormal to normal cells evidence physical anomalies and developmental delays similar to children with the full form, whereas children with a low ratio of abnormal to normal cells tend to be less severely handicapped.
3. *Trisomy 18 partial form:* Overall, children with this form tend to be less severely handicapped. They may have normal intelligence with mild to moderate learning disabilities (Udwin, 1994).

The first step in the treatment process is reliable detection, usually with ultrasound followed with amniocentesis (Yang et al., 1999). Associated abnormal sonographic signs often include hydramnios, intrauterine growth retardation, microcephaly, and spina bifida (Salihu, Boos, & Schmidt, 1997). The presence of choroid plexus cysts in fetal choroid plexus detected during second trimester ultrasound can also indicate the presence of Trisomy 18 and necessitate follow-up with amniocentesis (Burrows, Ramsden, & Frazer, 1993).

Parents need to receive genetic counseling on the expected prognosis. Families can also benefit from nonprofit organizations such as the Support Organization for Trisomy 18, 13, and other Related Disorders (SOFT). With Trisomy 18 full form, intensive medical treatment for life-threatening problems is necessary. For example, infants with feeding difficulties may require continual tube feeding to receive nourishment. Medical treatment for these surviving children and children with the Trisomy 18 mosaic type (severe form) will be ongoing. For optimal development, early and intensive physical, occupational, and speech therapy intervention is also recommended.

The special education accommodations and services for Trisomy 18 full form and severe mosaic type are provided under the diagnostic rubric of mental retardation or communication or motor skills disorders. These services will need to be individually tailored. For example, if the child is nonambulatory, all instructional environments including restrooms need to be wheelchair accessible, and educational personnel should be familiar with the student's daily care needs. Educational instruction should be multisensory, and supportive communication devices such as soundboards should be employed where appropriate.

Because children with Trisomy 18 mild mosaic and partial form who possess normal intellectual functioning are at increased risk for learning difficulties, neuropsychological and psychoeducational assessment is important. Careful attention should be paid to the acquisition of early reading and mathematics skills when the child is enrolled in prekindergarten through Grade 2 so that intervention can begin immediately. If the child meets formal criteria, special education services are provided under the learning disability category.

REFERENCES

Edwards, J. H., Hamden, D. G., Cameron, A. H., Crosse, V. M., & Wolff, O. H. (1960). A new trisomic syndrome. *Lancet, 1,* 787–793.

Burrows, A., Ramsden, G. H., & Frazer, M. I. (1993). Choroid plexus cysts in the fetal brain. *Australian and New Zealand Journal of Obstetrics and Gynaecology, 33,* 262–264.

Forrester, M. B., & Merz, R. D. (1999). Trisomies 13 and 18: Prenatal diagnosis and epidemiologic studies in Hawaii. *Genetic Testing, 3,* 335–340.

Pueschel, S. M., & Thurline, H. C. (1983). Chromosome disorders. In J. L. Matson & J. A. Mulick (Eds.), *Handbook of mental retardation.* New York: Pergamon Press.

Salihu, H. M., Boos, R., & Schmidt, W. (1997). Antenatally detectable markers for the diagnosis of autosomally trisomic fetuses in at-risk pregnancies. *American Journal of Perinatology, 14,* 257–261.

Smith, D. W. (1982). *Recognizable patterns of human malformation.* Philadelphia: W. B. Saunders.

Support Organization for Trisomy 18, 13 and other Related Disorders (SOFT). Retrieved from http://www.trisomy/org/info

Udwin, O. (1994). Edwards syndrome. Retrieved from http://www.cafamily.org.uk/Direct/e18.html

Yang, Y. H., Ju, K. S., Kim, S. B., Cho, Y. H., Lee, J. H., Lee, S. H., Choi, O. H., Chun, J. H., Kim, J. L., Kim, H. J., & Sohn, Y. S. (1999). The Korean collaborative study on 11,000 prenatal genetic amniocentesis. *Yonsei Medical Journal, 40,* 460–466.

Young, I. (1994). Edwards syndrome. Retrieved from http://www.cafamily.org.uk/Direct/e18.html

Louise O'Donnell
University of Texas Health Science Center–San Antonio
University of Texas at Austin

TRISOMY 21

Trisomy 21, or Down syndrome, is an autosomal chromosome abnormality. Down syndrome can result from three genetic errors in cell division. Over 90% of the cases constitute the full form, Trisomy 21. Instead of the normal pair, every cell in the body has three number 21 chromosomes. Mosaic Trisomy 21, present in 2–4% of the cases, results when the extra Chromosome 21 is present in some, but not all, cells. The remaining 2–4% of the Down syndrome cases are caused by a translocation. This occurs when cells, in addition to the normal complement of 46 chromosomes, have material from Chromosome 21 stuck or translocated onto another chromosome. With translocation Trisomy 21, the individual still has features associated with Down syndrome (National Institute of Child Health and Human Development [NICHD], 2000).

Although Trisomy 21 is a relatively common genetic birth defect, 75% of Trisomy 21 conceptions end in spontaneous abortion (Pediatric Database, 1994). For women under 30 years of age, the prevalence rates for Trisomy 21 range from 1 in 800 to 1 in 1,200 live births with 75% of all Trisomy 21 births born to these mothers. As maternal age increases, so does the probability of having a child with Trisomy 21. For example, at age 40 the incidence rate increases to 1 in 105, and at age 49, Trisomy 21 is present in approximately 1 in 12 live births (NICHD, 2000). Trisomy 21 occurs with equal frequency across all racial, ethnic, and socioeconomic groups. Each year in the United States, approximately 5,000 children are born with Trisomy 21, and there are approximately 350,000 families with at least one family member who has the syndrome (National Down Syndrome Society [NDSS], 2001).

Characteristics

1. Common facial characteristics present in Trisomy 21 include an upward-slanting outer side of the eye with small skin folds in the inner corner of the eye, a large protruding tongue that is furrowed with no central fissure, a flattened nose bridge, and small ears that fold over slightly at the top (Pueschel & Thurline, 1983). Other physical features include short, broad hands with a simian crease, incurving of the fifth finger with one furrow instead of two, and a larger than average gap between the large and second toes (Merck Manual of Diagnosis and Therapy [Merck], 2000). Individuals with Trisomy 21 are also often short in stature and evidence microcephaly.
2. Common health problems include heart defects, intestinal malformations, vision difficulties, and hearing loss due to fluid in the middle ear, a nerve defect, or both (NICHD, 2000). Children with Trisomy 21 are at increased risk for leukemia, thyroid dysfunction, bronchitis, and pneumonia. Seizure disorders also occur in 5–13% of the Down syndrome population (NICHD, 2000).
3. Mental retardation is present in all cases of Trisomy 21, although the degree of mental impairment can vary from the mild to severe range. The majority of individuals with Down syndrome have mild to moderate retardation. Dementia and accelerated memory loss often occurs when individuals are in their 40s (NICHD, 2000).

As Trisomy 21 is a genetic disorder, there currently is no treatment available, and efforts are often focused on treating the associated medical conditions. These can include chemotherapy to treat leukemia, neuroleptic medication for seizures, and if necessary surgery for heart, digestive, and orthopedic conditions. Parents of a newborn with unexpected Down syndrome should receive counseling and information and have the opportunity to contact a parental support group.

Children with Down syndrome achieve developmental milestones slower than do average children and can profit greatly from participation in early intervention programs that provide speech and occupational therapy as well as cognitive stimulation. School-age children will require special education accommodations and services. Depending on the particular needs of the child, special education may be provided in a mainstream classroom or in a classroom with others who have similar cognitive functioning. Although there are benefits and drawbacks associated with both options, inclusion in a regular classroom has become very common. As children with Down syndrome often have difficulties fitting in easily with normal peers, teachers and counselors are often needed to help facilitate this process.

There is wide variation in intellectual, social, and physical abilities among individuals with Trisomy 21. Most individuals with mild and some persons with moderate degrees of mental retardation can learn functional daily living skills including reading and can live and work semi-independently. Individuals with more severe mental impairment will require more supervision and support in their living and working environments. Life expectancy (approximately 55 years) is lower for individuals with Trisomy 21 due to higher than average rates of heart disease and acute leukemia (Merck, 2000).

In Trisomy 21, the extra genetic material leads to an overexpression of the genes that in turn leads to the associated phenotypical results. A number of current research efforts include identification of the genes found in the Down syndrome critical region (currently, 20 to 50 genes are estimated to be within this region) and their effects when overexpressed. Another promising research avenue includes the work of Moon and Pennington. Their neuropsychological test battery examines the functioning of the prefrontal cortex, hippocampus, and cerebellum in children with Down syndrome (NDSS, 2001).

REFERENCES

Leshin, L. (1997). Trisomy 21: The story of Down Syndrome. Retrieved from http://www.ds-health.com/trisomy.htm

Merck Manual of Diagnosis and Therapy. (2000). Congenital anomalies—Chromosomal abnormalities. Retrieved from http://www.merck.com/pubs/mmanual/section19/chapter261/2611.html

National Down Syndrome Society. (2001, March). About Down syndrome: General clinical and educational information. Retrieved from http://www.ndss.org.html

National Institute of Child Health and Human Development. (2000, June). Facts about Down syndrome. Retrieved from http://www.nicnd.nih.gov/publications/pubs/downsyndrome.down.html

Pediatric Database. (1994). Down syndrome. Retrieved from http://www.icondata.com/health/pedbase/files/DOWNSYND.html

Pueschel, S. M., & Thurline, H. C. (1983). Chromosome disorders. In J. L. Matson & J. A. Mulick (Eds.), *Handbook of mental retardation.* New York: Pergamon Press.

Louise O'Donnell
University of Texas Health Science Center–San Antonio

See also Down Syndrome

TRUNCUS ARTERIOSUS, PERSISTENT

Persistent truncus arteriosus is a congenital heart defect associated with a high mortality rate. In normal fetal development the truncus arteriosus divides into the aorta and pulmonary artery. If the truncus arteriosus persists beyond the fetal stage, a single arterial trunk arises from the normally formed ventricles, and blood from both ventricles will mix, affecting the pulmonary and systemic circulation. If the infant survives, pulmonary vascular obstructive disease often develops due to extreme hypertension (high blood pressure) in the lungs. This disorder is also often associated with ventricular septal defects. Persistent truncus arteriosus is also known as Buchanan syndrome, and approximately 35% of infants with persistent truncus arteriosus also have DiGeorge syndrome.

Persistent truncus arteriosus appears to affect male and female infants equally. No ethnic predilection is documented. In the United States persistent truncus arteriosus represents 1–2% of congenital heart defects in live born infants. Therefore, this disorder is present in approximately 5–15 infants per 100,000 live births.

Characteristics

1. Babies born with this condition have difficulty breathing; blood oxygen is low; and the skin has a bluish color (cyanosis).
2. The infant's appetite is adversely affected, resulting in slow weight gain and impeded growth.
3. Increased rate of respiration (tachypnea).
4. Congestive heart failure.
5. Enlarged heart.
6. Without surgery, only 50% of the affected infants will survive beyond 1 month, and 90% of infants will die within 6 months.
7. With surgery, the survival rate at a 10–20 year follow-up is above 80%.
8. As the child grows, repeated surgeries are necessary (reinterventions).

Treatment usually consists of surgical repair, with closure of the ventricular septal defect. This consists of consigning the common artery truck to the left ventricles and reconstructing the right ventricle outflow tract. If surgery takes place in the neonatal period, survival is dramatically increased. Children who have the surgical repair early in life often require further surgical intervention on the right ventricle tract, as this does not grow along with the child. Infants also showing signs of congestive heart failure are commonly treated with standard measures (e.g., digitalis and diuretic medicines).

Most children with a diagnosis of persistent truncus arteriosus can attend regular education classes following successful surgery. In some cases, students may have special education needs, which can be met under IDEA 1997 within the physical disability category. For example, the school may need to limit stair climbing or provide transportation. In some cases, pediatric cardiologists encourage children to do physical activity, within limits, to help keep their hearts fit (e.g., swimming and bicycling). However, in some cases, a pediatric cardiologist may advise a child to avoid strenuous activity. Children with this disorder may need to make regular visits to a cardiologist, and possibly have additional surgeries to correct additional problems. As the student may be away from school for medical reasons, school personnel need to be aware of the child's diagnosis and work closely with medical personnel to make appropriate educational accommodations.

Among individuals who survive the postoperative stage, the prognosis for persistent truncus arteriosus is good. Reinterventions, however, are essentially inevitable. Recent research has been exploring whether and when there is an optimum time to perform surgery (e.g., Shrivastava, 2000). More longitudinal research is needed to explore the outcome and effects of heart surgeries on individuals over a long period of time (e.g., Higgins & Reid, 1994).

REFERENCES

Higgins, S. S., & Reid, A. (1994). Common congenital heart defects: Long-term follow-up. *Nursing Clinics of North America, 29*(2), 233–248.

Shrivastava, S. (2000). Timing of surgery/catheter intervention in common congenital cardiac defects. *Indian Journal of Pediatrics, 67*(4), 273–277.

Rachel Toplis
University of Northern Colorado

TUBERCULOSIS

Tuberculosis (TB) is a disease caused by the organism *Mycobacterium tuberculosis,* also called tubercle bacilli (Centers for Disease Control and Prevention [CDC], 1994). Microscopic droplets containing tubercle bacilli may be expelled into the air when a person with infectious TB disease coughs or sneezes. Other people may inhale this air and become infected (New Jersey Medical School National Tuberculosis Center [NJMS], 1997). However, prolonged exposure to a person with TB disease is usually necessary for transmission to occur (National Institute of Allergy and Infectious Diseases [NIAID], 1999). Moreover, it is important to distinguish between TB infection and TB disease, as they refer to different presentations of TB. These terms are not used interchangeably in this text.

People infected with *M. tuberculosis* do not have symptoms of TB disease and cannot spread TB to others (CDC, 1994). Approximately 10% of people who have TB infection will develop the disease at some point, and the risk is greatest during the first two years of infection (NJMS, 1997). Some people who have TB infection have an increased chance of developing TB disease. This includes infants, young children, older adults, people with HIV infection, people who inject illicit drugs, people who are sick with other diseases that weaken the immune system, and people in close contact with a person who has infectious TB disease (CDC, 1994).

In order to determine whether a person has TB infection, a Mantoux tuberculin skin test (TST) is given. Diagnosis of TB disease is based also on the results of a chest X ray, a bacteriologic examination, and the individual's medical history (NJMS, 1997). However, these diagnostic measures may be inadequate when determining if a child has TB disease. Specifically, children display nonspecific clinical symptoms, and it may be difficult to interpret the skin tests and chest radiographs of children (Khan & Starke, 1995). Thus, the diagnosis of active TB disease in children typically occurs when the disease is found in an adult. This is of great concern because the adult may be transmitting the disease to others as well.

TB disease is the leading cause of death in the world from a single infectious organism. An estimated one third of the world's population is infected with TB bacterium, and approximately 10–15 million people in the United States are among them (NIAID, 1999). A total of 18,371 cases of TB disease in the United States were reported to the Centers for Disease Control and Prevention in 1998 (NIAID, 1999). More than 70% of the TB cases reported in 1993 were ethnic minorities (NJMS, 1997). The number of TB cases in children reported in the United States increased by 36% between 1985 and 1993 (NJMS, 1997).

Characteristics

TB infection

1. The human body prevents the bacteria from growing.
2. No symptoms.
3. Cannot spread TB to others.
4. Can develop TB disease later in life if not treated.

TB disease

1. Symptoms depend on part of body where TB bacteria are located.
2. TB in the lungs may cause a bad cough that lasts longer than 2 weeks, pain in the chest, and coughing up blood or sputum.
3. General symptoms include fatigue, weight loss, no appetite, chills, fever, and night sweating.
4. Highly infectious.

(Based on information cited in CDC, 1994)

Generally, the same methods are used for treating TB in adults and children. Individuals with TB infection receive preventive therapy, which typically consists of a daily regimen of isomiazid that lasts 6 months. It is recommended that children receive 9 months of preventive therapy (NJMS, 1997). Due to the increased likelihood of TB dissemination in infants and young children, treatment should be started as soon as the diagnosis is suspected (CDC, 1994). The required treatment for TB disease is at least 6 months, and the regimen includes at least two different drugs (NJMS, 1997). It is critical for both TB infection and TB disease patients to complete treatment. One effective strategy to ensure adherence to treatment is directly observed treatment (DOT), in which patients with TB infection or TB disease receive their antibiotic therapy under the supervision of a health service worker (CDC, 1994). This has resulted in high treatment completion rates.

A social stigma is attached to TB in general. For instance, children with TB disease likely would be placed in a hospital setting where they would not have close contact with anyone in order to prevent TB bacteria from spreading while being treated. This could be an anxiety-provoking and potentially traumatic experience for children with TB disease. When such children return to school, they may have a difficult time adjusting. Also, they may fall behind in schoolwork if treatment for TB has compromised school attendance. Ultimately, this experience may result in poor academic performance.

Future research should explore the etiology of TB infection. Improvements in diagnostic methods for children also should be a focus of study. Additionally, preventive measures should be examined.

REFERENCES

Centers for Disease Control and Prevention. (1994). Questions and answers about TB. Retrieved October 5, 2000, from http://www.cdc.gov/nchstp/tb/faqs/qa.htm

Khan, E. A., & Starke, J. R. (1995). Diagnosis of tuberculosis in children: Increased need for better methods. *Emerging Infectious Diseases, 1,* 115–123.

National Institute of Allergy and Infectious Diseases. (1999, July). Tuberculosis. Retrieved October 15, 2000, from http://www.niaid.nih.gov/factsheets/tb.htm

New Jersey Medical School National Tuberculosis Center. (1997, September 26). Tuberculosis. Retrieved October 5, 2000, from http://www.umdnj.edu/~ntbcweb/q%26aintro.htm

Eve N. Rosenthal
Karla Anhalt
Texas A&M University

TUBEROUS SCLEROSIS

Tuberous sclerosis is a dominantly inherited syndrome, with onset in the first decade of life, characterized pathologically by the presence of hamartomas in multiple organ systems (O'Callaghan, 1999). Tuberous sclerosis complex (TSC) is an autosomal dominant disorder characterized by the widespread development of distinctive tumors termed hamartomas (Van Slegtenhorst et al., 1997). The clinical features of epilepsy, learning difficulties, and skin signs (white spots, butterfly-like yellow-red nodular paranasal rash on cheeks and chin) are well known, but recent epidemiological and genetic research has begun to reveal the complexity of the condition (O'Callaghan, 1999). Tuberous sclerosis is a systemic disorder in which hamartomas occur in multiple organ systems, particularly the brain, skin, heart, lungs, and kidneys (O'Callaghan, 1999).

Compared with many other genetic diseases, tuberous sclerosis is quite common (O'Callaghan, Shiell, Osborne, & Martyn, 1998). The most recent and highest estimate of its prevalence was completed in the United Kingdom and resulted in 3.7 per 100,000 (O'Callaghan et al., 1998; Webb, Fryer, Osborne, 1996). This is also supported by American data (Wiedemann, Kunze, & Dibbern, 1992). A recent capture-recapture analysis of some of the U.K. data suggests that this survey failed to identify about half of the prevalent cases. The total population prevalence may therefore be as high as 8–9 per 100,000, which means that many people with tuberous sclerosis are receiving neither specialist medical supervision nor genetic counseling (O'Callaghan et al., 1998).

Linkage of TSC to Chromosome 9q34 was first reported in 1987, and this locus was denoted TSC1. Later studies provided strong evidence for locus heterogeneity and led to the identification of Chromosome 16p13 as the site of a second TSC locus (denoted TSC2; Van Slegtenhorst et al., 1997).

Characteristics

1. Variable cognitive abilities with over half of the affected individuals having normal intelligence. Mental retardation is frequently noted.
2. 90% of individuals with TSC have seizure disorders. Infants will have jackknife of salaam spasms, and onset is usually within the first two years of life.
3. Hamartomatous lesions and concomitant disabilities can develop in almost any organ except skeletal muscle (Webb et al., 1996).
4. Brain hamartomas (giant cell astrocytomas) frequently cause epilepsy, mental retardation, autism, attention-deficit/hyperactive disorder, or a combination of these conditions.

Treatment is symptomatic and varied depending on location and effects, and genetic counseling is recommended in all cases.

Special education services will most likely be needed because the cortical tubers (brain hamartomas) frequently cause epilepsy, mental retardation, autism, attention-deficit/hyperactive disorder, or a combination of these conditions (Gomez, 1988; Webb & Osborne, 1991). Children with this condition will most likely need ongoing medical attention with hospital stays that may interfere with school attendance. Medications associated with many of the physical conditions such as epilepsy may also have significant side effects that could interfere with memory, concentration, and learning. The special education team would have to monitor changes in academic progress as medical treatment is adjusted. Family counseling for chronic illness may also be needed by the child and family.

In terms of future research and prognosis, population-based studies are needed to answer questions about the potentially lethal complications in the renal and central nervous systems (O'Callaghan, 1999). The availability of sophisticated imaging techniques means that the lesions produced by this condition are now more clearly visualized and more often detected. For example, renal cysts and angiomyolipomas (hamartomas made up of blood vessels, smooth muscle, and fat) are often found in patients with tuberous sclerosis. Occasionally, they may bleed or compress healthy renal tissue, but usually they remain asymptomatic. There is a great need for medical professionals to learn how to identify those lesions that will cause problems later (O'Callaghan, 1999).

Current recommendations for aggressive intervention are based only on findings from small case series and may not be justified (O'Callaghan et al., 1998; Webb et al., 1996). Only long-term follow-up of a population-based sample of patients with tuberous sclerosis will establish which lesions are likely to become symptomatic and when, if at all, clinical intervention is best timed (O'Callaghan et al., 1998; Webb et al., 1996).

REFERENCES

Gomez, M. (1988). *Tuberous sclerosis.* New York: Raven.

O'Callaghan, F. J. (1999). Tuberous sclerosis. *British Medical Journal, 31,* 1019–1020.

O'Callaghan, F. J., Shiell, A. W., Osborne, J. P., & Martyn, C. N. (1998). Capture-recapture analysis to estimate the prevalence of tuberous sclerosis. *Lancet,* 351–1490.

Van Slegtenhorst, M., Hoogt, R., Hermans, C., Nellist, M., Verhoef, S., Lindhout, A., Van Den Ouweland, A., & Halley, D. (1997). Identification of the tuberous sclerosis gene TSC1 on chromosome 9q34. *Science, 277,* 805–808.

Webb, D. W., Fryer, A. E., & Osborne, J. P. (1996). Morbidity associated with tuberous sclerosis: A population study. *Developmental Child Neurology, 38,* 146–155.

Webb, D. W., & Osborne, J. P. (1991). Tuberous sclerosis. *Journal Medical Genetics, 28,* 417.

Wiedemann, H., Kunze, J., & Dibbern, H. (1992). *Atlas of clinical syndromes: A visual aid to diagnosis* (2nd ed.). St. Louis, MO: Mosby.

Michael La Conte
District 11 Public Schools
Colorado Springs, Colorado

TURNER SYNDROME

Turner syndrome is a noninherited, genetic disorder found in females that is caused by the complete absence (classic karyotype) or abnormal presentation (mosaicism) of the second X chromosome. Turner syndrome can also occur when there is structural abnormality or rearrangement of one or both of the X chromosomes.

Estimated prevalence rates of Turner syndrome range from 1 out of every 2,000 to 1 out of every 5,000 live female births. However, these figures are an underrepresentation of actual incidence rates because a high percentage (99%) of pregnancies with Turner syndrome end in spontaneous abortion during the first trimester (American Academy of Pediatrics, 1995). Turner syndrome occurs with equal frequency across racial and ethnic groups.

Characteristics

1. All individuals with Turner syndrome evidence significant growth retardation. After age 3, growth rate is significantly reduced, and adolescent pubertal growth spurt is absent. Accelerated ovarian dysgenesis prevents secondary sexual development and contributes to infertility.
2. Classic Turner syndrome anomalies include lymphedema, webbed neck, low posterior hair line, unusual ear shape and placement, and cubitus valgus.
3. Typical intellectual profiles consist of higher verbal IQ relative to performance IQ. Visual spatial processing, visual memory, and constructional deficits contribute to these differences. Some karyotypes have an increased risk for mental retardation. Academic problems, particularly in mathematics, are often present.
4. Behavior difficulties may include hyperactivity, shyness, poor peer relations, and low self-esteem.

Although there is great variability of symptom expression among affected persons, the total absence of the second X chromosome is strongly associated with increased skeletal, cardiac, and renal anomalies. Ongoing medical assessment throughout the life span is essential to monitor and/or provide treatment for 35 possible physical abnormalities (American Academy of Pediatrics, 1995). Any number of these difficulties have potential long-term deleterious impact. For example, abnormalities of facial bone structures predispose the development of middle ear infections that can lead to hearing loss and increase the possibility of language delay or disorder. A comprehensive listing of the physical anomalies associated with Turner syndrome and the American Academy of Pediatrics policy guidelines regarding health care for individuals with Turner syndrome are available online at http://www.aap.org.

Treatment for two of the most common symptoms associated with Turner syndrome (short stature and infertility) now includes administration of growth hormone, hormone replacement therapy to facilitate secondary sexual development, and assisted reproduction. Although these treatment regimens provide an increased quality of life, it is also equally important to address issues of self-esteem and relationships with peers through therapy and social skills intervention (Rickert, Fsam, Hassed, Hendon & Cunni, 1996).

Although not typically identified as a central feature of Turner syndrome, parent and teacher behavioral checklists often reveal problems with hyperactivity and impulsivity (Rovet, 1993), although children with Turner syndrome evidence wide variability in symptom expression and often meet the criteria for atypical attention disorder (Williams, Richman, & Yarbrough, 1991). A comprehensive treatment regimen may need to include a medication referral and will need to examine the impact of behavioral difficulties on the child's intellectual and academic progress.

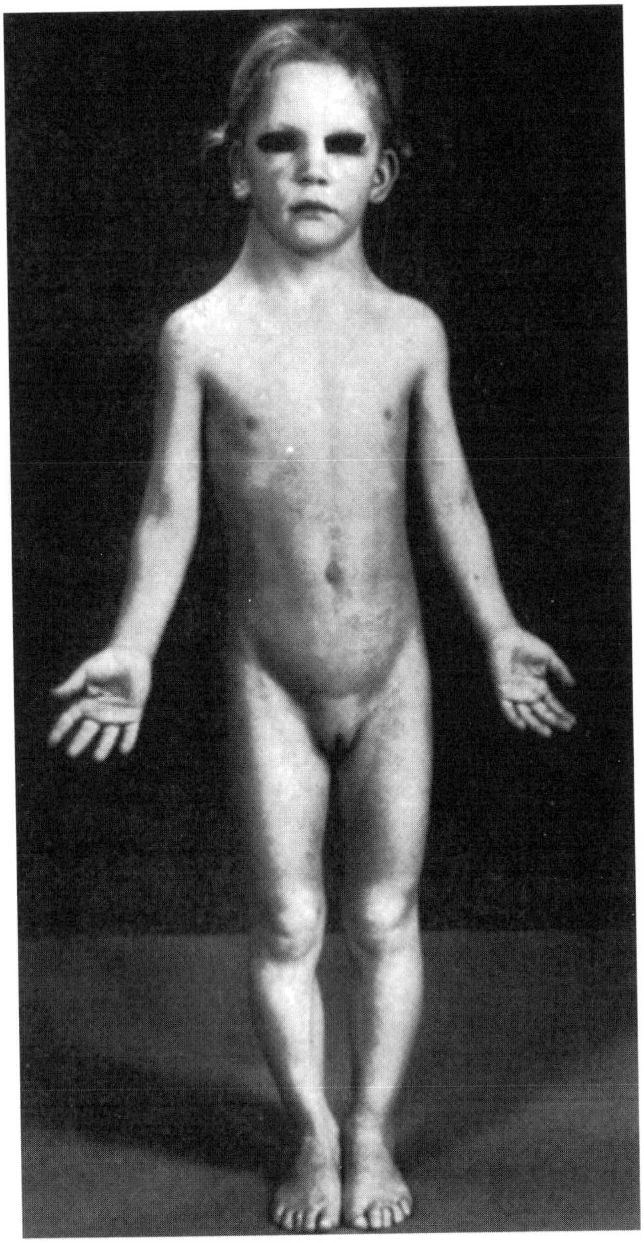

Turner Syndrome
Reprinted from *Clinical Syndromes,* Wiedemann and Kunze, 1997, by permission of the publisher Mosby

Given the wide range of physical and neurocognitive difficulties that may be associated with Turner syndrome, a comprehensive educational assessment is essential to ensure the timely and appropriate delivery of special education services for these children. Included in a comprehensive psychoeducational battery should be measures of intelligence, achievement, executive functioning, language, attention, memory, visual perception, and personality.

It is important to obtain an in-depth assessment of mathematics functioning because individuals with Turner syndrome on average perform two grade levels below current placement (Rovet, 1993). Computation difficulties can include slow retrieval of math facts along with poor implementation of step-wise calculation procedures (Buchanan, Pavlovic, & Rovet, 1998). In general, difficulties with mathematics were found to exist independently of visual-spatial deficits. Reading disabilities may also be present but were almost always found to coexist with mathematics disabilities (Rovet, 1995).

Children with Turner syndrome often qualify for special education services under a learning disability category and if significant attentional difficulties are present qualify under the Other Health Impairment category. Speech and language services may also be needed if language difficulties are present. Additionally, counseling as a related service may also be needed to address the psychosocial aspects of the disorder.

With early and appropriate medical, psychological, and academic intervention, individuals with Turner syndrome can live productive and fulfilling lives. Research continues within each major domain of the disorder. Most promising are the advances in behavioral genetics that shed light on the specific chromosomal abnormalities and their phenotypic expression.

REFERENCES

American Academy of Pediatrics. (1995). Health supervision for children with Turner syndrome. *Pediatrics, 96,* 1166–1173.

Buchanan, L., Pavlovic, J., & Rovet, J. (1998). A reexamination of the visuospatial deficit in Turner syndrome: Contributions of working memory. *Developmental Neuropsychology, 14,* 341–367.

Rickert, V., Fsam, S., Hassed, J., Hendon, A., & Cunni, C. (1996). The effects of peer ridicule on depression and self-image among adolescent females with Turner syndrome. *Journal of Adolescent Health, 19,* 34–38.

Rovet, J. F. (1993). The psychoeducational characteristics of children with Turner syndrome. *Journal of Learning Disabilities, 26,* 333–341.

Rovet, J. F. (1995). Turner syndrome. In B. P. Rourke (Ed.), *Syndrome of nonverbal learning disabilities: Neurodevelopmental manifestations* (pp. 351–371). New York: Guilford Press.

Williams, J., Richman, L., & Yarbrough, D. (1991). A comparison of memory and attention in Turner syndrome. *Journal of Pediatric Psychology, 16,* 585–593.

Louise O'Donnell
University of Texas Health Science Center–San Antonio
University of Texas at Austin

U

ULCERS

Ulcers are characterized by a persistent, burning pain in the abdomen as a result of a sore or lesion in the lining of the stomach or duodenum. Prevalence rates from the National Digestive Diseases Information Clearinghouse (NDDIC, 1998) indicate that about 4 million people are affected by ulcers, and that approximately 40,000 people have surgery for persistent problems, with complications resulting in death for 6,000 of them. Although ulcers can develop at any age, they are rare in teenagers, and even rarer in children.

> Characteristics
>
> 1. Persistent burning in the abdomen between the breastbone and naval.
> 2. Often occurs between meals and in the early morning hours.
> 3. Less common symptoms include nausea, vomiting, loss of appetite, and weight loss.
> 4. Bleeding may occur in the stomach, resulting in weakness and fatigue.

Ulcers may be diagnosed with an upper gastrointestinal series and X rays using a barium trace. In addition, an endoscopy may be performed under light sedation. Once an ulcer's presence and location has been confirmed, various tests may be performed for confirmation of the bacterium *Helicobacter pylori.* Tests include blood, breath, and stomach tissue. Before proceeding with treatment, it is important to rule out the possibility of nonsteroidal anti-inflammatory drugs (NSAIDs) related ulcers as well as nonulcer dyspepsia.

Etiology has historically been attributed to a number of causal factors but is believed to be primarily attributed to *H. pylori* bacteria that invade the lining of the stomach or duodenum (Ewald, 2000). Lifestyle factors such as smoking, alcohol, caffeine, and emotional stress may contribute to the exacerbation of symptoms through production of acid and the reoccurrence of ulcers. Physical stress, such as a severe injury, greatly increases the chance of ulcers as the immune system is overtaxed, combating a host of infectious agents. NSAIDs, such as aspirin, ibuprofen, and naproxen sodium, can make the stomach vulnerable to the harmful effects of acid and pepsin by impacting the stomach's ability to produce mucus and bicarbonate, which form a protective coating for the stomach lining.

H. pylori, a spiral-shaped bacterium found in the stomach, causes tissue damage by producing the enzyme urease. Urease neutralizes stomach acid, enabling the bacteria to survive. After penetrating the stomach's protective mucus lining, the bacteria make the stomach more susceptible to the harmful effects of hydrochloric acid and pepsin, which are naturally produced to aid in digestion. Local inflammation may occur, which may result in an ulcer. Whereas most people with *H. pylori* infection develop gastritis, an inflammation of the stomach lining, only a small number will have symptoms or problems related to the infection. It is unclear why some people have symptoms and others do not. *H. pylori* is more common in older adults, African Americans, Hispanics, and lower socioeconomic groups. *H. pylori* may be transmitted from person to person through contaminated food and water. Most individuals appear to be infected during childhood, with the infection of *H. pylori* lasting a lifetime.

Relative to the *H. pylori* causal hypothesis, Jefferson (1998) found in a meta-analysis of treatment studies that 20% of patients treated with antibiotics had a reoccurrence of ulcers within 6 months, despite a cure of infection and no report of NSAIDs use. This suggests that other factors may contribute to the development of ulcers.

Treatment is related to diagnosis with lifestyle change having little impact, other than stopping smoking, which has been related to reoccurrence. Acid blockers (Cimetidine, Famotidine, Ranitidine) and mucosa protection medications (Sulcralfate and Misoprostol) reduce symptoms. With the presence of *H. pylori,* antibiotics have the most dramatic effect in eradicating the ulcer. The National Institutes of Health indicate the most effective therapy as a two-week triple therapy, with a 90% success rate for both duodenal and stomach (not associated with NSAIDs) ulcers. This includes acid reducers, mucosal protectors, and antibiotics. In extreme cases (bleeding, perforation), surgery may be required with laparascopic procedures to be used in the future. This will hopefully prevent peritonitis, an inflammation of the abdominal cavity and wall.

Special education services for children may be warranted in extreme circumstances with services being provided under the umbrella of Other Health Impairment.

However, this is unlikely due to the success of current therapies in treating ulcers, as well as the infrequent occurrence in childhood and adolescence. Services may include a variety of supports focusing on accommodations and modifications in the regular education classroom and standardized test taking. Future research will hopefully determine why some people with *H. pylori* bacteria do not develop ulcers while others do and explore the hypothesized contribution of emotional stress.

REFERENCES

Ewald, P. (2000). *Plague time.* New York: Free Press.

Jefferson, T. C. (1998). Has the impact of helicobacter pylori therapy on ulcer recurrence in the United States been overstated? *Journal of the American Medical Association, 280,* 1466–1480.

National Digestive Diseases Information Clearinghouse. (1998). Stomach and duodenal ulcers. Retrieved from http://www.gastro.com/ulcers.htm

R. Brett Nelson
Diana L. Nebel
University of Northern Colorado

URTICARIA PIGMENTOSA

Urticaria pigmentosa (UP) is the most common form of mastocytosis, which is a disorder characterized by mast cell proliferation (increases in cells that contain histamine and heparin) and accumulation within various organs, most commonly the skin. It is a disease that produces skin lesions, intense itching, and hive formation at the site of the lesion upon rubbing. UP is also known as systemic mastocytosis and mastocytoma.

The cause of UP is still unknown, but the suggested etiology is probably an allergy specific to the skin in susceptible individuals. Allergens may be infections such as bacterial, viral, fungal, or parasitic. Allergies to certain foods can trigger UP, such as nuts, shellfish and seafood, chocolate, and dairy products. Certain drugs, such as penicillin, sulfa drugs, and barbiturates, may cause this condition. In some individuals physical agents may trigger UP. For example, cold, local heat, or exercise can induce the disorder.

Between 0.1% and 0.8% of new patients visiting dermatology clinics have some form of mastocytosis. Most reported cases are Caucasian, and the disorder affects females and males equally. Most cases are found in children; 75% of cases occur during infancy and early childhood. There is a second peak of incidence in adults around 30–40 years.

Characteristics

1. Skin lesions usually appear before age 2, although this disorder can occur at any age.
2. Appearance of lesions may be tan to dark brown, and they are found more often on the trunk than on the face and extremities. The number of lesions can vary from 1 lesion to over 1,000 lesions.
3. Welts or hives may form when lesions are rubbed or scratched.
4. In younger children, a blister may form over the lesion when it is rubbed.
5. Other symptoms less often associated with the UP form of mastocytosis are facial flushing, diarrhea, fast heart rate, headaches, and fainting (syncope).
6. In unusually severe cases, individuals may experience anaphylaxis, a severe reaction to stimuli such as insect bites and stings.

The prognosis for most patients with UP is excellent; therefore, treatment is conservative and aimed at symptom relief. It is suggested that patients avoid substances that induce mast cell mediator release such as crawfish, lobster, alcohol, spicy foods, hot beverages, and cheese. Patients should also avoid certain physical stimuli including emotional stress, temperature extremes, physical exertion, bacterial toxins, envenomation by insects to which the patient is allergic, and rubbing, scratching, or traumatizing the lesions.

Antihistamines may relieve some of the histamine-induced symptoms such as itching and flushing. Intralesional injections of small amounts of dilute corticosteroids may resolve skin lesions temporarily or indefinitely. However, this is only used in severe or persistent cases. Allergy testing may be indicated if the patient's history suggests an allergen-induced etiology.

School children diagnosed with UP will not be eligible for special services under IDEA 1997 if they appear to be benefiting from general education. These students may be able to access educational modifications and accommodations through Section 504 of the 1974 Rehabilitation Act. School personnel should be made aware of the physical stimuli and triggering substances to avoid for this student. Additionally, school personnel should be educated about the signs and symptoms of anaphylaxis, especially for patients with severe symptoms. On average, the main problem encountered by students with UP is the extreme itchiness and possible self-consciousness about the lesions. Students need to be encouraged not to scratch the lesions, as they may form welts or hives, to use prescribed medication when necessary, and most important, to avoid certain foods and possible allergens.

The prognosis for UP depends on age of onset. Most cases exhibited before 2 years of age are associated with excellent prognosis. These cases are often resolved by puberty. The number of lesions diminishes by approximately 10% per year. If the onset of the disease is after 10 years of age, the condition may be persistent and associated with systemic disease. If this is the case, other organs may be affected (e.g., the liver, spleen, and cardiovascular system). UP as a systemic disease carries a higher risk of malignant transformation (e.g., mast cell leukemia). This outcome is rare in most cases of UP. The most common prognosis for UP is that it disappears by puberty. It is considered a self-limiting benign disease.

Although advances have been made in recent years in understanding the pathogenesis of Urticaria Pigmentosa, as yet no effective treatment has been found (Hartmann & Henz, 2001). It has long been speculated that early onset and later juvenile/adult onset UP may be based on different pathogenetic mechanisms. New genetic findings indicate that this may be so. Further research is now investigating these possible differences (Hartmann & Metcalfe, 2000). For more information contact Medlineplus Health Information, National Library of Medicine, 8600 Rockville Pike, Bethesda MD 20894; http://www.nlm.nih.gov/medlineplus/healthtopics.html.

REFERENCES

Hartmann, K., & Henz, B. M. (2001). Mastocytosis: Recent advances in defining the disease. *British Journal of Dermatology, 144*(4), 682–695.

Hartmann, K., & Metcalfe, D. D. (2000). Pediatric mastocytosis. *Hematol Oncol Clin North Am, 14*(3), 625–640.

Rachel Toplis
University of Northern Colorado

USHER SYNDROME

Usher syndrome is a rare autosomal-recessive disorder manifested primarily by sensorineural hearing loss and retinitis pigmentosa. Although others described the syndrome earlier, it is named for Charles Usher, a British ophthalmologist who emphasized the role of heredity in the disorder (Usher, 1914). The degree of hearing loss in most affected individuals is severe to profound. Retinitis pigmentosa causes deterioration of the retina and progressive loss of vision, usually to blindness. Disturbances of balance occur with some types of Usher syndrome. Recent MRI evidence has indicated decreased brain and cerebellum size in a sample of Usher syndrome patients, suggesting a broader impact of the disorder than on the visual, auditory, and vestibular systems alone (Schaefer, Bodensteiner, Thompson, Kimberling, & Craft, 1998).

Usher syndrome is actually a group of conditions identified as three major types distinguished by age of onset and severity of symptoms. A fourth, X-linked type, is hypothesized. Although clinical symptoms present as three main types, gene localization studies have shown that one clinical type may be caused by any of several different genes located on different chromosomes. For example, seven different genes have been found that cause Usher syndrome Type 1 (Miner & Cioffi, 2001).

Usher syndrome affects an estimated 3–10 per 100,000 people worldwide. It is the most common disorder that causes both hearing and vision loss, and it accounts for more than half of the estimated 16,000 cases of deaf-blind individuals in the United States. Usher syndrome Types 1 and 2 cause approximately 10% of all cases of profound deafness in children (National Organization for Rare Disorders [NORD], 2001).

Characteristics

Usher Syndrome Type 1

1. Profound deafness from birth; hearing aids usually not effective
2. Severe balance problems
3. Onset of retinitis pigmentosa in infancy or early childhood, progressing to blindness

Usher Syndrome Type 2

1. Moderate to severe hearing loss from birth, especially for high frequencies
2. Usually able to benefit from hearing aids
3. Normal balance
4. Onset of retinitis pigmentosa in late childhood to teenage years; legally blind by early adulthood

Usher Syndrome Type 3

1. Normal hearing or mild hearing loss at birth
2. Onset in teenage years of progressive hearing loss, progressing to deafness by late adulthood
3. Mild balance disturbance
4. Retinitis pigmentosa onset around puberty; night blindness often initial symptom, progressing to legally blind by midadulthood

(Davenport, 2001; Department of Otolaryngology, Johns Hopkins University, 2001)

There is no known cure for Usher syndrome. Cochlear implants have shown significant benefits in young children (Young, Johnson, Mets, & Hain, 1995). A special form of vitamin A has been found to delay the progression of retinitis pigmentosa (NORD, 2001). Treatment of Usher syndrome primarily involves providing education and support services to optimize the functional ability of those affected by the condition. Prompt identification is important to allow initiation of treatment at the earliest opportunity.

Special education services are vital in helping individuals with Usher syndrome to cope with the often severe consequences of losing both vision and hearing. The progressive nature of the condition, coupled with onset in childhood, presents enormous challenges to successful adjustment. Treatment for the individual patient may include instruction in American Sign Language and tactile sign language; orientation and mobility training; Braille education; psychological, genetic, and career counseling; assistive devices; and support groups. Opportunities for children with the disorder to interact with successful adult Usher syndrome patients can be especially helpful.

The prognosis in Usher syndrome is variable depending on type and severity. However, with appropriate intervention, Usher syndrome patients may be able to attend college or receive vocational training and work in a wide variety of occupations. Loss of vision may progress sufficiently slowly that some individuals retain functional vision well into adulthood. Research is continuing into the genetic mechanisms of the disorder, with the hope of finding methods of prevention and treatment. Improving cochlear implant technology and the possibility of retinal tissue transplants are also being studied.

REFERENCES

Davenport, S. L. H. (2001). Usher syndrome. Retrieved from http://www.boystown.org/btnrh/deafgene.reg/usher-sx.htm

Department of Otolaryngology, Johns Hopkins University. (2001). What is Usher syndrome? Retrieved from http://www.med.jhu.edu/otolar/disorders/hearing/usher.html

Miner, I., & Cioffi, M. (2001). Usher syndrome in the school setting. Technical Assistance Center, Helen Keller National Center. Retrieved from http://www.tr.wosc.osshe.edu/DBLINK/usherfulltext.htm

National Organization for Rare Disorders. (2001). Usher syndrome. Retrieved from http://www.rarediseases.org

Schaefer, G. B., Bodensteiner, J. B., Thompson, J. N., Jr., Kimberling, W. J., & Craft, J. M. (1998). Volumetric neuroimaging in Usher syndrome: Evidence of global involvement. *American Journal of Medical Genetics, 79,* 1–4.

Usher, C. H. (1914). On the inheritance of retinitis pigmentosa, with notes of cases. *Royal London Ophthalmic Hospital Reports, 19,* 130–138.

Young, N. M., Johnson, J. C., Mets, M. B., & Hain, T. C. (1995). Cochlear implants in young children with Usher's syndrome. *Clinical Annals of Otology, Rhinology, and Laryngology, 166,* 342–345.

David R. Steinman
Austin Neurological Clinic
Department of Psychology
University of Texas at Austin

V

VARICELLA SYNDROME, CONGENITAL

When a pregnant woman contracts chicken pox (varicella), there is a 25% incidence of transmission of the infection to the fetus. However, a very small number of these babies will show evidence at birth that they were ever infected. Their condition is called congenital varicella syndrome (CVS).

Varicella-zoster virus (VZV), the causative agent of chicken pox, has an intense affinity for rapidly developing human tissues. This proclivity explains why VZV fetal infection at certain gestational ages can have devastating consequences. The period of pregnancy between the 8th and 20th week correlates with brisk growth of the extremities and maturation of the eyes, brain, and spinal cord. These structures are most likely to show the effects of VZV infestation.

This disorder occurs in only about 2% of infants delivered to women who had varicella at 8–20 weeks of gestation. Only 1–2 in 10,000 pregnant women have chicken pox. Therefore, CVS is a very rare phenomenon.

Characteristics

1. *Skin:* Cicatrix (zigzag scarring patterns), decreased pigmentation
2. *Eye:* Cataracts, underdeveloped optic nerve, unequal pupil size, microphthalmia (small eyeball)
3. *Brain:* Microcephaly (small head secondary to deficient brain growth), hydrocephaly, brain calcifications, complete failure of the brain to develop
4. *Spinal cord:* Shortened, malformed extremities; motor and sensory losses; anal-urinary sphincter dysfunction

Because active fetal VZV infection resolves long before birth, treatment of CVS-affected newborns with antiviral medication (acyclovir) is neither helpful nor indicated. Pregnant women with severe cases of varicella may be given acyclovia. The effect of this practice on the fetus is unknown, and its safety has been challenged.

Varicella zoster immune globulin (VZIG), which contains high levels of antibodies against VZV, is often given to susceptible pregnant women who are exposed to chicken pox to prevent their developing varicella. The benefits to the fetus of this practice are uncertain.

Because of the microcephaly and hydrocephaly, children with CVS may exhibit a variety of difficulties including learning difficulties and developmental delays. The severity of the difficulties depends on the amount of brain damage incurred. Because the severity and type of brain injury vary from one child to another, it is difficult to determine the exact cognitive sequelae and long-term prognosis. Providing the parents with counseling and education will enable them to be advocates for their child's educational need at an early age.

The prognosis for infants with CVS is largely dependent on gestational age at the time they acquired the infection. Infants affected from 16–20 weeks are most likely to have central and sensory nervous system damage, resulting in psychomotor retardation, seizure disorders, and blindness. Babies who are infected during the last few weeks of pregnancy generally have favorable outcomes.

The best strategy for eradicating CVS lies with the varicella vaccine (Varivax). Approved for use in the United States in 1995, this immunization is at least 90–95% effective in preventing infection when exposure to VZV occurs. The vaccine is given at 12–15 months of age. A booster dose is administered at 4 years of age. Ongoing studies demonstrate that this immunization scheme confers protection from VZV infection for at least two decades, with little evidence of waning immunity as vaccinated populations age.

REFERENCE

Myer, M. G., & Stanberry, L. R. (2000). Varicella-Zoster virus. In R. E. Behrman, R. M. Kleigman, & H. B. Jenson (Eds.), *Nelson's textbook of pediatrics* (16th ed., pp. 973–977). Philadelphia: W. B. Saunders.

Barry H. Davison
Ennis, Texas

Joan W. Mayfield
Baylor Pediatric Specialty Services
Dallas, Texas

VARICELLA ZOSTER

Varicella zoster is the virus that causes chicken pox. It is a mild but highly contagious disease that is contracted by exposure to someone while in the infectious stage. It is characterized by aches and fever followed by a blister-like rash. The rash typically starts on the trunk and then spreads to other parts of the body and will break and crust over. Symptoms usually occur form 11 to 20 days after exposure to the virus (Taylor-Robinson & Caunt, 1972).

The contagious stage of varicella zoster is from 1 to 2 days before the rash appears to 5 days after it appears. Once the blisters have dried up, the contagious stage is complete.

Characteristics

1. Headache and body aches
2. Fever that persists 2–4 days
3. Nausea, vomiting, or loss of appetite
4. Irritability or malaise
5. Blister-like lesions appearing typically 4–5 days after other symptoms (the lesions cause itching and will dry up and crust over at the end of the illness)

The treatment of varicella zoster is predominantly symptomatic. Normal treatment consists of medications such as those typically used for treating cold or flu symptoms and the use of topical solutions, such as calamine lotion, to relieve itching. It is not normally a fatal disease, but it often has more serious effects on infants and adults. A varicella zoster immune globulin (VZIG) can be administered to prevent or lessen the severity of the disease if given within 96 hr of exposure to the virus. This measure is usually reserved for high-risk patients such as those with a compromised immune system due to some other medical condition such as AIDS or leukemia or organ transplant patients. The varicella vaccine is currently available and should be administered between the ages of 12 and 18 months.

Varicella zoster is highly contagious, and those infected should be sheltered from others while in the infectious stage. School-age children should be excluded from school during this period. The prognosis for recovery in most children with a healthy immune system is good, and no special educational provisions or modifications are usually needed beyond the time of infection.

REFERENCE

Taylor-Robinson, D., & Caunt, A. E. (1972). Varicella virus. In *Virology monographs.* New York: Springer-Verlag.

Carol Schmitt
San Diego Unified School District

VASCULITIS

Vasculitis is the inflammation of the blood vessels, which can result in damage to the vessels and is usually associated with an allergic reaction to a drug or another foreign substance. There are many different forms of vasculitis. The different forms are named according to the organ, vessels, or system affected or to the clinical pattern.

The occurrence of vasculitis in the United States is rare, and the incidence is unknown. Vasculitis occurs more often in the Caucasian population and equally in males and females. The cause of vasculitis is unknown in approximately 50% of the cases, and the remaining 50% have various causes including allergic reaction, various infections, food or food additives, and Hepatitis B and C. Vasculitis may occur at any age, but may be called Henoch-Schönlein purpura in children and acute hemorrhagic edema in infants. Henoch-Schönlein purpura is the most common form of childhood vasculitis and is the inflammation of small blood vessels.

Characteristics

1. Fever and weight loss, which may develop over weeks to months
2. Pain in the extremities
3. Headache
4. Red or purple spots that appear on the skin (petechial purpura)
5. Abdominal pain (which usually occurs about 30 min after eating)
6. Pain in the joints with the knees and the ankles being the most commonly affected
7. Blisters on the skin
8. Itching or burning of the skin
9. Involving vessels that supply blood to organs (i.e., heart, lungs, kidneys, skin, and bowel)

Treatment consists of high doses of corticosteroids to help control the fever and to heal the vascular lesions. Antibiotics are also used in the treatment of vasculitis, but care must be exercised to ensure that the antibiotic is not causing an allergic reaction.

Individuals with more involved cases of vasculitis might qualify for special education services under the Physical Disability category. Students with hypersensitivity vasculitis typically would not qualify for special education services, although counseling may be beneficial. The counseling would be beneficial if the student was singled out because of the skin lesions. Homebound services may be warranted in order to prevent exposure to unnecessary infection.

With treatment, the prognosis for this disorder is generally good, and allergic vasculitis usually resolves with time. If the vasculitis affects the major organs, there is a greater chance of mortality. If there is no treatment, the 5-year survival rate is about 20%.

REFERENCES

Magglini, S., & Francisci, G. (1990). *Dictionary of medical syndromes* (3rd ed.). JB Lippincot.

Tierney, L., McPhee, S., & Papadakis, M. (2000). *Lange current medical diagnosis and treatment* (3rd ed.). New York: McGraw-Hill.

Wolff, K., & Winkelmann, R. (1980). *Vasculitis: Major problems in dermatology.* Philadelphia: W. B. Saunders.

Tammy Branan
University of Northern Colorado

VELOCARDIOFACIAL SYNDROME (SHPRINTZEN SYNDROME)

Velocardiofacial syndrome (VCFS) is a nondegenerative autosomal dominant disorder (National Institute on Deafness and Other Communication Disorders [NIDCD], 1996) that results in facial abnormalities, cardiovascular difficulties, learning disabilities, and neuropsychiatric problems (Phelps, 1998). VCFS also is known as Shprintzen syndrome, craniofacial syndrome, or conotruncal anomaly unusual face syndrome (NIDCD, 1996), although these syndromes are often classified as separate disorders with similar genetic deletions and overlapping behavioral phenotypes (Duke, McGuirt, Tamison, & Fasano, 2000).

The most common characteristic of VCFS is cleft palate. Other characteristics include heart problems, unusual facial features (wide nose, small ears, elongated face), learning problems, eye problems, feeding problems (especially nasal regurgitation resulting from the cleft palate), otitis media, hypoparathyroidism (low levels of the parathyroid hormone, a condition that can result in seizures), immunodeficiency, weak muscles, short stature, scoliosis, tapered fingers, structural brain anomalies, psychiatric disorders (i.e., attention-deficit/hyperactivity disorder, mood disorders, obsessive-compulsive disorder, oppositional defiant disorder, and specific phobias), and hypocalcemia (reduction of the blood calcium below normal (NIDCD, 1996; Wang, Woodin, Kreps-Falk, & Moss, 2000).

The etiology of the syndrome is unknown, although a link to a small deletion on Chromosome 22 (deletion 22q11) has been found in most children diagnosed with VCFS. Children who have a parent with VCFS generally have a 10–15% likelihood of acquiring the syndrome (NIDCD, 1996).

During the past decade, VCFS has been found to have a higher prevalence than once thought. It occurs in about 5–8% of children born with a cleft palate (NIDCD, 1996). NIDCD (1996) estimates that about 130,000 individuals are affected by VCFS in the United States. Wilson and colleagues (cited in Devriendt, Fryns, Mortier, Van Thienen, & Keymolen, 1998) report that 5% of the children diagnosed with a congenital heart defect also have VCFS. Overall, approximately 1 out of every 4,000 live births is diagnosed with VCFS (Devriendt et al., 1998).

Characteristics

1. Congenital onset
2. Motor, cognitive, and linguistic delays in infancy and early childhood
3. Presence of speech abnormalities (in addition to delays), including hoarseness, hypernasality, hyponasality, and articulation errors
4. Presence of feeding disorders, even in the absence of cleft palate or lip
5. Congenital heart defects
6. Relative impairment in visuospatial skills
7. Neuropsychiatric disorders (e.g., OCD, depression)

The majority of people with VCFS appear to function in the low average to borderline range of intelligence, with better developed verbal than nonverbal abilities (Wang et al., 2000); this is an interesting pattern of abilities, considering the significant speech delays and impairments children with VCFS often experience.

Based on the tremendous variability within the characteristics of VCFS, it is important to be flexible in designing any treatment regimen. Initial treatment may consist of surgery to correct any heart defects and to restore the cleft palate or lip so that normal feeding may occur. Also, speech and occupational therapy may be accessed to ameliorate some of the linguistic and motor delays, respectively.

Depending on the symptom severity, children with VCFS may be eligible to receive special education services in the schools. Children with VCFS may be eligible for services under the Individuals with Disabilities Education Act (IDEA) category of Emotional Disturbance if there is a psychiatric disorder (i.e., depression, anxiety) that is significantly affecting educational performance. Depending on the level of intellectual functioning, a child with VCFS may meet the criteria as a student with mental retardation. In addition, if a child has significant speech and motor delays, he would be eligible for services under the Speech or Language Impairment and Orthopedic Impairment categories of IDEA, respectively. If any congenital heart defects are present and significantly affect a child's ability to perform, he or she would be eligible for services under the Other Health Impaired category. Because there is a wide variability of symptom prevalence and manifestation, a child may be eligible for special services under several IDEA categories. Children with VCFS should be assessed to determine their patterns of strengths and weaknesses so that inappropriate expectations are not placed on them (Wang et al., 2000).

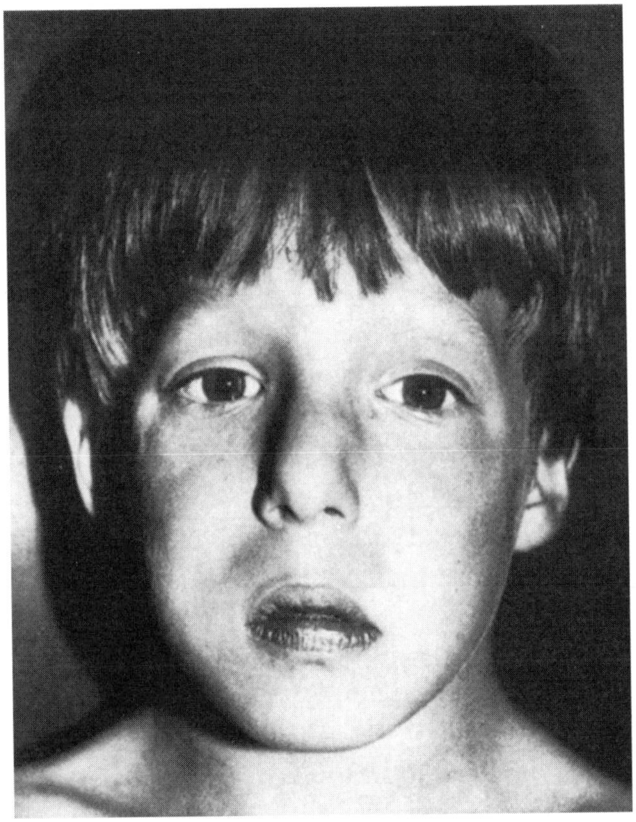

Velocardiofacial Syndrome
Reprinted from *Clinical Syndromes,* Wiedemann and Kunze, 1997, by permission of the publisher Mosby

The prognosis of individuals with VCFS is dependent on the symptoms they manifest, particularly as children. Because the disorder is not degenerative, a child with few symptoms may be able to lead a productive and effective life. Future research should focus on determining the etiology of the deletion on Chromosome 22 and developing treatments and interventions.

REFERENCES

Devriendt, K., Fryns, J. P., Mortier, G., Van Thienen, M. N., & Keymolen, K. (1998). *Journal of Medical Genetics, 35,* 789–790.

Duke, S. G., McGuirt, W. F., Tamison, J., & Fasano, M. B. (2000). Velocardiofacial syndrome: Incidence of immune cytopenias. *Archives of Otolaryngology: Head and Neck Surgery, 126,* 1141–1145.

National Institute on Deafness and Other Communication Disorders. (1996). Velocardiofacial syndrome. Retrieved from http://www.nidcd.nih.gov/health/pubs_vsl/velocario.htm

Phelps, L. (Ed.). (1998). *A guidebook for understanding and educating health-related disorders in children and adolescents.* Washington, DC: American Psychological Association.

Wang, P. P., Woodin, M. F., Kreps-Falk, R., & Moss, E. M. (2000). Research on behavioral phenotypes: Velocardiofacial syndrome (deletion 22q11.2). *Developmental Medicine and Child Neurology, 42,* 422–427.

Christine L. French
Texas A&M University

VENTRICULAR SEPTAL DEFECTS

Ventricular septal defects are heart defects that are present at birth. The lower two chambers of the heart (known as ventricles) are separated by the ventricular septum. Ventricular septal defects can occur in any portion of the ventricular septum. Blood returning from the lungs to the left ventricle flows to the right ventricle through the hole instead of being pumped into the aorta. The size and location of the defect determine the severity of the symptoms. This condition may be associated with other congenital heart defects or syndromes (e.g., Down syndrome). Ventricular septal defects may also be known as congenital ventricular defects and VSD. The exact cause of ventricular septal defects is not fully understood.

In the United States, the ventricular septal defect is the most common congenital heart defect in the first 3 decades of life. For every 1,000 live-born full-term infants, the incidence rate is 1.5–3.5. In premature infants, the incidence rate increases to 4.5–7.0 cases for every 1,000 live-born infants. Ventricular septal defect affects both male and female infants but is slightly more common in females than in males. Defects in the muscular portion of the ventricular septum are found in all ethnic groups; however, defects in the subpulmonary position are more common in the Asian population.

Characteristics

This condition is present at birth. It is most often diagnosed during a routine examination. Symptoms include

1. Shortness of breath
2. Paleness
3. Rapid breathing
4. Increased heart rate
5. Frequent respiratory infections

Complications include

1. Congestive heart failure
2. Infective endocarditis (infection of the heart walls or valves)

3. Aortic insufficiency
4. Arrhythmias
5. Failure to thrive (in infancy) and delayed growth and development

In many children, the opening is very small and produces no symptoms. These children do not have any physical or mental limitations that prevent them from being fully active. Many small defects will close developmentally without intervention. Pediatric cardiologists often encourage children with VSD to do physical activity to keep their hearts fit; however, activity should not be encouraged without the concurrence of the managing physician. For those defects that do not spontaneously close, the outcome is good with surgical repair. Repairing a ventricular septal defect with surgery usually restores the blood circulation to normal. Surgical repair of the defect should be done between the ages of 2 and 5 years. Complications may result if the defect is not treated. Although a child with ventricular septal defect can usually get through common childhood illnesses as safely as children with normal hearts, routine medical care is important.

Most children with ventricular septal defect can benefit from regular education and do not need restrictions. Most children can participate in healthful activities (e.g., swimming, bicycling, running, etc.). In some instances, a pediatric cardiologist may advise that a child avoid strenuous activities. In rare cases, a child may have some special education needs (e.g., the school may need to limit a child's stair climbing or provide special transportation). If this is the case, the child may qualify for services under the Individuals with Disabilities Education Act (IDEA; 1997) using the physical disability category or under Section 504 of the 1974 Rehabilitation Act.

Children with small to moderately sized ventricular septal defects have an excellent prognosis. Most openings have closed by 18 years of age. Infants and children with large ventricular septal defects have a good prognosis. Appropriate timing of surgical intervention leads to the best outcome. The majority of research appears to be focusing on producing effective surgical methods to treat this condition (Hisatomi, Taira, & Moriyama, 1999; Tabuchi, Mizuno, Kuriu, & Toyama, 2001). For more information and support concerning ventricular septal defects, contact Congenital Heart Anomalies, Support, Education, and Resources, 2112 North Wilkins Road, Swanton, OH 43558, (419) 825-5575, e-mail myer106w@wonder.em.cdc.gov or chaser@compuserve.com.

REFERENCES

Hisatomi, K., Taira, A., & Moriyama, Y. (1999). Is direct closure dangerous for treatment of doubly committed subarterial ventricular septal defect? *Annals of Thoracic Surgery, 67*(3), 758–759.

Tabuchi, N., Mizuno, T., Kuriu, K., & Toyama, M. (2001). Double patch technique for repairing postinfarction ventricular septal defect. *Japanese Journal of Thoracic and Cardiovascular Surgery, 49*(4), 264–266.

Rachel Toplis
University of Northern Colorado

VISUAL EFFICIENCY DISORDERS

Visual efficiency disorders consist of a variety of vision problems such as nearsightedness, farsightedness, astigmatism, teaming disorders, focusing disorders, and tracking disorders. The most common efficiency disorders are focusing, binocularity (eye teaming), and tracking. Near focusing and flexibility focusing are required for an individual to process visual information up close and to shift visual focus from near to far. Binocularity is the ability to converge or turn the eyes inward to maintain clear vision up close and diverge the eyes to keep far targets in clear vision. Eye tracking is the ability to move the eyes from point to point (e.g., moving the eyes smoothly and accurately along a line of print). Therefore, these types of visual disorders can have profound effects on a student's ability to achieve academically.

Visual efficiency disorders are highly underdiagnosed. At present, the standard school vision screening (the Snellen) emphasizes the student's ability to process letters of 20/20 size at 20 feet (visual acuity). Visual acuity allows the individual to see or discern details from a distance—for example, information on a blackboard. However, a student may have 20/20 vision and pass the vision screening, but the student may still have a visual efficiency disorder. Parent groups in California are currently supporting legislation that would require schools to test or screen for visual efficiency disorders (Parents Active for Vision Education [PAVE], 2002).

The National Society for the Prevention of Blindness estimates that 10 million children in the United States have undiagnosed vision problems and that 20–25% of children entering school have significant vision problems that affect academic progress (PAVE, 2002). The American Foundation for Vision Awareness estimates that vision disorders are the fourth most common disability in the United States (American Foundation for Vision Awareness [AFVA], 2002). Prevalence and incidence data have not been reported for gender and ethnicity, but some studies are indicating that children from backgrounds of low socioeconomic status are much more likely to have visual efficiency disorders. The reason for these statistics is not known at this time (PAVE, 2002).

Characteristics

General problem behaviors

1. Reduced reading comprehension
2. Holds reading materials very close
3. Rapidly tires when reading
4. Poor attention span

Focusing issues

1. Transient blur at near or distance
2. Headaches
3. Burning or itchy eyes

Teaming issues

1. Double vision
2. Covers one eye during seatwork or near-vision work

Tracking issues

1. Moves head back and forth while reading
2. Rereads or skips lines while reading
3. Loses place when copying from board
4. Must use marker to keep place

To accurately diagnose and treat visual efficiency disorders, students need to be referred for a comprehensive visual exam by a developmental optometrist or ophthalmologist. Therapeutic prisms and lenses or vision therapy is commonly used to manage visual efficiency disorders. Vision therapy consists of individually prescribed exercises to eliminate faulty skill patterns and rebuild them correctly. An example of an exercise could be using a pencil to circle nonsense words (that are arranged in lines) alphabetically. This exercise is timed, and over the course of therapy, the letters get smaller.

A student identified as having a vision efficiency disorder that is affecting the ability to achieve academically would probably not qualify for special education services under the Individuals with Disabilities Education Act (IDEA, 1997). However, classroom accommodations would most certainly be necessary for these students. Glasses may be required, and classroom recommendations may include utilizing larger print, offering preferential seating, allowing more time for near work (e.g., reading, providing postural supports and tilts for the table to create the optimum distance for near work—i.e., the center of the middle knuckle to the elbow, or the Harmon distance), and allowing the student to utilize auditory coping strategies for optimum learning.

At present, few investigations have directly addressed the prevalence and management of visual efficiency disorders in schools. However, some projects are underway, and there is likely to be an increase in research in this area in the near future (College of Optometrists in Vision Development [COVD], 2002). The prognosis for someone with a visual efficiency disorder is very good. Developmental optometrists suggest that in many cases, these disorders can be corrected with 6 weeks to 18 months of vision therapy, corrective lenses, or both.

The following organizations may be helpful to parents and professionals:

- Parents Active for Vision Education 4135 54th Place San Diego, CA 92105 http://www.pave-eye.com
- College of Optometrists in Vision Development 243 North Lindbergh Boulevard Suite 310 St. Louis, MO 63141

REFERENCES

American Foundation for Vision Awareness. (2002). Retrieved April 2002 from http://www.afva.com

College of Optometrists in Vision Development. (2002). Retrieved May 2002 from http://www.covd.org

Parents Active for Vision Education. (2002). Information on visual efficiency disorders. Retrieved April 2002, from http://www.pave-eye.com

Rachel Toplis
Elaine Fletcher-Janzen
University of Northern Colorado

VISUAL IMPAIRMENT

Visual impairment is loss of visual acuity, visual field, or both as a result of defect, disease, or injury to the organs of vision (eye, optic nerve, visual tract, and brain). Even with correction, ability to see is significantly below the level that allows normal visual access to information and the environment. The extent to which a visual impairment produces disability varies with the degree of vision loss, age of onset, ability to use other senses to supplement or substitute for vision, absence or presence of other disabilities, and diagnosis-prognosis.

Visual impairment is caused by medical problems, trauma, and hereditary conditions. Congenital etiologies include cataracts, retinopathy of prematurity, optic nerve disorders, glaucoma, anophthalmia (absence of the eye), microphthalmia (abnormally small eyes), aniridia (congenital absence of the iris), and retinoblastoma (malignant tumor of the retina). Recessive genes may cause later onset of vision loss in childhood (e.g., retinitis pigmentosa and macular degeneration). Acquired vision loss is often due to ocular trauma (penetrating injuries) or brain trauma (e.g., stroke, intracranial lesions), diabetic retinopathy, and retinal detachment.

Amblyopia, or lazy eye, results from strabismus (misalignment of the eyes) or anisometropia (unequal visual acuity in the two eyes) and occurs during early childhood. The brain suppresses the weaker image. Early childhood screening and medical, surgical, or optical treatment can prevent loss of binocular vision and depth perception.

Approximately 10 million people in the United States have been diagnosed with visual impairments. This number includes 93,600 school-aged individuals who are visually impaired or blind and 10,800 who are deaf and blind. About 90% have some usable vision (American Foundation for the Blind).

Characteristics

1. Approximate points on the vision loss continuum are acuity levels of 20/70 (mild), 20/200 (moderate), and 20/800 (severe). Profound vision loss includes CF (counts fingers at specified distance), HM (perceives hand movement at specified distance), LP (light perception, including light projection, which is the ability to orient to direction of a light source), and NLP or nil (no light perception or total blindness).
2. Even with severe to profound levels of low vision, children may perceive large shapes, high contrasts, and shadows in order to access the environment.
3. Children with severe to profound low vision and total blindness will require other senses (touch and hearing) in order to learn and will require training in orientation and mobility in order to travel safely and independently.
4. Loss of binocular vision and depth perception from amblyopia (lazy eye) can be prevented through screening and medical or surgical treatment in early childhood.

Special education placements and interventions vary with student needs. Infant and preschool programs provide early intervention. Some students are in general education classes in neighborhood schools with itinerant services by specialized teachers of the visually impaired (TVI) and orientation and mobility (O&M) instructors, general education accommodations, and other services if needed. Others are in self-contained classes or resource rooms in neighborhood schools. Those with severe multiple disabilities may attend specialized classrooms with itinerant vision services. Some, including those who are academically capable, attend specialized day schools or residential schools, with later transition to neighborhood schools. Additional services (occupational, physical, and speech-language therapy, remedial reading, and guidance in the form of school-psychology and counseling) help to overcome early developmental and functional delays (e.g., spatial concepts, language, self-help, emotional adjustment, and social functioning).

Levels of vision loss and their approximate visual acuities are mild (20/70), moderate (20/200), severe (20/800), and profound (CF, HM, LP). Total blindness is expressed as no light perception (NLP or nil).

Treatments for eye disorders include a variety of medical and surgical interventions in cases in which such treatments will have efficacy. Despite treatment, many eye disorders result in some impairment of vision. Some may lead to eventual profound or total vision loss.

Ability to use low vision effectively is influenced by qualitative factors (contrast sensitivity and need for lighting modifications). Functional improvement of low vision may be affected by the use of a variety of optical devices (e.g., magnifiers, telescopes, video-magnification systems, and computer software for screen magnification) and nonoptical strategies (e.g., large print, dark-line writing paper, book stands, preferential seating, and decreased or increased lighting). Access to curriculum for students with severe to profound vision loss is provided by the use of braille and auditory media (recorded books, electronic text with speech synthesizers, and braille displays for reading the computer screen). Decisions about appropriate learning media are based on individual variables, including the likelihood of further vision loss. Many students use braille, print, and auditory materials for different tasks.

Psychoeducational assessments must be done with care so that the student will not be penalized for the visual impairment. Scores on timed performance subtests—particularly those carrying bonus points for rapid completion of visual tasks—have been shown to vary with visual acuity and are not reliable indicators of intelligence. Such tests (if given) should be used for qualitative interpretation only, and they are useful for demonstrating the extent to which performance may decline when excessive demands are made on a faulty visual system. Many items in verbal tests also rely on the expectation of visual experience, and the results of these tests should also be interpreted with caution.

If there are no other disabilities, children with visual impairments who have the benefit of family support, specialized early intervention, and appropriate educational opportunities with qualified visual impairment professionals can be expected to overcome early developmental delays and to achieve academically to the same level as their sighted peers.

REFERENCES

American Foundation for the Blind. Retrieved from http://www.afb.org

Sattler, J. M., & Evans, C. A. (2001). Visual impairments. In J. M. Sattler (Ed.), *Assessment of children: Behavioral and clinical applications* (4th ed.). San Diego, CA: Sattler.

Carol Anne Evans
Elaine Clark
University of Utah

VITAMIN E DEFICIENCY

Vitamin E is an essential nutrient for maintaining the structural and functional integrity of the developing human nervous system, skeletal muscle, and the retina (Sokol, 1990). When vitamin E deficiency does occur, it strikes people who have diseases that prevent the absorption of dietary fats and fat-soluble nutrients.

Vitamin E functions as the prevention of the natural and continual process of deterioration of all body tissues. This deterioration is provoked by a number of causes; one such cause is toxic oxygen (Olendorf, Jeryan, & Boyden, 1999). Toxic oxygen can damage the membranes that form the boundaries of every cell. Vitamin E serves the body in protecting membranes from this kind of damage. The membranes are the most sensitive to toxic oxygen damage; therefore, the main symptom of vitamin E deficiency is damage to the nervous system. Vitamin E helps maintain the integrity of the circulatory and central nervous systems; is involved in the functioning of the kidneys, lungs, liver, and genitalia; and detoxifies poisonous materials absorbed by the body (Irons-George, 2001). Vitamin E deficiency rarely occurs and has been reported in only two situations: premature infants and patients who fail to absorb fat. Because of chronic malabsorption of vitamin E, children with cystic fibrosis, chronic cholestasis (file-flow obstruction), abetalipoproteinia, and short bowel syndrome are at risk for the development of neurological deficits caused by vitamin E deficiency. Premature infants may be at risk for vitamin E deficiency because they may be born with low tissue levels of the vitamin and because they have a poorly developed capacity for absorbing dietary sources (Olendorf et al., 1999). The best sources of vitamin E are vegetable and seed oils, sunflower seeds, nuts, whole grains, wheat germ, and leafy vegetables such as spinach.

Characteristics

1. Hemolytic anemia
2. Neurological and immunological abnormalities
3. Ataxia (poor muscle coordination with shaky movements)
4. Decreased sensation to vibration
5. Hyporeflexia
6. Limitation in upward gaze
7. Strabismus
8. Nyctalopia (night blindness)
9. Profound muscle weakness
10. Visual field constrictions
11. In severe cases, the inability to walk
12. With severe prolonged vitamin E deficiency, complete blindness, cardiac arrhythmia, and dementia

Treatment must be tailored to the underlying cause of the deficiency and may include oral or intramuscular vitamin supplementation. The treatment of vitamin E deficiency that occurs with malabsorption syndromes can be treated with weekly injections of 100 mg alpha-tocopherol that may continue for 6 months (Olendorf et al., 1999). Intramuscular administration is necessary when the deficiency occurs because of a low concentration of bile salts in the lumen of the small intestine; such patients are unable to absorb vitamin E taken orally. Vitamin E deficiency in premature infants may require treatment for only a few weeks. Patients receiving large doses of vitamin E may experience a halt in progression of the disease (Caplan & Collins, 2002).

The prognosis of vitamin E deficiency is usually reversible in the early stages, but it can have severe complications if allowed to progress. The more advanced the deficit of vitamin E, the more limited the response to therapy. Persons at risk for vitamin E deficiency should be periodically tested.

Research is being done on the absorption, transport, and tissue delivery of vitamin E in the human body. One goal is to define why vitamin E deficiency leads to neurological injury and what kind of vitamin E therapy to use with each fat malabsorption condition. Research has shown that vitamin E supplementation can significantly improve the immune response in healthy older persons. Research is being done to determine the effects of vitamin E in reducing the risk for coronary heart disease and prostate cancer and in slowing of the progression of Alzheimer's disease.

REFERENCES

Caplan, G. E., & Collins, T. (2002, Jan. 2). Vitamin E deficiency. Retrieved from http://www.emedicine.com/med/topic2382.htm

Irons-George, T. (2001). *Magill's medical guide* (2nd Rev. Ed.). Pasadena, CA: Salem Press.

Olendorf, D., Jeryan, C., & Boyden, K. (1999). *The Gale encyclopedia of medicine.* Farmington Hills, MI: Gale Research.

Sokol, R. J. (1990). Vitamin E and neurologic deficits. Retrieved from http://www.emedicine.com/med/topic2382.htm

Karen Wiley
University of Northern Colorado

VOICE DISORDERS

Voice disorders are defined as the abnormal production or the absence of vocal characteristics such as quality, pitch, loudness, resonance, and duration. The determination of the existence of a voice disorder takes into account the individual's age and sex (American Speech-Language-Hearing Association, 1993). Vocal quality refers to how well the vocal folds vibrate in synchrony. The pitch of one's voice can either be too high or too low and depends upon the mass, length, and tension of the vocal folds. Loudness refers the volume of the voice—too loud or too soft. Vocal resonance pertains to the degree that sounds are altered as they travel through the pharyngeal, oral, and nasal cavities. Disorders of nasal resonance are the most common and result in a voice that is characterized by too much nasal resonance (hypernasality) or too little nasal resonance (hyponasality).

According to Andrews (1986), about 6–9% of all school-aged children have voice disorders. The peak prevalence period is between the ages of 4 and 14 years (Marge, 1991). However, only approximately 1% of these children receive treatment services within the school system (Wilson, 1987).

The cause of voice disorders can be classified into three major categories. The first is organic voice disorders that are the result of structural or physiological disease. The second is psychogenic voice disorders, which are caused by a psychological condition such as a personality disorder or by poor habits of voice usage. The third category includes voice disorders that have an undetermined cause or origin (Pannbacker, 1984).

Voice disorders in children are most commonly due to vocal misuse and abuse. Shouting, excessive talking, screaming, and yelling are the primary ways that children abuse their voices. Vocal misuse occurs when the voice is used improperly, such as speaking too loudly or at an inappropriate high or low pitch. These behaviors can result in such pathological laryngeal conditions as inflammation of the vocal folds, chronic laryngitis, vocal nodules, vocal polyps and contact ulcers (National Institute on Deafness and Other Communication Disorders [NIDCD], 1999). Vocal nodules produce chronic hoarseness in 38–78% of children. Nodules are more common in boys than girls, with a ratio of approximately 2:1 or 3:1 (Gray & Smith, 1996).

Characteristics

1. Pitch that is too low or too high for age or sex
2. Volume that is too low or too high
3. Hyper- or hyponasality
4. Breathiness
5. Hoarseness
6. Harshness (Pannbacker, 1984)

When a vocal change or hoarseness is experienced for more than 2 weeks, an examination by a physician—specifically an otolaryngologist—should be sought. The otolaryngologist will examine the vocal folds in order to determine whether a medical condition is causing the voice problem. The vocal folds are examined via laryngoscopy or fiberoptic laryngoscopy. A referral to a speech-language pathologist may be made so that pitch, loudness, vocal quality, and vocal techniques such as breathing and pattern of voicing can be assessed. A treatment program will then be designed based upon these findings. In some instances, surgical intervention is necessary to remove the nodules, polyps, or contact ulcers (NIDCD, 1999).

Most of the disorders that result from vocal abuse and misuse are reversible. Treatment focuses on identifying and eliminating the vocal behaviors that lead to the voice disorder. A course of voice therapy can aid the individual in learning good vocal techniques (NIDCD, 1999). These services could be provided in the school setting by a speech-language pathologist under the umbrella of special education services.

Children with disorders of vocal abuse and misuse can be the most difficult to treat. This is because it is not always easy for them to identify and change their vocal behaviors. Most children do outgrow these disorders by the time they reach their teenage years (NIDCD, 1999). Typically, children who have voice disorders do not experience any related academic difficulties.

Research is currently being conducted in several areas. In-depth studies of the vocal folds themselves and how different types of stress affect their functioning are being carried out. Of special interest is in determining why particular vocal behaviors result in vocal nodules in some individuals and result in laryngitis, vocal polyps, or little to no voice change in others. The effectiveness of behavioral techniques is also being studied. Finally, the long-term impact of various medical and surgical treatments is being examined.

REFERENCES

Andrews, M. L. (1986). *Voice therapy for children.* White Plains, NY: Longman.

American Speech-Language-Hearing Association. (1993). Definitions of communication disorders and variations. *Asha, 35*(10), 40–41.

Gray, S. D., & Smith, M. E. (1996). Voice disorders in children. *NCVS Status and Progress Report, 10,* 133–149.

Marge, M. (1991). Introduction to the prevention and epidemiology of voice disorders. In T. S. Johnson (Ed.), *Seminars in Speech and Language, 12,* 49–72.

National Institute on Deafness and Other Communication Disorders. (1999). Health information: Voice, Speech, and Language. Bethesda, MD: Author. Retrieved August 31, 2000, from http://www.nih.gov/nidcd/health/vsl.htm

Pannbacker, M. (1984). Classification systems of voice disorders:

A review of the literature. *Language, Speech, and Hearing Services in Schools, 15,* 169–174.

Wilson, D. K. (1987). *Voice problems of children* (3rd ed.). Baltimore: Williams & Wilkins.

Theresa T. Aguire
Texas A&M University

VON WILLERBRANDS DISEASE

Von Willerbrands disease (VWD) is a common, mild type of congenital coagulopathy (bleeding disorders; Miller, Pearson, Baehner, & McMillan, 1978; Williams, Beutler, Ersler, & Rundles, 1972). VWD is thought to be associated with an X-linked autosomal dominant genetic disorder leading to a deficiency in the soluble clotting Factor VIII (antihemophilic factor) complex responsible for coagulatory responses. The prevalence of VWD has been approximated at 1% of the general population (Type I). Type III VWD, the most severe type, has an approximate prevalence of 1 in 1,000,000 births.

Characteristics

1. Uncontrollable internal or external bleeding
2. Exceptionally long or prolonged bleeding times
3. Potential joint damage
4. Psychological sequelae associated with a chronic medical illness
5. Psychosocial limitations as a result of medical condition
6. Reduced activity level

Although the disease has no direct cognitive consequences per se (except in cases of severe recurrent bleeding episodes), diseases transmitted through blood products (which are sometimes required in patients with VWD and hemophilia) has been known to cause neurocognitive impediments. The most prevalent in recent times have been the result of cognitive impairments caused by Hepatitis B or C or by horizontal transmission of HIV in VWD patients.

With regard to special education, these children are easily labeled under the Other Health Impaired label and are capable of receiving special services if they are required—particularly adaptations in their curriculum involving activities that may put these children at risk.

Future research should focus on the development of cost-effective treatments (c.f. Mannuci, 1977). The development of safer homeostatic interventions—particularly home-based interventions—also merit attention. Similarly, future treatments should maximize the functional status and quality of life of patients.

REFERENCES

Mannuci, P. M. (1977). DDAVP: A new pharmacological approach to the management of hemophilia and von Willerbrand's disease. *Lancet, 1,* 869.

Miller, D. R., Pearson, H. A., Baehner, R. L., & McMillan, C. W. (Eds.). (1978). *Smith's blood diseases of infancy and childhood.* St. Louis, MO: Mosby.

Williams, W. J., Beutler, E., Ersler, A. J., & Rundles, R. W. (1972). *Hematology.* New York: McGraw-Hill.

Antolin M. Llorente
Baylor College of Medicine
Houston, Texas

W

WAARDENBURG SYNDROME

Waardenburg syndrome (WS) is a hereditary, congenital disorder thought to be a variant of albinism (deficiency of pigmentation). Findings include widely spaced inner corners (canthi) of the eyes; defects in hair, skin, and iris pigmentation; and congenital sensorineural deafness. Two clinical types of WS have been identified. There is controversy regarding the existence of a Type III WS.

A mutation in the PAX3 gene on Chromosome 2 is associated with Type I WS. Type II WS is caused by a defective gene on chromosome 3. Type III WS has also been linked to abnormalities in the PAX3 gene.

The incidence of WS is 1–2 per 20,000 births. Male-to-female ratio is 1:1. The mode of inheritance is autosomal dominant. The majority of new cases (nonfamilial) are closely tied to advanced paternal age.

Characteristics

1. Widely spaced inner canthi with shortening of the opening of the eyelids (palpebral fissure). This finding is a constant feature in Type I WS. It is not seen in Type II disease.
2. Broad, high bridge of the nose. Underdeveloped sides (alae) of the nose (80%).
3. Flaring of the eyebrows around the base of the nose. Eyebrows may meet in the middle of the forehead (50%).
4. Partial albinism manifests as a white clump of hair in the midfrontal scalp, hypopigmented skin lesions, and hypochromic (pale blue) iris of the eye. Heterochromia irides (one brown and one blue iris) occurs in 25% of patients. Premature graying is also common and is usually complete by age 30.
5. Congenital deafness, usually secondary to defects in inner ear or auditory nerve development, is seen in 25% of Type I disease and 50% of individuals with Type II WS.
6. Occasional associated defects include cleft lip and cleft palate, congenital heart disease, gastrointestinal anomalies, scoliosis, and malformations of the female reproductive tract.
7. Type III WS (Klein-Waardenburg syndrome) is typified by all of the aforementioned features, plus malformations of the arm and hand. These features include abnormal shortening, joint contractures, fusion of the wrist bones, syndactyly (webbing of the fingers, with or without fusion), and undeveloped muscles.

Therapy for patients with WS involves regular auditory and ophthalmological assessments. Hearing deficits may not respond to assistive devices. Early diagnosis of deafness should prompt investigation of alternative means of communication (signing), should speech development be affected. Surgical correction of specific congenital anomalies involving the mouth, heart, and gut may be necessary. Because of the hereditary nature of WS (50% chance of recurrence in familial cases), genetic counseling should be made available for affected individuals.

There are no cognitive deficits associated with WS. If the child has hearing deficits, he or she is eligible to receive special support services. An early intervention program that provides speech and language therapy will help the child reach his or her language developmental milestones.

The prognosis for children with WS is good. The syndrome has no effect on life expectancy and is not associated with any defects in mental abilities. The astute clinician should be aware of the physical findings of WS and screen all infants thought to have WS for hearing deficits because delayed diagnosis of deafness can adversely affect overall outcome for the individual patient.

REFERENCES

Darmstadt, G. L. (2000). Hypopigmented lesions. In R. E. Behrman, R. M. Kleigman, & H. B. Jenson (Eds.), *Nelson textbook of pediatrics* (16th ed., p. 1986). Philadelphia: W. B. Saunders.

Jones, K. (1997). *Smith's recognizable patterns of human malformation* (5th ed.). Philadelphia: W. B. Saunders.

Pediatric Database. (1993). Waardenburg syndromes. Retrieved from http://www.icondata.com/health/pedbase/files/WAARDENB.HTM

National Organization for Rare Disorders. (2000). Waardenburg syndrome. Retrieved from http://www.stepstn.com/cgi-win/nord.exe?proc=GetDocument&rectype=0&recnum=430

Barry H. Davison
Ennis, Texas

Joan W. Mayfield
Baylor Pediatric Specialty Services
Dallas, Texas

WAGR SYNDROME

WAGR syndrome is a constellation of abnormalities that include Wilm's tumor, aniridia, genitourinary anomalies or gonadoblastoma, and mental retardation (WAGR). Wilms tumor is the most common form of childhood cancer and involves the kidneys (also known as nephroblastoma). Aniridia is the absence of the colored portion of the eye (the iris). Gonadoblastoma are cancer cells that form the testes in males and the ovaries in females. In order for a person to be diagnosed with WAGR syndrome, at least two of the conditions must be present, and in all but one case of WAGR syndrome, aniridia has been present. Therefore, the clinical representation will vary depending on the conditions present in the individual.

WAGR is a rare disorder that results from defects in Chromosome 11p and is thought to occur more often in males than in females. Currently, there is no known reason for the genetic mutations involved with this disorder. The severity of WAGR syndrome depends on the size and portion of the deletion on Chromosome 11p. There is deletion of part of Band 13 on Chromosome 11. WAGR syndrome can be diagnosed at birth. The most common physical feature associated with WAGR syndrome that is observable at birth is the absence of the colored portion of the eye. Another physical symptom that could be detected at birth is genitourinary abnormalities that may be present.

Characteristics

1. Either partial or complete absence of the colored portion of the eye
2. Presence of Wilms tumor
3. Genitourinary anomalies (i.e., renal dysplasias, horseshoe kidney, anomalies of the collecting system, pseudohermaphroditism, hypospadias, and cryptorchidism
4. Microcephaly
5. Mental retardation
6. Retardation of growth
7. Dysmorphism
8. Craniofacial dysostosis
9. Hypertension
10. Significant vision loss
11. Protruding lips

The prognosis for WAGR syndrome depends on the conditions that are present. Surgical removal of the tumor followed by both chemotherapy and radiotherapy following the surgery has been shown to be the most effective treatment. Studies have shown that patients have a better prognosis if the treatment is started when they are younger.

Individuals with WAGR syndrome would be identified for special education services under one of the following categories: physical disability, significant limited intellectual capacity, or multiple disability. The extent of the services will depend on the severity of the symptoms and on the number of conditions present.

Future research will probably revolve around the genetics involved in this syndrome. Some important goals include locating the exact location involved on Chromosome 11, looking at the way this syndrome is passed from generation to the next, and focusing on the factors that predispose an individual to develop Wilms tumor. Currently research is being done on the effects of chemotherapy and on the risk of developing a second tumor.

REFERENCES

Pavilack, M., & Walton, D. (1993). Genetics of aniridia: The aniridia-Wilm's tumor association. *International Ophthalmology Clinics, 33,* 77–84.

Pochedly, C., & Baum, E. (1984). *Wilm's tumor: Clinical and biological manifestations.* New York: Elsevier Science.

Urdang, L., & Swallow, H. (1983). *Mosby's medical and nursing dictionary.* Mosby.

Tammy Branan
University of Northern Colorado

See also Wilms Tumor

WALKER WARBURG SYNDROME

Walker Warburg syndrome is a type of congenital muscular dystrophy (CMD). Walker Warburg is the most severe type of CMD, affecting the muscles, eyes, and brain. It is also known as HARD ± E syndrome, which stands for hydrocephalus (an abnormal increase in the amount of cerebrospinal fluid within the cranial cavity), agyria (the condition of having a smooth cerebrum without convolutions), retina (abnormalities of the sensory membrane of the eye), dysplasia (abnormal growth or development of organs or cells in the body), and (if present) encephalocele (hernia of the brain). Walker Warburg syndrome is an autosomal recessive disorder, but at present there is no clear genetic linkage.

Walker Warburg syndrome is extremely rare. Thoene (1995) stated that only 60 cases had been reported in the medical literature. However, because of the wide range of brain and eye defects, the diagnosis is frequently not considered (Jones, 1997). There is some evidence that this syndrome affects females more than it does males.

Characteristics

1. Walker Warburg syndrome often presents with decreased fetal movement, excessive amounts of amniotic fluid (polyhydramnios), or both.
2. Severe hypotonia and weakness and mild spasticity are present at birth, along with a poor suck and cry.
3. Vision is poor, with possible ocular abnormalities (e.g., cataracts, retinal dysplasia and detachment, glaucoma).
4. Profound mental retardation and seizures are present.
5. Lissencephaly (malformations of the cerebellum).
6. Other symptoms are sometimes associated with Walker Warburg syndrome (e.g., cleft palate, cleft lip, and encephalocele).
7. Death usually occurs within the first few years. Those individuals who live beyond 5 years of age often have less severe mental retardation. However, seizures become increasingly common with age.

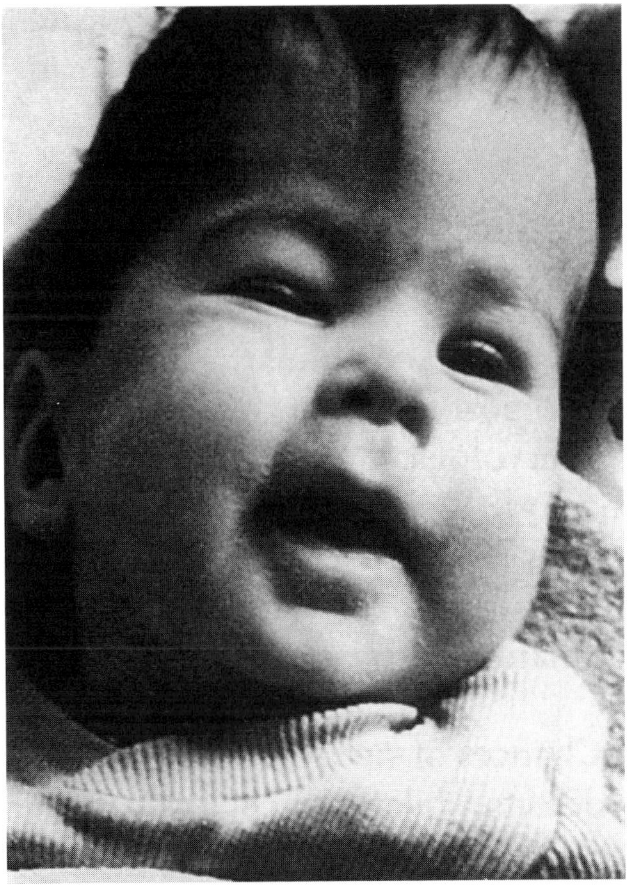

Walker Warburg Syndrome
Reprinted from *Clinical Syndromes*, Wiedemann and Kunze, 1997, by permission of the publisher Mosby

There is no specific treatment for Walker Warburg syndrome. If hydrocephalus is present, a shunt procedure may be necessary. Seizures may be controlled with mediation. Other treatment is symptomatic and supportive. For example, physical therapy is necessary to preserve muscle activity and allow for maximum functioning.

A student diagnosed with Walker Warburg syndrome is likely to be severely mentally retarded and therefore would qualify for special services under the Individuals with Disabilities Education Act (IDEA, 1997). Educational programs need to incorporate a variety of components, including physical therapy and speech-language pathologists, and make accommodations such as special transportation or shorter school day. Classroom arrangements will have to take into consideration mediations, special diets, and special equipment (e.g., assistive technology, augmentative-alternative communication devices). The life expectancy of a school-age individual with Walker Warburg syndrome is unknown. Therefore, the school personnel may find themselves in a death preparation or grief-counseling role.

For individuals diagnosed with Walker Warburg syndrome, death usually occurs within the 1st year, although rarely children will live up to 5 years. Research continues to try to identify the underlying genetic makeup of Walker Warburg syndrome (e.g., Zenker & Dorr, 2000). For more information on Walker Warburg syndrome, contact the Lissencephaly Network, Inc., 10408 Bitterroot Court, Fort Wayne, IN 46804, (219) 432-4310, home page: http://www.lissencephaly.org/

REFERENCES

Jones, K. L. (1997). *Smith's recognizable patterns of human malformation* (5th ed.). Philadelphia: W. B. Saunders.

Thoene, J. G. (Ed.). (1995). *Physicians guide to rare diseases* (2nd ed.). Dowden.

Zenker, M., & Dorr, H. G. (2000). A case associated with Walker Warburg syndrome phenotype and homozygous pericentric inversion 9: Coincidental or aetiological factor? *Acta Paediatr, 89*(6), 750–751.

Rachel Toplis
University of Northern Colorado

WANDERING SPLEEN (CONGENITAL)

Congenital wandering spleen is a very rare birth defect in which the ligaments that hold the spleen in its usual position in the upper left abdomen (splenic peritoneal attachments) are missing or underdeveloped (Rodkey & Macknin, 1992). Congenital wandering spleen has been observed in children from 3 months to 10 years old; the disorder is most commonly found in children who are younger than 1 year old. Wandering spleen is also sometimes called displaced spleen, drifting spleen, floating spleen, splenic ptosis, splenoptosis, or systopic spleen. Wandering spleen is extremely rare, with approximately 50 recorded cases in children under 10 years of age.

Acquired wandering spleen is an adult disorder that results from the relaxation of the splenic ligaments. Acquired wandering spleen affects females at a much higher rate than it does men (in part because pregnancy can lead to such muscle relaxations).

Although congenital wandering spleen can be asymptomatic, it is usually characterized by acute and chronic abdominal pain. Characteristic signs include the presence of a mobile mass with a notched edge; this mass is usually painless in the left upper quadrant (where there is resonance on percussion) but painful in other directions. A variety of imaging techniques can be used to diagnose wandering spleen, including computer tomography, magnetic resonance imaging, nuclear scans, and ultrasonography. Kanthan and Radhi (1999) argue that ultrasonography is the least invasive and the most effective diagnostic test for wandering spleen.

Characteristics

1. May be asymptomatic.
2. Acute or chronic abdominal pain.
3. Recurrent pancreatitis (e.g., Choi et al., 1996).
4. Other symptoms include having a bulging abdominal mass or distended stomach, bloating, constipation, fatigue, fever, nausea, vomiting, weight loss, and difficulty in urination.

Wandering spleen can be treated by observing for signs of compromised spleen functioning and trying to prevent activities that might further injure the spleen. However, Dawson and Roberts (1994) recommend against such a conservative management of the disease. They recommend an early splenoplexy, a surgery that attempts to place the spleen back into its correct position in the upper left abdomen. One risk with a splenoplexy is the breakdown of the suture fixture, which can lead to a recurrence of splenic torsion. Hirose et al. (1998) report the use of a laparascopic splenoplexy to treat wandering spleen, a procedure that is less invasive.

In the case of chronic abdominal pain or blood deficiencies, a splenectomy (removal of the spleen) may be chosen. This surgery is more commonly used in emergency situations because it poses the risk of complications such as life-threatening bacterial infections. Patients who undergo splenectomies are at an increased risk for serious infection for the rest of their lives.

It is unlikely that special education services would be needed for individuals with this disorder, other than possible assistance for pain management or depression resulting from a serious illness. A child with wandering spleen may also need to miss many days of school, particularly if surgery is needed.

Research is continually being conducted on genetic disorders such as wandering spleen, ranging from the Human Genome Project to more specific studies on possible surgical treatments.

REFERENCES

Choi, Y. H., Menken, F. A., Jacobson, I. M., Lombardo, F., Kazam, E., & Barie, P. S. (1996). Recurrent acute pancreatitis: An additional manifestation of the "wandering spleen" syndrome. *American Journal of Gastroenterology, 91*(5), 1034–1038.

Dawson, J. H., & Roberts, N. G. (1994). Management of the wandering spleen. *Australian & New Zealand Journal of Surgery, 64*(6), 441–444.

Hirose, R., Kitano, S., Bando, T., Ueda, Y., Sato, K., Yoshida, T., et al. (1998). Laparoscopic splenoplexy for pediatric wandering spleen. *Journal of Pediatric Surgery, 33*(10), 1571–1573.

Kanthan, R., & Radhi, J. M. (1999). The "true" splenic wanderer. *Canadian Journal of Gastroenterology, 13*(2), 169–171.

Rodkey, M. L., & Macknin, M. L. (1992). Pediatric wandering spleen: Case report and review of literature. *Clinical Pediatrics, 31*(5), 289–294.

James C. Kaufman
Educational Testing Service
Princeton, New Jersey

WEAVER SYNDROME

Weaver syndrome is an early overgrowth syndrome of unknown etiology. It is associated with accelerated development of bone and physical growth and is also accompanied by developmental delay, specific craniofacial manifestations, and bony abnormalities. It is also known as Weaver-Smith syndrome and WSS.

Weaver syndrome is rare; only 27 cases have been reported since Weaver first described the syndrome in 1974 (Pedlynx, May 2001). By a 3:1 ratio, males are more likely to be diagnosed with this syndrome than are females.

Characteristics

1. The age of onset is birth-infancy. Excessive growth is the first symptom.
2. Endocrine symptoms are excessive pre- and postnatal growth, excessive appetite, and thin-fine scalp hair.
3. Neurological symptoms are hypertonia (excessive muscular tension) and spasticity, delayed gross motor development, and hoarse or low-pitched cry in infancy.
4. Individuals with Weaver syndrome often exhibit behavioral problems and poor concentration. Temper tantrums are common.
5. Musculoskeletal symptoms are prominent finger pads, hyperextensible fingers, broad thumbs, dysplastic nails, and limited extension of joints (hips, knees, elbows, wrists, ankles). Other musculoskeletal symptoms that can be present are camptodactyly (a permanent bend of one or more fingers or joints), scoliosis (curve of the spine), talipes equinovarus (deformity of the foot resulting in walking on the toes and the outside of the foot), and tall stature.
6. Craniofacial symptoms are large, low-set ears; broad forehead; and micrognathia (abnormal smallness of one or both jaws). Other craniofacial symptoms may be long, accentuated philtrum (groove on the upper lip), macrocephaly (large head), strabismus, dysplastic ears, depressed nasal bridge, down-slanting palpebral fissures (space between the margins of the eyelids), and flat occiput (back part of the head).
7. Other symptoms are umbilical or inguinal hernia, cryptochidism (one or both testes fail to descend properly), excessive-loose skin on the neck and extremities, hyperbilirubinemia (excessive reddish-yellow pigmentation in the blood and bile that can cause jaundice).

At present, there is no known cure for the underlying disorder. Therefore, treatment is symptomatic and supportive (e.g., orthopedic interventions may be used to correct foot deformities, physical therapy may be required to address symptoms such as hypertonia, etc.).

A student entering school with a diagnosis of Weaver syndrome will probably qualify for special services under the Individuals with Disabilities Education Act (IDEA, 1997) within the other physical disability category. These students are likely to require extensive services, accommodations, and modifications. Physical therapy may be necessary, and transportation may be required. Students with Weaver syndrome may be developmentally delayed and may require accommodations to address this issue. Students may need extended periods of time away from school due to medical issues; therefore, arrangements may need to be made to help the student keep up with schoolwork. Because Weaver syndrome is associated with craniofacial abnormalities and other malformations of the bodily structure, students with this diagnosis may at various times require counseling (e.g., to come to terms with body image and identity).

Research is still attempting to identify the etiology of Weaver syndrome. Although most cases appear sporadic, there is some evidence of autosomal dominant inheritance of the disorder (e.g., Fryer, Smith, Rosenbloom, & Cole, 1997; Proud, Braddock, Cook, & Weaver, 1998). Autosomal dominant inheritance means that only one copy of the abnormal gene can be sufficient for expression of the disorder in offspring. Therefore, an affected person has a 50% chance of passing the trait on to a child.

REFERENCES

Fryer, A., Smith, C., Rosenbloom, L., & Cole, T. (1997). Autosomal dominant inheritance of Weaver syndrome. *Journal of Medical Genetics, 34*(5), 418–419.

Proud, V. K., Braddock, S. R., Cook, L., & Weaver, D. D. (1998). Weaver syndrome: Autosomal dominant inheritance of the disorder. *American Journal of Medical Genetics, 79*(4), 305–310.

Pedlynx. (2001). *Pediatric database.* Retrieved from http://www.icondata.com/health/pedbase/pedlynx.htm

Rachel Toplis
University of Northern Colorado

WEISMANN NETTER STUHL SYNDROME

The original name for this disorder was *toxopachyosteose diaphysaire tibio-peroniere.* Weismann Netter Stuhl syndrome is an extremely rare skeletal disorder that occurs as the result of abnormal development of the bone. This disorder, also referred to as dwarfism, is thought to be inherited as an autosomal or X-linked dominant genetic trait (Skeletal Dysplasia, Weismann-Netter Stuhl Type, 1990).

Reports are that males and females are affected in equal numbers. In dominant disorders such as this one, there is a 50% chance of the disorder's being transmitted from parent to offspring for each pregnancy, regardless of the sex of the resulting child. Age of onset is possibly prenatal, although the bowing of the legs is often not detected until the child begins to walk (Robinow & Johnson, 1988). Diagnosis may be difficult due to the lack of serious physical complications associated with the disorder (The National Organization for Rare Disorders [NORD], 1996). Most adolescent or adult cases that have been documented in the literature have been discovered incidentally because the patient was admitted to the hospital for other reasons (Skeletal Dysplasia, Weismann-Netter-Stuhl Type, 1990). In more recent literature, diagnosis of children has been difficult due to the fact that the cases were reported primarily in the French literature (Robinow & Johnson, 1988). In 1995, Tieder, Manor, Peshin, and Alon documented the difficulty in diagnosing the disorder: Although 79 cases had been reported in the literature, only 13 were pediatric cases. Of the 13 pediatric cases, only 2 had been reported in the English literature. Tieder et al. (1995) wanted to increase the awareness of the disorder among pediatric radiologists because of the difficulty in diagnosing. There is also a possibility that some cases of Weismann Netter Stuhl syndrome have been misdiagnosed throughout the years as either syphilis or healed rickets (Robinow & Johnson, 1988).

Characteristics

1. Short stature and bowing of the front of the long portions of the tibia (shinbone) and of the fibula (small bone below the knee).
2. Child may also exhibit bowing of the sides of the femur (thighbone), outward curvature of the tibia, or both.
3. The child will experience a delay in the onset of walking until the age of about 18 months or older.
4. Other bones in the body may be bowed, curved, or improperly developed.
5. Mild mental retardation has been detected in some cases.

There is very little discussion of treatment in the literature. Treatment should be symptomatic and supportive, possibly with genetic counseling for the child and the family (NORD, 1996).

Through the Individuals with Disabilities Education Act (IDEA, 1997), the child may be eligible for special education services under the categories of Orthopedic Impairment, Other Health Impaired, or Physical Disability. In the approximately 20% of the cases in which mental retardation is present, the child may also be eligible under the category of Mental Retardation, depending on the severity of the intellectual deficit. The child may require social support, occupational therapy, and other medical, social, or vocational services.

This disorder is not known to be debilitating or life threatening. Patients are expected to have a normal life span. Future research is documented in the area of surgical treatment for those who have bone disorders. The National Institutes of Health, through its Human Genome Project, is attempting to map every gene in the human body. It is hoped that such knowledge will lead to treatment of genetic and familial disorders.

REFERENCES

National Organization for Rare Disorders. (1996). Weismann Netter Stuhl syndrome. Retrieved July 2001, from http://www.rarediseases.org

Robinow, M., & Johnson, G. F. (1988). The Weismann-Netter syndrome. *American Journal of Medical Genetics, 29,* 573–579.

Skeletal dysplasia, Weismann Netter Stuhl type. (1990). In *Birth defects encyclopedia* (p. 1540). Dover, MA: Blackwell Scientific Publications.

Tieder, M., Manor, H., Peshin, J., & Alon, U. S. (1995). The Weismann-Netter, stuhl syndrome: A rare pediatric skeletal dysplasia. *Pediatric Radiology, 25,* 37–40.

Christine D. Cde Baca
University of Northern Colorado

WERDNIG-HOFFMANN DISEASE

Werdnig-Hoffmann disease (also known as infantile spinal muscular atrophy Type I, or SMA I) is a rare progressive neuromuscular degenerative disorder of infancy. SMA I is characterized by the wasting of the skeletal muscles caused by progressive deterioration of the motor nuclei within the lower brain stem and of the anterior horn cells of the spinal cord.

There are various forms of SMA with similar characteristics but different in pattern of inheritance, age of onset, severity, and prognosis. However, all forms are characterized by marked muscular weakness and hypotonia (Munsat, 1994). SMA I is the first of four main types of spinal muscle atrophy disorders, with onset occurring during fetal development (in utero) or at birth (congenital). SMA Type II (intermediate) symptoms manifest approximately between 6–12 months of age. SMA Type III (or Wohlfart-Kugelberg-Welander disease) can occur from 2–30 years of age. SMA Type IV, or Kennedy disease (bulbo-SMA) has an adult onset, from approximately 30 to 60 years of age (Beers & Berkow, 1999).

In most individuals, SMA I appears to be an inherited autosomal recessive trait, which means that both parents must be carriers of the gene for the disease for it to be expressed in the child (Heller, Alberto, Forney, & Schwartzman, 1996). SMAs are the second most common autosomal recessive disease in children (after cystic fibrosis) and the second most prevalent of the neuromuscular diseases (Heller et al., 1996). Incidence of SMA I in the United States is approximately 1 in 10,000 live births, which accounts for one fourth of all cases of SMA (Ben Hamida et al., 1994; Tsao & Armon, 2000). Incidence of SMA is higher in Saudi Arabia and Middle Eastern countries due to consanguinity (Munsat, 1994). The majority of cases of SMA occur in males (Munsat, 1994; Tsao & Arnon, 2000).

Characteristics

Werdnig-Hoffmann disease (SMA Type I, or acute infantile form)

1. May be a lack of fetal movement in the final months of pregnancy.
2. Age of onset is birth to 6 months of age.
3. Severe and rapid progression of symptoms.
4. Delayed milestones by 6 months of age.
5. Hypotonicity (low muscle tone, feeling flabby to the touch).
6. Severe weakness and muscle atrophy.
7. Unable to hold head up or sit without support.
8. Frog-shaped legs and bell-shaped chest.
9. Movement of extremities is limited to the hands and feet.
10. Absent reflexes.
11. Swallowing and feeding difficulties, with excessive drooling.
12. Weak cry.
13. Respiratory problems.

All types of spinal muscular atrophy

1. Muscle weakness and atrophy
2. Motor function loss
3. Skeletal deformities (usually scoliosis is most common)
4. Respiratory problems

Treatment of Werdnig-Hoffmann disease is symptomatic and supportive and should include antibiotic treatment of pneumonia and other respiratory infections that are associated with the disease. It is important that respiratory infections are treated early and aggressively because respiratory failure is the leading cause of death in children with SMA I, and it is unpredictable as to how many children with this form of SMA will live beyond the usual limit of 2 years of age (Munsat, 1994). Also, physical therapy, orthotic supports, and rehabilitation may prove beneficial in preventing scoliosis and contractures in patients with static or slowly progressive forms of SMA.

Due to the short life expectancy of children with SMA I, the majority will not live long enough to attend school. Children with SMA I will generally appear bright and alert and will readily respond to direct stimulation. Intelligence is normal for children with any of the types of spinal muscular atrophy disorders. Children who have Type II or III often perform well in school due to more exposure to adult conversations and extra effort they expend in academics to compensate for physical limitations. However, these children will need special provisions and assistance in the classroom (see Heller et al., 1996).

The prognosis for individuals with SMA Type I is poor because the disease is invariably fatal. Death occurs in 95% of children with SMA I by age 18 months, and the majority will succumb by 2 years of age. Indeed, this form of spinal muscular atrophy is the leading cause of infant death due to inherited conditions (Heller et al., 1996). The majority of deaths in children with SMA I is usually from respiratory failure, which is caused by the rapid and progressive weakening of the muscles. However, as previously mentioned, there are rare cases of children with SMA I who exceed the usual life expectancy. Parents are urged to speak frankly with their children's physicians regarding aggressive treatment, therapeutic goals, and uncertainty as to the immediate future for children with this form of SMA (Munsat, 1994).

Genetic studies have revealed that all types of SMA are caused by defects in genes located on the long arm (q) of Chromosome 5 (Carter, 1999). Recent breakthroughs have allowed for the reliable detection of SMA I via prenatal testing (Munsat, 1994). Furthermore, current genetic research is attempting to clone the gene for SMA and identify protein composition for more direct treatment of this disease (Munsat, 1994).

REFERENCES

Beers, M. H., & Berkow, R. (Eds.). (1999). *The Merck manual of diagnosis and therapy* (17th ed.). New Jersey: Merck.

Ben Hamida, C., Soussi-Yanicostas, N., Butler-Browne, G. S., Bejaoui, K., Hentati, F., & Ben Hamida, M. (1994). Biochemical and immunocytochemical analysis in chronic proximal spinal muscular atrophy. *Muscle Nerve, 17,* 400–410.

Carter, G. (1999). Rehabilitation management in neuromuscular disease. *Journal of Neurological Rehabilitation, 11,* 69–80.

Heller, K. A., Alberto, P. A., Forney, P. E., & Schwartzman, M. N. (1996). *Understanding physical, sensory, and health impairments: Characteristics and educational implications.* New York: Brooks/Cole.

Munsat, T. L. (1994). The spinal muscular atrophies. In S. Appel (Ed.), *Current neurology* (pp. 55–71). Mosby-Year Books.

Tsao, B., & Armon, C. (2000, December). Spinal muscular atrophy: Introduction. Retrieved from http://www.emedicine.com/neuro/topic631.htm

Andrea Holland
University of Texas at Austin

See also Neuropathy, Peripheral

WERNER SYNDROME

Werner syndrome (WS) is an autosomal recessive genetic disease that resembles premature aging (University of Washington, 2000). A genetic mutation on Chromosome 8, labeled WRN, is the cause of WS (National Institutes of Health [NIH], 1997). Although the disorder is not usually diagnosed until the third decade of life, the characteristic short stature and low body weight are present during childhood and adolescence (National Organization for Rare Disorders [NORD], 1999). Individuals with WS display clinical features that are similar to features of progeria. However, WS is characterized by a later age of onset, and many symptoms of WS are not manifested in progeria.

Werners syndrome is a rare disease that afflicts males and females at an equal rate (Salk, Fujiwara, & Martin, 1985). Estimates of the world prevalence of WS range between 1 and 22 cases per million people (Salk et al., 1985). Currently, the prevalence of WS in the United States is unknown. The prevalence of WS has been determined to be the highest in Japan, with an estimated 1 case per 20,000 to 40,000 people (J. Oshima, personal communication, December 14, 2000). The higher prevalence in Japan may be related to more frequent consanguineous marriages, which increases the rate for the pairing of recessive genes (Miller, 2000). Siblings of individuals with WS have approximately a 25 percent chance of having the disorder as well, but the likelihood of a sibling developing the disease is independent of birth order (Salk et al., 1985).

Characteristics

1. Short stature
2. Low weight relative to height
3. Premature graying and thinning of scalp hair
4. Facial abnormalities (e.g., beaked nose, unusually prominent eyes)
5. Voice changes (e.g., high-pitched, squeaky, or hoarse voice)
6. Loss of the layer of fat beneath the skin
7. Atrophy of muscle tissue
8. Degenerative skin changes (e.g., wrinkles)

Possible characteristics

1. Juvenile cataracts (bilateral)
2. Diabetes mellitus
3. Osteoporosis
4. Arteriosclerosis
5. Hypogonadism (e.g., secondary sexual underdevelopment, diminished fertility, testicular or ovarian atrophy)

Note. Based on information cited by the following authors: NORD (1999) and University of Washington (2000).

Due to its progressive and variable course, there is no universal treatment regimen for individuals afflicted with WS. A diversity of symptoms resembling premature aging may be displayed and increase the susceptibility to age-related diseases (NIH, 1997). A physician must treat the various medical problems that a person with WS may experience.

A diagnosis of WS may be accompanied by stress due to its degenerative nature and shortening of the life span. Reactions of sadness, anger, embarrassment, and loneliness may occur. Persons with WS may benefit from individual or family therapy. Support groups are also available; participation in such groups may decrease feelings of isolation.

Children with WS have an abnormally slow growth rate and may therefore become the object of teasing by their peers. This problem may lead the child to develop low self-esteem and become angry or lonely. The child's school performance could be negatively affected by these feelings, resulting in low academic achievement. If school personnel suspect that the child has a learning disability, they should consider whether the child's emotional problems better account for his or her low school achievement.

Persons diagnosed with WS have a poor prognosis. They will probably experience gradual physical deterioration and early onset of age-related disorders. Although the clinical features of WS resemble premature aging, individuals with WS are not susceptible to some medical conditions, such as Alzheimer's disease and hypertension (Yu et al., 1996). Future research should attempt to elucidate why certain age-related diseases are manifested in WS, while others are not. Additionally, epidemiological studies of WS should be conducted in order to determine current estimates of prevalence.

REFERENCES

Miller, R. W. (2000). National Cancer Institute: Division of cancer epidemiology and genetics. Retrieved December 13, 2000, from http://www-dceg.ims.nci.nih.gov/hgp/cgb/miller.html

National Institutes of Health. (1997, March 4). Statement of the director, national institute regarding aging on NIA's FY 1998 budget. Retrieved December 13, 2000, from http://www.dceg.ims.nci.nih.gov/hgp/cgb/miller.html

National Organization for Rare Disorders. (1999). Werner's syndrome. Retrieved November 5, 2000, from http://www.stepstn.com/cgi-win/nord.exe?proc=GetDocument&rectype=0&recNum=135

Salk, D., Fujiwara, Y., & Martin, G. M. (Eds.). (1985). *Werner's syndrome and human aging.* New York: Plenum Press.

University of Washington. (2000). Werner syndrome. Retrieved October 19, 2000, from http://www.pathology.washington.edu/werner/registry/diagnostic.html

Yu, C. E., Oshima, J., Fu, Y. H., Wijsman, E. M., Hisama, F., Alisch, R., et al. (1996, April 12). Positional cloning of the Werner's syndrome gene. *Science, 272,* 258–262.

Eve N. Rosenthal
Karla Anhalt
Texas A&M University

WHOOPING CHOUGH (PERTUSSIS)

Pertussis, also known as whooping cough, is an acute bacterial (*Bordatella pertussis*) infection of the cilia that line the air passages of the lower respiratory tract. Cilia are tiny, hairlike projections on cells that beat back and forth to help clear the respiratory system of mucus, bacteria, viruses, and dead cells. *Bordatella pertussis* interferes with the motion of the cilia. The debris accumulates and causes irritation in the respiratory tract and triggers coughing. It causes spasms (paroxysms) of uncontrollable coughing, followed by a sharp, high-pitched intake of air which creates the characteristic *whoop* for which the disease is named. Pertussis is very contagious and is spread by breathing in airborne droplets expelled from the nose or throat of an infected person or by direct contact with discharges from the nose or throat of an infected person.

Before the availability of pertussis vaccine, pertussis was one of the most common childhood diseases and a major cause of death in children in the United States. After the use of the pertussis vaccine, cases decreased by 99%, but about 5,000–7,000 cases per year are still reported in the United States. Incidence of pertussis has increased steadily since the 1980s (Center for Disease Control and Prevention, 2000). Approximately 38% of recognized cases occur in infants younger than 6 months of age, which stresses the need for early immunization. Pertussis can result in serious complications, including middle ear infections, pneumonia, convulsions (seizures), disorders of the brain, brief episodes of stopped breathing, and in 1% of the cases, death. Anyone can get pertussis, but children—especially unvaccinated or incompletely vaccinated infants under age 2—are at the most risk.

Characteristics

1. Incubation stage—symptoms appear between 6 and 21 days (average 7–10) after exposure to the bacteria.
2. Catarrhal stage—runny nose, low-grade fever, sneezing, and a mild cough similar to that from a common cold. Within 2 weeks, episodes of severe coughing develop.
3. Paroxysmal stage—rapid spasmodic coughing followed by a characteristic intake of breath that sounds like a *whoop.* During such an attack, the patient may become cyanotic (turn blue) due to the lack of air. Vomiting and exhaustion commonly follow the episode. The bouts of coughing can last from 1 to 2 months. Children and young infants, especially, appear very ill and distressed. The patient usually appears normal between attacks. Diagnosis of pertussis is suspected at this stage and can be confirmed by a throat culture.
4. Convalescent stage—spasms of coughing may occur, but will be less intense. This stage lasts about 3–4 weeks.
5. Infants under age 6 months, adolescents, immunized school children, and adults generally have milder symptoms without the typical whoop.

The treatment for pertussis is with the use of antibiotics (erythromycin). This treatment is limited because after the cilia are damaged, they cannot be repaired. It takes time for the cilia to grow back; until then, the patient has to wait and endure the symptoms. These antibiotics are used to prevent complicating infections and reduce the contagious period of the disease. Severe cases may require steroid treatments to reduce the severity of the disease. Hospitalization may be needed, and oxygen and mild sedation may be required to control coughing spells. Other supportive ways to help the patient to be more comfortable include monitoring liquids to prevent dehydration; resting in a quiet, dark room to decrease paroxysms; and suctioning the mucus.

The overall prognosis for a recovery is good in all age groups. Fewer than 1% of whooping cough cases end in death; this is usually in children who develop complications such as pneumonia and extreme weight loss. Special education services would probably not be needed unless long-term complications became evident.

The most effective measure to prevent the spread of pertussis is to maintain the highest level of immunization in children. Researchers are working on creating an adult vaccine to immunize adults.

REFERENCE

Center for Disease Control and Prevention. (2000, December). Pertussis. Retrieved from http://www.cdc.gov/ncidod/dbmd/diseaseinfo/pertussis_t.htm

Karen Wiley
University of Northern Colorado

WIEDEMANN RAUTENSTRAUCH SYNDROME

Wiedemann Rautenstrauch syndrome, a form of progeria, is also known as neonatal progeroid syndrome. Diagnostic criteria for this disorder also include lipoatrophy, which is a deficiency in or the absence of the layer of fat under the skin. Another feature is slow growth both pre- and postnatally. The most striking feature of the syndrome is the aged appearance at birth.

This condition is thought to be autosomal recessive, which means that the baby inherited from each parent the same defective gene for the same trait. The possibility of inheriting the same defective gene increases if the parents are related by blood. If both parents are carriers for a recessive disorder, the risk of transmitting the disease to children is 25%. The risk that those children will be carriers only, without showing symptoms, is 50% (National Organization for Rare Disorders [NORD], 2001). Research literature indicates no racial predilection, with reported cases of African American, Asian, Hispanic, and Caucasian patients (Pivnick et al., 2000).

This genetic disorder appears to affect males and females equally. The literature to date includes approximately 21 cases of Wiedemann Rautenstrauch syndrome, but there are several other forms of progeria and congenital disorders that share many of this syndrome's characteristics (NORD, 2001).

Characteristics

1. Aged appearance at birth.
2. Either deficiency or absences of the layer of fat under the skin, causing the skin to be abnormally thin, fragile, and wrinkled.
3. Mild to severe mental retardation with progressive neurological and neuromuscular abnormalities.
4. There may be neonatal incisors present that fall out during early infancy.
5. Child may have an abnormal accumulation of fatty deposits in the areas of the buttocks, genitals, and anus, as well as in the area between the ribs and hips.
6. Distinctive malformations of the head and facial area, including prominence in the forehead and sides of the skull, causing the head to appear abnormally large.
7. Small and underdeveloped bones in the face, with a beak-shaped nose that becomes more pronounced as the child ages.

Treatment should be individualized and symptom specific. Because prenatal detection of the disorder is possible through ultrasound, it is likely that pediatric specialist teams will be required immediately after birth and throughout life. The research literature documents four pairs of siblings among the 21 reported cases, suggesting that genetic counseling should be included as part of the treatment plan (National Organization for Rare Disorders, 2001).

Children with this disability would be eligible for special education services under Part H of the Individuals with Disabilities Education Act (IDEA, 1997), which includes children from birth to age 2. Intervention services are possible for children in this age group who encounter delays in cognitive, physical, communication, social-emotional, or adaptive development (McLean, Bailey, & Wolery, 1996).

Infants diagnosed with Wiedemann-Rautenstrauch syndrome usually die in early childhood, although there have been documented cases of survival into the early teens. The average life expectancy is somewhere between 9 and 15 months of age. Future research should be in the area of endocrine and lipid studies, as well as molecular studies of the genes that control lipid metabolism (Pivnick et al., 2000).

REFERENCES

McLean, M., Bailey, D., & Wolery, M. (1996). *Assessing infants and preschoolers with special needs.* Englewood Cliffs, NJ: Prentice Hall.

The National Organization for Rare Disorders. (2001). Wiedemann Rautenstrauch syndrome. Retrieved July 2001, from http://rarediseases.org

Pivnick, E., Angle, B., Kaufman, R., Hall, B., Pitukcheewanont, P., Hersh, J., et al. (2000). Neonatal progeroid (Wiedemann-Rautenstrauch) syndrome: Report of five new cases and review. *American Journal of Medical Genetics, 90,* 131–140.

Christine D. Cde Baca
University of Northern Colorado

WILDERVANCK SYNDROME

Wildervanck syndrome, sometimes called cervico-oculoacoustic syndrome, is a very rare disorder almost exclusively affecting females. Currently, Wilderbank syndrome is thought to be the result of random genetic mutations. According to the National Organization for Rare Disorders (NORD, 2000a), it is comprised of a triad of particular conditions: congenital deafness (caused by a malformed bone in the inner ear), Klippel-Feil syndrome (KFS), and Duane syndrome.

Klippel-Feil syndrome is characterized by a congenital fusion of at least two of the seven vertebrae in the neck area. Limited range of motion, low hairline on the back of the head, and shortened neck are typical of the disorder. Other anomalies that sometimes occur include renal, genital, respiratory, and heart malformations (National Institute of Neurological Disorders and Stroke, 2001).

The third contributor to Wildervanck syndrome is Du-

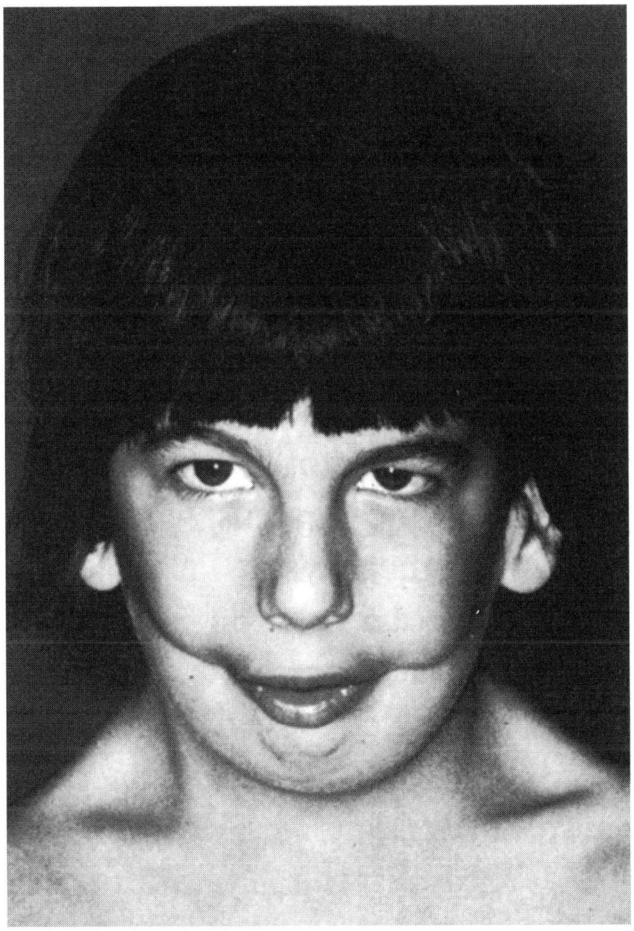

Wildervanck Syndrome
Reprinted from *Clinical Syndromes,* Wiedemann and Kunze, 1997, by permission of the publisher Mosby

ane syndrome. This congenital disorder limits the range of eye movement. Sometimes called Duane retraction syndrome, it affects one or both eyes, causing a retraction of the eyeball when it attempts to turn in a particular direction (NORD, 2000b).

Characteristics
1. Deafness
2. Duane syndrome (retraction of the eyeball when looking in a particular direction)
3. Klippel-Feil syndrome (fusion of at least two of the neck vertebrae)

Treatment may include physical therapy and surgery to stabilize the neck and increase mobility of the spine. It is recommended that those with Wildervanck syndrome be cautious about engaging in activities that may injure the neck because the neck is limited in its range of motion.

Within the school setting, children with Wildervanck syndrome are likely to need and qualify for a broad range of services, particularly modifications to address the hearing impairment. Preferential seating for vision impairment is in order; if vision problems are significant, a consultation with an orientation and mobility specialist may be warranted to determine the most appropriate means of working with the child. Physical activities may need to be adapted or avoided completely as per recommendation by the child's physician.

REFERENCES

National Institute of Neurological Disorders and Stroke. (2001). Klippel Feil syndrome information page. Retrieved from http://www.ninds.nih.gov/health_and_medical/disorders/klippel_feil.htm

National Organization for Rare Disorders. (2000a). Duane syndrome. Retrieved from http://www.stepstn.com/cgi-win/nord.exe?proc=GetDocument&rectype=0&recnum=224

National Organization for Rare Disorders. (2000b). Wildervanck syndrome. Retrieved from http://www.stepstn.com/cgi-win/nord.exe?proc=GetDocument&rectype=0&recnum=1001

Sharla Fasko
Rowan County Schools
Morehead, Kentucky

See also Duane Syndrome

WILLIAMS SYNDROME

Williams syndrome (WS) is characterized by distinctive facial features, cardiovascular disease, a specific cognitive profile, unique personality, cognitive impairments, and developmental delay. Elevated blood calcium levels and connective tissue abnormalities are also common. WS is a rare genetic disorder that occurs in 1 in 20,000 births. It is a disorder that is present at birth and affects both males and females in all ethnic groups. The disorder was first described by J. C. P. Williams of New Zealand in 1961. The cause was unknown at that time; however, in 1993, the genetic etiology was discovered. The disorder is a result of the deletion of a portion of the long arm of Chromosome 7 at Band q11.23, which contains the elastin gene (ELN). The elastin gene is a protein that provides strength and elasticity to the vessel walls (Morris, 1999). WS can occur sporadically in families, and the deletion can be maternal or paternal. The extent of the deletion varies, leaving no two individuals with exactly the same problems. If the disorder is suspected, it can be confirmed by a blood test using the technique called fluorescent in situ hybridization (FISH; Williams Syndrome Association).

Most WS children have birth weights lower than those

of their siblings and slower weight gain in the first few years. Many of these children are diagnosed failure to thrive. Feeding problems are often linked to low muscle tone, severe gag reflex, poor suck-swallow, and tactile defensiveness. Infants with WS often display an extended period of colic or irritability (Williams Syndrome Association) and developmental delays such as walking, talking, and toilet training are common.

Characteristics

1. Distinctive facial features (broad forehead, upturned nose, wide mouth, full lips, widely spaced teeth, small chin, puffiness around the eyes, small head, depressed nasal bridge
2. Cardiovascular disease
3. Specific cognitive profile
4. Unique personality characteristics described as over friendly and talkative
5. Cognitive impairments (usually mild retardation)
6. Developmental delays (sitting, walking, language; gross and fine motor skills)

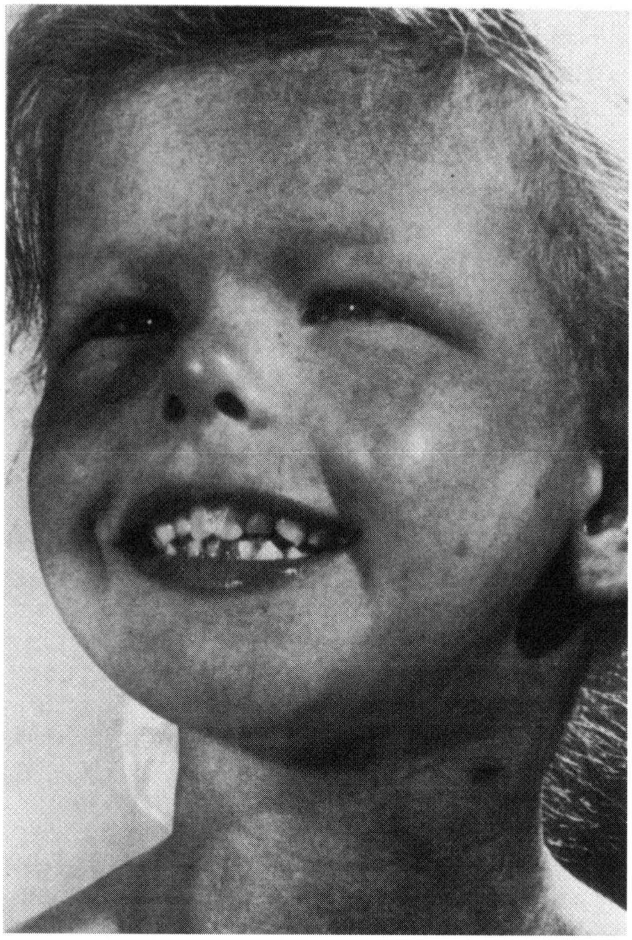

Williams Syndrome
Reprinted from *Clinical Syndromes,* Wiedemann and Kunze, 1997, by permission of the publisher Mosby

Children with WS have similar facial features that become more apparent with age. These children also tend to look more like other WS children than relatives (Lenhoff, Wang, Greenberg, & Bellugi, 1997). Some of the common characteristics observed are broad brow, upturned nose, wide mouth, full lips, widely spaced teeth, small chin, puffiness around the eyes, small head, and depressed nasal bridge. Young children usually have full cheeks and small, widely spaced teeth, whereas adults tend to have long faces and necks. Children with blue or green eyes may also have a starlike pattern in the iris.

The majority of WS children have some type of heart or blood vessel problem; the most common is the narrowing of the aorta (i.e., supravalvar aortic stenosis [SVAS]). SVAS occurs in about 75% of individuals with this syndrome (Morris, 1999). Elevated blood calcium levels, or hypercalcemia, is also common but often resolves during childhood. Another common feature of WS is connective tissue abnormalities. Children with WS often have low muscle tone and joint laxity. As children get older, joint stiffness occurs. Other associated symptoms included a hoarse, low-pitched voice; umbilical or inguinal hernias; and stomach problems. In children with WS, hearing is also more sensitive, and puberty occurs sooner than it does same-age peers (Morris, 1999).

Children with WS are often described as being overly friendly or excessively social. This behavior may be due in part to the fact that they tend to be unafraid of strangers, despite other anxieties. WS children show a distinct cognitive profile, with strength in auditory rote memory and expressive language and weakness in visual-spatial skill. Approximately 75% of individuals with WS score in the mild mental retardation range but range from severely impaired to low average (Morris, 1999). Intellectual delays and adaptive problems often affect these individuals' ability to function independently in the community; therefore, most adults live with parents or in group homes.

The management of WS requires a multidisciplinary approach that includes regular medical checkups and developmental as well as psychological evaluations. Consultation with speech and language pathologists and with occupational and physical therapists is often necessary in order to provide the best service possible. Prognosis largely depends on early diagnosis and early treatment. Genetic testing may be helpful, but research is still needed to determine which services are more likely to help a child with WS adapt to the environment. Presently, most children with WS who require special education services are often provided these under the categories of Intellectual Disability, Learning Disability, and Other Health Impaired (OHI). Children who do not require special education are likely to need accommodations in the classroom, given the high rate of learning and social problems. Vocational training is also critical and should be provided as early as possible. Because WS is a lifelong (and complex) condition, counseling should be offered to the child and to his or her family.

REFERENCES

Lenhoff, H. M., Wang, P. P., Greenberg, F., & Bellugi, U. (1997, December). Williams syndrome and the brain. *Scientific American*, 68–73.

Morris, C. A. (1999). Williams syndrome: GeneClinics. Medical genetics knowledge base. Retrieved from http://www.geneclinics.org/profiles/williams/details

Williams Syndrome Association. Retrieved from http://www.williams-syndrome.org/

Heidi Mathie
Elaine Clark
University of Utah

WILMS TUMOR

Wilms tumor (also known as nephroblastoma) is a malignant renal tumor and is the second most common extracranial solid tumor in children. In 80–90% of the cases, it occurs in the renal blastoma tissue. It usually is characterized by an asymptomatic abdominal mass and abdominal swelling.

Wilms tumor comprises approximately 6% of all pediatric cancers. It is diagnosed most commonly between 1 and 5 years of age, but the peak incidence is between 3 and 4 years. Wilms tumor rarely occurs in adolescents or adults. Approximately 600 to 700 new cases are diagnosed annually in the United States (Hinkle & Schwartz, 2001). It is slightly more prevalent in Black children than it is in White children by a ratio of approximately 10:9, but boys and girls are affected equally.

The exact cause is unknown, but approximately 38% of Wilms tumors are associated with a hereditary propensity (Nathan & Orkin, 1998). Several genes have been associated with Wilms tumor. The heredity type of the disease is likely to affect both kidneys and several sites in a single kidney. If prospective parents both have the recessive disorder of Wilms tumor, they have a 25% chance of transmitting the disease to their children. Congenital anomalies occur in 12–15% of children with Wilms tumor (Lanzkowsky, 2000). Wilms tumor may have no symptoms initially, but the child may begin to have weight loss, lethargy, hypertension, or blood in the urine. Abdominal swelling is often the most prominent later symptom and is occasionally accompanied by pain.

Characteristics

1. Wilms tumor comprises approximately 6% of pediatric cancers and occurs in the renal tissue.
2. Wilms tumor is most often characterized as an abdominal mass and is often asymptomatic.
3. Wilms tumor is the second most common extracranial tumor in children.
4. Treatment usually consists of a combination of surgery, chemotherapy, and radiation.
5. Cure rate with the current therapeutic regimen is 85%.

Treatment of Wilms tumor usually consists of a number of interventions. Most often, surgery is used to remove the affected kidney. Surgeons must take great care not to disturb the tumor and create tumor spillage. Often during the surgery, the abdominal cavity and lymph nodes are examined for the spread of the cancer. In addition, radiotherapy and chemotherapy are often used in conjunction with surgery. Unfortunately, radiation and chemotherapy can often have short-term untoward side effects such as nausea, vomiting, and (in some cases) suppression of bone marrow. Long-term undesirable side effects can include neuropsychological deficits.

Children undergoing surgery for Wilms tumor may require supportive, short-term educational modifications in order to help the child with postsurgery complications. These children also cannot engage in physical activities such as school sports. As with other cancers treated with chemotherapy and radiotherapy, there can be cognitive and educational side effects. Therefore, children with Wilms tumor may require special education intervention in order to deal with the learning problems resulting from chemotherapy and radiotherapy. Deficits in areas such as attention, memory, and previously acquired academic skills must be thoroughly evaluated. After comprehensive neuropsychological evaluation, any deficits should be identified, and specific remedial strategies should be implemented (Powers, Vannatta, Noll, Cool, & Stehbens, 1995).

The prognosis of Wilms tumor is usually dependent on the type of tumor (histopathology) and the stage of disease at diagnosis. Obviously, if the cancer has metastasized into other organs, prognosis is much worse. The cure rate is approximately 85% with the current therapeutic regimen. Children treated for Wilms tumor are considered cured if they survive for 2 years without any indication that the disease has returned. Future research appears to be directed toward finding genetic treatments for the disorder.

REFERENCES

Hinkle, A. S., & Schwartz, C. L. (2001). Cancers in childhood. In R. A. Hoekelman (Ed.), *Primary pediatric care* (4th ed., pp. 1359–1384). St. Louis, MO: Mosby.

Lanzkowsky, P. (2000). *Manual of pediatric hematology and oncology* (3rd ed.). New York: Academic Press.

Nathan, D. G., & Orkin, S. H. (1998). *Hematology of infancy and childhood* (5th ed.). Philadelphia: W. B. Saunders.

Powers, S. W., Vannatta, K. V., Noll, R. B., Cool, V. A., & Stehbens, J. A. (1995). Leukemia and other childhood cancers. In M. C. Roberts (Ed.), *Handbook of pediatric psychology* (2nd ed., pp. 310–326). New York: Guilford.

William A. Rae
Texas A&M University

See also Denys-Drash Syndrome; Wagr Syndrome

WILSON DISEASE

Wilson disease (WD), or hepatolenticular degeneration, is a rare autosomal recessive metabolic disease linked to Chromosome 13 (Schilsky & Sternlieb, 1998). It is caused by two mutant alleles of a putative copper transporter, STP7B. As a result of increased copper accumulation in the liver, brain, and corneal tissue, individuals with Wilson disease often suffer from cirrhosis of the liver, bilateral softening and degeneration of the basal ganglia, and brown pigmented rings in the periphery of the cornea, referred to as Kayser-Fleischer rings (International Hepatology Informatics Group, 1994; Sherlock & Dooley, 1993).

The disease is most commonly diagnosed in children, but symptoms can be manifested later on. In one third of all cases, the initial symptom is liver disease; however, the other two thirds present first with neurological or psychiatric symptoms (Akil & Brewer, 1995). These problems, however, are all a result of accumulated excess copper due to the liver's failure to metabolize and store the copper.

When the disease presents in young children, hepatic dysfunction is often quite severe with total organ failure being common. Most transplants for individuals with Wilson disease are performed between the ages of 10 and 15. It is less common for older individuals to have hepatic failure; most such individuals present with acute and milder symptoms of liver dysfunction (e.g., chronic hepatitis).

WD occurs at a rate of approximately 1 per 40,000 births; prevalence estimates are around 12–30 cases per million. All ethnic groups appear to be similarly affected by the disease (Lauterbach, 2000). On average, one fourth of full biological siblings of those with WD will also have the disease.

Characteristics

1. Hepatic manifestations include fatigue, nausea, anorexia, malnutrition, right upper quadrant pain, hepatomegaly, jaundice, edema, spontaneous bacterial peritonitis, variceal hemorrhage, endocrine abnormalities, delayed puberty, and gynecomastia.
2. Motor manifestations include dystonia, posturing, choreiform movements, resting and intention tremors, dysarthria, dysphagia, drooling, and abnormal gait.
3. Psychiatric manifestations include manic episodes, psychosis, disinhibition, emotional lability, irritability, and aggression; depression is especially common.
4. Kayer-Fleischer rings (i.e., copper deposits around the outer of the cornea) are common.
5. Children with a family history of chronic liver disease should be screened for Wilson disease, especially those who show cognitive abnormalities and speech slurring.

Treatment typically consists of methods to reduce the amount of copper in the liver and other tissues. Although a low-copper diet is recommended, more often than not a copper-chelating agent has to be administered (e.g., D-penicillamine). The chelating agent, however, has been shown to have serious side effects in 20–25% of patients (e.g., systemic lupus and a nephrotic syndrome). Trietine is an alternate treatment to D-penicillamine, and it is the drug of choice when neurological symptoms are exhibited. Zinc salt has also been used but only as a supplement. In cases of progressive liver disease such as chronic hepatitis and organ failure, liver transplants may be necessary (Shimizu, Yamaguchi, & Aoki, 1999). Prognosis is generally good after treatment is instituted; however, about 20% of patients who have to have transplants die in the 1st year following surgery (Schilsky & Sternlieb, 1998). Death can also occur from esophageal bleeding and infection (Sherlock & Dooley, 1993).

Children with Wilson disease may present with academic and behavioral symptoms before the diagnosis is actually made. These children may show a sudden deterioration in schoolwork, uncharacteristic and socially inappropriate behaviors, anxiety, and depression (Sternlieb & Scheinberg, 1993). Memory problems and lack of motor coordination may underlie some of these functional problems. In most cases, if accommodations are even needed, they are short term (e.g., providing the child with a homework manual or memory aide until treatment takes effect). These children should, however, be carefully evaluated by school psychologists and other ancillary staff (e.g., speech and language pathologists and occupational therapists) to determine the presence of persistent cognitive, motor, and behavior problems and to determine the need for services, including special education.

Parents and children need to be educated about the need to maintain proper diet and drugs to prevent a recurrence of symptoms. Further research is needed to facilitate early diagnosis because the delay in treatment can have devastating effects on the individual with Wilson disease. More information is also needed regarding the efficacy of certain therapies (e.g., special diets and supplements) and the potential deleterious effects of standard treatments, including D-penicillamine. Understanding the pathophysiology may also help researchers to understand such effects and to understand the development of various sequelae (in particular, behavioral and psychiatric symptoms) of Wilson disease.

REFERENCES

Akil, M., & Brewer, G. (1995). Psychiatric and behavioral abnormalities in Wilson's disease. *Advances in Neurology, 65*(11), 171–178.

International Hepatology Informatics Group. (1994). *Diseases of the liver and biliary tract.* New York: Raven Press.

Lauterbach, E. C. (Ed.). (2000). *Psychiatric management in neurological disease.* Washington, DC: American Psychiatric Press.

Schilsky, M., & Sternlieb, I. (1998). Wilson's disease. In G. Y. Wu & J. Isreal (Eds.), *Diseases of the liver and bile ducts* (pp. 285–292). Totowa, NY: Humana Press.

Sherlock, S., & Dooley, J. (Eds.). (1993). *Diseases of the liver and biliary system.* Cambridge, MA: Blackwell Scientific Publications.

Shimizu, N., Yamaguchi Y., & Aoki, T. (1999). Treatment and management of Wilson's disease. *Official Journal of the Japanese Pediatric Society, 41*(4), 419–422.

Sternlieb, I., & Scheinberg, I. (1993). Wilson's disease. In L. Schiff & E. Schiff (Eds.), *Diseases of the liver* (pp. 659–668). Philadelphia: J. B. Lippincott.

Heather Edgel
Elaine Clark
University of Utah

WINCHESTER SYNDROME

Winchester syndrome is thought to be a rare form of the mucopolysaccharidoses, a group of inherited metabolic disorders that are caused by a deficiency of specific lysosomal enzymes. These enzymes are needed to break down the long chains of sugar molecules (mucopolysaccharides) used to build connective tissues and organs in the body. As with mucopolysaccharidoses, some individuals with Winchester syndrome often lose oligosaccharide (a type of simple sugar) in the urine; this symptom assists in the diagnosis of this disorder (Dunger et al., 1987). Winchester syndrome is characterized by short stature and arthritis-like symptoms. Vision and skin disorders are often associated with this syndrome.

Winchester syndrome is a very rare disorder that is inherited as an autosomal recessive trait. Recessive inheritance occurs when both matching genes from the parent must be abnormal to produce the disease. If only one gene in the pair is abnormal, the disease is not manifested or is only mildly manifested; however, children can be carriers. Thoene (1995) reported only 10 identified cases. These cases occurred in individuals of Mexican, Indian, Puerto Rican, and Iranian descent. However, because the disorder is so rare, it is possible that other cases have gone undiagnosed or misdiagnosed.

Characteristics

1. Winchester syndrome usually becomes apparent at 2 years of age, when the joints swell and become stiff and painful. Shortening (contractures) of the joints can also occur.
2. The joints most often affected are fingers, elbows, knees, and feet.
3. Hypertrichosis (excessive hair growth) develops with thick leathery skin.
4. Lips and gums thicken, causing coarse facial features.
5. Short stature.
6. Loss of calcium may occur as the child grows, causing bones in ankles and feet to weaken.
7. Vision problems such as corneal opacities (opaque areas on the cornea, which block image formation on the retina) may develop.
8. Mental functioning is not usually affected.

Individuals with Winchester syndrome may benefit from physical therapy to promote the flexibility of joints and reduce immobility. Orthopedic procedures may help to reduce contractures. Individuals with Winchester syndrome may require mobility devices. Treatment may also consist of pain management and pain relief, but it tends to be symptomatic and supportive (e.g., laser surgery has had some success in reducing corneal opacities).

Students who enter school with a diagnosis of Winchester syndrome are likely to qualify for special services under the Individuals with Disabilities Education Act (IDEA, 1997) within the physical disability category. These students may need extensive modification to accommodate the physical limitations of the disorder. For example, classrooms and other areas within the school may need to be wheelchair accessible. Transportation to and from school and school functions may be required. Additionally, these students may require accommodations due to vision problems. Physical therapy may be an integral part of the student's day. Additionally, school staff may need to be cognizant of the limitations of the disability (e.g., how to use mobility and orthopedic devices). Students with Winchester syndrome may need to be educated in pain management techniques and may require individual counseling to come to terms with how the disorder may limit their daily experiences and affect their identity development and satisfaction with their bodily image. They may also require support and education to discover how to deal with the frustration they may experience from living with this type of disorder.

There has been little research published on this syndrome; most of the published research appears to be attempting to quantify and explain Winchester syndrome and how it is recognized and diagnosed (e.g., Al Ageel et al., 2000; Dunger et al., 1987; Prapanpoch, Jorgenson, Langlais, & Nummikoski, 1992). For more information on this syndrome, contact NIH/National Arthritis and Musculoskeletal and Skin Disease Information Clearinghouse, 1 AMS Circle, Bethesda, MD 20892, (301) 495-4484.

REFERENCES

Al Ageel, A., Al Sewairi, W., Edress, B., Gorlin, R. J., Desnick, R. J., & Martignetti, J. A. (2000). Inherited multicentric osteolysis with arthritis: A variant resembling Torg syndrome in a Saudi family. *American Journal of Medical Genetics, 93*(1), 11–18.

Dunger, D. B., Dicks-Mireaux, C., O'Driscoll, P., Lake, B., Ersser, R., Shaw, D. G., et al. (1987). Two cases of Winchester syndrome: with increased urinary oligosaccharide excretion. *European Journal of Pediatrics, 146*(6), 615–619.

Prapanpoch, S., Jorgenson, R. J., Langlais, R. P., & Nummikoski, P. V. (1992). Winchester syndrome: A case report and literature review. *Oral Surg Med Oral Pathol, 74*(5), 671–677.

Thoene, J. G. (1995). *Physicians' guide to rare diseases* (2nd ed.). Dowden Publishing Company.

Rachel Toplis
University of Northern Colorado

WOLF-HIRSCHHORN SYNDROME

Wolf-Hirschhorn syndrome is an extremely rare chromosomal disorder. It affects Chromosome 4, usually in the form of a partial deletion (absence of part of the short arm of Chromosome 4). The deletion of chromosomal material results in certain facial dysmorphic features and neurological manifestations. However, the amount of chromosomal material deleted varies from individual to individual. Large deletions are associated with more severe symptoms. Wolf-Hirschhorn syndrome is not usually inherited unless a parent is a translocation carrier (i.e., part of Chromosome 4 has been transferred to a different position). Cases of Wolf-Hirschhorn syndrome are more often a sporadic event. Wolf-Hirschhorn syndrome may also be known as Wolf syndrome; Wolf-Hirschhorn chromosome region (WHCR); partial deletion of the short arm of Chromosome 4; Chromosome 4, partial monosomy 4p; and 4p syndrome, partial.

The incidence rate of Wolf-Hirschhorn syndrome in the United States is 1 in 50,000 births. This syndrome appears to occur more frequently in females than in males, with a ratio of 2:1 (female to male). There is no ethnic group predilection based on the cases reported to date.

Characteristics

1. Wolf-Hirschhorn syndrome is usually detected in the newborn period because of dysmorphic features.
2. Facial dysmorphic features include extremely wide-set eyes; broad or beaked nose; a small head (microcephaly); low-set, malformed ears; and cleft lip, palate, or uvula.
3. Neurological manifestations include profound mental retardation, severe psychomotor retardation, and seizures.

There is no treatment for Wolf-Hirschhorn syndrome. Medical care is supportive and addresses the symptoms (e.g., seizure control). Because the amount of deleted chromosomal material varies, the severity and number of symptoms differ between individuals. Therefore, medical involvement also varies from near-normal maintenance to treatment of severe heart and other problems.

Students diagnosed with Wolf-Hirschhorn syndrome are likely to qualify for special services under the physical disability category of the Individuals with Disabilities Education Act (IDEA, 1997). The effect of this syndrome upon the individual can vary tremendously; some children walk, talk, and help in daily activities, whereas others may require constant care. Educational programs may need to incorporate a variety of components, from speech, language, and social skills development, to vocational development. Therefore, speech-language pathologists, physical therapists, and occupational therapists are a few examples of the professionals who may be needed to provide care to a child with Wolf-Hirschhorn syndrome. Students with this syndrome may require assistive technology and adaptive aids to increase their range of functioning. A variety of medical problems may accompany this syndrome (e.g., heart defects and seizures); therefore, school personnel should work together with medical personnel to plan and coordinate the necessary services.

The mortality rate for Wolf-Hirschhorn syndrome is estimated at 35% in the first 2 years of life. Stillbirths, perinatal deaths, and deaths due to heart defect, aspiration pneumonia, infection, or seizure are not uncommon in the 1st year of life. If the individual lives beyond infancy, they may show slow but continuous progress in development. However, the life expectancy for individuals with Wolf-Hirschhorn syndrome is unknown. Knowledge of Wolf-Hirschhorn syndrome in adults is limited; therefore, recent research has investigated the effects and characteristics of this disorder in an adult population (Marcelis et al., 2001). Research is also investigating how Wolf-Hirschhorn syndrome is differentially expressed in relation to the amount of chromosomal material deleted or missing (Wieczorek et al., 2000).

REFERENCES

Marcelis, C., Schrander-Stumpel, C., Engelen, J., Schoonbrood-Lenssen, A., Willemse, A., Beemer, F., et al. (2001). Wolf-Hirschhorn (4P-) syndrome in adults. *Genetics Counseling, 12*(1), 35–48.

Wieczorek, D., Krause, M., Majewski, F., Albrecht, B., Hoen, D., Riess, O., et al. (2000). Effect of the size of the deletion and clinical manifestation in Wolf-Hirschhorn syndrome: Analysis of 13 patients with a de novo deletion. *European Journal of Human Genetics, 8*(7), 519–526.

Rachel Toplis
University of Northern Colorado

WOLFRAM SYNDROME

Wolfram syndrome is a neurodegenerative disorder of early onset and is often referred to as the acronym DIDMOAD (diabetes insipidus, diabetes mellitus, optic atrophy, and deafness). This condition was first described by Wolfram and Wagener (1938, as cited in Inoue et al., 1998) to be the co-occurrence of diabetes mellitus and optic atrophy, which remain as the only symptoms necessary to diagnose Wolfram syndrome. Most patients, however, develop all of the conditions listed previously, with many displaying additional neurological abnormalities (Rando, Horton, & Layzer, 1992). From their own magnetic resonance imaging (MRI) studies and a review of the pathological and radiological studies of persons with Wolfram syndrome, Rando et al. (1992) discovered that the degree of brain atrophy found in such patients was greater than would be predicted from clinical presentation. Neural damage to the anterior visual pathway, hypothalamic nuclei, and the vestibulocochlear nuclei appear to correlate with key symptoms of optic atrophy, diabetes insipidus, and deafness (Rando et al., 1992).

Kinsley, Swift, Dumont, and Swift (1995) describe the clinical progression of Wolfram syndrome symptomology. In their study, diabetes mellitus was first diagnosed at a mean of 8.2 years of age and was usually the first indicator of Wolfram syndrome. Optic atrophy was determined at a mean of 13.1 years; consequently, legal blindness followed for many of the patients in a mean of 6.7 years. Although it was only present in about half of the patients, the mean age of onset for neurosensory hearing loss was 14.6, and diabetes insipidus was apparent at an average age of 15.5 years (Kinsley et al., 1995).

Genetic transmission of Wolfram syndrome is suspected to be through autosomal recessive means, although some researchers suggest that mitochondrial mutations may be implicated in some cases (Rotig et al., 1993, as cited in Polymeropoulous, Swift, & Swift, 1994). Polymeropoulous et al. (1994) linked the condition to DNA markers on the short arm of Chromosome 4. A group of researchers reported to have identified the gene WSF1 on Chromosome 4p, the mutation of which causes this disorder. This mutation results in the degeneration of insulin-secreting islet β-cells in the pancreas, causing early-onset diabetes mellitus (Inoue et al., 1998).

It is estimated that the prevalence of Wolfram syndrome is 1 in 100,000 (Washington University School of Medicine, 1998), and the disorder appears to affect men and women equally (Kinsley et al., 1995). An estimated 1% of the United States population are thought to be heterozygous carries of the mutated gene (Swift, Perkins, Chase, Sadler, & Swift, 1991). Furthermore, Swift et al. (1991) found that carriers of the gene may be at an eightfold risk over noncarriers for psychiatric hospitalization or suicide attempts. The rate of severe mental disorders in patients with Wolfram syndrome was found to be 25% and most commonly presented as depression, aggression, or organic brain syndrome (Swift, Sadler, & Swift, 1990). Furthermore, the authors asserted that these mental conditions were not purely a response to the physical illness and that the documented diffuse neurodegenerative processes may contribute to the high rate of comorbid psychiatric illness (e.g., Gregorios, 1989, as cited in Swift et al., 1990; Rando et al., 1992).

Characteristics

1. Optic atrophy
2. Diabetes mellitus
3. Diabetes insipidus
4. Neurosensory hearing loss
5. Urinary tract disease
6. Other neurological abnormalities, including ataxia, nystagmus, mental retardation, and seizures

Currently, no cure exists for this neurological degenerative disorder, and treatment revolves around symptom management. The diabetes mellitus is generally treated with insulin, and Kinsley et al. (1995) report that oral hypoglycemic medications have not met with long-term treatment success. Additionally, urinary tract symptoms may require self-catheterization, and antibiotics may prevent ensuing urinary tract infections. When psychiatric disorders are present in such patients, psychopharmacological agents may improve treatment compliance (Kinsley et al., 1995).

Wolfram syndrome is associated with a high mortality rate, with the expectation that 60% of the patients presenting with this constellation of symptoms will die by age 35

(Kinsley et al., 1995). In these patients, death may result from neurological degeneration or complications from urinary tract infection. Damage to lower brain stem centers controlling motor nuclei may cause some patients to choke on food, resulting in harm or even death (Kinsley et al., 1995). There is optimism, however, that recent research findings regarding the genetic contributions of Wolfram syndrome may shed some light on the mechanisms and possible therapies for both this condition and other more common forms of diabetes (University of Washington, 1998).

Students with Wolfram syndrome will qualify for special education services under Section 504 of the Rehabilitation Act of 1973 and under the Individuals with Disabilities Act (IDEA). The individualized educational program planning team may recommend assistive technology devices to aid the student with auditory and visual impairments that interfere with learning. Furthermore, medical support for the treatment of the student's diabetes must be organized. Teachers should be sensitive to the possibility of urinary tract infections, and the school should provide appropriate accommodations. The school district may also need to consider educational supports for any associated cognitive difficulties.

REFERENCES

Gregorios, J. D. (1989). Wolfram's syndrome with schizophrenia and central hypoventilation: a neuropathological study. *Journal of Neuropathology Experimental Neurology, 48,* 308.

Inoue, H., Tanizawa, Y., Wasson, J., Behn, P., Kalidas, K., Bernal-Mizrachi, E., et al. (1998). A gene encoding a transmembrane protein is mutated in patients with diabetes mellitus and optic atrophy (Wolfram syndrome). *Nature Genetics, 20,* 143–148.

Kinsley, B. T., Swift, M., Dumont, R. H., & Swift, R. G. (1995). Morbidity and mortality in the Wolfram syndrome. *Diabetes Care, 18*(12), 1566–1570.

Polymeropoulous, M. H., Swift, R. G., & Swift, M. (1994). Linkage of the gene for Wolfram syndrome to markers on the short arm of chromosome 4. *Nature Genetics, 8,* 95–97.

Rando, T. A., Horton, J. C., & Layzer, R. B. (1992). Wolfram syndrome: Evidence of a diffuse neurodegenerative disease by magnetic resonance imaging. *Neurology, 42,* 1220–1224.

Rotig, A., Cormier, V., Chatelain, P., Rene, F., Saudubray, J. M., Rustin, P., et al. (1993). Deletion of mitochondrial DNA in a case of early-onset diabetes mellitus, optic atrophy, and deafness. *Journal of Clinical Investigation, 9*(3), 1095–1098.

Swift, R. G., Perkins, D. O., Chase, C. L., Sadler, D. B., & Swift, M. (1991). Psychiatric disorders in 35 families with Wolfram syndrome. *American Journal of Psychiatry, 148,* 775–779.

Swift, R. G., Sadler, D. B., & Swift, M. (1990). Psychiatric findings in Wolfram syndrome homozygotes. *Lancet (North American Edition), 336*(8716), 667–669.

University of Washington School of Medicine. (1998). Researchers identify and isolate first gene for a form of insulin-dependent diabetes. Retrieved from http://www.sciencedaily.com/releases/1998/09/980929073115.htm

Wolfram, D. J., & Wagener, H. P. (1938). Diabetes mellitus and simple optic atrophy among siblings: Report of four cases. *Mayo Clinical Procedures, 13,* 715–718.

Sarah Schnoebelen
Margaret Semrud-Clikeman
University of Texas at Austin

WYBURN-MASON SYNDROME

Wyburn-Mason syndrome, also known as Bonnet-Dechaume-Blanc syndrome, is a rare condition that is characterized by arteriovenous malformations (i.e., abnormal communication between the arteries and veins) in the central nervous system and the retina. These malformations take the form of arteriovenous aneurysms, which are widenings of the walls of an artery and a vein with abnormal blood flow between the vessels. This condition is considered to be congenital, and it is passed on via autosomal dominant inheritance, which means that an affected person has a 50% chance of passing the trait to a child. In 1937, Bonnet et al. recognized the coexistence of retinal and cerebral arteriovenous malformations (AVMs). In 1943, Wyburn-Mason recorded cases of arteriovenous malformations of the midbrain, retina, and facial nevi and found that this syndrome may also be associated with mental changes in some cases.

Prior to 1973, only 43 cases had been reported in the literature. Between then and October 1998, a further 30 cases were described. Based on the literature available so far, there does not appear to be any race predilection. Additionally, males and females are equally likely to be affected.

Characteristics

1. Wyburn-Mason syndrome is characterized by vascular malformations of the brain and of the nerve-rich, innermost membranes of the eyes.
2. It typically presents with unilateral vascular abnormalities involving the facial structures, orbits, and brain; this means that the vascular (or blood vessel) abnormalities typically occur only on one side of the brain and face.
3. Symptoms of lowered vision (or blindness) typically appear in the second and third decades of life but may appear in the first.
4. Progressive protrusion of the eye may occur.
5. Chronic intermittent headaches.
6. Birthmarks or pigmented facial skin blemishes (facial nevi) may appear.
7. Mental changes may occur at this time as well, in some cases.

The discussions on the treatment and management of this particular syndrome are difficult to find in the literature. Usually the presenting symptoms are simply observed and documented. However, the National Organization for Rare Disorders (NORD) suggests contacting the National Aphasia Association for more information. (NAA, 156 Fifth Avenue, Suite 707, New York, NY 10010, 800-922-4622) for more information.

Wyburn-Mason syndrome is very rare. However, children diagnosed with this disorder would likely qualify for special education services within the visual impairment area. Depending upon the nature and impact (if any) of mental changes, the cognitive and social emotional changes would need to be addressed. Teachers and those working with the student need to be well informed about the illness and its symptoms. School staff will need to be able to deal with the manifestation of the illness as it presents itself in class. Because this syndrome is associated with intracranial vascular malformations, concern would arise from a neuropsychological viewpoint, and frequent assessments of current functioning (cognitive, motor, and social-emotional) would be recommended.

Most of the recent publications addressing this rare syndrome focus only on the clinical and radiological findings and do not discuss treatment. Considering the fact that patients have significant intracranial vascular malformations, more attention may be given to this syndrome in future neurological literature.

REFERENCES

Muthukumar, N., Sundaralingam, M., & Prabakara, M. (1998). Retinocephalic vascular malformation: Case report *British Journal of Neurosurgery, 12*(5), 458–460.

Patel, U., & Gupta, S. C. (1990). Wyburn-Mason syndrome. A case report and review of the literature. *Neuroradiology, 31*(6), 544–546.

Kathryn Zupancic
Rachel Toplis
University of Northern Colorado

X

X-LINKED HYDROCEPHALUS SYNDROME

X-linked hydrocephalus is one type of congenital hydrocephalus that results when circulation and absorption of the cerebrospinal fluid within the ventricles are impeded or impaired. The acronym HSAS was coined because stenosis of the aqueduct of Sylvius (a narrow passageway linking the third and fourth ventricles) was originally thought to be the causative agent of the disorder (Bickers & Adams, 1949). Edwards (1961) suggested that HSAS was due to an X-linked recessive gene, with primary transmission from mother to son. Poor developmental outcome (mental retardation and severe motor impairment) for shunted HSAS infants provided further support for genetic causation (Fransen, Lemmon, Van Camp, Coucke, & Willems, 1995; Halliday, Chow, Wallace, & Danks, 1986). Recent linkage studies have suggested that X-linked hydrocephalus is associated with mutations in the gene at Xq28 (Willems et al., 1992). Further studies have identified the mutated gene as a neural cell adhesion molecule L1 (L1CAM) that is thought to impair neuronal cell migration, neurite elongation, and fasciculation of axons (see Kenwrick, Jouet, & Donnai, 1996, for a review of the literature).

Although X-linked hydrocephalus is the most common form of genetically transmitted hydrocephalus, it is a relatively rare condition, occurring in approximately 1 in 30,000 male births (Kenwrick, Jouet, & Donnai, 1996). This condition often results in stillbirth or early mortality. For example, in a study of X-linked hydrocephalus cases that occurred over a 20-year period in Victoria, Australia, 18 of the 25 study babies were stillborn or died within 1–2 months (Halliday et al., 1986). This study also found that three fifths of the cases were males. There is no evidence available suggesting that specific racial or ethnic groups have a genetic predisposition for X-linked hydrocephalus.

Characteristics

1. Obviously a predominant feature of the disorder is the presence of congenital hydrocephalus and its subsequent deleterious impact on brain development. Some of the possible consequences include hypoplasia of the corpus callosum, along with reduced brain mass and disruptions of the myelination process (Fletcher, Brookshire, Bohan, Brandt, & Davidson, 1995). Larger ventricular enlargement is associated with early mortality (Kenwrick et al., 1996).
2. In the vast majority of surviving cases, significant mental deficits are present, with estimates of intellectual functioning at mental retardation ranging from severe to profound. Two studies from the early 1960s, however, reported IQs above 70 (Kenwrick et al., 1996).
3. Flexion deformity (adducted thumbs) is present in 50% of infants with X-linked hydrocephalus (Halliday et al., 1986).
4. Spasticity of the lower limbs is common, and in more severe cases, spastic quadriplegia is often present.
5. Additional neurological abnormalities reported include nystagmus, ptosis, optical atrophy, scoliosis, torticollis, lumbar lordosis, and seizures (Kenwrick et al., 1996).

In many (but not all) cases, the presence of hydrocephalus is detected during routine ultrasound testing. For infants who survive, valve insertion is an effective treatment to relieve the cranial pressure caused by the hydrocephalus and to increase life expectancy. However, significant developmental delays (intellectual, language, and motor retardation) are usually present. Parents need to receive genetic testing and counseling because the recurrence risk in X-linked hydrocephalus is 50% for subsequent brothers (Williems, Brouwer, Dijkstra, & Wilmink, 1987).

Children with severe and profound levels of mental impairment will require individually tailored special education accommodations and services. Provision of educational services for the majority of these children will be within the confines of a special education classroom for individuals with multiple handicaps. Educational instruction—preferably with a small student-to-teacher ratio—should be multisensory and supportive with communication devices such as soundboards employed where appropriate.

Many children with X-linked hydrocephalus have motor difficulties requiring the use of mobility devices (wheelchairs, walkers) to actively participate in their school environment. To maximize the child's educational gain and overall health, it is imperative that effective communication exists between school personnel and medical care providers. For example, educational personnel (with the school nurse as team leader) should be familiar with the student's special medical needs (shunt care). It is important that school personnel be able to recognize the signs of shunt infection (low-grade fever or redness or tenderness along the shunt) in order to alert the child's family and medical care providers.

The National Institute of Neurological Disorders and Stroke (NINDS) supports research that examines brain development. This research has a long-term goal that includes the prevention of X-linked hydrocephalus (NINDS, 2000). Included on the NINDS information web page is a list of support organizations.

REFERENCES

Bickers, D. S., & Adams, R. D. (1949). Hereditary stenosis of the aqueduct of Sylvius as a cause of congenital hydrocephalus. *Brain, 72,* 246–262.

Edwards, J. H. (1961). The syndrome of sex-linked hydrocephalus. *Archives of Disease in Childhood, 36,* 486–493.

Fletcher, J. M., Brookshire, B. L., Bohan, T. P., Brandt, M. E., & Davidson, K. C. (1995). Early hydrocephalus. In B. P. Rourke (Ed.), *Syndrome of nonverbal learning disabilities* (pp. 206–238). New York: Guilford.

Fransen, E., Lemmon, V., Van Camp, G., Coucke, P., & Willems, P. J. (1995). CRASH syndrome: Clinical spectrum of corpus callosum hypoplasia, retardation, adducted thumbs, spastic paraparesis and hydrocephalus due to mutations in one single gene, L1. *European Journal of Human Genetics, 3,* 273–284.

Halliday, J., Chow, C. W., Wallace, D., & Danks, D. M. (1986). X-linked hydrocephalus: A survey of a 20-year period in Victoria, Australia. *Journal of Medical Genetics, 23,* 23–31.

Kenwrick, S., Jouet, M., & Donnai, D. (1996). X-linked hydrocephalus and MASA syndrome. *Journal of Medical Genetics, 33,* 59–65.

National Institute of Neurological Disorders and Stroke. (2000, June). Hydrocephalus fact sheet. Retrieved from http://www.ninds.nih.gov/health_and_medical/disorders/hydrocephalus_fs.htm

Willems, P. J., Vits, L., Raeymaekers, P., Beuten, J., Coucke, P., Holden, J. J. A., et al. (1992). Further localization of X-linked hydrocephalus in the chromosome region Xq28. *American Journal of Human Genetics, 51,* 307–315.

Williems, P. J., Brouwer, O. F., Dijkstra, I., & Wilmink, J. (1987). X-linked hydrocephalus. *American Journal of Medical Genetics, 27,* 921–928.

Louise O'Donnell
University of Texas at Austin
University of Texas Health Science Center, San Antonio

X-LINKED LYMPHOPROLIFERATIVE SYNDROME (DUNCAN DISEASE, PURTILO SYNDROME)

X-linked lymphoproliferative syndrome (XLP) is an inherited immunodeficiency disorder characterized by one or more of three major phenotypic presentations. These presentations include a defective response to infection with the Epstein-Barr virus (EBV), acquired hypogammaglobulinemia, and malignant B-cell lymphoma (National Organization for Rare Disorders, 2001). Patients exhibit a range of symptoms, including life-threatening EBV infection, lymphoma or Hodgkins disease, suppressed bone marrow function with related immunodeficiency, aplastic anemia, and lymphohistiocytic disorder. In some cases, patients may have a proliferation of certain white blood cells (lymphocytes and histiocytes) in particular organs subsequent to an EBV infection. XLP can be associated with susceptibility to bruising and excessive bleeding because of a decrease in platelets (thrombocytopenia). The occurrence of a Burkitt type of malignant lymphoma in the ileocecal region should prompt for evaluation of XLP in the patient and family because it is a frequent finding in XLP.

Characteristics

1. Decreased immune response to Epstein-Barr virus (EBV), with susceptibility for life-threatening EBV infections
2. Acquired hypogammaglobulinemia
3. Development of malignant B-cell lymphomas
4. Normal range of intelligence
5. Decreased life span expectancy, with 50% mortality by age 10 and nearing 100% by the end of the fourth decade of life.

An X-linked recessive genetic disorder, it is fully expressed in males only, with a mutation in gene SH2D1A, SAP (DSHP), as well as similar diagnoses appearing in maternal male relatives. Carrier females may show atypical antibody response to early antigens but are otherwise asymptomatic. More than 272 cases from 80 kindred groups are listed in the University of Nebraska Medical Center's XLP Registry. Cases are reported from Germany, the United States, Great Britain, Scandinavia, New Zealand, Australia, France, and the Middle East (Buyse, 1990).

The EBV virus is common in the general population and typically causes infectious mononucleosis without significant complications. However, in XLP patients, there is a severely inadequate immune response to the EBV infection. Onset of symptoms is typically seen sometime between 6 months to 10 years of age. About half to two thirds of those with XLP will experience a life-threatening case of mononucleosis. Phenotypic variability of XLP is considerable both across individuals and kindred groups and within kindreds and over time within an individual. A fulminant infectious mononucleosis is not necessary for the development of malignant lymphoma or hypogammaglobulinemia. There is an unclear association between genotype, phenotype, and outcome. It appears that there may be environmental or other genetic factors that contribute to the pathogenesis of XLP (Sumegi et al., 2000).

Prognosis is poor, with 50% succumbing to complications of EBV infection, especially liver failure, by age 10. Although cause of early death is typically fatal infectious mononucleosis, cause of later death is associated with complications of other infections or hemorrhage. Lymphoma or Hodgkins disease, immunodeficiency, aplastic anemia, or lymphohistiocytic disorder can follow the acute EBV infection. Although fewer than 5% of individuals with this disorder survive fulminant hepatitis, those with isolated dysgammaglobulinemia have a higher survival rate (50%). Nevertheless, survival rate nears zero by the end of the fourth decade of life.

Genetic testing is available for diagnosis in affected males; it can also identify female carriers. Treatments include antiviral agents (e.g., acyclovir and interferon-alpha), high-dose IV gamma globulin, and bone marrow transplants. A recent promising treatment for reconstituting the immune system is umbilical cord stem cell transplantation (Ziegner et al., 2001). Those who develop the acquired hypogammaglobulinemia may benefit from prophylactic antibiotics and replacement immunoglobulin therapy. Early detection via genetic testing prior to EBV infection or other symptoms can offer the opportunity for prophylactic treatment along these lines as well. Those who develop lymphoma may receive traditional treatment with surgery, radiation, and chemotherapy. These latter patients (if not overtreated) show relatively good prognoses.

Children with XLP can be expected to display a normal range of intelligence. Special education services may be available due to Other Health Impairments or Physical Disability. School accommodations will focus on the physical symptoms of the disorder (e.g., fatigue, frequent illness due to infections). The vicissitudes of hepatic functioning may be associated with fluctuations in mental status. Vigilant hygiene practices and even possible limited contact with others may help to reduce the exposure of the child to the EBV virus and other infectious agents. Home schooling may be warranted for students with severely impaired immune systems. Caution regarding physical activity is warranted, given the vulnerability to bruising and tendency for excessive bleeding (hemorrhaging). Teachers and school personnel can be educated regarding the signs and symptoms of lymphoma and hypogammaglobulinemia to aid monitoring for symptoms' possible development.

REFERENCES

Buyse, M. L. (1990). *Birth defects encyclopedia.* Oxford, England: Blackwell Scientific Publications.

National Organization for Rare Disorders. (2001, May 7). Retrieved May 7, 2001 from http://www.stepstn.com/cgi-win/nord.exe?proc=GetDocument&rectype=0&recnum=729

Sumegi, J., Huang, D., Lanyi, A., Davis, J., Seemayer, T., Maeda, A., et al. (2000). Correlation of mutations of the SH2D1A gene and Epstein-Barr virus infection with clinical phenotype and outcome in x-linked lymphoproliferative disease. *Blood, 96*(9), 3118–3125.

Ziegner, U., Ochs, H., Schanen, C., Feig, S., Seyama, K., Futatani, T., et al. (2001). Unrelated umbilical cord stem cell transplantation for x-linked immunodeficiencies. *Journal of Pediatrics, 138*(4), 570–573.

Vicky Y. Spradling
Austin State Hospital

XERODERMA PIGMENTOSUM

Xeroderma pigmentosum (XP) is an autosomal recessive disorder characterized by extreme photosensitivity of the skin and eyes (Kraemer, 1990; Worobec-Victor, Shanker, Bene-Bain, & Solomon, 1988). Even minimal sun exposure can result in blistering of the skin, freckling, or both. The disorder is due to a defect in the ability of the cell to repair DNA damaged by ultraviolet (UV) radiation. The deficiency is in endonuclease activity, and individuals can be assigned to one of nine complementation groups: A through I (Worobec-Victor et al., 1988). In addition to UV radiation, these individuals also show hypersensitivity to certain chemical carcinogens, such as those found in cigarette smoke (Kraemer, 1990).

Characteristics

1. Infantile onset.
2. Hypersensitivity of the skin to sunlight, resulting in blistering, freckling, or both with minimal exposure.
3. Photophobia and atrophic changes to the anterior portion of the eye (conjunctivitis, corneal opacities, inflammatory masses, malignancies, and ectropion and entropion of the lids).
4. Development of benign, premalignant, and malignant tumors. Of the malignancies, basal cell carcinoma, squamous cell carcinoma, and melanoma are the most common.
5. Neurological involvement is seen in some cases; these symptoms include microcephaly, intellectual impairment, ataxia, spasticity, choreoathetosis, and a progressive neurological syndrome.

Progressive atrophic changes occur in cutaneous and oculocuteneous areas exposed to sunlight. Even a single brief exposure can lead to blistering. Individuals with XP have a 2,000 times greater frequency of developing cancer—particularly, basal cell, squamous, and melanoma. Metastases are common. A small but significant increase in the incidence of internal malignancies has been reported as well (Plon & Peterson, 1997). Cancer and secondary infection are frequent causes of death in XP individuals. Life expectancy is shortened, with death frequently occurring in childhood. There is a 70% probability of survival to age 40 years (Kraemer, 1990).

The incidence of XP is 1:250,000 in the United States and Western Europe. The incidence is higher in Japan at 1:40,000. Furthermore, in Japan there is a higher incidence of Group A, which is most often associated with severe neurological involvement. The DeSanctis-Cacchione syndrome refers to a subset of XP individuals (typically from Group A) with the most severe neurological symptoms including microcephaly, progressive mental retardation, choreoathetosis, cerebellar ataxia, diminished reflexes, spasticity, sensorineural deafness, seizures, dwarfism, and delayed sexual development (Worobec-Victor et al., 1988). Neurological involvement has also been reported in Group D, but the symptoms tend to have a later onset and are milder. The incidence of XP is equal for men and women. Incidence of XP is also typically higher in countries with a high rate of consanguinity.

Symptoms are typically evident in the newborn, and 50% of cases are diagnosed by 18 months of age; 75% are diagnosed by age 4 years (Kraemer, 1990). In addition to clinical diagnosis, XP may be diagnosed by studying fibroblasts derived from biopsy following UV radiation exposure (Worobec-Victor et al., 1988). This technique may also be used prenatally. Heterozygous carriers of XP tend to be clinically asymptomatic and cannot be consistently identified.

Treatment typically involves prevention of exposure to sunlight and other chemical carcinogens. Long hair can be helpful in shielding the neck and ears. Double layering of clothing and use of sunglasses are also helpful. Sunscreen should be used. A rather nocturnal lifestyle often develops to avoid sun exposure. As cancer or other cutaneous lesions occur, they should be treated through conventional means. Genetic counseling is difficult, as carriers are difficult to identify. For those with neurological involvement, a comprehensive neuropsychological evaluation is recommended to aid with educational and vocational planning. Specific speech, occupational, and physical therapies are often indicated in these cases. Psychological evaluation and intervention may also be indicated to help with issues of socialization due to the limitation of lifestyle and social opportunity imposed by XP. Support groups and involvement in activities such as nighttime camps may be very helpful with socialization issues (Xeroderma Pigmentosum Society, 2001). Issues of body image and longevity should also be assessed and treated as needed.

REFERENCES

Kraemer, K. H. (1990). Xeroderma pigmentosum. In M. L. Buyse (Ed.), *The birth defects encyclopedia.* Cambridge, England: Center for Birth Defects Information Services in association with Blackwell Scientific Publications.

Plon, S. E., & Peterson, L. E. (1997). Childhood cancer, heredity, and the environment. In P. A. Pizzo & D. G. Poplack (Eds.), *Principles and practice of pediatric oncology* (3rd ed.). Philadelphia: Lippincott-Raven.

Worobec-Victor, S. M., Shanker, D. B., Bene-Bain, M. A., & Solomon, L. M. (1988). Genodermatoses. In L. A. Schachner & R. C. Hansen (Eds.), *Pediatric dermatology.* New York: Churchill Livingstone.

Xeroderma Pigmentosum Society. (2001, May). Retrieved from http://www.xps.org

David M. Tucker
Rebecca Vaurio
Austin, Texas

See also DeSanctis-Cacchione Syndrome

XXX SYNDROME

XXX syndrome is a disorder in which affected females have three X chromosomes. It may also be referred to as Chromosome X, Triplo-X, and Chromosome 47, XXX karyotype. XXX syndrome was first described by P. A. Jacobs in the *Lancet* in 1959. It is the most frequent X chromosomal anomaly in females. The incidence of XXX syndrome is 0.3–1 per 1000 newborn females (Pedlynx, 2002).

This syndrome is very similar to XXXX syndrome, which has very similar clinical features, but it has lower incidence, with only 40 cases to date (Jones, 1997). Diagnosis for both conditions is confirmed by chromosomal analysis.

Characteristics

1. Hypertelorism
2. Tall stature (average height of 172 cm)
3. Widely spaced nipples
4. Webbed neck
5. Variable IQ, from superior to moderate-to-severe mental retardation
6. Transient gross motor delays
7. Speech and language delays
8. Fine motor delays
9. Coordination problems with awkwardness
10. Behavioral problems

11. Mild depression, conduct disorder, immature behavior, socializing problems
12. Occasional seizures

Treatment of this syndrome is multidisciplinary, utilizing professionals from pediatrics, endocrinology, neurology, and psychology. Genetic counseling is recommended, although no XXX daughter of an XXX mother has been reported.

Special education programming has been documented in 60% of cases due to frequent verbal learning and expressive language deficits. Behavior problems, including mild depression and conduct disorder, occur in 30% of cases (Jones, 1997). Due to the wide variability of symptoms with this syndrome, individualized assessment and treatment, as prescribed under special education guidelines, are quite appropriate. The prognosis for children with XXX syndrome is that they can expect to have normal life span (Pedlynx, 2002).

REFERENCES

Jones, K. L. (1997). *Smith's recognizable patterns of human malformation* (5th ed.). Philadelphia: W. B. Saunders.

Pedlynx. (2002). XXX syndrome. Retrieved from http://www.icondata.com/health/pedbase/files/XXXSYNDR.HTM

Elaine Fletcher-Janzen
University of Northern Colorado

XXXX SYNDROME

XXXX syndrome—also called Chromosome X, poly-X—is a genetic disorder in which affected females have four X chromosomes. It was first described by Carr, Barr, and Plunkett in a medical journal in 1961. The syndrome is due to successive nondisjunctive meiotic divisions within a parent, and the diagnosis is confirmed by genetic analysis (Jones, 1997).

The incidence of XXXX syndrome is rare; there have been about 40 cases reported. The age of onset is in childhood and the phenotype is quite variable, with some patients having faces suggestive of Trisomy 21 (Pedlynx, 2002).

Characteristics

Dysmorphisms

1. Hypertelorism
2. Upward-slanting palpebral fissures
3. Epicanthal folds
4. Midfacial hypoplasia
5. Micrognathia
6. Normal to tall stature
7. Narrow shoulder girdle
8. Fifth-finger clinodactyly
9. Simian crease

Neurological manifestations

1. IQ range from 30 to 80, with a mean of 55
2. Speech and language delays
3. Behavioral problems

Endocrine manifestations

1. Incomplete or absent sexual development
2. Variable amenorrhea with irregular menses
3. Possible fertility problems

Other manifestations

1. Congenital heart disease
2. Radioulnar synostosis

Treatment for XXXX syndrome is supportive and requires multidisciplinary professionals from the fields of pediatrics, endocrinology, neurology, and psychology. Genetic counseling is also prescribed for these patients and their families (Pedlynx, 2002).

The variety of sequelae for this disorder suggests that special education services would be needed for girls with XXXX syndrome. The average intellectual functioning of individuals with this disorder suggests that adaptive behavior and academic deficits would be present; it would therefore also identify the child for special education services under the mental retardation handicapping condition.

The prognosis for females with XXXX syndrome is dependent on appropriate and ongoing medical and educational monitoring and support.

REFERENCES

Carr, D. H., Barr, M. L., & Plunkett, E. R. (1961). An XXXX sex chromosome complex in two mentally defective females. *Canadian Medical Association Journal, 84,* 131.

Jones, K. L. (1997). *Smith's recognizable patterns of human malformation* (5th ed.). Philadelphia: W. B. Saunders.

Pedlynx. (2002). Online database: XXXX syndrome. Retrieved April 2002 from http://www.icondata.com/health/pedbase/files/XXXXSYND.HTM

Elaine Fletcher-Janzen
University of Northern Colorado

XYY SYNDROME

XYY syndrome is a tall-stature syndrome in males with an extra Y chromosome and is characterized by behavioral disorders that manifest in puberty. The main distinguishing characteristics of the syndrome are that the boys have tall stature (> 180 cm), behavior disorders in over 50% of cases, and delayed speech. This syndrome may be differentially diagnosed with Marfan syndrome, and there are no masculine or feminine characteristics specifically associated with this genotype (Theilgaard, 1984).

The incidence of XYY syndrome is about 1 per 1,000 newborn boys. However, epidemiological research with XYY syndrome has been historically insufficient due to the criteria with which genetic exploration has been carried out with some population groups that exhibit deviant or criminal behavior in contrast to the general population (Pirozynski, Scripcaru, Harmanschi, & Teodorescu, 1977). Indeed, a literature review by Ike (2000) reports that abnormal findings in XYY males often can be disputed because of bias, the cognitive and behavioral spectrum, biochemical variables, phenotypic predisposition, chance, legal loopholes, and environmental versus genetic contributions to crime. Ike (2000) suggests that most XYY carriers lead normal, productive lives. The apparent increased rate of XYY is most likely due to selective screening of children with behavioral problems.

Characteristics

1. Tall stature (< 180 cm)
2. Wide spectrum of intelligence scores
3. Labile affect
4. History positive for deviant behavior
5. Increased occurrence of minor anomalies such as acne, large head, asymmetrical cranium, strabismus, early varicosities of the lower leg, and leg ulcers

Hormonal therapy is an option for treatment if excessive growth is anticipated. In addition, behavioral problems and deviant behavior will most certainly require therapeutic support and guidance. Identification of cytogenetic abnormalities such as XYY syndrome has begun in high-risk populations in schools (Staley, Taylor, McGavran, & Meltesen, 1995).

Special education services would most likely be needed for speech-language delays and behavioral issues. Careful monitoring of behavioral plans and functional behavioral assessments will assist in maintaining the child in inclusive settings.

REFERENCES

Ike, N. (2000). Current thinking on XYY syndrome. *Psychiatric Annals, 30*(2), 91–95.

Pirozynski, T., Scripcaru, G., Harmanschi, A., & Teodorescu, F. (1977). XYY-syndrome: Clinical and behavioral typology. *Acta Psychiatrica Belgica, 77*(2), 197–215.

Staley, L., Taylor, A., McGavran, L., & Meltesen, L. (1995). Identification of cytogenetic abnormalities as a consequence of FMR-1 testing in schools. *Developmental Brain Dysfunction, 8*(4–6), 310–318.

Theilgaard, A. (1984). A psychological study of the personalities of XYY- and XXY-men. *Acta Psychiatrica Scandinavica, 69*(Suppl. 315), 1–133.

Elaine Fletcher-Janzen
University of Northern Colorado

Y

YAWS

Yaws is a chronic and contagious skin disease characterized by swollen, open sores; it primarily affects people living in rural, humid, and tropical climates. Yaws is characterized by three stages: primary, secondary, and tertiary.

Children under the age of 15 account for 75% of all new cases of yaws (Walker & Hay, 2000). The peak incidence of yaws is reported to occur between the ages of 6 and 10 years of age (Sehgal, Jain, Bhattacharya, & Thappa, 1994). Following the mass treatment programs sponsored by the World Health Organization (WHO) from 1957 to 1963, the incidence of yaws decreased dramatically from 50–100 million to fewer than 20 million cases in the 1970s. In 1997, an estimated 460,000 new cases of yaws was reported by the WHO, primarily in regions with poor hygiene and housing conditions, such as West Africa, Papua New Guinea, Indonesia, and the Solomon Islands (Nagreh, 1986). Among the reasons that yaws has yet to be completely eradicated include an underestimation of the number of untreated cases in the later stages of the disease and the prevalence of yaws in rural and remote populations (Aylward, Hennessey, Zegaria, Olive, & Cochi, 2000).

Yaws is very contagious. The most common route of transmission is when broken skin or open sores come into contact with an infected skin lesion. Three to 5 weeks after the initial infection, the first lesion, or mother yaw will appear, usually on the skin of the lower legs, which defines the primary stage of yaws. The primary lesion remains on the body, usually on the lower legs, for 2–9 months, by which time the lesion spontaneously disappears and scars form. Lesions marking the secondary stage are smaller and may appear as early as 1 month or as late as 24 months after the person is infected. Symptoms such as headache, fever, joint pains, and generalized lymphadenopathy may appear during the second stage of yaws. The symptoms persist for an average of 5 years, usually with interspersed latent periods. The tertiary phase is characterized by cutaneous plaque nodules, ulcers, and hyperkeratoses of the palms and soles, as well as by lesions involving the skull, sternum, tibia, or other bones. It is estimated that only 10% of those infected with yaws will ever experience the third stage (Sehgal et al., 1994).

The etiology of yaws is attributed to the *treponema pertenue* bacteria, which is similar in structure to the bacteria that causes syphilis to develop. However, unlike syphilis, yaws is nonvenereal and does not affect the cardiovascular or neurological systems (Sehgal et al., 1994). The mother yaw, characteristic of the primary phase, contains serous fluid with the treponemes; thus, diagnosis at this stage requires microscopic examination of the lesion for the bacteria (Nagreh, 1986). Because the treponemes are rarely present in skin lesions during the later stages, it is important to obtain an early diagnosis if possible (Chulay, 2000). In the later stages of yaws, diagnosis becomes increasingly more difficult because the skin lesions must be differentiated from lesions resulting from topical ulcers, sickle cell anemia, leprosy, tuberculosis, and so on. Yaws is not known to impair cognitive or educational functioning. Children from areas where yaws is known to exist should be forward with the teachers and nurses about their skin problems (Sehgal et al., 1994).

Characteristics

1. Infectious, chronic skin disease.
2. Primary stage symptoms include the presence of the primary skin lesion, usually on the lower legs.
3. Secondary and tertiary stage symptoms include additional lesions and ulcers on the palms and plantar surfaces. The skin, bone, and joints are also affected during these stages.

Yaws is easily treatable; however, issues of detection and eradication remain a large problem in some areas. Historically, penicillin has been the most effective treatment for curing yaws. Typically, a single dosage will cure the disease. However, in some areas, the penicillin treatment has shown to be ineffective and does not prevent the spread of yaws; thus, new treatments are needed. For example, Walker and Hay (2000) reported that penicillin treatment reportedly failed to cure yaws in areas of Papua New Guinea, possibly indicating the development of a strain of yaws resistant to penicillin. Prevention strategies can also be used to prevent the spread of yaws in the tropic areas.

REFERENCES

Aylward, B., Hennessey, K. A., Zegaria, N., Olive, J. M., & Cochi, S. (2000). When is a disease eradicable? 100 years of lessons learned. *American Journal of Public Health, 90,* 1515–1520.

Chulay, J. (2000). Treponema species (yaws, pinta, bejel). In G. L. Mandell, J. E. Bennet, & R. Dolin (Eds.), *Mandell, Douglas, and Bennett's principles and practice of infectious diseases* (5th ed., pp. 2490–2494). New York: Churchill Livingstone.

Nagreh, D. S. (1986). Yaws. *Cutis, 38,* 303–305.

Sehgal, V. N., Jain, S., Bhattacharya, S. N., & Thappa, D. M. (1994). Yaws: control eradication. *International Journal of Dermatology, 33,* 16–20.

Walker, S. L., & Hay, R. J. (2000). Yaws: A review of the last 50 years. *International Journal of Dermatology, 39,* 258–260.

Jennifer M. Gillis
Center for Educational Partnerships
University of California, Irvine

YUNIS-VARON SYNDROME

Yunis-Varon syndrome is a disorder that involves effects of varying degrees in growth and development of the skeletal, ectodermal, central nervous, and cardiovascular systems (Walch et al., 2000). Since the disorder's identification in 1983 by Yunis and Varon, there have been approximately 13 cases reported in the literature. Research suggests that the disorder may be inherited either as an X-linked dominant or an autosomal recessive trait (Garrett, Berry, Simpson, & Hall, 1990). In recessive disorders, the child inherits the same defective gene for the same trait from each parent.

Although the National Organization for Rare Disorders (NORD) reports that the disorder affects males and females in equal numbers, only 3 out of the 13 reported cases have been females. No race predilection is noted. The physical characteristics of the disorder are obvious at birth (NORD, 2001).

Characteristics

1. Craniofacial disproportion, with underdeveloped facial bones and an abnormally small jaw.
2. Absent or underdeveloped clavicles, thumbs, and great toes.
3. Fingers and toes may be webbed and are unusually short, small, thin, and pointed, with absence or underdevelopment of finger- and toenails.
4. Sparse scalp hair and absent or sparse eyebrows and eyelashes.
5. Short stature.
6. Low-set ears, possibly with absent lobes.
7. Thin, short upper lip.
8. Mental retardation.
9. Possible abnormalities of the heart, including enlargement or irregular heart rhythms.

Because only one of the cases identified in the literature survived past infancy, little is known about treatment. At birth, the children will likely exhibit signs of failure to thrive, including breathing and feeding difficulties (Garrett et al., 1990), and cardiac arrhythmia. Treatment at that time should be symptomatic and supportive, requiring the coordinated efforts of a team of specialists (NORD, 2001). In the case of the boy who survived past infancy, the treatment team included an oral surgeon and dentist because of the child's hypodontia, impacted canines, gingivitis, and other anomalies of the teeth and jaw (Lapeer & Fransman, 1992). As is the case with any genetic disorder, genetic counseling should be recommended as part of treatment.

Children with Yunis-Varon syndrome will likely qualify for special education services under the handicapping condition of Multiple Disabilities. The educational needs of the child will be extensive and ongoing.

Future research should be in the area of diagnosis of Yunis-Varon syndrome before birth, through ultrasound. The National Institute of Health, through the Human Genome Project, is currently researching genetic disorders. The goal of the program is to provide insight into the causes, treatment, and possible prevention of genetic disorders in the future (NORD, 2001).

REFERENCES

Garrett, C., Barry, A. C., Simpson, R. H., & Hall, C. M. (1990). Yunis-Varon syndrome with severe osteodysplasty. *Journal of Medical Genetics, 27,* 114–121.

Lapeer, G., & Fransman, S. L. (1992). Hypodontia, impacted permanent teeth, spinal defects, and cardiomegaly in a previously diagnosed case of the Yunis-Varon syndrome. *Oral Surgery Oral Medicine Oral Pathology, 73,* 456–460.

National Organization for Rare Disorders. (2001). Yunis-Varon syndrome. Retrieved August 2001 from http://www.rarediseases.org

Walch, E., Schmidt, M., Brenner, R., Emmons, E., Dame, C., Pontz, B., et al. (2000). Yunis-Varon syndrome: Evidence for a lysosomal storage disease. *American Journal of Medical Genetics, 95,* 157–160.

Christine D. Ramos
University of Northern Colorado

Z

ZAR

Zar is a culture-bound syndrome found mostly in Ethiopian, Somalian, and other Middle Eastern and North African societies (American Psychiatric Association [APA], 1994). Zar syndrome is psychiatric in nature and is closely related to notions of "spiritual possession" (Besmer, 1992, p. 124). Clinical manifestations of this disorder include dissociative episodes, apathy, withdrawal, and other erratic or bizarre behaviors.

There are no known prevalence or incidence studies on zar possession. However, there are ethnographic studies pertaining to this culture-bound syndrome that link the disorder to *buda,* or the evil eye, and—in the Ethiopian and Hausa communities of Northern Africa—to spiritual possession. Zar is apparently geographically defined to Middle Eastern and North African populations; however, zar possession has been documented in migrant Ethiopian populations in Israel. In one ethnographic study, Ethiopian women in Israel keep their newborns indoors to shield them from the *buda* of others looking at them. It is believed that *buda* leads to spiritual or zar possession (Hodes, 1997). Among the Hausa of northern Nigeria, those with zar possession are ridiculed because of the unusual behavior associated with zar possession and because of the cultural notion that zar affects "the unenlightened people" (Besmer, 1992, p. 124). Besmer (1992, p. 124) suggests that zar possession is linked to the "marginal social categories" and members of society who maintain differential inclusion. This syndrome is not linguistically limited, but it is linked closely to spiritual possession and possession cults of both geographic areas. Zar possession is more common in adult females; however, ethnographic evidence suggests that zar possession can occur as early as infancy (Hodes, 1997).

Characteristics

1. Dissociative episodes
2. Inappropriate shouting
3. Inappropriate laughing
4. Hitting head against a wall
5. Apathy
6. Refusal to eat or carry out daily tasks
7. Withdrawal

Historically, health care professionals have referred to zar possession as a culturally sanctioned condition, and there are no known treatments for this disorder within medical and psychiatric communities. However, within the social communities themselves, this disorder is not seen as pathological (APA, 1994). In terms of treatment, children and women are sent to the local shaman or local healers (Hodes, 1997). On many occasions, members of the community who have zar syndrome shun treatment from local healers and take membership in "spiritual cults" (Besmer, 1992, p. 126). Within these groups, ambiguous status is normalized and viewed from the perspective of "rituals of affliction" (Besmer, 1992, p. 125). Cult membership is also important in terms of family environment.

The need for differential diagnosis of this syndrome is evident in transient populations in that it is essential to determine the level of acculturation as well as family history when diagnosing zar syndrome. The overlap of this syndrome's presenting symptoms with those of other common psychiatric conditions in the United States requires cultural sensitivity on the part of the person conducting the evaluation. It is doubtful that special education services would be needed for a child exhibiting zar behaviors, but a lengthy duration would probably interfere with learning, and at some point intervention would be needed from an academic standpoint. The more unusual behaviors associated with zar would not be tolerated in most schools and would come to the attention of personnel. At this point, an acculturation assessment of the child and family would be necessary, and related services would have to be sensitive to the acculturation process of the student.

REFERENCES

American Psychiatric Association. (1994). *Diagnostic and statistical manual of mental disorders* (4th ed.). Washington, DC: Author.

Besmer, F. E. (1992). Horses, musicians, and gods: The Hausa cult of possession-trance. Retrieved from http://ets.umdl.umich.edu/cgi/e/ehraf/hraf-idx?type=html

Hodes, R. M. (1997). Cross-cultural medicine and diverse health beliefs: Ethiopians abroad. *Western Journal of Medicine, 166,* 29–36.

Kiely Ann Fletcher
Ohio State University

ZELLWEGER SYNDROME

Zellweger syndrome is a rare hereditary disorder characterized by decreased or missing peroxisomes in the liver, kidney, and brain cells. Manifestations include facial dysmorphology, opthamological and neurological abnormalities, hepatomegaly, and unusual problems in prenatal development.

This disease is present at birth and occurs equally between males and females. One Australian study indicated that it occurs once in 100,000 live births (United Leukodystrophy Foundation, 2000). However, more cases have occurred but have gone undiagnosed. Zellweger syndrome is inherited as an autosomal recessive trait. Both parents must be carriers, and each of their children will have a 25% chance of being affected. Carriers are completely healthy.

Characteristics

1. Infants with the disease often exhibit prenatal growth failure in spite of a normal period of gestation.
2. Syndrome can often be recognized at birth due to profound lack of muscle tone; some infants may be unable to move.
3. Other symptoms may include unusual facial characteristics, mental retardation, the inability to suck and swallow, and liver enlargement.
4. Vision problems, hearing problems, and congenital heart lesions occur less commonly.
5. Jaundice, gastrointestinal bleeding, or both due to deficiency of a coagulation factor in the blood can also occur.

Treatment of Zellweger syndrome is symptomatic and supportive. Often a multidisciplinary approach is taken in which pediatric, neurological, ophthalmological, cardiological, and other treatments are combined (Pedianet Disease Database, 2000). Genetic counseling can be of benefit to families with patients with this disorder. Infections should be guarded against carefully to avoid complications. Vitamin K may be needed to avoid abnormal bleeding. Experimental therapies with docosahexaenoic acid (DHA) are being studied. DHA is an essential fatty acid, which is deficient in patients with Zellweger syndrome. Another approach being tested is the administration of bile acids, such as cholic acid or chenodeoxycholic acid, which may be of help in respect to liver function (United Leukodystrophy Foundation, 2000). Supportive treatment may include occupational therapy, physical therapy, hearing aids, and modified nutrition intake.

If the child lives long enough to attend school, special education services for a child with Zellweger syndrome would be necessary on many levels. Because the child is likely to have some form of mental retardation, then the child would need modified education services tailored to his or her educational needs. Furthermore, the child would benefit from physical therapy and perhaps would need services outside the school setting in order to keep the child from acquiring an infection that could lead to death.

The prognosis for individuals with Zellweger syndrome is poor. Death usually occurs within 6 months after onset and may be caused by respiratory distress, gastrointestinal bleeding, or liver failure. Research is currently being done on genetic disorders, including leukodystrophies such as Zellweger syndrome. The goals of this research are to increase scientific understanding of these disorders and to find ways to prevent, treat, and cure them (National Institute of Neurological Disorders and Stroke, 2000).

REFERENCES

National Institute of Neurological Disorders and Stroke. (2000). Zellweger syndrome. Retrieved from http://www.ninds.nih.gov/health_and_medical/disorders/zellwege_doc.htm

Pedianet Disease Database. (2000). Zellweger's syndrome. Retrieved from http://www.pedianet.com/news/illness/disease/files/zellwege.htm

United Leukodystrophy Foundation. (2000). Zellweger syndrome. Retrieved from http://www.ulf.org/ulf/intro/index.htm

Sarah Compton
University of Texas at Austin

See also Cerebro-Hepato-Renal Syndrome; Leukodystrophy

ZOLLINGER-ELLISON SYNDROME

Zollinger-Ellison syndrome (ZES) is a rare digestive disorder that can cause tumors in the duodenum (top of small intestine) and pancreas and can cause stomach-duodenal ulcers (Drumm et al., 1988; Kumar & Spitz, 1984). Cancerous tumors secrete serum gastrin, causing the stomach to produce excessive acid, which is responsible for peptic ulcers. The actual cause of ZES is unknown, but it may be associated with an abnormal tumor-suppressing gene.

The prevalence of ZES is unknown. Tumors are cancerous in approximately 40–60% of individuals with ZES. Although ZES usually has a middle-age onset, cases have been reported in adolescents and young children. With regard to cognitive effects, sequelae associated with ZES are usually the result of problems seen in individuals suffering from a chronic disease, particularly diseases associated with pancreatic illnesses, as well as side effects associated with treatment or surgery to remove tumors caused by ZES (Drumm et al., 1988; Kumar & Spitz, 1984).

Characteristics

1. Duodenal or pancreatic tumors
2. Peptic ulcers as a result of elevated levels of gastrin
3. Diarrhea, fatigue, and vomiting
4. Weakness and nausea
5. Psychomotor retardation

With regard to special education, children and adolescents suffering from ZES usually qualify under an Other Health Impaired label. Future research should focus on finding the cause of ZES and on developing successful treatment interventions.

REFERENCES

Drumm, B., Rhoades, J. M., & Stringer, D. A. (1988). Peptic ulcer disease in children: Etiology, clinical findings, and clinical course. *Pediatrics, 82,* 410.

Kumar, D., & Spitz, L. (1984). Peptic ulceration in children. *Surgery, Gynecology and Obstetrics, 159,* 163.

Antolin M. Llorente
Baylor College of Medicine
Houston, Texas

SUBJECT AND SYMPTOM INDEX